IRISH
RECORDS

IRISH
RECORDS

SOURCES FOR FAMILY AND LOCAL HISTORY

by James G. Ryan, Ph.D.

Ancestry.

Ryan, James G., 1950-
    Irish records : sources for family and local history / by James G. Ryan.—Rev. ed.
        p. cm.
    Includes bibliographical references and index.
    ISBN 0-916489-76-0 (hardcover)
    1. Ireland—Genealogy—Bibliography. 2. Ireland—History, Local—Sources—Bibliography. I. Title.
Z5313.I7R83   1997
[CS483]
016.9415--dc21   97-11624

Irish Records: Sources for Family and Local History is available in Ireland exclusively from
The Flyleaf Press, 4 Spencer Villas, Glenageary, Co. Dublin, Ireland

© 1997 Ancestry Incorporated (USA)
and Flyleaf Press (Ireland)

Ancestry can be reached via the World Wide Web at http://www.ancestry.com

First printing 1997

10 9 8 7 6 5 4 3 2 1

Printed in the United States of America

To my family—
the best you could find

Contents

Preface

Although there are several guides to Irish family history records, most of them are organized according to the type of records they cover (e.g., parish records, wills, etc.) or according to the institution holding the records (e.g., Public Record Office holdings, etc.). Neither of these systems, however, is ideally suited to the needs of the genealogist or historian who is armed only with the information that a certain person came from a certain county on a certain (or uncertain) date.

Unfortunately, Irish family records are sparse. In the time period of greatest interest, the late eighteenth and early-to-middle nineteenth centuries, most of the Irish population (and particularly those who emigrated) lived as small tenant farmers or laborers. These activities required few written records. Even such events as births and marriages were not generally recorded by the state until 1864, and were not recorded by the Catholic church, in most cases, until after 1800. Because of this, every source of available information can be valuable. Indeed, many of the very best sources of information are those dealing with only one town or county. A detailed guide to these local sources is therefore very valuable.

This guide lists available records for each county in Ireland. They are listed, within each county, under the following headings: A Brief History; Census and Census Substitutes; Church Records; Commercial and Social Directories; Family History; Gravestone Inscriptions; Newspapers; Wills and Administrations; Miscellaneous Sources; and Research Sources and Services.

It is hoped that the result will be a more useful reference for the genealogist and historian.

James Ryan
Co. Dublin, Ireland
1997

Acknowledgments

This book is essentially a book of reference, and thanks are therefore primarily due to the hundreds of researchers and organizations to whose work it refers. Without their contributions this book would have no purpose. Thanks are also due to the following for providing illustrations and information: the National Library of Ireland for the parish maps, barony maps, and many other illustrations; the National Archives of Ireland for illustrations and for the use of their list of Church of Ireland parish records; the Representative Church Body Library; the Office of the Registrar General; the Family History Library of The Church of Jesus Christ of Latter-day Saints; and the Federation for Ulster Local Studies. Thanks are also due to the journals from which illustrations have been shown.

Thanks are due to the following for comments on parts of the draft manuscript: Mr. Michael Costello of the Kerry County Library, Mr. Jarlath Glynn of the Wexford County Library, Dr. Chris O'Mahoney of the Mid-west Archives, and Ms. Una Palcic of the Sligo Family Research Society.

I would also like to thank Rachel Devoy, Michelle Power, and Mary Cahill for typing the manuscript.

For the 1997 edition, I must further thank Brian Smith for his careful assistance in checking sources, and for many suggestions of improvements; to the heritage centers and libraries who sent me information and suggestions; and to the many reviewers and readers who pointed out necessary amendments.

Finally, I want to thank my wife, Kathryn, and my parents for their encouragement and comments on the drafts.

Introduction

How to Use This Guide

There are no definitive ways of ensuring success in family research. A researcher may start with a large amount of information on a family's vital data, names, and areas of residence, and find no further trace of the family in the available records. Alternatively, a persistent researcher with only the bare essentials of data may, through hard work and creative research, succeed in piecing together the history of the family. Initiative is an important ingredient in finding Irish roots, particularly where family details are sparse. Once the normal land and church record sources have been consulted, imaginative use of local historical accounts can produce further information about the family and its circumstances. These sources can point the way to other, more obscure records. In short, the more that is known about life in the area at the relevant period, the more one can try to imagine the ancestor's situation and the aspects of his or her life which might have been recorded.

Principles for Family Research

This guide is designed to facilitate family research by providing a comprehensive listing of all the record sources in the county from which an ancestor came. The objective of the family researcher is to add to the stock of information about his or her ancestors from the records available. This essentially means adding more "elements of identity" to one's ancestors. Elements of identity are names, dates, places, and relationships which distinguish one person from another and thus help to ensure that the researcher is following the right lines. For example, if a researcher knows only that his ancestor was a Michael Ryan born in Tipperary in the early 1830s, it would be virtually impossible to establish a definite family line. This is because there were many people of that name born at that time and place. If the exact birth date or place is known, then the possibilities are greatly improved.

The principles on which family research should be conducted are simple. First, researchers must work from what is already known to what is unknown and concentrate on adding to the known elements of identity of their ancestors. The best approach is to work on the ancestor about whom most is known. By adding new elements of identity to this person, more information will inevitably be found about other earlier relatives, siblings, etc. What the researcher should *not* do is to find a family of the same name in the ancestor's area and try to establish a link. Many Irish family names are associated with particular areas, and other families of the same name should therefore be expected to be found. An exception to this rule is where the name is very rare and a linkage therefore reasonable. Build from what is already known and, if the apparently "right" family is found, try to prove that it is not: for instance, look for evidence of the named person in Ireland after the ancestor left.

Second, the researcher should work from the more recent events in the ancestor's life to the less recent. As records generally improve with time, it may, for example, be easier to find a person's birth date by looking at death records and gravestone inscriptions. In the case of emigrant ancestors, both of these principles suggest that all possible information on the person in the immigrant country should be collected before attempting to trace ancestry in Ireland.

What the Records Can Indicate

The following is a guide to the information about elements of identity which various sources can provide.

Where Did They Live?

A precise "address" for an ancestor is one of the most valuable elements of identity, particularly in searching for ancestors with names which are locally very common. Records which provide both names and definite addresses are therefore very valuable ways of linking people with places. The two major records used for these purposes are *Griffith's Valuation* in the mid-1800s and the *Tithe Applotment Survey* (see Census and Census Substitutes) in the early 1800s. Both of these land occupancy records are indexed in the "Surname Index" compiled by the National Library of Ireland, which lists the householders and landholders recorded in *Griffith's Valuation*. By using this index, the researcher can trace a landholder to a precise holding. This index also shows whether landholders of that name are in the *Tithe Applotment Survey*. By examining the original records indicated in the index, the full names of those listed and the townland in which they lived can be established. Many heritage centers have now indexed the above land records and will provide a search for a fee.

For ancestors who lived in larger towns, a further useful source is the commercial directory. *Griffith's Valuation* also lists the householders in towns and villages. The *Tithe Applotment Survey*, however, only lists holders of certain types of agricultural land (see page 18).

For the latter part of the nineteenth century, a good source is the civil register of births, deaths, and marriages, which started in 1864 (see Civil Register of Birth, Marriage, and Death). If, for instance, it is known when the parent of an emigrant died, the death certificate (page 13) may give the family home address. Marriage certificates are particularly useful, as they give the addresses of both partners (page 12). Birth records also give the parents' address (page 11). The 1901 and 1911 censuses are also useful in locating a family holding.

There are a range of other censuses and census substitutes listed for each county, some of which have names arranged alphabetically and give addresses.

Who Were Their Relatives?

If an address has been found, the most obvious way of identifying other family members is to check local church records of birth and marriage. To do this it will be necessary to identify the church which served the area and consult its records, if they exist. This can be done using the guides in the Church Records section in each chapter. As a result of the Irish Genealogical Project, most counties have now established heritage centers (or equivalent), which have indexed parish records on computer (see the Research Sources and Services section in the county of interest). They can provide searches of their indexes for a specific ancestor.

After 1864, official certificates of death, birth, and marriage are also available (non-Catholic marriage certificates are available from 1845). Marriage certificates give the names of the bride's and groom's fathers. Death records are less useful since they only list the name of the person present at death, whose relationship to the deceased is often not stated. Birth records give names of parents (including mother's maiden name). The full list of details specified on each of these certificates is listed in the Civil Register of Birth, Marriage, and Death section. Other useful sources include gravestone inscriptions, wills, marriage license bonds, and birth, marriage, and death notices in newspapers. A few of the more detailed censuses also list entire households and give relationships of the residents. Finally, there are pedigrees and family histories (see Family Histories sections). These exist mainly for more prominent families. For such families, useful potential sources are the series of publications by Burke's, such as *Burke's Landed Gentry, Burke's Irish Family Records, Burke's Landed Gentry of Ireland*, etc. These appeared at various intervals and include detailed pedigrees of specific prominent families. If the families are large landowners or otherwise prominent members of society, they are likely to be listed in these, or in other local directories. People in either of these categories are also more likely to be mentioned in newspaper birth, death, marriage, or business notices.

What Were Their Occupations?

The range of possible occupations in the eighteenth and nineteenth centuries was far smaller than it is now, particularly in Ireland, where there was little industrialization. The majority of the population, and particularly of those who emigrated, were either small tenant farmers or laborers. A listing in *Griffith's Valuation* as a landholder (as distinct from just a householder) is a fair indication that the person concerned was a farmer (see page 189). Listings of laborers are very scarce, and generally only occur within estate records. If the ancestor was a tradesman or retailer, a commercial directory for the area may be a useful way to determine the exact nature of the business. It was also common for businesses to place advertisements in local newspapers. These can be a very valuable source of information.

Many of the directories listed in the records of each county also list various professionals separately, such as medical doctors, lawyers, clergy, and various categories of public officials (sheriffs, bailiffs, etc; see pages 239–241). Local public officials are also often listed in the reports and minute books of county and borough councils.

There are specific directories available for some occupations, particularly the professions and public officials.

For medical doctors, Croly's *Irish Medical Directory* (1843 and 1846) lists general practitioners and other medical graduates. This information is also available in the *Medical Directory for Ireland*, issued annually from 1852 to 1860, and in the *Irish Medical Directory*, which appeared annually from 1872.

The records of approximately 90,000 members of the Royal Irish Constabulary are held by the Public Record Office in London (Ref. HO 184.43), and a microfilm copy (Ref. MFA 24/1-16) is available at the NAI and at the LDS (films 856057-69, 852088-852110). Genealogical queries on members of southern Irish police forces may be directed to Garda Jim Herlihy, Garda Siochana, Blarney, Co. Cork, Ireland. The museum of the Garda Siochana, the police force of the Irish Republic, also has a home page, which is easily located by searching this name. Clergymen are also found in some directories: Catholic priests are listed in the *Irish Catholic Directory* (Dublin: Veritas Publications), issued annually from 1836. There are many other listings of priests in commercial directories (see page 37), in various diocesan history journals, and in local history journals. Church of Ireland ministers are listed in various publications: the *Ecclesiastical Registry of Ireland* by Samuel Lea (1814); *Irish Ecclesiastical Register*, issued in 1817, 1818, 1824, and 1827; the *Ecclesiastical Register* by J. Erck (1830); *Bourn's Churchman's Almanac and Irish Ecclesiastical Directory* (1841); *Irish Ecclesiastical Directory* (1841 and 1842); *Irish Clergy List* (1843); Oldham's *Clerical Directory of Ireland* (1858); and James Charles's *Irish Church Directory*, issued in 1862 and annually since then. Presbyterian church members are not well documented. The only specific directory is McComb's *Presbyterian Almanac* of 1857. Methodist clergymen are listed by Hill, Rev. William in *An Alphabetical Arrangement of all the Wesleyan Methodist Ministers and Preachers on Trial, in connection with the British Conferences*, London, 1885. Another useful source for graduates of all disciplines is *Alumni Dublinensis* by G.D. Burtchaell and T.N. Sadlier, Dublin, 1935, which lists graduates of Trinity College, Dublin. Further such references are in the section on Directories. Copies of these directories are available in various Irish and other libraries.

Irish Place-Names and Family Names

Place-Names

The majority of Irish place-names, and particularly townland names, are derived from the Gaelic, or Irish, language. Some components of these names, such as Bally- (town), -more (big) , or -beg (small), are particularly common. A good description of the origins of Irish place-names is given in P.W. Joyce's *Irish Names of Places* (1893) and *Irish Local Names Explained* (1884. Reprint. Baltimore: Genealogical Publishing Company, 1979). Because these names are ancient, there are often variations in the way in which they are spelled, particularly in earlier documents. Note, for instance, the variations in spelling between the names of many parishes and those of the corresponding Catholic parishes (e.g., Killadysert versus Kildysert).

It is not uncommon for researchers to know the name of the place of origin of their ancestor, and to find it is not listed in any guide. This may be because the name was taken down or remembered from the pronunciation used by an ancestor who may have been illiterate, Irish-speaking, or both. Thus the spelling will reflect the phonetics used. Examples include Mallah for Mallow, Carsaveen for Cahirciveen, etc. Some imagination is necessary to relate these names to their currently accepted forms. A knowledge of local accents is also very valuable in these situations.

There are several good sources for finding a place-name. In compiling censuses during the last century, for instance, indexes of townlands were compiled and have been published.

The *Alphabetical Index to the Towns and Townlands of Ireland* (Dublin: Alexander Thom and Company, 1877) lists townlands alphabetically and gives, for each, the parish, barony, county, and Poor Law Union to which it belongs. The parishes, baronies, and Poor Law Unions are also listed separately.

General Alphabetical Index to the Townlands and Towns, Parishes and Baronies of Ireland . . .1851 (Reprint. Baltimore: Genealogical Publishing Company, 1984) is based on the 1851 census and gives much the same information as the above index (see page 5).

Having found where an ancestor lived, some further background information on the area may be gleaned from the following publications:

A Topographical Dictionary of Ireland by Samuel Lewis (London, 1837) lists all the parishes, baronies, towns, villages, and counties in Ireland with local administrative details, an account of agriculture and industry, major local houses ("seats") and their owners, and other local information (see page 6).

William Shaw Mason's *A Statistical Account, or Parochial Survey of Ireland*, Dublin, 1814-19, and *Parliamentary Gazetteer of Ireland* (Fullerton and Company, 1846) also provide very useful local information.

Local history journals are also a good source of information on the history and other aspects of particular counties (see the section on Research Sources and Services below). The Irish Place-Names Commission in the Ordnance Survey Office, Phoenix Park, Dublin 8 can usually assist in finding the accepted vari-

>
> the enchantress Murna. When the wind blows strongly in certain directions, a loud whistling sound comes from some crevices in the rock, which can be heard distinctly half a mile off; and the peasantry who know nothing of such learned explanations, and care less, will tell you, among many other dim legends of the lady Murna, that this sound is the humming of her spinning wheel.
>
> III. The genitive of *ua* or *o* (a grandson) is *ui*, which is pronounced the same as *ee* or *y* in English; and consequently when a local name consists of a noun followed by a family name with *O* (such as O'Brien) in the genitive singular, the *ui* is usually (but not always) represented in anglicised names by *y*. This is very plainly seen in Cloonykelly near Athleague in Roscommon, *Cluain-Ui-Chealaigh*, O'Kelly's meadow; in Drumyarkin in Fermanagh (near Clones), O'Harkin's *drum* or hill-ridge. Cloonybrien, near Boyle in Roscommon, where a portion of the Annals of Lough Key was copied, is called in Irish *Cluain-I-Bhraoin*, O'Breen's meadow. Knockycosker, north of Kilbeggan in Westmeath, is written by the Four Masters *Cnoc-Ui-Choscraigh*, O'Cosgry's hill. The barony of Iraghticonor in the north of Kerry, is called in Irish *Oireacht-Ui-Chonchobhair*, O'Conor's *iraght* or inheritance.
>
> In the parish of Moycullen in Galway there is a townland, now called Gortyloughlin; but as we find it written Gurtyloughnane in an old county map, it is obvious that here *n* has been changed to *l*—a very usual phonetic corruption (1st Vol., Pt. I., c. III.), and that the Irish name is *Gort-Ui-Lachtnain*, the field of O'Lachtnan or O'Loughnane —a well-known family name. This townland includes the demesne and house of Danesfield, the name of which is an attempted translation of the

Extract from *The Origin and History of Irish Names of Places* by P. W. Joyce (Dublin: Gill & Son, 1893).

ant for difficult place-names where the above sources fail.

Maps are available for various periods and areas. Photocopies of *Griffith's Valuation* maps are available from the Valuation Office, 6 Ely Place, Dublin 2. These show the boundaries of the holdings of each of those listed in the survey itself. A full set of nineteenth-century maps of a wide range of scales are also available for consultation at the National Library of Ireland (NLI). The modern maps available are in metric sizes, a useful series being the 1:50,000 size, which is approximately equivalent to the old "half-inch" maps. These are available for all of Ireland from the Ordnance Survey Office, Phoenix Park, Dublin 8, or Ordnance Survey of Northern Ireland, Colby House, Stranmillis Court, Belfast BT9 8BJ, N. Ireland (Web site: http://www.nova.co.uk/nova/pages/map/htm). The archives of the Ordnance Survey are in the National Archives, and the index can be searched online through their home page (http://www.kst.dit.ie/nat-arch/os.html). These mainly contain documents and correspondence generated in the process of map-making. However, information on some landowners is inevitably included.

Family Names

Irish family names are mainly derived from Gaelic and Norman names. English and Scottish names are also common, particularly in the northern counties, but also occur elsewhere in the country. Most Scottish names are also derived from Gaelic. Huguenot, Palatine, and Jewish names also occur. To complicate the situation, many English surnames or family names were adopted by Irish families during the seventeenth and eighteenth centuries when Irish names were discouraged. MacGowan, for instance, became Smith, and McDarra became Oakes because these names either were English for, or sounded like, Irish language words with these meanings.

A common feature of Irish names is the "O" or "Mac" prefix. During the eighteenth and early nineteenth centuries, when the Irish language died away in most of the country, there was a gradual dropping of the "O" and, to a lesser extent, "Mc" from names. During the latter half of the century, when awareness of Gaelic heritage grew, these prefixes were restored. When searching Irish names it is therefore wise to check both forms (e.g., Sullivan and O'Sullivan, Neill and O'Neill).

The spelling of Irish surnames also varies. Although this occurs to some extent in Ireland (Keogh, Kehoe; O'Mara, O'Meara; O'Loughlin, O'Lochlann, O'Loghlen), it occurs to a much greater extent among Irish emigrants overseas (Ryan, Ryun, Ryne, Rion, etc.; Geraghty, Garritty, Gerritty, etc.). Thus it is often necessary to establish the accepted local spelling of a name before searching. A modern Irish telephone directory is one useful way to find the currently accepted forms of names. In general terms, the spelling form used currently in Ireland is more likely to be the form of spelling used in eighteenth- and nineteenth-century records. This is not always the case, however.

A good source for determining variants of family names is Edward McLysaght's *Surnames of Ireland* (Dublin: Irish Academic Press, 1985), as well as his other

CENSUS OF IRELAND

FOR THE YEAR

1851.

GENERAL ALPHABETICAL INDEX

TO THE

TOWNLANDS AND TOWNS OF IRELAND,

With the Number of the Sheet of the Ordnance Survey Maps in which they appear; the Areas of the Townlands in Statute Acres; the County, Barony, Parish, and Poor Law Union in which they are situated; also the Volume and Page of the Townland Census of 1851—which contain the Population and Number of Houses in 1841 and 1851, and the Poor Law Valuation in 1851.

*** The names of Towns are printed in SMALL CAPITALS, and those of *Islands* which are not Townlands in *Italics*.

No. of Sheet of the Ordnance Survey Maps.	Townlands and Towns.	Area in Statute Acres.	County.	Barony.	Parish.	Poor Law Union in 1857.	Townland Census of 1851, Part I.	
							Vol.	Page
		A. R. P.						
34	Abartagh .	34 2 32	Waterford .	Decies within Drum	Clashmore .	Youghal .	II.	351
97	Abberanville .	24 0 29	Galway .	Athenry .	Kiltullagh .	Loughrea .	IV.	4
93	Abbernadoorny .	62 3 27	Donegal .	Banagh .	Killymard .	Donegal .	III.	111
58	Abbert .	178 3 30a	Galway .	Tiaquin .	Monivea .	Tuam .	IV.	78
58, 59	Abbert Demesne .	1,293 2 21b	Galway .	Tiaquin .	Monivea .	Tuam .	IV.	78
4	Abbeville .	943 2 7	Tipperary, N.R.	Lower Ormond	Lorrha .	Borrisokane .	II.	285
118	Abbey .	27 0 22	Cork, W.R.	Bantry .	Kilmocomoge .	Bantry .	II.	119
116,117,125	Abbey .	334 3 28	Galway .	Leitrim .	Ballynakill .	Portumna .	IV.	50
58	Abbey .	875 3 7	Galway .	Tiaquin .	Abbeyknockmoy	Tuam .	IV.	75
56	Abbey .	222 3 21	Limerick .	Coshlea .	Kilflyn .	Kilmallock .	II.	240
13	Abbeycartron .	219 2 20	Longford .	Longford .	Templemichael .	Longford .	I.	160
16	Abbeycartron .	32 1 3	Roscommon .	Roscommon .	Elphin .	Strokestown .	IV.	209
18,19,22,23	Abbeyderg .	867 2 21	Longford .	Moydow .	Taghsheenod .	Ballymahon .	I.	162
21	ABBEYDORNEY T.	—	Kerry .	Clanmaurice .	O'Dorney .	Tralee .	II.	173
4	Abbeydown .	454 3 6	Wexford .	Scarawalsh .	Moyacomb .	Shillelagh .	I.	325
3	Abbey East .	301 0 12	Clare .	Burren .	Abbey .	Ballyvaghan .	II.	11
47	Abbeyfarm .	55 1 12	Limerick .	Kilmallock .	St.Peter's & St.Paul's	Kilmallock .	II.	250
42, 51	Abbeyfeale East .	1,350 3 23	Limerick .	Glenquin .	Abbeyfeale .	Newcastle .	II.	244
42	ABBEYFEALE T.	—	Limerick .	Glenquin .	Abbeyfeale .	Newcastle .	II.	244
42	Abbeyfeale West .	718 2 4c	Limerick .	Glenquin .	Abbeyfeale .	Newcastle .	II.	244
86	Abbeyfield .	18 0 36	Galway .	Kilconnell .	Kilconnell .	Ballinasloe .	IV.	40
107	Abbeygormacan .	94 1 18	Galway .	Longford .	Abbeygormacan .	Ballinasloe .	IV.	56
33	Abbeygrey or Monasternalea .	503 1 14	Galway .	Killian .	Athleague .	Mountbellew .	IV.	43
33	Abbeygrey or Monasternalea .	157 3 37	Galway .	Killian .	Killeroran .	Mountbellew .	IV.	44
20	Abbeygrove .	59 0 25	Kilkenny .	Gowran .	Blanchvilleskill .	Kilkenny .	I.	93
29	Abbeyhalfquarter .	247 0 29	Sligo .	Tireragh .	Kilmoremoy .	Ballina .	IV.	235
107	Abbey Island .	17 1 33	Donegal .	Tirhugh .	Kilbarron .	Ballyshannon .	III.	148
106	Abbey Island .	83 1 23	Kerry .	Dunkerron South	Kilcrohane .	Cahersiveen .	II.	183
20	Abbey Land .	9 0 3	Cavan .	Upper Loughtee	Urney .	Cavan .	III.	86
14	Abbeyland .	68 3 19d	Kildare .	Clane .	Clane .	Naas .	I.	53
40	Abbeyland .	144 2 3	Kildare .	Kilkea and Moone	Castledermot .	Athy .	I.	59
15, 20	Abbey Land .	9 0 11	Longford .	Ardagh .	Mostrim .	Granard .	I.	152
27	Abbeyland .	92 2 23	Meath .	Lower Duleek .	Duleek .	Drogheda .	I.	195
25	Abbeyland .	327 2 33	Meath .	Lower Navan .	Navan .	Navan .	I.	215
6, 7	Abbeyland .	75 1 25	Westmeath .	Corkaree .	Multyfarnham .	Mullingar .	I.	263
11	Abbeyland and Charlestown or Ballynamonaster .	230 1 6	Westmeath .	Moygoish .	Kilbixy .	Mullingar .	I.	279
100, 108	Abbeyland Great .	812 1 6	Galway .	Longford .	Clonfert .	Ballinasloe .	IV.	56
101	Abbeyland Little .	231 3 5	Galway .	Longford .	Clonfert .	Ballinasloe .	IV.	56
17	Abbeyland North .	26 0 8	Galway .	Dunmore .	Dunmore .	Tuam .	IV.	33
112	Abbey-lands .	20 3 14	Cork, E.R.	Kinsale .	Kinsale .	Kinsale .	II.	100

(a) Including 3A. 2R. 16P. water. (c) Including 6A. 3R. 5P. water.
(b) Including 12A. 3R. 24P. water. (d) Including 5A. 3R. 32P. water.

B

First page of the Townland and Towns Index from the *General Alphabetical Index to the Townlands and Towns, Parishes and Baronies of Ireland* (Dublin: Thom's, 1861).

exist: those of an ancient chapel at Rosslare, called St. Breoch's, or St. Bridget's, were taken down some years since.

ROSSLEA, or ROYSLEA, a village, in that part of the parish of CLONES which is in the barony of CLONKELLY, county of FERMANAGH, and province of ULSTER, 4 miles (N. N. E.) from Clones, on the road from Lisnaskea to Monaghan; containing 355 inhabitants. The place is romantically situated near the celebrated mountain of Carnmore, in a fine meadow district, several townlands of which are rich pasture land, especially those of Lisnabrack and Salloo, where vast numbers of oxen are annually fed for the English market. The village consists of one irregularly built street, containing 71 houses, and is connected with the new line of road on the mountain from Enniskillen to Belfast by a bridge over the river Fin. In the vicinity is Lake View, the residence of the Rev. T. Bogue, P. P., a beautiful villa, overlooking the lake of Island Hill and commanding a fine view of several other small lakes in the neighbourhood; it is surrounded with grounds tastefully laid out and richly embellished. Here is a flax-mill belonging to Mr. Lynch. Fairs are held on the 8th of every month; a constabulary police force is stationed here, and petty sessions and manorial courts are held in the court-house, a neat building in the centre of the village. The R. C. chapel is a very handsome edifice of stone, with a tower and campanile turret: the interior is highly embellished; the windows are enriched with stained glass, and over the altar-piece is a fine painting. Carnmore mountain is of lofty elevation, and abounds with wild and romantic scenery; from its summit are seen 32 lakes, including Lough Erne; and its deep glens are inhabited by a numerous class of peasantry of singular habits and of great originality of character.

ROSSLEE, a parish, in the barony of CARRA, county of MAYO, and province of CONNAUGHT, 6 miles (S. S. E.) from Castlebar, on the road to Hollymount; containing 886 inhabitants. The land is chiefly in pasture and under tillage; there is but little bog. Thomastown is the seat of T. V. Clendening, Esq.; Mount Pleasant, of G. Mahon, Esq.; Castle Lucas, of G. Ormsby, Esq.; and Lakemount, of J. O'Dowd, Esq. It is a rectory and vicarage, in the diocese of Tuam, forming part of the union of Balla: the tithes amount to £80. In the R. C. divisions it is part of the union or district of Balla. Here is a private school of about 30 boys and 20 girls. At Clogher Lucas are the ruins of an old castle.

ROSSMANOGUE, a parish, partly in the barony of SCARAWALSH, but chiefly in that of GOREY, county of WEXFORD, and province of LEINSTER, 5 miles (N. E.) from Ferns; containing 1211 inhabitants. This parish, which is situated on the river Bann, and is skirted by the high road from Camolin to Carnew, comprises 4451½ statute acres, as applotted under the tithe act, chiefly in tillage: on its border is a small red bog. It is a rectory, in the diocese of Ferns, forming part of the union and corps of the prebend of Tomb in the cathedral of Ferns: the tithes amount to £165. 4. 7¼; and there is a glebe of 14 acres. The church is in ruins. In the R. C. divisions it is part of the union or district of Camolin; the chapel is at Craneford, adjoining which is a residence for the priest. About 100 children

538

are educated in two private schools. The late Rt. Hon. George Ogle, of Bellevue, in this county, author of "Molly Asthore" and other admired ballads, received the earlier part of his education under the Rev. Mr. Millar, then rector of this parish.

ROSSMERE, ROSSMIRE, or ROSSMORE, a parish, partly in the barony of DECIES-without-DRUM, but chiefly in that of UPPERTHIRD, county of WATERFORD, and province of MUNSTER; containing, with the post-town of Kilmacthomas (which is separately described), 2484 inhabitants. It forms a narrow slip of land separating the portions of Upperthird barony; and within its limits, at Newtown, on the confines of the three baronies of Upperthird, Middlethird, and Decies-without-Drum, it was designed to build a new town, of which the streets were marked out and paved, but only a few houses were built, and these have since mostly gone to ruin. It is a vicarage, in the diocese of Lismore, and in the patronage of the Duke of Devonshire, in whom the rectory is impropriate: the tithes amount to £500, of which £300 is payable to the impropriator, and the remainder to the vicar. The church is a modern structure, towards the erection of which the late Board of First Fruits granted a loan of £750, in 1831; and there is a R. C. chapel. About 150 children are educated in two private schools; and there is a Sunday school under the superintendence of the curate.

ROSSNOWLOUGH, an ecclesiastical district, in the barony of TYRHUGH, county of DONEGAL, and province of ULSTER, 3 miles (N. W.) from Ballyshannon, on the west of the road to Donegal and on the sea coast; containing 1006 inhabitants. In the year 1830, nine townlands, comprising 2403½ statute acres, were separated from the parish of Drumholm and constituted the ecclesiastical district parish of Rossnowlough. It is a perpetual curacy, in the diocese of Raphoe, and in the patronage of the Vicar of Drumholm: the gross value of the benefice is £108. 8. 9., of which £75 is paid by the vicar, and £25 from Primate Boulter's fund; the remainder is the annual value of the glebe. The church was erected in 1831, by aid of a gift of £800 from the late Board of First Fruits. In the R. C. divisions it is in the district of Drumholm. About 360 children are educated in six public schools, of which one is supported by the trustees of Erasmus Smith's charity, one from Col. Robertson's endowment, and the remainder chiefly by subscription. There are also two private schools, in which are about 130 children; and two Sunday schools.

ROSSORY, a parish, partly in the barony of GLENAWLEY, but chiefly in that of MAGHERABOY, county of FERMANAGH, and province of ULSTER; containing, with part of the suburbs of Enniskillen, 4338 inhabitants. This parish, which is situated on the shores of Lough Erne, and on the roads leading respectively from Enniskillen to Sligo and Ballyshannon, comprises, according to the Ordnance survey, 7654 statute acres, of which 2302¼ are in the barony of Glenawley, and 5351¾ in Magheraboy: of these, about 494 acres are water, and by far the greater portion of the remainder is meadow and pasture. The land is of good quality, and that portion of it which is under tillage is in a state of profitable cultivation: there is a moderate proportion of bog, and limestone is quarried for agricul-

Description of various villages and civil parishes from *Topographical Dictionary of Ireland* by Samuel Lewis. London, 1837.

books, *Irish Families* and *More Irish Families*. Other sources include Robert Bell's *Book of Ulster Surnames*, Belfast, 1988; Robert E. Matheson's *Special Report on Surnames in Ireland together with Varieties and Synonyms of Surnames and Christian Names* (1901), reprinted by Genealogical Publishing Company of Baltimore (1968); and Rev. Patrick Woulfe's *Irish Names and Surnames* (1923), reprinted by the same company in 1993.

Administrative Divisions

An ancestor's address is a basic element of identity and can be an essential step in obtaining further information. To understand the components of the types of "addresses" commonly cited, it is necessary to know about the administrative areas used.

Many different administrative boundaries were used in Ireland for civil and ecclesiastical purposes. In most cases these divisions observe boundaries set up for other purposes, e.g., county boundaries, but others, such as diocese boundaries, tend to be unique. A short description of the different divisions is given below. A more detailed description is given by Dr. W. Nolan in a chapter of *Irish Genealogy—A Record Finder* (Dublin: Heraldic Artists, 1981).

Civil Divisions

The civil divisions are described below, starting from the smallest unit of land.

Townland

This is the smallest unit of land area used in Ireland. Their areas vary in size from less than ten acres to several thousand acres. Despite the name, these units do not necessarily contain towns; indeed, some have no occupants at all. There are approximately 64,000 townlands in Ireland, and they are the most specific "address" usually available for rural dwellers. They are generally organized into civil parishes.

Civil Parishes

These are important units for record purposes. They generally contain around twenty-five to thirty townlands, as well as towns and villages. There are approximately 2,500 civil parishes in the country. The guides to church records (see the section on Church Records below) list the parishes in each county, and they are also shown in the accompanying maps. Parishes are generally listed within each county, although they may also be divided by barony. In many cases civil parishes straddle county and barony boundaries. Another confusing aspect is that some civil parishes are in several geographically separate parts. This is indicated in the lists accompanying the maps in each chapter.

Barony

A barony is a portion of a county or a group of civil parishes. Historically the boundaries were defined by the Anglo-Normans, based on the Gaelic family territory or "tuath." Barony boundaries do not always conform to those of the civil parishes within them. There are 273 baronies in Ireland.

County

The county is a major and consistent division of land. The counties were gradually established by the English, starting at the time the Normans arrived. The first counties—Dublin, Kildare, and Louth—were established in the early thirteenth century, whereas the last counties, those of Ulster, were not established until after 1600. There are thirty-two counties, and these are formed into four provinces (see page 8).

Province

The four provinces of Ireland are Connaught, Leinster, Munster, and Ulster. Each comprises a number of counties.

Cities, Towns, Boroughs, and Wards

These are separate administrative areas of varying size. Many towns have several civil parishes, whereas some civil parishes have several townships. Other types of classifications of urban areas include the borough, which is a town with a corporation, or, alternatively, a town which sent a representative (i.e., an M.P.) to the Westminister Parliament. A ward is an administrative unit within a city or large town.

Poor Law Unions

These areas were set up under the Poor Law Relief Act (1838). Rates, land-based taxes, were collected within these areas for maintenance of local poor. They were named after a local large town, and do not always conform to county boundaries. The same districts later became used as General Registrar's Districts.

General Registrar's Districts

These districts, derived from Poor Law Unions (see above), are the areas within which births, deaths, and marriages were compiled.

Ecclesiastical Divisions

Church Parish

This is the basic area over which a parish priest or minister presided. Church of Ireland parishes generally conform to the civil parish boundaries. Catholic parish boundaries, which are generally larger, do not. The

The counties of Ireland, from *A New Genealogical Atlas of Ireland* by Brian Mitchell (Baltimore: Genealogical Publishing Co., 1986).

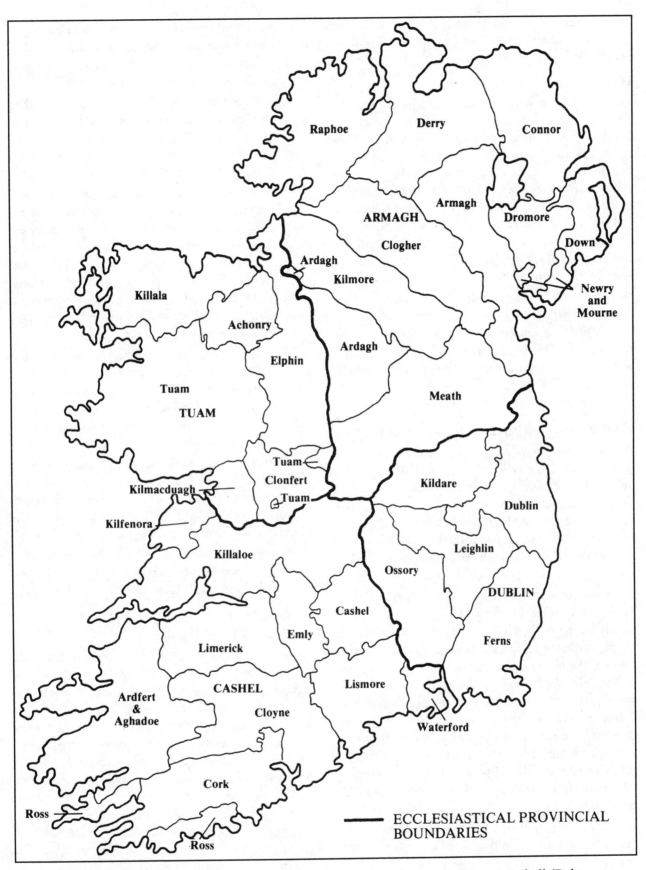

Church of Ireland dioceses, from *A New Genealogical Atlas of Ireland* by Brian Mitchell (Baltimore: Genealogical Publishing Co., 1986).

Church Records section in each chapter shows the Catholic parish(es) to which each civil parish belonged before 1880.

Diocese

The parishes of both the Catholic church and the Church of Ireland are organized into dioceses, each presided over by a bishop (see page 9). In both churches the dioceses are devised so as to include a certain number of church parishes. Thus the boundaries do not conform to county boundaries. Neither do the dioceses of the two churches conform to one another. Church of Ireland dioceses are important for record purposes such as administration of wills. The Church of Ireland diocese to which each civil parish belonged is shown in the Church Records section for each county.

Although Roman Catholic dioceses are less useful for record purposes, the Catholic diocese to which each church parish belonged can be determined from the *Irish Catholic Directory* (Dublin: Veritas Publications), which has been issued annually by the Catholic hierarchy since 1836. This also gives other details about chapels and priests in each Catholic parish.

Civil Register of Birth, Marriage, and Death

An important source of records not dealt with on a county basis is the civil register of births, marriages, and deaths. The central registration of non-Catholic marriages started in Ireland in 1845. However, the registration of births, marriages, and deaths for the entire population did not begin until 1864. These records are a very valuable source of information, despite their late start.

Civil records are collected within districts called registrar's districts (or General Registrar's Districts), which are generally named from a large town within them. If the townland of residence of an ancestor is known, the registrar's district (which is the same area as the Poor Law Union) can be obtained from one of the available indexes to towns and townlands (see Place-Names above). Note that some of the smaller registrar's districts were merged with surrounding districts at various times (e.g., Killala was merged with Ballina in 1917, and Donaghmore [Laois] was merged with Abbeyleix or Roscrea in 1887). A list of these changes is available in the GRO.

The categories of information which registrars were requested to provide on the three types of certificates is as follows:

Birth Certificates: (see page 11); provide date and place of birth; name (if any); sex; name, surname, and dwelling place of father; name, surname, and maiden surname of mother; rank or profession of father; signature, qualification, and residence of informant; when registered; signature of registrar; and baptismal name, if added after registration of birth, and date.

Marriage Certificates: (see page 12); state when married; names and surnames of bride and groom; ages; condition (i.e., bachelor, widow, etc.); rank or profession; residence(s) at time of marriage; fathers' names and surnames; and ranks or professions of fathers.

The church in which the marriage was performed and the names of two witnesses and the clergyman are also listed. Witnesses are commonly family members and may provide clues to family linkages. It is common for the age column to state merely "full age" (i.e., over twenty-one) rather than a specific age. For this reason, it is useful to note that "spinster" in the condition column refers to an unmarried girl of any age. In many cases it will be noted if a father is deceased.

Death Certificates: (see page 13); state date and place of death; name and surname; sex; condition (i.e., married, etc.); age last birthday; rank, profession, or occupation; certified cause of death and duration of illness; signature, qualification, and residence of informant; and when registered.

Certificates are available from: General Register Office, Joyce House, 8/11 Lombard Street, Dublin 2. Phone: 353-1-671 1863. Research can also be conducted. Microfilm copies of the registers are available at the LDS. The birth entries for the years 1864–68 are included in the International Genealogical Index.

A useful account of this source is "Irish Civil Registration" in *The Irish At Home and Abroad* 2 (1994/95), pp. 15–19.

Register of Land Deeds

A deed is simply a written and witnessed undertaking by one or more parties. Although it can refer to any legal undertaking (e.g., a name change), the vast majority relate to transfers of property. They generally refer to leases of land, but may also concern mortgages, sales, marriage settlements, or other arrangements. Although the collection of registered deeds at the Irish Registry of Deeds is complete from 1708, only a small proportion of deeds made between individuals were formally registered at this office. The registry is also difficult to search, and professional assistance is advisable. Nevertheless, it is worth searching. The Registry of Deeds is at King's Inns, Henrietta Street, Dublin 1.

The Registry is indexed both by the name of the grantor (i.e., the person granting the land) and by the name of the townland(s) within each county, and, in

A page from an 1864 Civil Registration of Births.

Superintendent Registrar's District of _Edenderry_

18 _64_ Marriage solemnized at the Roman Catholic Chapel of _Rhode_ in the Registrar's District of _Rhode_
in the Union of _Edenderry_ in the County of _Kings_

No.	When Married.	Name and Surname.	Age.	Condition.	Rank or Profession.	Residence at the Time of Marriage.	Father's Name and Surname.	Rank or Profession of Father.
11	21 July 1864	Michel Dunne	26	Bachelor	Baker	Rathangan Co. Kildare	Edwd Dunne	Farmer
		Elizth Taylor	21	Spinster	Farmer	Esker Kings Co	Thomas Taylor	Farmer

Married in the Roman Catholic Chapel of _Rhode_ according to the Rites and Ceremonies of the Roman Catholic Church by me, _Laurence Whelan P.P._

This Marriage was solemnized between us, { _Michael Dunne_ _Elizth Taylor_ } in the Presence of us, { _Larry Ennis_ _John Mulvany_ Clerk }

18 ____ Marriage solemnized at the Roman Catholic Chapel of ____
in the Union of ____ in the Registrar's District of ____
in the County of ____

No.	When Married.	Name and Surname.	Age.	Condition.	Rank or Profession.	Residence at the Time of Marriage.	Father's Name and Surname.	Rank or Profession of Father.

A page from an 1866 Civil Registration of Marriages.

Superintendent Registrar's District _____ Registrar's District _____

18__. DEATHS Registered in the District of _____ in the Union of _____ in the County of _____

No.	Date and Place of Death.	Name and Surname.	Sex.	Condition.	Age last Birthday.	Rank, Profession, or Occupation.	Certified Cause of Death, and Duration of Illness.	Signature, Qualification, and Residence of Informant.	When Registered.	Signature of Registrar.

A page from an 1865 Civil Registration of Deaths.

some cases, barony. Many deeds contain valuable genealogical information, particularly leases made for the term of the life of specified persons. The witnesses to deeds were commonly relations of the parties concerned, and this relationship is often stated on the deed.

A description of the Registry and its genealogical value is given by Rosemary ffolliott in *Irish Genealogy— A Record Finder*, Heraldic Artists, Dublin. The surname and place-name index and copy memorials are also available on film at the LDS.

Description of Types of Records Listed for Each County

Since the first edition of this book, many new sources have come to light. More significantly, a very large proportion of the material available for Irish research has been indexed by the heritage centers which now exist in almost all Irish counties. In each county, both old and new family history sources and research contacts are presented in the following sections: A Brief History; Census and Census Substitutes; Church Records; Commercial and Social Directories; Family History; Gravestone Inscriptions; Newspapers; Wills and Administrations; Research Sources and Services; and Miscellaneous Sources. The significance and content of each of the above sections is explained below.

A Brief History

This section of each chapter is intended to give a general background to the local effects of the events affecting social and family history. It also describes other local events and factors of relevance to the family researcher. Emphasis is given to events which caused significant changes in population or family structure, e.g., wars, plantations, and the famine. The major family names associated with each county are also listed.

Census and Census Substitutes

This section includes censuses and various types of census substitutes, i.e., records which are not official censuses but fulfill the same function by listing local inhabitants. The different types of census substitutes are described below. Official censuses are described first, then each other type in the approximate chronological order of its occurence.

Official Government Censuses

A full census of the entire population of Ireland was first conducted in 1821 and subsequently at ten-year intervals. Although the statistical information from each census is available, few individual household returns for the entire country are available for any years other than 1901 and 1911. The individual household returns for the censuses of 1861 to 1891 were deliberately destroyed by government order (either to protect confidentiality or to make paper during the shortage of the First World War). Almost all of the returns for 1821 to 1851 were burned in the fire which destroyed the Public Record Office in 1922. Some remnants remain. The returns for 1901 and 1911 are a very valuable source of information, providing name, age, and relationship to the head of household of each resident person (see page 15). Also recorded is the county of birth of each member of the household. This is particularly useful in attempting to trace those who migrated within the country. The 1911 returns also note, for each couple, the number of children born and the number then living.

Indexes to some counties have been published (see Longford and Fermanagh), while heritage centers in other counties have indexes which will be searched for a fee.

The remaining census returns are housed in the National Archives, Bishop Street, Dublin 2; and in Public Record Office of Northern Ireland, 66 Balmoral Avenue, Belfast BT9 6NY, Northern Ireland.

Pension Claim Forms

A source which is based on the government censuses is the old age pension claim form. When old age pensions were introduced in 1908, individuals needed to show proof of age. However, civil registration only started in 1864. Many people applied for certificates to prove that they were listed (with age) on the census of 1841 (or 1851). These censuses existed until 1921. The claim forms (see Leitrim chapter for illustration) show applicant's name and expected entry on census, as well as the information found by the PRO staff. They are available at NAI, PRONI, and at SLC (films 0258525-48 and 0993085-108).

Civil Survey 1654–6

This survey was a preliminary description of the land-ownership of Ireland prior to its redistribution by the English Parliament following the defeat of the rebelling Irish Catholics in 1641. There was a massive confiscation of their lands, which were redistributed to English adventurers (those who had provided the funds to raise the army which put down the rebellion), to soldiers (as payment for services), and other groups. Commissioners were appointed and examined under oath the "most able and ancient inhabitants of the country." They pro-

CENSUS OF IRELAND, 1901.

(Two Examples of the mode of filling up this Table are given on the other side.)

FORM A.

No. on Form B.

RETURN of the MEMBERS of this FAMILY and their VISITORS, BOARDERS, SERVANTS, &c., who slept or abode in this House on the night of SUNDAY, the 31st of MARCH, 1901.

No.	NAME and SURNAME (Christian Name)	(Surname)	RELATION to Head of Family	RELIGIOUS PROFESSION	EDUCATION	AGE (Years)	AGE (Months)	SEX	RANK, PROFESSION, OR OCCUPATION	MARRIAGE	WHERE BORN	IRISH LANGUAGE	If Deaf and Dumb; Blind; Imbecile or Idiot; or Lunatic.
1	Mathew	Schreider	Head of fam	Jew	Cannot Read or Write not English	60		M.	Hebrew Teacher	Married	Russia		
2	Hannah	Shreider	Wife	Jewess	do not English	53		F.		Married	Russia		
3	Elias	Shreider	Son	Jew	read + write	24		M.	Dental Mechanic	not married	Russia		
4	Rosie	Shreider	Daughter	Jewess	read + write	19		F.		not married	Russia		
5	Leah	Schreider	Daughter	Jewess	read + write	14		F.		unmarried	Russia		

I hereby certify, as required by the Act 63 Vic., cap. 6, s. 6 (1), that the foregoing Return is correct, according to the best of my knowledge and belief.

Thomas Kelly P.C. 109ᵃ *(Signature of Enumerator.)*

I believe the foregoing to be a true Return.

Mathew Shreider his mark X *(Signature of Head of Family):*

A return from the 1901 census for the Schreider household, Dublin.

The Parrish of Killincoole

Is bounded on the east with the river of Castle Ring, on the south with the parrish of Derver and Dromiskin, on the west and north with the parrish of Lowth.

The tythes of the said parish both great and small were in the yeare 1640 in the possession of Arlander Usher Clerk as Incumbent there, being presented thereto by Pattrick Gernon of Killingcoole, patron of the said parrish. The said tythes with tenne acres of glebe land, and one howse and backside with a pidgeon howse in Killincoole, were worth in the yeare 1640.   50li per annum

In this parrish is conteyned the townes of: Allerdstowne, Killincoole and Whiterath

					li		
Henry Gernon of Miltowne th' one moytie and Pattrick Barnwall of Allardstowne the other moytye thereof Free lands	Allerdstowne 4 tates	280	Arrable 275 pasture 5		70	00	00

Bounded on the east with the river of Castle-Ring, on the south and southwest with the lands of Derver and Killincoole, on the west with the lands of Cordery and Whiterath, and on the north with Grange and Whiterath, A castle, a farme howse and divers cabbins, the said castle and towne belonging to Pattrick Barnwall.

					li		
Pattrick Gernon of Killincoole free lands 120 ac. p(ai)d 10s. per annum	Killincoole 3 tates	180	Arrable 170 pasture 10		40	00	00

Bounded on the east with the lands of Allardstowne, on the south with the lands of Derver, on the west with the lands of Rahessine and on the north with the lands of Allards- towne and Corderrye. The walls of 2 castles the tymber thereof being burnt, a ruinows mill, an old chappell and cabbins.

					li		
Stephen Taaffe of Athelare	Whiterath 2 tates	100	Arrable 80 pasture 20		25	00	00
10s. per annum che(ife) *These above named*							

Bounded on the east with the lands of Grange and Allerdstowne, on the south with the lands of Corderye and Allerdstowne, on the lands of Grange. A castle unroofed Noe commons in this parrish.

An extract from a copy of the Civil Survey giving a description and names of the landowners of the parish of Killincoole, County Louth, in 1654–56. From *Civil Survey*, vol. 10 (Dublin: R. C. Simington, Irish Manuscripts Commission, 1961).

duced a survey of landholders and also of the ancient boundaries, place-names, and antiquities of three provinces. The Civil Survey lists the owners of land in 1640. The parts which survive have been published by the Irish Manuscripts Commission, and the originals are in the NAI (see illustration above).

Books of Survey and Distribution

These are a compilation of the above survey and others conducted subsequently. It lists both the 1640 proprietors of lands and the owners following their "distribution." The further changes made in the Cromwellian resettlement of 1659, and at the Restoration of the British monarchy, are also noted. Four volumes have been published by the Irish Manuscripts Commission, and the remaining sets are in the NAI (see page 17).

Hearth Money Rolls

Starting in the 1660s, a tax was levied on Ireland based on the number of hearths in each house. Hearth Money Rolls have not survived for all counties, but those that do give householders' names in each parish. They are held in various archives and many have been published in periodicals (see page 198).

Subsidy Rolls

This was a form of tax levied, starting in the 1660s, on all those whose goods amounted to over £3 value or who had land of over £1 annual valuation. These lists are less comprehensive than Hearth Money Rolls, since the poor are excluded, but are valuable nonetheless. These are held in various archives, and many have been published in local history periodicals.

Muster Rolls

These are lists of men available for military purposes, i.e., as militia, yeomen, etc. The lists generally consist only of names and type of arms available. Addresses are not usually given. An example of a 1630 muster roll is in the Donegal chapter. Although there are many histories and other sources about specific military units, they usually only give names of officers (see page 488). Muster rolls provide names of all the men.

PARISH OF CLONTOUSKERT

BALLINTOBBER BARONY

County of Roscomon : Parish of Clontouskert : Ballintobber Bar :

No. of Reference in ye Alphabett	Proprietors Names Anno: 1641	Denominations	Number of Acres unprofittable	Numbr. of Acres profittable	No. of profittable Acres disposed of on ye Acts	To whom soe disposed wth their Title whether by Decree, Certificate or Patent, References to ye Record thereof	No. of ye Book or Roll & of ye Page or Skin
16	Tirlogh mc Dowell ..	Tulloghfusoge 1 : Cart. in Cooleshaghteny 1 qr:	—	015..0..00	015..0..00	Wm. Dellamare ⧸	
17	Gillernow mc: Dermot Hanley :: / Rory Ballow mc: Teig Hanley :: ..	Corry 1: Cartron of Cooleshaghteny containing of arrable Land ½ a Cart: / ½ a Cart:	—	028..0..00	028..0..00		

County of Roscomon   Ballintobber Baro : Parish of Clontouskert

No. of Reference in ye Alphabett	Proprietors Names Anno: 1641	Denominations	Number of Acres unprofittable	Numbr. of Acres profittable	No. of profittable Acres disposed of on ye Acts	To whom soe disposed wth their Title whether by Decree, Certificate or Patent, References to ye Record thereof	No. of ye Book or Roll & of ye Page or Skin
18	Henry Dillon in Keile and Shanballyloske.. / Turlogh oge mc Dowell here	Gallagmaghery ½ a qr. Cont. of Arrable Land 1: Cart:: / 1: Cart.	—	058..0..00	033..0..00	Wm. Dellamare ⧸	
19	Hugh oge ò Connor in Eden / In Garryduffe in Gologhmaghry	Galloghmaghry ye other ½ Quart. containing of Arrable Land .. / 1 Cart: / 1 Cart :/In Magalla : 8 qrs.	ǀ	084..0..00	102..0..00 / 7..0..00	Nicholas Mahon *Plus*	
20	Xtopher Delahide .. :: / Thomas Dillon .. ::	Carrowbane : 1 qr. containing of arrable .. :: / ½ gn: / ½ gn:	—	021..0..00	021..0..00		
21	Tumultogh Boy hanly ..	Two gneeves of Carrowbane Cont. of arrable Land .. :: / more of Pasturable Wood —ibm—	005..0..00	013..0..00 / 016..0..00	013..0..00 / 016..0..00	Wm. Dellamare ⧸	

Extract from a copy of the *Books of Survey and Distribution* showing the 1641 landowners in the parish of Clontouskert, Co. Roscommon, and the persons to whom the properties were subsequently granted. R.C. Simington, *Books of Survey and Distribution*, vol. 1. Dublin: Irish Manuscripts Commission, 1949.

Census of Ireland (1659)

This gives the names of "tituladoes" (those with title to land) and total number of persons overall. It also lists the numbers of families in each barony with Irish names. Copies are in the RIA, and they have been published by the Irish Manuscripts Commission.

Catholic Qualification Rolls and Converts

After 1692 a series of so-called "Penal Laws" were enacted which severely restricted the rights of Catholics in land and property ownership and almost all other areas of activity. These restrictions were gradually lifted toward the end of the eighteenth century for those Catholics who took an oath of allegiance and thereby "qualified." In 1778, for example, those taking the oath could take long-term land leases. In 1782 it allowed the buying and selling of land by Catholics. The rolls consist of those taking the oath. They are published in the *59th Report of the Deputy Keeper of Public Records of Ireland* (DKPRI), which is held in the NLI, NAI, and elsewhere (see page 431).

Some Catholics also converted to Protestantism, and are listed in Eileen O'Byrne's *The Convert Rolls: 1703–1838*, Dublin, S.O., 1981.

Religious Censuses

In several dioceses and in some parishes, censuses of parishioners were taken, in some cases for ecclesiastical administration purposes and in others for security reasons (since Catholic or "popish" was at many times in Irish history equated to "rebel"). The censuses vary widely in quality and accuracy. Copies are held in various archives and have been published in several sources. Perhaps the largest such census was commissioned in 1766, when each Church of Ireland minister was requested to provide a listing of the members of each denomination in his parish. Although some were completed as requested, many ministers provided only the details on Church of Ireland parishioners, and omitted Catholics, Presbyterians, etc. Others provided a complete survey of all local inhabitants, including family names and the numbers of children in the household. Those available are listed in relevant chapters.

Freeholders Lists

A freeholder was one who held land for the duration of his life or for that of a specified individual(s), as distinct from short-term leaseholders or annual rent payers. The significance of freeholder status is that they were entitled to vote. Lists are available for many counties at various periods. Where available, they usually give the address, sometimes the occupation, and occasionally voting tendency (see page 69).

1796 Spinning Wheel Premiums

During the late eighteenth century, the Linen Board attempted to encourage the growth of flax in Ireland. One innovative mechanism was to offer a free spinning wheel for every acre of flax planted in the year 1796. The list of those who received spinning wheels provides the name and parish of residence of over 52,000 persons. It is particularly useful for Northern counties, where the linen industry was strongest, but includes most counties. It is available in the NLI (Ref. IR 677 L3), PRONI, and LDS Family History Library, and microfiche copies of individual counties can be purchased from several sources.

Tithe Applotment Survey

Tithes were a form of tax payable by all religious denominations for maintenance of the Church of Ireland, which was the "established" (state-recognized) church until 1867. Between 1823 and 1837 a valuation was conducted to determine the tithe payable by each eligible local landholder. Tithes were only payable on certain types of land, and the tithe applotment survey is therefore far from comprehensive. It does not include any urban inhabitants, for instance. However, it is a valuable source. The surnames in the survey have been indexed (see *Griffith's Valuation*). The originals are in the NAI. Lists of tithe defaulters for 1831 are also available, and are being indexed by S. McCormac. Copies of the indexes will be made available in NAI and NLI; see *Irish Roots* 1 (1997): 25–28. (See page 326.)

Griffith's—and Other—Valuations

Between 1848 and 1864, all of the land of Ireland was surveyed for the purpose of establishing the level of rates (local tax) to be paid by each landholder or leaseholder. *Griffith's Valuation* lists each land- or householder in the country, giving the townland and description of the property (e.g., land; house; house and land; or house, outoffices/outbuildings, and land). It also lists the landlord and the annual valuation. Because of the shortage of other records, this is a very important substitute census, although it obviously does not cover all inhabitants of an area. It is particularly important in emigrant family research, as it was carried out during a period when much emigration occurred, and thus it can form a useful link between the information available about the local origins of an emigrant ancestor and the Irish records. The names occurring in both *Griffith's Valuation* and the *Tithe Applotment Survey* books

ARMAGH.

Houses of the Yearly Value of £.10 and upwards.

No.	Inhabitants' Names.	Yearly Value.		No.	Inhabitants' Names.	Yearly Value.	
		£.	s.			£.	s.
	Lower English-street:				Lower English-st.—*cont*^{d.}		
1	Francis M'Cormick	10	–	114	John Lyle	12	–
39	Hugh Lynch	10	–	121	Samuel Thompson	11	–
40	John Duff	10	10	128	John M'Elroy	10	–
41	Henry Mooney	10	–				
42	Patrick Cunningham	10	–		Upper English-street:		
53	Bernard Quin	10	–	1	William Caldwell	24	10
54	John Garland	10	–	2	Edward Parker	24	–
57	Edward Murphy	10	–	3	Peter M'Kee	20	–
58	Peter Kelly	10	–	4	James Donnelly	22	–
59	James M'Elroy	12	–	5	Sarah M'Glone	19	–
64	John Woods	10	–	6	Edward Hynes	30	–
65	James Donoghue	13	–	7	Patrick Downey	15	–
66	Owen Farley	10	–	8	Edward Corvin	18	–
68	James Dunne	12	–	9	Thomas Craig	45	–
70	Margaret Williamson	10	–	10	Arthur Branigan	19	–
71	Andrew Johnson	10	–	11	Bernard Hagan	19	–
73	John Allen	10	–	12	George Barnes	24	–
74	Peter M'Caghey	14	–	13	Miss Atkinson	30	–
76	Johnson Nelson	22	–	14	James F. Bell	50	–
77	John Williams	30	–	15	William Blacker	100	–
78	James Vogan	34	–	16	Mrs. Lyle	70	–
79	John Graham	16	–	17	John M'Kinstry	90	–
80	Patrick Corvin	15	–	18	R. J. Thornton	100	–
81	Michael M'Bride	19	–	19	Robert C. Hardy	70	–
82	Patrick Carberry	10	–	20	Leonard Dobbin, jun.	100	–
83	Patrick Devlin	19	–	21	John Stanley	130	–
–	Patrick Stores	10	–	22	James Moore	40	–
84	James Dickson	19	–	23	Mrs. Dundass	24	–
85	Robert Caldwell	29	10	24	James Rickard	60	–
86	John Evatt	10	–	25	Hugh Freanor	55	–
87	Cathrine Donnelly	12	–	26	Dr. Vogan	60	–
89	James Feely	14	–	27	Matthew Bell	130	–
90	Patrick M'Kew	12	–	28	Messrs. Colville	63	–
92	James Bennett, jun.	40	–	29	Robert Cochrane	50	–
93	James Starr	18	–	30	James Smyth	50	–
94	Ditto	15	–	31	Robert M'Endow	55	–
95	William Walker	20	–	32	Samuel Gardner	50	–
96	Joshua Vogan & Co.	160	–	33	Ditto	75	–
97	Edward M'Donald	15	–	34	Mrs. Dundass	45	–
98	William Jones	10	–	35	Alexander Bright	20	–
99	Eleanor Steele	10	–	36	Greer & Mackay	70	–
100	William O'Neill	10	10	37	William Rogers	120	–
101	Robert Garvey	10	–	38	John Adams	90	–
104	Patrick M'Manus	12	–	39	William Carroll	40	–
106	John Downey	10	–	40	Ulster Bank	90	–
111	Francis Sleaven	12	–	41	Vogan & Matthews	55	–

An extract from tables showing the holders of houses of more than £10 annual valuation in the town of Armagh. This is a sample of the information on ratepayers and voters presented to the Select Committee on Fictitious Votes, 1837. From *Parliamentary Papers*, Appendix G, 1837, 2 (1).

have been indexed for each county in the surname index compiled by the National Library of Ireland. Microfilmed copies are available in several libraries. A more easily used, although less detailed, index to *Griffith's Valuation* is available for Dublin, Cork, and Belfast cities and for certain other counties. This index, on microfilm, is compiled by All Ireland Heritage Inc. (Vienna, VA). It is available in NLI and NAI. In addition, local heritage centers have indexed the *Griffith's Valuation* for most counties and will search it for a fee. Valuations continue to be made on property, and the information can be valuable in tracking changes of ownership. An account of these records is given by D. A. Radford in "Irish Valuation Records," *The Irish At Home and Abroad* 1 (Winter 1993/94): 7–10. (See page 167.)

Local Censuses and Map Indexes

There are detailed censuses for some towns and districts, the reasons for which are sometimes obscure. Detailed maps, particularly estate maps, of some towns also give the names of landholders shown (see pages 204, 289).

Lists of Freemen

In medieval cities, members of all trade corporations had to be freemen of the city, a status conferred by the corporation (city council). In later centuries, the status of freeman of specified cities and towns was given to persons whom the city wished to honor. They were therefore generally prominent citizens or visitors. However, as this status also conferred voting rights, it was abused in some cities so as to admit voters for certain candidates or parties. Few Catholics were made freemen during the eighteenth century. Lists of Freemen generally contain few personal details.

Rate Books (or Poor Law Rate Books)

Under the Poor Law Relief Act (1838), landholders were required to contribute to programs to help the poor in their area. The funds ran the local workhouse or went to "outdoor relief." Districts, called Poor Law Unions, were set up for collection and distribution of these contributions, or "rates." These ratepayers would generally be the holders of property of a certain annual valuation. The books list the ratepayers by area, their holding, and valuation.

Workhouse Records

Workhouses for the "relief of the destitute poor" were built as a result of the Poor Relief (Ireland) Act of 1838, commonly known as the Poor Law. The poor within each Poor Law Union were fed and sheltered in the workhouse in return for basic work. The records of many of these are excellent, providing the names of those entering and leaving on a daily basis, and also of the persons availing of assisted emigrations. The records are located in various local and national libraries, and many are on film in the LDS library.

Estate Rentals

The vast majority of small farmers and town-dwellers rented their properties from large landowners, many of whom lived abroad. The records of these estates can include details of their tenants. The records are scattered and highly variable in value. Only a small number of the available rentals are listed in this book. Estate rentals will often list only the estate's principal tenants, i.e., those from whom the estate directly collected rent. These tenants would, in turn, have rented to subtenants.

To trace estate rentals, it is first necessary to find the name of the ancestor's landlord, through *Griffith's Valuation*, for instance. A search for the estate records or family papers can then be made. Richard J. Hayes's *Manuscript Sources for the History of Irish Civilisation* (NLI) is one valuable listing of estate papers. Many estate papers are held in the National Archives, National Library, PRONI, and in county libraries. Other estate papers and records in private hands are listed in *Analecta Hibernica*, volumes 15, 20, and 25, and (for Cork/Kerry) in Eugene O'Casey's *O'Kief, Coshe Mang and Slieve Luachra*. From 1849 to 1885 the estates of insolvent owners were sold at public auction. Auction notices generally listed properties and tenants' names. These records of "encumbered estates," indexed by landlord's name, are available in the NLI and NAI (see below).

Encumbered Estates

Between 1848 and 1880, about three thousand bankrupt estates (5 million acres) were sold at public auction. These were sold through an Encumbered Estates Court, which later became the Landed Estates Court. Descriptions or prospectuses of the estates sold at these auctions are available, and many contain lists of the sitting tenants and details of their leases. They are in the NLI and at the LDS on films 0258793–0258850.

Voters Lists

Lists of voters (or Election Poll Books) are available for various periods, particularly in the large towns and cities. Note, however, that the vote was restricted for much of this period. A listing and description of such sources is given by B.W. Walker and K.W. Hoppen in *Irish Book Lore* 3 (1) and 4 (2). A large number of lists relating to those entitled to vote was also produced as evidence for the "Commission on Fictitious Votes" in 1837 and 1838. These include lists of freemen, marksmen

**The Percentage of Members of Each of the Major Religions in
Each County in the Census of 1861**

County	Catholic	Protestant	Presbyterian	Methodist
Province of Connaught (population 913,135)				
Galway	96.5	3.0	0.2	0.2
Leitrim	89.8	9.1	0.3	0.8
Mayo	96.8	2.6	0.4	0.2
Roscommon	96.1	3.6	0.2	0.1
Sligo	90.1	8.4	0.7	0.6
Province of Ulster (population 1,914,236)				
Antrim	27.5	20.2	47.6	2.4
Armagh	48.8	30.9	16.2	3.2
Cavan	80.5	14.9	3.5	0.9
Derry	45.3	16.9	35.1	0.6
Donegal	75.1	12.6	11.0	1.0
Down	32.3	20.5	44.5	1.4
Fermanagh	56.5	38.4	1.8	3.3
Tyrone	56.5	21.9	19.5	1.6
Monaghan	73.4	14.0	12.0	0.3
Province of Leinster (population 1,457,635)				
Carlow	88.4	10.9	0.2	0.3
Dublin	75.5	20.9	1.8	0.7
Kildare	87.0	11.5	1.0	0.4
Kilkenny	94.9	4.8	0.2	0.1
Laois	88.3	10.7	0.3	0.5
Longford	90.4	8.6	0.8	0.1
Louth	91.5	6.9	1.3	0.3
Meath	93.6	5.9	0.4	0.1
Offaly	88.8	10.1	0.4	0.4
Westmeath	92.1	7.0	0.4	0.2
Wexford	90.4	8.9	0.2	0.3
Wicklow	81.0	17.7	0.3	0.8
Province of Munster (population 1,513,558)				
Clare	97.8	2.0	0.1	0.1
Cork	90.7	8.0	0.3	0.5
Kerry	96.7	3.1	0.1	0.5
Limerick	94.7	4.5	0.3	0.3
Tipperary	94.3	5.1	0.2	0.2
Waterford	95.1	3.9	0.4	0.2

Source: *Irish Church Records* (Dublin: Flyleaf Press, 1992).

```
        Dec 20   MACLATCHY Mary, of Moses, Newry, servant
            21   AICKEN Mary, of Robert
            25   SCOTT Agnus, of Andrew
1780 Jan  1   HARRISON Mary, of James
       Feb  7   AICKIN Elizabeth, of John
            20   BRANNEN Elizabeth, of John
1781 Oct  5   TOWNLEY Esther, of James, Newry, Grocer and Merchant
             5   COMBS Mary, of William, Newry, Glazier
             5   MITCHELL Mary, of John, Newry, sadler
             5   NELSON Anne, of . . . , Sugar Island, Smith
       Nov 11   TOWNLEY Samuel, of Samuel, junr, Newry, merchant
            22   ROBISON Thomas, of Andrew, Rockhamilton, linen draper
            23   McGUFFIN Letty, of Richard, Newry, shoemaker
            23   GLENN Mary, of George, Newry, Flaxdresser
            26   ANDERSON John, of John, Newry, woollen draper
            28   CALBREATH Matthew, of James, Newry, Hardware merchant
       Dec  4   McKINSTRY Robert, of William, Canal Street, Carpenter
            11   PETTY Samuel, of Samuel, High Street, Shoemaker
            12   CUNINGHAM Isabella, of Edward*, Derrylecka, farmer
                        *This person's father was a Roman Catholic, his mother a
                        Dissenter, he alone of all the children embraced the
                        Protestant Faith
            13   WHARTON . . . . , of George, Derrylecka, Weaver
            16   MOORE John, of Joseph, Benagh, Weaver
                 BELL Mary, of Robert, Newry, Apothecary

1782 Jan  9   McMINN Archibald, of James, Desart, farmer
            11   GREER Deborah, of William, Newry (Liberty), Gent
            13   McCULLOCH John, of William, Scott's Park, Labourer
            20   HARLAND Mary, of Samuel, Pollock's Green, Bleacher
            20   BETTERTON Juliana, of Thos Wm, Newry, Dancing Master and Player
            24   DAVIDSON Jane, of Arthur, Newry, Chandler
            30   LITTLE John, of William, Altnaveagh, Farmer
            30   RIGGS Mary, of Alexr, Cloghoran, Farmer
            30   THOMPSON George, of Ross, Liberty, Merchant
            31   HALL John, of . . . . , High Street, Breeches-maker
       Feb  2   BROWN Peter, of Samuel, Pound Street, Slater
             9   PATTY Samuel, of George, High Street, Gardener
            10   GRAHAM Margaret, of Gerard, Derrylackah, Weaver
            11   AIKINS James, of John, Sugar Island, Cabinet maker
            18   DODDS Catherine, of John, Crobane, weaver
            21   . . . . William, of . . . . High Street, servant
       Mch  4   EAGER George, of David, Canal Street
             5   TATE . . . , of David, Creeve, Bailif
             8   McMURRAY John, of . . . . , Canal Street, Guager
            10   POLLOCK Elizabeth, of Alexander, High Street, Shoemaker
```

Extract of baptisms from a transcript of the "Registers of the First Presbyterian Church of Newry, Co. Down 1779–1796," *Irish Ancestor* 11 (1) (1979).

(those entitled to vote by making a mark rather than a signature), and other lists for some towns.

Church Records

Because of the relative lack of other comprehensive sources of information, church records are the most important source of information on Irish family relationships. The value, quality, and accessibility of church records of each denomination is discussed in *Irish Church Records* (Dublin: Flyleaf Press, 1992), and briefly discussed below. Other useful guides to location of registers are John Grenham's *Tracing Your Irish Ancestors* (Dublin: Gill and McMillan, 1992), and Brian Mitchell's *A Guide to Irish Parish Registers*, Baltimore, 1988.

Church of Ireland (Protestant or Episcopalian) Records

These records generally start earlier than Catholic records, the earliest being 1619. Although there was a legal obligation on the Church of Ireland to keep records from 1634, in practice most began after 1750. In 1876 a law was enacted that all Church of Ireland registers be sent for safekeeping to the Public Record Office (PRO) in Dublin. This was later amended to allow ministers with suitable storage to keep their own registers. Other ministers sent copies, or kept copies, of their books. Almost all of the registers sent to the PRO, approximately half of those in existence, were destroyed in a fire in 1922.

Copies of available records have been compiled since then and are kept either in the NAI, in the custody of the local clergyman, or, in a few cases, in the Library of the Representative Church Body (RCB), which is the administrative body for the Church of Ireland. In Northern Ireland, the PRONI has over two hundred parish registers. Both RCB and PRONI have published guides to their holdings. Note also that non-Catholic marriages have been registered by the state from 1845, when the Church of Ireland, Presbyterian, or other minister was made a state registrar. These records are in the General Register Office. Details on Church of Ireland parishes are listed under each county. A full account of the range of Church of Ireland records is given by R. Refausse in *Irish Church Records* (Dublin: Flyleaf Press, 1992, pp. 41–68). Also, some records in different parts of Ireland have been indexed by Mark Williams' Anglican Record Project. The results of this project are available in RCBL and in the Society of Genealogists (London). In addition, a series of (mainly Dublin) registers were published by the Parish Register Society and are widely available.

Presbyterian Records

Presbyterians in Ireland are very predominantly located in Ulster. In the 1861 census, for instance, over ninety-six percent of Presbyterians were in this province, and particularly in the counties of Antrim, Derry, and Down (see page 21). Presbyterian records generally do not begin until after 1819, from which year Presbyterian ministers were required to keep records (see page 22). However, because marriages in Presbyterian churches or kirks were not recognized until 1845, many Presbyterian marriages took place in the Church of Ireland. Also, the Presbyterian church rarely kept burial records. Note also that there are several branches of Presbyterianism. A full account of the origins and significance of these different groups, and a full list of the records of Presbyterian churches, is given by Dr. Christine Kinealy in *Irish Church Records* (Dublin: Flyleaf Press, 1992, pp. 69–106). Presbyterian congregations and their ministers are detailed in *History of Congregations in the Presbyterian Church in Ireland 1610–1982* (Belfast: Presbyterian Historical Society of Ireland, 1982).

Baptist Records

The Baptist community in Ireland was always very small, and numbered only 4,237 in 1861. Their records are not available in a central repository, but are preserved within each church. The Irish Baptist Historical Society, 117 Lisburn Road, Belfast BT9 7AF, can assist with parish addresses, etc. They also publish a journal. An account of the origins and record-keeping practices of the Baptist church is given by H.D. Gribbon in *Irish Church Records* (Dublin: Flyleaf Press, 1992, pp. 183–191).

Huguenot Church Records

Although effectively an Anglican church, many of the French emigré Huguenots maintained their own churches in Ireland for generations after their arrival. The records of three Dublin churches (the earliest being 1668) are contained in volumes 7 and 14, and of Portarlington in volume 19, of the Proceedings of the Huguenot Society of London. The records of other Huguenot groups either do not exist, or are included in the local Church of Ireland records. A full account of the origins and records of the various Huguenot communities is given by Vivienne Costello in *Irish Church Records* (Dublin: Flyleaf Press, 1992, pp. 171–182).

Quaker Records

The Religious Society of Friends, or Quaker, communities arguably have the best records of any Irish religious group. Quakers have been active in Ireland since 1653,

Marriage register of the South Parish (St. Finbar's), Cork City, 1775, from *Irish Church Records* (Dublin: Flyleaf Press, 1992).

and established meetings in many parts of the country. Their records are now located at either the Dublin Friends Historical Library (DFHL) or, for Ulster, at the Ulster Archives Committee at Lisburn (4 Magheralave Rd., Lisburn, Co. Antrim, N. Ireland BT28 3BD). Records are also available in the LDS on films 0571395-98. A full account of the origins and records of the Quakers in Ireland is given by Richard Harrison in *Irish Church Records* (Dublin: Flyleaf Press, 1992, pp. 15-

40). Another source is Olive Goodbody's *Guide to Irish Quaker Records 1654–1860* (Dublin: IMC, 1967). The classical history of Quakers is John Rutty's *A History of the Rise and Progress of the People called Quakers in Ireland from the year 1653 to 1700* (London: Phillips, 1800).

Methodist Records

Research on Methodists requires some understanding of the complex interrelationships between the various

Methodist groups in Ireland, and with the Church of Ireland. Methodist records are found at various archives, and in their original circuit premises. The Wesley Historical Society (Aldersgate House, 9-11 University Road, Belfast) is a major source of information on Irish Methodism. A full account of the origins and records of Irish Methodism is given by Marion G. Kelly, Honorary Archivist of this society, in *Irish Church Records* (Dublin: Flyleaf Press, 1992, pp. 139-161).

Jewish Records

Although the early Jewish population of Ireland is very small (only 393 were recorded in the 1861 census and 5,381 in 1891), they have been prominent in Irish politics and public life. The records are mainly preserved within the Irish Jewish Museum in Dublin. An account of the Jewish communities is Louis Hyman's *A History of the Jews in Ireland*, London/Jerusalem, 1972.

Roman Catholic Church Records

Church records are undoubtedly the most important record source for Catholics. However, most rural Catholic churches do not begin records until after 1820. This is because of restrictions on the Catholic church by the Penal Laws, internal church disorganization, poverty of many rural parishes, and other factors. Urban records tend to be earlier, but even here few begin before 1760. Nevertheless, there are early records for individual parishes in almost all parts of the country. The reasons for the significant variability in existence and content of Catholic records are given by this author in *Irish Church Records* (Dublin: Flyleaf Press, 1992, pp. 107-138). The records themselves are highly variable in terms of legibility of handwriting, level of detail, and state of preservation. At worst, the handwriting can be virtually illegible, written in Latin using the writer's own abbreviations, giving only the most basic information, e.g., date followed by (baptism) "Patrick of James and Honora Murphy." In addition, the ink may be faded, and the register book may be torn at the edges, overwritten, or have pages missing. At best, the records are written in beautiful copperplate handwriting in neat columns, giving full details (dates, names, and residences) in well-preserved books. All possible combinations of these variables will be found. Names of witnesses are almost always given, and these may sometimes give clues to other family associations. (See page 24.)

Almost all Catholic record books have been microfilmed and are held by the National Library and at the Family History Library in Salt Lake City. However, not all are available for consultation by researchers. Some dioceses require that the specific permission of the Bishop be obtained to consult these microfilms. Some of the LDS films are available through their branch libraries. There is also a major program, organized by the Irish Genealogical Project, to index these records. The indexed records are held in local heritage centers (or equivalent), who will search their indexes for a fee. The records of most Irish counties have now been indexed, and the contact details for the relevant center are indicated in each chapter.

If it is necessary to contact a Catholic parish, the priests' names and full contact details are listed in the *Irish Catholic Directory* (Dublin: Veritas Publications), which is issued annually.

A common problem in research is to ascertain which church an ancestor attended. The Roman Catholic Records section lists all of the civil parishes in each county and indicates the Catholic church which its inhabitants are likely to have attended. This information has been gleaned from a range of sources, but principally Lewis's *Topographical Dictionary of Ireland*, 1837, and the "tentative list" provided in the introductory pages of the "Surname Index" to *Griffith's Valuation* and the *Tithe Applotment Survey* compiled by the National Library of Ireland.

A sample entry of information given in the Roman Catholic Church Records section and a discussion of the relevance of each of the items of information is given below:

Civil Parish: Ballymoney
Map Grid: 12
RC Parish: Ballymoney and Derrykeighan
Diocese: CR
Earliest Record: b. 3.1853; m. 4.1853; d. 1879
Status: LC; NLI (mf); Indexed by UHF (b/m to 1900; d. to 1887)

Civil Parish: Lists all of the civil parishes in each county in alphabetical order. The common alternate names for civil parishes are also indicated. Note that there are many different spellings of some of these parishes.

Map Grid: Lists the reference number of the civil parish on the county map at the end of each county section. The parishes are listed in sequence (left to right and top to bottom) within each of the baronies in the county.

RC Parish: This indicates the Catholic church which the inhabitants of this civil parish are likely to have attended. Note that the Catholic parish name is often not the same as the civil parish name. Indeed, individual civil parishes may be served by several Catholic parishes or vice versa.

NOBILITY AND GENTRY.

Note.—The private Residents of the Professional and Trading Classes will be found under their respective heads.

Achmuty (Mrs. S.) 23, *Rutland-str.*
Acton (Miss M.) 77, *Stephen's-gr. S*
Adair (Mrs.) 64, *Mount-street,* and *Belgrove, Monasterevan.*
Adams (Mrs. Isabella) 2, *Russell-st.*
Adams (Sam. esq.) 45, *Eccles-street.*
Adamson (J. esq.) 55, *Aungier-str.*
Adamson (Rev. A.S.) 14, *Blackhall-st.*
Agar (Wm. esq.) 4, *Molesworth-str.*
Airey (Maj. Gen.) 14, *Merr.-sq. N.*
Alexander (Robert, sen. esq.) 12, *Merrion-square,* and *Seapoint.*
Alexander (Sir Wm.) *Booterstown.*
Alexander (W.J.esq.) 16, *Fitz-sq.W.*
Alexander (W. esq.) 4, *up. Baggot-s.*
Alexander (W. esq.) 1, *Richmond-pl.*
Allen (Captain) 3, *Richmond-street.*
Allen (Edm. esq.) 3, *low. Fitzw.-str.*
Allen (Lieu.Col.) 36, *l. Gardiner's-s.*
Allen (Lord Viscount) 10, *Merrion-square, S.*
Allen (Rich. esq.) 24, *Eccles-street.*
Anderson (E.esq.) 33, *up.Gloucester-s.*
Anderson (Mrs.) 15, *Charlemont-st.*
Anderson (Mrs.) 18, *Mount-street.*
Anderson (Mrs. M.) 12, *Cuffe-str.*
Anderson (Mrs.) 148, *Mecklb.-str.*
Anderson (Rob. esq.) 22, *Brunsw.-s.*
Annesley (Hon.Fra.) 29, *Molesw.-st.*
Annesley (Rev. Mr.) 2, *S. Cumb.-st.*
Anson (Hon. G.) 3d Guards, *Dublin Castle.*
Arabin (Henry, esq.) 12, *Clare-str.* and *Corka, Clondalkin.*
Archbold (Miss E.) 39, *Gloucester-st.*
Archdall (John, esq.) *Merrion-str.*
Archdall (Hon.Mrs.M)1, *Kildare-p. Castle Archdall, Co. Fermanagh.*
Archer (Ald.) 9, *Gardiner's-place.*
Archer (Mrs.) 65, *Stephen's-gr. S.*
Archer (John esq.) *North-wall.*
Ardagh (Dean of) 26, *Harcourt-st.*

Armagh (Archd. of) 7, *Mer.-sq. E.* and *Aughnacloy.*
Armit (John, esq.) 1, *Kildare-street,* and *Newtown-park.*
Armitage (Mrs.) 45, *Bishop-street.*
Armstrong (Capt.) 17, *Prussia-str.*
Armstrong (Col.) 73, *Mount-street.*
Armstrong (Colonel) *Merrion-str.*
Armstrong (E. esq.)51, *Dominick-st*
Armstrong (Mrs. D.) 12, *l. Dorset-st*
Armstrong (Mrs.) 43, *up. Rutl.-str.*
Armstrong (Rev. Mr.)32, *Hardw.-st.*
Armstrong (R. esq.) *up. Baggot-str.*
Armstrong (Tho. esq.) 41, *Bless.-st.*
Arnold (Jas. esq.) 45, *up. Rutland-st.* and *Banbridge, Co. Down.*
Arran (Dowager Countess of) 21, *Kildare-street.*
Arthure (B. esq.) 42, *Dominick-str.*
Arthure (Mrs.) 8, *Charlemont-str.*
Arthure (Mrs. J.) 9, *Gloucester-str.*
Ashe (Major) 4, *up. Rutland-street.*
Ashe (Mrs.) 24, *Mount-street.*
Ashe (Mrs. W.) 45, *Leeson-street.*
Ashworth (J. esq.) 5, *S. Cumb.-str.*
Ashworth (R. esq.) 16, *Mer.-sq. N.*
Atkinson (John, esq.) 1, *Ely-place.*
Atkinson(John,esq.)3, *Blessington-st.*
Atkinson (Jos. esq.) 34, *gt. Ship-st.*
Attorney-General (Rt. Hon. the) 27, *Steph.-gr. N. & Carysfort-park.*
Austin (Colonel) *Dublin Castle.*
Aylmer (Lord) *Royal Hospital.*
Aylmer (Mrs. Cath.) 1, *Eccles-str.*
Aylmer (Mrs. E.) 24, *Queen-street,*
Aylward (Nich. esq.) 9, *Temple-str.* and *Shankhill Castle, Co. Kilkenny.*
B.
Babington(Mrs.T.)14, *Blessington-s.*
Bacon (James C.esq.) 27, *Temple-str.*
Bacon (Miss S.) 8, *gt. Ship-street.*
Bagot (Mrs. D.) 36, *Leeson-street.*

A list of nobility and gentry from *Wilson's Dublin Directory* for the year 1820.

If the relevant church is not within the civil parish, this column will refer the reader to the appropriate church and civil parish. Thus "see Rathcormack" means that Rathcormack church serves the inhabitants of this civil parish, and that it is detailed opposite the civil parish of the same name. If the church parish does not have the same name as the civil parish, it will be referred to, for example, as "Ovens, see Athnowen." This means that the name of the church is Ovens, and that it is detailed opposite the civil parish of Athnowen.

In some cases, a civil parish may be served by several surrounding church parishes. In this case the column will state, for example, "part Skibereen, see Creagh; part Caheragh." This means that part of the parish is served by the church of Skibereen, which is described opposite the civil parish of Creagh, and that another part is served by Caheragh church, which is described opposite the civil parish of the same name.

Diocese: Lists the Church of Ireland (not Catholic) diocese to which the civil parish belonged prior to 1880. This is relevant to tracing probate records. (Inevitably there have been some changes in boundaries which cannot be adequately accounted for here. If the civil parish of interest is on the boundary of two dioceses, it may be necessary to check records for both dioceses.)

Earliest Record: Lists the earliest record of each of the three types of record in the order of baptism, marriage, and death/burial. The records are listed by the (month and) year of the starting record. Records which start after 1880 are generally not microfilmed, and indexing by heritage centers ends at 1900. If the records of the church which serves the area of interest start too late to be of value, it may be useful to check the other surrounding churches. A late start to the records may suggest that the church did not exist before the records started and that a different church was attended at the time.

Missing Dates: Lists the dates for which the records are missing, specifically the month and year in which the records stopped and then resumed, e.g., 2.1865-8.1878 means that the records stop at some date in February 1865 and resume at some date in August 1878. As can be seen, there are very often extensive gaps in the records, due, for instance, to lost or damaged records, or to the negligence or unavailability of the priest.

Status: Gives the location of the records and their status in regard to indexation, publication, etc. Virtually all Catholic records are still in local custody (LC) in their original parishes. However, since most records have been indexed, it is no longer necessary to contact the priests for searches. They are also available on microfilm in the NLI and the LDS libraries. The location of the indexing centers is indicated in each chapter in the Research Services section. They can also be accessed on the Internet at http://www.mayo-ireland.ie/roots.htm.

Commercial and Social Directories

Ireland has a good selection of commercial directories. These list the various tradesmen, professionals, gentry, and, in some cases, inhabitants of towns and cities.

The most comprehensive directories are: *Commercial Directory of Ireland*, Manchester: J. Pigot, 1820; *City of Dublin and Hibernian Provincial Directory*, Manchester: James Pigot & Co., 1824; and *Royal National Commercial Directory of Ireland*, Manchester: Slater's, 1846, 1856, 1870, and 1881. These cover most large towns in the country, and are available in many libraries and in microfiche editions. There are also many local directories, some of which are excellent, with detailed lists of occupants by street. Others will only list the more prominent citizens. The earlier directories, in particular, concentrated on the more prominent persons and the "big houses." An example is the rare Ambrose Leet's *Directory to the market towns, villages, gentlemen's seats and other noted places*, Dublin, 1814. Gentlemen's residences can also be found in other sources, such as Samuel Lewis's *A Topographical Dictionary of Ireland*, London, 1837 (reprinted by Genealogical Publishing Co., Baltimore). (See page 6.)

Most commercial directories include lists of local public officials, magistrates, and gentry (see page 26), and most have a list of tradesmen. Some of the better directories also include a house-by-house list of occupants on each street and are therefore very valuable in locating urban dwellers. In some cases the directories also list the major farmers in the immediate vicinity of the town.

Directories are particularly good for Dublin (see illustrations in the Dublin chapter). There are annual directories from 1755 to the present day. From 1755 to 1815 *The Treble Almanack* included only merchants and traders; from 1815 to 1834 it contained nobility and gentry as well. In that year, Pettigrew and Oulton's *Dublin Almanac* began with a house-to-house listing of the main streets, and from 1835 it also contained an alphabetical list of individuals. This directory ceased publication in 1849, but in the meantime Thom's *Directory* had begun. This contained all of the lists in Pettigrew and Oulton's and other additional information. It has been published every year up to the present.

There are also directories of specific occupations and trades. The clerical and medical directories have been mentioned earlier, but other directories should also be checked, particularly if an ancestor had a trade that might have been centrally organized through a guild or organization.

Copies of the national directories and the Dublin directories are available in many libraries. Some local directories, however, are very rare and only available in NLI or TCD Library. As many have been abstracted in local history journals, you should check the Census Substitutes section for a possible reference.

Family History

An ideal scenario for many is to find that their ancestors have been described in detail by some previous researcher. Although this is rarely the case, the possibility always exists. Published histories usually deal

THE INSCRIPTIONS OF MAGHEROSS CEMETERY

by

Rev. Pádraig Ó Mearáin

In the southern end of the town of Carrickmacross stand the remains of a church destroyed in the rebellion of 1641 and rebuilt in 1682. Surrounding this church is the ancient grave-yard of Magheross. Although P. S. Ó Dalaigh in "Sketches of Farney" mentions a headstone dated 1651, the oldest one that we discovered was dated 1664. The last burial in the grave-yard was in 1955.

The references at the end are to the numbers of the tomb-stones.

1. Elizabeth Connolly of Killough, who died at Carrickma-cross October 5th 1855, aged 70 Yrs.

   This stone is erected by the surviving members of the family whom she served devotedly and faithfully for 46 years. Close beside whose burial ground at her own re-quest her remains are now interred.

2. John Clarke of Carrickmacross, aged 85 years. Also his Father. His mother Mary died 28th Dec. 1895, aged 85 years. R.I.P.

   (on the other side)

   And his brothers John, died 7th Nov. 1882. Aged 35 years. Patrick, died 20th April 1890. Aged 55 years. R.I.P.

3. Here lies the body of Patrick Mc. Cabe. He died in January 7th 1775 aged 68 years.
   Erected by Peter Mc Cabe.

4. This stone was erected by Francis Merron, Box, in memory of his father Patrick Merron who departed this life.

5. Erected by Phillip Duffy in memory of his mother who de-parted this life 26th Jany 1827 aged 56 years.
   Requiescat in Pace.

6. I. H. S. John Mc Adden died in ye year of Our Lord 1794.

7. Here lyeth the body of Thomas Marron who departed this life November ye 8th 1774 aged 48 years. This stone was erected by Nean Marron wife to the said Thomas Marron who departed this life. Feb.ry in the 56th year of her age. Also the body of Alexdr. Howes who departed this life July 3rd 1772 in the 7th year of his age.

8. This stone was erected by Henry Carrol in memory of his

Transcripts from "Gravestone Inscriptions from the Cemetery of Magheross near Carrickmacross, Co. Monaghan," *Clogher Record 5* (1) (1963).

Butter in casks, 5l. 12s. 6d. to 00s. od. per cwt. of 112l.
Ditto in bowls 0l. 1s. 1d. to 1s. 1hd. per lb. of 16 oz.
Green Pork . 0l. 43s. 0d. to 48s. od. per cwt. 112lb.
Bacon . . 5l. 16s. 8d. to 00s. od. per ditto.
Apple Potatoes 0l. 9s. 5d. to 00s. od. per ditto.
Black ditto . 0l. 8s. 6d. to 00s. od. per ditto.
New ditto . 0l. 8s. od. to 8s. 8d per ditto.

Price of Meat at New Market.

Beef . 8d. to 10d. per lb. | Pork . 0d. to 5d. per lb.
Mutton 7d. to 10hd. per lb. | Fed Veal 8d. to 9d. per do.
Lamb . 5s. od. to 6s. 6d. per quarter.

Patrick-street Market.

Beef . 6d. to 8d. per lb. | Pork 4d. to 5d. per lb.
Mutton 7d. to 9d. ditto. | Veal 6hd. to 8d. ditto.
Lamb 4s. 10hd. to 6s. 6d. per quarter.

Price of Potatoes and Eggs at the Little Green.

Apple Potatoes . . . . 9s. 2hd. per cwt.
Black ditto . . . . . . 8s. 1hd. per ditto.
Eggs (six score to a hundred) . . . 6s. 6d. to 8s. 1hd.

Price of Potatoes on George's Quay.

Apple . . 9s. 6d. to 0s. od. per cwt. of 112lb.
Black . . 8s. 1hd. to 0s. od. ditto.

Price of Coals on Sir John's and City Quay.

Whitehaven . 32s. to 0s. | Harrington . 37s. to 0s.
Chester . . 31s. to 0s. | Wilmington . 30s. to 3s.

Price of Butter at the Crane on Usher's-quay.

Butter in casks . 5l. 12s. to 5l. 18s. per cwt.

Price of Hydes at the City Crane, Bonham-street.

Dry Hides, 8d. per lb.; ditto Kipps, 9d. per lb.; ditto Calf-skins, 13d. per lb.; Green Ox hides, 50s. to 56s. per cwt.; Salted Hides, 45s. per cwt.; Salted Calf-skins 7d. per lb.; ditto Kipps, 6d. per lb.

DUBLIN MARKET NOTE FOR WEEK ENDING SEPTEMBER 4.

		from s.	from d.	to s.	to d.	Mid. P s.	Mid. P d.
696	Wheat, per Bar 20 Stone,	50	0	91	0	77	0
9411	Flour, per Cwt............	25	0	52	0	0	0
6 5	Bere, per Bar............	22	0	27	6	24	11½
0	Barley, per Bar..........	0	0	0	0	0	0
1341	Oats, per Bar............	28	6	41	0	36	0½
350	Oatmeal, per Cwt.........	32	0	88	0	34	7
0	Peas.....................	0	0	0	0	0	0
	SOLD TO BAKERS ONLY,						
13	Barrels of Wheat.........	80	0	91	0	86	0
5452	Cwt. of Flour............	42	0	52	0	48	4½

Average Price of Wheat and Flour, 12l. 8d. per Sack.

Receipts......... 5400 { 1st, from 51s. 0d. to 52s. 0d. / 2d, from 40s. 0d. to 50s. 0d.

MEETING OF CREDITORS.

At the Royal Exchange, Dublin, at the hour of two o'clock
This Day:

John Carr, Mountrath, Queen's County, dividend, W. J. Moore, Agent, Robert Armstrong, Assignee.

John Hubert Moore, Dublin, final dividend, Benjamin Kearney, Agent.

BIRTH—On Wednesday last, at Stamer Park, co. Clare, the lady of Colonel Cullen, of the Leitrim Militia, of a son and heir—At Ards-house, County Donegal, the Lady of Robert Montgomery, Esq. of a son.—On Friday last, the Lady of James Bushell, Esq. of Clonmel, of a daughter.

MARRIED—On Thursday last, the Rev. Henry Allen, to Susanna, daughter of the late Dr. Ryan, of Killaloe.—In Liverpool, Mr. Patrick O'Neil, of Youghall, to Miss Rhodes, of Liverpool.—At Cork, Lieutenant James Coote, of the Royal Navy, to Eliza, eldest daughter of Mathias Smith, of Blackrock, Esq.—At St. Martin's, in the West Indies, Lieutenant Tucker, of the Royal Artillery, to Miss Richardson, niece of the President of the Council of that Island.

DIED—At Strangways, in the County Kilkenny, Miss Sarah White, daughter of the late Mr. Charles White, of this City.—At Harold's-Cross, at the advanced age of 102, Thomas Madden, formerly of Kilrush, Co. Clare, a respectable Grazier.—At Kilworth, on the 26th Inst. Mrs. Murphy, wife to Patrick Murphy, Esq. of said place.—On the 15th Inst. in London, Lieutenant-Colonel Armstrong, formerly of Lisgoole, County Fermanagh, Aide-de-Camp to his Royal Highness the Duke of York. The estimation in which Colonel Armstrong's public character was held, will be best explained by a referrence to the confidential and exalted situations which he successfully filled under the Marquis Wellesley in India, and subsequently in Portugal and England.

IRISH STOCKS

Bank Stock.................................		—
Government Debentures...........	3½ per Cent.	71¼
Do. Stock................................	3½ per Cent.	71¼
Government Debs......................	5 per Cent.	100¼
Do. Stock................................	5 per Cent.	99½
Grand Canal Stock....................		—
Grand Canal Loan......................	4 per Cent.	—
Ditto..	6 per Cent.	99¼

DUBLIN: Printed by WILLIAM PORTER, *No. 72, Grafton-street, where all communications will be*

From the *Irish Farmers Journal and Weekly Intelligencer*, 5 September 1812.

with the more prominent families, or "gentry," of Ireland. The publications listed in the Family History section are those which either refer to a family from one specific county or part of a county, or refer to families which are particularly linked with one county. There are many other references to specific families in local history publications and other sources (see page 297). Many of these publications are author-published and can be difficult to trace. NLI, SLC, and TCD have good collections. For more prominent families, the series of publications by Burke's, such as *Landed Gentry of Ireland*, London, 1899, and *Irish Family Records*, London, 1976, contain detailed pedigrees of prominent, mainly Anglo-Irish, families. For older Gaelic families, a useful source is O'Hart's *Irish Pedigrees*, Dublin, 1876 and 1880.

Gravestone Inscriptions

These can be a very useful source of information as, in many cases, they indicate relationships or give the ages or birth dates of those interred. In some cases the same graveyard is used for many generations, even after the family has moved elsewhere. They are extensively researched in some counties (e.g., Wicklow, Wexford, Cork, and Down) and virtually unresearched in others. The records have been published in a wide variety of sources (see page 28). A major source is the *Journal of the Association for the Preservation of the Memorials of the Dead*, which published from 1888-1916 (SLC films 127952-54; 1279285).

The records list the name of the graveyard and the place of publication or availability of the transcriptions. Unfortunately, the name of the graveyard is not always the name of the town or even of a local townland. Graveyards are often on ancient monastic sites which predate other boundary names. The location of most is determinable with the *Index to Townlands* (see the Place-Names section above). In each chapter the available records are listed by townland (or graveyard) name. Where possible, the general location is indicated. A useful general source is Brian Mitchell's *A Guide to Irish Churches and Graveyards*, 1990.

Newspapers

The earliest known Irish newspaper was published in 1649. During the eighteenth century the numbers increased greatly, and by the nineteenth century most large towns had at least one newspaper, and some towns had several. By 1900 Dublin had seen the publication of some seventy different newspaper titles, and Belfast had seen forty.

The availability of newspapers is often difficult to trace. Many newspaper issues do not exist at all, particularly those from the eighteenth century. Newspapers occasionally changed their names or their base of publication or even stopped publishing for long periods.

In this guide the main newspapers for each county are listed. Also listed are the holdings of each paper in the National Library of Ireland, which has one of the best collections of Irish newspapers; in the British Library, London; and in some county libraries. In many cases the local county library will have good runs of the local newspapers. Useful sources of information on Irish newspapers include the British Library's Newsplan Report on Irish Newspapers, and *The Waterloo Directory of Irish Newspapers and Periodicals, 1800-1900* by John S. Northern, North Waterloo Academic Press, 1986.

Announcements of marriages, deaths, and births are the most obvious items of interest in these newspapers. However, these occur primarily only after the mid-eighteenth century. Individual papers differed in their policy on advertisements; some contained many, others few. The policy also changed over the lives of some newspapers. Birth, marriage, and death notices, as might be expected, usually refer to the middle and upper classes. The birth notices tend to be less valuable, since the name of the child and even the mother is usually not given. Birth notices often take the form "At Bandon, County Cork, the wife of John Barry Esq., of a daughter." On the other hand, marriage announcements are very valuable. There was a widespread practice of city newspapers repeating the notices appearing in provincial newspapers, often in an abridged form. If a notice of a rural "event" is found in a city newspaper, it is usually wise to check some of the local papers, as more details may be found. Many papers did not place these small advertisments in one regular column but inserted them throughout the paper where space allowed.

If the area from which an ancestor came is known, then it is obviously useful to choose a newspaper published close to that area. For this reason the town of publication of each paper is shown. If no success is obtained with the most local paper, check papers from surrounding counties. A look through items such as court notices and other general advertisements in issues of these papers will usually tell quickly whether they contain entries from the area of interest to the researcher.

Basic news items are rarely of interest, since names are not frequently given, other than in court cases, etc. Advertisements are an important source of information for tradesmen and other businessmen (see page 29).

Wills, Administrations, and Marriage Licenses

Wills are legal documents detailing the wishes of deceased persons as to the division of their property. Administrations are legal documents setting out the decisions of a court as to division of the property of those who died without making a will. Marriage licensing was a system to ensure that there was no impediment to a marriage. The groom (usually) would lodge a sum of money as surety and receive a marriage license.

Wills

These are a particularly valuable source of genealogical information. They can contain detailed information on relationships between many members of a family group, together with other information on the residences, occupations, history, and circumstances of the family. They are therefore well worth finding if they exist. Until 1858

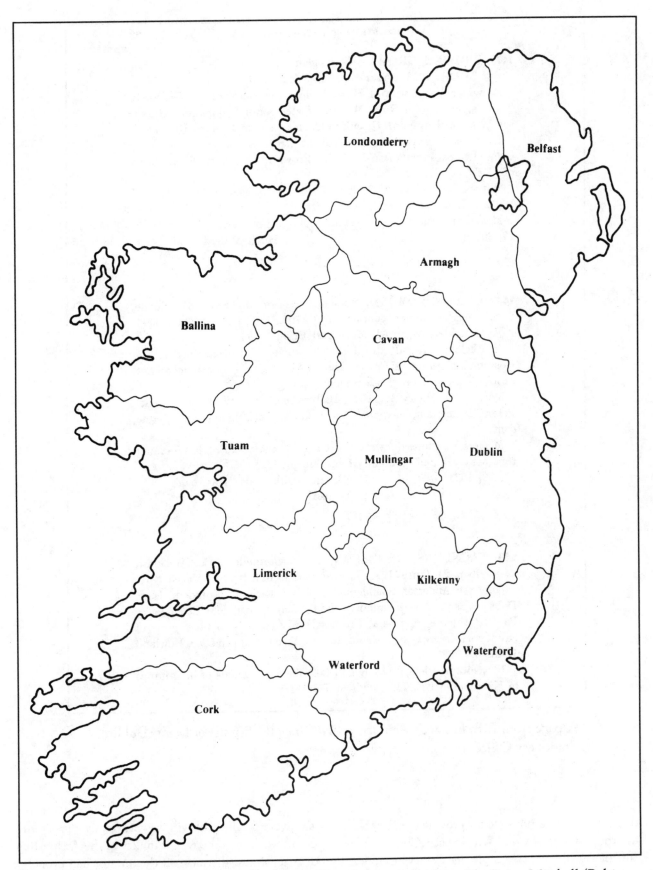

The Probate districts of Ireland, from A *New Genealogical Atlas of Ireland* by Brian Mitchell (Baltimore: Genealogical Publishing Co., 1986).

147   BROWNE, THOMAS, Cork, gent.
        28 Dec. 1713. Narrate, 1 p., 8 March 1717.
   Daughter Mary, wife of Hugh Millerd the younger.   Grandson
Thomas, son of said Hugh Millerd. Sister Sarah Humpston. Grandson William Kingsmill. Grandson Thomas, son of Edward Browne.
   Evan Davis, clerk, tenant in Browne Street. A rent charge formerly granted to St. Peter's Parish, Cork. Brown Street, North East Marsh of Cork.
   Witnesses: William Olliffe, Theodore Rheda, merchant, and William Lane, gent., all of Cork city.
   Memorial witnessed by: William Olliffe, Ed. Barns.
21, 30, 10695   Hugh Millerd (seal)

148   DILLON, EDMOND, Billogh, parish of Ragharoe, B. Athlone,
        Co. Roscommon, gent. 18 July 1708. Full, 1 p., 13 March 1717.
   My daughters Winifred, Mary and Bridget (heir).
   My beloved friend Mr. Joseph Sproule, Gortmacassaughy, Co. Roscommon, gent., and Garrett Dillon, Athleag, said county, merchant, exors. Lands in Co. Roscommon.
   Witnesses: Henry Magawly, Ballynahome, Co. Westmeath, gent., Peter Chamberlain, Maynooth, Co. Kildare, gent., Simon Smith, same, gent.
   Memorial witnessed by: John Gregson, clerk to Bruen Worthington, notary public, Dublin, Hen. Buckley.
21, 38, 10714   Bridget Dillon als. Kavanagh
             her mark (seal)

149   SAUNDERS, ANDERSON, Newtownsaunders, Co. Wicklow,
        Esq., 24 Jan. 1717. Narrate, part in full, 1 p., 13 March 1717.
   Only son Anderson Saunders. Nephews Richard Saunders, Isaac Dobson, Esq., Morley Saunders, Esq., Robert Saunders Esq., Jeffry Paul, Rathmore, Esq., and Francis Hardy (who is to take name of Saunders if he inherits). Exors. Isaac Dobson, Esq., and Mr. Rowland Bradstock.
   Newtownsaunders, and lands in Co. Wicklow. Lands of inheritance in Kingdom of Ireland. Lands in Tipperary.

A page from P. B. Eustace's *Abstracts of Wills from the Registry of Deeds* (Dublin: Stationery Office, 1956).

the church was responsible for proving (i.e., establishing the validity) of wills. Within each Church of Ireland diocese there was a *Consistorial Court* which proved wills of those who had been residents within the diocese and whose property was also within the diocese. However, if the testator's property in another diocese was over £5 value, the will was proven by a *Prerogative Court*, which was the responsibility of the Archbishop of Armagh. Furthermore, if the testator had property in England, the will was also proved in the English court at Canterbury and a copy proved in Armagh. These records may also be checked. Recent immigrants to Ire-

A page from Sir A. Vicar's *Index to the Prerogative Wills of Ireland 1536–1810* (Dublin, 1897).

land, in particular, may have retained property in England.

One of the circumstances in which a will might have been proved in the Prerogative Court is if the testator had land which straddled the border of two dioceses. In the guide to Catholic church records in each county, the Church of Ireland diocese in which each civil parish is located is shown. From this, and the accompanying map, it can be seen if the land is on the border of another diocese. The other major circumstance in which a testator's will might be in the Prerogative Court is if he or she was wealthy and therefore had property or goods elsewhere in the country.

After 1858, wills were proved in probate districts, and a principal registry was established in Dublin to handle local wills, as well as those cases which could not be decided within a single district. The probate districts are shown on page 31.

Most of the actual will documents (of all types) were destroyed in the fire at the Public Record Office in 1922. The records which are now available are of three types:

Wills

Only a few wills survived the PRO fire, but further wills and copies have since been obtained and form the current NAI collection. The PRONI also has an extensive collection, and a microfilm of the card index is available in the LDS. See page 35 for other collections.

Will Abstracts

Many local or family historians have examined wills of certain families or areas over the centuries. Their notes on the contents of these wills, called abstracts, are available in the NAI and/or other libraries. These abstracts vary in their detail depending on the purpose for which they were made. They usually contain the testator's name and address, date of will and probate, executor's name, and the names of the major beneficiaries. The relationship of beneficiaries to the testator is also often indicated. Major abstract collections include Betham's *Abstracts of Prerogative Wills 1536–1800* (NAI, SLC) and the three volumes of *Registry of Deeds Dublin–Abstracts of Wills* by Beryl Eustace (volumes I and II) and Ellis and Eustace (volume III; see page 32). These are abstracts of wills deposited at the Registry of Deeds. Another reference is Rev. Wallace Clare's *A Guide to Copies and Abstracts of Irish Wills*, 1930, reprinted in 1989.

Will Indexes

The major set of indexes to Irish wills are the books originally used in the PRO as a guide to finding the wills among their collection. These are now in the NAI. The indexes to consistorial wills survived the fire, although some were damaged. These are in the NAI and are arranged alphabetically by family and Christian name; they give the address (in some cases occupation) and year of probate. The indexes to consistorial wills have been published in various places. The major source is the series of volumes edited by Gertrude Thrift (London: W.P.W. Phillimore, 1909–20. Reprint. Genealogical Publishing Company, 1970). (See page 152.) Other sources include the 26th and 30th reports of the DKPRI,

and local history journals. The sources for indexes are indicated in the relevant section in each county.

Prerogative will indexes are arranged alphabetically by testator's name and also give the address, occupation, and year of probate. They are in two series, the first up to 1810, and the second from 1811 to 1857. The first series has been published as *Index to the Prerogative Wills of Ireland 1536–1810*, edited by Sir Arthur Vicars (1897. Reprint. Baltimore: Genealogical Publishing Company, 1967). (See page 33.) The indexes are also available in the NAI.

Administrations

If a person died without making a will, the above two courts also had responsibility for deciding on the distribution of the deceased's property to family and creditors. Having made its decision, the court acted by appointing an administrator (usually a next of kin or major creditor) to distribute the estate of the deceased in the manner set down. The administrator entered a bond for a sum of money as surety that he would do so (hence Administration Bonds). Most of the records of these courts perished in the 1922 fire, but the following are available:

Administrations

Those available are the Prerogative Administrations of 1684–88, 1748–51, and 1839, and the Consistorial Grant Books (see Administration Bonds below).

Abstracts of Administrations

In many of the collections listed in the Major Repositories of Wills and Administration Records section, both wills and administrations have been abstracted. Abstracts of approximately five thousand pre-1802 administrations were made by Betham. The originals are at the NAI, while an indexed copy is at the Genealogical Office. These abstracts contain deceased's name, address, occupation, date of grant, and to whom made. The Prerogative Court of Canterbury also granted administrations, and these are included with the wills in the records for 1828–39 available at the NAI.

Administration Bonds (see Administrations above)

No original bonds survived the fire. However, the grant books, into which the grants were copied, survive for the dioceses of Cashel (1840–45), Ossory (1848–58), and a damaged copy for Derry and Raphoe (1812–21).

Marriage Licenses

Civil registration of Irish marriages began in 1845 for non-Catholic marriages and in 1864 for Catholics. Until its disestablishment in 1857, the Church of Ireland was responsible for granting permission to marry. The church used two methods to ensure that neither party had already been married: publishing of "banns," which gave three weeks' public notice of intention to marry so that objections could be made, and marriage license bonds, in which the groom (usually) paid a sum of money as surety that there was no reason not to marry. This sum was theoretically to insure the church against any damages which might be sought at a later date if it turned out there was an existing impediment to the marriage. Although publishing of banns was a less expensive mechanism, their publication became socially undesirable among most Catholics, and almost all couples purchased a marriage license. There is extensive evidence to suggest that many poor couples did not marry in the church because of the costs involved. "Private" clerics or "couple-beggars" offered a cheap alternative and performed many thousands of marriages in the early nineteenth century.

Few records of banns exist. Likewise, the original marriage license bonds have not survived. However, indexes and some abstracts of marriage license bonds and grants (the official permission to marry) survive. The indexes give the names of bride and groom and the year of the marriage. The existing records are shown in the relevant section for each county.

Major Repositories of Probate Records

The LDS library has a good collection of copies (on film and otherwise) from the collections listed below. This collection is detailed in *Irish Probates Register* (LDS, 1979: 941.5 P2gs). Specific items are listed within each chapter.

National Archives

(See page 37.) This is the largest collection of Irish wills anywhere. It includes wills which survived the 1922 fire, copies and originals which have been deposited since, and various collections of will abstracts. The following are the surviving will books held in the NAI:

1. Prerogative Wills for the years 1664-84; 1706-08 (surnames beginning with A-W); 1726-28 (A-W); 1728-29 (A-W); 1777 (A-L); 1813 (K-Z); 1834 (A-E).

2. Consistorial Wills. The individual Consistorial Courts varied as to the care which they took of wills deposited with them. In 1857 the PRO was entrusted with keeping the will documents. When the staff began to assemble the wills, the number of wills actually received from each court varied greatly. None produced all the wills they should have had, few provided many

wills before 1780, and some produced very few from any period. Only one consistorial will survived the 1922 fire. The surviving will books are for Connor (1818-20 and 1853-58) and Down (1850-58). All of the indexes survive (see the Wills and Administrations section) and are available at the NAI and on film at SLC.

Of particular note among the NAI's collections of abstracts are the Betham Prerogative Will Abstracts. In 1860 Sir William Betham organized the indexing of prerogative wills according to testator's names. He also wrote out brief genealogical abstracts of almost all the pre-1800 wills—amounting to some 37,500 abstracts. The general card index in the NAI covers the wills and will copies and most abstract collections. Abstract collections which are independently indexed in the NAI include the Crossle Collection (mainly seventeenth- and eighteenth-century, with an emphasis on the northwestern counties), and the Jennings Collection of Waterford wills and administrations.

3. The *Irish Will Registers* compiled by the Inland Revenue Commissioners, London, are available from 1828-39 (except part of 1834). They give the names and addresses of testator and executors; dates of will, decease, and probate; main legacies; and names of beneficiaries. This is a very valuable reference for the period 1828-39. The *Indexes to Irish Will Registers* compiled by the Inland Revenue Commissioners in London for the years 1828-79 are also available in the NAI.

Genealogical Office

The GO collection is mainly pre-1800, and many are arranged in series dealing with particular families. These are referenced in the Hayes's *Manuscript Sources for the History of Irish Civilisation* (in the NLI and other archives). The GO collection is not indexed, and thus it is somewhat difficult to determine its exact contents. A general index is in *Analecta Hibernica*, volume 17.

Registry of Deeds

The Registry of Deeds has a collection of almost 1,500 wills which were deposited in connection with land transfers, particularly regarding disputed legacies of land. These wills have been abstracted and published by the Irish Manuscripts Commission as *Registry of Deeds, Dublin, Abstracts of Wills* volume 1, 1708-45 and volume 2, 1746-88, edited by P.B. Eustace (1954-56). Volume 3, 1785-1832, was edited by E. Ellis and P.B. Eustace (1984).

National Library of Ireland

There are many collections of wills relating to specific families and areas held here. They are not separately indexed. However, Hayes's *Manuscript Sources for the History of Irish Civilisation* indexes all NLI holdings by name, area, etc.

Research Sources and Services

This section lists various sources of information which the family researcher can access in Dublin, Belfast, or in the county of interest.

Journals

For many counties in Ireland there is a wealth of detailed local history available to the family researcher. The articles in these journals include detailed histories of specific parishes or townlands, information on local families and institutions, and accounts of the local effects of various events (contemporary accounts of the 1798 rebellion and of the Great Famine being particularly common). For some counties, such as Cork and Galway, journals have been published for over one hundred years. In some, the volumes are indexed by the places and persons mentioned. Copies are available in NLI and Trinity College Library and elsewhere. Many will accept queries from researchers. In short, all sorts of local historical detail is available in most counties, which may either explain certain events in an ancestor's history or point toward other avenues for research.

Apart from the local journals, there are also the following journals which cover local or family history in all of Ireland, or in a significant part. Specialist publications of interest include:

Irish Roots, Belgrave Publications, Belgrave Avenue, Cork; Ph/Fax: 021 500067.

North Irish Roots, c/o Dept. of Education, QUB, 69 University Street, Belfast BT7 1HL.

Familia (mainly Northern interest), c/o Ulster Historical Foundation (see following pages).

Irish Genealogist, c/o Julian Walton, Woodlands, Halfway House, Waterford.

Irish Ancestor (publication now ceased).

Irish Family History Society Journal, PO Box 36, Naas, Co. Kildare.

Irish Family Links, 162a Kingsway, Dunmurry, Belfast BT17 9AD.

The Septs, Irish Genealogical Society, POB 16585, St. Paul, MN 55116-0585, USA.

O'Lochlainn's Irish Family Journal, Box 7575, Kansas City, MO 64116, USA.

The Irish at Home and Abroad, Dept. IR, POB 521806, Salt Lake City, UT 84152, USA.

Libraries and Information Sources

In most counties, the major repository of information is the county library. Virtually all of these have local history or local studies sections, generally in the main branch library. Some have very extensive collections of local interest. County and city library contact details are given in each chapter. A useful guide to 155 Irish archives is *Directory of Irish Archives* by S. Helferty and R. Refausse (Dublin: Irish Academic Press, 1988).

The major repositories of Irish family history records are in Dublin and Belfast. The records in Dublin relate to all of Ireland, but more particularly to the twenty-six counties of the Republic of Ireland. Those in Belfast relate to the six counties of Northern Ireland and, in some cases, to those Ulster counties which are not within "Northern Ireland" (i.e., Cavan, Donegal, and Monaghan). In the USA, the major repository is the Family History Library in Salt Lake City. This is arguably the biggest single collection of Irish family history material anywhere. Their holdings are also available through the LDS family history centers worldwide. The library also has a range of computer databases designed to help researchers. They can be contacted at the Family History Library, 35 North West Temple, Salt Lake City, UT 84150; Web site: www.lds.org.

The major archives and family-history-related organizations located in Dublin are the following:

National Library of Ireland (NLI)
Kildare St.
Dublin 2
Ph: 353-1-6618811
http://www.hea.ie/natlib/homepage.html

Holdings include: *Griffith's Valuation*, including list of householders in each county; Catholic parish registers (microfilm copies of most Catholic registers for all parts of Ireland); local and commercial directories; newspapers (microfilm and original copies of Irish newspapers); estate papers and records; maps; old photographs; and many other sources.

National Archives (NAI)
Bishop Street
Dublin 8
Ph: 353-1-4783711
http://147.252.133.152/nat-arch/

The National Archives was formed by merger of the Public Record Office, State Paper Office, and other state archives. Its holdings of family history sources include the original *Tithe Applotment Survey* books for twenty-six counties and copies of the books for northern Irish counties; census returns for 1901 and 1911 and the surviving parts of other censuses; and copies and originals of some surviving Church of Ireland parish registers (see also Representative Church Body Library). The

INDEX TO CLERGY OF ROMAN CATHOLIC CHURCH.

NAME, DIOCESE, AND POST TOWN.

Ahern, Michael, Cloyne, Macroom
Ahern, M., Cloyne, Youghal
Ahern, Richard, Cloyne, Mallow
Allen, James, Ard. and Clon., enamore, Longford
Allman, J., Kerry, Castle Island
Ambrose, James, Cork, Monktown
Ambrose, Robert, Limerick, Newcastle
Anderson, Terence, Dublin, Presb., Seville-place
Ansbro, Laurence, Tuam, Dromgriffin
Ashlin, Stephen, Cloyne, Doneraile
Atkinson, Joseph, Ard. and Clon., Longford
Aylward, Edward, Ferns, Wexford
Aylward, James, Ferns, Enniscorthy
Aylward, Patrick, Ossory, Kilkenny
Bambuck, P., Elphin, Roscommon
Barrett, John, Tuam, Headford
Barrett, P., Killaloe, Dunkerrin
Barrett, R., Cork, Cork
Barrett, T. Cork, Kinsale
Barron, Michael, Waterford, Waterford
Barry, D. Cloyne, Mallow
Barry, Edward, Cloyne, Rathcormack
Barry, James, Cloyne, Middleton
Barry, John, Cloyne, Carrigtoohill
Barry, John, Cloyne, Inniscarra
Barry, John, Cork, Glounthaune R. S. O.
Barry, Michael, Emly, Kilcooly, Thurles
Barry, Patrick, Killaloe, Roscrea
Barry, Robert, Meath, Dunsany
Darton, J., Kerry, Kenmare
Barton, Luke, Meath, Castle Geoghegan
Barton, P., Kerry, Castletown-Bere
Baxter, James, Dublin, Lucan
Beatson, H., Down and Connor, Belfast
Beauchamp, John, Kildare and Leighlin, Borris
Beasley, J. J., Kerry, Castletown-Bere
Beechinor, J., Cloyne, Charleville
Begley, John, Limerick, Shanagolden
Begley, John, Tuam, Tuam
Behan, Hugh, Meath, Trim
Benson, Francis, Achonry, Ballaghadereen
Bergin, James, Kildare, Philipstown
Bermingham, Peter, Clogher, Carrickmacross
Bernard, D., Cork, Bandon
Biggins, R., Tuam, Clifden
Birch, J., Ossory, Knocktopher
Blake, Patrick, Raphoe, Dunfanaghy
Blake, Richard, Meath, Navan
Blaney, P. Derry, Draperstown
Bodkin, Joseph, Clonfert, Kilrickill
Boggan, J. Ferns, Skreen, Gorey
Boggan, L. Ferns, Duncormick, Wexford
Bolger, David, Ferns, Wexford
Bolger, M., Kildare and Leighlin, Hacketstown
Bolger, P., Kildare, Bancroft
Bollasty, Patrick, Meath, Drumconrath, Ardee
Booth, W. J., Armagh, Drogheda
Bourke, John, Cashel, Bruff
Bourke, Joseph, Dublin, Presb., Aughrim-st.
Bourke, Rd., Kildare & Leighlin, Bagenalstown
Bourke, Sylvester, Dublin, Donnybrook
Bourke, Thomas, Dublin, Presb., Harrington-st.
Bourke, William, Killaloe, Kildysart
Bowden, J., Ossory, Kilkenny
Bowe, John, Ossory, Gowran
Bowe, Thomas, Ossory, Kilkenny
Bowes, John, Clonfert, Ballinasloe
Bowes, T. Clonfert, Killimore
Bowes, Bernard, Clonfert, Kilrickill
Bowler, Thomas, Cloyne, Youghal
Boylan, John, Kilmore, Kilnaleck
Boylan, Pk., Clogher, Silverstream, Monaghan
Boylan, T., Ardagh, Drumshambo
Boyle, Hugh, Derry, Victoria Place, Derry
Boyle, John, Raphoe, Falcarragh, Letterkenny
Boyle, John, Killala, Ballina
Boyle, Joseph, Raphoe, Dunfanaghy
Boyle, Patrick, Down, Crossgar
Boyle, Thomas, Derry, Garvagh
Boyle, T., Armagh, Drogheda
Bracken, Michael, Meath, Tullamore
Bracken, W., Meath, Tullamore
Bradley, William, Derry, Castledawson
Brady, Joseph, Derry, Strabane
Brady, Bernard, Meath, Dunboyne
Bradley, Bernard, Kilmore, Swanlinbar
Brady, E., Kilmore, Kinlough
Brady, Eugene, Kilmore, Bawnboy
Brady, F., Kilmore, Carrigallen
Brady, J., Dublin, Blackrock
Brady, James, Dublin, 47, Westland-row
Brady, Jas., Ardagh, Keadue, Car.-on-Shan.
Brady, John, Kilmore, Belturbet
Brady, Michael, Dublin, Presb., Seville-place
Brady, P. Kilmore, Ballinamore
Brady, Patrick, Annagh, Dundalk
Brady, Patrick, Kilmore, Kilnaleck
Brady, Peter, Kilmore, Cootehill
Brady, Terence, Kilmore, Bailieborough
Brady, Thomas, Kilmore, Cootehill
Brady, William, Ardagh and Clonmacnoise, Street, Rathowen
Brannan, F., Kilmore, Garrison
Brannan, J., Dublin, 7, Eblana-av., Kingstown
Brannan, M., Castlerea
Breagey, J., Armagh, Dundalk
Breen, J., Kildare, Ballickmoyler, Carlow
Breen, James, Dublin, Dundrum
Breen, John, Limerick, Athea
Breen, M., Cloyne, Newmarket

Breen, M., Killaloe, Shinrone
Breen, P., Clogher, Irvinestown
Breen, William, Dublin, St. Margarets
Brennan, Denis, Armagh, Drogheda
Brennan, Edward, Ossory, Piltown
Brennan, Edward, Ossory, Rathdowney
Brennan, Edwd., Kildare & Leighlin, Mountrath
Brennan, Geoffrey, Down & Connor, Killough
Brennan, Henry, Ossory, Waterford
Brennan, Hugh, Ardagh, Drumcong, Car.-on-Sh.
Brennan, J., Elphin, Riverstown, Ballymote
Brennan, James, Ossory, Swinford
Brennan, James, Dublin, 47, Westland-row
Brennan, M., Kildare, Stradbally
Brennan, Patrick, Killaloe, Carrigaholt
Brennan, P., Dublin, Glasnevin
Brennan, P. J., Dublin, Skerries
Brennan, Thomas, Ossory, Castlecomer
Breslan, James, Armagh, Coal Island
Bresnahan, Daniel, Limerick, Limerick
Brie, J., Kerry, Killarney
Briody, John, Ard. and Clon., Killoe, Longford
Briody, P., Ardagh, Carrick Fines, Granard
Briody, Patrick, Meath, Athboy
Brislane, P., Killala, Inniscrone, Ballina
Brock, William, Killaloe, Arran-quay
Brogan, John, Meath, Oldcastle
Brophy, Thomas, Ossory, Waterford
Brosnahan, Timothy, Killaloe, Kilkee
Brosnan, P., Kerry, Castlemaine
Brosnan, Very Rev. Thade, Kerry, Cahirciveen
Brosnan, Thomas, Kerry, Tralee
Brosnan, T., Kerry, Tralee
Brown, D., Cloyne, Killinardrisk
Brown, D., Cloyne, Mallow
Brown, Patrick, Kerry, Tralee
Browne, D., Cloyne, Macroom
BROWNE, Most Rev. JAMES, D.D., *Bishop* of Ferns, St. Peter's College, Wexford
Browne, James, Cloyne, Macroom
Browne, John, Ferns, Duncannon, Gorey
Browne, Lawrence, Killaloe, Doonbeg
Browne, Thomas, Limerick, Limerick
Browne, William, Waterford, Waterford
BROWNRIGG, Most Rev. ABRAHAM, D.D., *Bishop*, Ossory, Kilkenny
Buchanan, George, Meath, Summerhill
Buckley, C., Cloyne, Buttevant
Buckley, Timothy, Cloyne, Mallow
Buckley, W., Killaloe, Feakle
Buglar, Michael, V.G., Killaloe, Birr
Burdon, D., Cloyne, Buttevant
Burke, David, Down, Loughgiel, Clough
Burke, E. W., Kildare, Bagenalstown
Burke, Edward, Dublin, 83, Stephen's-green
Burke, Edmond, Emly, Kilcooly, Thurles
Burke, J., Tuam, Dunmore
Burke, J. Kerry, Tralee
Burke, James, Waterford, Newcastle, Clonmel
Burke, John, Ross, Timoleague
Burke, J., Kilfenora, Lisdoonvarna
Burke, Mat., Achonry, Swinford
Burke, Michael, Tuam, Ballyhaunis
Burke, Michael, Ardagh, Killoe, Longford
Burke, Thomas, Kilmacduagh, Kilcolgan
Burke, Timothy, Emly, Kilnaule
Burke, Thaddeus, Waterford, Car.-on-Suir
Burke, Tobias, Wat. & Lis., Passage, Waterford
Burke, Wm., Watf. & Lis., Kilmacthomas
Burns, J. V., Down, Belfast
Burton, John, Cloyne, Doneraile
Busher, John, Ferns, Tinahely, Rathdrum
Busher, Thomas, Ferns, Newtownbarry
Butler, M. J., Dublin, Balbriggan
Butterfield, M., Dublin, Presb., Haddington-rd.
Butterly, P., Dublin, Inchicore
Byrne, Charles, Meath, Moate
Byrne, Daniel, Kildare and Leighlin, Carlow
Byrne, Eugene, Dub., 7, Eblana-av., Kingstown
Byrne, F., Armagh, Forkhill
Byrne, George, Kildare and Leighlin, Newbridge
Byrne, J., Kildare and Leighlin, Carlow
Byrne, James, Dromore, Lurgan
Byrne, J. Dublin, Glendalough, Rathdrum
Byrne, John, Armagh, Ardee
Byrne, John, Dublin, 59, Eccles-street
Byrne, John, Kildare & Leighlin, Clonegal
Byrne, Laurence, Armagh, Portadown
Byrne, M., Dublin, Baldoyle
Byrne, Michael, Clonfert, Taghmaconnell
Byrne, Michael, Limerick, Newcastle West
Byrne, Patrick, Waterford & Lismore, Lismore
Byrne, Patrick, Kildare, Rathangan
Byrne, Patrick, Waterford, Clonmel
Byrne, Peter J., Armagh, Dungannon
Byrne, Richard, Kildare and Leigh, Rathvilly
Byrne, Thomas, Dublin, Arklow
Byrne, Wm., Kildare, Coolkenno, Tullow
Byrnes, James, Emly, Galbally, Tipperary
Byrne, W., Dublin, Cuttlestown
Caffrey, Joseph, Dublin, Fairview
Cahalan, Joseph, Clonfert, Kiltulla, Athenry
Cahill, Cornelius, Cloyne, Glanworth
Cahill, F. Ardagh, Cloone, Mohill
Cahill, Henry, Tuam, Ballyglunin
Cahill, John, Ossory, Knocktopher
Cahill, P., Ardagh, Abbeylara, Granard
Cahill, Richard, Emly, Tipperary
Cahill, T., Ard. & Clonmac., Dromahair
Cahill, Thomas, Ferns, Ballymore, Killinick
Cahill, William, Ossory, Piltown

Cahir, James, Killaloe, Miltownmalbay
Callaghan, A., Achonry, Foxford
Callan, Patrick, Clogher, Annyalla, Monaghan
Callanan, Jonas, Ross, Rosscarbery
Callanan, Jonas, Ross, Timoleague
Callanan, Michael, Waterford, Kilmacthomas
Callary, Michael, Meath, Skryne, Tara
Callary, Philip, Meath, Drogheda
Calligan, M. Killaloe, Killaloe
Campbell, A., Derry, Kileter, Castlederg
Campbell, J., Down, Belfast
Campbell, Joseph, Clogher, Iniskeen
Campbell, P., Dromore, Loughbrickland
Campbell, Patrick, Kilfenora, Liscannor
Campion, Peter, Kildare & Leighlin, Whitehall
Canning, John, Tuam, Westport
Cannon, J. C., Raphoe, Termon
Canton, Joseph, Tuam, Athenry
Cantwell, James, Emly, Killenaule
Cantwell, John, Wat. & Lismore, Clashmore
Cantwell, Patrick, Meath, Enfield
Cantwell, Walter, Emly, Tipperary
Canty, Michael, Limerick, Kilmallock
Canty, Thomas, Emly, Tipperary
Carberry, J., Meath, Collinstown
Carberry, Philip, Dublin, Rathdrum
Carbery, Thomas, Dublin, Ballytore
Carey, James, Killaloe, Corofin
Carey, Jeremiah, Cork, Carrigaline
Carey, John, Meath, Ballymahon
Carey, Joseph, Meath, Garristown
Carey, Michael, Killaloe, Ennis
Carey, Michael, Killaloe, Scariff
Carlin, James, Dromore, Newry
Carlos, Luke, Elphin, Frenchpark
Carmody, James, Kerry, Castleisland
Carmody, Thomas, Kerry, Castletown-Bere
Carolan, F., Armagh, Forkhill
Carolan, P., Dublin, Ballymore-Eustace
Carraher, B., Armagh, Forkhill
Carrick, John, Limerick, Loughill
Carrick, Robert, Dublin, Finglas
Carrigan, Patrick, Ossory, Callan
Carrigan, W., Ossory, Jenkinstown
Carroll, F., Dublin, Presb. Francis-street
Carroll, James, Limerick, Newcastle West
Carroll, John, Ossory, Waterford
Carroll, John, Down and Connor, Coleraine
Carroll, John, Ossory, Kilkenny
Carroll, Luke, Kilmore, Mullagh
Carroll, M., Limerick, Newcastle
Carroll, P., Limerick, Croom
Carver, John, Cloyne, Castletownroche
Casey, John, Waterford, Lismore
Casey, Christopher, Meath, Churchtown, Naas
Casey, Francis L., Cork, Passage West
Casey, James, Elphin, Athleague, Roscommon
Casey, John, Kerry, Cahirciveen
Casey, Michael, Waterf. and Lism. Cappoquin
Casey, P., Waterford and Lismore, Dungarvan
Casey, Thomas, Meath, Kells
Casey, William, Limerick, Abbeyfeale
Cashel, John, Ardagh, Moate
Casserly, James, Ard. & Clon., Clondra, Longford
Cassidy, Edward, Raphoe, Donegal
Cassidy, Francis, Kilmacduagh, Loughrea
Cassidy, F., Rossmuch, Oughterard
Cassidy, J., Cork, Cork
Cassidy, John, Meath, Slane
Cassidy, Thomas, Meath, Longwood
Cassidy, William, Derry, Muff, Donegal
Cassin, W., Ossory, Kilkenny
Caulfield, Patrick, Tuam, Hollymount
Cavanagh, Bartholomew, Tuam, Ballyhaunis
Cavanagh, D. Ferns, Adamstown, Enniscorthy
Cavanagh, M., Ferns, Blackwater, Gorey
Cavanagh, M. Ferns, Ballywilliam, New Ross
Clancy, James, Killaloe, Lerrha
Clancy, John, Emly, Cashel
Clarke, John, Armagh, Dunleer
Clarke, M., Killala, Easky
Clarke, Michael, Dublin, Wicklow
Clarke, Michael, Killala, Killala
Clarke, Owen, Armagh, Donaghmore, Dungannon
Clarke, Patrick, Armagh, Dundalk
Clarke, Patrick, Kilmore, Bailieborough
Clarke, Patrick, Meath, Kingscourt
Clarke, Thomas, Kilmore, Ballinagh
Clavin, James, Meath, Moynalty
Cleary, Denis, Killaloe, O'Callaghan's Mills
Cleary, John, Ferns, Clonroche
Cleary, Michael, Emly, Templemore
Clifford, Edmond, Limerick, Newcastle West
Clifford, Patrick, Clogher, Fintona
Cloney, Silvester, Ferns, Skreen, Gorey
Cloney, Thomas, Ferns, Tagoat
Cloney, Thomas, Ferns, Bridgetown, Wexford
Clune, James, Killaloe, Mountshannon
Cody, Michael, Ossory, Castlecomer
Coen, M., Tuam, Athenry
Coffey, Fras., Dublin, Presb., Arran Quay
COFFEY, Most Rev J., *Bishop of Kerry*, Killarney
Coghlan, J., Cork, Blackrock, Cork
Coghlan, Jas., Clonfert, Loughrea
Coghlan, J., Cork, Bandon
Coghlan, W, Cloyne, Charleville
Coghlan, William, Cloyne, Mallow
Coghlan, W., Cloyne, Charleville
Coglan, J., Waterford, Lismore
Coglan, D., Clonfert, Aughrim
Cole, Dermot, Meath, Navan

NAI also has many manuscripts of relevance to family and local history, such as estate records, court records, and other government papers. The records which were originally in the State Paper Office are those of the British administration of Ireland, e.g., records of convicts who were transported, records of the 1798 Rebellion, Fenian Rising, and many others.

Genealogical Office (GO)

42 Kildare St.
Dublin 2
Ph: 353-1-6618811

This office is now part of the National Library of Ireland and incorporates the State Heraldic Museum and the Office of the Chief Herald. The institution has been in existence continuously since 1552, assigning and ratifying coats of arms for individuals and institutions. The office has a large range of material on family pedigrees, wills, funeral entries (biographies of noblemen who died from 1552 to 1700), and operates a genealogical research service.

General Register Office

Joyce House, 8–11 Lombard St.
Dublin 2
Ph: 353-1-6711863

This office contains all of the official records of births, marriages, and deaths for all counties since records began in 1864. It also has non-Catholic marriage records from April 1845 to 1864. A public research room is available where the indexes to these records can be consulted. A fee is charged for searching.

The Registry of Deeds

Henrietta Street
Dublin 1
Ph: 353-1-8732233
http://www.irlgov.ie/landreg/

Houses original deeds deposited since 1708.

Representative Church Body Library (RCBL)

Braemor Park
Rathgar, Dublin 14
Ph: 353-1-4923979

The Representative Church Body Library is the library of the Church of Ireland (the Anglican or Protestant Episcopal Church in Ireland) and is, *inter alia*, the principal repository for the parish records of this church in the Republic of Ireland. Records from parishes in Northern Ireland, which are not retained in parish custody, are deposited in the Public Record Office of Northern Ireland in Belfast.

It holds parish records, biographical material of the Church of Ireland clergy, census records, marriage and testamentary material, and general research papers and books relevant to the Church of Ireland. These include original records for almost three hundred parishes, almost half of which are parochial registers dating from the late seventeenth century (exclusively for the Republic of Ireland).

Dublin Friends Historical Library

Swanbrook House, Morehampton Road
Dublin 4
Ph: 353-1-6687157

Has records of Quaker meeting houses in Munster, Leinster, and Connaught. Research is conducted for a fee. A profile of their holdings is in *Irish Roots* 3 (1996).

Irish Family History Foundation

Ph: 353-1-4783711
http://www.mayo-ireland.ie/roots.htm

This organization is not an archive, but is the coordination body for the Irish Genealogical Project (IGP), which has established a network of government-approved research centers throughout Ireland. These centers have indexed millions of records since 1990, and provide research services based on these databases, and other records.

Trinity College Library (TCD)

Dublin 2
Ph: 353-1-6772941

This large library has a fine collection of manuscripts, newspapers, and many examples of illuminated manuscripts and other treasures.

Royal Irish Academy (RIA)

19 Dawson St.
Dublin

Has a large collection of manuscript and printed sources.

Family History Centre

The Willows, Finglas Rd.
Dublin 11
Ph: 353-1-8309960

This is one of 1,500 branches of the Family History Library of The Church of Jesus Christ of Latter-day Saints, headquartered in Salt Lake City. It has a significant collection of microfilmed family history sources. There is also a branch in Cork (Sarsfield Road, Wilton, Cork, Ph: (021) 874858) and Belfast (see below). A profile of their holdings is in *Irish Roots* 4 (1993).

Dept. of Folklore

University College Dublin
Belfield, Dublin 4
Ph: 353-1-693244

Has interesting collections of documents and tapes relating to folklore and customs in various parts of the country.

In Belfast the archives available are the following:

Public Record Office of Northern Ireland (PRONI)
66 Balmoral Avenue
Belfast BT9 6NY
Ph: 00441-0232-661621
http://www.nics.gov.uk/proni/pro_home.htm

Holds the official records from Northern Ireland government departments from ca. 1830, as well as records of NI courts, local authorities, and other public bodies. It also has large collections of private papers, including estate papers, copies of all surviving Church of Ireland (Episcopalian) parish registers for Northern Ireland, and also registers for some Presbyterian and Roman Catholic churches. A profile of their holdings is in *Irish Roots* 4 (1992) or on their home page (see address above). The PRONI catalog is in the LDS on films 0247316-20 and 0258549-0258622.

Northern Ireland Registrar-General's Office
Oxford House
Chichester Street
Belfast BT1 4HL

Has records of births, marriages, and deaths from 1864 (and of non-Catholic marriages from 1845) for the Northern counties.

Presbyterian Historical Society
Church House
Fisherwick Place
Belfast BT1 6DW

Has many of the oldest Presbyterian church registers in the province. These may be consulted by arrangement at the Library, Assembly College, Botanic Avenue, Belfast BT7 1JT.

Society of Friends Library
4 Magheralave Road
Lisburn, Co. Antrim BT28 3BD, N. Ireland

Holds records of Quaker meeting houses in Ulster.

Family History Centre
403 Hollywood Rd.
Belfast 4
Ph: 0044-1232-768250

This is a branch of the Family History Library of The Church of Jesus Christ of Latter-day Saints. It has a significant collection of microfilmed family history sources. A profile of holdings is in *Irish Roots* 4 (1993).

Research Services
Because of the accessibility of the archives and records described above, some of the major research services are located in Dublin and Belfast. These perform research for all parts of the country, although Belfast research centers tend to concentrate on the Northern counties. In most counties there are also heritage centers which have indexed the local parish records and other local records, and provide a research service. These centers are described in the Research Sources and Services section in the relevant county.

Most full-time researchers are members of the Association of Professional Genealogists of Ireland (APGI). A full list of their members (and specialties) can be obtained from APGI c/o Genealogical Office, Kildare Street, Dublin 2. Both the NAI and NLI also have lists of researchers. *Research services in Dublin include:*

Gorry Research
12 Burrow Road
Sutton, Dublin 13
Ph: 353-1-8393942

Hibernian Research Company Ltd.
24 Balnagowan
Palmerstown Park
Rathmines, Dublin 6
Ph: 353-1-4966522; fax: 353-1-4973011

Dr. J. Ryan
4 Spencer Villas
Glenageary, Co. Dublin
Ph: 353-1-2806228

In Northern Ireland, most professional researchers are affiliated to APGI (see above) and/or to the Association of Ulster Genealogists and Record Agents (AUGRA). A list of their members can be obtained from the Secretary, c/o Glen Cottage, Glenmachan Road, Belfast BT4 2NP. *Research services in Northern Ireland include:*

Ulster Historical Foundation
Balmoral Buildings, 12 College Square East
Belfast BT1 6DD
Ph: (1232) 332288

Irish World
See Irish World office in relevant county in Research Services section.

Societies
There is great interest in local history in Ireland, as is shown by the numbers of local history societies listed in each chapter. Researchers may be interested to join local societies, or place queries or articles in their newsletters or journals. Although a few societies have permanent headquarters and libraries, most do not and are dependent on voluntary local secretaries. Local history societies are affiliated either to the Federation of Local History Societies, c/o Rothe House, Kilkenny, Co. Kilkenny, or to The Federation of Ulster Local Studies, 8 Fitzwilliam Street, Belfast

BT9 6AW. Continually updated lists of member societies can be obtained from these organizations.

Family history societies also exist. These are listed in the relevant county. Most of the Irish genealogical societies and organizations are affiliated to the Council of Irish Genealogical Organizations (CIGO), whose secretary, Des Clarke, can be contacted c/o 21 St. Brigid's Grove, Killester, Dublin 5. CIGO cannot undertake research, nor is it open to individual members.

The Irish Family History Society is a national society and can be contacted at PO Box 36, Naas, Co. Kildare; home page: http://www.mayo-ireland.ie/geneal/ifhissoc.htm. They publish the *Irish Family History Society Journal*.

In the USA, the Irish Genealogical Society (POB 16585, St. Paul, MN 55116-0585, USA) specifically caters to Irish family history interests. They publish *The Septs*. Many other UK, US, and Australian societies also frequently cover Irish-interest topics.

Miscellaneous Sources

In this section, records of genealogical interest which do not easily fall into the other categories are presented. These include a varied assortment of articles dealing with social issues, emigration, lists of public officials, and other useful background information.

A Brief History of Ireland

Some general background information about Irish history will be useful in understanding the nature and value of the record sources listed in this book. This section, therefore, outlines some of the major events which have affected Irish family and social history.

Current evidence suggests that the earliest arrival of people in Ireland was approximately 6500 B.C. A number of independent waves of further migrants followed this early invasion. The exact origins of the earlier arrivals are not known, but the bulk of the later arrivals were Celtic, part of the same racial stock as now also inhabit Scotland, Wales, Cornwall, and Brittany in France. These people developed a rich culture in Ireland.

In the old Gaelic cultural system, families and their territories were very closely linked. Indeed, the Gaelic name of a territory and of its people were the same, "tuath." It is therefore possible to identify precisely the territories of the ruling families (O'Neills, O'Briens, O'Connors, etc.). Other families were associated with these ruling families as doctors, lawyers, scribes, historians, etc., and can also be linked with particular territories. For example, the Maguires, ruling family of the area which is now Fermanagh, were associated with the O'Husseys (bards), the O'Keenans (historians), O'Cassidys (physicians), O'Breslins (lawyers), etc. These territories gradually broke down as the families were dispossessed and new land divisions were imposed by English rule. However, families are generally still well represented in their ancient territories.

The native language of the country is Gaelic, or Irish. Although the Irish language is still spoken in some parts of Ireland and is one of the official languages of the Irish Republic, English is the primary language of the country. Most Gaelic family and place-names are based on Gaelic language forms.

The first significant new arrivals to Ireland within recorded history were the Norse and Danish Vikings, who arrived in the eighth and ninth centuries, first to raid and later to settle and trade. Many coastal ports, including Waterford, Wexford, and Dublin, were largely developed by these Vikings. Up to and following the defeat of the Vikings by the native Irish in 1014, there was widespread integration of these peoples into the native population. These Scandinavian settlers did not use family names which were traditionally passed from father to son as in most of Europe, and as a result, there is little evidence of Viking influence in current family names. Exceptions include the names Sweetman, Harold, and Doyle.

In the twelfth century Ireland was invaded and largely conquered by the Normans, descendants of a mixed Scandinavian-Frankish people who had earlier conquered England and Wales. In time, however, the Normans also became totally integrated with the Irish people, adopting the native dress, customs, and language. Norman names such as Burke, Roche, Fitzgerald, etc., are now among the most common in Ireland.

England nominally controlled all of Ireland from the time of the Norman invasion. In practice, however, for several centuries, English law only applied in an area around Dublin called the "Pale." The extent of the Pale varied during this time, but generally included the current counties of Dublin and parts of Kildare, Meath, Wicklow, and Louth.

In the mid-sixteenth century, Henry VIII began the Tudor "reconquest" of Ireland, gaining the submission of many of the Gaelic chieftains in return for assurances that they would retain lordship of their ancestral territories. He also began the process of destroying Gaelic culture by outlawing Irish language, dress, and even hairstyle!

Gaelic Ireland did not give up easily, however, and English rule was only tentatively maintained over many areas from within fortified garrisons. In Ulster, particularly, the O'Neills and O'Donnells fought the "nine years' war" with England. This ended with O'Neill's defeat in 1603. The subsequent departure of O'Neill and most of the leading chieftains of Ulster opened the way for the era of "plantation" of Irish territories. In a plantation, the native people were removed from their lands and replaced by colonists from England, Scotland, or Wales. This policy was pursued in Ulster with good success. Success was not total, however, because there were not enough planters to occupy all of the areas to be planted and not enough labor to work them. Thus, significant numbers of the native populations stayed in their traditional territories as tenants and laborers. The plantations elsewhere in Ireland had moderate or little success. These plantation schemes are more fully dealt with in the histories of the affected counties.

In 1641 there was a further rebellion by the Catholic population of Ireland, which included the Gaelic and "Old English" or Norman people. The Catholics set up a rival parliament in Kilkenny, which ruled Ireland for some years. This rebellion was finally defeated by Oliver Cromwell in 1649 and was followed by massive confiscation of land and the forced transplantation of many Catholics to the province of Connaught. Many of the defeated soldiers and others made homeless by the war were transported to the West Indies. The Irish confiscated lands were redistributed to various "adventurers" (those who had financed Cromwell's army), to officers in this army, and to others favored by the English establishment. The bulk of the population, however, continued to live where they had previously, albeit under new landlords.

From the family history viewpoint, this period is significant, because the process of confiscation and redistribution required extensive surveys of the land and its owners. Many of these surveys survive.

In order to increase the numbers of Protestant settlers in Ireland, various encouragements were offered to immigrants of that faith. The earliest of these was "an act to encourage Protestant settlers to settle in Ireland," passed in 1662. This helped the influx of French Huguenots into Ireland, particularly after the Revocation of the Edict of Nantes gave them cause to leave France. Many Huguenots were tradesmen, such as goldsmiths, weavers, etc., and many became very successful merchants.

In 1690 James II and William of Orange, contenders for the throne of England, fought a war in Ireland, with Catholic support going to James. The war resulted in a defeat for King James, and had a number of devastating consequences for Irish Catholics. The first was that huge numbers of the soldiers who had fought in King James's army were forced to flee overseas. By one estimate, half a million soldiers joined the armies of France and other continental European countries in the fifty years following the end of this war.

Although the Catholic army had negotiated honorable surrender terms (the "Treaty of Limerick") which guaranteed that there would be no general repression of Catholics, this treaty was not honored. Instead, a series of "Penal Laws" were enacted by the English parliament which severely restricted Catholic entry to certain trades, their right to land ownership and inheritance, and many other rights. By the beginning of the eighteenth century it is estimated that only about five percent of Ireland was owned by Catholics.

The Penal Laws are very significant from a family history viewpoint, as they had the effect of reducing the number and variety of records relating to Catholic families. By restricting the activities of the Roman Catholic church, and by limiting the numbers and rights of its priests, the Penal Laws, in effect, hindered the keeping of comprehensive records. By reducing Catholic rights to own land, they also removed Catholic families from inclusion in land records, such as deeds and leases. The Penal Laws also restricted Catholics from entering public office, removed their voting rights, and in general impoverished them, thus cutting down the range of records which they might be expected to have left. For this reason, the eighteenth century is known as the "silent century" in Irish family research.

The Penal Laws also applied in some respects to Presbyterians. These laws were a major cause of the migration of Presbyterians from Ireland to North America and Canada in the eighteenth century. These were the so-called Scots-Irish, the Scottish who were settled in the plantation of Ulster beginning in 1609.

Inspired by the French Revolution of 1789, a new nationalist movement, the United Irishmen, arose in Ireland toward the end of the eighteenth century. This movement culminated in a rebellion in 1798. The rebellion was sporadic, however, and was quickly put down.

The major period of emigration from Ireland started about 1780, but the event which forced the major emigration from Ireland was the Great Famine of 1845 to 1847. The conditions which produced this famine are complex. Briefly: Ireland underwent great social change during the eighteenth century. Agriculture developed rapidly in response to the demand from Britain for food. The increase in tillage required an increased workforce, and thus there was a period of relative prosperity for smallholders and laboring classes. Another significant development was that the Irish peasantry became increasingly reliant on the potato as their staple food. Since an entire family could support itself on a small area of land, a social revolution occurred. The average age at marriage dropped as it became possible for younger men to support a family by renting a small amount of land on which to grow potatoes (to eat) and cereals (to sell for rent money).

During the nineteenth century there was a consequent large increase in population. In 1687 it is estimated that the population was around 2.2 million. By 1725 it had exceeded three million, and by 1772 it was almost 3.6 million. In 1781 it was just over four million, and from then until 1820 the rate of increase was approximately seventeen percent per decade. The population grew to over eight million in 1841, the highest it had ever been (or has been since). The two major factors which were to significantly change this situation were (a) a decline in the value of agricultural produce and (b) the increasingly common destruction of the potato crop by potato blight.

During most of the period of this rapid population increase, the Irish agricultural economy was heavily dependent on export of cereals to England. When the Napoleonic wars ended in 1814, food prices dropped. This meant that smallholdings became increasingly less viable, as the small areas planted in cereals were unable to produce enough return to pay the rent. This resulted in large-scale unemployment of the laboring classes, and evictions of many smallholders.

The final blow to these smallholders, however, was the increasing incidence of potato blight, a fungal disease which attacks potatoes. The crop partially failed many times between 1800 and 1845. However, in the four years between 1845 and 1848, the crop failed three times, causing what became known as the Great Famine. The result was the death of a million people by starvation or disease, and a flood of emigration.

It is estimated that in 1847 alone, around 230,000 people left Ireland for North America and Australia and further thousands for Britain. Some two million left between 1845 and 1855, and the process of emigra-

tion continued for the remainder of the century and beyond. Between 1845 and 1925 approximately 4.75 million Irish people went to the United States, 70,000 to Canada, and 370,000 to Australia. From its peak of over eight million in 1841, the population by 1926 had fallen to four million, and is currently around five million.

For those Catholic Irish who remained in Ireland, rights to land, voting, etc., were gradually restored. Toward the end of the nineteenth century, the movement for self-government for Ireland, either as a separate parliament within the United Kingdom ("Home Rule") or as an independent state, grew. In 1916 a rebellion began which finally resulted in the establishment of an independent Irish state in 1921.

Until 1921, all of Ireland was within the "United Kingdom of Great Britain and Ireland." In that year, twenty-six of the thirty-two counties became independent, and later became the Republic of Ireland. Six counties, Antrim, Armagh, Down, Fermanagh, Derry (or Londonderry), and Tyrone, remain part of the United Kingdom. As the records of interest to researchers are generally pre-1921, most relevant public records derive from the British administration of Ireland. There are many detailed histories of Ireland available. For the period from 1800 onward, a useful general history is *Ireland Since the Famine* by F.S.L. Lyons, 1971.

Emigration to the United States and Britain has continued at varying levels ever since the early eighteenth century. In some parts of the country, where the initial level of emigration was high, it became a tradition. Even when the economic situation in Ireland had improved, the attraction of America, in particular, remained. Indeed, in some parts of the country going to America meant reunion with as many family members and friends as were left behind. In his book *20 Years a-Growing*, Maurice O'Sullivan, a native of one such high-emigration area, considers his options of going to Dublin or America to work. He imagines his sister's advice from America to "come out here where your own people are, for if you go to Dublin you will never see any of your kinsfolk again!"

Almost none of these events in Irish history affected all counties equally. The local effects in each county are discussed in the county history given at the beginning of each chapter.

Bibliography

Guides and How-To Books

Begley, Donal F., ed. *Irish Genealogy: A Record Finder.* Dublin: Heraldic Artists, 1981.

Falley, Margaret Dickson. *Irish and Scotch-Irish Ancestral Research.* Evanston, Ill.: the author, 1961–2.

Grenham, John. *Tracing Your Irish Ancestors: The Complete Guide.* Dublin: Gill & McMillan, 1992.

McCarthy, Tony. *The Irish Roots Guide.* Dublin: Lilliput Press, 1991.

O'Connor, Michael. *A Guide to Tracing Your Kerry Ancestors.* Dublin: Flyleaf Press, 1995.

Sources

Hayes, Richard. *Manuscript Sources for the History of Irish Civilisation.* 11 vols. Boston: G. & K. Hall & Co., 1965.

_____. *Periodical Sources for the History of Irish Civilisation.* 9 vols. Boston: G. & K. Hall & Co., 1970. Supplement (3 vols.), 1979.

Helferty, Seamus, and R. Refausse. *Directory of Irish Archives.* Dublin: Irish Academic Press, 1988.

Phillimore, W.P.W., and Gertrude Thrift, eds. *Indexes to Irish Wills.* Reprint. Baltimore: Genealogical Publishing Co., 1970.

Ryan, James G., ed. *Irish Church Records–Their History, Availability, and Use.* Dublin: Flyleaf Press, 1992.

Vicars, Sir Arthur, ed. *Index to the Prerogative Wills of Ireland, 1536–1810.* 1897. Reprint. Baltimore: Genealogical Publishing Co., 1967.

Family Names and Place-Names

General Alphabetical Index to the Townlands and Towns, Parishes, and Baronies of Ireland. Reprint. Baltimore: Genealogical Publishing Co., 1984.

Matheson, Sir Robt. E. *Special Report on Surnames in Ireland.* Dublin: Thom's, 1909. Reprint. Baltimore: Genealogical Publishing Co., 1988.

McLysaght, Edward. *Bibliography of Irish Family History.* 2nd ed. Dublin: Irish Academic Press, 1982.

_____. *Irish Families–Their Names, Arms, and Origins.* Dublin: Irish Academic Press, 1985 (and further titles in this series: *More Irish Families*, etc.).

_____. *The Surnames of Ireland.* 6th ed. Dublin: Irish Academic Press, 1985.

Mitchell, Brian. *New Genealogical Atlas of Ireland.* Baltimore: Genealogical Publishing Co., 1986.

Nolan, W. *Tracing the Past: Sources for Local Studies in the Republic of Ireland.* Dublin: Geography Publications, 1982.

Woulfe, Rev. Patrick. *Sloinnte Gaedeal is Gall–Irish Names and Surnames.* Ireland, 1923. Reprint. Baltimore: Genealogical Publishing Co., 1993.

Irish History and Emigration

Filby, P.W., and Mary K. Meyer, eds. *Passenger and Immigration Lists Index.* Detroit: Gale Research, 1981. (Lists over 1,000 published lists of Irish immigrants to the U.S.)

_____. *Passenger and Immigration Lists Bibliography.* Detroit: Gale Research, 1988. (Lists over 2,500 published lists of Irish immigrants to the U.S.)

Glazier, Ira A., ed. *The Famine Emigrants: Lists of Irish Emigrants Arriving at the Port of New York, 1846–51.* 7 vols. Baltimore: Genealogical Publishing Co., 1983–6.

Harris, Ruth-Ann, and D.M. Jacobs, eds. *The Search for Missing Friends: Irish Immigrant Advertisements in the Boston Pilot.* Vols I–III. Boston: New England Historic Genealogical Society, 1989–93.

Lyons, F.S.L. *Ireland Since the Famine.* London: Fontana, 1973.

Abbreviations Used in the Text and Tables

AA	Armagh Ancestry
A&A	Ardfert and Aghadoe (Diocese)
AC	Achonry (Diocese)
ACM	Armagh County Museum
AD	Ardagh (Diocese)
Add.	Additional
AM	Armagh
Anglican Rec. Proj.	Anglican Record Project
Archiv. Hib.	Archivum Hibernum
b.	birth/born
BBHC	Brú Ború Heritage Centre
BL	British Library
BPL	Belfast Public Library
ca.	circa (i.e., approximately)
CA	Cashel (Diocese)
CCAR	Cork City Ancestral Research Ltd.
CF	Clonfert (Diocese)
CG	Clogher (Diocese)
CGP	Carlow Genealogical Project
CHGC	Cavan Heritage and Genealogy Centre
CI	Church of Ireland (Protestant or Episcopalian)
CK	Cork (Diocese)
Clare HC	Clare Heritage Centre
Co.	County
C of I	Church of Ireland
CR	Connor (Diocese)
CY	Cloyne (Diocese)
d.	death/died
DA	Donegal Ancestry
DE	Derry (Diocese)
DFHL	Dublin Friends Historical Library
DGC	Derry Genealogy Centre
DHC	Duhallow Heritage Centre
DHG	Dublin Heritage Group
DKPRI	Deputy Keeper of Public Records of Ireland (Report of . . .)
DLHC	Dun Laoghaire Heritage Centre
DR	Dromore (Diocese)
DU	Dublin (Diocese)
DW	Down (Diocese)

Ed.	Edited or Edition
Eire-Ir.	Eire-Ireland
EL	Elphin (Diocese)
EM	Emly (Diocese)
FE	Ferns (Diocese)
FHG	Fingal Heritage Group
FHL	Friends Historical Library
GC-Derry	Genealogy Centre-Derry
GCL	Galway County Library
Gen.	Genealogy/genealogical
GFHS	Galway Family History Soc.
GO	Genealogical Office
GRO	General Register Office
HC	Heritage Centre
Hist.	Historical
HMSO	Her Majesty's Stationery Office (UK)
IGP	Irish Genealogical Project
IGRS	Irish Genealogical Research Society
ISBN	International Standard Book Number
J. or Jnl.	Journal
K&K	Killaloe and Kilfenora (Diocese)
KA	Killala (Diocese)
KAS	Kilkenny Archaeological Society
KD	Kildare (Diocese)
KF	Kilfenora (Diocese)
KGC	Killarney Genealogical Centre
KHP	Kildare Heritage Project
KL	Killaloe (Diocese)
KM	Kilmore (Diocese)
KMC	Kilmacduagh (Diocese)
LA	Limerick Archives
LC	local custody (records are held by local church)
LDS	Family History Library of The Church of Jesus Christ of Latter-day Saints, Salt Lake City, Utah, and branches
LE	Leighlin (Diocese)
LHC	Leitrim Heritage Centre
LHL	Linen Hall Library (Belfast)
LK	Limerick (Diocese)
LMGC	Longford Museum and Genealogical Centre

LOFHR	Laois-Offaly Family History Research Centre
LS	Lismore (Diocese)
m.	marriage/married
ME	Meath (Diocese)
mf	microfilm
MFCI	reference for microfilm records at NAI
MHC	Mallow Heritage Centre
misc.	miscellaneous
MNFHRC	Mayo North Family History Research Centre
Mon. Anc.	Monaghan Ancestry Ltd.
MP	Member of Parliament (i.e., British/Westminster)
ms/s or Ms/s	manuscript/s
N&M	Newry and Mourne (Diocese)
NAI	National Archives of Ireland
n.d.	not dated/no date
NLI	National Library of Ireland
no/s.	number/s
N.S.	New Series
OS	Ossory (Diocese)
p/p.	page/s
Parl.	Parliament/parliamentary
Ph	phone
PHSA	Presbyterian Historical Society Archives
PO	Post Office
PRO	Public Record Office (now National Archives)
PRO(m)	Public Record Office (microfilm)
PRONI	Public Record Office of Northern Ireland
Pub.	published/publisher

QUB	Queens University, Belfast
RA	Raphoe (Diocese)
RC	Roman Catholic
RCB	Representative Church Body
RCBL	Representative Church Body Library
RHGS	Roscommon Heritage and Genealogical Society
RIA	Royal Irish Academy
RO	Ross (Diocese)
s (as in 20s)	shilling (e.g., 20 shillings)
SEELB	South East Education and Library Board (N. Ireland)
SHGS	Sligo Heritage and Genealogy Society
SLC	Genealogical Library, Salt Lake City, Utah
SMFRC	South Mayo Family Research Centre
SO	Stationery Office (Publisher of Irish Government Documents and Papers)
Soc.	Society
Soc. Gen.	Society of Genealogists (London)
SPO	State Paper Office (now part of NAI)
TCD	Trinity College Dublin
THU	Tipperary Heritage Unit
TNFHF	Tipperary North Family History Foundation
TU	Tuam (Diocese)
UHF	Ulster Historical Foundation
Vol/s.	Volume/s
WA	Waterford (Diocese)
WHRC	Wexford Heritage Research Centre
Wicklow HC	Wicklow Heritage Centre
WCHC	West Cork Heritage Centre
WHL	Waterford Heritage Limited

Abbreviations of Periodicals and References

Anal.Hib.
  Analecta Hibernica

Archiv. Hib.
  Archivum Hibernicum

Derry Hist. Soc. J.
  Derry Historical Society Journal

Donegal Ann.
  Donegal Annual

Dublin Hist. Rec.
  Dublin Historical Record

Gen.
  Genealogist

Hist. Mss. Comm. Rep.
  Historical Manuscripts Commission Report

Ir. Anc.
  Irish Ancestor

Ir. Gen.
  Irish Genealogist

Ir. Hist. Stud.
  Irish Historical Studies

J. Ass. Pres. Mem. Dead
  Journal of the Association for the Preservation of
  Memorials of the Dead

J. Ballinteer FHS
  Journal of Ballinteer Family Historical Society

JCHAS
  Cork Historical and Archaeological Society Journal

J. Cork Hist. & Arch. Soc.
  Cork Historical and Archaeological Society Journal

J. Galway Arch. Hist. Soc.
  Journal of Galway Archaeological and Historical
  Society

J. Kildare Arch. Hist. Soc.
  Journal of Kildare Archaeological and Historical
  Society

J. Louth Arch. Hist. Soc.
  Journal of Louth Archaeological and Historical Society

J. Waterford & S.E. Ire. Arch. Soc.
  Journal of the Waterford and South East Ireland
  Archaeological Society

Kerry Arch. Mag.
  Kerry Archaeological Magazine

L. Gur Hist. Soc. J.
  Lough Gur Historical Society Journal

Louth Arch. J.
  Louth Archaeological Journal

N. Munster Antiq. J.
  North Munster Antiquarian Journal

OCM
  O'Kief, Coshe Mang and Slieve Luachra

Parl. Papers
  Parliamentary Papers

R.S.A.I.
  Journal of the Royal Society of Antiquarians of Ireland

Ulster Gen. & Hist. Guild
  Ulster Genealogical and Historical Guild

Ulster J. Arch.
  Ulster Journal of Archaeology

County Antrim

A Brief History

Antrim is on the northeastern coast of Ireland. The major towns are Carrickfergus, Ballymena, Lisburn, Ballycastle, Larne, and the city of Belfast, which straddles the border of Antrim and Down. For practical purposes, many Belfast records, particularly church records, are listed together in the appendix.

Under the old Gaelic system, this area was part of the territory of the O'Neills, and was called Dalriada. The other major Gaelic families were the McQuillans and O'Quinns. Some "gallowglass," or mercenary families from Scotland, settled in Antrim in the thirteenth and fourteenth centuries. These included the McDonnells, Bissels (who became McKeowns), MacNeills, and McAllisters. Two Connaught families, the O'Haras and MacClearys, also migrated to Antrim at this period. The county was little affected by the Norman invasion, and the ruling families of the county maintained their independence for several centuries.

In 1594 the major tribes of Ulster, led by Hugh O'Neill, rebelled against English rule. This rebellion lasted until 1603, when the Ulster tribes were finally defeated. Following the defeat and departure of O'Neill and the heads of the major clans, Antrim, like most of the rest of Ulster, was "planted" with settlers from Britain. Antrim was one of the first counties planted, in advance of the main Ulster plantation, which began in 1609. In about 1605, the Lord Deputy, Arthur Chichester, acquired the castle and lands of Belfast. Subsequently, he ruthlessly exterminated the inhabitants of these estates and planted them with English settlers. These came mainly from Devon, Lancashire, and Cheshire, and included families named Bradshaw, Bradford, Watson, Taylor, Walker, Jackson, Wilson, Johnson, and Young.

Also in the early 1600s, English and Scottish adventurers, such as Clotworthy and Upton, were given confiscated lands in Antrim on the understanding that they would bring over settlers to their new estates. The now common occurrence of names such as Boyd, Fraser, Lindsay, Johnson, Morrison, Patterson, and Maxwell is due to the Scottish settlers brought to the county by these adventurers.

The objectives of plantation, i.e., the clearance of the native population and its replacement by British subjects, were most successfully achieved in this county. Many of the native people were removed from the county altogether. As the native Irish population was predominantly Catholic, the Scottish usually Presbyterian, and the English generally Protestant, the proportions of these religions among the population can, in very general terms, be used to estimate the origins of the inhabitants of the county. When religious affiliation was first determined in the census of 1861, the respective proportions of Catholic, Presbyterian, and Protestant in Antrim were twenty-eight, twenty, and forty-eight percent.

Antrim, like the other northeastern counties, became a center of the linen industry. The industry was particularly developed by the arrival in the county of many French Huguenot weavers from 1685 onward. These Huguenots settled in particular in Lisburn and Belfast, and their introduction of French looms and other innovations began a period of prosperity for the industry. By 1700, Belfast had a population of two thousand.

As in the other northern counties, many northern Presbyterians or so-called Scots-Irish left Antrim during the eighteenth and early nineteenth centuries because of the repression of Presbyterians under the Penal Laws (see the introduction), which were primarily intended to repress Catholicism. In the late eighteenth century, Belfast was the center of the Society of the United Irishmen, which was a movement of Catholics and Presbyterians against this repression.

Belfast City is arguably the only city in Ireland to have felt the full effects of the industrial revolution. The city developed rapidly in the nineteenth century, largely based on the linen industry and on heavy industry such as shipbuilding. Its rapid growth resulted in further immigration of people from Scotland, northern England, and rural Ireland. By the end of the nineteenth century, its population had grown to 300,000.

The county is one of the few whose population has increased since the Great Famine. This is largely due to the growth of Belfast City and surrounding towns. Apart from Dublin, the population of County Antrim is the most urbanized in Ireland. Because of this, commercial directories are particularly valuable sources of information. Some of the 1857 census returns have also survived. The northern, and non-urbanized, parts of the county are largely agricultural, and also have important fishing ports.

In 1921, the county was one of those which remained in the United Kingdom when the Irish Free State was formed.

Census and Census Substitutes

1614-15

Names of Masters and Merchants trading in and out of Carrickfergus. *Carrickfergus & District Hist. J.* 2, 1986 (date of entry, name, qualification, ship, and tonnage).

1635-1796

"The Roll of Freemen—Belfast." In *The Townbook of the Corporation of Belfast 1613-1816*, 215-17. SLC film 0990294.

1642

Muster Roll. PRONI T8726/2; SLC film 897012.

1643

"Tax List for Belfast." In *The Townbook of the Corporation of Belfast 1613-1816*, 25-27. SLC film 0990294.

1659

"Census" of Ireland. Edited by S. Pender. Dublin: Stationery Office, 1939. NLI I6551. SLC film 924648.

1660-69

"Hearth Money and Poll Tax returns for Co. Antrim" by S.T. Carlton. Pub. by PRONI.

1663-69

Subsidy Roll. PRONI T307.

1666

Hearth Money Roll. NAI film 2745; NLI ms. 9584. NLI P 207.

Subsidy Roll. PRONI T.3022/4/1.

1669

Hearth Money Roll. PRONI T307; NLI ms. 9584 (index on 9585).

"Extracts from Hearth Money Roll for Parishes of Ramoan, Culfreightrin and Rathlin." *The Glynns* 1 (1973): 10-15.

"Extracts from Glenarm Barony." *The Glynns* 5 (1977): 15-16.

1719

"Map of Glenarm" (including names and holdings of the Earl of Antrim's Tenants in the Town and Adjoining Lands). *The Glynns* 9 (1981): 52-61.

1720

List of Landed Gentry in Down and Antrim. RIA ms. 24 K 19.

1734

A religious census of the Barony of Cary. *The Glynns* 21 (1993): 65-76; 22 (1994): 53-58. (Parishes of Ballintoy, Culfeightrin, Ramoan, Armoy, and part of Billy and Derrykeighan; gives townland, chief tenant, and householders.)

Map Showing Residents of Ballymoney. SLC film 990232.

1740

Protestant householders in parishes of Ahoghill, Armoy, Ballintoy, Ballymena, Ballymoney, Bellewillen, Billy, Clogh, Drumaul, Dunean, Dunkegan, Dunluce, Finvoy, Kilraghts, Loghall, Manybrooke, Rasharkin, Rathlin, and Ramoan. GO 559; SLC film 100249; RCB Library. PRONI T808/15258.

1744

"List of Voters in Belfast." In *The Townbook of the Corporation of Belfast, 1613-1816*, 246-300.

1766

Parishes of Ahoghill and Ballynure. RCB Library. MS 23 NAI M.2476 (1). SLC film 1279330.

Parish of Ballintoy. GO 536; SLC film 258517 or 100173; PRONI T808/15264.

All above parishes on NLI ms. 4173.

1779

Map of Glenarm, including tenants' names. *The Glynns* 9 (1981).

1796

See Co. Mayo 1796 (List of Catholics . . .).

Spinning Wheel Premium list. See introduction.

1798

List of Persons who Suffered Losses During '98 Rebellion. NLI JLB 94107 (approximately 140 names, addresses, and occupations).

1799–1800

Militia Pay Lists and Muster Rolls, PRONI T.1115/1 A and B.

1803

Inhabitants of Ballintoy. SLC 941.61/B7 K2c.

1804–10

Old Ballymoney residents. *North Irish Roots* 2 (3) (1989) (name, occupation, and religion, by street).

1813

Census of Ballyeaston Congregation (Presbyterian) covering Ballycor, Donagore, Glenwhirry, Grange of Doagh, Kilbride, and Rashee. SLC (fiche) 6026299 and (mf) 100173.

1820

List of Lisburn householders. PRONI T679/107–112. (Householder's name and no. in household.)

1821

Government census, various fragments. Thrift Abstracts, NAI. SLC film 824240.

1824–34

Tithe Applotment Survey (see introduction).

1832–36

"List of Excise License Holders and Applicants in Belfast, Lisburn, and Carrickfergus" (names, occupations, and address). *Parl. Papers* 1837/38, 13 (2): Appendix 10, 13.

1832–37

Belfast Poll Book. PRONI D2472.

1832–65

"Historical sketch of Parliamentary elections in Belfast . . . till 1865." (Names and addresses of voters, and of those on the register who did not vote in 1865.) Belfast: Banner of Ulster Office, 1865, p. 194.

1833–39

Mitchell, Brian. *Irish Emigration Lists 1833–1839*. Lists of emigrants extracted from the ordnance survey memoirs. Baltimore, 1989. 118 pp. Indexed.

1834

Registered Freeholders, Leaseholders, and Householders of Carrickfergus. Court of Quarter Sessions, 1834. SLC film 990408.

1837

"Lists of Freemen (since 1831) of Carrickfergus." *Parl. Papers* 1837, 11 (1): Appendix B1; 1837/38, 13 (2): Appendix 3.

"List of Applicants for the Vote in Borough of Belfast." *Parl. Papers* 1837, 11 (2): Appendix 7, 235–45 (gives 772 names, residences, occupations).

"Occupants of Lisburn, Arranged by Street, Giving Property Values." *Parl. Papers* 1837, 11 (1): Appendix G, 211–15.

1838

"Lists of Marksmen (illiterate voters) in Belfast" (over 250 names, occupations, and residences). *Parl. Papers* 1837, 11 (1): Appendix A3; 1837/38, 13 (2): Appendix 4.

1839

List of Persons who obtained Game Certificates in Ulster, Roscommon, Longford, Leitrim, Sligo, Mayo, and Galway. PRONI T688.

1841

Extracts from the Government Census Relating to the Families Johnston, McShane, and Thompson. SLC film 824240.

1845–78

Persons admitted into, and discharged from, Larne Workhouse (with index). PRONI; SLC film 0993083–4.

1848

Applications for registration as Electors. Dublin: Pilkington, 1849. SLC film 993156.

1851

Government Census Extracts: parishes of Aghagallon (townlands of Montiaghs, Tamnyrane, and Tiscallen only), Aghalee, Ahohill (townland of Craigs only), Ballinderry, Ballymoney (townland of Garryduff only), Carncastle, Clough, Craigs, Dunaghy, Grange of Killyglen, Killead (townlands from Ardmore to Carnagliss only), Kilwaughter, Larne, Rasharkin (townlands from Killydonnelly to Tehorny only), Tickmacreevan. NAI CEN 1851/2-13; SLC films 597143-53, 597108-13. These records can also be directly searched on an Internet site established by the North of Ireland Family History Society (http://brigit.os.qub.ac.uk/nifhs/census/).

1852

Names and addresses of the electors of Belfast (alphabetically arranged; gives names and addresses of voters and how they voted). Belfast: W&G Agnew, 1852, 92 pp.

1854

List of persons entitled to vote. SLC film 993156.

1855

Belfast Register of Electors, PRONI BELF5/1/1/1-2.

1856/57

Register of Persons Entitled to Vote in general election (arranged alphabetically by barony; gives over nine thousand names, addresses, nature of qualification to vote, location of freehold, etc.). NLI ILB 324.

1857

List of the electors of Belfast (arranged alphabetically in wards; gives names of voters and how they voted). Belfast: Daily Mercury, 1857, 68 pp.

1859

Voters in Lisburn By-Election of February 1863. *Lisburn Hist. Soc. J.* 6 (Winter 1986-7) (name and street).

1861-62

Griffith's Valuation (see introduction).

1863

Names and addresses of voters at the Lisburn election. No place of publication, 1863, 10 pp, LHL.

1865

List of the voters of Belfast. (Arranged alphabetically; gives names and addresses of voters.) BPL.

1868

Names and addresses of Belfast voters from the general election. (Arranged alphabetically in wards.) Belfast: H. Adair, 1869, 168 pp.

Alphabetical list of voters and non-voting electors (and addresses). Belfast: publisher not stated, 1868, 96 pp, BPL.

1871

Creggan Upper. Archiv. Hib. 3.

1901

Census. NAI (see introduction). SLC (mf).

1911

Census. NAI. SLC film 857372.

Church Records

Church of Ireland

See the introduction for a description of Church of Ireland records and their major repositories. Many C of I records were lost in the PRO fire of 1922. These are indicated as "Lost." However, as C of I records were effectively state records, the records of marriage (from 1845) are also in the General Registrar's Office. Many are still in local custody (LC), while others are in one of a variety of other archives (e.g., RCBL or NAI). The parish registers of Antrim are being indexed by the Ulster Historical Foundation (see Research Services at the end of the chapter). A search of the index will be conducted by this center for a fee. For registers within the city of Belfast, see also the further registers in the appendix.

Aghalee
Earliest Records: b. 1782; m. 1782; d. 1782
Status: LC; SLC film 908817 (b. 1812-18; m. 1812-45; d. 1811-74)

Ahoghill
Earliest Records: b. 1811; m. 1811; d. 1811
Status: LC

Ardclinis
Status: Lost

Ballinderry
Earliest Records: b. 1805; m. 1840; d. 1805
Status: LC

Ballintoy
Earliest Records: b. 1776; m. 1776
Status: LC; SLC 941.61/B7 K2c (1776-1843)

Ballyclug
Earliest Records: b. 1841
Status: LC

Ballyeaston
Status: Lost

Ballymena (Kirkinriola)
Earliest Records: b. 1815; m. 1807; d. 1780
Status: LC; SLC film 990408

Ballymire
Earliest Records: b. 1812; m. 1825; d. 1840
Missing Dates: m. 1830-45; d. 1841-51
Status: LC

Ballymoney
Earliest Records: b. 1807
Status: LC; SLC film 908674; index on 883747

Ballyrashane
Status: Lost

Ballyscullion (Grange)
Status: Lost

Ballysillan
Earliest Records: b. 1826; m. 1825; d. 1827
Status: LC

Belfast Cathedral
Earliest Records: m. 1874-1893
Status: RCBL (mf)

Billy
Status: Lost

Carnmoney
Earliest Records: b. 1788; m. 1789; d. 1845
Status: LC; SLC (mf) 0990097 or 990488 (b. 1788-1879; m/d. 1791-1855)

Carrickfergus
Earliest Records: b. 1740; m. 1740; d. 1837
Status: LC

Christchurch
Earliest Records: b. 1837; m. 1837; d. 1837
Status: LC

Christchurch (Belfast)
Status: LC

Christchurch (Lisburn)
Earliest Records: b. 1849
Status: LC

Craigs
Earliest Records: b. 1839; m. 1841; d. 1841
Status: LC

Culfeightrin
Status: Lost

Cushendun
Status: Lost

Derryaghey (Lisburn)
Earliest Records: b. 1696; m. 1696; d. 1696
Missing Dates: b. 1739-70; m. 1739-1826; d. 1739-1826
Status: LC; Pub. by W.N.C. Barr & W.C. Kerr, Lisburn, 1981 (with index)

Derrykeighan
Status: Lost

Donegore
Status: Lost

Drummaul (Randalstown)
Earliest Records: b. 1823; m. 1823; d. 1823
Status: LC

Drumtullagh
Status: Lost

Dunaghy
Status: Lost

Duneane
Status: Lost

Dunluce (Bushmills)
Earliest Records: b. 1809; m. 1826; d. 1826
Status: LC

Dunseverick
Earliest Records: b. 1832; m. 1833; d. 1833
Status: LC

Falls, Lower (or St. Luke Belfast)
Status: Lost

Falls, Upper Belfast
Earliest Records: b. 1855
Status: LC

Finvoy
Earliest Records: b. 1811; m. 1812; d. 1811
Status: LC

Gartree
Status: Lost

Glenavy
Earliest Records: b. 1707; m. 1813; d. 1707
Status: LC

Glynn
Earliest Records: b. 1838; m. 1842; d. 1838
Status: LC

Inver and Larne
Earliest Records: b. 1806; m. 1817; d. 1826
Status: LC

Islandmagee
Status: Lost

Jordanstown
Earliest Records: b. 1878
Status: LC; RCBL (mf) (b. 1878-1974)

Kilbride and Donegore
Status: Lost

Kilbride
Status: Lost

Kildolla
Status: Lost

Killagan
Status: Lost

Killead
Status: Lost

Killwaughter and Carncastle
Status: Lost

Lambeg
Earliest Records: b. 1810; m. 1810; d. 1810
Status: LC

Layde
Earliest Records: b. 1826; m. 1826; d. 1826
Status: LC

Lisburn or Blaris
Earliest Records: b. 1639; m. 1661; d. 1661
Missing Dates: b. 1647–60
Status: LC

Lisnagarvey
Earliest Records: b. 1637; m. 1637
Status: LC; Published by RCBL (1996) (b/m 1637–1646)

Magdalen Asylum (Belfast)
Earliest Records: b. 1855
Status: LC

Magheragall
Earliest Records: b. 1771; m. 1772; d. 1772
Status: LC

Mariners Chapel (Belfast)
Earliest Records: b. 1868
Status: LC

Muckamore
Earliest Records: b. 1847; d. 1847
Status: LC

Newtown Crommelin
Status: Lost

Portglenone
Status: Lost

Raloo
Status: Lost

Ramoan
Status: Lost

Rasharkin
Status: Lost

Rathlin
Status: Lost

St. Andrews (Belfast)
Status: Lost

St. Anne's (Belfast)
Earliest Records: b. 1745; m. 1745; d. 1745
Status: LC; NLI (mf); Indexed by UHF (to 1900)

St. George (Belfast)
Earliest Records: b. 1818; m. 1818
Status: LC; Indexed by UHF (to 1900)

St. John (Belfast)
Earliest Records: b. 1853
Status: LC

St. John Malone (Belfast)
Earliest Records: b. 1839; m. 1842
Status: LC

St. Mark (Belfast)
Earliest Records: b. 1856
Status: LC

St. Mary (Belfast)
Earliest Records: b. 1867; d. 1860
Status: LC

St. Mathew (Belfast)
Earliest Records: b. 1847; m. 1859; d. 1887
Status: LC; NLI (mf); Indexed by UHF (to 1900)

St. Mathew (Lisburn)
Status: Lost

St. Paul (Belfast)
Status: Lost

St. Philip Drew Memorial (Belfast)
Earliest Records: no records pre-1872
Status: LC

Skerry
Earliest Records: b. 1805; m. 1805; d. 1805
Status: LC

Stoneyford (Derryagney)
Earliest Records: b. 1845
Status: LC

Templecorran
Earliest Records: b. 1848; d. 1856
Status: LC

Templepatrick
Earliest Records: b. 1827; m. 1827; d. 1827
Status: LC; SLC (mf) 0883875 (1831–1875)

Tickmacrevan (Glenarm)
Earliest Records: b. 1788; m. 1788; d. 1846
Status: LC

Trinity (Belfast)
Earliest Records: b. 1844
Status: LC

Whitehouse
Earliest Records: b. 1840
Status: LC

Methodist

An account of the Methodist church in Ireland is given in the introduction. Methodist churches existed in Belfast, Ballymena, Ballycastle, Lisburn, and Portaferry. For registers in the city of Belfast, see the appendix.

Parish: Downpatrick
Earliest Record: b/m/d 1827
Status: LC; NLI (mf); Indexed by UHF (to 1900)

Presbyterian

An account of Presbyterian records is given in the introduction. These registers rarely contain death records, and occasionally have only records of births. This is indicated where appropriate. All are held in the local parish unless otherwise indicated. The Presbyterian registers of Antrim are being indexed by the Ulster Historical Foundation (see Research Services at the end of the chapter). A search of the index will be conducted for a fee. Copies of many are also held at the Public Record Office of Northern Ireland (PRONI). For further registers in Belfast, see also the appendix.

Ahogill
Starting Date: b. 1835; m. 1836
Status: LC; PRONI MIC 1P/64, 95 and 136

Antrim 1st and 2nd
Starting Date: b/m 1850
Status: LC; PRONI MIC 1P/3 and 346

Armoy
Starting Date: b. 1842; m. 1815
Status: LC; PRONI MIC 1P/290

Ballycarney
Starting Date: 1832
Status: LC; PRONI MIC 1P/330

Ballycastle
Starting Date: b/m 1829
Status: LC; PRONI MIC 1P/115

Ballyeaston 1st and 2nd
Starting Date: b/m 1813
Status: LC; PRONI MIC 1P/24 and 124

Ballylinney (Ballyclare)
Starting Date: b. 1837; m. 1837
Status: LC; PRONI MIC 1P/327 (1851-); SLC (mf) 973220 (b/m. 1837-) (Index SLC film 0883875-84)

Ballymena 1st and West
Starting Date: b. 1824; m. 1825
Status: LC; PRONI MIC 1P/105 and 144

Ballymena Wellington St.and High Kirk
Starting Date: b. 1863; m. 1845
Status: LC; PRONI MIC 1P/27

Ballymoney (First, Trinity and St. James)
Starting Date: b/m/d. 1807

Status: LC; PRONI MIC 1P/35, 266 and 363; SLC film 0908674 (b/m/d. 1807-98)

Ballynure
Starting Date: b. 1819; m. 1827
Status: LC; PRONI MIC 1P/103

Ballywat
Starting Date: b. 1867; m. 1845
Status: LC; PRONI MIC 1P/379

Ballyweaney
Starting Date: b. 1862; m. 1845
Status: LC; PRONI MIC 1P/82

Ballywillan
Starting Date: b. 1816; m. 1862
Status: LC; PRONI MIC 1P/368

Ballymacarrett (Belfast)
Starting Date: 1837
Status: LC

Ballysillan
Starting Date: 1839
Status: LC

Belfast (Fisherwick Place)
Starting Date: 1810
Status: LC

Belfast (Rosemary St.)
Starting Date: 1722
Status: LC

Benurden
Starting Date: b. 1864; m. 1864
Status: LC; PRONI MIC 1P/19

Broadmills (Lisburn)
Starting Date: 1824

Broughshane 1st and 2nd
Starting Date: b. 1836; m. 1845
Status: LC; PRONI MIC 1P/76 and 77

Buckna
Starting Date: b. 1841; m. 1845
Status: LC; PRONI MIC 1P/322

Bushvale
Starting Date: b. 1858; m. 1848
Status: LC; PRONI MIC 1P/362

Cairncastle
Starting Date: b/m. 1832
Status: LC; PRONI MIC 1P/328

Carnalbanagh
Starting Date: b/m. 1862
Status: LC; PRONI MIC 1P/351

Carnmoney
Starting Date: b/m. 1708
Status: LC; PRONI MIC 1P/137 (b/m. 1819-); SLC (mf) 994085 (b. 1799-1869; m. 1708-1871)

Carrickfergus 1st
Starting Date: b. 1823; m. 1840
Status: LC; PRONI MIC 1P/157

Castlereagh
Starting Date: 1807
Status: LC

Cliftonville
Starting Date: 1825
Status: LC

Clough
Starting Date: b. 1865; m. 1873
Status: LC; PRONI MIC 1P/312

Cloughwater
Starting Date: b. 1852; m. 1845
Status: LC; PRONI MIC 1P/320

Connor (Ballymena)
Starting Date: b. 1819; m. 1845
Status: LC; PRONI MIC 1P/162

Crumlin
Starting Date: b. 1836; m. 1846
Status: LC; PRONI MIC 1P/125

Cullybackey (Cunningham Memorial)
Starting Date: b. 1812; m. 1813
Status: LC; PRONI MIC 1P/88

Cushendall
Starting Date: b. 1854; m. 1853
Status: LC; PRONI MIC 1P/352

Cushendun
Starting Date: b. 1854; m. 1853
Status: LC; PRONI MIC 1P/352

Donegore
Starting Date: b. 1806; m. 1806
Status: LC; PRONI MIC 1P/79 and 153; SLC film 908674 (b. 1806-41)

Drumbo (Lisburn)
Starting Date: 1764
Status: LC

Drumneagh
Starting Date: b. 1864; m. 1845
Status: LC; PRONI MIC 1P/374

Dundonald (Belfast)
Starting Date: 1678
Status: LC

Dundron (Belfast)
Starting Date: 1829
Status: LC

Dunloy
Starting Date: b. 1841; m. 1842
Status: LC; PRONI MIC 1P/117

Dunluce
Starting Date: b. 1865; m. 1845
Status: LC; PRONI MIC 1P/367

Finvoy
Starting Date: b/m 1843
Status: LC; PRONI MIC 1P/321

Gilnahirk (Belfast)
Starting Date: 1797
Status: LC

Glenarm
Starting Date: b. 1836
Status: LC; PRONI MIC 1P/350

Glenwherry (Ballymena)
Starting Date: b/m 1845
Status: LC; PRONI MIC 1P/151

Grange (Toomebridge)
Starting Date: b/m 1824
Status: LC; PRONI MIC 1P/375

Islandmagee (2nd)
Starting Date: b/m 1829
Status: LC; PRONI MIC 1P/326 and 337

Kilruaght (Ballymoney)
Starting Date: 1836
Status: LC

Larne (1st and 2nd)
Starting Date: b. 1813; m. 1846
Status: LC; PRONI MIC 1P/263 and 335

Lisburn (1st, Railway St. and Sloan St.)
Starting Date: b. 1813; m. 1824
Status: LC; PRONI MIC 1P/74, 159 and 263

Loughmourne
Starting Date: b. 1848; m. 1863
Status: LC; PRONI MIC 1P/161

Lylehill (Templepatrick)
Starting Date: b. 1830; m. 1889
Status: LC; PRONI MIC 1P/98

Magheragall
Starting Date: b. 1878; m. 1845
Status: LC; PRONI MIC 1P/81

Maghamorne
Starting Date: b/m 1880
Status: LC; PRONI MIC 1P/349

Mosside
Starting Date: b/m 1842
Status: LC; PRONI MIC 1P/91

Muckamore
Starting Date: b. 1861; m. 1845
Status: LC; PRONI MIC 1P/277

Newtowncrommelin
Starting Date: b. 1835; m. 1836
Status: LC; PRONI MIC 1P/319

Portglenone 1st, 2nd, and 3rd
Starting Date: b. 1826; m. 1822
Status: LC; PRONI MIC 1P/24, 334 and 357

Portrush
Starting Date: 1843
Status: LC

Raloo (Larne)
Starting Date: b. 1842; m. 1841
Status: LC; PRONI MIC 1P/354

Ramoan
Starting Date: m. 1845
Status: LC; PRONI MIC 1P/366

Randalstown
Starting Date: b. 1853; m. 1845
Status: LC; PRONI MIC 1P/86 and 99

Rasharkin
Starting Date: b. 1834; m. 1845
Status: LC; PRONI MIC 1P/292

Templepatrick
Starting Date: b/m 1831
Status: LC; PRONI MIC 1P/325; SLC (mf) 0990082
(1831–1910)

Toberleigh
Starting Date: b. 1829; m. 1845
Status: LC; PRONI

Woodburn
Starting Date: b. 1820; m. 1821
Status: LC; PRONI MIC 1P/160

Roman Catholic

Approximately ninety-five percent of the Catholic parish registers of this county have been indexed by the Ulster Historical Foundation (UHF; see Research Services at the end of the chapter). A search of the index will be conducted by the relevant center for a fee. These are noted below. Microfilm copies of all registers are also available in the National Library of Ireland (NLI), and through the LDS library system.

Civil Parish: Aghagallon
Map Grid: 80
RC Parish: Aghagallon and Ballinderry
Diocese: CR
Earliest Record: b. 4.1828; m. 5.1828; d. 3.1828
Missing Dates: 7.1848–5.1872
Status: LC; NLI (mf); Indexed by UHF

Civil Parish: Aghalee
Map Grid: 81
RC Parish: see Aghagallon
Diocese: DR

Civil Parish: Ahoghill
Map Grid: 29 and 30
RC Parish: Ahoghill

Diocese: CR
Earliest Record: b. 1833; m. 1833; d. 1833
Missing Dates: d. few, ends 1863
Status: LC; NLI (mf); Indexed by UHF (1864–1900)

Civil Parish: Antrim
Map Grid: 48
RC Parish: Antrim
Diocese: CR
Earliest Record: b. 1.1874
Status: LC; NLI (mf); Indexed by UHF

Civil Parish: Ardclinis
Map Grid: 18
RC Parish: see Layde; also part Carnlough, see Tickmacrevan
Diocese: CR

Civil Parish: Armoy
Map Grid: 6
RC Parish: Armoy
Diocese: CR
Earliest Record: b. 4.1848; m. 5.1848
Missing Dates: 3.1842–10.1873; 1.1872–11.1873
Status: LC; NLI (mf); Indexed by UHF

Civil Parish: Ballinderry
Map Grid: 79
RC Parish: see Aghagallon
Diocese: CR

Civil Parish: Ballintoy
Map Grid: 2
RC Parish: Ballintoy
Diocese: CR
Earliest Record: b. 4.1872; m. 5.1872
Status: LC; NLI (mf); Indexed by UHF

Civil Parish: Ballyclug
Map Grid: 33
RC Parish: Ballymena, see Kirkinriola
Diocese: CR

Civil Parish: Ballycor
Map Grid: 47
RC Parish: Ballyclare, see Belfast
Diocese: CR

Civil Parish: Ballylinny
Map Grid: 59 and 61
RC Parish: part Ballyclare, see Belfast; part Carrickfergus
Diocese: CR

Civil Parish: Ballymartin
Map Grid: 70
RC Parish: part Ballyclare, see Belfast; part Antrim
Diocese: CR

Civil Parish: Ballymoney (see also Co. Derry)
Map Grid: 12
RC Parish: Ballymoney and Derrykeighan
Diocese: CR

Earliest Record: b. 3.1853; m. 4.1853; d. 1879
Status: LC; NLI (mf); Indexed by UHF (b/m to 1900;
d. to 1887)

Civil Parish: Ballynure
Map Grid: 57
RC Parish: part Larne; part Carrickfergus
Diocese: CR

Civil Parish: Ballyrashane
Map Grid: 10
RC Parish: Portrush, see Ballywillin
Diocese: CR

Civil Parish: Ballyscullion (see Co. Derry)
Map Grid: 40
RC Parish: see Duneane
Diocese: DE

Civil Parish: Ballywillin
Map Grid: 7
RC Parish: Portrush and Bushmills
Diocese: CR
Earliest Record: b. 7.1844; m. 5.1848
Status: LC; NLI (mf); Indexed by UHF

Civil Parish: Belfast (1)
RC Parish: Ballyclare
Diocese: CR
Earliest Record: b. 7.1869; m. 2.1870
Status: LC; NLI (mf); Indexed by UHF

Civil Parish: Belfast (2)
RC Parish: Whitehouse, see Templepatrick
Diocese: CR

Civil Parish: Billy
Map Grid: 9
RC Parish: see Ballintoy
Diocese: CR

Civil Parish: Blaris (also in Co. Down)
Map Grid: 84
RC Parish: Lisburn
Diocese: CR
Status: No records available

Civil Parish: Camlin
Map Grid: 75
RC Parish: see Glenavy
Diocese: CR

Civil Parish: Carncastle
Map Grid: 36
RC Parish: part Glenarm, see Tickmacrevan; part
Larne
Diocese: CR

Civil Parish: Carnmoney
Map Grid: 65
RC Parish: part Greencastle; part Whitehouse, see
Belfast
Diocese: CR

Civil Parish: Carrickfergus
Map Grid: 66
RC Parish: Carrickfergus, see Larne for pre-1828
records
Diocese: CR
Earliest Record: b. 12.1820; m. 9.1821
Missing Dates: b. 2.1841–3.1852; m. 10.1840–
4.1852
Status: LC; Indexed by UHF (to 1900)

Civil Parish: Connor
Map Grid: 35
RC Parish: Braid or Glenravel, see Skerry; part
Randalstown, see Drummaul
Diocese: CR
Earliest Record: b. 9.1878; m. 11.1878
Status: LC; NLI (mf); Indexed by UHF

Civil Parish: Craigs
Map Grid: 27
RC Parish: see Rasharkin
Diocese: CR

Civil Parish: Cranfield
Map Grid: 45
RC Parish: see Duneane
Diocese: CR

Civil Parish: Culfeightrin
Map Grid: 4
RC Parish: Culfeightrin
Diocese: CR
Earliest Record: b. 7.1825; m. 1.1839
Missing Dates: b. 5.1867–1.1868; m. 6.1844–8.1845
Status: LC; NLI (mf); Indexed by UHF (b. 1848–
1900; m. 1894–1900)

Civil Parish: Derryaghy
Map Grid: 78
RC Parish: Hannastown, Rock, and Derryaghy
Diocese: CR
Earliest Record: b. 1848; m. 1848
Status: LC; NLI (mf); Indexed by UHF (to 1900)

Civil Parish: Derrykeighan
Map Grid: 11
RC Parish: see Ballymoney
Diocese: CR

Civil Parish: Donegore
Map Grid: 49
RC Parish: see Antrim
Diocese: CR

Civil Parish: Drumbeg
Map Grid: 73A
RC Parish: see Derryaghy
Diocese: DW

Civil Parish: Drummaul
Map Grid: 42

RC Parish: Randalstown
Diocese: CR
Earliest Record: b. 10.1825; m. 10.1825; d. 1837
Missing Dates: b. 9.1854-8.1855, 1.1868-9.1871; m. 5.1854-5.1858, 11.1867-1871
Status: LC; NLI (mf); Indexed by UHF (to 1900); d. to 1848

Civil Parish: Dunaghy
Map Grid: 25
RC Parish: Glenravel, see Skerry
Diocese: CR

Civil Parish: Duneane
Map Grid: 44
RC Parish: Duneane (Toomebridge)
Diocese: CR
Earliest Record: b. 5.1834; m. 5.1835
Missing Dates: m. 2.1847-10.1847
Status: LC; NLI (mf); Indexed by UHF (to 1900)

Civil Parish: Dunluce
Map Grid: 8
RC Parish: part Portrush, see Ballywillin
Diocese: CR

Civil Parish: Finvoy
Map Grid: 20
RC Parish: Dunloy and Cloughmills
Diocese: CR
Earliest Record: b. 6.1860; m. 6.1877; d. 4.1877
Missing Dates: b. 6.1860, 12.1876-4.1877; m. 12.1876; d. 4.1877
Status: LC; NLI (mf); Indexed by UHF (m. to 1900)

Civil Parish: Glenavy
Map Grid: 77
RC Parish: Glenavy and Killead
Diocese: CR
Earliest Record: b. 5.1849; m. 3.1848
Status: LC; NLI (mf); Indexed by UHF (to 1900)

Civil Parish: Glenwhirry
Map Grid: 34
RC Parish: Braid, see Skerry
Diocese: CR

Civil Parish: Glynn
Map Grid: 56
RC Parish: see Larne
Diocese: CR

Civil Parish: Grange of Ballyscullion
Map Grid: 41
RC Parish: see Duneane
Diocese: CR

Civil Parish: Grange of Doagh
Map Grid: 51
RC Parish: Ballyclare, see Belfast
Diocese: CR

Civil Parish: Grange of Drumtullagh
Map Grid: 5
RC Parish: see Ballintoy
Diocese: CR

Civil Parish: Grange of Dundermot
Map Grid: 24
RC Parish: Dunloy and Cloughmills, see Finvoy
Diocese: CR

Civil Parish: Grange of Inispollen
Map Grid: 16
RC Parish: Craiga and Cushleak (Cushendon), see also Culfeightrin
Diocese: CR
Earliest Record: b. 1834; m. 1845
Status: LC; NLI (mf); Indexed by UHF (to 1900)

Civil Parish: Grange of Killyglen
Map Grid: 38
RC Parish: see Larne
Diocese: CR

Civil Parish: Grange of Layd
Map Grid: 15
RC Parish: Cushendun, see Grange of Innispollen
Diocese: CR

Civil Parish: Grange of Muckamore
Map Grid: 67
RC Parish: see Antrim
Diocese: CR

Civil Parish: Grange of Nilteen
Map Grid: 52
RC Parish: see Antrim
Diocese: CR

Civil Parish: Grange of Shilvodan
Map Grid: 43
RC Parish: Braid, see Skerry
Diocese: CR

Civil Parish: Inver
Map Grid: 54
RC Parish: see Larne
Diocese: CR

Civil Parish: Island Magee
Map Grid: 53
RC Parish: see Larne
Diocese: CR

Civil Parish: Kilbride
Map Grid: 50
RC Parish: see Antrim
Diocese: CR

Civil Parish: Killagan
Map Grid: 21
RC Parish: part Dunloy, see Finvoy; part Glenravel, see Skerry

Diocese: CR

Civil Parish: Killead
Map Grid: 68 and 69
RC Parish: see Glenavy
Diocese: CR

Civil Parish: Kilraghts
Map Grid: 13
RC Parish: see Ballymoney
Diocese: CR

Civil Parish: Kilroot
Map Grid: 40
RC Parish: see Duneane
Diocese: CR

Civil Parish: Kilwaughter
Map Grid: 37
RC Parish: see Larne
Diocese: CR

Civil Parish: Kirkinriola
Map Grid: 28 and 30
RC Parish: Ballymena (Kirkinriola); also part Ahogill
Diocese: CR
Earliest Record: b. 1.1848; m. 1.1840; d. 1852
Missing Dates: m. 7.1842–1.1847
Status: LC; NLI (mf); Indexed by UHF (to 1900)

Civil Parish: Lambeg
Map Grid: 73
RC Parish: see Derryaghy
Diocese: CR

Civil Parish: Larne
Map Grid: 39
RC Parish: Larne, see Carrickfergus for post-1828
Diocese: CR
Earliest Record: b. 8.1821; m. 9.1821
Status: LC; NLI (mf); Indexed by UHF

Civil Parish: Layd or Layde
Map Grid: 17
RC Parish: Cushendall (Layde and Ardclinis); also part Cushendun, see Grange of Innispollen
Diocese: CR
Earliest Record: b. 4.1838; m. 7.1837
Missing Dates: b. 3.1844–1.1858; m. 5.1844–3.1860
Status: LC; NLI (mf); Indexed by UHF (b. 1858–1900; m. 1860–1900)

Civil Parish: Loughguile
Map Grid: 14
RC Parish: Loughguile or Loughile
Diocese: CR
Earliest Record: b. 1842; m. 1825; d. 1870
Status: LC; NLI (mf); Indexed by UHF (to 1900)

Civil Parish: Magheragall
Map Grid: 82

RC Parish: see Derryaghy
Diocese: CR

Civil Parish: Magheramesk
Map Grid: 83
RC Parish: see Aghagallon
Diocese: CR

Civil Parish: Newton Crommelin
Map Grid: 22
RC Parish: see Rasharkin
Diocese: CR

Civil Parish: Portglenone
Map Grid: 26
RC Parish: Portglenone (Ahoghill before 1864)
Diocese: CR
Earliest Record: b. 1.1864; m. 2.1864
Status: LC; NLI (mf); Indexed by UHF (to 1900)

Civil Parish: Racavan
Map Grid: 32
RC Parish: Braid, see Skerry
Diocese: CR

Civil Parish: Raloo
Map Grid: 55
RC Parish: see Larne
Diocese: CR

Civil Parish: Ramoan
Map Grid: 3
RC Parish: Ramoan (Ballycastle)
Diocese: CR
Earliest Record: b. 10.1838; m. 10.1838
Status: LC; NLI (mf); Indexed by UHF (to 1900)

Civil Parish: Rasharkin
Map Grid: 23
RC Parish: Rasharkin
Diocese: CR
Earliest Record: b. 8.1848; m. 7.1848
Status: LC; NLI (mf); Indexed by UHF (to 1900)

Civil Parish: Rashee
Map Grid: 46
RC Parish: Ballyclare, see Belfast
Diocese: CR

Civil Parish: Rathlin
Map Grid: 1
RC Parish: see Ramoan
Diocese: CR

Civil Parish: Shankill
Map Grid: 72
RC Parish: Greencastle, see Templepatrick
Diocese: CR

Civil Parish: Skerry
Map Grid: 31
RC Parish: Glenravel or Braid

Diocese: CR
Earliest Record: b. 7.1825; m. 6.1825; d. 1825
Missing Dates: b. 9.1856–2.1864; m. 9.1832–
10.1878
Status: LC; NLI (mf); Indexed by UHF (to 1900)

Civil Parish: Templecorran
Map Grid: 58
RC Parish: see Larne
Diocese: CR

Civil Parish: Templepatrick
Map Grid: 56, 62, 63, 64, and 71
RC Parish: Greencastle (Whitehouse); also part
Ballyclare (see Belfast)
Diocese: CR
Earliest Record: b. 3.1854; m. 4.1854
Status: LC; NLI (mf); Indexed by UHF (to 1900)

Civil Parish: Tickmacrevan (1)
Map Grid: 19
RC Parish: part Carnlough; part Glenarm (see below)
Diocese: CR
Earliest Record: b. 12.1825
Missing Dates: b. 3.1854–6.1857, 12.1862–6.1865
Status: LC; NLI (mf); Indexed by UHF (b. 1857–
1900; m. 1869–1900)

Civil Parish: Tickmacrevan (2)
Map Grid: 19
RC Parish: Glenarm (Tickmacrevan)
Diocese: CR
Earliest Record: b. 1784; m. 1859
Status: LC; NLI (mf); Indexed by UHF (to 1900)

Civil Parish: Tullyrusk
Map Grid: 76
RC Parish: see Glenavy
Diocese: CR

Commercial and Social Directories

1807–8
Joseph Smith's Belfast Directories of 1807 and 1808.
Reprinted as *Merchants in Plenty*, J.R.R. Adams, ed.
Ulster Hist. Foundation, 1992. 94 pp.

1819
*Thomas Bradshaw's General and Commercial Directory
for 1819*. Finlay, 1819. Covers only Belfast and Lisburn,
giving history, index of merchants and traders, and a
general name index.

1820
Belfast Almanac contains lists of streets and thorough-
fares and an alphabetical list of traders and their addresses.

Joseph Smyth's *Directory of Belfast and its Vicinity*
covers parts of Antrim.

1824
J. Pigot's *City of Dublin and Hibernian Provincial Direc-
tory* includes traders, nobility, gentry, and clergy lists of
Antrim, Ballycastle, Ballymena, Ballymoney, Belfast,
Carrickfergus, Larne, Lisburn, Portglenone, and
Randalstown.

1835
William T. Matier's *Belfast Directory* contains lists of
traders, merchants, and gentry, arranged alphabetically,
and also a list of prominent people in the surrounding
areas.

1839
Matthew Martin's *Belfast Directory* contains alphabetical list of gentry, merchants, and traders; a list of persons classified by professions and trades; residents of
each house on the principal streets; and a list of noblemen and gentry residing in the county.

1841
A further edition of the above *Belfast Directory* covers
Antrim, Ballymena, Belfast, Carrickfergus, Crumlin,
and Lisburn. SLC film 258724.

1842
Third edition of the *Belfast Directory* covers Antrim,
Ballymena, Belfast, Carrickfergus, Crumlin, Larne, and
Lisburn. SLC film 258725.

1850
James Alexander Henderson's *Belfast Directory* contains
an alphabetical list of nobility and gentry in and about
Belfast; a list of the principal houses on the principal
streets; an alphabetical list of gentry, merchants, and
traders; a list of persons classified by trades; and covers
Belfast and the suburbs of Ballymacarrett, Holywood,
Whiteabbey, and Whitehouse.

1852
Henderson's *Belfast and Province of Ulster Directory* has
lists of inhabitants, traders, etc., in and around the towns
of Antrim, Ballycastle, Ballymoney, Carrickfergus,
Larne, Lisburn, and Randalstown.

1854
Further edition of above covering Antrim, Ballyclare,
Ballycastle, Ballymena, Ballymoney, Bushmills,
Carrickfergus, Crumlin, Dromara, Glenarm, Larne,

Lisburn, and Randalstown. Further editions in 1856, 1858, 1861, 1863, 1868, and 1870.

1856

Slater's *Royal National Commercial Directory of Ireland* lists nobility, gentry, clergy, traders, etc., in Antrim, Ballycastle, Ballyclare, Ballymena, Ballymoney, Belfast, Carrickfergus, Crumlin and Glenavy, Cushendall, Glenarm, Larne, Lisburn, Portglenone, and Randalstown.

1860

Hugh Adair's *Belfast Directory* lists the residents of main Belfast streets and of the suburbs of Ardoyne, Ligoniel, Ballynafeigh, Ballymacarrett, Dundonald, the Knock, Newtownbreda, Sydenham, Whiteabbey, and Whitehouse.

1865

R. Wynne's *Business Directory of Belfast* covers Antrim, Ballymena, Ballymoney, Carrickfergus, Larne, Lisburn, and Portrush.

1870

Slater's *Directory of Ireland* contains trade, nobility, and clergy lists for Antrim, Ballycastle, Ballyclare, Ballymena, Ballymoney, Belfast, Carrickfergus, Crumlin and Glenavy, Cushendall, Glenarm, Larne, Lisburn, Portglenone, Portrush, Randalstown, and Whiteabbey.

1877

Revised edition of Henderson's *Belfast and Province of Ulster Directory* covers Antrim, Ballyclare, Ballycastle, Ballymena, Ballymoney, Bushmills, Carnlough, Carrickfergus, Crumlin, Dromara, Glenarm, Larne, Lisburn, and Randalstown. Further editions in 1880, 1884, 1887, 1890, 1894, and 1900.

1881

Slater's *Royal National Commercial Directory of Ireland* contains lists of traders, clergy, nobility, and farmers in adjoining parishes of the towns of Antrim, Ballycastle, Ballyclare, Ballymena, Ballymoney, Belfast, Carrickfergus, Glenarm, Larne, Lisburn, Portrush, Randalstown, and Whiteabbey.

1887

The *Derry Almanac* covers Portrush.

1888

Bassett's *Book of Antrim* (does not cover Belfast).

1894

Slater's *Royal National Directory of Ireland* lists traders, police, teachers, farmers, and private residents in each of the towns, villages, and parishes of the county.

Family History

"The Agnews in Co. Antrim." *Ulster J. Arch.* 7, 2nd ser. (1901): 166–71.

Bigger, F. *The Magees of Belfast and Dublin.* Belfast, 1916.

"Caters of Irish Quarter, Carrickfergus." *Ir. Anc.* 10 (1) (1978): 31–33.

"Chiefs of the Antrim MacDonnells Prior to Sorley Boy." *Ulster J. Arch.* 7, 1st ser. (1859): 247–59.

"The Clan of the MacQuillins of Antrim." *Ulster J. Arch.* 8, 1st ser. (1860): 251–68.

Copies of census returns for the following families and years: McNeil, 1821—NAI film 5446 (4); Hamilton, 1821, 31, 41, 51—NAI film 5246 (9, 12); Moat, 1821, 31, 41, 51—NAI film 5246 (6), 5247 (1), 5248 (14, 35, 37), 5249 (5); Melance, 1831—NAI film 5247 (3); Martin, 1841—NAI film 5248 (13); Jamison, 1851—NAI film 5249/32.

"Gleanings in Family History from the Antrim Coast, The MacNaghtens and MacNeills." *Ulster J. Arch.* 8, 1st ser. (1860): 127–44.

"Gleanings in Family History from the Antrim Coast, The McAuleys and MacArtneys." *Ulster J. Arch.* 8, 1st ser. (1860): 196–210.

Hamilton—see McNeil.

Higginson, Thomas Boyd. *Descendants of the Rev. Thomas Higginson* (b. Ballinderry, Co. Antrim, 1700). London: Research Publishing Co., 1958.

Hill, George. *Historical Account of the MacDonnells of Antrim.* Belfast, 1873. Facsimile ed. pub. by Glens of Antrim Historical Soc., 1976.

Hope, Sir T. *Memoirs of the Fultons of Lisburn.* 1903.

Martin—see McNeil.

McDonnell, Hector. *The Wild Geese of the Antrim MacDonnells.* Irish Academic Press, 1996.

"The McKinleys of Conagher, Co. Antrim, and their Descendants, with Notes about the President of the United States." *Ulster J. Arch.* 3, 2nd ser. (1897): 167–70.

Melance—see McNeil.

Moat—see McNeil.

"Notes on the Stewart Family of Co. Antrim." *J. Ass. Pres. Mem. Dead* 7 (1907–09): 701.

"Notices of the Clan Iar Vor, Clan-Donnell Scots, Especially of the Branch Settled in Ireland." *Ulster J. Arch.* 9, 1st ser. (1861–62): 301–17.

"The Sitlington Family of Dunagorr, Co. Antrim." *Ulster J. Arch.* 15, 2nd ser. (1909): 161–72.

Walsh, Micheline. *The MacDonnells of Antrim and on the Continent* (text of O'Donnell lecture). Dublin, 1960.

Wray—see Co. Donegal.

Gravestone Inscriptions

A major source for this county are the volumes in the series *Gravestone Inscriptions–Co. Antrim*, published by the Ulster Historical Foundation. The foundation also published a series on *Gravestone Inscriptions–Belfast*. Graveyards within Belfast would also contain inscriptions of relevance to Antrim families.

Ardclinis: *The Glynns* 4 (1976): 11–16.

Ballycarley N.S. Presbyterian: Gravestone Inscriptions, Co. Antrim, Vol. 2.

Ballyclare Presbyterian: SLC (mf) 0918004 and 558361.

Ballygarvan R.C.: Gravestone Inscriptions, Co. Antrim, Vol. 2.

Ballykeel: Gravestone Inscription Series, Co. Antrim, Vol. 1.

Ballyvallagh: Gravestone Inscriptions, Co. Antrim, Vol 2.

Balmoral: Gravestone Inscription Series–Belfast, Vol. 3.

Balmoral Friends Burial Ground: Gravestone Inscription Series–Belfast, Vol. 3.

Bunamargy: IGRS Collection, GO; SLC film 477615.

Carnmoney Holy Evangelist (C of I), Newtown Abbey. North of Ireland Family Hist. Soc. 1994. ISBN: 0-9524698-0-4.

Culfeightrin: *Ir. Anc.* 2 (2) (1970).

Derryiaghy–Christ Church, by W.N.C. Barr, 1980. ISBN: 0- 950718-0-17.

Dunmurry First Presbyterian: SLC film 87997.

Friar's Bush (Miltown): Gravestone Inscription Series–Belfast, Vol. 2.

Glynn: Gravestone Inscription Series, Co. Antrim, Vol. 2.

Grange of Doagh: SLC film 251934.

Hannahstown–St. Joseph's. A history of the parish of St Joseph's, Hannahstown 1826-1993, detailing the names of the graves . . . and notable landowning families. *Ulster Journal*, 1993.

Islandmagee: Gravestone Inscriptions, Co. Down, Vol. 2.

Killycrappin: *The Glynns* 5 (1977): 11–14.

Kilmore: *The Glynns* 4 (1976): 11–16.

Kilroot: Gravestone Inscription Series, Co. Antrim, Vol. 2.

Lambeg: Cassidy, William. *Inscriptions on Old Tombstones in Lambeg Churchyard, Lisburn (1626-1837)*. SLC film 990442.

Lisburn Cathedral: Carmody, W.P. *Lisburn Cathedral and its Past Rectors*. 1926.

Magheragall: *Family Links* 1 (2) (1981): 31–32; and 1 (3) (1982): 26–32.

Malone Presbyterian: Gravestone Inscription Series–Belfast, Vol. 3.

Milltown: Gravestone Inscription Series–Belfast, Vol. 2.

Raloo C of I, Pres., N.S. Pres: Gravestone Inscriptions, Co. Antrim, Vol. 2.

Shankill: Gravestone Inscription Series–Belfast, Vol. 1.

Templecorran: Gravestone Inscription Series, Co. Antrim, No. 2.

Newspapers

One of the best early papers for this county is the *Belfast Newsletter*, which began publication in 1737. The availability of this and all other Belfast newspapers is listed in the appendix.

The South Eastern Education and Library Board (SEELB; see Library Sources at the end of the chapter) has a collection of local papers, and has also been compiling and publishing indexes to articles and persons and places mentioned.

Title: *Ballymena Advertiser*
Published in: Ballymena, ca. 1867–92
BL Holdings: 6.1873–7.1892

Title: *Carrickfergus Advertiser*
Published in: Carrickfergus, 1883–current
BL Holdings: 4.1884–1.1931; 10.1946–current

Title: *Larne Times and Weekly Telegraph* (continued as *Larne Times* in 1936, and *East Antrim Times* in 1962)
Published in: Larne, 1891–current
NLI Holdings: 4.1910–12.1915; 6.1921–current
BL Holdings: 1.1893–12.1929; 1.1931–current

Title: *Larne Weekly Reporter*
Published in: Larne, 1881–1904
BL Holdings: 3.1865–3.1861; 4–11.1881; 4.1884–3.1904

Title: *Lisburn Herald*
Published in: Lisburn, 1891–1969
NLI Holdings: 7 Jan. 1905–3 Aug. 1940
BL Holdings: 9.1891–9.1969

Title: *Lisburn Standard*
Published in: Lisburn, 1876–1959
BL Holdings: odd numbers 1878, 1884; 5.1885–12.1924; 1–10.1925; 1.1927–5.1959

Title: *North Antrim Standard*
Published in: Ballymoney, 1887–1922
NLI Holdings: 8.1890–10.1922
BL Holdings: 8.1890–12.1920; 3.1921–10.1922

Title: *Northern Herald* (continued as *Ballymoney Northern Herald* in 1862)
Published in: Ballymoney, 1860–63
NLI Holdings: 10.1860–1.1863
BL Holdings: 7.1862–1.1863

Wills and Administrations

A discussion of the types of records, where they are held, and of their availability and value is given in the Wills and Administrations section of the introduction. The availability of prerogative wills, administrations, and marriage license records is also described in the relevant parts of the same section. Where available, published sources of these records are given in the Miscellaneous Sources section.

Pre-1858 Wills and Administrations

Prerogative Wills. See the introduction.

Consistorial Wills. County Antrim is mainly in the diocese of Connor, with one parish in each of the dioceses of Derry, Down, and Dromore. The guide to Catholic parish records in this chapter shows the diocese to which each civil parish belonged. The wills of residents of each diocese were usually proven within that diocese (see Wills section in the introduction for exceptions). The following records survive:

Wills

Connor (1818–20 and 1853–58) and Down (1850–58). NAI; Derry (1612–1858), see Co. Derry; Down (1646–1858), see Co. Down; Dromore (1678–1858), see Co. Down.

Abstracts

Stewart-Kennedy notebooks contain about five hundred seventeenth- to nineteenth-century abstracts, particularly from Down and Connor dioceses, and mainly for testators named Stewart, Clarke, Cunningham, Kennedy, and Wade. TCD Library.

Indexes

Connor 1680–1856 (A–L) and 1636–1857 (M–Y). Also 1810–58 in a volume of combined wills and administrations.

Post-1858 Wills and Administrations

County Antrim was served by the District Registry of Belfast. The surviving records are kept in the PRONI and SLC films 930388 and -9; 930328–94.

Marriage Licenses

Indexes

Down, Connor, and Dromore (1721–1845). NAI; SLC film 100867.

Miscellaneous Sources

Agnew, Jean. *Belfast Merchant Families of the 17th Century.* Dublin: Fourcourts Press, 1996. (Profile of thirty merchant families.)

Cox, Robert R. *A History of the Parish of Kilbride (Diocese of Connor).* 1959, 121 pp.

"Demographic Study of . . . Rathlin Island, 1841–1964." *Ulster Folk* 117 (1971): 70–80.

Dubourdieu, John. *Statistical Survey of the County of Antrim, with Observations of the Means of Improvement.* Dublin: Graisberry & Campbell (for the RDS), 1812.

Dubourdieu, Rev. J. *Statistical Survey of the County of Antrim.* 1812.

Heatley, Fred. *The Story of St. Patrick's, Belfast 1815–1977.* (Includes biographies of the Catholic clergy of Belfast ca. 1677–1866.) Portglenone: Bethlehem Abbey, ca. 1978, 104 pp.

High Sheriffs of the County of Antrim 1603–1854 (name and residence). *North Irish Roots* 2 (3) (1989).

"Maps of Carrickfergus." *Ulster J. Arch.* 2 (1895): 2–3.

Millin, S. Shannon. *Sidelights on Belfast History.* Contains many valuable extracts from primary sources and section of biographies of important Belfastmen. Belfast: W&G Baird, 1932.

"Nineteenth-Century Co. Antrim Immigrant Families of the Burgh of Campelltown." *The Glynns* 13 (1985): 27–31 (biographical details).

O'Kane, W. "Surnames of Co. Antrim." *Irish Roots* 3 (1993): 30–31.

Provisional list of pre-1900 School Registers in the PRONI. *Ulster Gen. & Hist. Guild* 9 (1986): 60–71. Lists registers and PRONI reference numbers for all NI counties.

Richardson, James N. *Reminiscences of "Friends" in Ulster.* Useful biography source. Particularly stong on the Lisburn area. Gloucester: Bellows, ca. 1911.

Sharkie, B.S. *Co. Antrim Bibliography.* Belfast, 1984.

Sibbett, R.M. *On the Shining Bann. Records of an Ulster Manor.* (A history of Portglenone and district.) Belfast: Baird, 1928, 208 pp.

Watson, Charles. *The Story of the United Parishes of Glenavy, Camlin and Tullyrusk; together with Short Accounts of the History of the Different Denominations in the Union.* Ballynahinch, 1892 (reprinted in 1982).

"The Will Book of the Ballyhagan Meeting of the Society of Friends." *Ir. Gen.* 2 (8) (1950): 225–39.

Research Sources and Services

Journals

Carrickfergus Historical Society Journal (1985–present)

The Corran (published by Larne and District Historical Society, 1975–present)

Down and Connor Historical Society Magazine, NL Ir. 94115 (sic)

East Belfast Historical Society Journal, NI Ir. 94115 e 3

The Glynns (published by Glens of Antrim Historical Society, 1975–present)

Lisburn Historical Society Journal (1978–present)

North Belfast Historical Magazine (1984–present)

North Irish Roots

Outline Annual (published by West Belfast Historical Society, 1977–present)

Libraries and Information Sources

Family History Centre, 403 Holywood Road, Belfast 4. Ph: (012327) 68250. This center is a branch of the Family History Library run by The Church of Jesus Christ of Latter-day Saints. It has filmed many of the major Irish record sources, and also has an extensive collection of other materials, such as the 1901 census, *Tithe Applotment Books, Griffith's Valuation*, and civil registration indexes.

Irish and Local Studies Department, Central Library, Royal Avenue, Belfast BT1 1EA, Ph: (01232) 243233

Lisburn Museum, Assembly Buildings, Market Square, Lisburn, Co. Antrim

North Eastern Education and Library Board, Area Library, Demesne Avenue, Ballymena, Co. Antrim. Ph: (01266) 4153123

South Eastern Education and Library Board, Library and Information Service, Windmill Hill, Ballynahinch, Co. Down BT48 8DH. Ph: (01238) 566400; Fax: (01238) 565072. The Irish and Local Studies section has a very extensive collection of local history materials, particularly relating to Down and South Antrim. These include maps, photographs, newspapers, and periodicals. The library has also published materials of local relevance, including indexes to local newspapers and source lists for local industries, towns, and events.

Ulster-American Folk Park Library. See Libraries in Co. Tyrone chapter

Research Services

See Research Services in Belfast in the introduction.

Irish World, The Museum, Castle Street, Ballycastle, Co. Antrim. Ph: (012657) 63858

Ulster Historical Foundation. Balmoral Buildings, 12 College Sq. East, Belfast BT1 6DD. Ph: (1232) 332288; Fax: (1232) 239885; e-mail: @uhf.dnet.co.uk; Internet: http://www.unite.net/customers/uhf. This is a non-profit organization established in 1956 (as the Ulster-Scot Historical Society) to promote interest in Ulster history and genealogy. In 1975 it changed its name to reflect its wider genealogical activities. It provides extensive genealogical research services, publishes a journal *(Familia)* and books, and is also the official Irish Genealogical Project (see introduction)

center for indexing the records of Antrim and Down (including Belfast). Researchers are advised to contact the center for an updated list of registers and other sources indexed. Research services are conducted for a fee, and interested researchers can also join the UHF-founded Ulster Genealogical and Historical Guild, which provides a directory of research interests and a subscription to *Familia–Ulster Genealogical Review*.

Societies

Abbey Historical Society, Mr. Robert Armstrong, 196 Merville Garden Village, Newtownabbey, Co. Antrim BT37 9TR. Ph: (01232) 854141

Antrim Historical Society, Dr. Bob Foy, 13 Inishgarry Park, Antrim BT41 4LA. Ph: (01849) 468031

Ballyclare Historical Society, Mr. Jim Cardwell, 5 Highgrove Avenue, Ballyclare, Co. Antrim BT39 9XL. Ph: (01960) 322039

Carrickfergus and District Historical Society, Mr. Robin Cameron, 33 Upper Road, Greenisland, Co. Antrim BT38 8RH. Ph: (01232) 863187

Carrickfergus Gasworks Preservation Society Ltd., Mr. Paul Logan, 33 Cable Road, Whitehead, Carrickfergus, Co. Antrim BT38 9PZ. Ph: (01960) 378651

Glens of Antrim Historical Society, Mrs. B.P. McKay, Gruig, Cushendall, Co. Antrim BT44 OST. Ph: (01266) 771180. Publishes *The Glynns*

Islandmagee and Dist. Conservation Society, Mr. Joe Waring, 9 Middle Road, Islandmagee, Larne, Co. Antrim BT40 3SL. Ph: (01960) 373413

Larne and District Folklore Society, Mr. Sam Cross, President, 24 Mill Road, Larne, Co. Antrim BT40 3BS. Ph: (01574) 276385. Publishes *The Corran*

Lisburn Historical Society, Mrs. P. Farr, 1 Ballyvannon Road, Upper Ballinderry, Lisburn, Co. Antrim BT28 2LB. Ph: (01846) 422158

North of Ireland Family History Society, Queens University of Belfast, Dept. of Education, 69 University Street, Belfast BT7 1HL. Publishers of *North Irish Roots*

North West Archaeological and Historical Society, Mrs. Vivian Smyth, 11 Ballybogey Road, Ballymoney, Co. Antrim BT53 6QD. Ph: (012656) 67668

Randalstown Historical Society, Mr. A. Houston, 48 Shanes Street, Randalstown, Co. Antrim BT41 2AA. Ph: (01849) 472874

Royal Ulster Academy Association, Ms. Roberta Hunter, 118 Saintfield Road, Lisburn, Co. Antrim BT27 5PG. Ph: (01846) 638565

Templecorran Historical Society, Rev. Dr. J.W. Nelson, Drumcorran, 102 Carrickfergus Road, Larne, Co. Antrim BT40 3JX. Ph: (01574) 272600

Antrim Civil Parishes as Numbered on Map

1. Rathlin
2. Ballintoy
3. Ramoan
4. Culfeightrin
5. Grange of Drumtullagh
6. Armoy
7. Ballywillin
8. Dunluce
9. Billy
10. Ballyrashane
11. Derrykeighan
12. Ballymoney
13. Kilraghts
14. Loughguile
15. Grange of Layd
16. Grange of Inispollen (Layd)
17. Layd
18. Ardclinis
19. Tickmacrevan
20. Finvoy
21. Killagan
22. Newtown Crommelin
23. Rasharkan
24. Grange of Dundermot
25. Dunaghy
26. Portglenone
27. Craigs
28 and 30. Kirkinriola
29 and 30. Ahoghill
31. Skerry
32. Racavan
33. Ballyclug
34. Glenwhirry
35. Connor
36. Carncastle
37. Kilwaughter
38. Killyglen
39. Larne
40. Ballyscullion
41. Grange of Ballyscullion

42. Drummaul (3 pts.)
43. Shelvodan Grange
44. Duneane
45. Cranfield
46. Rashee
47. Ballycor
48. Antrim
49. Donegore
50. Kilbride
51. Grange of Doagh
52. Grange of Nilteen
53. Island Magee
54. Inver
55. Raloo
56. Glynn
57. Ballynure
58. Templecorran
59 and 61. Ballylinny
60. Kilroot
56, 62, 63, 64, and 71. Templepatrick (2 pts.)
65. Carnmoney
66. Carrickfergus or St. Nicholas
66. St. Nicholas or Carrickfergus
67. Grange of Muckamore
68 and 69. Killead
70. Ballymartin
72. Shankill (2 pts.)
73. Lambeg (2 pts.)
73A. Drumbeg
74. Belfast
75. Camlin
76. Tullyrusk
77. Glenavy
78. Derryaghy
79. Ballinderry
80. Aghagallon
81. Aghalee
82. Magheragall
83. Magheramesk
84. Blaris

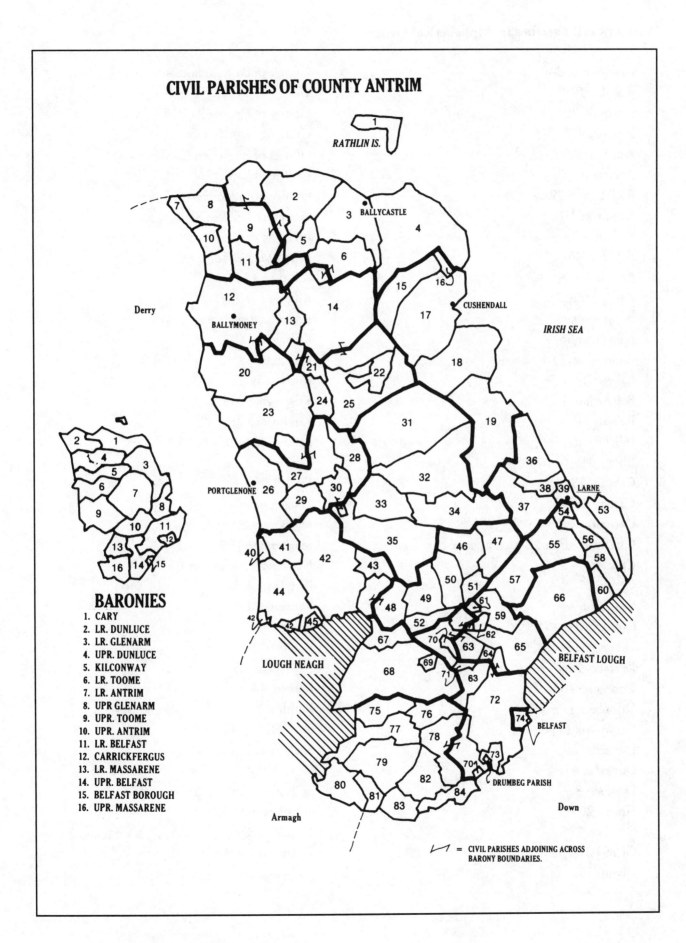

CIVIL PARISHES OF COUNTY ANTRIM

RATHLIN IS.

BALLYCASTLE

Derry

BALLYMONEY

CUSHENDALL

IRISH SEA

PORTGLENONE

LARNE

BARONIES

1. CARY
2. LR. DUNLUCE
3. LR. GLENARM
4. UPR. DUNLUCE
5. KILCONWAY
6. LR. TOOME
7. LR. ANTRIM
8. UPR GLENARM
9. UPR. TOOME
10. UPR. ANTRIM
11. LR. BELFAST
12. CARRICKFERGUS
13. LR. MASSARENE
14. UPR. BELFAST
15. BELFAST BOROUGH
16. UPR. MASSARENE

LOUGH NEAGH

BELFAST LOUGH

BELFAST

DRUMBEG PARISH

Armagh

Down

⌐ = CIVIL PARISHES ADJOINING ACROSS
      BARONY BOUNDARIES.

Antrim Civil Parishes in Alphabetical Order

Aghagallon: 80

Aghalee: 81

Ahoghill: 29

Antrim: 47

Ardclinis: 18

Armoy: 6

Ballinderry: 79

Ballintoy: 2

Ballyclug: 32

Ballycor: 46

Ballylinny: 58

Ballymartin: 70

Ballymoney: 12

Ballynure: 56

Ballyrashane: 10

Ballyscullion: 39

Ballywillin: 7

Belfast: 74

Billy: 9

Blaris: 84

Camlin: 75

Carncastle: 35

Carnmoney: 65

Carrickfergus or St. Nicholas: 66

Connor: 34

Craigs: 27

Cranfield: 44

Culfeightrin: 4

Derryaghy: 78

Derrykeighan: 11

Donegore: 48

Drumbeg: 73

Drummaul (3 pts.): 41

Dunaghy: 25

Duneane: 43

Dunluce: 8

Finvoy: 20

Glenavy: 77

Glenwhirry: 33

Glynn: 55

Grange of Ballyscullion: 40

Grange of Doagh: 50

Grange of Drumtullagh: 5

Grange of Dundermot: 24

Grange of Inispollen (Layd): 16

Grange of Layd: 5

Grange of Muckamore: 67

Grange of Nilteen: 51

Inver: 53

Island Magee: 52

Kilbride: 49

Killagan: 21

Killead: 68 and 69

Killyglen: 37

Kilraghts: 13

Kilroot: 59

Kilwaughter: 36

Kirkinriola: 28

Lambeg (2 pts.): 72

Larne: 38

Layd: 17

Loughguile: 14

Magheragall: 82

Magheramesk: 83

Newtown Crommelin: 22

Portglenone: 26

Racavan: 31

Raloo: 54

Ramoan: 3

Rasharkan: 23

Rashee: 45

Rathlin: 1

Shankill (2 pts.): 71

Shelvodan Grange: 42

Skerry: 30

St. Nicholas or Carrickfergus: 66

Templecorran: 57

Templepatrick (2 pts.): 56, 62, 63, 64, and 71

Tickmacrevan: 19

Tullyrusk: 76

County Armagh

A Brief History

County Armagh was part of the old Gaelic territory of Uriel or Oriel. The town of Armagh was the ancient seat of the High Kings of Ulster and has also been the ecclesiastical capital of Ireland for some 1500 years.

The main Gaelic families associated with the area are O'Neill, O'Hanlon, MacCann, MacMahon, O'Keelaghan, McPartlan, MacVeagh, O'Heany, MacSherry, MacAlinden, O'Mulcreevy, O'Heron, O'Garvey, O'Loughran, O'Rogan, O'Hoey, and McEntee or McGinty. Most of these are still much in evidence in the county. Although the Normans invaded Armagh following their invasion of Ireland in the twelfth century, they did not exercise effective control because of the power of the Gaelic families. This situation of independence from English rule continued for several centuries.

The O'Neill rebellion in 1594 led to the emigration of Hugh O'Neill and the major families of Ulster, the confiscation of their territories, and, in 1609, the English plantation of Ulster by "adventurers" (see Co. Antrim).

Among the English adventurers given land in Armagh at this time were the families of Acheson, Brownlow, St. John, McHenry, and Blacker. The plantation of Ulster, which also took place in Cavan, Donegal, Derry, Fermanagh, and Tyrone, was largely successful. Thousands of settlers, of all social classes, came to Armagh from Scotland and England during the early seventeenth century. The names of the Scottish settlers who came to the county include Boyd, Fraser, Lindsay, Johnston, Morrison, Patterson, and Maxwell. The English settler names include Bradshaw, Bradford, Watson, Taylor, Walker, Jackson, Wilson, Johnson, and Young.

The native population was predominantly Catholic, the Scottish were usually Presbyterian, and English were of the of the Protestant faith. The proportions of these religions among the population can, in very general terms, be used to estimate the origins of the inhabitants of the county. When religious affiliation was first determined in the census of 1861, the respective proportions of Catholic, Presbyterian, and Protestant were 49, 31, and 16 percent.

The Penal Laws, enacted in the 1690s following the accession of the Protestant King William to the English throne, were mainly aimed at restriction of the rights of Catholics. However, they also included various measures which disadvantaged Presbyterians. As a result many Ulster Presbyterians, the so-called Scots-Irish or Ulster Scots, emigrated to North America during the eighteenth century.

During the seventeenth and eighteenth centuries Armagh became a major center of Ulster's linen industry, particularly around the town of Lurgan. This industry and other farming activities made the county relatively prosperous during the seventeenth and eighteenth centuries. By the nineteenth century the population had grown to over 200,000 making it one of the most densely populated in the country. The population density was 511 people to the square mile at the peak population (232,000) in 1841.

The county was relatively less affected than others by the Great Famine of 1845-47, although it still reduced the population by around 15 percent between 1841 and 1851.

In 1921 the county was one of those which remained in the United Kingdom when the Irish Free State was formed. The main towns are Armagh, Portadown, Lurgan, Tanderagee, and Keady.

Census and Census Substitutes

1602

"First Census of the Fews." *Louth Arch. J.* 8 (2) (1934): 136–38.

1612–13

"Survey of Undertakers Planted in Armagh" (names, acreages allotted, and account of the progress of each). *Hist. Mss. Comm. Rep.* (Hastings mss.) 4 (1947): 159–82.

1630

"Census of Men and Arms on Settlers' Estates" (names and arms, arranged under name of "undertakers"). *Seanchas Ardmhacha* 5 (2) (1970): 401–17.

Muster Roll of Armagh. Armagh Co. Library NLI. P206. PRONI D1759/3C/1.

1631

Muster Roll. PRONI T934; BL add. ms. 4770.

1634

Copy of Subsidy Roll, NAI. M. 2471, 2745.

1641

Book of Survey and Distribution (extract for Creggan parish). *Louth Arch. J.* 8 (2) (1934): 142–46. PRONI T 370/A and D 1854/1/8. SLC film 1279327.

1654–1703

Books of Survey and Distribution. ACM M96, F7; SLC film 1279356.

1659

"Census" of Ireland. Edited by S. Pender. Dublin: Stationery Office, 1939. NLI I6551 Dub. SLC film 924648.

"Extract for Fews Baronies." *Louth Arch J.* 8 (2) (1934): 149–52.

1660

Poll Tax Abstracts. SLC film 1279356.

1661

Books of Survey and Distribution, PRONI T 370/A and D 1854/1/8.

1663–64

Hearth Money Roll for Orior Barony. *Louth Arch. J.* 7 (3) (1931): 419–431.

1664–65

Co. Armagh Householders. *Seanchas Ardmhacha* 3 (1) (1958): 96–142.

Hearth Money Roll. GO ms. 538; NLI ms. 9586/9856; PRONI T604; NAI m2741, 2745; also printed in *Anal. Hib.* 8 (1936): 121–202; SLC film 100181.

"Extract for Barony of Fewes." *Louth Arch. J.* 8 (2) (1934): 152–56.

1669

"Hearth Money Roll for Parish of Lisburn and Adjoining Parts of Parishes of Magheragall and Magheramesk." *Down & Connor Hist. Soc.* 7 (1936): 85–92.

"Extracts for parish of Aghagallon and adjoining parts of parishes of Magheragall and Magheramesk." *Down & Connor Hist. Soc.* 6 (1934): 52–54.

"Early Census of Glenravel" (parishes of Dunaghy and Skerry). *Down & Connor Hist. Soc.* 5 (1933): 59.

1670–71

Franciscan Petition Lists (Diocese of Armagh; names only of Gentry and principal inhabitants). *Seanchas Ardmhaca* 15 (1) (1992): 186–216.

1689

Protestants attainted by James II. PRONI T.808/14985. SLC film 1279332; ACM P8.

1737

Tythe Payers of Drumcree (from records of rector). NLI I 920041 P1.

1738

A List of the Freeholders of Co. Armagh ca. 1738. NLI: P206 and Armagh Co. Museum.

1740

Protestant Householders in Parishes of Creggan, Derrynoose, Loughgall, Lurgan, Mullaghbrack, Shankill, and Tynan. GO 539; NAI 1A 46 100; RCB Library; SLC film 258517. PRONI T808/15258.

1753

County Armagh Poll Book. GO MS 443; NAI M 4878; PRONI T808/14936. Ref. 1 324 411307. SLC film 1279327; ACM P8. Belfast Central Library. Contains the names of 1181 voters, valuation and situation of their freeholds, and residences.

1755

Poll Book for Co. Armagh. GO ms. 443; SLC film 100181, 258500.

1766

Reference, i.e., a list of holdings and occupiers, to a plan of Armagh City. Armagh Public Library.

BARONY OF O'NEILAND-EAST.

No.	Freeholder's Name.	Place of Abode.	Name of Landlord and Residence.	Value of Freehold	Description.	Situation	Names of Lives or other Tenure.	Date of Registry.
601	Kirk, Robert	Tullygally	Wm. Brownlow, Esq. Lur-[gan		same	Tullygally	Myself, David and William Kirk	August 25, 1813
602	Kirk, Samuel	Lurgan	same		Lands	same	David, William and Jonathan Kirk	same
603	Kelly, Richard	Aughacammon	same		Houses & Land	Aughacammon	Anne Cartless	same
604	Kirk, David	Tullygally	same		Land	Tullygally	Myself, William and Jonathan Kirk	same
605	Kennedy, Hugh	Lurgan	same		A House	Lurgan	Hugh and John Kennedy	same
606	Kirk, Samuel	same	same		same	same	Myself, James and William Carroll	same
607	Kennedy, George	Knocknashane	same		Houses & Land	Knocknashane	George and Anne Kennedy, and Richard Eustice	same
608	Kane, Roger	Turmoyra	same		House & Land	Turmoyra	Prince Augustus, Adol. Frederick, & Henry McAvoy	same
609	Kelly, Arthur	Cornikinigan	same		same	Cornikinigan	same — Michael Kelly	same
610	Kane, Owen	Turmoyra	same		Houses & Land	Turmoyra	same — Thomas Kano	same
611	Kennedy, John	Lurgan	Charles Brownlow, Esq.	FORTY SHILLINGS.	House & Land	Lurgan	John, Jane and Lucy Kennedy	March 2, 1816
612	Kean, Richard	Crossmacahly	Mr. Sparrow, Tandragee		Houses & Land	Crossmacahly	Richard Kane	August 11, 1817
613	Kelly, John	Lisnisky			same	Lisnisky	Samuel Kelly	Sep. 1, 1817
614	Kirk, David	Monbrief	Charles Brownlow, Esq.		same	Monbrief	Prince Augustus, Adol. Frederick, Thomas Brown	Nov. 3, 1817
615	Kerr, James	Legacorry	same		House & Land	Legacorry	Myself, Jane and Rebecca Kerr	same
616	Kelly, John	Kinigo	Joseph Greer, Moy		Houses & Land	Kinigo	William, Mary and Margaret Hare	same
617	Kerr, Owen	Lissaconan	Charles Brownlow, Esq		same	Lissaconan	Henry Pedlow	same
618	Kelly, Richard	Aughacammon	same		House & Land	Aughacammon	Anne Castles	August 26, 1818
619	Kane, Patrick	Turmoyra	same		same	Turmoyra	Prince Augustus, Adol. Frederick, Henry McAvoy	same
620	Kirk, David	Monbrief	same		same	Monbrief	same — Thomas Buron	same
621	Kennedy, George	Knocknashane	same		same	Knocknashane	Myself, James and John Kennedy (my sons)	same
622	Kane, Owen	Turmoyra	same		Houses & Land	Turmoyra	Prince Augustus, Adol. Frederick, Thos. Kane	same
623	Kelly, Arthur	Cornikinigan	same		House & Land	Cornikinigan	same — Michael Kelly	same
624	Kirk, Barrack	Tegnevin	same		same	Tegnevin	James Taylor	same
625	Kelly, John	Kinigo	same		Land	Kinigo	Prince Augustus, Adol. Frederick, David Graham	same
626	Kennedy, John	Lurgan	same		Houses	Lurgan	John, Jane and Lucy Kennedy	same
627	Kelly, Arthur	same	same		same	same	Arthur, Catherine and Henry Kelly	same
628	Kerr, Owen	Lissaconan	same		Houses & Land	Lissaconan	Henry Pedlow, sen.	same
629	Kirk, David	Tullygally	same		same	Tullygally	Charles Brownlow, Barrack Kirk, and Brownlow Kirk	August 31, 1818
630	Kirk, Robert	same	same		House & Land	same	Myself, David and William Kirk	Nov. 19, 1818
631	Kean, Charles	Taisin	Miss Sparrow, Tandragee		Houses & Land	Taisin	Anne Kean	Jan. 11, 1819
632	Kirk, Samuel	Lurgan	Wm. Brownlow, Esq. Lur-[gan		Houses	Lurgan	Renewable for ever	August 25, 1813
633	Levingstone, Wm.	Legacorry	same		House & Land	Legacorry	William Livingstone, John and John McCollem	same
634	Lowndale, Thos. sen	Drumnakairn	same		Houses & Land	Drumnakairn	Prince Augustus, Adol. Frederick, Geo. Lowndale	same
635	Love, Patrick	Aughavillan	same		House & Land	Aughavillan	Myself	same
636	Lynass, William	Taberburney	same		same	Taberburny	Prince Augustus, Adol. Frederick, Thomas Lynass	same
637	Latherdale, John	Ballyblough	same		Lands	Ballyblough	Richard Chapman, and Shottle Jackson	same
638	Lavery, James	Donnygreagh	same		House & Land	Donnygreagh	The Rev. Brownlow Ford	same
639	Lynass, Alexander	Ballyblough	same		Houses & Land.	Ballyblough	Prince Augustus, Augustus, and Adolphus Frederick	same
640	Lynass, Joseph	Tullygally	same		same	Tullygally	William and Jonathan Kirk	same
641	Larkin, Terence	Kinigo	James Ford, Esq.		House & Land	Kinigo	Donald Cobb, and John Corr	same
642	Lowndale, Thomas	Drumnakarn	Wm. Brownlow, Esq. Lur-[gan		same	Drumnakairn	Prince Augustus, Adol. Frederick, and Patrick Farfy	same
643	Larkin. John	Killaughey	same		same	Killaughey	Myself	same
644	Levingstone, John	Legacorry	same		same	Legacorry	Wm. (my son) Jane (my daughter) & James McMurry	same
645	Lynch, William	Boconnell	same		Houses & Land	Boconnell	William Lynch	same

Extract from the Barony of O'Neilland East, Co. Armagh, of the "Return of Registered Freeholders of £20 and 40 shillings from First January 1813 to First January 1820." NLI IR 94116 al.

Appendix (G.)

A RETURN of the several HOUSES in the Towns in *Ireland*, which Return MEMBERS to serve in PARLIAMENT; specifying the Streets in which each is situated, its Number, and the Name of the Occupant; together with the Annual Value of each, as estimated and returned by the Valuators appointed to make the Annual Applotment of Rates and Taxes for Municipal Purposes, either under the Provisions of the Act 9 Geo. 4, c. 82, or of any Local or Private Acts passed for the Regulation of these Towns, or of the New Valuation Act, where it has come into operation.

ARMAGH.

Houses of the Yearly Value of £. 10 and upwards.

No.	Inhabitants' Names.	Yearly Value.		No.	Inhabitants' Names.	Yearly Value.	
		£.	s.			£.	s.
	Lower English-street :				Lower English-st.—*cont*ᵈ.		
1	Francis M'Cormick	10	–	114	John Lyle	12	–
39	Hugh Lynch	10	–	121	Samuel Thompson	11	–
40	John Duff	10	10	128	John M'Elroy	10	–
41	Henry Mooney	10	–				
42	Patrick Cunningham	10	–		Upper English-street :		
53	Bernard Quin	10	–	1	William Caldwell	24	10
54	John Garland	10	–	2	Edward Parker	24	–
57	Edward Murphy	10	–	3	Peter M'Kee	20	–
58	Peter Kelly	10	–	4	James Donnelly	22	–
59	James M'Elroy	12	–	5	Sarah M'Glone	19	–
64	John Woods	10	–	6	Edward Hynes	30	–
65	James Donoghue	13	–	7	Patrick Downey	15	–
66	Owen Farley	10	–	8	Edward Corvin	18	–
68	James Dunne	12	–	9	Thomas Craig	45	–
70	Margaret Williamson	10	–	10	Arthur Branigan	19	–
71	Andrew Johnson	10	–	11	Bernard Hagan	19	–
73	John Allen	10	–	12	George Barnes	24	–
74	Peter M'Caghey	14	–	13	Miss Atkinson	30	–
76	Johnson Nelson	22	–	14	James F. Bell	50	–
77	John Williams	30	–	15	William Blacker	100	–
78	James Vogan	34	–	16	Mrs. Lyle	70	–
79	John Graham	16	–	17	John M'Kinstry	90	–
80	Patrick Corvin	15	–	18	R. J. Thornton	100	–
81	Michael M'Bride	19	–	19	Robert C. Hardy	70	–
82	Patrick Carberry	10	–	20	Leonard Dobbin, jun.	100	–
83	Patrick Devlin	19	–	21	John Stanley	130	–

An extract from tables showing the holders of houses of more than £10 annual valuation in the town of Armagh. This is a sample of the information on ratepayers and voters presented to the Select Committee of Fictitious Votes, 1837. From *Parliamentary Papers*, Appendix G, 1837, 2 (1).

"Religious Census of Parish of Creggan." GO ms. 537; SLC film 100173; *Louth Arch. J.* 8 (2) (1934): 156-62. Also Parliamentary Returns 657 in NAI.

1770

List of inhabitants of Armagh City. SLC film 258621. PRONI T1288/1, Armagh Pub. 9/5/20, NLI Ms. 7370.

1793-1908

Armagh Militia Records, Armagh Co. Library, NLI P. 1014.

1796

"List of Flax Growers of Armagh" (with background to the industry). *Ulster Gen. & Hist. Guild Newsletter* 1 (7) (1981): 204-16. (Gives names in each parish; also NLI.)

Surname index for the 1796 Spinning Wheel Premium entitlement lists. All-Ireland Heritage, Inc., 1986. 12 microfiches.

See Co. Mayo 1796 (list of Catholics).

1799-1800

Militia Pay Lists and Muster Rolls, PRONI T1115/2A-C.

1802

"Game-license Holders." *Ir. Anc.* 8 (1) (1976): 35-39.

1813-30

Registered Freeholders of 20s and 40s, Baronies of O'Neilland E. and Upper Orior (1,372 and 1,471 names respectively, arranged alphabetically with residence, location of freehold, etc.). NLI IR 352, p. 2. PRONI T862.

Barony of Tureny (395 names), Lower Fews (1,250 names), Upper Fews (365 names). NLI IR 94116 A1.

Lists of Freeholders. SLC film 993156, 279324.

1821

Government Census Remnants for Parish of Kilmore (townlands of Balleney, Corcreevy, Crewcat, Derryhale, Drumnahushin, Listeyborough, and Maynooth). PRONI T450; SLC film 258511, 258621.

Extract of Derryhale (townland in par. Kilmore) published in *Ulster Folklife* 7 (1961): 41-50. (All named with ages.)

Family Compositions and Occupations in Kilmore Parish. *North Irish Roots* 3 (1): 27-36.

1821-31

A List of the Registered Freeholders of Co. Armagh (also listing by barony—except Orior lower—for 1813-20). PRONI T862.

1825-35

Tithe Applotment Survey (see introduction).

1830-39

Armagh Freeholders. ACM M87, F7; SLC film 1279330.

1833

Extracts of Kilmore Parish Tithe Applotments. NLI I920041 P1.

1834

Mullabrack Parish List (from Tythepayers lists of 1834). NLI I 920041 P1.

1834-37

"Occupants of Armagh, Arranged by Street within 2 Sections" (over and under £10 value). *Parl. Papers* 1837, 11 (1): Appendix G, 176-91.

1837

Marksmen (i.e., illiterate voters), Armagh Borough, *Parliamentary Papers* 1837, Reports from Committees, Vol. 11 (I), Appendix A.

1839

"Freeholders and Leaseholders in Armagh, Tiranny, O'Neiland West, and O'Neiland East." *Commercial Telegraph* 27 (960) (3 Oct. 1839). PRONI T808/14961.

List of Persons who obtained Game Certificates in Ulster. PRONI T688.

1843

Voters List. NAI 1842/85.

1847

"Castleblayney Poor Law Rate Book." *Clogher Record* 5 (1) (1963): 131-48 (ratepayers in each townland in Castleblayney Poor Law Union).

1851-73

Co. Armagh—Persons entitled to vote. ACM D7; SLC film 1279325.

1852

Registry of Voters in Armagh, Lower Fews, Tiranny, O'Neiland E. and W., Upper Fews, Lower and Upper Orior. SLC film 258499 and Belfast Public Library.

1859

List of persons who voted at the election for the borough of Armagh, May 1859, 1 page. Gives names and religious denominations of voters and how they voted. Armagh Museum and PRONI.

1864

Griffith's Valuation (see introduction).

1901

Census. NAI. SLC (mf).

1911

Census. NAI.

Church Records

Church of Ireland

See the introduction for a description of C of I records and their major repositories. Many C of I records were lost in the PRO fire of 1922. These are indicated as "Lost." However, as Church of Ireland records were effectively state records, the records of marriage (from 1845) are also in the General Registrar's Office. Many are still in local custody (LC), while others are in one of a variety of other archives (e.g., RCBL or NAI). Some of the registers of this county have been indexed by Armagh Ancestry (see Research Services) and will be searched for a fee. These are indicated "Indexed by AA."

Acton
Earliest Records: m. 1845-
Status: LC; indexed by AA (to 1900)

Aghavilly
Earliest Records: b. 1844-76; d. 1846-76
Status: LC

Annaghmore
Earliest Records: b. 1856-; d. 1859-
Status: LC

Armagh
Earliest Records: b. 1750-; m. 1750-; d. 1750
Status: LC; indexed by AA (to 1900)

Armaghbreague
Earliest Records: m. 1845-1922
Status: LC

Baleek
Status: Lost

Ballymore (Tandragee)
Earliest Records: b. 1783-1871; m. 1783-1845; d. 1783-1871
Status: LC

Ballymoyer
Earliest Records: b. 1820-75; m. 1820-45; d. 1836-75
Status: LC

Camlough
Earliest Records: b. 1832-76; m. 1835-45; d. 1833-77
Status: LC

Charlemont (Loughgall)
Status: Indexed by AA (to 1900)

Clare (Ballymore)
Status: Indexed by AA (to 1900)

Creggan
Earliest Records: b. 1808-75; m. 1808-39; d. 1808-75
Status: LC

Derrynoose
Earliest Records: b. 1822-75; m. 1822-45; d. 1835-75
Status: LC; Indexed by AA (to 1900)

The Diamond
Earliest Records: b. 1848-77
Status: LC; Indexed by AA (m. 1910-1922 only)

Drumbanagher
Earliest Records: b. 1838-79; m. 1838-45; d. 1838-79
Status: LC

Drumcree
Earliest Records: b. 1780-1875; m. 1780-1845; d. 1780-1875
Status: LC; Indexed by AA (to 1900)

Eglish
Earliest Records: b. 1803-; m. 1804-; d. 1803-
Status: LC; Indexed by AA (to 1900)

Forkhill
Status: Lost

Grange
Earliest Records: b. 1780-; m. 1780-; d. 1780-
Status: LC; Indexed by AA (to 1900)

Keady
Earliest Records: b. 1780-1871; m. 1780-1845; d. 1813-1881
Status: LC

Kilclooney
Earliest Records: b. 1832-75; m. 1835-45; d. 1837-75
Status: LC; Indexed by AA (to 1900)

Kildarton
Status: Indexed by AA (to 1900)

Killeavy or Mullaghglass
Status: Lost

Killylea (Tynan)
Earliest Records: b. 1845–75; d. 1845–75
Status: LC; Indexed by AA (to 1900)

Kilmore
Earliest Records: b. 1789–1879; m. 1798–1845; d. 1824–79
Status: LC; Indexed by AA (to 1900)

Lisnadill
Status: Indexed by AA (to 1900)

Loughgall
Earliest Records: b. 1706–1875; m. 1706–1845; d. 1706–1875
Missing Dates: b. 1730–78; m. 1730–78; d. 1730–78
Status: LC; Indexed by AA (to 1900)

Loughgilly
Earliest Records: b. 1804–75; m. 1804–45; d. 1804–75
Status: LC; Indexed by AA (to 1900)

Meigh
Status: Lost

Milltown
Earliest Records: b. 1840–75; m. 1840–45; d. 1815–75
Status: LC

Moyntaghs or Ardmore
Earliest Records: b. 1822–75; m. 1822–45; d. 1822–75
Status: LC

Mullaghbrack
Earliest Records: b. 1622–1826; m. 1622–1826; d. 1622–1826
Status: NLI Ms 2669 (Leslie manuscript); Indexed by AA (to 1900)

Mullavilly
Earliest Records: b. 1821–74; m. 1821–45; d. 1821–75
Status: LC; Indexed by AA (to 1900)

Newry
Existing Records: b. 1784–1864; m. 1784–1864; d. 1784–1864
Status: NLI Ms 2202–34 (Leslie manuscript)

Newtown Hamilton
Existing Records: b. 1622–1826; m. 1622–1826; d. 1622–1826
Status: NLI Ms 2669 (Leslie manuscript)

Portadown
Earliest Records: b. 1826–76; m. 1827–45
Status: LC

Richhill (Kilmore)
Status: Indexed by AA (to 1900)

St. Saviour Portadown
Earliest Records: b. 1858–72; d. 1862–76
Status: LC

Seagoe
Earliest Records: b. 1683–1865; m. 1683–1845; d. 1683–1875
Missing Dates: b. 1713–53; m. 1713–53; d. 1713–53
Status: LC

Tynan
Earliest Records: b. 1686–1875; m. 1683–1845; d. 1683–1875
Missing Dates: b. 1725–1805; m. 1724–1807; d. 1724–1807
Status: LC; Indexed by AA (to 1900)

Presbyterian

An account of Presbyterian records is given in the introduction. These registers rarely contain death records, and occasionally have only records of births. This is indicated where appropriate. Many of the Presbyterian registers of Armagh have been indexed by Armagh Ancestry (see Research Services at the end of the chapter). A search of the index will be conducted for a fee. Copies of some are in the PRONI at the call reference given below. Those indexed by Armagh Ancestry are noted below as "Indexed by AA."

Ahorey (Loughgall)
Starting Date: b. 1834–; m. 1834–
Status: LC; Indexed by AA (to 1900); PRONI MIC IP/353

Armagh
Starting Date: b. 1707–; m. 1707–
Status: Indexed by AA (to 1900); PRONI MIC IP/4 and 281

Armaghbrague
Starting Date: b. 1908–; m. 1840–
Status: Indexed by AA (to 1900); PRONI MIC IP/297

Bellville
Starting Date: b. 1863–; m. 1875–
Status: Indexed by AA (to 1900); PRONI MIC IP/271

Bessbrook
Starting Date: 1854

Cladymore
Starting Date: 1848
Status: Indexed by AA (to 1900)

Clare (Tandragee)
Starting Date: b. 1824; m. 1825
Status: LC; Indexed by AA (to 1900); PRONI MIC IP/50

Creggan
Starting Date: 1835
Status: LC

Cremore
Starting Date: 1831
Status: LC; Indexed by AA (to 1900)

Donacloney (Lurgan)
Starting Date: 1798
Status: LC

Drumbanagher
Starting Date: 1832
Status: LC

Drumhillory
Starting Date: b/m. 1829
Status: Indexed by AA (m. 1845 to 1900); PRONI MIC IP/286

Druminnis
Starting Date: m. 1846
Status: Indexed by AA (to 1900); PRONI MIC IP/286

Gilford
Starting Date: 1843

Keady (Temple)
Starting Date: b. 1838; m. 1845
Status: LC; Indexed by AA (to 1900); PRONI MIC IP/71

Kingmills (Whitecross)
Starting Date: 1842
Status: LC

Knappagh
Starting Date: 1842
Status: LC; Indexed by AA (to 1900)

Lislooney
Starting Date: 1836
Status: Indexed by AA (to 1900)

Loughgall
Starting Date: b. 1842; m. 1845
Status: LC; Indexed by AA (to 1900); PRONI MIC IP/287

Lurgan
Starting Date: b. 1746; m. 1845
Status: LC; Indexed by AA (to 1900); PRONI MIC IP/71 and 109

Markethill (1st)
Starting Date: 1821
Status: LC; Indexed by AA (to 1900)

Middleton
Starting Date: m. 1847
Status: Indexed by AA (to 1900)

Mountnorris
Starting Date: b. 1810; m. 1804
Status: Indexed by AA (to 1900); PRONI MIC IP/29

Newmills (see Portadown)

Newtownhamilton
Starting Date: 1823
Status: LC

Portadown
Starting Date: b. 1839; m. 1838
Status: LC; Indexed by AA (to 1900); PRONI MIC IP/52 and 269

Poyntzpass
Starting Date: b. 1840; m. 1850
Status: LC; Indexed by AA (to 1900)

Redrock
Starting Date: b. 1808; m. 1812
Status: Indexed by AA (from 1845); PRONI MIC IP/285

Richhill
Starting Date: b. 1848; m. 1845
Status: LC; Indexed by AA (to 1900); PRONI MIC IP/372

Tandragee
Starting Date: b. 1830; m. 1835
Status: LC; Indexed by AA (to 1900); PRONI MIC IP/258

Tartaraghan
Starting Date: b. 1853; m. 1845
Status: LC; Indexed by AA (to 1900); PRONI MIC IP/288

Tassagh
Starting Date: m. 1845
Status: LC; Indexed by AA (to 1900)

Tullyallen
Starting Date: b/m. 1795
Status: LC; Indexed by AA (to 1900); PRONI MIC IP/29 (m. 1834–1885)

Vinecash (Portadown)
Starting Date: m. 1838
Status: LC; Indexed by AA (to 1900)

Methodist

An account of the Methodist church in Ireland is given in the introduction. Methodist churches existed in several areas of Co. Armagh. In 1795 there were churches at the following locations: Armagh, Bluestone, Charlemount, Clanmaine, Derryanville, Lurgan, Mullyhead, Scotch St., and Tanderagee. The Methodist records of Newry circuit, 1830-65, are described in *Seanchas Ardmhacha* 1977, Vol. 7, No. 2.

Armagh
Starting Date: m. 1863
Status: Indexed by AA (m. 1863-1922)

Blackwatertown
Starting Date: m. 1899
Status: Indexed by AA (m. 1899-1920)

Cranagill
Starting Date: m. 1884
Status: Indexed by AA (m. 1884-1920)

Markethill
Starting Date: m. 1866
Status: Indexed by AA (m. 1884-1920)

Richhill
Starting Date: m. 1886
Status: Indexed by AA (m. 1866-1920)

Tandragee
Starting Date: m. 1863
Status: Indexed by AA (m. 1863-1920)

Tullyroan
Starting Date: m. 1899
Status: Indexed by AA (m. 1899-1920)

Roman Catholic

Note that most of the Catholic parish registers of this county have been indexed by Armagh Ancestry and/or Armagh Records Centre (see Research Services at the end of the chapter). A search of the index will be conducted for a fee. Those indexed are noted below as "Indexed by AA."

Microfilm copies of all registers are also available in the National Library of Ireland (NLI), and through the LDS library system.

Civil Parish: Armagh
Map Grid: 14
RC Parish: Armagh
Diocese: AM
Earliest Record: b. 7.1796; m. 1.1802
Missing Dates: m. 5.1803-1.1817
Status: LC; NLI (mf); Indexed by AA (to 1900)

Civil Parish: Ballymore
Map Grid: 21
RC Parish: Ballymore and Mullaghbrack (Tandragee)
Diocese: AM
Earliest Record: b. 1798; m. 10.1843
Missing Dates: b. 1803-1830; 11.1856-6.1859; 11.1856-7.1859
Status: LC; NLI (mf); Indexed by AA (to 1900)

Civil Parish: Ballymyre
Map Grid: 23
RC Parish: see Loughgilly
Diocese: AM

Civil Parish: Clonfeacle (see also Co. Tyrone)
Map Grid: 3
Diocese: AM
RC Parish: Clonfeacle (Moy)
Diocese: AM
Earliest Record: b. 10.1814; m. 11.1814
Missing Dates: b. 3.1840-8.1840
Status: LC; NLI (mf); Indexed by AA (to 1900)

Civil Parish: Creggan (see also Co. Louth)
Map Grid: 25
RC Parish: Creggan Upper (Crossmaglen)
Diocese: AM
Earliest Record: b. 8.1796; m. 8.1796
Missing Dates: b. 1.1803-9.1812, 5.1829-5.1845; m. 2.1803-12.1812, 7.1829-5.1845, 3.1870-5.1871
Status: LC; NLI (mf); Indexed by AA (to 1900)

Civil Parish: Derrynoose
Map Grid: 15
RC Parish: Derrynoose (Keady)
Diocese: AM
Earliest Record: b. 1814; m. 1808; d. 1823
Missing Dates: b. 1820-1822; 1831; 1.1837-12.1846; m. 1815-1822; 1834-45; d. ends 4.1851
Status: LC; NLI (mf); Indexed by AA (to 1900)

Civil Parish: Drumcree
Map Grid: 5
RC Parish: Portadown (Drumcree)
Diocese: AM
Earliest Record: b. 1.1844; m. 2.1844; d. 5.1863
Missing Dates: m. 11.1863-7.1864; d. 12.1863-6.1864
Status: LC; NLI (mf); Indexed by AA (to 1900)

Civil Parish: Eglish
Map Grid: 11
RC Parish: Eglish
Diocese: AM
Earliest Record: b. 1.1862; m. 1.1862; d. 1877
Status: LC; NLI (mf); Indexed by AA (to 1900)

Civil Parish: Forkhill
Map Grid: 28
RC Parish: Forkhill (Mullaghbawn)
Diocese: AM
Earliest Record: b. 1.1845; m. 1.1844
Status: LC; NLI (mf); Indexed by AA (to 1900)

Civil Parish: Grange
Map Grid: 13
RC Parish: see Armagh
Diocese: AM

Civil Parish: Jonesborough
Map Grid: 29
RC Parish: see Co. Louth
Diocese: AM

Civil Parish: Keady
Map Grid: 16
RC Parish: see Derrynoose
Diocese: AM

Civil Parish: Kilclooney
Map Grid: 20
RC Parish: Ballymacnab, see Lisnadill
Diocese: AM

Civil Parish: Kildarton
Map Grid: 17
RC Parish: see Armagh
Diocese: AM

Civil Parish: Killevy (1)
Map Grid: 26
RC Parish: part Killeavy, Lower (Bessbrook); part
Killeavy, Upper, see below
Diocese: AM
Earliest Record: b. 1.1835; m. 1.1835; d. 8.1858
Missing Dates: m. 12.1862-5.1874
Status: LC; NLI (mf); Indexed by AA (to 1900)

Civil Parish: Killevy (2)
Map Grid: 26
RC Parish: Killeavy, Upper (Cloghogue)
Diocese: AM
Earliest Record: b. 10.1832; m. 11.1832
Status: LC; NLI (mf); Indexed by AA (to 1900)

Civil Parish: Killevy (3)
Map Grid: 26
RC Parish: Dromintee
Diocese: AM
Earliest Record: b. 6.1853; m. 11.1853
Status: LC; NLI (mf); Indexed by AA (to 1900)

Civil Parish: Killyman
Map Grid: 2
RC Parish: Dungannon, see Drumglass, Co. Tyrone
Diocese: AM

Civil Parish: Kilmore
Map Grid: 6
RC Parish: Kilmore (Mullavilly or Richill)
Diocese: AM
Earliest Record: b. 1.1845; m. 1.1845
Status: LC; NLI (mf); Indexed by AA (to 1900)

Civil Parish: Lisnadill
Map Grid: 19
RC Parish: Ballymacnab (Kilcluney)
Diocese: AM
Earliest Record: b. 1820; m. 1.1844
Status: LC; NLI (mf); Indexed by AA (to 1900)

Civil Parish: Loughgall
Map Grid: 14
RC Parish: Loughgall and Tartaraghan
Diocese: AM

Earliest Record: b. 1.1835; m. 8.1833
Missing Dates: b. 8.1852-10.1854, 5.1858-9.1859;
m. 1.1854-2.1860
Status: LC; NLI (mf); Indexed by AA (to 1900)

Civil Parish: Loughgilly
Map Grid: 22
RC Parish: Loughgilly (Whitecross)
Diocese: AM
Earliest Record: b. 5.1825; m. 2.1825
Missing Dates: b. 12.1844-2.1849; m. 11.1844-
2.1849
Status: LC; NLI (mf); Indexed by AA (to 1900)

Civil Parish: Magheralin
Map Grid: 10
RC Parish: see Co. Down
Diocese: DR

Civil Parish: Montiaghs
Map Grid: 7
RC Parish: Seagoe, see Seagoe
Diocese: DR

Civil Parish: Mullaghabawn
see: Forkhill

Civil Parish: Mullaghbrack
Map Grid: 18
RC Parish: see Ballymore
Diocese: AM

Civil Parish: Newtownhamilton
Map Grid: 24
RC Parish: Creggan, Lower (Cullyhanna)
Diocese: AM
Earliest Record: b. 2.1845; m. 2.1845
Status: LC; NLI (mf); Indexed by AA (to 1900)

Civil Parish: Newry
Map Grid: 27
RC Parish: see Newry, Co. Down
Diocese: N&M

Civil Parish: Seagoe
Map Grid: 8
RC Parish: Seagoe or Derrymacash, see also
Dromore, Co. Down; also part Portadown, see
Drumcree
Diocese: DR
Earliest Record: b. 9.1836; m. 10.1836; d. 4.1837
Status: LC; NLI (mf); Indexed by AA (to 1900)

Civil Parish: Shankill
Map Grid: 9
RC Parish: Lurgan, see also Dromore, Co. Down
Diocese: DR
Earliest Record: b. 9.1822; m. 1822; d. 1825
Status: LC; NLI (mf); Indexed by AA (to 1900)

Civil Parish: Tartaraghan
Map Grid: 1
RC Parish: see Loughgall
Diocese: AM

Civil Parish: Tynan
Map Grid: 12
RC Parish: Tynan (Middletown)
Diocese: AM
Earliest Record: b. 6.1822; m. 6.1822
Missing Dates: b. 8.1834-8.1838, 7.1842-7.1845; m. 10.1834-6.1845
Status: LC; NLI (mf); Indexed by AA (to 1900)

Commercial and Social Directories

1819
Thomas Bradshaw's *General Directory . . .* covers Newry, Armagh, and gives an alphabetical list of the traders in Armagh, Lurgan, Markethill, Portadown, and Tandragee.

1820
J. Pigot's *Commercial Directory of Ireland* contains information on the gentry, nobility, and traders in and around the town of Armagh.

1824
J. Pigot's *City of Dublin and Hibernian Provincial Directory* includes traders, nobility, gentry, and clergy lists for Armagh, Blackwatertown, Lurgan, Portadown, and Tanderagee.

1841
Mathew Martin's *Belfast Directory* contains an alphabetical list of traders, merchants and gentry, residents of the principal streets, and the noblemen and gentry in and around the towns of Armagh, Lurgan, Portadown, and Waringstown.

1842
A further edition of the above, covering the same towns.

1846
Slater's *National Commercial Directory of Ireland* lists nobility, clergy, traders, etc., in Armagh, Blackwatertown, Loughgall, Lurgan and Moira, Portadown, and Tanderagee.

1852
Henderson's *Belfast and Province of Ulster Directory* has lists of inhabitants, traders, etc., in and around the towns of Armagh, Blackwatertown, Lurgan, and Portadown.

1856
Slater's *Royal National Commercial Directory of Ireland* lists nobility, gentry, clergy, traders, etc., in Armagh, Keady, Middletown, Richill, Tynan and Markethill, Blackwatertown and Loughgall, Lurgan, Moira and Waringstown, Portadown, and Tanderagee.

1865
R. Wynne's *Business Directory of Belfast* covers Armagh, Lurgan, and Portadown.

1870
Slater's *Directory of Ireland* contains trade, nobility, and clergy lists for Armagh, Crossmaglen, Lurgan, Moy, Newtown Hamilton, Portadown, and Tanderagee.

1877
A further edition of Henderson's *Belfast and Province of Ulster Directory* covers Armagh, Blackwatertown, Keady, Lurgan, Moira, Portadown, Richill, Tanderagee, Waringstown, and Donaghcloney. Further editions in 1880, 1884, 1890, 1894, and 1900.

1881
Slater's *Royal National Commercial Directory of Ireland* contains lists of traders, clergy, nobility, and farmers in adjoining parishes of the towns of Armagh, Crossmaglen, Lurgan, Moy, Newtown Hamilton, Portadown, and Tanderagee.

1883
Farrell's *County Armagh Directory and Almanac* contains street directories for Armagh and alphabetical lists for the towns of Lurgan, Portadown, Richill, and Tanderagee.

1888
G.H. Bassett's *Book of Antrim* contains a variety of local information and history, as well as a directory of Armagh town and of all the postal districts in the county.

1894
Slater's *Royal National Directory of Ireland* lists traders, police, teachers, farmers, and private residents in each of the towns, villages, and parishes of the county.

Family History

Pedigrees of Atkinson, Beck, Chambers, Cole, Jackson, and Pilleys or Pillows. SLC film 1279354.

Pedigrees of Anderson, Burleigh, Hollingsworth, McAlindon, McBride, Peebles, Whaley, Woodhouse, and Smith. SLC film 1279327.

"Blaney of Lurgan, Co. Armagh." *Ir. Anc.* 3 (1) (1971): 32–39.

"The Descendants of Robert McCann of Cloghoge, Co. Armagh." *Ir. Anc.* 5 (1): 1–6.

Phillips, Sir T. *Pedigree of Molyneux of Castle Dillon, Co. Armagh.*

"Obins of Castleobins." Pedigree in *Swanzy Notebooks.* RCB Library, Dublin.

O'Neill, Hovenden, Stronge—See Miscellaneous Sources.

Gravestone Inscriptions

Creggan: *Seanchas Ardmhacha* 6 (2) (1972): 309–32.

Kilclooney: SLC film 1279354.

Mullaghabrack: ACM F6 and SLC film 1279384.

St. Patrick's: ACM P8 and SLC film 1279356.

Sandy Hill (Armagh City): *Seanchas Ardmhacha* 11 (2) (1985): 395–434.

Newspapers

Title: *Armagh Guardian*
Published in: Armagh, 1844–1982
BL Holdings: 12.1844–in progress

Title: *Armagh Standard* (incorporated with *Ulster Gazette*)
Published in: Armagh, 1879–1909
BL Holdings: 4.1844–6.1909

Title: *Lurgan Gazette*
Published in: Lurgan, 1861–74

Title: *Lurgan Mail* (continued as *Lurgan and Craigavon Mail* in 1977, and as *Lurgan Mail* in 1983)
Published in: Lurgan, 1890–current
NLI Holdings: 12.1904–10.1977
BL Holdings: 12.1897–in progress (except 1926)

Title: *Lurgan Times and Portadown Recorder*
Published in: Lurgan, 1877–1915
BL Holdings: 5.1879–5.1915

Title: *Portadown (Weekly) News* (continued as *Portadown and Lurgan News* from 1872–90)
Published in: Portadown, 1859–current
NLI Holdings: 1.1899–10.1956
BL Holdings: 4–10.1859; 11.1859–5.1822; 6.1872–12.1925; 1927; 1.1929–10.1956

Title: *Ulster Gazette* (continued as *Armagh Gazette* in 1850)
Published in: Armagh, 1844–current
NLI Holdings: 11.1879–12.1913; 6.1921–9.1940; 1.1950–in progress
BL Holdings: 10.1844–1924

Wills and Administrations

A discussion of the types of records, where they are held, and their availability and value is given in the Wills section of the introduction. The availability of prerogative wills, administrations, and marriage license records is also described in the relevant parts of the same section.

Pre-1858 Wills and Administrations

Prerogative Wills. See the introduction.

Consistorial Wills. County Armagh is mainly in the diocese of Armagh; four parishes are in Dromore and one in Newry and Mourne. The guide to Catholic parish records in this chapter shows the diocese to which each civil parish belonged. The wills of residents of each diocese were usually proven within that diocese (see the Wills section of the introduction for exceptions). The following records survive:

Wills

See the introduction.

Abstracts

"Quaker Wills from the Lisburn Meeting." *Ir. Gen.* (1950). Johnson collection of Will abstracts—Armagh library.

Indexes

Co. Armagh Will index (1610–1811) ACM M74 and 98 (vol. 1–5), F7; SLC film 1279384. Dromore 1678–1858 with the Peculiar of Newry and Mourne 1727–1858; Armagh 1666–1837 (A–L) and 1677–1858 (M–Y); also the District of Drogheda 1691–1846.

Post-1858 Wills and Administrations

This county was served by the District Registry of Armagh. The surviving records are kept in the PRONI and at LDS on SLC films 917201; 917484–93; 917906–16. Belfast District Will Books (1871–92): SLC films 930328–39; 930381–94.

Marriage Licenses

Indexes

Armagh Diocesan Marriage Licenses (1727–1845) NAI; SLC films 100859–860 and 930388–89. Dromore Marriage License Bonds (1721–1844) NAI; SLC film 100867.

Miscellaneous Sources

"Ballentaken-Beragh in the 17th Century." *Seanchas Ardmhaca* 10 (2) (1982): 455–501.

Coote, Sir Charles. *Statistical Survey of the County of Armagh.* Royal Dublin Society (1804).

"Life and Times of Fr. Edmund Murphy, Killeavy 1680." *Louth Arch. J.* 7 (3) (1931): 336–81. (Lists many residents of Killeavy RC parish in Killevy civil parish.)

Marshall, John J. *History of the Parish of Tynan, Co. Armagh.* With Notices of the O'Neill, Hovenden, Stronge, and other Families connected with the district. Dungannon: Tyrone Printing Co., 1932.

The Migration of Ulster Catholics to Connaught 1795–96 (addendum). *Seanchas Ardmhaca* 12 (1) (1986).

Provisional list of pre-1900 School Registers in the PRONI. *Ulster Gen. & Hist. Guild* 9 (1986): 60–71. Lists registers and PRONI reference numbers for all NI counties.

"Some Lists of Mid-18th-Century Linen-drapers in S.E. Ulster." *Ir. Anc.* 11 (1) (1979): 9–14.

Stuart, James. *Historical Memoirs of the City of Armagh (1819).* Edited by the Rev. A. Coleman. 1900.

"The Survey of Armagh and Tyrone, 1622." *Ulster J. Arch.* 23 (1960): 126–37; 27 (1964): 140–54.

Workhouse records: Lurgan Union (1841–1910). PRONI and SLC film 259166–72.

Research Sources and Services

Journals

Breifne (see Co. Cavan)

Craigavon Hist. Soc. Review (1972–present)

Down & Connor Hist. Soc. Journal

North Irish Roots (published by North of Ireland Family History Society)

Seanchas Ardmhaca (published by Armagh Diocesan Historical Society, 1954–present)

Seanchas Dhroim Mor (journal of the Dromore Diocesan Historical Society)

Libraries and Information Sources

Armagh County Museum (abbreviated ACM in text), The Mall East, Armagh BT61 9BE, N. Ireland. Ph: (01861) 523070; fax: (01861) 522631. This is a branch of the Ulster Museum, and has a large collection of local historical and biographical material, mainly dealing with Armagh. Much of the collection has been microfilmed by SLC. Open to researchers by appointment.

Irish and Local Studies Dept., Central Library, Royal Avenue, Belfast BT1 1EA

Southern Library Board Headquarters, Brownlow Road, Craigavon, Co. Armagh

Ulster-American Folk Park Library; see Libraries in Co. Tyrone chapter

Research Services

See Research Services in Belfast in the introduction.

Armagh Ancestry, 42 English Street, Armagh, N. Ireland, BT61 7AB. Ph: (01861) 521802; Fax: (01861) 510033. Has computer index of all Armagh Catholic church registers pre-1900; all Co. Armagh civil marriages pre-1922; some Presbyterian church registers pre-1900. Further Presbyterian registers, Church of Ireland registers, and pre-1922 death records are being indexed. Researchers are advised to contact the center for an updated list of registers and other sources indexed. Research services are conducted for a fee.

Armagh Record Centre, Ara Coeli, Armagh BT61 7GY. Ph: (01861) 522981. This is the record center for the Catholic Archdiocese of Armagh. They have indexed all of the Catholic records of the diocese, which covers both the counties Armagh and Louth.

Societies

Armagh Diocesan Historical Society/Cumann Seanchais Ardmhacha, Dr. J.B. Walsh, 14 Ashley Park, Armagh

Armagh Natural History and Phil. Society, Mr. Victor Whitcroft, 23 Charlemont Gardens, Armagh BT61 9BB. Ph: (01861) 523130

Craigavon Historical Society, Mr. John Trimble, 103 Drumgor Park, Craigavon, Co. Armagh BT65 4AH. Ph: (01762) 343326

Creggan Historical Society, Mrs. Geraldine Hanratty, Teer, Crossmaglen, Newry, Co. Armagh BT35 9BB. Ph: (01693) 868064

Keady and District Historical Society, Ms. Kathleen Quinn, 25 Armagh Road, Keady, Armagh BT60 3TN. Ph: (01861) 531255

Markethill and District Historical Society, Mrs. Pearl Ross, Ross Insurance Services, Main Street, Markethill, Co. Armagh BT60 1PL. Ph: (01861) 551818

North of Ireland Family History Society, Queens University of Belfast, Dept. of Education, 69 University Street, Belfast BT7 1HL. Publishers of *North Irish Roots*

Armagh Civil Parishes as Numbered on Map

1. Tartaraghan
2. Killyman
3. Clonfeacle (2 pts.)
4. Loughgall
5. Drumcree
6. Kilmore
7. Montiaghs
8. Seagoe
9. Shankill
10. Magheralin
11. Eglish
12. Tynan
13. Grange
14. Armagh
15. Derrynoose
16. Keady
17. Kildarton
18. Mullaghbrack
19. Lisnadill
20. Kilclooney
21. Ballymore
22. Loughgilly
23. Ballymyre
24. Newtownhamilton
25. Creggan
26. Killevy
27. Newry
28. Forkhill
29. Jonesborough

Armagh Civil Parishes in Alphabetical Order

Armagh: 14
Ballymore: 21
Ballymyre: 23
Clonfeacle (2 pts.): 3
Creggan: 25
Derrynoose: 15
Drumcree: 5
Eglish: 11
Forkhill (2 pts.): 28
Grange: 13
Jonesborough: 29
Keady: 16
Kilclooney: 20
Kildarton: 17
Killevy: 26
Killyman: 2
Kilmore: 6
Lisnadill: 19
Loughgall: 4
Loughgilly: 22
Magheralin: 10
Montiaghs: 7
Mullaghbrack: 18
Newry (5 pts.): 27
Newtownhamilton: 24
Seagoe: 8
Shankill: 9
Tartaraghan: 1
Tynan: 12

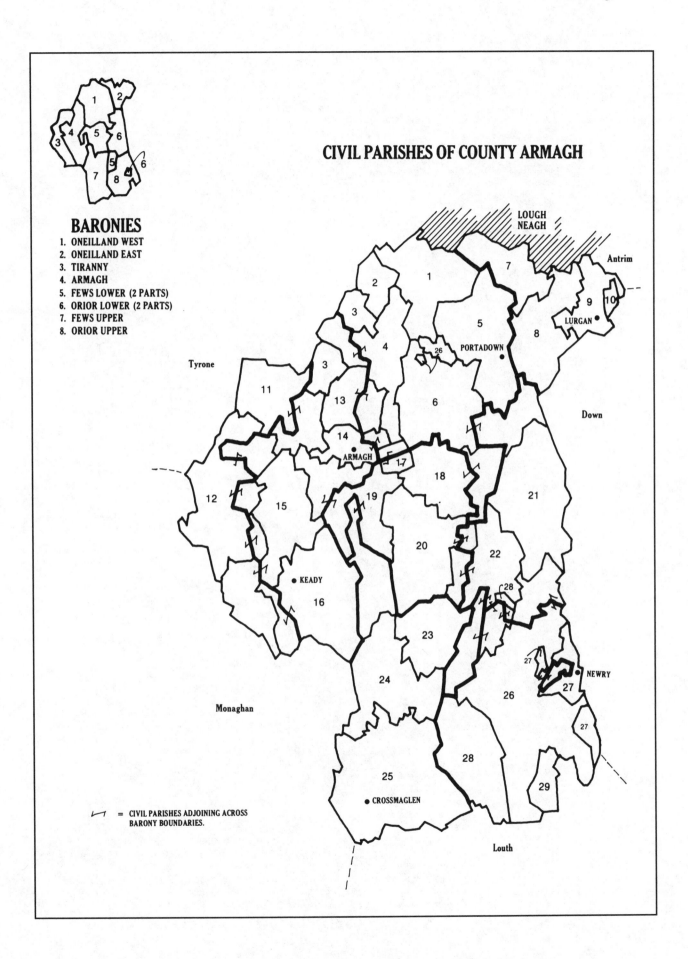

BARONIES

1. ONEILLAND WEST
2. ONEILLAND EAST
3. TIRANNY
4. ARMAGH
5. FEWS LOWER (2 PARTS)
6. ORIOR LOWER (2 PARTS)
7. FEWS UPPER
8. ORIOR UPPER

CIVIL PARISHES OF COUNTY ARMAGH

LOUGH NEAGH

Antrim

Tyrone

Down

Monaghan

Louth

LURGAN

PORTADOWN

ARMAGH

KEADY

NEWRY

CROSSMAGLEN

⌐⌐ = CIVIL PARISHES ADJOINING ACROSS
BARONY BOUNDARIES.

County Carlow

A Brief History

This inland Leinster county contains the towns of Carlow, Muinebeag (or Bagenalstown), Tullow, Leighlinbridge, and Rathvilly.

County Carlow was formerly part of the territory of Ui Kinsellaigh. The major families of the county were Kavanagh, O'Ryan of Idrone, O'Nolan of Forth, O'Neill, and O'Hayden. Following the Norman invasion, the county was taken by their leader, Strongbow, and castles were built at Carlow town, Leighlin, and Tullow. The English administration gradually lost its power elsewhere in the county to the powerful McMurrough Kavanaghs, who allied themselves with the O'Byrnes and O'Tooles in Wicklow. These native chieftains continued to hold varying degrees of control over the county for several centuries.

The town of Carlow was an important Norman stronghold during the Middle Ages. In 1361 it was walled to protect it from the neighboring Gaelic chieftains. It was repeatedly attacked, and was captured in 1405 by the McMurrough Kavanaghs (see Wexford) and in 1567 by the O'Moores (see Laois). Although a plan for a plantation of the county was put forward during the reign of James I, it was not acted on.

In 1641 the county joined the rebellion of the Catholic Confederacy (see the introduction), but the Carlow rebels were finally defeated by Ireton, one of Cromwell's generals, in 1650. Of the English and Norman families who settled in Carlow at various times, the most prominent were Bruen, Butler, Bagenal, Best, Brown, Bunbury, Burton, and Tallon.

The county was relatively badly affected by the Great Famine of 1845-47. The population in 1841 was 86,000, and by 1851 had fallen by twenty-one percent, to 68,000. Of these people, over 10,000 died of starvation or other causes between 1845 and 1850, and further thousands emigrated.

County Carlow is now an important agricultural center, with an extensive sugarbeet and cereal industry. The current population is around 40,000.

Census and Census Substitutes

1641
Book of Survey and Distribution. NLI MS 971.

1659
"Census" of Ireland. Edited by S. Pender. Dublin: Stationery Office, 1939. NLI I 6551. SLC film 924648.

1669
"Householders of the Parish of Carlow." *J. Kildare Arch. Soc.* 10 (1918-21): 255-57 (gives names on four streets).

1739
"Tenants of the Lordship of Carlow." *J. Kildare Arch. Soc.* 12 (2) (1937): 99-101.

1767
"Co. Carlow Freeholders." *Ir. Gen.* 12 (1) and (2) (1980): 46-47.

1775
Catholic Qualification Roll Extracts (ninety-three names, addresses, and occupations). 59th Report. DKPRI: 50-84.

1798
List of Persons who Suffered Losses During '98 Rebellion. NLI 94107 (approximately three hundred names, addresses, and occupations).

1821

Extracts from the Government Census for Fennagh Parish Relating Only to the Surnames Clowry, Foley, White, Lennon, Rigney, and Gregor. SLC film 100158.

1824–26

List of labourers and observations on their work. Castletown, Co. Carlow. NLI Ms 19, 448.

1821–37

Tithe Applotment Survey (see introduction).

1832–37

"List of Voters Registered in the Borough of Carlow." *Parl. Papers* 11 (2) (1837): 193–96 (over four hundred names and street addresses).

1835

List of electors, 167 pp. This is handwritten and gives names and addresses of voters. NLI Ms 16899.

1837

Marksmen (illiterate voters) in Parliamentary boroughs: Carlow, *Parliamentary Papers* 11 (1) (1837): Appendix A.

1843

Voters List. NAI 1843/55.

1846

Ratepayers in Barragh Electoral Division (names in each townland, description of property, and rate due). NLI film P4547.

1852–53

Griffith's Valuation (see introduction).

1858–59

Census of the RC parish of Bagenalstown. Included in parish register (see civil parish of Dunleckney).

1901

Census. NAI (see introduction). SLC film 812107–16.

1911

Census. NAI.

Church Records

Church of Ireland

See the introduction for a description of Church of Ireland records and their major repositories. Many C of I records were lost in the PRO fire of 1922. These are indicated as "Lost." However, as Church of Ireland records were effectively state records, the records of marriage (from 1845) are also in the General Registrar's Office. Many are still in local custody (LC), while others are in other archives (e.g., RCBL or NAI). Some of the records are indexed by Carlow Genealogy Project (see Research Services at the end of the chapter). These are indicated as "Indexed by CGP."

Ardoyne
Status: Lost

Barragh
Earliest Records: b. 1799–; m. 1799–; d: 1799–
Missing Records: b. 1806–30; m. 1806–29; d. 1806–37
Status: LC; Indexed by Anglican Rec. Proj. at RCBL, Soc. of Gen. (b. 1799–1805, 1831–79; m. 1799–1805, 1830–1903; d. 1799–1805, 1838–78)

Bilboa
Earliest Records: m. 1846–
Status: RCBL (m. 1846–1956)

Carlow
Earliest Records: b. 1689–1885; m. 1689–1915; d. 1698–1894
Status: RCBL (b. 1689–1885; m. 1689–1915; d. 1698–1894); Indexed by CGP (b/m. 1689–1900); NAI Ms 1073 (b/m/d. 1698–1835) and GO 578 (extracts b/m/d. 1744–1816)

Clonagoose or Borris
Earliest Records: m. 1846–
Status: RCBL (m. 1846–1954)

Clonegal—see Co. Wexford

Clonmelsh
Earliest Records: m. 1846–
Status: RCBL (m. 1846–1934)

Clonmore
Earliest Records: b. 1826–; m. 1826–; d. 1827–
Status: LC (copy of earlier records)

Cloydagh
Status: Lost

Dunleckney
Earliest Records: b. 1791–; m. 1791–; d. 1791–
Status: LC; RCBL (b/d. 1791–1837 and m. 1791–1957)

Fenagh
Earliest Records: b. 1809–; m. 1809–; d. 1809–
Status: LC

Hackettstown
Earliest Records: b. 1799; m. 1799; d. 1799
Status: LC (copy)

Kellistown (Kellitstown)
Earliest Records: m. 1854–
Status: RCBL (m. 1854–1917)

Killeshin (see Carlow)
Earliest Records: b. 1824–; m. 1824–; d. 1824–
Status: LC

Kiltennel (New Ross)
Earliest Records: b. 1837–; m. 1837–; d. 1837–
Status: RCBL (b. 1837–75; m. 1837–1950; d. 1837–1957)

Kinneagh
Status: Lost

Lorum
Existing Records: m. 1845–
Status: RCBL (m. 1845–1954)

Myshall
Earliest Records: b. 1814–; m. 1815–; d. 1816–
Status: LC

Nurney
Existing Records: m. 1845–
Status: RCBL (m. 1845–1954)

Old Leighlin
Earliest Records: b. 1781–; m. 1790–; d. 1781–
Status: RCBL (b. 1781–1813; m. 1790–1855; d. 1781–1813)

Painestown (Carlow)
Earliest Records: b. 1833–; m. 1833–; d. 1833–
Status: LC

Rathvilly
Earliest Records: b. 1826–75; m. 1826–45; d. 1826–75
Status: LC

St. Annes
Earliest Records: b. 1859–
Status: LC

St. Mullins
Status: Lost

Staplestown
Status: Lost

Straboe (see Rathvilly)

Tullow
Earliest Records: b. 1696–; m. 1700–; d. 1700–
Status: RCBL (b. 1696–1844; m. 1700–1843; d. 1700–1844)

Tullowmagimma
Status: Lost

Urglin-Rutland Church (Carlow)
Earliest Records: b. 1710–; m. 1715–; d. 1715–
Status: LC

Wells
Earliest Records: b. 1870–; m. 1803–; d. 1802
Status: RCBL (b. 1870–1957; m. 1803–1915; d. 1802)

Methodist

Methodist churches existed in Carlow at Carlow Town and Collierty. See the introduction for more details.

Roman Catholic

Carlow Genealogy Project (CGP) is computer-indexing all of the church records of the county. They will be providing a service starting in mid-1997 (see Research Services at the end of the chapter). Carlow County Heritage Society also has a card index of these records (also see Research Services). Microfilm copies of all registers are also available in the National Library of Ireland (NLI), and through the LDS library system.

Civil Parish: Agha
Map Grid: 32
RC Parish: Leighlinbridge
Diocese: LE
Earliest Record: b. 1.1783; m. 2.1783
Missing Dates: b. 10.1786–12.1819; m. 1.1788–1.1820, 2.1827–7.1827
Status: LC; NLI (mf); Indexing by CGP in progress

Civil Parish: Aghade
Map Grid: 43 (2 parts)
RC Parish: see Ballon
Diocese: LE

Civil Parish: Ardoyne
Map Grid: 23
RC Parish: see Ardoyne, Co. Wicklow
Diocese: LE

Civil Parish: Ardristan
Map Grid: 25
RC Parish: Tullow, see Tullowphelim
Diocese: LE

Civil Parish: Ballinacarrig or Staplestown
Map Grid: 6
RC Parish: Tinryland, see Tullowmagimma
Diocese: LE

Civil Parish: Ballon
Map Grid: 42
RC Parish: Ballon
Diocese: LE
Earliest Record: b. 1.1785; m. 8.1782; d. 8.1825
Missing Dates: b. 9.1795–7.1816; m. 12.1795–8.1816; d. 12.1834–1.1861
Status: LC; NLI (mf); Indexing by CGP in progress

Civil Parish: Ballycrogue
Map Grid: 7
RC Parish: Tinryland, see Tullowmagimma
Diocese: LE

Civil Parish: Ballyellin
Map Grid: 36
RC Parish: Bagenalstown, see Dunleckney
Diocese: LE

Civil Parish: Baltinglass
Map Grid: 13
RC Parish: see Baltinglass, Co. Wicklow
Diocese: LE

Civil Parish: Barragh
Map Grid: 45
RC Parish: Clonegal, see Moyacomb
Diocese: LE

Civil Parish: Carlow
Map Grid: 4
RC Parish: Carlow
Diocese: LE
Earliest Record: b. 6.1774; m. 11.1769
Missing Dates: b. many gaps to 1820; m. 8.1786–1.1820
Status: LC; NLI (mf); Indexing by CGP in progress

Civil Parish: Clonmelsh
Map Grid: 5
RC Parish: Leighlinbridge, see Agha
Diocese: LE

Civil Parish: Clonmore
Map Grid: 22
RC Parish: Clonmore
Diocese: LE
Earliest Record: b. 11.1819; m. 2.1813
Missing Dates: m. 2.1833–5.1833
Status: LC; NLI (mf); Indexed by Wicklow HC (to 1900), see Co. Wicklow

Civil Parish: Clonygoose
Map Grid: 37
RC Parish: part Borris; part Bagenalstown, see Dunleckney
Diocese: LE
Earliest Record: b. 5.1782; m. 1.1782
Missing Dates: b. 12.1813–2.1825; m. 12.1813–2.1825, 11.1868–2.1869
Status: LC; NLI (mf); Indexing by CGP in progress

Civil Parish: Cloydagh
Map Grid: 26
RC Parish: Leighlinbridge, see Agha
Diocese: LE

Civil Parish: Crecrin (see also Co. Wicklow)
Map Grid: 21

RC Parish: see Clonmore
Diocese: LE

Civil Parish: Dunleckney
Map Grid: 33
RC Parish: Bagenalstown
Diocese: LE
Earliest Record: b. 1.1820; m. 1.1820
Status: LC; NLI (mf); Indexing by CGP in progress

Civil Parish: Fennagh
Map Grid: 24
RC Parish: part Myshall; part Ballon
Diocese: LE

Civil Parish: Gilbertstown
Map Grid: 40
RC Parish: see Ballon
Diocese: LE

Civil Parish: Grangeford
Map Grid: 9
RC Parish: Tullow, see Tullowphelim
Diocese: LE

Civil Parish: Hacketstown (see also Co. Wicklow)
Map Grid: 19
RC Parish: Hacketstown
Diocese: LE
Earliest Record: b. 8.1820; m. 8.1820
Missing Dates: b. 4.1823–7.1826, 9.1826–10.1827; m. 12.1827–3.1829, 9.1870–2.1877
Status: LC; NLI (mf); Indexing by CGP in progress

Civil Parish: Haroldstown
Map Grid: 18
RC Parish: see Hacketstown
Diocese: LE

Civil Parish: Kellistown
Map Grid: 8
RC Parish: see Ballon
Diocese: LE

Civil Parish: Killerrig
Map Grid: 3
RC Parish: part Tullowphelim; part Leighlinbridge, see Agha
Diocese: LE

Civil Parish: Killinane
Map Grid: 30
RC Parish: Leighlinbridge, see Agha
Diocese: LE

Civil Parish: Kiltegan
Map Grid: 15
RC Parish: see Hacketstown
Diocese: LE

Civil Parish: Kiltennell
Map Grid: 38

RC Parish: Borris, see Clonygoose
Diocese: LE

Civil Parish: Kineagh
Map Grid: 12
RC Parish: part Castledermot, see Co. Kildare; part Rathvilly
Diocese: DU

Civil Parish: Lorum
Map Grid: 36
RC Parish: Bagenalstown, see Dunleckney

Civil Parish: Moyacomb (see also Cos. Wicklow and Wexford)
Map Grid: 46
RC Parish: Clonegal
Diocese: FE
Earliest Record: b. 1.1833; m. 2.1833
Status: LC; NLI (mf); Indexing by CGP in progress

Civil Parish: Myshall
Map Grid: 44
RC Parish: Myshall
Diocese: LE
Earliest Record: b. 2.1822; m. 9.1822
Missing Dates: b. 5.1846–10.1846; m. 1.1845–2.1846
Status: LC; NLI (mf); Indexing by CGP in progress

Civil Parish: Nurney
Map Grid: 31
RC Parish: Bagenalstown, see Dunleckney
Diocese: LE

Civil Parish: Old Leighlin
Map Grid: 28
RC Parish: Leighlinbridge, see Agha
Diocese: LE

Civil Parish: Painestown (see also Co. Kildare)
Map Grid: 1
RC Parish: see Carlow
Diocese: LE

Civil Parish: Rahill
Map Grid: 11
RC Parish: see Rathvilly
Diocese: LE

Civil Parish: Rathmore
Map Grid: 17
RC Parish: see Rathvilly
Diocese: LE

Civil Parish: Rathvilly
Map Grid: 14
RC Parish: Rathvilly
Diocese: LE
Earliest Record: b. 10.1797; m. 10.1800
Missing Dates: b. 1.1813–6.1813; m. 2.1812–6.1813
Status: LC; NLI (mf); Indexing by CGP in progress

Civil Parish: St. Mullin's (1) (see also Co. Wexford)
Map Grid: 47
RC Parish: St. Mullin's (2)
Diocese: LE
Earliest Record: b. 5.1796; m. 6.1796
Missing Dates: b. 3.1810–1.1812, 3.1814–1.1820; m. 2.1807–10.1807, 3.1813–1.1820, 11.1871–2.1872
Status: LC; NLI (mf); Indexing by CGP in progress

Civil Parish: Slyguff
Map Grid: 34
RC Parish: part Borris, see Clonygoose; part Bagenalstown, see Dunleckny
Diocese: LE

Civil Parish: Straboe
Map Grid: 16
RC Parish: see Rathvilly; also Tullow, see Tullowphelim
Diocese: LE

Civil Parish: Templepeter
Map Grid: 41
RC Parish: see Ballon
Diocese: LE

Civil Parish: Tullowcreen
Map Grid: 27
RC Parish: Leighlinbridge, see Agha
Diocese: LE

Civil Parish: Tullowmagimma
Map Grid: 10
RC Parish: Tinryland
Diocese: LE
Earliest Record: b. 3.1813; m. 6.1813
Status: LC; NLI (mf); Indexing by CGP in progress

Civil Parish: Tullowphelim
Map Grid: 20
RC Parish: Tullow
Diocese: LE
Earliest Record: b. 8.1763; m. 5.1775
Missing Dates: b. 1.1781–1.1798, 1.1802–6.1807; m. 2.1776–1.1799, 2.1800–6.1807, 5.1830–11.1830
Status: LC; NLI (mf); Indexing by CGP in progress

Civil Parish: Ullard
Map Grid: 39
RC Parish: Graignamanagh, see Co. Kilkenny
Diocese: LE

Civil Parish: Urglin
Map Grid: 2
RC Parish: part Tullow; part Tinryland, see Tullowmagimma
Diocese: LE

Civil Parish: Wells
Map Grid: 29
RC Parish: Leighlinbridge, see Agha
Diocese: LE

Commercial and Social Directories

1788

Richard Lucas' *General Directory of the Kingdom of Ireland* contains lists of traders in Carlow, Old Leighlin, and Leighlinbridge. Also reprinted in *Ir. Gen.* 3 (10) (1965): 392-416.

1820

J. Pigot's *Commercial Directory of Ireland* contains information on the gentry, nobility, and traders in and around the town of Carlow.

1824

J. Pigot's *City of Dublin and Hibernian Provincial Directory* includes traders, nobility, gentry, and clergy lists for the towns of Carlow, Hacketstown, Leighlinbridge, and Tullow.

1839

T. Shearman's *New Commercial Directory for the Cities of Waterford and Kilkenny, Towns of Clonmel, Carrick-on-suir, New Ross, and Carlow.* Lists traders, gentry, etc.

1840

F. Kinder's *New Triennial and Commercial Directory for 1840, '41 and '42.* Contains lists of traders, nobility, and others for Carlow town (rare volume).

1846

Slater's *National Commercial Directory of Ireland* lists nobility, clergy, traders, etc., in Carlow, Hacketstown, Leighlinbridge, Bagenalstown and Royal Oak, and Tullow.

1856

Slater's *Royal National Commercial Directory of Ireland* lists nobility, gentry, clergy, traders, etc., in Carlow, Hacketstown, Leighlinbridge, Bagenalstown, Borris and Royal Oak, and Tullow.

1870

Slater's *Directory of Ireland* contains trade, nobility, and clergy lists for Bagenalstown and Leighlinbridge, Carlow, Hacketstown, and Tullow.

1881

Slater's *Royal National Commercial Directory of Ireland* contains lists of traders, clergy, nobility, and farmers in adjoining parishes of the towns of Bagenalstown and Leighlinbridge, Borris and Old Leighlin, Carlow and Graigue, Hacketstown, and Tullow.

1886

Francis Guy's *Postal Directory* of Munster lists gentry, clergy, traders, principal farmers, teachers, police, etc., in each postal district, and magistrates, clergy, and the professions for the whole county.

1894

Slater's *Royal National Commercial Directory of Ireland* lists traders, police, teachers, farmers, and private residents in each of the towns, villages, and parishes of the county.

Family History

"The Blackneys of Ballyellen" (Co. Carlow). *Ir. Gen.* 3 (1957-58): 44-45, 116.

King, J.A. "The Breens of Co. Carlow." *Irish Roots* (1) (1993): 24-25.

Cullen—Biographical Material. *Reportorium* 1 (1) (1955): 213-27.

"The Early Cullen Family." *Reportorium* 1 (1): 185-202.

"The Dillons of Carlow." *Ir. Gen.* 3 (7) (1962): 245-48.

"The Family of the MacMurrough Kavanaghs." *Carloviana* 1 (3) (1954): 13-16.

Copies of 1841 Census Returns for McCall Family. NAI film 5248 (10).

Bewley, Sir Edward. *The Rudkins of the Co. Carlow.* Exeter, 1905; also *Gen.* N.S. 11 (1905): 145-62.

"The Vigors of Leighlinbridge." *Carloviana* 2 (8) (1980).

"Vigors Papers" (Burgage, Co. Carlow). *Anal. Hib.* 20 (302): 10.

Gravestone Inscriptions

A series of "Carlow Tombstone Inscriptions" has been published by Muintir Na Tire, Borris, Co. Carlow, four volumes to date.

Ballicopagan: Carlow Tombstone Inscriptions, Vol. 2.

Ballyellen: Carlow Tombstone Inscriptions, Vol 4. SLC film 6342811.

Ballymurphy: Carlow Tombstone Inscriptions, Vol. 3.

Borris: Carlow Tombstone Inscriptions, Vol. 2.

Clonagoose: Carlow Tombstone Inscriptions, Vol. 2.

Dunleckney: SLC film 6342811.

Kellymount: Carlow Tombstone Inscriptions, Vol 4. SLC film 6342811.

Kilcullen: Carlow Tombstone Inscriptions, Vol. 3.

Killedmond: Carlow Tombstone Inscriptions, Vol. 3.

Kiltennel: Carlow Tombstone Inscriptions, Vol. 3.

A
TOPOGRAPHICAL DICTIONARY
OF
IRELAND.

HAC

HACKETSTOWN, a market-town and parish, partly in the barony of BALLYNACOR, county of WICKLOW, but chiefly in that of RATHVILLY, county of CARLOW, and province of LEINSTER, 6¾ miles (S. E.) from Baltinglass, on the road from Wicklow to Carlow; containing 4434 inhabitants. In 1798 it sustained two attacks from the insurgent forces, one on the 25th of May, which was successfully repulsed by the yeomanry and a detachment of the Antrim militia; the other on the 25th of June, when a body of insurgents, amounting to several thousands, advanced against it at five in the morning. The garrison, consisting of 170, mostly yeomen, marched out to meet them, but, after a few volleys, were obliged to retreat, the cavalry by the road to Clonmore, and the infantry, 120 in number, into the barrack, where they maintained their position throughout the day behind a breastwork in the rear of it. The town was fired in several places by the rebels, who, after various ineffectual attempts to force an entrance to the barrack and a garrisoned house by which it was flanked, retreated, and in the night the garrison retired on Tullow. The town, which consists of 131 houses, is situated on a rising ground, below which flows a branch of the Slaney, and commands fine views. It is a constabulary police station, and has a penny post to Baltinglass, and a dispensary. A patent was granted in 1635, by Chas. I., to the Earl of Ormonde for a market on Wednesday and fairs on the Tuesday after Nov. 1st, and the Thursday after Trinity Sunday. The market is now held on Thursday, but only during the summer months from March to August, for the sale of meal and potatoes; and the fairs are on Jan. 13th, the first Thursday in Feb., March 12th, April 13th, May 4th, June 2nd, July 13th, Aug. 21st, Sept. 18th, Oct. 17th, the third Thursday in November, and Dec. 21st.

The parish comprises 31,570 statute acres, of which 11,954 are applotted under the tithe act: about one-sixth of the land is arable, nearly one-half pasture, and the remainder bog and waste; the latter is chiefly situated in the eastern part of the parish, and large blocks of granite are dispersed throughout. The principal seats are Woodside, the residence of S. Jones, Esq.; Ballyhelane, of J. Brownrigg, Esq.; and Ballasallagh House, of

VOL. II.—1

HAG

J. Hogier, Esq. The living is a rectory, in the diocese of Leighlin, episcopally united in 1693 to the vicarage of Haroldstown, and in the patronage of the Bishop: the tithes amount to £553. 16. 11., and of the benefice to £619. 15. 11. The glebe-house was erected in 1819, by a gift of £300 and a loan of £500 from the late Board of First Fruits; the glebe comprises 8½ acres. The church is a neat building, with a square embattled tower surmounted with pinnacles, which was erected and the church roofed anew, in 1820, by a gift of £600 and a loan of £500 from the late Board of First Fruits; it has recently been repaired by a grant of £559 from the Ecclesiastical Commissioners. In the churchyard is a monument to the memory of Capt. Hardy, who was killed in 1798 while defending the town. In the R. C. divisions it is the head of a union or district, comprising the parishes of Hacketstown and Moyne, and parts of Haroldstown, Clonmore, and Kiltegan; and containing chapels at Hacketstown, Killamote, and Knockanana. Near the church is a very neat place of worship for Wesleyan Methodists, recently erected. The parochial school is supported by the rector and a small payment from the scholars; and there is a national school in the R. C. chapel-yard.

HAGGARDSTOWN, a parish, in the barony of UPPER DUNDALK, county of LOUTH, and province of LEINSTER, 2 miles (S.) from Dundalk, on the road from Dublin to Belfast; containing, with the village of Blackrock, 1011 inhabitants. This parish comprises 1400¼ statute acres, according to the Ordnance survey, nearly the whole of which is very excellent land and under tillage. It is a rectory, in the diocese of Armagh, entirely impropriate in T. Fortescue, Esq.: the tithes amount to £178. 16. 3½. There is neither church, glebe-house, nor glebe. In the R. C. divisions it is the head of a union or district, also called Kilcurley, which comprises the parishes of Haggardstown, Heynstown, Ballybarrack, Philipstown, Dunbin, and part of Baronstown: a handsome chapel was erected here in 1833, and there is another at Baronstown. Here is a school of about 150 children; and there are some remains of the old church and also of an ancient castle.

B

Description of Hacketstown, County Carlow, from A *Topographical Dictionary of Ireland* by Samuel Lewis (London, 1837).

Linkardstown: IGRS Collection, GO.

New Cemetery: Carlow Tombstone Inscriptions, Vol. 2.

Paulstown: Carlow Tombstone Inscriptions, Vol 4. SLC film 6342811.

Rathanna: Carlow Tombstone Inscriptions, Vol. 3.

St. Michaels: Carlow Tombstone Inscriptions, Vol. 1.

St. Mullins: Carlow Tombstone Inscriptions, Vol. 1.

Wells: Carlow Tombstone Inscriptions, Vol 4. SLC film 6342811.

Newspapers

The earliest paper published in Carlow is the *Carlow Morning Post*, published starting in 1817. Newspapers from surrounding counties should be consulted for periods before its publication.

Title: *Carlow Independent*
Published in: Carlow, 1875–82
BL Holdings: 6.1879–1.1882

Title: *Carlow Morning Post*
Published in: Carlow, 1817–35
NLI Holdings: 12.1817–5.1820; 1.1828–1.1835
BL Holdings: 1–5 and 11–12.1833; 1.1834–1.1835

Title: *Carlow Nationalist and Leinster Times* (continued as *Nationalist and Leinster Times* in 1885)
Published in: Carlow, 1883–current
NLI Holdings: 9.1883–in progress
BL Holdings: 9.1883–in progress

Title: *Carlow Post*
Published in: Carlow, 1853–78
NLI Holdings: odd numbers 1858–77
BL Holdings: 10.1853–5.1878

Title: *Carlow Sentinel*
Published in: Carlow, 1832–1920
NLI Holdings: 12.1847–11.1853; 11.1847–2.1881; 8.1883–8.1888; 1.1885–12.1913
BL Holdings: 1.1832–10.1820

Title: *Carlow Standard*
Published in: Carlow, 1832–32
NLI Holdings: 1–4.1832
BL Holdings: 1–4.1832

Title: *Carlow Vindicator*
Published in: Carlow, 1892–c.1898
BL Holdings: 1–2.1892

Title: *Carlow Weekly News*
Published in: Carlow, 1858–63
BL Holdings: 3.1858–10.1863

Title: *Leinster Reformer*
Published in: Carlow, 1839–41
NLI Holdings: 10.1839–7.1841
BL Holdings: 10.1839–7.1841

Wills and Administrations

A discussion of the types of records, where they are held, and their availability and value is given in the Wills section of the introduction. The availability of prerogative wills, administrations, and marriage license records is also described in the relevant parts of the same section. Where available, published sources of these records are given in the Miscellaneous Sources section.

Pre-1858 Wills and Administrations

Prerogative Wills. See the introduction.

Consistorial Wills. County Carlow is mainly in the diocese of Leighlin, with one parish in Ferns diocese and one in Dublin diocese. The guide to Catholic parish records in this chapter shows the diocese to which each civil parish belonged. The wills of residents of each diocese were usually proven within that diocese (see Wills section for exceptions and those which might have survived).

Indexes

Leighlin (1642–1858). Those to 1800 have been published by Phillimore; Ferns—see Co. Wexford; Dublin—see Co. Dublin.

Post-1858 Wills and Administrations

County Carlow was served by the District Registry of Kilkenny. The surviving records are kept in the NAI. Will books (1858–95): NAI and SLC 1000943-5. Index to Leighlin Intestate Administrations: Supplement to *Ir. Anc.* 1972. SLC film 990403.

Marriage Licenses

Indexes

Leighlin and Ferns (1691–1845). NAI; GO ms. 612-17 (more complete); SLC film 100169-172 and 100870-71. Dublin—see Co. Dublin.

Miscellaneous Sources

Hood, S.E. Marriage in Ireland before the Famine: Case Study of Rathvilly Parish. *J. West Wicklow Historical Soc.* 3 (1989): 33–40.

Brophy, M. *Carlow Past and Present.* Carlow, 1888.

Coleman, James. Bibliography of counties Carlow, Kilkenny, and Wicklow. *Waterford & S. E. Ir. Arch. Soc. J* 11 (1907), 8, 126, NL, Ir 794105 W 1.

Coyle, James. *The Antiquities of Leighlin.*

Hore, H.J. *The Social State of the Southern and Eastern Counties of Ireland in the Sixteenth Century.* 1870.

MacSuibhne, P. *'98 in Carlow.* Carlow, 1974.

MacSuibhne, P. *Clonegal Parish (Carlow).* Carlow, 1975.

O'Toole, ed. *The Parish of Ballon, Co. Carlow.* 1933.

Ryan, John. *The History and Antiquities of the County Carlow*. Dublin, 1833.

Research Sources and Services

Journals
Carlow Past and Present
Carloviana

Libraries and Information Sources
Carlow County Library, Dublin Street, Carlow. Ph: (0503) 31126. The local history section has a good selection of local interest publications.

Research Services
Carlow Genealogy Project, Old School, College St., Carlow. Ph: (0503) 30850. This project is computer-indexing all of the church, and eventually other, records of the county. They will be providing a service starting in mid-1997. Researchers are advised to contact the project for an updated list of registers, and other sources, indexed.

Carlow County Heritage Society, Kennedy St., Carlow Town, Ireland. Ph: (0503) 42399. The society has card indexes of almost all of the church records of the county, and a large collection of relevant reference sources, estate papers, etc. They will conduct local research for a fee.

Irish Origins Research Agency, College Road, Kilkenny. Ph: (056) 21483; fax: (056) 64777. Genealogical research service, specializing in counties Kilkenny, Carlow, Tipperary, Wexford, and Waterford.

See also Research Services in Dublin in the introduction.

Societies
Carlow County Heritage Society (publishes *Carlow Past and Present*), Mr. Michael Purcell, 4 Kennedy St., Carlow

Old Carlow Society, Ms. Rose Murphy, 38 Kennedy Street, Carlow, Co. Carlow (publishers of *Carloviana*)

Tullowphelim Historical Society, Mr. John Keogh, 56 Dublin Road, Tullow, Co. Carlow

West Wicklow Historical Society, Ms. Maeve Baker, Ladystown, Rathvilly, Co. Carlow (publishers of *West Wicklow Historical Society Journal*)

Carlow Civil Parishes as Numbered on Map

1. Painestown
2. Urglin
3. Killerrig (2 pts.)
4. Carlow
5. Clonmelsh (2 pts.)
6. Ballinacarrig
7. Ballycrogue
8. Kellistown (2 pts.)
9. Grangeford
10. Tullowmaggimma
11. Rahill
12. Kineagh
13. Baltinglass
14. Rathvilly
15. Kiltegan
16. Straboe
17. Rathmore
18. Haroldstown
19. Hacketstown
20. Tullowphelim
21. Crecrin
22. Clonmore
23. Ardoyne (2 pts.)
24. Fennagh (4 pts.)
25. Ardristan
26. Cloydagh
27. Tullowcreen
28. Old Leighlin
29. Wells (2 pts.)
30. Killinane (2 pts.)
31. Nurney
32. Agha
33. Dunleckny
34. Sliguff (2 pts.)
35. Lorum
36. Ballyellin (5 pts.)
37. Clonygoose
38. Kiltennell
39. Ullard (2 pts.)
40. Gilbertstown (2 pts.)
41. Templepeter
42. Ballon
43. Aghade
44. Myshall
45. Barragh
46. Moyacomb
47. St. Mullins

BARONIES

1. CARLOW
2. RATHVILLY
3. IDRONE WEST
4. IDRONE EAST
5. FORTH
6. ST. MULLINS UPR.
7. ST. MULLINS LR.

CIVIL PARISHES OF COUNTY CARLOW

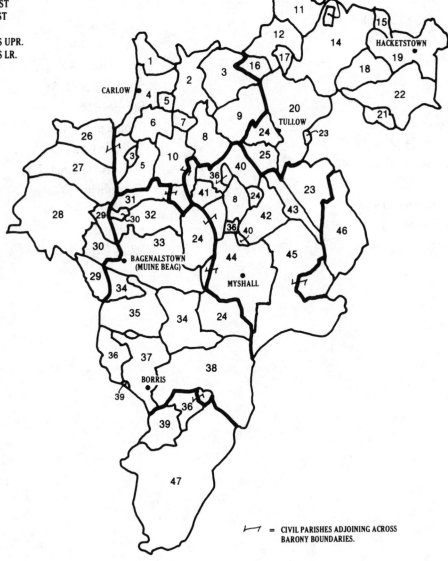

⊢⊣ = CIVIL PARISHES ADJOINING ACROSS
BARONY BOUNDARIES.

Carlow Civil Parishes in Alphabetical Order

Agha: 32
Aghade: 43
Ardoyne (2 pts.): 23
Ardristan: 25
Ballinacarrig: 6
Ballon: 42
Ballycrogue: 7
Ballyellin (5 pts.): 36
Baltinglass: 13
Barragh: 45
Carlow: 4
Clonmelsh (2 pts.): 5
Clonmore: 22
Clonygoose: 37
Cloydagh: 26
Crecrin: 21
Dunleckny: 33
Fennagh (4 pts.): 24
Gilberstown (2 pts.): 40
Grangeford: 9
Hacketstown: 19
Haroldstown: 18
Kellistown (2 pts.): 8

Killerrig (2 pts.): 3
Killinane (2 pts.): 3
Kiltegan: 15
Kiltennell: 38
Kineagh: 12
Lorum: 36
Moyacomb: 46
Myshall: 44
Old Leighlin: 28
Painestown: 1
Rahill: 11
Rathmore: 17
Rathvilly: 14
St. Mullins: 47
Sliguff (2 pts.): 34
Straboe: 16
Templepeter: 41
Tullowcreen: 27
Tullowmagimma: 10
Tullophelim: 20
Ullard (2 pts.): 39
Urglin: 2
Wells (2 pts.): 29

County Cavan

A Brief History

Originally part of the ancient kingdom of Breifne, this inland Ulster county contains the towns of Cavan, Bailieborough, Virginia, Belturbet, and Ballyjamesduff.

This part of Breifne was ruled by the O'Reillys, whose base was the town of Cavan. Other families associated with the county are (Mc)Brady, O'Mulleady, McGowan (often anglicized as Smith), O'Farrelly, McKiernan, O'Curry, O'Clery, and McIlduff. The O'Reillys retained control over the county for several centuries after the arrival of the Normans in Ireland in 1169. This was due both to the skill of their cavalry and also to the difficulty of the Cavan terrain, with its forests, bogs, and lakes.

The boundaries of the county of Cavan were established by the English in 1584, and the county was divided into baronies. Most of these were given to different branches of the O'Reillys, with two baronies controlled by the McKernons and McGowans. During the late sixteenth century, the O'Reillys and their Cavan allies joined the rebellion of O'Neill against the English (see Co. Tyrone).

Following the defeat of the rebels, the land in the county was confiscated and "planted" with English and Scottish settlers in 1609. This was done by granting portions of the county to adventurers (such as Auchmuty) who, in return, undertook to settle an agreed number of English or Scottish families. Pynnar's Survey of the progress of the Ulster plantation during its early stages shows that 286 families were planted in Cavan. The native population retained large parts of the county, however, as there were not enough settlers willing to come to the county.

In 1641 the Catholics in the county, again led by an O'Reilly, joined the Catholic Confederacy (see Co.

Kilkenny) in rebellion. This rebellion was finally defeated by Cromwell in 1649, and was followed by further confiscations and granting of land in Cavan to English soldiers and others.

The relative proportions of people of Irish, Scottish, and English extraction can, in very general terms, be estimated from the relative proportions of Catholics, Presbyterians, and Episcopalians (Protestants) in the county. In 1861, when the census first collected this information, the respective proportions were eighty-one, four, and fifteen percent respectively.

The county was badly affected by the Great Famine of 1845-47. In 1841 the population was 243,000, and by 1851 it had fallen by almost thirty percent, to 174,000. Around 25,000 people died of starvation or disease between 1845 and 1850. Further thousands migrated to the cities or emigrated. The population of the county is now around 55,000.

Census and Census Substitutes

1584
Fiants—legal records listing the names of the principal people living in various districts. Lurgan parish fiants. In *Briefne Antiq. Soc. J.* Vol. 1 and Crosserlough Parish in Vol. 2.

1612-13
"Survey of Undertakers Planted in Cavan." (Names, acreages allotted, and account of the progress of each.) *Hist. Mss. Comm. Rep.* (Hastings Mss.) 4 (1947): 159-82.

1630
Muster Roll, ca. 1630. PRONI T934; BL add.ms. 4770; printed in *Breifne* 5 (18) (1977-78) NLI. P.206.

A typical cabin of a smallholder in the area of Ballinaught, County Cavan, in 1835. From *The Miseries and Beauties of Ireland* by Jonathan Binns (London, 1837).

1641

Book of Survey and Distribution (see introduction). (On microfilm and photocopy.) Articles on Killinkere Parish, Crosserlough, Munterconnaght and Castlerahan, Lurgan, and Virginia are in *Breifne Antiq. Soc. J.* Vols 1–3; copies also in Cavan Co. Library and NAI.

1659

"Census" of Ireland. Ed. by S. Pender. Dublin: Stationery Office, 1939. NLI I6551. SLC film 924648.

1664

Hearth Money Roll for Parishes of Killeshandra, Kildallan, Killenagh, Templeport, Tomregan. PRONI 184. Cavan Co. Library.

Hearth Money Roll for Barony of Castlerahan in *Breifne* 7(25) (1987): 489–497.

Articles on parishes of Killeshandra, Kildallan, Templeport, Tomregan, and Killinagh are in *Breifne* 1960; on Killinkere, Lurgan, and Mullagh in *Breifne* Vol. 1; on Castlerahan and Munterconnaght in *Breifne* Vol. 2; and on Crosserlough in *Breifne* Vol. 3.

1703–04

"Robert Craigies Co. Cavan Tenants." *Ir. Anc.* 8 (2): 86–87 (parishes of Kildallan and Killeshandra).

1726–27

Lists of Protestant householders in parishes of: BallyMcAleny alias Scrabie (8 names), BallyMcHugh (6 names), and Drumlumman (9 names). Edgeworth family papers NAI M 1502 (names-only list compiled for "the charitable distribution of religious books").

1761

Poll-Book for Co. Cavan (lists 1,137 freeholders). PRONI T1522; Cavan Co. Library, Local Studies Dept.

1766

Religious Census Transcripts. Householders in the parishes of: Kinawley; GO 536, and (Protestant householders only) in NAI M2476 and RCB Ms.23; Lavey, Protestant householders in. GO 537 and RCB Ms. 23;. Lurgan, Protestant householders in NAI M2476 and GO 537 and RCB Ms. 23. Munterconnaught, Protestant householders in NAI M2476 and GO 537 and RCB Ms.23. All details on SLC films 258517 and 100173. Also published in *Breifne* (1961).

1796

See Co. Mayo 1796 (List of Catholics).

1796

Spinning Wheel Premium List. (See introduction.)

1802

"Protestants in Enniskeen Parish." *Ir. Anc.* 5 (2) (1973).

1813-21

List of Freeholders of Co. Cavan (over five thousand names, addresses, situation of freeholds, etc., alphabetically listed within baronies). NLI IR94119 c2.

1814

"A Census of Protestant Children in Parishes of Drung and Larah, in C of I Parish Register." *Ir. Anc.* 10 (1) (1978): 33-37.

1821

Government Census Remnants: Parishes of Annageliffe, Ballymacue, Castlerahan, Castleterra, Crosserlough, Denn, Drumloman, Drung, Kilbride, Kilmore, Kinawley, Larah, Lavey, Lurgan, Mullagh, Munterconnaught. NAI CEN 1821/1-15; SLC films 597154-158. Indexed by Cavan Heritage and Genealogy Centre. (See Research Services.)

1823-27

Tithe Applotment Survey (see introduction).

1824-1826

Clippings from national and provincial newspapers (including the Cavan Herald) on the "2nd" or "New" Reformation in Cavan, with lists of those who conformed to the Established Church; Cavan. Co. Library.

1825

Registry of Freeholders. Jas. O'Brien: Cavan, 1826 (name, residence, and landlord on barony basis). Cavan Co. Library, Local Studies Dept.

1825-32

List of those Registered to Keep Arms (covers 1799-1833, but mainly 1825-32; gives over 1,500 names, alphabetically within baronies, residence, type of arms, etc.). NLI ILB 04 P12. Cavan Co. Library.

1839

List of Persons who obtained Game Certificates in Ulster PRONI T688.

1841

Government Census Remnants: Killeshandra parish, except townlands of Corranea, Glebe, and Drumberry. PRO; SLC films 100831-838. NAI CEN 1841/1, NLI P 5349. Cavan Co. Library; also *Breifne* 1976.

1841

Abstracts of 1841 census returns of Killeshandra for the names Bigger, Johnston, Kenny, Morrow, Noble, Sheridan, Venton and Weir, *Irish Family History* 9 (1993): 62-86.

1843

Voters List. NAI 1843/71.

1856-57

Griffith's Valuation (see introduction).

Pre-1861

An undated list of the inhabitants of the Barony of Castlerahan is contained in the Catholic church records of Killinkere (list was probably compiled between 1842 and 1861). (See civil parish of Killinkere.)

1880

Tenants in the Barony of Clankee, giving name, quality of land and rent, tenure, etc. Cavan. Co. Library.

1881-1892

Tenant Purchasers of the Castlecoole Estate 1881-1892. (146 Names and Properties.) In *The History of 2 Ulster Manors*. Earl of Belmore. London/Dublin 1903: 449-451.

1890

Dogs Regulation Act, 1890: A list of licencees. Cavan Co. Library.

1901

Census. NAI, Cavan Co. Lib; indexed by CHGC—see Research Services. SLC films 812117-31; 588841-49.

1911

Census. NAI.

Church Records

Church of Ireland

See the introduction for a description of Church of Ireland records and their major repositories. Many Church of Ireland records were lost in the PRO fire of 1922. These are indicated as "Lost." However, as Church of Ireland records were effectively state records, the records of marriage (from 1845) are also in the General Registrar's Office. Many are still in local custody (LC), while others are in one of a variety of other archives (e.g., RCBL or NAI). Some of the parish registers of this county have been indexed by the Cavan Heritage and Genealogy Centre (see Research Services at the end

BARONY OF CASTLERAHAN.

No.	Name of Freeholder.	Place of Abode.	Situation of Freehold.	Name of Landlord.	Value of freehold.	Name of Lives or other Tenure.	Place and Date of Registry.
1	Bell, Mathias	Derrylaghen.	Derrylaghen.	H. B. Wilson, Esq.		John Magill, Sen.	Cavan, 22d February, 1813.
2	Boylan, John	same.	same.	same.		Connor Maguire.	same.
3	Byers, Robert	same.	same.	same.		John Magill, Sen.	same.
4	Brady, Nicholas	Drummalard.	Drummalard.	Colonel Sankey.		His Royal Highness the Duke of York.	Mt. Nugent, 22d Dec. 1813.
5	Brady, Patrick	Drummolats.	Drummolats.	same.		same.	same.
6	Brady, Patrick	same.	same.	same.		same.	same.
7	Brady, Michael	same.	same.	same.		same.	same.
8	Byers, James	same.	same.	same.		same.	same.
9	Bran, John	Carrickashall.	Carrickashall.	Colonel Sankey.	_FORTY SHILLINGS._ / £20.	Duke of Clarence.	
10	Ray, Thomas	Corneen.	Corneen.	Lord Farnham.		James Clearkin, and James O'Neil.	Cavan, 30th July, 1814.
11	Brady, Charles	Killcully.	Killcully.	his own.		....	Do. 5th August, 1814.
12	Brady, Andrew	Dromony.	Dromony.	Lord Farnham.		Chas. Coote, Jas. & Robt. Saunderson.	same.
13	Byrne, Charles	same.	same.	same.		Chas. Coote, Jas. Saunderson, & Lessee.	same.
14	Byers, Robert	Galloubragh.	Galloubragh.	same.		Hugh Porter.	same.
15	Blackstock, John	Cladaugh.	Cladaugh.	same.		George, John, and William Blackstock.	same.
16	Blackstock, Geo.	same.	same.	same.		same.	same.
17	Byers, Robt. Jun.	same.	same.	same.		William, David, and John Byers.	same.
18	Byers, William	same.	same.	same.		William, Esther, and William Byers.	same.
19	Byers, John	Galuabragher.	Galuabragher.	same.		Hugh Porter.	same.
20	Byers, Hugh	same.	same.	same.		....	same.
21	Brady, Patrick	Corneen.	Corneen.	same.		James Clearkin.	same.
22	Byers, Robert	Tevenaman.	Tevenaman.	same.		Robert and John Byers.	same.
23	Brady, Owen	Lisnagerill.	Lisnagerill.	same.		Owen Brady, and Hugh and Phillip Tully.	same.
24	Burrowes, Hugh	Pottle.	Pottle.	same.		Thomas Hawthorn.	Do. 16th August, 1814.
25	Boylan, Michael	same.	same.	same.		same.	same.
26	Boylan, James	same.	same.	same.		same.	same.
27	Boylan, Matthew	same.	same.	same.		same.	same.
28	Boylan, James	same.	same.	same.		same.	same.
29	Boylan, Owen	same.	same.	same.		same.	same.
30	Boylan, Patrick	Pollareagh.	Pollareagh.	same.		Park. & Hugh Cosgrove, & Patt. Boylan.	same.
31	Blackstock, John	Cladaugh.	Cladaugh.	same.		George, William, and John Blackstock.	same.
32	Briady, Jeremiah	Drumini-shillen.	Druminishillen.	Mr. Norton.		Abraham Strong.	Mt. Nugent, 21st Oct. 1814.
33	Briady, James	same.	same.	same.		....	same.
34	Briady, Thomas	same.	same.	same.		same.	same.
35	Briady, John	same.	same.	same.		same.	same.
36	Brady, John	Aghaca-hell.	Ballintemple.	same.		Charles Brady.	same.
37	Boylan, Matthew	Mullacaslin.	Mullacaslin.	same.		Duke of Clarence.	Do. 30th November, 1814.
38	Boylan, William	Tonylion.	Tonylion.	same.		same.	same.
39	Boylan, Bryan	same.	same.	same.		same.	same.
40	Boylan Luke, Jun.	same.	same.	same.		same.	same.
41	Boylan, Luke	same.	same.	same.		same.	same.
42	Boylan, Phillip	same.	same.	same.		same.	same.
43	Boylan, Bryan	same.	same.	same.		same.	same.
44	Boylan, James	same.	same.	same.		same.	same.
45	Boylan, Bryan	same.	same.	same.		same.	same.

Extract from "A list of the Freeholders registered in County Cavan since First of January 1813 with those of £50 and £20 previously registered." NLI IR 94119 c2.

of the chapter). A search of the index will be conducted by the center for a fee. Those indexed are noted as "Indexed by CHGC."

Annagelliffe
Earliest Records: b. 1804–; m. 1804–; d. 1804–
Status: LC; Indexed by CHGC (to 1899)

Annagh (Belturbet or Cloverhill)
Earliest Records: b. 1804–; m. 1801–; d. 1803–
Status: LC; RCBL (mf) (b. 1804–1985; m. 1801–1916; d. 1803–1985); Indexed by CHGC (1803–1899)

Ashfield
Earliest Records: b. 1821–; m. 1820–; d. 1818–
Missing Records: d. 1828–55
Status: LC; RCBL (mf) (b. 1821–1907; m. 1820–56; d. 1818–1985); NAI M 5077–8 (b. 1821–76)

Bailieborough
Earliest Records: b. 1824–; m. 1809–; d. 1809–
Status: LC; RCBL (mf) (b. 1824–1985; m. 1809–1915; d. 1809–1915)

Ballintemple
Earliest Records: b. 1880–; m. 1845–; d. 1880–
Status: LC; RCBL (mf) (b. 1880–1955; m. 1845–1952; d. 1880–1971)

Ballyjamesduff and Castlerahan
Earliest Records: b. 1877–; m. 1845–; d. 1879–
Status: LC; RCBL (mf) (b. 1877–1986; m. 1845–1955; d. 1879–1985); Indexed by CHGC (to 1899)

Ballymachugh
Earliest Records: b. 1816–; m. 1815–; d. 1816–
Status: LC; RCBL (mf) (b. 1816–76; m. 1815–47; d. 1816–75); Indexed by CHGC (to 1899)

Belturbet—see Annagh
Billis (Virginia)
Earliest Records: b. 1840–
Status: LC; RCBL (mf) (1851–1900)

Castleterra (Ballyhaise)
Earliest Records: b. 1800–; m. 1785–; d. 1820–
Status: LC; Indexed by CHGC (to 1899)

Cloverhill
Earliest Records: b. 1860–; m. 1860–
Status: LC; Indexed by CHGC (to 1899)

Crosserlough—see Kildrumferton
Denn
Earliest Records: b. 1879–; m. 1845–; d. 1879–
Status: LC; RCBL (mf) (b. 1879–1982; m. 1845–1954; d. 1879–1986); Indexed by CHGC (to 1899)

Dernakesh
Earliest Records: b. 1837–; m. 1837–; d. 1837–
Status: LC; RCBL (mf) (b. 1837–1905; m. 1837–42; d. 1837–1985)

Derryheen
Earliest Records: b. 1879–; m. 1846–; d. 1879–
Status: LC; RCBL (mf) (b. 1879–1984; m. 1846–1917; d. 1879–1985); Indexed by CHGC (to 1899)

Derrylane
Earliest Records: b. 1845–; m. 1846–; d. 1875–
Status: LC; RCBL (mf) (b. 1845–1917; m. 1846–1945; d. 1875–1958)

Dowra
Earliest Records: b. 1877–
Status: LC; RCBL (mf) (b. 1877–91)

Drumgoon (Cootehill)
Earliest Records: b. 1802–; m. 1802–; d. 1825–
Missing Records: b. 1815–24; m. 1815–24
Status: LC; RCBL (mf) (b/d from 1825 only)

Drumlane
Earliest Records: b. 1874–; m. 1845–; d. 1877–
Status: LC; RCBL (mf) (b. 1874–1985; m. 1845–1932; d. 1877–1982); Indexed by CHGC (to 1899)

Drumlumman
Status: Lost

Drung
Earliest Records: b. 1785–; m. 1785–; d. 1785–
Status: LC; Indexed by CHGC (to 1899); SLC film 897355

Enniskeen
Status: Lost

Kildallan (Ballyconnell); see also Tomregan
Earliest Records: b. 1810–; m. 1812–; d. 1785–
Status: LC; RCBL (from b. 1856, m. 1845, and d. 1877)

Kildrumferton (Crosserlough)
Earliest Records: b. 1801–; m. 1801–; d. 1803–
Status: LC; RCBL (mf) (b. 1801–75; m. 1801–52; d. 1803–75); Indexed by CHGC (to 1899)

Kildrumsherdan (Kilsherdoney)
Earliest Records: b. 1796–; m. 1796–; d. 1797–
Status: LC; RCBL (mf) (b. 1796–1982; m. 1796–1845; d. 1797–1829)

Killeshandra
Earliest Records: b. 1735–; m. 1735–; d. 1735–
Status: LC; RCBL (mf) (b. 1735–1982; m. 1735–1955; d. 1735–1955)

Killinagh
Status: Lost

Killinkere
Earliest Records: b. 1878–; m. 1845–; d. 1877–
Status: LC; RCBL (mf) (b. 1878–99; m. 1845–98; d. 1877–1901)

Killoughter (Redhills)
Earliest Records: b. 1827–; m. 1827–; d. 1827–
Status: LC; RCBL (mf) (b. 1827–1982; m. 1827–45; d. 1827–1905)

Kilmore (Cavan)
Earliest Records: b. 1702–; m. 1702–; m. 1845–
Status: LC; RCBL (mf) (b. 1702–1950; m. 1702–1930; m. 1845–1970)

Kinawley (see also Swanlinbar)
Earliest Records: b. 1761–; m. 1761–; d. 1761–
Status: LC; RCBL (mf) (b. 1761–1972; m. 1761–1935; d. 1761–1966)

Kingscourt
Earliest Records: m. 1845–
Status: RCBL (m. 1845–1949)

Knockbride (see also Bailieborough)
Earliest Records: b. 1825–; m. 1825–; d. 1825–
Status: LC; RCBL (mf) (b. 1825–1917; m. 1825–1930; d. 1825–1971)

Larah (see Drung for early entries)
Status: Lost

Lavey
Status: Lost

Loughan (Castlekeeran)
Earliest Records: m. 1880–
Status: RCBL (mf) (m. 1880–1891)

Lurgan (see also Billis)
Earliest Records: b. 1831–; m. 1831–; d. 1831–
Status: LC; RCBL (mf) (b. 1831–1902; m. 1831–1900; d. 1831–1901)

Moybologue
Earliest Records: m. 1878–
Status: RCBL (m. 1878–1956)

Mullagh
Earliest Records: b. 1877–; m. 1946–; d. 1877–
Status: LC; RCBL (mf) (b. 1877–1984; m. 1946–48; d. 1877–1986)

Munterconnaught
Earliest Records: b. 1857–; m. 1845–; d. 1857–
Status: LC; RCBL (mf) (b. 1857–1901; m. 1845–99; d. 1857–1901)

Quivy
Earliest Records: b. 1854–1938; m. 1857–1940
Status: LC; RCBL (mf) (b. 1854–1938; m. 1857–1940); Indexed by CHGC (to 1899)

St. John—see Annagh

Scrabby
Status: Lost

Shercock
Earliest Records: b. 1881–; m. 1846–; d. 1881–
Status: LC; RCBL (mf) (b. 1881–1979; m. 1846–1955; d. 1881–1976)

Swanlinbar (see also Kinawley)
Earliest Records: b. 1798–; m. 1798–; d. 1798–
Status: RCBL (b. 1798–1863; m. 1798–1952; d. 1798–1883)

Templeport
Earliest Records: b. 1796–; m. 1796–; d. 1797–
Status: LC; copy also RCBL (b. 1837; m. 1845–1954; d. 1878–1906)

Tomregan (Ballyconnell)
Earliest Records: b. 1797–; m. 1797–; d. 1805–
Status: LC; RCBL (mf) (b. 1797–1984; m. 1797–1913; d. 1805–1986)

Presbyterian

An account of Presbyterian records is given in the introduction. Many of the Presbyterian registers of Cavan have been indexed by Cavan Heritage and Genealogy Centre and one by Leitrim Heritage Centre (see Research Services at the end of the chapter). A search of the index will be conducted for a fee. Those indexed are noted below as "Indexed by CHGC."

Bailieborough (1st and 2nd)
Starting Date: b. 1861; m. 1745
Status: LC; PRONI MIC 1P/145 and 143

Ballyhobridge
Starting Date: b. 1840
Status: LC

Ballyjamesduff
Starting Date: b. 1826; m. 1845
Status: LC; PRONI MIC 1P/268; Indexed by CHGC (to 1899)

Bellasis
Starting Date: b. 1877; m. 1845
Status: LC; PRONI MIC 1P/267; Indexed by CHGC (to 1899)

Belturbet
Starting Date: b. 1845; m. 1858
Status: LC; PRONI MIC 1P/272

Carrigallen
Starting Date: b. 1837–; m. 1845
Status: LC; PRONI MIC 1P/163

Cavan
Starting Date: b. 1851
Status: LC

Cootehill (1st and 2nd)
Starting Date: b. 1822; m. 1845
Status: LC; PRONI MIC 1P/177 and 178; Indexed by CHGC (1st to 1899)

Corglass
Starting Date: b. 1861–; m. 1845
Status: LC; PRONI MIC 1P/145

Corlea
Starting Date: b. 1836–; m. 1835
Status: LC; PRONI MIC 1P/158

Corraneary (Coronary)
Starting Date: b. 1764; m. 1846
Status: LC; PRONI MIC 1P/179; Indexed by CHGC (to 1899)

Drumkeerin (Co. Cavan)
Earliest Records: b. 1797–; m. 1835–; d. 1880–
Status: LC; Indexed by Leitrim Heritage Centre (to 1900); PRONI MIC IP/166

Killeshandra
Starting Date: b. 1841; m. 1741
Status: LC; PHSA (m. 1743); PRONI MIC 1P/164

Kilmount
Starting Date: b. 1866; m. 1862
Status: LC; PRONI MIC 1P/213

Seafin
Starting Date: m. 1846
Status: LC; PRONI MIC 1P/144

Smithborough
Starting Date: b. 1868; m. 1883
Status: LC; PRONI MIC 1P/200

Methodist

Methodist churches existed in County Cavan at Bally-Hays (Ballyhaise), Ballyconnell, Belturbet, Cavan, and Cootehill. See the introduction for information on finding records.

Roman Catholic

Note that most of the Catholic parish registers of this county have been indexed by the Cavan Heritage and Genealogy Centre (see Research Services at the end of the chapter). A search of the index will be conducted by the center for a fee. Those indexed are noted as "Indexed by CHGC."

Microfilm copies of all registers are also available in the National Library of Ireland (NLI), and through the LDS library system.

Civil Parish: Annagelliff
Map Grid: 13
RC Parish: Cavan (Urney and Annagelliffe)
Diocese: KM
Earliest Record: b. 7.1812; m. 7.1812
Missing Dates: b. 7.1859–1.1860
Status: LC; NLI (mf); Indexed by CHGC (to 1899)

Civil Parish: Annagh (1)
Map Grid: 16
RC Parish: Anna West; also Anna East, see below
Diocese: KM
Earliest Record: b. 1845; m. 1847; d. 1.1849
Status: LC; NLI (mf); Indexed by CHGC (to 1899 b/m only)

Civil Parish: Annagh (2)
Map Grid: 16
RC Parish: Anna East
Diocese: KM
Earliest Record: b. 11.1845; m. 7.1847
Status: LC; NLI (mf); Indexed by CHGC (to 1899)

Civil Parish: Bailieborough
Map Grid: 23
RC Parish: Killann or Kinawley
Diocese: KM
Earliest Record: b. 1.1835; m. 1.1835
Missing Dates: b. 11.1849–1.1868; m. 2.1850–1.1868
Status: LC; NLI (mf); Indexed by CHGC (to 1899)

Civil Parish: Ballintemple
Map Grid: 26
RC Parish: Ballintemple
Diocese: KM
Earliest Record: b. 10.1862; m. 10.1862
Status: LC; NLI (mf); Indexing by CHGC planned

Civil Parish: Ballymachugh
Map Grid: 28
RC Parish: Drumlumman South and Ballymachugh
Diocese: AD
Earliest Record: b. 11.1837; m. 12.1837; d. 12.1837
Missing Dates: b. 8.1873–5.1857; m. 6.1873–2.1876; d.9.1869–2.1876
Status: LC; NLI (mf); Indexing by CHGC in progress

Civil Parish: Castlerahan
Map Grid: 32
RC Parish: Castlerahan
Diocese: KM
Earliest Record: b. 2.1752; m. 9.1751
Missing Dates: b. 7.1771–2.1773, 11.1776–11.1814,
8.1820–10.1828, 5.1841–8.1854; m. 6.1771–2.1773,
2.1775–11.1814, 6.1820–5.1832, 11.1841–8.1855
Status: LC; NLI (mf); Indexed by CHGC (to 1899)

Civil Parish: Castleterra
Map Grid: 11
RC Parish: Castleterra (Castletara)
Diocese: KM
Earliest Record: b. 6.1763; m. 7.1763
Missing Dates: b. 6.1809–4.1862; m. 4.1793–
10.1808; ends 6.1809
Status: LC; NLI (mf); Indexed by CHGC (to 1899)

Civil Parish: Crosserlough
Map Grid: 30
RC Parish: Crosserlough
Diocese: KM
Earliest Record: b. 10.1843; m. 10.1843; d. 10.1843
Status: LC; NLI (mf); Indexed by CHGC (to 1899)

Civil Parish: Denn
Map Grid: 14
RC Parish: Denn
Diocese: KM
Earliest Record: b. 10.1856; m. 10.1856
Missing Dates: b. many gaps; m. ends 10.1858
Status: LC; NLI (mf); Indexed by CHGC (to 1899)

Civil Parish: Drumgoon
Map Grid: 19
RC Parish: Drumgoon
Diocese: KM
Earliest Record: b. 2.1829; m. 3.1829
Status: LC; NLI (mf); Indexed by CHGC (to 1899)

Civil Parish: Drumlane
Map Grid: 6
RC Parish: Drumlane
Diocese: KM
Earliest Record: b. 1.1836; m. 9.1870
Status: LC; NLI (mf); Indexed by CHGC (to 1899)

Civil Parish: Drumlumman
Map Grid: 27
RC Parish: Mullahoran (Loughduff and
Drumlumman North)
Diocese: AD
Earliest Record: b. 1.1859; m. 1.1859; d.2.1859
Status: LC; NLI (mf); Indexing by CHGC planned

Civil Parish: Drumreilly (see Co. Leitrim)
Map Grid: 4

RC Parish: Drumreilly (see Co. Leitrim)
Diocese: AD

Civil Parish: Drung
Map Grid: 17
RC Parish: Killesherdany and Drung
Diocese: KM
Earliest Record: b. 6.1803; m. 7.1803
Missing Dates: b. 11.1814–11.1826, 4.1849–
10.1855, 2.1860–1.1867; m. 1.1814–1.1835,
5.1835–1843, 4.1849–10.1855
Status: LC; NLI (mf); Indexing by CHGC in progress

Civil Parish: Enniskeen (see also Co. Meath)
Map Grid: 24
RC Parish: Kingscourt and Enniskeen
Diocese: ME
Earliest Record: b. 10.1838; m. 8.1838; d.9.1846
Missing Dates: 8.1854–1.1864
Status: LC; NLI (mf); Indexing by CHGC in progress

Civil Parish: Kilbride
Map Grid: 29
RC Parish: Kilbride (see Co. Meath)
Diocese: ME

Civil Parish: Kildallan
Map Grid: 7
RC Parish: Kildallan and Tomregan
Diocese: KM
Earliest Record: b. 4.1867; m. 1.1867
Status: LC; NLI (mf); Indexed by CHGC (to 1899)

Civil Parish: Kildrumsherdan
Map Grid: 18
RC Parish: Killesherdiney (see Drung)
Diocese: KM

Civil Parish: Killashandra
Map Grid: 8
RC Parish: Killeshandra
Diocese: KM
Earliest Record: b. 1.1835; m. 1.1835; d. 1.1835
Missing Dates: b. 8.1844–3.1845; m. 9.1840–8.1849;
d.5.1852–9.1868
Status: LC; NLI (mf); Indexing by CHGC planned

Civil Parish: Killinagh (1)
Map Grid: 1
RC Parish: see also Glangevlin below
Diocese: KM
Earliest Record: b. 1867; m. 1867; d. 1875
Status: LC; NLI (mf); Indexed by CHGC (to 1899)

Civil Parish: Killinagh (2)
Map Grid: 1
RC Parish: Glangevlin
Diocese: KM

Earliest Record: b. 1867; m. 1867
Status: LC; NLI (mf); Indexed by CHGC (to 1899)

Civil Parish: Killinkere
Map Grid: 31
RC Parish: Killinkere (see also Mullagh after 1842)
Diocese: KM
Earliest Record: b. 5.1766; m. 12.1766
Missing Dates: b. 10.1790-1.1842, 4.1862-3.1864;
m. 8.1789-1.1842, 11.1861-6.1864
Status: LC; NLI (mf); Indexing by CHGC planned

Civil Parish: Kilmore
Map Grid: 12
RC Parish: Kilmore
Diocese: KM
Earliest Record: b. 5.1859; m. 5.1859; d.5.1859
Status: LC; NLI (mf); Indexed by CHGC (to 1899)

Civil Parish: Kinawley
Map Grid: 3
Diocese: KM
RC Parish: Kinawley (also in Co. Fermanagh)
Earliest Record: b. 1835; m. 1835; d. 1852
Status: LC; Indexed by CHGC (to 1899 and d. to
1857)

Civil Parish: Knockbride
Map Grid: 21
RC Parish: Knockbride
Diocese: KM
Earliest Record: b. 5.1835; m. 1.1835; d. 1.1835
Status: LC; NLI (mf); Indexing by CHGC in progress

Civil Parish: Larah
Map Grid: 20
RC Parish: Larah, Upper and Lower
Diocese: KM
Earliest Record: b. 5.1876
Status: LC; NLI (mf); Indexing by CHGC in progress

Civil Parish: Lavey
Map Grid: 15
RC Parish: Lavey
Diocese: KM
Earliest Record: b. 1867; m. 1867
Status: LC; NLI (mf); Indexing by CHGC in progress

Civil Parish: Loughan or Castlekeeran (see Co. Meath)
Map Grid: 36
RC Parish: Carnaross, see Loughan, Co. Meath

Civil Parish: Lurgan
Map Grid: 33
RC Parish: Lurgan
Diocese: KM
Earliest Record: b. 1.1755; m. 2.1755
Missing Dates: b. with gaps, 8.1795-11.1821; m.

8.1770-1.1773, 9.1780-11.1821
Status: LC; NLI (mf); Indexed by CHGC (to 1899)

Civil Parish: Moybolgue
Map Grid: 25
RC Parish: Moybolgue (see Kilmainham, Co. Meath)
Diocese: KM

Civil Parish: Mullagh
Map Grid: 34
RC Parish: Mullagh (see Killinkere for earlier records)
Diocese: KM
Earliest Record: b. 6.1842; m. 7.1842; d.9.1842
Missing Dates: d. ends 2.1857
Status: LC; NLI (mf); Indexing by CHGC in progress

Civil Parish: Munterconnaught
Map Grid: 35
RC Parish: see Castlerahan
Diocese: KM

Civil Parish: Scrabby
Map Grid: 9
RC Parish: Granard (see Co. Longford)
Diocese: AD

Civil Parish: Shercock
Map Grid: 22
RC Parish: Killann (see Bailieborough)
Diocese: KM

Civil Parish: Templeport (1)
Map Grid: 2
RC Parish: Templeport; also Corlough, see below;
also Glangevlin, see Killinagh (2)
Diocese: KM
Earliest Record: b. 9.1836; m. 11.1836; d.2.1827
Missing Dates: d. ends 12.1845
Status: LC; NLI (mf); Indexed by CHGC (to 1899)

Civil Parish: Templeport (2)
Map Grid: 2
RC Parish: Corlough
Diocese: KM
Earliest Record: b. 1877; m. 1877; d. 1827
Missing Dates: d. ends 12.1845
Status: LC; NLI (mf); Indexed by CHGC (to 1899)

Civil Parish: Tomregan (see also Co. Fermanagh)
Map Grid: 5
RC Parish: Tomregan (see Kildallan)
Diocese: KM

Civil Parish: Urney
Map Grid: 10
RC Parish: Cavan (see Annagelliff)
Diocese: KM

Commercial and Social Directories

1824

J. Pigot's *City of Dublin and Hibernian Provincial Directory* includes lists of traders, nobility, gentry, and clergy in Bailieboro, Ballyconnell, Belturbet, Cavan, Cootehill, Killeshandra, and Kingscourt.

1846

Slater's *National Commercial Directory of Ireland* lists nobility, clergy, traders, etc. in Bailieborough, Ballyconnell, Belturbet, Cavan, Cootehill, Killeshandra, and Kingscourt.

1852

Henderson's *Belfast and Province of Ulster Directory* has lists of inhabitants, traders, etc. in and around Cavan town.

1854

Further edition of above covers the towns of Bailieboro, Belturbet, Cavan, and Cootehill. Further issues in 1856, 1858, 1861, 1863, 1865, 1868, 1870, 1877, 1880, 1884, 1890, 1894, 1900.

1856

Slater's *Royal National Commercial Directory of Ireland* lists nobility, gentry, clergy, traders, etc. in Bailieboro, Ballyconnell, Belturbet, Cavan, Cootehill, Killeshandra, and Kingscourt.

1870

Slater's *Directory of Ireland* contains trade, nobility, and clergy lists for Bailieborough, Ballyconnell, Bawnboy, Swanlinbar, Ballyjamesduff, Belturbet, Cavan, Cootehill, Killeshandra, and Kingscourt.

1881

Slater's *Royal National Commercial Directory of Ireland* contains lists of traders, clergy, nobility, and farmers in adjoining parishes of the towns of Bailieborough, Kingscourt, Ballyconnell, Bawnboy, Swanlinbar, Ballyjamesduff, Belturbet, Cavan, Cootehill, and Killeshandra.

1894

Slater's *Royal National Directory of Ireland* lists traders, police, teachers, farmers, and private residents in each of the towns, villages, and parishes of the county.

Family History

Adams, W. *A Genealogical History of Adams of Cavan.* London, 1903.

"The Babingtons of Cavan." *Breifne* 5 (21) (1982–83).

"Baker of Co. Cavan." Pedigree in *Swanzy Notebooks.* RCB Library, Dublin.

"Burrows of Stradone." Pedigree in *Swanzy Notebooks.* RCB Library, Dublin.

"Colkin of Cavan." Pedigree in *Swanzy Notebooks.* RCB Library, Dublin.

Historical and Genealogical Records of the Coote Family. Lausanne, 1900.

Brief Genealogies of the Families Corry, Crawford, Auchinleck, Dane, Rampain, and Leslie, in *The History of 2 Ulster Manors.* Earl of Belmore, London/Dublin, 1903.

"Some Account of the Family of French of Belturbet." *Ulster J. Arch.* 2nd ser. 8 (1902): 155–60.

Swanzy, H.B. *The Families of French of Belturbet and Nixon of Fermanagh.* Dublin, 1908.

Gill family of Cavan. SLC film 1279327.

"Humphreys of Knockfad, Co. Cavan." *Ir. Anc.* 13 (2) (1981): 88–89.

Copies of 1841 census returns of Keaney family. NAI film 5248(6).

"Kernan of Ned, Co. Cavan." *Ir. Gen.* 4 (4) (1971): 323–30.

Kernan, J.D. *Notes on the Descendants of John Kernan of Ned, Co. Cavan.* 3rd ed. Englewood, N.J., 1969.

"Moore of Moyne Hall." Pedigree in *Swanzy Notebooks.* RCB Library, Dublin.

"Moore of Tullyvin." Pedigree in *Swanzy Notebooks.* RCB Library, Dublin.

Lyons, J. *Historical Sketch of the Nugent Family.* Ladestown, 1853.

"Nugent Papers" (Mount Nugent, Co. Cavan). *Anal. Hib.* 20: 125–215.

Carney, James, ed. *A Genealogical History of the O'Reilly's.* Written in the eighteenth century by Eoghan O'Raghallaigh and incorporating the earlier work of Dr. Fitzsimons, Vicar-General of the Diocese of Kilmore. Dublin, 1959. SLC film 994070.

"The O'Reilly's and McQuaids of Lisdoagh." *Breifne* 8 (2) (1991): 489–495.

"The O'Reilly's of Corlattylannan and Their Relations." *Breifne* 8 (4) (1994): 489–495.

"The O'Reilly's of East Breifne, circa 1250–1450." *Breifne* 8 (2) (1991): 155–180.

"Parr of Co. Cavan." Pedigree in *Swanzy Notebooks.* RCB Library, Dublin.

"Perrott of Co. Cavan." Pedigree in *Swanzy Notebooks.* RCB Library, Dublin.

"Wilton of Co. Cavan." Pedigree in *Swanzy Notebooks*. RCB Library, Dublin.

Gravestone Inscriptions

The Cavan Heritage and Genealogy Centre has indexes to many graveyards and gravestone inscriptions in the county; these are indicated "Indexed by CHGC." They should be contacted (see Research Services at the end of the chapter) for an updated list. The published and archive sources are:

Annagelliffe: (Cavan Parish) *Breifne* 6 (24) (1986): 408-417.

Ballanagh (C of I): GO Ms. 622,107.

Ballyconnell (RC and C of I): *Breifne* 7 (25) (1986): 498-512.

Ballintemple. Indexed by CHGC.

Billis: GO Ms. 622, 182.

Bruskey. Indexed by CHGC.

Callowhill: *Breifne* 5 (21) (1982-83).

Castlerahan: *Breifne* 2 (3) (1925-26).

Castlerahan Old. Indexed by CHGC.

Cathedral (Cavan Parish): *Breifne* 6 (24) (1986): 408-417.

Castletara. Indexed by CHGC.

Cavan: see Cathedral.

Cloone (St. Michaels): *Seanchas Ardmhacha* 10 (1) (1980/81): 63-84.

Clonosey. Indexed by CHGC.

Crosserlough New. Indexed by CHGC.

Crosserlough Old. Indexed by CHGC.

Crosserlough: *Breifne* 5 (17) (1976) and IGRS Collection. GO.

Crosskeys. Indexed by CHGC.

Denn: *Breifne* 2 (2) (1924).

Denn (Old): *Breifne* 8 (4) (1994): 497-512. Indexed by CHGC.

Darver: *Breifne* 1 (3) (1922). Indexed by CHGC.

Drumlane: *Breifne* 5 (19) (1979).

Drumgoon Old. Indexed by CHGC.

Drumkilly. Indexed by CHGC.

Drung. Indexed by CHGC.

Gallon. Indexed by CHGC.

Kilbride. Indexed by CHGC.

Kill Cemetery Kilnaleck. Indexed by CHGC.

Killaghduff. Indexed by CHGC.

Killinagh Old. Indexed by CHGC.

Killoughter. Indexed by CHGC.

Kildrumfertan: *Breifne* 2 (8) (1965).

Kilsherdany: *Breifne* 7 (26) (1988): 605-616.

Knocktemple. Indexed by CHGC.

Laragh Old. Indexed by CHGC.

Lavey Lower. Indexed by CHGC.

Lavey Upper. Indexed by CHGC.

Lavey: GO Ms. 622, 181; and *Breifne* 8 (1) (1989/90): 136-142.

Lurgan: *Breifne* 1 (4) (1961). Indexed by CHGC.

Magherintemple: *Breifne* 2 (6) (1963).

Munterconnacht: *Breifne* 3 (1) (1927-28).

Old Rossory. Appendix to *A short History of Rossory Parish* by Mary Rogers, p. 24, n.d.

Raffoney. Indexed by CHGC.

St. Mary's Abbey (Cavan Parish): *Breifne* 6 (24) (1986): 408-417.

St. Mogue's Island. Indexed by CHGC.

Templeport: *Breifne* 4 (14) (1971).

Urney (Cavan Parish): *Breifne* 6 (24) (1986): 408-417.

Virginia. Indexed by CHGC.

Newspapers

Title: *Anglo-Celt*
Published in: Cavan, 1846-current
Note: Breaks in publication between 1847 and 1864
NLI Holdings: 2.1846-4.1858; 12.1864-11.1873; 1.1885-12.1886; 1.1887-in progress
BL Holdings: 2.1846-4.1858; 12.1864-11.1869; 7.1870-11.1873; 5.1889-12.1919; 1.1921-in progress. Also Cavan Co. Library 1846-date.

Title: *Cavan Observer*
Published in: Cavan, 1857-64
BL Holdings: 7.1857-10.1864 (except 1-6.1858)

Title: *Cavan Weekly News*
Published in: Cavan, 1864-1907
NLI Holdings: 2.1871-12.1895; odd nos. 1898; 12.1904-7.1907
BL Holdings: 12.1864-7.1907. Cavan Co. Library.

Wills and Administrations

A discussion of the types of records, where they are held, their availability and value is given in the Wills section of the introduction. The availability of prerogative wills, administrations, and marriage license records is also described in the relevant parts of the same section. Where available, published sources of these records are given in the Miscellaneous Sources section.

Pre-1858 Wills and Administrations

Prerogative Wills. See the introduction.

Consistorial Wills. County Cavan is mainly in the diocese of Kilmore, with three parishes in each of the dioceses of Meath and Ardagh. The guide to Catholic parish records in this chapter shows the diocese to which each civil parish belonged. The wills of residents of each diocese were usually proven within that diocese (see the Wills section for exceptions). The following records survive:

Wills

See the introduction.

Abstracts

The Upton papers contain abstracts of Cavan family wills, RIA Library; The Swanzy Will Abstracts cover mainly Clogher and Kilmore, RCB Library.

Indexes

Kilmore Fragments (1682-1858) published by Smyth-Wood. Index to Ardagh Wills: *Ir. Anc.* 1971 (supplement). SLC film 824242.

Post-1858 Wills and Administrations

County Cavan was served by the District Registry of Cavan. The surviving records are kept in the NAI. Cavan Will Books: NAI and SLC film 597717 (1856-73) and SLC film 100927/8 (1858-1899).

Marriage Licenses

Indexes

Kilmore, Ardagh, and Meath (1691-1845). NAI; SLC films 100869.

Miscellaneous Sources

Shirley, Evelyn Philip. *Some Account of the Territory or Dominion of Farney, in the Province and Earldom of Ulster.* London: Wm. Pickering, 1845.

Gillespie, R., ed. "Cavan; Essays on the History of an Irish County." Dublin: Irish Academic Press, 1995.

"The Management of the Farnham Estates (Co. Cavan) During the Nineteenth Century." *Breifne* 4 (16) (1973-75): 531-60.

O'Connell, P. *The Diocese of Kilmore, its History and Antiquities.* 1937.

Smyth, T.S. *The Civil History of the Town of Cavan.* Cavan, 1934.

"Sources for Cavan Local History." *Breifne* 5 (18) (1977-78): 1.

"The Volunteer Companies of Ulster 1778-1793, III Cavan." *Irish Sword* 7 (1906): 308-09 (officers' names only).

Research Sources and Services

Journals

Breifne (published by Breifne Historical Society, 1958-present)

Heart of Breifne (published by Mrs. Anna Sexton, Grousehall Post Office, Bailieboro, Co. Cavan)

Breifne Antiquarian Society Journal

Libraries and Information Sources

Cavan County Library, Farnham Street, Cavan, Ph: (049) 31799. The library has a sizable collection of local history materials, including books, directories, newspapers, periodicals, photographs, and estate papers.

Research Services

Co. Cavan Heritage and Genealogy Centre, Cana House, Farnham St., Cavan, Ph: (049) 61094. This center is the official IGP center for the county and is indexing all of the family history records of the county. They have already indexed most of the church registers and many gravestone inscriptions. Researchers are advised to contact the center for an updated list of sources indexed. Those already indexed are indicated in the relevant sections of this chapter. The center offers a search service for a fee.

See also Research Services in Dublin in the introduction.

Societies

Breifne Historical Society, Mrs. Bridie Fay-Kennedy, Castle View, Clowninny, Belturbet, Co. Cavan, Ph: 00 353 49 22355

Cavan Civil Parishes as Numbered on Map

1. Killinagh
2. Templeport
3. Kinawley
4. Drumreilly
5. Tomregan
6. Drumlane
7. Kildallan
8. Killashandra (2 pts.)
9. Scrabby
10. Urney (2 pts.)
11. Castleterra
12. Kilmore
13. Annagelliff
14. Denn
15. Lavey
16. Annagh
17. Drung (2 pts.)
18. Kildrumsherdan
19. Drumgoon
20. Laragh
21. Knockbride
22. Shercock
23. Bailieborough
24. Enniskeen
25. Moybolgue
26. Ballintemple
27. Drumlumman
28. Ballymachugh
29. Kilbride
30. Crosserlough
31. Killinkere
32. Castlerahan
33. Lurgan
34. Mullagh
35. Munterconnaught
36. Loughan (Castlekeeran) (2 pts.)

Cavan Civil Parishes in Alphabetical Order

Annagelliff: 13
Annagh: 16
Bailieborough: 23
Ballintemple: 26
Ballymachugh: 28
Castlerahan: 32
Castleterra: 11
Crosserlough: 30
Denn: 14
Drumgoon: 19
Drumlane: 6
Drumlumman: 27
Drumreilly: 4
Drung (2 pts.): 17
Enniskeen: 24
Kilbride: 29
Kildallan: 7
Kildrumsherdan: 18
Killashandra (2 pts.): 8
Killinagh: 1
Killinkere: 31
Kilmore: 12
Kinawley: 3
Knockbride: 21
Laragh: 20
Lavey: 15
Loughan (Castlekeeran) (2 pts.): 36
Lurgan: 33
Moybolgue: 25
Mullagh: 34
Munterconnaught: 35
Scrabby: 9
Shercock: 22
Templeport: 2
Tomregan: 5
Urney (2 pts.): 10

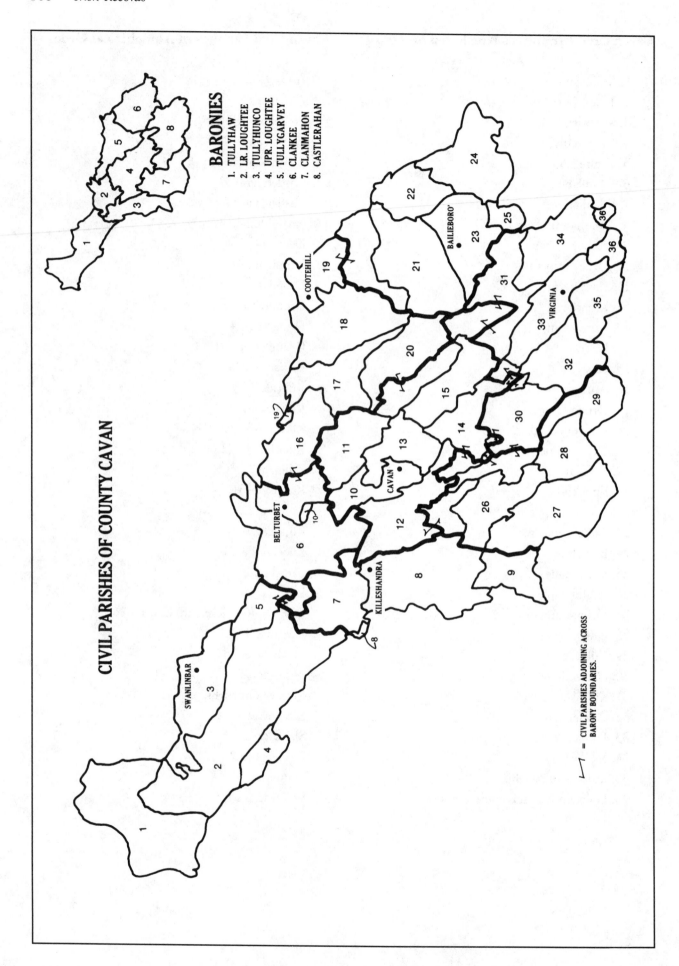

CIVIL PARISHES OF COUNTY CAVAN

BARONIES

1. TULLYHAW
2. LR. LOUGHTEE
3. TULLYHUNCO
4. UPR. LOUGHTEE
5. TULLYGARVEY
6. CLANKEE
7. CLANMAHON
8. CASTLERAHAN

∖ = CIVIL PARISHES ADJOINING ACROSS BARONY BOUNDARIES.

County Clare

A Brief History

This Munster county occupies the area between the lower parts of the Shannon River and the west coast. It contains the towns of Ennis, Kilkee, Killaloe, and Kilrush.

In the old Gaelic system the county was part of the Kingdom of Thomond. The major families were those of O'Loughlin, McNamara, and McMahon, and the chief family was the O'Briens. Together, these families are generally referred to as the Dalcassian families.

The O'Briens were a major force in Thomond from earliest times. The Danish vikings raided this county on many occasions during the ninth to eleventh centuries, establishing settlements in Limerick and on Inniscattery Island. They were finally defeated early in the eleventh century by one of the most famous of the O'Briens, Brian Boru, who also led the Irish army which defeated the powerful Danes of Dublin at the Battle of Clontarf in 1014 (see the introduction).

Following the Norman invasion, the area was granted to Norman knights, but the Clare chieftains kept them from holding any substantial power in the county. In 1275 it was granted to Thomas de Clare, who attempted to take control of the county but was totally defeated by the O'Briens. The O'Briens were later made Earls of Thomond and thereby remained the major force in the county for centuries. Despite the failure of Thomas de Clare or his successor to take control of the Thomond territories, the county was nevertheless named after the family when its boundaries were established by the English administration in 1565. Initially it was made part of Connaught, but in 1602 the county was joined with the province of Munster.

The major Norman settlements in the county were at Clare town and at Bunratty. The Norman inhabitants of these towns were either gradually expelled from the county by the Gaelic families, or else adopted the Irish way of life. The Norman castle at Bunratty, for instance, was captured by the O'Briens in 1355 and held by them until the seventeenth century. In the fifteenth century, the O'Briens rebuilt the castle on the same site, and this castle, restored and refurbished, is now open to the public.

Following the defeat of the 1641 rebellion of the Catholic Confederacy (see the introduction and Co. Kilkenny), this county was one of those which was set aside to accomodate the "delinquent proprietors," i.e., those proprietors whose land was confiscated because they did not actively oppose the rebellion. Parts of the holdings of the existing Clare landholders were confiscated to accommodate these newcomers.

The county was badly affected by the Great Famine of 1845-47. The population was 286,000 in 1841, and by 1851 had been reduced to 212,000. Over 50,000 people died between 1845 and 1850, and thousands emigrated, many to Australia. Between 1851 and 1855, for example, over 37,000 people emigrated from the county. The decline in population continued for the remainder of the century, so that by 1891 the population was 124,000. It is currently around 88,000.

County Clare has one of the best local sources of family history research in the form of the Clare Heritage Centre, located in Corofin (see the Research Sources and Services section).

Census and Census Substitutes

1636-1703

Books of Survey and Distribution, Co. Clare. Abstracts of various surveys and documents relating to land ownership. Simington, R.C. Dublin: Stationery Office, 1955. SLC 941.5 B4b.

1641

Proprietors of Co. Clare (Book of Survey and Distribution). NAI; NLI ms. 963; also published by Irish Manuscripts Commission, 1967.

1659

"Census" of Ireland. Edited by S. Pender. Dublin: Stationery Office, 1939. NLI P.5556. SLC film 924648.

1666–8

Grantees of Co. Clare (same source as 1641 proprietors).

1745

List of Voters at the Parliamentary Election in Clare. TCD ms. 2059.

1778

"Extracts from Minute Book of Ennis Volunteers" (with index of those named). *N. Munster Antiq. J.* 6 (4) (1952): 143–151.

1799

"Gentlemen of the Counties of Clare and Limerick Who Were in Favour of the Union in 1799." *Ir. Anc.* 14 (1) (1982): 30–32.

1803–21

"Game Licenses in Co. Clare." *Ir. Anc.* 14 (2) (1982): 95–98.

1814–43

Tithe Applotment Survey (see introduction).

1829

List of Freeholders. GO ms. 443; NLI P5556. SLC film 1440951.

1834

Rental of the Roxton Estate, Inchiquin Barony. NAI film 5764.

1837

Marksmen (illiterate voters) in parliamentary boroughs: Ennis. *Parliamentary Papers* 11 (1): Appendix A.

1843

Voters List. NAI 1843/68.

1850

Deaths in Kilrush and Ennistymon workhouses, hospitals, infirmaries, March 1850–March 1851. NL, Accounts and Papers. *Parliamentary Papers* 49 (484): 1–47.

1855

Griffith's Valuation (see introduction). Indexed by Clare HC and Clare County Library.

1866

Census of Kilfenora Catholic Parish (included in parish record—see Church Records section). NLI P.2440.

1901

Census. NAI (see introduction). SLC films 588850–75 and 812374–75.

1911

Census. NAI (see introduction).

Church Records

Church of Ireland

See the introduction for a description of Church of Ireland records and their major repositories. Many C of I records were lost in the PRO fire of 1922. These are indicated as "Lost." However, as Church of Ireland records were effectively state records, the records of marriage (from 1845) are also in the General Registrar's Office. Many are still in local custody (LC), while others are in one of a variety of other archives (e.g., RCBL or NAI). Most of the LC records have been indexed by Clare Heritage Centre (see Research Services). This is indicated below as "Indexed by Clare HC."

Parish: Clare Abbey (or Clare)
Earliest Records: m. 1845–
Status: RCBL (m. 1845–1901)

Parish: Clondegad
Earliest Records: m. 1845–; d. 1882–
Status: RCBL (m. 1845–1885; d. 1882–1915)

Parish: Clonlea
Earliest Records: b. 1879–; m. 1845–; d. 1877–
Status: RCBL (b. 1879–1947; m. 1845–1946; d. 1877–1951)

Parish: Drumcliff (Ennis)
Earliest Records: b. 1744–; m. 1744–; d. 1744–
Status: LC; NAI MFCI I, M5222 (b. 1744–1870; m. 1744–1845; d. 1744–1869); Indexed by Clare HC (to 1900)

Parish: Feakle
Earliest Records: b. 1845–
Status: Indexed by Clare HC (to 1900)

Parish: Kildysert
Earliest Records: b. 1881–; m. 1847–; d. 1882–
Status: RCBL (b. 1881–1920; m. 1847–1918; d. 1882–1915)

Parish: Kilfarboy (Miltown)
Earliest Records: b. 1879-; m. 1845-
Status: RCBL (m. 1845-1957); Indexed by Clare HC
(b. to 1900)

Parish: Kilfenora
Earliest Records: m. 1853-
Status: RCBL (m. 1853-1918)

Parish: Kilfiddane (see Kilmurry)

Parish: Kilfieragh or Kilfearagh (Kilkee) (also see Kilrush)
Existing Dates: b. 1829; m. 1829, 1845-
Status: RCBL (m. 1845-1954); NAI M5244 (b/m.
1829)

Parish: Kilfinaghty (Sixmilebridge)
Earliest Records: b. 1879-; m. 1862-
Status: RCBL (m. 1862-1939); Indexed by Clare HC
(to 1900)

Parish: Kilfintinan (no records)

Parish: Kilkeedy
Status: Lost

Parish: Killaloe
Earliest Records: b. 1679-; m. 1682-; d. 1683-
Status: LC; NAI MFCI 5, M5222 (b. 1679-1872; m.
1682-1845; d. 1683-1873); Indexed by Clare HC (b.
to 1900)

Parish: Killard
Earliest Records: m. 1848-
Status: RCBL (m. 1848-1933)

Parish: Killinaboy or Kilnaboy (Corofin)
Earliest Records: b. 1799-; m. 1802-; d. 1821-
Status: RCBL (b. 1799-1931; m. 1802-1961; d.
1821-1831); Indexed by Clare HC (b. to 1900)

Parish: Killonaghan
Status: Lost

Parish: Kilmaley
Status: Lost

Parish: Kilmanaheen
Earliest Records: b. 1886-; m. 1845-
Status: RCBL (b. 1886-1972; m. 1845-1920)

Parish: Kilmurry
Earliest Records: b. 1889-; m. 1845-; d. 1892-
Status: RCBL (b. 1889-1918; m. 1845-1905; d.
1892-1954)

Parish: Kilnaboy (see Killinaboy)

Parish: Kilnasoolagh (Newmarket)
Earliest Records: b. 1731-; m. 1799-; d. 1786-
Status: RCBL (b. 1731-1829; m. 1746-1954; d.
1739-1829); NAI MFCI 2, 5, M5222 (b. 1731-
1874; m. 1799-1844; d. 1786-1876)

Parish: Kilrush
Earliest Records: b. 1741-; m. 1766-; d. 1743-
Status: RCBL (b. 1741-1841; m. 1766-1841; d.
1743-1841); NAI MFCI 4, 5, M5235, 5240 (b.
1741-1872; m. 1760-1845; d. 1742-1873); Indexed
by Clare HC (b. 1842 to 1900)

Parish: Kilseily
Earliest Records: b. 1881-; m. 1848-; d. 1877-
Status: RCBL (b. 1881-1915; m. 1848-1905; d.
1877-1951)

Parish: Kiltenanlea
Status: Lost

Parish: Newquay
Status: Lost

Parish: O'Briensbridge
Status: Lost

Parish: Ogonneloe
Earliest Records: b. 1807-; m. 1807-; d. 1836-
Status: NAI MFCI 5 (b. 1807-1870; m. 1807-1865;
d. 1836-1875); Indexed by Clare HC (b. 1845 to
1900).

Parish: Quin
Earliest Records: b. 1907-; m. 1845-; d. 1906-
Status: RCBL (b. 1907-1954; m. 1845-1915; d.
1906-1927)

Parish: Rathbourney
Status: Lost

Parish: Sixmilebridge (see Kilfinaghty)

Parish: Tomgraney (Bodyke)
Earliest Records: b. 1845-
Status: LC; Indexed by Clare HC (b. to 1900)

Parish: Tulla
Earliest Records: b. 1845-1900
Status: LC; Indexed by Clare HC (b. to 1900)

Roman Catholic

All of the Catholic records have been indexed by Clare
Heritage Centre (see Research Services at the end of the
chapter). This is indicated below as "Indexed by Clare
HC." Microfilm copies of all registers are also available
in the National Library of Ireland (NLI), and through
the LDS library system.

Civil Parish: Abbey
Map Grid: 3
RC Parish: see Carron
Diocese: KF

Civil Parish: Bunratty
Map Grid: 76
RC Parish: Newmarket, see Kilnasoolagh
Diocese: KL

Civil Parish: Carron
Map Grid: 10
RC Parish: Carron
Diocese: KF
Earliest Record: b. 10.1853; m. 11.1856
Status: LC; NLI (mf); Indexed by Clare HC

Civil Parish: Clareabbey
Map Grid: 45
RC Parish: Clareabbey
Diocese: KL
Earliest Record: b. 12.1853; m. 1.1854
Status: LC; NLI (mf); Indexed by Clare HC

Civil Parish: Clondagad
Map Grid: 46
RC Parish: Clondegad (Ballynacally)
Diocese: KL
Earliest Record: b. 10.1846; m. 11.1846
Status: LC; NLI (mf); Indexed by Clare HC

Civil Parish: Clonlea
Map Grid: 49
RC Parish: O'Callaghan's Mills, see Killuran
Diocese: KL

Civil Parish: Clonloghan
Map Grid: 71
RC Parish: Newmarket, see Kilnasoolagh
Diocese: KL

Civil Parish: Clonrush
Map Grid: 38
RC Parish: Clonrush
Diocese: KL
Earliest Record: b. 7.1846; m. 1.1846
Status: LC; NLI (mf); Indexed by Clare HC

Civil Parish: Clooney (1) (near Rath)
Map Grid: 18
RC Parish: Ennistymon, see Kilmanaheen
Diocese: KF

Civil Parish: Clooney (2) (near Tulla)
Map Grid: 30
RC Parish: see Quin

Civil Parish: Doora
Map Grid: 31
RC Parish: Doora
Diocese: KL
Earliest Record: b. 3.1821; m. 1.1823
Status: LC; NLI (mf); Indexed by Clare HC

Civil Parish: Drumcliff
Map Grid: 43
RC Parish: Ennis
Diocese: KL
Earliest Record: b. 3.1841; m. 4.1837
Status: LC; NLI (mf); Indexed by Clare HC

Civil Parish: Drumcreehy
Map Grid: 2
RC Parish: Glanaragh
Diocese: KF
Earliest Record: b. 9.1854
Status: LC; NLI (mf); Indexed by Clare HC

Civil Parish: Drumline
Map Grid: 72
RC Parish: Newmarket, see Kilnasoolagh
Diocese: KL

Civil Parish: Dysert
Map Grid: 25
RC Parish: Dysert and Ruan
Diocese: KL
Earliest Record: b. 8.1845; m. 7.1846
Status: LC; NLI (mf); Indexed by Clare HC

Civil Parish: Feakle (1)
Map Grid: 33
RC Parish: Feakle Lower; also Killanena, see below
Diocese: KL
Earliest Record: b. 4.1860; m. 9.1860
Status: LC; NLI (mf); Indexed by Clare HC

Civil Parish: Feakle (2)
Map Grid: 33
RC Parish: Killanena (Caher Feakle)
Diocese: KL
Earliest Record: b. 2.1842; m. 1.1842
Missing Dates: m. 2.1861–11.1862
Status: LC; NLI (mf); Indexed by Clare HC

Civil Parish: Feenagh
Map Grid: 73
RC Parish: Six-Mile-Bridge, see Kilfinaghta
Diocese: KL

Civil Parish: Gleninagh
Map Grid: 1
RC Parish: Glanaragh, see Drumcreehy
Diocese: KF

Civil Parish: Inagh
Map Grid: 24
RC Parish: Inagh
Diocese: KL
Earliest Record: b. 2.1850; m. 4.1850
Missing Records: m. 7.1865–9.1865
Status: LC; NLI (mf); Indexed by Clare HC

Civil Parish: Inishcronan
Map Grid: 27
RC Parish: Crusheen (Inchicronan)
Diocese: KL
Earliest Record: b. 2.1860
Status: LC; NLI (mf); Indexed by Clare HC

Civil Parish: Inishcaltra
Map Grid: 38

RC Parish: see Clonrush
Diocese: KL

Civil Parish: Kilballyowen
Map Grid: 57
RC Parish: Cross or Kilballyowen
Diocese: KL
Earliest Record: b. 2.1878; m. 3.1878
Status: LC; NLI (mf); Indexed by Clare HC

Civil Parish: Kilchreest
Map Grid: 63
RC Parish: Clondegad, see Clondagad
Diocese: KL

Civil Parish: Kilconry
Map Grid: 75
RC Parish: Newmarket, see Kilnasoolagh
Diocese: KL

Civil Parish: Kilcorney
Map Grid: 9
RC Parish: see Carron
Diocese: KF

Civil Parish: Kilfarboy
Map Grid: 39
RC Parish: Milltown Malbay (Kilfarboy)
Diocese: KL
Earliest Record: b. 11.1831; m. 11.1856
Missing Dates: m. 12.1858-2.1859
Status: LC; NLI (mf); Indexed by Clare HC

Civil Parish: Kilfearagh
Map Grid: 56
RC Parish: Kilkee
Diocese: KL
Earliest Record: b. 3.1869
Status: LC; NLI (mf); Indexed by Clare HC

Civil Parish: Kilfenora
Map Grid: 16
RC Parish: Kilfenora
Diocese: KL
Earliest Record: b. 6.1836; m. 12.1865
Missing Dates: b. 5.1847-9.1854
Status: LC; NLI (mf); Indexed by Clare HC

Civil Parish: Kilfiddane
Map Grid: 62
RC Parish: Kilfidane (Coolmeen)
Diocese: KL
Earliest Record: b. 8.1868; m. 1.1869
Status: LC; NLI (mf); Indexed by Clare HC

Civil Parish: Kilfinaghta
Map Grid: 74
RC Parish: Six-Mile-Bridge
Diocese: KL
Earliest Record: b. 12.1828; m. 1.1829
Missing Dates: b. 8.1839-12.1839; m. 8.1839-

5.1904, 12.1864-2.1865
Status: LC; NLI (mf); Indexed by Clare HC

Civil Parish: Kilfintinan
Map Grid: 77
RC Parish: Cratloe
Diocese: KL
Earliest Record: b. 11.1802; m. 1.1822
Status: LC; NLI (mf); Indexed by Clare HC

Civil Parish: Kilkeedy
Map Grid: 20
RC Parish: Kilkeedy
Diocese: KL
Earliest Record: b. 2.1833; m. 2.1871
Missing Dates: b. 1866-1870
Status: LC; NLI (mf); Indexed by Clare HC

Civil Parish: Killadysert
Map Grid: 64
RC Parish: Kildysert
Diocese: KL
Earliest Record: b. 7.1829; m. 1.1867
Status: LC; NLI (mf); Indexed by Clare HC

Civil Parish: Killaloe
Map Grid: 53
RC Parish: Killaloe
Diocese: KL
Earliest Record: b. 5.1828; m. 2.1829
Status: LC; NLI (mf); Indexed by Clare HC

Civil Parish: Killard
Map Grid: 41
RC Parish: Kilkee, see Kilfearagh
Diocese: KL

Civil Parish: Killaspuglonane
Map Grid: 14
RC Parish: Liscannor, see Kilmacrehy
Diocese: KF

Civil Parish: Killeany
Map Grid: 8
RC Parish: Killeany, Killymoon, and Killileagh
Diocese: KF
Earliest Record: b. 6.1854; m. 1.1860
Status: LC; NLI (mf); Indexed by Clare HC

Civil Parish: Killeely (see also Co. Limerick)
Map Grid: 78
RC Parish: Parteen and Meelick
Diocese: KL
Earliest Record: b. 9.1831; m. 7.1814
Missing Dates: m. 12.1819-2.1821; 1.1836-2.1847
Status: LC; NLI (mf); Indexed by Clare HC

Civil Parish: Killilagh
Map Grid: 12
RC Parish: see Killeany
Diocese: KF

Civil Parish: Killimer
Map Grid: 65
RC Parish: Killimer
Diocese: KL
Earliest Record: b. 1.1859; m. 2.1859
Status: LC; NLI (mf); Indexed by Clare HC

Civil Parish: Killinaboy
Map Grid: 21
RC Parish: Corofin
Diocese: KL
Earliest Record: b. 4.1819; m. 1.1818
Missing Dates: b. 1.1837; m. 2.1844-1.1859
Status: LC; NLI (mf); Indexed by Clare HC

Civil Parish: Killofin
Map Grid: 66
RC Parish: Kilmurryibricken, see Kilmurryibrickane
Diocese: KL

Civil Parish: Killokennedy
Map Grid: 51
RC Parish: part Broadford, see Kilseily; part Doonass, see Kiltenanlea
Diocese: KL

Civil Parish: Killonaghan
Map Grid: 5
RC Parish: Glanaragh, see Drumcreehy
Diocese: KF

Civil Parish: Killone
Map Grid: 44
RC Parish: Killone, see Clareabbey for earlier records
Diocese: KL
Earliest Record: b. 1.1863; m. 2.1863
Status: LC; NLI (mf); Indexed by Clare HC

Civil Parish: Killuran
Map Grid: 48
RC Parish: O'Callaghan's Mills (also called Kilkishen)
Diocese: KL
Earliest Record: b. 1.1835; m. 1.1835
Status: LC; NLI (mf); Indexed by Clare HC

Civil Parish: Kilmacduane
Map Grid: 55
RC Parish: Kilmacduane (Cooraclare)
Diocese: KL
Earliest Record: b. 1.1854; m. 5.1853
Status: LC; NLI (mf); Indexed by Clare HC

Civil Parish: Kilmacrehy
Map Grid: 13
RC Parish: Liscannor
Diocese: KF
Earliest Record: b. 6.1843; m. 2.1866
Status: LC; NLI (mf); Indexed by Clare HC

Civil Parish: Kilmaleery
Map Grid: 70

RC Parish: Newmarket, see Kilnasoolagh
Diocese: KL

Civil Parish: Kilmaley
Map Grid: 42
RC Parish: Inch and Kilmaley
Diocese: KL
Earliest Record: b. 9.1828
Missing Dates: b. ends 2.1873
Status: LC; NLI (mf); Indexed by Clare HC

Civil Parish: Kilmanaheen
Map Grid: 17
RC Parish: Ennistymon
Diocese: KF
Earliest Record: b. 1.1870
Status: LC; NLI (mf); Indexed by Clare HC

Civil Parish: Kilmihil
Map Grid: 60
RC Parish: Kilmihil
Diocese: KL
Earliest Record: b. 3.1849; m. 1.1849
Status: LC; NLI (mf); Indexed by Clare HC

Civil Parish: Kilmoon
Map Grid: 6
RC Parish: see Killeany
Diocese: KF

Civil Parish: Kilmurryclonderlaw
Map Grid: 40
RC Parish: Kilmurry (or Kilmurry McMahon)
Diocese: KL
Earliest Record: b. 11.1845; m. 9.1837; d. 11.1844
Missing Dates: d. ends 4.1848
Status: LC; NLI (mf); Indexed by Clare HC

Civil Parish: Kilmurryibrickane
Map Grid: 61
RC Parish: Kilmurryibricken (Mullagh)
Diocese: KL
Earliest Record: b. 4.1839; m. 9.1855
Status: LC; NLI (mf); Indexed by Clare HC

Civil Parish: Kilmurrynegaul
Map Grid: 69
RC Parish: Six-Mile-Bridge, see Kilfinaghta
Diocese: KL

Civil Parish: Kilnamona
Map Grid: 26
RC Parish: see Inagh
Diocese: KL

Civil Parish: Kilnasoolagh
Map Grid: 67
RC Parish: Newmarket
Diocese: KL
Earliest Record: b. 4.1828; m. 1.1828
Status: LC; NLI (mf); Indexed by Clare HC

Civil Parish: Kilnoe
Map Grid: 37
RC Parish: Kilnoe and Tuamgraney (Bodyke)
Diocese: KL
Earliest Record: b. 11.1832; m. 11.1832
Status: LC; NLI (mf); Indexed by Clare HC

Civil Parish: Kilraghtis
Map Grid: 29
RC Parish: see Doora
Diocese: KL

Civil Parish: Kilrush
Map Grid: 59
RC Parish: Kilrush
Diocese: KL
Earliest Record: b. 8.1827; m. 1.1829
Missing Dates: b. 12.1831–1.1833
Status: LC; NLI (mf); Indexed by Clare HC

Civil Parish: Kilseily
Map Grid: 50
RC Parish: Broadford
Diocese: KL
Earliest Record: b. 1.1844; m. 2.1844
Status: LC; NLI (mf); Indexed by Clare HC

Civil Parish: Kilshanny
Map Grid: 15
RC Parish: Kilshanny
Diocese: KF
Earliest Record: b. 6.1854; m. 1.1860
Status: LC; NLI (mf); Indexed by Clare HC

Civil Parish: Kiltenanlea
Map Grid: 54
RC Parish: Doonass and Trugh
Diocese: KL
Earliest Record: b. 7.1851; m. 9.1851
Status: LC; NLI (mf); Indexed by Clare HC

Civil Parish: Kiltoraght
Map Grid: 19
RC Parish: see Kilfenora
Diocese: KF

Civil Parish: Moyarta
Map Grid: 58
RC Parish: Carrigaholt (Moyarta)
Diocese: KL
Earliest Record: b. 2.1853; m. 1.1852
Status: LC; NLI (mf); Indexed by Clare HC

Civil Parish: Moynoe
Map Grid: 35
RC Parish: Scariff and Moynoe
Diocese: KL
Earliest Record: b. 5.1852; m. 11.1852
Status: LC; NLI (mf); Indexed by Clare HC

Civil Parish: Noughaval
Map Grid: 11
RC Parish: see Carron
Diocese: KF

Civil Parish: O'Briens-Bridge
Map Grid: 52
RC Parish: see Kiltenanlea
Diocese: KL

Civil Parish: Ogonnelloe
Map Grid: 47
RC Parish: Ogonnelloe
Diocese: KL
Earliest Record: b. 3.1832; m. 2.1857
Missing Dates: b. ends 2.1869; m. ends 2.1869
Status: LC; NLI (mf); Indexed by Clare HC

Civil Parish: Oughtmanna
Map Grid: 4
RC Parish: see Carron
Diocese: KF

Civil Parish: Quin
Map Grid: 32
RC Parish: Quin (Clooney)
Diocese: KL
Earliest Record: b. 1.1816; m. 1.1833
Status: LC; NLI (mf); Indexed by Clare HC

Civil Parish: Rath
Map Grid: 22
RC Parish: part Glanaragh, see Drumcreehy; part Corofin, see Killinaboy
Diocese: KL

Civil Parish: Rathborney
Map Grid: 7
RC Parish: Glanaragh, see Drumcreehy
Diocese: KF

Civil Parish: Ruan
Map Grid: 23
RC Parish: see Dysert
Diocese: KL

Civil Parish: St. Munchin's
Map Grid: 79
RC Parish: see Limerick-St. Munchin's in Limerick chapter
Diocese: KL

Civil Parish: St. Patrick's (see also Co. Limerick)
Map Grid: 80
RC Parish: Parteen, see Killeely
Diocese: LK

Civil Parish: Templemaley
Map Grid: 28
RC Parish: see Doora
Diocese: KL

Civil Parish: Tomfinlough
Map Grid: 68
RC Parish: Newmarket, see Kilnasoolagh
Diocese: KL

Civil Parish: Tomgraney
Map Grid: 34
RC Parish: Tuamgraney, see Kilnoe
Diocese: KL

Civil Parish: Tulla
Map Grid: 36
RC Parish: Tulla
Diocese: KL
Earliest Record: b. 1.1819; m. 1.1819
Status: LC; NLI (mf); Indexed by Clare HC

Commercial and Social Directories

1788

Richard Lucas's *General Directory of the Kingdom of Ireland* contains lists of traders in Ennis. Reprinted in *Ir. Gen.* 4 (1) (1968): 37–46.

1824

J. Pigot's *City of Dublin and Hibernian Provincial Directory* includes traders, nobility, gentry, and clergy lists of Ennis, Killaloe, and Kilrush.

1842

Directory of Kilkee (street directory with householders and number and types of rooms per house). Kilkee: H. Hogan. NLI Ir 61312 h1.

1846

Slater's *National Commercial Directory of Ireland* lists nobility, clergy, traders, etc., in Ennis, Kilkee, Killaloe, Kilrush, and Tulla.

1856

Slater's *Royal National Commercial Directory of Ireland* lists nobility, gentry, clergy, traders, etc., in Ennis, Ennistymon, Kilkee, Killaloe, Kilrush, Milltown Malbay, and Tulla.

1866

G.H. Bassett's *Directory of the City and County of Limerick and of the Principal Towns in the Cos. of Tipperary and Clare* has trader lists for Killaloe, Ennis, and Kilrush, and an alphabetical list of the gentry in County Clare.

1870

Slater's *Directory of Ireland* contains trader, nobility, and clergy lists for Ennis, Ennistymon, Kilkee, Killaloe, Kilrush, Miltown Malbay, Newmarket-on-Fergus, Sixmilebridge and Cratloe, and Tulla.

1881

Slater's *Royal National Commercial Directory of Ireland* contains lists of traders, clergy, nobility, and farmers in adjoining parishes of the towns of Ennis, Ennistymon, Kilkee, Killaloe, Kilrush, Milltown Malbay, Newmarket-on-Fergus, and Tulla.

1886

Francis Guy's *Postal Directory* of Munster lists gentry, clergy, traders, principal farmers, teachers, and police sergeants in each postal district of the county and has a listing of magistrates, clergy, and the professions for the whole county.

1893

Francis Guy's *Directory of Munster* contains lists of traders and farmers in each of the postal districts of the county and a general alphabetical index to persons in the whole county.

1894

Slater's *Royal National Directory of Ireland* contains lists of traders, police, teachers, farmers, and private residents in each of the towns, villages, and parishes of the county.

Family History

"An O'Brien family in France." *Ir. Gen.* 8 (2) (1991): 207–209.

"The Butlers of Co. Clare." *N. Munster Antiq. J.* 6 (1952): 108–29; 7 (1953): 153–67; 7 (2) (1955): 19–45.

Census Returns Relating to Following Families and Years: Brooks (1841) NAI film 5248 (1); Ryan (1851) NAI film 5249 (66, 67).

"Colpoys of Ballycarr" (Co. Clare). *R.S.A.I.* 27 (1898): 71–72.

"The Cratloe O'Briens." *Ir. Gen.* 6 (1) (1980): 48–53.

"The Families of Corcomroe." *N. Munster Antiq. J.* 17 (1975): 21–30.

"Finucane of Co. Clare." *Ir. Anc.* 1 (1) (1969): 1–11; 1 (2): 144.

History of Kenny, Lysaght, O'Loghlen, and related Clare families. NLI ms. 2109–2110.

"The McNamara Name." *The Other Clare* 5 (1981).

"Nihell of Co. Clare and Co. Limerick." *Ir. Anc.* 4 (1972): 496–506.

O'Brien, Ivar. *O'Brien of Thomond–The O'Briens in Irish History: 1500–1865.* Phillimore, 1986.

O'Croinin, R. *O'Dea-Ua Deaghaid–A Rebel Clan.* Ballinakella Press, 1992.

"The O'Davorens of Cahermacnaughten, Burren, Co. Clare." *N. Munster Antiq. J.* 2 (1912-13): 63-93, 149-64.

O'Donoghue, John. *Historical Memoir of the O'Briens, With Notes, Appendix and a Genealogical Table of their Several Branches.* Dublin: Hodges, Smith & Co., 1860.

"O'Halloran of Ballyainveen." *N. Munster Antiq. J.* 5 (4) (1948): 102-06; 7 (3) (1956): 12-17 (gives diary of births/marriages, etc. from 1758-1912).

The O'Shaughnessys of Munster. See Family History—Co. Galway.

"The Sarsfields of Co. Clare." *N. Munster Antiq. J.* 3 (1914-15): 92-107, 170-90, 328-43.

"The Studderts of Kilkishen." *The Other Clare* 4 (1980).

Twigge, R.W. *The Pedigrees of MacConmara of . . . Co. Clare with Some Family Reminiscences.* 1908.

Gravestone Inscriptions

Clare Heritage Centre has indexed eighty Clare graveyards and will conduct a search for a fee (see Research Sources and Services section).

Killaloe Cathedral: Year Book of St. Flannan's Cathedral.

Newspapers

The town of Ennis was the center of newspaper publishing in this county. However, because of its proximity to Limerick city, many of the Limerick city newspapers also contain material of relevance to the south of County Clare. An index to biographical notices in Limerick, Ennis, Clonmel, and Waterford newspapers up to 1821 (50,000 items) is available on microfiche from Ms. R. ffolliott, Glebe House, Fethard, Co. Tipperary. Copies are in NLI, Waterford Municipal Library, and elsewhere. In addition, the NLI and Clare Co. Library hold the Dunboyne Collection of newspaper clippings, which covers Clare trials, town commission affairs, and church affairs from 1824 to 1879.

Title: *Clare Advertiser*
Published in: Kilrush, 1868-88
NLI Holdings: 1.1870-5.1873 (odd nos.); 3.1881-12.1885

Title: *Clare Freeman and Ennis Gazette*
Published in: Ennis, 1853-1884
NLI Holdings: 1878-84 (odd nos.)
BL Holdings: 2.1853-1.1884

Title: *Clare Independent and Tipperary Catholic Times* (continued as *Independent and Munster Advertiser* in 1881)
Published in: Ennis, 1876-85
NLI Holdings: 8.1876-12.1885
BL Holdings: 1.1877-12.1885

Title: *Clare Journal and Ennis Advertiser*
Published in: Ennis, 1807-1917
Index of b/m/d. to 1900 available from Clare Heritage Centre
NLI Holdings: 1.1807-9.1809 (incomplete); 1.1854-12.1876; 1-7.1886 (odd nos.); 8.1886-4.1917
BL Holdings: 1.1828-4.1917
Clare Co. Library Holdings: 1840-1880, 1896-1915

Title: *Ennis Chronicle* (continued as *Ennis Chronicle and Clare Advertiser* in 1802)
Published in: Ennis, 1789-1831
NLI Holdings: 1789-92; 1794-97; 1800-11; 1814; 1816; 1818; 1820; 1825-27; 1831
BL Holdings: 1.1828-11.1831
Clare Co. Library Holdings: 1.1828-11.1831
Indexed (1827) in OCM Vol. 11

Title: *Kilrush Herald and Kilkee Gazette*
Published in: Kilrush, 1874-1922
BL Holdings: 6.1874-3.1880; 5.1889-6.1922

Wills and Administrations

A discussion of the types of records, where they are held, and their availability and value is given in the Wills and Administrations section of the introduction. The availability of prerogative wills, administrations, and marriage license records is also described in the relevant parts of the same section. Where available, published sources of these records are given in the Miscellaneous Sources section.

Pre-1858 Wills and Administrations

Prerogative Wills. See the introduction.

Consistorial Wills. County Clare is mainly in the diocese of Killaloe, with two baronies in Kilfenora and four parishes in Limerick. The guide to Catholic parish records for this county shows the diocese to which each civil parish belonged. The wills of residents of each diocese were usually proven within that diocese (see the Wills section for exceptions). The following records survive:

Wills

O'Loughlen Wills (Co. Clare). NLI P2543.

Abstracts

Westropp's "Notes on Clare" manuscripts contain abstracts from Clare and Limerick. RIA Library. Molony Will Abstracts: GO Ms. 450-466 and SLC films 257780 and 100148-50.

Indexes

Killaloe and Kilfenora fragments survive from 1653-1858. Those to 1800 have been published by Phillimore. Limerick—see Co. Limerick.

Post-1858 Wills and Administrations

County Clare was served by the District Registry of Limerick. The surviving records are kept in the NAI and are on SLC films 100946 and -7. Clare Heritage Centre also has a collection of wills and copies.

Marriage Licenses

Marriage Licenses: Diocese of Killaloe (1680–1762). GO Ms. 688; SLC film 100239.

Indexes

Killaloe (1691–1845) PRO; SLC film 100869.

Bonds

Killaloe (1680–1720) and (1760–62). *Ir. Gen.* 5 (5) (1978): 580–590.

Grants

Killaloe. *Ir. Gen.* 5 (6) (1979): 710–19.

Miscellaneous Sources

"Businessmen of Ennis, Co. Clare Early in the Napoleonic Wars." *Ir. Anc.* 16 (1) (1984): 6–8.

Coffey, Thomas. *The Parish of Inchicronan (Crusheen).* Ballinakella Press, 1993. ISBN: 0-946538-131.

Dunboyne Collection of Newscuttings (NLI ms. 3321–79); covers trials, town commissions, and church affairs from 1824–28 and 1842–79 (at County Library).

Dutton, Hely. *A Statistical Survey of County Clare.* Royal Dublin Society, 1808.

"Emigration from County Clare." *N. Munster Antiq. J.* 17 (1975): 69–76.

"Emigration from the Workhouse at Ennistymon, Co. Clare." *Ir. Anc.* 13 (2) (1981): 79–82.

Frost, J. *History and Topography of Co. Clare to the Beginning of the 18th Century.* 1893; reprinted 1978.

"Funeral Entries from Co. Clare in the 17th Century." *N. Munster Antiq. J.* 17 (1975): 63–67 (records of twelve prominent deaths).

Gwynn, A., and O.F. Gleeson. *A History of the Diocese of Killaloe.* Dublin, 1962.

Hugh, W. L. Weir. *Houses of Clare.* Ballinakella Press, 1986. (Gives major houses, associated families, features and history.)

"Magistrates of Co. Clare 1819." *Ir. Anc.* 8 (1): 16–17.

"Magistrates of Co. Clare 1837." *Ir. Anc.* 7 (2): 99–100.

"The Moravian Brethren and Their Church at Corofin." *The Other Clare* 3 (1979): 27–28.

Murphy, Ignatius. *A Starving People–Life and Death in West Clare 1845–51.* Dublin: Irish Academic Press, 1995.

Poor Law Records of County Limerick, Clare and Tipperary. *N. Munster Antiq. J.* Supplement to Vol.

21, 1979. SLC fiche 6035640.

"Schoolmasters in Killaloe Diocese (1808)." *N. Munster Antiq. J.* 11 (1968): 57–63.

"Some Observations on Thomond Surnames." *N. Munster Antiq. J.* 5 (1) (1946): 11–14.

Starkey, Mgt. "Families in Co. Clare: 1864–1880" (indexed abstracts from civil records). Vienna, VA: Starkey, 1990. SLC film 1696528.

White, Rev. P. *History of Co. Clare and of the Dalcassian Clans of Tipperary, Limerick and Galway.* Limerick, 1893.

Research Sources and Services

Journals

Dalgcais
The Other Clare
The North Munster Antiquarian Journal

Libraries and Information Sources

Clare County Library has a Local Studies Centre located at The Manse, Harmony Row, Ennis, Co. Clare, Ph: (065) 21616, ext. 271; fax: (065) 42462. It is a research center and reference library with an extensive collection of local material, including books (approximately two thousand titles on the history, etc., of the county); photographs (from 1870); maps; estate records; local govt. records; folklore collection; and local newspapers from 1824.

Research Services

Clare Heritage Centre, Corofin, Co. Clare. Ph: (065) 37955. This is the oldest and most comprehensive such center in the country, having been founded in 1982 by the late Dr. Ignatius Cleary. It provides research service on Clare families, and has indexes to all Clare Catholic and Church of Ireland parishes, land records, civil records, tombstone inscriptions, some newspapers, wills, workhouse records, convict trials, and ship's passenger lists. Researchers are advised to contact the center for an updated list of sources, indexed. Research is conducted for a fee.

See also Research Services in Dublin in the introduction.

Societies

Clare Archaeological and Historical Society, Mr. John Culliney, Ballyalia, Ennis, Co. Clare

Killaloe Heritage Society, Ms. Lesley Mawson, Hill Road, Killaloe, Co. Clare

North Clare Historical Society, Ms. Frances Madigan, Circular Road, Ennistimon, Co. Clare

Shannon Archaeological Society, Ms. Mary Quinn, Showgrounds, Drumbiggil, Co. Clare

Clare Civil Parishes as Numbered on Map

1. Gleninagh
2. Drumcreehy
3. Abbey
4. Oughtmama (5 pts.)
5. Killonaghan
6. Kilmoon
7. Rathborney
8. Killeany
9. Kilcorney
10. Carran
11. Noughaval
12. Killilagh
13. Kilmacrehy (2 pts.)
14. Killaspuglonane
15. Kilshanny
16. Kilfenora
17. Kilmanaheen
18. Clooney (NB: 2 parishes of this name—see 30)
19. Kiltoraght
20. Kilkeedy
21. Killinaboy
22. Rath
23. Ruan
24. Inagh
25. Dysert (NB: 2 parishes of this name—see 18)
26. Kilnamona (2 pts.)
27. Inchicronan
28. Templemaley
29. Kilraghtis
30. Clooney
31. Doora (2 pts.)
32. Quin
33. Feakle
34. Tomgraney
35. Moynoe
36. Tulla
37. Kilnoe
38. Inishcaltra
39. Kilfarboy
40. Kilmurry (NB: 3 parishes of this name)
41. Killard
42. Kilmaley
43. Drumcliff
44. Killone
45. Clareabbey
46. Clondagad
47. Ogonnelloe
48. Killuran
49. Clonlea
50. Kilseily
51. Killokennedy
52. O'Briensbridge (2 pts.)
53. Killaloe
54. Kiltenanlea
55. Kilmacduane (2 pts.)
56. Kilfearagh
57. Kilballyowen
58. Moyarta
59. Kilrush
60. Kilmihil
61. Kilmurry (NB: 3 parishes of this name)
62. Kilfiddane
63. Kilchreest
64. Killadysart
65. Killimer
66. Killofin
67. Kilnasoolagh
68. Tomfinlough
69. Kilmurry (NB: 3 parishes of this name)
70. Kilmaleery
71. Clonloghan
72. Drumline
73. Feenagh
74. Kilfinaghta
75. Kilconry
76. Bunratty
77. Kilfintinan
78. Killeely
79. St. Munchin's
80. St. Patrick's

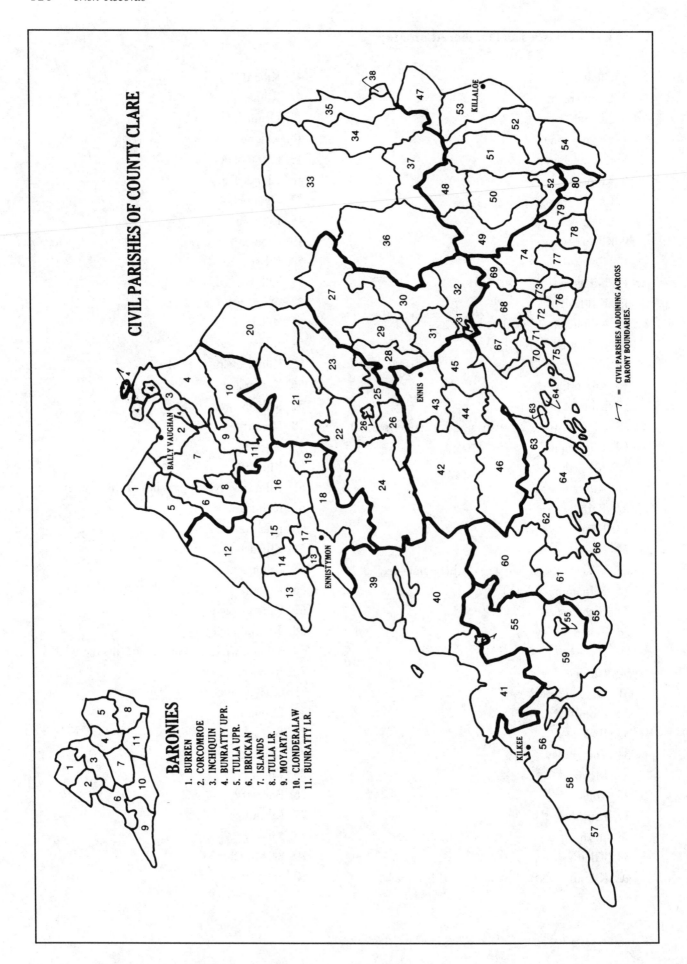

CIVIL PARISHES OF COUNTY CLARE

BARONIES
1. BURREN
2. CORCOMROE
3. INCHIQUIN
4. BUNRATTY UPR.
5. IBRICKAN
6. ISLANDS
7. TULLA LR.
8. TULLA UPR.
9. MOYARTA
10. CLONDERALAW
11. BUNRATTY LR.

⌐ = CIVIL PARISHES ADJOINING ACROSS
BARONY BOUNDARIES.

Clare Civil Parishes in Alphabetical Order

Abbey: 3
Bunratty: 76
Carran: 10
Clareabbey: 45
Clondagad: 46
Clonlea: 49
Clonloghan: 71
Clooney: 30
Clooney: 18
Doora (2 pts.): 31
Drumcliff: 43
Drumcreehy: 2
Drumline: 72
Dysert: 25
Feakle: 33
Feenagh: 73
Gleninagh: 1
Inagh: 24
Inchicronan: 27
Inishcaltra: 38
Kilballyowen: 57
Kilchreest: 63
Kilconry: 75
Kilcorney: 9
Kilfarboy: 39
Kilfearagh: 56
Kilfenora: 16
Kilfiddane: 62
Kilfinaghta: 74
Kilfintinan: 77
Kilkeedy: 20
Killadysart: 64
Killaloe: 53
Killard: 41
Killaspuglonane: 14
Kileany: 8
Killeely: 78
Killilagh: 12
Killimer: 65
Killinaboy: 21

Killofin: 66
Killokennedy: 51
Killonaghan: 5
Killone: 44
Killuran: 48
Kilmacduane (2 pts.): 55
Kilmacrehy (2 pts.): 13
Kilmaleery: 70
Kilmaley: 42
Kilmanaheen: 17
Kilmihil: 60
Kilmoon: 6
Kilmurry: 40
Kilmurry: 61
Kilmurry: 69
Kilnamona (2 pts.): 26
Kilnasoolagh: 67
Kilnoe: 37
Kilraghtis: 29
Kilrush: 59
Kilseily: 50
Kilshanny: 15
Kiltenanlea: 54
Kiltoraght: 19
Moyarta: 58
Moynoe: 35
Noughaval: 11
O'Briensbridge (2 pts.): 52
Ogonnelloe: 47
Oughtmama (5 pts.): 4
Quin: 32
Rath: 22
Rathborney: 7
Ruan: 23
St. Munchin's: 79
St. Patrick's: 80
Templemaley: 28
Tomfinlough: 68
Tomgraney: 34
Tulla: 36

County Cork

A Brief History

This Munster county is the largest in Ireland. The major towns in the county are Cork city, Mallow, Mitchelstown, Youghal, Kanturk, Cobh, Fermoy, Kinsale, Clonakilty, Skibbereen, Bantry, and Bandon.

Before the establishment of the county system, the area of the present County Cork was divided between the territories of Desmond, Muskerry, and Corca Laoidhe. The major Gaelic families in the county were McCarthy, O'Keefe, Murphy, O'Mahony, O'Callaghan, O'Donovan, O'Driscoll, and O'Riordan.

The city of Cork itself was founded in the sixth century by the establishment of a monastery and school on the site by St. Finbarr. This grew into a considerable town. In the early ninth century the Norse Vikings raided and later settled in the town, established it as a trading post, and merged with the local inhabitants.

Following the Norman invasion in the twelfth century, the county was granted to the Norman knights Fitzstephen and De Cogan. These brought over further Anglo-Norman settlers, but the colony never extended much beyond the area around the present Cork city. Like the Norsemen, the Normans in the county gradually merged with the native Irish and adopted the Irish way of life. Gradually, over the succeeding centuries, the power and holdings of the individual Norman families increased by war and intermarriage. The main names of Norman extraction now found in the county are Barry, Roche, Cogan, and Nagle.

The power of many of these Norman and Gaelic families was broken after they supported the unsuccessful revolt of the Earl of Desmond in the late sixteenth century. This resulted in the confiscation of the bulk of the holdings of these families and their distribution, in 1583, to English adventurers. During what is known as the Plantation of Munster, around 15,000 people were brought over and settled in Cork and neighboring counties. Most of these settlers left again during Hugh O'Neill's war with the English (see Co. Tyrone), and particularly on the approach of his army into Munster in 1598. Although some returned again after his defeat, the plantation was largely a failure. Further English settlers came in the 1650s following the defeat of the 1641 rebellion (see the introduction).

In the Great Famine of 1845-47, County Cork was one of the most severely affected areas. The population, which peaked at 854,000 in 1841, had fallen to 650,000 in 1851. Almost 150,000 people died between 1845 and 1850, and further thousands emigrated. The population is currently around 404,000.

Currently, the twenty most common names in Cork are O'Sullivan, Murphy, McCarthy, Mahoney, O'Donovan, Walsh, O'Brien, O'Callaghan, O'Leary, Crowley, Collins, O'Driscoll, O'Connell, Barry, Cronin, Buckley, Daly, Sheehy, O'Riordan, and Kelliher.

Census and Census Substitutes

1641

Survey of Houses in Cork City, listing tenants and possessors; NAI Quit Rent Office Papers.

1641

Book of Survey and Distribution (proprietors in 1641, grantees in 1666-68), NL MS 966-7. Also published as "Extracts from Civil Survey of Cork" (which gives name, religion, and townland of proprietors in each parish) in *J. Cork Hist. & Arch. Soc.* 37 (146) (1932): 83-89; 38 (147) (1933): 39-45; 38 (148) (1933): 72-79; 39 (149) (1934): 33-36; 39 (150) (1934): 79-84; 40 (151) (1935): 43-48; 40 (152) (1935): 91-94; 51 (153) (1936): 37-41; 51 (154) (1936): 97-104.

1654

Proprietors in parishes of Aghabullog, Aghina, Aglish, Ballinaboy, Ballyvorney, Carnaway, Carrigrohanbeg, Clondrohid, Currykippane, Desertmore, Donoughmore, Drishane, Garrycloyne, Granagh, Inchigeelagh, Inniscarra, Kilbonane, Kilcolman, Kilcorny, Kilmihil, Kilmurry, Kilnamartyr, Knockavilly, Macloneigh, Macroom, Matehy, Moviddy, Templemichael, Whitechurch. *Civil Survey*, R.C. Simington. Irish Manuscripts Commission, Vol. VI; SLC film 973123.

Cork city, with North and South suburbs and liberties. *Civil Survey*, R.C. Simington. Irish Manuscripts Commission, Vol. 6; SLC film 973123.

1659

"Census" of Ireland, edited by S. Pender. Dublin: Stationery Office, 1939. SLC film 924648.

1662–67

Subsidy Rolls, Condons and Clangibbons baronies (extracts), NAI M.4968. Also NAI Ms. 2636, 2643.

1663–64

Valuation of Cork City in *Civil Survey* Vol. 6 (see above). SLC film 973123.

1700–1752

Freemen, Cork City. NAI M.4693.

1730–31

"Debtors in Cork Gaol" (over fifty names, addresses, occupations). *J. Cork Hist. & Arch. Soc.* 47 (165) (1942): 9–23.

1753 and after

Householders in St. Nicholas parish, Cork City, in C. of I. register.

1757

Jephson, M.D. "Male, Able-bodied Protestants in Parishes of Brigown, Castletown Roche, Clonmeen, Farrihy, Glanworth, Kilshannig, Marshallstown, Roskeen." Appendix (4) in *An Anglo-Irish Miscellany* (1964).

1761

Militia List of Cos. Cork. . . . GO Ms 680.

1766

Religious Census of All Householders (see introduction) in Parishes of Aghada, Ardagh, and Clonpriest (names of householder's wife and children), Ballyhea, Ballyhooly and Killathy, Britway, Carrigdownane, Castlelyons, Castlemartyr, Castletown Roche, Churchtown, Clenor, Clonfert, Clondrohid, Clondullane, Clonmeen, Ruskeen and Kilcummy, Clonmult and Kilmahon, Cloyne and Ballintemple, Coole, Farrihy, Templemologga, Kildorrery, Nathlash, Garrycloyne, Whitechurch and Grenagh, Glanworth, Inniscarra and Matehy, Killogrohanbeg, Kilnamartyr, Kilshannig, Kilworth and Macrony, Knockmourne and Ballynoe, Lisgoold and Ballykeary, Litter, Macroom, Magourney and Kilcolman, Mallow, Marshalstown, Midleton, Mourne Abbey, Shandrum, Youghal. NAI m 5036a. SLC film 101781.

Householders of Rathbarry and Ringrone. NAI 1A 46 49. SLC film 100173.

Householders of Castletownroche. GO Ms 437 and RCB Ms 23.

"Householders of Dunbulloge (Carrignavar)." *J. Cork. Hist. & Arch. Soc.* 51 (173) (1946): 69–77.

"Householders of Kilmichael" (with notes on the names and their current status in the area). *J. Cork Hist. & Arch. Soc.* 26 (124) (1920): 69–73.

1768

Tenant Farmers on the Barrymore Estate (Barrymore Barony). *J. Cork Hist. & Arch. Soc.* 51 (173) (1946): 31–40 (name, townland, and holding).

1770

Rental of Bennett Estate (notes on sixty-eight properties, mainly in Cork city and surroundings, with details of each, and mentioning previous tenants [to 1690s] and neighbors, etc.) NLI film P288.

1771–72

"Debtors in Cork Gaol" (over 150 names). *J. Cork Hist. & Arch. Soc.* 47 (165) (1942): 9–23.

1773–1800

Catholic Qualification Roll Extracts (139 names, addresses, and occupations). 59th Report DKPRI: 50–84. Also Qualification Rolls (1773–1800). NAI and SLC films 100889–891.

1783

List of Freemen and Freeholders Who Voted in 1783 City of Cork Election (gives names and occupations). NLI P2054.

1793 et seq.

Householders in St. Anne's (Shandon) Parish (list for valuation purposes) in Year 1793 and of Additional Houses Built in Years 1804, 1809, 1821, 1832, 1837, 1844, 1853. *J. Cork Hist. & Arch. Soc.* 47 (165): 87–111 (names and addresses with value of holding).

The following is a list of debtors in the Cork City Marshalsea and the County Gaol in 1730-31.

Baily, George	Cork	Ropemaker
Barber, Peter	City	Cooper
Beneson, Robert	Gourtey Cross (Croom) ?	Yeoman
Bonn, Henry	Currivolly, Co. Cork	Gent
Bryan, William	Cork City	Merchant
Butler, William	Cork City	Nailor
Callaghan, Morgan	Killeen, North Liberties	Dairyman
Callan, Teig	Baulan, Co. Cork	Yeoman
Cantlan, Nicholas	Cork City	Taylor
Carthy, James	Cork City	Clothier
Clancy, Thomas	Gloun, Rousk, Cork	Yeoman
Coleman, Thomas	Limerick City	Weaver
Collins, Denis	Cork City	Sawyer
Conan, David	Ballyhouly	Malster
Connell, Bart.	Rathmacully, South Liberties	Farmer
Connell, *Eleanor*	Cork City	Widow
Coppinger, Thomas	Cork	Merchant
Crowley, Florence	Cork City	Porter
Doyle, Edward	Cork (Youghal)	Mariner
Evans, *Catherine*	Cork City	Mealwoman
Field, Stephen	Fairlain (now Wolfe Tone St.)	Mariner
Fling, Darby	Cork City	Miller

A list of the debtors imprisoned in Cork jails in 1730-31. Such lists were prepared for presentation at the quarter sessions of the courts. They were also posted in the jail. From *Journal of the Cork Hist. and Arch. Soc.* (1942).

1817

A List of the Freemen at Large of the City of Cork (arranged alphabetically, gives occupations only). NLI P722.

1821

Co. Cork Game Licenses. *Ir. Gen.* 8 (1): 79-81.

1823-37

Tithe Applotment Survey (see introduction).

1830

The Census of the Parish of St. Mary Shandon, Cork (circa 1830). *J. Cork Hist. & Arch. Soc.* 49 (169) (1944): 10-18. SLC 941. 5/A1/59 (gives names of house-owners, other details not related to names).

1830-37

Names, in Alphabetical Order, of Some Householders in the City of Cork (120 names, addresses and occupations). Reports from Committees. *Parl. Papers* 1837-38, 13 (2): 554-57.

1832-37

Several Lists of Householders in Cork Classified by Valuation and Voting Status (giving residence and occupation for Appendixes 1 and 7). *Parl. Papers* 1837/38, 13 (1): Appendixes 1-5, 301-14; 7-9, 318-23.

1834

List of Protestant Parishioners (including children's names) in Ballymoden, Town of Bandon, Arranged by street. NLI ms. 675.

Protestant families in Magourney. Casey, Albert. *O'Kief, Coshe Mang, and Slieve Luachra* Vol. 14: 493; SLC film 832809.

1835

Occupants of Houses of Over £5 Valuation in Youghal (arranged alphabetically with description and value of premises). *Parl. Papers* 1837, 11 (1): Appendix G, 239-49.

The Youghal Poll-Books of 1835 and 1837. Gives names, addresses, and occupations of voters and how they voted. In Youghal Corporation Records at Cork Archives. The 1835 list is published in *J. Cork Hist. & Arch. Soc.* 83 (238) (1978): 106-46; 1837 list in *J. Cork Hist. & Arch. Soc.* 84 (239) (1979): 15-43.

1836/49/52

Census of Kingwilliamstown Estate, Co. Cork

		BOROUGH OF YOUGHAL.	
Number.	N A M E.	R E S I D E N C E.	OCCUPATION.
1	William Ahern - -	North Main-street - - -	labourer.
2	John Barry - -	Knockavirry - - - -	farmer.
3	Daniel Buckly -	North Main-street - - -	shopkeeper.
4	Edmond Bowler -	Friar's-street - - - -	labourer.
5	William Conway -	North Main-street - - -	skinner.
6	John Connor -	South Main-street - - -	shopkeeper.
7	Michael Coleman -	North Main-street - - -	tailor.
8	Cornelius Hurley- -	ditto - - - - -	victualler.
9	Michael Hallahan -	ditto - - - - -	baker.
10	James Hallahan -	Meat Shamble-lane - -	shopkeeper.
11	James Kinneary -	Copper-alley - - - -	farmer.
12	Denis Kenealy -	Cross-lane - - - -	gardener.
13	Richard Moore -	South Main-street - - -	shoemaker.
14	James M'Guire -	North Main-street - - -	wheelwright.
15	John M'Guire -	Knockavirry - - - -	farmer.
16	Darby M'Grath -	Windmill-lane - - - -	carman.
17	Garrett Meade -	North Main-street - - -	victualler.
18	John Murphy -	Fish Shamble-lane - -	dealer.
19	Maurice Nagle -	North Main-street - - -	baker.
20	Robert Power -	Cock-lane - - - -	weaver.
21	John Prendergast, sen.-	North Main-street - - -	publican.
22	Daniel Quinlan -	Nile-street - - - -	shoemaker.
23	John Ronayne -	ditto - - - - -	tailor.
24	Edmond Seward -	South Main-street - - -	fisherman.
25	John Sullivan - -	Mall-lane - - - -	tailor.
26	John Frihey - -	Shambles-lane - - -	publican.

28 February 1837.   *James Chatterton,* Clerk of the Peace.

Registered voters in the Borough of Youghal, County Cork, who were registered as "Marksmen" (i.e., who could vote by making their mark rather than a signature). This information was prepared as evidence for the Select Committee on Fictitious Votes, 1837. From *Parliamentary Papers* 1837, 2 (1): Appendix G.

(Nohavaldaly Parish) (see also 1849–51). SLC film 101767.

1837

Occupants of Bandon (Bridge) Arranged by Street, Giving Property Values. *Parl. Papers* 1837, 11 (1): Appendix G, 191–98.

List of Nonresident Freemen, City of Cork (mainly Cork Co.). *Parl. Papers* 1837–38, 13 (1): 315–17.

Several Lists of Waste and Poor in Various Parishes in the City of Cork. *Parl. Papers* 1837–38, 13 (1): Appendix 9(2), 10, 11: 323–34.

1838

List of Marksmen (illiterate voters) in Cork City, Mallow, Youghal, Kinsale (gives names, residences, and oc-

cupations). *Parl. Papers* 1837/38, 13 (1): Supplemental Appendixes, 5–15; 1837, 13 (2), Appendix 4.

1841

Untitled list of voters at the Cork election of 1841. Gives names, addresses, place of freehold, leasehold, etc. Printed in *Minutes of the Proceedings of the select committee on the Cork County election . . .* , H.C. 1842 (271), VI: 1–214 (Poll book is Appendix, pp. 177–214).

1842

Voters List. NAI 1842/26 (Cork West Riding) and NAI 1842/23 (Cork East Riding).

1845–46

Members of Ballineen Agricultural Society 1845/46. *J. Cork. Hist. & Arch. Soc.* 51 (173) (1946): 52–60.

1849-51

Emigrants from Kingwilliamstown (Ballydesmond; part of Nohavaldaly; gives names, ages, and relationships of 191 people with dates of departure, arrival, etc.). In E. Ellis, *Emigrants from Ireland 1847-52* (Baltimore: Genealogical Publishing Co., 1977), 42-53.

1850

Kingswilliamstown Census (1849, 1850, and 1852). SLC film 101767.

1851

Government Census Remnants: Parish of Kilcrumper (except the townlands of Glenwood, Lisnallagh, and Loughnakilly); Parish of Kilworth; Parish of Leitrim (except the townlands of Ballymamudthogh, Cronahil, and Propogue); the townlands of Castle Cooke, Kilclogh, Macrony, and Shanaclure in the parish of Macrony. NAI M 4685.

1851-53

Griffith's Valuation (see introduction).

1901

Census. NAI (see introduction).

1911

Census. NAI.

Church Records

Church of Ireland

See the introduction for a description of Church of Ireland records and their major repositories. Many Church of Ireland records were lost in the PRO fire of 1922. These are indicated as "Lost." However, as Church of Ireland records were effectively state records, the records of marriage (from 1845) are also in the General Registrar's Office. Many are still in local custody (LC), while others are in one of a variety of other archives (e.g., RCBL or NAI). Indexes of some parish records have been published in O'Casey's *O'Kief, Coshe Mang and Sleive Luachra* (here abbreviated OCM). Several heritage centers are involved in indexing parish records from different parts of this large county (see Research Services, etc.). Duhallow Heritage Centre has already indexed some registers. Those indexed are noted as "Indexed by Duhallow HC." There is also an index to Cloyne marriages before 1845 on SLC film 924578.

Abbeymahon

Earliest Records: b. 1782-; m. 1738-; d. 1732-
Status: RCBL (b. 1782-1852; m. 1738-1852; d. 1732-1852); NAI MFCI 18 and 20 (b. 1827-1873)

Abbeystrewery

Earliest Records: b. 1788-
Status: LC; NAI MFCI 32 (b. 1788-1915)

Aghabulloge

Earliest Records: b. 1807-; m. 1808-; d. 1808-
Status: LC; NAI M 5067 (b. 1807-77; m. 1808-1843; d. 1808-1879); m. indexed in OCM Vol. XIV

Aghada

Earliest Records: b. 1730-; m. 1730-; d. 1730-
Status: LC; NAI M 6075-77a, 6201, MFCI 20, 30, 36 (b. 1730-1921; m. 1730-1915; d. 1730-1924)

Aghadown

Status: Lost

Aglish

Status: Lost

Ahern or Aghern

Status: Lost

Ardagh

Status: Lost

Ardfield

Earliest Records: b. 1832; m. 1843; d. 1834-36
Status: LC

Athnowen and Kilnagleary

Status: Lost

Ballinaboy

Status: Lost

Ballinadee

Status: Lost

Ballintemple or Churchtown

Status: Lost

Ballyclough or Ballyclogh

Earliest Records: b. 1831; m. 1831; d. 1831
Status: LC; NAI M 5047 (b. 1831-1900; m. 1831-1948; d. 1831-1900); m. 1845-1898 indexed by Duhallow HC; SLC film 597159

Ballycotton

Status: Lost

Ballydehob (chapel of ease to Skull)

Earliest Records: b. 1826-75
Status: LC

Ballyhea

Earliest Records: b. 1777-; m. 1777-; d. 1777-
Status: LC; Indexed by Duhallow HC (b. 1777-1799; m. 1777-1779; d. 1777-1779); SLC film 962669

Ballyhooly

Earliest Records: b. 1789; m. 1808; d. 1791
Status: LC; Indexed by Duhallow HC (b. 1894-1900); SLC film 596420 (extracts 1789-1892)

Ballymartle
Earliest Records: b. 1785-; m. 1761-; d. 1785-
Status: LC; NAI M 5081 (b. 1799-1868; d. 1800-1876)

Ballymodan
Earliest Records: b. 1695-; m. 1695-; d. 1695-
Status: RCBL (b. 1695-1878; m. 1695-1958; d. 1695-1878)

Ballymoney
Earliest Records: b. 1782-; m. 1786-; d. 1800-
Status: LC; NAI MFCI 19 (b. 1805-71; m. 1805-74; d. 1805-73)

Ballyvoe
Status: Lost

Ballyvourney
Earliest Records: b/m/d. 1845-1935
Status: LC; Indexed in OCM Vol. II; SLC film 596420 (extracts 1789-1892)

Berehaven (Killaconenagh)
Earliest Records: b. 1787-; m. 1784-; d. 1796-
Status: LC; NAI M 6051, MFCI 25 (b. 1787-1872; m. 1784-1844; d. 1796-1873)

Blackrock
Earliest Records: b. 1828; m. 1828; d. 1830
Status: RCBL (b. 1828-1897; m. 1828-1981; d. 1830-1946); NAI MFCI 19 (to 1872 for b. and d., and 1844 for m.)

Bridgetown and Kilcummer
Earliest Records: b. 1859-
Status: LC; NAI M 5083 (b. 1859-71); Indexed by Duhallow HC; SLC film 596420

Brigown
Earliest Records: b. 1751-; m. 1775-; d. 1775-
Status: LC; NAI MFCI 21 and M6044 (b. 1751-1870; m. 1775-1848; d. 1775-1871)

Brinny
Earliest Records: b. 1797-; m. 1797-; d. 1797-
Status: LC; RCBL (transcript) and NAI MFCI 28 (b. 1797-1884; m. 1797-1844; d. 1797-1844)

Buttevant
Earliest Records: b. 1873-; m. 1845-; d. 1867-
Status: OCM Vol. XI (b. only); Indexed by Duhallow HC (to 1900); SLC film 596420 (extracts 1789-1892)

Caheragh
Earliest Records: b. 1836-; m. 1837-; d. 1860-
Status: LC; NAI MFCI 19 (b. 1836-1871; m. 1837-1843; d. 1860-1878)

Caherconlish
Status: Lost

Canaway
Earliest Records: m. 1845-
Status: RCBL (m. 1845-1872)

Carrigaline
Earliest Records: b. 1724-; m. 1726-; d. 1808-
Status: RCBL (b. 1724-56, m. 1726-92); NAI MFCI 19, NAI M 6001, 6028 (b. 1724-1871; m. 1791-1871; d. 1808-1879)

Carrigleamleary
Earliest Records: m. 1848-
Status: OCM Vol. XIV (m. 1848-1871); Indexed by Duhallow HC

Carrigrohanbeg
Earliest Records: b. 1791-; m. 1787-; d. 1789-
Status: LC

Carrigtohill
Earliest Records: b. 1776-1875; m. 1779-1955; d. 1776-1843
Status: LC; NAI MFCI 24 (b. 1776-1875; m. 1779-1844; d. 1776-1843); RCBL (m. 1848-1955)

Castlehaven or Castletownsend
Status: Lost

Castlelyons
Status: Lost

Castlemagner
Earliest Records: m. 1849-
Status: Indexed by Duhallow HC (to 1899)

Castletownroche
Earliest Records: b. 1728-; m. 1728-; d. 1733-
Status: NAI M 5048, 5083 (b. 1728-1928; m. 1728-1893; d. 1733-1803); Indexed by Duhallow HC (b. 1842-1900; m. 1845-1900)

Castleventry
Earliest Records: b. 1825-; m. 1825-; d. 1825-
Status: LC (copy)

Catherlog or Caherlag
Earliest Records: m. 1870-
Status: RCBL (m. 1870-1955)

Churchtown or Bruhenny
Earliest Records: b. 1806; m. 1808; d. 1826
Status: NAI; SLC film 596420 (extracts 1806-1872)

Clenor
Earliest Records: b. 1813; m. 1814; d. 1814
Status: NAI (Grove-White Abstracts); SLC film 596420 (extracts 1813-1876)

Clondrohid
Earliest Records: b. 1770-; m. 1848-; d. 1778-

Status: LC (copy); also RCBL (m. 1848–1984); OCM
Vol. II (m. 1848–1884)

Clondulane
Status: Lost

Clonfert (Newmarket)
Earliest Records: b/m/d. 1771
Status: LC; OCM Vol. XIV (m. 1845–47); Indexed by
Duhallow HC (from 1845); SLC film 596421
(extracts)

Clonmeen
Earliest Records: b. 1889–; m. 1848–; d. 1892–
Status: LC; Indexed by Duhallow HC (to 1896, 1862,
and 1896 respectively); SLC film 596421

Clonmel (Cobh or Queenstown)
Earliest Records: b. 1761–; m. 1761–; d. 1761–
Status: LC; NAI MFCI 28 and 29 (b. 1761–1870; m.
1761–1845; d. 1761–1870)

Clonmult
Status: Lost

Clonpriest
Earliest Records: m. 1851–
Status: LC; NAI M 5114 (m. 1851–1870)

Cloyne
Earliest Records: b. 1708–; m. 1708–; d. 1708–
Status: NAI MFCI 30, and M 6072 and 6036 (b.
1708–1871; m. 1708–1845; d. 1708–1871)

Cobh (see Clonmel)

Cork City: Holy Trinity
Earliest Records: b. 1644–; m. 1643–; d. 1644–
Status: LC; NAI MFCI 21, 22 (b. 1664–1871; m.
1643–1845; d. 1644–1885); also 1643–1668 register
published by R. Caulfield, Cork, 1877; SLC film
596421 (extracts)

Cork City: St. Anne, Shandon
Earliest Records: b. 1772–; m. 1772–; d. 1779–
Status: LC; NAI MFCI 25, 26, 27; M 6053, 6059 (b.
1772–1871; m. 1772–1845; d. 1779–1882)

Cork City: St. Brendans
Status: Lost

Cork City: St. Edmunds
Status: Lost

Cork City: St. Finnbarr
Status: Lost

Cork City: St. Lappan
Status: Lost

Cork City: St. Luke
Earliest Records: b. 1837–
Status: NAI MFCI 27 (b. 1837–1874)

Cork City: St. Mary (Shandon)
Earliest Records: b. 1802–; m. 1802–; d. 1802–
Status: LC; NAI MFCI 22, M 6049, 5064 (b. 1802–
1878; m. 1802–1840; d. 1802–1878)

Cork City: St. Michael, Blackrock
Earliest Records: b. 1828; m. 1837; d. 1803
Status: LC

Cork City: St. Nicholas
Earliest Records: b. 1725–; m. 1726–; d. 1726–
Status: LC; NAI MFCI 23, 24, 25, M 6047 (b.
1725–1870; m. 1726–1845; d. 1726–1870)

Cork City: St. Paul
Status: Lost

Cork City: St. Peter
Status: Lost

Corkbeg
Earliest Records: b. 1836–; m. 1838–; d. 1836–
Status: LC; NAI MFCI 36 (b. 1836–1872; m. 1838–
1850; d. 1836–1874)

Creagh
Status: Lost

Cullen
Earliest Records: b. 1779–; m. 1775–; d. 1779–
Status: NAI MFCI 6 (b. 1779–1876; m. 1775–1851;
d. 1779–1873)

Desertserges
Earliest Records: b. 1811–1871; m. 1811–1845; d.
1811–1872
Status: LC; NAI MFCI 27, 28 (b. 1811–1871; m.
1811–1845; d. 1811–1872)

Doneraile and Templeroan
Earliest Records: b. 1730–; m. 1730–; d. 1730–
Status: LC; OCM Vol. XIV (b. 1869–1952); Indexed
by Duhallow HC; SLC film 962669

Donoughmore
Earliest Records: m. 1847–; d. 1899–
Status: LC; OCM Vol. XV (m. 1847–1937); Indexed
by Duhallow HC

Douglas
Earliest Records: b. 1789–; m. 1792–; d. 1789–
Status: RCBL (b. 1789–1818; m. 1792–1893; d.
1790) and NAI MFCI 29 (b. 1789–1877; m. 1792–
1845; d. 1789–1871)

Drimoleague
Earliest Records: b. 1802–; m. 1802–11; d. 1802–
Status: NAI MFCI 31, M 6086 (b. 1802–1871; m.
1802–1811; d. 1802–1872)

Drinagh
Status: Lost

Drishane
Earliest Records: b/m. 1792; d. 1793
Status: LC (from 1877); NAI (Grove-White Abstracts); SLC film 596421 (extracts 1813–1876); Indexed by Duhallow HC (b. 1900–; m. 1890–; d. 1896–)

Dromdaleague
Earliest Records: b. 1812–; m. 1730–; d. 1730–
Status: LC

Dromtarriffe
Earliest Records: b. 1825; m/d. 1828
Status: LC; OCM Vol. I (m. 1849–1913); Indexed by Duhallow HC (to 1900); SLC film 596421 (extracts)

Dunderrow
Earliest Records: b. 1805–; m. 1799–; d. 1823–
Status: LC (copy)

Dungourney
Earliest Records: b. 1825–; m. 1826–; d. 1826–
Status: LC (copy) and RCBL (m. 1850–1954)

Durrus and Kilcrohane
Status: Lost

Fanlobbus
Earliest Records: b. 1855–; d. 1853–
Status: LC; NAI M 5110 (b. 1855–71; d. 1853–71)

Farihy
Status: Lost

Fermoy
Earliest Records: b. 1802–; m. 1803–; d. 1805–
Status: NAI MFCI 25 (b. 1802–1873; m. 1803–1845; d. 1805–1871)

Frankfield
Earliest Records: m. 1847–
Status: RCBL (m. 1847–1955)

Garrycloyne
Status: Lost

Glanworth
Earliest Records: b. 1808; m/d. 1811
Status: NAI (Grove-White Abstracts); SLC film 596421 (extracts)

Glengarriff
Earliest Records: b. 1863–
Status: LC; NAI M 5113 (b. 1863–1913)

Gortroe
Status: Lost

Holy Trinity (see Cork City–Holy Trinity)

Ightermurragh
Status: Lost

Inch
Earliest Records: b. 1815–; m. 1644–; d. 1644–
Status: LC; NAI M 6077b (m. 1847–1948)

Inchigeelagh
Earliest Records: b. 1900; m. 1845–1865
Status: RCBL (b. 1900; m. 1845–1865)

Inchinabackey
Status: Lost

Inniscarra
Earliest Records: b. 1820–; m. 1820–; d. 1820–
Status: LC; NAI MFCI 25 (b. 1820–71; m. 1820–44; d. 1820–72); also OCM Vol. XIV (to 1901)

Innishannon
Earliest Records: b. 1693–; m. 1693–; d. 1693–
Status: LC; RCBL (to 1844 for b./d.and to 1911 for m.); NAI MFCI 28, 29 (b. 1696–1871; m. 1693–1844; d. 1693–1879)

Inniskenny
Status: Lost

Kanturk
Earliest Records: b. 1818; m. 1819; d. 1820
Status: LC; Indexed by Duhallow HC (b/m. to 1900; d. 1879); SLC film 596421 (extracts 1818–1876)

Kilbolane
Earliest Records: m. 1846–; d. 1881–
Status: LC; Indexed by Duhallow HC (m. to 1894; d. to 1900)

Kilbrin and Liscarroll
Earliest Records: m. 1845–
Status: LC; Indexed by Duhallow HC (m. 1845–1898)

Kilbritain
Earliest Records: b. 1832–; m. 1830–
Status: RCBL (b. 1832–1876; m. 1830–1868)

Kilbrogan
Earliest Records: b. 1752–; m. 1753–; d. 1707–
Status: LC; NAI MFCI 29, M 6065 (b. 1752–1871; m. 1753–1845; d. 1707–1877)

Kilcaskin
Status: Lost

Kilcoe
Status: Lost

Kilcredan
Status: Lost

Kilcrohane (see Durrus)

Kilcully
Earliest Records: b. 1844
Status: LC

Kilcummer (see Bridgetown)

Kilgariffe
Status: Lost

Killaconenagh (see Berehaven)

Killanully
Earliest Records: b. 1831–; d. 1836–
Status: LC; NAI M 6029, 6030 (b. 1831–1874; d. 1836–1877)

Killaspugmullane
Status: Lost

Killeagh
Earliest Records: b. 1782–; m. 1776–; d. 1782–
Status: LC; NAI M 5144 (b. 1782–1870; m. 1776–1879; d. 1782–1884); RCBL (b. 1782–1863; m. 1778–1840; d. 1787–1868)

Killowen
Earliest Records: b. 1833–; d. 1851–
Status: LC; NAI MFCI 28 (b. 1833–1874; d. 1851–1972)

Kilmacabea
Status: Lost

Kilmahon
Earliest Records: m. 1808–
Status: NAI M 6046 (m. 1808–1944)

Kilmaloda
Status: Lost

Kilmeen
Earliest Records: b. 1806; m. 1806; d. 1844
Status: LC

Kilmichael
Status: Lost

Kilmocomoge
Status: Lost

Kilmoe
Status: Lost

Kilnagleary (see Athnowen)

Kilnemartyr
Status: Lost

Kilroan or Ballydelougher (Ringrone)
Earliest Records: b. 1885–; m. 1846–
Status: RCBL (b. 1885–1920; m. 1846–1920)

Kilshannig
Earliest Records: b. 1731–; m. 1731–; d. 1731–
Status: LC; NAI MFCI 18, M 6031 (b. 1731–1877; m. 1731–1846; d. 1731–1876); OCM (b. 1731–1865–Vol. XI and m. 1845–1915; d. 1855–1958–Vol. XIV); Indexed by Duhallow HC

Kilworth
Status: Lost

Kinneigh
Earliest Records: b. 1794–; m. 1814–; d. 1815–
Status: LC; NAI M 6038 (b. 1794–1877; m. 1814–1844; d. 1815–1870)

Kinsale
Earliest Records: b. 1684–; m. 1688–; d. 1685–
Status: LC; NAI MFCI 30, 31 and M 6071 (b. 1684–1871; m. 1688–1864; d. 1685–1872)

Knockavilly
Earliest Records: b. 1837–; m. 1844–; d. 1837–
Status: RCBL (b. 1837–1883; m. 1844–1848; d. 1837–1883); NAI MFCI 28 (b. and m. only)

Knockmourne
Status: Lost

Knocktemple (see Kilbolane)

Leighmoney
Earliest Records: b. 1869–
Status: RCBL (b. 1869–1943)

Liscarroll (see Kilbrin)

Lisgoold
Earliest Records: b. 1847–; d. 1850–
Status: NAI; SLC film 59642 (to 1875)

Lislee
Earliest Records: b. 1809–; m. 1809–; d. 1823–
Status: NAI MFCI 18, 20, M 6041 (b. 1809–1890; m. 1809–1844; d. 1823–1889)

Litter
Earliest Records: b/m/d. 1811–
Status: NAI; SLC film 596422 (to 1876)

Macroom
Earliest Records: b. 1727–; m. 1737–; 1736; d. 1727–
Status: LC; NAI M 5138 (m. to 1837; b./d. to 1835); OCM Vol. VIII and XIV

Magourney
Earliest Records: b. 1757–; m. 1756–; d. 1758–
Status: NAI M 5118 (b. 1757–1876; m. 1756–1844; d. 1758–1876)

Mallow
Earliest Records: b. 1783–; m. 1793–; d. 1783
Status: LC; NAI MFCI 18, 19 (b./d. 1793–1871; m. 1793–1863); also OCM Vol. XI (b./m./d. 1783–1867), Vol. XV (m. 1867–1932) and Vol. XIV (m. 1845–1867); Indexed by Duhallow HC; SLC film 596422 (extracts 1776–1839)

Marmullane
Earliest Records: b. 1801–1873; m. 1797–1954; d. 1801–1873
Status: RCBL (b. 1801–73, m. 1802–1954; d. 1803–

73); NAI MFCI 29, 32 (b. 1801–1873; m. 1797–1843; d. 1801–1873)

Marshallstown
Earliest Records: b. 1831; m. 1832; d. 1849
Status: Most lost; Extracts in Grove-White Collection at NAI and SLC film 596422

Midleton
Earliest Records: b. 1699–; m. 1728–; d. 1696–
Status: RCBL (b. 1699–1881; m. 1728–1823; d. 1696–1877); NAI M 5119 (b. 1810–1883; m. 1811–1881; d. 1809–1883)

Mageely
Status: Lost

Mogeesha
Earliest Records: b. 1852
Status: LC

Monanimy
Earliest Records: b. 1812; m. 1814; d. 1824
Status: Indexed by Duhallow HC (m. 1845–1879); Extracts in Grove-White Collection (NAI) and SLC film 596422 (extracts 1812–1878)

Monkstown
Earliest Records: b. 1842–; m. 1841–; d. 1842–
Status: NAI MFCI 30 (b. 1842–1872; m. 1841–1844; d. 1842–1903)

Mourneabbey (see also Rahan)
Earliest Records: b. 1807; m. 1811; d. 1807
Status: LC; OCM Vol. XV (m. 1847–1937); Indexed by Duhallow HC (b. 1832–1884; m. 1847–1898); Extracts in Grove-White Collection (NAI) and SLC film 596422 (extracts 1807–1877)

Moviddy
Status: Lost

Murragh
Earliest Records: b. 1750–; m. 1739–; d. 1784–
Status: NAI MFCI 27, M 6056, 6060, 6063 (b. 1750–1876; m. 1739–1876; d. 1784–1876)

Nathlash
Earliest Records: b. 1812–; m. 1813–; d. 1813–
Status: LC; b. 1844–1868; Indexed by Duhallow HC

Nohaval
Earliest Records: b. 1846–; d. 1846–
Status: NAI M 6033, 6039 (b. 1846–1870; d. 1846–1875)

Queenstown (see Clonmel)

Rahan
Earliest Records: b. 1773–; m. 1773–; d. 1773–
Status: OCM Vol. XIV (m. 1847–1859); also m. 1847–1891 indexed by Duhallow HC; extracts in Grove-White Collection (NAI) and SLC film 596422 (extracts 1773–1871)

Rathbarry
Status: Lost

Rathclarin
Earliest Records: b. 1780–; m. 1780–; d. 1792–
Status: RCBL (b. 1780–1875; m. 1780–1849; d. 1792–1875)

Rathcooney
Earliest Records: b. 1750–; m. 1749–; d. 1750–
Status: RCBL (b. 1750–1897; m. 1749–1854; d. 1750–1853); NAI MFCI 24, 25 (b. 1750–1871; m. 1749–1849; d. 1750–1853)

Rathcormack
Status: Lost

Ringcurran or Rincurran
Earliest Records: b. 1793–; m. 1793–; d. 1827; 1849–
Status: NAI MFCI 30, M 6070 (b. 1793–1870; m. 1793–1829; d. 1827; 1849–1872)

Ringrone (see Kilroan)

Ross Cathedral (Rosscarbery)
Earliest Records: b. 1690–; m. 1704–; d. 1669–
Status: NAI MFCI 19 (b. 1690–1871; m. 1704–1845; d. 1669–1870)

Rostellan
Status: Lost

Rushbrook
Earliest Records: b. 1866–
Status: NAI M 6073 (b. 1866–1872)

Shandrum
Status: Lost

Schull or Skull (see also Ballydehob)
Earliest Records: b. 1826–
Status: NAI MFCI 25 (b. 1826–1873)

Templebredy
Status: Lost

Templemartin
Earliest Records: b. 1845–; d. 1845–
Status: NAI MFCI 24, M 6048 (b. 1845–1879; d. 1845–1879)

Templemichael
Earliest Records: b. 1845–
Status: RCBL (b. 1845–1853)

Templenacarriga
Earliest Records: d. 1883–
Status: RCBL (d. 1883–1932)

Templeomalus
Status: Lost

Templeroan (see Doneraile)

Templetrines
Status: Lost

Timoleague
Earliest Records: b. 1827-
Status: LC; RCBL (b. 1827-1878)

Tracton
Status: Lost

Tullagh
Status: Lost

Tullylease
Earliest Records: m. 1860
Status: Indexed by Duhallow HC

Wallstown
Status: Lost

Whitechurch
Status: Lost

Youghal
Earliest Records: b. 1665-; 1666-; d. 1665-
Missing: b./m./d. 1720-27
Status: LC; NAI MFCI 19, 20 (b. 1665-1871; 1666-1842; d. 1665-1871)

Quaker

An account of Quaker records is given in the introduction. Cork Meeting records (b. 1625-1860; m. 1679-1860; d. 1664-1860) and Youghal Meeting records (b. 1661-1839; m. 1652-1839; d. 1675-1839) are in FHL (Dublin) and on SLC film 571398.

Cork
Earliest Records: b. 1653-
Status: DFHL; OCM Vol. XI, pp. 1921-1924 (b. 1653-1860)

Bandon
Earliest Records: b. 1672-; m. 1672-; d. 1672-
Status: DFHL; OCM Vol. XI, pp. 1925-44 (b. 1672-1713; m. 1672-1713; d. 1672-1713)

Youghal
Earliest Records: b. 1659-; m. 1659-; d. 1659-
Status: DFHL; OCM Vol. XI (b. 1659-1839; m. 1659-1839; d. 1659-1839)

Presbyterian

An account of Presbyterian records is given in the introduction. These registers rarely contain death records, and occasionally have only records of births. This is indicated where appropriate. Note also that the records of marriage (from 1845) are in the General Registrar's Office. Indexing of these records by local heritage centers (see Research Services at end of chapter) is planned. They should be contacted for an update on progress.

Bandon
Starting Date: 1842

Cork
Starting Date: 1832

Cobh (Queenstown)
Starting Date: 1847

Roman Catholic

Note that many of the Catholic parish registers of this county have been indexed by the several heritage centers in this large county (see Research Services at the end of the chapter). A search of the index will be conducted by the relevant center for a fee. The centers in the county currently offering a service are Mallow Heritage Centre (MHC) and Duhallow Heritage Centre (DHC), while two other centers, Cork City Ancestral Research Ltd. (CCAR) and West Cork Heritage Centre (WCHC), are currently compiling indexes. Those indexed are noted below as "Indexed by Mallow HC" or "Duhallow HC" as appropriate. Microfilm copies of all registers are also available in the National Library of Ireland (NLI), and through the LDS library system.

Civil Parish: Abbeymahon
Map Grid: S66
RC Parish: see Donoughmore (2)
Diocese: RO

Civil Parish: Abbeystowry
Map Grid: S52
RC Parish: part Skibbereen, see Creagh; part Caheragh
Diocese: RO

Civil Parish: Aghabulloge
Map Grid: N48
RC Parish: Coachford or Aghabullogue
Diocese: CY
Earliest Record: b. 1.1820; m. 1.1820
Status: LC; NLI (mf); Indexed by Mallow HC

Civil Parish: Aghacross
Map Grid: E32a
RC Parish: see Kildorrery
Diocese: CY

Civil Parish: Aghada
Map Grid: E105
RC Parish: Aghada
Diocese: CY
Earliest Record: b. 1792; m. 1785
Missing Dates: b. 3.1837-3.1838
Status: LC; NLI (mf); Indexed by Mallow HC

Civil Parish: Aghadown
Map Grid: S55
RC Parish: Aghadown or Aughadown
Diocese: RO

Earliest Record: b. 6.1822; m. 10.1822
Missing Dates: m. 2.1865–1880
Status: LC; NLI (mf); Indexing in progress

Civil Parish: Aghern
Map Grid: E69
RC Parish: Conna, see Knockmourne
Diocese: CY

Civil Parish: Aghinagh
Map Grid: N50
RC Parish: Aghinagh
Diocese: CK
Earliest Record: b. 4.1848.; m. 1848
Status: LC; NLI (mf); Indexed by Mallow HC

Civil Parish: Aglish
Map Grid: N56
RC Parish: Ovens, see Athnowen
Diocese: CK

Civil Parish: Aglishdrinagh
Map Grid: N24
RC Parish: Ballyhea, see Ballyhea
Diocese: CY

Civil Parish: Ardagh
Map Grid: E87
RC Parish: see Killeagh

Civil Parish: Ardfield
Map Grid: S61
RC Parish: Ardfield and Rathbarry
Diocese: RO
Earliest Record: b. 1.1801; m. 5.1800
Missing Dates: b. 1.1802–1.1803; m. 1812–16
Status: LC; NLI (mf); Indexing in progress

Civil Parish: Ardnageehy
Map Grid: E42
RC Parish: Watergrasshill
Diocese: CK
Earliest Record: b. 1.1836
Status: LC; NLI (mf); Indexing in progress

Civil Parish: Ardskeagh
Map Grid: E2
RC Parish: part Ballyhay, see Ballyhea; part
Charleville, see Rathgoggan
Diocese: CY

Civil Parish: Athnowen
Map Grid: N57
RC Parish: Ovens
Diocese: CK
Earliest Record: b. 9.1816; m. 9.1816
Missing Dates: b. 9.1833–10.1834; m. 8.1833–
10.1834, 2.1837–1.1839
Status: LC; NLI (mf); Indexing in progress

Civil Parish: Ballinaboy
Map Grid: N70, S25, and E85
RC Parish: Ballinhassig
Diocese: CK
Earliest Record: b. 3.1821; m. 7.1821
Status: LC; NLI (mf); Indexing in progress

Civil Parish: Ballinadee
Map Grid: N46 and S74
RC Parish: Courcey's Country (Ballinspittal)
Diocese: CK
Earliest Record: b. 9.1819; m. 9.1819
Missing Dates: b. 11.1854–1.1858
Status: LC; NLI (mf); Indexing in progress

Civil Parish: Ballintemple
Map Grid: E108
RC Parish: see Cloyne
Diocese: CY

Civil Parish: Ballycaraney or Ballycurrany
Map Grid: E53
RC Parish: see Lisgoold
Diocese: CY

Civil Parish: Ballyclough
Map Grid: N34
RC Parish: Kilbrin and Ballyclough
Diocese: CY
Earliest Record: b. 8.1807; m. 1.1805
Missing Dates: m. 1.1828
Status: LC; NLI (mf); Indexed by Mallow HC

Civil Parish: Ballydeloher
Map Grid: E59
RC Parish: Glounthaune, see Caherlag
Diocese: CK

Civil Parish: Ballydeloughy
Map Grid: E12
RC Parish: Ballindangan, see Glanworth
Diocese: CY

Civil Parish: Ballyfeard
Map Grid: S29
RC Parish: see Clontead
Diocese: CK

Civil Parish: Ballyfoyle
Map Grid: S35
RC Parish: see Tracton
Diocese: CK

Civil Parish: Ballyhea
Map Grid: N20 and E1
RC Parish: Ballyhea, Empheric, and Cooline; also part
Charleville, see Rathgoggan
Diocese: CY
Earliest Record: b. 1.1809; m. 6.1811
Status: LC; NLI (mf); Indexed by Mallow HC

Civil Parish: Ballyhooly
Map Grid: E27
RC Parish: see Castletownroche
Diocese: CY

Civil Parish: Ballymartle
Map Grid: S26
RC Parish: see Clontead
Diocese: CK

Civil Parish: Ballymodan
Map Grid: S20
RC Parish: Bandon; also part Kilbrittain
Diocese: CK
Earliest Record: b. 1.1794; m. 1.1794
Status: LC; NLI (mf); Indexing in progress

Civil Parish: Ballymoney
Map Grid: S70
RC Parish: part Dunmanway, see Fanlobbus; part
Enniskeane, see Killowen
Diocese: CK

Civil Parish: Ballynoe
Map Grid: E70
RC Parish: Ballynoe or Conna, see Knockmourne
Diocese: CY

Civil Parish: Ballyoughtera
Map Grid: E94
RC Parish: part Imogeela, see Mogeely (2); part
Midleton
Diocese: CY

Civil Parish: Ballyspillane
Map Grid: E62
RC Parish: see Midleton
Diocese: CY

Civil Parish: Ballyvourney
Map Grid: N38
RC Parish: Ballyvourney
Diocese: CY
Earliest Record: b. 1810–; m. 1871–
Missing Dates: m. 12.1829 onward destroyed by fire
Status: LC; NLI (mf); Indexed by Mallow HC; and
OCM Vol. II (index to b. 1810–1868)

Civil Parish: Barnahely
Map Grid: S41
RC Parish: Passage, see Marmullane
Diocese: CK

Civil Parish: Bohillane
Map Grid: E99
RC Parish: Ballymacoda, see Kilmacdonagh
Diocese: CY

Civil Parish: Bregoge
Map Grid: N31
RC Parish: see Buttevant
Diocese: CY

Civil Parish: Bridgetown
Map Grid: E25
RC Parish: see Castletownroche
Diocese: CY

Civil Parish: Brigown
Map Grid: E33
RC Parish: Mitchelstown
Diocese: CY
Earliest Record: b. 1.1792; m. 1.1822
Missing Dates: b. 7.1801–9.1814
Status: LC; NLI (mf); Indexed by Mallow HC

Civil Parish: Brinny
Map Grid: S17
RC Parish: see Inishannon
Diocese: CK

Civil Parish: Britway
Map Grid: E50
RC Parish: see Castlelyons
Diocese: CY

Civil Parish: Buttevant
Map Grid: N32
RC Parish: Buttevant
Diocese: CY
Earliest Record: b. 7.1814; m. 7.1814
Status: LC; NLI (mf); Indexed by Mallow HC

Civil Parish: Caheragh
Map Grid: S46
RC Parish: Caheragh
Diocese: CK
Earliest Record: b. 6.1818; m. 6.1818
Missing Dates: m. 8.1858–11.1858
Status: LC; NLI (mf); Indexing in progress

Civil Parish: Caherduggan
Map Grid: E8
RC Parish: see Doneraile
Diocese: CY

Civil Parish: Caherlag
Map Grid: E60
RC Parish: Glounthaune
Diocese: CK
Earliest Record: b. 8.1864; m. 10.1864
Status: LC; NLI (mf); Indexing in progress (CCAR)

Civil Parish: Cannaway
Map Grid: N55
RC Parish: see Kilmurry
Diocese: CK

Civil Parish: Carrigaline (1)
Map Grid: E84 and S38
RC Parish: Douglas; also part Passage, see
Marmullane; see also below
Diocese: CK

Earliest Record: b. 11.1812; m. 11.1812
Status: LC; NLI (mf); Indexing in progress (CCAR)

Civil Parish: Carrigaline (2)
Map Grid: E84 and S38
RC Parish: Carrigaline and Templebrigid
Diocese: CK
Earliest Record: b. 1.1826; m. 1.1826
Status: LC; NLI (mf); Indexing in progress (CCAR)

Civil Parish: Carrigdownane
Map Grid: E13
RC Parish: see Kildorrery
Diocese: CY

Civil Parish: Carrigleamleary
Map Grid: E15
RC Parish: Annakissy, see Clenor
Diocese: CY

Civil Parish: Carrigrohane
Map Grid: N64 and E78
RC Parish: Ballincollig and Ballinora
Diocese: CK
Earliest Record: b. 1.1820; m. 1.1825
Missing Dates: b. 3.1828-8.1828; m. 2.1828-8.1828,
11.1857-10.1873
Status: LC; NLI (mf); Indexing in progress

Civil Parish: Carrigrohanebeg
Map Grid: N58
RC Parish: see Innishcarra
Diocese: CY

Civil Parish: Carrigtohill
Map Grid: E61
RC Parish: Carrigtwohill
Diocese: CY
Earliest Record: b. 12.1817; m. 11.1817
Status: LC; NLI (mf); Indexed by Mallow HC

Civil Parish: Castlehaven (1)
Map Grid: S53
RC Parish: Barryroe East; also Castlehaven, see below
Diocese: RO
Earliest Record: b. 8.1804; m. 11.1771
Status: LC; NLI (mf); Indexing in progress

Civil Parish: Castlehaven (2)
Map Grid: S53
RC Parish: Castlehaven
Diocese: RO
Earliest Record: b. 10.1842; m. 10.1842; d. 10.1842
Status: LC; NLI (mf); Indexing in progress

Civil Parish: Castlelyons
Map Grid: E44
RC Parish: Castlelyons
Diocese: CY
Earliest Record: b. 8.1791; m. 1.1830
Missing Dates: 1829

Status: LC; NLI (mf); Indexing in progress

Civil Parish: Castlemagner
Map Grid: N10
RC Parish: Castlemagner
Diocese: CY
Earliest Record: b. 5.1832; m. 5.1832
Status: LC; NLI (mf); Indexed by Mallow HC and
DHC

Civil Parish: Castletownroche
Map Grid: E17
RC Parish: Castletownroche
Diocese: CY
Earliest Record: b. 8.1811; m. 9.1811
Status: LC; NLI (mf); Indexing in progress

Civil Parish: Castleventry
Map Grid: S13
RC Parish: see Kilmeen (1)
Diocese: RO

Civil Parish: Churchtown
Map Grid: N27
RC Parish: see Liscarroll
Diocese: CY

Civil Parish: (Cape) Clear Island
Map Grid: S58
RC Parish: Rath and the Islands, see Tullagh
Diocese: RO

Civil Parish: Clenor
Map Grid: E16
RC Parish: Killavullen or Annakissy
Diocese: CY
Earliest Record: b. 6.1806; m. 7.1805
Status: LC; NLI (mf); Indexed by Mallow HC

Civil Parish: Clondrohid
Map Grid: N39
RC Parish: Clondrohid
Diocese: CY
Earliest Record: b. 1807; m. 1807
Missing Dates: b. 10.1843-6.1844; m. 6.1847-
1.1848
Status: LC; NLI (mf); Indexed by Mallow HC

Civil Parish: Clondulane
Map Grid: E38a
RC Parish: see Fermoy
Diocese: CY

Civil Parish: Clonfert (1)
Map Grid: N1
RC Parish: Newmarket; also Kanturk, see below
Diocese: CY
Earliest Record: b. 11.1821; m. 1.1822
Missing Dates: b. 10.1865-3.1866; m. 9.1865-3.1866
Status: LC; NLI (mf); Indexed by Mallow HC and
DHC

Civil Parish: Clonfert (2)
Map Grid: N1
RC Parish: Kanturk
Diocese: CY
Earliest Record: b. 7.1822; m. 2.1824; (and Kanturk
Workhouse b. 9.1844-)
Status: LC; NLI (mf); Indexed by Mallow HC and
DHC

Civil Parish: Clonmeen
Map Grid: N13
RC Parish: Banteer or Clonmeen, see also
Castlemagner
Diocese: CY
Earliest Record: b. 1828; m. 1828
Status: LC; NLI (mf); Indexed by Mallow HC and by
DHC

Civil Parish: Clonmel
Map Grid: E66
RC Parish: St. Colman's Cathedral, Cobh
(Queenstown)
Diocese: CK
Earliest Record: b. 1812; m. 9.1812
Missing Dates: b. 6.1842-7.1842
Status: LC; NLI (mf); Indexing in progress (CCAR)

Civil Parish: Clonmult
Map Grid: E58
RC Parish: Castlemartyr, see Mogeely (2)
Diocese: CY

Civil Parish: Clonpriest
Map Grid: E91
RC Parish: see Youghal
Diocese: CY

Civil Parish: Clontead
Map Grid: S84
RC Parish: Clontead and Ballymartle (Belgooly)
Diocese: CK
Earliest Record: b. 4.1836; m. 4.1836
Status: LC; NLI (mf); Indexing in progress (WCHC);
b. 1822-1823; 1859-1900; m. 1870-1900 (OCM
Vol. II)

Civil Parish: Cloyne
Map Grid: E98
RC Parish: Cloyne
Diocese: CY
Earliest Record: b. 9.1791; m. 2.1786
Missing Dates: b. 11.1793-10.1803
Status: LC; NLI (mf); Indexing in progress (CCAR)

Civil Parish: Coole
Map Grid: E45
RC Parish: see Castlelyons
Diocese: CY

Civil Parish: Cooliney
Map Grid: N23

RC Parish: see Ballyhea
Diocese: CY

Civil Parish: Corbally
Map Grid: N66
RC Parish: Ballincollig, see Carrigrohane
Diocese: CK

Civil Parish: Corcomohide
Map Grid: N18
RC Parish: see Co. Limerick

Civil Parish: Corkbeg
Map Grid: E107
RC Parish: see Aghada
Diocese: CY

Civil Parish: Cork (city) (1)
Map Grid: E80
RC Parish: Cathedral (North Parish)
Diocese: CK
Earliest Record: b. 7.1748; m. 7.1748
Missing Dates: m. 5.1764-4.1765
Status: LC; NLI (mf); Indexing in progress (CCAR)

Civil Parish: Cork (city) (2)
Map Grid: E80
RC Parish: South Parish, see St. Finbar
Diocese: CK

Civil Parish: Cork (city) (3)
Map Grid: E80
RC Parish: St. Patrick's
Diocese: CK
Earliest Record: b. 10.1831; m. 7.1832
Status: LC; NLI (mf); Indexing in progress (CCAR)

Civil Parish: Cork St. Nicholas
Map Grid: E80
RC Parish: Blackrock
Diocese: CK
Earliest Record: b. 7.1810; m. 9.1810
Missing Dates: b. and m. 5.1811-2.1832, 8.1837-
2.1839, 6.1839-1.1848
Status: LC; NLI (mf); Indexing in progress (CCAR)

Civil Parish: Cork St. Pauls
Map Grid: E80
RC Parish: see Cork St. Peters
Diocese: CK

Civil Parish: Cork St. Peters
Map Grid: E80
RC Parish: St. Peters and St. Pauls
Diocese: CK
Earliest Record: b. 4.1766; m. 4.1766
Missing Dates: b. 10.1766-11.1780, 9.1803-1.1809;
m. 9.1766-10.1780, 10.1803-1.1809, 8.1810-
7.1814, 8.1817-5.1834
Status: LC; NLI (mf); Indexing in progress (CCAR)

Civil Parish: Creagh
Map Grid: S56
RC Parish: Skibbereen
Diocese: RO
Earliest Record: b. 3.1814; m. 11.1837
Status: LC; NLI (mf); Indexing in progress (WCHC)

Civil Parish: Cullen (1) (Duhallow)
Map Grid: N11
RC Parish: part Dromtarriff; part Millstreet, see Drishane
Diocese: A&A

Civil Parish: Cullen (2) (Kinalea)
Map Grid: S27
RC Parish: Ballymartle (see Clontead)
Diocese: CK

Civil Parish: Currykippane
Map Grid: E75
RC Parish: Cathedral, see Cork (city) (1)
Diocese: CK

Civil Parish: Dangandonovan
Map Grid: E88
RC Parish: see Killeagh
Diocese: CY

Civil Parish: Derryvillane
Map Grid: E11
RC Parish: see Glanworth
Diocese: CY

Civil Parish: Desert
Map Grid: S79
RC Parish: Clonakilty, see Kilgarriff
Diocese: RO

Civil Parish: Desertmore
Map Grid: N61
RC Parish: Ovens, see Athowen
Diocese: CK

Civil Parish: Desertserges
Map Grid: S71
RC Parish: Enniskeane and Desertserges; also part Bandon, see Ballymodan
Diocese: CK
Earliest Record: b. 11.1794 (separate registers for Enniskeane and Desertserges); m. 9.1794
Status: LC; NLI (mf); Indexing in progress

Civil Parish: Donaghmore (1) (Ibane and Barryroe Barony)
Map Grid: S68
RC Parish: Donaghmore; also Barryroe, see Castlehaven
Diocese: CY
Earliest Record: b. 4.1803; m. 1.1790
Status: LC; NLI (mf); Indexing in progress

Civil Parish: Donaghmore (2) (East Muskerry Barony)
Map Grid: N49
RC Parish: part Aghabulloge; part Glountane, see Kilshannig

Civil Parish: Doneraile
Map Grid: E5
RC Parish: Doneraile
Diocese: CY
Earliest Record: b. 4.1815; m. 1.1815
Status: LC; NLI (mf); Indexed by Mallow HC

Civil Parish: Drimoleague (Dromdaleague)
Map Grid: S50
RC Parish: Drimoleague
Diocese: CK
Earliest Record: b. 7.1817; m. 7.1817
Missing Dates: m. 11.1863–12.1876, 1878
Status: LC; NLI (mf); Indexing in progress

Civil Parish: Drinagh
Map Grid: S51
RC Parish: see Drimoleague
Diocese: CK

Civil Parish: Drishane
Map Grid: N36
RC Parish: Millstreet (Cullen)
Diocese: A&A
Earliest Record: b. 12.1853; m. 1.1855
Status: LC; NLI (mf); Indexing in progress

Civil Parish: Dromdowney
Map Grid: N35
RC Parish: see Ballyclough
Diocese: CY

Civil Parish: Dromtarriff
Map Grid: N12
RC Parish: Dromtarriff
Diocese: A&A
Earliest Record: b. 2.1832; m. 1.1832
Status: LC; NLI (mf); Indexing in progress

Civil Parish: Dunbulloge
Map Grid: E41
RC Parish: Glanmire, see Rathcooney
Diocese: CK

Civil Parish: Dunderrow
Map Grid: N68 and S24
RC Parish: see Kinsale
Diocese: CK

Civil Parish: Dungourney
Map Grid: E57
RC Parish: Castlemartyr, see Mogeely (2)
Diocese: CY

Civil Parish: Dunisky
Map Grid: N44

RC Parish: see Kilmichael
Diocese: CK

Civil Parish: Dunmahon
Map Grid: E20
RC Parish: see Glanworth
Diocese: CY

Civil Parish: Durrus
Map Grid: S45
RC Parish: see Kilcrohane
Diocese: CK

Civil Parish: Fanlobbus
Map Grid: S9
RC Parish: Dunmanway
Diocese: CK
Earliest Record: b. 6.1818; m. 6.1818
Status: LC; NLI (mf); Indexing in progress

Civil Parish: Farahy
Map Grid: 37
RC Parish: see Kildorrery
Diocese: CY

Civil Parish: Fermoy
Map Grid: E38
RC Parish: Fermoy
Diocese: CY
Earliest Record: b. 1.1828; m. 5.1828; (also Fermoy
Workhouse baptisms from 4.1854)
Missing Dates: 8.1848-1.1849
Status: LC; NLI (mf); Indexing in progress

Civil Parish: Garrankinnefeake
Map Grid: E97
RC Parish: see Aghada
Diocese: CY

Civil Parish: Garrycloyne
Map Grid: N54
RC Parish: Blarney
Diocese: CY
Earliest Record: b. 8.1791; m. 9.1778
Missing Dates: b. 6.1792-2.1821, 1.1826-10.1826;
m. 3.1813-2.1821, 11.1825-12.1826
Status: LC; NLI (mf); Indexed by Mallow HC

Civil Parish: Garryvoe
Map Grid: E100
RC Parish: Ballymacoda, see Kilmacdonagh

Civil Parish: Glanworth
Map Grid: E18
RC Parish: Glanworth and Ballindangan
Diocese: CY
Earliest Record: b. 1.1836; m. 1.1836
Status: LC; NLI (mf); Indexed by Mallow HC

Civil Parish: Gortroe
Map Grid: E49

RC Parish: see Rathcormack
Diocese: CY

Civil Parish: Grenagh
Map Grid: N72
RC Parish: Grenagh, see Mourneabbey for pre-1840
records
Diocese: CY
Earliest Record: b. 4.1840; m. 4.1840
Status: LC; NLI (mf); Indexed by Mallow HC

Civil Parish: Hackmys
Map Grid: N22
RC Parish: Charleville, see Rathgoggan
Diocese: CY

Civil Parish: Holy Trinity (Christchurch)
Map Grid: E80
RC Parish: part St. Peters and St. Paul; part
Blackrock, see Cork-St. Nicholas
Diocese: CK

Civil Parish: Ightermurragh
Map Grid: E95
RC Parish: Ballymacoda, see Kilmacdonagh
Diocese: CY

Civil Parish: Imphrick
Map Grid: N29 and E4
RC Parish: see Ballyhea
Diocese: CY

Civil Parish: Inch
Map Grid: E103
RC Parish: see Aghada
Diocese: CY

Civil Parish: Inchigeelagh
Map Grid: N42 and S6
RC Parish: Iveleary (Inchigeela)
Diocese: CK
Earliest Record: b. 1816; m. 1816.; b. 1863-1900; m.
1816-1900 (OCM Vol. II)
Status: LC; NLI (mf); Indexing in progress

Civil Parish: Inchinabacky
Map Grid: E65
RC Parish: see Midleton
Diocese: CY

Civil Parish: Inishcarra
Map Grid: N52
RC Parish: Inishcarra
Diocese: CY
Earliest Record: b. 7.1814; m. 8.1814
Missing Dates: b. 9.1844-1.1845
Status: LC; NLI (mf); Indexed by Mallow HC

Civil Parish: Inishannon
Map Grid: S22
RC Parish: Inishannon
Diocese: CK

Earliest Record: b. 8.1825; m. 8.1825
Status: LC; NLI (mf); Indexing in progress

Civil Parish: Inishkenny
Map Grid: N69 and E83
RC Parish: Ballincollig, see Carrigrohane
Diocese: CK

Civil Parish: Island
Map Grid: S62
RC Parish: part Clonakilty, see Kilgarriff; part
Rathbarry, see Ardfield
Diocese: RO

Civil Parish: Kilbolane (see also Co. Limerick)
Map Grid: N17
RC Parish: Freemount, see Knocktemple
Diocese: CY

Civil Parish: Kilbonane
Map Grid: N60
RC Parish: see Kilmurry
Diocese: CK

Civil Parish: Kilbrin
Map Grid: N7
RC Parish: see Ballyclough
Diocese: CK

Civil Parish: Kilbrittain
Map Grid: S73
RC Parish: Kilbrittain
Diocese: CK
Earliest Record: b. 8.1810
Status: LC; NLI (mf); Indexing in progress

Civil Parish: Kilbrogan
Map Grid: S19
RC Parish: Bandon, see Ballymodan
Diocese: CK

Civil Parish: Kilbroney
Map Grid: N30
RC Parish: see Buttevant
Diocese: CY

Civil Parish: Kilcaskan (see also Co. Kerry)
Map Grid: S2
RC Parish: Glengarriffe, see Kilmacomoge
Diocese: RO

Civil Parish: Kilcatherine
Map Grid: S1
RC Parish: Eyeries
Diocese: RO
Earliest Record: b. 4.1843; m. 2.1824
Status: LC; NLI (mf); Indexing in progress

Civil Parish: Kilcoe
Map Grid: S48
RC Parish: see Aghadown
Diocese: RO

Civil Parish: Kilcorcoran
Map Grid: N6
RC Parish: Kanturk, see Clonfert
Diocese: CY

Civil Parish: Kilcorney
Map Grid: N37
RC Parish: see Clonmeen
Diocese: CY

Civil Parish: Kilcredan
Map Grid: E101
RC Parish: Lady's Bridge, see Kilmacdonagh
Diocese: CY

Civil Parish: Kilcrohane
Map Grid: S44
RC Parish: Muintervara or Durrus
Diocese: CK
Earliest Record: b. 5.1820; m. 2.1819
Status: LC; NLI (mf); Indexing in progress

Civil Parish: Kilcrumper
Map Grid: E21
RC Parish: part Fermoy; part Kilworth
Diocese: CY

Civil Parish: Kilcully
Map Grid: E74
RC Parish: Glanmire, see Rathcooney
Diocese: CK

Civil Parish: Kilcummer
Map Grid: E26
RC Parish: see Castletownroche
Diocese: CY

Civil Parish: Kildorrery
Map Grid: E30
RC Parish: Kildorrery
Diocese: CY
Earliest Record: b. 5.1824; m. 1.1803
Missing Dates: b. 9.1853 onward
Status: LC; NLI (mf); Indexed by Mallow HC

Civil Parish: Kilfaughnabeg
Map Grid: S14
RC Parish: see Kilmacabea
Diocese: RO

Civil Parish: Kilgarriff
Map Grid: S75
RC Parish: Clonakilty
Diocese: RO
Earliest Record: b. 8.1809; m. 1.1811
Status: LC; NLI (mf); Indexing in progress

Civil Parish: Kilgrogan
Map Grid: N28
RC Parish: see Liscarroll
Diocese: CY

Civil Parish: Kilgullane
Map Grid: E34
RC Parish: see Glanworth
Diocese: CY

Civil Parish: Kilkerranmore
Map Grid: S59
RC Parish: part Rosscarbery, see Ross; part Kilmeen;
part Rathbarry, see Ardfield

Civil Parish: Killaconenagh
Map Grid: S4
RC Parish: Castletownbere, see Kilnamanagh
Diocese: RO

Civil Parish: Killanully
Map Grid: E86 and S39
RC Parish: Douglas, see Carrigaline (1)
Diocese: CK

Civil Parish: Killaspugmullane
Map Grid: E51
RC Parish: Watergrasshill, see Ardnageehy
Diocese: CK

Civil Parish: Killathy
Map Grid: E28
RC Parish: see Castletownroche
Diocese: CY

Civil Parish: Killeagh
Map Grid: E90
RC Parish: Killeagh
Diocese: CY
Earliest Record: b. 3.1829; m. 11.1822
Status: LC; NLI (mf); Indexed by Mallow HC

Civil Parish: Killeenemer
Map Grid: E19
RC Parish: see Glanworth
Diocese: CY

Civil Parish: Killowen
Map Grid: S18
RC Parish: see Desertserges
Diocese: CK

Civil Parish: Kilmacabea
Map Grid: S11
RC Parish: Kilmacabea
Diocese: RO
Earliest Record: b. 6.1832; m. 7.1832
Missing Dates: m. 2.1865-5.1865
Status: LC; NLI (mf); Indexing in progress (WCHC)

Civil Parish: Kilmacdonagh
Map Grid: E96
RC Parish: Ballymacoda and Lady's Bridge
Diocese: CY
Earliest Record: b. 11.1835; m. 9.1835
Status: LC; NLI (mf); Indexed by Mallow HC

Civil Parish: Kilmaclenan
Map Grid: N33
RC Parish: see Ballyclough
Diocese: CY

Civil Parish: Kilmacomogue (1)
Map Grid: S5
RC Parish: Glengarriffe
Diocese: CK
Earliest Record: 7.1822
Status: LC; NLI (mf); Indexing in progress (WCHC)

Civil Parish: Kilmacomogue (2)
Map Grid: S5
RC Parish: Bantry
Diocese: CK
Earliest Record: 7.1822 (parts of 1788, 1791-92,
1794-99, 1808-09, 1812-14, and 1822-24 also
exist); 5.1788
Missing Dates: 12.1857-1.1872
Status: LC; NLI (mf); Indexing in progress (WCHC)

Civil Parish: Kilmahon
Map Grid: E104
RC Parish: see Cloyne
Diocese: CY

Civil Parish: Kilmaloda
Map Grid: S72
RC Parish: see Timoleague
Diocese: RO

Civil Parish: Kilmeen (1) (W. Carbery)
Map Grid: S10
RC Parish: Kilmeen
Diocese: RO
Earliest Record: b. 8.1821
Status: LC; NLI (mf); Indexing in progress (WCHC)

Civil Parish: Kilmeen (2) (Duhallow)
Map Grid: N5
RC Parish: Boherbue (also Co. Kerry)
Diocese: A&A
Earliest Record: b. 7.1833; m. 3.1863
Missing Dates: b. 12.1860-2.1863
Status: LC; NLI (mf); Indexing in progress (WCHC)

Civil Parish: Kilmichael
Map Grid: N45 and S7
RC Parish: Kilmichael
Diocese: CK
Earliest Record: b. 10.1819; m. 1.1819
Missing Dates: m. 2.1850-1.1851
Status: LC; NLI (mf); Indexing in progress (MHC)

Civil Parish: Kilmoe
Map Grid: S49
RC Parish: Goleen (West Schull)
Diocese: CK
Earliest Record: b. 1.1827; m. 1.1827
Status: LC; NLI (mf); Indexing in progress (WCHC)

Civil Parish: Kilmoney
Map Grid: S42
RC Parish: see Carrigaline

Civil Parish: Kilmonogue
Map Grid: S32
RC Parish: see Clontead
Diocese: CK

Civil Parish: Kilmurry
Map Grid: N47
RC Parish: Kilmurry
Diocese: CK
Earliest Record: b. 6.1786; m. 1.1812
Missing Dates: b. 1803-05 mutilated
Status: LC; NLI (mf); Indexing in progress (MHC)

Civil Parish: Kilnagleary
Map Grid: N63 and E82
RC Parish: Ballincollig, see Carrigrohane
Diocese: CK

Civil Parish: Kilnagross
Map Grid: S77
RC Parish: Clonakilty, see Kilgarriff
Diocese: RO

Civil Parish: Kilnamanagh
Map Grid: S3
RC Parish: Castletownbere
Diocese: RO
Earliest Record: b. 9.1819; m. 7.1819
Status: LC; NLI (mf); Indexing in progress (WCHC)

Civil Parish: Kilnamartry
Map Grid: N40
RC Parish: Kilnamartyra
Diocese: CY
Earliest Record: b. 1.1803; m. 1.1803
Missing Dates: m. 6.1833-9.1939
Status: LC; NLI (mf); Indexed by Mallow HC

Civil Parish: Kilpatrick
Map Grid: S31
RC Parish: see Tracton
Diocese: CK

Civil Parish: Kilphelan
Map Grid: E35
RC Parish: Mitchelstown, see Brigown
Diocese: CY

Civil Parish: Kilquane (1)
Map Grid: E3
RC Parish: see Kilquane, Co. Limerick

Civil Parish: Kilquane (2)
Map Grid: E50
RC Parish: Glounthaune, see Caherlag
Diocese: CK

Civil Parish: Kilroan
Map Grid: S82
RC Parish: Courcey's, see Ballinadee
Diocese: CK

Civil Parish: Kilroe
Map Grid: N8
RC Parish: Kanturk, see Clonfert (2)
Diocese: CY

Civil Parish: Kilshanahan
Map Grid: E48
RC Parish: Watergrasshill, see Ardnageehy
Diocese: CK

Civil Parish: Kilshannig
Map Grid: N16
RC Parish: Glountane or Glantane, also Kilpadder.
Not to be confused with Glounthaune (see Caherlag).
Specific Kilshannig reg. 1842-1850 bound into
Glantane register.
Diocese: CY
Earliest Record: b. 5.1829; m. 1858
Missing Dates: b. 8.1844-5.1847
Status: LC; NLI (mf); Indexed by Mallow HC

Civil Parish: Kilsillagh
Map Grid: S69
RC Parish: Barryroe, see Castlehaven (1)
Diocese: RO

Civil Parish: Kilworth
Map Grid: E36
RC Parish: Kilworth
Diocese: CY
Earliest Record: b. 9.1829; m. 10.1829
Status: LC; NLI (mf); Indexing in progress

Civil Parish: Kinneigh
Map Grid: S8
RC Parish: part Enniskeane, see Desertserges; part
Murragh
Diocese: CK

Civil Parish: Kinnure
Map Grid: S33
RC Parish: see Tracton
Diocese: CK

Civil Parish: Kinsale
Map Grid: S85
RC Parish: Kinsale
Diocese: CK
Earliest Record: b. 1.1805; m. 8.1828
Missing Dates: b. 7.1806-1.1815
Status: LC; NLI (mf); Indexing in progress (WCHC)

Civil Parish: Knockavilly
Map Grid: N67 and S21
RC Parish: see Inishannon
Diocese: CK

Civil Parish: Knockmourne
Map Grid: E68
RC Parish: Conna
Diocese: CY
Earliest Record: b. 9.1834; m. 1834
Missing Dates: b. 9.1844–12.1845
Status: LC; NLI (mf); Indexed by Mallow HC

Civil Parish: Knocktemple
Map Grid: N3
RC Parish: Milford or Freemount
Diocese: CY
Earliest Record: b. 9.1827; m. 10.1827
Missing Dates: b. 3.1840–1.1858 (except 7.1843–12.1843)
Status: LC; NLI (mf); Indexed by Mallow HC

Civil Parish: Lackeen
Map Grid: N26
RC Parish: see Liscarroll
Diocese: CY

Civil Parish: Leighmoney
Map Grid: S28
RC Parish: see Inishannon
Diocese: CK

Civil Parish: Leitrim
Map Grid: E39
RC Parish: see Kilworth
Diocese: CY

Civil Parish: Liscarroll
Map Grid: N25
RC Parish: Churchtown or Liscarroll
Diocese: CY
Earliest Record: b. 3.1812; m. 2.1813
Status: LC; NLI (mf); Indexed by Mallow HC

Civil Parish: Liscleary
Map Grid: S40
RC Parish: Douglas, see Carrigaline (1)
Diocese: CK

Civil Parish: Lisgoold
Map Grid: E54
RC Parish: Lisgoold
Diocese: CY
Earliest Record: b. 7.1807; m. 10.1821
Status: LC; NLI (mf); Indexed by Mallow HC

Civil Parish: Lislee
Map Grid: S67
RC Parish: Barryroe, see Castlehaven (1)
Diocese: RO

Civil Parish: Lismore and Mocollop
Map Grid: E40
RC Parish: see Co. Waterford
Diocese: LS

Civil Parish: Litter
Map Grid: E29
RC Parish: see Fermoy (also, Templenoe village is in Castletownroche parish)
Diocese: CY

Civil Parish: Little Island
Map Grid: E63
RC Parish: Glounthaune, see Caherlag
Diocese: CK

Civil Parish: Macloneigh
Map Grid: N43
RC Parish: see Kilmichael
Diocese: CK

Civil Parish: Macroney
Map Grid: E37
RC Parish: see Kilworth
Diocese: CY

Civil Parish: Macroom
Map Grid: N41
RC Parish: Macroom
Diocese: CY
Earliest Record: b. 9.1805; m. 1.1780
Missing Dates: b. 11.1843–12.1843
Status: LC; NLI (mf); Indexing in progress

Civil Parish: Magourney
Map Grid: N51
RC Parish: see Aghabulloge
Diocese: CY

Civil Parish: Mallow
Map Grid: N15 and E14
RC Parish: Mallow
Diocese: CY
Earliest Record: b. 1.1809; m. 4.1757
Missing Dates: b. 7.1809–6.1817, 2.1818–8.1820, 12.1828–4.1832; m. 11.1823–8.1825, 7.1828–4.1832
Status: LC; NLI (mf); Indexed by Mallow HC

Civil Parish: Marmullane
Map Grid: S36
RC Parish: Passage
Diocese: CK
Earliest Record: b. 4.1795; m. 4.1795
Missing Dates: m. 5.1831–5.1832
Status: LC; NLI (mf); Indexing in progress

Civil Parish: Marshalstown
Map Grid: E32
RC Parish: Mitchelstown, see Brigown
Diocese: CY

Civil Parish: Matehy
Map Grid: N53
RC Parish: see Inishcarra
Diocese: CY

Civil Parish: Midleton
Map Grid: E93
RC Parish: Midleton
Diocese: CY
Earliest Record: b. 9.1819; m. 10.1819
Status: LC; NLI (mf); Indexed by Mallow HC

Civil Parish: Mogeely (1) (Kinnatalloon)
Map Grid: E71
RC Parish: Conna, see Knockmourne

Civil Parish: Mogeely (2)
Map Grid: E89
RC Parish: Imogeela (Castlemartyr)
Diocese: CY
Earliest Record: b. 2.1835; m. 9.1833
Status: LC; NLI (mf); Indexed by Mallow HC

Civil Parish: Mogeesha
Map Grid: E64
RC Parish: see Carrigtohill
Diocese: CY

Civil Parish: Monanimy
Map Grid: E24
RC Parish: Killavullen, see Clenor
Diocese: CY

Civil Parish: Monkstown
Map Grid: S37
RC Parish: Passage, see Marmullane
Diocese: CY

Civil Parish: Mourneabbey
Map Grid: N71 and E22
RC Parish: part Mourne Abbey (Ballinamona), see
also Mallow
Diocese: CY
Earliest Record: b. 1.1829; m. 10.1829
Status: LC; NLI (mf); Indexed by Mallow HC

Civil Parish: Moviddy
Map Grid: N59
RC Parish: see Kilmurry
Diocese: CK

Civil Parish: Murragh
Map Grid: S15
RC Parish: Murragh
Diocese: CK
Earliest Record: b. 1.1834; m. 1.1834
Status: LC; NLI (mf); Indexing in progress

Civil Parish: Myross
Map Grid: S54
RC Parish: see Castlehaven (2) (church)
Diocese: RO

Civil Parish: Nohaval
Map Grid: S34
RC Parish: see Tracton
Diocese: CK

Civil Parish: Nohavaldaly
Map Grid: N4
RC Parish: part Boherbue, see Kilmeen (2); part
Clonfert
Diocese: A&A

Civil Parish: Rahan
Map Grid: E23
RC Parish: part Mallow; part Ballinamona, see
Mourneabbey
Diocese: CY

Civil Parish: Rathbarry
Map Grid: S60
RC Parish: see Ardfield
Diocese: RO

Civil Parish: Rathclarin
Map Grid: S78
RC Parish: see Kilbritain

Civil Parish: Rathcooney
Map Grid: E73
RC Parish: Glanmire
Diocese: CK
Earliest Record: b. 11.1806; m. 1.1803
Missing Dates: b. 9.1816-5.1818; m. 5.1817-5.1818
Status: LC; NLI (mf); Indexing in progress

Civil Parish: Rathcormack
Map Grid: E43
RC Parish: Rathcormack
Diocese: CY
Earliest Record: b. 1.1792; m. 1.1829
Status: LC; NLI (mf); Indexing in progress

Civil Parish: Rathgoggan
Map Grid: N21
RC Parish: Charleville
Diocese: CY
Earliest Record: b. 5.1827; m. 8.1774
Missing Dates: m. 11.1792-11.1794, 7.1822-6.1827
Status: LC; NLI (mf); Indexing in progress

Civil Parish: Rincurran
Map Grid: S86
RC Parish: see Kinsale
Diocese: CK

Civil Parish: Ringrone
Map Grid: S81
RC Parish: Courcey's, see Ballinadee
Diocese: CK

Civil Parish: Rosscarbery (Ross)
Map Grid: S12
RC Parish: Rosscarbery
Diocese: RO
Earliest Record: b. 11.1814; m. 1.1820
Status: LC; NLI (mf); Indexing in progress

Civil Parish: Rosskeen
Map Grid: N14
RC Parish: see Castlemagner
Diocese: CY

Civil Parish: Rostellan
Map Grid: E102
RC Parish: see Aghada
Diocese: CY

Civil Parish: St. Anne, Shandon
Map Grid: E77
RC Parish: part Cathedral, see Cork (city) (1); part SS Peter and Paul, see Cork St. Peter

Civil Parish: St. Finbar
Map Grid: N62 and E79
RC Parish: St. Finbar's South; also part SS Peter and Paul, see Cork St. Peter
Diocese: CK
Earliest Record: b. 8.1756; m. 3.1775
Missing Dates: b. 1.1757-7.1760; 9.1763-3.1774; 7.1777-1.1789
Status: LC; NLI (mf); Indexing in progress (CCAR)

Civil Parish: St. Mary, Shandon
Map Grid: E76
RC Parish: Cathedral, see Cork (city) (1)

Civil Parish: St. Michael
Map Grid: E46
RC Parish: see Templemichael
Diocese: CK

Civil Parish: St. Natlash
Map Grid: E10
RC Parish: see Kildorrery
Diocese: CY

Civil Parish: St. Nicholas
Map Grid: N65 and E81
RC Parish: see Cork
Diocese: CK

Civil Parish: St. Pauls
Map Grid: E80
RC Parish: see Cork
Diocese: CK

Civil Parish: St. Peters
Map Grid: E80
RC Parish: see Cork

Civil Parish: Shandrum
Map Grid: N19
RC Parish: Shandrum; see also Ballyhea
Diocese: CY
Earliest Record: b. 3.1829; m. 1829
Status: LC; NLI (mf); Indexed by Mallow HC

Civil Parish: Skull
Map Grid: S47

RC Parish: Skull
Diocese: CK
Earliest Record: b. 10.1807; m. 2.1809
Missing Dates: b. 9.1815-1.1816; m. 11.1815-1.1816, 11.1832-2.1833, 9.1870-1.1871
Status: LC; NLI (mf); Indexing in progress (WCHC)

Civil Parish: Subulter
Map Grid: N9
Old name: see Ballyclough
Diocese: CY

Civil Parish: Templebodan
Map Grid: E55
RC Parish: see Lisgoold
Diocese: CY

Civil Parish: Templebreedy
Map Grid: S43
RC Parish: see Carrigaline (church)
Diocese: CK

Civil Parish: Templebryan
Map Grid: S76
RC Parish: see Clonakilty, see Kilgarriff
Diocese: RO

Civil Parish: Templemartin
Map Grid: S16
RC Parish: part Bandon, see Ballymodan
Diocese: CK

Civil Parish: Templemichael
Map Grid: S23
RC Parish: Glanmire, see Rathcooney
Diocese: CK

Civil Parish: Templemolaga
Map Grid: E31
RC Parish: see Kildorrery
Diocese: CY

Civil Parish: Templenacarriga
Map Grid: E56
RC Parish: see Lisgoold
Diocese: CY

Civil Parish: Templeomalus
Map Grid: S63
RC Parish: Clonakilty, see Kilgarriff
Diocese: RO

Civil Parish: Templequinlan
Map Grid: S64
RC Parish: see Clonakilty, see Kilgarriff
Diocese: RO

Civil Parish: Templeroan
Map Grid: E6
RC Parish: see Doneraile
Diocese: CY

Civil Parish: Temple Robin (Great Island)
Map Grid: E67
RC Parish: Cobh, see Clonmel
Diocese: CY

Civil Parish: Templetrine
Map Grid: S80
RC Parish: Courcey's, see Ballinadee
Diocese: CK

Civil Parish: Templeusque
Map Grid: E47
RC Parish: Glanmire, see Rathcooney
Diocese: CK

Civil Parish: Timoleague
Map Grid: S65
RC Parish: Timoleague; also Barryroe, see
Castlehaven
Diocese: RO
Earliest Record: b. 11.1842; m. 4.1843
Status: LC; NLI (mf); Indexing in progress

Civil Parish: Tisaxon or Teighsasson
Map Grid: S83
RC Parish: see Kinsale
Diocese: CK

Civil Parish: Titeskin (Kilteskin)
Map Grid: E106
RC Parish: see Cloyne
Diocese: CY

Civil Parish: Trabolgan
Map Grid: E109
RC Parish: see Aghada
Diocese: CY

Civil Parish: Tracton
Map Grid: S30
RC Parish: Tracton Abbey
Diocese: CK
Earliest Record: b. 12.1802; m. 6.1840
Status: LC; NLI (mf); Indexing in progress

Civil Parish: Tullagh
Map Grid: S57
RC Parish: Inisherkin is part of Rath; remainder is in
Skibbereen, see Creagh
Diocese: RO
Earliest Record: b. 7.1818; m. 1.1819
Missing Dates: b. 9.1851–2.1852; m. 8.1851–
10.1851
Status: LC; NLI (mf); Indexing in progress (WCHC)

Civil Parish: Tullilease
Map Grid: N2
RC Parish: Freemount, see Knocktemple
Diocese: CY

Civil Parish: Wallstown
Map Grid: E9
RC Parish: Killavullen, see Clenor
Diocese: CY

Civil Parish: Whitechurch
Map Grid: N73 and E72
RC Parish: Blarney, see Garrycloyne
Diocese: CY

Civil Parish: Youghal
Map Grid: E92
RC Parish: Youghal
Diocese: CY
Earliest Record: b. 9.1803; m. 12.1801
Missing Dates: 6.1862–6.1866
Status: LC; NLI (mf); Indexing in progress

Commercial and Social Directories

1787

Richard Lucas's *General Directory of the Kingdom of Ireland* contains lists of traders in Bandon, Cork, Cobh, Innishannon, Kinsale, Passage, and Youghal. Also reprinted in *The Irish Genealogist* 4 (1): 37–46.

1797

J. Nixon's *Cork Almanac* contains lists of merchants and traders in the city.

1809

Holden's *Triennial Directory* covers the city of Cork and has alphabetical lists of traders.

1810

West's *Directory of Cork* contains lists of gentry, traders, and professionals.

1812

Connor's *Cork Directory* contains alphabetical lists of merchants and traders. Also issued in 1817, 1821, 1826, and 1828.

1817

Gentlemens and Citizens Cork Almanac, published by Geary, gives lists of physicians, bankers, clergy, and public officials.

1820

J. Pigot's *Commercial Directory of Ireland* contains information on the gentry, nobility, and traders in and around the towns of Bandon, Cork, Kinsale, and Youghal.

1824

J. Pigot's *City of Dublin and Hibernian Provincial Directory* includes traders, nobility, gentry, and clergy lists of Bandon, Bantry, Castlelyons, Castlemartyr, Charleville, Clonakilty, Cloyne, Cork, Cobh, Doneraile, Fermoy, Kanturk, Kilworth, Kinsale, Macroom, Mallow, Midleton, Millstreet, Mitchelstown, Newmarket, Rathcormac, Skibbereen, and Youghal.

1842

General Directory of the City and County of Cork, with a separate alphabetical listing for city and county of nobility, gentry, and clergy. NLI.

1844

General P.O. Directory of Cork contains general alphabetical directory and trades directory of Cork and list of gentry and traders for each of the following: Ballincollig, Ballinhassig, Ballydehob and Skibbereen, Bandon, Bantry, Blackrock, Buttevant, Carrigaline, Castlelyons, Castlemartyr, Castletown, Castletownroche, Castletownsend, Charleville, Clonakilty, Cloyne, Coachford, Cove, Crookstown, Doneraile, Douglas, Dunmanway, Enniskeane, Fermoy, Glanmire, Glounthaun, Inniscarra, Innoshannon, Kildorrery, Killeagh, Killinardish, Kanturk, Kinsale, Kilworth, Macroom, Mallow, Rathcormac, Rosscarbery, Shanagarry, Skibbereen, Tallow, Timoleague, Unionhall, Watergrasshill, Whitegate, and Youghal.

1846

Slater's *National Commercial Directory of Ireland* lists nobility, clergy, traders, etc. in Ballincollig, Bandon and Innishannon, Bantry, Charleville, Clonakilty, Cloyne and Castlemartyr, Cork, Cove, Doneraile, Fermoy, Kanturk, Kilworth, Kinsale, Macroom, Mallow, Midleton, Millstreet, Mitchelstown, Newmarket, Rathcormac, Skibbereen and Castletownsend, and Youghal.

1856

Slater's *Royal National Commercial Directory of Ireland* lists nobility, gentry, clergy, traders, etc. in Ballincollig, Bandon and Innishannon, Bantry and Glengariff, Charleville, Clonakilty, Cloyne and Castlemartyr, Cork, Doneraile, Dunmanway, Fermoy, Kanturk, Kilworth, Kinsale, Macroom, Mallow, Midleton, Millstreet, Mitchelstown, Newmarket, Passage and Monkstown, Queenstown (Cove), Rathcormac and Castlelyons, Ross, Skibbereen, Castletownsend and Baltimore, Skull and Ballydehob, and Youghal.

1870

Slater's *Directory of Ireland* contains trade, nobility, and clergy lists for Ballincollig, Bandon, Bantry, Charleville, Clonakilty, Cloyne and Castlemartyr, Cork, Doneraile, Dunmanway, Fermoy, Kanturk, Kilworth, Kinsale, Macroom, Mallow, Midleton, Millstreet, Mitchelstown, Newmarket, Passage, Queenstown (Cobh), Rathcormac and Castlelyons, Rosscarbery, Skibbereen and Ballydehob, and Youghal.

1875

Guy's *Directory of the City and County of Cork* gives residents, traders, and large farmers in each postal district. Issued annually to 1913.

1881

Slater's *Royal National Commercial Directory of Ireland* contains lists of traders, clergy, nobility, and farmers in adjoining parishes of the towns of Bandon, Bantry and Glengariff, Charleville, Clonakilty, Cloyne and Castlemartyr, Cork, Dunmanway, Fermoy, Kanturk, Kinsale, Macroom, Mallow, Midleton, Millstreet, Mitchelstown, Newmarket, Passage and Monkstown, Queenstown (Cove), Rathcormac and Castlelyons, Rosscarbery, Skibbereen, Castletownsend and Leap, Skull and Ballydehob, and Youghal.

1886

Francis Guy's *Postal Directory* of Munster lists gentry, clergy, traders, principal farmers, teachers, and police sergeants in each postal district of the county and has a listing of magistrates, clergy, and the professions for the whole county. Issued annually from 1889.

1893

Francis Guy's *Directory of Munster* lists traders and farmers in each of the postal districts of the county and a general alphabetical index to persons in the whole county.

1894

Slater's *Royal Directory of Ireland* lists traders, police, teachers, farmers, and private residents in each of the towns, villages, and parishes of the county.

Family History

"Co. Cork Families 1630-5." *J. Cork Hist. & Arch. Soc.* 204 (1961): 126-29, 635-38; 205 (1962): 36-40; 1638-57: 206 (1962): 139-43; (1951): 126-29.

Gillman, Herbert Webb. "The Chieftains of Pobal-I-Callaghan, Co. Cork." *J. Cork Hist. & Arch. Soc.* N.S. 3 (1897): 201-20.

"Barrymore." *J. Cork Hist. & Arch. Soc.* N.S. 5 (1899): 1–17, 77–92, 153–68, 209–24; 6 (1900): 1–11, 65–87, 129–46, 193–209; 7 (1901): 1–16, 65–80, 129–38; 8 (1902): 1–17, 129–50.

"Chinnery of Co. Cork." *Ir. Anc.* 7 (2) (1975): 67–69.

"George Chinnery, 1774–1852, With Some Account of his Family and Genealogy." *J. Cork Hist. & Arch. Soc.* N.S. 37 (1932): 11–21; 38 (1933): 1–15.

Rylands, J.P. *Some Account of the Clayton Family of Thelwall, Co. Chester, Afterwards of St. Dominick's Abbey, Doneraile, and Mallow, Co. Cork.* Liverpool, 1880.

"Cole of Co. Cork." *Gen.* 3 (1879): 289–91.

Cole, R.L. *The Cole Family of West Carbery.* Belfast, 1943.

"Conner Papers." (Manch, Co. Cork.) *Anal. Hib.* 15: 153–59.

"The Conran Family of Co. Cork." *Ir. Gen.* 3 (9): 341–50.

Copinger, W.A. *A History of the Copingers or Coppingers of Co. Cork.* Manchester, 1882.

"The Cotter Family of Rockforest, Co. Cork." *J. Cork Hist. & Arch. Soc.* N.S. 43 (1938): 21–31.

"Notes on the Cotter Family of Rockforest, Co. Cork." *J. Cork Hist. & Arch. Soc.* N.S. 14 (1908): 1–12.

"A Genealogical Note on the Family of Cramer or Coghill." *J. Cork Hist. & Arch. Soc.* N.S. 16 (1910): 66–81, 143.

"Crone of Co. Cork." *Ir. Anc.* 1 (2) (1969): 77–88.

de Barry. *Etude sur l'histoire des Bary-Barry.* Vieux-Dieu-Les Anvers, 1927.

de Bary, Alfred. *De l'origine des Barry d'Irlande.* Guebwiller, 1900.

"The Family Register of John Dennehy of Fermoy." *Ir. Gen.* 1 (1) (1937): 23–25.

"The Denny Family." In *History of Co. Kerry,* 242–60. Dublin, 1910.

"Dennys of Cork." *J. Cork Hist. & Arch. Soc.* N.S. 28 (1922): 45–46.

"The Drews of Mocollop Castle." *J. Cork Hist. & Arch. Soc.* 24 (1918): 4–6.

"The Fleetwoods of the Co. Cork." *R.S.A.I.* 38 (1908): 103–25.

"Gray of Cork City and Lehana." *Ir. Anc.* 7 (1) (1975): 11.

"Gray of Co. Cork." Pedigree in *Swanzy Notebooks.* RCB Library, Dublin.

"The Harmons of Cork." *Ir. Gen.* 3 (12): 524–28.

"The Herricks of Co. Cork." *Ir. Gen.* 3 (8): 291–98.

"The Family of Jackson of Wooldale in the Co. of Cork." *Gen.* N.S. 37 (1920): 29–33.

"The Origins of Co. Cork Kingstons." *J. Cork Hist. & Arch. Soc.* 76 (1981): 75–99.

Trimble, D. *The Kingston Family in Co. Cork.* 1929.

The Family of Limerick of Schull, Co. Cork. 1909. Also printed in *J. Cork Hist. & Arch. Soc.* N.S. 13: 120–27.

Day, Robert. "Loftus Family Record." *J. Cork Hist. & Arch. Soc.* N.S. 2 (1896): 491–92.

"Longfield Papers." (Longueville, Co. Cork.) *Anal. Hib.* 115: 135–42.

"The Longs of Muskerry and Kinalea." *J. Cork Hist. & Arch. Soc.* N.S. 51 (1946): 1–9.

"The Pedigree and Succession of the House of MacCarthy Mor." *R.S.A.I.* 51 (1921): 32–48.

"The Clann Carthaigh (McCarthy)." *Kerry Arch. Mag.* 1 (1908–12): 160–79, 195–208, 233–51, 320–38, 385–402, 447–66; 2 (1912–14): 3–24, 53–74, 105–22, 181–202; 3 (1914–16): 55–72, 123–39, 206–26, 271–92; 4 (1917): 207–14.

MacCarthy, D. *Historical Pedigree of the MacCarthys.* Exeter, 1880.

McCarthy, Samuel T. *The MacCarthys of Munster.* Dundalk, 1922.

"MacCarthys of Drishane." *J. Cork Hist. & Arch. Soc.* 23 (1917): 114–15.

"The MacFinnin MacCarthys of Ardtully." *J. Cork Hist. & Arch. Soc.* N.S. 2 (1896): 210–14.

"Some McCarthys of Blarney and Ballea." *J. Cork Hist. & Arch. Soc.* N.S. 59 (1954): 1–10, 82–88; 60 (1955): 1–5, 75–79.

"The Lords of Ella: the Macdonoghs of Duhallow." *J. Cork Hist. & Arch. Soc.* 3 (1894): 157–62.

Leabhar Chlainn Suibhne: an Account of the MacSweeney Families in Ireland, with Pedigree. Edited by Rev. Paul Walsh. Dublin, 1920.

Sweeney, R. Mingo. *Sween, Clan of the Battle-axe, a Brief History of the MacSweeney (Mac Suibhne) Galloglass.* Prince Edward Island: Bonshaw, 1968.

"The Co. Cork Ancestry of the Maddens of Australia." *Ir. Anc.* 16 (1): 14–20.

"The Nagles of Mount Nagle (Co. Cork)." *Ir. Gen.* 2 (1954): 337–48.

O'Connell, Basil. "The Nagles of Mount Nagle (Co. Cork) and Later of Jamestown and Dunower, Barts." *Ir. Gen.* 3 (1955): 377–89.

"A Defeated Clan, (The O'Crowleys)." *J. Cork Hist. & Arch. Soc.* N.S. 36 (1931): 24–28.

"O'Crowley Pedigree from the Carew Mss. and Other Sources." *J. Cork Hist. & Arch. Soc.* N.S. 35 (1930): 89.

"The O'Crowleys of Coill t-Sealbhaigh." *J. Cork Hist. & Arch. Soc.* N.S. 56 (1951): 91–94; 57 (1952): 1–6, 105–09; 58 (1953): 7–11.

Burke, J. "The O'Driscolls and Other Septs of Corca Laidh." *J. Cork Hist. & Arch. Soc.* N.S. 16 (1910): 24–31.

"The O'Heas of South-west Cork." *J. Cork Hist. & Arch. Soc.* N.S. 51 (1951): 97–107.

"A History of the O'Mahony Septs of Kinelmeky and Ivagha." *J. Cork Hist. & Arch. Soc.* N.S. 12 (1906): 183–95; 13 (1907): 27–36, 73–80, 105–15, 182–92; 14 (1908): 12–21, 74–81, 127–41, 189–99; 15 (1909):

7-18, 63-75, 118-26, 184-96; 16 (1910): 9-24, 97-113.

"The O'Mullanes." *J. Cork Hist. & Arch. Soc.* N.S. 48 (1953): 97.

"The O'Mullanes and Whitechurch." *J. Cork Hist. & Arch. Soc.* N.S. 48 (1953): 20-21.

"The O'Regans of Carbery." *J. Cork Hist. & Arch. Soc.* N.S. 63 (1958): 18-22.

The O'Shaughnessys of Munster. See Family History—Co. Galway.

"History of the O'Sullivans." *J. Cork Hist. & Arch. Soc.* 4 (1898): 120-31, 207-12, 255-78.

Sullivan, T.D. *Bantry, Berehaven and the O'Sullivan Sept.* Dublin, 1908.

"Admiral Penn, William Penn, and Their Descendants in Co. Cork." *J. Cork Hist. & Arch. Soc.* N.S. 14 (1908): 105-14, 177-89.

"The Penroses of Woodhill." *J. Cork Hist. & Arch. Soc.* 241, 242 (1980).

Ffolliott, Rosemary. *The Pooles of Mayfield and Other Irish Families: Nisbett; Meade; Flemings.* With illus. and genealogical tables. Dublin: Hodges, 1958.

Pratt, John. *The Family of Pratt of Gawsworth and Carrigrohane, Co. Cork.* 1925.

"Puxleys of Dunboy, Co Cork." *Irish Family History* 5 (1989): 7-16.

"The Pynes of Co. Cork." *Ir. Gen.* 6 (6) (1985): 696-710; 7 (1) (1986): 31-50; 7 (2) (1987): 229-244.

"Some Account of the Roberts Family of Kilmoney." *J. Cork Hist. & Arch. Soc.* N.S. 24 (1929): 107-10.

"Roche Papers (Co. Cork)." *Anal. Hib.* 15: 143-52.

Donnelly, Eithne. "The Roches, Lords of Fermoy." *J. Cork Hist. & Arch. Soc.* N.S. 38 (1933): 86-91; 39 (1934): 38-40, 57-68; 40 (1935): 37-42, 63-73; 41 (1936): 2-28, 78-84; 42 (1937): 40-52.

"A Cork Branch of the Rochford Family." *J. Cork Hist. & Arch. Soc.* N.S. 21 (1915): 112-20.

Ffolliott, Rosemary. *Rogers of Lota and Ashgrove.* Cork family—late eighteenth to mid-nineteenth century. Cork, 1967. Offprint from *J. Cork Hist. & Arch. Soc.*, 75-80.

"Notes on the Family of Ronayne, or Ronan, of Cos. Cork and Waterford." *J. Cork Hist. & Arch. Soc.* N.S. 22 (1916): 56-63, 109-14, 178-85; 23 (1917): 93-104, 142-52.

"The Rumley Family of Cork." *J. Cork Hist. & Arch. Soc.* N.S. 7 (1901): 127.

"The Family of Sarsfield." *Herald and Genealogist* 2 (1865): 205-15.

Caulfield. "Records of the Sarsfield Family of the County Cork." *J. Cork Hist. & Arch. Soc.* N.S. 21 (1915): 82-91, 131-36.

"Notes on the Pedigree of Sherlock of Mitchelstown, Co. Cork." *J. Cork Hist. & Arch. Soc.* N.S. 12 (1906): 50-51.

"The Descent of the Somervilles of Drishane." *Ir. Gen.* 5 (6) (1979): 704-09.

Somerville, E.E., and Boyle Townshend Somerville, comps. *Records of the Somerville Family of Castlehaven and Drishane, from 1174 to 1904.* Cork, 1940.

"The Somervilles and Their Connections in Cork." *J. Cork Hist. & Arch. Soc.* N.S. 47 (1942): 30-33.

"The Southwells." *J. Cork Hist. & Arch. Soc.* 18 (1912): 141-49.

"Spread of Co. Cork." *Ir. Anc.* 2 (2) (1970): 102-11.

"Notes on the Stamers Family." *J. Cork Hist. & Arch. Soc.* N.S. 3 (1897): 152-53, 193-94, 232, 304.

Berry, Henry F. "The Old Youghal Family of Stout." *J. Cork Hist. & Arch. Soc.* N.S. 23 (1917): 19-29.

MacLir, Mananaan. *The Synans of Doneraile.* Cork, 1909.

Townshend, R., and D. Townshend. *An Officer of the Long Parliament and His Descendants. An Account of the Life and Times of Colonel Richard Townshend of Castletown (Castle Townshend) and a Chronicle of His Family.* London, 1892.

"The Trants." *J. Cork Hist. & Arch. Soc.* 243, 244 (1981).

"The Trants: an Enterprising Catholic Family in 18th Century Co. Cork." *J. Cork Hist. & Arch. Soc.* 86 (1981): 21-29.

Fitzgerald-Uniacke, R.G. "The Uniackes of Youghal." *J. Cork Hist. & Arch. Soc.* N.S. 3 (1894): 113-16, 146-52, 183-91, 210-21, 232-41, 245-55.

Vickery, Louise E., and Rice, B. *Vickery of Evansville, Indiana 1850-1987: the Descendants of William Warner Vickery and Elizabeth Wolfe from Southwest Cork, Ireland.* Evansville, Indiana, 1987: 408.

"The Wallis Family of Drishane." *J. Cork. Hist. & Arch. Soc.* N.S. 67 (1962): 48-51.

"The Waters or Walter Family of Cork." *J. Cork Hist. & Arch. Soc.* N.S. 31 (1926): 7-78; 32 (1927): 17-23, 104-13; 33 (1928): 35-41; 34 (1929): 36-42, 97-105; 35 (1930): 36-43, 102-13; 36 (1931): 26-38, 76-86; 37 (1932): 35-41.

"Wrixon of Co. Cork." Pedigree in *Swanzy Notebooks.* RCB Library, Dublin.

Gravestone Inscriptions

Those records in the *Journal of the Cork Historical and Archaeological Society* (here indicated as *J. Cork Hist. & Arch. Soc.*) are in the series "The Gravestone Inscriptions of Co. Cork" Nos. I to XI. All are indexed by name and place. The series of volumes entitled *O'Kief, Coshe Mang, and Slieve Luachra* by Albert Casey (abbreviated as OCM below) also contains many records, all of which are indexed.

Adrigole: Berehaven Inscriptions, Cork Co. Library, SLC film 994078.

Aghinagh: *J. Cork Hist. & Arch. Soc.* 216 (1967): 93-100.

Ballaghaboy: Berehaven Inscriptions, Cork Co. Library, SLC film 994078.

Ballinacurra: *J. Cork Hist. & Arch. Soc.* 254 (1990).

Ballyclough: OCM Vol. VIII (1965).

Ballycurrany: *J. Cork Hist. & Arch. Soc.* 237 (1978): 78-82.

Ballymodan, RC: Genealogical Survey of Bandon, 1985 (see West Cork Heritage Centre).

Ballymadan (St. Peters, CI): Genealogical Survey of Bandon, 1985 (see West Cork Heritage Centre).

Ballymartle: *J. Cork Hist. & Arch. Soc.* 253 (1989).

Ballyvourney: OCM Vol. VI (1963).

Bandon (St. Patrick's, RC): Genealogical Survey of Bandon, 1986 (see Ballymodan).

Brinny (Bandon, CI): Genealogical Survey of Bandon, 1986 (see Ballymodan).

Carrigohanebeg: *J. Cork Hist. & Arch. Soc.* 218 (1968): 175-81.

Carrigtwohill: Few records in *J. Cork Hist. & Arch. Soc.* 211 (1965): 26-32.

Castlemagner: OCM Vol. VI (1963).

Clanlaurence: Berehaven Inscriptions, Cork Co. Library, SLC film 994078.

Clondrohid: OCM Vol. VI (1963).

Clonfert: OCM Vol. VI (1963).

Clonmeen: OCM Vol. VII (1964): 233, 234; (1976): 95-117; 235 (1977): 11-29 (Lyre and Banteer).

Clonmult: *J. Cork Hist. & Arch. Soc.* 219 (1969): 34-39.

Cobh (Old Churchyard): Published by Great Island Hist. Soc. c/o L. Cassidy, 1 Park View, Cobh, Co. Cork.

Cullen: OCM Vol. VI (1963) and *J. Cork Hist. & Arch. Soc.* 253 (1989).

Dangandonovan: *J. Cork Hist. & Arch. Soc.* 229 (1974): 26-58.

Desertmore: *J. Cork Hist. & Arch. Soc.* 219 (1969): 34-39.

Drishane: OCM Vol. V (1963).

Dromagh: OCM Vol. VIII (1965).

Dromtariffe: OCM Vol. VI (1963).

Drumlave: Berehaven Inscriptions, Cork Co. Library, SLC film 994078.

Dunderrow: *J. Cork Hist. & Arch. Soc.* 224 (1971): 110-27.

Dursey Island: Berehaven Inscriptions, Cork Co. Library, SLC film 994078.

Fermoy: *Irish Sword* 51 (1977); 53 (1979) (military stones only).

Inchigeela: OCM Vol. VI (1963) (see Ballymodan).

Kilbeg (Bandon, CI): Genealogical Survey of Bandon, 1985 (see Ballymodan).

Kilbrin: OCM Vol. VIII (1965).

Kilbrogan (RC): Genealogical Survey of Bandon, 1985 (see Ballymodan).

Kilbrogan: Genealogical Survey of Bandon, 1985 (see Ballymodan, CI).

Kilcatherine: Berehaven Inscriptions, Cork Co. Library, SLC film 994078.

Kilcorney: OCM Vol. VII (1964).

Kilcrea Friary: *J. Cork Hist. & Arch. Soc.* 217 (1968): 1-30.

Kilcummin: OCM Vol. VI (1963).

Killaconenagh: Berehaven Inscriptions, Cork Co. Library, SLC film 994078.

Killeagh: *J. Cork Hist. & Arch. Soc.* 226 (1972): 76-104; 227 (1973): 40-65.

Kilnaglory: *J. Cork Hist. & Arch. Soc.* 220 (1969): 184-87.

Kilnamanagh: Berehaven Inscriptions, Cork Co. Library, SLC film 994078.

Kilnamartyra: OCM Vol. VI (1963).

Kilmeen (Barony of Dunhallow): OCM Vol. VI (1963).

Kilmonoge: *J. Cork Hist. & Arch. Soc.* 251 (1987): 113-117.

Kinsale (CI): Available from M. McCarthy, 2 Lr. O'Connell Street, Kinsale, Co. Cork.

Lisgoold: *J. Cork Hist. & Arch. Soc.* 237 (1978): 59-65.

Macloneigh: OCM Vol. VIII (1965).

Macroom: OCM Vol. VIII (1965).

Mallow: OCM Vol. VIII (1965).

Mologga: *Ir. Gen.* 2 (12) (1955): 390-92.

Nohovaldaly: OCM Vol. VIII (1965).

Rossmacowen: Berehaven Inscriptions, Cork Co. Library, SLC film 994078.

St. Finbarr's: Robinson, Rev. Andrew C. *St. Finbarr's Cathedral*, 1897.

St. Peters Churchyard: *J. Cork Hist. & Arch. Soc.* 252 (1988).

Tisaxon: *J. Cork Hist. & Arch. Soc.* 222 (1970): 143-57.

Titeskin: *J. Cork Hist. & Arch. Soc.* 221 (1970): 56-57.

Tullylease: OCM Vol. VIII (1965).

Youghal: Field, W.G. *The Handbook of Youghal.* (1896; reprinted 1973.) Contains inscriptions from the Collegiate Church.

Newspapers

A card index to biographical notices in Cork and Kerry newspapers from 1756 to 1827 is available in the Library of University College, Cork. Microfiche copies of this are available in the NLI, the Library of University College, Dublin, the New York Public Library, and SLC film 537921/2. Microfiche copies are also available from the compiler, Ms. R. ffolliott, Glebe House, Fethard, Co. Tipperary.

Title: *Constitution* or *Cork Morning Post* (continued as *Cork Constitution* in 1873)
Published in: Cork, 1823-1924
NLI Holdings: 6.1823-12.1827; 1829; 1831-34; 10.1873-7.1922; 1924
BL Holdings: odd numbers 1823; 1.1826-10.1873; 10.1873-12.1924
Indexed (1756-1827) in ffolliot Index

Title: *Cork Advertiser* (continued as *Constitution* in 1823)
Published in: Cork, 1799-1824
NLI Holdings: 1-8.1799; 1800; 1-10.1801; 3-12.1803; 2-12.1804; 4-12.1806; 1-8.1807; 11.1811-12.1816; 9.1818-5.1819; 12.1822-6.1823
BL Holdings: odd numbers 1810, 1813, 1823, 1824
Indexed (1756-1827) in ffolliot Index

Title: *Cork Examiner*
Published in: Cork, 1841-current
NLI Holdings: 8.1841-12.1896; 3.1897-5.1910; 7.1910-in progress
BL Holdings: 8.1841-in progress
Cork City Library Holdings: 8.1841-1924 and 1957-in progress
Abstracts from 1923-48 are in OCM Vol. XV 2331-2457

Title: *Cork Herald* (continued as *Cork Daily Herald* from 1860)
Published in: Cork, 1856-1901
NLI Holdings: 1870-84; 1896-7.1901
BL Holdings: 4.1858-7.1901

Title: *Hibernian Chronicle* (later *Cork Mercantile Chronicle*)
Published in: Cork, 1769-1818
Cork City Library Holdings: 1769-1818
Indexed (1756-1827) in ffolliot Index; Index (1803-1818) held by IGRS, London

Title: *Munster Advertiser*
Published in: Cork, 1839-41
NLI Holdings: 4.1839-5.1841
BL Holdings: 4.1839-5.1841

Title: *Peoples Press and Cork Weekly Register*
Published in: Cork, 1834-36
BL Holdings: 9.1834-2.1836

Title: *Skibbereen and West Carbery Eagle*
Published in: Skibbereen, 1857-1929
NLI Holdings: 5.1881-12.1884; 4.1899-7.1922; 8.1927-12.1928
BL Holdings: 9.1861-10.1870; 1.1871-7.1922

Title: *Southern Reporter* (continued as *Irish Daily and Southern Reporter* in 1871)
Published in: Cork, 1807-73
NLI Holdings: 6.1807-8.1808; 5.1811-12.1813; 1.1817-4.1819; 1824; 1826; 1827; 1829-7.1832; 1834; 1848; 4.1856-12.1873

BL Holdings: 1.1823-12.1871; odd numbers 1872 and 1873
Indexed (1756-1827) in ffolliot Index

Title: *Southern Star*
Published in: Skibbereen, 1864-current
NLI Holdings: 6.1921-11.1962
BL Holdings: 2-7.1864; odd numbers 1892; 12.1892-3.1918; 4.1919

Wills and Administrations

A discussion of the types of records, where they are held, their availability, and value is given in the Wills section of the introduction. The availability of prerogative wills, administrations, and marriage license records is also described in the relevant parts of the same section. Where available, published sources of these records are given in the Miscellaneous Sources section.

Pre-1858 Wills and Administrations

Prerogative Wills. See introduction.

Consistorial Wills. County Cork is in the dioceses of Cork, Cloyne, Ross, Lismore, Ardfert and Aghadoe, and Limerick. The guide to Catholic parish records in this chapter shows the diocese to which each civil parish belonged. The wills of residents of each diocese were usually proven within that diocese (see the Wills section for exceptions). The following records survive:

Wills
See introduction.

Abstracts
See introduction; also McSwiney papers: Abstracts mainly from Cork and Kerry (RIA library); Pre-1800 abstracts from Cork and Cloyne, GO, see *Anal. Hib.* 17 (1949).

The Welply Will Abstracts in the RCBL contain extracts from 1,682 Munster wills, mainly from Cork. Index contains name, date of will and (usually) probate, residence. Index in *Ir. Gen.* from Vol. 6 (6) 1985 to Vol. 7 (1) 1986.

Indexes
Cloyne (exist for 1621-1858), NAI. The following have been published: (1621-1800) by Phillimore (see introduction); (1621-1858) OCM Vol. VIII (1965); (1547-1628) in *J. Cork Hist. & Arch. Soc.* (1895); Cork and Ross (1548-1858) published to 1800 by Phillimore, also in OCM Vol. VIII (1965). Also, wills from 1548-1833 from the Cork Registry published in *J. Cork Hist. & Arch. Soc.* 1895-98; Lismore—see Co. Waterford; Limerick—see Co. Limerick; Ardfert—see Co. Kerry.

136   *Cloyne Wills, 1621-1800.*

		Date of Probate.
Hemington, Thomas, Newmarket		1770
Hendley (*or* Headly), Catherine (widow), Mount Rivers		1791
„ Roger, Ballyvoluck		1736
Henesy, James, Killshaney		1741
„ Laurence, Ballymaloobeg ...		1781
Hennebry, Maurice, Blarny		1740
Hennessy, George, BallymcMoy (Monition) ...		1779
„ (*or* Henessy), Honor (widow), Richardstown...		1777
„ John, Park		1726
„ (*or* Henessy), Peter, Richardstown ...		1777
Hennesy, John, Killmahan		1740
Herbert, William, ship " Speke "		1780
Herlihy, William, Shanacloune		*1726
„ *See also* Hearlihy and Hierlihy.		
Hewitt, Anne (widow), Castlelyons		*1727
Hickey, William, Mallow		1766
Hicky, Andrew, Castle Redmond		1791
„ Dennis, Ballyganhedagh		1757
„ John oge		1654
Hierlihy (*or* Herlihy), Daniel, Cove		1791
Higgins, Richard, Cork		1780
Hilgrove, Francis, Burgess		1795
Hill, Thomas, Coolegilly		1680
Hindes, John, Kineagh		1629
Hobbs, John, Curroghanyearla		1775
Hodder, John, Bridgetown		1673
„ Margery (widow), Coolemore		1677
„ William, Coolemore		1665
Hodge, John, Middleton		1679
„ William, H.M.S. "Bridgewater"		1749
Hogan, Daniel, Kilcronatt		1775
„ Denis, Newmarket		1682
Hogben, Robert, Barriscourt		1654
Holland, Francis, Dromclogh		1680
„ Susanna (widow), Castleblah		1772
Holmes, Thomas, Ardrabegg		*1753
„ „ Longstown		1774
„ William, Fedane		1687
Homan, Robert, Gortbofinny		1787
Honner, John, Maddam (Copy) (Original in Prerogative)		1670
Honohane, Lyonell, Broghill		1712
Hood, Daniel, Mallow		*1729

A page of will indexes for the dioceses of Cloyne, from
Phillimore's *Indexes to Irish Wills* (London, 1910).

Post-1858 Wills and Administrations

County Cork was served by the District Registry of Cork. The surviving records are kept in the NAI and in SLC on films 597718-21 (1858-68) and 100929-42 (1858-1897).

Marriage Licenses

Indexes

Cloyne (1630-1845) NAI; SLC films 100863 and 908143 (1630-1800). Cork and Ross (1623-1845) NAI; SLC films 100864-866. Lismore—see Co. Waterford.

   Published in:

Green, T.G.H. Index to the Marriage License bonds of the Diocese of Cloyne, 1630-1800. Cork: Guy and Co., 1899-1900.

Gillman, H.W., ed. Index to the Marriage License bonds of the Diocese of Cork and Ross, 1623-1750. Cork: Guy and Co., 1896-97.

Miscellaneous Sources

Cadogan, Tim. "Surnames of Co. Cork." Irish Roots (3) 1994: 14-15.

Cadogan, Tim, and Tony McCarthy. Tracing your Cork Ancestors. Flyleaf Press, 4 Spencer Villas, Glenageary, Dublin.

Diarmuid O'Murchadha. Family Names of County Cork. Cork: Collins Press, 1996. ISBN: 0-9-7606-3-X.

"Co. Cork Families 1630-5." J. Cork Hist. & Arch. Soc. 204 (1961): 126-29, 635-38; 205 (1962): 36-40; 1638-57: 206 (1962): 139-43; (1951): 126-29.

"Agnes Townsend's Notebook." Ir. Anc. 8 (2) (1976): 96-113 (general birth and death information from West Cork area).

"A Brief Directory of the City of Cork 1758 and 1769-1770." Ir. Gen. 1 (8) (1940): 254-59.

Caulfield, Richard. The Council Book of the Corporation of Kinsale from 1652 to 1800. Guildford: Billings, 1879.

Coombes, James. A History of Timoleague and Barryroe. Timoleague: Muintir na Tire, 1969.

Cusack, M.F. A History of the City and County of Cork. Dublin, 1875.

Donnelly, J.S. Land and People of 19th Century Cork. London, 1975.

Gibson, Rev. C.B. History of the County and City of Cork. 2 vols. 1861.

"Honorary Freemen of Cork 1690-1946." J. Cork Hist. & Arch. Soc. 52 (175): 74-86.

"Mallow Testamentary Records." Ir. Anc. 1 (1) (1969): 52-59.

"Maps and Plans of Cork Interest." J. Cork Hist. & Arch. Soc. 73 (1968): 72-73.

"The Memorandum Book of David Rochfort. 1750s to 1794." J. Cork Hist. & Arch. Soc. 203 (1961): 55-64 (death and marriage records in Garrettstown, Co. Cork). Addendum. 205 (1962): 54-56.

O'Flanagan and Buttimer, eds. Cork History and Society: Interdisciplinary Essays on the History of an Irish County. Dublin: Geography Publications, 1994.

"Register of Boys at St. Stephens Hospital (School) 1773-1802." J. Cork Hist. & Arch. Soc. 195 (1957): 46-55 (gives name, age of entry, departure, and to whom apprenticed or other fate of each boy).

Smith, Charles. The Ancient and Present State of the County and City of Cork (1750).

"Some Marriage Announcements from The Cork Mercantile Chronicle for 1806." Ir. Gen. 1 (12) (1942): 356-61.

"Some Notices of Early French Refugees in Cork." J. Cork Hist. & Arch. Soc. 24 (117) (1918): 8-15.

Townsend, Rev. H. A General and Statistical Survey of the County of Cork. 2 vols. 1815.

White, James Grove. "Historical and Topographical Notes on Buttevant, Mallow, etc." Supplement to Cork Historical and Archaeological Society's Journal. 1905-10.

Research Sources and Services

Journals
Journal of Cork Historical and Archaeological Society

Libraries and Information Sources

Cork City Library, Grand Parade, Cork. Ph: (021) 277110. Has an extensive local history section with a particular interest in Cork City. This includes books, journals, photographs, and local newspapers.

Cork County Library, Farranlea Road, Cork. Ph: (021) 46499. Has an extensive collection of material related to the history, topography, etc., including books, directories, newspapers, periodicals, photographs, and estate papers. The Local Studies Dept. will answer queries on local history matters. However, they have no access to church records other than those published in secondary sources.

Cork Archives Institute (formerly the Cork Archives Council), at Christ Church Centre, South Main Street, Cork. Ph: (021) 277809. Holds Cork Corporation and County Council records, and also a large range of family, company, trade union, society, and individual papers, mainly from nineteenth- and twentieth-century Cork.

Family History Center, Sarsfield Road, Wilton, Cork. Ph: (021) 874858. This center is a branch of the Family History Library run by The Church of Jesus Christ of Latter-day Saints. It has filmed many of the major Irish record sources and also has an extensive collection of other materials, such as the 1901 census, Tithe Applotment Books, Griffith's Valuation, and Civil Registration indexes.

Research Services

There are several research centers involved in indexing local sources and providing research services. Many of the registers of the county have been indexed, and these centers are actively working on the remainder. Researchers are advised to contact the centers for updated lists of registers and other sources indexed.

Cork City Ancestral Research Ltd. (CCAR), Cork Co. Library, Farranlea Road, Cork. Ph: (021) 46499. Was established in 1994 to index family history material for the Cork City area (i.e., all parishes within three to six miles of the City). It expects to offer a research service based on this index starting in 1997.

Mallow Heritage Centre, 27-19 Bank Place, Mallow, Co. Cork. Ph: (022) 21778. Has indexed Catholic and some Church of Ireland records for the Northern parts of the county. It offers a research service based on this index. The parishes which are indexed by this center are noted as "Indexed by MHC" in the text.

West Cork Heritage Centre (WCHC), Bandon, Co. Cork. Ph: (023) 44566. (West and South Cork records.) This center is in the process of indexing records for the western parts of the county. A search of the Church of Ireland records already indexed can be conducted for a fee.

Duhallow Heritage Centre, O'Keefe Institute, Newmarket, Co. Cork. Ph: (029) 60713. Is not a member of the Irish Family History Foundation or the Irish Genealogical Project (see introduction). However, it has indexes to records of some parishes in the west of the county, and will conduct research for a fee. The parishes which are indexed by this center are noted as "Indexed by DHC" in the text.

See also Research Services in Dublin in the introduction.

Societies

Ardmore Local History Society, Mr. James T. Quanin, Garry Rhu, Windsor Hill, Glounthaune, Co. Cork

Banndon-Cumman Seachais, Mr. Patrick J. Cunniffe, Bawnishal, Harehill, Bandon, Co. Cork

Bantry Historical and Archaeological Society, Mrs. Kathleen O'Riordan, 4 Newtown, Bantry, Co. Cork

Beara Historical Society, Mr. Connie Murphy, N.T., East End, Castletownbere, Co. Cork

Blackpool Historical Society, Mr. Donal O'Sullivan, Shalom, Mount Desert, Lee Road, Cork

Canovee Historical and Archaeological Society, Mr. Denis Long, Glenville House, Farnanes, Co. Cork

Charleville and District Historical Society, Mr. Patrick Collins, Cooline, Charleville, Co. Cork

Cloich na Coillte-Cumann Seanchais, Mr. Michael Donovan, Tubbereen Road, Clonakilty, Co. Cork

Cork Historical and Archaeological Society, Ms. Rosalie Mulvey, Sonas, Farranleer, Co. Cork

Duhallow Heritage Society, Mr. Timmie O'Shea, O'Keefe Institute, Newmarket, Co. Cork

Great Island Historical Society, Mr. Patrick Healy, Ardeen, Norwood Park, Cobh, Co. Cork

Kinsale Local History Society, Mr. Gearoid McCarthy, Pike Road, Kinsale, Co. Cork

Mallow Field Club, Mr. John Caplice, Old Dromore, Mallow, Co. Cork

Mizen Peninsula Archaeological and Historical Society, Ms. Deirdre Collins, Poll An Uisce, High Street, Schull, Co. Cork

O'Mahony Society, Mr. Gerard McCarthy, Pike Cross, Kinsale, Co. Cork

Youghal Heritage Society, Mr. Kelly, De Valera Street, Youghal, Co. Cork

Cork—Southwest—Civil Parishes as Numbered on Map

1. Kilcatherine
2. Kilcaskan
3. Kilnamanagh
4. Killaconenagh
5. Kilmacomoge
6. Inchigeelagh
7. Kilmichael
8. Kinneigh
9. Fanlobbus
10. Kilmeen
11. Kilmacabea
12. Ross
13. Castleventry (3 pts.)
14. Kilfaughnabeg
15. Murragh
16. Templemartin
17. Brinny
18. Killowen
19. Kilbrogan
20. Ballymodan

21. Knockavilly
22. Inishannon
23. Templemichael
24. Dunderrow (2 pts.)
25. Ballinaboy
26. Ballymartle
27. Cullen
28. Leighmoney
29. Ballyfeard
30. Tracton
31. Kilpatrick (2 pts.)
32. Kilmonoge
33. Kinure
34. Nohaval
35. Ballyfoyle
36. Marmullane
37. Monkstown
38. Carrigaline (2 pts.)
39. Killanully
40. Liscleary (2 pts.)
41. Barnahely
42. Kilmoney
43. Templebreedy
44. Kilcrohane
45. Durrus
46. Caheragh (2 pts.)
47. Skull
48. Kilcoe
49. Kilmoe
50. Dromdaleague
51. Drinagh
52. Abbeystrowry (2 pts.)
53. Castlehaven

54. Myross
55. Aghadown
56. Creagh (2 pts.)
57. Tullagh
58. Clear Island
59. Kilkerranmore
60. Rathbarry (2 pts.)
61. Ardfield (2 pts.)
62. Island (9 pts.)
63. Templeomalus
64. Templequinlan
65. Timoleague
66. Abbyemahon
67. Lislee
68. Donaghmore
69. Kilsillagh
70. Ballymoney
71. Desertserges
72. Kilmaloda
73. Kilbrittain
74. Ballinadee
75. Kilgarriff
76. Templebryan (2 pts.)
77. Kilnagross
78. Rathclarin
79. Desert
80. Templetrine
81. Ringrone (2 pts.)
82. Kilroan
83. Tisaxon
84. Clontead
85. Kinsale
86. Ringcurran (2 pts.)

Cork—Southwest—Civil Parishes in Alphabetical Order

Abbeymahon: 66
Abbeystrowry (2 pts.): 52
Aghadown: 55
Ardfield (2 pts.): 61
Ballinaboy: 25
Ballinadee: 74

Ballyfeard: 29
Ballyfoyle: 35
Ballymartle: 26
Ballymodan: 20
Ballymoney: 70
Barnahely: 41

Brinny: 17
Caheragh (2 pts.): 46
Carrigaline (2 pts.): 38
Castlehaven: 53
Castleventry (3 pts.): 13
Clear Island: 58
Clontead: 84
Creagh (2 pts.): 56
Cullen: 27
Desert: 79
Desertserges: 71
Donaghmore: 68
Drinagh: 51
Dromdaleague: 50
Dunderrow (2 pts.): 24
Durrus: 45
Fanlobbus: 9
Inchigeelagh: 6
Inishannon: 22
Island (9 pts.): 62
Kilbrittain: 73
Kilbrogan: 19
Kilcaskan: 2
Kilcatherine: 1
Kilcoe: 48
Kilcrohane: 44
Kilfaughnabeg: 14
Kilgarriff: 75
Killaconenagh: 4
Killanully: 39
Kilkerranmore: 59
Killowen: 18
Kilmacabea: 11
Kilmacomoge: 5
Kilmaloda: 72
Kilmeen: 10
Kilmichael: 7

Kilmoe: 49
Kilmoney: 42
Kilmonoge: 32
Kilnagross: 77
Kilnamanagh: 3
Kilpatrick (2 pts.): 31
Kilroan: 82
Kilsillagh: 69
Kinneigh: 8
Kinsale: 85
Kinure: 33
Knockavilly: 21
Leighmoney: 28
Liscleary (2 pts.): 40
Lislee: 67
Marmullane: 36
Monkstown: 37
Murragh: 15
Myrosa: 54
Nohaval: 34
Rathbarry (2 pts.): 60
Rathclarin: 78
Ringcurran (2 pts.): 86
Ringrone (2 pts.): 81
Ross: 12
Skull: 47
Templebreedy: 43
Templebryan (2 pts.): 76
Templemartin: 16
Templemichael: 23
Templeomalus: 63
Templequinlan: 64
Templetrine: 80
Timoleague: 65
Tisaxon: 83
Tracton: 30
Tullagh: 57

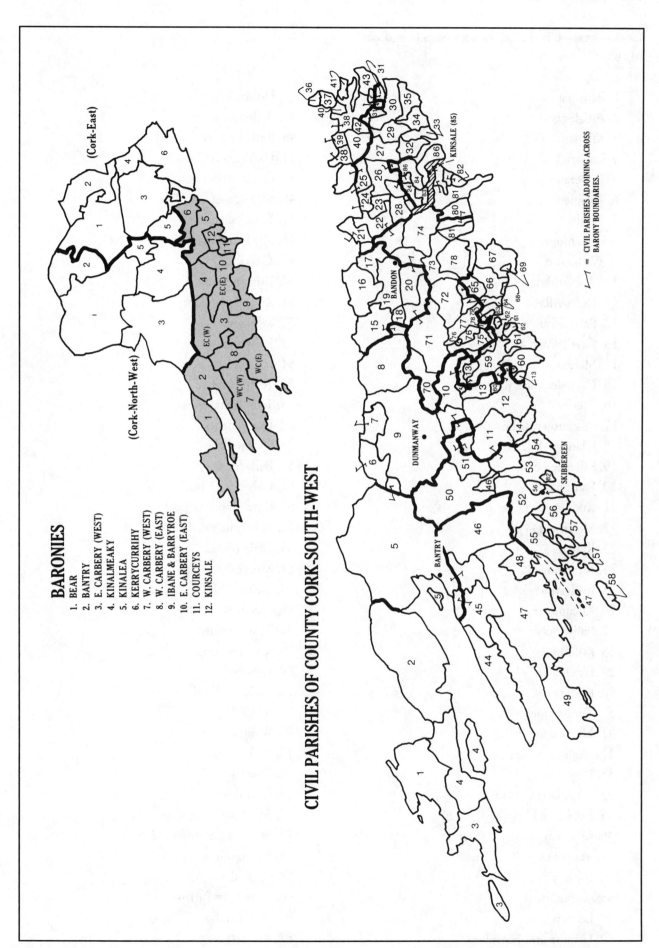

BARONIES

1. BEAR
2. BANTRY
3. E. CARBERY (WEST)
4. KINALMEAKY
5. KINALEA
6. KERRYCURRIHY
7. W. CARBERY (WEST)
8. W. CARBERY (EAST)
9. IBANE & BARRYROE
10. E. CARBERY (EAST)
11. COURCEYS
12. KINSALE

(Cork-East)

(Cork-North-West)

CIVIL PARISHES OF COUNTY CORK-SOUTH-WEST

⌐ = CIVIL PARISHES ADJOINING ACROSS BARONY BOUNDARIES.

Cork—East—Civil Parishes as Numbered on Map

1. Ballyhea
2. Ardskeagh
3. Kilquane
4. Imphrick
5. Doneraile
6. Templeroan
7. Farahy
8. Caherduggan
9. Wallstown
10. St. Nathlash
11. Derryvillane
12. Ballydeloughy
13. Carrigdownane
14. Mallow
15. Carrigleamleary
16. Clenor
17. Castletownroche
18. Glanworth (2 pts.)
19. Killeenemer
20. Dunmahon
21. Kilcrumper (2 pts.)
22. Mournabbey
23. Rahan
24. Monanimy
25. Bridgetown
26. Kilcummer
27. Ballyhooly
28. Killathy
29. Litter
30. Kildorrery
31. Templemolaga
32. Marshalstown
32a. Aghacross
33. Brigown
34. Kilgullane (2 pts.)
35. Kilphelan (2 pts.)
36. Kilworth
37. Macroney
38. Fermoy
38a. Clondulane
39. Leitrim
40. Lismore and Mocollop

41. Dunbulloge
42. Ardnageehy
43. Rathcormack
44. Castlelyons (2 pts.)
45. Coole
46. St. Michael's
47. Templeusque
48. Kilshanagahan
49. Gortroe
50. Britway (2 pts.)
51. Killaspugmulane
52. Kilquane
53. Ballycurrany
54. Lisgoold
55. Templebodan
56. Templenacarriga
57. Dungourney
58. Clonmult
59. Ballydeloher
60. Caherlag (2 pts.)
61. Carrigtohill (2 pts.)
62. Ballyspillane
63. Little Island
64. Mogeesha
65. Inchinabacky
66. Clonmel
67. Templerobin
68. Knockmourne
69. Aghern
70. Ballynoe
71. Mogeely
72. Whitechurch
73. Rathcooney
74. Kilcully
75. Currykippane
76. St. Mary's Shandon
77. St. Ann's Shandon (2 pts.)
78. Carrigrohane
79. St. Finbar's
80. Cork City Parishes
81. St. Nicholas
82. Kilnagleary

83. Inishkenny
84. Carrigaline (2 pts.)
85. Ballinaboy (2 pts.)
86. Killanully
87. Ardagh
88. Dangandonovan
89. Mogeely
90. Killeagh
91. Clonpriest
92. Youghal
93. Midleton
94. Ballyoughtera (2 pts.)
95. Ightermurragh

96. Kilmacdonagh
97. Garrankinnefeake
98. Cloyne (4 pts.)
99. Bohillane
100. Garryvoe
101. Kilcredan
102. Rostellan (2 pts.)
103. Inch (3 pts.)
104. Kilmahon (2 pts.)
105. Aghada
106. Titeskin (2 pts.)
107. Corkbeg
108. Ballintemple
109. Trabolgan

Cork—East—Civil Parishes in Alphabetical Order

Aghacross: 32a
Aghada: 105
Aghern: 69
Ardagh: 87
Ardnageehy: 42
Ardakeagh: 2
Ballinaboy: 85 (2 pts.)
Ballintemple: 108
Ballycurrany: 53
Ballydeloher: 59
Ballydeloughy: 12
Ballyhay: 1
Ballyhooly: 27
Ballynoe: 70
Ballyoughtera: 94 (2 pts.)
Ballyspillane: 62
Bohillane: 99
Bridgetown: 25
Brigown: 33
Britway: 50 (2 pts.)
Carrigdowane: 13
Caherduggan: 8
Caherlag: 60 (2 pts.)
Carrigaline: 84 (2 pts.)
Carrigleamleary: 15

Carrigrohane: 78
Carrigtohill: 61 (2 pts.)
Castlelyons: 44 (2 pts.)
Castletownroche: 17
Clenor: 16
Clondulane: 38a
Clonmel: 66
Clonmult: 58
Clonpriest: 91
Cloyne: 98 (4 pts.)
Coole: 45
Corkbeg: 107
Cork City Parishes: 80
Currykippane: 73
Dangandonovan: 88
Derryvillane: 11
Doneraile: 5
Dunbulloge: 41
Dungourney: 57
Dunmahon: 20
Farahy: 7
Fermoy: 36
Garrankinnefeake: 97
Garryvoe: 100
Glanworth: 18 (2 pts.)

Gortroe: 49

Ightermurragh: 95

Imphrick: 4

Inch: 103 (3 pts.)

Inchinabacky: 65

Inishkenny: 83

Kilcredan: 101

Kilcummer: 26

Kildorrery: 30

Kilgullane: 34 (2 pts.)

Killanully: 86

Killaspugmullane: 51

Killathy: 28

Killeagh: 90

Killeenemer: 19

Kilmacdonagh: 96

Kilmahon: 104 (2 pts.)

Kilnagleary: 82

Kilphelan: 35 (2 pts.)

Kilquane: 3

Kilquane: 52

Kilshanahan: 48

Kilworth: 36

Knockmourne: 68

Leitrim: 39

Lisgoold: 54

Lismore and Mocollop: 40

Litter: 29

Little Island: 63

Macroney: 37

Mallow: 14

Marshalstown: 32

Midleton: 93

Mogeely: 71

Mogeely: 89

Mogeesha: 64

Monanimy: 24

Mournabbey: 22

Rahan: 23

Rathcooney: 73

Rathcormack: 43

Rostellan: 102 (2 pts.)

St. Ann's–Shandon: 77 (2 pts.)

St. Finbar's: 79

St. Mary's–Shandon: 76

St. Michael's: 46

St. Nathlash: 10

St. Nicholas: 81

Templebodan: 55

Templemolaga: 31

Templenacarriga: 56

Templeroan: 6

Templerobin: 67

Templeusque: 47

Titeskin: 106 (2 pts.)

Trabolgan: 109

Wallstown: 9

Whitechurch: 72

Youghal: 92

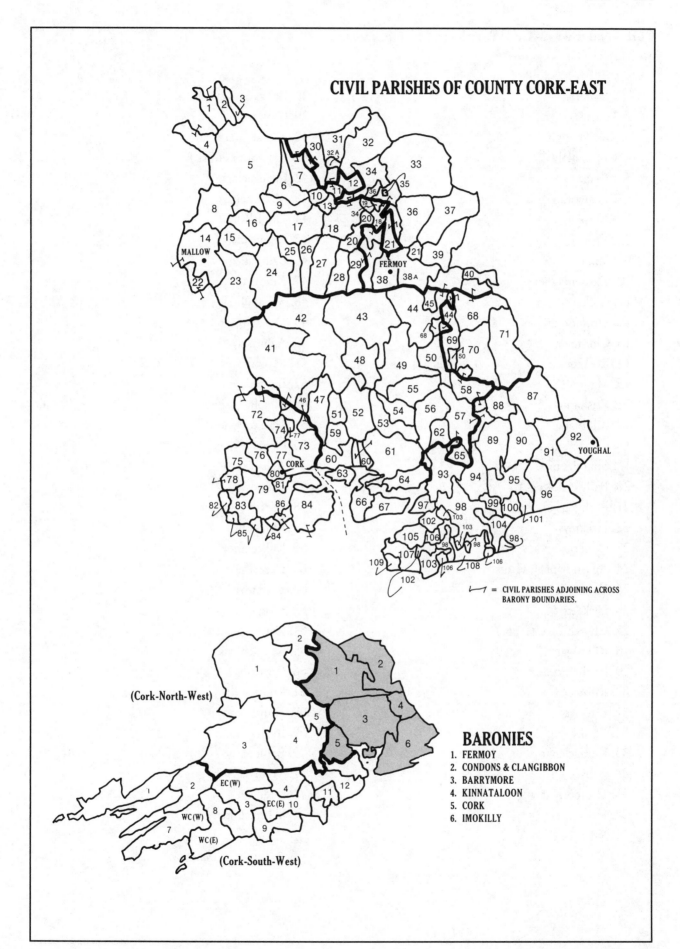

CIVIL PARISHES OF COUNTY CORK-EAST

⌐⌐ = CIVIL PARISHES ADJOINING ACROSS
BARONY BOUNDARIES.

(Cork-North-West)

(Cork-South-West)

BARONIES

1. FERMOY
2. CONDONS & CLANGIBBON
3. BARRYMORE
4. KINNATALOON
5. CORK
6. IMOKILLY

Cork—Northwest—Civil Parishes as Numbered on Map

1. Clonfert
2. Tullylease
3. Knocktemple
4. Nohavadaly
5. Kilmeen
6. Kilcorcoran
7. Kilbrin
8. Kilroe
9. Subulter
10. Castlemagner
11. Cullen
12. Dromtarriff
13. Clonmeen
14. Roskeen
15. Mallow
16. Kilshanig
17. Kilbolane
18. Corcomohide
19. Shandrum
20. Ballyhea (4 pts.)
21. Rathgoggan
22. Hackmys
23. Cooliney
24. Aglishdrinagh (2 pts.)
25. Liscarroll
26. Lackeen
27. Churchtown (2 pts.)
28. Kilgrogan
29. Imphrick
30. Kilbroney
31. Bregoge
32. Buttevant
33. Kilmaclenan
34. Ballyclogh
35. Dromdowney
36. Drishane
37. Kilcorney
38. Ballyvourney
39. Clondrohid
40. Kilnamartry
41. Macroom (4 pts.)
42. Inchigeelagh
43. Macloneigh
44. Dunisky
45. Kilmichael
46. Ballinadee
47. Kilmurry
48. Aghabulloge
49. Donaghmore
50. Aghinagh
51. Magourney
52. Innishcarra
53. Matehy
54. Garrycloyne
55. Cannaway
56. Aglish
57. Athnowen
58. Carrigrohanebeg
59. Moviddy
60. Kilbonane
61. Desertmore
62. St. Finbar's
63. Kilnaglory
64. Carrigrohane
65. St. Nicholas
66. Corbally
67. Knockavilly
68. Dunderrow
69. Inishkenny
70. Ballinaboy
71. Mourne Abbey
72. Grenagh
73. Whitechurch

Cork—Northwest—Civil Parishes in Alphabetical Order

Aghabulloge: 48
Aghinagh: 50
Aglish: 56
Aglishdrinagh (2 pts.): 24
Athnowen: 57
Ballinaboy: 70
Ballinadee: 46
Ballyclogh: 34
Ballyhea (4 pts.): 20
Ballyvourney: 38
Bregoge: 31
Buttevant: 32
Cannaway: 55
Carrigrohane: 64
Carrigrohanebeg: 58
Castlemagner: 10
Churchtown (2 pts.): 27
Clondrohid: 39
Clonfert: 1
Clonmeen: 13
Cooliney: 23
Corbally: 66
Corcomohide: 18
Cullen: 11
Desertmore: 61
Donaghmore: 49
Drishane: 36
Dromdowney: 35
Dromtarriff: 12
Dunderrow: 68
Dunisky: 44
Garrycloyne: 54
Grenagh: 72
Hackmys: 22
Imphrick: 29
Inchigeelagh: 42
Inishkenny: 69

Innishcarra: 52
Kilbolane: 17
Kilbonane: 60
Kilbrin: 7
Kilbroney: 30
Kilcorcoran: 6
Kilcorney: 37
Kilgrogan: 28
Kilmaclenan: 33
Kilmeen: 5
Kilmichael: 45
Kilmurry: 47
Kilnagleary: 63
Kilnamartry: 40
Kilroe: 8
Kilshannig: 16
Knockavilly: 67
Knocktemple: 3
Lackeen: 26
Liscarroll: 25
Macloneigh: 43
Macroom (4 pts.): 41
Magourney: 51
Mallow: 15
Matehy: 53
Mourne Abbey: 71
Moviddy: 59
Nohavadaly: 4
Rathgoggan: 21
Roskeen: 14
Shandrum: 19
St. Finbar's: 62
St. Nicholas: 65
Subulter: 9
Tullylease: 2
Whitechurch: 73

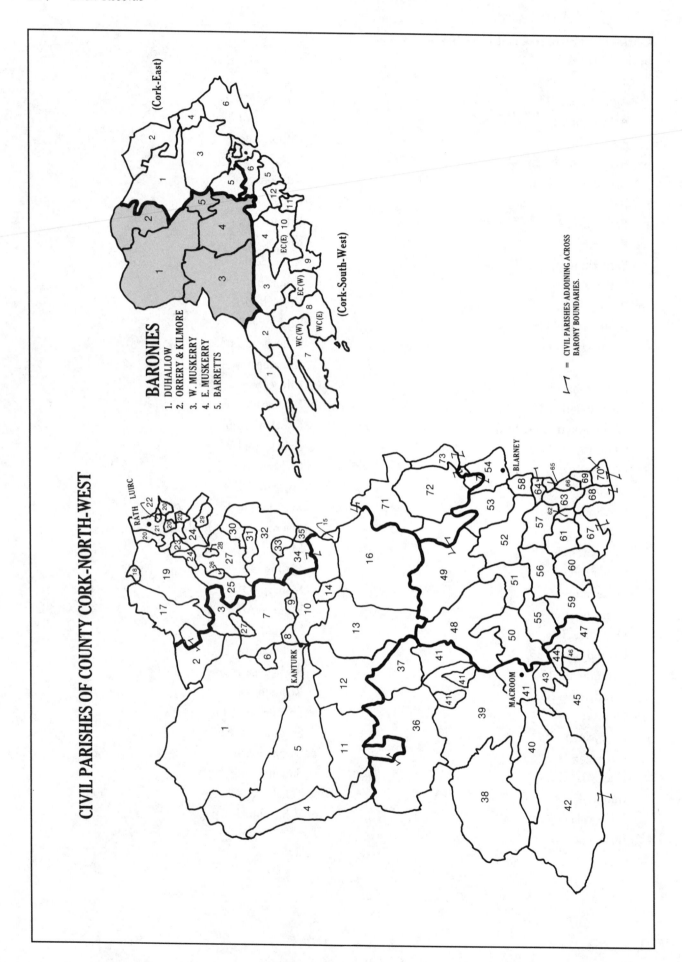

CIVIL PARISHES OF COUNTY CORK-NORTH-WEST

BARONIES
1. DUHALLOW
2. ORRERY & KILMORE
3. W. MUSKERRY
4. E. MUSKERRY
5. BARRETTS

⌐ = CIVIL PARISHES ADJOINING ACROSS BARONY BOUNDARIES.

(Cork-East)

(Cork-South-West)

County Derry

A Brief History

This Ulster county contains the city of Derry (or Londonderry) and the towns of Coleraine, Limavady, Magherafelt, and Portstewart.

In the old Gaelic system, much of Derry was in the old territory of Tirowen. The area was mainly the territory of the O'Cahans or O'Kanes. Other families associated with the area include O'Connor, O'Donnell, O'Mullan, McCloskey, O'Hegarty, O'Corr, McGurk, McRory, (O')Diamond, McCrilly, McGilligan, O'Deery, and McColgan.

The city of Derry dates back to the foundation of a monastery on the site in A.D. 546. The growth of the monastery and the surrounding settlement made Derry an important town. The town was repeatedly raided by the Danish vikings during the ninth to eleventh centuries.

Neither Derry city nor the old kingdom of Tirowen were affected by the Norman invasion and, like most of the rest of Ulster, it retained its independence from English rule until the beginning of the seventeenth century.

In 1600, during the rebellion of O'Neill and O'Donnell (see the introduction and Co. Tyrone) and their allies, the city of Derry was taken by English forces. Following the final defeat of the rebellion, most of the county was confiscated from its owners and given to "adventurers" and others for the purpose of planting it with English and Scottish settlers. The O'Cahans were one of the few native families who retained property in the county. Ulster was also divided into counties, and Derry was, for a time, known as the county of Coleraine.

In 1609 the plantation of Ulster began, and huge areas of Ulster were set aside for the use of settlers from Britain. In an effort to ensure the effective settlement of the new county of Coleraine, it was offered as a business venture to the city of London. Accordingly, in 1613 the county was renamed Londonderry and formally handed over to the city of London by King James. The city decided to administer the county by dividing it among twelve trade guilds of London, each of which was responsible for the development of its own area.

The London guilds were, by most accounts, less than enthusiastic about the scheme, and there were consequently not as many English settlers as the plantation organizers had expected. By some accounts there were more Irish tenants in the county than in any other. Consequently, the London company was heavily fined in 1635 for failing to honor their commitment to plant the county. Nevertheless, a large colony of Protestants was brought into Derry, and the fortification of the city was completed by 1618.

Among the common settler names in the county are those of Elliott, Campbell, Anderson, Baird, Thompson, McClintock, Hamilton, Browne, Barr, Stewart, Smith, Johnston, Irwin, Morrison, Young, and White.

In 1641 the native Irish joined the general rebellion of Irish Catholics. The rebellion was defeated and those involved were dealt with severely.

During the Williamite wars of the early 1690s, the city of Derry became a stronghold for the Protestants of the North and withstood a seven-month siege by Jacobite forces.

A general indication of the relative proportions of those of English, Scottish, or native Irish extraction in the county can be gauged from their religious persuasions. In 1861, when the census first ascertained religion, the relative proportions of Catholics (Irish), Protestants (English), and Presbyterians (Scottish) were forty-five, seventeen, and thirty-five percent respectively.

The Penal Laws were specifically enacted at the beginning of the eighteenth century to suppress Catholics, but they also affected Presbyterians. For this reason, there was considerable emigration of the Presbyterians, or so-called Scots-Irish, from Derry and other Ulster counties during the eighteenth century.

During the Great Famine, County Derry was not as badly affected as others. The population was 222,000 in 1841, and by 1851 it had fallen to 192,000. Derry was an important port of emigration at this time, and there was extensive migration to the city as a result of the famine.

Following the foundation of an independent Irish State in 1921, Derry was one of the six Ulster counties which was kept within the United Kingdom. The name Derry continues to be used in reference to the city and county by most of the population of Ireland. The name Londonderry should also be referred to by researchers.

Census and Census Substitutes

1609-1629

Londonderry and the London Companies. A survey and other documents submitted to King Charles I by Sir Thomas Phillips. Edited by D.A. Chart. Belfast: H.M.S.O., 1928.

1618

Survey of Derry, City and County, and Coleraine, etc., with Names of Undertakers, Servitors, and Principal Natives. TCD ms. 864 (F.I.9).

1628

Houses and Families in Londonderry, 15 May 1628. Edited by Rev. R.G.S. King, Londonderry: "Sentinel" Office, 1936. SLC films 1363860 and 990087; NLI IR 94112 L1.

1642/43

Muster Roll. SLC 941.5/M23m.

1654-56

The Civil Survey A.D. Counties of Donegal, Londonderry and Tyrone. Vol. 3. With returns of church lands for the three counties. Robert C. Simington, Dublin, SO, 1937.

1659

"Census" of Ireland. Edited by S. Pender. Dublin: Stationery Office, 1939. NLI I6551. SLC film 924648.

1662

Extracts from Subsidy Rolls. PRONI T716 (1-17).

1663

Hearth Money Roll. PRONI T307; NLI ms. 9584 (index on 9585).

1740

Protestant Householders in the Parishes of Aghadowy, Anlow, Artrea, Arigall, Ballinderry, Ballynascreen, Ballyscullion, Balten, Banagher, Beleaghron, Belerashane, Belewillin, Boveva, Coleraine, Comber, Desart, Desartlin, Desartmartin, Drummacose, Dunboe, Dungiven, Faughanvale, Glendermot, Killcranoghen, Killowen, Killylagh, Kilrea, Lissan, Macosquin, Maghera, Magherafelt, Tamlaghtfinlaggan, Tamlagh O' Creely, Tamlatard, Tamloght, Templemore, and Termoneny. GO 539; SLC films 100182 and 1279327.

Magherafelt householders alone are in NAI M2809.

1752-et seq.

Lists of tenants from various townlands in Derry appear in *Sth. Derry Hist. Soc. J.* 1 (2) 1981/82 as follows: Ballyheifer and Ballylifford (1752, 1795, 1812, 1825, 1845, 1859, 1900, and 1930) p. 167-176; Ballymilligan and Aghaskin (1752, 1778, 1795, 1812, 1825, 1845, 1859, 1900, and 1930) p. 312-320.

1761

Militia List, Cos. Limerick, Cork, Tipperary, Kerry, Derry, Louth, Wicklow, Monaghan, Roscommon, Down, Donegal, Dublin, Tyrone. GO Ms 680.

1766

Householders of Parishes of Artrea, Desertlyn, and Magherafelt. SLC film 258517 (except Desertlin). NAI Parl. Returns 650, 659, and 674 respectively.

Householders of Parishes of Artrea, Bovevagh, Derryloran, Desertmartin, and Magherafelt. GO 536 and RCB Ms 23; also SLC films 100173 and 1279330 (except Bovevagh).

Protestant householders of Parishes of Ballynascreen, Banagher, and Dungiven (only) and all householders for Bovevagh, Desertmartin, Drumachose, and Inch. SLC film 258517 and NAI M2476.

Householders of Parish of Desertmartin. RCB M23, SLC film 258517; *Sth. Derry Hist. Soc. J.* 1 (3) (1982/83): 221-224.

Householders of Inch. NAI M2476 and RCB M23.

Householders of Derryloran. NAI Parl. Return 665, GO 536 and RCB Ms 23.

Name	Address	Name	Address
Gubbin Patrick	Middle Rd	Hay Rev G	Shipquay St
Guiggan Patrick	Fergusons Lane	Hays	Richmond St
Haffin John	Foyle St	Hayshaw Mrs	Widows Row
Hagan	Nailors Row	Hazlett Samuel	Ship-Quay
Hagan Bernard	Creevagh Lower	Hazlett William	Kilkea
Hagan James	Bishop St Without	Hazlett William	Shipquay St
Hagan John	Bennetts Lane	Heaney Nicholas	Bennetts Lane
Hagan Patrick	Kilkea	Heany Edward	Bogside St
Hagan Patrick	Nailors Row	Heffernan Robert	Priests Lane
Hall John (2)	Waterloo Place	Hegarty	Fahan St
Hall Mrs	Cunningham Row	Hegarty	Long Tower
Halliday James	Bishop St Without	Hegarty	New Gate off Wapping
Halliday Patrick	Bishop St Without	Hegarty	Wapping
Halliday Tristam	Shantallow	Hegarty Christopher	Fahan St
Hamilton (2)	Ship-Quay	Hegarty Daniel	Foyle St
Hamilton	Thomas St	Hegarty Hugh	Cow Bog
Hamilton David	Bishop St	Hegarty James	Barrack Row
Hamilton Dr	Ferryquay St	Hegarty John	Bishop St Without
Hamilton Dr	Richmond St	Hegarty John	Horse Barrack
Hamilton James	Fahan St	Heggarty	Rossville St
Hamilton John	Bennetts Lane	Henderson Dr	Ballymagrorty
Hamilton John	Fahan St	Henderson Rev W	St Columbs Court
Hamilton John	Foyle St	Henderson William	Ferryquay St
Hamilton John	William St	Henry Barney	William St
Hamilton Mrs	Bogside St	Heslip Edward	William St
Hampton Moss	Ferryquay St	Higgans	St Columbs Wells
Hanigan Neil	Bennetts Lane	Hill John	Diamond
Hanley James	Bogside St	Hill Marcus S	East Wall
Hannigan	Rossville St	Hindman John	Diamond
Harkan Denis	Bridge St	Hindman John S	Foyle St
Harkan Patrick	William St	Hinds Patrick	Foyle Alley
Harkin Bernard	Creggan St	Hinds William	Society St
Harkin Robert	Henrietta St	Hoghey James	Barrack Row
Harkin William	Abbey St	Holland John	Sugar House Lane
Harkin William (2)	William St	Hooton Charles	Fahan St
Harl Robert	Abbey St	Horner Frances	Magazine St
Harlin	Wapping	Horner Francis	Abbey St
Harrigan	Thomas St	Horner Francis	Rossville St
Harrigan Bryan	Abbey St	Horner Leonard	Shipquay St
Harrigan Edward	Horse Barrack	Huffington John	Diamond
Harrigan James	Strand Rd	Huffington William	Cunningham Lane
Harris William	Ballingard	Huffington William	St Columbs Court
Hart General	Culmore	Hughs Miss	Cunningham Row
Hart William	Bishop St Without	Hunter James	Cow Bog
Hart William	Shantallow	Hunter William	Abbey St
Hartford John	Bishop St Without	Hunter William	Ship-Quay
Harvey Henry	Sugar House Lane	Hurlin Daniel	Rossville St
Harvey Richard	Mullennan	Hush Samuel	Orchard Lane
Harvey Thomas	Magazine St	Hutrick Mathew	Nailors Row
Haslett Mrs	Nailors Row	Hutton James	Bogside St
Haslitt	Richmond St	Hyde James (2)	Society St
Hassan James	Weavers Court	Inigly Michael	Bogside St
Hassan John	Long Tower	Irwine Robert	Bishop St Without
Hassan Thomas	Thomas St	Jameson	Long Tower
Hasson	Wapping	Johnston	Rossville St
Hastings Mrs	Wapping	Johnston William	Rossville St
Hattrick J	Cow Bog	Jones Daniel	Fahan St
Hattrick James	Ballingard	Kean James	Cow Bog
Hattrick Joshua	Creggan	Kearney Daniel	Bogside St
Hattrick Robert	Bogside St	Kearney Hugh	East Wall
Haverty James	St Columbs Wells	Kearney James (2)	Fergusons Lane
Havlin Thomas	Wapping Lane	Kearney John	Cow Bog

Sample page of householders in the 1832 Valuation of Derry from "The First and Second Valuations of the City of Derry" (Derry Youth and Community Workshop, 1984).

Householders of Artrea. *Sth. Derry Hist. Soc. J.* 1 (1980/81): 54-61.

Householders of Magherafelt. *Sth. Derry Hist. Soc. J.* 1 (2) (1981/82): 146-152.

1796

See Mayo 1796 (List of Catholics).

Spinning Wheel Premium List (see introduction). SLC film 1419442.

Census of the Presbyterian Congregation of Garvagh first. (In Garvagh Presbyterian Register.)

1797-1800

Muster Rolls of Co. Derry. SLC film 993910.

1803

Census for Faughanvale, Co. Londonderry. *Ulster Gen. & Historical Guild Newsletter* 1 (10) (1984): 324-332.

1808-13

Freeholders List (alphabetical list, A-L only). NAI film M6199.

1821

Extracts from the Government Census Relating Mainly to the Surnames Johnston, McShane, and Thompson. PRO; SLC film M824240.

1823-38

Tithe Applotment Survey (see introduction).

1829

Census of Protestants in Chapel of the Woods Parish. PRONI T308.

Magherafelt Tithe Applotments. *Sth. Derry Hist. Soc. J.* 1 (2) (1981/82): 153-152.

1830

Register of Freeholders of City and County. PRONI D834.

1831

Government census remnants. Mf. copy at PRONI (surname index at Genealogy Centre, Derry). See Research Services at end of chapter.

1831-34

Government Census Remnants. Derry is one of the counties for which some returns survive (see introduction). Parishes of Aghadowey, Aghanloo, Agivey, Arboe, Artrea, Ballinderry, Balteagh, Banagher, Ballyaughran, Ballymoney, Ballynascreen, Ballyrashane, Ballyscullion, Ballywillin, Bovevagh, Clondermot, Coleraine, Cumber, Desertlyn, Derryloran, Desertmartin, Desertoghill, Drumachose, Dunboe, Dungiven, Errigal, Faughanvale, Kildollagh, Kilrea, Kilcronaghan, Killelagh, Killowen, Lissane, Maghera, Magherafelt, Macosquin, Tamlaght, Finlagan, Tamlaght O'Crilly, Tamlaghtard, Templemore, and Termoneeny. NAI CEN 1831-4/1-44; Mf copy at PRONI; SLC films 597160-63. This census (38,000 heads of households) has been indexed by the Genealogy Centre, Derry; see Research Services at end of chapter and SLC film 874437 (b. 1826-66; m. 1826-45; d. 1826-78).

1831-32

The First Valuation of the City of Derry, Parish of Templemore (gives 1,656 householders' names with street address). Derry Youth and Community Workshop, 1984. NAI and SLC fiche 6342808.

1832

A list of persons who voted at the Coleraine Borough election. Gives names and occupations of voters. Printed single sheet in NAI Outrage Papers 1832/2188.

Petition of Co. Derry Flax-growers, with signatures. NAI ms.

City of Londonderry Registry. Clerk of the peace's poll-book. Names, addresses, and occupations of voters. PRONI.

1832-36

Names of Holders of Applications for Licenses to Sell Liquor in Londonderry and Coleraine (names and addresses). *Parl. Papers* 1837/38, 13 (2): Appendix 10.

1833-34

Emigrants to America from Londonderry Co. (compiled by Rev. R.J. Stanley; SLC 973 A1 5).

1833-39

Irish Emigration Lists. Brian Mitchell, 1989. Lists of Emigrants extracted from the Ordnance Survey memoirs for counties Londonderry and Antrim. Baltimore, 1989. SLC 941.6 W2m.

1837

List of Those Made Freemen of Londonderry and Coleraine since 1831 (seventy-five names, occupations, and residences). *Parl. Papers* 1837, 11 (1): Appendix B1; 1837/38, 13 (2): Appendix 3.

Name and Residence of Aldermen, Burgesses and Freemen of Coleraine 1831-37 (fifty-one names). *Parl. Papers* 1837, 11 (2): 279-80.

Occupants of Coleraine, Arranged by Street, Giving Property Values. *Parl. Papers* 1837, 11 (1) Appendix G: 198-202.

Occupants of Londonderry, Arranged by Street (giving valuation of property). Also List of Names and Residences (arranged by street) of those exempted from Local Tax (with reasons). *Parl. Papers* 1837, 11 (1) Appendix G: 216-25.

1838

Lists of Marksmen (illiterate voters) in Londonderry and Coleraine (ninety-seven names, occupations, and residences). *Parl. Papers* 1837, 11 (1): Appendix A3; 1837/38, 13 (2): Appendix 4.

1839

List of persons who obtained Game Certificates in Ulster. PRONI T 688.

1840

Census of the Presbyterian Congregation of Garvagh. (In Garvagh Presbyterian Register.)

1841 and 1851

Extracts from Government Censuses Pertaining to Old Age Pension Claims. NAI; SLC films 258538-41.

1842

Voters List. NAI 1842/69.

1847

Protestants at Fallaghy. PRONI D2098.

1847-49

Emigrants from Derry Port. By Dessie Baker (Port of Derry Ship List for J. & J. Cooke's line). 107 pp. (Name and place-name index.) Derry, 1985.

Ship list from Cooke's Line. Dessie Baker. Penn.: Closson Press, 1985. SLC 973 W3po.

1847-81

Irish Passenger Lists. By Brian Mitchell. Lists of passengers sailing from Derry to America on ships of the J. & J. Cooke Line and the McCorkell Lines. Baltimore, 1988.

1850

Census of the Presbyterian Congregation of Magilligan. (In Magilligan Presbyterian Register.)

1858

The Second Valuation *(Griffith's Valuation)* of the City of Derry (gives 2,923 names with street of residence in parishes of Glendermott and Templemore). Derry Youth and Community Workshop, 1984.

1858-59

Griffith's Valuation (see introduction).

1864-71

Company List of Passengers to Sail from Londonderry (1864-71; gives name, address, occupation, and age). PRONI D2892/1/4; *Ulster Gen. & Hist. Guild J.* 1 (3) (1979): 80-90.

1868

List of voters in 1868 general election for the city of Londonderry. Arranged alphabetically under (a) how they voted and (b) religion (gives name, address, occupation). NLI JP733. Magee College Library, Derry. PRONI.

1868

State of the poll at the general election for the city of Londonderry, 20 Nov. 1868. (Londonderry: John Hempton, 1868, 36 pp.) Gives names, addresses, religion, and occupations of many. Magee College Library, Derry.

1870

State of the poll at the election for the city of Londonderry. (Londonderry: John Hempton, 1870, 35 pp.) (Names, addresses, and religion.) Queens University Library, Belfast.

Voters at the election in Londonderry. (Londonderry: Sentinel Office, 1870, 33 pp.; names, addresses, religion, and occupations.) Presbyterian Historical Society Library, Belfast.

1901

Census. NAI (see introduction).

1911

Census. NAI (see introduction).

Church Records

Church of Ireland

See the introduction for a description of Church of Ireland records and their major repositories. Many C of I records were lost in the PRO fire of 1922. These are indicated as "Lost." However, as Church of Ireland records were effectively state records, the records of marriage (from 1845) are also in the General Registrar's Office. In this county, most are still in local custody (LC).

Aghadowey
Status: No pre-1870 entries

Aghanloo
Status: No pre-1870 entries

Agherton (Ballyaghran)
Status: No pre-1870 entries

Arboe
Earliest Records: b. 1775-1813 and 1824-; m. 1773-1812 and 1825-
Status: LC

Ardtrea (Artrea)
Earliest Records: b. 1811; m. 1811; d. 1811
Status: LC

Ballinderry
Earliest Records: b. 1802; m. 1803; d. 1802
Status: LC; also pub. by Zara Mettam; SLC film 824282 (1802-70)

Ballyeglish (in Artrea Parish)
Earliest Records: b. 1868; d. 1868
Status: LC

Ballymoney
Earliest Records: b. 1807; m. 1807; d. 1807
Status: LC

Ballyrashane
Status: No pre-1870 entries

Ballynascreen (Draperstown)
Earliest Records: b. 1808; m. 1825-26, 1828-; d. 1824
Status: LC

Ballyscullion
Status: No pre-1870 entries

Balteagh
Status: No pre-1870 entries

Ballywillian
Earliest Records: b. 1826; m. 1827; d. 1837
Status: LC

Banagher (Derry)
Earliest Records: b. 1821; m. 1827; d. 1837
Status: LC

Bovevagh
Status: No pre-1870 entries

Camus-Juxta-Bann (Macosquin)
Status: No pre-1870 entries

Carrick
Status: No pre-1870 entries

Castledawson (in Magherafelt parish)
Earliest Records: b. 1846; d. 1846
Status: LC

Castlerock (in Dunboe parish)
Earliest Records: b. 1870; m. 1871; d. 1874
Status: LC

Clonmany
Status: Lost

Clooney (formed from Glendermot parish)
Earliest Records: b. 1867; d. 1867
Status: LC

Coleraine
Earliest Records: b. 1769; m. 1769; d. 1769
Status: LC

Culmore (in Templemore parish)
Earliest Records: b. 1867; m. 1865; d. 1868
Status: LC; RCB (mf.) (b. 1867-1920; m. 1865-1935)

Cumber, Upper
Earliest Records: b. 1811-18 and 1826-; m. 1811-14 and 1837-; d. 1837-
Status: LC

Cumber, Lower
Earliest Records: b. 1806; m. 1806; d. 1825 and 1855-
Status: LC

Derry Cathedral (St. Columb's or Templemore)
Earliest Records: b. 1642; m. 1649; d. 1642-1775 and 1829-
Missing Records: d. 1776-1828
Status: LC (1642-1703 is published by Parish Register Society, Dublin, 1910); SLC film 599241

Derry City (Christ Church)
Earliest Records: b. 1855
Status: LC

Derry—Free Church (Christ Church)
Earliest Records: b. 1855
Status: LC

Derry—St. Augustine's
Status: No pre-1870 entries

Derryloran
Earliest Records: b. 1797; m. 1797; d. 1795
Status: LC

Desertlyn (Moneymore)
Earliest Records: b. 1797; m. 1797; d. 1798
Status: LC

Desertmartin
Earliest Records: b. 1785; m. 1784-1830, 1832-; d. 1783-88, 1829, 1842-
Status: LC

Desertoghill
Status: No pre-1870 entries

Draperstown (see Ballynascreen)

Drumachose (Limavady)
Earliest Records: b. 1729-52, 1804-32 and 1837-;

m. 1728–53, 1814–35 and 1838–; d. 1729–36, 1823–32 and 1837–
Status: LC; SLC film 496750 (b. 1730–52, 1804–98; m. 1730–50, 1805–45; d. 1730–76, 1822–81)

Dunboe
Earliest Records: b. 1839; m. 1845; d. 1845
Status: LC

Dungiven
Earliest Records: b. 1795; m. 1795–1826, 1828–; d. 1824
Status: LC

Errigal
Status: No pre-1870 entries

Faughanvale
Earliest Records: b. 1802; m. 1802; d. 1802
Status: LC

Formoyle or Fermoyle
Earliest Records: b. 1860; m. 1844; d. 1864
Status: LC

Glendermot or Clondermott
Earliest Records: b. 1810; m. 1808; d. 1828
Status: LC

Glenely
Status: Lost

Kilcronaghan
Earliest Records: b. 1790; m. 1748; d. 1828–29 and 1831–
Status: LC

Kildollagh
Status: No pre-1870 entries

Killelagh
Status: No pre-1870 entries

Killowen
Earliest Records: b. 1824; m. 1824; d. 1825–30 and 1843–
Status: LC

Kilrea
Earliest Records: b. 1801; m. 1802–05 and 1829–; d. 1802–04 and 1829–
Status: LC; SLC film 908817 (1829–62)

Learmount
Earliest Records: b. 1832; m. 1833; d. 1832
Status: LC

Lissan
Earliest Records: b. 1753–; m. 1744–; d. 1753–
Missing Records: b. 1796–1803; m. 1794–1816; d. 1796–1802
Status: LC

Maghera
Earliest Records: b. 1785; m. 1798; d. 1809
Status: LC

Magherafelt
Earliest Records: b. 1718–; m. 1720; d. 1716–
Missing Records: b. 1794–1798; d. 1772–1798
Status: LC

Moville, Upper
Earliest Records: b. 1814; m. 1814; d. 1815
Status: LC

Six Towns (in Ballynascreen parish)
Status: No pre-1870 entries

St. Augustine's (Derry), see Derry—St. Augustine's

Tamlaght
Earliest Records: b. 1801–; m. 1829; d. 1834
Missing Records: b. 1808–1820
Status: LC; also pub. by Zara Mettam; SLC film 824282

Tamlaghtard
Earliest Records: b. 1747–; m. 1747–; d. 1747–
Missing Records: b. 1776–1819, 1841–1843; m. 1776–1819; d. 1776–1819, 1841–
Status: LC

Tamlaght Finlagan
Earliest Records: b. 1796; m. 1796; d. 1796
Status: LC

Tamlaght O'Crilly (Lower)
Status: No pre-1870 entries

Tamlaght O'Crilly (Upper)
Status: No pre-1870 entries

Templemore—see Derry Cathedral

Termoneeny
Earliest Records: b. 1821–; m. 1821–38; d. 1833–
Missing Records: b. 1840–1845; m. 1839–; d. 1834–1845
Status: LC

Woods Chapel (formed from Artrea parish)
Earliest Records: b. 1807; m. 1808; d. 1808
Status: LC

Presbyterian

Note that many of the Presbyterian parish registers of this county have been indexed by the Genealogy Centre, Derry (see Research Services at the end of the chapter). A search of the index will be conducted by the center for a fee. Those indexed are noted as "Indexed by DGC." Copies of some registers are in the Presbyterian Historical Society Archives (PHSA) and/or on microfilm in the PRONI. Generally, the original records are still in the local custody of the parish (LC).

Aghadowey
Starting Date: b. 1855; m. 1845
Status: LC; PRONI MIC 1P/123

Ballyarnett
Starting Date: 1848
Status: LC; Indexed by DGC

Ballygoney
Starting Date: 1834
Status: LC

Ballykelly
Starting Date: b. 1826; m. 1699
Status: LC; PRONI MIC 1P/208

Ballylintagh (dissolved 1883)
Starting Date: 1872
Status: LC

Ballyrashane
Starting Date: b. 1863; m. 1846
Status: LC; PRONI MIC 1P/70

Ballywatt (2nd Ballyrashane)
Starting Date: b. 1867; m. 1845
Status: Indexed by DGC

Ballywillan
Starting Date: b. 1862; m. 1846
Status: LC

Balteagh
Starting Date: m. 1845
Status: LC; PRONI MIC 1P/228

Banagher
Starting Date: b. 1834; m. 1845
Status: LC; PRONI MIC 1P/227

Bellaghy (1st and 2nd)
Starting Date: b. 1862; m. 1845
Status: LC; PRONI MIC 1P/377

Boveedy (Kilrea)
Starting Date: b. 1841; m. 1842
Status: LC; PRONI MIC 1P/18

Bovevagh
Starting Date: b. 1818; m. 1842; d. 1870
Status: LC; Indexed by DGC; PRONI MIC 1P/229

Castledawson
Starting Date: b. 1809; m. 1805
Status: LC; PRONI MIC 1P/90

Castlerock
Starting Date: 1875
Status: Indexed by DGC

Churchtown
Starting Date: b. 1840; m. 1845
Status: LC; PRONI MIC 1P/347

Claggan
Starting Date: 1848
Status: LC

Coagh
Starting Date: b. 1839; m. 1845
Status: LC

Coleraine 1st
Starting Date: 1845
Status: LC; PRONI MIC 1P/54; Indexed by DGC

Coleraine 2nd or New Row
Starting Date: b. 1842; m. 1809
Status: LC; PRONI MIC 1P/31; Indexed by DGC; Families of the Congregation 1831 compiled by Judith E. Wight (nd) SLC 941 62/C1k28w

Coleraine 3rd or Terrace Row
Starting Date: b. 1862; m. 1845
Status: LC; PRONI MIC 1P/101

Crossgar (Coleraine)
Starting Date: b. 1839; m. 1846
Status: LC

Culnady
Starting Date: b. 1882; m. 1864
Status: LC

Cumber Lower (Claudy)
Starting Date: b. 1827; m. 1843
Status: LC; PRONI MIC 1P/147; PHSA

Cumber Upper
Starting Date: 1834
Status: LC; PRONI MIC 1P/148; PHSA

Curran
Starting Date: m. 1845
Status: LC; PRONI MIC 1P/338

Derramore (Limavady)
Starting Date: 1825
Status: LC

Derry 1st
Starting Date: 1825
Status: LC; PRONI MIC 1P/150; Indexed by DGC

Derry 2nd or Strand
Starting Date: b. 1845; m. 1847
Status: LC; PRONI MIC 1P/293; Indexed by DGC

Derry 3rd or Terrace Row
Starting Date: b. 1838; m. 1837
Status: LC

Derry 4th or Carlisle Road
Starting Date: b. 1838; m. 1839
Status: LC; PRONI MIC 1P/67; Indexed by DGC

Draperstown
Starting Date: b. 1876; m. 1845
Status: LC; PRONI MIC 1P/343

Dromore
Starting Date: b. 1889; m. 1869
Status: LC; PRONI MIC 1P/373

Drumachose (Limavady)
Starting Date: 1837
Status: Indexed by DGC

Dunboe 1st (Coleraine)
Starting Date: b. 1805; m. 1845
Status: LC

Dunboe 2nd
Starting Date: b. 1835; m. 1837
Status: LC; PRONI MIC 1P/149

Dungiven
Starting Date: b. 1835; m. 1839
Status: LC

Faughanvale (Eglinton)
Starting Date: b. 1819; m. 1845
Status: LC; PRONI MIC 1P/190; Indexed by DGC

Garvagh 1st
Starting Date: b/m. 1795
Status: LC; PRONI MIC 1P/257

Garvagh 2nd or Main Street
Starting Date: b/m. 1830; d. 1853
Status: LC; PRONI MIC 1P/17

Garvagh 3rd (dissolved 1908)
Starting Date: b. 1872; m. 1864
Status: LC

Glendermott 1st and 2nd
Starting Date: 1855
Status: LC

Gortnessy (Derry)
Starting Date: b. 1839; m. 1845
Status: LC; PRONI MIC 1P/189; Indexed by DGC

Killaigh (Coleraine)
Starting Date: 1805
Status: LC; PHSA

Kilrea
Starting Date: b/m. 1825
Status: LC; PRONI MIC 1P/53 and 261

Largy
Starting Date: b. 1848; m. 1845
Status: LC; PRONI MIC 1P/180

Lecumpher (Moneymore)
Starting Date: 1825
Status: LC

Limavady 1st
Starting Date: 1832
Status: LC; PRONI MIC 1P/34

Limavady 2nd
Starting Date: 1845
Status: LC

Macosquin
Starting Date: b. 1823; m. 1885
Status: LC

Maghera
Starting Date: b. 1843; m. 1843; d. 1861
Status: LC; PRONI MIC 1P/376

Magherafelt 1st
Starting Date: b. 1703; m. 1769
Status: Indexed by DGC

Magherafelt—Union Road
Starting Date: 1868
Status: LC

Magilligan
Starting Date: 1814
Status: LC; PRONI MIC 1P/215

Moneydig
Starting Date: b. 1857; m. 1852
Status: LC; PRONI MIC 1P/93

Moneymore 1st
Starting Date: b/m. 1827
Status: LC; PRONI MIC 1P/339; Indexed by DGC

Moneymore 2nd
Starting Date: b. 1845; m. 1868
Status: LC; PRONI MIC 1P/340; Indexed by DGC

Myroe
Starting Date: b. 1850; m. 1845
Status: LC

Portrush
Starting Date: b. 1843; m. 1846
Status: LC

Portstewart
Starting Date: 1829
Status: LC

Ringsend
Starting Date: b. 1871; m. 1845
Status: LC

Saltersland
Starting Date: b. 1847; m. 1845
Status: LC

Swatragh
Starting Date: No pre-1900 registers
Status: LC

Tobermore
Starting Date: b. 1860; m. 1845
Status: LC; PRONI MIC 1P/344

Waterside
Starting Date: 1866
Status: LC

Roman Catholic

Note that most of the Catholic parish registers of this county have been indexed by the Genealogy Centre in Derry (see Research Services at the end of the chapter). A search of the index will be conducted by the center for a fee. Those indexed are noted as "Indexed by GC-Derry."

Microfilm copies of all registers are also available in the National Library of Ireland (NLI), and through the LDS library system.

Civil Parish: Aghadowey
Map Grid: 20
RC Parish: see Coleraine; also part Errigal
Diocese: DE

Civil Parish: Aghanloo
Map Grid: 8
RC Parish: Newtown Limavady (Drumachose, Tamlaght Finlagin, and Aghanloo)
Diocese: DE
Earliest Record: b. 12.1855; m. 4.1856; d. 5.1859
Missing Dates: d. ends 12.1869
LC; NLI (mf); Indexed by GC-Derry (to 1900)

Civil Parish: Agivey
Map Grid: 21
RC Parish: see Coleraine
Diocese: DE

Civil Parish: Ardboe
Map Grid: 46
RC Parish: see Ardboe, Co. Tyrone
Diocese: DE

Civil Parish: Artrea
Map Grid: 42
RC Parish: Artrea and Desertlin (Moneymore)
Diocese: AM
Earliest Record: b. 1.1832; m. 4.1830
Missing Dates: b. 3.1834-1.1838, 2.1843-11.1854; m. 7.1843-11.1854, ends 2.1869
LC; NLI (mf); Indexing by GC-Derry planned

Civil Parish: Ballinderry
Map Grid: 48
RC Parish: Ballinderry
Diocese: AM

Earliest Record: b. 12.1826; m. 1.1827
Missing Dates: b. 10.1838-9.1841
LC; NLI (mf); Indexing by GC-Derry planned

Civil Parish: Ballyaghran
Map Grid: 2
RC Parish: see Coleraine
Diocese: CR

Civil Parish: Ballymoney
Map Grid: 6
RC Parish: see Co. Antrim
Diocese: CR

Civil Parish: Ballynascreen
Map Grid: 36
RC Parish: Ballynascreen or Draperstown (see Dungiven for pre-1834 records)
Diocese: DE
Earliest Record: b. 11.1825; m. 11.1825; d. 11.1825
Missing Dates: b. 2.1834-6.1836; d. ends 4.1832
LC; NLI (mf); Indexed by GC-Derry (to 1900)

Civil Parish: Ballyrashane
Map Grid: 4
RC Parish: see Co. Antrim
Diocese: CR

Civil Parish: Ballyscullion
Map Grid: 39
RC Parish: Bellaghy, see also Magherafelt
Diocese: DE
Earliest Record: b. 9.1844; m. 9.1844
LC; NLI (mf); Indexed by GC-Derry (to 1900)

Civil Parish: Ballywillin
Map Grid: 1
RC Parish: see Coleraine; also see Co. Antrim
Diocese: CR

Civil Parish: Balteagh
Map Grid: 12
RC Parish: see Errigal
Diocese: DE

Civil Parish: Banagher
Map Grid: 15
RC Parish: Feeny (or Banagher)
Diocese: DE
Earliest Record: b. 1.1848; m. 12.1851
LC; NLI (mf); Indexed by GC-Derry (to 1900)

Civil Parish: Bovevagh
Map Grid: 13
RC Parish: part Banagher; part Dungiven
Diocese: DE

Civil Parish: Carrick
Map Grid: 11
RC Parish: Newtown Limavady, see Aghanloo
Diocese: DE

Page 20.

Births and Baptismes in August, 1655.

Ann, the daughter of Hugh Powell, borne July 19th, bap. Aug. 2th.
Ralph, the son of Richard Ball of the bogs side, bap. 3th.
Moses, the son of William Hamilton, baptized the 3th.
Jane, the daughter of John Hunter, baptized the 9th.
Robert, the son of George Holcraft, labourer, bap. the 10th.
James, the son of Hugh McGrañaghan of Taghboine, bap. 16th.
Margarett, the daughter of Andrew Miller, bap. the 16th.
Elizabeth, the daughter of Theophilus Davis, borne August the
    eleventh, baptized the 16th.
John, the son of William Colewell of Clendermott pish, bap. 19th.
Isabell, the daughter of Robert Lion, baptized the 30th.
James, the son of George Heggerty baptized the 30th.
Thomas, son of Thomas Colwell born Aug. 11th, bap. 30th.
Jennett, daughter of John King born Aug 22th, bap. the 30th.

Birthes and Baptismes in September 1655.

James, son of James Hill, borne and baptized Sep. y[e] 1st.
Bryan, the son of Turlagh O Devin, baptized the 1st.
Ellinor, the daughter of Donnogh Tooll, baptized the 1st.
Barbara, the daughter of John Graham, borne the 1st, bap. 6th.
Wentworth, son of Wentworth Boucher, souldier, bap. the 11th.
Anne, daughter of Richard Hancie, souldier, baptized Sep. 20th.
Joseph, the son of William Richards, borne and bap. the 23th.
John, the son of Neale McNicholls, borne and bap. 24th.
Mary, the daughter of John Robbinson, bor. 16, bap. 25th.
Margarett, the daughter of Thomas Grier, bor. and bap. 26th.

Birthes and baptismes in October 1655.

James, the son of Andrew Cunningham, bor. Sep. 23th, bap. Octo. 4th.
Manus, son of Henry McKauthery, porter, bap. Octob. y[e] 7th.
Daniell, son of Thomas Radley, baptized October the 15th.
Elizabeth, the daughter of Alphord Ripley, bor. 12th, bap. 18th.
William, the son of Mr William Tuckey, bor. October 17th, bap. 21th.
John, son of John Heard of Clendermott parish, bap. 22th.
George, son of James Neeper of Cumber parish, bap. 26th.
Jennett, the daughter of William Davis of Doñoghedy, bap. 26th.
Sara, the daughter of Thomas Zanchy, souldier, bap. the 28th.
Henry, the son of Humphrey Godfrey, bor. October the 21th, bap.
    30th.
James, the son of James Davis, souldier, baptized the 30th.

Page 28.

Birthes and Baptismes, November 1655.

James, the son of Thomas Hickes, souldier, baptized Nov. y[e] 10th.
Mul Muřey, the son of Hugh McSwyne of Killegh, bap. Novem-
    ber 10th.
Thomas, the son of John Stoyle of this parish, baptized the 11th.
Jennett, the daughter of John Mitchell of Birt, baptized the 12th.
Thomas, the son John Reinalds of Clendermott parish, bap. the
    15th.
James, son of Edward Erwyne of Clendermott parish, bap. the 15th.

Extract from a published copy of the baptismal register of Templemore, County
Derry, 1655, from the "Register of Derry Cathedral . . ." (Dublin: Parish Register
Society, 1910).

Civil Parish: Clondermot
Map Grid: 27
RC Parish: Glendermot (Waterside)
Diocese: DE
Earliest Record: b. 1.1864; m. 1.1864
LC; NLI (mf); Indexing by GC-Derry planned

Civil Parish: Coleraine
Map Grid: 3
RC Parish: Coleraine
Diocese: CR
Earliest Record: b. 5.1848; m. 5.1848
LC; NLI (mf); Indexed by GC-Derry (to 1900)

Civil Parish: Cumber Lower
Map Grid: 28
RC Parish: part Glendermot, see Clondermot; part
Cumber, see below

Civil Parish: Cumber Upper
Map Grid: 30
RC Parish: Cumber Upper and Learmount (Claudy)
Diocese: DE
Earliest Record: b. 5.1863; m. 9.1863
LC; NLI (mf); Indexed by GC-Derry (to 1900)

Civil Parish: Derry City
Map Grid: 25
RC Parish: see Templemore
Diocese: DE

Civil Parish: Derryloran
Map Grid: 45
RC Parish: see Desertcreat, Co. Tyrone
Diocese: AM

Civil Parish: Desertlyn
Map Grid: 44
RC Parish: part Artrea; part Magherafelt
Diocese: AM

Civil Parish: Desertmartin
Map Grid: 40
RC Parish: Desertmartin and Kilcronaghan
Diocese: DE
Earliest Record: b. 11.1848; m. 11.1848; d. 11.1848
LC; NLI (mf); Indexed by GC-Derry (to 1900)

Civil Parish: Desertoghill
Map Grid: 23
RC Parish: see Kilrea; also part Errigal
Diocese: DE

Civil Parish: Drumachose
Map Grid: 10
RC Parish: Newtown Limavady, see Aghanloo
Diocese: DE

Civil Parish: Dunboe
Map Grid: 16
RC Parish: Dunboe, Macosquin and Aghadowey

(Coleraine)
Diocese: DE
Earliest Record: b. 8.1843
LC; NLI (mf); Indexing by GC-Derry planned

Civil Parish: Dungiven
Map Grid: 14
RC Parish: Dungiven, see also Ballynascreen
Diocese: DE
Earliest Record: b. 7.1847; m. 9.1864; d. 3.1870
Missing Dates: d. ends 12.1871
LC; NLI (mf); Indexed by GC-Derry (to 1900)

Civil Parish: Errigal
Map Grid: 22
RC Parish: Errigal (Garvagh)
Diocese: DE
Earliest Record: b. 4.1846; m. 2.1873
LC; NLI (mf); Indexed by GC-Derry (to 1900)

Civil Parish: Faughanvale
Map Grid: 26
RC Parish: Faughanvale and Lower Cumber (Creggan)
Diocese: DE
Earliest Record: b. 9.1863; m. 11.1860
LC; NLI (mf); Indexed by GC-Derry (to 1900)

Civil Parish: Formoyle
Map Grid: 18
RC Parish: Magilligan, see Tamlaghtard; also Dunboe
Diocese: DE

Civil Parish: Kilcronaghan
Map Grid: 37
RC Parish: see Desertmartin
Diocese: DE

Civil Parish: Kildollagh
Map Grid: 5
RC Parish: see Coleraine
Diocese: CR

Civil Parish: Killelagh
Map Grid: 33
RC Parish: part Errigal; part Maghera
Diocese: DE

Civil Parish: Killowen
Map Grid: 17
RC Parish: see Coleraine
Diocese: DE

Civil Parish: Kilrea
Map Grid: 32
RC Parish: Kilrea and Desertoghill
Diocese: DE
Earliest Record: b. 8.1846; m. 8.1846; d. 8.1846
Missing Dates: m. ends 8.1865
LC; NLI (mf); Indexed by GC-Derry (to 1900)

Civil Parish: Learmont
Map Grid: 31
RC Parish: see Cumber Upper
Diocese: DE

Civil Parish: Lissan
Map Grid: 43
RC Parish: Lissan, see Co. Tyrone
Diocese: AM

Civil Parish: Londonderry City
Map Grid: 25
RC Parish: see Templemore; also Glendermot, see Clondermot
Diocese: DE

Civil Parish: Loughermore
Map Grid: 29
RC Parish: see Cumber Upper
Diocese: DE

Civil Parish: Macosquin
Map Grid: 19
RC Parish: part Coleraine; part Dunboe
Diocese: DE

Civil Parish: Maghera
Map Grid: 34
RC Parish: Maghera and Killylough; part Termoneeny
Diocese: DE
Earliest Record: b. 3.1841; m. 5.1841; d. 5.1848
Missing Dates: 5.1853-10.1857
LC; NLI (mf); Indexed by GC-Derry (to 1900)

Civil Parish: Magherafelt
Map Grid: 41
RC Parish: Magherafelt and Ardtrea
Diocese: AM
Earliest Record: b. 1.1834; m. 1.1834
Missing Dates: b. 7.1857-1.1858; m. 4.1857-2.1858
LC; NLI (mf); Indexing by GC-Derry planned

Civil Parish: Tamlaght
Map Grid: 47
RC Parish: see Co. Tyrone
Diocese: AM

Civil Parish: Tamlaghtard
Map Grid: 7
RC Parish: Tamlaghtard or Magilligan
Diocese: DE
Earliest Record: b. 9.1863; m. 10.1863; d. 9.1863
LC; NLI (mf); Indexed by GC-Derry (to 1900)

Civil Parish: Tamlaght Finlagan
Map Grid: 9
RC Parish: Newtown Limavady, see Aghanloo
Diocese: DE

Civil Parish: Tamlaght O'Crilly
Map Grid: 35

RC Parish: Greenlough; also part Kilrea
Earliest Record: b. 1845; m. 1846
Diocese: DE
LC; NLI (mf); Indexed by GC-Derry (to 1900)

Civil Parish: Templemore
Map Grid: 24
RC Parish: Templemore (St. Columb's, Long Tower, Derry)
Diocese: DE
Earliest Record: b. 10.1823; m. 11.1823
Missing Dates: b. 9.1826-9.1836, 4.1863-1.1864; m. 9.1826-3.1835, 7.1836-1.1841, 11.1851-1.1854
LC; NLI (mf); Indexed by GC-Derry (to 1900)

Civil Parish: Termoneeny
Map Grid: 38
RC Parish: Termoneeny (Lavey)
Diocese: DE
Earliest Record: b. 11.1871; m. 12.1873
LC; NLI (mf); Indexed by GC-Derry (to 1900)

Commercial and Social Directories

1820

J. Pigot's *Commercial Directory of Ireland* contains information on the gentry, nobility, and traders in and around the towns of Coleraine and Londonderry.

1824

J. Pigot's *City of Dublin and Hibernian Provincial Directory* includes traders, nobility, gentry, and clergy lists of Castledawson, Coleraine, Dungiven, Kilrea, Londonderry, Maghera, Magherafelt, Moneymore, and Newtown-Limavady.

1842

Matthew Martin's *Belfast Directory* contains an alphabetical list of traders, merchants, and gentry, residents of the principal streets, and the nobility and gentry in and around the towns of Castledawson, Coleraine, Magherafelt, and Moneymore.

1846

Slater's *National Commercial Directory of Ireland* lists nobility, clergy, traders, etc., in Castledawson and Bellaghy, Coleraine, Portstewart, Bushmills and Port Ballintrae, Dungiven, Garvagh and Ballinameen, Kilrea, Londonderry, Maghera, Magherafelt, Moneymore and Coagh, and Newtown-Limavady.

1852

Henderson's *Belfast and Province of Ulster Directory* has lists of inhabitants, traders, etc., in and around the towns of Castledawson, Coleraine, Londonderry, and Maghera.

1854

Further edition of above extended to cover Castledawson, Coleraine, Londonderry, Maghera, Magherafelt, Moneymore. Further editions were issued in 1856, 1858, 1861 (with the addition of Newtown-Limavady), 1865, 1868, 1870, 1877, 1880, 1884, 1894, and 1900.

1856

Slater's *Royal National Commercial Directory of Ireland* lists nobility, gentry, clergy, traders, etc., in Castledawson and Bellaghy, Coleraine, Portstewart, Bushmills and Port Ballintrae, Dungiven, Garvagh and Ballinameen, Kilrea, Londonderry, Maghera, Magherafelt, Moneymore and Coagh, and Newtown-Limavady.

1865

R. Wynne's *Business Directory of Belfast* also covers Coleraine, Londonderry, Newtown-Limavady, Maghera, and Moneymore.

1870

Slater's *Directory of Ireland* contains trade, nobility, and clergy lists for Castledawson, Coleraine, Dungiven, Garvagh, Kilrea, Londonderry, Maghera, Magherafelt, Moneymore, and Newtown-Limavady.

1881

Slater's *Royal National Commercial Directory of Ireland* contains lists of traders, clergy, nobility, and farmers in adjoining parishes of the towns of Coleraine, Dungiven, Kilrea, Limavady, Londonderry, Maghera, Magherafelt, Moneymore, and Coagh.

1887

Derry Almanac of Coleraine, Dungiven, Kilrea, Londonderry, Limavady, and Portstewart.

1894

Slater's *Royal National Directory of Ireland* lists traders, police, teachers, farmers, and private residents in each of the towns, villages, and parishes of the county.

Family History

Beresford Family Papers (1800–1922). PRONI DOD 519 and SLC film 247312.

Boyle. *Genealogical Memoranda Relating to the Family of Boyle of Limavady.* Londonderry, 1903.

"Entries from the Family Bible of Alexander and Esther Crookshank. *Ir. Anc.* 9 (2) (1977): 1–2.

Bewley, Sir Edmund. *The Folliotts of Londonderry and Chester.* 1902.

Gage Family Papers (1610–1837). PRONI; SLC film 248301.

Abercorn Papers—Hamilton family (1250–1942). PRONI DOD 669; SLC film 248300.

Kennedy, F.E. *A Family of Kennedy of Clogher and Londonderry ca. 1600–1938.* Taunton, 1938.

Macausland Family Papers (1250–1942). PRONI DOD 669; SLC film 248300.

MacRory, R.A. *The Past—MacRorys of Duneane, Castle-Dawson, Limavady, and Belfast.* Belfast, n.d.

"Some Account of the Sept of the O'Cathains of Ciannachta Glinne-Geimhin. Now the O'Kanes of the Co. of Londonderry." *Ulster J. Arch.* 3 (1855): 1–8, 265–72; 4 (1856): 139–48.

The O'Doherty Information Pack: History and Genealogy. Derry Youth and Community Workshop, 1985.

"Richardson of Somerset." Pedigree in *Swanzy Notebooks.* RCB Library, Dublin.

Wray—see Co. Donegal, Family Histories section.

Gravestone Inscriptions

Aghanloo C of I. *Irish Family Links.* 1985, 2 (3): 15, 1, 9.

Aghanloo Old. *Irish Family Links.* 1985, 2 (3): 15, 1, 9.

Ballykelly. *Irish Family Links.* 1985, 2 (3): 15, 1, 9.

Ballykelly (2). *Irish Family Links.* 1985, 2 (4): 12–14, 19–22.

Ballykelly Presbyterian. *Irish Family Links.* 1985, 2 (4): 12–14, 19–22.

Balteagh Presbyterian. *Irish Family Links.* 1985, 2 (4): 12–14, 19–22.

Churchill (Ballinderry). *Sth. Derry Hist. Soc. J.* 1 (3) 1982/83: 325–328.

Derramore Presbyterian. *Irish Family Links.* 1985, 2 (4): 12–14, 19–22.

Draperstown (Presbyterian Congregation Church). Published by Ballynascreen Historical Society, 1982.

Drumachose Old. *Irish Family Links.* 1985, 2 (4): 12–14, 19–22.

Drumachose Presbyterian. *Irish Family Links.* 1985, 2 (5): 19–24.

Eglish (Loup). *Sth. Derry Hist. Soc. J.* 1 (2) 1980/81: 122–129.

Eglish (Gort, Ballinderry). *Sth. Derry Hist. Soc. J.* 1 (3) 1982/83: 329–330.

Glendermot (Old) (Derry). Pub. by Sheelagh and David Dodd, Londonderry, 1988. SLC 941.62/L1 v3t.

Largy Presbyterian. *Irish Family Links.* 1985, 2 (5): 19–24.

Limavady First Presbyterian. *Irish Family Links.* 1985, 2 (5): 19–24.

Limavady Reformed Presbyterian. *Irish Family Links.* 1985, 2 (5): 19–24.

Limavady RC. *Irish Family Links.* 1985, 2 (5): 19–24.

Limavady-St. Canice's RC. *Irish Family Links*. 1985, 2 (5): 19-24.

Maghera and Magherafelt area. Published in *South Derry Historical Society Journal*.

Magilligan Presbyterian. *Irish Family Links*. 1986, 2 (6): 19-24.

Magilligan RC. *Irish Family Links*. 1986, 2 (6): 19-24.

Myroe Presbyterian. *Irish Family Links*. 1986, 2 (6): 19-24.

St. Canice's RC. *Irish Family Links*. 1986, 2 (6): 19-24.

St. Finlough's RC. *Irish Family Links*. 1985, 2 (4): 12-14, 19-22.

Tamlaghtard C of I. *Irish Family Links*. 1986, 2 (6): 19-24.

Tamlaghtfinlagan. *Irish Family Links*. 1985, 2 (4): 12-14, 19-22.

Coleraine-St. Patrick's Church. In Henry, Sam. *The Story of St. Patrick's Church, Coleraine, Its History, Heraldry, Sculptured Stones, Stained Glass, Old Families and Alliances, Architecture and Traditions*. Coleraine: Coleraine Chronicle, n.d. (c.1940s).

Newspapers

Derry has a good series of papers. An indexed set of abstracts of cuttings from *Derry Journal* is in the GO (Reynell Coll. Ms 446A) and SLC film 100159. Also, Irish Genealogical Abstracts from *Derry Journal* (1772-1784; by Donald M. Schlegel; Baltimore, 1990) has indexed birth, death, marriage, and legal notices. SLC 941.62 B3sd.

Title: *Coleraine Chronicle* (continued as *Chronicle* in 1967)
Published in: Coleraine, 1844-current
NLI Holdings: 1.1905-11.1967
BL Holdings: 4.1844-in progress

Title: *Coleraine Constitution* (continued as *Northern Constitution* in 1908)
Published in: Coleraine, 1875-current
NLI Holdings: 1.1905-6.1908; 10.1908-in progress
BL Holdings: 4.1877-10.1908; 10.1908-in progress

Title: *Londonderry Chronicle*
Published in: Derry, 1829-72
NLI Holdings: 2-10.1829
BL Holdings: 2-10.1829

Title: *Londonderry Guardian*
Published in: Derry, 1857-71
BL Holdings: 9.1857-9.1871
Derry Central Library Holdings: 1857-71 (microfilm)

Title: *Londonderry Journal* (continued as *Derry Journal* in 1880)
Published in: Derry, 1772-current
NLI Holdings: 1.1772-4.1796; 1.1798-12.1809;
1810-1818; 1820-1.1827; 9.1829-1836; 9.1837-12.1847; 1.1848-10.1851; 1852-1855; 9.1860-12.1861; 1858; 1859; 7.1862-12.1863; 1864; 1865; 1866; 9.1933-in progress
BL Holdings: 1.1835-7.1869; 1.1870-in progress
Derry Central Library Holdings: 1825-current (early issues on microfilm)

Title: *Londonderry Sentinel* (continued as *Sentinel* in 1974)
Published in: Derry, 1829-current
NLI Holdings: 1.1885-12.1911; 1913; 6.1921-7.1945; 1.1954-5.1974; 7.1924-in progress
BL Holdings: 9.1829-10.1854; 1.1856-7.1869; 1.1870-12.1925; 7.1926-in progress
Derry Central Library Holdings: 1829-current (early issues on microfilm)

Title: *Londonderry Standard* (continued as *Derry Standard* in 1888)
Published in: Derry, 1836-1964
NLI Holdings: 1.1853-12.1924; 1.1950-12.1963
BL Holdings: 11.1836-7.1869; 1.1870-1.1964
Derry Central Library Holdings: 1836-current (early issues on microfilm)

Wills and Administrations

A discussion of the types of records, where they are held, their availability, and their value is given in the Wills section of the introduction. The availability of prerogative wills, administrations, and marriage license records is also described in the relevant parts of the same section. Where available, published sources of these records are given in the Miscellaneous Sources section.

Pre-1858 Wills and Administrations

Consistorial Wills. County Derry is mainly in the diocese of Derry, with some parishes in Connor and Armagh dioceses. The guide to Catholic parish records in this chapter shows the diocese to which each civil parish belonged. The wills of residents of each diocese were usually proven within that diocese (see Wills section for exceptions). The following records survive:

Wills
Only for Connor Diocese—see Co. Antrim.

Abstracts
See the introduction.

Indexes
Derry (1612-1858) published by Phillimore; Connor—see Co. Antrim; Armagh—see Co. Armagh.

Post-1858 Wills and Administrations

County Derry was served by the District Registry of Londonderry. The surviving records are kept in the PRONI. Records include: Londonderry District Will Book (1858-1899). PRONI; SLC films 930300, 942216-22.

Marriage Records

Indexes

Armagh (1727-1845) NAI and PRONI; SLC films 100859-60. Connor (1721-1845) NAI and PRONI; SLC film 100867. Index to Belfast, Londonderry, and Armagh Wills and Administrations (1900-1909 for Derry) PRONI; SLC film 930388.

Miscellaneous Sources

O'Kane, Willie. "Surnames of Co. Derry." *Irish Roots* (2) (1993): 30-31.

Colby, Thomas, ed. "Ordnance Survey of the County of Londonderry." Volume 1. "Memoir of the City and North Western Liberties of Londonderry." "Parish of Templemore." Dublin: Hodges & Smith, 1837.

Derry–Sources for Family History. Mitchell. Genealogy Centre, Derry, 1992.

"Derry Clergy List 1631." *Derriana* (1980): 9-13. SLC film 994003.

Desertmartin Estate Rental 1877-1886. PRONI D3262 (tenants, holdings, and rent, with some comments).

Kernohan, J.W. *The County of Londonderry in Three Centuries, with Notices of the Ironmonger's Estate.* Belfast: the author, 1921.

"Mortality in Magherafelt, County Derry in the Early Eighteenth Century." *Ir. Hist. Stud.* 19 (1974): 125-35.

Provisional list of pre-1900 School Registers in the PRONI. *Ulster Gen. & Hist. Guild.* 9 (1986): 60-71. Lists registers and PRONI reference numbers for all NI counties.

"Popish Clergy in Derry 1704." *Derriana* (1980): 14-25.

"Priests of Derry 1820-1905." *Derriana* (1980): 26-34.

Simpson, Robert. *The Annals of Derry, showing the Rise and Progess of the Town from the earliest accounts on Records to the Plantation under King James I-1613. And thence of the City of Londonderry to the Present Time.* Londonderry: Hempton, 1847.

A memoir explanatory of the chart and survey of the county of Londonderry. George Vaughan Sampson. London, 1814.

An historical account of the plantation in Ulster at the commencement of the seventeenth century, 1608-1620. George Hill. Shannon, 1877.

City on the Foyle. Sam Hughes. Londonderry, 1984.

Derriana: Essays and occasional verses chiefly relating to the Diocese of Derry by Most Reverend Dr. O'Doherty. Dublin, 1902.

Derry, A City Invincible. Brian Mitchell. Eglinton, 1990.

Derry Clergy and Parishes. James B. Leslie. Enniskillen, 1937.

Derry, Donegal and Modern Ulster, 1790-1921. Desmond Murphy. Londonderry, 1981.

Historical Gleanings from County Derry and some from Fermanagh. Sam Martin. Dublin, 1955.

Londonderry and the Donegal Highlands. London: Ward, Lock & Co., 1921.

North West Ulster. Alastair Rowan. London, 1979.

Notes on the place-names of the parishes and townlands of the county of Londonderry. Alfred Moor Munn. Londonderry, 1925.

On the Banks of the Foyle, Historical photographs of Victorian and Edwardian Derry. Brian Mitchell. Belfast, 1989.

Ordnance Survey of the country of Londonderry, Volume 1–Memoir of the city and Northwest Liberties of Londonderry, Parish of Templemore. Colonel Colby. Dublin, 1837.

Siege City, The Story of Derry and Londonderry. Brian Lacy. Belfast, 1990.

Statistical Survey of the County of Londonderry. Rev. George Vaughan Sampson. Dublin, 1802. SLC film 924934.

The Londonderry Plantation 1609-1641. T.W. Moody. Belfast, 1939.

The Londonderry Plantation 1609-1914. James Stevens Curl. Chichester, 1986.

The Maiden City and the Western Ocean. Sholto Cooke. Dublin, n.d.

The Siege of Derry. Patrick Macroy. London, 1980.

The Siege and History of Londonderry. John Hempton. Londonderry, 1861.

Ulster's Historic City, Derry Londonderry. T.H. Mullin. Coleraine, 1986.

Workhouse Records: Records of Limavady Union Workhouse (1864-1927). PRONI; SLC film 259176. Records of Magherafelt Union Workhouse (1842-1899). PRONI; SLC film 259179-80.

Research Sources and Services

Journals

Derriana (published by the Derry Diocesan Historical Society, 1978-present)

South Derry Historical Society Journal (1980-present)

Benbradagh (Dungiven parish magazine)

North Irish Roots (published by North of Ireland Family History Society)

Libraries and Information Sources

Central Library, 35 Foyle Street, Derry BT48 6AL, N. Ireland. Ph: (01504) 266888. The Local Studies department has an extensive collection of local materials, including maps, photographs, and newspapers.

Ulster-American Folk Park Library. See Libraries in Co. Tyrone chapter.

Research Services

Genealogy Centre, 4–22 Butcher St., Derry BT48 6HL, N. Ireland. Ph: (01504) 373177 or 261967. Fax: (01504) 374818. This is the major center in the county for family history material. It has compiled a database of one million records on Co. Derry and the Inishowen peninsula of Donegal. The center has indexed all of the Catholic parish records (pre-1900) and many Presbyterian registers, as well as civil marriage registers, passenger lists, gravestone inscriptions, and a range of census substitutes. Researchers are advised to contact the center for an updated list of registers, and other sources, indexed. Research is conducted for a fee.

Irish World, 6C Coleraine Road, Maghera BT46 EBN, N. Ireland. Ph: (0648) 43187

See also Research Services in Belfast in the introduction.

Societies

North of Ireland Family History Society, Queens University of Belfast, Dept. of Education, 69 University Street, Belfast BT7 1HL. Publishers of *North Irish Roots*

Ballinascreen Historical Society, Mr. Graham Mawhinney, Labby, Draperstown, Magherafelt, Co. Derry, BT45 7BE. Ph: (01648) 28514

Coleraine Historical Society, Miss Peggy Voles, 16 Millbank Avenue, Portstewart, Co. Derry, BT55 7DQ. Ph: (01265) 832636

Desertmartin Local History Group, Ms. Alice Gribbin, Annagh, Desertmartin, Magherafelt, Co. Derry, BT45 5NB. Ph: (01648) 32844

Killultagh Historical Society, Mrs. Pearl Hutchinson, 11 Drumagarner Road, Kilrea, Coleraine, Co. Derry, BT51 5TB. Ph: (01849) 422494

Kilrea Local History Group, Mrs. Pearl Hutchinson, 11 Drumagarner Road, Kilrea, Coleraine, Co. Derry, BT51 5TB. Ph: (01266) 540517

Londonderry Naturalists Field Club, Mrs. Amy Moore, 11 Rossdowney Park, Derry, BT47 1NR. Ph: (01504) 42258

Moneyneena Local History Group, Mr. Mickey Joe Callagher, 30 Cloane Road, Draperstown, Magherafelt, Co. Derry, BT45 7EF. Ph: (01648) 28864

Roe Valley Historical Society, Mrs. Marty Tierney, Beaupre, 108 Roe Mill Road, Limavady, Co. Derry, BT49 9BE. Ph: (015047) 63204

Derry Civil Parishes as Numbered on Map

1. Ballywillin
2. Ballyaghran
3. Coleraine
4. Ballyrashane
5. Kildollagh
6. Ballymoney (2 pts.)
7. Tamlaghtard (Magilligan)
8. Aghanloo
9. Tamlaght Finlagan
10. Drumachose
11. Carrick
12. Balteagh
13. Bovevagh (2 pts.)
14. Dungiven
15. Banagher
16. Dunboe
17. Killowen
18. Formoyle
19. Macosquin
20. Aghadowey
21 Agivey
22. Errigal
23. Desertoghill
24. Templemore
25. Derry

26. Faughanvale
27. Clondermot
28. Cumber Lr.
29. Loughermore
30. Cumber Upp.
31. Learmont
32. Kilrea
33. Killelagh
34. Maghera (2 pts.)
35. Tamlaght O'Crilly
36. Ballynascreen
37. Kilcronaghan
38. Termoneeny
39. Ballyscullion
40. Desertmartin
41. Magherafelt
42. Artrea (or Ardtrea)
43. Lissan
44. Desertlyn
45. Derryloran (2 pts.)
46. Arboe
47. Tamlaght
48. Ballinderry

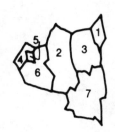

CIVIL PARISHES OF COUNTY DERRY

BARONIES

1. LIBERTIES OF COLERAINE
2. KEENAGHT
3. COLERAINE
4. LIBERTIES OF DERRY
5. CITY OF DERRY
6. TIRKEERAN
7. LOUGHINSHOLIN

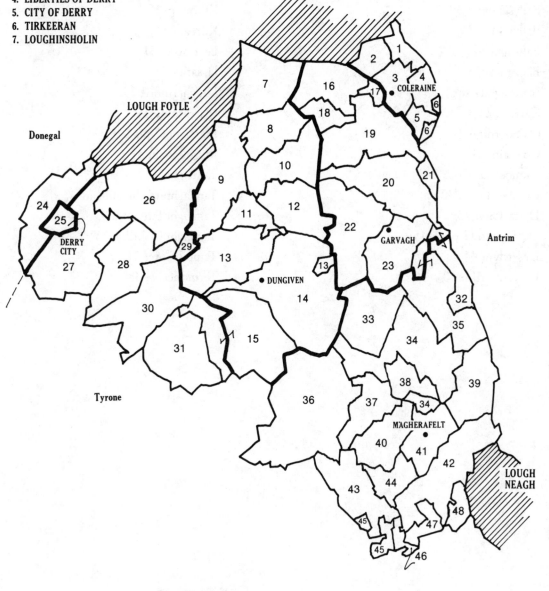

⊢⊓ = CIVIL PARISHES ADJOINING ACROSS
BARONY BOUNDARIES.

Derry Parishes in Alphabetical Order

Aghadowey: 20

Aghanloo: 8

Agivey: 21

Arboe: 46

Artrea: 42

Ballinderry: 48

Ballyaghran: 2

Ballymoney (2 pts.): 6

Ballynascreen: 36

Ballyrashane: 4

Ballyscullion: 39

Ballywillin: 1

Balteagh: 12

Banagher: 15

Bovevagh (2 pts.): 13

Carrick: 11

Clondermot: 27

Coleraine: 3

Cumber Lr.: 28

Cumber Upp.: 30

Derry City: 25

Derryloran (2 pts.): 45

Desertlyn: 44

Desertmartin: 40

Desertoghill: 23

Drumachose: 10

Dunboe: 16

Dungiven: 14

Errigal: 22

Faughanvale: 26

Formoyle: 18

Kilcronaghan: 37

Kildollagh: 5

Killelagh: 33

Killowen: 17

Kilrea: 32

Learmont: 31

Lissan: 43

Loughermore: 29

Macosquin: 19

Maghera (2 pts.): 34

Magherafelt: 41

Tamlaght: 47

Tamlaghtard (Magilligan): 7

Tamlaght Finlagan: 9

Tamlaght O'Crilly: 35

Templemore: 24

Termoneeny: 38

County Donegal

A Brief History

This Ulster coastal county, which is largely bog and mountain land, contains the towns of Letterkenny, Donegal, Ballyshannon, Lifford, Stranorlar, Killybegs, and Bundoran.

County Donegal was known as the Kingdom of Tirconnell in the old Irish administrative system. It was the territory of the powerful O'Donnell family. The other major families in the county were O'Boyle, O'Doherty, O'Friel, O'Sheil, MacWard, McLoughlin, McDunlevy, McGillespie, MacRearty, McGrath, McGonagle, O'Mulholland, O'Harkin, O'Derry, and O'Strahan. The McSweeneys, also a relatively common name in the county, were a gallowglass, or mercenary, family who arrived in the county in the thirteenth century.

This county was little affected by the Norman invasion in the twelfth century, and it was not until the late sixteenth century that the English gained any foothold. This was lost again in 1592 when the O'Donnells, under their chief Red Hugh O'Donnell, joined with the O'Neills in a rebellion against the English. This rebellion ended in the defeat of the Ulster Chieftains in 1602, and the county was subsequently included in the plantation of Ulster. Under this scheme, the lands were confiscated from the native Irish owners and given to undertakers, i.e., to persons who were granted land on the agreement that they would bring over settlers from England or Scotland.

Among the common settler names in the county are those of Elliott, Campbell, Anderson, Baird, Thompson, McClintock, Hamilton, Browne, Barr, Stewart, Smith, Johnston, Irwin, Morrison, Young, and White.

A general indication of the proportion of native Irish, Scottish, and English can be estimated from the religious persuasions of the inhabitants, as the native Irish were generally Catholic, the Scottish Presbyterian, and the English Protestant or Episcopalian. In 1861, when the census first ascertained religion, the proportions of each religion were seventy-five, eleven, and thirteen percent respectively.

In the eighteenth century the county remained relatively remote. Contemporary maps show few roads in the county, and the accounts of various travelers tell of the unique customs of some of its people.

The Penal Laws were specifically enacted at the beginning of the eighteenth century to suppress Catholics. However, they also disadvantaged Presbyterians. For this reason, there was considerable emigration of the so-called Scots-Irish from Donegal and other Ulster counties during the eighteenth century.

The density of population on the arable land in County Donegal was one of the highest in the country in the early nineteenth century. The county was not as badly affected as many others in the Great Famine of 1845-47. The population was 296,000 in 1841, and by 1851 it had fallen to 255,000. Almost 28,000 people died in the county between 1845 and 1850, and further thousands emigrated.

Census and Census Substitutes

1612-13

Survey of Undertakers Planted in Donegal (names, acreages allotted, and account of the progress of each). *Hist. Mss. Comm. Rep.* (Hastings Mss.) 4 (1947): 159-82.

1630

Muster Roll. BL add. ms. 4770; printed in *Donegal Annual* 10 (2) (1972): 124-49.

1642

Muster Roll. SLC film 897012.

1654

Civil Survey, Vol. 3.

1654–1656

"The Civil Survey A.D." Robert C. Simington. Counties of Donegal, London-Derry, Tyrone. Vol III. With returns of church lands for the three counties. Dublin: Stationery Office, 1937.

1659

"Census" of Ireland. Edited by S. Pender. Dublin: Stationery Office, 1939. NLI 16551. SLC film 924648.

1663–65

Hearth Money Roll Extracts. NAI film 2473.

1665

Hearth Money Roll. GO 538; NLI ms. 9583/4; SLC film 100181, 258502. Lists have been printed for the following parishes in *The Laggan and its Presbyterianism*, by A.G. Lecky (1905): Taughboyne (p. 89); Clonleigh (p. 91); Raphoe (and Convoy) (p. 92); Donoughmore (p. 93); Stranorlar (p. 94); Leck (p. 94).

1669

Subsidy Roll (Kilmacrenan, Raphoe, Taghboyne, Tirhugh). SLC film 258502; PRONI T307.

1718

"William Connolly's Ballyshannon Estate." *Donegal Ann.* 33 (1981): 27–44 (gives tenants and holdings in 1718 and 1726, with comments).

1726

See William Connolly, 1718.

1730

"The Murray of Broughton Estate (Southwest Donegal)." *Donegal Ann.* 12 (1) (1977): 22–39 (lists holdings and tenants, with comments).

1740

Protestant Householders in Parishes of Cloncaha, Clonmeny, Culdaff, Desertegney, Donagh, Fawne, Movill, and Templemore. GO MS539; SLC film 100182.

1761

Militia List of Cos . . . Donegal, etc. GO MS 680.

1761–75

Electors of Donegal. SLC film 100181; GO ms. 442.

1761–88

List of Freeholders. NLI ms. 787/8; and Donegal Ancestry (see Research Services at end of chapter).

1766

Census of householders of the Parish of Donaghmore. NAI film 207/208.

Protestant householders in Parish of Leck. NAI M 2476; RCB Ms 23, SLC film 258517. Also published as "Protestant Householders in Leck Parish" in *The Laggan and its Presbyterianism*. A.G. Lecky, 1905.

1766

Protestant householders in Donaghmore and Derry, NAI M207-8. Protestant householders in Raphoe and Leck, NAI M2476 and RCB Ms. 23.

1770

Names of Owners of Freeholds Entitled to Vote ca. 1770. NLI Ms. 987–88.

1782

"Inhabitants of Culdaff Parish." *300 Years in Inishowen.* A.I. Young, 1929, pp. 159–60.

1794

"Householders in St. Johnston (Parish of Taughboy)." In *The Laggan and its Presbyterianism*. A.G. Lecky (1905) 1: 89.

1794

Tenants on Abercorn Estate (Laggan) in *The Laggan and its Presbyterianism*. A.G. Lecky: 1905, Appendix I.

1796

Spinning Wheel Premium List (see introduction).

1799

"Protestant Householders in the Parish of Templecrone, Co. Donegal" (list of church wardens of the parish for 1775-90). *Ir. Anc.* 16 (2) (1984): 78–79.

1802–03

"Protestants in Part of Culdaff Parish." (Fourteen of thirty-three townlands). In A.I. Young, *300 Years in Inishowen*, 1929, pp. 186–87.

1819–28

Rent Rolls of the Pettigo Estate of Charles Leslie in the Barony of Tirhugh and Civil Parish of Templecarn. Detailed rental by townland. NLI Ms 5811.

1823–30

Tenants and workers of the Fort Stewart Estate (Area of

134   DONEGAL ANNUAL

No Armes
_____

[f182ᵛ] Barony de Rapho
         The Lady Conningham Widdow of Sir James Conningham.
         undertaker of 2,000 acres, her men and armes.

William Conningham	Richard Leaky
James Calquahan	Robert Staret
Andrew mcCorkill	John mcIihome
John mcCorkill	Sallomon Giffin
Tobias Hood	David Reed
James Davye	Donnell mcDonnell
Peter Starret	Alexander Carlell
John mcquchowne	William Gafeth
James Knox	
Adam Garvance	Swords onely
	_____
Swords and Pikes	Gilbert Highgate
_____	Patrick Porter
James mcAdowe	Robert Hasta
ffyndlay Ewing	William Gambell
Dunkan mcffarlan	John Hunter
Ninian ffoulton	John Crawfford
James Scot	Robert Johnston
William Rankin	Henry Smyth
Daniell Ramsay	William Boyes
Martin Galbreath	David Ramsay
Patrick Porter	William Steward
	Robert Crafford
Swords and Snaphances	[f183ᵛ] James Conningham
	Andrew Conningham
_____	John Crafford
William mcIltherne	John Hunter
David Walker	John Wilson
John Barbor	James Bredyne
	Mungo Davy
Swords and Calleuers	William Richey
_____	John mcIlhome
James Makee	Henry Hunter
	John mcHutchon
Sword and halbert	James Rankin
_____	William Killy
f183 Andrew George	Robert Pots
James mcIlman	William Gambell
Michaell Rot(h?)es	John Lyone
Patrick Miller	James Knox 66
Robert Muntgomery	
Alexander Conningham	

Extract from a County Donegal muster roll of 1630. It shows the fighting men
available to Lady Conningham, an undertaker in the Barony of Raphoe, and their
arms. From *Donegal Annual* 10 (2) (1972).

Ramelton—Civil Parishes of Aughnish and Tullyfern). Held by Donegal Ancestry (see Research Services at end of chapter).

1825–36

Tithe Applotment Survey (see introduction). Indexed by Donegal Ancestry (see Research Services at end of chapter).

1832–36

Rent Rolls of the Pettigo Estate of Charles Leslie in the Barony of Tirhugh and Civil Parish of Templecarn. Detailed rental by townland. NLI Ms 5812.

1839

List of Persons who obtained Game Certificates in Ulster . . . . PRONI T 688. SLC film 100179.

1843

Voters List. NAI 1843/56.

1852–64

Vaccination Register for Milford. NLI Ms. 9767 (in the GRO). (Child's name, date of vaccination, address, and age.)

1852–72

Vaccination Register for Rathmullen. NLI Ms. 9976 (in the GRO). (Child's name, date of vaccination, address, and age.)

1857

Griffith's Valuation (see introduction). Indexed by Donegal Ancestry (see Research Services at end of chapter).

1858–69

Rental of Earl of Leitrim Estate, Barony of Kilmacrenan. NLI ms. 5175-5178.

c.1875–1902

List of all inhabitants of parish of Conwall (some with years of birth). RCB P206/8/1a.

1901

Census. NAI (see introduction). Indexing in progress by Donegal Ancestry (see Research Services at end of chapter); Stranorlar Parish index is in *Donegal-Stranorlar Parish Roots Book*. Noel Farrell, Longford, 1996.

1911

Census. NAI. Stranorlar Parish index is in *Donegal-Stranorlar Parish Roots Book*. Noel Farrell, Longford, 1996.

Church Records

Church of Ireland

See the introduction for a description of Church of Ireland records and their major repositories. Many C of I records were lost in the PRO fire of 1922. These are indicated as "Lost." However, as Church of Ireland records were effectively state records, the records of marriage (from 1845) are also in the General Registrar's Office. Many are still in local custody (LC), while others are in one of a variety of other archives (e.g., RCBL or NAI). Most of the parish registers of this county have been indexed by Donegal Ancestry (see Research Services at the end of the chapter). A search of the index will be conducted for a fee. Those indexed are noted below as "Indexed by DA."

Aghanunshin
Earliest Records: b. 1878–; m. 1845–; d. 1878–
Status: LC; RCBL (m. 1845-1971 only)

All Saints, Taughboyne
Earliest Records: b. 1877–; m. 1845–; d. 1820
Status: LC; Indexed by DA (to 1899)

Ardara
Earliest Records: b. 1829–; m. 1854–; d. 1876–
Status: LC; RCBL (mf) (b. 1829-1954; m. 1854-1956; d. 1876-1984); Indexed by DA (to 1899)

Ballintra (see Drumholm)

Ballyshannon (see Kilbarron and Finner)

Burt
Earliest Records: b. 1829-1913; m. 1829-1929; d. 1829-1941
Status: LC; RCBL (mf) (b. 1829-1913; m. 1829-1929; d. 1829-1941); Indexed by DA (to 1899)

Carndonagh (see Donagh)

Castlefin (see Donaghmore)

Cloncha
Status: Lost

Clondahorky
Earliest Records: b. 1871–; m. 1845–; d. 1884–
Status: LC; RCBL (mf) (b. 1871-1906; m. 1845-1915; d. 1884-1926); Indexed by DA (to 1899)

Clondevaddock
Earliest Records: b. 1794–; m. 1794–; d. 1794–
Status: LC; Indexed by DA (to 1899)

Clonleigh
Earliest Records: b. 1872–; m. 1845–; d. 1877–
Status: LC; RCBL (mf) (b. 1872-1983; m. 1845-1956; d. 1877-1984)

VALUATION OF TENEMENTS.

PARISH OF KILLYBEGS, LOWER.

67

No. and Letter of Reference to Map.		Names.		Description of Tenement.	Area.			Rateable Annual Valuation.		Total Annual Valuation of Rateable Property.
		Townland and Occupiers.	Immediate Lessors.					Land.	Buildings.	
					A. R. P.	£ s. d.	£ s. d.	£ s. d.		
		DRUMBARRAN. (*Ord. S. 73 & 82.*)								
1	{a}{b}	James Evans,	Rev. G. N. Tredennick	House, offices, and land, / Corn-mill and kiln,	21 0 20	13 10 0	4 10 0 / 12 0 0	} 30 0 0
2		Thomas Mullowney,	Same,	Land,	1 0 10	1 0 0	—	1 0 0
3		Francis M'Clinchy,	Same,	Land,	1 2 30	1 10 0	—	1 10 0
4		Charles Gallagher,	Same,	Land,	0 3 15	1 0 0	—	1 0 0
5	{	Thomas Dwyer, / Charles Morough,	} Same,	Land,	7 1 30	{ 1 15 0 / 1 15 0	—	{ 1 15 0 / 1 15 0
6		James M'Hugh,	Same,	Land,	2 1 20	1 2 0	—	1 2 0
7	A	John Maginly (*Shane*),	Same,	Land,	1 2 5	0 13 0	—	} 2 10 0
—	B				3 2 35	1 17 0	—	
8	{	James Dorian, / Charles Morough,	} Same,	Land,	2 3 15	{ 0 15 0 / 0 15 0	—	{ 0 15 0 / 0 15 0
9		Sidney Bresland,	Same,	Land,	1 2 0	0 15 0	—	0 15 0
10		Bernard Magrorty,	Same,	Land,	6 0 22	3 10 0	—	3 10 0
—	a	Patrick Shevlin,	Same,	House and garden,	0 0 24	0 3 0	0 5 0	0 8 0
—	b	James M'Hugh,	Same,	House and garden,	0 0 24	0 3 0	0 12 0	0 15 0
11		William Walker,	Same,	Land,	3 0 35	1 15 0	—	1 15 0
12		Thomas Maloney,	Same,	Land,	4 0 0	2 5 0	—	2 5 0
13		John Boyle,	Same,	Land,	2 2 0	1 10 0	—	1 10 0
14		John O'Donnell,	Same,	Land,	2 3 20	1 10 0	—	1 10 0
15		Dudley O'Donnell,	Same,	Land,	5 0 30	2 10 0	—	2 10 0
—	a	James M'Afee,	Same,	Garden,	0 1 0	0 5 0	—	0 5 0
—	b	National school-house and play ground,	(*See Exemptions.*)					
—	c	Unoccupied,	Rev. Geo. N. Tredennick	House,	—		0 10 0	0 10 0
16		Patrick Shevlin,	Same,	Land,	2 1 10	1 5 0	—	1 5 0
17		Michael Fisher,	Same,	Land,	3 1 5	2 0 0	—	2 0 0
18		Charles Gallagher,	Same,	Land,	3 0 15	2 0 0	—	2 0 0
19		Blakeney Gubbins,	Same,	Land,	1 2 30	1 0 0	—	1 0 0
—	a	William Tredennick,	Same,	Ice-house,	—	—	0 5 0	0 5 0
20		John Crimley,	Same,	Land,	2 1 0	1 5 0	—	1 5 0
—	a	John Sheeran,	Same,	Land,	0 3 15	0 15 0	—	0 15 0
		TOWN OF ARDARA. MAIN-STREET.						
21	1	R. C. Chapel, yard, and grave-yard,	(*See Exemptions*).					
—	2	Teague Bresland,	Rev. Geo. N. Tredennick	House, offices, & sm. gar.	—	—	3 0 0	3 0 0
—	3	James Dorian,	Same,	House, office, & sm. gar.	—	—	3 5 0	3 5 0
—	4	Unoccupied,	James Dorian,	House (*in progress*),	—	—		
—	5	Patrick Gillespie,	Charles Gallagher,	House & small garden,	—	—	1 5 0	1 5 0
—	6	Charles Gallagher,	Same,	House & small garden,	—	—	1 5 0	1 5 0
—	7	John Boyle,	Rev. Geo. N. Tredennick	House & small garden,	—	—	2 15 0	2 15 0
—	8		John Boyle,	Ruins,	—	—	—	
—	9	Myles Sweeney,	Rev. Geo. N. Tredennick	House, office, & sm. gar.	—	—	1 10 0	1 10 0
—	10	James Heraghty,	Same,	House & small garden,	—	—	1 5 0	1 5 0
—	11	Patrick Kennedy,	Same,	House and garden,	0 0 8	0 2 0	2 13 0	2 15 0
—	12	Francis M'Hugh,	Francis M'Glenchy,	House, office, & garden,	0 0 7	0 2 0	3 13 0	3 15 0
—	13	Manus M'Glenchy,	Rev. Geo. N. Tredennick	House,	—	—	1 10 0	1 10 0
—	14	John Dever,	Same,	House, office, & garden,	0 0 8	0 2 0	3 13 0	3 15 0
—	15	Henry Morrisson,	Same,	House, office, & garden,	0 0 8	0 2 0	2 18 0	3 0 0
—	16	Andrew Mackey,	Same,	House & small garden,	—	—	2 5 0	2 5 0
—	17	John Coen,	Same,	House & small garden,	—	—	1 0 0	1 0 0
—	18	William Given,	Archibald Bicley,	House & small garden,	—	—	0 15 0	0 15 0
—	19	Patrick Bresland,	Charles Gallagher,	House, yard, & sm. gar.	—	—	1 0 0	1 0 0
—	20	Dudly O'Donnell,	Owen Craig,	House and office,	—	—	1 0 0	1 0 0
—	21	Patrick Kelly,	Denis Bresland,	House,	—	—	0 15 0	0 15 0
—	22	John Sweeney,	Same,	House & small garden,	—	—	0 15 0	0 15 0
—	23	Unoccupied,	Patrick Boyle,	Ho. (*in progress*) & gar.	0 0 7	0 2 0	—	0 2 0
—	24	Mary Manelis,	Rev. Geo. N. Tredennick	House, offices, & garden,	0 0 8	0 2 0	1 8 0	1 10 0
—	25	John Gallagher,	Patrick Boyle,	House,	—	—	1 0 0	1 0 0
—	26	Charles Gallagher,	Rev. Geo. N. Tredennick	Ho., off., yd., & sm. gar.	—	—	10 10 0	10 10 0
—	27	James Dwyer,	John Evans,	House,	—	—	1 10 0	1 10 0
—	28	Neal Sharp,	Same,	House,	—	—	1 0 0	1 0 0
—	29	John Campbell,	Rev. Geo. N. Tredennick	House,	—	—	0 10 0	0 10 0
—	30	Thomas Manelis,	Same,	House,	—	—	0 10 0	0 10 0
—	31	John Shevlin,	Same,	House,	—	—	0 10 0	0 10 0
—	32	Peter Carolan,	Same,	House,	—	—	0 10 0	0 10 0

A page from the *Griffith's* or *Primary Valuation of Ireland* showing some of the land and lease-holders in the parish of Killybegs Lower, County Donegal.

Convoy
Earliest Records: b. 1871–; m. 1845–; d. 1881–
Status: LC; RCBL (mf) (b. 1871–1981; m. 1845–1902; d. 1881–1981); Indexed by DA (to 1899)

Conwal
Earliest Records: b. 1876–; m. 1845–; d. 1878–
Status: RCBL (b. 1876–1971; m. 1845–1988; d. 1878–1906)

Craigadooish
Earliest Records: d. 1871–
Status: LC; RCBL (mf) (d. 1871–1907)

Culedaff
Earliest Records: b. 1875–; m. 1845–; d. 1876–
Status: LC; RCBL (mf) (b. 1875–1911; m. 1845–1921; d. 1876–1980)

Desertegny
Earliest Records: b. 1790–; m. 1813–; d. 1803–
Missing Records: m. 1831–43; d. 1804–32
Status: LC; RCBL (mf) (m. 1848–1929; d. 1879–1981); Indexed by DA (b/d. 1878–1899; m. 1845–1899)

Donagh (or Carndonagh)
Status: Lost

Donaghmore
Earliest Records: b. 1818–; m. 1817–; d. 1824–
Status: LC; RCBL (mf) (b. 1818–1902; m. 1817–1955; d. 1824–1892); Indexed by DA (to 1899)

Donegal
Earliest Records: b. 1808–; m. 1812–; d. 1812–
Status: LC; Indexed by DA (to 1899)

Drumholm (Ballintra)
Earliest Records: b. 1719; m. 1691; d. 1696
Status: LC; Indexed by DA (b/d. to 1873; m. to 1869)

Dunboe
Status: Lost

Dunfanaghy
Earliest Records: b. 1873–; m 1875–; d. 1873–
Status: LC; RCBL (mf) (b/m. 1853–82); Indexed by DA

Dunlewey
Earliest Records: b. 1853–; m. 1853–
Status: LC; RCBL (mf) (m. 1853–82); Indexed by DA (m. to 1882)

Fahan, Upper
Earliest Records: b. 1762–; m. 1814–; d. 1832–
Status: LC; RCBL (mf) (b. 1762–1921; m. 1814–1909; d. 1832–1934); Indexed by DA (to 1899)

Fahan, Lower
Earliest Records: b. 1817–; m. 1818–; d. 1822–
Status: LC; RCBL (mf); Indexed by DA (to 1899)

Finner
Earliest Records: b. 1815; m. 1815; d. 1815
Status: LC

Gartan
Earliest Records: b. 1881–; m. 1845–
Status: RCBL

Glenalla
Earliest Records: b. 1871–; m. 1871–; d. 1906–
Status: LC; RCBL (mf) (b. 1871–1983; m. 1871–1951; d. 1906–1981); Indexed by DA (b/m. to 1899)

Glencolumbkille
Earliest Records: b. 1827–; m. 1845–; d. 1828–
Status: LC; RCBL (mf) (b. 1827–1984; m. 1845–1954; d. 1828–1975); Indexed by DA (to 1899)

Gleneely
Earliest Records: b. 1872–; m. 1859–
Status: LC; RCBL (mf) (b. 1872–1981; m. 1859–1954)

Glenties
Earliest Records: b. 1898–; m. 1856–; d. 1898–
Status: LC; RCBL (mf) (b. 1898–1972; d. 1898–1982); Indexed by DA (to 1899)

Goland Chapel of Ease
Earliest Records: b. 1847–1854
Status: LC

Gweedore
Earliest Records: b. 1880–; m. 1855–; d. 1881–
Status: LC; RCBL (mf) (b. 1880–1980; m. 1855–1952; d. 1881–1982); Indexed by DA (to 1899)

Inch
Earliest Records: b. 1868–; m. 1846–; d. 1868–
Status: LC; RCBL (mf) (b. 1868–1951; m. 1846–1946; d. 1868–1965); Indexed by DA (to 1899)

Inniskeel
Earliest Records: b/m/d. 1699–1700, 1818–
Status: LC; NAI M5749 (to 1864); RCBL (mf) (b. 1852–1948; d. 1852–1983); Indexed by DA (b/d. to 1899; m. to 1851)

Inver
Earliest Records: b. 1805–; m. 1805–; d. 1818–
Status: LC; Indexed by DA (to 1899)

Kilbarron (Ballyshannon)
Earliest Records: b. 1785; m. 1785; d. 1785
Status: LC

Kilcar
Earliest Records: b. 1819–; m. 1819–; d. 1818–
Status: LC; RCBL (mf) (b. 1819–1957; m. 1819–1938; d. 1818–1930); Indexed by DA (to 1899)

Killaghtee
Earliest Records: b. 1873–; m. 1857–; d. 1874–
Status: LC; Indexed by DA (to 1899)

Killea
Earliest Records: b. 1877–; m. 1845–; d. 1880–
Status: LC; RCBL (mf) (b. 1877-1922; m. 1845-1931); Indexed by DA (to 1899)

Killybegs
Earliest Records: b. 1787–; m. 1810–; d. 1806–
Missing Records: b. 1797-1808; m. 1840-1863
Status: LC; RCBL (mf) (b. 1809-1983; m. 1810-1944; d. 1806-1984); Indexed by DA (to 1899)

Killygarvan (Rathmullan)
Earliest Records: b. 1706–; m. 1707–; d. 1706
Status: LC; Indexed by DA (to 1899)

Killymard
Earliest Records: b. 1880–; m. 1845–; d. 1819
Status: LC; Indexed by DA (to 1899)

Kilmacrennan
Earliest Records: b. 1818–; m. 1828–; d. 1819-1823
Status: LC; Indexed by DA (to 1899)

Kilteevogue
Earliest Records: b. 1818–; m. 1845–; d. 1825–
Status: LC; RCBL (mf) (b. 1818-1979; m. 1845-1896; d. 1825-1921)

Laghey
Earliest Records: b. 1877–; m. 1847–; d. 1877–
Status: LC; Indexed by DA (b/d. to 1899; m. to 1871)

Leck
Earliest Records: b. 1878–; m. 1846–; d. 1878–
Status: RCBL (b. 1878-1975; m. 1846-1959; d. 1878-1900)

Lettermacaward
Earliest Records: b. 1889–; m. 1890–; d. 1890–
Status: LC; RCBL (mf) (b. 1889-1982; d. 1890-1981); Indexed by DA (to 1899)

Lough Eske
Earliest Records: b. 1876–
Status: LC; Indexed by DA (to 1899)

Meenglass
Earliest Records: m. 1864–
Status: LC; RCBL (mf) (m. 1864-1963)

Mevagh
Earliest Records: b. 1876–; m. 1877–; d. 1846–
Status: LC; Indexed by DA (to 1899)

Milford
Earliest Records: b. 1879–; m. 1860–; d. 1902– Status: LC; RCBL (mf) (b. 1880-1981; m. 1860-1949; d. 1902-1976); Indexed (b. and m. only) by DA

Monellan
Earliest Records: b. 1833–; m. 1836–; d. 1849–
Status: LC; Indexed by DA (to 1899)

Mount Charles (or Mountcharles)
Earliest Records: b. 1877–; m. 1861–
Status: LC; Indexed by DA (to 1899)

Moville Lower
Status: Lost

Muff
Earliest Records: b. 1803–; m. 1804–; d. 1847–
Status: LC; RCBL (mf) (b. 1837-1986; m. 1837-1956; d. 1847-1875)

Newtowncunningham
Earliest Records: b. 1877–; m. 1845–; d. 1820–
Status: LC; RCBL (mf) (b. 1877-1937; m. 1845-1897; d. 1820-1955)

Ramelton
Earliest Records: b. 1788–; m. 1873–
Status: LC

Raphoe
Earliest Records: b. 1771–; m. 1771–; d. 1771–
Status: LC; Indexed by DA (to 1899)

Rathmullan (see Killygarvan)

Raymochy
Earliest Records: b. 1844–; m. 1845–; d. 1878–
Status: LC; RCBL (mf) (b. 1844-1986; m. 1845-1982; d. 1878-1986)

Raymunterdoney
Earliest Records: b. 1878–; m. 1845–; d. 1880–
Status: LC; Indexed by DA (to 1899)

Rossnowlagh
Earliest Records: b. 1879–; m. 1845–
Status: LC; Indexed by DA (to 1899)

Stranorlar
Earliest Records: b. 1821–; m. 1821–; d. 1821–
Status: LC

Taughboyne
Earliest Records: b. 1820–; m. 1836–; d. 1836–
Status: LC; RCBL (mf) (b. 1820-1983; m. 1836-1906; d. 1836-1982); Indexed by DA (to 1899)

Templecarn
Earliest Records: b. 1825–; m. 1825–; d. 1825–
Status: LC; RCBL (mf) (b. 1825-1936; m. 1825-1906; d. 1825-1905)

Templecrone
Earliest Records: b. 1878–; m. 1849–; d. 1879–
Status: LC; RCBL (mf) (b. 1878-1982; d. 1879-1980); Indexed by DA (to 1899)

Tullaghobegley
Earliest Records: b. 1848–; m. 1845–; d. 1850–
Status: LC; Indexed by DA (to 1899)

Tullyaughnish (Ramelton)
Earliest Records: b. 1798–; m. 1798–; d. 1798–
Status: LC; RCBL (mf) (b. 1798–1983; m. 1798–1935; d. 1798–1983); Indexed by DA (to 1899)

Methodist

Methodist churches were located in several parts of the county from 1795 (see the introduction). No death records were maintained. Several of the Methodist registers have been indexed by Donegal Ancestry (see Research Services at the end of the chapter). A search of the index will be conducted for a fee. Those indexed are noted below as "Indexed by DA."

Ardara and Dunkinelly
Earliest Records: b. 1860–; m. 1863–
Status: LC; Indexed by DA (to 1899)

Ballintra Circuit
Earliest Records: b. 1835–; m. 1864–
Status: LC; Indexed by DA (to 1899)

Inishowen
Earliest Records: b. 1862–; m. 1873–
Status: LC; Indexed by DA (to 1899)

Ramelton Mission
Earliest Records: b. 1829–1867
Status: LC; Indexed by DA (to 1899)

Presbyterian

An account of Presbyterian records is given in the introduction. These registers rarely contain death records, and occasionally have only records of births. This is indicated where appropriate. Many of the Presbyterian registers of Donegal have been indexed by Donegal Ancestry (see Research Services at the end of the chapter). A search of the index will be conducted for a fee. Those indexed are noted below as "Indexed by DA."

Ballindrait
Starting Date: 1819
Status: LC; Indexed by DA; PRONI MIC 1P/185

Ballylennon (First)
Starting Date: 1829 (d. from 1830)
Status: LC; Indexed by DA; PRONI MIC 1P/207

Ballylennon (Second)
Starting Date: 1845 (b. only)
Status: LC; Indexed by DA

Ballyshannon
Starting Date: 1836
Status: LC; Indexed by DA; PRONI MIC 1P/5

Buncrana
Starting Date: 1836
Status: LC; Indexed by DA; PRONI MIC 1P/32

Burt
Starting Date: 1833
Status: LC; Indexed by DA; PRONI MIC 1P/33

Carndonagh
Starting Date: 1830
Status: LC; Indexed by DA; PRONI MIC 1P/237

Carnone (Raphoe)
Starting Date: 1834
Status: LC; Indexed by DA; PRONI MIC 1P/221

Carrigart
Starting Date: 1844
Status: LC; Indexed by DA; PRONI MIC 1P/216

Convoy
Starting Date: 1822 (d. from 1859)
Status: LC; Indexed by DA; PRONI MIC 1P/220

Crossroads
Starting Date: 1811 (d. from 1854)
Status: LC; Indexed by DA; PRONI MIC 1P/259

Donegal (First and Second)
Starting Date: 1824
Status: LC; Indexed by DA; PRONI MIC 1P/6

Donoughmore (Castlefin)
Starting Date: 1835
Status: LC; Indexed by DA; PRONI MIC 1P/217

Drumholm
Starting Date: 1845 (b. only)
Status: LC; Indexed by DA

Dunfanaghy
Starting Date: 1830
Status: LC; Indexed by DA; PRONI MIC 1P/152

Fannet
Starting Date: 1827
Status: LC; Indexed by DA; PRONI MIC 1P/232

Gortlee Reformed
Starting Date: 1872 (b. only)
Status: LC; Indexed by DA; PRONI MIC 1P/226

Greenbank
Starting Date: 1862
Status: LC; Indexed by DA

Killymarde
Starting Date: 1845 (d. only)
Status: LC; Indexed by DA

Kilmacrennan
Starting Date: 1846
Status: LC; Indexed by DA; PRONI MIC 1P/141

Knowhead (Muff)
Starting Date: 1826
Status: LC; Indexed by DA; PRONI MIC 1P/141

Letterkenny (First, Second, and Third)
Starting Date: 1821
Status: LC; Indexed by DA; PRONI MIC 1P/222, 223, and 225

Malin
Starting Date: 1845
Status: LC; Indexed by DA; PRONI MIC 1P/236

Milford
Starting Date: 1838
Status: LC; Indexed by DA; PRONI MIC 1P/244

Monreagh (Derry)
Starting Date: 1845
Status: LC; Indexed by DA; PRONI MIC 1P/233

Moville
Starting Date: 1833
Status: LC; Indexed by DA; PRONI MIC 1P/241

Newtowncunningham
Starting Date: 1808
Status: LC; PRONI MIC 1P/188

Pettigo
Starting Date: 1844
Status: LC; PRONI MIC 1P/66

Ramelton (First, Second, and Third)
Starting Date: 1806 (d. from 1830 in Ramelton Third)
Status: LC; Indexed by DA; PRONI MIC 1P/142

Raphoe (First) (Ramelton Reformed Church)
Starting Date: 1829
Status: LC; Indexed by DA; PRONI MIC 1P/1, 183, and 184

Rathmullan
Starting Date: 1845
Status: LC; PRONI MIC 1P/231

Ray (First and Second)
Starting Date: 1829
Status: LC; PRONI MIC 1P/186 and 187

St. Johnston (Ramelton Reformed Church)
Starting Date: 1838
Status: LC; Indexed by DA; PRONI MIC 1P/206

Stranorlar
Starting Date: 1821
Status: LC; PRONI MIC 1P/218

Trentagh or Trenta (Ramelton Reformed Church)
Starting Date: 1836 (d. from 1843)
Status: LC; Indexed by DA; PRONI MIC 1P/224

Urney (Ramelton Reformed Church)
Starting Date: 1845 (b. only)
Status: LC; Indexed by DA

Roman Catholic

Note that some of the Catholic parish registers of this county have been indexed by Donegal Ancestry (see Research Services at the end of the chapter). Indexing of the remainder of these parishes is under way. Many of the Inishowen parishes (i.e., Diocese of Derry) have also been indexed by the Genealogy Centre in Derry (see Research Services at the end of the Derry chapter). A search of these indexes will be conducted by either center for a fee. Those indexed are noted below as "Indexed by DA" or "by GC-Derry," as appropriate. Microfilm copies of all registers are also available in the National Library of Ireland (NLI), and through the LDS library system.

Civil Parish: Aghanunshin
Map Grid: 18
RC Parish: Aghanunshin, see Aughnish
Diocese: RA

Civil Parish: Allsaints
Map Grid: 29
RC Parish: see Taughboyne
Diocese: RA

Civil Parish: Aughnish
Map Grid: 16
RC Parish: Aughnish
Diocese: RA
Earliest Record: b. 11.1873; m. 12.1873
Status: LC; NLI (mf); Indexed by DA (to 1881)

Civil Parish: Barr of Inch (see Mintiaghs)

Civil Parish: Burt
Map Grid: 25
RC Parish: Burt, Inch, and Fahan
Diocese: DE
Earliest Record: b. 11.1859; m. 1.1856; d. 4.1860
Missing Dates: d. ends 7.1866
Status: LC; NLI (mf); Indexed by GC-Derry (to 1900)

Civil Parish: Clonca
Map Grid: 1
RC Parish: Malin
Diocese: DE
Earliest Record: b. 11.1856; m. 4.1870
Status: LC; NLI (mf); Indexed by GC-Derry (to 1900)

Civil Parish: Clondahorky
Map Grid: 10
RC Parish: Dunfanaghy
Diocese: RA
Earliest Record: b. 10.1877; m. 1.1879
Status: LC; NLI (mf); Indexing planned by DA

Civil Parish: Clondavaddog
Map Grid: 7
RC Parish: Clondavaddog (Tamney)
Diocese: RA
Earliest Record: b. 2.1847; m. 2.1847; d. 2.1847
Missing Dates: b. 3.1871–5.1873; m. ends 7.1869; d. ends 2.1869
Status: LC; NLI (mf); Indexing planned by DA

Civil Parish: Clonleigh
Map Grid: 35
RC Parish: Clonleigh (Lifford)
Diocese: DE
Earliest Record: b. 4.1773; m. 8.1788
Missing Dates: b. 2.1795–1.1836, 5.1837–3.1853; m. 9.1781–1843
Status: LC; NLI (mf); Indexed by GC-Derry (to 1900)

Civil Parish: Clonmany
Map Grid: 2
RC Parish: Clonmany
Diocese: DE
Earliest Record: b. 1.1852
Status: LC; NLI (mf); Indexed by GC-Derry (to 1900)

Civil Parish: Convoy
Map Grid: 36
RC Parish: see Raphoe
Diocese: RA

Civil Parish: Conwal
Map Grid: 17
RC Parish: Conwal and Leck (Letterkenny)
Diocese: RA
Earliest Record: b. 5.1853; m. 5.1853
Missing Dates: b. 12.1862–3.1868; m. 11.1863–2.1877
Status: LC; NLI (mf); Indexing planned by DA

Civil Parish: Culdaff
Map Grid: 4
RC Parish: Culdaff
Diocese: DE
Earliest Record: b. 1.1838; m. 1.1849
Missing Dates: b. 11.1841–6.1847
Status: LC; NLI (mf); Indexed by GC-Derry (to 1900)

Civil Parish: Desertegny
Map Grid: 20
RC Parish: Buncrana (Desertegny and Lower Fahan)
Diocese: DE
Earliest Record: b. 12.1864; m. 11.1871
Status: LC; NLI (mf); Indexed by GC-Derry (to 1900)

Civil Parish: Donagh
Map Grid: 3
RC Parish: Carndonagh or Donagh
Diocese: DE
Earliest Record: 1.1847
Status: LC; NLI (mf); Indexed by GC-Derry (to 1900)

Civil Parish: Donaghamore
Map Grid: 39
RC Parish: Donaghmore (Killygordon)
Diocese: DE
Earliest Record: b. 11.1840; m. 4.1846
Status: LC; NLI (mf); Indexing planned by DA

Civil Parish: Donegal
Map Grid: 48
RC Parish: Donegal (Tawnawilly Mts.)
Diocese: RA
Earliest Record: b. 12.1872; m. 1.1882
Status: LC; NLI (mf); Indexing planned by DA

Civil Parish: Drumhome
Map Grid: 49
RC Parish: Drumhome (Ballintra)
Diocese: RA
Earliest Record: b. 6.1866; m. 8.1866
Status: LC; NLI (mf); Indexing planned by DA

Civil Parish: Fahan Lower
Map Grid: 21
RC Parish: see Desertegny
Diocese: DE

Civil Parish: Fahan Upper
Map Grid: 22
RC Parish: see Burt
Diocese: DE

Civil Parish: Gartan
Map Grid: 14
RC Parish: Termon and Gartan
Diocese: RA
Earliest Record: b. 1862; m. 1862; d. 1862
Status: LC; NLI (mf); Indexing planned by DA

Civil Parish: Glencolumbkille
Map Grid: 42
RC Parish: Glencolumbkille
Diocese: RA
Earliest Record: b. 1860; m. 1860; d. 1860
Status: LC; NLI (mf); Indexing planned by DA

Civil Parish: Inch
Map Grid: 24
RC Parish: see Burt
Diocese: DE

Civil Parish: Inishkeel
Map Grid: 28
RC Parish: Glenties
Diocese: RA
Earliest Record: b. 10.1866; m. 11.1866
Status: LC; NLI (mf); Indexing planned by DA

Civil Parish: Inishmacsaint
Map Grid: 52
RC Parish: see Co. Fermanagh
Diocese: CG

Civil Parish: Inver
Map Grid: 46
RC Parish: Inver
Diocese: RA
Earliest Record: b. 1.1861; m. 2.1861
Missing Dates: m. 6.1867-11.1875
Status: LC; NLI (mf); Indexed by DA (to 1900)

Civil Parish: Kilbarron
Map Grid: 51
RC Parish: Kilbarron
Diocese: RA
Earliest Record: b. 11.1854; m. 1.1858
Status: LC; NLI (mf); Indexing planned by DA

Civil Parish: Kilcar
Map Grid: 43
RC Parish: Kilcar
Diocese: RA
Earliest Record: b. 1.1848
Status: LC; NLI (mf); Indexing planned by DA

Civil Parish: Killaghtee
Map Grid: 45
RC Parish: see Killybegs Upper
Diocese: CG

Civil Parish: Killea
Map Grid: 33
RC Parish: see Taughboyne
Diocese: RA

Civil Parish: Killybegs Lower
Map Grid: 41
RC Parish: Ardara
Diocese: RA
Earliest Record: b. 1.1869; m. 6.1867
Status: LC; NLI (mf); Indexing planned by DA

Civil Parish: Killybegs Upper
Map Grid: 44
RC Parish: Killybegs and Killaghtee
Diocese: RA
Earliest Record: b. 1.1845; m. 9.1857
Missing Dates: b. 4.1847-10.1850, 10.1853-7.1857
Status: LC; NLI (mf); Indexing planned by DA

Civil Parish: Killygarvan
Map Grid: 13
RC Parish: Killygarvan
Diocese: RA
Earliest Record: b. 10.1868; m. 2.1873
Status: LC; NLI (mf); Indexing planned by DA

Civil Parish: Killymard
Map Grid: 47
RC Parish: Killymard
Diocese: RA
Earliest Record: b. 9.1874
Status: LC; NLI (mf); Indexing planned by DA

Civil Parish: Kilmacrenan
Map Grid: 15
RC Parish: Kilmacrenan
Diocese: RA
Earliest Record: b. 11.1862
Status: LC; NLI (mf); Indexing planned by DA

Civil Parish: Kilteevoge
Map Grid: 37
RC Parish: Kilteevoge (Cloghan)
Diocese: RA
Earliest Record: b. 12.1855; m. 11.1855
Missing Dates: b. 4.1862-4.1870; m. 3.1862-5.1870
Status: LC; NLI (mf); Indexing planned by DA

Civil Parish: Leck
Map Grid: 30
RC Parish: see Conwal
Diocese: RA

Civil Parish: Lettermacaward
Map Grid: 27
RC Parish: Lettermacaward, see Templecrone
Diocese: RA

Civil Parish: Mevagh
Map Grid: 11
RC Parish: Mevagh
Diocese: RA
Earliest Record: b. 1.1871
Status: LC; NLI (mf); Indexing planned by DA

Civil Parish: Mintiaghs or Barr of Inch
Map Grid: 19
RC Parish: Buncrana, see Desertegny
Diocese: DE

Civil Parish: Moville Lower
Map Grid: 5
RC Parish: Moville Lower
Diocese: DE
Earliest Record: b. 11.1847; m. 11.1847; d. 11.1847
Missing Dates: d. ends 7.1854
Status: LC; NLI (mf); Indexed by GC-Derry (to 1900)

Civil Parish: Moville Upper
Map Grid: 6
RC Parish: Iskaheen and Moville Upper
Diocese: DE
Earliest Record: 9.1858
Status: LC; NLI (mf); Indexed by GC-Derry (to 1900)

Civil Parish: Muff
Map Grid: 23
RC Parish: Iskaheen, see Moville Upper
Diocese: DE

Civil Parish: Raphoe
Map Grid: 34
RC Parish: Raphoe
Diocese: RA

Earliest Record: b. 2.1876; m. 2.1876
Status: LC; NLI (mf); Indexing planned by DA

Civil Parish: Raymoghy
Map Grid: 31
RC Parish: see Taughboyne
Diocese: RA

Civil Parish: Raymunterdoney
Map Grid: 9
RC Parish: part Clondahorky; part Tullaghobegley
Diocese: RA

Civil Parish: Stranorlar
Map Grid: 38
RC Parish: Stranorlar
Diocese: RA
Earliest Record: b. 1860; m. 1860; d. 1860
Status: LC; NLI (mf); Indexing planned by DA

Civil Parish: Taughboyne
Map Grid: 32
RC Parish: All Saints, Raymoghy, and Taughboyne
Diocese: RA
Earliest Record: b. 12.1843; m. 11.1843
Status: LC; NLI (mf); Indexing planned by DA

Civil Parish: Templecarn (see also Co. Fermanagh)
Map Grid: 50
RC Parish: Pettigo
Diocese: RA
Earliest Record: b. 3.1851; m. 1.1836
Status: LC; NLI (mf); Indexing planned by DA

Civil Parish: Templecrone
Map Grid: 26
RC Parish: Dungloe
Diocese: RA
Earliest Record: b. 11.1876
Status: LC; NLI (mf); Indexing planned by DA

Civil Parish: Tullaghobegley (1)
Map Grid: 8
RC Parish: Tullaghbegley East and Raymunterdoney; also Tullaghbegley West, see below
Diocese: RA
Earliest Record: b. 11.1849; m. 8.1861; d. 11.1849
Missing Dates: 4.1861–11.1871; ends 8.1869
Status: LC; NLI (mf); Indexing planned by DA

Civil Parish: Tullaghobegley (2)
Map Grid: 8
RC Parish: Tullaghbegley West
Diocese: RA
Earliest Record: b. 1.1868
Status: LC; NLI (mf); Indexing planned by DA

Civil Parish: Tullyfern
Map Grid: 12
RC Parish: see Killygarvan
Diocese: RA

Civil Parish: Urney
Map Grid: 40
RC Parish: Urney, see Co. Tyrone
Diocese: DE

Commercial and Social Directories

1824

J. Pigot's *City of Dublin and Hibernian Provincial Directory* includes traders, nobility, gentry, and clergy lists of Ballybofey, Ballyshannon, Donegal, Letterkenny, Lifford, Pettigo, Raphoe, and Stranorlar.

1839

Directory of the Towns of Sligo, Enniskillen, Ballyshannon . . . etc., gives an alphabetical list of nobility, gentry, clergymen, and traders listed by trades and alphabetically. Covers the towns of Ballyshannon, Donegal, Stranorlar, and Ballybofey.

1846

Slater's *National Commercial Directory of Ireland* lists nobility, clergy, traders, etc., in Ballyshannon and Bundoran, Buncrana, Donegal, Killybegs and Dunkineely, Letterkenny, Lifford and Castlefinn (the latter under Strabane, Co. Tyrone), Moville, Raphoe, Rathmelton, Stranorlar, and Ballybofey.

1854

Henderson's *Belfast and Province of Ulster Directory* covers the towns of Ballyshannon and Lifford. Further editions were issued in 1856, 1858, 1861, 1863, 1865, 1868, 1870, 1877, 1880, 1884, 1890, 1894, and 1900.

1870

Slater's *Directory of Ireland* contains trade, nobility, and clergy lists for Ballyshannon, Buncrana, Donegal, Dunfanaghy, Glenties and Ardara, Killybegs, Letterkenny and Manorcunningham, Lifford, Moville, Pettigoe, Raphoe and Convoy, Ramelton, and Stranorlar.

1881

Slater's *Royal National Commercial Directory of Ireland* contains lists of traders, clergy, nobility, and farmers in Ballyshannon, Buncrana and Clonmany, Donegal, Dunfanaghy, Glenties and Ardara, Killybegs, Letterkenny and Manorcunningham, Lifford, Moville, Pettigoe, Raphoe, Ramelton, Stranorlar and Ballybofey.

1891

The Derry Almanac and Directory has traders lists for the towns of Ardara, Ballintra, Ballybofey, Ballyshannon, Buncrana, Carndonagh, Carrigans,

Castlefin, Donegal, Donemana, Dunfanaghy, Glenties, Killygordon, Letterkenny, Lifford, Manorcunningham, Milford, Mountcharles, Moville, Ramelton, Raphoe, Rathmullen, Stranorlar, and St. Johnstown. <u>Produced annually starting in 1891.</u>

1894

Slater's *Royal National Directory of Ireland* lists traders, police, teachers, farmers, and private residents in each of the towns, villages, and parishes of the county.

Family History

"Abstracts of Some Boyd Wills." *Ir. Anc.* 9 (1) (1977): 53–55.

Crawford, R. *The Crawfords of Donegal and How They Came There.* Dublin, 1886.

"The Dickson and Connolly Families of Ballyshannon." *Donegal Annual* 4 (1959): 111–17.

"The Dills of Fanad." *Donegal Annual* 34 (see also Patton).

Doherty—see Co. Derry Family History section.

Downey—see Co. Sligo Family History section.

Early, Samuel S. *A History of the Family of Early in America: The Ancestors and Descendants of Jeremiah Early Who Came from Donegal.* New York, 1896.

Harvey, G.H. *The Harvey Families of Inishowen, Co. Donegal . . .* Folkestone, 1927.

Hewetson, John. "Hewetson of Ballyshannon, Donegal." *R.S.A.I.* 40 (1910): 238–43.

Irwin—see Co. Fermanagh Family History section.

Nesbitt of Woodhill. Pedigree in *Swanzy Notebooks.* RCB Library, Dublin.

"The O'Briens of Glencolumbkille." *Ir. Gen.* 7 (1) (1986): 51–53.

"O'Cannons of Tirchonaill." *Donegal Annual* 12 (2) (1978): 280–315.

"Notes on the O'Peatains of Donegal, Mayo, and Roscommon." *Ir. Gen.* 4 (4) (1971): 303–07.

"The Pattons and Dills of Springfield." *Donegal Annual* 11 (1) (1974).

Trench, C.V. *The Wrays of Donegal, Londonderry, and Antrim.* Oxford, 1945.

Young, A. *Three Hundred Years in Inishowen, Being More Particularly an Account of the Family of Young of Culdaff.* Belfast, 1929.

Gravestone Inscriptions

Assaroe Abbey: *Donegal Annual* 3 (3) (1957).

Assaroe (Ballyshannon): Indexed by Donegal Ancestry.

Aughanunshin: Indexed by Donegal Ancestry.

Balleeghan (Manorcunningham): Indexed by Donegal Ancestry.

Ballyshannon (St. Annes, C of I): in *Donegal Annual* 12 (2) (1978): 320–58 and *Family Links* 1 (2) (1981): 11–18 and 1 (4) (1982): 31–39. Also indexed by Donegal Ancestry.

Bruckless: Indexed by Donegal Ancestry.

Carne (Pettigo): *Donegal Annual* 4 (1989): 135–156; also indexed by Donegal Ancestry.

Clonleigh: Indexed by Donegal Ancestry.

Finner: In *Where Erne and Drowes Meet the Sea*, by Rev. P.O. Gallachair, 1961.

Gartan: Indexed by Donegal Ancestry.

Inver and Old Inver: Indexed by Donegal Ancestry.

Killaghtee and Old Killaghtee: Indexed by Donegal Ancestry.

Killybegs-St. Catherine's: Indexed by Donegal Ancestry.

Killydonnell (Ramelton): Indexed by Donegal Ancestry.

Kilmacrennan: Indexed by Donegal Ancestry.

Kilmonaster: Indexed by Donegal Ancestry.

Leck: Indexed by Donegal Ancestry.

Magheragallon—Old Graveyard: *Irish Family History* 5 (1989): 94–100.

Raphoe: Indexed by Donegal Ancestry.

Raymoghy: Indexed by Donegal Ancestry.

Tullaghobegley: Indexed by Donegal Ancestry.

Tullyaughnish: Indexed by Donegal Ancestry.

Newspapers

The newspapers published within this county start relatively late. However, many biographical notices for Donegal are included in the Derry newspapers, particularly the *Londonderry Journal*, which began in 1772. The newspapers published in the county are:

Title: *Ballyshannon Herald*
Published in: Ballyshannon, 1831–73
BL Holdings: 1.1832–12.1873

Title: *Donegal Independent*
Published in: Ballyshannon, 1884–1927
NLI Holdings: 1.1885–6.1907; 8–9.1927
BL Holdings: 4.1884–6.1907; 2.1908–4.1921

Title: *Donegal Vindicator*
Published in: Ballyshannon, 1889–1956
NLI Holdings: 1.1906–5.1912; 6.1921–9.1956
BL Holdings: 2.1889–12.1920; odd numbers 1928; 10.1928–9.1956

Title: *The Liberator*
Published in: Ballyshannon, 1839
BL Holdings: 1–11.1839

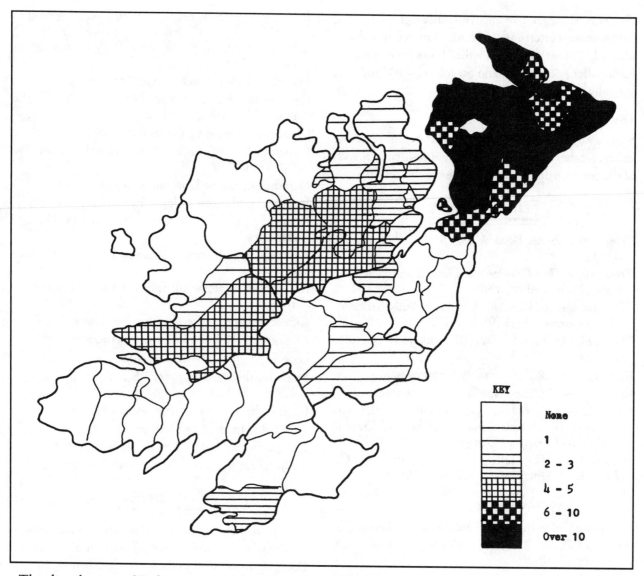

The distribution of Dohertys paying hearth tax in County Donegal in 1665 (by parish). From "The O'Doherty Information Pack" (Derry Youth and Community Workshop, 1985).

Wills and Administrations

A discussion of the types of records, where they are held, their availability, and their value is given in the Wills section of the introduction. The availability of prerogative wills, administrations, and marriage license records is also described in the relevant parts of the same section. Where available, published sources of these records are given in the Miscellaneous Sources section.

Pre-1858 Wills and Administrations

Prerogative Wills. See the introduction.

Consistorial Wills. County Donegal is mainly in the diocese of Raphoe, with two baronies in Derry and two parishes in Clogher. The guide to Catholic parish records

in this chapter shows the diocese to which each civil parish belonged. The wills of residents of each diocese were usually proven within that diocese (see the Wills section for exceptions). The following records survive:

Wills

See the introduction.

Abstracts

See the introduction.

Indexes

Raphoe (1684–1858) Vol. 5 of *Irish Wills* . . . Phillimore, 1920; Derry—see Co. Derry; Clogher—see Co. Tyrone.

Post-1858 Wills and Administrations

County Donegal was served by the District Registry of Londonderry. The surviving records are kept in the NAI. Londonderry District Will Books: NAI; SLC films 930300, 942216-942223.

Marriage Licenses

Indexes

Raphoe (1661-1750). NAI; SLC film 100872. Clogher (1709). NAI; SLC film 100861. Index to Raphoe Marriage License Bonds, by R. ffolliott (1710-1755 and 1817-1830). *Ir. Anc.* (Supplement, 1969); SLC film 873655.

Miscellaneous Sources

Duffy, Godfrey F. *A Guide to Tracing your Donegal Ancestors.* Dublin: Flyleaf Press, 1996. ISBN: 0-9508466 6-X.

Nolan, William, Liam Ronayne, and Mairead Dunleavy, eds. *Donegal History and Society—Interdisciplinary Essays on the History of an Irish County.* Geography Publications, 1995. ISBN: 0906602-459.

Donegal-Stranorlar Parish Roots Book. Noel Farrell, Longford, 1996.

Gallagher, B. *Arranmore Links: the families of Arranmore.* Ireland, 1986. (Genealogies of island families.) SLC 941.63/T3 D2gb.

The Parish of Donagh, a list of parish priests. (1400-1975, small biographies.) *Donegal Annual* 42 (1990): 13-16.

Spears, Arthur. "Surnames of Co. Donegal." *Irish Roots* (2) (1995): 27-29.

Dolan, L. *Land War and Eviction in Derryveagh 1840-1865.* Dundalk, 1980.

"Further Notes on the High Sheriffs of Co. Donegal." *Ir. Gen.* 2 (6) (1948): 165-76.

"Kinship and Land Tenure on Tory Island." *Ulster Folk* 12 (1966): 1-17.

Lucas Leslie, W. *Mevagh Down the Years. A History of Carrigart, Downings, Glen and the Surrounding District.* 2nd ed.

Lucas Leslie, W. *More about Mevagh.* Ballyshannon: Donegal Democrat, 1965.

"The Muster Roll of ca. 1630: Co. Donegal." *Donegal Annual* 10 (2) (1972): 124-49.

"Some Notes on the High Sheriffs of Co. Donegal." *Ir. Gen.* 1 (6) (1939): 179-84.

Tory Island, 1841-1964. Parts 1 and 2. *Ir. J. Med. Sci.* 7th ser. 1 (1) (1968): 19-24, 63-72 (discusses trends in population size).

"Two Early Seventeenth-Century Maps of Donegal." *R.S.A.I.* 94 (1964): 199-202.

"A Demographic Study of Tory Island and Rathlin Island, 1841-1964." *Ulster Folk* 17 (1971): 70-80.

Young, A.I. *300 Years in Inishowen.* Belfast, 1929.

O'Gallchobair. *History of Landlordism in Donegal.* Ballyshannon, 1975.

"Volunteer Companies of Ulster 1778-1793." *Irish Sword* 7 (29) (1966): 309-12 (officers' names only).

Research Sources and Services

Journals

Donegal Annual (published by County Donegal Historical Society, 1947-present)

North Irish Roots (published by North of Ireland Family History Society)

Libraries and Information Sources

Donegal Local Studies, Central Library and Arts Centre, Lower Main Street, Letterkenny, Co. Donegal. Ph: (074) 24950; fax: (353) 74 24950. The library has a collection of local history materials, including books, directories, newspapers, periodicals, photographs, and estate papers. It also has Assisted Passenger lists to Sydney and passenger lists to America (1811-1817 and 1847-71).

Donegal County Council, County Archive Centre, The Courthouse, The Diamond, Lifford, Co. Donegal. Ph: Letterkenny 21968. This archive holds a large variety of records of public bodies in the county, including records of boards of guardians, rural district councils, etc. It also contains a number of manuscripts and sets of private papers.

Ulster-American Folk Park Library. See Libraries in Co. Tyrone chapter.

Research Services

Donegal Ancestry, Old Meeting House, Back Lane, Ramelton, Letterkenny, Co. Donegal. Ph/Fax: (074) 51266. This center is the official IGP center for the county. It has indexed most of the Presbyterian and Church of Ireland registers of the county, and is currently working to index further Catholic registers. It has also indexed other local records, such as Hearth Money Rolls, 1901 census, Murray Stewart Estate Records, Assisted Passenger Lists, Spinning Wheel Premium Lists, etc. Researchers are advised to contact the center for an updated list of registers and other sources, indexed. The center will conduct a search of their database for a fee.

Genealogy Centre, 4-22 Butcher St., Derry BT48 6HL, Northern Ireland. Ph: (01504) 373177; fax: (1504) 374818. This center is mainly concerned with Derry. However, it also has records for the Inishowen peninsula of Donegal. Research is conducted for a fee.

See also Research Services in Dublin in the introduction.

Societies

Donegal Historical Society, c/o Mrs. Kathleen Emerson, 61 Cluain Barron, Ballyshannon, Co. Donegal. Ph: (00) (353) 72 51267 (publishers of *Donegal Annual*)

Clogher Historical Society, Mr. J.I.D. Johnston, Corick, Clogher, Co. Tyrone. This society publishes the *Clogher Record*, which deals with the social, church, political, archaeological, and genealogical history of the diocese of Clogher. This covers a small part of Donegal around Ballyshannon, as well as Monaghan, Fermanagh, and South Tyrone. The journal is a particularly important source of information on these counties.

North of Ireland Family History Society, Queens University of Belfast, Dept. of Education, 69 University Street, Belfast BT7 1HL. Publishers of *North Irish Roots*

Donegal Civil Parishes as Numbered on Map

1. Clonca
2. Clonmany
3. Donagh
4. Culdaff (3 pts.)
5. Moville Lower (2 pts.)
6. Moville Upper
7. Clondavoddog
8. Tullaghobegley
9. Raymunterdoney (4 pts.)
10. Clondahorky
11. Mevagh
12. Tullyfern
13. Killygarvan
14. Gartan
15. Kilmacrenan (3 pts.)
16. Augnish (2 pts.)
17. Conwal
18. Aghanunshin
19. Mintiaghs or Bar of Inch
20. Desertegny
21. Fahan Lower
22. Fahan Upper
23. Muff
24. Inch
25. Burt
26. Templecrone
27. Lettermacaward
28. Inishkeel
29. All Saints
30. Leck (2 pts.)
31. Raymoghy
32. Taughboyne
33. Killea
34. Raphoe
35. Clonleigh
36. Convoy
37. Kilteevoge
38. Stranorlar
39. Donaghmore
40. Urney
41. Killybegs Lower (2 pts.)
42. Glencolumbkille
43. Kilcar
44. Killybegs Upper
45. Killaghtee (2 pts.)
46. Inver
47. Killymard (2 pts.)
48. Donegal
49. Drumhome
50. Templecarn
51. Kilbarron
52. Inishmacsaint

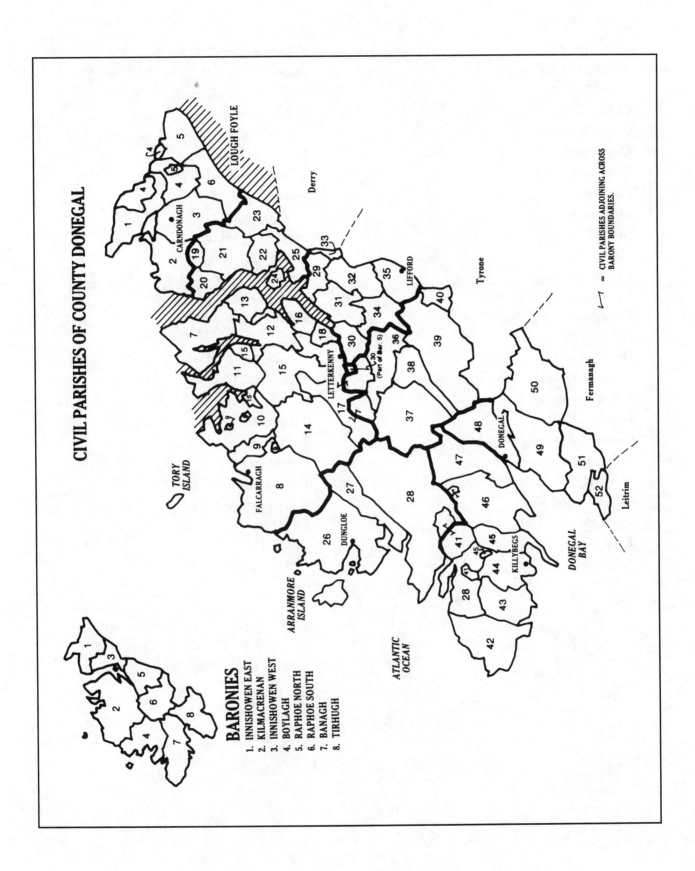

CIVIL PARISHES OF COUNTY DONEGAL

LOUGH FOYLE

Derry

Tyrone

Fermanagh

Leitrim

LIFFORD

LETTERKENNY

CARNDONAGH

DONEGAL

KILLYBEGS

DUNGLOE

FALCARRAGH

TORY ISLAND

ARRANMORE ISLAND

ATLANTIC OCEAN

DONEGAL BAY

= CIVIL PARISHES ADJOINING ACROSS BARONY BOUNDARIES.

30 (Part of Bar. 5)

BARONIES
1. INNISHOWEN EAST
2. KILMACRENAN
3. INNISHOWEN WEST
4. BOYLAGH
5. RAPHOE NORTH
6. RAPHOE SOUTH
7. BANAGH
8. TIRHUGH

Donegal Civil Parishes in Alphabetical Order

Aghanunshin: 18

All Saints: 29

Augnish (2 pts.): 16

Burt: 25

Clonca: 1

Clondahorky: 10

Clondavaddog: 7

Clonleigh: 35

Clonmany: 2

Convoy: 36

Conwal: 17

Culdaff (3 pts.): 4

Desertegny: 20

Donagh: 3

Donaghmore: 39

Donegal: 48

Drumhome: 49

Fahan Lower: 21

Fahan Upper: 22

Gartan: 14

Glencolumbkille: 42

Inch: 24

Inishkeel: 28

Inishmacsaint: 52

Inver: 46

Kilbarron: 51

Kilcar: 43

Killaghtee (2 pts.): 45

Killea: 33

Killybegs Lower (2 pts.): 41

Killybegs Upper: 44

Killygarvan: 13

Killymard (2 pts.): 47

Kilmacrenan (3 pts.): 15

Kilteevoge: 37

Leck (2 pts.): 30

Lettermacaward: 27

Mevagh: 11

Mintiaghs or Bar of Inch: 19

Moville Lower (2 pts.): 5

Moville Upper: 6

Muff: 23

Raphoe: 34

Raymoghy: 31

Raymunterdoney (4 pts.): 9

Stranorlar: 38

Taughboyne: 32

Templecarn: 50

Templecrone: 26

Tullaghobegley: 8

Tullyfern: 12

Urney: 40

County Down

A Brief History

County Down was the first Ulster county to be colonized by the Normans. The knight John de Courcey took the area around Downpatrick after the Norman invasion. The county was formed around 1300, and later came into the possession of the De Lacys. Most of this county came to be known as the Earldom of Ulster during this period. One of the few Norman families who settled in the county is Savage. The major Gaelic families were O'Neill, McGuinness, McQuillan, McCartan, and MacGilmore.

In 1569, Sir Thomas Smith unsuccessfully attempted to bring English settlers into the Ards Peninsula and County Down. Hugh O'Neill, the major Ulster chieftain, began a general rebellion in Ulster in 1594 (see Co. Tyrone). On the defeat of O'Neill, his lands and those of his allies were confiscated and divided among English and Scottish "adventurers." A well-planned plantation of Ulster began in 1609, involving the introduction to the province of thousands of settlers. These were brought in by adventurers who, in return for title to the land, brought in a specified number of settlers to their estates.

One Scottish adventurer, James Hamilton, brought over ten thousand Scots to northwest Down. Scottish names such as Boyd, Fraser, Johnston, Lindsay, Morrison, Patterson, and Maxwell are consequently common in Down. English adventurers in Down who brought over English families included Annesley, Hill, and Montgomery. These settlers brought the names Wilson, Johnson, Young, Taylor, Walker, Jackson, Watson, Bradshaw, and Bradford to Ulster. The new settlers developed a prosperous linen industry in Down and surrounding counties. The industrial center of Belfast also grew rapidly during the eighteenth and nineteenth centuries.

The relative proportions of people of Gaelic/Norman, Scottish, and English extraction can, in very general terms, be estimated from the proportions of Catholic, Presbyterian, and Episcopalian (Protestant) in the county. In 1841 the respective proportions were thirty-two, forty-five, and twenty-one percent.

County Down was less badly affected by the Great Famine than many others. One of its effects, however, was a large exodus from the rural areas to the city of Belfast, part of which is in County Down. The population of Down in 1841 was 368,000. In 1851 this had been reduced by approximately eleven percent. Of these, 46,000 died, mainly in the years 1847–50. The level of emigration from the county was among the lowest in Ireland: only six percent of the population, versus a national average of 11.4 percent.

During the remainder of the nineteenth century, the town of Belfast and other towns in the county grew enormously. Some notes on the history of Belfast are included in the history of County Antrim. Belfast's prosperity attracted further immigration of workers from rural Ireland and Scotland to the city and to the outlying towns of the county. In 1921, Down was one of the six counties which remained part of the United Kingdom when an independent Irish state was formed.

Census and Census Substitutes

1631

Muster Roll of Co Down. SLC film 990025.

1642

Muster Roll for Parts of Co. Down. PRONI 7563; SLC film 897012.

No.	Denominations	No. of Feet in front	Rear	Depth	Principall Tenants	Tenants in possession	Half year's Rent at May, 1708.	Nature of the Improvements and Observations.
	IRISH QUARTER							**Irish Street** on the West side
1a	Old wall, orchard & garden	184	184	436				
1b	Bowling Green	192		square				
2a	Hutchinson's house & back side }	42	38	78	Seneca Hadzor	Do.	5 10 0	This with Prior's Island pays £20 ye ann.
2b	Hutchinson's Garden	184		square				
3	Wast Tent. unbuilt	44	44	78	Wash house			
4	McLeland's ½ Tent	30	30	84	Do. S. Hadzor has it for ye present	for building		On it a tite mud wall House, now used as a Barn
5	Wm. Irwyn's Tent.	64	53	90	Jno. McGrady & Rob. McKewn	Do.	0 10 0	An ordinary Mudd Wall Cabbin
6	Glencrosses Tent.	52	52	95	Waste unbuilt			
7	Margery Coots Tent.	60	34	448	Jno Curry & Jno McKeaten		1 8 0	A mudd wall Thatchd House, out of repair
8	Rider's Tenement	82	70	446	Francis Rider	Wm. Peery	1 3 4	A range of Clay and Stone wall thatchd Houses and 3 back Cabbins
9	Wm. McCrea's Tent.	42	42	440	Widow McCrea	Do.	1 3 4	A low Stone Wall House, Back House and Spring Well
10	Russell's Tenemt.	40	40	435	Wm. Thompson	Dr. Alex. Mercer	0 11 8	A stone wall slated House, 2½ story high, 2 back Houses, & a Wel
11 }	Widow Dounan's Tents.	44	44	436	Thos. Lautherdale	Do.	0 14 0 }	An old low stone wall thatchd House and 2 back houses
12					John Connor	Do.	0 11 8	
13	McKearly's Tent.	48	37	435	Pat Smith	Do.	1 0 0	A good stone wall house and new back house, all thatchd
14 }	Widow Eager's Tent.	43	37	436	Thos. Eager	{ Alex McCrery / John Coghran }	0 18 4	A strong stone wall thatched House with Malt House and Kiln backward
15 }								

An extract showing the principal tenants and sub-tenants, and descriptions of their properties, in the Irish Quarter of Downpatrick, 1708. From a "Survey of the Town of Downpatrick," an appendix to *The City of Downe* by R. E. Parkinson (Belfast, 1927).

1659

"Census" of Ireland. Edited by S. Pender. Dublin: Stationery Office, 1939. NLI I6551. SLC film 924648.

1660

Poll Tax abstracts of Co. Down. SLC film 993164; PRONI.

1663

Subsidy Roll. SLC film 1279356; ACM M9; PRONI T307, T1046; NLI 9584/5.

1669

Rent Roll of Downpatrick. Ms. Add. 3822 Cambridge Univ. Library (mf).

1698

Poll Tax Return: Newry and Mourne. PRONI T1046.

1708

"Householders in the Town of Downpatrick." In R.E. Parkinson, *The City of Downe*, pp. 151–62.

1720

List of Landed Gentry in Co. Down and Antrim. RIA ms. 24 K 19.

1740

List of Protestants in Parishes of Kilbroney and Seapatrick. NLI ms. 4173.

1761

Militia List Cos. . . . Down, etc. GO Ms 680.

1766

Householders of Parishes of Kilbroney and Seapatrick. RCB Library ms. 23; NLI ms. 4173; SLC film 1279330.

Householders of Lurgan, part of Parish of Shankill. Transcript with names of householders is at NAI M2476 and RCB Ms 23.

1796

See Co. Mayo 1796 ("List of Catholics").

Spinning Wheel Premium List (see introduction).

1796–1811

List of Freeholders in Barony of Upper Iveagh. SLC film 258701.

1798

List of Persons Who Suffered Losses in '98 Rebellion. NLI JLB 94107 (approximately 180 names, addresses, and occupations).

1813–24

List of Freeholders in the County. SLC film 258701.

1817

Rental of the Estate of Chichester Fortescue in Barony of Lr. Iveagh, Co. Down. Lists 189 tenants in townlands of Tonaghmore, Ballykelly, Ballygunaghan, Drumnavaddy, and Ballycross. NAI M3610.

1821–51

Extracts from the Government Censuses (1821, 1831, 1841, and 1851) for the Parish of Anahilt, Mainly Referring to the Name "Hanna." SLC film 258608; PRONI.

1823–37

Tithe Applotment Survey (see introduction).

1832

List of Freeholders on the Marquis of Londonderry's Estate. SLC film 258713.

1832–36

"Names of Holders of, and Applicants for, Licences to Sell Liquor in Downpatrick and Newry" (names and addresses). *Parl. Papers* 1837/38, 13 (2): Appendix 10.

1837

"Occupants of Newry, Arranged in 2 Lists" (valuations over and under £5 by street). *Parl. Papers* 1837 11 (1): Appendix G, 225–39.

1838

"Lists of Marksmen [illiterate voters] of Downpatrick and Newry" (names, occupations, and residences). *Parl. Papers* 1837 11 (1): Appendix A3; 1837/38, 13 (2): Appendix 4.

1839

List of Persons who obtained Game Certificates in Ulster. PRONI T 688.

1842

Voters List. NAI 1842/113.

1843

List of the Ballycopeland Presbyterian Congregation (Parish of Donaghadee). In *Millisle and Ballycopeland Presbyterian Church*, pp. 117–21.

1851

List of all inhabitants in parish of Scarva, with their ages (also lists of Church of Ireland members in 1858, 1860, 1861). RCB Library Ms. 65.

Rental of the estates of David S. Ker, Esq. for year ending Nov. 1851. Lists tenant names and holdings in thirty-one townlands. SEELB (see Library Sources at end of chapter).

1851/61

Census of Presbyterian Parishoners in Loughlinisland Parish (names, addresses, relationships, and some comments). *Family Links* 1 (5) (1982): 5–11; 1 (7) (1983): 9–14.

1852/57

Two Poll-Books for Co. Down. (1) for baronies of Dufferin, Kiniarty, Lecale, Mourne, Newry and Upper Iveagh. (2) for Lower Iveagh, Upper Castlereagh, Lower Castlereagh and Ards. Lists voters by townland, religion. Freeholders are recorded separately. PRONI (Downshire papers, D 671/02/5.6 and 7.8). SLC film 993158.

1856

"Tenants on Anglesey Estate" (parish of Newry; Townlands of Sheeptown, Derrylacka, Crobane, Dysert). *Louth Arch. J.* 12 (2) (1950): 151–53.

1857

Poll Book of electors of Co. Down. PRONI; SLC film 993159.

1858/60/61

Scarva C of I members (see 1851).

1863–64

Griffith's Valuation (see introduction).

1868

An alphabetically arranged list of electors who voted, and those who did not, at an election held in Newry on 20th November 1868. Gives names, addresses, and religious denominations of voters. Newry: Newry Telegraph Office, 1868. PRONI.

1891–99

Register of the inhabitants of Killyleagh. Copy held by SEELB (see Library Sources at end of chapter).

1901

Government Census. NAI (see introduction). SLC (mf).

1911

Government Census. NAI.

1914

Rental of the estate of Col. J.V. Nugent, Portaferry. Tenant names and holdings for seventeen townlands and large area of town of Portaferry. SEELB mf. (see Library Sources at end of chapter).

Church Records

Church of Ireland

See the introduction for a description of Church of Ireland records and their major repositories. Many C of I records were lost in the PRO fire of 1922. These are indicated as "Lost." However, as Church of Ireland records were effectively state records, the records of marriage (from 1845) are also in the General Registrar's Office. Many are still in local custody (LC), while others are in one of a variety of other archives (e.g., RCBL or NAI). The parish registers of this county are being indexed by the Ulster Historical Foundation (see Research Services at the end of the chapter). A search of the index will be conducted by the foundation for a fee. Marriage records from a range of parishes in the county were abstracted and published (nd) by Zara Mettam and are available on SLC film 824282.

Aghaderry (Loughbrickland)
Earliest Records: b. 1816; m. 1814; d. 1816
Status: LC

Annaduff
Status: Lost

Annahilt
Status: Lost

Annalong (Castlewellan)
Earliest Records: b. 1857; d. 1857
Status: LC

Ardglass
Status: Lost

Ardkeen
Earliest Records: b. 1746; m. 1746; d. 1746
Status: LC

Ardquin
Status: Lost

Ballee (Downpatrick)
Earliest Records: b. 1792; m. 1792; d. 1792
Status: LC

Ballyculter
Earliest Records: b. 1777; m. 1812; d. 1812
Status: LC

Ballyhalbert
Earliest Records: b. 1852; d. 1852
Status: LC

Ballymacarret
Earliest Records: b. 1827; m. 1827
Status: LC

Ballynahinch (see Magheradrool)

Ballyphilip (Portsterry)
Earliest Records: b. 1745; m. 1745; d. 1745
Status: LC

Ballywalter or Whitechurch
Earliest Records: b. 1844; d. 1844
Status: LC

Bangor
Earliest Records: b. 1803; m. 1805; d. 1815
Status: LC

Blaris (Lisburn)
Earliest Records: b. 1637–; m. 1639–; d. 1629–
Status: RCB (mf)

Castlewellan
Status: Lost

Clonallan
Status: Lost

Clonduff
Earliest Records: b. 1782; m. 1786; d. 1782
Status: LC

Comber
Earliest Records: b. 1683; m. 1683; d. 1683
Status: LC

Donaghadee
Earliest Records: b. 1778; m. 1778; d. 1778
Status: LC

Donaghcloney
Earliest Records: b. 1697; m. 1697; d. 1697
Status: LC

Donaghmore
Earliest Records: b. 1783; m. 1795; d. 1784
Status: LC

Down (Patrick)
Earliest Records: b. 1750; m. 1752; d. 1752
Status: LC

Dromara
Status: Lost

Dromore
Earliest Records: b. 1784; m. 1784; d. 1784
Status: LC; SLC films 496515 and 496723

Drumballyroney
Earliest Records: b. 1831; m. 1831; d. 1831
Status: LC

Drumbeg
Earliest Records: b. 1823; m. 1823; d. 1823
Status: LC

Drumbo
Earliest Records: b. 1791; m. 1791; d. 1791
Status: LC

Drumgooland
Earliest Records: b. 1779; m. 1779; d. 1779
Missing Dates: d. 1791–1838
Status: LC

Dundela
Earliest Records: b. 1864
Status: LC

Dundonald
Earliest Records: b. 1811; m. 1811; d. 1823
Status: LC

Dunsford
Status: Lost

Garvaghy
Status: Lost

Gilford
Earliest Records: b. 1869
Status: LC

Glencraig
Earliest Records: b. 1858
Status: LC

Grey Abbey
Earliest Records: b. 1807
Status: LC

Groomsport
Status: Lost

Hillsborough
Earliest Records: b. 1777; m. 1782; d. 1823
Status: LC

Hollymount
Status: Lost

Hollywood
Earliest Records: b. 1806; m. 1806; d. 1806
Status: LC

Inch
Earliest Records: b. 1767; m. 1764; d. 1788
Missing Records: m. 1765-90
Status: LC

Innishargy
Earliest Records: b. 1783; m. 1783; d. 1783
Status: LC

Kilbroney
Earliest Records: b. 1814; m. 1818; d. 1814
Status: LC

Kilclief
Status: Lost

Kilkeel
Earliest Records: b. 1816; m. 1816; d. 1816
Status: LC

Killaney
Earliest Records: b. 1858; d. 1865
Status: LC

Killinchy
Earliest Records: b. 1819; m. 1819; d. 1819
Status: LC

Killyleagh
Earliest Records: b. 1830; m. 1830; d. 1836
Status: LC; Published (b. 1835–81) by D. Stewart, Dublin, 1940; SLC film 928510

Kilmegan
Earliest Records: b. 1823; m. 1823; d. 1823
Status: LC

Kilmood
Earliest Records: b. 1822; m. 1822; d. 1793
Status: LC

Knockbreda
Earliest Records: b. 1784; m. 1784; d. 1784
Status: LC

Knocknamuckley
Earliest Records: b. 1838; m. 1838; d. 1853
Status: LC

Loughin Island
Earliest Records: b. 1760; m. 1760; d. 1760
Missing Dates: b. 1807–20; m. 1807–20; d. 1807–20
Status: LC

Maghera
Status: Lost

Magheradrool
Status: Lost

Magherahamlet
Status: Lost

Magheralin
Earliest Records: b. 1692; m. 1692; d. 1692
Status: LC

Magherally
Status: Lost

Moira
Earliest Records: b. 1845; d. 1845
Status: LC

Newcastle
Earliest Records: b. 1843; d. 1845
Status: LC

Newry
Earliest Records: b. 1822; m. 1784; d. 1824
Status: LC; SLC film 259218 (1784–1901)

Newtownards
Status: Lost

Rathmullan
Status: Lost

St. John Kilwarlin
Status: Lost

St. Patricks, Newry (see Newry)

Saintfield
Earliest Records: b. 1724; m. 1724; d. 1798
Missing Dates: b. 1758–97; m. 1751–97
Status: LC

Saul
Status: Lost

Scarvagh
Status: Lost

Seapatrick
Earliest Records: b. 1802; m. 1802; d. 1835
Status: LC

Shankill
Earliest Records: b. 1681; m. 1676; d. 1675
Status: LC

Tullynakill
Status: Lost

Tullylish
Earliest Records: b. 1820; m. 1820; d. 1849
Status: LC; SLC film 547238 (1820–33)

Tyrella
Earliest Records: b. 1839; m. 1844; d. 1839
Status: LC

Warrenpoint
Earliest Records: b. 1825; m. 1826
Status: LC

Presbyterian (for Belfast, see also appendix)

An account of Presbyterian records is given in the introduction. These registers rarely contain death records, and occasionally have only records of births. This is indicated where appropriate. All are held in the local parish unless otherwise indicated. The Presbyterian registers of Down are being indexed by the Ulster Historical Foundation (see Research Services at the end of the chapter). A search of the index will be conducted for a fee. Copies of many are also held at the Public Record Office of Northern Ireland (PRONI).

Anaghlone (Banbridge)
Starting Date: 1839

Anahilt (Hillsborough)
Starting Date: 1780

Annalong
Starting Date: 1840

Ardaragh (Newry)
Starting Date: 1804

Ballydown (Banbridge)
Starting Date: 1809

Ballygilbert
Starting Date: 1841

Ballygraney (Bangor)
Starting Date: 1838

Ballynahinch
Starting Date: 1841

Ballyroney (Banbridge)
Starting Date: 1831

Ballywater
Starting Date: 1824

Banbridge
Starting Date: 1756

Bangor
Starting Date: 1833

Carrowdore (Greyabbey)
Starting Date: 1843

Clarkesbridge (Newry)
Starting Date: 1833

Clonduff (Banbridge)
Starting Date: 1842

Clough (Downpatrick)
Starting Date: 1836

Cloughey
Starting Date: 1844

Comber
Starting Date: 1847

Conligh (Newtownards)
Starting Date: 1845

Donaghadee
Starting Date: 1822

Downpatrick
Starting Date: 1827

Dromara
Starting Date: 1810
Status: Records (1810-73) published, nd; SLC film 496273

Dromore
Starting Date: 1834

Drumbanagher (Derry)
Starting Date: 1832

Drumgooland
Starting Date: 1833

Drumlee (Banbridge)
Starting Date: 1826

Edengrove (Ballynahinch)
Starting Date: 1829

Glastry
Starting Date: 1728

Groomsport
Starting Date: 1841

Hillsborough
Starting Date: 1832

Kilkeel
Starting Date: 1842

Killinchy
Starting Date: 1835

Killyleagh
Starting Date: 1693

Kilmore (Crossgar)
Starting Date: 1833

Kirkcubbin
Starting Date: 1785
Status: LC; SLC film 883748 (b. 1778-1826; m. 1781-1845)

Leitrim (Banbridge)
Starting Date: 1837

Lissera (Crossgar)
Starting Date: 1809

Loughagherry (Hillsborough)
Starting Date: 1801

Loughbrickland
Starting Date: 1842

Magherally (Banbridge)
Starting Date: 1837

Millisle
Starting Date: 1773

Mourne (Kilkeel)
Starting Date: 1840

Newry
Starting Date: 1809
Status: Some records published in *Ir. Anc.* 11 (1) and 11 (2) (1979)

Newtownards
Starting Date: 1833

Portaferry
Starting Date: 1634

Raffrey (Crossgar)
Starting Date: 1843
Status: SLC film 990494 (b. 1843-85; m. 1845-77)

Rathfriland
Starting Date: 1804

Rostrevor
Starting Date: 1851

Saintfield
Starting Date: 1831
Status: SLC film 990494 (b. 1724-54; m. 1724-50)

Scarva
Starting Date: 1807

Seaforde
Starting Date: 1826

Strangford
Starting Date: 1846

Tullylish (Gilford)
Starting Date: 1813

Warrenpoint
Starting Date: 1832

Methodist

An account of Methodist records is given in the introduction. The following records occur:

Down Circuit (Matthew Lanktree Register)
Record Dates: 1815-1849
Status: NAI 1A 36 102; SLC film 100873; Pub. in
Gaelic Gleanings Vol. II (V)

Roman Catholic

Note that ninety-five percent of the Catholic parish registers of this county have been indexed by the Ulster Historical Foundation (see Research Services at the end of the chapter). A search of the index will be conducted by them for a fee. Microfilm copies of all registers are also available in the National Library of Ireland (NLI), and through the LDS library system.

Civil Parish: Aghaderg
Map Grid: 50
RC Parish: Loughbrickland and Sisagade, see also
Dromore
Diocese: DR
Earliest Record: b. 1.1816; m. 2.1816; d. 9.1838
Missing Dates: d. 11.1840-1.1843
Status: LC; NLI (mf); Indexed by UHF

Civil Parish: Annaclone
Map Grid: 51
RC Parish: Annaclone

Diocese: DR
Earliest Record: b. 9.1834; m. 5.1851; d. 4.1851
Status: LC; NLI (mf); Indexed by UHF

Civil Parish: Annahilt
Map Grid: 36
RC Parish: see Magheradrool
Diocese: DR

Civil Parish: Ardglass
Map Grid: 48
RC Parish: Ardglass, see Dunsfort
Diocese: DW

Civil Parish: Ardkeen
Map Grid: 13
RC Parish: Kircubbin
Diocese: DW
Earliest Record: b. 1.1828; m. 1.1828
Missing Dates: b. 11.1838-6.1852; m. 6.1839-
6.1852
Status: LC; NLI (mf); Indexed by UHF

Civil Parish: Ardquin
Map Grid: 15
RC Parish: see Ballyphilip
Diocese: DW

Civil Parish: Ballee
Map Grid: 45
RC Parish: Ballee, see Saul
Diocese: DW

Civil Parish: Ballyculter
Map Grid: 44
RC Parish: part Saul; part Kilclief
Diocese: DW

Civil Parish: Ballyhalbert (St. Andrew)
Map Grid: 12
RC Parish: Kircubbin, see Ardkeen
Diocese: DW

Civil Parish: Ballykinler
Map Grid: 66
RC Parish: see Tyrella
Diocese: DW

Civil Parish: Ballyphilip
Map Grid: 18
RC Parish: Ballyphilip and Portaferry
Diocese: DW
Earliest Record: b. 3.1843
Status: LC; NLI (mf); Indexed by UHF

Civil Parish: Ballytrustan
Map Grid: 16
RC Parish: see Ballyphilip
Diocese: DW

Civil Parish: Ballywalter
Map Grid: 10

RC Parish: Ballygalget
Diocese: DW
Earliest Record: b. 1.1828; m. 6.1852
Missing Dates: b. 4.1835-6.1852, 2.1864-11.1866; m. 9.1866-3.1867
Status: LC; NLI (mf); Indexed by UHF

Civil Parish: Bangor
Map Grid: 7
RC Parish: see Newtownards
Diocese: DW

Civil Parish: Blaris (also in Co. Antrim)
No records survive

Civil Parish: Bright
Map Grid: 69
RC Parish: Bright, Rossglass, and Killough
Diocese: DW
Earliest Record: b. 11.1856; m. 11.1856
Status: LC; NLI (mf); Indexed by UHF

Civil Parish: Castleboy
Map Grid: 14
RC Parish: see Ardkeen
Diocese: DW

Civil Parish: Clonallan
Map Grid: 54
RC Parish: Clonallon, see Warrenpoint
Diocese: DR

Civil Parish: Clonduff
Map Grid: 62
RC Parish: Clonduff
Diocese: DR
Earliest Record: b. 9.1850; m. 8.1850; d. 7.1850
Status: LC; NLI (mf); Indexed by UHF

Civil Parish: Comber
Map Grid: 4
RC Parish: see Newtownards
Diocese: DW

Civil Parish: Donaghadee
Map Grid: 8
RC Parish: see Newtownards
Diocese: DW

Civil Parish: Donaghcloney
Map Grid: 33
RC Parish: see Tullylish
Diocese: DR

Civil Parish: Donaghmore
Map Grid: 52
RC Parish: Donaghmore
Diocese: DR
Earliest Record: b. 5.1835; m. 9.1825; d. 10.1840
Missing Dates: d. ends 1871
Status: LC; NLI (mf); Indexed by UHF

Civil Parish: Down
Map Grid: 65
RC Parish: Downpatrick
Diocese: DW
Earliest Record: b. 10.1851; m. 2.1853; d. 8.1851
Status: LC; NLI (mf); Indexed by UHF

Civil Parish: Dromara
Map Grid: 58
RC Parish: Dromara; part Ballynahinch, see Magheradrool
Diocese: DR
Earliest Record: b. 1.1844; m. 1.1844; d. 1.1844
Status: LC; NLI (mf); Indexed by UHF

Civil Parish: Dromore
Map Grid: 35
RC Parish: Dromore and Garvaghy (also contains marriages, 1827-1843, for Aghaderg, Seagoe, Tullylish, Shankill, etc.)
Diocese: DR
Earliest Record: b. 3.1843; m. 9.1821; d. 11.1821
Missing Dates: d. 1.1845-11.1847
Status: LC; NLI (mf); Indexed by UHF

Civil Parish: Drumballyroney
Map Grid: 59
RC Parish: see Annaclone
Diocese: DR

Civil Parish: Drumbeg
Map Grid: 22
RC Parish: Lisburn, see Blaris
Diocese: DW

Civil Parish: Drumbo
Map Grid: 23
RC Parish: Lisburn, see Blaris
Diocese: DW

Civil Parish: Drumgath or Drumcath
Map Grid: 53
RC Parish: Rathfryland, Drumgath, and Barnmeen
Diocese: DR
Earliest Record: b. 4.1829; m. 7.1837; d. 6.1837
Status: LC; NLI (mf); Indexed by UHF

Civil Parish: Drumgooland (1)
Map Grid: 60
RC Parish: Drumgooland Upper (Leitrim); also Drumgooland Lower, see below
Diocese: DW
Earliest Record: b. 5.1827; m. 8.1827; d. 5.1828
Status: LC; NLI (mf); Indexed by UHF

Civil Parish: Drumgooland (2)
Map Grid: 60
RC Parish: Drumgooland Lower (Gargory)
Diocese: DW
Earliest Record: b. 3.1832; m. 4.1832; d. 3.1832
Status: LC; NLI (mf); Indexed by UHF

Civil Parish: Dundonald
Map Grid: 2
RC Parish: see Newtownards
Diocese: DW

Civil Parish: Dunsfort
Map Grid: 47
RC Parish: Dunsfort and Ardglass (also contains
birth and marriages from 4.1845-2.1848 for
Derraghy, Hannahstown, and Rockwilliam)
Diocese: DW
Earliest Record: b. 2.1848; m. 2.1848; d. 2.1848
Status: LC; NLI (mf); Indexed by UHF

Civil Parish: Garvaghy
Map Grid: 57
RC Parish: part Dromore; part Annaclone
Diocese: DR

Civil Parish: Grey Abbey
Map Grid: 9
RC Parish: Ballygalget, see Ballywalter
Diocese: DW

Civil Parish: Hillsborough
Map Grid: 30
RC Parish: see Blaris
Diocese: DW

Civil Parish: Holywood
Map Grid: 1
RC Parish: Holywood
Diocese: DW
Earliest Record: b. 11.1866; m. 5.1867
Status: LC; NLI (mf); Indexed by UHF

Civil Parish: Inch
Map Grid: 42
RC Parish: see Kilmore
Diocese: DW

Civil Parish: Inishargy
Map Grid: 11
RC Parish: Kircubbin, see Ardkeen
Diocese: DW

Civil Parish: Kilbroney
Map Grid: 56
RC Parish: Kilbroney (Rostrevor)
Diocese: DR
Earliest Record: b. 1.1808; m. 1.1808; d. 1.1808
Status: LC; NLI (mf); Indexed by UHF

Civil Parish: Kilclief
Map Grid: 46
RC Parish: Kilclief and Strangford
Diocese: DW
Earliest Record: b. 1.1866; m. 11.1865
Missing Dates: b. 7.1867-10.1870; m. 10.1868-
1.1871
Status: LC; NLI (mf); Indexed by UHF

Civil Parish: Kilcoo (1)
Map Grid: 63
RC Parish: Kilcoo; also Ballymoney, see below; also
part Maghera
Diocese: N and M
Earliest Record: b. 10.1832
Status: LC; NLI (mf); Indexed by UHF

Civil Parish: Kilcoo (2)
Map Grid: 63
RC Parish: Ballymoney
Diocese: N and M
Earliest Record: b. 3.1853; m. 4.1853
Status: LC; NLI (mf); Indexed by UHF

Civil Parish: Kilkeel (1)
Map Grid: 71
RC Parish: Lower Mourne (Glasdrummond); also
Upper Mourne, see below
Diocese: DW
Earliest Record: b. 8.1842; m. 9.1839
Missing Dates: m. 11.1866-8.1867
Status: LC; NLI (mf); Indexed by UHF

Civil Parish: Kilkeel (2)
Map Grid: 71
RC Parish: Upper Mourne (Kilkeel)
Diocese: DW
Earliest Record: b. 7.1839; m. 5.1839
Status: LC; NLI (mf); Indexed by UHF

Civil Parish: Killaney
Map Grid: 25
RC Parish: see Killinchy
Diocese: DW

Civil Parish: Killinchy
Map Grid: 26
RC Parish: Carrickmannan and Saintfield
Diocese: DW
Earliest Record: b. 10.1837; m. 10.1845
Status: LC; NLI (mf); Indexed by UHF

Civil Parish: Killyleagh
Map Grid: 27
RC Parish: see Kilmore
Diocese: DW

Civil Parish: Kilmegan (1)
Map Grid: 61
RC Parish: Kilmegan (Castlewellan); also Drumaroad,
see below
Diocese: N and M
Earliest Record: b. 1.1853; m. 5.1853
Status: LC; NLI (mf); Indexed by UHF

Civil Parish: Kilmegan (2)
Map Grid: 61
RC Parish: Drumaroad and Clannaraghan
Diocese: N and M

Earliest Record: b. 1.1853; m. 5.1853
Status: LC; NLI (mf); Indexed by UHF

Civil Parish: Kilmood
Map Grid: 5
RC Parish: see Newtownards
Diocese: DW

Civil Parish: Kilmore
Map Grid: 40
RC Parish: Kilmore (Crossgar)
Diocese: DW

Civil Parish: Knockbreda
Map Grid: 20
RC Parish: see Holywood
Diocese: DW

Civil Parish: Lambeg
Map Grid: 21
RC Parish: see Blaris
Diocese: CR

Civil Parish: Loughinisland
Map Grid: 41
RC Parish: Loughinisland
Diocese: DW
Earliest Record: b. 1806; m. 11.1805; d. 11.1805
Missing Dates: all end 10.1852
Status: LC; NLI (mf); Indexed by UHF

Civil Parish: Maghera
Map Grid: 64
RC Parish: Bryansford and Newcastle (Maghera)
Diocese: DW
Earliest Record: b. 2.1845; m. 3.1845; d. 4.1860
Status: LC; NLI (mf); Indexed by UHF

Civil Parish: Magheradrool
Map Grid: 38
RC Parish: Ballynahinch and Dunmore
Diocese: DR
Earliest Record: b. 5.1827; m. 3.1829
Status: LC; NLI (mf); Indexed by UHF

Civil Parish: Magherahamlet
Map Grid: 39
RC Parish: Ballynahinch, see Magheradrool
Diocese: DR

Civil Parish: Magheralin
Map Grid: 32
RC Parish: Magheralin, Moira, and Aughalee
Diocese: DR
Earliest Record: b. 1815; m. 1815; d. 1815
Status: LC; NLI (mf); Indexed by UHF

Civil Parish: Magherally
Map Grid: 37
RC Parish: see Tullylish
Diocese: DR

Civil Parish: Moira
Map Grid: 29
RC Parish: see Magheralin
Diocese: DR

Civil Parish: Mullaghbawn (see Forkhill, Co. Armagh)

Civil Parish: Newry
Map Grid: 70
RC Parish: Newry
Diocese: N and M
Earliest Record: b. 9.1818; m. 1820; d. 11.1818
Missing Dates: b. 11.1819-5.1820; m. 5.1825-8.1825; d. 1862 (index of baptisms from 1858)
Status: LC; NLI (mf); Indexed by UHF

Civil Parish: Newtownards
Map Grid: 3
RC Parish: Newtownards, Comber and Donaghadee
Diocese: DW
Earliest Record: b. 6.1864
Status: LC; NLI (mf); Indexed by UHF

Civil Parish: Rathmullan
Map Grid: 68
RC Parish: see Bright
Diocese: DW

Civil Parish: St. Andrews
Map Grid: 12
RC Parish: Kircubbin, see Ardkeen
Diocese: DW

Civil Parish: Saintfield
Map Grid: 24
RC Parish: Saintfield, see Killinchy
Diocese: DW

Civil Parish: Saul (1)
Map Grid: 43
RC Parish: Saul and Ballee; also Ballyalter, see below
Diocese: DW
Earliest Record: b. 5.1868; m. 5.1868
Status: LC; NLI (mf); Indexed by UHF

Civil Parish: Saul (2)
Map Grid: 43
RC Parish: Ballyculter and Ballee
Diocese: DW
Earliest Record: b. 1.1844; m. 8.1843
Missing Dates: b. 5.1864-11.1870
Status: LC; NLI (mf); Indexed by UHF

Civil Parish: Seapatrick
Map Grid: 49
RC Parish: Banbridge; part Tullylish
Diocese: DR
Earliest Record: b. 1.1843; m. 7.1850; d. 7.1850
Status: LC; NLI (mf); Indexed by UHF

Civil Parish: Shankill
Map Grid: 28
RC Parish: see Magheralin
Diocese: DR

Civil Parish: Slanes
Map Grid: 17
RC Parish: see Ballyphilip
Diocese: DW

Civil Parish: Tullylish
Map Grid: 34
RC Parish: Tullylish, see also Dromore
Diocese: DR
Earliest Record: b. 1.1833; m. 1.1833; d. 1.1833
Missing Dates: b. 8.1844-4.1846; m. 4.1844-2.1845
Status: LC; NLI (mf); Indexed by UHF

Civil Parish: Tullynakill
Map Grid: 6
RC Parish: see Newtownards
Diocese: DW

Civil Parish: Tyrella
Map Grid: 67
RC Parish: Tyrella and Ballykinler
Diocese: DW
Earliest Record: b. 4.1854; m. 7.1854
Status: LC; NLI (mf); Indexed by UHF

Civil Parish: Warrenpoint
Map Grid: 55
RC Parish: Warrenpoint (Clonallon)
Diocese: DR
Earliest Record: b. 11.1826; m. 11.1825
Missing Dates: b. ends 1.1869
Status: LC; NLI (mf); Indexed by UHF

Civil Parish: Witter
Map Grid: 19
RC Parish: see Ballyphilip
Diocese: DW

Commercial and Social Directories

1740

A Directory of Belfast. *North Irish Roots* 4 (2) 1993 (mainly freemen of Belfast).

1807/08

Joseph Smith's Belfast Directories. Reprinted as *Merchants in Plenty*. J.R.R. Adams, ed. Ulster Historical Foundation, 1992, pp. 94.

1819

Thomas Bradshaw's *General Directory of Newry, Armagh . . . etc.* gives an alphabetical listing of the traders in Banbridge, Rathfriland, Rostrevor, Kilkeel, and Warrenpoint.

Thomas Bradshaw's *General and Commercial Directory* covers only Belfast and Lisburn, giving history, index of merchants and traders, and a general-name index. Published by Finlay, 1819.

1820

J. Pigot's *Commercial Directory of Ireland* contains information on the gentry, nobility, and traders in and around the town of Newry.

1820

Thomas Bradshaw's *General Directory of Portadown, Waringstown, Banbridge, Warrenpoint, Rostrevor, Kilkeel, Rathfriland and others*. Newry, 1819.

1824

J. Pigot's *City of Dublin and Hibernian Provincial Directory* includes traders, nobility, gentry, and clergy lists of Ballynahinch, Banbridge, Bangor, Castlewellan, Comber, Donaghadee, Downpatrick, Dromore, Gilford, Hillsborough, Killileigh, Loughbrickland, Newry, Newtownards, Portaferry, Rathfryland, Rosstrevor, Saintfield, Strangford, and Warrenpoint.

1841

Mathew Martin's *Belfast Directory* contains alphabetical lists of gentry, merchants, traders, street lists, and a list of noblemen and gentry in and around the towns of Banbridge, Bangor, Comber, Downpatrick, Dromore, Hillsborough, Holywood, and Killileagh.

1842

Further edition of Martin's *Belfast Directory* covers Banbridge, Bangor, Castlewellan, Comber, Crawfordsburn, Donaghadee, Downpatrick, Dromore, Hillsborough, Holywood, Killileagh, Kircubbin, Newtownards, Portaferry, Rathfriland, Saintfield, and Strangford.

1846

Slater's *National Commercial Directory of Ireland* lists nobility, clergy, traders, etc., in Ballynahinch, Banbridge, Bangor, Castlewellan, Clough and Newcastle, Comber, Donaghadee, Downpatrick, Dromore, Gilford and Loughbrickland, Hillsborough, Killyleagh, Newry, Newtownards, Portaferry, Strangford and Kircubbin, Rathfryland, Saintfield, Warrenpoint, and Rosstrevor.

1852

Henderson's *Belfast and Province of Ulster Directory* has lists of inhabitants, traders, etc., in and around the towns of Ardglass, Ballynahinch, Banbridge, Bangor, Donaghadee, Downpatrick, Dromore, Hillsborough, Newry, Newtownards, and Saintfield.

1854

A further edition of Henderson's *Directory* covers Ardglass, Ballynahinch, Banbridge, Bangor, Castlewellan, Comber, Donaghadee, Downpatrick, Dromore, Gilford, Hillsborough, Holywood, Killyleagh, Loughbrickland, Newcastle, Newry, Newtownards, Rathfriland, Rosstrevor, Saintfield, and Strangford. Further editions in 1856, 1858, 1861 (Kilkeel included from this date), 1863, 1865, 1868 (Laurencetown included from this date), 1870, 1877, 1880, 1884, 1890, 1894, and 1900.

1856

Slater's *Royal National Commercial Directory of Ireland* lists nobility, gentry, clergy, traders, etc., in Ballynahinch, Banbridge, Bangor, Castlewellan, Comber, Donaghadee, Downpatrick, Dromore, Gilford, Loughbrickland and Laurencetown, Hillsborough, Kilkeel, Killyleagh, Newry, Newtownards and Grey Abbey, Portaferry, Strangford and Kircubbin, Rathfryland, Saintfield, Warrenpoint, and Rosstrevor.

1865

Wynne's *Directory of Ballynahinch, Banbridge, Bangor, Comber, Downpatrick, Donaghadee, Dromore, Hillsborough, Holywood, Newry, Newtownards, Rathfriland, and Warrenpoint.*

1870

Slater's *Directory of Ireland* contains trade, nobility, and clergy lists for Ballynahinch, Banbridge, Bangor, Castlewellan, Comber, Donaghadee, Downpatrick, Dromore, Gilford, Hillsborough, Hollywood, Kilkeel, Killyleagh, Newry, Newtownards, Portaferry, Rathfryland, Saintfield, Warrenpoint, and Rosstrevor.

1881

Slater's *Royal National Commercial Directory of Ireland* contains lists of traders, clergy, nobility, and farmers in adjoining parishes of the towns of Ballynahinch and Saintfield, Banbridge, Bangor, Castlewellan, Donaghadee, Downpatrick, Dromore, Holywood, Kilkeel, Newry, Newtownards, Portaferry, Rathfryland, Warrenpoint, and Rosstrevor.

1883

S. Farrell's *County Armagh Directory and Almanac* has a street directory for Newry.

1886

G.H. Bassett's *County Down One Hundred Years Ago* lists traders, etc., in the borough of Newry.

1894

Slater's *Royal National Directory of Ireland* lists traders, police, teachers, farmers, and private residents in each of the towns, villages, and parishes of the county and in many of the suburbs of Belfast which are in Co. Down.

1916

Newtownards and Co. Down Illustrated Almanac and Directory lists householders in Newtownards, Ballygowan, Ballywalter, Carrowdore, Comber, Donaghadee, Greyabbey, Killinchy, Kirkcubbin, Portaferry and Saintfield.

1918

Newtownards and Co. Down Illustrated Almanac and Directory lists householders, as in 1916 edition.

Family History

Crossle, Philip. *Histories of Newry families prior to 1910.* PRONI; SLC films 259195-259219.

"Surnames of the Upper Ards." *Family Links* 1 (1) (1981): 13-22.

(Barcroft/Malcolmson) "A Quaker Wedding at Lisburn, Co. Down 1867." *Ir. Anc.* 1392 (1981): 90-92.

Nine generations: a history of the Andrews family, Millers of Comber. I. Andrews, 1958.

"The Bradshaws of Bangor and Mile-Cross, in the Co. of Down." *Ulster J. Arch.* 2nd Ser. 8 (1902): 4-6, 55-57.

Fisher, F.O., ed. *Memoirs of the Camacs of Co. Down with some account of their predecessors.* 1897.

"Clenlow of Co. Down." Pedigree in *Swanzy Notebooks.* RCB Library, Dublin.

"Cossett of Co. Down." Pedigree in *Swanzy Notebooks.* RCB Library, Dublin.

Brett, C.E.B. *Long Shadows Cast Before: Nine Lives in Ulster, 1625-1977.* Bartholomew, 1978. ISBN: 07028 1058-4.

Moffett, P. *The Dunville family of Redburn House, Holywood 1757-1940.*

Hamilton, J. *The Hamilton manuscripts: containing some account of the settlement of the territories of the Upper Clandboye, Great Ardes, and Dufferin . . . .* Archer & Sons, 1867.

Hamilton, R.W. *A short family and personal history.* J.V. Hamilton, 1995.

"Henry of Co. Down." Pedigree in *Swanzy Notebooks.* RCB Library, Dublin.

Danne, E.F. Notes on the Family of Magennis, Formerly Lords of Iveagh, Newry and Mourne. Salt Lake City, 1878.

Guinness, Henry S. "Magennis of Iveagh." R.S.A.I. 62 (1932): 96–102.

Linn, Richard. Pedigree of the Magennis (Guinness) Family of North Ireland and of Dublin. Christchurch, N.Z., 1897.

McGiffert, J. The McGiffert Letters (of Killyleagh). 1983.

Montgomery, W. The Montgomery manuscripts: (1603–1706) compiled from family papers. J. Cleeland, 1869.

Wilson, I. Neills of Bangor. The author, 1982.

Hartigan, A.S. The Family of Pollock of Newry. Folkestone, n.d.

"Quinn of Newry." Pedigree in Swanzy Notebooks. RCB Library, Dublin.

Osbourne, M.J. Rea/Rae of Ballynahinch, Holywood and allied families. Univ. of California, 1980.

Public Record Office of Northern Ireland: Twenty-one volumes (approximately 2000 documents), papers and correspondence of the Roden family. Newcastle, Co. Down.

James, H.E. The Rose-Cleland Family. The author, 1984.

Savage-Armstrong, G.F. The ancient and noble family of the Savages of the Ards with sketches of English and American branches. Marcus Ward, 1888.

A genealogical history of the Savage family in Ulster. Chiswick Press, 1906.

Altpeter, L.H. Ancestors and descendants of Alexander Sloane Killyleagh, Co. Down in Ireland. The author, 1986.

Elder, L.C. The Smillies of Ballynahinch: a genealogy. The author, 1985.

"Smith of Co. Louth and Co. Down." Pedigree in Swanzy Notebooks. RCB Library, Dublin.

"Stothard of Co. Down." Pedigree in Swanzy Notebooks. RCB Library, Dublin.

Stranaghan family, Co. Down 1800–1950. N.p., 1990.

"Waddell of Co. Down." Pedigree in Swanzy Notebooks. RCB Library, Dublin.

West—see Co. Wicklow.

Gravestone Inscriptions

Many of the graveyards in this county have been recorded in the series "Gravestone Inscriptions Series—Co. Down," edited by R.S.J. Clarke and published by the Ulster Historical Foundation from 1966–84 in nineteen volumes. A separate series is also available for Belfast. Most of the gravestone inscriptions of the county have also been indexed by the Ulster Historical Foundation, who will conduct a search for a fee. SLC 941.65v3c.

Aghlisnafin: "Gravestone Series—Down," No. 9.

Annahilt: "Gravestone Series—Down," No. 18.

Ardkeen: "Gravestone Series—Down," No. 13.

Ardglass: "Gravestone Series—Down," No. 8.

Ardquin: "Gravestone Series—Down," No. 18.

Baileysmill: "Gravestone Series—Down," No. 2.

Ballee: "Gravestone Series—Down," No. 8.

Balligan: "Gravestone Series—Down," No. 14.

Balloo: "Gravestone Series—Down," No. 17.

Ballyblack: "Gravestone Series—Down," No. 12.

Ballycarn: "Gravestone Series—Down," No. 3.

Ballycopeland: "Gravestone Series—Down," No. 16.

Ballycranbeg: "Gravestone Series—Down," No. 13.

Ballycruttle: "Gravestone Series—Down," No. 8.

Ballyculter: "Gravestone Series—Down," No. 8.

Ballydown: "Gravestone Series—Down," No. 20.

Ballygalget: "Gravestone Series—Down," No. 13.

Ballygowan: "Gravestone Series—Down," No. 5.

Ballyhalbert: "Gravestone Series—Down," No. 15.

Ballyhemlin: "Gravestone Series—Down," No. 14.

Ballykinler: "Gravestone Series—Down," No. 9.

Ballymacashen: "Gravestone Series—Down," No. 6.

Ballymageogh: "Gravestone Series—Down," No. 10.

Ballymartin: "Gravestone Series—Down," No. 10.

Ballynahinch: "Gravestone Series—Down," No. 9.

Ballyphilip: "Gravestone Series—Down," No. 13.

Ballytrustan: "Gravestone Series—Down," No. 13.

Ballydown: "Gravestone Series—Down," No. 20.

Banbridge: "Gravestone Series—Down," No. 20.

Barr: J.D. Cowam. An Ancient Irish Parish. 1914.

Belfast: "Gravestone Inscriptions—Belfast," Vol. 1, 1982; Vol. 2, 1984; Vol 3., 1986; Vol. 4, 1991.

Blaris: "Gravestone Series—Down," No. 5.

Boardmills: "Gravestone Series—Down," No. 2.

Breda: "Gravestone Series—Down," No. 1.

Bright: "Gravestone Series—Down," No. 8.

Cargacreevy: "Gravestone Series—Down," No. 18.

Carrowdore: "Gravestone Series—Down," No. 14.

Carryduff: "Gravestone Series—Down," Nos. 1 and 18.

Castlereagh: "Gravestone Series—Down," No. 1.

Clandeboye: "Gravestone Series—Down," No. 17.

Clare: "Gravestone Series—Down," No. 20.

Cloghy: "Gravestone Series—Down," No. 14.

Clough: "Gravestone Series—Down," No. 9.

Comber: "Gravestone Series—Down," No. 5.

Copeland Island: "Gravestone Series—Down," No. 16.

Donaghadee: "Gravestone Series—Down," No. 16.

Donaghcloney: Edward D. Atkinson. An Ulster Parish. 1898.

Donaghmore: J.D. Cowan. An Ancient Irish Parish. 1914.

Downpatrick: "Gravestone Series—Down," Nos. 7 and 21.

Dromara: "Gravestone Series–Down," No. 19.

Dromore: "Gravestone Series–Down," No. 19.

Drumaroad: "Gravestone Series–Down," No. 9.

Drumbeg: "Gravestone Series–Down," No. 3.

Drumbo: "Gravestone Series–Down," Nos. 1, 4, and 18.

Dundonald: "Gravestone Series–Down," No. 2.

Dunsfort: "Gravestone Series–Down," No. 8.

Edenderry: "Gravestone Series–Down," No. 3.

Eglantine: "Gravestone Series–Down," No. 18.

Gilnahirk: "Gravestone Series–Down," No. 18.

Glasdrumman: "Gravestone Series–Down," No. 10.

Glastry: "Gravestone Series–Down," No. 15.

Gransha: "Gravestone Series–Down," No. 1.

Greyabbey: "Gravestone Series–Down," No. 12.

Groomsport: "Gravestone Series–Down," No. 17.

Hillhall: "Gravestone Series–Down," No. 1.

Hillsborough: "Gravestone Series–Down," No. 18.

Holywood: "Gravestone Series–Down," No. 14.

Inch: "Gravestone Series–Down," Nos. 7 and 21.

Inishargy: "Gravestone Series–Down," No. 14.

Kilcarn: "Gravestone Series–Down," No. 5.

Kilclief: "Gravestone Series–Down," No. 8.

Kilhorne: "Gravestone Series–Down," No. 10.

Kilkeel: "Gravestone Series–Down," No. 10.

Killarney: "Gravestone Series–Down," No. 2.

Killaresy: "Gravestone Series–Down," No. 6.

Killinakin: "Gravestone Series–Down," No. 6.

Killinchy: "Gravestone Series–Down," Nos. 5 and 6.

Killough: "Gravestone Series–Down," No. 8.

Killybawn: "Gravestone Series–Down," No. 1.

Killyleagh: "Gravestone Series–Down," Nos. 6, 7, and 21.

Killysuggan: "Gravestone Series–Down," No. 5.

Kilmegan: "Gravestone Series–Down," No. 9.

Kilmood: "Gravestone Series–Down," No. 5.

Kilmore: "Gravestone Series–Down," No. 3.

Kilwarlin: "Gravestone Series–Down," No. 18.

Kircubbin: "Gravestone Series–Down," No. 12.

Knock: "Gravestone Series–Down," No. 4.

Knockbrecken: "Gravestone Series–Down," Nos. 1 and 18.

Knockbreda: "Gravestone Series–Down," No. 2.

Lawrencetown: "Gravestone Series–Down," No. 20.

Legacurry: "Gravestone Series–Down," No. 2.

Lisbane: "Gravestone Series–Down," No. 13.

Lisburn Cathedral: SLC film 251934.

Lisburn (Christ Church): SLC film 560159.

Loughaghery: "Gravestone Series–Down," No. 18.

Loughinisland: "Gravestone Series–Down," Nos. 9 and 12.

Magheradrool: "Gravestone Series–Down," Nos. 9 and 12.

Magherahamlet: "Gravestone Series–Down," No. 9.

Magherally: "Gravestone Series–Down," No. 19.

Banbridge: "Gravestone Series–Down," No. 20.

Maze: "Gravestone Series–Down," No. 18.

Millisle: "Gravestone Series–Down," No. 16.

Moira: "Gravestone Series–Down," No. 18.

Moneyrea: "Gravestone Series–Down," No. 1.

Mourne: "Gravestone Series–Down," No. 10.

Movilla: "Gravestone Series–Down," No. 11.

Moyallon: "Gravestone Series–Down," No. 20.

Newtownards: "Gravestone Series–Down," No. 11.

Old Court: "Gravestone Series–Down," No. 8.

Portaferry: "Gravestone Series–Down," No. 13, and *Portaferry Gravestone Inscriptions*, Byers Business Services, 1988.

Rademan: "Gravestone Series–Down," No. 3.

Raffrey: "Gravestone Series–Down," No. 5.

Saintfield: "Gravestone Series–Down," No. 3.

Rathmullan: "Gravestone Series–Down," No. 9.

Ravara: "Gravestone Series–Down," No. 5.

Saul: "Gravestone Series–Down," Nos. 7, 8, and 21.

Seaforde: "Gravestone Series–Down," No. 9.

Seapatrick: "Gravestone Series–Down," No. 20.

Slanes: "Gravestone Series–Down," No. 14.

Tamlaght: "Gravestone Series–Down," No. 10.

Templepatrick: "Gravestone Series–Down," No. 14.

Tullylish: "Gravestone Series–Down," No. 20.

Tullymacnous: "Gravestone Series–Down," No. 6.

Tullynakill: "Gravestone Series–Down," No. 1.

Waringstown: Edward D. Atkinson. *An Ulster Parish.* 1898.

Whitechurch: "Gravestone Series–Down," No. 15.

Newspapers

The best early source for this county is the *Newry Journal,* published in the 1770s and 1780s. However, there are few copies of this newspaper in existence. See the appendix for newspapers published in Belfast; many of these covered events and carried notices of relevance to several of the surrounding counties. The South Eastern Education and Library Board (SEELB; see Library Sources at the end of the chapter) has a collection of local papers, and has also been compiling and publishing indexes to articles and persons and places mentioned.

Title: *County Down Spectator*
Published in: Bangor 3 June 1904–current
NLI Holdings: 6.1921–in progress
BL Holdings: 6.1904–in progress (with gaps 1917–1924)

SEELB holds 1904-in progress, and also publish an index to 1904-1964

Title: *Downpatrick Recorder*
Published in: Downpatrick, 1836-current
NLI Holdings: 12.1836-in progress
BL Holdings: 12.1836-in progress
SEELB holds 12.1836-in progress, and also publish an index to 1836-1886

Title: *Downshire Protestant*
Published in: Downpatrick, 1855-62
BL Holdings: 7.1855-9.1862

Title: *Newry Commercial Telegraph* (continued as *Newry Telegraph* in 1877)
Published in: Newry, 1812-1970
NLI Holdings: 1814-91 (odd numbers); 4.1858-12.1913; 1.1950-6.1970
BL Holdings: 1.1828-7.1877; 7.1877-9.1922; 1.1923-12.1927; 7.1928-6.1970

Title: *Newry Examiner* (continued as *Dundalk Examiner*)
Published in: Newry, 1830-80
NLI Holdings: 1.1852-12.1857
BL Holdings: 1.1832-8.1880

Title: *Newry Herald and Down, Armagh and Louth Journal*
Published in: Newry, 1858-64
BL Holdings: 1.1858-12.1864

Title: *Newry Journal* (Jones)
Published in: Newry, ca. 1770-c.1776

Title: *Newry Journal* (Stevenson)
Published in: Newry, ca. 1774-1788

Title: *Newry Reporter*
Published in: Newry, 1867-current
NLI Holdings: 6.1921-9.1922; 1.1923-in progress
BL Holdings: 11.1867-5.1901; 6.1901-9.1922; 1.1923-6.1925; 1.1926-in progress

Title: *Newry Standard* (continued as *Belfast and Newry Standard* in 1882 and as *Newry and Belfast Standard* in 1891)
Published in: Newry, 1879-99
NLI Holdings: 6.1879-4.1882; 5.1882-11.1891; 12.1891-6.1899
BL Holdings: 5.1889-6.1899

Title: *Newtownards Chronicle*
Published in: Newtownards, 1873-current
NLI Holdings: 6.1921-in progress
BL Holdings: 1.1874-in progress
SEELB holds 1873-in progress, and also publish an index to 1873-1900

Title: *North Down Herald* (continued as *Northern Herald* in 1926)
Published in: Bangor, ca. 1880-1957
NLI Holdings: 6.1921-2.1957
BL Holdings: 1.1898-12.1925; 1.1926-3.1939; 5.1952-1957

Title: *Northern Star*
Published in: Belfast, 1.1792-5.1797
NLI Holdings: 1793-1795; 1796-5.1797 (odd numbers)
BL Holdings: 1.1792-12.1796 (with gaps)
SEELB holds all issues and has published an index

Wills and Administrations

A discussion of the types of records, where they are held, and their availability and value is given in the Wills section of the introduction. The availability of prerogative wills, administrations, and marriage license records is also described in the relevant parts of the same section. Where available, published sources of these records are given in the Miscellaneous Sources section.

Pre-1858 Wills and Administrations

Prerogative Wills. See the introduction.

Consistorial Wills. County Down is in the dioceses of Down, Dromore, Newry, and Mourne (four parishes) and Connor (two parishes). The guide to Catholic parish records in this chapter shows the diocese to which each civil parish belonged. The wills of residents of each diocese were usually proven within that diocese (see the Wills section for exceptions). The following records survive:

Wills

Connor (1818-20, 1853-58); Down (1850-58).

Abstracts

See the introduction; Stewart-Kennedy notebooks—see Co. Antrim.

Indexes

Down (1646-1858) none published; Dromore (1678-1858); Newry and Mourne (1727-1858) published in 1858 by Phillimore; Connor—see Co. Antrim.

Post-1858 Wills and Administrations

County Down was served by the District Registry of Belfast. The surviving records are kept in the PRONI. Other published records:

"Administrations from the Peculiar of Newry and Mourne." *Ir. Anc.* 1 (1) (1969): 41-42.

Belfast District Will Books (1858-1872). PRONI; SLC films 917960-917971.

Marriage Licenses

Indexes

Down, Connor, and Dromore (1721-1845). NAI; SLC film 100867.

Miscellaneous Sources

"Administrations From the Peculiar of Newry and Mourne." *Ir. Anc.* 1 (1) (1969): 41–42.

Agnew, Jean. *The Merchant Community of Belfast, 1660–1700.* Dublin: Fourcourts Press, 1996. (Profile of thirty merchant families.)

"The Census of 1901 and 1911 for Copeland Island." *J. Bangor Hist. Soc.* 1 (1981).

"Killyleagh and District Branch Records." J. McGiffert (Member No. 72). *North Irish Roots* 2 (5): 191.

"Maps of the Mountains of Mourne." *Ulster J. Arch.* 8 (1902): 133–37.

Parkinson, R.E. *The City of Downe from its Earliest Days.* Belfast: Erskine Mayne, 1927. Reprint of the 1927 end. Bangor: Fairview Pub., 1977.

Provisional list of pre-1900 School Registers in the PRONI. *Ulster Gen. & Hist. Guild* 9 (1986): 60–71. Lists registers and PRONI reference numbers for all NI counties.

"Some Lists of Mid-18th-Century Linen Drapers in S.E. Ulster." *Ir. Anc.* 11 (1) (1979): 9–14.

Stevenson, J. *Two Centuries of Life in County Down, 1600–1800.*

Surnames of Co. Down. *Irish Roots* (1) (1996): 22–23.

Young, R. *Historical Notices of Old Belfast.* 1896.

Barry, J. *Hillsborough: a parish in the Ulster Plantation.* 3rd ed. William Mullan, 1982.

Canavan, T. *Frontier town: an illustrated history of Newry.* Blackstaff Press, 1989. ISBN: 085640-430-6.

Carr, P. *The most unpretending of places: a history of Dundonald, Co. Down.* White Row Press, 1987. ISBN: 187013-200-9.

Crowe, W. *Haughton, Bridges to Banbridge.* Dundalgan Press, 1980.

Dubourdieu, J. Rev. *Statisical survey of the County Down.* Graisberry and Campbell, 1802.

Irwin, David. *Tide and times in the 'Port: a narrative history of the County Down village of Groomsport.* Groomsport Presbyterian Church, 1993.

James, W.V. *Strangford, the forgotten past of Strangford village.* Northern Whig, 1994.

Linn, R. *A History of Banbridge.* Banbridge Cronicle Press, 1935.

McCavery, T. *Newtown: a history of Newtownards.* White Row Press, 1994. ISBN: 1832170-70-X.

McCorry, F.X. *Lurgan, an Irish provincial town, 1610–1970.* Inglewood Press, 1993. ISBN: 095221-610-8.

McCullough, S. *Ballynahinch: centre of Down.* Ballynahinch Chamber of Commerce, 1968.

O'Laverty, J. Rev. *An historical account of the diocese of Down and Connor.* 5 vols. M.H. Gill, 1880.

Reeves, W. Rev. *Ecclesiastical antiquities of Down, Connor and Dromore.* Hodges and Smith, 1847.

Wilson, A.M. *Saint Patrick's Town.* Isabella Press, 1995. ISBN: 095270-910-4.

Wolseley, H.H. Rev. *Statistical account of the parish of Saintfield in the County of Down (1815).* Transcription. 1908.

Workhouse Records: Records of Clogher Union Workhouse (1842–49). PRONI; SLC film 259162–3; Records of Downpatrick Union Workhouse (1847–1901). PRONI; SLC film 259159–61; Records of Downpatrick Union Workhouse (1868–1903). PRONI; SLC film 259159–61; Records of Lurgan Union Workhouse (1841–1910). PRONI; SLC film 259166–72.

Research Sources and Services

Journals

Ards Upper Historical Society Journal (1967–present)

Lecale Miscellany (published by Lecale Historical Society, 1983–present)

Familia–Ulster Genealogical Review (published by Ulster Historical Foundation, 1978–present)

Old Newry Journal (published by Old Newry Society, 1977–present)

East Belfast Historical Society Journal (1981–present)

Saintfield Heritage (published by Saintfield Heritage Society in 1982)

Seanchas Ardmhacha (see Co. Armagh)

North Irish Roots (published by North of Ireland Family History Society)

Libraries and Information Sources

South Eastern Education and Library Board, Library and Information Service, Windmill Hill, Ballynahinch, Co. Down BT48 8DH. Ph: (01238) 566400; fax: (01238) 565072. The Irish and Local Studies section has a very extensive collection of local history materials, particularly relating to Down and South Antrim. These include maps, photographs, newspapers, and periodicals. The library has also published materials of local relevance, including indexes to local newspapers and source lists for local industries, towns, and events.

Family History Centre, 403 Holywood Road, Belfast 4. Ph: (0232) 768250. This center is a branch of the Family History Library run by The Church of Jesus Christ of Latter-day Saints. It has filmed many of the major Irish record sources, and also has an extensive collection of other materials, such as the 1901 census, *Tithe Applotment Books, Griffiths Valuation,* civil registration indexes, etc. It is open to all researchers.

Bangor Visitors and Heritage Centre, Town Hall, Bangor, Co. Down

Down Museum, Southwell Building, The Mall, Downpatrick, Co. Down

Ulster-American Folk Park Library. See Libraries in Co. Tyrone chapter

Research Services

See Research Services in Belfast in the introduction.

Ulster Historical Foundation, Balmoral Buildings, 12 College Sq. East, Belfast BT1 6DD. Ph: (1232) 332288; fax: (1232) 239885. E-mail: uhf.dnet.co.uk. Internet: http://www.unite.net/customers/uhf. This is a non-profit organization established in 1956 (as the Ulster-Scot Historical Society) to promote interest in Ulster history and genealogy. In 1975 it changed its name to reflect its wider genealogical activities. It provides extensive genealogical research services, publishes a journal *(Familia)* and books, and is also the official Irish Genealogical Project (see the introduction) center for indexing the records of Antrim and Down (including Belfast). Researchers are advised to contact the center for an updated list of registers and other sources indexed. Research services are conducted for a fee, and interested researchers can also join the UHF-founded Ulster Genealogical and Historical Guild, which provides a directory of research interests and a subscription to *Familia–Ulster Genealogical Review.*

Societies

North of Ireland Family History Society, Queens University of Belfast, Dept. of Education, 69 University Street, Belfast BT7 1HL. Publishers of *North Irish Roots*

Ards Art Club, Mr. R.L.M. Payne, 3 Galla Way, Rosehill, Newtownards, Co. Down, BT23 4JR. Ph: (01247) 813486

Ards Historical Society, Mr. T.R. Ward, 1 Bowmount Park, Newtownards, Co. Down, BT23 3SS. Ph: (01247) 815063

Banbridge and District Historical Society, Ms. Angela Dillon, 7 Forthill Avenue, Banbridge, Co. Down, BT32 3JF. Ph: (018206) 25872

Bangor Historical Society, Mr. Paul McKay, 19 Kensington Park, Bangor, Co. Down, BT20 3RF. Ph: (01247) 465150

Bay-Burn Historical Society, Mr. Adrian Hencarelli, 10 Meadow Park, Crawfordsburn, Bangor, Co. Down, BT19 1JN. Ph: (01247) 852676

Burren Heritage Association, Mrs. Margaret Harty, 35 Clonallon Road, Burren, Warrenpoint, Newry, Co. Down, BT34 3PH. Ph: (016937) 72698

Downe Society, Mrs. R. Wheeler, 2 Finnebrogue Road, Downpatrick, Co. Down, BT30 9AA. Ph: (01396) 612730

Downpatrick Railway Society, Mr. Neil Hamilton, c/o The Railway Station, Market Street, Downpatrick, Co. Down, BT30 6LZ. Ph: (01396) 615779

Dromore and District Historical Group, Mrs. Alison Hutchinson, Bridgehill Cottage, 28 Milebush Road, Ballymacormick, Dromore, Co. Down, BT25 IRU. Ph: (01846) 692603

Friends of Down County Museum, c/o The Museum, The Mall, English Street, Downpatrick, Co. Down, BT30 6AH. Ph: (01396) 615218

The Glen Abbey Historical Society, Mr. R.J. Trayte, 2 Cuan Gardens, Greyabbey, Newtownards, Co. Down, BT22 2QG. Ph: (01247) 788263

Kilkeel Art Society, Mrs. Mary Clark, 35 Aughnaloopy Road, Kilkeel, Newry, Co. Down, BT34 4HQ. Ph: (01693) 762589

Lecale Historical Society, Mrs. P.D. McCullough, Down Lodge, 9 Castleward Road, Strangford, Downpatrick, Co. Down, BT30 7LY. Ph: (01396) 881428

Mourne Local Studies Group, Mr. H.M. McCalden, 15 Mill Vale, Kilkeel, Newry, Co. Down, BT34 4YL. Ph: (01693) 765041

Mullaghbawn Folklore and Historical Society, Mrs. Nora McCoy, Ard-na-Greine, Mullaghbawn, Newry, Co. Down, BT35 9RA. Ph: (01693) 888278

Newcastle and District Gardening Society, Mr. R. Whatmough, Clock House, Dundrum, Newcastle, Co. Down, BT33 ONE. Ph: (01396) 751311

Newcastle Art Society, Ms. Ann K. Smith, Garrybeg, 2 Shimna Park, Newcastle, Co. Down, BT33 OED. Ph: (01396) 722679

Newcastle Field Club, Mr. Thomas P. Walsh, 41 Shievenamaddy Avenue, Newcastle, Co. Down, BT33 ODS. Ph: (01396) 723587

Old Newry Society, Mr. Irwin Major, 47 Crieve Court, Newry, Co. Down, BT34 2PE. Ph: (01693) 63385

Poyntzpass and District Historical Society, Mrs. B. Heron, St. Jude's, William Street, Poyntzpass, Newry, Co. Down, BT35 6SS. Ph: (01762) 318435

Rathfriland Historical Society, Mrs. Maude Harbinson, 34 Downpatrick Street, Rathfriland, Newry, Co. Down, BT34 5DQ. Ph: (018206) 30204

Ulster Folklife Society, Ms. Linda M. Ballard, Ulster Folk and Transport Museum, Cultra, Holywood, Co. Down, BT18 OEU. Ph: (01232) 428428

Upper Ards Historical Society, Dr. Daryl Birkett, Buena Vista, 2 Ballyfounder Road, Portaferry, Newtownards, Co. Down, BT22 1RE. Ph: (012477) 28058

Warrenpoint Historical Group, Ms. Eileen McPolin, SummerHill, Warrenpoint, Newry, Co. Down, BT34 3JB.

Down Civil Parishes as Numbered on Map

1. Hollywood
2. Dundonald
3. Newtownards
4. Comber
5. Kilmood
6. Tullynakill
7. Bangor
8. Donaghadee
9. Grey Abbey
10. Ballywalter (2 pts.)
11. Inishargy
12. St. Andrews (Ballyhalbert)
13. Ardkeen
14. Castleboy (2 pts.)
15. Ardquin
16. Ballytrustan (4 pts.)
17. Slanes
18. Ballyphillip
19. Witter (2 pts.)
20. Knockbreda
21. Lambeg
22. Drumbeg
23. Drumbo
24. Saintfield (2 pts.)
25. Killaney
26. Killinchy
27. Killyleagh
28. Shankill
29. Moira
30. Hillsborough
31. Blaris
32. Magheralin
33. Donaghcloney
34. Tullylish
35. Dromore
36. Annahilt
37. Magherally
38. Magheradrool
39. Magherahamlet
40. Kilmore
41. Loughinisland
42. Inch
43. Saul (2 pts.)
44. Ballyculter (2 pts.)
45. Ballee
46. Kilclief (4 pts.)
47. Dunsforth
48. Ardglass
49. Seapatrick (3 pts.)
50. Aghaderg
51. Annaclone
52. Donaghmore
53. Drumcath
54. Clonallan
55. Warrenpoint
56. Kilbroney
57. Garvaghy
58. Dromara
59. Drumballyroney
60. Drumgooland
61. Kilmegan
62. Clonduff
63. Kilcoo
64. Maghera
65. Down
66. Ballykinler
67. Tyrella
68. Rathmullan (2 pts.)
69. Bright
70. Newry (2 pts.)
71. Kilkeel

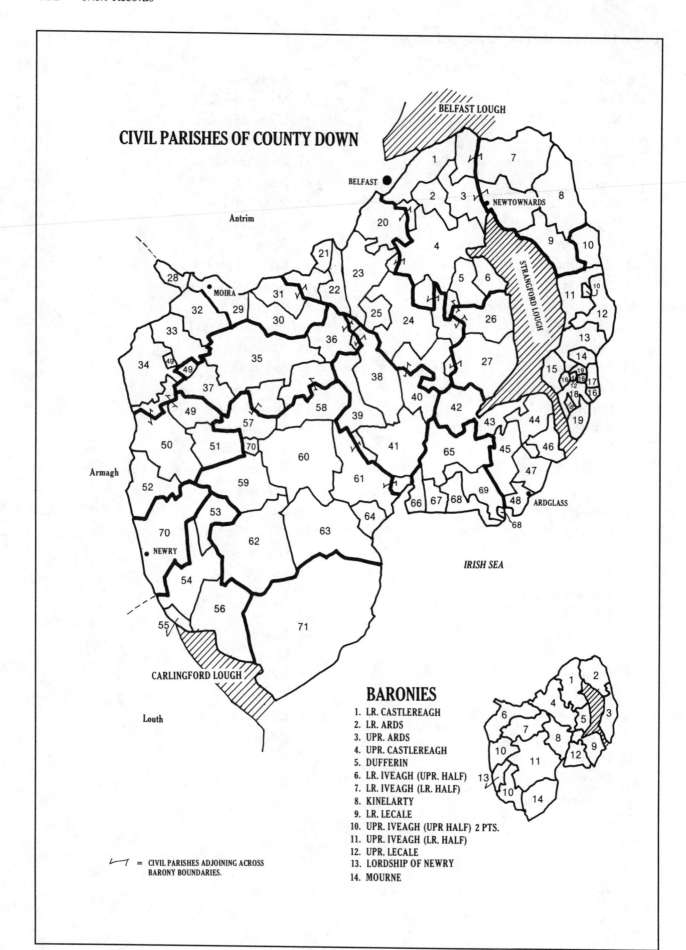

CIVIL PARISHES OF COUNTY DOWN

BELFAST LOUGH

BELFAST

Antrim

NEWTOWNARDS

STRANGFORD LOUGH

MOIRA

ARDGLASS

Armagh

NEWRY

IRISH SEA

CARLINGFORD LOUGH

Louth

BARONIES

1. LR. CASTLEREAGH
2. LR. ARDS
3. UPR. ARDS
4. UPR. CASTLEREAGH
5. DUFFERIN
6. LR. IVEAGH (UPR. HALF)
7. LR. IVEAGH (LR. HALF)
8. KINELARTY
9. LR. LECALE
10. UPR. IVEAGH (UPR HALF) 2 PTS.
11. UPR. IVEAGH (LR. HALF)
12. UPR. LECALE
13. LORDSHIP OF NEWRY
14. MOURNE

⌐⌐ = CIVIL PARISHES ADJOINING ACROSS
      BARONY BOUNDARIES.

Down Civil Parishes in Alphabetical Order

Aghaderg: 50
Annaclone: 51
Annahilt: 36
Ardglass: 48
Ardkeen: 13
Ardquin: 15
Ballee: 45
Ballyculter (2 pts.): 44
Ballykinler: 66
Ballyphillip: 18
Ballytrustan (4 pts.): 16
Ballywalter (2 pts.): 10
Bangor: 7
Blaris: 31
Bright: 69
Castleboy (2 pts.): 14
Clonallan: 54
Clonduff: 62
Comber: 4
Donaghadee: 8
Donaghcloney: 33
Donaghmore: 52
Down: 65
Dromore: 35
Dromara: 58
Drumcath: 53
Drumballyroney: 59
Drumbeg: 22
Drumbo: 23
Drumgooland: 60
Dundonald: 2
Dunsforth: 7
Garvaghy: 57
Grey Abbey: 9
Hillsborough: 30
Hollywood: 1

Inch: 42
Inishargy: 11
Kilbroney: 56
Kilclief (4 pts.): 46
Kilcoo: 63
Kilkeel: 71
Killaney: 25
Killinchy: 26
Killyleagh: 27
Kilmegan: 61
Kilmood: 5
Kilmore: 40
Knockbreda: 20
Lambeg: 21
Loughinisland: 41
Maghera: 64
Magheralin: 32
Magherally: 37
Magheradrool: 38
Magherahamlet: 39
Moira: 29
Newry (2 pts.): 70
Newtownards: 3
Rathmullan (2 pts.): 68
Saul (2 pts.): 43
Saintfield (2 pts.): 24
St. Andrews (Ballyhalbert): 12
Seapatrick (3 pts.): 49
Shankill: 28
Slanes: 17
Tullylish: 34
Tullynakill: 6
Tyrella: 67
Warrenpoint: 55
Witter (2 pts.): 19

County Dublin

A Brief History

The earliest accounts of Dublin city go back as far as A.D. 140, when Ptolemy mentioned a settlement on this site. The major development of the city began in the eighth century, when the Vikings, or Norsemen, established a settlement which developed into a powerful Viking base. The power of the Dublin Norsemen lasted until 1014, when they were defeated at the Battle of Clontarf by the native Irish, led by Brian Boru (see Co. Clare). However, the Vikings remained in much of the county, particularly north of the city. The Vikings did not use hereditary surnames or family names, and therefore their influence is not obvious in the family names which exist in the county.

In 1169, the Normans made Dublin the center of their activities following their successful invasion of Ireland. It has remained the effective seat of government almost ever since. The north of the county was granted to the Norman Hugh de Lacy in the thirteenth century. Other Anglo-Norman families who settled in the county include those of Baggot, Sarsfield, Luttrell, Delahyde, Talbot, Barnewall, St. Lawrence, Cruise, Archbold, and Segrave. The city grew considerably during the fourteenth to sixteenth centuries, despite the continuing attacks by the O'Tooles and O'Byrnes of Wicklow (see Co. Wicklow) and the O'Moores and O'Carrolls (see counties Laois and Offaly).

As the seat of English administration of Ireland, Dublin was largely a Protestant city from the fifteenth to seventeenth centuries. In 1644 the total population of the city was only around eight thousand. By 1682, when the rebellion of Irish Catholics (see Co. Kilkenny) had been defeated and English power was imposed on most of the country, the population of Dublin was estimated at 60,000. Extensive growth outside the walls of the old city was occurring at this time. By 1728 the population was 146,000, and by the end of the century it was over 170,000. The influx of people to Dublin included English administrators, as well as people from all over Ireland. There have also been influxes of Huguenot, Jewish, and other peoples from abroad.

The eighteenth century was the great period of growth in Dublin city, when the great streets were laid out and many of the great public buildings established. In this period, Dublin was one of the great cities of Europe. In 1800, however, the Irish Parliament was amalgamated with the Westminster Parliament in London. As a consequence, Dublin lost much of its glamour, and many of the gentry moved to London. Although it was the administrative capital, the city did not develop extensive heavy industry, as did Belfast. The population continued to grow, however, and by 1841 it had reached over 230,000.

The population expanded during the Great Famine of 1845-47, due to migration of people from other badly affected parts of the country. The population of Dublin county was 372,000 in 1841, and by 1851 this had grown to 405,000. There were, however, over 75,000 deaths in the city between 1845 and 1850, and thousands emigrated through Dublin port. The number of natives of the county who emigrated was relatively low: less than four percent of the population, compared to eighteen percent in Tipperary and Clare. The city's population grew only slowly during the remainder of the century, but has grown rapidly since the foundation of the Irish state. The current population is over one million.

Census and Census Substitutes

1468-85
Freemen of the City of Dublin. SLC film 100228; GO Ms. 490/493, NLI Ms. 76-79.

1610–24

Some inhabitants of City of Dublin. *Dun Laoghaire Gen. Soc. J.* 1 (1) (1992): 278–31; 1 (2) (1992): 39–43.

1621

"List of Householders in St. John's Parish Who Were Rated for Parish Cess." Appendix 2 in the "Registers of St. John's, 1619–1699." *Parish Register Society* 1 (1906): 273; SLC film 82407.

1646

"List of Householders for St. John's Parish." *Parish Register Society* 1 (1906): 276; SLC film 824047.

1652

Inhabitants of the Baronies of Newcastle and Uppercross, districts of Ballyfermot, Balliowen, Ballidowde, Belgard, Bellemount, Blundestown, Butterfield, Carranstown, Crumlin, Dalkey, Deane Rath, Esker, Feddenstown, Finstown, Gallanstown, Great Katherins, Irishtown, Killnemanagh, Killiney, Kilmainham, Kilmactalway, Kilshock, Loughstown, Lucan, Milltown, Nangor, Nealstown, Newcastle, Newgrange, Newland, Oldbawn, Palmerstown, Rathgar, Rathfarnham, Rowlagh (Ranelagh), Rockstown, Shankill, Symon, Tallaght, Templeogue, and Terenure (gives names, ages, occupations, and relationships). NAI M2476. Published in *Ir. Gen.* 7 (4): 496–504; 8 (1): 3–14; 8 (2): 162–174; 8 (3): 322–332; and 8 (4): 498–529.

1654–56

Civil Survey. Robert C. Simington, Irish Manuscripts Commission, Vol. 7. SLC film 973123.

1659

"Census" of Ireland. Edited by S. Pender. Dublin: Stationery Office, 1939. NLI I6551. SLC film 924648.

1663–64

Hearth Money Roll. *Kildare Arch. Soc. J.* 10 (5): 245–54; 11 (1): 386–466 (also covers parts of Kildare).

Extracts for Parish of Taney in J. Ballinteer FHS Vol. 1 (1): 29–30.

1665

Rental of lands and other city dues for approx. sixty Dublin streets. 57th Rept. of DKPRI (1936): Appendix 4, 526–558.

1680

Dublin City Pipe Water Accounts. *Ir. Gen.* 7 (2) (1987): 201–204.

1684

Principal Inhabitants of Dublin. *Ir. Gen.* 8 (1): 49–57.

1687

"List of Householders in St. John's Parish." *Parish Register Society* 1 (1906): 277; SLC film 824047.

1704/5

Dublin City Pipe Water Accounts. *Ir. Gen.* 9 (1) (1994): 76–88. (Lists relevant householders alphabetically, with trade and address.)

1761

Alphabetical list of freemen and freeholders that polled at the election of members to represent the city of Dublin. Dublin, for Peter Wilson, 1761. NLI I6551 DUBL.

Militia List Cos. . . . Dublin, etc. Go Ms 680.

1766

Religious Census of Parishes of Crumlin—GO 537 and RCB Ms 23; Castleknock—RCB Ms37; Taney—NAI M2478; SLC film 258517.

1767

List of Freeholders in Co. Dublin. NAI film M 4912.

Voters List for Dublin City. (Dublin: Jas. Hunter, 1767.) NLI I6551 Dubl; NAI M 4878.

1774–1824

"Alphabetical List of the Freemen of the City of Dublin." *Ir. Anc.* 15 (1) and (2) (1983): 2–133; also NLI ILB. 94133 D2.

1775

Catholic Qualification Roll Extracts (ninety-eight names, addresses, and occupations). 59th Reprint DKPRI, 50–84.

1776

Rent Roll for Pavement Tax in Merrion Square. Gilbert Library. Ms.117. (A list of the inhabitants of Merrion Street and surrounding streets.)

1776–92

Records of Admission of Freemen to Corporation of Saddlers, Upholders, Coach and Harness Makers, etc. Dublin, NLI Ms. 82.

1777–1830

"Brethren Admitted to the Guild of Smiths, Dublin, by Marriage Right, 1777–1830." Reports from Committees. *Parl. Papers* 1837, Vol. 2 (2) (480): 182.

1778–82

"The Catholic Merchants, Manufacturers and Traders of Dublin, 1778–1782." *Reportorium* 2 (2) (1960): 298–323 (compiled from Catholic qualification rolls—gives name, trade, and address).

1779–1825

Bolger, (Brian) Papers. Papers of Brian Bolger, Dublin quantity surveyor. Alphabetical listing of some 1800 persons for whom work was conducted, with address and type of work done. NAI Open Access.

1784

Employees of the Irish Post Office. *Dun Laoghaire Gen. Soc. J.* 5 (1) (1996) (250 names).

1792–1837

"Names of All Persons Admitted to Dublin Trade Guilds (apothecaries, bakers, barbers, surgeons, carpenters, smiths, merchants, tailors, etc.), 1792–1837." *Parl. Papers* 1837, 11 (161–91): Appendix 3 (gives names and those of some fathers and fathers-in-law).

1793–1810

Census of Protestants in Castleknock. SLC film 100225 and Go Ms 495.

1798

List of Persons who Suffered Losses in '98 Rebellion. NLI JLB 94107 (approximately one hundred names, addresses, and occupations).

1801

Protestants in parishes of Clonsilla and Mulhuddart (with children's ages). GO 495.

1807

Tradesmen employed by the Board of Works, Dublin. *Dun Laoghaire Gen. Soc J.* 4 (2) (1995) (names and trade description).

1816

Rental (tenant list) of the estate of the city of Dublin. Appendix 8 to *History of the City of Dublin*, by Warburton, Whitelaw, and Walsh. London, 1818.

1821

Government Census Extracts for Dublin City and Tallaght for Selected Surnames. SLC film 100158; NAI.

1823–37

Tithe Applotment Survey (see introduction).

1826

"Labourers on Account" 1826. NAI–SPO OP/588t/727 (1522 names, including boys of ten–sixteen years).

"List of Food Recipients on Public Account." NAI–SPO OP/588s/726. (1,004 names.)

The above two lists are indexed in *Weavers and Related Trades in Dublin*. Dun Laoghaire Genealogical Society, 1995. ISBN: 1-898471-15-0.

1830

Dublin City and County Freeholders (contains names and addresses). NLI ms. 11.847. (Domville Papers.)

1831

Householders in St. Bride's Parish (possibly based on 1831 government census). NLI P1994, original in St. Werburgh's, Dublin.

1832

"Number and Names of Freemen Registered as Voters, City of Dublin." *Parl. Papers* 1837, 2 (1): 159–75 (2,678 names only).

List of the voters at an election of December, 1832, to elect representatives for the University of Dublin, in parliament. Dublin: R.M. Tims, 1833, pp. 32. Gives names, addresses, and qualifications of voters. NLI P.650.

1832–36

"An Alphabetical List of the Registered Voters in Parliamentary Elections for the City of Dublin." *Parl. Papers* 1837, 11 (2) (480): 1–145 (names, occupations or "gent," residence, etc., given alphabetically by year of registration).

"Names and Residences of Persons in Dublin Receiving Liquor Licenses." *Parl. Papers* 1837, 11 (1) Appendix 2: 250.

1832, '35, '37

Alphabetical list of the Constituency (Voters) of Dublin with residence, qualification and profession. Dublin: Pettigrew and Oulton, 1837. (Approx. 11,000 names.)

1835–37

Dublin County Freeholders and Leaseholders and how they voted, 1835, 1837, and 1852. NLI ms. 9363.

1835–37

Alphabetical list of £50, £20, and £10 freeholders and leaseholders, arranged in baronies. Dillon MacNamara (Dublin: Richard Grace, 1835, pp. 88). Gives names, addresses and qualifications of voters in 1832, 1835, and 1837. NLI Ms 9363.

1837–80

Register of Marriages of Baptist Church, Abbey Street, Dublin. Register of Members of Baptist Chapel, Harcourt Street, 1887–1928. NLI p 5647.

1838–72

Register of Births of Baptist Church, Abbey Street, Dublin. Register of Members of Baptist Chapel, Harcourt Street, 1887–1928. NLI p 5647.

1841

Mirror of the Dublin election . . . arranged in street lists. . . . Dublin: W.H. Dyott, 1841, pp. 296. Gives names, addresses, occupations, and qualifications. NLI Ir 94133 d.15.

1841–77

Register of Deaths of Baptist Church, Abbey Street, Dublin. Register of Members of Baptist Chapel, Harcourt Street, 1887–1928. NLI p 5647.

1842

List of voters at the city of Dublin election. Dublin: Shaw Brothers, 1842, pp. 27. Gives names, addresses, occupation, and qualification. NLI Ir 32341 d. 29.

1843

Voters List. NAI 1843/52.

1844/50

List of householders in Parish of St. Peter. RCB Library P45/15/1 and 2.

1848–54

Griffith's Valuation, see introduction. The parishes of Dublin city are not included in the Index to Surnames, but are in: Surname Index to the 1854 *Griffith's Valuation* of the City of Dublin, Ireland (microform). Vienna, VA: All-Ireland Heritage, Inc., 1986. Available at NAI and NLI.

"Griffiths Valuation: Alphabetical Index to Michaels Parish, 1848." *Dun Laoghaire Gen. Soc J.* 4 (3) (1995).

1851

List of heads of families in the 1851 Census of Dublin City, compiled by D.A. Chart. NAI CEN 1851/18/1–2. (Gives the name of each head of household alphabetically by street.)

Head of Families in 1851 Census for Newmarket, St. Lukes Parish and Frederick St. Lr. *Familia* 2 (2) (1986).

1852 (see also 1835–37)

Lists of registered voters of county Dublin. Dublin:

Browne and Nolan, 1852, pp. 140. Gives names and addresses of voters. NLI Ms 9363.

List of voters, Co. Dublin, July 1852. Dublin: n.p., 1852, pp. 94. Gives names, addresses, and religion of some. UCD Pamphlets no. 5328.

1853

Memorial from 140 Catholic Parishioners of Clondalkin seeking a new priest. Cullen Papers 46/1/3, Dublin Diocesan Archives.

1857

City of Dublin election, March 1857. List of electors. Dublin: Browne & Nolan, 1857, pp. 76. Gives names and addresses of voters and how they voted. BL 809 N. 33; NLI Ir 32341 d.30; TCD Gall. BB 15 30a.

Names of the electors at the college election, 1857, pp. 63. Hand-written; gives names, addresses, and qualifications of voters. NLI Ms 199.

1859

May 1859. List of electors for City of Dublin election. Dublin: Shannon & McDermott, 1859, pp. 277. Gives names and addresses of voters. BL 809. f. 42; NLI Ir 32341 d.25.

1864–1885

Vaccinations Register for the Registrar's Districts of Bray and Rathmichael 1864–1885. NAI L.B.G. 137 L2 (child's name, age, date of vaccination, parent or guardian, and address).

1865

List of the registered voters of County of Dublin. Dublin: Browne & Nolan, 1865, 150 pp. Gives names and addresses. TCD research floor.

List of electors 1865 . . . . Dublin: J. Atkinson, 1865, pp. 272. Gives names and addresses of voters. NLI Ir 32341 d. 15.

1868

List of electors for the year 1868 . . . . Dublin: Browne & Nolan, 1868, pp. 361. (Gives names and addresses of voters.) Also in NLI Ir 32341 d. 16; TCD Gall. NN 4 22. Also "City of Dublin election, Nov. 18th, 1868" by Tudor S. Bradburne. Dublin: J. Atkinson, 1869, pp. 272. SLC fiche 6343075.

1901

Census. NAI (see introduction).

1911

Census. NAI.

Church Records

Church of Ireland

See the introduction for a description of Church of Ireland records and their major repositories. Many C of I records were lost in the PRO fire of 1922. These are indicated as "Lost." However, as Church of Ireland records were effectively state records, the records of marriage (from 1845) are also in the General Registrar's Office. Many are still in local custody (LC), while others are in one of a variety of other archives (e.g., RCBL or NAI). Some of the parish registers of Dublin City and County have been indexed by several heritage groups: Fingal Heritage Group, Dublin Heritage Group, and Dun Laoghaire Heritage Centre (see Research Services at the end of the chapter). A search of the index will be conducted by the relevant center for a fee. Those indexed are noted as "Indexed by FHG, DHG," etc., as appropriate.

Arbour Hill Barracks
Earliest Records: b. 1848–; d. 1847–
Status: RCB Library

Baggotrath
Earliest Records: b. 1865–1923; m. 1882–1923
Status: RCB Library

Balbriggan, Balrothery, and Balscadden
Earliest Records: b. 1839; m. 1840; d. 1821
Status: LC; Indexed by FHG; RCBL

Balgriffin
Earliest Records: b. 1820; m. 1846; d. 1821
Status: RCB Library

Balrothery, see Balbriggan

Balscadden, see Balbriggan

Beggar's Bush Barracks
Earliest Records: b. 1868–1921
Status: RCB Library

Bookerstown
Earliest Records: b. 1824; m. 1824
Status: RCB Library

Castleknock
Earliest Records: b. 1709–1959; m. 1710–1956; d. 1710–1963
Status: RCB Library; GO Ms. 495; SLC film 992664 (1768–1871)

Christ Church Cathedral
Earliest Records: b. 1740; m. 1717; d. 1710
Status: RCB Library

Clonmethan, see Kilsallaghan

Clonsilla
Earliest Records: b. 1830–1901; m. 1831–1956; d. 1831–1902
Status: RCB Library; GO Ms. 495; SLC film 992664 (1830–1871)

Cloughran or Cloghran (Coolock)
Earliest Records: b. 1782–; m. 1738–; d. 1732–
Status: RCB Library (b. 1782–1852 and 1870–91; m. 1738–1852 and 1858–75; d. 1732–1852 and 1872–1938); indexed (b. 1782–1864) by Anglican Rec. Proj. in RCBL and Soc. Gen. (London); SLC film 897365 (b. 1732–1864)

Crumlin—St. Mary's
Earliest Records: d. 1740–1830
Status: published in Register Section of *Irish Memorials Assoc. J.* Vol. 12; GO Ms. 495; SLC film 990093 (b/d. to 1864; m. to 1845)

Dalkey
Earliest Records: b. 1877; m. 1872
Status: RCB Library

Donabate
Earliest Records: b. 1811; m. 1814; d. 1817
Status: Indexed by FHG; RCB Library

Donnybrook
Earliest Records: b. 1712–1957; m. 1712–1956; d. 1712–1873
Status: RCB Library

Dun Laoghaire—Christ Church
Earliest Records: b. 1852–1867; m. 1875–1956
Status: RCB Library

Dun Laoghaire—Mariners
Earliest Records: b. 1843–1970; m. 1875–1972
Status: RCB Library

Female Penitentiary
Earliest Records: b. 1879–1907
Status: RCB Library

Finglas
Earliest Records: b. 1658; m. 1666; d. 1664
Status: RCB Library; b/m/d. records 1685–1684 in *Ir. Gen.* 9 (2): 202–209; SLC film 992663

Holmpatrick (Skerries)
Earliest Records: b. 1779; m. 1800; d. 1786
Status: Indexed by FHG; RCB Library

Irishtown
Earliest Records: b. 1812–1973; m. 1824–1956; d. 1807–1866
Status: RCB Library (b. 1812–1973)

Killiney
Earliest Records: b. 1829; d. 1831
Status: RCB Library

212

1834 Feby 28

February first Christopher Banks & Margaret Kennedy.

Feb. 1 Thomas Donnelly & Anne Baptist

Feb. 2 Richard Taylor & Eliza Barbour

Feb. 2 Thomas Cavanagh & Anne Larvin.

Feb. 3 William Howe & Eliza McMullen.

Feb. 3 Edward Ellis & Jane Leslie

Feb. 4 John Luke & Mary Walsh.

Feb. 4 Patrick McCabe & Catharine Lee.

Feb. 4 Michael Lawlor & Charlotte Farrell.

Feb. 4 Richard Moore & Julia Byrne.

Feb. 4 George O'Brien & Esther Kennedy.

Feb. 5 Thomas Healy & Margaret Dunigan.

Feb. 5 James White & Mary A. Brade

Feb. 6 Mathew Noble & Eliza Smith.

Feb. 6 Michael Church Crew & King Light Dr. Mary English

Feb. 7 Wm. Haidsworth P. 12 Boy Long. Bridget McDermott

Feb. 8 Edward Anderson Wright & Miss Elizabeth Bateman

Feb. 8 Abraham Fagan & Esther Gannon.

Feb. 8 Nathaniel Hurst & Miss Amelia Goodison

213 1834

Feb. 9 Robert Barnett & Bridget Dutton.

Feb. 9 Justin Milbern Esq & Miss Elizabeth Calvert.

Feb. 9 Francis Shea & Anne Clifford.

Feb. 10 Thomas Gannon & Anne Moore.

Feb. 10 Henry Gordon & Catherine Horton.

Feb. 10 John Gore & Dr. Tessars & Catharine Barton.

Feb. 10 Thomas McCoy & Jane Parsley.

Feb. 10 John Platt Esq. & Dr. Reg. Mary A. Anderson.

Feb. 10 John Gallion & Mary Kelly Kilkenny

Feb. 11 John Cavanagh & Anne McKean

Feb. 11 John Rea & Rebecca Leitch.

Feb. 11 Mr. Miles Magrath & Mrs. Hannah Kelly

Feb. 11 Mr. Nicholas Hopkins & Miss Mary A. Fitzsimons.

Feb. 11 James Gray & Lydia Young.

Feb. 11 Edward Burke & Elizabeth Hopson.

Feb. 11 Rd. Norton & Elizabeth Lawrence.

Feb. 11 Richard Regan & Betty Flanigan.

Feb. 11 James Kelly & Betty Leonard.

Feb. 11 Mr. Wm. Buchanan & Miss Elizabeth Sargent.

Feb. 11 George Sutton & Julia Sullivan

Extract, from February 1834, of the records of the German Church, Poolbeg Street, Dublin, showing marriages performed by the Reverend Schulze. The records of marriages and baptisms in this church (now extinct) from 1806 to 1835 are in the Office of the Registrar General, Dublin.

Kilmainham
Earliest Records: b. 1857-1982; m. 1861-1981; d. 1807-1866
Status: RCB Library

Kilsallaghan, Clonmethan, and Naul
Earliest Records: b. 1806; m. 1847; d. 1817
Status: LC; Indexed by FHG

Kilternan
Earliest Records: b. 1817-1895; m. 1817-1954; d. 1817-1936
Status: RCB Library

Lusk
Earliest Records: b. 1809; m. 1809; d. 1822
Status: Indexed by FHG; RCB Library

Malahide
Earliest Records: b. 1822-1871; m. 1825-1935; d. 1822-1876
Status: RCB Library

Missions to Seamen
Earliest Records: b. 1961-1981
Status: RCB Library

Molyneux Chapel
Earliest Records: b. 1871-1926
Status: RCB Library

Monkstown
Earliest Records: m. 1669
Status: *Parish Reg. Soc.* Vol. 6; SLC film 883748

Mulhuddert
Earliest Records: m. 1871-1944
Status: RCB Library

Naul, see Kilsallaghan

Newcastle-Lyons
Earliest Records: b. 1768; m. 1772; d. 1776
Status: RCB Library

Pigeon House Fort
Earliest Records: b. 1872-1901
Status: RCB Library

Portmarnock
Earliest Records: b. 1820-1876; m. 1825-1951; d. 1820-1875
Status: RCB Library

Portobello Barracks
Earliest Records: b. 1857-1869
Status: RCB Library

Raheny
Earliest Records: b. 1816; m. 1817; d. 1815
Status: RCB Library

Richmond Barracks
Earliest Records: b. 1857-1922
Status: RCB Library

St. Andrew's
Earliest Records: b. 1877; m. 1845
Status: RCB Library; also m. 1810-1819 published in Register Section of *Irish Memorials Assoc. J.* Vol. 12

St. Ann's
Earliest Records: b. 1719; m. 1799; d. 1722
Status: RCB Library (b. 1873-1938; m. 1845-1978; d. 1780-1816); GO Ms. 577; SLC film 100226

St. Audeon's
Earliest Records: b. 1672-1916; m. 1673-1947; d. 1673-1885
Status: RCBL; also b. 1672-1692 published in Register Section of *Irish Memorials Assoc. J.* Vol. 12

St. Bride's
Earliest Records: b. 1633; m. 1845-1887
Status: RCB Library; b. 1633-1714 in *Ir. Gen.* 6 (6): 711-723; 7 (1): 17-30; 7 (2): 205-228; and 7 (3): 358-377

St. Catherine's
Earliest Records: b. 1699-1966; m. 1679-1966; d. 1679-1898
Status: RCB Library

St. George's
Earliest Records: b. 1794-1875; m. 1794-1956; d. 1824-1908
Status: RCB Library

St. James's
Earliest Records: b. 1730-1963; m. 1742-1963; d. 1742-1989
Status: RCB Library; SLC film 962524

St. John's
Earliest Records: b. 1619-1878; m. 1619-1878; d. 1619-1850
Status: RCB Library; GO Ms. 577; SLC film 100226

St. Kevin's
Earliest Records: b. 1883-1980; m. 1884-1977
Status: RCB Library

St. Luke's
Earliest Records: b. 1713-1974; m. 1716-1973; d. 1716-1974
Status: RCB Library

St. Mark's
Earliest Records: b. 1730-1971; m. 1730-1971; d. 1733-1923
Status: RCB Library

St. Mary's
Earliest Records: b. 1697–1872; m. 1697–1880; d. 1700–1858
Status: RCB Library

St. Mathias
Earliest Records: b. 1867–1955; m. 1873–1955
Status: RCB Library

St. Michan's
Earliest Records: b/d. 1701
Status: GO Ms. 577; SLC film 100226 (1701–24)

St. Nicholas Within
Earliest Records: b. 1671–1866; m. 1671–1850; d. 1671–
Status: RCB Library; Indexed by DHG; d. 1825–1863 records are in *Irish Memorials Assoc. J.* Vol. 12; SLC film 990093

St. Nicholas Without
Earliest Records: b. 1694; m. 1699; d. 1694
Status: RCB Library

St. Patrick's
Earliest Records: d. 1801
Status: GO Ms. 701; SLC film 257807

St. Paul's
Earliest Records: b. 1698; m. 1699; d. 1702
Status: RCB Library; d. 1702–1718 published in Register Section of *Irish Memorials Assoc. J.* Vol. 13 (1): 360–390; GO Ms. 577; SLC film 100226

St. Peter
Earliest Records: b. 1669; m. 1670; d. 1670
Status: RCB Library

St. Stephen
Earliest Records: b. 1837; m. 1862
Status: RCB Library

St. Thomas
Earliest Records: b. 1740; m. 1740; d. 1740
Status: RCB Library; Index (by R. Refausse) published by RCBL, 1994; SLC film 990209

St. Werburgh
Earliest Records: b/m/d. 1704
Status: RCB Library

Sandymount
Earliest Records: b. 1850
Status: RCB Library

Santry
Earliest Records: b. 1753; m. 1754; d. 1753
Status: Pub. (nd), SLC films 962187, 883674

Swords
Earliest Records: b/m. 1703
Status: LC; Indexed by FHG

Whitechurch
Earliest Records: b/d. 1824; m. 1827
Status: RCB Library

Presbyterian

An account of Presbyterian records is given in the introduction. These registers rarely contain death records, and occasionally have only records of births. This is indicated where appropriate. Many of the Presbyterian registers have been indexed by the heritage centers in Dublin City and County (see Research Services at the end of the chapter). A search of the indexes will be conducted by the relevant center for a fee.

Arran Quay
Earliest Records: b. 1731; m. 1731
Status: LC; Indexing by FHG in progress

Clontarf
Earliest Records: b. 1836
Status: LC; Indexed by FHG

Eustace Street
Earliest Records: b. 1653–1867
Status: LC; SLC film 100238

Lucan
Earliest Records: b. 1886–1900
Status: LC; Indexed by DHG

Strand Street
Earliest Records: b. 1767–1867
Status: LC; SLC film 100238

Abbey Church
Earliest Records: b. 1777
Status: LC

Ormond Quay
Earliest Records: b. 1787
Status: LC

Methodist

An account of the Methodist church in Ireland is given in the introduction. There are several congregations in Dublin, and several registers have been indexed by the heritage centers serving the county (see Research Services section).

Clontarf
Earliest Records: b. 1876; m. 1870
Status: LC; Indexed by FHG

Skerries
Earliest Records: m. 1889
Status: LC; Indexed by FHG

Baptist

See the introduction for an account of Baptist records. The following published records are available for Dublin:

Kingstown Congregational Church—Membership Roll. In *Dun Laoghaire Gen. Soc.* 2 (1) (1993): 31–37.

Kingstown Congregational Church—m. 1849-51; d. 1849-61; in *Dun Laoghaire Gen. Soc.* 2 (2) (1993): 70–74.

Kingstown Congregational Church—Baptismal Register. In *Dun Laoghaire Gen. Soc.* 3 (1) (1994): 19–23.

Roman Catholic

Note that many of the Catholic parish registers of this county have been indexed by one of the heritage centers in the county (see Research Services at the end of the chapter). A search of the index will be conducted by the relevant center for a fee. The centers in the county currently offering a service are Fingal Heritage Group (FHG), Dublin Heritage Group (DHG), and Dun Laoghaire Heritage Centre (DLHC), while other centers are currently compiling indexes. Those indexed are noted below. Microfilm copies of all registers are also available in the National Library of Ireland (NLI) and through the LDS library system. Several city and south county parishes are neither filmed nor indexed. Requests for searches can be made to the church. Addresses are available in the *Catholic Directory*, issued annually. Parishes in Dublin county are listed first and those in Dublin city later.

Civil Parish: Aderrig
Map Grid: 49
RC Parish: see Lucan
Diocese: DU

Civil Parish: Artaine
Map Grid: 39
RC Parish: see Clontarf
Diocese: DU

Civil Parish: Baldongan
Map Grid: 5
RC Parish: Skerries, see Holmpatrick
Diocese: DU

Civil Parish: Baldoyle
Map Grid: 36
RC Parish: Baldoyle
Diocese: DU
Earliest Record: b. 12.1784; m. 1.1785
Missing Dates: b. 12.1800-8.1806; m. 12.1800-8.1806, 11.1815-5.1818, 11.1824-1.1826
Status: LC; NLI (mf); Indexed by FHG

Civil Parish: Balgriffin
Map Grid: 34
RC Parish: see Baldoyle
Diocese: DU

Civil Parish: Ballyboghil
Map Grid: 14

RC Parish: see Finglas
Diocese: DU

Civil Parish: Ballyfermot
Map Grid: 59
RC Parish: part Palmerstown, part Clondalkin

Civil Parish: Ballymadun
Map Grid: 10
RC Parish: see Garristown

Civil Parish: Balrothery
Map Grid: 2
RC Parish: Balrothery and Balbriggan
Diocese: DU
Earliest Record: b. 10.1816; m. 2.1817
Status: LC; NLI (mf); Indexed by FHG

Civil Parish: Balscaddan
Map Grid: 1
RC Parish: see Balrothery
Diocese: DU

Civil Parish: Booterstown (1)
Map Grid: 71
RC Parish: Booterstown; also Blackrock and Dundrum, see below
Diocese: DU
Earliest Record: b. 1755; m. 1756
Status: LC; NLI (mf); Indexed by DLHC

Civil Parish: Booterstown (2)
Map Grid: 71
RC Parish: Blackrock
Diocese: DU
Earliest Record: b. 1850; m. 1922
Status: LC; Indexed by DLHC

Civil Parish: Castleknock
Map Grid: 26
RC Parish: Blanchardstown
Diocese: DU
Earliest Record: b. 12.1774; m. 1.1775
Status: LC; NLI (mf); Indexing by DHC in progress

Civil Parish: Chapelizod
Map Grid: 27
RC Parish: see Clondalkin
Diocese: DU

Civil Parish: Cloghran (near Castleknock)
Map Grid: 23
RC Parish: see Castleknock
Diocese: DU

Civil Parish: Cloghran (near Santry)
Map Grid: 31
RC Parish: see Clontarf (Coolock for later records)
Diocese: DU

Civil Parish: Clondalkin
Map Grid: 58
RC Parish: Clondalkin
Diocese: DU
Earliest Record: b. 5.1778; m. 6.1778
Missing Dates: b. 4.1800-8.1809; m. 2.1800-8.1812
Status: LC; NLI (mf); Indexed by DHG

Civil Parish: Clonmethan
Map Grid: 12
RC Parish: Rolestown, see Killossery
Diocese: DU

Civil Parish: Clonsilla
Map Grid: 25
RC Parish: see Castleknock
Diocese: DU

Civil Parish: Clontarf
Map Grid: 46
RC Parish: Clontarf
Diocese: DU
Earliest Record: b. 1774; m. 1774
Status: LC; Indexed by FHG

Civil Parish: Clonturk (Drumcondra)
Map Grid: 38
RC Parish: Fairview, see Clontarf for earlier records
Diocese: DU
Earliest Record: b. 6.1879; m. 6.1879
Status: LC; NLI (mf); Indexed by FHG

Civil Parish: Coolock
Map Grid: 35
RC Parish: Coolock, see Clontarf for earlier records
Diocese: DU
Earliest Record: b. 1879; m. 1879
Status: LC; Indexed by FHG

Civil Parish: Cruagh
Map Grid: 66
RC Parish: see Rathfarnham
Diocese: DU

Civil Parish: Crumlin
Map Grid: 62
RC Parish: see Rathfarnham
Diocese: DU

Civil Parish: Dalkey
Map Grid: 78
RC Parish: Dalkey; earlier records in Kingstown, see Monkstown
Diocese: DU
Earliest Record: b. 1861; m. 1894
Status: LC; Indexed by DLHC

Civil Parish: Donabate
Map Grid: 17
RC Parish: Donabate
Diocese: DU

Earliest Record: b. 11.1760; m. 1.1761
Missing Dates: b. 12.1807-7.1824; m. 6.1805-2.1869
Status: LC; NLI (mf); Indexed by FHG

Civil Parish: Donnybrook
Map Grid: 68
RC Parish: part Donnybrook, see Donnybrook–Dublin City section; part Booterstown
Diocese: DU

Civil Parish: Drimnagh
Map Grid: 61
RC Parish: see Clondalkin
Diocese: DU

Civil Parish: Dublin City
RC Parish: see separate listing below and map at end of chapter

Civil Parish: Esker
Map Grid: 50
RC Parish: see Lucan, Palmerstown, and Clondalkin
Diocese: DU

Civil Parish: Finglas
Map Grid: 24
RC Parish: Finglas and St. Margaret's
Diocese: DU
Earliest Record: b. 2.1784; m. 11.1757
Missing Dates: m. 7.1760-12.1784
Status: LC; NLI (mf); Indexed by FHG

Civil Parish: Garristown
Map Grid: 7
RC Parish: Garristown
Diocese: DU
Earliest Record: b. 1.1857; m. 7.1857
Status: LC; NLI (mf); Indexed by FHG

Civil Parish: Glasnevin
Map Grid: 37
RC Parish: part St. Michan's (Dublin city); part Finglas
Diocese: DU

Civil Parish: Grallagh
Map Grid: 8
RC Parish: see Garristown
Diocese: DU

Civil Parish: Grangegorman
Map Grid: 43
RC Parish: St. Paul's (Dublin city)
Diocese: DU

Civil Parish: Hollywood
Map Grid: 9
RC Parish: see Garristown; also Balrothery
Diocese: DU

Civil Parish: Holmpatrick or Skerries
Map Grid: 3
RC Parish: Skerries
Diocese: DU
Earliest Record: b. 10.1751; m. 6.1751
Status: LC; NLI (mf); Indexed by FHG

Civil Parish: Howth
Map Grid: 42
RC Parish: Howth, see Baldoyle for earlier records
Diocese: DU
Earliest Record: b. 1890; m. 1890
Status: LC; Indexed by FHG

Civil Parish: Kilbarrack
Map Grid: 41
RC Parish: see Baldoyle
Diocese: DU

Civil Parish: Kilbride
Map Grid: 53
RC Parish: see Clondalkin
Diocese: DU

Civil Parish: Kilgobbin
Map Grid: 79
RC Parish: see Taney
Diocese: DU

Civil Parish: Kill
Map Grid: 77
RC Parish: Cabinteely; see also Booterstown
Diocese: DU
Earliest Record: b. 1859; m. 1859
Status: LC; Indexed by DLHC

Civil Parish: Killeek
Map Grid: 20
RC Parish: see Finglas
Diocese: DU

Civil Parish: Killester
Map Grid: 45
RC Parish: see Clontarf
Diocese: DU

Civil Parish: Killiney
Map Grid: 80
RC Parish: Kingstown (Dun Laoghaire)—see Monkstown

Civil Parish: Killossery
Map Grid: 15
RC Parish: Rowlestown (see also Garristown)
Diocese: DU
Earliest Record: b. 1.1857; m. 1.1857
Status: LC; NLI (mf); Indexed by FHG

Civil Parish: Kilmactalway
Map Grid: 51
RC Parish: see Lucan and Clondalkin
Diocese: DU

Civil Parish: Kilmacud
Map Grid: 73
RC Parish: see Booterstown
Diocese: DU

Civil Parish: Kilmahuddrick
Map Grid: 52
RC Parish: see Clondalkin
Diocese: DU

Civil Parish: Kilsallaghan
Map Grid: 19
RC Parish: part Finglas; part Rowlestown, see Killossery
Diocese: DU

Civil Parish: Kiltiernan
Map Grid: 81
RC Parish: Sandyford, see Taney
Diocese: DU

Civil Parish: Kilsaley
Map Grid: 32
RC Parish: see Baldoyle
Diocese: DU

Civil Parish: Leixlip
Map Grid: 47
RC Parish: see Co. Kildare
Diocese: DU

Civil Parish: Lucan
Map Grid: 48
RC Parish: Lucan
Diocese: DU
Earliest Record: b. 9.1818; m. 9.1818
Missing Dates: b. 7.1834-8.1835, 8.1842-2.1849, ends 1.1862; m. 9.1842-2.1849
Status: LC; NLI (mf); Indexed by DHG

Civil Parish: Lusk (1)
Map Grid: 4
RC Parish: Lusk; also Rush, see below
Diocese: DU
Earliest Record: b. 9.1757; m. 11.1757
Missing Dates: b. 8.1801-3.1802, 12.1835-8.1856; m. 1.1801-3.1802, 12.1835-3.1856
Status: LC; NLI (mf); Indexed by FHG

Civil Parish: Lusk (2)
Map Grid: 4
RC Parish: Rush
Diocese: DU
Earliest Record: b. 9.1785; m. 9.1785
Missing Dates: b. 12.1796-12.1799; m. 4.1810-8.1813
Status: LC; NLI (mf); Indexed by FHG

Civil Parish: Malahide
Map Grid: 28
RC Parish: Malahide; see Swords for early records

Earliest Record: b. 12.1763; m. 10.1763
Missing Records: b/m. 8.1777–6.1802
Diocese: DU
Status: LC; NLI (mf); Indexed by FHG

Civil Parish: Monkstown (1)
Map Grid: 75
RC Parish: Monkstown—earlier records in Kingstown (see below); also Glasthule (see below); also see Booterstown; also Cabinteely, see Kill
Diocese: DU
Earliest Record: b. 1865; m. 1881
Status: LC; Indexed by DLHC

Civil Parish: Monkstown (2)
RC Parish: Dun Laoghaire (Kingstown)
Earliest Record: b. 1769; m. 1769
Status: LC; NLI (mf); Indexed by DLHC

Civil Parish: Monkstown (3)
RC Parish: Glasthule
Earliest Record: b. 1865; m. 1865
Status: LC; Indexed by DLHC

Civil Parish: Mulhuddart
Map Grid: 22
RC Parish: see Castleknock
Diocese: DU

Civil Parish: Naul
Map Grid: 6
RC Parish: see Balrothery
Diocese: DU

Civil Parish: Newcastle
Map Grid: 54
RC Parish: see Saggart
Diocese: DU

Civil Parish: Old Connaught
Map Grid: 83
RC Parish: see Monkstown; also Bray, see Co. Wicklow
Diocese: DU

Civil Parish: Palmerston
Map Grid: 11
RC Parish: Rowlestown, see Killossery
Diocese: DU

Civil Parish: Palmerstown
Map Grid: 57
RC Parish: Palmerstown
Diocese: DU
Earliest Record: b. 8.1798; m. 9.1837
Missing Dates: b. 12.1799–9.1837, ends 1862; m. ends 9.1857
Status: LC; NLI (mf); Indexed by DHG

Civil Parish: Portmarnock
Map Grid: 33

RC Parish: see Baldoyle
Diocese: DU

Civil Parish: Portraine
Map Grid: 18
RC Parish: see Donabate
Diocese: DU

Civil Parish: Raheny
Map Grid: 40
RC Parish: see Clontarf
Diocese: DU

Civil Parish: Rathcoole
Map Grid: 55
RC Parish: see Saggart
Diocese: DU

Civil Parish: Rathfarnham (1)
Map Grid: 69
RC Parish: Rathfarnham; also Terenure, see below
Diocese: DU
Earliest Record: b. 1777; m. 1777
Status: LC; NLI (mf); Indexed by DHG

Civil Parish: Rathfarnham (2)
Map Grid: 69
RC Parish: Terenure
Diocese: DU
Earliest Record: b. 1870; m. 1894
Status: LC; to be indexed by DHG

Civil Parish: Rathmichael
Map Grid: 82
RC Parish: see Taney; also Kingstown, see Monkstown
Diocese: DU

Civil Parish: Saggart
Map Grid: 56
RC Parish: Saggart
Diocese: DU
Earliest Record: b. 10.1832; m. 5.1832
Status: LC; NLI (mf); to be indexed by DHG

Civil Parish: St. Mark's
Map Grid: 67
RC Parish: Donnybrook, see Donnybrook, Dublin City section
Diocese: DU

Civil Parish: St. Margaret's
Map Grid: 29
RC Parish: see Finglas
Diocese: DU

Civil Parish: St. Peter's (1)
Map Grid: 64
RC Parish: Rathmines, see St. Nicholas Without, Dublin City section, for earlier records; also Rathgor, see below

Diocese: DU
Earliest Record: b. 1823; m. 1823
Status: LC; to be indexed by DHG

Civil Parish: St. Peter's (2)
Map Grid: 64
RC Parish: Rathgar, see Rathmines for earlier records
Diocese: DU
Earliest Record: b. 1874; m. 1874
Status: LC; NLI (mf); to be indexed by DHG

Civil Parish: Santry
Map Grid: 30
RC Parish: see Clontarf; also part Finglas
Diocese: DU

Civil Parish: Skerries (see Holmpatrick)

Civil Parish: Stillorgan
Map Grid: 74
RC Parish: see Booterstown
Diocese: DU

Civil Parish: Swords
Map Grid: 16
RC Parish: Swords
Diocese: DU
Earliest Record: b. 12.1763; m. 10.1763
Missing Dates: b. 7.1777–6.1802; m. 6.1777–6.1802
Status: LC; NLI (mf); Indexed by FHG

Civil Parish: Tallaght
Map Grid: 65
RC Parish: see Rathfarnham; also part Saggart
Diocese: DU

Civil Parish: Taney (1)
Map Grid: 70
RC Parish: Taney or Sandyford; also part Dundrum, see below
Diocese: DU
Earliest Record: b. 8.1856; m. 8.1856
Status: LC; Indexed by DLHC

Civil Parish: Taney (2)
Map Grid: 70
RC Parish: Dundrum
Diocese: DU
Earliest Record: b. 1861; m. 1861
Status: LC; NLI (mf); Indexed by DLHC

Civil Parish: Tully
Map Grid: 76
RC Parish: see Monkstown; also part Taney (1)
Diocese: DU

Civil Parish: Ward
Map Grid: 21
RC Parish: see Finglas
Diocese: DU

Civil Parish: Westpalstown
Map Grid: 13
RC Parish: see Ballyboghill
Diocese: DU

Civil Parish: Whitechurch
Map Grid: 72
RC Parish: see Rathfarnham (1)
Diocese: DU

Dublin City (all are in Dublin diocese)

Civil Parish: Christ Church
RC Parish: Michael and John's, see St. Michael

Civil Parish: Donnybrook (1)
RC Parish: Sandymount, see Donnybrook (3) for earlier records
Earliest Record: b. 1865; m. 1865
Status: LC; to be indexed by DHG

Civil Parish: Donnybrook (2)
RC Parish: Donnybrook
Earliest Record: b. 1871; m. 1877
Status: LC; to be indexed by DHG

Civil Parish: Donnybrook (3)
RC Parish: Haddington Road (St. Mary's)
Earliest Record: b. 1798; m. 1798
Status: LC; Indexed by DHG

Civil Parish: St. Andrew
RC Parish: St. Andrew; also part St. Michael and St. John
Earliest Record: b. 1.1742; m. 2.1742
Status: LC; NLI (mf); Indexed by DHG

Civil Parish: St. Audoen
RC Parish: St. Audoen
Earliest Record: b. 12.1778; m. 2.1747
Missing Dates: b. 12.1799–6.1800, 9.1856–6.1878; m. 8.1785–1.1800
Status: LC; NLI (mf); partially indexed by DHG

Civil Parish: St. Anne
RC Parish: See St. Andrew

Civil Parish: St. Bartholomew
RC Parish: see Donnybrook (3)

Civil Parish: St. Bridget's
RC Parish: part Michael and John; part St. Nicholas Without

Civil Parish: St. Catherine
RC Parish: St. Catherine
Earliest Record: b. 5.1740; m. 5.1740
Missing Dates: b. 2.1794–12.1979, 7.1866–6.1871; m. 12.1792–2.1794, 7.1794–12.1799
Status: LC; NLI (mf); to be indexed by DHG

Civil Parish: St. George
RC Parish: see St. Mary's

Civil Parish: St. James
RC Parish: St. James
Earliest Record: b. 9.1742; m. 1754
Missing Dates: b. 9.1798–1.1803; m. 1755–10.1804
Status: LC; NLI (mf); to be indexed by DHG

Civil Parish: St. John
RC Parish: Michael and John, see St. Michael

Civil Parish: St. Luke
RC Parish: see St. Nicholas Without

Civil Parish: St. Mark
RC Parish: mainly St. Andrew

Civil Parish: St. Mary (1)
RC Parish: St. Mary's Pro-Cathedral; also part St. Michan
Earliest Record: b. 1734; m. 1734
Status: LC; to be indexed by DHG

Civil Parish: St. Mary (2)
RC Parish: Seville Place; also North William Street, see below; see St. Mary (1) for earlier records
Earliest Record: b. 7.1853; m. 6.1856
Status: LC; to be indexed by DHG

Civil Parish: St. Mary (3)
RC Parish: St. Agatha's—North William Street; see St. Mary (1) for earlier records
Earliest Record: b. 12.1852; m. 1.1853
Status: LC; NLI (mf); to be indexed by DHG

Civil Parish: St. Michael
RC Parish: Michael and John
Earliest Record: b. 1.1768; m. 1.1784 (marriage index 1743–1842) in register
Status: LC; NLI (mf); Indexed by DHG

Civil Parish: St. Michan
RC Parish: St. Michan; also part St. Paul
Earliest Record: b. 1726; m. 1726
Status: LC; NLI (mf); to be indexed by DHG

Civil Parish: St. Nicholas Within
RC Parish: part Michael and John, see St. Michael; part St. Nicholas Without

Civil Parish: St. Nicholas Without (1)
RC Parish: St. Nicholas Without (Francis St.); also Harrington St., see below
Earliest Record: b. 1.1742; m. 9.1767; d. 4.1829
Missing Dates: b. 8.1752–1.1767; m. 12.1801–11.1824; d. 5.1856–11.1857
Status: LC; NLI (mf); Indexed by DHG

Civil Parish: St. Nicholas Without (2)
RC Parish: Harrington St. (St. Kevin's)
Earliest Record: b. 1865
Status: LC; to be indexed by DHG

Civil Parish: St. Patrick
RC Parish: see St. Nicholas Without

Civil Parish: St. Paul (1)
RC Parish: St. Paul; also part St. Michan
Earliest Record: b. 1731; m. 1731
Status: LC; NLI (mf); to be indexed by DHG

Civil Parish: St. Paul (2)
RC Parish: Cabra, see St. Paul for earlier records
Earliest Record: b. 1909; m. 1856
Status: LC; to be indexed by DHG

Civil Parish: St. Peter
RC Parish: part St. Michael and St. John; part St. Nicholas Without; part St. Andrew

Civil Parish: St. Thomas'
RC Parish: see St. Mary

Civil Parish: St. Werburgh
RC Parish: Michael and John, see St. Michael

Commercial and Social Directories

1751

Wilson's *Alphabetical List of Names and Places of Abode of the Merchants and Traders of the City of Dublin.*

1752

Similar list published as supplement to *Gentleman's and Citizen's Almanac.* Further edition in 1753.

1755

Merchants and traders list in *Gentlemans and Citizens Almanac* (renamed the *Treble Almanac* in 1787). Lists of lawyers and medical practitioners were also added, as well as lists of city officials, faculty of the College of Surgeons and Physicians, clergy, and city guild officers. A list of nobility and gentry was added in 1815 and gradually enlarged from then on. Issued annually to 1837.

1820

J. Pigot's *Commercial Directory of Ireland* contains information on the gentry, nobility, and traders in and around Dublin.

1824

J. Pigot's *City of Dublin and Hibernian Provincial Directory* includes traders, nobility, gentry, and clergy lists of Dublin, Howth, Lucan, and Swords.

1834

Pettigrew and Oulton's *Dublin Almanac and General Register of Ireland* has lists of merchants and traders of various other categories. It also has a list of residents of

86 *Merchants and Traders.* **SAL**

Rourke (John) Boot and Shoemaker, 4, S. gt. George's-street.
Rourke (Thomas) Watch and Clock-maker, 4, Inns-quay.
Rowan and Hamilton, Lace and Muslin-warehouse, 37, Abbey-street.
Rowe (Mary) Paper-maker, 17, Cook-street.
Roycraft (Thomas) Wine-cooper, 141, Abbey-street.
Roycroft (Michael) Cabinet-maker, 18, Fisher's-lane.
Russell and Taylor, Woollen-drapers, 24, Eustace-street.
Russell (Bernard) Whip-maker, 49, Bridgefoot-street.
Russell (Catherine) Haberdasher, 53, Stephen-street.
Russell (Christopher and Peter) Carpenters, Buckingham-street.
Russell (Henry) Merchant-tailor, 6, John's-lane.
Russell (James) Linen-printer and Dyer, Marrowbone-lane.
Russell (James F.) Clothier, 9, Ardee-street.
Russell (John) Builder and Carpenter, 11, Russel-place, Mountjoy-square.
Russell (John) Linen-manufacturer, 92, Coombe.
Russell (John) Cooper, 11, lit. Britain-street.
Russell (John and Co.) Merchants, 106, Townsend-street.
Russell (Newhold) Linen-draper, 8, low. Bridge-street.
Russell (Samuel) Painter, 8, gt. Strand-street.
Russell (Wm. and Francis) Merchants, 19, Meath-street.
†Rutherford (John) Merchant, 59, Abbey-street.
Ryan (Charles) Apothecary, 7, Church-street.
Ryan (Edward) Glover and Breeches-maker, 31, Denmark-streets.
Ryan (Edward) Haberdasher, 36, Golden-lane.
Ryan (Edward) Tailor, 12, Crow-street.
Ryan (Denis) Stone-cutter, Swift's-alley.
Ryan (James and Edward) Linen-drapers, 14, low. Bridge-street.
†Ryan (James) Merchant, 77, Marlborough-street.
Ryan (John) Timber-merchant, 15, Hanbury-lane, & 6, S. Earl-street.
Ryan (Laurence) Perfumer, 109, Capel-street.
Ryan (Michael) Victualler, Cole's-lane-market.
Ryan (Pierce) Linen-draper, 99, Bride-street.
Ryan (Richard) Painter and Glazier, 7, N. King-street.
Ryan (Simon) Skinner, 17, Watling-street.
Ryan (Thomas) Silk-manufacturer, 42, Castle-street.
Ryan (Thomas) Baker, 161, Church-street.
Ryan (Tim.) Skinner, 59, Watling-street.
Ryan (William) Haberdasher, 10, Castle-street.
Ryder (Andrew) Silk-manufacturer, 5, W. Hanover-street.
Ryder (John) Grocer, 91, Dorset-street.
Ryden (Michael) Baker, 6, Moore-street.
Ryder (Patrick) Baker, 107, Abbey-street.

Extract from a list of the merchants and traders of Dublin, 1808, in Wilson's *Dublin Directory for the Year 1808.*

Sankey (John) Sheriff's-peer and Merchant, 1, *Fitzwilliam-square, N.*
Sargent (Henry) Tailor, 37, *Bolton-street*
Satchwell (M.) Silk-manufacturer, 84, *Dame-street.*
Sattell (James) Fencing Academy, 34, *Bachelor's-walk.*
Saul (Edward) Merchant, 31, *gt. Britain-street,* and *Commercial-buildings.*
Saul (Francis) Silk, Poplin and Tabinet-manufacturer, 12, *Spitalfields.*
Saul (James) Woollen-draper, 4, *High-street.*
Saunders (George) Merchant-tailor, 10, *Cork-hill.*
Saunders (John) Slater, 4, *low. Digges-street.*
Saunders (William) Carpenter, 56, *Mecklenburgh-street.*
Savage (Andrew) Carpenter and Builder, 134, *N. King-street.*
Savage (Arthur and Son) Apothecaries and Druggists, 30, *Meath-street.*
Savage (Henry) Trimming & Ribbon-manufacturer, 11, *Wormwood-gt.*
Savage (Sylvester) Brazier, 105, *Thomas-street.*
Scaif, Willis and Co. Merchant-tailors, 11, *Kildare-street.*
Scallan (William) Carpenter and Builder, 3, *Pembroke-street.*
Scanlan (Daniel) Corn-chandler, 11, *Camden-street.*
Scanlan (M.) Paper-maker, 8, and 9, *Cook-street.*
Scanlan (Patrick) Merchant, 21, *Eustace-street.*
Scarlet (James) Iron-monger, 67, *Pill-lane.*
Schooles (Alexander) Apothecary, 107, *Capel-street.*
Scott & Co. Army-clothiers & Accoutrement-makers, 33, *Dawson-st.*
Scott and Son, Watch-makers, 41, *Grafton-street.*
Scott (John) Carpenter, 41, *Montgomery-street.*
Scott (John) Silk-throwster, 37, *New-street.*
Scott (John) Timber-merchant, 54, *Townsend-street.*
Scott (Samuel) Merchant, 37, *low. Gardiner-street.*
Scott (Thomas) Apothecary and Chymist, 8, *Kevin's-port, Camden-street.*
Scott (William) Cabinet-maker and Upholder, 44, *Stafford-street.*
Scully (E.) Tailor, 33, *Exchequer-street.*
Scully (James) Merchant-tailor, 4, *Pitt-street.*
Scully (John) Merchant-tailor, 58, *Dominick-street.*
Scully (M.) Broker, 40, *Tighe-street.*
Scully (Timothy) Turner, 22, and 8, *Ash-street.*
Scurlog (Gregory) Wine-merchant, 44, *Dominick-street.*
Seabrooke (Geo. & Co.) Fur and Straw-plat-warehouse, 11, *Crow-street.*
Seale (Edward) Baker, 13, *Smock-alley.*
Seaver (John) Currier, 29, *Back-lane.*
Seaver (Stev.) Dutch Consul & Merchant, 54, *Abbey-street.*
Seed (Richard) Watch-maker, 20, *Bride-street.*
Segrave (Nicholas) Delf and Glass-seller, 111, *Dorset-street.*
Segrave (Patrick) Manufacturing Jeweller, 87, *Dame-street.*
Segrave (Richard) Tallow-chandler, 110, *gt Britain-street.*
Segrave (Thomas) Tobacconist and Tallow-chandler, 1, *Kevin-street.*
Sellors (James) Wholesale Hardware-merchant, 19, *W. New-row.*
Semple (John) Sheriff's-peer and Builder, 21, *Marlborough-street.*
Shallow (Mathew) Dry-cooper, 14, *up. Liffey-street.*

An extract from a list of merchants and traders in *Wilson's Dublin Directory for the Year 1820.*

LINEN-HALL FACTORS.

Alexander and Garretts, Office, 4, *Lurgan-street.*
Bastiville (Richard) 16, *Bolton-street*
Beggs, Jameson and Co. Office, 6, *Lurgan-street.*
Brady (James and George) Office, 127, *Linen-hall.*
Chambers, Todd and Co. Office, entrance off *N. Fred.-street.*
Clarke (James) 4, *Granby-row.*
Christie (James M.) Office, *Linen-h.*
Clibborn (Edward) 42, *York-street.*
Coile (Bernard & Co.) 10, *Linen-hall-s.*
Courtney (John) 10, *Linen-hall-str.*
Courtney (William) 1, *Yarn-hall-str*
Coulson (John & William) *Linen-hall.*
Dick (Sam. & Co.) 13, *Linen-hall-st.*
Egan (Constantine) 25, *Beresford-st*
Gardiner, Cusack & Co. *Linen-hall.*
Hall (Alexander) *Linen-hall.*
Harkness (W. & Co.) 22, *Dominick-s*
Hawthorne (Wm.) 5, *Lurgan-str.*

Johnston and Boyle, *Linen-hall.*
Knox (John) 5, *N. Anne-street.*
Knox (Wm.) 4, *Blessington-street.*
Leckey (John) 7, *N. Anne-street.*
Maguire (Alex.) Office, 58, *Bolton-st*
M'Kiernan (Hugh) 2, *Linen-hall.*
Mc. Mullen and Magrane, 20, *N. Anne-street.*
Meade (Mat.) 3, *Lisburn-street.*
Mills and Chambers, *Lisburn-str.*
Nicholson (John) *Linen-hall.*
Nolan and Taaffe, *Linen-hall.*
Ogilby (James & Son) 18, *Prussia-st*
Pepper and Locke, 26, *N. Anne-st.*
Pim (Tobias) 67, *Aungier-street.*
Richardson (R. & T.) 56, *Bolton-str.*
Salmon (Mich.) Office, *Linen-hall.*
Shaw and Carroll, 13, *Granby-row*
Stanley (John) *Linen-hall.*
Stott and Son, 36, *Dom.-str.*
Thompson (John) 167, *N. King-st*
Wolfenden (Wm.) 2, *up. Dorset-st*

PAWN-BROKERS.

Adams (Thomas) 117, *Thomas-street.*
Anderson (John) 18, *gt. Longford-st*
Barnier (Jos.) 22, *Stephen-street.*
Bonham (Edw.) 199, *gt. Britain-str*
Booth (H.) 68, *Fleet-street,* and 49, *Bishop-street.*
Burrows (Robert) 25, *Denmark-str.*
Byrne (John) 28, *Townsend-street.*
Campbell (Pat) 28, *Chancery-lane.*
Carpenter (John) 76, *Bride-street.*
Cooney (James) 127, *Francis-street.*
Dillon (Robert) *Bride-street.*
Dooley (Timothy) 11, *Beresford-st.*
Douglass (Rich.) 16, *Meath-street*
Dunn (William) 13, *Phœnix-street.*
Eades (Wm. Geo.) 4, *Johnson's-pl*
Fannin (Thomas) 41, *York-street.*

Fenton (Joseph) 8, *Townsend-street*
Fox (Thomas) 46, *Francis-street.*
Gregor (George) 89, *Bride-street.*
Harris (Thomas) 43, *gt. Britain-str.*
Henderson (Prud.) 15, *Montague-st.*
Hickey (Laurence) 12, *Moore-str.*
Hunter (James) 3, *Smock-alley.*
Langan (John) 67, *Church-street.*
Locke (Henry) 34, *Coombe.*
M'Namara (J.) 12, *Usher's-court.*
M'Namara (John) 5, *Jervis-street.*
Miller (John H.) 11, *Exchequer-str.*
Muley (Thomas) 11, *Greek-street.*
Murphy (Thomas) 96, *Coombe.*
O'Hara (Mathias) 52, *King-str. S.*
Parker (Stephen) 2, *St. Andrew-str.*
Pearson (Eliza) 7, *Pitt-street.*

An extract from the list of Dublin linen-hall factors and pawnbrokers in *Wilson's Dublin Directory for the Year 1820.*

1430   DUBLIN STREET DIRECTORY.

- 4 *Inspectors of Weights and Measures*
  —James Ryan and John M'Evoy,
  res. 6 Strandville avenue,   35*l.*
- 5 Bennett, M. tailor,   11*l.*
- 6 Ruins
- 7 Mooney, J. G. & Co. (limited), wine
  and spirit merchants, and 8,   40*l.*

..........*here Pitt-street intersects*..........

- 8 Mooney, J. G. & Co. (limited), wine
  and spirit merchants, and 7,   20*l.*

————

3 S.—Hatch-street, Lower.
From Leeson-street to Harcourt-street.
P. St. Peter.—Fitzwilliam W.

- 1 Duffy, Christopher, esq.   35*l.*
- 2 Andrews, Miss   45*l.*
- 3 Walsh, Miss,   40*l.*
- 4 Williams, Alexander, artist and
  musician, R.H.A.   40*l.*
- 5 Longfield, Mrs. George,   45*l.*
- 6 Macartney, Miss,   40*l.*
  ,, Peebles, Miss
- 7 Trench, F. N. Le Poer, Q.C.   45*l.*
- 8 Geoghegan, Jacob T. barrister, 45*l.*
- 9 Hart, Henry Chichester, esq.   46*l.*
- 10 Carey, Mrs.   45*l.*
- 11 Bennett, Miss, professor of the
  pianoforte,   45*l.*
- 12 Wilson, Herbert, barrister,   45*l.*
- 13 Campion, Wm. Bennett, Q.C. 2nd
  Sergeant-at-law,   45*l.*
- 14 Stanley, Robert H. barrister, 45*l.*
  ,, Stanley, Mrs.
- 15 Ryan, A. L. solicitor, commissioner
  for oaths, Offices—24 St. Andrew
  street   45*l.*
- 16 Roberts, Mrs.
  ,, Roberts, William C. esq.

.......*here Earlsfort-terrace intersects*......

- 20 Murland, Mrs.   60*l.*
  ,, Beckett, W. H. esq.
- 21 Verner, Miss Harriet,   48*l.*
- 22 Edge, J. Samuel, barrister,   48*l.*
  ,, Edge, Miss
- 23 Sullivan, William, barrister,   48*l.*
- 24 Patton, Mrs.   36*l.*
  ,, Patton, Miss C.
- 25 Murray, William D. esq.   35*l.*
- 26 Sheil, Richard H. barrister,   37*l.*
- 27 Leeper, Charles, esq.   35*l.*
- 28 Stubbs, William C. barrister, 38*l.*
- 29 Pierce, John, esq.   18*l.*
- 30 Archer, Mr.   18*l.*
- 31 Stubbs, Miss
- 31A McKnight, Mr. horse dealer, 18*l.*
- 32 Holland, Johnston, builder and
  contractor—res. Raglan house,
  Rathgar,   8*l.*
  ,, Holland, George

3 S.—Hatch-street, Upper.
From Earlsfort-terrace to Harcourt-st.
P. St. Peter.—Fitzwilliam W.

- 1 Gillman, Daniel, esq.   60*l.*
  ,, Gillman, Herbert R. esq.
  ,, Gillman, Sylvester, esq.
- 2 Owen, Mrs. Frances,   50*l.*
  Bonded Stores—W. & A. Gilbey,
          180*l.*

4 S.—Hawkins-street.
From D'Olier-street to Burgh-quay.
P. St. Mark.—Trinity W.

- 1 Gallaher & Co. tobacco manufacturers at Belfast. Branch house
  for south-west of Ireland—Wm.
  Hilles, agent, and 17 D'Olier-
  street,   43*l.*
- 2 Vacant,   24*l.*
- 3 Flynn, Mr. John,   24*l.*
  ,, *Central Loan Office*—W. Watson,
  manager
- 4 Whelan, Mr. John,
- 5 Farrelly, John, & Son, saddlers &
  harness makers,   41*l.*
- 6, 7 and 8 Goods entrance, *Junior
  Army and Navy* stores,   28*l.* 26*l.*
- 9 Foran, Mrs. tobacconist,   11*l.*
  ,, Dolan, J. shell-fish stores
  ,, Penfold, William
- 10 *Alliance Gas Co.* stores,   22*l.*
.......*here Leinster Market intersects*......
- 11 Commins, Thomas, wine and spirit
  mer. & 10 Leinster-market,   40*l.*
- 12 Fry, O. and R. general commission
  agents, flour, cheese, ling, herring
  and butter stores,   100*l.*
  ,, Matterson and Sons, Limerick
  ,, Baron Liebig's Extract of Malt
  ,, M'Call, John, & Co. London
  ,, Moir, J. and Son
  ,, Hay & Co. Lerwick
  ,, *Edwards' Dessicated Soap*
  ,, Libby, M'Neill & Libby, Chicago
  ,, *Limerick Dairy Co.*
  ,, White, T. H. and Co. and Belfast
  ,, *Condensed Milk Co. of Ireland*
  ,, Fry, Oliver, merchant—res. 7
  Ailesbury-road, Merrion
  ,, Fry, Richard, merchant—res. 8
  Elton-park, Sandycove
- 13 MacMullen, Shaw, and Co. flour
  merchants, & 12 Burgh-quay
  ,, Smyth, P. J. & Co.—office, 14
.......*here Burgh-quay intersects*.......
- 14 Smyth, Patrick J. and Co. sacking
  merchants,   28*l.*
- 14A Gallagher, Alfred H.   28*l.*
.......*here Poolbeg-street intersects*......
- 16 *Alliance Gas Co.*   100*l.*
  THE LEINSTER HALL (Concert Hall)
  —Michael Gunn, esq. proprietor
  —res. 69 Merrion-square
- 17A *Alliance and Consumers' Gas Co.*
  stove department
- 17 & 18 *Boys' Home* — Mrs. Macnamara, superintendent
- 19 Meagher, Philip, tea and wine
  merchant, and 1 & 2 Townsend-st.

1 E.—Hawthorn-avenue.
*Off Church-road, North-strand.—North
Dock W.*
Nine small cottages

1 E.—Hawthorn-terrace.
*Church-road, North-strand.—North
Dock W.*

- 1 Brough, Mr. John,   11*l.*
- 2 Smyth, Mrs.   8*l.*
- 3 Brownell, Mr. J.   8*l.*
- 4 Irwin, Mr. J. B.   10*l.*
- 5 Dempsey, Mr. Patrick,   10*l.*
- 6 Rocliffe, James,   10*l.*
- 7 Potter, James, engineer,   10*l.*
- 8 M'William, John, mariner,   10*l.*
- 9 M'William, Mr. Alexander,   8*l.*
- 10 O'Gier, Mr. A. V.   8*l.*

- 11 Hill, Mr. J.   8*l.*
- 12 Robertson, Mr. W.   8*l.*
- 13 Sanderson, Mr. T.   8*l.*
- 14 Buchanan, W. bottle maker,   8*l.*
- 15 M'Cormick, J. carpenter,   8*l.*
- 16 Rowe, Robert R. ship steward,   8*l.*
- 17 Vacant,   7*l.*
- 18 Vacant,   7*l.*
- 19 Walsh, Mrs.   7*l.*
- 20 Vance, Mr. W.   7*l.*
- 21 Willis, Mr. William,   10*l.*
- 22 Furlong, Mr. Michael,   9*l.*
- 23 Lynch, Mr. M.   9*l.*
- 24 Kennedy, Mr. T.   9*l.*
- 25 Casey, Mrs.   9*l.*
- 26 Cashmore, Robert, glass cutter,   9*l.*
- 27 M'Carthy, Bryan, late R.N.   9*l.*
- 28 Bratton, Mr. Henry James,   9*l.*
- 29 Harbron, Mr. W. J.   14*l.*
- 30 Tenements,   12*l.*
- 31 Adams, Mr. Harvey,   12*l.*
- 32 Tenements,   9*l.*

3 N.—Hay-market.
From Smithfield to Queen-street.
P. St. Michan.—Arran-quay W.

- 1 and 2 Petrie, Wm. sack merchant
  and sack hirer; agents for Lip-
  man and Co. hessian and sack
  manufacturers, Dundee—res. 30
  North Summer-street,   26*l.* 7*l.*
- 3 Doyle, Gerald, stores,   5*l.*
- 4 M'Quaid, John, cattle exporter, and
  Stormanstown, Glasnevin
- 5 and 6 Tenements,   each 13*l.*
.........*here Burgess-lane intersects*.........
- 7 and 8 Vacant,   8*l.*, 13*l.*
- 9 Cullen, Mrs. dairy,   12*l.*
.. ..*here Queen-street intersects*.........
  Weigh-house No. 5,   5*l.*
- 10 & 11 Doyle, James, and Son, coach
  factory
- 12 Hackett, William, & Son, farming
  implement manufacturers,   12*l.*
  ,, Bergin, Jeremiah, factor
- 13 Vacant,   5*l.*
- 14 Tenements,   15*l.*
- 15 Osborne, G. T. & Co. corn, hay and
  potato factors,   6*l.*

3 N.—Hendrick-lane.
From Benburb-street to Hendrick-place.
P. St. Paul.—Arran-quay W.

- 1 and 2 Tenements,   6*l.* 10*l.*
- 3 O'Brien, James, car owner,   7*l.*
- 4 and 5 Vacant,   35*l.*
.........*here Hendrick-street intersects*.....
- 6 Tenements,   2*l.*
- 7 Tenements
- 8 Tenements,   2*l.*
- 9 Devine, Mrs. provision dealer
- 10 and 11 M'Govern, M. grocer

3 N.—Hendrick-street.
From Queen-street to Hendrick-place.
P. St. Paul.—Arran-quay W.

- 1 to 4 Tenements,   12*l.*, 4*l.*, 9*l.*
- 5 Baird, Mr. John,   9*l.*
- 6 to 11 Tenements,   11*l.* to 15*l.*
- 12 Fletcher, Wm. upholsterer,   11*l.*
  METHODIST CHURCH — Rev. R.
  Hazelton, minister
.......*here Hendrick-lane intersects*......
- 14 Tenements
- 15 Tenements,   12*l.*
- 16, 17, & 18 Judd, Brothers, hide and
  sheep skin tanners,   40*l.*
- 19 to 23 Tenements,   6*l.* to 11*l.*
- 24 Clarke, George, stores,   11*l.*

An extract from the Directory of Residents of Dublin Streets from *Thom's Official Directory of the United Kingdom of Great Britain and Ireland* for 1893. Also shown is the street location, the registration district for births, deaths, and marriages, and the house valuation.

each of the main streets. The residents of rented houses, of which there were many, were generally not listed, these premises being referred to as tenements. The scope of the directory was gradually increased over the years to include the suburbs. Issued annually to 1849.

1844

Alexander Thom's *Irish Almanac and Official Directory* has the same categories of lists as Pettigrew and Oulton. It rapidly expanded annually to include the Dublin suburbs. Issued annually to present.

1846

Slater's *National Commercial Directory of Ireland* lists nobility, clergy, traders, etc., in Balbriggan and Skerries, Blackrock, Booterstown, Dalkey, Dublin, Howth, Kingstown (Dun Laoghaire), Monkstown, Swords, Malahide, and Williamstown.

1850

Henry Shaw's *New City Pictorial Directory of Dublin City* has a list of residents of the main streets, an alphabetical list of residents, and lists of attorneys and barristers. It also has interesting line drawings of the street fronts, showing shop names, etc.

1856

Slater's *Royal National Commercial Directory of Ireland* lists nobility, gentry, clergy, traders, etc., in Balbriggan and Skerries, Dublin and Kingstown (Dun Laoghaire), Howth, Swords, and Malahide.

1870

Slater's *Directory of Ireland* contains trade, nobility, and clergy lists for Balbriggan and Skerries, Dalkey, Dublin, Dundrum, Howth, Rathfarnham, Swords, and Malahide.

1881

Slater's *Royal National Commercial Directory of Ireland* contains lists of traders, clergy, nobility, and farmers in adjoining parishes of the towns of Balbriggan and Skerries, Donabate and Malahide, Dublin, Howth and Baldoyle, Rathfarnham, and Swords.

1894

Slater's *Royal National Directory of Ireland* lists traders, police, teachers, farmers, and private residents in Dublin city and in each of the towns, villages, and parishes of the county.

1911

Porters Post Office Guide and Directory of Kingstown, Blackrock, Killiney and neighborhood–1911.

1912

Porters Guide and Directory for North Co. Dublin gives occupations of heads of households in Artane, Balbriggan, Baldoyle, Blanchardstown, Castleknock, Chapelozid, Clondakin, Clontarf, Coolock, Donabate, Donnycarney, Dollymount, Drumcondra, Finglas, Fairview, Garristown, Glasnevin, Howth, Inchicore, Kilbarrack, Lucan, Lusk, Malahide, Mulhuddart, Phoenix Park, Portmarnock, Raheny, Rathfarnham, Rush, Skerries and Swords.

Family History

"Acton Papers" (Stradbrook, Co. Dublin). *Anal. Hib.* 25: 3–13.

"Arnoldi of Dublin, 27 Entries in the Family Bible." *J. Ass. Pres. Mem. Dead* 8 (1910–12): 71.

Barton, Bertram Francis. *Some account of the family of Barton drawn from manuscripts and records.* Dublin: Cahill & Co., 1902.

"Barnewall." *Ir. Gen.* 5 (2) (1975): 181–85.

"The Barnewalls of Turvey." *Reportorium* 1 (2) (1956): 336–41.

"The Bathes of Drumcondra." *Reportorium* 1 (2) (1956): 328–30.

"The Brocas Family, Notable Dublin Artists." *University Review* 2 (6) (1959): 17–25.

"Notes on the Cooke, Ashe and Swift Families, All of Dublin." *J. Ass. Pres. Mem. Dead* 9 (1912–16): 503.

"Corballis/Corbally families of Co. Dublin." *Irish Family History* 8 (1992): 84–93.

"Cusack Family of Meath and Dublin." *Ir. Gen.* 5 (3) (1976): 298–313; 5 (4) (1977): 464–70; 5 (5) (1978): 591–600; 5 (6) 1979: 673–84; 6 (2) (1981): 130–53; 6 (3) (1982): 285–98.

"Dix Family of Dublin, Entries from Family Bible." *J. Ass. Pres. Mem. Dead* 11 (1921–25): 490.

"The Dexters of Dublin and Annfield, Co. Kildare." *Ir. Anc.* 2 (1) (1970): 31–42.

"Fagans of Feltrim." *Reportorium* 2 (1) (1958): 103–06.

"The Falkiners of Abbotstown, Co. Dublin." *J. Kildare Arch. Hist. Soc.* 8 (1915–17): 331–63.

"The Fitz Rerys, Welsh Lords of Cloghran, Co. Dublin." *J. Louth Arch. Soc.* 5 (1921): 13–17.

"The Fitzwilliams of Merrion." *Reportorium* 2 (1) 1958: 88–96.

Genealogical Memoir of the Family of Talbot of Malahide, Co. Dublin. 1829.

"Notes on the Family of Grierson of Dublin." *Ir. Gen.* 2 (1953): 303–37.

"The Hollywoods of Artane." *Reportorium* 1 (2) 1956: 341–44.

"Kingsbury of Dublin." Pedigree in *Swanzy Notebooks.* RCB Library, Dublin.

"Law Family of Dublin." Pedigree. *J. Ass. Pres. Mem. Dead* 11 (1921-25): 444.

"The Lawless Family." *Reportorium* 1 (2) (1956): 344-50.

Bigger, F. *The Magees of Belfast and Dublin.* Belfast, 1916.

"Moore of Rutland Square, Dublin." Pedigree in *Swanzy Notebooks.* RCB Library, Dublin.

"A Moorhouse Family of Dublin, Carlow, and Kildare." *Ir. Anc.* 9 (1) (1977): 15-18.

"Nottinghams of Ballyowen." *Reportorium* 1 (2) 1956: 323-24.

"Pemberton of Dublin." *Ir. Anc.* 11 (1) (1979): 14-26.

"The Plunketts of Dunsoghly." *Reportorium* 1 (2) (1956): 330-36.

"Plunketts of Portmarnock." *Reportorium* 2 (1) (1958): 106-08.

"An Early Dublin Candlemaker: History of the Family of Rathborne, Chandlers, Dublin." *Dublin Hist. Record* 14 (1957): 66-73.

"The Scurlocks of Rathcredan." *Reportorium* 1 (1) (1955): 79-80.

"Segraves of Cabra." *Reportorium* 1 (2) (1956): 324-28.

A Genealogical History of the Family of Sirr of Dublin. London, 1903.

"Talbot de Malahide." *Reportorium* 2 (1) (1958): 96-103.

"The Talbots of Belgard." *Reportorium* 1 (1) (1955): 80-83.

Tweedy, Owen. *The Dublin Tweedys: The Story of an Irish Family 1650-1882.* London, 1956.

Tyrrell, J.H. *Genealogical History of the Tyrrells of Castleknock in Co. Dublin, Fertullagh in Co. Westmeath, and Now of Grane Castle, Co. Meath.* London, 1904.

"The Tyrrells of Castleknock." *R.S.A.I.* 76 (1946): 151-54.

"The Wolverstons of Stillorgan." *Reportorium* 2 (2) (1960): 243-45.

Gravestone Inscriptions

Indexing of gravestone inscriptions is in progress by various groups. Notable among the resulting series of publications are *Memorials of the Dead–Dublin City and County,* by Michael T. S. Egan and Richard Flatman, published by the Irish Genealogical Research Society (noted below as *Memorials of the Dead–Dublin*). A very useful account of the graveyards of Dublin and the status of their records is given in *Directory of Graveyards in the Dublin Area–an Index and Guide to Burial Records,* Dublin Public Libraries, 1988, ISBN: 0-9468410-6-3.

Abbotsown: *Ir. Gen.* 6 (6) (1985): 824-827; and 7 (1) (1986): 124-128; and *Memorials of the Dead–Dublin,* Vol. 3.

Aderrig: *J. Assoc. Pres. Mem. Dead.* 10: 191 and *J. Ir. Mem. Assoc.* 11: 155.

Artane (1100s-1700): *J. Ir. Mem. Assoc.* 11: 409-413.

Balbriggan (St. George's): *J. Ass. Pres. Mem. Dead* 3: 62-64; 8: 277; and *Memorials of the Dead–Dublin,* Vol. 6.

Ballybough (Jewish): In Hyman, L. (1972) and Shillman, B. (1945).

Balyboughal: *Memorials of the Dead–Dublin,* Vol. 6.

Ballyfermot (St. Lawrence): Unpublished survey available from Mr. Pat Johnson, Curator, Dublin Corporation Civic Museum, Sth. William St., Dublin 2.

Ballymadun (1800-): *J. Ir. Mem. Assoc.* 6: 217-221; and *Memorials of the Dead–Dublin,* Vol. 5.

Balrothery: *Memorials of the Dead–Dublin,* Vol. 6.

Balrothery Union: *Memorials of the Dead–Dublin,* Vol. 6.

Balscadden (New and Old): *Memorials of the Dead–Dublin,* Vol. 6.

Bluebell (Old, 1713-): *Memorials of the Dead–Dublin,* Vol. 3.

Bremore (Balbriggan): *Memorials of the Dead–Dublin,* Vol. 6.

Bullys Acre: see Kilmainham.

Chapelizod: *Ir. Gen.* 5 (4) (1977): 490-505.

Chapelmidway (Kilsallaghan): *Memorials of the Dead–Dublin,* Vol. 5.

Cloghran: Adams, Rev. Benjamin W. *History and Description of Santry and Cloghran Parishes.* 1883.

Cloghran: *Memorials of the Dead–Dublin,* Vol. 4.

Cloghran-Hidart: *Memorials of the Dead–Dublin,* Vol. 4.

Clonmethan (Oldtown): *Memorials of the Dead–Dublin,* Vol. 5.

Colmanstown (1743-): *Memorials of the Dead–Dublin,* Vol. 3.

Cruagh (Rathfarnham): *Memorials of the Dead–Dublin,* Vol. 4.

Christ Church Cathedral–Dublin City: Finlayson, Rev. *Inscriptions on the Monuments . . . in Christ Church Cathedral.* Dublin, 1878.

Dalkey: *Ir. Gen.* 5 (2) (1975): 250-55.

Damastown (Hollywood): *Memorials of the Dead–Dublin,* Vol. 5.

Deans Grange (Blackrock): Two volumes of inscriptions published in *Dun Laoghaire Gen. Soc.* (1994 and 1996).

Donnybrook (ca. 800-1993): compiled by Danny Parkinson. 1993. *Dublin Family Hist. Soc.* 2 (1988).

Esker: *Ir. Gen.* 6 (1): 54-58.

Esker (Old), Lucan: *Memorials of the Dead–Dublin,* Vol. 2.

Finglas (C of I): *J. Ir. Memorials Assoc.* (Parish Register Section) 1926-31.

Garristown: *Memorials of the Dead–Dublin,* Vol. 5.

Goldenbridge, Inchicore (1829): *Memorials of the Dead–Dublin*, Vol. 1.

Grallagh (Naul): *Memorials of the Dead–Dublin*, Vol. 5.

Grange, The (Baldoyle): *Memorials of the Dead–Dublin*, Vol. 4.

Hollywood (Naul): *Memorials of the Dead–Dublin*, Vol. 6.

Inchicore—see Goldenbridge.

Irishtown: *Ir. Gen.* 7 (4): 599–614.

Kilbride (Baldonnell): *Memorials of the Dead–Dublin*, Vol. 2, and *Ir. Gen.* 6 (3): 81.

Kilgobbin (New): *Memorials of the Dead–Dublin*, Vol. 3.

Kilgobbin (Old): *Memorials of the Dead–Dublin*, Vol. 2.

Killeek: *Memorials of the Dead–Dublin*, Vol. 5.

Killiney (old graveyard): *Ir. Gen.* 4 (6) (1973): 647–48.

Killossery: *Memorials of the Dead–Dublin*, Vol. 5.

Kilmactalway (Castle Bagot) (Baldonnell): *Memorials of the Dead–Dublin*, Vol. 2, and *Ir. Gen.* 6 (3): 378–81.

Kilmahuddrick: *Ir. Gen.* 6 (3): 378–81, and *Memorials of the Dead–Dublin*, Vol. 2.

Kilmainham, Royal Hospital: Bullys Acre and Royal Hospital graveyards. *History and Inscriptions.* Sean Murphy. Dublin: Divelina Publications, 1989. ISBN: 9512611-0.

Kilsallaghan: *Memorials of the Dead–Dublin*, Vol. 4.

Kilternan Old: *Memorials of the Dead–Dublin*, Vol. 2.

Kill o' the Grange: *Ir. Gen.* 4 (5) (1972): 507–14.

Leixlip: *Ir. Gen.* 4 (2) (1969): 110–16.

Loughtown Lower: *Ir. Gen.* 6 (3): 378–81.

Loughtown Lower (Religeen-Newcastle): *Memorials of the Dead–Dublin*, Vol. 2.

Lucan: *Ir. Gen.* 5 (6) (1976): 763–67.

Merrion (Merrion Rd.): *Memorials of the Dead–Dublin*, Vol. 2.

Merrion Row (Huguenot): *Memorials of the Dead–Dublin*, Vol. 2.

Monkstown: *Ir. Gen.* 4 (3) (1970): 201–02; 4 (4) (1971); also pub. by Danny Parkinson, Dublin, 1988.

Mount Jerome: Records from 1837-1965 are in the LDS Family History Centre (see Library and Information Sources at the end of the chapter).

Mount St. Joseph (Clondakin): *Memorials of the Dead–Dublin*, Vol. 2.

Mulhuddart (Old): *Memorials of the Dead–Dublin*, Vol. 4.

Naul: *Memorials of the Dead–Dublin*, Vol. 5.

Newcastle: *Ir. Gen.* 6 (2) (1981): 219–26.

Newcastle (C of I and RC): *Memorials of the Dead–Dublin*, Vol. 2.

Palmerstown: *Ir. Gen.* 4 (5) (1978): 650–53.

Palmerstown (Oldtown): *Memorials of the Dead–Dublin*, Vol. 4.

Rathcoole: *Ir. Gen.* 6 (4) (1983): 523–25.

Rathcoole (C of I): *Memorials of the Dead–Dublin*, Vol. 2.

Rathfarnham: *Ir. Gen.* 7 (2) (1987): 293–306.

Saggart (New, 1895-, and Old, 1711-): *Memorials of the Dead–Dublin*, Vol. 3.

Santry: Adams, Rev. Benjamin W. *History and Description of Santry and Cloghran Parishes.* 1883.

"St. Andrew's, Westland Row" (names on coffin plates). *Ir. Gen.* 5 (1) (1974): 131–39.

St. Catherine's. *Memorial Inscriptions from St. Catherine's Church and Graveyard.* Sean Murphy. Dublin: Divelina Publications, 1987. ISBN: 09512611-18.

St. Doolough's: *Ir. Gen.* 7 (1) (1986): 124–128.

St. James's Graveyard: *Memorial Inscriptions.* Published by St. James's Graveyard Project, 1988. NAI.

St. Mary's (Lucan): *Memorials of the Dead–Dublin*, Vol. 2.

St. Matthew's (C of I): *Memorials of the Dead–Dublin*, Vol. 2.

St. Paul (C of I): *R.S.A.I.* 104 (1974): 368–69. "SS. Peter and John" (names on coffin plates). *Ir. Gen.* 5 (3) (1976).

Tallaght: *Ir. Gen.* 4 (1) (1968): 29–36.

Taney: Ball, F. Elrington. *The Parish of Taney.* 1895.

Templeogue (Old): *Memorials of the Dead–Dublin*, Vol. 2.

Westpalstown (Oldtown): *Memorials of the Dead–Dublin*, Vol. 5.

The Ward: *Memorials of the Dead–Dublin*, Vol. 4.

Whitechurch (New) (Rathfarnham): *Memorials of the Dead–Dublin*, Vol. 4.

Whitechurch (Old) (Rathfarnham): *Memorials of the Dead–Dublin*, Vol. 3; and *Ir Gen.* 8 (1) (1990): 111–121.

Newspapers

Arguably the best Dublin newspapers for the eighteenth century are *Faulkner's Dublin Journal*, the *Freemans Journal*, *Dublin Hibernian Journal*, and the *Dublin Evening Post*. In the nineteenth century, further useful papers began publication, including the *Dublin Morning Post*, *Dublin Evening Herald*, and *Dublin Evening Mail*. A card index to biographical notices in *Faulkner's Dublin Journal* from 1763-71 is held in the National Library of Ireland.

Title: *Constitution and Church Sentinel* ·
Published in: Dublin, 1849-53
BL Holdings: 4.1849-5.1853

Title: *Dublin Courant*
Published in: Dublin, 1702-25; N.S. 1744-50
NLI Holdings: odd numbers 1703, 1705; 6.1744-2.1752; many issues missing

BL Holdings: odd numbers 1718-20, 22, 1.1723-12.1725; 4.1744-3.1750

Title: *Correspondent*
Published in: Dublin, 1806-61
Note: continued as *Dublin Correspondent* in 1822; *Evening Packet and Correspondent* in 1828; *Evening Packet* in 1860
NLI Holdings: 11.1806-12.1861
BL Holdings: 11.1806-4.1810; odd numbers 1810-11, 1813-16, 1820; 1-12.1823; odd numbers 1825, 26

Title: *Dublin Chronicle*
Published in: Dublin, 1762-1817
Note: breaks in publication
NLI Holdings: 1.1770-12.1771; 5.1787-12.1793; odd numbers 6.1815-1817
BL Holdings: 5.1787-4.1792; 5-12.1793

Title: *Dublin Evening Mail* (continued as *Evening Mail*)
Published in: Dublin, 1823-1962
NLI Holdings: 2.1823-7.1962
BL Holdings: 2.1823-2.1928

Title: *Dublin Evening Post*
Published in: Dublin, 1732-37 and 1778-1875
NLI Holdings: 6.1732-1.1737; 2.1778-8.1875
BL Holdings: 6.1732-7.1734; 7.1737-7.1741; 8.1778-7.1753; 10.1783-12.1785; 1787; 1789; 1792; 1794; 5-6.1795; 1.1796-12.1797; 1.1804-12.1810; odd numbers 1813, 14; 1.1815-8.1875

Title: *Dublin Gazette* (continued as *Iris Oifiguil*)
Published in: Dublin, 1705-current
Note: government notices only
NLI Holdings: 11.1706-12.1727; 3.1729-4.1744; 6.1756-12.1759; 1760; 1762; 1763; 1765; 1766; 1767; 1-7.1775; 1776-88; 1790-1921

Title: *Dublin Gazette and Weekly Courant*
Published in: Dublin, 1703-28
NLI Holdings: odd numbers 1708

Title: *Dublin Intelligence*
Published in: Dublin, 1690-1725 (at various times under different managements)
NLI Holdings: 9.1690-5.1693
BL Holdings: odd numbers 1708-12, 1723-25

Title: *Dublin Journal* (see *Faulkner's Dublin Journal*)

Title: *Dublin Mercury* (continued as *Hoey's Dublin Mercury* in 1770)
Published in: Dublin, 1704-75
NLI Holdings: 12.1722-5.1724; 1-9.1726; 1-9.1742; 3-9.1770; 9.1770-4.1773
BL Holdings: 1-9.1742; 3.1766-4.1773

Title: *Dublin Morning Post* (continued as *Carricks Morning Post* in 1804-21)
Published in: Dublin, ca. 1804-32
NLI Holdings: 4.1814-1831
BL Holdings: odd numbers 1824-26; 1.1830-5.1832

Title: *Evening Freeman*
Published in: Dublin, 1831-71
NLI Holdings: 8.1831-7.1836; 4-12.1844; 1845-9.1847; odd numbers 1848; 2.1858-59
BL Holdings: 1.1831-6.1871

Title: *Evening Irish Times*
Published in: Dublin, ca. 1860-1921
NLI Holdings: 4.1896-3.1900; 7.1900-3.1901; 7.1901-1907; 1911-6.1915
BL Holdings: 10.1880-10.1921

Title: *Evening Herald*
Published in: Dublin, 1786-1814; new series 1891-in progress
NLI Holdings: 5.1786-12.1789; 1.1806-12.1809; odd numbers 1810; 1.1812-6.1814
BL Holdings: 5.1786-12.1789; odd numbers 1807, 1813; 12.1891-in progress

Title: *Evening Packet* (incorporated with *Dublin Evening Mail*)
Published in: Dublin, 1828-62
BL Holdings: 1.1828-4.1929; 9.1829-3.1862

Title: *Evening Telegraph*
Published in: Dublin, 1871-1924
NLI Holdings: 10.1884-12.1924
BL Holdings: 7.1871-11.1873; 8.1875-5.1916; 1.1919-12.1924

Title: *Faulkner's Dublin Journal*
Published in: Dublin, 1725-1825
NLI Holdings: 1.1726-7.1735; 5.1736-1782; 1787-90; 1.1791-4.1825
BL Holdings: odd numbers 1726, 1739-40; 3.1741; 8-12.1744; 3.1748-3.1750; 3.1751-12.1764; 12.1765-12.1768; odd numbers 1782-84, 1792; 1-12.1796; odd numbers 1798, 99, 1803; 10.1804-12.1810; odd numbers 1813-14, 1817; 12.1819-12.1821

Title: *Freeman's Journal* or *Public Register*
Published in: Dublin, 1763-1924
BL Holdings: odd numbers 1784; odd numbers 1823-1833; 1.1837-12.1924
LDS Holdings: 1763-1793; films 0993905-19
Biographical notices from this paper are currently being indexed by Dublin Heritage Group

Title: *General Advertiser*
Published in: Dublin, 1804-1924
NLI Holdings: 9.1804-11.1820; odd numbers 1837; 2.1841-12.1851; 1853-54, 1857-61; 1864; 1866-67; 1869-70; 1874-12.1877; 1.1880-1890; 1892-3.1924
BL Holdings: 10.1838-12.1840 (with gaps); odd numbers 1841, 1846; 12.1846-7.1914; 1.1915-12.1923

Title: *Impartial Occurrences* (continued as *Peu's Occurrences* in 1714)
Published in: Dublin, 1704-80
NLI Holdings: 12.1704-2.1706; 12.1718-1748;

1751-1755; 1.1756-5.1757; 4-12.1768
BL Holdings: 1.1705-2.1706; odd numbers 1714, 1719, 1740; 1.1741-12.1742; 1.1744-12.1749; 1.1752-12.1753; 1.1756-12.1758; 1761
Title: *The Irish Times*
Published in: Dublin, 1859-current
Note: evening and weekly versions listed under *Evening Irish Times* and *Weekly Irish Times*
NLI Holdings: 3.1859-in progress
BL Holdings: 3.1859-in progress (except part of 11.1871)
Title: *Kingstown Gazette*
Published in: Kingstown Dun Laoghaire, old series 1857-58; new series 1868-69
BL Holdings: 12.1857-1.1858; 5.1868-7.1869
Title: *Magee's Weekly Packet*
Published in: Dublin, 1777-93
NLI Holdings: 6.1777-3.1895; 3.1787-8.1790; 8.1792-8.1793
BL Holdings: 6-10.1777; 11.1777-3.1785; odd numbers to 1793
Title: *Morning Mail*
Published in: Dublin, 1870-1912
NLI Holdings: 2.1870-12.1883
BL Holdings: 3.1871-6.1880; 12.1896-8.1912 (with gaps)
Title: *Morning Register*
Published in: Dublin, 1824-43
NLI Holdings: 10.1824-1.1843
BL Holdings: 10.1824-1.1843
Title: *Nation* (continued as *Daily Nation* and *Weekly Nation*)
Published in: Dublin, 1842-1900
NLI Holdings: 10.1842-7.1891; 6.1896-9.1900
BL Holdings: 10.1824-7.1848; 9.1849-7.1891; 6.1896-9.1900
Title: *Patriot* (continued as *Statesman and Patriot* in 1828)
Published in: Dublin, ca. 1810-29
NLI Holdings: 7.1810-1815; 1818-10.1828; 11.1829-5.1829
BL Holdings: 1.1823-10.1828
Title: *Saunder's Newsletter* (continued as *Saunder's Irish Daily News* in 1878)
Published in: Dublin, 1755-1879
NLI Holdings: odd numbers 1767-91; 3.1773-12.1787; 1.1789-3.1795; 2.1796-12.1802; 4.1804-12.1806; 1.1808-11.1809; 1812-18; 1820-11.1879
BL Holdings: 3.1773-12.1787; 1789; 1.1793-12.1794; 1795; 1.1797-12.1811; 1.1813-12.1815; 1.1817-11.1879
Title: *The Warder* (continued as *Sport's Mail* and *Irish Weekly Mail* in 1921)
Published in: Dublin, 1821-1939
NLI Holdings: 3.1821-9.1938

BL Holdings: 3.1822-9.1939 (except 1930)
Title: *Weekly Freeman's Journal* (continued as *Weekly Freeman, National Press*, and *Irish Agriculturist* in 1892)
Published in: Dublin, ca. 1817-1924
NLI Holdings: 1-7.1818; 3-7.1830; 1.1834-4.1840; 6.1880-12.1882; 5.1883-3.1892; 4.1892-12.1893; 1.1895-12.1913; 6.1914-12.1924
BL Holdings: 10.1821-12.1831; 1.1838-3.1892; 4.1892-12.1924
Title: *Weekly Irish Times* (continued as *Times Pictorial* in 1941)
Published in: Dublin, 1875-1941
NLI Holdings: odd numbers 1875; 1.1883-6.1886; 1.1906-11.1941
BL Holdings: 6.1875-12.1920; 1.1922-11.1941

Wills and Administrations

A discussion of the types of records, where they are held, and their availability and value is given in the Wills section of the introduction. The availability of prerogative wills, administrations, and marriage license records is also described in the relevant parts of the same section. Where available, published sources of these records are given in the Miscellaneous Sources section.

Pre-1858 Wills and Administrations
Prerogative Wills. See the introduction.
Consistorial Wills. County Dublin is entirely in the diocese of Dublin. The guide to Catholic parish records in this chapter shows the diocese to which each civil parish belonged. The wills of residents of each diocese were usually proven within that diocese (see the Wills section for exceptions). The following records survive:

Wills
See the introduction.

Abstracts
See the introduction.

Indexes
Dublin and Glendalough (1536-1858) published in the appendices to the 26th and 30th reports of the DKPRI of 1895 and 1899, respectively. The 26th and 30th reports of the DKPRI also index marriage licenses for the Dublin and Glendalough diocese.

Post-1858 Wills and Administrations
Dublin County was served by the District Registry of Dublin (Principal Registry). The surviving records are kept in the NAI.

Other collections include:

Lane-Poole contain fifty-two will abstracts of the seventeenth to nineteenth centuries from Dublin and Wicklow. These are in NLI (ms. 5359) and also published in *Ir. Gen.* 8 (4) (1993): 610-617.

Quaker Wills from Dublin and East Leinster. Society of Friends Library, Dublin.

Marriage Licenses

Indexes

Dublin (1672) NAI; SLC 100867.

Original Bonds, Dublin (1749-1813) indexed by males, surnames beginning with A only. NAI; SLC 101770.

Abstracts

Fisher's Abstracts (1638-1800), indexed separately for bride and groom, by surname, gives groom's name and address, bride's name and address, and date of marriage: GO MS 134-38 and SLC film 100226.

Listing of Dublin (1638-1800). Phillip's listing, by both bride and grooms' surnames, of all marriage licenses granted, and intended place of marriage. GO MS 473-75; SLC 100227.

Miscellaneous Sources

Ryan, James. *A Guide to Tracing your Dublin Ancestors.* Dublin: Flyleaf Press, 1988.

Directory of Graveyards in the Dublin Area–an Index and Guide to Burial Records in Dublin City and County. Dublin Public Libraries, 1988. ISBN: 0-9468410-6-3.

Clark, Mary. "Sources for Genealogical Research in Dublin Corporation Archives." *Ir. Gen.* 7 (2) (1987): 291-2.

Ball, F.E. *History of County Dublin.* 4 vols. Dublin, 1920. Reprint, 1979.

"Catalogue of the names of the Chief Magistrates of Dublin (Provosts, Bailiffs, Mayors and Sheriffs) from 1308 to 1816." Appendix 9, *History of the City of Dublin,* by Warburton, Whitelaw, and Walsh. London, 1818.

Gardiners Dublin. *A History and Topography of Mountjoy Square and Environs.* National Council for Education Awards, 1991. ISBN: 0-905717-37-6.

Costello, Peter. *Dublin Churches.* Dublin, 1989. ISBN: 0-7171-1700-6.

Census Search applications. Barony of Rathdown, Co. Dublin. *Dun Laoghaire Gen. Soc J.* 5 (1) (1996). (All details from green forms–see introduction.)

Clark, Mary, and Raymond Refausse. *Directory of Historic Dublin Guilds.* Dublin Public Libraries, 1993.

Clark, Mary. "The Dublin Guild of Carpenters 1656." *Ir. Gen.* 8 (3) 322-332 and 8 (4) 498-529.

D'Alton, J. *The History of Co. Dublin.* Dublin, 1838. Reprint. Cork: Tower, 1976.

Pearson, P. *Dun Laoghaire–Kingstown.* Dublin: O'Brien Press, 1991.

Gilbert, J. *A History of the City of Dublin.* 3 vols. Reprint. Dublin, 1972.

"The Huguenots in Dublin." *Dublin Hist. Rec.* 8 (1945-46): 110-34.

"Liberty of St. Sepulchre–1586-1590 Court Book." Herbert Wood, ed. *R.S.A.I.,* 1930.

"The Manor of Lucan and the Restoration Land Settlement, 1660-1688." *Dublin Hist. Rec.* 21 (1966-67): 139-43.

Smyth, Hazel P. *The Town of the Road.* Pale Publishing, 1994. (A history of Booterstown.)

Goodbody, Rob. *On the Borders of the Pale.* Pale Publishing, 1993. (A history of Stepaside, Kilgobbin, and Sandyford.)

O'Sullivan, P. *Newcastle-Lyons: A Parish of the Pale.* Dublin: Geography Publications, 1985.

Henry, Brian. *Dublin Hanged–Crime, Law Enforcement and Punishment in Late-Eighteenth-Century Dublin.* Irish Academic Press, 1994.

Refausse, Raymond, ed. *Register of the Parish of St. Thomas, Dublin, 1740-1791.* RCBL, 1994.

"Succession Lists of Parish Priests in Dublin Diocese 1771-1960." *Dublin Hist. Rec.* 3 (1) (1962): 178-90.

Warburton, J.W., Rev. J. Whitelaw, and Rev. R. Walsh. *A History of the City of Dublin. From the earliest account to the present time; to which is added biographical notices of eminent men and copious appendices of its population, revenue, commerce and literature.* London: Cadell, 1818.

Weavers and Related Trades in Dublin 1826. Sean Magee, ed. Dun Laoghaire Gen. Soc., 1995. ISBN: 1-898471-15-0.

Abstracts of the Acts of the Assembly of the City of Dublin from A.D. 1539 to A.D. 1752. Gilbert Library. Ms. 57-60.

Assembly Rolls of the City of Dublin from 1660 to 1687, from 1788 to 1803. Gilbert Library. Ms 46-53.

O'Donnell, E.E. *The Annals of Dublin.* Wolfhound Press, 1987. ISBN: 086327-1499.

Douglas Bennett Encyclopedia of Dublin. Gill & Macmillan, 1991.

DeCourcy, J.W. *The Liffey in Dublin.* Gill & Macmillan, 1996.

Dublin Street Names–Dated and Explained. C.T. McCready, Dublin, 1892.

Charters and Documents of the Guild of the Holy Trinity or Merchant Guild of Dublin, A.D. 1438-1824. Gilbert Library. Ms. 78-79.

Charters and Documents of the Dublin Corporation of Cutlers, Painters, Stainers, and Stationers, also of the Dublin Guild of Bricklayers. Gilbert Library. Ms. 81.

Documents of the Guild of Tailors of Dublin, A.D. 1296-1753. Gilbert Library. M. 80.

Dublin, Memorandum Rolls of the City of Dublin from 26 Henry VI. Gilbert Library. Ms. 54-55.

Dublin, Index to transcripts of Memorandum Rolls of the City of Dublin, A.D. 1447 to A.D. 1660. Gilbert Library. Ms. 56.

Dublin, Monday Books of the City of Dublin, A.D. 1567-1712. Gilbert Library. Ms. 44-45.

Dublin, Register of ye Mayors of Dublin. Gilbert Library. Ms. 85.

Dublin, Transcript (A) of the Book of Charters belonging to the City of Dublin . . . from 1667 . . . to 1767. Gilbert Library. Ms. 71-73.

Research Sources and Services

Journals
Dublin Historical Record
Reportorium Novum (Dublin Diocesan History)

Libraries and Information Sources
National Library, Kildare Street, Dublin 2 (see introduction)

Dublin Public Libraries. There are twenty-seven branches in Dublin city (run by Dublin Corporation), and ten in Dublin county (run by the county councils). Almost all libraries have a local studies section, but the Gilbert Library (see below) has the major collection of materials relating to Dublin city. Dublin Corporation Public Libraries has also published a series of guides of relevance to family history, such as *How to Trace Your Family History* (1994); *Directory of Local and Family History Societies* (1990); *Directory of Graveyards* (1990); and *Some Eminent Dubliners* (1988).

Gilbert Library, 138-142 Pearse Street, Dublin 2. Ph: (01) 677 7662. This library has the best collection of books and documents on Dublin. The library houses several collections of papers donated by individuals (including the founder, Sir John Gilbert) and a very extensive collection of early newspapers, periodicals, directories, papers of Dublin private and public organizations, trade unions and guilds, etc.

Dun Laoghaire—Rathdown Public Library, Lower Georges Street, Dun Laoghaire, Co. Dublin. Ph: (01) 2801254/2801147; fax: (01) 2846141. This library has an extensive collection relating to the South County Dublin area.

LDS Family History Centre, The Willows, Finglas Rd., Dublin 11. Ph: (01) 8309960 (the center) or (01) 2883312 (director—Tom Milligan). This center is run by The Church of Jesus Christ of Latter-day Saints. Although established for the use of church members, non-members who wish to do their own research are welcome, and there are no charges. The library cannot conduct research for others. It holds an extensive collection of microfiche copies of civil records; indexes of birth and death (1864-1958) and marriages (1845-1958), as well as certificates for some years; records from Mount Jerome graveyard (1837-1965); and other Dublin and national sources.

Research Services
Fingal Heritage Group (FHG), Carnegie Library, North Street, Swords, Co. Dublin. Ph: (01) 8403629/ 8400080; fax: 8405175. This is the official IGP center for the area of Fingal, which covers almost all of the northern part of Co. Dublin. This center has indexed many of the Catholic and Church of Ireland records, and is working on the remainder and on Presbyterian records. It has also indexed Roll-books of the Old Borough School and St. Colmcille School in Swords; the 1901 census for Swords and Lusk; vaccination records from 1864; and gravestone inscriptions from the graveyards managed by Dublin County Council. Researchers are advised to contact them for an updated list of registers, and other sources, indexed. They will conduct research on their indexes for a fee.

Dublin Heritage Group (DHG), 2nd Floor, Cumberland House, Fenian St., Dublin 2. Ph: (01) 6619000; fax: (01) 6761628; e-mail: dublin.city.libs@iol.ie. This is the official IGP center for Dublin city and the southwestern part of Co. Dublin. This center is indexing the church and other relevant records of this area. Those already indexed are indicated in the section on church records. They are also compiling databases on Dublin vernacular architecture, the Dublin Fire Brigade, and are indexing the *Freeman's Journal* newspaper. Researchers are advised to contact the group for an updated list of registers, and other sources, indexed. They will conduct research on their indexes for a fee.

Dun Laoghaire Heritage Centre (DLHC), Moran Park House, Dun Laoghaire, Co. Dublin. Ph: (01) 2806961; fax: (353) 1 2806969. This is the official IGP center for Dun Laoghaire and the south of Co. Dublin. This center is indexing the church and other relevant records of this area. Those already indexed are indicated in the section on church records. Researchers are advised to contact the center for an updated list of registers, and other sources, indexed. They will conduct research on their indexes for a fee.

Also see Research Services in Dublin in the introduction.

Societies
Balbriggan Historical Society, Ms. Emma Barton, Bruc na h-Aille, Westown, Naul, Co. Dublin

Ballinteer Family History Society, c/o 29 The View, Woodpark, Ballinteer, Dublin 16

Clondalkin Historical Society, Mr. Peter Ging, Lareston, Monastary Road, Clondalkin, Dublin 22

Clontarf Historical Society, Mr. Jack Leake, 93 Seafield Road, Clontarf, Dublin 3

Crumlin Historical Society, Sister Rosario, St. Agnes Convent, Crumlin, Dublin 12

Dun Laoghaire Genealogical Society, 14 Rochestown Park, Dun Laoghaire, Co. Dublin

Dun Laoghaire Historical Society, Mr. Colin Scudds, 7 Northumberland Park, Dun Laoghaire, Co. Dublin

Loughshinny and Rush Historical Society, Mrs. Margaret McCann, Don Bosco, Harbour Road, Rush, Co. Dublin

Mount Merrion Historical Society, Ms. Sheila Casey, 38 The Rise, Mount Merrion, Blackrock, Co. Dublin

Old Dublin Society, The Secretary, Civic Museum, 58 South William Street, Dublin 2

Raheny Heritage Society, The Secretary, 68 Raheny Park, Raheny, Dublin 5

Skerries Historical Society, Ms. Betty Balcome, 63 The Townparks, Skerries, Co. Dublin

Tallaght Historical Society, Mrs. Patricia Moran, 7 Bancroft Park, Tallaght, Dublin 24

Dublin Civil Parishes as Numbered on Map

1. Balscadden
2. Balrothery
3. Skerries or Holmpatrick
4. Lusk
5. Baldongan
6. Naul
7. Garristown
8. Grallagh
9. Hollywood
10. Ballymadun
11. Palmerston
12. Clonmethan
13. Westpalstown
14. Ballyboghil
15. Killossery
16. Swords
17. Donabate
18. Portraine
19. Kilsallaghan
20. Killeek
21. Ward
22. Mulhuddart
23. Cloghran (Castleknock barony)
24. Finglas
25. Clonsilla
26. Castleknock
27. Chapelizod
28. Malahide
29. St. Margaret's
30. Santry
31. Cloghran (Coolock barony)
32. Kilsaley
33. Portmarnock
34. Balgriffin
35. Coolock
36. Baldoyle
37. Glasnevin
38. Clonturk
39. Artane
40. Raheny
41. Kilbarrack
42. Howth

43. Grangegorman
44. St. George's
45. Killester
46. Clontarf
47. Leixlip
48. Lucan
49. Aderrig
50. Esker
51. Kilmactalway
52. Kilmahuddrick
53. Kilbride
54. Newcastle
55. Rathcoole
56. Saggart
57. Palmerstown
58. Clondalkin
59. Ballyfermot
60. St. James'
61. Drimnagh
62. Crumlin
63. St. Catherine's
64. St. Peter's
65. Tallaght
66. Cruagh
67. St. Mark's
68. Donnybrook
69. Rathfarnham
70. Taney
71. Booterstown
72. Whitechurch
73. Kilmacud
74. Stillorgan
75. Monkstown
76. Tully
77. Kill
78. Dalkey
79. Kilgobbin
80. Killiney
81. Kiltiernan
82 Rathmichael
83. Old-Connaught

CIVIL PARISHES OF COUNTY DUBLIN

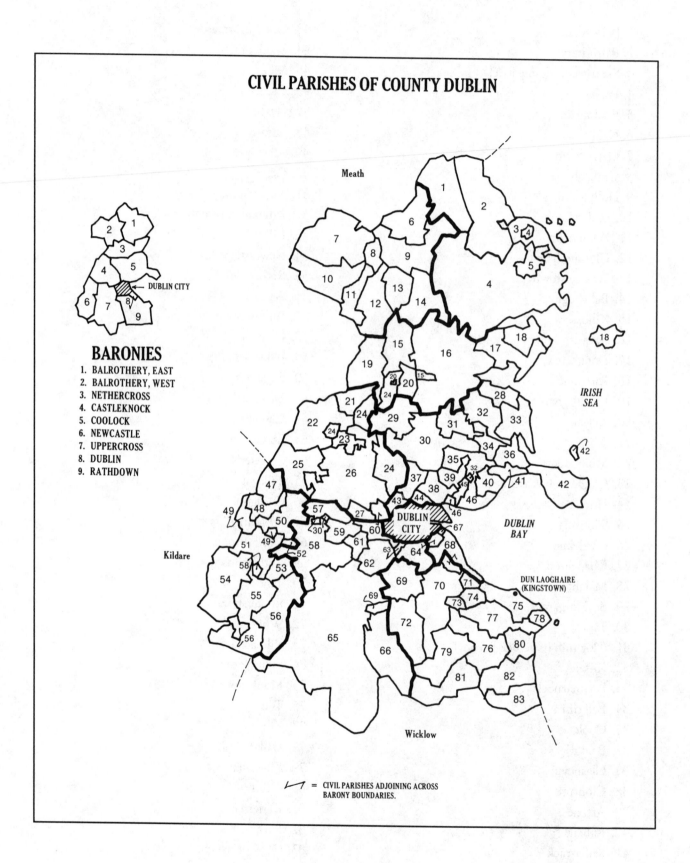

BARONIES

1. BALROTHERY, EAST
2. BALROTHERY, WEST
3. NETHERCROSS
4. CASTLEKNOCK
5. COOLOCK
6. NEWCASTLE
7. UPPERCROSS
8. DUBLIN
9. RATHDOWN

DUBLIN CITY

Meath

Kildare

Wicklow

IRISH SEA

DUBLIN BAY

DUN LAOGHAIRE (KINGSTOWN)

↳⌐ = CIVIL PARISHES ADJOINING ACROSS BARONY BOUNDARIES.

Dublin Civil Parishes in Alphabetical Order

Aderrig: 49

Artane: 39

Baldongan: 5

Baldoyle: 36

Balgriffin: 34

Ballyboghil: 14

Ballyfermot: 59

Ballymadun: 10

Balrothery: 2

Balscadden: 1

Booterstown: 71

Castleknock: 26

Chapelizod: 27

Cloghran (Castleknock barony): 23

Cloghran (Coolock barony): 31

Clondalkin: 58

Clonmethan: 12

Clonsilla: 25

Clontarf: 46

Clonturk: 38

Coolock: 35

Cruagh: 66

Crumlin: 62

Dalkey: 78

Donabate: 17

Donnybrook: 68

Drimnagh: 61

Esker: 50

Finglas: 24

Leixlip: 47

Lucan: 48

Garristown: 7

Glasnevin: 37

Grallagh: 8

Grangegorman: 43

Hollywood: 9

Holmpatrick or Skerries: 3

Howth: 42

Kilbarrack: 41

Kilbride: 53

Kilgobbin: 79

Kill: 77

Killeek: 20

Killester: 45

Killiney: 80

Killossery: 15

Kilmactalway: 51

Kilmacud: 73

Kilmahuddrick: 52

Kilsaley: 32

Kilsallaghan: 19

Kiltiernan: 81

Lusk: 4

Malahide: 28

Mulhuddart: 22

Monkstown: 75

Newcastle: 54

Naul: 6

Old-Connaught: 83

Palmerston: 11

Palmerstown: 57

Portmarnock: 33

Portraine: 18

Raheny: 40

Rathcoole: 55

Rathfarnham: 69

Rathmichael: 82

Saggart: 56

Santry: 30

St. Catherine's: 63

St. George's: 44

St. James': 60

St. Margaret's: 29

St. Mark's: 67

St. Peter's: 64

Skerries or Holmpatrick: 3

Stillorgan: 74

Swords: 16

Tallaght: 65

Taney: 70

Tully: 76

Ward: 21

Westpalstown: 13

Whitechurch: 72

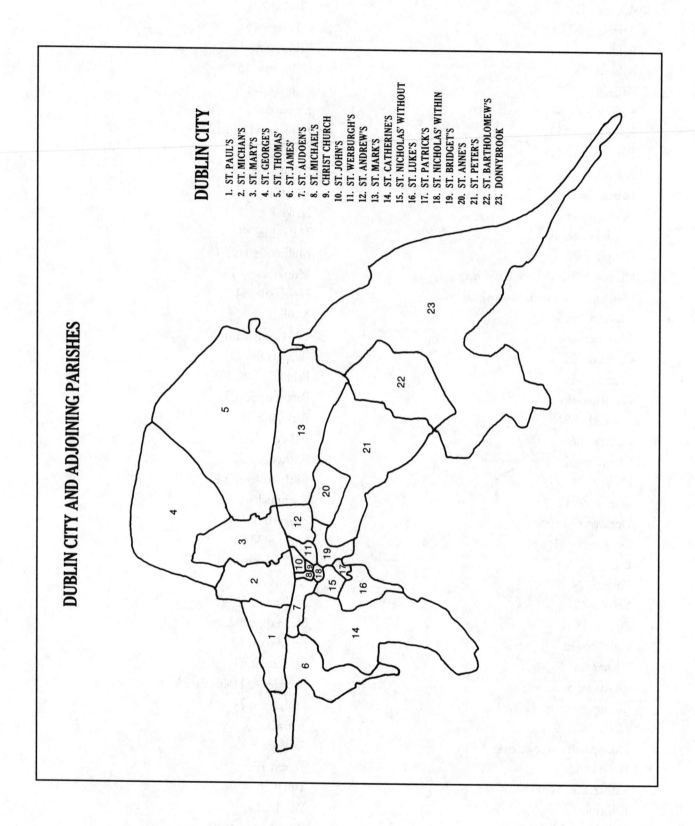

DUBLIN CITY AND ADJOINING PARISHES

DUBLIN CITY

1. ST. PAUL'S
2. ST. MICHAN'S
3. ST. MARY'S
4. ST. GEORGE'S
5. ST. THOMAS'
6. ST. JAMES'
7. ST. AUDOEN'S
8. ST. MICHAEL'S
9. CHRIST CHURCH
10. ST. JOHN'S
11. ST. WERBURGH'S
12. ST. ANDREW'S
13. ST. MARK'S
14. ST. CATHERINE'S
15. ST. NICHOLAS' WITHOUT
16. ST. LUKE'S
17. ST. PATRICK'S
18. ST. NICHOLAS' WITHIN
19. ST. BRIDGET'S
20. ST. ANNE'S
21. ST. PETER'S
22. ST. BARTHOLOMEW'S
23. DONNYBROOK

County Fermanagh

A Brief History

This Ulster county contains the towns of Enniskillen, Kesh, Irvinestown, and Lisnaskea.

County Fermanagh was historically the territory of the Maguires and was partly in the Gaelic Kingdom of Oriel. Other families associated with the county include Rooney (or Mulrooney), Muldoon, McKernan, Devine, McDonnell, Flanagan, Bannon, Owens, Fee, Corrigan, Hussey, Whelan, Corcoran, and Breslin.

In the twelfth and thirteenth centuries, the Normans made several unsuccessful attempts to conquer Fermanagh. The Maguires and the other local chieftains allied themselves to the powerful O'Neills of Tyrone and remained independent for four centuries. The Maguires dominated this territory from the beginning of the fourteenth century. In the early sixteenth century, they nominally submitted to the English crown, but in practice they retained control over the county.

Toward the end of the sixteenth century, the English began making various administrative demands on the county and establishing administrators for various purposes. Accordingly, in 1593 the chief of the Maguires rebelled and expelled all the English from the county. He later joined with O'Neill in the general Ulster rebellion.

After the defeat of the O'Neills and the emigration of most of the Ulster chieftains, Fermanagh was planted with settlers, along with most of the Ulster counties. English and Scottish "undertakers" were appointed; they obtained land in return for an "undertaking" to plant a specified number of English or Scottish families. Among the English undertakers were Flowerden, Blennerhassett, Archdale, Warde, Barton, Hunings, Wirral, Bogas, Calvert, and Sedborough. The Scottish undertakers included Hume, Hamilton, Gibb, Lindsey, Fowler, Dunbar, Balfour, Wishart, Moneypenny, Trayle, and

Smelholme. Among the other families who obtained lands in the county at this time were ffolliott, Atkinson, Cole, Gore, Davys, Harrison, and Mistin. The O'Neills and Maguires and some of the other Gaelic families were also granted small portions of land.

Many of the native families either obtained lands in the county or else remained as tenants or servants on the planted lands. Many of those planted left again, and the general picture was that the plantation was of mixed success in this county.

In 1641, the Maguires again led the county in support of the Catholic revolt, and many of the new settlers were driven out, or, in some cases, killed. Following the defeat of the rebellion, further lands in the county were confiscated and given to planters. The Brooke family got their lands at this time, as well as Montgomery, Leonard, Wyatt, and Balfour.

Following the Williamite wars of the 1690s, the Fermanagh planters began to replace the native families with laborers from England and Scotland. Many of these left again, but nevertheless, the county did gradually become more English and less Irish.

The 1609 plantation and the subsequent arrivals of laborers and farmers have introduced many English and Scottish names to the county. These include Johnson, Patterson, Armstrong, Morrison, Elliott, Graham, Irvine, Thompson, Noble, Carson, Forster, Hamilton, and Boyd.

In the eighteenth century, the Penal Laws further deprived Catholics of lands and rights. Although primarily intended to restrict Catholic privileges, the laws also adversely affected the rights of Presbyterians. Thus there was a steady emigration of Presbyterians, the so-called Scots-Irish, during this century. The origins of the inhabitants can, in very general terms, be shown by their religion, as the natives are generally Catholic, the English Protestant, and the Scottish Presbyterian. In 1861, when religious persuasion was first determined in the census, the relative proportions of the three were fifty-seven, thirty-eight, and two percent, respectively. Livingstone's history of the county gives an analysis of Fermanagh families from the voters list of 1962. The families are indicated as British (B), Gaelic (G), Gaelic names associated with Fermanagh (GF), or of mixed origin (M). The twenty-five most common families in 1962, in order of their abundance, are: Maguire (GF), Johnston (B), Armstrong (B), MacManus (GF), Elliott (B), McCaffrey (GF), O'Reilly (G), Smith (M), Murphy (G), Graham (B), Irvine (B), Gallagher (G), Cassidy (GF), Owens (GF), Beatty (M), Thompson (B), MacBryan/ Breen (GF), Noble (B), Duffy (G), Dolan (G), Morris (B), Woods (G), McElroy (GF), Monaghan (GF), and Corrigan (GF).

A Web site on the history of Fermanagh during the Great Famine is at http://www.nua.ie/dagda/ Fermanagh/Roslea/story/famineInFermanagh.html.

Census and Census Substitutes

1612–13

"Survey of Undertakers Planted in Fermanagh" (names, acreages allotted, and account of the progress of each). *Hist. Mss. Comm. Rep.* (Hastings Mss.) 4 (1947): 159–82.

1625

"A Fermanagh Survey." *Clogher Record* 2 (2) (1958): 293–310 (account of the plantations; only major landholders named).

1631

Muster Roll. In *History of Enniskillen*, by W. C. Trimble, 198–219; SLC film 1341267; PRONI T934; BL add. ms. 4770.

1632–36

Balfour Estate Rentals; Baronies of Coole; Magherastephana (part) and Knockninny. *Clogher Record* 12 (1): 92–109.

1659

"Census" of Ireland. Edited by S. Pender. Dublin: Stationery Office, 1939. NLI I6551. SLC film 924648.

1665

Hearth Money Roll. NAI film 2472; NLI ms. 9583.

The Roll for Barony of Lurg. *Clogher Record* 2 (1) (1957): 207–14.

1761/88

Lists of resident freeholders in Fermanagh. NLI Ms 787/8; GO Ms 442; SLC film 100181.

1766

Householders of Parishes of Derryvullan. RCBL Ms. 23; SLC film 100173, 258517. NAI M2476 and GO 536.

Householders of Devenish, Kinawley and Rossory. GO 536; SLC film 258517, 100173. NAI M 2476 (Kinawley and Rossory are also on RCBL Ms. 23).

1785

Male Protestants of Seventeen Years and Upwards in Clogher Diocese (civil parishes of Magheracloone and Trory). SLC film 258517.

1788

List of Freeholders. GO ms. 442; PRONI T543; SLC films 100181 and 1279356.

1796

Spinning Wheel Premium List (see introduction).

Also see Co. Mayo 1796 (List of Catholics).

1821

Government Census Remnants: Parish of Aghalurcher and Parish of Derryvullan. SLC film 597733, 596418. NAI CEN 1821/16–17.

1823–37

Tithe Applotment Survey (see introduction).

1832–37

"Voters (i.e., householders and burgesses) in Enniskillen" (285 names). Reports from Committees. *Parl. Papers* 1837/38, 13 (2): Appendix 8.

"Names of £50, £20, and £10 Freeholders and Leaseholders in Fermanagh" (1,838 names). *Parl. Papers* 1837, 11 (1): Appendix A1, 7–21.

"List of Voters Registered in the Borough of Enniskillen." *Parl. Papers* 1837, 11 (2): 201–03. (284 names and residences.)

1839

List of persons who obtained Game Certificates in Ulster . . . . PRONI T 688.

1841 and 1851

Extracts from Government Census for Old Age Pension Claims. NAI; SLC film 258537.

1842

Voters List. NAI 1842/114.

1850–51

A census of thirty-two townlands of Galloon parish (forming the C of I parish of Sallaghy), conducted by Rev. William Bredin. PRONI D 2098.

1851

Extracts from Government Census for the Townland of Clonee, in Parish of Drumkeeran. NAI CEN 1851/ 13/1; SLC film 100858.

1862

Griffith's Valuation of County Fermanagh (see introduction). NLI, NAI. Surname index available on microfiche from All-Ireland Heritage Inc., 1986; also in NLI and NAI.

1901

Census. NAI (see introduction). A full index to this census (on microfiche) is available from Largy Books, PO Box 6023, Fort McMurray, Alberta T9H 4W1, Canada. Ph: (403) 791-1750. SLC films 836597-660, 836117-28.

1911

Census. NAI.

Church Records

Church of Ireland

See the introduction for a description of Church of Ireland records and their major repositories. Many C of I records were lost in the PRO fire of 1922. These are indicated as "Lost." However, as Church of Ireland records were effectively state records, the records of marriage (from 1845) are also in the General Registrar's Office. Many are still in local custody (LC), while others are in one of a variety of other archives (e.g., RCBL or NAI). Most of the parish registers of this county can be searched by Heritage World (see Research Services at the end of the chapter) for a fee.

Aghadrum
Earliest Records: b. 1821–; m. 1821–; d. 1821–
Status: LC

Aghalurcher (Lisnaskea)
Earliest Records: b. 1867–; m. 1845–; d. 1870–
Status: LC; RCBL (mf)

Aghaveagh (or Aghavea)
Earliest Records: b. 1815–; m. 1815–; d. 1815–
Status: LC; RCBL (mf) (b. 1857-83; m. 1853-1907; d. 1859-)

Belleek
Earliest Records: b. 1820–; m. 1823–; d. 1822–
Status: LC; RCBL (mf)

Bohoe
Status: Lost

Clabby
Earliest Records: b. 1862
Status: LC

Cleenish
Earliest Records: b. 1886-1947; m. 1845-1934; d. 1886-1922
Status: LC; RCBL (mf)

Clones (Aghadrimsee)
Earliest Records: b. 1829-1927; m. 1829-1935; d. 1829-1890
Status: LC; RCBL (mf)

Coolaghty
Earliest Records: b. 1835; m. 1844
Status: LC

Derrybrusk
Status: Lost

Derryvullan North
Earliest Records: b. 1803; m. 1803; d. 1803
Status: LC

Derryvullan South
Status: Lost

Devenish
Earliest Records: b. 1800; m. 1800; d. 1800
Status: LC

Drumkeeran
Earliest Records: b. 1873–; m. 1845–
Status: RCBL (mf) and LC (b/m/d. 1801)

Drummully
Earliest Records: b. 1802; m. 1812; d. 1812
Status: LC

Enniskillen
Earliest Records: b. 1667–; m. 1668–; d. 1667–
Status: LC; RCBL (extracts to 1789); GO 578 and SLC film 992663 (extracts for b/m/d. 1666-1826)

Galloon
Earliest Records: b. 1798; m. 1798; d. 1798
Status: LC

Garrison
Earliest Records: b. 1879–; m. 1849–; d. 1877–
Status: LC; RCBL (mf)

Garvary
Status: Lost

Innismacsaint
Earliest Records: b/m/d. 1660-1672, 1800–
Status: LC; NAI M5148; GO 578; SLC film 992663

Killesher
Earliest Records: b. 1798; m. 1798; d. 1798
Status: LC

Kiltumon
Earliest Records: b. 1861
Status: LC

Kinawley
Earliest Records: b. 1761; m. 1761; d. 1761
Status: LC

Lisbellaw
Status: Lost

Lisnaskea
Earliest Records: b. 1804; m. 1804; d. 1804
Status: LC

Magheracross
Earliest Records: b. 1800; m. 1800; d. 1800
Status: LC

Magheraculmoney
Earliest Records: b. 1767; m. 1767; d. 1767
Status: LC

Maguiresbridge
Earliest Records: b. 1840; m. 1840; d. 1840
Status: LC

Muckross
Status: Lost

Mullaghadun
Earliest Records: b. 1819–; m. 1819–; d. 1819–
Status: LC; RCBL (mf) (to 1836 for b., 1927 for m/d.)

Mullaghfad
Earliest Records: b. 1878–; m. 1906–
Status: LC; RCBL (mf)

Rossory
Earliest Records: b. 1799; m. 1799; d. 1799
Status: LC

Sallaghy
Status: Lost

Slavin
Status: Lost

Templecarn
Earliest Records: b. 1825; m. 1825; d. 1825
Status: LC

Tempo
Earliest Records: b. 1836; m. 1836; d. 1836
Status: LC

Trory, St. Michael
Earliest Records: b. 1779; m. 1779; d. 1835
Status: LC

Presbyterian

An account of Presbyterian records is given in the introduction. These registers rarely contain death records, and occasionally have only records of births. This is indicated where appropriate. All are held in the local parish unless otherwise indicated. Copies of many are also held at the Public Record Office of Northern Ireland (PRONI).

Aughentaine
Starting Date: 1836
Status: LC; PRONI MIC 1P/80

Ballyhobridge
Starting Date: 1846
Status: LC; PRONI MIC 1P/274

Cavanleck
Starting Date: 1819
Status: LC; PRONI MIC 1P/80

Enniskillen
Starting Date: 1819
Status: LC; PRONI MIC 1P/282

Irvinestown
Starting Date: 1842
Status: LC; PRONI MIC 1P/66

Lisbellaw
Starting Date: 1851
Status: LC; PRONI MIC 1P/284

Maguiresbridge
Starting Date: 1845
Status: LC; PRONI MIC 1P/69

Pettigo
Starting Date: 1844

Tempo
Starting Date: 1845
Status: LC; PRONI MIC 1P/9

Roman Catholic

Note that most of the Catholic parish registers of this county have been indexed by Irish World (see Research Services at the end of the chapter). A search of the index will be conducted by the center for a fee. Those indexed are noted as "Indexed by Irish World." Microfilm copies of all registers are also available in the National Library of Ireland (NLI), and through the LDS library system.

Civil Parish: Aghalurcher
Map Grid: 17
RC Parish: Aghalurcher (Lisnaskea)
Diocese: CG
Earliest Record: b. 10.1835
Status: LC; NLI (mf); Indexed by Irish World

Civil Parish: Aghavea
Map Grid: 16
RC Parish: Aghavea or Aghintaine
Diocese: CG
Earliest Record: b. 3.1862; m. 5.1866
Status: LC; NLI (mf); Indexed by Irish World

Civil Parish: Belleek
Map Grid: 2
RC Parish: Templecarn (Pettigoe)
Diocese: CG
Earliest Record: b. 3.1851; m. 1.1836
Status: LC; NLI (mf); Indexed by Irish World

Civil Parish: Boho
Map Grid: 13
RC Parish: Derrygonnelly, see Devenish (2)
Diocese: CG

Civil Parish: Cleenish
Map Grid: 14
RC Parish: Cleenish
Diocese: CG
Earliest Record: b. 12.1835; m. 4.1866
Missing Dates: b. 9.1839-2.1859
Status: LC; NLI (mf); Indexed by Irish World

Civil Parish: Clones (see also Co. Monaghan)
Map Grid: 18
RC Parish: Rosslea
Diocese: CG
Earliest Record: b. 1.1862; m. 1.1862
Status: LC; NLI (mf); Indexed by Irish World

Civil Parish: Currin
Map Grid: 19
RC Parish: Currin, Killeevan, and Aughabog
Diocese: CG
Status: LC; NLI (mf); Indexed by Irish World

Civil Parish: Derrybrusk
Map Grid: 11
RC Parish: see Enniskillen (2)
Diocese: CG

Civil Parish: Derryvullan
Map Grid: 5
RC Parish: see Enniskillen
Diocese: CG

Civil Parish: Devenish (1)
Map Grid: 7
RC Parish: Devenish (Irvinestown); also
Derrygonnelly, see below
Diocese: CG
Earliest Record: b. 11.1846; m. 12.1851
Status: LC; NLI (mf); Indexed by Irish World

Civil Parish: Devenish (2)
Map Grid: 7
RC Parish: Derrygonnelly (Botha)
Diocese: CG

Earliest Record: b. 2.1853
Status: LC; NLI (mf); Indexed by Irish World

Civil Parish: Drumkeeran
Map Grid: 1
RC Parish: see Magheraculmoney
Diocese: CG

Civil Parish: Drummully (see also Co. Monaghan)
Map Grid: 23
RC Parish: part Galloon
Diocese: CG

Civil Parish: Enniskillen (1)
Map Grid: 12
RC Parish: Tempo (Pobal); also Enniskillen, see below
Diocese: CG
Earliest Record: b. 11.1845; m. 10.1845
Status: LC; NLI (mf); Indexed by Irish World

Civil Parish: Enniskillen (2)
Map Grid: 12
RC Parish: Enniskillen
Diocese: CG
Earliest Record: b. 1838; m. 2.1818
Missing Dates: b. 10.1870-8.1871
Status: LC; NLI (mf); Indexed by Irish World

Civil Parish: Galloon
Map Grid: 22
RC Parish: Galloon
Diocese: CG
Earliest Record: b. 1.1853; m. 5.1847
Missing Dates: b. 2.1859-6.1863
Status: LC; NLI (mf); Indexed by Irish World

Civil Parish: Inishmacsaint (see also Co. Donegal)
Map Grid: 6
RC Parish: Inishmacsaint; also part Derrygonnelly,
see Devenish
Diocese: CG
Earliest Record: b. 7.1860; m. 1.1860
Status: LC; NLI (mf); Indexed by Irish World

Civil Parish: Killesher
Map Grid: 15
RC Parish: Killesher
Diocese: KM
Earliest Record: b. 9.1855; m. 9.1855; d. 9.1855
Status: LC; NLI (mf); Indexed by Irish World

Civil Parish: Kinawley
Map Grid: 20
RC Parish: Kinawley
Diocese: KM
Earliest Record: b. 12.1835; m. 12.1835; d. 4.1853
Missing Dates: m. 3.1857-1.1870
Status: LC; NLI (mf); Indexed by Irish World

Civil Parish: Magheracross
Map Grid: 9
RC Parish: see Enniskillen (1)
Diocese: CG

Civil Parish: Magheraculmoney
Map Grid: 4
RC Parish: Culmaine or Magheraculmoney (Ederney)
Diocese: CG
Earliest Record: b. 8.1836; m. 11.1837
Status: LC; NLI (mf); Indexed by Irish World

Civil Parish: Rossory
Map Grid: 8
RC Parish: see Enniskillen (2)
Diocese: CG

Civil Parish: Templecarn
Map Grid: 3
RC Parish: see Belleek
Diocese: CG

Civil Parish: Tomregan
Map Grid: 21
RC Parish: see Co. Cavan
Diocese: KM

Civil Parish: Trory
Map Grid: 10
RC Parish: see Enniskillen

Commercial and Social Directories

1824

J. Pigot's *City of Dublin and Hibernian Provincial Directory* includes traders, nobility, gentry, and clergy lists of Churchill, Enniskillen, Irvinestown, and Maguiresbridge.

1839

Sligo Independent Sligo/Derry Directory lists Enniskillen traders, etc. GO Ms 626; SLC film 100179.

1841

Martin's *Belfast Directory* lists residents of principal streets, gentry, and traders in Enniskillen and Irvinestown.

1846

Slater's *National Commercial Directory of Ireland* lists nobility, clergy, traders, etc., in Enniskillen, Lisnaskea, Maguiresbridge and Brookeborough, and Lowtherstown.

1848

MacCloskie, Charles. *The Handbooks or Directory for the County of Fermanagh.* Armagh: The Guardian Office. Lists householders of main towns of Fermanagh.

1880

Lowe's *Fermanagh Directory and Household Almanac.* Lists householders of main towns of Fermanagh.

1852

Henderson's *Belfast and Province of Ulster Directory* has lists of inhabitants, traders, etc., in and around the town of Enniskillen. Further editions were issued in 1854, 1856, 1858, 1861, 1863, 1865, 1868, 1870, 1877, 1880, 1884, 1890, 1894, and 1900.

1856

Slater's *Royal National Commercial Directory of Ireland* lists nobility, gentry, clergy, traders, etc., in Enniskillen, Lisnaskea, and Lowtherstown.

1870

Slater's *Directory of Ireland* contains trade, nobility, and clergy lists for Enniskillen, Lisnaskea, Maguiresbridge and Brookeborough, and Lowtherstown.

1880

Lowe's *Fermanagh Directory and Household Almanac* lists householders of Belleek, Brookborough, Belcoo, Derrygonnelly, Irvinestown, Lisbellaw, Newtownbutler, Pettigo, Rosslea, Ederney, Lack, Maguiresbridge, Tempo, Kesh, Enniskillen. New Edition. Republished. Belfast: Friars Bush Press, 1990. ISBN: 0946872-295.

1881

Slater's *Royal National Commercial Directory of Ireland* contains lists of traders, clergy, nobility, and farmers in adjoining parishes of the towns of Enniskillen, Lisnaskea, and Lowtherstown.

1891

Derry Almanac and Directory has a list of traders in Enniskillen (published annually thereafter).

1894

Slater's *Royal National Directory of Ireland* lists traders, police, teachers, farmers, and private residents in each of the towns, villages, and parishes of the county.

Family History

Each of the Fermanagh families is briefly documented in *The Fermanagh Story*, by P. Livingstone, and *Cumann Seanchais Clochair*, 1969.

Archdale, Henry Blackwood. Memoirs of the Archdales with the descents of some allied families. Enniskillen: *Impartial Reporter*, 1925.

"Bredin of Drumcagh, Co. Fermanagh." Pedigree in *Swanzy Notebooks*. RCB Library, Dublin.

Brooke, Victor. A memoir of his life and extracts from his letters. Oscar Leslie Stephen. London: John Murray, 1894.

Internet information on Cassidy is at http://expo.nua.ie/dagda/families/cassidy.html.

Lowry-Corry, Somerset Richard. *The History of the Corry Family of Castlecoole.* London: Longmans, Green & Co., 1891.

Cole, Maud Lowry. *Memoirs of Sir (Galbraith) Lowry Cole.* London: Macmillan & Co., 1934.

"Clogherici: the Connollys of Fermanagh and Co. Monaghan." *Clogher Record* 2 (1957): 172–76.

"Coulson of Belmont." Pedigree in *Swanzy Notebooks.* RCB Library, Dublin.

Downey—see Co. Sligo.

"Fawcett of Co. Fermanagh." Pedigree in *Swanzy Notebooks.* RCB Library, Dublin.

"Fiddes of Co. Fermanagh." Pedigree in *Swanzy Notebooks.* RCB Library, Dublin.

Fuller, J.F. *Pedigree of the Hamilton Family of Fermanagh and Tyrone.* London, 1889.

Belmore, Earl of. "Monea Castle: Co. Fermanagh, and the Hamiltons." *Ulster J. Arch.* 2nd ser. 1 (1895): 195–208, 256–77.

Swanzy, Henry Biddall. *Some account of the family of Hassard with a list of descendants in England and Ireland.* Dublin: Alex. Thom & Co., 1903.

"The Irwins of Fermanagh and Donegal." *Ir. Gen.* 1 (1941): 278–83.

"The Johnstons of Correnney, Co. Fermanagh." *Ir. Gen.* 1 (1941): 321.

Swanzy, Henry Biddall. *The families of French of Belturbet and Nixon of Fermanagh and their descendants.* Dublin: Alex. Thom & Co., 1908.

Ua Duinnin, An t'Athair P. *The Maguires of Fermanagh.* Dublin: Gill, 1917, p. 140.

Internet information on Maguire is at http://skynet.ul.ie/~ger/maguire/history.html.

"Ovens of Fermanagh." Pedigree in *Swanzy Notebooks.* RCB Library.

"Ramadge." *Clogher Record* 10 (1) 1979.

Swanzy, H.B. *Later History of the Family of Rosborough of Mullinagoan, Co. Fermanagh.* 1897.

Moran, T. Whitley. *The Whitleys of Enniskillen.* Hoylake, 1962.

Steele, John Haughton. *Genealogy of the Earls of Erne.* Edinburgh: T&A Constable, 1910.

Gravestone Inscriptions

Irish World (see Research Services at the end of the chapter) has indexed a huge range of gravestone inscriptions from graveyards in Tyrone and Fermanagh. The full list is not included here for reasons of space. This index can be searched for a fee. Other sources of gravestone inscriptions are:

Aghalurcher: *Clogher Record* 2 (2) (1958): 328–52.

Aghavea: *Clogher Record* 4 (1): 95–112; 4 (2) (1960–61).

Devenish (St. Molaise's and Devenish Abbey): MacKenna, Rev. J. E., and F. Bigger. *Devenish, Its History, Antiquities and Traditions.* 1897.

Donagh: *Clogher Record* 1 (3) (1955): 141–48.

Drumully: *Clogher Record* 1 (2) (1954): 35–38.

Enniskillen: Dundas, W. H. *Enniskillen Parish and Town.* 1913.

Galoon: *Clogher Record* 10 (2) (1980): 264–68.

Holywell: *Clogher Record* 2 (1) (1957): 138–47.

Kinawley: *Clogher Record* 1 (4) (1956): 161–65.

Monea: Steele, Rev. William B. *The Parish of Devenish, Co. Fermanagh.* 1937.

Templenafrin: *Clogher Record* 2 (1) (1957): 138–47.

Tullynageeran: *Clogher Record* 2 (3) (1959): 521–23.

Newspapers

Title: *Enniskillen Advertiser*
Published in: Enniskillen, 1864–76
BL Holdings: 7.1864–9.1876

Title: *Enniskillen Chronicle* (continued as *Fermanagh Mail and Enniskillen Chronicle* in 1885)
Published in: Enniskillen, 1808–93
NLI Holdings: odd numbers 1808–11; 1.1824–5.1849; odd numbers 1885; 1.1886–12.1892
BL Holdings: 1.1824–5.1849; 8.1849–11.1850; 3.1851–7.1893

Title: *Fermanagh News*
Published in: Enniskillen, 1894–1920
NLI Holdings: 1.1905–6.1907; 1.1972–in progress
BL Holdings: 7.1896–6.1907; 10.1907–5.1920

Title: *Fermanagh Times*
Published in: Enniskillen, 1880–1949
NLI Holdings: 9.1921–4.1949
BL Holdings: 3.1880–4.1949 (except 1930)

Title: *Impartial Reporter*
Published in: Enniskillen, 1825–current
NLI Holdings: 1.1894–12.1902
BL Holdings: 5.1825–5.1873; 4.1879–12.1925; 1.1927–in progress

Wills and Administrations

A discussion of the types of records, where they are held, and their availability and value is given in the Wills section of the introduction. The availability of prerogative wills, administrations, and marriage license records is also described in the relevant parts of the same section. Where available, published sources of these records are given in the Miscellaneous Sources section.

Pre-1858 Wills and Administrations

Prerogative Wills. See the introduction.

Consistorial Wills. County Fermanagh is mainly in the diocese of Clogher, with three parishes in the diocese of Kilmore. The guide to Catholic parish records in this chapter shows the diocese to which each parish belonged. The wills of residents of each diocese were usually proven within that diocese (see the Wills section for exceptions). The following records survive:

Wills

See the introduction.

Abstracts

See the introduction.

Indexes

Clogher (1661–1858); Kilmore—see Co. Cavan. Index to Kilmore Diocesan Wills, pub. by P. Smythe-Wood; SLC film 990068.

Post-1858 Wills and Administrations

County Fermanagh was served by the District Registry of Armagh. The surviving records are kept in the PRONI. Armagh District Will Books (1858–1900). PRONI; SLC films 917201, 917484–92, 917906–16. Other collections are "Upton Papers," abstracts from Cavan, Longford, and Westmeath, RIA Library.

Marriage Licenses

Indexes

Clogher (1709–1866). NAI; SLC film 100862. Kilmore (1691–1845). NAI; SLC film 100869.

Miscellaneous Sources

"English Settlement in Co. Fermanagh, 1610–1640." *Clogher Record* 10 (1) (1979): 137–43.

Maguire, Thomas. *Fermanagh–Its native chiefs and clans.* Omagh: S. D. Montgomery, 1954.

"High Sheriffs of Fermanagh, 1605–1903." Appendix U. *The History of Two Ulster Manors.* Earl of Belmore. London/Dublin, 1903.

Livingstone, Peader. *The Fermanagh Story. A documented history of the County Fermanagh from the earliest times to the present day.* Clogher Historical Society, 1974.

Provisional list of pre-1900 School Registers in the PRONI. *Ulster Gen. & Hist. Guild* 9 (1986): 60–71. Lists registers and PRONI reference numbers for all NI counties.

"The Scotch Settlement of Co. Fermanagh, 1610–30." *Clogher Record* 9 (2) (1976/78): 367–73.

"The Volunteer Companies of Ulster, 1778–1793, 6 Fermanagh." *Irish Sword* 8 (31): 92–94 (some offic-

ers' names only).

Workhouse Records: Records of Enniskillen Union Workhouse (1845–1913). PRONI; SLC film 259148 –53; Records of Irvinestown Union Workhouse (1845–1918). PRONI; SLC film 259187–90.

Research Sources and Services

Journals

Clogher Record (published by Clogher Historical Society—see below)

North Irish Roots (published by North of Ireland Family History Society)

Libraries and Information Sources

Fermanagh Divisional Library, Hall's Lane, Enniskillen, Co. Fermanagh BT74 7DR, N. Ireland. Ph: (01365) 322886; fax: (01365) 324685. The Irish and Local History department holds an extensive collection of material of local interest. A "Local History Services" guidebook is available, which details the extent of these holdings. The holdings include a range of books on local subjects, photographs, maps, journals, directories, family and parish histories, and newspapers.

Fermanagh County Museum, Castle Barracks, Enniskillen, Co. Fermanagh

Ulster-American Folk Park Library. See Libraries in Co. Tyrone chapter

Research Services

See Research Services in Belfast in the introduction.

Heritage World, 26 Market Sq., Dungannon, Co. Tyrone BT70 1AB. Ph: (018687) 24187; fax: (01868) 752141; e-mail: irishwld@gpo.iol.ie. Homepage: http://www.iol.ie/irishworld/. This organization is the official IGP indexing center for Fermanagh and Tyrone. It has compiled one of the largest databases of family history information in the country. This includes church records, gravestone inscriptions from seven hundred graveyards, civil records of birth, death, and marriage, census and land records, etc. The database can be searched for a fee. They have also published books on local history subjects, and produce coats of arms and related products. Researchers are advised to contact the center for an updated list of registers, and other sources, indexed. Research will be conducted for a fee.

Societies

Clogher Historical Society, Mr. J. I. D. Johnston, Corick, Clogher, Co. Tyrone. This society publishes *Clogher Record*, which deals with the social, church, political, archaeological, and genealogical history of the diocese of Clogher. This covers Co. Fermanagh, as well as Monaghan, South Tyrone, and a small part of Donegal around Ballyshannon. The journal is a particularly important source of information on these counties, as can be seen from the number of references to its pages in this chapter.

North of Ireland Family History Society, Queens University of Belfast, Dept. of Education, 69 University Street, Belfast BT7 1HL. Publishers of *North Irish Roots*

Belcoo and District Historical Society, Ms. Margaret M. Gallagher, The Enterprise Centre, Railway Road, Belcoo, Co. Fermanagh. Ph: (01365) 386536

Fermanagh Naturalists' Field Club, Mr. Edmund Richey, Algeo Drive, Enniskillen, Co. Fermanagh BT74 6JL. Ph: (01365) 322104

Fermanagh Civil Parishes as Numbered on Map

1. Drumkeeran
2. Belleek
3. Templecarn
4. Magheraculmoney
5. Derryvullan (5 pts.)
6. Inishmacsaint
7. Devenish
8. Rossorry
9. Magheracross (3 pts.)
10. Trory (3 pts.)
11. Derrybrusk (3 pts.)
12. Enniskillen (3 pts.)
13. Boho (2 pts.)
14. Cleenish
15. Killesher
16. Aghavea (2 pts.)
17. Aghalurcher (2 pts.)
18. Clones (2 pts.)
19. Currin
20. Kinawley
21. Tomregan
22. Galloon
23. Drummully (2 pts.)

Civil Parishes in Alphabetical Order

Aghavea (2 pts.): 16
Aghalurcher (2 pts.): 17
Belleek: 2
Boho (2 pts.): 13
Cleenish: 14
Clones (2 pts.): 18
Currin: 19
Derrybrusk (3 pts.): 11
Derryvullan (5 pts.): 5
Devenish: 7
Drumkeeran: 1
Drummully (2 pts.): 23
Enniskillen (3 pts.): 12
Galloon: 22
Inishmacsaint: 6
Killesher: 15
Kinawley: 20
Magheracross (3 pts.): 9
Magheraculmoney: 4
Rossorry: 8
Trory (3 pts.): 10
Templecarn: 3
Tomregan: 21

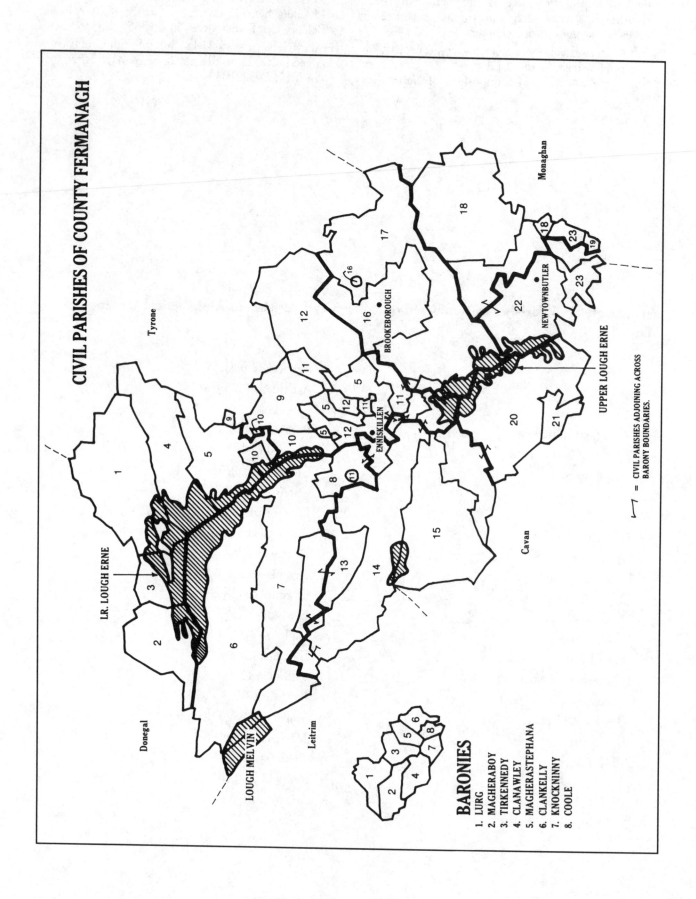

CIVIL PARISHES OF COUNTY FERMANAGH

Tyrone

Monaghan

18

17

16

BROOKEBOROUGH

18

23

19

NEWTOWNBUTLER

23

22

12

11

9

5

5

12

11

11

ENNISKILLEN

20

21

10

10

12

5

12

UPPER LOUGH ERNE

9

10

4

10

8

11

LR. LOUGH ERNE

5

15

Cavan

3

7

13

2

6

14

Donegal

Leitrim

LOUGH MELVIN

$\sqcap$ = CIVIL PARISHES ADJOINING ACROSS
BARONY BOUNDARIES.

BARONIES

1
2
3
5
6
4
7
8

1. LURG
2. MAGHERABOY
3. TIRKENNEDY
4. CLANAWLEY
5. MAGHERASTEPHANA
6. CLANKELLY
7. KNOCKNINNY
8. COOLE

County Galway

A Brief History

The county of Galway is on the west coast and contains the city of Galway and the towns of Tuam, Ballinasloe, Athenry, and Loughrea. The east of the county is relatively good farmland, while the west, the area known as Connemara, is rocky and barren. In this area, and on the offshore islands, particularly the Aran islands, the Irish language is still the everyday language.

Before the redivision of the country into counties, the west of the county was the territory of Iar-Connacht. The major Gaelic families of the county were O'Halloran, O'Daly, O'Kelly, O'Flaherty, O'Malley, O'Madden, O'Fallon, O'Naughton, O'Mullaly, and O'Hynes.

The town of Galway was a prominent trading port from early times. It was also reputed to be one of the landmarks in the ancient division of Ireland (in the second century A.D.) into the northerly half, Leath-Cuin, controlled by Conn-Cead-Cathac, and the southerly Leath-Mogha, controlled by Eoghan, King of Munster. The fortunes of the town from earliest times have been documented in Hardiman's *History of Galway*. The city was destroyed on several occasions by local raids, fire, and by Danish Vikings, but was rebuilt. After the Norman invasion, the whole Kingdom of Connaught, including Galway, was granted to Richard de Burgo, or Burke. However, because of the power of the existing chieftains, de Burgo only took control of part of the south of the county. One of the families who arrived with the Burkes were the Birminghams. Another family which settled in the north of the county was the Joyces. The part of the county in which they settled is still known as "Joyce's country." The de Burgos fortified the town of Galway and established it as a major center, trading with Spain and Portugal. The Normans gradually assimilated with the local people and, apart from the town of Galway itself, adopted Irish custom and dress.

The fourteen major merchant families in the city, known as the "Tribes of Galway," were Athy, Blake, Bodkin, Browne, Darcy, Deane, Font, French, Joyce, Kirwan, Lynch, Martin, Morris, and Skerrett. These families dominated Galway town, which became a center of commercial activity in the province. As the power of the English receded in the province of Connaught, the town remained a bastion of English customs and language. The county of Galway and the other Connaught counties were established in 1584 by Sir Henry Sidney. Many of the native and Norman chieftains submitted at this time and promised their allegiance to the English crown.

The Catholics of Galway joined the general rebellion of the Catholic Confederacy (see Co. Kilkenny) in 1641. The city itself was a stronghold of the rebels, but was finally taken by the Parliamentarians after a nine-month siege in 1652. The town and county suffered badly in the aftermath of this rebellion. It is calculated that over one third of the population perished through famine, disease, or at the hands of the victorious English parliamentary forces. In addition, over one thousand people were taken and sold as slaves to the West Indies.

Although the estates of the leaders of this rebellion were confiscated and given to English adventurers and soldiers, many of these properties were returned after the restoration of King Charles.

County Galway was very badly affected by the Great Famine of 1845–47. The population, which in 1841 was 442,000, had fallen to 322,000 by 1851. Over 73,000 people died in the county between 1845 and 1850, and approximately eleven percent of the population emigrated in the succeeding five years. Through continued emigration, the population fell to 215,000 by 1891, and is approximately 172,000 today. An excellent detailed history of Galway is available on an Internet site at http://www.wombat.ie/galwayguide/archive.cgi/history/hardiman.

Census and Census Substitutes

1574

"Galway Castles and Owners in 1574." *J. Galway Arch. & Hist. Soc.* 1 (2) (1901): 109–23.

1585

"The Compossicion Booke of Conought." The written account between the landowners of Connaught and the Crown, for the purpose of obtaining title and rent. Dublin: Stationery Office, 1936.

1599

Description of the County of Galway with the Names of the Principal Inhabitants. NLI P1707.

1636–1703

Books of Survey and Distribution, County of Galway. Abstracts of various surveys and instruments of title. R.C. Simington. Dublin: Stationery Office, 1962.

1640

"Irish Papist Proprietors in Galway Town." In *History of the Town and County of Galway* by James Hardiman, Dublin, 1820. Appendix 7; SLC film 990403.

1657

"English Protestant Proprietors." In *History of the Town and County of Galway* by James Hardiman, Dublin, 1820. Appendix 7; SLC film 990403.

1659

"Census" of Ireland. Ed. by S. Pender. Dublin: Stationery Office, 1939. NLI I6551. SLC film 924648.

1727

"A Galway Election List." *J. Galway Arch. & Hist. Soc.* 35 (1976): 105–28 (lists all entitled to vote, i.e., Protestants, and also classified list according to trade; some comments, e.g., "Popish wife," etc.).

1749

"Census of Elphin Diocese; householders, occupations, number and religion of children and number of servants in parishes of Ahascragh, Athleague, Ballynakill,

Drimatemple, Dunamon, Kilbegnet, Kilcroan, Killian, Killosolan." NAI M 2466; SLC film 101781.

1775

"Catholic Qualification Roll Extracts" (eighty-four names, addresses, and occupations). 59th Report DKPRI: 50–84.

1791

"Survey of the Town of Loughrea." *J. Galway Arch. & Hist. Soc.* 23 (3) (1951): 95–110 (gives names of residents on each street and size of holding).

1794

"Names of Roman Catholic Freemen of Galway Town." *J. Galway Arch. & Hist. Soc.* 9 (1) (1915): 62–64 (gives list of three hundred names only).

1798

"List of Convicted Rebels from Galway." *J. Galway Arch. & Hist. Soc.* 25 (3, 4) (1953): 104–33 (list of 130 names, occupations, addresses, and fate).

"List of Persons who Suffered Loss in '98 Rebellion." NLI JLB 94107 (approximately one hundred names, addresses, and occupations).

1801–06

"Inhabitants of Killalaghten Catholic Parish." Included in parish records of Cappataggle (see Killalaghten). NLI P2431.

1805

"Tenants of J.P. Smyth at Gort, Co. Galway in 1805." *Ir. Anc.* 14 (1) (1982): 20–21.

1810–1819

"Index to Persons in . . . Account books of C. St. George, Oranmore." *Ir. Gen.* 7 (1) (1986): 101–112.

1821

"Government Census Remnants: parishes of Aran, Athenry, Kilconickney, Kilconerin, Killimoredaly, Kilreekil, Kiltullagh and Lickerrig." Medlycott. NAI CEN 1821/18–25 and SLC film 597734.

Extracts from 1821 Government Census for Galway City. *Utah Gen. and Hist. Mag.* 4 (1918): 75–79.

1821–29

Marriages in the Roman Catholic Diocese of Tuam, 1821–1829. Indexed. USA: Heritage Books, 1993. Original in NLI film P4222.

1824–44

Tithe Applotment Survey (see introduction).

Houses, &c.	Proprieters in 1640, Irish Papists.	Proprietors in 1657, Eng. Protestants.	Yearly value, if to be let for years.		
			£.	s.	d.
A thatched house.	John Blake Fitz-Robert.	——	0	8	0
Do.	Thomas Browne.	Captain Bird.	1.	5	0
A dwelling-house, covered with slate, three stories, with a yard.	Stephen Browne.	Thomas Williams.	7	10	0
Ditto, two stories,—a thatched house backward, one story high, with a back-side.	Thomas Nolan.	George Duffett.	12	0	0
Do. two stories, with do.	Do.	Thomas Marshell.	11	10	0
Two do. three stories, with do.	John Martin Fitz-Geffery.	Blanerhassett Wells.	13	0	0
Do. with back-house slated, one story	Do.	George Burwast.	16	0	0
Do. three stories,—a back-house slated, three stories, and a yard.	Mathew Martyn.	Thomas Symper.	14	0	0
A dwelling-house thatched, one story	James Lynch Fitz-Marcus.	Jarvis Hines.	1	15	0

A SCHEDULE CONTAINING A SURVEY AND VALUATION OF SOE MANY OF THE HOUSES IN THE TOWN OF GALWAY, WITH THE GARDENS, ORCHARDS AND EDIFICES, AND THEIR APPURTENANCES, AS ARE SET OUT PURSUANT TO SAID ADDITIONAL ACT.

Extract from a list of houses in the town of Galway showing their proprietors ("Irish Papists") before the Catholic Rebellion of 1641, and in 1656, when most of the properties had been confiscated and given to English adventurers and soldiers—i.e., "English Protestants." From *The History of the Town and County of Galway from the Earliest Period to the Present Time* by James Hardiman (Dublin, 1820).

1827

Protestant Parishioners of Aughrim (names of parents and children, plus ages of latter in Aughrim C of I parish register). NAI film 5359. NAI Ms 359.

1832-36

"Names of Holders and of Applicants for Licenses to Sell Liquor in Galway" (names and addresses). *Parl. Papers* 1837/38, 13 (2): Appendix 10.

1834

Parochial census of Kinvara. Held by Galway Family Hist. Soc. West (see Research Services at end of chapter).

1837

"List of those Made Freemen of Galway Since 1831" (names, occupations, and residences). *Parl. Papers* 1837, 2 (1): Appendix B1; 1837/38, 13 (2): Appendix 3.

The Names and Residences of Several Persons in the City of Galway who Were Discharged from Payment of Rates and Taxes. Reports from Committees. *Parl. Papers* 1837, 11 (1) (39): 206-10.

"Occupants of Galway, Arranged by Street, Giving Property Values." *Parl. Papers* 1837, 11 (1): Appendix G, 206-10.

1839

List of persons who obtained Game Certificates in Galway. PRONI T 688.

1839-46

"List of Subscribers to RC Chapel at Dunmore" (gives names, townlands, and subscription). In Catholic Church Records of Dunmore. NLI P4211.

1848-49

"Emigrants from Irvilloughter and Boughill" (parts of Ahascragh and Taghboy respectively—names, ages, and relationships of 410 people, dates of departure and arrival). In Ellis, E. *Emigrants from Ireland 1847-52*. Baltimore: Genealogical Publishing Co., 1977, pp. 22-41.

1853-56

Griffith's Valuation (see introduction).

1884/95

Parochial census of Spiddal. Held by Galway Family Hist. Soc. West (see Research Services at end of chapter). Contains information similar to 1901 government census.

1901

Census. NAI (see introduction). SLC (mf).

1911
Census. NAI.

Church Records

Church of Ireland

Many Church of Ireland records were lost in the PRO fire of 1922 (see introduction). These are indicated as "Lost." However, as C of I records were effectively state records, the records of marriage (from 1845) are also in the General Registrar's Office. Many are still in local custody (LC), while others are in one of a variety of other archives (e.g., RCBL or NAI). Many of the Galway parish registers have been indexed by the county's two heritage centers, East Galway Family History Society and Galway Family History Society West (see Research Services). The centers will conduct searches of their indexes for a fee. Those indexed are noted as "Indexed by East GFHS" or "by GFHS West." Also, the Aughrim Parish History Project is indexing twenty-three of the registers of Clonfert diocese in East Galway. Details are available from Canon T. Sullivan, The Rectory, Aughrim, Ballinasloe, Co. Galway. Ph./fax: (353) 905 73849.

Ahascragh
Earliest Records: b. 1785-1872; m. 1785-1859; d. 1787-1875
Status: LC; NAI MFCI 6, M5354; SLC film 962187

Annaghdown
Status: Lost

Ardrahan
Earliest Records: b. 1804-; d. 1857-
Status: LC; NAI M5253/4 (b. 1804-71; d. 1857-79); SLC film 990092 (1804-75)

Arran
Status: Lost

Athenry
Earliest Records: b. 1796-; m. 1796-; d. 1795-
Status: LC; NAI M5147B (1796-1827); also Indexed by GFHS West (1826-1900); SLC film 924521 (1795-1828) and SLC film 1279207-09 (1858-1919)

Aughrim
Earliest Records: b. 1814-; m. 1814-; d. 1822-
Status: LC; NAI MFCI 6 (b. 1814-75; m. 1814-42; d. 1822-72)

Ballinacourty
Earliest Records: b. 1834
Status: LC

Ballinakill
Earliest Records: b. 1775-; m. 1792-; d. 1803-
Status: RCBL; also NAI MFCI 31 (b. 1852-72; d. 1852-78); Indexed by GFHS West (1831-1900); SLC film 1279258 (1852-1964)

Ballinasloe—see Creagh

Ballymacward
Status: Lost

Castleblakeney
Status: Lost

Castlekirke
Earliest Records: b. 1879-1925; d. 1879-1963
Status: RCBL

Clifden (Omey)
Earliest Records: b. 1831-; m. 1831-; d. 1832-
Status: LC; NAI MFCI 35; M6088 (b. to 1887, m. to 1844, and d. to 1900); also Indexed (to 1900) by GFHS West; SLC film 1279258

Clonfert
Status: Lost

Clontuskart
Earliest Records: d. 1843-
Status: LC; NAI M5353 (to 1870)

Creagh (Ballinasloe)
Earliest Records: b. 1809-; m. 1808-; d. 1823-
Status: LC; also NAI MFCI 6, M5360 (b. 1809-73; m. 1808-45; d. 1824-71)

Dononaughta
Status: Lost

Dunmore
Earliest Records: b. 1884-1914; m. 1846-1903; d. 1887-1938
Status: RCBL

Errislanon
Status: Lost

Errismore
Status: Lost

Eyrecourt
Status: GO 701 (extracts); SLC film 257807

Headford
Earliest Records: b. 1888-; m. 1845-; d. 1885-
Status: RCBL

Inniscaltra
Earliest Records: b. 1851-; d. 1851-
Status: LC; NAI MFCI 4, M5234 (1851-74)

Kilcolgan
Status: Lost

Kilconickny
Status: Lost

Kilconnell
Status: Lost

Kilconla
Earliest Records: m. 1846-1906
Status: RCBL

Kilcummin
Earliest Records: b. 1812–; m. 1812–; d. 1812–
Status: LC; NAI MFCI 33 and LC (b/m/d 1812–76);
also Indexed to 1900 by GFHS West

Kilkerrin
Status: Lost

Killannin
Earliest Records: b. 1844–
Status: LC

Killeraght
Earliest Records: m. 1846–1936
Status: RCBL

Killererin
Earliest Records: b. 1811–28; m. 1818–28; d. 1818
Status: RCBL (extracts)

Killinane
Status: Lost

Killyon and Kilroran
Status: Lost

Kilmacduagh
Earliest Records: b. 1787–; m. 1811–; d. 1827–
Status: LC

Kilmoylan
Earliest Records: b. 1866
Status: RCBL

Kiltormer
Status: Lost

Lickmolassy
Earliest Records: b. 1766–; m. 1762–; d. 1800–
Status: LC

Loughrea
Earliest Records: b. 1747–; m. 1747–; d. 1747–
Status: LC; also NAI MFCI 5, M5222 (b. 1808–73;
m. 1819–45; d. 1819–72)

Monivea
Earliest Records: b. 1874–; d. 1881–
Status: LC; NLI (mf); Indexed (to 1900) by GFHS
West

Moylough
Earliest Records: b. 1826–1922; m. 1823–1844; d.
1843–1940
Status: RCBL; also NAI MS 7924 (b. 1762–1804; m.
1828); NAI MFCI 35 (b. 1827–1922; m. 1826–44; d.
1847–1919)

Moyrus (Beauchamp)—see Roundstone

Omey—see Clifden

Rahoon
Status: Lost

Renvyle
Earliest Records: b. 1884–; m. 1869–; d. 1871–
Status: RCBL; also Indexed (to 1900) by GFHS West

Ross
Earliest Records: m. 1856–1950
Status: RCBL

Roundstone (Moyrus or Beauchamp)
Earliest Records: b. 1841–; m. 1845–; d. 1849–
Status: LC; NAI MFCI 35 (to 1871); also Indexed (to
1900) by GFHS West; SLC film 1279212 (1852–
1910)

St. Nicholas (Galway)
Earliest Records: b. 1792–; m. 1792–; d. 1838–
Status: LC

Sellerna
Earliest Records: b. 1897–; m. 1857–; d. 1849–
Status: RCBL; also Indexed (to 1900) by GFHS West

Taughmaconnell
Earliest Records: b. 1852–; d. 1845–
Status: LC; NAI M5279 (b. 1852–88; d. 1845–79)

Tuam
Earliest Records: b. 1808–; m. 1808–; d. 1808–
Status: LC; also NAI MFCI 7, M5351/2 (b. 1818–
71; m. 1831–40; d. 1829–75); also Indexed (to 1900)
by GFHS West

Tynagh
Status: Lost

Methodist

An account of Methodist records is given in the introduction. Some of the records have been indexed by the
Galway heritage centers (see Research Services at the
end of the chapter).

Ballinasloe
Records: b. 1834–1900
Status: LC; Indexed by East GFHS

Clifden
Records: b. 1865–; m. 1866–1888
Status: LC; NLI (mf); Indexed by GFHS West

Galway
Records: b. 1836–; m. 1866–
Status: LC; NLI (mf); Indexed by GFHS West

Oughterard
Records: b. 1860–69
Status: LC; NLI (mf); Indexed by GFHS West

Salthill
Records: m. 1886–1888
Status: LC; NLI (mf); Indexed by GFHS West

Presbyterian

An account of Presbyterian records is given in the introduction. These registers rarely contain death records,
and occasionally have only records of births. Some registers have been indexed (see Research Services at the
end of the chapter).

Ballinasloe
Records: b. 1846–; m. 1848
Status: LC; Indexed by East GFHS (to 1900)

Galway
Starting Date: b. 1833; m. 1849
Status: LC; Indexed by GFHS West (to 1900)

Roman Catholic

Note that most of the Catholic parish registers of this county have been indexed by one of the two heritage centers in the county, East Galway Family History Society and Galway Family History Society West (see Research Services at the end of the chapter). The centers will conduct searches of their indexes for a fee. Those indexed are noted as "Indexed by East GFHS" or by "GFHS West" as appropriate. Also note the publication "Marriages in the Roman Catholic Diocese of Tuam, 1821–1829," Heritage Books, 1993. This is an index of NLI film P4222 which lists approximately four thousand marriages not included in the individual parish registers. Microfilm copies of all registers are also available in NLI, and through the LDS library system.

Civil Parish: Abbeygormacan
Map Grid: 112
RC Parish: Mullagh and Killoran (Abbeygormacan)
Diocese: CF
Earliest Record: b. 2.1859; m. 4.1863
Status: LC; NLI (mf); Indexed (to 1900) by East GFHS

Civil Parish: Abbeyknockmoy
Map Grid: 41
RC Parish: Abbeyknockmoy
Diocese: TU
Earliest Record: m. 1821–; m. 1844–; d. 1847–48
Status: LC; NLI (mf); Indexed (to 1900) by GFHS West

Civil Parish: Addergoole
Map Grid: 10
RC Parish: Addergoole and Liskeevey (Miltown)
Diocese: TU
Earliest Record: b. 8.1858; m. 1.1821
Status: LC; NLI (mf); Indexed (to 1900) by GFHS West

Civil Parish: Ahascragh
Map Grid: 78
RC Parish: Ahascragh and Caltra
Diocese: EL
Earliest Record: b. 1.1840; m. 1.1866
Status: LC; NLI (mf); Indexed (to 1900) by East GFHS

Civil Parish: Annaghdown
Map Grid: 36
RC Parish: Annaghdown (Corrandulla)

Diocese: TU
Earliest Record: b. 9.1834; m. 3.1834
Missing Dates: b. 9.1869–2.1875; m. 11.1868–2.1875
Status: LC; NLI (mf); Indexed (to 1900) by GFHS West

Civil Parish: Ardrahan
Map Grid: 66
RC Parish: Ardrahan
Diocese: KMC
Earliest Record: b. 5.1839; m. 3.1845; d. 1878
Missing Dates: b. 3.1846–11.1866; m. 2.1850–2.1867
Status: LC; NLI (mf); Indexed (to 1900) by GFHS West

Civil Parish: Athenry
Map Grid: 69
RC Parish: Athenry
Diocese: TU
Earliest Record: b. 8.1858; m. 8.1821
Status: LC; NLI (mf); Indexed (1858–1900) by GFHS West

Civil Parish: Athleague (see also Co. Roscommon)
Map Grid: 49
RC Parish: Athleague and Fuerty
Diocese: EL
Earliest Record: b. 1.1808; m. 6.1808; d. 1.1807
Missing Dates: b. 5.1828–8.1834, 7.1864–1.1865; m. 2.1834–3.1836; d. ends 1837
Status: LC; NLI (mf); Indexed by RHGC (see Co. Roscommon)

Civil Parish: Aughrim
Map Grid: 77
RC Parish: Aughrim and Kilconnell
Diocese: CF
Earliest Record: b. 3.1828; m. 1829; d. 1825
Status: LC; NLI (mf); Indexed (to 1900) by East GFHS

Civil Parish: Ballinchalla
Map Grid: 6
RC Parish: see Cong, Co. Mayo
Diocese: TU

Civil Parish: Ballindoon (1)
Map Grid: 4
RC Parish: Omey and Ballindoon (Clifden); also Ballyconneely, see below
Diocese: CF
Earliest Record: b. 1.1838; m. 9.1839
Missing Dates: b. 10.1855–7.1856; m. 5.1855–8.1858
Status: LC; NLI (mf); Indexed (to 1900) by GFHS West

Civil Parish: Ballindoon (2)
Map Grid: 4

RC Parish: Ballyconneely
Earliest Dates: b. 1864-; m. 1864-; d. 1869-1877
Status: LC; NLI (mf); Indexed by GFHS West

Civil Parish: Ballinrobe
Map Grid: 5
RC Parish: see Ballinrobe, Co. Mayo
Diocese: TU

Civil Parish: Ballymacward
Map Grid: 46
RC Parish: Ballymacward (Clonkeenkerrill)
Diocese: CF
Earliest Record: b. 1856; m. 1885
Status: LC; NLI (mf); Indexed (to 1900) by East GFHS

Civil Parish: Ballynacourty
Map Grid: 56
RC Parish: Ballynacourty, see Oranmore
Diocese: TU

Civil Parish: Ballynakill (1) (Killian)
Map Grid: 50
RC Parish: Killian and Killeroran; also Mountbellew, see Moylough
Diocese: TU
Dates: b. 1869-; m. 1869-
Status: LC; NLI (mf); Indexed by GFHS West

Civil Parish: Ballynakill (2) (Ballymoe)
Map Grid: 19
RC Parish: Glinsk and Kilbegnet (Creggs)
Diocese: CF
Earliest Record: b. 9.1836; m. 11.1836; d. 9.1836
Missing Dates: b. 6.1848-3.1849; m. 4.1865-7.1865; d. ends 9.1839
Status: LC; NLI (mf); Indexing planned by GFHS West

Civil Parish: Ballynakill (3) (Ballynahinch)
Map Grid: 1
RC Parish: Ballynakill (Letterfrack and Tullycross); also part Kilbride and Ballynakill, see below
Diocese: TU
Earliest Record: b. 7.1869; m. 7.1869
Status: LC; NLI (mf); Indexed by GFHS West

Civil Parish: Ballynakill (4) (Ballynahinch)
Map Grid: 1
RC Parish: Kilbride
Diocese: TU
Earliest Record: b. 12.1853
Status: LC; NLI (mf); Indexed by GFHS West

Civil Parish: Ballynakill (5) (Leitrim)
Map Grid: 105
RC Parish: Abbey and Duniry; see also Ballynakill (6)
Diocese: CF
Earliest Record: b. 4.1839; m. 1870
Missing Dates: b. 10.1851-6.1855, 12.1857-2.1859
Status: LC; NLI (mf); Indexed by East GFHS

Civil Parish: Ballynakill (6) (Leitrim)
Map Grid: 105
RC Parish: Woodford
Diocese: CF
Earliest Record: b. 4.1821; m. 4.1821
Missing Dates: b. 11.1843-3.1851, 8.1861-4.1865, 9.1868-2.1869; m. 10.1833-3.1851, 7.1861-7.1865, 2.1869-2.1871
Status: LC; NLI (mf); Indexed by East GFHS

Civil Parish: Beagh
Map Grid: 90
RC Parish: Beagh (Shanaglish)
Diocese: KMC
Earliest Record: b. 1.1855; m. 3.1849
Missing Dates: m. 2.1850-5.1860
Status: LC; NLI (mf); Indexed by East GFHS; b. 1855/56 can be accessed on the Internet at http://members.aol.com/LABATH/births.htm

Civil Parish: Belclare
Map Grid: 30
RC Parish: Kilmoylan and Cummer, see Cummer
Diocese: TU

Civil Parish: Boyounagh
Map Grid: 18
RC Parish: Boyounagh (Glenamaddy)
Diocese: TU
Earliest Record: b. 10.1838; m. 10.1838
Missing Dates: b. 6.1858-12.1859, 10.1863-10.1865
Status: LC; NLI (mf); Indexed by East GFHS

Civil Parish: Bullaun
Map Grid: 91
RC Parish: Bullaun, Grange, and New Inn
Diocese: CF
Earliest Record: b. 10.1827; m. 10.1827
Missing Dates: b. 4.1840-8.1841
Status: LC; NLI (mf); Indexed by East GFHS

Civil Parish: Cargin
Map Grid: 31
RC Parish: Headford, see Killower

Civil Parish: Claregalway
Map Grid: 55
RC Parish: Claregalway
Diocese: TU
Earliest Record: b. 11.1849; m. 11.1849; d. 11.1849
Missing Dates: d. ends 11.1876
Status: LC; NLI (mf); Indexed by GFHS West

Civil Parish: Clonbern
Map Grid: 22
RC Parish: see Kilkerrin
Diocese: TU

Civil Parish: Clonfert
Map Grid: 111
RC Parish: Clonfert, Meelick, and Eyrecourt
Diocese: CF

Earliest Record: b. 11.1849; m. 11.1849; d. 11.1849
Status: LC; NLI (mf); Indexed by East GFHS

Civil Parish: Clonkeen
Map Grid: 45
RC Parish: see Ballymacward

Civil Parish: Clonrush
Map Grid: 107
RC Parish: see Co. Clare
Diocese: KL

Civil Parish: Clontuskert
Map Grid: 81
RC Parish: Clontuskert
Diocese: TU
Earliest Record: b. 10.1827; m. 10.1827; d. 10.1827
Missing Dates: b. 10.1868–3.1870; m. 10.1868–3.1870; d. ends 10.1868
Status: LC; NLI (mf); Indexed by East GFHS

Civil Parish: Cong
Map Grid: 8
RC Parish: see Co. Mayo
Diocese: TU

Civil Parish: Cummer
Map Grid: 34
RC Parish: Kilmoylan and Cummer
Diocese: TU
Earliest Record: b. 12.1835; m. 10.1813
Missing Dates: b. 8.1860–8.1872
Status: LC; NLI (mf); Indexed by GFHS West

Civil Parish: Donaghpatrick
Map Grid: 26
RC Parish: Donaghpatrick and Kilcoona
Diocese: TU
Earliest Record: b. 4.1844; m. 4.1844
Missing Dates: b. 6.1844–11.1849, 6.1861–8.1863; m. 12.1846–12.1849, 6.1861–9.1863
Status: LC; NLI (mf); Indexed by GFHS West

Civil Parish: Donanaghta
Map Grid: 115
RC Parish: see Clonfert
Diocese: CF

Civil Parish: Drumacoo
Map Grid: 62
RC Parish: see Kilcolgan
Diocese: KMC

Civil Parish: Drumatemple
Map Grid: 17
RC Parish: see Ballintober, Co. Roscommon
Diocese: EL

Civil Parish: Dunamon
Map Grid: 21
RC Parish: Glinsk, etc., see Ballynakill (Ballymoe)
Diocese: CF

Civil Parish: Duniry
Map Grid: 103
RC Parish: Ballinakill, see Ballynakill (Leitrim)
Diocese: CF

Civil Parish: Dunmore
Map Grid: 11
RC Parish: Dunmore
Diocese: TU
Earliest Record: b. 3.1833; m. 3.1833
Missing Dates: b. 3.1846–12.1847, 10.1859–9.1877; m. 9.1860–1.1861
Status: LC; NLI (mf); Indexed by GFHS West

Civil Parish: Fahy
Map Grid: 114
RC Parish: Fahy and Quansboro (Kilquain)
Diocese: CF
Earliest Record: b. 1873; m. 1876
Status: LC; NLI (mf); Indexed by East GFHS

Civil Parish: Fohanagh
Map Grid: 71
RC Parish: Fohenagh and Kilgerrill
Diocese: CF
Earliest Record: b. 8.1827; m. 8.1827; d. 8.1827
Status: LC; NLI (mf); Indexed by East GFHS

Civil Parish: Grange
Map Grid: 74
RC Parish: see Bullaun
Diocese: CF

Civil Parish: Inishbofin
Map Grid: 106
RC Parish: see Ballynakill (Ballynahinch)
Diocese: TU
Earliest Record: b. 1867–; m. 1867–
Status: LC; NLI (mf); Indexed by GFHS West

Civil Parish: Inisheer
Map Grid: 84
RC Parish: Aran Islands
Diocese: TU
Earliest Record: b. 1872; m. 1872
Status: LC; NLI (mf); Indexed by GFHS West

Civil Parish: Inishmaan
Map Grid: 83
RC Parish: Aran Islands; see Inisheer

Civil Parish: Inishmore
Map Grid: 82
RC Parish: Aran Islands, see Inisheer

Civil Parish: Isertkelly
Map Grid: 93
RC Parish: see Kilchreest
Diocese: CF

Civil Parish: Kilbarron
Map Grid: 108

RC Parish: see Clonrush
Diocese: KL

Civil Parish: Kilbeacanty
Map Grid: 89
RC Parish: Kilbeacanty
Diocese: KMC
Earliest Record: b. 8.1854
Status: LC; NLI (mf); Indexed by East GFHS

Civil Parish: Kilbegnet
Map Grid: 20
RC Parish: Glinsk and Kilbegnet, see Ballynakill (2) (Ballymoe)
Diocese: EL

Civil Parish: Kilbennon
Map Grid: 13
RC Parish: Kilconla and Kilbennon
Diocese: TU
Earliest Record: b. 3.1872; m. 1872
Status: LC; NLI (mf); Indexed by GFHS West

Civil Parish: Kilchreest
Map Grid: 95
RC Parish: Kilchreest (Isertkelly)
Diocese: CF
Earliest Record: b. 2.1855; m. 2.1865
Status: LC; NLI (mf); Indexed by East GFHS

Civil Parish: Kilcloony
Map Grid: 80
RC Parish: Ballinasloe (Creagh and Kilclooney)
Diocese: CF
Earliest Record: b. 1820; m. 1820; d. 1825
Status: LC; NLI (mf); Indexed by East GFHS

Civil Parish: Kilcolgan (Ballindereen)
Map Grid: 63
RC Parish: Ballindereen and Kilcolgan (and Drumacoo and Killeenavara)
Diocese: KMC
Earliest Record: b. 11.1854; m. 1.1871
Status: LC; NLI (mf); Indexed (to 1900) by GFHS West

Civil Parish: Kilconickny
Map Grid: 68
RC Parish: Kilconickny, etc., see Kilconieran
Diocese: CF

Civil Parish: Kilconieran
Map Grid: 61
RC Parish: Carrabane (Kilconickny, Kilconieran, and Lickerrig)
Diocese: CF
Earliest Record: b. 7.1831; m. 7.1831
Status: LC; NLI (mf); Indexed by East GFHS

Civil Parish: Kilconly
Map Grid: 12
RC Parish: see Kilbennon
Diocese: TU

Civil Parish: Kilconnell
Map Grid: 72
RC Parish: see Aughrim
Diocese: CF

Civil Parish: Kilcooly
Map Grid: 100
RC Parish: Leitrim (Kilcooly and Kilmeen)
Diocese: CF
Earliest Record: b. 5.1815; m. 5.1815; d. 5.1815
Missing Dates: b. 6.1829-9.1850; m. 6.1829-12.1846; d. 6.1829-12.1846
Status: LC; NLI (mf); Indexed by East GFHS

Civil Parish: Kilcoona
Map Grid: 33
RC Parish: see Donaghpatrick
Diocese: TU

Civil Parish: Kilcroan
Map Grid: 16
RC Parish: Glinsk, see Ballynakill (Ballymoe)
Diocese: EL

Civil Parish: Kilcummin (1)
Map Grid: 23
RC Parish: Rosmuc; also Carraroe, see below
Diocese: TU
Earliest Record: b. 8.1840; d. 1863
Status: LC; NLI (mf); Indexed by GFHS West

Civil Parish: Kilcummin (2)
Map Grid: 23
RC Parish: Carraroe (Killeen)
Diocese: TU
Earliest Record: b. 8.1853; m. 1853
Status: LC; NLI (mf); Indexed by GFHS West

Civil Parish: Kilcummin (3)
Map Grid: 23
RC Parish: Kilcummin and Oughterard
Diocese: TU
Earliest Record: b. 6.1809; m. 7.1809; d. 3.1827
Missing Dates: b. 8.1821-3.1827; m. 2.1816-3.1827; d. ends 2.1874
Status: LC; NLI (mf); Indexed by GFHS West

Civil Parish: Kilgerrill
Map Grid: 79
RC Parish: see Fohanagh
Diocese: CF

Civil Parish: Kilkerrin
Map Grid: 39
RC Parish: Kilkerrin and Clonberne
Diocese: TU
Earliest Record: b. 8.1853; m. 1884
Status: LC; NLI (mf); Indexed by East GFHS

Civil Parish: Kilkilvery
Map Grid: 29
RC Parish: Killursa, etc., see Killower
Diocese: TU

Civil Parish: Killaan
Map Grid: 75
RC Parish: see Bullaun
Diocese: CF

Civil Parish: Killalaghten
Map Grid: 76
RC Parish: Cappataggle and Kilriekhill
Diocese: CF
Earliest Record: b. 1799; m. 1806; d. 1806
Missing Dates: b/m/d. 5.1827-9.1827
Status: LC; NLI (mf); Indexed by East GFHS

Civil Parish: Killannin
Map Grid: 24
RC Parish: Killanin (Rosscahill)
Diocese: TU
Earliest Record: b. 1834; m. 1.1875; d. 1881
Status: LC; NLI (mf); Indexed by GFHS West

Civil Parish: Killeany
Map Grid: 32
RC Parish: Killursa, etc., see Killower
Diocese: KMC

Civil Parish: Killeely
Map Grid: 58
RC Parish: see Kinvarradoorus
Diocese: KMC

Civil Parish: Killeenadeema
Map Grid: 96
RC Parish: Kilnadeema and Aile
Diocese: CF
Earliest Record: b. 5.1836; m. 4.1836
Status: LC; NLI (mf); Indexed by East GFHS

Civil Parish: Killeenavarra
Map Grid: 65
RC Parish: see Kilcolgan
Diocese: KMC

Civil Parish: Killeeney
Map Grid: 59
RC Parish: Castlegar
Diocese: KMC
Earliest Records: b. 1827-; m. 1827-; d. 1829-
Status: LC; NLI (mf); Indexed by GFHS West

Civil Parish: Killererin
Map Grid: 35
RC Parish: Killererin
Diocese: TU
Earliest Record: b. 6.1870; m. 2.1851
Missing Dates: m. 8.1858-10.1870
Status: LC; NLI (mf); Indexed by GFHS West

Civil Parish: Killeroran
Map Grid: 48
RC Parish: see Killian
Diocese: EL

Civil Parish: Killian
Map Grid: 47
RC Parish: Ballygar (Killian and Killeroran)
Diocese: EL
Earliest Record: b. 4.1804; m. 4.1804; d. 5.1804
Missing Dates: b. 7.1833-10.1844; m. 2.1843-
10.1844; d. 9.1829-10.1844, ends 1859
Status: LC; NLI (mf); Indexed by East GFHS

Civil Parish: Killimorbologue
Map Grid: 116
RC Parish: Killimorbologue and Tiranascragh
Diocese: CF
Earliest Record: b. 1831; m. 1831
Missing Dates: m. 1842-50
Status: LC; NLI (mf); Indexed by East GFHS

Civil Parish: Killimordaly
Map Grid: 73
RC Parish: Killimordaly and Kiltullagh
Diocese: CF
Earliest Record: b. 9.1839; m. 8.1839
Missing Dates: m. 4.1874-1.1877
Status: LC; NLI (mf); Indexed by East GFHS

Civil Parish: Killinan
Map Grid: 94
RC Parish: see Kilchreest
Diocese: CF

Civil Parish: Killinny
Map Grid: 86
RC Parish: Killursa, etc., see Killower
Diocese: TU

Civil Parish: Killogilleen
Map Grid: 67
RC Parish: Killogilleen, etc., see Killora
Diocese: CF

Civil Parish: Killora
Map Grid: 60
RC Parish: Craughwell (Killogilleen and Killora)
Diocese: KMC
Earliest Record: b. 11.1847; m. 1847; d. 1847
Status: LC; NLI (mf); Indexed by East GFHS

Civil Parish: Killoran
Map Grid: 109
RC Parish: see Abbeygormacan
Diocese: CF

Civil Parish: Killoscobe
Map Grid: 42
RC Parish: Menlough (Killascobe)
Diocese: TU
Earliest Record: b. 7.1867; m. 6.1807
Missing Dates: m. 7.1819-11.1825, 6.1847-7.1849
Status: LC; NLI (mf); Indexed by East GFHS

Civil Parish: Killosolan
Map Grid: 43

RC Parish: Caltra, see Ahascragh
Diocese: EL

Civil Parish: Killower
Map Grid: 27
RC Parish: Headford; Killursa and Killower
Diocese: TU
Earliest Record: b. 1880; m. 1880
Status: LC; NLI (mf); Indexed by GFHS West

Civil Parish: Killursa
Map Grid: 28
RC Parish: see Killower
Diocese: TU

Civil Parish: Kilmacduagh
Map Grid: 88
RC Parish: Kilmacduagh and Kiltartan
Diocese: KMC
Earliest Record: b. 2.1848; m. 12.1853
Status: LC; NLI (mf); Indexed by East GFHS

Civil Parish: Kilmalinoge
Map Grid: 120
RC Parish: Portumna (Kilmalinoge and Lickmolassey)
Diocese: CF
Earliest Record: b. 10.1830; m. 10.1830
Status: LC; NLI (mf); Indexed by East GFHS

Civil Parish: Kilmeen
Map Grid: 99
RC Parish: see Kilcooly
Diocese: TU

Civil Parish: Kilmoylan
Map Grid: 37
RC Parish: see Cummer
Diocese: TU

Civil Parish: Kilquain
Map Grid: 113
RC Parish: see Fahy
Diocese: CF

Civil Parish: Kilreekil
Map Grid: 98
RC Parish: see Killalaghten
Diocese: CF

Civil Parish: Kiltartan
Map Grid: 87
RC Parish: Kiltartan, see Kilmacduagh
Diocese: KMC

Civil Parish: Kilteskil
Map Grid: 101
RC Parish: see Killeenadeema
Diocese: CF

Civil Parish: Kilthomas
Map Grid: 97
RC Parish: Peterswell (Kilthomas)
Diocese: KMC

Earliest Record: b. 1.1854; m. 1.1856
Status: LC; NLI (mf); Indexed by East GFHS

Civil Parish: Kiltormer
Map Grid: 110
RC Parish: Laurencetown (Kiltormer and Oghill)
Diocese: CF
Earliest Record: b. 3.1834; m. 2.1834
Missing Dates: b. 7.1860-5.1862; m. 5.1860-9.1860
Status: LC; NLI (mf); Indexed by East GFHS

Civil Parish: Kiltullagh
Map Grid: 70
RC Parish: see Killimordaly
Diocese: CF

Civil Parish: Kinvarradoorus
Map Grid: 85
RC Parish: Kinvara
Diocese: KMC
Earliest Record: b. 6.1831; m. 7.1831
Missing Dates: b. 5.1837-6.1843, 8.1853-7.1854; m. 5.1837-6.1843, 8.1853-7.1854
Status: LC; NLI (mf); Indexed by GFHS West

Civil Parish: Lackagh
Map Grid: 38
RC Parish: Lackagh
Diocese: TU
Earliest Record: b. 7.1842; m. 9.1841; d. 1858
Missing Dates: b. 9.1847-3.1848; m. 12.1847-9.1853
Status: LC; NLI (mf); Indexed by GFHS West

Civil Parish: Leitrim
Map Grid: 102
RC Parish: see Kilcooly
Diocese: CF

Civil Parish: Lickerrig
Map Grid: 64
RC Parish: Craughwell, see Killora
Diocese: KMC

Civil Parish: Lickmolassy
Map Grid: 119
RC Parish: see Kilmalinoge
Diocese: CF

Civil Parish: Liskeevy
Map Grid: 9
RC Parish: see Addergoole
Diocese: TU

Civil Parish: Loughrea
Map Grid: 92
RC Parish: Loughrea (St. Brendan's Cathedral)
Diocese: CF
Earliest Record: b. 1810; m. 1820; d. 1817
Status: LC; NLI (mf); Indexed by East GFHS

Civil Parish: Meelick
Map Grid: 118

RC Parish: see Clonfert
Diocese: CF

Civil Parish: Monivea
Map Grid: 44
RC Parish: part Athenry; part Abbeyknockmoy
Diocese: TU

Civil Parish: Moycullen (1)
Map Grid: 25
RC Parish: Moycullen; also Spiddal, see below
Diocese: CF
Earliest Record: b. 1.1786; m. 1.1786; d. 1.1786
Missing Dates: b. 3.1823-1.1837, 5.1841-10.1843; m. 1.1823-10.1843, 10.1848-2.1849; d. 1.1823-11.1848
Status: LC; NLI (mf); Indexed by GFHS West (from 1848)

Civil Parish: Moycullen (2)
Map Grid: 25
RC Parish: Spiddal
Diocese: CF
Earliest Record: b. 2.1861; m. 4.1873; d. 4.1873
Status: LC; NLI (mf); Indexed by GFHS West

Civil Parish: Moylough
Map Grid: 40
RC Parish: Moylough and Mountbellew
Diocese: TU
Earliest Record: b. 1.1848; m. 11.1848
Missing Dates: b. 7.1870-1.1871
Status: LC; NLI (mf); Indexed by East GFHS

Civil Parish: Moyrus (1)
Map Grid: 3
RC Parish: Carna or Moyrus; also Roundstone, see below
Diocese: TU
Earliest Record: b. 12.1853; m. 9.1852
Status: LC; NLI (mf); Indexed by GFHS West

Civil Parish: Moyrus (2)
Map Grid: 3
RC Parish: Roundstone
Earliest Records: b. 1872; m. 1872
Status: LC; NLI (mf); Indexed by GFHS West

Civil Parish: Omey
Map Grid: 2
RC Parish: see Ballindoon

Civil Parish: Oranmore
Map Grid: 52
RC Parish: Oranmore
Diocese: TU
Earliest Record: b. 3.1833; m. 5.1833; d. 1.1833
Missing Dates: m. 7.1838-8.1848; d. 12.1837-1848
Status: LC; NLI (mf); Indexed by GFHS West

Civil Parish: Rahoon
Map Grid: 53
RC Parish: Rahoon

Diocese: TU
Earliest Record: b. 1806; m. 1806; d. 1806
Missing Dates: b. 1.1845-4.1845; m. ends 12.1832; d. ends 7.1826
Status: LC; NLI (mf); Indexed by GFHS West

Civil Parish: Ross
Map Grid: 7
RC Parish: Clonbur (Ross); see also Cong, Co. Mayo
Diocese: TU
Earliest Records: b. 1853; m. 1853
Missing Dates: b. 4.1871-1.1873
Status: LC; NLI (mf); Indexed by GFHS West

Civil Parish: St. Nicholas (Galway Town)
Map Grid: 54
RC Parish: St. Nicholas Cathedral
Diocese: TU
Earliest Record: b. 3.1723; m. 1789; d. 1789
Missing Dates: b. 3.1725-2.1814
Status: LC; NLI (mf); Indexed by GFHS West

Civil Parish: Stradbally
Map Grid: 57
RC Parish: Clarinbridge or Kilcornan
Diocese: KMC
Earliest Record: b. 8.1854; m. 6.1837
Status: LC; NLI (mf); Indexed by GFHS West

Civil Parish: Taghboy
Map Grid: 51
RC Parish: Dysart and Tisara, see Dysart, Co. Roscommon
Diocese: EL

Civil Parish: Templetogher
Map Grid: 15
RC Parish: see Boyounagh
Diocese: TU

Civil Parish: Tiranascragh
Map Grid: 117
RC Parish: see Killimorebologue
Diocese: CF

Civil Parish: Tuam
Map Grid: 14
RC Parish: Tuam
Diocese: TU
Earliest Record: b. 3.1790; m. 1.1790
Missing Dates: b. 7.1804-10.1811, 10.1857-10.1858; m. 3.1832-10.1832
Status: LC; NLI (mf); Indexed by GFHS West

Civil Parish: Tynagh
Map Grid: 104
RC Parish: Tynagh
Diocese: CF
Earliest Record: b. 5.1809; m. 5.1816
Missing Dates: b. 12.1842-9.1846; m. 12.1842-9.1846
Status: LC; NLI (mf); Indexed by East GFHS

Commercial and Social Directories

1820

J. Pigot's *Commercial Directory of Ireland* contains information on the gentry, nobility, and traders in and around the city of Galway.

1824

J. Pigot's *City of Dublin and Hibernian Provincial Directory* includes traders, nobility, gentry, and clergy lists of Ballinasloe, Eyrecourt, Galway, Gort, Loughrea, and Tuam.

1846

Slater's *National Commercial Directory of Ireland* lists nobility, clergy, traders, etc., in Athenry, Ballinasloe, Castleblakeney, Clifden, Dunmore, Eyrecourt, Galway, Gort, Headford, Loughrea, Portumna, and Tuam.

1856

Slater's *Royal National Commercial Directory of Ireland* lists nobility, gentry, clergy, traders, etc., in Athenry, Ballinasloe, Clifden, Dunmore, Eyrecourt, Galway, Gort, Headford, Loughrea, Portumna, and Tuam.

1870

Slater's *Directory of Ireland* contains trade, nobility, and clergy lists for Athenry, Ballinasloe, Clifden, Dunmore, Eyrecourt, Galway, Gort, Headford, Loughrea, Portumna, and Tuam.

1881

Slater's *Royal National Commercial Directory of Ireland* contains lists of traders, clergy, nobility, and farmers in adjoining parishes of the towns of Athenry, Ballinasloe, Clifden, Eyrecourt, Galway, Gort, Loughrea, Portumna, and Tuam.

1894

Slater's *Royal National Directory of Ireland* lists traders, police, teachers, farmers, and private residents in each of the towns, villages, and parishes of the county.

Family History

Pedigrees of Clare, Galway, and Limerick families. GO Ms. 520; SLC film 257821.

Orpen, Goddard H. "Notes on the Bermingham Pedigree." *J. Galway Arch. & Hist. Soc.* 9 (1915-16): 195-205.

Knox, H. "The Bermingham Family of Athenry." *J. Galway Arch. & Hist. Soc.* 10 (1917-18): 139-54.

"The Burkes of Marble Hill." *J. Galway Arch. & Hist. Soc.* 8 (1913-14): 1-11.

"Portumna and the Burkes." *J. Galway Arch. & Hist. Soc.* 6 (1909): 107-09.

"Seanchus na mBurcach and Historia et Genealogia Familae De Burgo." *J. Galway Arch. & Hist. Soc.* 13 (1926-27): 50-60, 101-37; 14 (1928-29): 310-51, 142-66.

"Some Notes on the Burkes." *J. Galway Arch. & Hist. Soc.* 1 (1900-01): 1966-67.

Burke—see also De Burgo.

Blake, Martin J. "Families of Daly of Galway with Tabular Pedigrees." *J. Galway Arch. & Hist. Soc.* 13 (1926-27): 140.

"The De Burgo Clans of Galway." *J. Galway Arch. & Hist. Soc.* 1 (1900-01): 123-31; 3 (1903-04): 46-58; 4 (1905-06): 55-62.

Family History of the Donnellys and Crushells, Belmont, Galway. Nepal, 1987. SLC 941.74/B4 D2d.

Hartigan, A.S. *A Short Account of the Eyre Family of Eyre Court, and Eyre of Eyreville, in Co. Galway.* Reading, n.d.

Hayes-McCoy, Marguerite. "The Eyre Documents in University College, Galway." *J. Galway Arch. & Hist. Soc.* 20: 57-74; 21: 71-95; 23: 147-53 (1942-49).

"The Joyces of Merview." *Ir. Gen.* 9 (1) (1994): 89-113; 9 (2) (1995).

Kenney, J.F. *Pedigree of the Kenney Family of Kilclogher, Co. Galway.* Dublin, 1868.

"Profile of the Larkin Family: 1787-1983." *Irish Family Links* 2 (2) (1984): 26-28.

Blake, Martin J. "Pedigree of Lynch of Lavally, County Galway." *J. Galway Arch. & Hist. Soc.* 10 (1917-18): 66-69.

Lynch, E. *Genealogical Memoranda Relating to the Family of Lynch.* London, 1883.

Lynch Record, containing biographical sketches of men of the name Lynch, 16th century to 20th century. New York, 1925.

Lynch, John. "Account of the Lynch Family and of the Memorable Events of the Town of Galway." *J. Galway Arch. & Hist. Soc.* 8 (1913-14): 76-93.

"Mahon Papers" (Castlebar, Co. Galway). *Anal. Hib.* 25: 77-93.

"Notes on the Mills Family of Headford, Co. Galway and Roscommon." *J. Ass. Pres. Mem. Dead* 10: 241.

Genealogy of the O'Malleys of the Owals. Philadelphia, 1913.

O'Malley, Sir Owen. "Note on the O'Malley Lordship at the Close of the XVIth Century." *J. Galway Arch. & Hist. Soc.* 24 (1950-51): 27-57.

"O'Malleys Between 1607 and 1725." *J. Galway Arch. & Hist. Soc.* 25 (1952): 32-46.

"The O'Maolconaire Family." *J. Galway Arch. & Hist. Soc.* 29 (1940-41): 118-46.

"The O'Maolconaire Family." *J. Galway Arch. & Hist. Soc.* 20 (1942–43): 82–88.

Walsh, Rev. Paul. "The Learned Family of O'Maelconaire." In *Irish Men of Learning.* Dublin, 1947.

"O'Shaughnessy of Gort (1543–1783): Tabular Pedigree." *J. Galway Arch. & Hist. Soc.* 7 (1911–12): 53.

Feheny, John P.M. *The O'Shaughnessys of Munster.* Cork: Iverus Publications, 1996. (Covers the origins of the family in Galway and the spread into Clare, Limerick, Cork, and Tipperary.)

Gravestone Inscriptions

Galway Family History Society West (GFHS West) has abstracts of gravestone inscriptions from a large number of graveyards in their area. The society will search this index for a fee. Those available from GFHS West (showing graveyard and civil parish) are:

Abbeyknockmoy–Abbey RC; Indexed by GFHS West

Abbeyknockmoy–Moore Graveyard; Indexed by GFHS West

Abbeyknockmoy–New Cemetery; Indexed by GFHS West

Abbeyknockmoy–Old Abbey Cemetery; Indexed by GFHS West

Abbeyknockmoy–Tobair Padraig Cemetery; Indexed by GFHS West

Aghyart (Moylough) Cemetery; Indexed by GFHS West

Aran–Kilmurvey Cemetery; Indexed by GFHS West

Aran Cenotaphs (Aran) Cemetery; Indexed by GFHS West

Aran–Killeany Cemetery; Indexed by GFHS West

Aran–Na Seacht Teampaill Cemetery; Indexed by GFHS West

Ardbear (Clifden) Cemetery; Indexed by GFHS West

Athenry–Dominican Cemetery; Indexed by GFHS West

Ballybrit (Castlegar) Cemetery; Indexed by GFHS West

Barraderry (Kilcummin) Cemetery; Indexed by GFHS West

Bohermore–Galway City Cemetery; Indexed by GFHS West

Bushypark (Rahoon) Cemetery; Indexed by GFHS West

Carrowbrown (Castlegar) Cemetery; Indexed by GFHS West

Castlegar Cemetery; Indexed by GFHS West

Cill Ronain (Aran) Cemetery; Indexed by GFHS West

Claregalway RC (Claregalway) Cemetery; Indexed by GFHS West

Claregalway Abbey (Claregalway) Cemetery; Indexed by GFHS West

Claretuam (Cummer) Cemetery; Indexed by GFHS West

Clarinbridge (Clarinbridge) Cemetery; Indexed by GFHS West

Clifden C of I (Clifden) Cemetery; Indexed by GFHS West

Clifden–Franciscan Bros. (Clifden) Cemetery; Indexed by GFHS West

Clifden RC (Clifden) Cemetery; Indexed by GFHS West

Clifden Town (Clifden) Cemetery; Indexed by GFHS West

Creevaghbawn (Killererin) Cemetery; Indexed by GFHS West

Errislannan C of I (Clifden) Cemetery; Indexed by GFHS West

Errislannan Manor (Clifden) Cemetery; Indexed by GFHS West

Eskerstephena (Moylough) Cemetery; Indexed by GFHS West

Galway City–Bohermore; Indexed by GFHS West

Galway City–Castlelawn (Ballinfoyle); Indexed by GFHS West

Galway City–Forthill; Indexed by GFHS West

Galway City–Mervue-St. James; Indexed by GFHS West

Galway City–Methodist; Indexed by GFHS West

Galway City–St. Nicholas; Indexed by GFHS West

Galway City–The Abbey; Indexed by GFHS West

Inishbofin (Inishbofin); Indexed by GFHS West

Kilconly (Kilconly); Indexed by GFHS West

Kill (Clifden); Indexed by GFHS West

Killascobe (Menlough, Ballinasloe); Indexed by GFHS West

Killeany (Aran); Indexed by GFHS West

Killeelly (Oranmore); Indexed by GFHS West

Killeen (Castlegar); Indexed by GFHS West

Killeeneen (Oranmore); Indexed by GFHS West

Killererin (Killererin); Indexed by GFHS West

Kilmacduagh: *Irish Ancestor* 7 (1) (1975): 26–34

Kilmurvey (Aran); Indexed by GFHS West

Lettermore–Chuigeal; Indexed by GFHS West

Lettermore–Relig Ghleann na Cuaichigh; Indexed by GFHS West

Lettermore–Sean Bhaile; Indexed by GFHS West

Lettermore–Tra Baine; Indexed by GFHS West

Menlo (Castlegar); Indexed by GFHS West

Mervue–St. James; Indexed by GFHS West

Monivea RC (Monivea); Indexed by GFHS West

Monivea C of I (Monivea); Indexed by GFHS West

Monivea–Franciscan Graveyard (Monivea); Indexed by GFHS West

Mountbellew; Indexed by GFHS West

Oranmore New Cemetery; Indexed by GFHS West

Oughterard C of I (Kilcummin); Indexed by GFHS West

Rahoon–Galway; Indexed by GFHS West

Shanaglish (Beagh Parish); accessible on the Internet at http://members.aol.com/LABATH/cembeagh.htm

Tuam—St. Mary's; Indexed by GFHS West

Newspapers

Unfortunately, there were not very many newspapers published in Galway, and surviving copies of those published are rare. The *Connaught Journal* is the best of the early (1813) surviving papers. The Galway County Library (GCL; see Library Sources at the end of the chapter) also has a good collection of local newspapers, mainly on microfilm.

Title: *Ballinasloe Independent* (see *Western Argus*)

Title: *Connaught Champion*
Published in: Galway, 1904–1911

Title: *Connaught Journal*
Published in: Galway, 1793–1840
NLI Holdings: 1793; 1795; 1823–36; odd numbers 1839, 1840
BL Holdings: 1.1823–12.1836; 2–12.1840
GCL Holdings: 1793–1840

Title: *Connaught Patriot*
Published in: Tuam, 1859–69
BL Holdings: 8.1859–12.1864; 10.1865–3.1869

Title: *Connaught People*
Published in: Ballinasloe, 1882–86
BL Holdings: 4.1884–9.1886

Title: *Connaught Tribune*
Published in: Galway, 1909–1983

Title: *Galway American*
Published in: Galway, 1862–1863
GCL Holdings: 1862–1863

Title: *Galway Express*
Published in: Galway, 1853–1920
NLI Holdings: 1.1853–10.1918; 3.1919–9.1920
BL Holdings: 1.1853–12.1918; 3.1919–9.1920
GCL Holdings: 1853–1920

Title: *Galway Free Press*
Published in: Galway, 1832–35
NLI Holdings: 1.1832–3.1835
BL Holdings: 1.1832–3.1835
GCL Holdings: 1832–35

Title: *Galway Independent Paper*
Published in: Galway, ca. 1825–32
NLI Holdings: 1.1829–3.1832
BL Holdings: 1.1829–3.1832
GCL Holdings: 1829–32

Title: *Galway Mercury*
Published in: Galway, 1844–60
NLI Holdings: 10.1844–3.1860

BL Holdings: 10.1844–3.1860
GCL Holdings: 1844–1860

Title: *Galway Observer*
Published in: Galway, 1881–1966
NLI Holdings: 1902; 1917–21; 8.1927–10.1966
BL Holdings: odd numbers 1882–84; 6.1889–8.1923; 2.1925–10.1966
GCL Holdings: 1882–1966

Title: *Galway Packet*
Published in: Galway, 1852–54
NLI Holdings: 4.1852–12.1854
BL Holdings: 4.1852–12.1854
GCL Holdings: 1852–1854

Title: *Galway Patriot*
Published in: Galway, 1835–39
NLI Holdings: 7.1835–10.1839
BL Holdings: 7.1835–10.1839
GCL Holdings: 1835–1839

Title: *Galway Press*
Published in: Galway, 1860–1861
GCL Holdings: 1860–1861

Title: *Galway Standard*
Published in: Galway, 1841–1843
GCL Holdings: 1841–1843

Title: *Galway Vindicator*
Published in: Galway, 1841–99
NLI Holdings: 7.1841–12.1844; 3–12.1845; 1846–55; 2.1856–12.1858; 1.1859–12.1898; 1–11.1899
BL Holdings: 7.1841–12.1844; 3.1845–12.1855; 2.1856–1.1876; 2.1876–11.1899
GCL Holdings: 1841–1899 (with gaps, as for NLI)

Title: *Galway Weekly Advertiser*
Published in: Galway, 1823–43
NLI Holdings: 1.1823–5.1843
BL Holdings: 1.1823–5.1843
GCL Holdings: 1.1823–5.1843

Title: *Tuam Herald* (continued as *Herald and Western Advertiser* in 1955)
Published in: Tuam, 1837–1955
NLI Holdings: 5.1837–9.1955 (with gaps)
BL Holdings: 5.1837–9.1955 (with gaps)

Title: *Tuam News and Western Advertiser*
Published in: Tuam, 1871–1904
NLI Holdings: 1.1882–12.1904 (with gaps)
BL Holdings: 6.1871–7.1873; 4.1884–1.1896

Title: *Western Argus and Ballinasloe Independent*
Published in: Ballinasloe, 1828–33
NLI Holdings: 4.1828–12.1829; 2.1830–1.1833
BL Holdings: 4.1828–10.1829; odd numbers 1830; 7.1830–1833
GCL Holdings: 1828–1833

Title: *Western News*
Published in: Ballinasloe, 1877–1926

NLI Holdings: 10–12.1898; 3.1901–7.1903; 7.1904–12.1926

BL Holdings: 11.1878–11.1877; 2.1888–1.1892; 12.1899–12.1902

Title: *Western Star and Ballinasloe Advertiser*
Published in: Ballinasloe, 1845–1902
NLI Holdings: 10.1845–12.1866; 1.1867–8.1869; 12.1888–5.1902
BL Holdings: 10.1845–8.1869; 12.1888–5.1902

Wills and Administrations

A discussion of the types of records, where they are held, and their availability and value is given in the Wills section of the introduction. The availability of prerogative wills, administrations, and marriage license records is also described in the relevant parts of the same section. Where available, published sources of these records are given in the Miscellaneous Sources section.

Pre-1858 Wills and Administrations

Prerogative Wills. See the introduction.

Consistorial Wills. County Galway is mainly in the diocese of Tuam, but also in Elphin, Kilmacduagh, and Clonfert. The guide to Catholic parish records in this chapter shows the diocese to which each civil parish belonged. The wills of residents of each diocese were usually proven within that diocese (see the Wills section for exceptions). The following records survive:

Wills

See the introduction.

Abstracts

See the introduction; also GO ms. 707 has many abstracts from Diocese of Tuam, Clonfert, and Kilmacduagh.

Indexes

Tuam (1648–1858), Elphin (1650–1858), Kilmacduagh and Clonfert (1663–1858) published to 1800 by Phillimore; also in *Clonfert and Kilmacduagh* by P. Smythe-Wood, 1977. SLC 941.5 A1 56. Crossle Will Indexes GO Ms. 416, SLC film 100175. Tuam Wills by P. Crossle (1641–1741) SLC film 257807.

Post-1858 Wills and Administrations

County Galway was served by the District Registry of Tuam. The surviving records are kept in the NAI. Tuam District Will Books (1858–1901): NAI and SLC films 100949–50.

Marriage Licenses

Indexes

Tuam (1661–1750). NAI; SLC film 100872. Elphin (1740–1850). NAI; SLC film 100868. Clonfert (1691–1845). NAI; SLC film 100869. Clonfert Marriage License Bonds, Wills, and Administrations: *Ir. Anc.* 1970 (Supplement) and SLC film 990403.

Miscellaneous Sources

"The Ethnography of the Aran Islands, Co. Galway." *R. Ir. Acad. Proc.* 3rd ser., 2 (1891–93): 827–29.

"The Ethnography of Inishbofin and Inishshark, Co. Galway." *R. Ir. Acad. Proc.* 3 (1893–96): 360–80.

Moran, G., and R. Gillespie, eds. *Galway: History and Society–Interdisciplinary Essays on the History of an Irish County.* Geography Publications, 1996.

"The Ethnography of Carna and Mweenish in the Parish of Moyruss, Connemara." *R. Ir. Acad. Proc.* 6 (1900–02): 503–34.

"The Composition of the Galway Gentry." *Ir. Gen.* 7 (1) (1986): 81–96.

Hardiman, J. *History of the Town and County of Galway.* Dublin, 1820. Reprint. 1978.

White, Rev. P. *History of Clare and Dalcassian Clans of Tipperary, Limerick and Galway.* Dublin, 1893.

Kavanagh, M.A. *Bibliography of the County Galway.* Galway, 1965; SLC film 990403.

Murphy, M., and J.R. Reilly. *Marriages in the Roman Catholic Diocese of Tuam, Ireland, 1821–1829.* USA: Heritage Books, 1993.

Tuam RC Diocese. Register of marriages in each Deanery for parts of 1821 and 1822, with additions in many parishes to 1829. NLI film P4222.

"Mayors, Sheriffs and other Public Officials of Galway Town. 1274–1820." In *History of the Town and County of Galway* by J. Hardiman. Dublin, 1820, pp. 197–232.

McLochlainn, J. *A Historical Summary of the Parish of Ahascragh, Caltra and Castleblakeny.* Ballinasloe, 1979.

O'Sullivan, M.D. *Old Galway.* Cambridge, 1942.

"The Tribes of Galway." *Ir. Gen.* 2 (4) (1946): 99–106.

Villiers-Tuthill, Kathleen. "History of Clifden 1810–1860." *Connaught Tribune* 1982, 1992.

Tadhg MacLochlainn. *A Short History of the Parish of Killure, Fohenagh and Kilgerril.* Galway, 1975.

Research Sources and Services

Journals

Journal of the Galway Archaeological and Historical Society
Galway Roots–Clanna na Gaillimhe. ISSN: 0791-8526 (1993)

Libraries and Information Sources

Galway County Library, Galway. Ph: (091) 62471

Research Services

See Research Services in Dublin in the introduction.

Galway Family History Society West Ltd., Unit 3, Venture Centre, Liosbaun Estate, Tuam Road, Galway. Ph: (091) 756737. This is the official IGP center for Galway City and the western part of Co. Galway. This center has indexed all of the church records of the area and is in the process of indexing other major records of relevance to family history. Those already indexed are indicated in the section on church records. They also have unique access to parochial censuses of Kinvara (1834) and Spiddal (1884 and 1895). Researchers are advised to contact the center for an updated list of registers, and other sources, indexed. They will conduct research on their indexes for a fee.

East Galway Family History Society, Woodford Heritage Centre, Woodford, Co. Galway. Ph: (0509) 49309; fax: (353) 509 49309. This center is the official center for the eastern part of Co. Galway. It has indexed most of the Catholic church records and is working on the records of other denominations. It also has access to the other major sources for the area, such as *Griffith's Valuation*, the 1901 census, and civil records of birth, marriage, and death (many of which have also been indexed). Researchers are advised to contact the center for an updated list of registers, and other sources, indexed. The center has also published several guides on the area. Local research, and searches of the indexed records, will be conducted for a fee.

Societies

Galway Archaeological and Historical Society, Mr. Peadar O'Dowd, Business Studies Department, Regional Technical College, Galway

Glenamaddy Arts and Historical Society, Ms. Brid Morgan, Sonnagh House, Glenamaddy, Co. Galway

Moycullen Historical Group, Ms. Treasa McMahon, Moycullen Community Office, Moycullen, Co. Galway

Old Galway Society, Ms. Elizabeth Byrnes, Merville by the Bridge, Oranmore, Co. Galway

Galway Civil Parishes as Numbered on Map

1. Ballynakill
2. Omey
3. Moyrus
4. Ballindoon
5. Ballinrobe
6. Ballinchalla
7. Ross
8. Cong
9. Liskeevy (2 pts.)
10. Addergoole (3 pts.)
11. Dunmore
12. Kilconla
13. Kilbennon
14. Tuam
15. Templetogher
16. Kilcroan
17. Drumatemple
18. Boyounagh
19. Ballynakill
20. Kilbegnet
21. Dunamon

22. Clonbern
23. Kilcummin (4 pts.)
24. Killannin (2 pts.)
25. Moycullen
26. Donaghpatrick
27. Killower (2 pts.)
28. Killursa
29. Kilkilvery
30. Belclare (3 pts.)
31. Cargin
32. Killeany
33. Kilcoona
34. Cummer
35. Killererin
36. Annaghdown
37. Kilmoylan
38. Lackagh
39. Kilkerrin
40. Moylough
41. Abbeyknockmoy
42. Killoscobe

43. Killosolan
44. Monivea
45. Clonkeen
46. Ballymacward
47. Killian
48. Killeroran
49. Athleague
50. Ballynakill
51. Taghboy
52. Oranmore
53. Rahoon
54. St. Nicholas
55. Claregalway
56. Ballynacourty (2 pts.)
57. Stradbally
58. Killeely
59. Killeeney
60. Killora
61. Kilconierin
62. Drumacoo
63. Kilcolgan (2 pts.)
64. Lickerrig (2 pts.)
65. Killeenavara
66. Ardrahan
67. Killogilleen
68. Kilconickny
69. Athenry
70. Kiltullagh
71. Fohanagh
72. Kilconnell
73. Killimordaly
74. Grange
75. Killaan
76. Killalaghten
77. Aughrim
78. Ahascragh
79. Kilgerrill
80. Kilcloony
81. Clontuskert
82. Inishmore
83. Inishmaan
84. Inisheer
85. Kinvarradoorus
86. Killinny
87. Kiltartan
88. Kilmacduagh
89. Kilbeacanty
90. Beagh
91. Bullaun
92. Loughrea
93. Isertkelly
94. Killinan
95. Kilchreest
96. Killeenadeema
97. Kilthomas
98. Kilreekill
99. Kilmeen
100. Kilcooly
101. Kilteskill
102. Leitrim
103. Duniry
104. Tynagh (2 pts.)
105. Ballynakill
106. Inishbofin
107. Clonrush
108. Kilbarron
109. Killoran
110. Kiltormer
111. Clonfert
112. Abbeygormacan
113. Kilquain
114. Fahy
115. Donanaghta
116. Killimorbologue
117. Tiranascragh
118. Meelick
119. Lickmolassy
120. Kilmalinogue

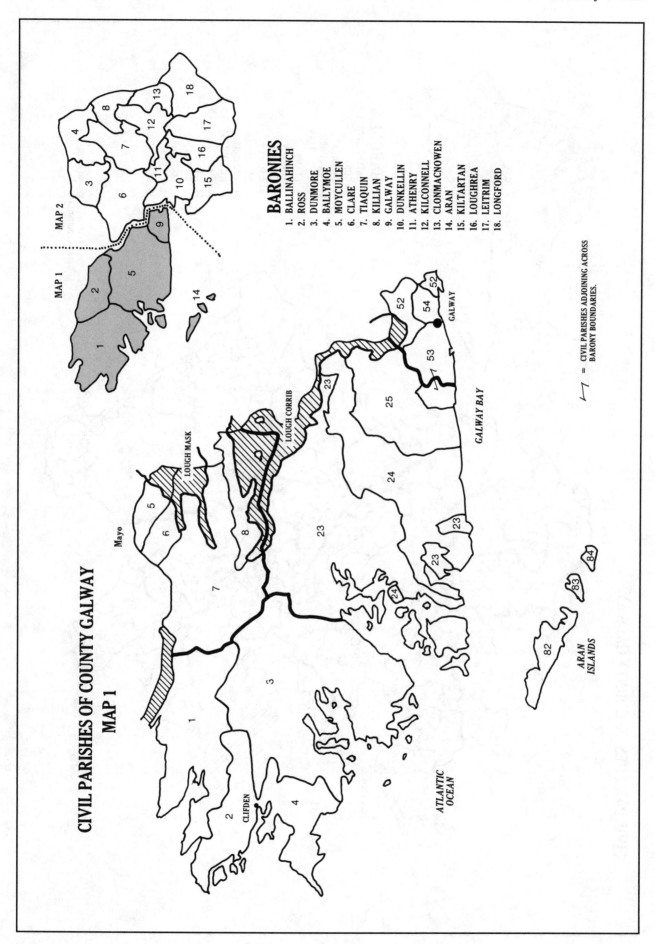

CIVIL PARISHES OF COUNTY GALWAY
MAP 1

BARONIES

1. BALLINAHINCH
2. ROSS
3. DUNMORE
4. BALLYMOE
5. MOYCULLEN
6. CLARE
7. TIAQUIN
8. KILLIAN
9. GALWAY
10. DUNKELLIN
11. ATHENRY
12. KILCONNELL
13. CLONMACNOWEN
14. ARAN
15. KILTARTAN
16. LOUGHREA
17. LEITRIM
18. LONGFORD

= CIVIL PARISHES ADJOINING ACROSS BARONY BOUNDARIES.

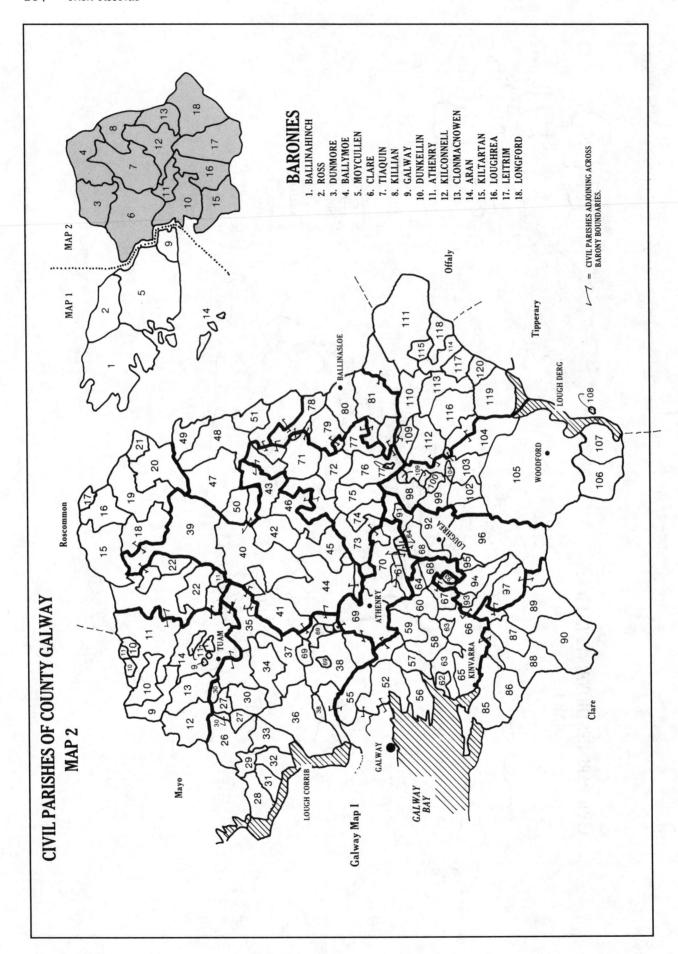

CIVIL PARISHES OF COUNTY GALWAY
MAP 2

BARONIES
1. BALLINAHINCH
2. ROSS
3. DUNMORE
4. BALLYMOE
5. MOYCULLEN
6. CLARE
7. TIAQUIN
8. KILLIAN
9. GALWAY
10. DUNKELLIN
11. ATHENRY
12. KILCONNELL
13. CLONMACNOWEN
14. ARAN
15. KILTARTAN
16. LOUGHREA
17. LEITRIM
18. LONGFORD

⌐ = CIVIL PARISHES ADJOINING ACROSS
     BARONY BOUNDARIES.

Galway Civil Parishes Listed Alphabetically

Abbeygormacan: 112

Abbeyknockmoy: 41

Addergoole (3 pts.): 10

Ahascragh: 78

Annaghdown: 36

Ardrahan: 66

Athenry: 69

Athleague: 49

Aughrim: 77

Ballinchalla: 6

Ballindoon: 4

Ballinrobe: 5

Ballymacward: 46

Ballynacourty (2 pts.): 56

Ballynakill: 1

Ballynakill: 19

Ballynakill: 50

Ballynakill: 105

Beagh: 90

Belclare (3 pts.): 30

Boyounagh: 18

Bullaun: 91

Cargin: 31

Claregalway: 55

Clonbern: 22

Clonfert: 111

Clonkeen: 45

Clonrush: 107

Clontuskert: 81

Cong: 8

Cummer: 34

Donaghpatrick: 26

Donanaghta: 115

Drumacoo: 62

Drumatemple: 17

Dunamon: 21

Duniry: 103

Dunmore: 11

Fahy: 114

Fohanagh: 71

Grange: 74

Inishbofin: 106

Inisheer: 84

Inishman: 83

Inishmore: 82

Isertkelly: 93

Kilbarron: 108

Kilbeacanty: 89

Kilbegnet: 20

Kilbennon: 13

Kilchreest: 95

Kilcloony: 80

Kilcolgan (2 pts.): 63

Kilconickny: 68

Kilconierin: 61

Kilconla: 12

Kilconnell: 72

Kilcooly: 100

Kilcoona: 33

Kilcroan: 16

Kilcummin (4 pts.): 23

Kilgerrill: 79

Kilkerrin: 39

Kilkilvery: 29

Killaan: 75

Killalaghten: 76

Killanin (2 pts.): 24

Killeany: 32

Killeely: 58

Killeenadeema: 96

Killeenavara: 65

Killeeney: 59

Killererin: 35

Killeroran: 48

Killian: 47

Killimorbologue: 116

Killimordaly: 73

Killinan: 94

Killinny: 86

Killogilleen: 67

Killora: 60

Killoran: 109

Killoscobe: 42

Killosolan: 43

Killower (2 pts.): 27

Killursa: 28

Kilmacduagh: 88

Kilmalinogue: 120

Kilmeen: 99

Kilmoylan: 37

Kilquain: 113

Kilreekill: 98

Kiltartan: 87

Kilteskil: 101

Kilthomas: 97

Kiltormer: 110

Kiltullagh: 70

Kinvarradoorus: 85

Lackagh: 38

Leitrim: 102

Lickerrig (2 pts.): 64

Lickmolassy: 119

Liskeevy (2 pts.): 9

Loughrea: 92

Meelick: 118

Monivea: 44

Moycullen: 25

Moylough: 40

Moyruss: 3

Omey: 2

Oranmore: 52

Rahoon: 53

Ross: 7

St. Nicholas: 54

Stradbally: 57

Taghboy: 51

Templetogher: 15

Tiranascragh: 117

Tuam: 14

Tynagh (2 pts.): 104

County Kerry

A Brief History

The county of Kerry is on the southwestern coast of Ireland. Its major towns are Tralee, Listowel, Castleisland, Killarney, Caherciveen, Dingle, and Ballybunion. Before the division of Ireland into counties, this area formed part of the Gaelic territory of Desmond. The major Gaelic families included O'Connor Kerry, O'Driscoll, O'Donoghue, O'Falvey, O'Shea, O'Kelleher, Moriarty, O'Mahoney, and O'Connell. Following the Norman invasion, the county was granted to Robert Fitzstephen and Milo de Cogan. However, because of the power of the native chieftains, they were unable to take possession of the county.

The Norman conquest of the more easterly parts of Munster, however, drove the McCarthys and O'Sullivans of those parts to Kerry, displacing some of the resident families. Although the chief of the McCarthys nominally submitted to Henry II in 1172, the McCarthys and the other chieftains effectively retained their lands and control of much of the county.

Parts of the county did come under the chieftainship of Norman families by other means. Raymond Fitzgerald, ancestor of the present Fitzmaurice family, was granted the area around Lixnaw (or Clanmaurice) by one of the McCarthys in return for assistance in a dispute. John Fitzthomas also obtained large parts of Kerry by marriage. Apart from Fitzgerald and Fitzmaurice, the other families which became established in Kerry after the Norman invasion were Cantillon, Stack, Ferriter, Brown, Clifford, Cromwell, Hussey, and Trant. Fitzthomas was an ancestor of the Fitzgeralds, who were made Earls of Desmond in 1329 and maintained control of Desmond for centuries.

By the mid-fourteenth century, the three major families in the county were Fitzgerald, Fitzmaurice, and McCarthy.

By the late sixteenth century, the lands of Kerry and Cork began to attract the attention of English "adventurers," who approached the English crown to give them title to these lands. A huge scheme of confiscation of Munster lands was planned. This alarmed the Irish and Norman chieftains, who protested against the scheme. Their formal protests failed, and in 1580 the Earl of Desmond rebelled against the English. He was eventually defeated after a bloody war which devastasted much of Desmond. The people of Munster suffered greatly after this rebellion, both from the savagery of the troops and from the famine which resulted from their destruction of crops and property. The power of the Fitzgeralds never recovered after this. Thousands of those made homeless during this rebellion were gathered together and transported to the West Indies. After the rebellion, the estates of all the rebels were confiscated and distributed among English adventurers, in particular Blennerhassett, Browne, Herbert, Champion, Holly, Denny, and Conway. Among the settlers who obtained grants from these adventurers were the families of Spring, Rice, Morris, and Gunn.

Following the defeat of the 1641 rebellion, further parts of the county were granted to English adventurers, in particular Sir William Petty. Many of the settlers brought in at this time (the 1670s) left again during the Williamite wars, when the Irish forces again took control of the county. The names of the pre-1641 and post-1641 owners of land are listed in the Book of Survey of Distribution and in the Civil Survey.

The county was relatively badly affected by the Great Famine of 1845-47. The population was 294,000 in 1841, and had dropped by nineteen percent in 1851. During the main years of the famine, 1845-50, approximately 32,000 people died. Furthermore, between 1851 and 1855, 44,000 people, or seventeen percent of the population, emigrated.

The eastern part of the county, particularly the northeast, is rich agricultural land, while the more westerly parts are mountainous.

The major industries are agriculture, fishing, and tourism. The lakes of Killarney, for instance, have been a tourist attraction since the early nineteenth century.

Census and Census Substitutes

1586

The Desmond Survey. A survey of the Earl of Desmond's lands, giving names of leaseholders, placenames, and the sizes of holdings. Printed in *The Kerryman* newspaper, August through October 1927; also available at NAI Ms M.5037.

1622

An unpublished Survey of the Plantation of Munster in 1622. Robert Dunlop, R.S.A.I. 4 (1924): 136–139. Names proprietors and number of leaseholders in Denis Vale (Tralee), Island of Kerry, Soflymricahill, Mullahriff, Killorglin, and Ballymacdonnell. BM Mss Sloane 4756 f.80 names the leaseholders.

1641

List of Proprietors of Land: Books of Survey and Distribution. NLI ms. 970.

1657

"Parishes of Dysart, Killury, Rathroe." *Civil Survey.* Vol. 4. Clanmaurice Barony. R.C. Simington. Stationery Office, 1938. Also in *Kerry Arch. Mag.* 1 (6) (1911): 357–68; SLC film 973122.

1659

"Census" of Ireland. Edited by S. Pender. Dublin: Stationery Office, 1939. NLI I6551. SLC film 924648.

1666–68

"New Grantees of Lands" (see source listed in 1641 above).

1761

Militia List, Counties Kerry, etc. Go Ms 680.

1775

"Catholic Qualification Roll Extracts" (103 names, addresses, and occupations). 59th Report DKPRI, 50–84.

1796

Spinning Wheel Premium Lists (see introduction; lists 950 Kerry names).

1799

A list of 300 prominent Roman Catholics petitioning the Lord Lieutenant. Gives name and address (parish, town or townland). *Dublin Evening Post*, 9 June 1799.

1821

Government Census Remnants: Parish of Kilcummin. RIA; McSwiney Papers (Parcel F, No. 3); SLC film 596418.

1823–37

Tithe Applotment Survey (see introduction). Copies of Tithe Applotment Returns are also found in OCM (see introduction); Barony of Magunihy in vol. 7 and Barony of Trughanacmy in vol. 8.

1834

"Census of the Parishes of Prior and Killemlagh." *J. Kerry Arch. Hist. Soc.* 8 (1975): 114–35.

1835

"Tralee Borough election, January 1835." Gives names, occupations, religion of voters and how they voted. NAI–SPO–Outrage Papers 1835/158; also in *J. Kerry Arch. Hist. Soc.* 19 (1986): 73–79.

"A Census of the Catholic Parish of Ferriter" (comprising civil parishes of Dunquin, Dunurlin, Ferriter, Kilmalkedar, Kilquane, and Marhin). *J. Kerry. Arch. Hist. Soc.* 7 (1974): 37–70 (both above list householders in each townland, and total males and females in each household).

1852

Griffith's Valuation (see introduction).

1901

Census. NAI (see introduction). J. King's "Co. Kerry Past and Present" is a partial index to this census. SLC (mf).

1911

Census. NAI.

Church Records

Church of Ireland

See the introduction for a description of Church of Ireland records and their major repositories. Many C of I records were lost in the PRO fire of 1922. These are indicated as "Lost." However, as Church of Ireland records were effectively state records, the records of marriage (from 1845) are also in the General Registrar's Office. Some are still in local custody (LC), while others

126 PÁDRAIG DE BRÚN

Population returun of the Parish of Keelimila Barony of Iueragh County of Kerry as enumerated in the month of December 1834

Townlands	M.	F.	Tot.
BOLUS			
William Cronin	5	4	9
Daniel Leary	4	6	10
William Casey	3	2	5
John Sullivan	3	2	5
Daniel Hartnett	5	2	7
Cornelius Kelly	3	2	5
Michael Burke	2	1	3
Darby Currane	2	2	4
Maurice Currane	2	2	4
John Currane	2	2	4
Denis Currane	3	1	4
Daniel Gallivan	2	2	4
John Sughrue	5	2	7
Thomas Moore	2	3	5
	43	33	76
[all Catholics]			
Houses		14	

	M.	F.	Tot.
John Goggin	4	3	7
Michael Shea	1	3	4
James FitzGerald	3	4	7
	25	23	48
[all Catholics]			
Houses		7	
TUREEN			
Daniel Foley	5	1	6
Timothy Foley	2	3	5
Patrick Casey	2	2	4
Michael Burke	5	4	9
Daniel Connor	1	1	2
	15	11	26
[all Catholics]			
Houses		5	

DUCALLA	M.	F.	Tot.
Darby Murphy	2	2	4
Daniel Murphy	2	3	5
John Murphy	2	2	4
Daniel Sullivan	1	2	3
Maurice Sullivan	1	1	2
John Keating	4	1	5
Denies Sullivan	1	1	2
Daniel Sullivan	1	2	3
William Goggin	1	2	3
	15	16	31
[all Catholics]			
Houses		9	

KEELŌNCAH[38]	M.	F.	Tot.
Daniel Murphy	4	3	7
Maurice Sullivan	3	3	6
Eugene Sullivan	3	2	5[39]
Cornelius Sullivan	2	2	4
Darby Sullivan	2	3	5
Cornelius Connor	1	1	2
	15	14	29
[all Catholics]			
Houses		6	

ALAHEE[37]	M.	F.	Tot.
John Sullivan	5	4	9
William Murphy	2	4	6
Barth^w Murphy	6	1	7
Patrick Mahoney	4	4	8

AHERT	M.	F.	Tot.
Patrick Sullivan	7	3	10
Thomas Currane	4	3	7
Michael Connell	4	4	8
Michael Keary	3	5	8
Thomas Currane	4	3	7

37. Allaghee More in Ordnance Survey; see also note 44.
38. *Sic*; also spelt thus in totals. Cf. note 84.
39. Corrected from '3'.

Extract from a census of County Kerry, parishes of Prior and Killemlagh, in December 1834. From *J. Kerry Arch. and Hist. Soc.* 8 (1975).

are in one of a variety of other archives (e.g., RCBL or NAI).

Aghadoe
Earliest Records: b. 1838–; m. 1840–; d. 1838–
Status: LC; NAI M5974 (b. 1838–78; m. 1840–61; d. 1838–81)

Aghavallin
Earliest Records: b. 1872; m. 1811; d. 1873
Status: LC

Aghlish
Status: Lost

Ardfert
Status: Lost

Ballincuslane (see Ballycuslane)

Ballybunion (Liselton)
Earliest Records: b. 1840–; d. 1840–
Status: LC; NAI MFCI 17 (b. 1840–81; d. 1840–75)

Ballycuslane
Status: Lost

Ballyheige
Status: Lost

Ballymacelligot
Earliest Records: b. 1817–; m. 1817–; d. 1817–
Status: LC; NAI MFCI 17, M5991 (b/m/d. 1817–56)

Ballynacourty
Earliest records: b. 1803–77; m. 1803–45; d. 1803–77
Status: LC

Ballynahaglish
Status: Lost

Ballyseedy
Earliest Records: b. 1830–; d. 1831–
Status: LC; and NAI MFCI (b. 1830–78; d. 1831–78)

Caher
Earliest Records: b. 1878–1947; m. 1847–76
Status: RCBL

Castleisland
Earliest Records: b. 1835–77; m. 1836–76; d. 1836–75
Status: LC; NAI M5986 (b. 1835–71; m. 1836–48; d. 1836–75)

Cloghane
Status: Lost

Dromod and Prior
Earliest Records: b. 1820–; m. 1827–; d. 1833–
Status: LC; and NAI M5093 (m. 1822–42)

Duagh
Status: Lost

Glenbeigh
Status: Lost

Kenmare
Earliest Records: b. 1818–73; m. 1819–1950; d. 1818–49
Status: RCBL; Indexed by Anglican Rec. Proj. (m. 1819–1950)

Kilbonane (see Mollahiffe)

Kilconly (see Aghavallin)

Kilcrohane (see also Templenoe)
Earliest Records: m. 1846–1930
Status: RCBL

Kilcummin (see Killarney)

Kilflynn
Status: Lost

Kilgarrylander (see Kiltallagh)

Kilgarvan
Earliest Records: b. 1811–50; m. 1812–1947; d. 1819–1960
Status: RCBL; Indexed by Anglican Rec. Proj. (b. 1811–50; m. 1812–1947; d. 1819–50, 1878–1960)

Kilgobban
Earliest Records: b. 1713–; m. 1713–; d. 1713–
Missing Dates: b/m/d. 1755–1806
Status: LC; b/d. 1806–1875 published in *Kerry Evening Post* April 1910 and m. 1806–1845 in October 1913

Killarney
Earliest Records: b. 1785–1900; m. 1792–1900
Status: OCM Vols 5, 6, 7, 8, and 14

Killeentierna or Disert
Status: Lost

Killeny
Status: Lost

Killorglin
Earliest Records: b. 1840–; m. 1837–; d. 1837–
Status: LC; NAI TAB 12/63 (b. 1840; m. 1837–40; d. 1837)

Killury and Rattoo
Earliest Records: b. 1803; m. 1803; d. 1802
Status: LC

Kilmackelogue or Tuosist (see Kenmare)

Kilmalkedar
Status: Lost

Kilmoiley (see also Ballyheige)
Status: Lost

Kilmore
Earliest Records: b. 1826–1960; m. 1850–1925
Status: RCBL

Kilnaughtin
Earliest Records: b. 1793–1871; m. 1793–1845; d. 1793–1873
Status: LC; and NAI MFCI 17 (b. 1785–1871; m. 1785–1845; d. 1786–1873)

Kilshenane (see Kilflynn)

Kiltallagh
Status: Lost

Knockane
Status: Lost

Liselton (see Ballybunion)

Listowel
Earliest Records: b. 1790–1875; m. 1790–1845; d. 1790–1875
Status: LC; and NAI MFCI 17, M 5970 (b. 1835–72; m. 1835–45; d. 1836–71)

Mollahiffe
Status: Lost

Ratass (see Tralee)
Status: Lost

Rattoo (see Killury)

Templenoe (see also Kilcrohane)
Earliest Records: m. 1849–1920
Status: RCBL

Tralee (Ratass)
Earliest Records: b. 1771–; m. 1771–; d. 1771–
Status: LC; and NAI MFCI 14 (b. 1771–1872; m. 1796–1850; d. 1805–80)

Valentia
Earliest Records: b. 1826–; d. 1826–
Status: LC; and NAI M5988/9 (b. 1826–72; d. 1826–77)

Ventry
Status: Lost

Presbyterian

An account of Presbyterian records is given in the introduction. These registers rarely contain death records, and occasionally have only records of births.

Tralee
Starting Date: 1840

Roman Catholic

The Catholic parish registers of this county are being indexed by Killarney Genealogical Centre Ltd. (KGC; see Research Services at the end of the chapter). When completed, a search of the index will be conducted by the center for a fee. Microfilm copies of all registers are also available in the National Library of Ireland (NLI), and through the LDS library system.

Civil Parish: Aghadoe
Map Grid: 79
RC Parish: Killarney (Fossa); also part Glenflesk, see Killaha
Diocese: A and A
Earliest Record: b. 1.1857; m. 1.1858
Status: LC; NLI (mf); Indexing in progress by KGC

Civil Parish: Aghavallen
Map Grid: 2
RC Parish: Ballylongford
Diocese: A and A
Earliest Record: b. 3.1823; m. 6.1826
Missing Dates: b. 5.1838–10.1869; m. few records to 1837
Status: LC; NLI (mf); Indexing in progress by KGC

Civil Parish: Aglish
Map Grid: 75
RC Parish: Firies, see Kilnanare
Diocese: A and A

Civil Parish: Annagh
Map Grid: 53
RC Parish: part Tralee; part Ballymacelligott
Diocese: A and A

Civil Parish: Ardfert
Map Grid: 25
RC Parish: Ardfert and Spa
Diocese: A and A
Earliest Record: (only scattered records to 1835); b. 3.1819; m. 2.1822
Missing Dates: b. 1846–1859; m. 1846–1859
Status: LC; NLI (mf); Indexing in progress by KGC

Civil Parish: Ballincuslane
Map Grid: 56
RC Parish: Knocknagoshel; also part Castleisland
Earliest Record: b/m. 1850
Status: LC; NLI (mf); Indexing in progress by KGC

Civil Parish: Ballinvoher
Map Grid: 40
RC Parish: Annascaul, see Kilgobban; also part Ballyferriter, see Kilmalkedar
Diocese: A and A

Civil Parish: Ballyconry
Map Grid: 8
RC Parish: Ballybunion, see Killeheny
Diocese: LK

Civil Parish: Ballyduff
Map Grid: 28
RC Parish: Castlegregory, see Killiney
Diocese: A and A

Civil Parish: Ballyheigue
Map Grid: 16
RC Parish: Ballyheigue
Diocese: A and A

Earliest Record: b. 12.1857; m. 1.1858
Status: LC; NLI (mf); Indexing in progress by KGC

Civil Parish: Ballymacelligott
Map Grid: 49
RC Parish: Ballymacelligott
Diocese: A and A
Earliest Record: b. 10.1868; m. 11.1868
Status: LC; NLI (mf); Indexing in progress by KGC

Civil Parish: Ballynacourty (Ballinacourty)
Map Grid: 39
RC Parish: Annascaul, see Ballinvoher
Diocese: A and A

Civil Parish: Ballynahaglish
Map Grid: 45
RC Parish: Spa (earlier records in Ardfert)
Diocese: A and A
Earliest Record: b. 11.1866; m. 1.1867
Status: LC; NLI (mf); Indexing in progress by KGC

Civil Parish: Ballyseedy
Map Grid: 54
RC Parish: see Ballymacelligott
Diocese: A and A

Civil Parish: Brosna
Map Grid: 52
RC Parish: Brosna
Diocese: A and A
Earliest Record: b. 3.1866–75, IGI; b. 1866–1900; m. 1872–1900, OCM vol. 8
Status: LC; NLI (mf); Indexing in progress by KGC

Civil Parish: Caher
Map Grid: 65
RC Parish: Cahirciveen
Diocese: A and A
Earliest Record: b/m. 11.1846
Status: LC; NLI (mf); Indexing in progress by KGC

Civil Parish: Castleisland
Map Grid: 51
RC Parish: Castleisland
Diocese: A and A
Earliest Record: b. 4.1823–72; m. 10.1822–1900, OCM Vols 4, 6, and 7
Missing Dates: b. 8.1869–2.1870; m. 8.1858–2.1859
Status: LC; NLI (mf); Indexing in progress by KGC

Civil Parish: Cloghane
Map Grid: 27
RC Parish: part Castlegregory, see Killiney; also part Dingle
Diocese: A and A

Civil Parish: Clogherbrien
Map Grid: 46
RC Parish: Mainly Tralee; part Ardfert
Diocese: A and A

Civil Parish: Currans
Map Grid: 59
RC Parish: see Killeentierna and also Ballymacelligott
Diocese: A and A

Civil Parish: Dingle
Map Grid: 35
RC Parish: Dingle
Diocese: A and A
Earliest Record: b. 2.1825; m. 5.1821
Missing Dates: b. 4.1837–9.1837
Status: LC; NLI (mf); Indexing in progress by KGC

Civil Parish: Dromod
Map Grid: 70
RC Parish: Dromod (Waterville)
Diocese: A and A
Earliest Record: b. 2.1850; m. 1.1850
Status: LC; NLI (mf); Indexing in progress by KGC

Civil Parish: Duagh
Map Grid: 15
RC Parish: Duagh (also part Listowel)
Diocese: A and A
Earliest Record: (some gaps in early 1850s); b. 1.1819; m. 1.1832
Status: LC; NLI (mf); Indexing in progress by KGC

Civil Parish: Dunquin
Map Grid: 41
RC Parish: Ballyferriter, see Kilmalkedar
Diocese: A and A

Civil Parish: Dunurlin
Map Grid: 32
RC Parish: Ballyferriter, see Kilmalkedar
Diocese: A and A

Civil Parish: Dysert (Trughenackmy)
Map Grid: 61
RC Parish: see Killeentierna
Diocese: A and A

Civil Parish: Dysart (Clanmaurice)
Map Grid: 13
RC Parish: part Lixnaw, see Kilcarragh; part Listowel
Diocese: A and A

Civil Parish: Fenit
Map Grid: 44
RC Parish: Ardfert; also Spa, see Ballynahaglish
Diocese: A and A

Civil Parish: Finuge
Map Grid: 14
RC Parish: see Listowel; also part Lixnaw, see Kilcarragh
Diocese: A and A

Civil Parish: Galey
Map Grid: 6
RC Parish: part Listowel; part Lisselton
Diocese: A and A

Civil Parish: Garfinny
Map Grid: 36
RC Parish: see Dingle
Diocese: A and A

Civil Parish: Glanbehy (Glanbeigh)
Map Grid: 67
RC Parish: Glenbeigh
Diocese: A and A
Earliest Record: b. 3.1830; m. 3.1830
Missing Dates: b. 8.1837-6.1841; m. ends 2.1835
Status: LC; NLI (mf); Indexing in progress by KGC

Civil Parish: Kenmare
Map Grid: 84
RC Parish: Kenmare, see also Tuosist
Diocese: A and A
Earliest Record: b. 1.1819; m. 1.1819
Missing Dates: m. 3.1824-1.1826, 7.1838-1.1839
Status: LC; NLI (mf); Indexing in progress by KGC

Civil Parish: Kilbonane
Map Grid: 74
RC Parish: Milltown
Diocese: A and A
Earliest Record: b. 10.1825; m. 10.1821
Missing Dates: b. 9.1840-10.1841; m. 11.1832-10.1842
Status: LC; NLI (mf); Indexing in progress by KGC

Civil Parish: Kilcaragh
Map Grid: 19
RC Parish: Lixnaw
Diocese: A and A
Earliest Record: b. 8.1810; m. 1.1810
Missing Dates: b. 2.1845-6.1848; m. 6.1852-8.1856
Status: LC; NLI (mf); Indexing in progress by KGC

Civil Parish: Kilcaskan (see Co. Cork)
Map Grid: 87
RC Parish: Glengarriffe (see Kilmacomogue)
Diocese: RO

Civil Parish: Kilcolman
Map Grid: 62
RC Parish: Milltown, see Kilbonane
Diocese: A and A

Civil Parish: Kilconly
Map Grid: 1
RC Parish: Ballybunion, see Killeheny
Diocese: A and A

Civil Parish: Kilcredane
Map Grid: 76
RC Parish: Firies, see Kilnanare
Diocese: A and A

Civil Parish: Kilcrohane (1)
Map Grid: 82
RC Parish: Sneem (Ballybeg); also Cahirdaniel, see below

Diocese: A and A
Earliest Record: b. 8.1845; m. 2.1858
Missing Dates: b. 11.1848-11.1857
Status: LC; NLI (mf); Indexing in progress by KGC

Civil Parish: Kilcrohane (2)
Map Grid: 82
RC Parish: Cahirdaniel
Diocese: A and A
Earliest Record: b. 2.1831; m. 5.1831
Status: LC; NLI (mf); Indexing in progress by KGC

Civil Parish: Kilcummin
Map Grid: 77
RC Parish: Kilcummin West; also part Glenflesk, see Killaha
Diocese: A and A
Earliest Record: b. 1.1821; m. 1.1823 OCM Vol 5
Missing Dates: b. 8.1859-11.1859; m. 9.1859-2.1873
Status: LC; NLI (mf); Indexing in progress by KGC

Civil Parish: Kildrum
Map Grid: 43
RC Parish: see Dingle
Diocese: A and A

Civil Parish: Kilfeighny
Map Grid: 20
RC Parish: Abbeydorney, see O'Dorney
Diocese: A and A

Civil Parish: Kilflyn
Map Grid: 24
RC Parish: Abbeydorney, see O'Dorney
Diocese: A and A

Civil Parish: Kilgarrylander
Map Grid: 57
RC Parish: Castlemaine, see Kiltallagh
Diocese: A and A

Civil Parish: Kilgarvan
Map Grid: 85
RC Parish: Kilgarvan
Diocese: A and A
Earliest Record: b. 4.1818; m. 11.1818
Missing Dates: m. 4.1864-9.1864
Status: LC; NLI (mf); Indexing in progress by KGC

Civil Parish: Kilgobban
Map Grid: 31
RC Parish: Cappaclough (Annascaul)
Diocese: A and A
Earliest Record: b. 4.1829; m. 5.1829
Missing Dates: b. 3.1834-3.1837, 3.1839-10.1857; m. 6.1835-5.1837, 10.1837-9.1855
Status: LC; NLI (mf); Indexing in progress by KGC

Civil Parish: Killaha
Map Grid: 81
RC Parish: Glenflesk

Diocese: A and A
Earliest Record: b. 9.1821; m. 2.1831
Status: LC; NLI (mf); Indexing in progress by KGC

Civil Parish: Killahan
Map Grid: 17
RC Parish: Abbeydorney, see O'Dorney
Diocese: A and A

Civil Parish: Killarney
Map Grid: 80
RC Parish: Killarney; also part Glenflesk, see Killaha
Diocese: A and A
Earliest Record: b. 8.1792; m. 8.1792
Missing Dates: b. 3.1854–5.1854; m. 5.1851–1.1858
Status: LC; NLI (mf); Indexing in progress by KGC

Civil Parish: Killeentierna
Map Grid: 60
RC Parish: Killeentierna
Diocese: A and A
Earliest Record: b. 6.1801; m. 6.1803, OCM Vols 4 and 6
Missing Dates: b. 12.1809–7.1823; m. 2.1828–6.1830
Status: LC; NLI (mf); Indexing in progress by KGC

Civil Parish: Killehenny
Map Grid: 4
RC Parish: Ballybunion
Diocese: A and A
Earliest Record: b. 11.1831; m. 2.1837
Status: LC; NLI (mf); Indexing in progress by KGC

Civil Parish: Killemlagh
Map Grid: 68
RC Parish: see Prior
Diocese: A and A

Civil Parish: Killinane
Map Grid: 66
RC Parish: see Caher
Diocese: A and A

Civil Parish: Killiney
Map Grid: 30
RC Parish: Castlegregory; also part Annascaul, see Kilgobban
Diocese: A and A
Earliest Record: b. 12.1828; m. 2.1829
Status: LC; NLI (mf); Indexing in progress by KGC

Civil Parish: Killorglin
Map Grid: 63
RC Parish: Killorglin, see also Glanbeigh
Diocese: A and A
Earliest Record: LC
Status: LC; NLI (mf); Indexing in progress by KGC

Civil Parish: Killury
Map Grid: 11
RC Parish: Causeway
Diocese: A and A

Earliest Record: b. 12.1782; m. 2.1809
Missing Dates: b. 7.1786–11.1806, 11.1819–7.1820; m. 5.1845–2.1846
Status: LC; NLI (mf); Indexing in progress by KGC

Civil Parish: Kilmalkedar
Map Grid: 34
RC Parish: (Kilmelchidar) Ballyferriter
Diocese: A and A
Earliest Record: b. 1.1807; m. 1.1808
Status: LC; NLI (mf); Indexing in progress by KGC

Civil Parish: Kilmoyly
Map Grid: 22
RC Parish: see Ardfert
Diocese: A and A

Civil Parish: Kilnanare
Map Grid: 73
RC Parish: Firies
Diocese: A and A
Earliest Record: b. 1.1871; m. 1.1830
Status: LC; NLI (mf); Indexing in progress by KGC

Civil Parish: Kilnaughten
Map Grid: 3
RC Parish: Tarbert and Ballylongford; see also Aghavallen
Diocese: A and A
Earliest Record: b. 10.1859; m. 7.1859
Status: LC; NLI (mf); Indexing in progress by KGC

Civil Parish: Kilquane
Map Grid: 26
RC Parish: Ballyferriter, see Kilmalkedar
Diocese: A and A

Civil Parish: Kilshinane (Kilshenane)
Map Grid: 21
RC Parish: part Lixnaw, see Kilcarragh; part Listowel
Diocese: A and A

Civil Parish: Kiltallagh
Map Grid: 58
RC Parish: Castlemaine
Diocese: A and A
Earliest Record: b. 2.1804; m. 2.1804
Missing Dates: b. 7.1813–1.1815, 10.1817–4.1818
Status: LC; NLI (mf); Indexing in progress by KGC

Civil Parish: Kiltomy
Map Grid: 18
RC Parish: Lixnaw, see Kilcarragh
Diocese: A and A

Civil Parish: Kinard
Map Grid: 37
RC Parish: see Dingle
Diocese: A and A

Civil Parish: Knockane
Map Grid: 71
RC Parish: Tuogh, see also Killorglin

Diocese: A and A
Earliest Record: b. 3.1844; m. 1.1843
Status: LC; NLI (mf); Indexing in progress by KGC

Civil Parish: Knockanure
Map Grid: 10
RC Parish: Moyvane, see Murhir
Diocese: A and A

Civil Parish: Lisselton
Map Grid: 5
RC Parish: Ballydonohoe and Ballybunion, see Killehenny
Diocese: A and A

Civil Parish: Listowel
Map Grid: 9
RC Parish: Listowel
Diocese: A and A
Earliest Record: (many gaps to 1856); b. 8.1802; m. 1.1837
Status: LC; NLI (mf); Indexing in progress by KGC

Civil Parish: Marhin
Map Grid: 33
RC Parish: Ballyferriter, see Kilmalkedar
Diocese: A and A

Civil Parish: Minard
Map Grid: 38
RC Parish: see Dingle
Diocese: A and A

Civil Parish: Molahiffe
Map Grid: 72
RC Parish: Firies, see Kilnanare
Diocese: A and A

Civil Parish: Murhir
Map Grid: 7
RC Parish: Moyvane
Diocese: A and A
Earliest Record: b. 7.1855; m. 10.1855
Status: LC; NLI (mf); Indexing in progress by KGC

Civil Parish: Nohaval (Nohoval)
Map Grid: 55
RC Parish: see Ballymacelligott
Diocese: A and A

Civil Parish: Nohavaldaly
Map Grid: 78
RC Parish: Boherboy (Boherbue)
Diocese: A and A
Earliest Record: b. 7.1833; m. 3.1863; Boherbue: b. 1860-1900; 1863-1900 OCM Vols 2 and 11
Missing Dates: b. 12.1860-2.1863
Status: LC; NLI (mf); Indexing in progress by KGC

Civil Parish: O'Brennan
Map Grid: 50
RC Parish: see Ballymacelligot
Diocese: A and A

Civil Parish: O'Dorney
Map Grid: 23
RC Parish: Abbeydorney
Diocese: A and A
Earliest Record: b. 10.1835; m. 1.1837
Missing Dates: b. 9.1844-2.1851; m. 7.1859-11.1859
Status: LC; NLI (mf); Indexing in progress by KGC

Civil Parish: Prior
Map Grid: 69
RC Parish: Prior (Ballinskelligs)
Diocese: A and A
Earliest Record: b. 1.1832; m. 1.1832
Status: LC; NLI (mf); Indexing in progress by KGC

Civil Parish: Ratass
Map Grid: 48
RC Parish: part Ballymacelligott; part Tralee
Diocese: A and A

Civil Parish: Rattoo
Map Grid: 12
RC Parish: Causeway, see Killury
Diocese: A and A

Civil Parish: Stradbally
Map Grid: 29
RC Parish: Castlegregory, see Killiney
Diocese: A and A

Civil Parish: Templenoe
Map Grid: 83
RC Parish: see Kenmare
Diocese: A and A

Civil Parish: Tralee
Map Grid: 47
RC Parish: Tralee (St. John's)
Diocese: A and A
Earliest Record: b. 1.1772; m. 2.1774
Status: LC; NLI (mf); Indexing in progress by KGC

Civil Parish: Tuosist
Map Grid: 86
RC Parish: Tuosist
Diocese: A and A
Earliest Record: b. 4.1844
Status: LC; NLI (mf); Indexing in progress by KGC

Civil Parish: Valentia
Map Grid: 64
RC Parish: Valentia
Diocese: A and A
Earliest Record: b. 3.1825; m. 2.1827
Missing Dates: b. 7.1864-5.1867; m. 4.1856-1880
Status: LC; NLI (mf); Indexing in progress by KGC

Civil Parish: Ventry
Map Grid: 42
RC Parish: see Dingle
Diocese: A and A

Commercial and Social Directories

1824

J. Pigot's *City of Dublin and Hibernian Provincial Directory* includes traders, nobility, gentry, and clergy lists of Dingle, Kenmare, Killarney, Listowel, Tarbert, and Tralee.

1846

Slater's *National Commercial Directory of Ireland* lists nobility, clergy, traders, etc., in Castleisland, Dingle, Kenmare, Killarney, Listowel, Milltown, Tarbert, and Tralee.

1856

Slater's *Royal National Commercial Directory of Ireland* lists nobility, gentry, clergy, traders, etc., in Cahirciveen and Valentia, Castleisland, Dingle, Kenmare, Killarney, Listowel, Milltown, Tarbert, Tralee, and Blennerville.

1870

Slater's *Directory of Ireland* contains trade, nobility, and clergy lists for Cahirciveen and Valentia, Castleisland, Dingle, Kenmare, Killarney, Listowel, Milltown and Castlemaine, Tarbert and Ballylongford, and Tralee.

1881

Slater's *Royal National Commercial Directory of Ireland* contains lists of traders, clergy, nobility, and farmers in adjoining parishes of the towns of Cahirciveen and Valentia, Castleisland, Dingle, Kenmare, Killarney, Listowel, Milltown and Castlemaine, Tarbert and Ballylongford, and Tralee.

1886

Francis Guy's *Postal Directory of Munster* lists gentry, clergy, traders, principal farmers, teachers, and police in each postal district and a listing of magistrates, clergy, and the professions for the county. SLC film 1559399.

1893

Francis Guy's *Postal Directory of Munster* lists traders and farmers in each of the postal districts of the county, and a general alphabetical index to persons in the whole county.

1894

Slater's *Royal National Directory of Ireland* lists traders, police, teachers, farmers, and private residents in each of the towns, villages, and parishes of the county.

Family History

Denny, H.L.L. *A Handbook of County Kerry Family History, Biography, etc.* Tralee: Co. Kerry Society, 1923.

Bernard, J.H. *The Bernards of Kerry.* Dublin, 1922.

"The Blennerhassets of Kerry: Earlier English Stock." *Kerry Arch. Mag.* 5 (1919): 34-39.

"Richard Cantillon de Ballyheigue." *Studies* 11 (1932): 105-22.

Conway—see Mahony.

"The Conways of Kerry." *Kerry Arch. Mag.* 5 (1920): 71-91.

"Notes on the Families of . . . Denny of Tralee." *J. Ass. Pres. Mem. Dead* 7 (1907-09): 373.

Eagar, F. *The Eagar Family of Co. Kerry.* Dublin, 1860.

"The Fitzmaurices of Duagh, Co. Kerry." *Ir. Gen.* 3 (1): 25-35.

"The Fitzmaurices, Lords of Kerry." *J. Cork Arch. Hist. Soc.* n.s., 26 (1920): 10-18.

"The Fitzmaurices of Kerry." *Kerry Arch. Mag.* 3 (1970): 23-42.

Marquis of Lansdowne. *Glanerought and the Petty-Fitzmaurices.* London, 1937.

Fuller, J.F. *Some Descendants of the Kerry Branch of the Fuller Family.* Dublin, 1880.

Fuller, J.F. *Pedigree of the Family of Fuller of Cork, Kerry, and Halstead.* 1909.

King, J. "The Fuller Family." In *History of Co. Kerry.* Dublin, 1910: 208-11, 346-52.

Hewson, John. *Hewsons of Finuge, Kerry, of Royal Descent.* 1907.

Pielou, P.L. *The Leslies of Tarbert, Co. Kerry and their Forbears.* Dublin, 1935.

"The Mahonys of Kerry." *Kerry Arch. Mag.* 4 (1917-18): 171-90, 223-35.

"Markham of Nunstown and Callinafercy, Co. Kerry." *Ir. Anc.* 16 (2) (1984): 60.

Marquis of Ruvigny and Raineval. *Morris of Ballybeggan and Castle Morris, Co. Kerry.* 1904.

"Murphys of Muskerry." *J. Cork Hist. Arch. Soc.* 219 (1969): 1-19.

King, J. "The O'Moriarty Family." In *History of Co. Kerry.* Dublin, 1935: 265-79.

MacCarthy, S. "Three Kerry Families: O'Mahony, Conway and Spotswood." *Folkestone* (1923).

Orpen, G.H. *The Orpen Family: Richard Orpen of Killowen, Co. Kerry, with Some Researches into the Early History of his Forebears.* Frome, 1930.

Palmer, A.H. *Genealogical and Historical Account of the Palmer Family of Kenmare, Co. Kerry.* 1872.

"The Pierse Family of Co. Kerry." *Kerry Arch. Mag.* 5 (1972): 14-32.

Spotswood—see Mahony.

A Handbook of
County Kerry Family History,
Biography, &c.,

BY

The Rev. H. L. L. DENNY, M.A., F.S.G.,

Author of 'Anglo-Irish Genealogy,' 'Memorials of an Ancient House,' 'The Manor of Hawkesbury,' Etc., Etc.

(Ancient Seal of the Borough of Tralee)

Compiled for the Archæological Group

OF

The County Kerry Society.

MCMXXIII.

BRIGGS & MACLEAN, PRINTERS, BK-THEE.

SELECTIONS

FROM

OLD KERRY RECORDS,

Historical and Genealogical,

WITH

INTRODUCTORY MEMOIR, NOTES, AND APPENDIX.

BY

MARY AGNES HICKSON.

London

PRINTED BY WATSON & HAZELL,
28, CHARLES STREET, HATTON GARDEN.

1872.

Title pages from two major sources of Kerry family history.

McCarthy, S. "The Trant Family." *Folkestone* 1924; supplement, 1926.

"Trant Family." *Kerry Arch. Mag.* 2 (1914): 237-62; 3 (1914): 20-38; 5 (1919): 18-26.

King, J. "The Trant Family." In *History of Co. Kerry*. Dublin, 1911.

Gravestone Inscriptions

The major series of gravestone inscriptions in this county are those included in volumes 6 and 8 of the series *O'Kief, Coshe Mang and Slieve Luachra* by Albert Casey *(OCM)*. Seven graveyards have also been indexed by the Finuge Heritage Survey (see Research Sources and Services), and will be searched by them for a fee.

Aghadoe: OCM 6 (1963)

Aglish: OCM 6 (1963)

Ardcrone—Currans: OCM 6 (1963)

Ardfert: OCM 8 (1965) and extracts in *Kilkenny Arch Soc. J.* 2 (1852-3): 128-133

Ballybunion: OCM Vol. 11

Ballymacelligott: OCM Vol. 8 and 11

Brosna: OCM Vol. 6 (1963)

Castleisland (C of I): OCM Vol. 6 (1963)

Clogherbrien: OCM Vol. 8 (1963)

Cordal (Killeentierna): OCM Vol. 6 (1963)

Currans: OCM Vol. 6 (1963)

Dingle: *J. Ass. Pres. Mem. Dead* and extracts in *Kilkenny Arch Soc. J.* 2 (1852-3): 128-133

Duagh (RC): Finuge Heritage Survey; OCM Vols 8 and 11

Duagh—St. Brigid's: OCM Vols 8 and 11

Dysert (Castelisland): OCM Vol. 6 (1963)

Finuge: Finuge Heritage Survey

Firies: OCM Vol. 6 (1963)

Fossa Cemetery and Church (Killarney): OCM Vol. 6 (1963)

Galey: Finuge Heritage Survey

Garfinny: *J. Ass. Pres. Mem. Dead* and extracts in *Kilkenny Arch Soc. J.* 2: 128-133

Glenflesk (Kilcummin): OCM Vol. 6 (1963)

Gneeveguilla (Kilcummin): OCM Vol. 6 (1963)

Kilbannivane (Castelisland): OCM Vol. 6 (1963)

Kilcummin (RC): OCM Vol. 6 (1963)

Kilcummin—St. Agatha's: OCM Vol. 6 (1963)

Killarney and Muckross Abbey: OCM Vol. 6 (1963)

Kilmurry (Castelisland): OCM Vol. 6 (1963)

Kilsarcon (Dysert East): OCM Vol. 6 (1963)

Kilshanane: Finuge Heritage Survey

Kilnanare: OCM Vol. 6 (1963)

Killarney New Cemetery: OCM Vol. 6 (1963)

Killarney (C of I): OCM Vol. 6 (1963)

Killarney RC Cathedral: OCM Vol. 6 (1963)

Killeentierna: OCM Vol. 6 (1963)

Killorglin: OCM Vols 8 and 11

Kilquane: OCM Vol. 6 (1963)

Kiltomey: extracts in *Kilkenny Arch Soc. J.* 2: 128-133

Lisselton: *J. Ass. Pres. Mem. Dead*

Listowel (RC): OCM Vol. 11

Listowel—St. John's (C of I): OCM Vol. 8

Muckross Abbey (Killarney): OCM Vol. 6 (1963)

Molahiffe (RC): OCM Vol. 6 (1963)

Nohoval: OCM Vols 6, 8, and 11

O'Brennan: OCM Vols 8 and 11

Rathmore (Kilcummin): OCM Vol. 6 (1963)

Rathmore, Old (Killarney): OCM Vol. 6 (1963)

Spa (Tralee): OCM Vol. 11

Tralee (RC): OCM Vols 8 and 11

Tralee Abbey (RC): *J. Ass. Pres. Mem. Dead*

Ventry (C of I): Extracts in *Kilkenny Arch Soc. J.* 2: 128-133

Newspapers

Kerry has several excellent newspaper sources. In addition, papers from surrounding counties of Limerick and Cork also extensively reported Kerry events and people. These should be consulted as well. There are several indexes to events in papers covering Kerry. These include "Co. Kerry and Cork Birth, Marriages and Deaths and Miscellaneous Events" (1781-1821), compiled by Basil O'Connell and printed in OCM Vol. 8. A card index to biographical notices in Cork and Kerry newspapers (1754 to 1827) is in the library of University College, Cork. Microfiche copies of this are in the NLI, the library of University College, Dublin, the New York Public Library, and on SLC film 537921/2. Biographical notices from the *Kerry Evening Post* (1828-64) are listed in OCM Vol. 6, and the Nash collection of Kerry newspaper cuttings is in the LDS Family History Library, Mf. 0477616.

Title: *Chute's Western Herald* (continued as *Western Herald* in 1828)
Published in: Tralee, 1791-1835
NLI Holdings: 1791-1823 (with gaps); 1.1824-9.1829; 10.1828-5.1835
BL Holdings: 1-9.1828; 10.1828-3.1830; 3.1830-5.1835

Title: *Kerry Evening Post*
Published in: Tralee, 1813-1917
NLI Holdings: odd numbers 1813-24; 1.1828-9.1917
BL Holdings: odd numbers 1813-24; 1.1828-9.1917 (see also card index above)

Indexed in OCM Vols 6, 11, and 15

Title: *Kerry Examiner and Munster General Observer*
Published in: Tralee, 1840–56
NLI Holdings: 8.1840–3.1856 (with gaps)
BL Holdings: 8.1840–10.1849; 3.1850–8.1854;
1.1855–3.1856

Title: *Kerry Independent*
Published in: Tralee, 1880–84
NLI Holdings: 10.1880–7.1884 (with gaps)
BL Holdings: 10.1880–7.1884 (with gaps)

Title: *Kerry News*
Published in: Tralee, 1894–1939
NLI Holdings: 8.1927–6.1941
BL Holdings: 1.1894–8.1920; 8.1927–12.1929;
1.1931–7.1939

Title: *Kerry Star*
Published in: Tralee, 1861–63
NLI Holdings: 5.1861–3.1863
BL Holdings: 5.1861–3.1863

Title: *Kerry Weekly Reporter and Commercial Advertiser*
(continued as *Kerry Reporter* in 1927)
Published in: Tralee, 1883–1936
NLI Holdings: 2.1883–8.1920; 8.1927–12.1935
BL Holdings: 2.1883–8.1920; 8.1927–2.1936

Title: *Tralee Chronicle* (continued as *Tralee Chronicle and Killarney Echo* in 1857)
Published in: Tralee, 1843–81
NLI Holdings: 3.1843–5.1881
BL Holdings: 3.1843–10.1848; 1849–5.1881

Title: *Tralee Mercury*
Published in: Tralee, 1829–39
NLI Holdings: 2.1829–12.1836; 2.1837–7.1839
BL Holdings: 2.1829–12.1836; 2.1837–7.1839

Wills and Administrations

A discussion of the types of records, where they are held, and their availability and value is given in the Wills section of the introduction. The availability of prerogative wills, administrations, and marriage license records is also described in the relevant parts of the same section. Where available, published sources of these records are given in the Miscellaneous Sources section.

Pre-1858 Wills and Administrations

Prerogative Wills. See the introduction.

Consistorial Wills. County Kerry is mainly in the diocese of Ardfert, with one parish in the diocese of Limerick and one in Ross. The guide to Catholic parish records in this chapter shows the diocese to which each civil parish belonged. The wills of residents of each diocese were usually proven within that diocese (see the Wills section for exceptions). The following records survive:

Wills

See the introduction.

Abstracts

See the introduction.

The Welply Will Abstracts in the RCBL contain extracts from 1,682 Munster wills, mainly from Cork. Index contains name, date of will and (usually) probate, and residence. Index in *Ir. Gen.* 6 (6) 1985 to 7 (1) 1986.

Indexes

Ardfert (1690–1858) published to 1800 by Phillimore, and to 1858 in OCM 5 (1962); see also counties Limerick and Cork.

Post-1858 Wills and Administrations

County Kerry was served by the District Registries of Limerick (Baronies of Clanmaurice and Iraghticonnor) and Cork (rest of county). The surviving records are kept in the NAI. These comprise:

Original Wills (1900–1960), Will Books (1858–1900), Probate Grants, Administration Grants, and Wills and Administration indexes. The Will Books (1858–1888) are also published in OCM Vols 11 and 14 and are on microfilm in the LDS Family History Library. The Cork District Wills (1858–1897) are on films 100929–42, and Limerick District Wills (1858–1888) are on SLC film 100946–7. Other probate sources are described in O'Connor's *A Guide to Tracing Your Kerry Ancestors* (see Miscellaneous Sources).

Marriage Licenses

Indexes

Limerick (1691–1845) NAI; SLC film 100869. Ross (1623–1845) NAI; SLC film 100864–66.

Miscellaneous Sources

O'Connor, Michael H. *A Guide to Tracing Your Kerry Ancestors.* Dublin: Flyleaf Press, 1994. ISBN: 0-9508466-5-1.

O'Connor, Tommy. "Surnames of Co. Kerry." *Irish Roots* 3 (1995): 12–13.

Cusack, N. *History of the Kingdom of Kerry.* London, 1871.

Denny, Rev. L.L. *A Handbook of County Kerry Family History, Biography etc.* Compiled for the Archaeological Group of the County Kerry Society, 1923.

Hickson, M.A. *Selections from Old Kerry Records Historical and Genealogical.* 2 vols. London, 1872–74.

The Godfrey Papers, Abstracts of Deeds 1800–1839. *Kerry Arch. Hist. Soc. J.* 21 (1988): 42–101 (indexed);

Abstracts 1850–1858, 23 (1990): 46–68.

Kenmare Estates: Rent Rolls for Lord Viscount Kenmare's Estates in Kerry, Limerick, and Bantry, Co. Cork. NAI; SLC films 101772-9.

Some Lists of Kerry Priests—1750-1835. *Kerry Arch. Hist. Soc. J.* 18 (1985): 83–169.

King, J. *County Kerry, Past and Present–Handbook to Local and Family History.* Dublin, 1931. Reprint. Mercier Press, 1984. (Includes index to 1901 census.)

"Land Tenure in Kenmare and Tuosist 1696-1716." *Kerry Arch. Hist. Soc. J.* 10 (1977).

O'Kief, Coshe Mang and Slieve Luachra. Compiled and published by Albert O'Casey, 16 vols. Includes "Genealogies of North Cork and East Kerry" in Vol. 7.

Smith, C. *The Ancient and Present State of the County of Kerry.* Dublin, 1756.

"Some Kerry Wild Geese." *Ir. Gen.* 2 (8) (1950): 250–54.

"A View of the State of Agriculture in the County of Kerry" (1800). *Kerry Arch. Hist. Soc. J.* 1 (1968): 81–100.

Stack, M.A. *A Bibliography of Co. Kerry.* Thesis for fellowship of the Library Association of Ireland, 1968.

Bary, Valerie. *Houses of Kerry* (detailing major houses and associated families). Ballinakella Press, 1994.

Research Sources and Services

Journals

Kerry Archaeological Magazine
Journal of Kerry Archaeological and Historical Society
Kenmare Literary and Historical Society Journal

Libraries and Information Sources

Kerry County Library, Moyderwell, Tralee, Co. Kerry. Ph: (066) 21200.

Research Services

See Research Services in Dublin in the introduction.

Finuge Heritage Survey, Teach Siamsa, Finuge, Lixnaw, Co. Kerry. Ph: (068) 40243. This has an index of parish registers and gravestones for Listowel and Lixnaw.

Killarney Genealogical Centre Ltd. (KGC), Cathedral Walk, Killarney, Co. Kerry. Ph: (064) 35946. This is the designated IGP center for Co. Kerry and is indexing the church and other records of the county. Researchers are advised to contact the center for an updated list of registers, and other sources, indexed. Research is conducted for a fee.

Kerry Diocesan Genealogical Centre, c/o Fr. Ciaran O'Shea, Castleisland, Co. Kerry. Ph: (066) 41598

Societies

Cumman Luachra Ciarrai Thoir, Mrs. Eileen Fleming, Gneeveguilla, Rathmore, Co. Kerry

Kenmare Literary and Historical Society, Ms. Nancy Price, Cahir, Kenmare, Co. Kerry

Kerry Archaeological Society, Ms. Kathleen Brown, c/o Kerry Co. Library, Tralee, Co. Kerry

Valentia Heritage Society, Mrs. Clare Ring, Knightstown, Valentia Island, Co. Kerry

Kerry Civil Parishes as Numbered on Map

1. Kilconly
2. Aghavallen
3. Kilnaughten
4. Killehenny
5. Lisselton
6. Galey
7. Murher
8. Ballyconry
9. Listowel
10. Knockanure
11. Killury

12. Rattoo
13. Dysert (note also 61)
14. Finuge
15. Duagh
16. Ballyheigue
17. Killahan
18. Kiltomy
19. Kilcaragh
20. Kilfeighny
21. Kilshenane
22. Kilmoyly

23. O'Dorney
24. Kilflyn
25. Ardfert
26. Kilquane
27. Cloghane
28. Ballyduff
29. Stradbally
30. Killiney
31. Kilgobban
32. Dunurlin
33. Marhin
34. Kilmalkedar
35. Dingle
36. Garfinny
37. Kinard
38. Minard
39. Ballynacourty
40. Ballinvoher
41. Dunquin
42. Ventry
43. Kildrum
44. Fenit
45. Ballynahaglish
46. Clogherbrien
47. Tralee
48. Ratass
49. Ballymacelligott
50. O'Brennan
51. Castleisland
52. Brosna
53. Annagh
54. Ballyseedy
55. Nohoval

56. Ballincuslane
57. Kilgarrylander
58. Kiltallagh
59. Currans
60. Killeentierna
61. Dysert (note also 13)
62. Kilcolman
63. Killorglin
64. Valentia
65. Caher
66. Killinane
67. Glanbeigh
68. Killemlagh
69. Prior
70. Dromod
71. Knockane
72. Molahiffe
73. Kilnanare
74. Kilbonane
75. Aglish
76. Kilcredane
77. Kilcummin
78. Nohovaldaly
79. Aghadoe
80. Killarney
81. Killaha
82. Kilcrohane
83. Templenoe
84. Kenmare
85. Kilgarvan
86. Tuosist
87. Kilcaskan

Kerry Civil Parishes in Alphabetical Order

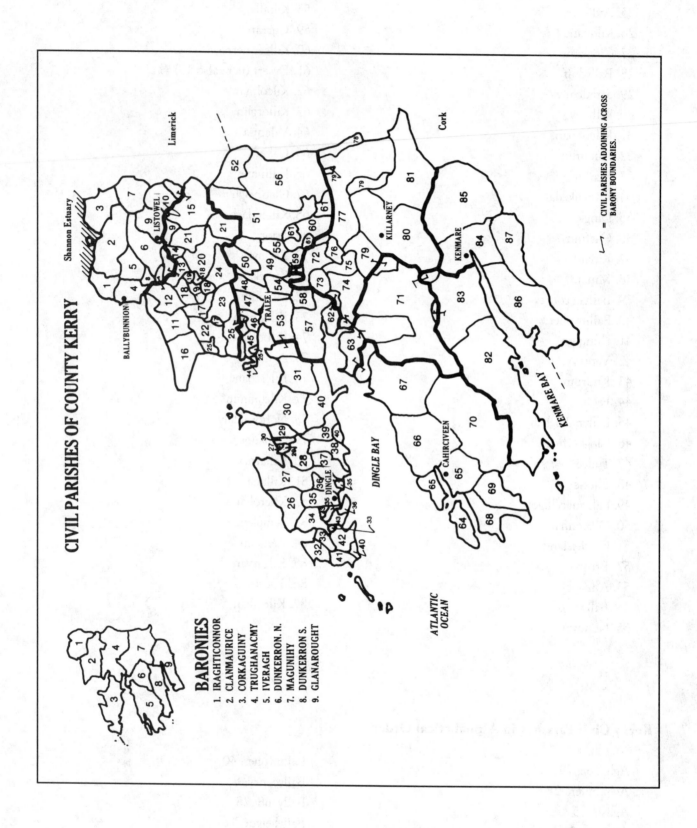

CIVIL PARISHES OF COUNTY KERRY

BARONIES

1. IRAGHTICONNOR
2. CLANMAURICE
3. CORKAGUINY
4. TRUGHANACMY
5. IVERAGH
6. DUNKERRON. N.
7. MAGUNIHY
8. DUNKERRON S.
9. GLANAROUGHT

⌐ = CIVIL PARISHES ADJOINING ACROSS
     BARONY BOUNDARIES.

Ballynahaglish: 45
Ballyseedy: 54
Brosna: 52
Caher: 65
Castleisland: 51
Cloghane: 27
Clogherbrien: 46
Currans: 59
Dingle: 35
Dromod: 70
Duagh: 15
Dunquin: 41
Dunurlin: 32
Dysert: 61
Dysert: 13
Fenit: 44
Finuge: 14
Galey: 6
Garfinny: 36
Glanbeigh: 67
Kenmare: 84
Kilbonane: 74
Kilcaragh: 19
Kilcaskan: 87
Kilcolman: 62
Kilconly: 1
Kilcredane: 76
Kilcrohane: 82
Kilcummin: 77
Kildrum: 43
Kilfeighny: 20
Kilflyn: 24
Kilgarrylander: 57
Kilgarvan: 85
Kilgobban: 31
Killaha: 81
Killahan: 17
Killarney: 80

Killeentierna: 60
Killehenny: 4
Killemlagh: 68
Killinane: 66
Killiney: 30
Killorglin: 63
Killury: 11
Kilmalkedar: 34
Kilmoyly: 22
Kilnanare: 73
Kilnaughten: 3
Kilquane: 26
Kilshenane: 21
Kiltallagh: 58
Kiltomy: 18
Kinard: 37
Knockane: 71
Knockanure: 10
Lisselton: 5
Listowel: 9
Marhin: 33
Minard: 38
Molahiffe: 72
Murher: 7
Nohoval: 55
Nohovaldaly: 78
O'Brennan: 50
O'Dorney: 23
Prior: 69
Ratass: 48
Rattoo: 12
Stradbally: 29
Templenoe: 83
Tralee: 47
Tuosist: 86
Valentia: 64
Ventry: 42

County Kildare

A Brief History

Kildare is a relatively small inland county in Leinster. It is forty-two miles from north to south and twenty-six miles from east to west, and contains the towns of Naas, Newbridge, Maynooth, Kildare, and Athy. The county derives its name from Cill-Dara, the Church of Oak, which is said to have been built in the fifth century. In pre-Norman times, the county was partly the territory of Hy-Kaelan, which was the territory of the O'Byrnes, and Hy-Murray, the territory of the O'Tooles. The Cullens, Dowlings, and McKellys were also families of this county.

During the peak of their power in the tenth century, the Vikings of Dublin extended their territory to the northeast of Kildare. The town of Leixlip derives its name from the Vikings: the name means "Salmon Leap" in Old Norse.

Following the Norman invasion, the county was granted to the Fitzgeralds. The O'Byrnes and O'Tooles were displaced into Wicklow, where they continued to raid the Norman-occupied area called "the Pale" (see Co. Wicklow) for centuries. Other Norman families who settled in Kildare included Birmingham, Sutton, Aylmer, Wogan, Sherlock, White, and Eustace. The Fitzgeralds became a major force in Ireland in the Middle Ages. Their base was at Maynooth castle in the county. The family's power was reduced by an ill-conceived rebellion by "Silken Thomas" Fitzgerald in 1536.

Following the defeat of the rebellion of the Catholic Confederacy of 1641 (see Co. Kilkenny), Cromwell confiscated the lands of many of the Norman families in the county in 1654. Some of these estates were restored by Charles II in 1662-64. Following the Williamite war of 1689-91, many of these landholders again lost their lands, some of which were planted with settlers.

The county was less affected by the Great Famine of 1845-47 than many others. A relatively high proportion of the county was in pasture rather than in potato crops at this time. The population in 1841 was 114,000, and by 1851 it had fallen to 96,000. Of the difference, about 14,000 died and the remainder emigrated.

The county is mainly agricultural, and is also a major center of the horse-racing and bloodstock industry.

Census and Census Substitutes

1600

"The Principal Gentry of the County Kildare in the Year 1600." Walter Fitzgerald. *J.K.A.S.* 3 (2) (1900): 118–122. A comprehensive list of the most important Kildare families is given.

1641

"Book of Survey and Distribution." *Kildare Arch. Soc. J.* 10 (1918-21): 197-205, 221-30.

1654-56

"The Civil Survey," vol. 3, county of Kildare. Robert C. Simington. Dublin: Stationery Office, 1952. SLC film 973123.

1659

"Census" of Ireland. Edited by S. Pender. Dublin: Stationery Office, 1939. NLI I6551. SLC film 924648.

1663

"Hearth Money Roll" (for some areas). *Kildare Arch. Soc. J.* 10 (5): 245-54; 11 (1): 386-466.

1700

"Claimants of Lands in Co. Kildare." *Kildare Arch. Soc. J.* 9 (1918-21): 331-57.

1766

"Protestant Householders and household numbers of Parishes of Ballybought, Ballymore-Eustace, Coghlanstown, Tipperkevin and Yeaganstown." SLC film 0100173, RCB M 37.

"Catholic Householders of Parish of Kilrush," published as "Collections relating to the Diocese of Kildare and Leighlin." Vol. 1. Rev. M. Comerford. Dublin, 1884, p. 272.

"Parish of Ballycommon." *Kildare Arch. Soc. J.* 7 (4) (1913): 274-76.

1772

"Gentlemen of Kildare, Spring Assizes 1772." Faulkner's Journal for 9 Feb. 1773. *J.K.A.S.* 12 (2) (1937): 105. A list of names and residences.

1775

"Catholic Qualification Roll Extracts" (forty-five names, addresses, and occupations). 59th Report DKPRI: 50-84.

1779

"Persons Willing to Join Naas Volunteers." *Kildare Arch. Soc. J.* 11 (1) (1930): 467-68.

1798

List of Persons Who Suffered Losses in '98 Rebellion. NLI JLB 94107 (approximately 320 names, occupations, and addresses).

1804

"Yeomanry Order Book (Millicent, Co. Kildare)." *Kildare Arch. Soc. J.* 13 (4) (1953): 211-19 (gives names and addresses of officers and men).

1808

"Grand Jury Panel for Kildare." *Kildare Arch. Soc. J.* 12 (3) (1938): 128-30 (names and addresses).

1821

Extracts from the Government Census for Naas, Mainly Dealing with the Surname Tracey. SLC film 100158.

1823-37

Tithe Applotment Survey (see introduction).

1837

Alphabetical List of Registered Voters. NLI ms. 1398.

1840

Census of Castledermot Parish. Names of householders and families (not age) in each townland or street of Castledermot parish. NLI P 3511.

1843

Voters List. NAI 1843/53.

1847

County of Kildare election . . . August 1847. Dublin: D. Corbet, n.d., p. 23. Gives names of voters (listed by barony). PRONI Leinster Papers, D3078/3/34.

1851

Griffith's Valuation (see introduction).

1859-63

"Tenants on Aylmer Estate, Donadea Castle." *Kildare Arch. Soc. J.* 7 (1912): 411-16 (eighty-three names and addresses).

1901

Census. NAI (see introduction). SLC films 840922-38.

1911

Census. NAI.

Church Records

Church of Ireland

See the introduction for a description of Church of Ireland records and their major repositories. Many C of I records were lost in the PRO fire of 1922. These are indicated as "Lost." However, as Church of Ireland records were effectively state records, the records of marriage (from 1845) are also in the General Registrar's Office. Many are still in local custody (LC), while others are in one of a variety of other archives (e.g., RCBL or NAI). Many of the parish registers of this county have been indexed by the Kildare Heritage Project (KHP; see Research Services at the end of the chapter). A search of the index will be conducted by the center for a fee. Those indexed are noted as "Indexed by KHP."

Athy
Earliest Records: b. 1669-; m. 1675-; d. 1669-
Status: LC; NAI MFCI 78 (b. 1669-1880; m. 1675-1891; d. 1669-1850); Indexed by KHP

Attanagh
Status: Lost

Ballinafagh or Ballynafagh
Earliest Records: b. 1876-1954; m. 1851-1957; d. 1877-1964
Status: RCBL

Ballaghmoon (see Castledermot)

Ballymore-Eustace
Earliest Records: b. 1838-; m. 1840-; d. 1832-

468

The following persons are willing to serve as Volunteers in the District of Naas and to associate themselves in a troop of Dragoons and to arm, mount and acoutre themselves :—

1. Lord Visc. Allen
2. Hon. Richard Allen.
3. William Eustace.
4. John Mt. Gomery.
5. William Mt. Gomery.
6. David Burtchel.
7. Bartholomew Callan.
8. Richard Archbold.
9. Charles Geoghagan.
10. Henry Haydon.
11. Thomas Dunn.
12. James Martin.
13. Martin Dunty.
14. Laurence Dunty.
15. Andrew Carthy.
16. Gerald Archbold.
17. Grantham Gale.
18. John Plunket.
19. James Moilsey.
20. John Highland.
21. William Tracy.
22. Edward Dunn.
23. Edward Wilson.
24. Samuel Whelan.
25. Christopher Nagle.
26. Maurice Fitzgerald.
27. William Moore.
28. James Ennis.
29. Thomas Browne.
30. Robert Day.
31. Pat. Cosgrave.
32. Edward Scully.
33. Bart. Martin.
34. Pat Lyons.
35. . . . .
36. James Meaghan.
37. Pat Corcoran.
38. James O'Reilly.
39. Charles Fitzgerald.
40. Mathew Dodd.
41. Dennis Rafter.
42. Timothy Holden.
43. James Owens.
44. Edward Collogan.
45. James Magee.
46. . . . . Renolds.
47. Terence Dunn.
48. John Fennel.
49. Theady Kilroy.
50. John Burke.
51. Richard Mooney.
52. James Eustace.
53. Robert Graydon.

We approve of the above list, and are willing and desirous to serve and associate with them. However, we express a doubt whether it be legal to arm some of them above gentleman who profess the roman catholick Religion.

Sept. 20th, 1779.

ROBERT GRAYDON.
WILLIAM EUSTACE.

In the troop of light horse the following persons have associated since the former lists were approved by your Grace, and have been approved of by Mr. Nevill and your humble Servant :—viz.,

Arthur Wolfe.
James Cusack.
Maurice Peppard Warren.
William S. Wolfe.

John Wolfe.

THESE LISTS APPROVED OF BY ME.
LEINSTER, G.

A list of persons in the District of Naas, County Kildare, who declared themselves willing to serve as volunteers in 1779. From *J. Kildare Arch. Soc.* 11 (1) (1930).

Status: LC; NAI MFCI 86 (b. 1838-79; m. 1840-79; d. 1832-79); Indexed by KHP

Ballysax
Earliest Records: b. 1830-; m. 1841-; d. 1834-
Status: LC; NAI MFCI 71 (b. 1830-1939; m. 1841-59; d. 1834-1982) and NAI M5140-5 (m. 1859-1903); Indexed by KHP

Ballysonnon or Ballyshannon
Status: Most records lost; Indexed by KHP (m. from 1845)

Carnalway
Earliest Records: b. 1805; m. 1805; d. 1805
Status: LC; Indexed by KHP (from 1846)

Carogh
Status: Lost

Castlecarbery
Earliest Records: b. 1804-; m. 1805-; d. 1805-
Status: LC; NAI MFCI 66 (b. 1804-1902; m/d. 1805-48)

Castledermot
Earliest Record: b. 1701; m. 1701; d. 1708
Status: GO ms. 142 (abstracts 1701-1780); SLC film 100235

Celbridge or Kildrought
Earliest Records: b. 1777-1977; m. 1777-1975; d.

1787–1882

Status: RCBL; and NAI MFCI 88 (b. 1777–1881; m. 1777–1843; d. 1787–1882)

Clane

Earliest Records: b. 1802–; m. 1804–; d. 1804–

Status: LC; RCBL (m. 1850–1956; d. 1906–47); and NAI M5953 (b. 1802–46; m. 1804–81; d. 1804–1906); Indexed by KHP

Clonaslee

Earliest Records: b. 1814–1982; m. 1814–44; d. 1816–1982

Status: LC; NAI MFCI 69 (b. 1814–1982; m. 1814–44; d. 1816–1982)

Clonsast (Newbridge)

Earliest Records: b. 1805–1983; m. 1804–57; d. 1806–1983

Status: LC; NAI MFCI 63; Indexed by KHP (from 1845)

Curragh Camp and Newbridge Garrison

Earliest Records: b. 1856–; m. 1890–; d. 1869–

Status: NAI M 5050–5; also RCBL (b. 1867–1922)

Donadea

Earliest Records: b. 1890–1968; m. 1846–1939; d. 1892–1920

Status: RCBL

Edenderry or Monasteroris

Earliest Records: b/m/d. 1678–1754

Status: NAI M 5111

Feighcullen

Status: Lost

Fontstown

Earliest Records: b. 1814–40; m. 1811–56; d. 1811–69

Status: RCBL

Great Connell and Ladytown

Status: Lost

Harristown (Monasterevin)

Earliest Records: b. 1666–; m. 1799–; d. 1802–

Status: LC; NAI M5111 (b. 1666–1917; m. 1799–1883; d. 1802–1983)

Kilberry

Status: Lost

Kilcock

Status: Lost

Kilcullen

Earliest Records: b. 1778–; m. 1819–; d. 1779–

Status: LC; also NAI MFCI 71 (b. 1778–1982; m. 1779–1839; d. 1778–1982); Indexed by KHP

Kildare

Earliest Records: b. 1801–; m. 1801–; d. 1801–

Status: LC; NAI MFCI 70 (b. 1801–1962; m. 1801–45; d. 1801–69); Indexed by KHP

Kill

Earliest Records: b. 1814–; m. 1820–; d. 1814–

Status: LC; NAI MFCI 68 (b. 1814–84; m. 1820–44; d. 1814–79)

Killishee

Status: Lost

Kilmeague or Lullymore

Status: Lost

Lackagh

Earliest Records: b/m/d. 1829–

Status: LC; also NAI MFCI 70 (b. 1829–82; m. 1829–64; d. 1829–79)

Lea

Earliest Records: b. 1830–52; m. 1841; d. 1842–86

Status: RCBL

Leixlip

Earliest Records: b. 1778–; m. 1781–; d. 1778–

Status: LC; NAI MFCI 90 (b. 1778–1879; m. 1781–1876; d. 1778–1879)

Maynooth or Laraghbryan

Earliest Records: b. 1774–; m. 1792–; d. 1792–

Status: LC; and NAI MFCI 42 (m. 1839–70)

Monasterevin—see Harristown

Monasteroris—see Edenderry

Morristownbiller and Old Connell

Status: LC; Indexed by KHP (m. from 1845)

Naas

Earliest Records: b. 1679–; m. 1742–; d. 1679–

Status: LC; NAI MFCI 68 (b. 1679–1882; m. 1742–1848; d. 1679–1891)

Narraghmore

Status: Lost

Newbridge—see Clonsast

Newbridge Garrison—see Curragh

Nurney

Status: Lost

Rathangan

Status: Lost

Rathmore

Status: Lost

Straffan (see also Celbridge)

Earliest Records: b. 1838–81; m. 1838–1950; d. 1841–1940

Status: RCBL; and NAI MFCI 88 (b. 1838–81; m. 1838; d. 1841–1940); Indexed by KHP

Taghadoe—see Maynooth

Thomastown

Status: Lost

Timahoe (see Ballinafagh)

Timolin
Earliest Records: b. 1802-; m. 1800-; d. 1803-
Status: LC; also NAI MFCI 84 (b. 1802-74; m. 1800-97; d. 1803-1984)

Tipperkevin
Status: Lost

Presbyterian

There are two Presbyterian congregations in Co. Kildare: Athy and Nass. These congregations had a strong Scottish element in them. Baptism and marriage registers for Athy begin in 1854; baptism and marriage registers for Naas begin in 1860. These are at The Manse in Naas. There were no burial registers kept by these congregations. An account of Presbyterian records is given in the introduction.

Roman Catholic

Some of the Catholic parish registers of this county have been indexed by the Kildare Heritage Project (KHP; see Research Services at the end of the chapter). A search of the index will be conducted by the project for a fee. Those indexed are noted below as "Indexed by KHP" as appropriate. Microfilm copies of all registers are also available in the National Library of Ireland (NLI), and through the LDS library system.

Civil Parish: Ardkill
Map Grid: 10
RC Parish: see Carbury
Diocese: KD

Civil Parish: Ardree
Map Grid: 104
RC Parish: see Churchtown
Diocese: DU

Civil Parish: Ballaghmoon
Map Grid: 115
RC Parish: see Castledermot
Diocese: DU

Civil Parish: Ballybought
Map Grid: 81
RC Parish: see Ballymore-Eustace

Civil Parish: Ballybrackan
Map Grid: 86
RC Parish: see Monastervin
Diocese: KD

Civil Parish: Ballymany
Map Grid: 63
RC Parish: Newbridge, see Greatconnell
Diocese: KD

Civil Parish: Ballymore-Eustace
Map Grid: 77
RC Parish: Ballymore-Eustace

Diocese: DU
Earliest Record: b. 3.1779; m. 10.1779
Missing Dates: b. 4.1796-1.1797; m. 6.1796-5.1797
Status: LC; NLI (mf); Indexed by Wicklow HC (to 1900)—see Co. Wicklow

Civil Parish: Ballynadrumny
Map Grid: 1
RC Parish: Balyna
Diocese: KD
Earliest Record: b. 10.1785; m. 11.1797
Missing Dates: b. 7.1803-8.1807, 10.1811-1.1815, 2.1815-1.1818; m. 4.1799-11.1801, 1.1802-10.1807, 10.1811-1.1815, 2.1815-3.1818
Status: LC; NLI (mf); Indexed by KHP (to 1899)

Civil Parish: Ballynafagh
Map Grid: 30
RC Parish: Downings, see Carragh
Diocese: KD

Civil Parish: Ballysax
Map Grid: 64
RC Parish: Suncroft, see Carn (for Army Camp records see Curragh Camp)
Diocese: KD

Civil Parish: Ballyshannon
Map Grid: 92
RC Parish: Suncroft, see Carn
Diocese: KD

Civil Parish: Balraheen
Map Grid: 16
RC Parish: see Clane
Diocese: KD

Civil Parish: Belan
Map Grid: 107
RC Parish: see Castledermot
Diocese: KD

Civil Parish: Bodenstown
Map Grid: 36
RC Parish: see Kill
Diocese: KD

Civil Parish: Brannockstown
Map Grid: 78
RC Parish: see Kilcullen
Diocese: DU

Civil Parish: Brideschurch
Map Grid: 35
RC Parish: see Carragh
Diocese: KD

Civil Parish: Cadamstown
Map Grid: 4
RC Parish: Balyna, see Ballynadrumny
Diocese: KD

Civil Parish: Carbury
Map Grid: 9

RC Parish: Carbury
Diocese: KD
Earliest Record: b. 10.1821; m. 11.1821; d. 2.1869
Status: LC; NLI (mf); Indexing in progress

Civil Parish: Carn
Map Grid: 65
RC Parish: Suncroft
Diocese: KD
Earliest Record: b. 3.1805; m. 5.1805
Status: LC; NLI (mf); Indexing in progress

Civil Parish: Carnalway
Map Grid: 75
RC Parish: Newbridge, see Greatconnell
Diocese: DU

Civil Parish: Carragh
Map Grid: 34
RC Parish: Carragh (Downings)
Diocese: KD
Earliest Record: b. 6.1849; m. 2.1850
Status: LC; NLI (mf); Indexed by KHP (to 1899)

Civil Parish: Carrick
Map Grid: 5
RC Parish: Balyna, see Ballynadrumny
Diocese: KD

Civil Parish: Castledermot
Map Grid: 111
RC Parish: Castledermot
Diocese: DU
Earliest Record: b. 11.1789; m. 11.1789
Status: LC; NLI (mf); Indexed by KHP (to 1899)

Civil Parish: Castledillon
Map Grid: 46
RC Parish: Celbridge, see Straffan
Diocese: DU

Civil Parish: Churchtown
Map Grid: 96
RC Parish: Athy
Diocese: DU
Earliest Record: b. 3.1837; m. 4.1837
Status: LC; NLI (mf); Indexed by KHP (to 1899)

Civil Parish: Clane
Map Grid: 33
RC Parish: Clane
Diocese: KD
Earliest Record: b. 3.1785; m. 4.1825
Missing Dates: b. 9.1785-2.1786, 7.1786-12.1788, 4.1789-2.1825; m. 6.1828-11.1829
Status: LC; NLI (mf); Indexing in progress

Civil Parish: Clonaglish
Map Grid: 48
RC Parish: see Kill
Diocese: DN

Civil Parish: Cloncurry (near Kilcock)
Map Grid: 12
RC Parish: see Kilcock
Diocese: KD

Civil Parish: Cloncurry (near Rathangan)
Map Grid: 56
RC Parish: see Kildare
Diocese: KD

Civil Parish: Clonshanbo
Map Grid: 15
RC Parish: see Kilcock
Diocese: DU

Civil Parish: Coghlanstown
Map Grid: 76
RC Parish: see Ballymore-Eustace
Diocese: DU

Civil Parish: Confey
Map Grid: 21
RC Parish: Maynooth, see Laraghbryan
Diocese: DU

Civil Parish: Curragh Camp (civil parish of Ballysax)
Map Grid: 64
RC Parish: Curragh Camp
Earliest Record: b. 8.1855; m. 9.1855
Status: LC; NLI (mf); Indexing in progress

Civil Parish: Davidstown
Map Grid: 99
RC Parish: see Narraghmore
Diocese: DU

Civil Parish: Donadea
Map Grid: 18
RC Parish: Maynooth, see Laraghbryan
Diocese: KD

Civil Parish: Donaghcumper
Map Grid: 44
RC Parish: Celbridge, see Straffan
Diocese: KD

Civil Parish: Donaghmore
Map Grid: 22
RC Parish: Celbridge, see Straffan
Diocese: KD

Civil Parish: Downings
Map Grid: 31
RC Parish: Caragh, see Carragh
Diocese: KD

Civil Parish: Duneany
Map Grid: 84
RC Parish: see Monasterevin
Diocese: KD

Civil Parish: Dunfierth
Map Grid: 7

RC Parish: see Carbury
Diocese: KD

Civil Parish: Dunmanoge
Map Grid: 110
RC Parish: see Castledermot
Diocese: DU

Civil Parish: Dunmurraghill
Map Grid: 17
RC Parish: Maynooth, see Laraghbryan
Diocese: KD

Civil Parish: Dunmurry
Map Grid: 59
RC Parish: see Kildare
Diocese: KD

Civil Parish: Feighcullen
Map Grid: 68
RC Parish: see Kilmeage
Diocese: KD

Civil Parish: Fontstown
Map Grid: 93
RC Parish: see Narraghmore
Diocese: KD

Civil Parish: Forenaghts
Map Grid: 52
RC Parish: see Kill
Diocese: DU

Civil Parish: Gilltown
Map Grid: 79
RC Parish: part Kilcullen; part Ballymore-Eustace
Diocese: DU

Civil Parish: Graney
Map Grid: 113
RC Parish: part Castledermot; part Baltinglass, Co.
Wicklow
Diocese: DU

Civil Parish: Grangeclare
Map Grid: 58
RC Parish: see Kildare
Diocese: KD

Civil Parish: Grangerosnolvan
Map Grid: 106
RC Parish: see Castledermot
Diocese: DU

Civil Parish: Greatconnell
Map Grid: 72
RC Parish: Newbridge
Diocese: KD
Earliest Record: b. 8.1786; m. 8.1786
Missing Dates: b. 1.1795-1.1820, 8.1832-1.1834; m.
1.1795-1.1820
Status: LC; NLI (mf); Indexed by KHP (to 1899)

Civil Parish: Harristown
Map Grid: 89
RC Parish: Athy, see Churchtown
Diocese: KD

Civil Parish: Haynestown
Map Grid: 53
RC Parish: see Kill
Diocese: DU

Civil Parish: Hortland (see Scullogestown)

Civil Parish: Jago
Map Grid: 80
RC Parish: Ballymore-Eustace
Diocese: DU

Civil Parish: Johnstown
Map Grid: 41
RC Parish: see Kill
Diocese: KD

Civil Parish: Kerdiffstown
Map Grid: 39
RC Parish: part Newbridge, see Greatconnell; part
Kill

Civil Parish: Kilberry
Map Grid: 95
RC Parish: see Churchtown
Diocese: DU

Civil Parish: Kilcock
Map Grid: 13
RC Parish: Kilcock
Diocese: KD
Earliest Record: b. 7.1771; m. 8.1816
Missing Dates: b. 12.1786-8.1816, 12.1826-
10.1831; m. 9.1822-7.1834
Status: LC; NLI (mf); Indexing in progress

Civil Parish: Kilcullen
Map Grid: 94
RC Parish: Kilcullen
Diocese: DU
Earliest Record: b. 10.1777; m. 5.1786
Missing Dates: b. 9.1818-4.1829, 9.1840-1.1857; m.
11.1806-4.1810, 10.1816-5.1829, 11.1831-4.1836,
6.1840-1.1857
Status: LC; NLI (mf); Indexed by KHP (to 1899)

Civil Parish: Kildangan
Map Grid: 87
RC Parish: see Monasterevin
Diocese: KD

Civil Parish: Kildare
Map Grid: 61
RC Parish: Kildare (for Army Camp records see
Curragh Camp)
Diocese: KD
Earliest Record: b. 11.1815; m. 11.1815
Status: LC; NLI (mf); Indexed by KHP (to 1899)

Civil Parish: Kildrought
Map Grid: 26
RC Parish: Celbridge, see Straffan
Diocese: DU

Civil Parish: Kilkea
Map Grid: 109
RC Parish: see Castledermot
Diocese: DU

Civil Parish: Kill
Map Grid: 50
RC Parish: Kill and Lyons; also part Newbridge, see
Greatconnell
Diocese: DU
Earliest Record: b. 1813; m. 1813
Status: LC; NLI (mf); Indexed by KHP (to 1899)

Civil Parish: Killadoon
Map Grid: 27
RC Parish: Celbridge, see Straffan
Diocese: DU

Civil Parish: Kilashee (or Killishy)
Map Grid: 73
RC Parish: Newbridge, see Greatconnell

Civil Parish: Killelan
Map Grid: 108
RC Parish: see Castledermot
Diocese: DU

Civil Parish: Killybegs
Map Grid: 32
RC Parish: see Carragh
Diocese: KD

Civil Parish: Kilmacredock
Map Grid: 23
RC Parish: Maynooth, see Laraghbryan
Diocese: DU

Civil Parish: Kilmeage
Map Grid: 66
RC Parish: Allen and Milltown
Diocese: KD
Earliest Record: b. 10.1820; m. 10.1820
Missing Dates: b. ends 10.1852
Status: LC; NLI (mf); Indexed by KHP (to 1899)

Civil Parish: Kilmore
Map Grid: 8
RC Parish: part Carbury; part Balyna, see
Ballynadrumny
Diocese: KD

Civil Parish: Kilpatrick
Map Grid: 11
RC Parish: see Carbury
Diocese: KD

Civil Parish: Kilrainy
Map Grid: 2

RC Parish: Balyna, see Ballynadrumny
Diocese: DU .

Civil Parish: Kilrush
Map Grid: 91
RC Parish: Suncroft, see Carn
Diocese: KD

Civil Parish: Kilteel
Map Grid: 51
RC Parish: Blessington, see Co. Wicklow
Diocese: DU

Civil Parish: Kineagh
Map Grid: 112
RC Parish: part Castledermot; part Rathvilly, see Co.
Carlow
Diocese: DU

Civil Parish: Knavinstown or Kevinstown
Map Grid: 83
RC Parish: see Kildare
Diocese: KD

Civil Parish: Lackagh
Map Grid: 82
RC Parish: part Monasterevin; part Kildare
Diocese: KD

Civil Parish: Ladytown
Map Grid: 71
RC Parish: see Carragh
Diocese: KD

Civil Parish: Laraghbryan
Map Grid: 20
RC Parish: Maynooth and Leixlip
Diocese: DU
Earliest Record: b. 8.1814; m. 1.1806
Status: LC; NLI (mf); Indexing in progress

Civil Parish: Leixlip
Map Grid: 24
RC Parish: Maynooth
Diocese: DU

Civil Parish: Lullymore
Map Grid: 54
RC Parish: see Kildare
Diocese: DU

Civil Parish: Lyons
Map Grid: 47
RC Parish: see Kill
Diocese: DU

Civil Parish: Mainham
Map Grid: 19
RC Parish: see Clane
Diocese: KD

Civil Parish: Monasterevin
Map Grid: 85
RC Parish: Monasterevin and Kildangan

Diocese: KD
Earliest Record: b. 1.1819; m. 9.1819
Status: LC; NLI (mf); Indexing in progress

Civil Parish: Moone
Map Grid: 103
RC Parish: see Castledermot
Diocese: DU

Civil Parish: Morristownbiller
Map Grid: 69
RC Parish: Newbridge, see Greatconnell
Diocese: DU

Civil Parish: Mylerstown
Map Grid: 3
RC Parish: Balyna, see Ballynadrumny
Diocese: DU

Civil Parish: Naas
Map Grid: 40
RC Parish: Naas
Diocese: KD
Earliest Record: b. 3.1813; m. 2.1813; d. 3.1861
Status: LC; NLI (mf); Indexed by KHP (to 1899)

Civil Parish: Narraghmore
Map Grid: 101
RC Parish: Narraghmore
Diocese: DU
Earliest Record: b. 4.1827; m. 10.1827
Missing Dates: b. 7.1846-5.1853; m. 8.1840-7.1842,
7.1846-1.1853
Status: LC; NLI (mf); Indexing in progress

Civil Parish: Nurney (1) (near Carrick)
Map Grid: 6
RC Parish: Balyna, see Ballynadrumny
Diocese: KD

Civil Parish: Nurney (2) (near Harristown)
Map Grid: 90
RC Parish: Monasterevin and Kildangan, see
Monasterevin
Diocese: KD

Civil Parish: Oldconnell
Map Grid: 70
RC Parish: Newbridge, see Greatconnell
Diocese: KD

Civil Parish: Oughterard
Map Grid: 49
RC Parish: see Kill
Diocese: DU

Civil Parish: Painestown
Map Grid: 114
RC Parish: Painestown, Co. Carlow
Diocese: LE

Civil Parish: Pollardstown
Map Grid: 62

RC Parish: Allen and Milltown, see Kilmeage
Diocese: KD

Civil Parish: Rathangan
Map Grid: 55
RC Parish: Rathangan (see Kildare for earlier records)
Diocese: KD
Earliest Record: b. 1880; m. 1880; d. 1888
Status: LC; NLI (mf); Indexed by KHP (to 1899)

Civil Parish: Rathernan
Map Grid: 67
RC Parish: Allen and Milltown, see Kilmeage
Diocese: KD

Civil Parish: Rathmore
Map Grid: 43
RC Parish: Blessington, see Co. Wicklow
Diocese: DU

Civil Parish: St. John's (also Co. Offaly)
Map Grid: 98
RC Parish: Athy, see Churchtown
Diocese: DU

Civil Parish: St. Michaels
Map Grid: 97
RC Parish: Athy, see Churchtown
Diocese: DU

Civil Parish: Scullogestown (or Hortland)
Map Grid: 14
RC Parish: see Kilcock
Diocese: KD

Civil Parish: Sherlockstown
Map Grid: 38
RC Parish: Kill and Lyons, see Kill
Diocese: KD

Civil Parish: Stacumny
Map Grid: 45
RC Parish: Celbridge, see Straffan
Diocese: DU

Civil Parish: Straffan
Map Grid: 28
RC Parish: Straffan
Diocese: DU
Earliest Record: b. 1.1857
Status: LC; NLI (mf); Indexing in progress

Civil Parish: Taghadoe
Map Grid: 25
RC Parish: Maynooth, see Laraghbryan
Diocese: DU

Civil Parish: Tankardstown (also Co. Laois)
Map Grid: 105
RC Parish: Athy, see Churchtown
Diocese: DU

Civil Parish: Thomastown
Map Grid: 57

RC Parish: see Kildare
Diocese: KD

Civil Parish: Timahoe
Map Grid: 29
RC Parish: see Clane
Diocese: KD

Civil Parish: Timolin
Map Grid: 102
RC Parish: see Castledermot
Diocese: DU

Civil Parish: Tipper
Map Grid: 42
RC Parish: part Naas; part Kill
Diocese: DU

Civil Parish: Tipperkevin
Map Grid: 74
RC Parish: see Ballymore-Eustace
Diocese: DU

Civil Parish: Tully
Map Grid: 60
RC Parish: Kildare and Rathangan, see Kildare
Diocese: DU

Civil Parish: Usk
Map Grid: 100
RC Parish: see Narraghmore
Diocese: DU

Civil Parish: Walterstown
Map Grid: 88
RC Parish: see Kildare
Diocese: KD

Civil Parish: Whitechurch
Map Grid: 37
RC Parish: see Kill
Diocese: KD

Society of Friends (Quakers)

Kildare Quakers attended the monthly meetings at Carlow, Dublin, Edenderry, Mountmellick, and Wicklow. The heritage center is currently indexing the Carlow monthly meeting records. The original registers are at the Friends Library in Dublin. There was also a Quaker school in Ballitore, Co. Kildare. The pupil registers from 1726 to 1836 were published (see Research Sources and Services).

Meeting: Carlow
Earliest Records: b. 1607–1859; m. 1649–1847; d. 1655–1860
Status: FHL mf. 571395

Meeting: Dublin
Earliest Records: b. 1606–1861; m. 1631–1872; d. 1664–1860
Status: FHL mf. 571395-6

Meeting: Edenderry
Earliest Records: b. 1612–1846; m. 1652–1810; d. 1680–1860
Status: FHL mf. 571396

Meeting: Mountmellick
Earliest Records: b. 1613–1860; m. 1650–1860; d. 1648–1860
Status: FHL mf. 571397

Meeting: Wicklow
Earliest Records: b. 1627–1817; m. 1640–1859; d. 1654–1859
Status: FHL mf. 571398

Commercial and Social Directories

1788

Richard Lucas's *General Directory of the Kingdom of Ireland* contains lists of traders in Athy. Reprinted in *Ir. Gen.* 3 (10) (1965): 392–416.

1824

J. Pigot's *City of Dublin and Hibernian Provincial Directory* includes traders, nobility, gentry, and clergy lists of Athy, Celbridge, Kilcock, Kilcullen, Kildare, Leixlip, Maynooth, Monasterevin, Naas, and Rathangan.

1846

Slater's *National Commercial Directory of Ireland* lists nobility, clergy, traders, etc., in Athy, Celbridge, Leixlip and Lucan, Kilcullen, Kildare, Maynooth and Kilcock, Monasterevin, Naas, and Rathangan.

1856

Slater's *Royal National Commercial Directory of Ireland* lists nobility, gentry, clergy, traders, etc., in Athy, Celbridge, Leixlip and Lucan, Kilcullen, Kildare, Maynooth and Kilcock, Monasterevin, Naas and Newbridge, and Rathangan.

1870

Slater's *Directory of Ireland* contains trade, nobility, and clergy lists for Athy, Kilcullen, Kildare, Maynooth and Kilcock, Monasterevin, Naas, Newbridge, and Rathangan.

1881

Slater's *Royal National Commercial Directory of Ireland* contains lists of traders, clergy, nobility, and farmers in adjoining parishes of the towns of Athy, Celbridge, Kildare, Maynooth and Kilcock, and Naas.

1894

Slater's *Royal National Directory of Ireland* lists traders, police, teachers, farmers, and private residents in each of the towns, villages, and parishes of the county.

Family History

"Alen of St. Wolstan's." *J. Kildare Arch. and Hist. Soc.* 1 (1892-95): 340-41.

"An Account of the Family of Alen, of St. Wolstan's, Co. Kildare." *J. Kildare Arch. and Hist. Soc.* 4 (1903-05): 95-110; 5 (1906-08): 344-47.

"Ladytown and the Allens." *J. Kildare Arch. and Hist. Soc.* 9 (1918-21): 60-69.

"The Aylmer Family." *J. Kildare Arch. and Hist. Soc.* 1 (1893-95): 295-307; 3 (1899-1902): 169-78; 4 (1903-05): 179-83.

"The Boylan Family of Carbury Area." *J. Kildare Arch. and Hist. Soc.* 14 (3) 1968.

"The Breretons of Co. Carlow and Co. Kildare." *Ir. Anc.* 3 (1971): 10-26, 124.

Dexter—see Co. Dublin.

McCann, P.D. *The Dooney Family of Co. Kildare and New Zealand.* 1977 (c/o De la Salle Provincialate, 121 Howth Road, Dublin).

"The Eustace Family and Their Lands in Co. Kildare." *J. Kildare Arch. and Hist. Soc.* 13 (6): 270-87; 13 (7): 307-41; 13 (8): 364-413.

"The Eustaces of Co. Kildare." *J. Kildare Arch. and Hist. Soc.* 1 (1891-95): 115-30.

"The House of Eustace." *Reportorium Novum* 2 (2) (1960): 245-56.

"The Family of Fish of Castlefish, Co. Kildare." *Ir. Anc.* 14 (1) 1982.

"The Family of Flatesbury, of Ballynascullogue and Johnstown, Co. Kildare." *J. Kildare Arch. and Hist. Soc.* 4 (1903): 87-94.

"Kilcullen New Abbey and the FitzEustaces." *J. Kildare Arch. and Hist. Soc.* 12 (1935-45): 217-21.

"The Fitzgeralds of Ballyshannon (Co. Kildare), and Their Successors Thereat." *J. Kildare Arch. and Hist. Soc.* 3 (1899-1902): 425-52.

"The Hewetsons of Co. Kildare." *R.S.A.I.* 39 (1909): 146-63.

"The Lattin and Mansfield Families, in the Co. Kildare." *J. Kildare Arch. and Hist. Soc.* 3 (1899-1902): 186-90.

Dunlop, R. *Plantation of Renown. The Story of the La Touche Family of Harristown and the Baptist Church at Brannockstown in Co. Kildare.* N.p., 1970.

"The La Touche Family of Harristown, Co. Kildare." *J. Kildare Arch. and Hist. Soc.* 7 (1912-14): 33-40.

"Lawe of Leixlip." *J. Kildare Arch. and Hist. Soc.* 6 (1909-11): 730-39.

"The Lockes of Athgoe." *Reportorium* 1 (1) (1955): 76-79.

"Mansfield Papers (Co. Kildare)." *Anal. Hib.* 20: 92-125.

Moorhouse—see Co. Dublin.

"The Nuttalls of Co. Kildare." *J. Kildare Arch. and Hist. Soc.* 8 (1915-17): 180-84.

"The O'More Family of Balyna in the Co. Kildare, ca. 1774." *J. Kildare Arch. and Hist. Soc.* 9 (1918-21): 227-91, 318-30.

Dundrum, E. O'H. *The O'Reillys of Templemills, Celbridge . . . with a Note on the History of the Clann Ui Raghallaigh in General.* Dublin, 1941.

Prince, T. *Account of the Palmer Family of Rahan, Co. Kildare.* New York, 1903.

"Patrick Sarsfield, Earl of Lucan, with an Account of His Family and Their Connection with Lucan and Tully." *J. Kildare Arch. and Hist. Soc.* 4 (1903-05): 114-47.

"Notes on the Family of Sherlock: from State Papers and Official Documents." *J. Kildare Arch. and Hist. Soc.* 2 (1896-99): 33-47; 6 (1909-11): 155-59.

"The Family of Tone." *J. Kildare Arch. and Hist. Soc.* 12 (1935-45): 326-29.

Wolfe, George. "The Wolfe Family of Co. Kildare." *J. Kildare Arch. and Hist. Soc.* 3 (1899-1902): 361-67.

Wolfe, R. *Wolfes of Forenaghts, Blackhall, Baronrath, Co. Kildare, and Tipperary.* Guildford, 1893.

"The Extinct Family of Young of Newtown-O'More, Co. Kildare." *J. Kildare Arch. and Hist. Soc.* 3 (1899-1902): 338.

Gravestone Inscriptions

The county library has a collection of gravestone inscriptions compiled by various local groups and individuals. These are on file at the Kildare County Library. For a listing of what is available, see Kiely, Newman, and Ruddy's *Tracing Your Ancestor in County Kildare.* This work has a "list and map of burial grounds in County Kildare" which shows a rough map keyed to the cemetery name. If necessary, inscriptions can be accessed through the Kildare Heritage Project (see Research Services).

An article on "Memorial Inscriptions in Co. Kildare" is in *J. Kildare Arch. Hist. Soc.* 16: 510-527; Naas-St. David's (C of I) is in *Irish Family History* 9 (1993): 39-54. Other transcripts can be found in the collections of the Genealogical Office (GO MS 622: Athy, p. 89; Ballyshannon, p. 108; Fontstown, p. 148-9; Harristown, p. 126; and Mageneys, p. 108). This Genealogical Office manuscript is also on microfilm through the FHL (#257819, item 1).

Newspapers

There are no early newspapers published within this county. Those from the surrounding counties—especially Dublin—should be consulted, depending on their proximity to the area of interest.

An index is being compiled by Kildare County Library (see Library Services at the end of the chapter). It has currently been indexed (with some gaps) from 1896 to 1971. Searches of the index will be conducted for a fee.

Title: *Kildare Observer*
Published in: Naas, 1879-1935
NLI Holdings: 4.1879-6.1890; 1.1892-3.1897 (with gaps); 1.1899-5.1935
BL Holdings: 10.1880-1.1921; 5.1921-12.1924; 1.1926-12.1929; 1.1931-5.1935

Title: *Leinster Express*
Published in: Naas, 1868-73 and 1874-1947

Title: *Leinster Leader*
Published in: Naas, 1880-current
NLI Holdings: 1.1881-in progress
BL Holdings: 11.1882-in progress

Wills and Administrations

A discussion of the types of records, where they are held, and their availability and value is given in the Wills section of the introduction. The availability of prerogative wills, administrations, and marriage license records is also described in the relevant parts of the same section. Where available, published sources of these records are given in the Miscellaneous Sources section.

Pre-1858 Wills and Administrations

Prerogative Wills. See the introduction.

Consistorial Wills. Wills and administrations (pre-1858) were probated in the Church of Ireland dioceses of Dublin, Kildare, or Leighlin. Only one parish is in Leighlin. The original records were destroyed in the 1922 fire; however, the indexes survive and are at the National Archives, with microfilm copies at the Friends Historical Library (FHL). The guide to Catholic parish records in this chapter shows the diocese to which each civil parish belonged. The wills of residents of each diocese were usually proven within that diocese (see the Wills section for exceptions). The following records survive:

Wills

See the introduction. Also, an account of Kildare diocesan wills has been published in *J. Kildare Arch. Hist.*

Soc. 12 (3) (1938): 115-123; 12 (4) (1939): 188-189; 12 (5) (1940-41): 222-225; 12 (6) (1940-41): 269-272.

Abstracts

See the introduction. Also, the Betham Collection (NAI) has abstracts of most wills from 1661 to 1826 for names beginning A-K, and to 1824 for those beginning K-S. These are in the NAI (Ms. 1A 44 22); also abstracts of wills, 1661-1826, from Phillips Manuscripts, A-K and L-S, are in the Friends Historical Library (FHL), Mf. 101027.

Indexes

Dublin—see Co. Dublin; see also the article "Index to the Wills of the Diocese of Kildare, in the Public Records Office of Ireland" (now the National Archives, or NAI) by Sydney Cary, editor, in *J. Kildare Arch. Hist. Soc.* 4 (6) (1905): 473-491; also the indexes (1661-1800) to all dioceses are published in Phillimore and Thrift's *Indexes to Irish Wills*, vol. 1 (also in FHL Mf. 1426012, item 11). Indexes to Wills (1652-1858) for Leighlin diocese are in the FHL (Mf. 100916).

Administration Bonds for Kildare diocese (1679-1840 and 1770-1848) are in the FHL (Ms. 100962); those for Leighlin Diocese (1694-1845) are also in FHL (Mf. 100963).

Post-1858 Wills and Administrations

This county was served by the District Registry of Dublin. The surviving records are kept in the NAI, but almost all were destroyed in the 1922 fire.

Marriage Licenses

Original Marriage Records
Kildare (1845-65). NAI; SLC film 100873.

Indexes

Kildare (1740-1850). NAI; SLC film 100868.
"Index to Kildare Marriage License Bonds." Transcribed by Guillamore O'Grady. *J. Kildare Arch. Hist. Soc.* (A-C) 11 (2) (1931): 43-58; (D-I) 11 (3) (1932): 114-133; (J-O) 12 (1) (1935): 12-29; (P-) 12 (2) (1937): 74-98.

For marriage licenses in Dublin diocese, see Co. Dublin.

Miscellaneous Sources

Kiely, K., M. Newman, and J. Ruddy. *Tracing Your Ancestors in County Kildare.* Kildare Co. Library, 1992.

"Family History Research in Co. Kildare." *Irish Family History* 6 (1990): 70-78.

Kavanagh, Michael V. *A Bibliography of the History of County Kildare in Printed Books.* Droichead Nau, Co.

Kildare: Kildare County Council, 1976.

Costello, Con. *Looking Back: Aspects of History, Co. Kildare.* Naas, Co. Kildare: Leinster Leader Ltd., 1988.

The Roll of the Quaker School at Ballitore, County Kildare. E.J. McAuliffe. (Pupil registers, 1726–1836.) Irish Academic Press, 1984.

Kavanagh, Michael V. *A Bibliography of the History of Co. Kildare in Printed Books.* Indexed. Kildare, 1976, pp. 328.

"Prosperous Landlords and Tenants." *Kildare Arch. Soc. J.* 16: 241–263.

"The High Sheriffs of Co. Kildare (1286–1897)." *J. Kildare Arch. Hist. Soc.* 2 (1896–99): 253–76.

O'Loan, J. "The Manor of Cloncurry, Co. Kildare, and the Feudal System of Land Tenure in Ireland." *Ir. Dept. Agric. J.* 58 (1961): 14–36.

"Schools of Kildare and Leighlin A.D. 1775–1835." Rev. M. Brenan. Dublin: Gill, 1935.

"Statistical Survey of the County of Kildare with Observations on the Means of Improvement; drawn up for the consideration, and by direction of The Dublin Society." Thomas James Rawson, Esq. Dublin: Graisberry for the Dublin Society, 1807, p. xiii, xviii, 237.

"The Pre-Famine Population of Some Kildare Towns, with an Additional Note on the Population of Some Rural Areas." *J. Kildare Arch. Hist. Soc.* 14 (4) (1969): 444–51.

Research Sources and Services

Journals
Kildare Archaeological Society Journal

Libraries and Information Sources
Kildare County Library, Athgarvan Road, Newbridge, Co. Kildare. Ph: (045) 431486/431109. This library has a very extensive collection of local and family history materials and has been very actively promoting the collection and indexation of relevant sources. It has published a bibliography of local printed materials and a guide to family history sources (see Miscellaneous Sources). Both sources detail the holdings of the library. The library is also directly associated with the Kildare Heritage Project (see Research Services). The library is involved in indexing the local *Leinster Leader* newspaper. This project has already indexed 1896 to 1971. Enquiries to Old Library, Basin St., Naas, Co. Kildare. Ph: (045) 879275.

Research Services
Kildare Heritage Project (KHP) c/o Kildare County Library, Athgarvan Road, Newbridge, Co. Kildare. Ph: (045) 433602; fax: (353) 45 432940; e-mail: capinfo@iol.ie. This center is the official IGP center for the county. It has indexed many of the Catholic and Church of Ireland registers of the county and is currently working to index further registers. Researchers are advised to contact the center for an updated list of registers, and other sources, indexed. It also has access to the significant local history collection of Kildare County Library, which includes a unique set of indexed gravestone inscriptions (some of which have been compiled by KHP), newspapers, land records, the 1901 census, etc. The center will conduct a search of their database for a fee.

See also Research Services in Dublin in the introduction.

Societies
Athy Museum Society, Mr. Frank Taaffe, Ardreigh House, Athy, Co. Kildare

Curragh Historical Society, Mr. Oliver McCrossan, McSwiney Road, Curragh Camp, Co. Kildare

Donadea Local History Group, Mr. Des O'Leary, Donadea, Naas, Co. Kildare

Kildare Archaeological Society, Mrs. Elizabeth Connolly, Newington House, Christianstown, Newbridge, Co. Kildare

Naas Local History Group, Ms. Frances Murphy, St. Martin's, Kilbelin, Newbridge, Co. Kildare

Newbridge Local History Group, Ms. Mary Ryan, Hawkfield, Newbridge, Co. Kildare

Kildare Civil Parishes as Numbered on Map

1. Ballynadrumny
2. Kilrainy
3. Mylerstown
4. Cadamstown
5. Carrick
6. Nurney
7. Dunfierth
8. Kilmore
9. Carbury
10. Ardkill
11. Kilpatrick
12. Cloncurry
13. Kilcock
14. Scullogestown
15. Clonshanbo
16. Balrasheen
17. Dunmurraghill
18. Donadee
19. Mainham
20. Laraghbryan
21. Confey
22. Donaghmore
23. Kilmacredock
24. Leixlip
25. Taghadoe
26. Kildrought
27. Killadoon
28. Straffan
29. Timahoe
30. Ballynafagh
31. Downings
32. Killybegs
33. Clane
34. Carragh
35. Brideschurch
36. Bodenstown
37. Whitechurch
38. Sherlockstown
39. Kerdiffstown
40. Naas
41. Johnstown
42. Tipper
43. Rathmore
44. Donaghcumper
45. Stacumney
46. Castledillon
47. Lyons (2 pts.)
48. Cloneglish (2 pts.)
49. Oughterard
50. Kill (2 pts.)
51. Kilteel
52. Forenaghts
53. Hainestown
54. Lullymore
55. Rathangan (2 pts.)
56. Cloncurry
57. Thomastown
58. Grangeclare
59. Dunmurry
60. Tully (3 pts.)
61. Kildare (2 pts.)
62. Pollardstown
63. Ballymany
64. Ballysax
65. Carn
66. Kilmeage
67. Rathernan (2 pts.)
68. Feighcullen (2 pts.)
69. Morristownbiller
70. Oldconnell
71. Ladytown (2 pts.)
72. Greatconnell
73. Killashee
74. Tipperkevin
75. Carnalway
76. Coghlanstown
77. Ballymoreustace
78. Brannockstown
79. Gilltown
80. Jago
81. Ballybought
82. Lackagh
83. Kevinstown
84. Duneeny (2 pts.)

CIVIL PARISHES OF COUNTY KILDARE

Meath

Dublin

Offaly

RATHANGAN

NAAS

NEWBRIDGE

MONASTEREVIN

KILDARE

Wicklow

ATHY

Laois

Carlow

BARONIES

1. CARBURY
2. IKEATHY & OUGHTERANY
3. NORTH SALT
4. CLANE
5. NORTH NAAS
6. SOUTH SALT
7. EAST OFFALY
8. CONNELL
9. SOUTH NAAS
10. WEST OFFALY
11. KILCULLEN
12. NARRAGH & REBAN WEST
13. NARRAGH & REBAN EAST
14. KILKEA & MOONE

⌐ = CIVIL PARISHES ADJOINING ACROSS
BARONY BOUNDARIES.

85. Monasterevin
86. Ballybracken
87. Kildangan
88. Walterstown
89. Harristown
90. Nurney
91. Kilrush
92. Ballyshannon
93. Fontstown (2 pts.)
94. Kilcullen
95. Kilberry
96. Churchtown
97. St. Michael's
98. St. John's (4 pts.)
99. Davidstown (2 pts.)
100. Usk

101. Narraghmore
102. Timolin
103. Moone (2 pts.)
104. Ardree
105. Tankardstown
106. Grangerosnolvan
107. Belan
108. Killelan (4 pts.)
109. Kilkee
110. Dunmanoge
111. Castledermot
112. Kinneagh (2 pts.)
113. Graney (2 pts.)
114. Painestown
115. Ballaghmoon

Kildare Civil Parishes in Alphabetical Order

Ardkill: 10
Ardree: 104
Ballaghmoon: 115
Ballybought: 81
Ballybracken: 86
Ballymany: 63
Ballymoreustace: 77
Ballynadrumny: 1
Ballynafagh: 30
Ballysax: 64
Ballyshannon: 92
Balrasheen: 16
Belan: 107
Bodenstown: 36
Brannockstown: 78
Brideschurch: 35
Cadamstown: 4
Carbury: 9
Carn: 65
Carnalway: 75
Carragh: 34
Carrick: 5
Castledermot: 111

Castledillon: 46
Churchtown: 96
Clane: 33
Cloncurry: 56
Cloncurry: 12
Cloneglish (2 pts.): 48
Clonshanbo: 15
Coghlanstown: 76
Confey: 21
Davidstown (2 pts.): 99
Donadee: 18
Donaghcumper: 44
Donaghmore: 22
Downings: 31
Duneeny (2 pts.): 84
Dunfierth: 7
Dunmanoge: 110
Dunmurraghill: 17
Dunmurry: 59
Feighcullen (2 pts.): 68
Fontstown (2 pts.): 93
Forenaghts: 52
Gilltown: 79

Graney (2 pts.): 113
Grangeclare: 106
Grangerosnolvan: 58
Greatconnell: 78
Hainestown: 53
Harristown: 89
Jago: 80
Johnstown: 41
Kerdiffstown: 39
Kevinstown: 83
Kilberry: 95
Kilcock: 13
Kilcullen: 94
Kildangan: 87
Kildare (2 pts.): 61
Kildrought: 26
Kilkee: 109
Kill (2 pts.): 50
Killadoon: 27
Killashee: 73
Killelan (4 pts.): 108
Killybegs: 32
Kilmacredock: 23
Kilmeage: 66
Kilmore: 8
Kilpatrick: 11
Kilrainy: 2
Kilrush: 9
Kilteel: 51
Kineagh (2 pts.): 112
Lackagh: 82
Ladytown (2 pts.): 71
Lullymore: 54
Laraghbryan: 20
Leixlip: 24

Lyons (2 pts.): 47
Mainham: 19
Monasterevin: 85
Moone (2 pts.): 103
Morristownbiller: 69
Mylerstown: 3
Naas: 40
Narraghmore: 101
Nurney: 6
Nurney: 90
Oldconnell: 70
Oughterard: 49
Painestown: 114
Pollardstown: 62
Rathangan (2 pts.): 55
Rathernan (2 pts.): 67
Rathmore: 43
Scullogestown: 14
Sherlockstown: 38
St. John's (4 pts.): 98
St. Michael's: 97
Stacumney: 45
Straffan: 28
Taghadoe: 25
Tankardstown: 105
Thomastown: 57
Timolin: 102
Timahoe: 29
Tipper: 42
Tipperkevin: 74
Tully (3 pts.): 60
Usk: 100
Walterstown: 88
Whitechurch: 37

County Kilkenny

A Brief History

In the old Gaelic territorial system, this county formed the bulk of the Kingdom of Ossory. The major Gaelic families in the county were the Walshes, the O'Brennans, and the O'Dunphys. After the Norman invasion, a number of Norman families settled in Kilkenny and have been associated with the county ever since. These include Archer, Grace, Forestal, Comerford, Cantwell, Shortall, Wandesford, Rothe, Archdeacon ("Gaelicized" as Cody), and Butler. As elsewhere, these Normans became "more Irish than the Irish." The Sweetman family, which is of Norse origin, is also associated with the county.

Kilkenny City was probably founded by the establishment of a monastery there in 1052. The Norman invaders built a large castle on this site in 1195. The city acted as the parliamentary seat for Ireland on many occasions from the thirteenth to sixteenth centuries. In 1366, the English-controlled Parliament passed the infamous "Statutes of Kilkenny" in an attempt to prevent the adoption of the Irish lifestyle by the Normans. These statutes made it treasonable for a Norman to marry an Irishwoman or to adopt the dress, language, or customs of the Irish. The native Irish were also prohibited from living in walled towns. These statutes failed completely in their aims.

In the early seventeenth century, when English power had greatly receded in Ireland, Kilkenny City became the meeting place of an independent Irish government, called the Confederation of Kilkenny, set up in opposition to the English-controlled Dublin Parliament. A general rebellion by those represented at this parliament, which began in 1641 and lasted until 1650, resulted in confiscation of the lands of these rebels and their redistribution to English soldiers and adventurers.

The county has very good agricultural soils and had a generally well-developed system of agriculture in the early nineteenth century, including a large dairy industry. Kilkenny was relatively badly affected by the Great Famine. The population in 1841 was 202,400, and in 1861 had fallen to 124,500. There were some 27,000 deaths in the county between 1845 and 1850.

The current population of the county is approximately 71,000. The major towns are Kilkenny, Callan, Graiguenamanagh, Thomastown, and Castlecomer. The county is still a major dairying area, while Kilkenny City now has many industries and is the center of Irish design because of the government's establishment there of the Kilkenny Design Centre. In regard to records, the county has a long-established local history society, the Kilkenny Archaeological and Historical Society, whose library is a valuable local archive.

Census and Census Substitutes

1537-1628

"Corporation Book of Irish Town of Kilkenny." *Anal. Hib.* 28 (1978): 1-78 (lists public officials, corporation members, etc.).

1569

Names of Gentlemen of Co. Kilkenny. Lambeth Palace Library, London. Ms. 611; NLI P1699.

1654-56

Books of Survey and Distribution, Kilkenny City—Vol. 6. Abstracts of various surveys and documents relating to land ownership. Simington, R.C. Dublin: Stationery Office, 1955. SLC film 973123.

1659

"Census" of Ireland. Edited by S. Pender. Dublin: Stationery Office, 1939. NLI I6551. SLC film 924648.

1664

Hearth Money Roll for parishes of Agherney, Aghavillar, Bellaghtobin, Belline, Burnchurch, Callan, Castleinch, Clone, Coolaghmor, Coolcashin, Danganmore, Derrinahinch, Dunkitt, Earlstown, Eynk, Fartagh, Inishnagg and Stonecarthy, Jerpoint, Kells, Kilbecon and Killahy, Kilcolm, Kilferragh, Kilkredy, Killamerry, Killaloe, Killree, Kilmoganny, Kiltacaholme, Knocktopher and Kilkerchill, Mucklee and Lismatigue, Outrath, Rathbach, Rathpatrick, Tullaghanbrogue, Tullaghmaine, Tullahaght, Urlingford. Transcript in the Carrigan Mss., Kilkenny. In *Ir. Gen.* 5 (1) (1974): 33–47 (baronies of Ida, Knocktopher, and Kells); 5 (2) (1975): 169–80 (rest of the county). SLC film 100158.

1702

List of Male Householders in Kilkenny City, comprising Catholics of St. Mary's Hightown Ward, and both Catholics and Protestants of St. Canice's Ingate and Outgate, city of Kilkenny. NAI 1A 55 82.

1747

Freeholders and Leaseholders of Co. Kilkenny. SLC 941.89 R2k.

1766

Catholic Householders in Portnascully. SLC film 100158, GO 683-4.

1775

Names of Co. Kilkenny Landholders and representatives. GO ms. 443; SLC film 100181.

Catholic Qualification Roll Extracts (189 names, addresses, and occupations). 59th Report DKPRI: 50-84.

1785

Freeholders of Kilkenny (selected surnames only). GO Ms. 685; SLC film 100158.

1786–1809

Freeholders of Barony of Iverk. GO Ms. 684; SLC film 100158.

1797

"Chief Inhabitants of the Parishes of Graiguenamanagh and Knocktopher." *Ir. Anc.* 10 (2) (1978): 73-76.

1798

List of Persons Who Suffered Losses in '98 Rebellion. NLI JLB 94107 (approximately 250 names, addresses, and occupations).

1809–19

A List of Co. Kilkenny Freeholders, 1809-1819. NLI ms. 14181.

1819

A Survey of Tullaroan (or Grace's Parish), Co. Kilkenny. Wm. S. Mason. Dublin, 1819. (Lists townlands and main proprietors, quality of land, and produce.)

1821

"Government Census Remnants: Parishes of Aglish and Portnascully." *Ir. Anc.* 8 (2) (1976): 113-24; *Ir. Gen.* 5 (3) (1976): 383-93. Parish of Pollrone. *Ir. Gen.* 5 (4) (1977): 522-26; SLC film 100158. Parishes of Clonmore, Fiddown, Kilmacow, Muckalee, Owning, Rathkieran, Tubrid, Tybroughney, Ullid and Whitechurch. *Ir. Gen.* 5 (5) (1978): 643-49. All of the above also on GO Ms. 683/4. SLC film 100158.

1822–30

Lists of Applicants for the Vote. Division of Kilkenny (1,285 names) and Thomastown (2,525 names). (Gives names, occupations, residence, description of property, etc.) NLI ILB 324 Kilkenny.

1823–38

Tithe Applotment Survey (see introduction). List of tithe defaulters for 1831 (compiled by S. McCormac) is in NAI and NLI; see *Irish Roots* (1) 1997: 25-28.

1831

"Government Census Remnants: Parish of Aglish" (possibly not complete). Walsh-Kelly Transcripts GO 683-4. SLC film 100158.

"Clergy Relief Fund." Tithe Defaulters in Grangesilvia. *Ir. Gen.* 8 (1) (1990): 82-102. (Names, occupations, residences and tithe arrears.)

1832–36

"Names of Holders and Applicants for Licenses to Sell Liquor in Kilkenny" (names and addresses). *Parl. Papers* 1837/38, 13 (2): Appendixes 10 and 13.

1837

"List of those Made Freemen of Kilkenny Since 1831" (names, addresses, and occupations). *Parl. Papers* 1837, 11 (1): Appendix B1; 1837/38, 13 (2): Appendix 3.

1841

"Government Census Remnants: Townlands of Aglish North and South and Portnascully, Parish of Aglish." *Ir. Anc.* 9 (1) (1977): 44-47; SLC film 100158.

Praysers: Thomas Phelan, Thomas Dwygine, Thomas Carran.
Porters; Dennis Caghell, William Longe, Donogheh O'Loghman.
The rates of vittles to continue as the last yere.
Free burgesses admitted: David Pembroke, Thomas Corran.

(This yere uppon the seccond of July, 1574, the Lord Deputy directed his letters unto Master Robert Poore, then being Portrive of the Irishtoune, therein requyring him to repayre unto his Honour to show what he had in the mayntenance of that xorporaction of meetre land commonly called the cross of meetre land; which thing he performed accordingly. The proceedings of this suite you shall find in sixte leaf of this booke).[1]

fol. 35b. Thomas Seix, Portrive, the 11th of Octobre, 1574.
Sargente: Robert Roth.
Constables: Micholas Lawles, Thomas Carran, Edmund Browne, William Hoyne.
Bayliffs: Walter Roth, fitz Oliver, Dennise Carran.
(Free burgess admitted: Nicholas Fleming).[2]
Proctors: Geffry Roth, Thomas Dullany.
Auditors: Morgan Kealy, Richard Poore, Thomas Dullany, John Hoyne.
Praysers: John Dywy, Robert Roth, fitz David, Thomas Deegin.
Porters: Dennise Caghell, Patrick Brenen, Dennise Loghman, James Stackboll.
The rates of all kinde of vittles of beefe, bread, and ale, fish, tallow, (the wages of) laborers and artificers, to continue as affore is concluded the yere John Busher was Portrive.
David Pembrocke, sworne Portrive the 11th of Octobre, 1575.
Officers appointed:
Sargente: Robert Roth.
Constables: William Donogh, John Morphy, Thomas Hoyne, William Breckley.
Bayliffs: Dennise Kelly, John Fleming.
Proctors: James Kenedy, Edward Browne.
Auditors: Richard Poore, John Dowly, Richard Mooney, Thomas Dullany.
Prayers: William Brenagh, Derby Pysan, Thomas Dwigin.
Porters: John Galvan, Dennise Davyn Loghman.
(Free burgesses admitted: Thomas Raghtor, William Donogho, Lawrence Walsh, Dennise Call.)
Sessors: Dennise Davyne, Robert Kyvan, Danyell O'Teyne, Robert Kelly.

Extract from the "Corporation Book of the Irish Town of Kilkenny, 1537–1628," giving the names of various corporation officers. From *Analecta Hibernica* 23 (1978).

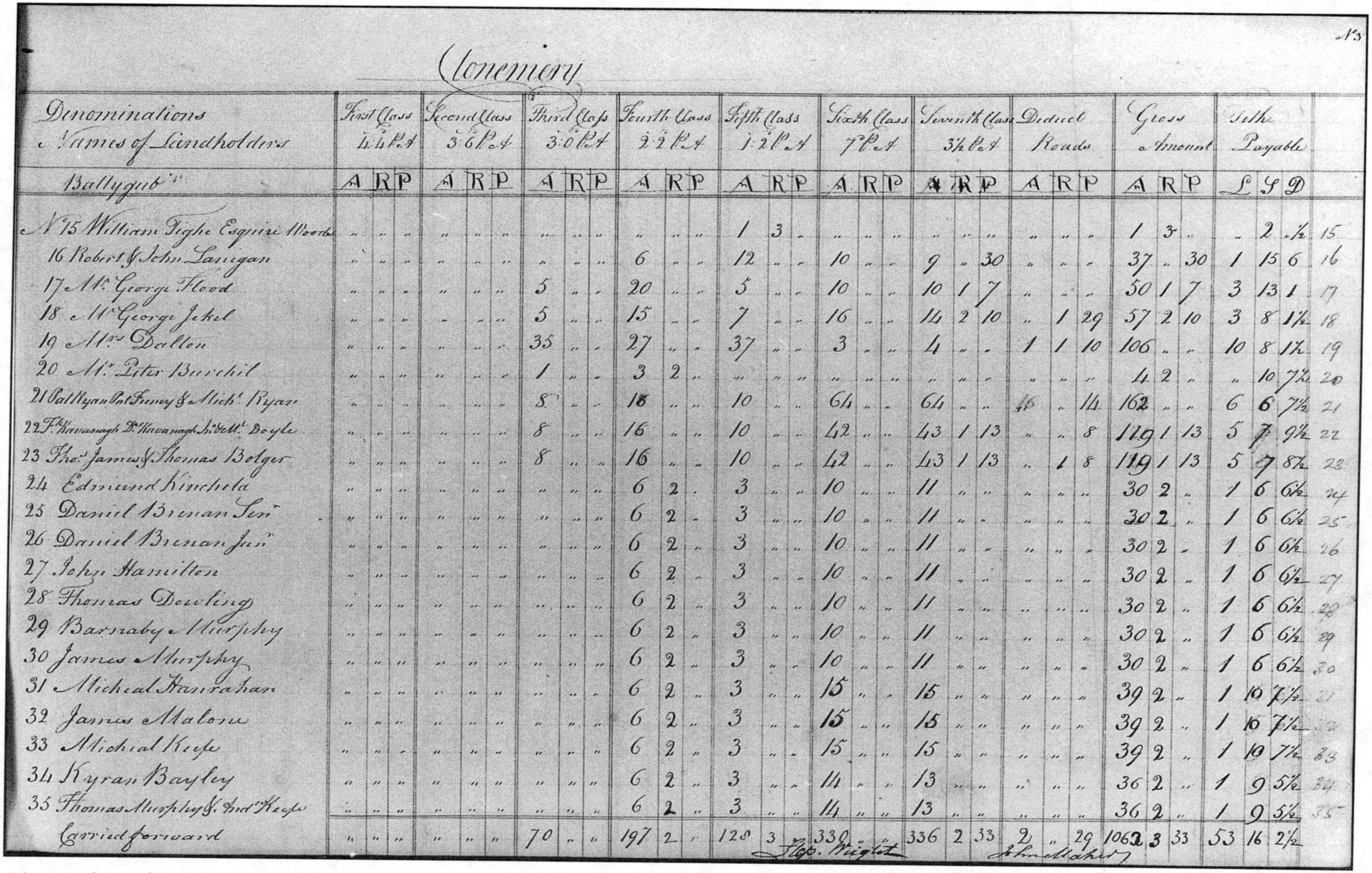

No. 3

Clonemery

Denominations / Names of Landholders	First Class 4:4 P A	Second Class 3:6 P A	Third Class 3:0 P A	Fourth Class 2:2 P A	Fifth Class 1:2 P A	Sixth Class 7 P A	Seventh Class 3½ P A	Deduct Roads	Gross Amount	Tithe Payable	
Ballygub	A R P	A R P	A R P	A R P	A R P	A R P	A R P	A R P	A R P	£ S D	
No. 15 William Fighe Esquire Moore					1 3				1 3	2 ½	15
16 Robert & John Lanigan				6	12	10	9 . 30		37 . 30	1 15 6	16
17 Mr. George Flood			5	20	5	10	10 1 7		50 1 7	3 13 1	17
18 Mr. George Jekel			5	15	7	16	14 2 10	. 1 29	57 2 10	3 8 1½	18
19 Mrs. Dallon			35	27	37	3	4	1 1 10	106	10 8 1½	19
20 Mr. Peter Burchil			1	3 2					4 2	10 7½	20
21 Pat Ryan Pat Finney & Michl. Ryan			8	18	10	64	64	16 . 14	162	6 6 7½	21
22 Fr. Kavanagh Dr. Kavanagh & Wm. Doyle			8	16	10	42	43 1 13	. . 8	119 1 13	5 7 9½	22
23 Thos. James & Thomas Bolger			8	16	10	42	43 1 13	. 1 8	119 1 13	5 7 8½	23
24 Edmund Kinchela				6 2	3	10	11		30 2	1 6 6½	24
25 Daniel Brenan Senr.				6 2	3	10	11		30 2	1 6 6½	25
26 Daniel Brenan Junr.				6 2	3	10	11		30 2	1 6 6½	26
27 John Hamilton				6 2	3	10	11		30 2	1 6 6½	27
28 Thomas Dowling				6 2	3	10	11		30 2	1 6 6½	28
29 Barnaby Murphy				6 2	3	10	11		30 2	1 6 6½	29
30 James Murphy				6 2	3	10	11		30 2	1 6 6½	30
31 Micheal Hanrahan				6 2	3	15	15		39 2	1 10 7½	31
32 James Malone				6 2	3	15	15		39 2	1 10 7½	32
33 Micheal Keefe				6 2	3	15	15		39 2	1 10 7½	33
34 Kyran Bayley				6 2	3	14	13		36 2	1 9 5½	34
35 Thomas Murphy & Andw. Keefe				6 2	3	14	13		36 2	1 9 5½	35
Carried forward			70	197 2	120 3	330	336 2 33	2 . 29	1062 3 33	53 16 2½	

Jos. Wright   John Maher

A page from the *Tithe Applotment Survey* showing the tithe-payers of the townland of Ballygub, Parish of Clonamery, County Kilkenny, in 1829.

"Government Census Remnants of Rathkyran" (Rathcurby and Ballymountain townlands only). Walsh-Kelly Transcripts GO 683-4. SLC film 100158.

1842

Voters List. NAI 1842/79.

1849-50

Griffith's Valuation (see introduction).

1851

"Government Census Remnants: Parishes of Aglish, Portnascully and Rathkieran." *Ir. Anc.* 9 (2) (1977): 129-33. SLC film 100158.

Aglish, Portnascully (Clasharow townland only), and Rathkyran (Ballincurra and Ballymountain townlands only). Walsh-Kelly Transcripts GO 683-4.

1901

Census. NAI (see introduction). SLC films 840939-53, 0843001-6.

1911

Census. NAI.

Church Records

Church of Ireland

See the introduction for a description of Church of Ireland records and their major repositories. Many C of I records were lost in the PRO fire of 1922. These are indicated as "Lost." However, as Church of Ireland records were effectively state records, the records of marriage (from 1845) are also in the General Registrar's Office. Many are still in local custody (LC), while others are in one of a variety of other archives (e.g., RCBL or NAI). Most of the registers of this county have been indexed by Kilkenny Archaeological Society (see Research Services at the end of the chapter). A search of the index will be conducted by them for a fee. Those indexed are noted below as "Indexed by KAS."

Aghour or Freshford
Earliest Records: b/m/d. 1846
Status: Indexed by KAS (to 1900)

Ballinamare
Status: Lost

Bilboa
Earliest Records: b. 1845-
Status: LC; Indexed by KAS (to 1900)

Blackrath
Earliest Records: b. 1811-; d. 1845-
Status: LC

Burnchurch
Earliest Records: b. 1881-; d. 1882-
Status: RCBL (to 1941+)

Callan
Earliest Records: b. 1892-; m. 1846-; d. 1894-
Status: RCBL (to 1954+)

Castlane or Whitechurch (Castle Archdall)
Status: Lost

Castlecomer
Earliest Records: b. 1799-1839; m. 1799-1845; d. 1799-1901
Status: RCBL; Indexed by KAS (to 1900)

Castlecomer Colliery
Earliest Records: b. 1838-; m. 1839-; d. 1861-
Status: RCBL (b. 1838-58; m. 1839-44); Indexed by KAS (to 1900)

Clara (see St. John Kilkenny)

Clonmantagh
Status: Lost

Clonmore
Earliest Records: b. 1817-; m. 1820-; d. 1822-
Status: LC; NAI M5086 (b. 1817-1906; d. 1822-1921); SLC film 990092 (b. 1817-1874; d. 1817-1871)

Donoughmore (see Odagh)

Dunkitt (including Gaulskill and Kilcollum)
Status: Lost

Dunmore
Earliest Records: b. 1839-; m. 1838-; d. 1842-
Status: LC

Eirke
Status: Lost

Ennisnag
Status: Lost

Fertagh
Earliest Records: b. 1797-; m. 1797-; d. 1797-
Status: LC

Fiddown
Status: Lost

Gowran
Earliest Records: b. 1885-; m. 1845-
Status: RCBL (to 1956+)

Graiguenamanagh
Earliest Records: b. 1804-; m. 1846-
Status: RCBL (b. 1804-05; m. 1846-1933)

Grangesylvae
Earliest Records: b. 1803-; m. 1803-; d. 1806-
Status: LC and RCBL (m. 1850-1921)

Inchyolaghan
Status: Lost

Innistiogue
Earliest Records: b. 1797–; m. 1797–; d. 1797–
Status: LC

Jerpoint (with Thomastown)
Status: Lost

Kells
Status: Lost

Kilbecon
Status: Lost

Kilfane
Status: Lost

Killamery
Status: Lost

Kilmacow
Status: Lost

Kilmanagh
Earliest Records: b. 1784–; m. 1784–; d. 1784–
Status: LC

Kilmocahill (see also Shankill)
Earliest Records: m. 1848–
Status: RCBL (m. 1848–1864)

Kilmoganny
Earliest Records: b. 1782; m. 1782; d. 1782
Status: LC

Knocktopher
Earliest Records: b. 1884–; m. 1849–; d. 1887–
Status: RCBL (b. 1884–1959; m. 1849–1940; d. 1887–1983)

Listerlin
Status: Lost

Macully or Kilculliheen
Status: Lost

Mothel
Earliest Records: b. 1810–; m. 1811–; d. 1817–
Status: RCBL (b. 1810–1843; m. 1811–1950; d. 1817–1842); Indexed by KAS (to 1900)

Odagh
Earliest Records: b/m. 1848–
Status: LC; Indexed by KAS (to 1900)

Powerstown
Earliest Records: m. 1854
Status: RCBL

Rathcool
Earliest Records: b. 1836–; m. 1842
Status: RCBL (b. 1835–44, m. 1842); Indexed by KAS (to 1844 and 1800, respectively)

Rathkieran Church
Status: Lost

Rower or The Rower
Earliest Records: b. 1888–; m. 1849–; d. 1883–

Status: RCBL (b. 1888–1943; m. 1849–1937; d. 1883–1985)

St. Canice (Kilkenny City)
Earliest Records: b. 1789–; m. 1789–; d. 1789–
Status: LC; Indexed by KAS

St. John (Kilkenny City)
Status: Lost

St. Mary's and St. Patrick (Kilkenny City)
Earliest Records: b. 1732–; m. 1732–; d. 1732–
Status: LC; GO Ms. 685 and SLC film 100158

Shankill or St. Kill (see also Kilmocahill)
Earliest Records: m. 1845–
Status: RCBL (m. 1845–1950)

Stamcarty (see Kells)

Tascoffin (see also Mothel)
Earliest Records: m. 1853–
Status: RCBL (m. 1853–1880)

Thomastown
Earliest Records: b. 1895–; m. 1845–; d. 1870–
Status: RCBL (b. 1895–1965; m. 1845–1949; d. 1870–1987)

Treadingstown
Status: Lost

Ullard (Graigue up to ca. 1833)
Earliest Records: m. 1857–
Status: RCBL

Roman Catholic

Note that most of the Catholic parish registers of this county have been indexed by Kilkenny Archaeological Society (see Research Services at the end of the chapter). A search of the index will be conducted by them for a fee. Those indexed are noted below as "Indexed by KAS." Microfilm copies of all registers are also available in the National Library of Ireland (NLI), and through the LDS library system.

Civil Parish: Abbeyleix
Map Grid: 14
RC Parish: part Abbeyleix, Co. Laois; part Ballyragget, see Donaghmore
Diocese: LE

Civil Parish: Aghaviller
Map Grid: 104
RC Parish: Aghaviller
Diocese: OS
Earliest Record: b. 10.1847; m. 2.1848
Status: LC; NLI (mf); Indexing planned by KAS

Civil Parish: Aglish
Map Grid: 140
RC Parish: Mooncoin, see Pollrone
Diocese: OS

Civil Parish: Aharney (see also Co. Laois)
Map Grid: 10
RC Parish: Lisdowney
Diocese: OS
Earliest Record: b. 5.1817; m. 9.1771
Missing Dates: b. 10.1853-4.1854; m. 4.1778-11.1828, 8.1853-11.1853
Status: LC; NLI (mf); Indexing planned by KAS

Civil Parish: Arderra
Map Grid: 136
RC Parish: Mooncoin, see Pollrone
Diocese: OS

Civil Parish: Attanagh (see also Co. Laois)
Map Grid: 13
RC Parish: Ballyragget, see Donaghmore
Diocese: OS

Civil Parish: Balleen
Map Grid: 7
RC Parish: Lisdowney, see Aharney
Diocese: OS

Civil Parish: Ballinamore
Map Grid: 38
RC Parish: see Freshford
Diocese: OS

Civil Parish: Ballybur
Map Grid: 52
RC Parish: part Danesfort; part St. Canice's
Diocese: OS

Civil Parish: Ballycallan
Map Grid: 41
RC Parish: Ballycallan
Diocese: OS
Earliest Record: b. 5.1820; m. 7.1820
Status: LC; NLI (mf); Indexed by KAS (to 1911)

Civil Parish: Ballygurrin
Map Grid: 119
RC Parish: Slieverue, see Rathpatrick
Diocese: OS

Civil Parish: Ballylarkin
Map Grid: 32
RC Parish: see Freshford
Diocese: OS

Civil Parish: Ballylinch
Map Grid: 83
RC Parish: see Thomastown
Diocese: OS

Civil Parish: Ballytarsney
Map Grid: 135
RC Parish: Mooncoin, see Pollrone
Diocese: OS

Civil Parish: Ballytobin
Map Grid: 97

RC Parish: see Dunnamaggan
Diocese: OS

Civil Parish: Blackrath
Map Grid: 66
RC Parish: part St. John's, part Gowran
Diocese: OS

Civil Parish: Blanchvilleskill
Map Grid: 74
RC Parish: see Gowran
Diocese: OS

Civil Parish: Borrismore
Map Grid: 6
RC Parish: see Urlingford
Diocese: OS

Civil Parish: Burnchurch
Map Grid: 56
RC Parish: part Danesfort; part Freshford; part Mooncoin, see Pollrone; part Ballyhale, see Derrynahinch
Diocese: OS

Civil Parish: Callan
Map Grid: 47
RC Parish: Callan; also part Ballycallan
Diocese: OS
Earliest Record: b. 1.1821; m. 1.1821
Status: LC; NLI (mf); Indexing planned by KAS

Civil Parish: Castlecomer (1)
Map Grid: 15
RC Parish: Castlecomer; also see Clough below
Diocese: OS
Earliest Record: b. 1.1812; m. 8.1842
Missing Dates: b/m. 10.1818-12.1828
Status: LC; NLI (mf); Indexing planned by KAS

Civil Parish: Castlecomer (2)
Map Grid: 15
RC Parish: Clough
Earliest Record: b. 1832; m. 1830
Missing Dates: b. 1857
Status: LC; NLI (mf); Indexed by KAS (to 1911)

Civil Parish: Castleinch (or Incholaghan)
Map Grid: 51
RC Parish: see St. Patrick's
Diocese: OS

Civil Parish: Clara
Map Grid: 70
RC Parish: Clara; see also Gowran
Diocese: OS
Earliest Record: b. 1779-; m. 1778
Status: LC; NLI (mf); Indexed by KAS (to 1890)

Civil Parish: Clashacrow
Map Grid: 36
RC Parish: see Freshford
Diocese: OS

Civil Parish: Clomantagh
Map Grid: 28
RC Parish: part Urlingford; part Freshford
Diocese: OS

Civil Parish: Clonamery
Map Grid: 112
RC Parish: see Inistioge
Diocese: OS

Civil Parish: Clonmore
Map Grid: 131
RC Parish: Mooncoin, see Pollrone
Diocese: OS

Civil Parish: Columkille
Map Grid: 89
RC Parish: see Thomastown
Diocese: OS

Civil Parish: Coolaghmore
Map Grid: 93
RC Parish: see Callan
Diocese: OS

Civil Parish: Coolcashin
Map Grid: 8
RC Parish: Lisdowney, see Aharney
Diocese: OS

Civil Parish: Coolcraheen
Map Grid: 22
RC Parish: part Conahy, see Grangemaccomb; part Muckalee
Diocese: OS

Civil Parish: Danesfort
Map Grid: 57
RC Parish: Danesfort and Cuffe's Grange
Diocese: OS
Earliest Record: b. 1.1819; m. 1.1824
Status: LC; NLI (mf); Indexing planned by KAS

Civil Parish: Derrynahinch
Map Grid: 106
RC Parish: Ballyhale; also Mullinavat, see Kilbeacon
Diocese: OS
Earliest Record: b. 8.1823
Status: LC; NLI (mf); Indexing planned by KAS

Civil Parish: Donaghmore
Map Grid: 18
RC Parish: Ballyragget
Diocese: OS
Earliest Record: b. 1801; m. 4.1856
Missing Dates: b. 1806–1855; (b. indexed by KAS to 1911)
Status: LC; NLI (mf); Indexing planned by KAS

Civil Parish: Dunbell
Map Grid: 73
RC Parish: see Gowran
Diocese: OS

Civil Parish: Dungarvan
Map Grid: 81
RC Parish: see Gowran
Diocese: OS

Civil Parish: Dunkitt
Map Grid: 121
RC Parish: see Kilmacow
Diocese: OS

Civil Parish: Dunmore
Map Grid: 26
RC Parish: see Muckalee (1)
Diocese: OS

Civil Parish: Dunnamaggan
Map Grid: 98
RC Parish: Dunnamaggan
Diocese: OS
Earliest Record: b. 9.1826; m. 10.1826
Missing Dates: b. 6.1840–4.1843; m. 6.1842–2.1843
Status: LC; NLI (mf); Indexing planned by KAS

Civil Parish: Durrow (see also Co. Laois)
Map Grid: 11
RC Parish: part Ballyragget, see Donaghmore
Diocese: OS

Civil Parish: Dysart
Map Grid: 21
RC Parish: see Muckalee (1)
Diocese: OS

Civil Parish: Dysartmoon
Map Grid: 113
RC Parish: see Rosbercon
Diocese: OS

Civil Parish: Earlstown
Map Grid: 59
RC Parish: see Callan
Diocese: OS

Civil Parish: Ennisnag
Map Grid: 60
RC Parish: see Danesfort
Diocese: OS

Civil Parish: Erke (see also Co. Laois)
Map Grid: 1
RC Parish: Johnstown, see Fertagh
Diocese: OS

Civil Parish: Famma
Map Grid: 91
RC Parish: see Thomastown
Diocese: OS

Civil Parish: Fertagh (1)
Map Grid: 4
RC Parish: Johnstown
Diocese: OS
Earliest Record: b. 8.1814; m. 2.1851
Status: LC; NLI (mf); Indexing planned by KAS

Civil Parish: Fertagh (2)
Map Grid: 4
RC Parish: Galmoy
Diocese: OS
Earliest Record: b. 6.1861; m. 9.1861
Status: LC; NLI (mf); Indexing planned by KAS

Civil Parish: Fiddown
Map Grid: 128
RC Parish: Owning and Templeorum
Diocese: OS
Earliest Record: b. 10.1803; m. 8.1815; d. 9.1803
Missing Dates: m. 11.1849–1.1851; d. 3.1806–8.1808, ends 6.1815
Status: LC; NLI (mf); Indexing planned by KAS

Civil Parish: Freshford
Map Grid: 33
RC Parish: Freshford; also part Ballyragget, see Donaghmore
Diocese: OS
Earliest Record: b. 1.1773; m. 8.1775
Missing Dates: b. 8.1797–3.1800; m. 11.1779–2.1801
Status: LC; NLI (mf); Indexed by KAS (to 1911)

Civil Parish: Garranamanagh
Map Grid: 29
RC Parish: see Freshford
Diocese: OS

Civil Parish: Gaulskill
Map Grid: 122
RC Parish: see Kilmacow
Diocese: OS

Civil Parish: Glashare (see also Co. Laois)
Map Grid: 2
RC Parish: Johnstown, see Fertagh (1)

Civil Parish: Gowran
Map Grid: 71
RC Parish: Gowran and Clara
Diocese: OS
Earliest Record: b. 1.1809; m. 1.1810
Status: LC; NLI (mf); Indexed by KAS (to 1911)

Civil Parish: Graiguenamanagh
Map Grid: 86
RC Parish: Graignamanagh
Diocese: LE
Earliest Record: b. 4.1838; m. 7.1818
Status: LC; NLI (mf); Indexing planned by KAS

Civil Parish: Grange
Map Grid: 50
RC Parish: see St. Patrick's
Diocese: OS

Civil Parish: Grangekilree
Map Grid: 58
RC Parish: see Dunnamaggan
Diocese: OS

Civil Parish: Grangemaccomb
Map Grid: 19
RC Parish: Conahy
Diocese: OS
Earliest Record: b. 6.1832; m. 6.1832
Status: LC; NLI (mf); Indexed by KAS (to 1911)

Civil Parish: Grangesilvia
Map Grid: 76
RC Parish: Paulstown, see Kilmacahill
Diocese: LE

Civil Parish: Inistioge
Map Grid: 92
RC Parish: Inistioge and Clodiagh
Diocese: OS
Earliest Record: b. 12.1810 (2 registers); m. (The Rower) 1881; 1.1827
Status: LC; NLI (mf); Indexed by KAS (to 1911)

Civil Parish: Jerpointabbey
Map Grid: 88
RC Parish: see Thomastown
Diocese: OS

Civil Parish: Jerpointchurch
Map Grid: 102
RC Parish: see Thomastown
Diocese: OS

Civil Parish: Jerpointwest
Map Grid: 108
RC Parish: part Thomastown; part Mullinavat, see Kilbeacon

Civil Parish: Kells
Map Grid: 95
RC Parish: part Danesfort; part Ballyhale, see Derrynahinch
Diocese: OS

Civil Parish: Kilbeacon
Map Grid: 110
RC Parish: Mullinavat
Diocese: OS
Earliest Record: b. 2.1843; m. 5.1843

Civil Parish: Kilbride
Map Grid: 117
RC Parish: Slieverue, see Rathpatrick
Diocese: OS

Civil Parish: Kilcoan
Map Grid: 118
RC Parish: Slieverue, see Rathpatrick
Diocese: OS

Civil Parish: Kilcolumb
Map Grid: 123
RC Parish: Slieverue, see Rathpatrick
Diocese: OS

Civil Parish: Kilculliheen
Map Grid: 140a

RC Parish: Slieverue, see Rathpatrick
Diocese: OS

Civil Parish: Kilcooly
Map Grid: 34
RC Parish: Gortnahoe, see Buolick, Co. Tipperary
Diocese: CA

Civil Parish: Kilderry
Map Grid: 67
RC Parish: see St. John
Diocese: OS

Civil Parish: Kilfane
Map Grid: 85
RC Parish: see Thomastown
Diocese: OS

Civil Parish: Kilferagh
Map Grid: 54
RC Parish: see St. Patrick's
Diocese: OS

Civil Parish: Kilkeasy
Map Grid: 105
RC Parish: Ballyhale, see Derrynahinch
Diocese: OS

Civil Parish: Kilkieran
Map Grid: 63
RC Parish: Templeorum, see Fiddown
Diocese: OS

Civil Parish: Killahy (1) (Barony of Cranagh)
Map Grid: 35
RC Parish: see Freshford
Diocese: OS

Civil Parish: Killahy (2) (Barony of Knocktopher)
Map Grid: 109
RC Parish: see Kilmacow
Diocese: OS

Civil Parish: Killaloe
Map Grid: 48
RC Parish: see Ballycallan
Diocese: OS

Civil Parish: Killamery
Map Grid: 96
RC Parish: Windgap
Diocese: OS
Earliest Record: b. 8.1822; m. 9.1822
Status: LC; NLI (mf); Indexing planned by KAS

Civil Parish: Killarney
Map Grid: 79
RC Parish: see Thomastown
Diocese: OS

Civil Parish: Kilmacahill
Map Grid: 72
RC Parish: Paulstown and Goresbridge
Diocese: LE
Earliest Record: b. 7.1824; m. 1.1824

Missing Dates: b. 4.1846-5.1852; m. 11.1869-2.1870
Status: LC; NLI (mf); Indexing planned by KAS

Civil Parish: Kilmocar
Map Grid: 20
RC Parish: part Ballyragget, see Donaghmore; part Conahy, see Grangemaccomb
Diocese: OS

Civil Parish: Kilmacow
Map Grid: 138
RC Parish: Kilmacow
Diocese: OS
Earliest Record: b. 7.1858; m. 8.1858; d. 6.1858
Status: LC; NLI (mf); Indexing planned by KAS

Civil Parish: Kilmademoge
Map Grid: 27
RC Parish: see Muckalee (1)
Diocese: OS

Civil Parish: Kilmadum
Map Grid: 62
RC Parish: see St. John
Diocese: OS

Civil Parish: Kilmaganny
Map Grid: 100
RC Parish: see Dunnamaggan
Diocese: OS

Civil Parish: Kilmakevoge
Map Grid: 124
RC Parish: Glenmore
Diocese: OS
Earliest Record: b. 3.1831; m. 1.1831
Status: LC; NLI (mf); Indexing planned by KAS

Civil Parish: Kilmanagh
Map Grid: 40
RC Parish: see Ballycallan
Diocese: OS

Civil Parish: Kilmenan
Map Grid: 17
RC Parish: Ballyragget, see Donaghmore
Diocese: OS

Civil Parish: Kilree
Map Grid: 99
RC Parish: see Dunnamaggan
Diocese: OS

Civil Parish: Knocktopher
Map Grid: 103
RC Parish: Ballyhale, see Derrynahinch
Diocese: OS

Civil Parish: Lismateige
Map Grid: 107
RC Parish: part Templeorum, see Fiddown; part Aghaviller
Diocese: OS

Civil Parish: Listerlin
Map Grid: 115
RC Parish: see Rosbercon
Diocese: OS

Civil Parish: Mallardstown
Map Grid: 94
RC Parish: see Callan
Diocese: OS

Civil Parish: Mayne
Map Grid: 23
RC Parish: Conahy, see Grangemaccomb
Diocese: OS

Civil Parish: Mothell
Map Grid: 24
RC Parish: see Muckalee (1)
Diocese: OS

Civil Parish: Muckalee (1) (Barony of Fassadinin)
Map Grid: 25
RC Parish: Muckalee
Diocese: OS
Earliest Record: b. 10.1801; m. 4.1809
Missing Dates: b. 9.1806–6.1840; m. 11.1857–2.1858
Status: LC; NLI (mf); Indexed by KAS (to 1911)

Civil Parish: Muckalee (2) (Barony of Knocktopher)
Map Grid: 130
RC Parish: part Mooncoin, see Pollrone; part Aghaviller
Diocese: OS

Civil Parish: Odagh
Map Grid: 39
RC Parish: part Freshford; part Conahy, see Grangemaccomb
Diocese: OS

Civil Parish: Outrath
Map Grid: 53
RC Parish: see St. Patrick's
Diocese: OS

Civil Parish: Owning
Map Grid: 127
RC Parish: Templeorum, see Fiddown
Diocese: OS

Civil Parish: Pleberstown
Map Grid: 90
RC Parish: see Thomastown
Diocese: OS

Civil Parish: Pollrone
Map Grid: 134
RC Parish: Mooncoin
Diocese: OS
Earliest Record: b. 12.1797; m. 1.1772
Missing Dates: m. 3.1783–1.1789, 2.1814–2.1816,
9.1836–1.1837
Status: LC; NLI (mf); Indexing planned by KAS

Civil Parish: Portnascully
Map Grid: 139
RC Parish: Mooncoin, see Pollrone
Diocese: OS

Civil Parish: Powerstown
Map Grid: 82
RC Parish: see Graiguenamanagh
Diocese: LE

Civil Parish: Rathaspick
Map Grid: 16
RC Parish: see Co. Laois
Diocese: LE

Civil Parish: Rathbeagh
Map Grid: 30
RC Parish: Lisdowney, see Aharney
Diocese: OS

Civil Parish: Rathcoole
Map Grid: 64
RC Parish: see St. John
Diocese: OS

Civil Parish: Rathkieran
Map Grid: 133
RC Parish: Mooncoin, see Pollrone
Diocese: OS

Civil Parish: Rathlogan
Map Grid: 5
RC Parish: Johnstown, see Fertagh
Diocese: OS

Civil Parish: Rathpatrick
Map Grid: 125
RC Parish: Slieverue
Diocese: OS
Earliest Record: b. 11.1766; m. 2.1766; d. 12.1766
Missing Dates: m. 5.1778–5.1791, 7.1801–10.1801; d. ends 11.1799
Status: LC; NLI (mf); Indexing planned by KAS

Civil Parish: Rosbercon
Map Grid: 116
RC Parish: Rosbercon
Diocese: OS
Earliest Record: b. 4.1817; m. 1.1835
Missing Dates: b. 6.1819–1.1821, 3.1825–1.1830
Status: LC; NLI (mf); Indexed by KAS (to 1910)

Civil Parish: Rosconnell (see also Co. Laois)
Map Grid: 12
RC Parish: Ballyraggett, see Donaghmore
Diocese: OS

Civil Parish: Rossinan
Map Grid: 111
RC Parish: see Kilmacow
Diocese: OS

Civil Parish: The Rower
Map Grid: 114
RC Parish: see Inistioge
Diocese: OS

Civil Parish: St. Canice's
Map Grid: 42
RC Parish: St. Canice's, Kilkenny
Diocese: OS
Earliest Record: b. 4.1768; m. 6.1768
Status: LC; NLI (mf); Indexing planned by KAS

Civil Parish: St. John (1)
Map Grid: 43
RC Parish: St. John's, Kilkenny; also Kilkenny Workhouse, see below
Diocese: OS
Earliest Record: b. 1.1789; m. 6.1789
Missing Dates: b. 7.1830-2.1842; m. 7.1830-4.1842
Status: LC; NLI (mf); Indexed by KAS (to 1911)

Civil Parish: St. John (2)
Map Grid: 43
RC Parish: Kilkenny Workhouse
Earliest Record: b. 4.1876
Status: LC; NLI (mf); Indexing planned by KAS

Civil Parish: St. Martin's
Map Grid: 69
RC Parish: see St. Patrick's
Diocese: OS

Civil Parish: St. Mary's
Map Grid: 44
RC Parish: St. Mary's, Kilkenny
Diocese: OS
Earliest Record: b. 1.1754; m. 1.1754; d. 1.1754
Missing Dates: b. 8.1782-8.1784; d. ends 7.1787
Status: LC; NLI (mf); Indexed by KAS (to 1910)

Civil Parish: St. Maul's
Map Grid: 45
RC Parish: see St. Canice's
Diocese: OS

Civil Parish: St. Patrick's
Map Grid: 46
RC Parish: St. Patrick's, Kilkenny
Diocese: OS
Earliest Record: b. 8.1800; m. 7.1801
Status: LC; NLI (mf); Indexing planned by KAS

Civil Parish: Shanbogh
Map Grid: 120
RC Parish: see Rosbercon
Diocese: OS

Civil Parish: Shankill
Map Grid: 68
RC Parish: Paulstown, see Kilmacahill
Diocese: LE

Civil Parish: Sheffin
Map Grid: 9
RC Parish: Lisdowney, see Aharney
Diocese: OS

Civil Parish: Stonecarthy
Map Grid: 61
RC Parish: see Dunnamaggan
Diocese: OS

Civil Parish: Thomastown
Map Grid: 84
RC Parish: Thomastown and Tullaherin
Diocese: OS
Earliest Record: b. 6.1782; m. 1.1786
Missing Dates: b. 9.1809-1.1810; m. 8.1806-5.1810
Status: LC; NLI (mf); Indexed by KAS (to 1911)

Civil Parish: Tibberraghny
Map Grid: 129
RC Parish: Templeorum, see Fiddown
Diocese: OS

Civil Parish: Tiscoffin
Map Grid: 65
RC Parish: see Gowran
Diocese: OS

Civil Parish: Treadingstown
Map Grid: 77
RC Parish: see Danesfort
Diocese: OS

Civil Parish: Tubbrid
Map Grid: 132
RC Parish: Mooncoin, see Pollrone
Diocese: OS

Civil Parish: Tubbridbritain
Map Grid: 31
RC Parish: see Urlingford
Diocese: OS

Civil Parish: Tullaghanbrogue
Map Grid: 49
RC Parish: see St. Patrick's
Diocese: OS

Civil Parish: Tullaherin
Map Grid: 80
RC Parish: see Thomastown
Diocese: OS

Civil Parish: Tullahought
Map Grid: 101
RC Parish: Windgap, see Killamery
Diocese: OS

Civil Parish: Tullamaine
Map Grid: 55
RC Parish: see Callan
Diocese: OS

Civil Parish: Tullaroan
Map Grid: 37
RC Parish: Tullaroan
Diocese: OS
Earliest Record: b. 3.1843; m. 4.1843
Status: LC; NLI (mf); Indexing planned by KAS

Civil Parish: Ullard (see also Co. Carlow)
Map Grid: 87
RC Parish: see Graiguenamanagh
Diocese: LE

Civil Parish: Ullid
Map Grid: 137
RC Parish: see Kilmacow
Diocese: OS

Civil Parish: Urlingford
Map Grid: 3
RC Parish: Urlingford (Graine)
Diocese: OS
Earliest Record: b. 5.1805; m. 5.1805
Missing Dates: m. 9.1870–2.1871
Status: LC; NLI (mf); Indexing planned by KAS

Civil Parish: Wells
Map Grid: 75
RC Parish: Leighlinbridge, see Agha, Co. Carlow
Diocese: LE

Civil Parish: Whitechurch
Map Grid: 126
RC Parish: Templeorum, see Fiddown
Diocese: OS

Civil Parish: Woolengrange
Map Grid: 78
RC Parish: see Danesfort
Diocese: OS

Commercial and Social Directories

1788

Richard Lucas's *General Directory of the Kingdom of Ireland* contains lists of traders in Kilkenny and Thomastown.

1820

J. Pigot's *Commercial Directory of Ireland* contains information on the gentry, nobility, and traders in and around the town of Kilkenny.

1824

J. Pigot's *City of Dublin and Hibernian Provincial Directory* includes traders, nobility, gentry, and clergy lists of Ballyragget, Callan, Castlecomer, Kilkenny, and Thomastown.

1839

T. Shearman's *New Commercial Directory for the Cities of Waterford and Kilkenny, Towns of Clonmel, Carrick-on-Suir, New Ross and Carlow* lists traders, gentry, etc.

1840

F. Kinder's *New Triennial and Commercial Directory for the Years 1840, '41 and '42* lists traders, nobility, etc., in Kilkenny City (very rare volume).

1846

Slater's *National Commercial Directory of Ireland* lists nobility, clergy, traders, etc., in Ballyragget, Callan, Castlecomer, Durrow, Kilkenny, and Thomastown.

1856

Slater's *Royal National Commercial Directory of Ireland* lists nobility, gentry, clergy, traders, etc., in Ballyragget, Callan, Castlecomer, Durrow, Kilkenny, and Thomastown.

1870

Slater's *Directory of Ireland* contains trade, nobility, and clergy lists for Ballyragget, Callan, Castlecomer, Durrow, Kilkenny, and Thomastown.

1881

Slater's *Royal National Commercial Directory of Ireland* contains lists of traders, clergy, nobility, and farmers in adjoining parishes of the towns of Callan, Castlecomer, Durrow, Kilkenny, and Thomastown.

1884

G.H. Bassett's *Kilkenny City and County Guide and Directory* of Ballyhale, Ballyragget, Bennett's Bridge, Callan, Castlecomer, Clonmantagh, Cuff's Grange, Dungarvan, Ferrybank, Freshford, Glenmore, Goresbridge, Gowran, Graigue, Inistioge, Jenkinstown, Johnstown, Johnswell, Kells, Kilfane, Kilkenny, Kilmacow, Kilmanagh, Kilmoganny, Knocktopher, Luke's Well, Mooncoin, Mullinavat, Piltown and Fiddown, Rosbercon, Slieverue, Stonyford, The Rower, Thomastown, Three Castles, Tullaroan, Tullogher, Urlingford, Whitehall, and Windgap. Dublin: Sealy, 1884.

1894

Slater's *Royal National Directory of Ireland* lists traders, police, teachers, farmers, and private residents in each of the towns, villages, and parishes of the county.

Family History

Anderson, A.L.B. *The Andersons of Co. Kilkenny.* Simla, 1931.

"An Inquiry into the Origin of the Family of Archer in Kilkenny, with Notices of Other Families of the Name in Ireland." *R.S.A.I.* 9 (1867): 220-32.

"The Bourchier Tablet in the Cathedral Church of St. Canice, Kilkenny, with Some Account of That Family." *R.S.A.I.* 34 (1904): 365-79; 35 (1905): 21-33.

"Bryan's of Jenkinstown." *Old Kilkenny Review* 2 (3) 1981.

"Some Notice of the Family of Cowley in Kilkenny." *R.S.A.I.* 2 (1852): 102-14.

"Edwards of Newtown, Co. Kilkenny." *J. Cork Hist. Arch. Soc.* N.S. 34 (1929): 100-05.

"The Family of Gall Burke, of Gallstown, in the Co. of Kilkenny." *R.S.A.I.* 6 (1860): 97-120.

Fitzgerald—see Geraldines.

"Fitzpatricks of Ossory." *Old Kilkenny Review* 2 (3) 1981.

"The Geraldines of the Co. Kilkenny." *R.S.A.I.* 22 (1892): 358-76; 23 (1893): 179-86, 408-20; 32 (1902): 128-31.

"Memoirs of the Family of Grace." Grace Sheffield. The Graces were a leading Kilkenny family, and the "Memoirs" are an important source for Kilkenny local history. London, 1823.

"The Origin of the Grace Family of Courtstown, Co. Kilkenny, and of Their Title to the Tullaroan Estate." *R.S.A.I.* 30 (1900): 319-24; 32 (1902): 64-67.

"The Helshams of Kilkenny." *Old Kilkenny Review* 2 (4) (1982): 319-27.

"Hewetson of the Co. Kilkenny." *R.S.A.I.* 39 (1909): 369-92.

Kenealy, M. "The Parish of Aharney and the Marum Family." *Old Kilkenny Review* 1976.

"Memorials of the Family of Langton of Kilkenny." *R.S.A.I.* 8 (1864): 59-108.

"Loftus Papers (Cos. Kilkenny and Wexford)." *Anal. Hib.* 25: 31-55.

Brennan, T.A. *A History of the O'Brennans of Idough, Co. Kilkenny.* New York, 1975.

Morris, H.F., and T. Reade-Duncan. "The Reades of Cos. Tipperary and Kilkenny." *Ir. Gen.* 8 (1) (1990): 15-44; 8 (3): 336-364.

"The Family of Rothe of Kilkenny." *R.S.A.I.* 17 (1886): 501-37, 620-54.

"The Sullivans: A Notable Nineteenth-Century Kilkenny Family." *Old Kilkenny Review* 16 (1954): 23-32.

"Tobin of Caherlesk." *Ir. Gen.* 5 (6) (1979): 760-62.

"The Wall Family in Ireland 1170-1970." Hubert Gallwey. Naas: Leinster Leader Co., 1970.

McCall, H.B. *The Story of the Family of Wandesforde of Kirklington and Castlecomer.* London, 1904.

Gravestone Inscriptions

Kilkenny Archaeological Society (see Research Services) has indexed most of the gravestones in the county. These include all of the Kilkenny City graveyards and some thirty of those in other parts. The inscriptions are in the society's library, and can also be searched by the society's search service (for a fee). Published sources include:

Knocktopher: *Kilkenny Gravestone Inscriptions* 1; Kilkenny Arch. Soc., 1988.

St. Canice's Cathedral: Graves, Rev. James, and J.G.A. Prim. *The History, Architecture and Antiquities of the Cathedral Church of St. Canice, Kilkenny.* 1857.

St. Canice's Cathedral (Kilkenny): *Stone in St. Canice's Cathedral . . . Incised Stones and Panels in Relief.* Bennettsbridge, Co. Kilkenny: Annamult Lithographs (Chap. Book 1), 1978.

St. Mary's, Kilkenny: *Old Kilkenny Review* (1979-81).

Tullamaine: held by Kilkenny Archaeological Society (see Research Sources and Services).

Newspapers

The best early source for this county is *Finn's Leinster Journal*, although this newspaper did not contain many detailed biographical notices.

Title: *Finn's Leinster Journal*
Published in: Kilkenny, 1767-1965
NLI Holdings: 1.1767-12.1776; 1778-89; 12.1789-1799; 1801-08; 1.1818-1828

Title: *Kilkenny and Wexford Express* (see also Co. Wexford, *County of Wexford Express*)
Published in: Kilkenny, 1878-1907
BL Holdings: 2.1878-4.1905; 6-11.1907

Title: *Kilkenny Journal*
Published in: Kilkenny, 1830-1965
NLI Holdings: 5.1830-12.1845; 1.1847-11.1851; 1.1859-12.1965
BL Holdings: 1.1832-3.1924; 5.1935-12.1965 (except 12.1849-12.1893)

Title: *Kilkenny People*
Published in: Kilkenny, 1892-current
NLI Holdings: odd numbers 1922; 8.1927-in progress
BL Holdings: 10.1895-12.1922; 1.1924-12.1925; 1.1927-12.1929; 3-11.1930; 1.1931-in progress

Title: *Moderator* (continued as *Kilkenny Moderator* in 1829 and as *Moderator* in 1920)
Published in: Kilkenny, ca. 1775-1924
NLI Holdings: 1814-19; 7.1815-8.1822; 12.1832-11.1843; 1845 (with gaps); 4.1849-11.1851 (with gaps); 1905-19

BL Holdings: 2.1825; 1.1828-12.1919; 1.1920-12.1924

Wills and Administrations

A discussion of the types of records, where they are held, and their availability and value is given in the Wills section of the introduction. The availability of prerogative wills, administrations, and marriage license records is also described in the relevant parts of the same section. Where available, published sources of these records are given in the Miscellaneous Sources section.

Pre-1858 Wills and Administrations

Prerogative Wills. See the introduction.

Consistorial Wills. County Kilkenny is mainly in the diocese of Ossory, with nine parishes in Leighlin and one in Cashel diocese. The guide to Catholic parish records in this chapter shows the diocese to which each civil parish belonged. The wills of residents of each diocese were usually proven within that diocese (see the Wills section for exceptions). The following records survive:

Wills

See the introduction.

Abstracts

See the introduction. The Walsh-Kelly Papers in the GO include mainly Ossory wills. GO ms. 683-6. Carrigan Manuscripts: Administration Wills and Abstracts from Ossory and Leighlin Dioceses. NLI P903; indexed in *Ir. Gen.* 4 (3) (1970): 221-42; abstracts also in *Old Kilkenny Review* 3 (5) (1988): 503-520 (sixty-six pre-1922 will abstracts). Also, the intestate administrations from Ossory (1660-1803) and Leighlin (1702-1802) were published in *Ir. Gen.* 4 (5) (1972): 477-89.

Indexes

Ossory (1536-1858) published to 1800 by Phillimore. Leighlin—see Co. Carlow. Ossory Administration Bonds (1660-1857). GO Ms. 618; SLC film 100172.

Post-1858 Wills and Administrations

This county was served by the District Registry of Kilkenny. The surviving records are: Kilkenny District Will Books (1858-1895). NAI; SLC film 100943-5.

Marriage Licenses

Original Marriage Records
Kildare (1845-65). NAI; SLC film 100873.

Indexes

Kildare (1740-1850). NAI; SLC film 100868. Dublin—see Co. Dublin.

Ossory Marriage Licenses: *Ir. Gen.* 8 (3) (1992): 393-428.

Ossory Marriage Licenses 1739-1804: *Ir. Gen.* 8 (1): 122-143; 8 (2) (1991): 239-267.

Index to Marriage License Bonds of Ossory, Ferns, and Leighlin (1691-1845). GO Ms. 612-617; SLC film 100169-72.

Miscellaneous Sources

Nolan, Pat. A *Guide to Genealogical Sources in and for Kilkenny City and County*. Irish Origins, 1995.

Burtchaell, G.D. *Genealogical Memoirs of the Members of Parliament for the County and City of Kilkenny*. Dublin, 1888.

The Register of Kilkenny College (1684-1769). NLI P4545.

The Register and Accounts of St. Kieran's College (1811-1858). NLI P 973.

Hogan, W. *History and Antiquities of Kilkenny County and City*. Kilkenny, 1893.

Comerford, Patrick. "The Early Society of Friends and Their History in Kilkenny." *Old Kilkenny Review* 25 (1973): 68-75.

Nolan, W. *Fassadinin: Land, Settlement and Society in Southeast Ireland 1600-1850*. Dublin: Geography Publications, 1979.

Silverman, M., and P.H. Gulliver. *In the Valley of the Nore—Social History of Thomastown, Co. Kilkenny 1840-1983*. Dublin: Geography Publications, 1986.

O'Kelly, O. *The Place-Names of Co. Kilkenny*. 1985.

O'Kelly, O. *A History of Co. Kilkenny*. Donegal, 1969.

Nolan, W. *Kilkenny History and Society*. Dublin: Geography Publications, 1989.

Tighe, William. *Statistical Observations relative to the County of Kilkenny, made in the years 1800 and 1801*. Dublin: Graisberry and Campbell, 1802, pp. xvi, 6444, 119.

Whelan, K., and W. Nolan. *Kilkenny History and Society*. Dublin: Geography Publications, 1990.

"Bibliography of Counties Carlow, Kilkenny and Wicklow." *Waterford & S.E. Ireland Arch. Soc.* I, 11 (1907/8): 126-133.

"Kilkenny Deeds, 1785-1879." (List of deeds deposited in NAI.) *Old Kilkenny Review* 2 (4) (1982): 393-400.

Callan Tenant Protection Society. Published by Callan Heritage Society. N.d.

"Co. Kilkenny Priests in Newfoundland." *Old Kilkenny Review* 3 (3) (1986): 242-255 (twenty-one small biographies).

"Church Wardens of Castlecomer 1799-1847." *Deenside*, Christmas 1990, p. 21.

Research Sources and Services

Journals

Old Kilkenny Review

Deenside

Kilkenny and South-East of Ireland Archaeological Review

Libraries and Information Sources

Kilkenny County Library, 6 Johns Quay, Kilkenny. Ph: (056) 22021/22606; fax: (056) 63384. The local studies section of this library has an extensive collection of materials relating to the local and family history of Kilkenny. These include newspapers (1767–current), journals, local authority records, minute books of the Boards of Guardians, County and City Presentments, etc. The local studies collection is being prepared for presentation on a World Wide Web site.

Research Services

See Research Services in Dublin in the introduction.

Irish Origins Research Agency, College Road, Kilkenny. Ph: (056) 21483; fax: (056) 64777. Genealogical research service, specializing in counties Kilkenny, Carlow, Tipperary, Wexford, and Waterford.

Kilkenny Archaeological Society, Rothe House, Kilkenny. Ph: (056) 22893. This is the official IGP center for Kilkenny and will have indexed all of the church registers of the county by 1997. It has also indexed gravestone inscriptions and the householders index to the 1901 census. Researchers are advised to contact the center for an updated list of registers, and other sources, indexed. A search will be conducted for a fee.

Kilkenny Archives Ltd. This organization has been set up to hold the papers of Kilkenny families and businesses. It is currently looking for sponsors to match support from the Office of Public Works. When received and archived, the family papers will be available for study. The organization can be contacted c/o the secretary, John Kirwan, Rothe House, Kilkenny, Ireland.

Societies

Kilkenny Archaeological Society, Rothe House, Kilkenny, Co. Kilkenny (publishers of *Old Kilkenny Review*). The society is one of the most active local history organizations in the country and has an excellent library and publications. It also operates the genealogical indexing and search service for the county (see above).

Tullagherin Heritage Society, Mr. Edward Law, Bishopslough, Bennettsbridge, Co. Kilkenny

Kilkenny Civil Parishes as Numbered on Map

1. Erke
2. Glashare
3. Urlingford
4. Fertagh (2 pts.)
5. Rathlogan
6. Borrismore
7. Balleen
8. Coolcashin
9. Sheffin
10. Aharney
11. Durrow
12. Rosconnell
13. Attanagh
14. Abbeyleix (2 pts.)
15. Castlecomer
16. Rathaspick
17. Kilmenan
18. Donaghmore
19. Grangemacomb

20. Kilmocar
21. Dysart
22. Coolcraheen
23. Mayne
24. Mothell
25. Muckalee
26. Dunmore
27. Kilmademoge
28. Clomantagh
29. Garranamanagh
30. Rathbeagh
31. Tubbridbritain
32. Ballylarkin
33. Freshford (2 pts.)
34. Kilcooly
35. Killahy
36. Clashacrow
37. Tullaroan
38. Ballinamore

39. Odagh
40. Kilmanagh
41. Ballycallan
42. St. Canice's (2 pts.)
43. St. John's
44. St. Mary's
45. St. Maul's
46. St. Patrick's
47. Callan
48. Killaloe (2 pts.)
49. Tullaghanbrogue
50. Grange
51. Castleinch (Inchyolaghan)
52. Ballybur
53. Outrath
54. Kilferagh
55. Tullamaine
56. Burnchurch
57. Danesfort
58. Grangekilree
59. Earlstown
60. Ennisnag
61. Stonecarthy
62. Kilmadum
63. Kilkieran
64. Rathcoole (2 pts.)
65. Tiscoffin
66. Blackrath (2 pts.)
67. Kilderry
68. Shankill
69. St. Martin's
70. Clara
71. Gowran
72. Kilmacahill
73. Dunbell
74. Blanchvilleskill
75. Wells
76. Grangesilvia
77. Treadingstown (2 pts.)
78. Woolengrange (3 pts.)
79. Killarney
80. Tullahieran
81. Dungarvan
82. Powerstown

83. Ballylinch
84. Thomastown
85. Kilfane
86. Graiguenamanagh
87. Ullard
88. Jerpointabbey
89. Columbkille
90. Pleberstown
91. Fanna
92. Inistiogue
93. Coolaghmore
94. Mallardstown
95. Kells
96. Killamery
97. Ballytobin
98. Dunnamaggan (2 pts.)
99. Kilree
100. Kilmaganny
101. Tullahought
102. Jerpointchurch (2 pts.)
103. Knocktopher
104. Aghaviller
105. Kilkeasy
106. Derrynahinch
107. Lismeteige
108. Jerpointwest (3 pts.)
109. Killahy
110. Kilbeacon
111. Rossinan
112. Clonamery
113. Dysartmoon
114. The Rower
115. Listerlin
116. Rosbercon
117. Kilbride
118. Kilcoan
119. Ballygurrin
120. Shanbogh
121. Dunkitt
122. Gaulskill
123. Kilcolumb
124. Kilmakevoge
125. Rathpatrick
126. Whitechurch

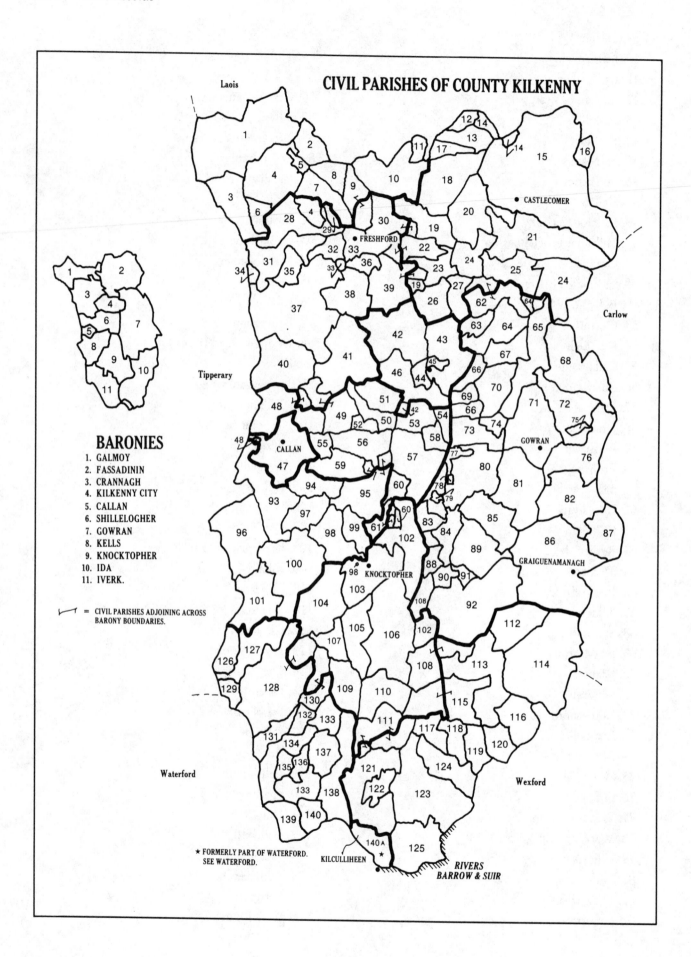

CIVIL PARISHES OF COUNTY KILKENNY

BARONIES
1. GALMOY
2. FASSADININ
3. CRANNAGH
4. KILKENNY CITY
5. CALLAN
6. SHILLELOGHER
7. GOWRAN
8. KELLS
9. KNOCKTOPHER
10. IDA
11. IVERK.

= CIVIL PARISHES ADJOINING ACROSS
BARONY BOUNDARIES.

★ FORMERLY PART OF WATERFORD.
SEE WATERFORD.

RIVERS
BARROW & SUIR

127. Owning
128. Fiddown
129. Tibberaghney
130. Muckalee
131. Clonmore
132. Tubbrid
133. Rathkieran (2 pts.)

134. Pollrone
135. Ballytarsney
136. Arderra
137. Ullid
138. Kilmacow
139. Portnascully
140. Aglish

Kilkenny Civil Parishes in Alphabetical Order

Abbeyleix (2 pts.): 14
Aghaviller: 104
Aglish: 140
Aharney: 10
Arderra: 136
Attanagh: 13
Balleen: 7
Ballinamore: 38
Ballybur: 52
Ballycallan: 41
Ballygurrin: 119
Ballylarkin: 32
Ballylinch: 83
Ballytarsney: 135
Ballytobin: 97
Blackrath (2 pts.): 66
Blanchvilleskill: 74
Borrismore: 6
Burnchurch: 56
Callan: 47
Castlecomer: 15
Castleinch (Inchyolaghan): 51
Clara: 70
Clashacrow: 36
Clomantagh: 26
Clonamery: 112
Clonmore: 131
Collaghmore: 93
Columbkille: 89
Coolcashin: 8
Coolcraheen: 22

Danesfort: 57
Derrynahinch: 106
Donaghmore: 18
Dunbell: 73
Dungarvan: 81
Dunkitt: 121
Dunmore: 26
Dunnamaggan (2 pts.): 98
Durrow: 11
Dysart: 21
Dysartmoon: 113
Earlstown: 59
Ennisnag: 60
Erke: 1
Fanna: 91
Fertagh (2 pts.): 4
Fiddown: 128
Freshford (2 pts.): 33
Garranamanagh: 29
Gaulskill: 122
Glashare: 2
Gowran: 71
Graiguenamanagh: 86
Grange: 50
Grangekilree: 58
Grangemacomb: 19
Grangesilvia: 76
Inistiogue: 92
Jerpointabbey: 88
Jerpointchurch (2 pts.): 102
Jerpointwest (3 pts.): 108

Kells: 95

Kilbeacon: 110

Kilbride: 117

Kilcoan: 118

Kilcolumb: 123

Kilcooly: 34

Kilderry: 67

Kilfane: 85

Kilferagh: 54

Kilkeasy: 106

Kilkieran: 63

Killahy: 109

Killahy: 35

Killaloe (2 pts.): 46

Killamery: 96

Killarney: 79

Kilmacahill: 72

Kilmacow: 138

Kilmademoge: 27

Kilmadum: 62

Kilmaganny: 100

Kilmakevoge: 124

Kilmanagh: 40

Kilmenan: 17

Kilree: 99

Kilmocar: 20

Knocktopher: 103

Listerlin: 115

Lismeteige: 107

Mallardstown: 94

Mayne: 23

Mothell: 24

Muckalee: 25

Muckalee: 130

Odagh: 39

Outrath: 53

Owning: 127

Pleberstown: 90

Pollrone: 134

Portnascully: 139

Powerstown: 82

Rathaspick: 16

Rathbeagh: 30

Rathcoole (2 pts.): 64

Rathkieran (2 pts.): 133

Rathlogan: 5

Rathpatrick: 125

Rosbercon: 116

Rosconnell: 12

Rossinan: 111

Shanbogh: 120

Shankill: 68

Sheffin: 9

St. Canice's (2 pts.): 42

St. John's: 43

St. Martin's: 69

St. Mary's: 44

St. Maul's: 45

St. Patrick's: 46

Stonecarthy: 51

The Rower: 114

Thomastown: 84

Tibberaghney: 129

Tiscoffin: 65

Treadingstown (2 pts.): 77

Tubbrid: 132

Tubbridbritain: 31

Tullaghanbrogue: 49

Tullahieran: 80

Tullahought: 101

Tullamaine: 55

Tullaroan: 37

Ullard: 87

Ullid: 137

Urlingford: 3

Wells: 75

Whitechurch: 126

Woolengrange (3 pts.): 78

County Laois

A Brief History

This small county is in the midlands of Ireland and contains the towns of Portlaoise (formerly Maryborough), Mountmellick, Portarlington, Abbeyleix, Rathdowney, and Durrow. In ancient times, the present county was partly in the Kingdom of Laois and partly in Ossory. The county was formed by the English in 1547 and named Queen's County. Its name was changed back to Laois (sometimes also called Leix) in 1922 after the formation of the Irish Free State.

The major families in this area were the O'Moores and O'Dunnes. Other families included the Lawlors, (O')Dowlings, (O')Deevys or Devoys, (O')Dorans, McEvoys, (O')Dempseys, (O')Brophys, (O')Deegans, (O')Tynans, (Mc)Cashins, (O')Mulhalls, and (Mac)Crossons.

The area was granted to the Fitzpatricks after the Norman conquest. Although the Fitzpatricks maintained control over a small part of the county, the O'Moores gradually regained power over much of the present County Laois and were undisputed rulers during the fifteenth and early sixteenth centuries. The tribes of Laois and Offaly continued to raid the English-controlled area around Dublin during this time. As a result, the English decided to invade the counties in 1547.

After the successful invasion, a major fort was built at Portlaoise on the site of an O'Moore stronghold. This was first named Fort Protector and later Maryborough. Because of continued resistance to English rule and attacks on the fort, it was decided to clear the counties of natives and bring in English settlers. This was begun in 1556, making it the first plantation of Ireland. The plantation was fiercely resisted by the native tribes and was only partially successful. The seven families which were most influential in this settlement were those of Cosby, Hartpole, Barrington, Bowen, Hetherington, Ruish, and Ovington.

In the early seventeenth century, the families of Piggott, Parnell, Coote, Prior, and Pole settled in the county, and later in the century, the families Vesey, Johnson, Dawson, Staples, and Burrowes were granted lands in the county.

The town of Mountmellick had a considerable Quaker population in the eighteenth and nineteenth centuries. There was also a large Huguenot population in the county, particularly in Portarlington. In 1696, this town and its surrounding area were granted by King William to one of his victorious Huguenot generals. A colony of Huguenot soldiers were subsequently planted there and developed a thriving town.

The county was relatively badly affected by the Great Famine of 1845–47. The population was 154,000 in 1841 and had dropped by twenty-eight percent in 1851. Over 18,000 people died of disease and starvation between 1845 and 1850, and many thousands emigrated. The current population of the county is approximately 52,000.

Census and Census Substitutes

1599

Names of Principal Inhabitants. Lambeth Palace Library, London ms. 635; NLI film P1707.

1641

Books of survey and distribution. Abstracts of various surveys and documents relating to land ownership. Simington, R.C. Dublin: Stationery Office, 1955.

1659

"Census" of Ireland. Edited by S. Pender. Dublin: Stationery Office, 1939. NLI I6551. SLC film 924648.

1664

"Hearth Money Rolls" for parishes of Kilkenny and Moyanna. NAI Thrift Abstracts 3737.

1668/9

"Hearth Money Rolls" for parishes of Maryborough and Upper Ossory. NAI Thrift Abstracts 3738.

1760

Queen's County Poll Book.

1758–75

"List of Freeholders of Co. Leix." GO ms. 443; SLC film 100181; published in *Kildare Arch. Soc. J.* 8 (1915): 309–27 (gives name, address, and date of registration).

1766

Householders of Parish of Lea. RCB Library; SLC film 258517.

1775

Catholic Qualification Roll Extracts (948 names, addresses, and occupations). 59th Report DKPRI: 59–84.

1779

"List of High Sheriffs, Grand Jury, and Gentlemen of Queen's Co." *Freeman's J.* 17 (13) 23 Sept. 1779; SLC film 993912.

1783–90

Rent Roll for County Leix. GO Ms. 660 and SLC film 100220.

1819

"Survey, Valuation and Census of Barony of Portnehinch." Although it does not give names, it gives detailed breakdown of farms, ages, religion and occupations of inhabitants, rents, etc. NLI.

1821

Extracts from Government Census for the Parish of Aghaboe, Mainly Dealing with the Name Kelly. NAI; SLC film 100158.

1823–38

Tithe Applotment Survey (see introduction).

1832 and 1840

Owners and occupiers of Lea Parish. NLI 4723/4.

1844

List of Persons Having Licenses to Keep Arms, Division of Ballinakill (baronies of Cullenagh, Upper Ossory, and Maryborough West). (Gives 433 names arranged alphabetically, with occupations, residences, and types of arms.) NLI ILB 04 P12.

1847

List of Voters in Queen's Co. up to 1847 (mainly 1838–47). (Gives approximately one thousand names arranged alphabetically by barony, with occupation, residence, location of freehold, etc.) NLI ILB 04 P12.

1850–51

Griffith's Valuation (see introduction).

1901

Census. NAI (see introduction).

1911

Census. NAI.

Church Records

Church of Ireland

See the introduction for a description of Church of Ireland records and their major repositories. Many C of I records were lost in the PRO fire of 1922. These are indicated as "Lost." However, as Church of Ireland records were effectively state records, the records of marriage (from 1845) are also in the General Registrar's Office. Many are still in local custody (LC), while others are in one of a variety of other archives (e.g., RCBL or NAI). Some of the parish registers of this county have been indexed by the Laois/Offaly Family History Research Centre (see Research Services at the end of the chapter). A search of the index will be conducted by the center for a fee. Those indexed are noted as "Indexed by LOFHR."

Abbeyleix
Earliest Records: b. 1781–; m. 1781–; d. 1781–
Status: LC

Aghavoe (District Church in Aghavoe Parish)
Status: Lost

Aghmacart and Bordwell
Status: Lost

Attanagh
Status: Lost

Ballyadams
Status: Lost

QUEEN'S COUNTY.

DIVISION OF BALLINAKILL.

A LIST OF PERSONS WHO HAVE OBTAINED

LICENSES TO KEEP ARMS,

AT A GENERAL QUARTER SESSIONS OF THE PEACE, HELD AT

ABBEYLEIX, ON THE 1st & 15th JANUARY, 1844.

No.	Name, Addition, Residence, and Barony.	No. and Description of Arms Registered.
1	Abbott Francis of the Swan, farmer, barony of Upper Ossory	one gun and one pistol.
2	Atkinson Richard of Rathdowney, do.	one gun.
3	Alley Peter T. of Donamore, gentleman, do.	2 guns, 1 double-barrelled gun, 2 pistols, 2 blunderbusses, 1 sword and 1 bayonet
4	Abbott Thomas K. of Borris-in-Ossory, yeoman, do.	two pistols.
5	Brennan, William of Knockbawn, farmer, barony of Cullenagh	one gun.
6	Bailey Thomas A. of Thornbury, gentleman, do.	3 guns, 2 pistols, and 1 blunderbuss.
7	Bowe Timothy of Clonking, do.	one gun.
8	Boate Mary of Boley, do.	one gun and one pistol.
9	Bland John Thomas of Blandsfort, gentleman, do.	3 guns, 2 pistols, 2 blunderbusses, 2 swords and two bayonets.
10	Bannon John of Scotchrath, farmer, barony of Maryborough West	one double gun, 4 muskets and 2 swords.
11	Brownlow William of Knapton, esquire, barony of Cullenagh	1 double gun, 4 muskets and 2 swords.
12	Betts Clement of Abbeyleix, tailor, do.	one gun.
13	Betts George, jun. of Abbeyleix, gentleman, do.	one gun.
14	Bell Wellington of Ballyeagle, esquire, do.	one gun, one pistol, and one cane sword.
15	Bolton George of Abbeyleix, attorney at law, do.	three guns and two pistols.
16	Betts James of Ballyking, farmer, do.	one gun, two pistols and one sword.
17	Bagnell John H. of Attans, clerk, barony of Upper Ossory,	4 guns, 2 pistols, three swords, 2 bayonets
18	Bergin John of Tubberboe, farmer, do.	6 blunderbusses, and 1 rifle.
19	Bond Robert of Rathdowney, do.	one single-barrel fowling-piece.
20	Bergin Timothy of Balaguage, farmer, do.	two guns.
20½	Byrne Edward of Abbeyleix, shopkeeper, barony of Cullenagh	one gun.
21	Belton John Pepper of Penfield, gentleman, barony of Upper Ossory	one gun and one pistol.
22	Biggs William of Borris Castle, esquire, do.	one gun, two pistols, and one blunderbuss.
23	Bates Robert of Borris-in-Ossory, do.	seven guns, 1 double & 2 single pistols.
24	Boland James of Spring-hill, do.	one flint gun.
25	Bond George of Spring-hill, do.	two pistols
26	Bennet John of Aghavoe, farmer, do.	one gun
27	Bond William of Lisduffe, do.	one gun and two pistols
28	Brophy Michael of Donaghmore, do.	two pistols.
29	Beresford Rev. James Isaac, Rector of Donaghmore, do.	one pistol
		three guns, one pistol and one blunderbuss
30	Comerford Edward of Ballynakill, gentleman, barony of Cullenagh	three guns and one sword.
31	Campion, William of Docrey, farmer, do.	one gun.
32	Claxton John of Corbally, farmer, barony of Maryborough West	one gun and one gun.
33	Case Thomas of Raheenabrogue, farmer, barony of Cullenagh	two guns.
34	Case William of Raheenabrogue, farmer, do.	two guns, two pistols, and one sword.
35	Case Allen of Newtown, farmer, do.	two guns.
36	Carrick Robert of Rathdowney, barony of Upper Ossory	one gun.
37	Caldbeck Richard of Ballacolla, gentleman, do.	one gun and one case of pistols.
38	Cummins Lawrence of Oldglass, farmer, do.	one pistol.
39	Craig William of Ballacolla, inn-keeper, do.	two guns, two pistols, and three swords
40	Costigan Michael of Ballynany, farmer, do.	one gun.
41	Cooper Mathew of Coolrain, farmer, do.	one gun and one pistol.
42	Connors Denis of Mountsalem, farmer, do.	one gun
43	Campion James of Badger-hill, farmer, do.	one gun
44	Cornelius Henry of Castletown, esquire, do.	two guns and four pistols.
45	Cuddy Patrick of Derrylahane, do.	one gun
46	Conrahy Bernard of Marymount, farmer, barony of Upper Ossory	one gun.
47	Cuddy Martin of Comras, farmer, barony of Upper Ossory	two guns.
48	Case Allen of Newtown, farmer, barony of Cullenagh	one gun.

No.	Name, Addition, Residence, and Barony.	No. and Description of Arms Registered.
51	Coyle Mary of C. of Cullenagh, farmer, barony of Cullenagh	one pistol and two blunderbusses.
52	Case Thomas of Abbeyleix, shopkeeper, do.	one gun two pistols and one bayonet.
53	Crowley Mathias Morgan, of Durrow, barony of Upper Ossory	1 double and 1 single gun and two pistols.
54	Cantwell Joseph of Kile, farmer, do.	two pistols.
55	Carr Henry of Kylebeg, farmer, do.	two pistols and one bayonet.
56	Cantwell Jacob of Kylebeg, farmer, do.	one gun and two pistols.
57	Cantwell George of Knockanoran, farmer, do.	one gun.
58	Chaplain Samuel of Woodview, farmer, do.	one gun two pistols and one blunderbuss.
59	Clarke Benjamin T. of Durrow, do.	one gun and two pistols.
60	Cole Samuel of Dairyhill, farmer, do.	one gun.
61	Chamberlain Joseph of Mullamore, farmer, do.	2 guns two pistols and two blunderbusses.
62	Chamberlain Joseph of Knockfinn, farmer, do.	one gun.
63	Chrystal George of Charleville, do.	one gun.
64	Claxton Langley of Cloncourse, farmer, do.	one gun and one pistol.
65	Carroll Charles of Graiguevalla, do.	one gun and two pistols.
66	Carter John of Coran, farmer, do.	two guns.
67	Curran Daniel of Kiladooley, farmer, do.	one gun.
68	Carter Isaac of Rathmakelofy, farmer, do.	one gun.
69	Comerford John of Bawnaghra, farmer, do.	one gun and two pistols.
70	Dobbs James of Abbeyleix, gentleman, barony of Cullenagh	one gun.
71	Dunne Francis of Moyadd, farmer, do.	one gun and one pistol.
72	Dunne Peter of Knockbawn, farmer, do.	one gun.
73	Delany Patrick of Ballynakill, do.	two pistols.
74	Deegan Lawrence of Ballynakill, do.	one gun one blunderbuss and one dagger.
75	Doran Michael of Cashel, farmer, do.	one gun.
76	Dowling James of Cappanaclough, farmer, barony of Maryborough West	one gun.
77	Dowling Patrick of Cappanaclough, farmer, do.	one gun.
78	Dunne Lyndon of Ballinakill, gentleman, barony of Cullenagh	two guns and one dagger.
79	Duffe Henry of Aughinacross, farmer, do.	one gun.
80	Dagge Thomas of Boulybawn, farmer, do.	one gun one pistol and one dagger.
81	Dooley Sylvester of Kill, farmer, barony of Upper Ossory	one pistol.
82	Dooley John jun. of Ralish, farmer, barony of Cullenagh	one gun.
83	Dooley John sen. of Kill, farmer, do.	one gun.
84	Doxey Thomas of Millbrook, gentleman, M.D. & J.P. do.	three guns and two pistols.
85	Dobbs Henry of Cullenagh, caretaker, do.	one gun and two pistols.
86	Dundas William John of Farnaley, esquire, do.	one gun three pistols and one blunderbuss.
87	Delany William of Durrow, esquire J.P., barony of Upper Ossory	one gun four pistols and one blunder'buss.
88	Delaney John of Cappanellan, farmer, barony of Upper Ossory	one gun.
89	Dagge Robert of Castlewood, farmer, do.	one gun and two pistols.
90	Delaney Denis of Aharney, farmer, do.	one gun.
91	Dunne Edward of Aharney, farmer, do.	one double and one single barrelled gun.
92	Delaney Edmund Scully of Durrow, gentleman, do.	one gun.
93	Delaney Mathew of Castledenning farmer, do.	4 guns 2 pistols and 2 blunderbusses
94	Dugdale John of Donamore, miller, do.	two pistols.
95	Dann Edward of Coolrain, farmer, do.	one gun and two pistols.
96	Despard Edward of Caher, farmer, do.	one gun.
97	Dunne James of Castletown, gentleman, do.	two guns.
98	Despard William W. of Donore, esquire, justice of the peace, do.	one gun.
99	Despard Richard of Donore, esquire, same barony	one gun, one pistol, and one blunderbuss.
100	Dann Robert of Coolrain, farmer, do.	one gun.
101	Delaney Denis of Strahard, farmer, do.	one pistol.
102	Delaney Martin of Crunagh, farmer, do.	one gun.
103	Delaney Michael of Coalsmancurragh, farmer, do.	one gun and two pistols.
104	Delaney John of Borris-in-Ossory, shopkeeper, do.	one gun and two pistols.

A list of persons in Queen's County (now County Laois) who were licensed to keep arms in 1844.

Ballyfin (with Clonenagh)
Earliest Records: b. 1821–; m. 1821–; d. 1821–
Status: LC; Indexed by LOFHR (to 1899 and 1980
respectively)

Ballyroan
Status: Lost

Bordwell (see Aghmacart)

Borris-in-Ossory
Status: Lost

Castlebrack (see Oregan)

Castletown (Killeban)
Earliest Records: b. 1802–; m. 1802–; d. 1802–
Status: LC

Clonenagh (union including Ballyfin, Mountrath, and Roskelton)
Earliest Records: b. 1749–; m. 1749–; d. 1749–
Status: LC

Coolbanagher
Earliest Records: b. 1802–; m. 1802–; d. 1802–
Status: LC; also NAI MFCI 69 (b. 1802–90; m.
1802–45; d. 1802–72)

Corclone
Status: Lost

Donoughmore
Status: Lost

Durrow
Earliest Records: b. 1731–; m. 1731–; d. 1731–
Status: LC; RCBL (transcript: b. 1731–1841; m/d.
1731–1836); NLI Ms 2670 (b/m/d. 1731–41); NAI
M 5056-8 (b/m/d. 1808–75)

Dysertgallen
Status: Lost

Killeban (Castletown District)
Earliest Records: b. 1802–; m. 1802–; d. 1802–
Status: LC

Killeban (Mayo District)
Earliest Records: b. 1830–; m. 1826–; d. 1828–
Status: LC

Killermagh
Status: Lost

Lea
Earliest Records: b. 1801–; m. 1801–; d. 1801–
Status: LC; NAI MFCI 72 (b. 1801–90; m/d. 1801–
69)

Maryborough (Portlaoise)
Earliest Records: b. 1793–; m. 1794–; d. 1794–
Status: LC; Indexed by LOFHR (to 1899)

Mayo
Earliest Records: b. 1830–; m. 1826–; d. 1828–
Status: LC

Mountmellick (see also Coolbanagher and Oregan)
Earliest Records: b. 1840–; m. 1840–; d. 1840–
Status: LC; NAI MFCI (b/d. 1840–1982; m. 1840–
56)

Mountrath (with Clonenagh)
Earliest Records: b. 1749–; m. 1749–; d. 1749–
Status: LC

Offerlane
Earliest Records: b. 1807–; m. 1807–; d. 1807–
Status: LC

Oregan—see Rosenallis

Portarlington
Earliest Records: b. 1694–; m. 1694–; d. 1694–
Status: LC; NAI MFCI 72 (b. 1694–1972; m. 1694–
1812; d. 1694–1983); SLC film 962137

Portlaoise (Maryborough)
Earliest Records: b. 1793–; m. 1793–; d. 1793–
Status: LC; Indexed by LOFHR

Rathaspect
Status: Lost

Rathdowney
Earliest Records: b. 1756–; m. 1756–; d. 1756–
Status: LC

Rathsaran
Earliest Records: b. 1810–; m. 1810–; d. 1810–
Status: LC

Roscrea
Earliest Records: b. 1784–; m. 1792–; d. 1792–
Status: LC; NAI MFCI 3, M5222 (b. 1784–1878; m.
1792–1845; d. 1792–1872)

Rosenallis or Oregan
Earliest Records: b. 1801–; m. 1801–; d. 1801–
Status: LC; NAI MFCI 69 (b. 1801–1976; m. 1801–
71; d. 1801–1972)

Roskelton (with Clonenagh)
Earliest Records: b. 1826–; m. 1826–; d. 1826–
Status: LC

St. Paul's (French Church, Portarlington)
Earliest Records: b. 1694–; m. 1694–; d. 1694–
Status: LC; see Huguenot records section in introduction

Skeirke
Status: Lost

Straboe (see Maryborough)

Stradbally
Earliest Records: b. 1772–; m. 1776–; d. 1826–
Status: LC

Timahoe
Earliest Records: b. 1845–; m. 1850–; d. 1856–
Status: LC

Timogue
Status: Lost

Methodist

Methodist churches existed in Mountmellick, Mountrath, and Portarlington. See the introduction for information on sources and access. An account of Portlaoise Methodist Church was published in Mountmellick; Besprint, 1983. SLC 941.87/M1 K2pm.

Presbyterian

An account of Presbyterian records is given in the introduction. These registers rarely contain death records, and occasionally have only records of births.

Mountmellick
Starting Date: 1849

Roman Catholic

Note that most of the Catholic parish registers of this county have been indexed by by the Laois/Offaly Family History Research Centre (see Research Services at the end of the chapter). A search of the index will be conducted by the center for a fee. Those indexed are noted as "Indexed by LOFHR." Microfilm copies of all registers are also available in the National Library of Ireland (NLI), and through the LDS library system.

Civil Parish: Abbeyleix
Map Grid: 41
RC Parish: Abbeyleix; also part Ballyragget, see Donaghmore, Co. Kilkenny
Diocese: LE
Earliest Record: b. 6.1824; m. 7.1824
Missing Dates: b. 8.1830-1.1838, 12.1849-4.1850; m. 7.1830-1.1838
Status: LC; NLI (mf); Indexed by LOFHR (to 1899)

Civil Parish: Aghaboe
Map Grid: 23
RC Parish: Aghaboe
Diocese: OS
Earliest Record: b. 1795; m. 7.1794
Missing Dates: b. 1802-1803, 1813, 6.1825-6.1826; m. 2.1807-11.1816, 8.1824-8.1825, 8.1846-6.1850
Status: LC; NLI (mf); Indexed by LOFHR (to 1899)

Civil Parish: Aghmacart
Map Grid: 32
RC Parish: see Durrow
Diocese: OS

Civil Parish: Aharney
Map Grid: 36
RC Parish: Lisdowney, see Aharney, Co. Kilkenny
Diocese: OS

Civil Parish: Ardea
Map Grid: 5

RC Parish: see Rosenallis
Diocese: KD

Civil Parish: Attanagh
Map Grid: 37
RC Parish: Ballyragget, see Donaghmore, Co. Kilkenny
Diocese: KD

Civil Parish: Ballyadams
Map Grid: 43
RC Parish: Ballyadams
Diocese: LE
Earliest Record: b. 1.1820; m. 1.1820
Status: LC; NLI (mf); Indexing planned by LOFHR

Civil Parish: Ballyroan
Map Grid: 38
RC Parish: part Ballinakill, see Dysartgallen; part Abbeyleix
Diocese: LE

Civil Parish: Bordwell
Map Grid: 29
RC Parish: see Aghaboe
Diocese: OS

Civil Parish: Borris or Maryborough
Map Grid: 10
RC Parish: Portlaoise (formerly Maryborough)
Diocese: LE
Earliest Record: b. 5.1826; m. 4.1826. d. 1876
Status: LC; NLI (mf); Indexed by LOFHR (to 1909, 1899, and 1916, respectively)

Civil Parish: Castlebrack
Map Grid: 1
RC Parish: Rosenallis and Mountmellick, see Rosenallis

Civil Parish: Clonenagh and Clonagheen (1)
Map Grid: 9
RC Parish: Ballyfin (Cappinrush); also Mountrath and Raheen, see below
Diocese: LE
Earliest Record: b. 10.1824; m. 8.1819
Status: LC; NLI (mf); Indexed by LOFHR (1862 to 1899)

Civil Parish: Clonenagh and Clonagheen (2)
Map Grid: 9
RC Parish: Mountrath
Diocese: LE
Earliest Record: b. 10.1823; m. 6.1827; d. 1882
Status: LC; NLI (mf); Indexed by LOFHR (to 1899)

Civil Parish: Clonenagh and Clonagheen (3)
Map Grid: 9
RC Parish: Raheen
Diocese: LE
Earliest Record: b. 4.1819; m. 1.1820; d. 1884
Status: LC; NLI (mf); Indexed by LOFHR (b/m. to 1899; d. to 1925)

Civil Parish: Cloydagh
Map Grid: 53
RC Parish: Leighlinbridge, see Agha, Co. Carlow
Diocese: LE

Civil Parish: Coolbanagher
Map Grid: 6
RC Parish: part Portarlington, see Lea; part
Mountmellick, see Rosenallis
Diocese: KD

Civil Parish: Coolkerry
Map Grid: 31
RC Parish: part Aghaboe; part Rathdowney
Diocese: OS

Civil Parish: Curraclone
Map Grid: 18
RC Parish: see Stradbally
Diocese: LE

Civil Parish: Donaghmore
Map Grid: 25
RC Parish: see Rathdowney
Diocese: OS

Civil Parish: Durrow (see also Co. Kilkenny)
Map Grid: 33
RC Parish: Durrow
Diocese: OS
Earliest Record: b. 1.1789; m. 7.1811
Status: LC; NLI (mf); Indexed by LOFHR (to 1899)

Civil Parish: Dysartenos
Map Grid: 14
RC Parish: Portlaoise, see Borris
Diocese: LE

Civil Parish: Dysartgallen
Map Grid: 42
RC Parish: Ballinakill
Diocese: LE
Earliest Record: b. 10.1794; m. 10.1794; d. 1794
Missing Dates: b. 3.1815-1.1820, 5.1820-11.1820,
9.1872-4.1877; m. 2.1815-1.1820, 7.1820-11.1820,
11.1875-5.1877
Status: LC; NLI (mf); Indexed by LOFHR (b/m. to
1899; d. to 1815)

Civil Parish: Erke
Map Grid: 27
RC Parish: see Co. Kilkenny
Diocese: OS

Civil Parish: Fossy (or Timahoe)
Map Grid: 40
RC Parish: part Ballyadams; part Stradbally
Diocese: LE

Civil Parish: Glashare
Map Grid: 35
RC Parish: see Co. Kilkenny
Diocese: LE

Civil Parish: Grangemonk (see Monksgrange)

Civil Parish: Kilcolmanbane
Map Grid: 13
RC Parish: Portlaoise, see Borris
Diocese: LE

Civil Parish: Kilclonbrook or Kilcolmanbrack
Map Grid: 39
RC Parish: see Stradbally
Diocese: LE

Civil Parish: Kildellig
Map Grid: 28
RC Parish: see Aghaboe
Diocese: OS

Civil Parish: Killaban
Map Grid: 49
RC Parish: Arles; also part Ballyadams; also part
Doonane, see Rathaspick
Diocese: LE
Earliest Record: b. 1821; m. 1821; d. 1821
Status: LC; NLI (mf); Indexed by LOFHR (to 1899)
(entries from 1821 to 1856 are arranged by townland)

Civil Parish: Killenny
Map Grid: 15
RC Parish: Portlaoise, see Borris
Diocese: LE

Civil Parish: Killermagh
Map Grid: 30
RC Parish: see Aghaboe
Diocese: OS

Civil Parish: Killeshin
Map Grid: 51
RC Parish: Graigue and Killeshin
Diocese: LE
Earliest Record: b. 11.1819; m. 1.1822
Missing Dates: b. 10.1845-8.1846
Status: LC; NLI (mf); Indexed by CGC (b. 1799-
1900; see Co. Carlow)

Civil Parish: Kilmanman
Map Grid: 2
RC Parish: Clonaslee
Diocese: KD
Earliest Record: b. 1.1849; m. 2.1849; d. 1892
Status: LC; NLI (mf); Indexed by LOFHR (to 1906,
1899, and 1970, respectively)

Civil Parish: Kilteale
Map Grid: 12
RC Parish: Portlaoise, see Borris
Diocese: LE

Civil Parish: Kyle
Map Grid: 21
RC Parish: Kyle and Knock
Diocese: OS

Earliest Record: b. 1.1845; m. 2.1846
Status: LC; NLI (mf); Indexing planned by LOFHR

Civil Parish: Lea
Map Grid: 7
RC Parish: Portarlington
Diocese: KD
Earliest Record: b. 1.1820; m. 11.1822; d. 1904
Status: LC; NLI (mf); Indexed by LOFHR (to 1899)

Civil Parish: Maryborough (see Borris)
Map Grid: 19
RC Parish: Portlaoise—see Borris
Diocese: LE

Civil Parish: Monksgrange (or Grangemonk)
Map Grid: 48
RC Parish: Arles, see Killaban
Diocese: LE

Civil Parish: Moyanna
Map Grid: 16
RC Parish: see Stradbally
Diocese: LE

Civil Parish: Offerlane (1)
Map Grid: 8
RC Parish: Castletown; also Cormorass, see below
Diocese: OS
Earliest Record: b. 9.1772; m. 9.1784
Missing Dates: b. 5.1816–5.1831; m. 5.1816–2.1831, 2.1855–9.1857
Status: LC; NLI (mf); Indexing planned by LOFHR

Civil Parish: Offerlane (2)
Map Grid: 8
RC Parish: Cormorass or Comeris
Diocese: OS
Earliest Record: b. 5.1816; m. 1.1820
Missing Dates: b. 3.1830–10.1838, gaps 1838–1850; m. 3.1830–8.1839, 2.1842–8.1846
Status: LC; NLI (mf); Indexing planned by LOFHR

Civil Parish: Rathaspick (see also Co. Kilkenny)
Map Grid: 47
RC Parish: Doonane (see also Ballyadams)
Diocese: LE
Earliest Record: b. 6.1843; m. 5.1843
Status: LC; NLI (mf); Indexed by LOFHR (to 1899)

Civil Parish: Rathdowney
Map Grid: 24
RC Parish: Rathdowney
Diocese: OS
Earliest Record: b. 7.1763; m. 5.1769
Missing Dates: b. 11.1781–9.1782, 7.1789–5.1790, 11.1791–4.1810, 9.1810–6.1839; m. 11.1781–9.1782, 7.1789–9.1789, 11.1791–1.1808, 5.1808–10.1839
Status: LC; NLI (mf); Indexed by LOFHR (b. to 1900)

Civil Parish: Rathsaran
Map Grid: 26
RC Parish: see Rathdowney
Diocese: OS

Civil Parish: Rearymore
Map Grid: 3
RC Parish: part Clonaslee, see Kilmanman; part Rosenallis
Diocese: KD

Civil Parish: Rosconnell
Map Grid: 34
RC Parish: Ballyraggett, see Donaghmore, Co. Kilkenny
Diocese: LE

Civil Parish: Rosenallis (1)
Map Grid: 4
RC Parish: Rosenallis; also Mountmellick, see below
Diocese: KD
Earliest Record: b. 10.1765; m. 10.1765; d. 10.1824
Missing Dates: b. 1.1777–2.1782, 8.1782–8.1823; m. 6.1777–2.1782, 6.1782–7.1823, 7.1859–1.1865; d. ends 9.1827
Status: LC; NLI (mf); Indexed by LOFHR (b/m. to 1901, 1899; d. 1921–1987 only)

Civil Parish: Rosenallis (2)
Map Grid: 4
RC Parish: Mountmellick
Diocese: KD
Earliest Record: b. 1.1814; m. 2.1814; d. 1890
Missing Dates: m. 4.1843–7.1843
Status: LC; NLI (mf); Indexed by LOFHR (to 1899 and 1948, respectively)

Civil Parish: St. John (see Co. Kildare)
Map Grid: 44
RC Parish: Athy, see Churchtown, Co. Kildare
Diocese: LE

Civil Parish: Shrule
Map Grid: 50
RC Parish: Arles, see Killaban
Diocese: LE

Civil Parish: Skirk (Skeirke)
Map Grid: 22
RC Parish: see Rathdowney
Diocese: OS

Civil Parish: Sleaty
Map Grid: 52
RC Parish: Graigue and Killeshin, see Killeshin
Diocese: LE

Civil Parish: Straboe
Map Grid: 11
RC Parish: Portlaoise, see Borris
Diocese: LE

Civil Parish: Stradbally
Map Grid: 17
RC Parish: Stradbally
Diocese: LE
Earliest Record: b. 1.1820; m. 1.1820; d. 1893
Missing Dates: m. 6.1849–2.1851
Status: LC; NLI (mf); Indexed by LOFHR (to 1899, 1899, and 1983, respectively)

Civil Parish: Tankardstown
Map Grid: 46
RC Parish: Athy, see Churchtown, Co. Kildare
Diocese: LE

Civil Parish: Tecolm
Map Grid: 45
RC Parish: see Ballyadams
Diocese: LE

Civil Parish: Timahoe—see Fossy

Civil Parish: Timogue
Map Grid: 19
RC Parish: see Stradbally
Diocese: LE

Civil Parish: Tullomoy
Map Grid: 20
RC Parish: see Ballyadams
Diocese: LE

Commercial and Social Directories

1788

Richard Lucas's *General Directory of the Kingdom of Ireland* contains lists of traders in Mountmellick and Portarlington. Reprinted in *Ir. Gen.* 3 (10) (1965): 392–416.

1824

J. Pigot's *City of Dublin and Hibernian Provincial Directory* includes traders, nobility, gentry, and clergy lists of Ballinakill, Durrow, Maryborough, Mountrath, Mountmellick, Portarlington, and Stradbally.

1846

Slater's *National Commercial Directory of Ireland* lists nobility, clergy, traders, etc., in Ballinakill, Maryborough, Mountmellick, Mountrath, Portarlington, and Stradbally.

1856

Slater's *Royal National Commercial Directory of Ireland* lists nobility, gentry, clergy, traders, etc., in Ballinakill, Maryborough, Mountmellick, Mountrath, Portarlington, Rathdowney and Donaghmore, and Stradbally.

1870

Slater's *Directory of Ireland* contains trade, nobility, and clergy lists for Abbeyleix, Maryborough, Mountmellick, Mountrath, Portarlington, Rathdowney, and Stradbally.

1881

Slater's *Royal National Commercial Directory of Ireland* contains lists of traders, clergy, nobility, and farmers in adjoining parishes of the towns of Abbeyleix, Ballinakill, Ballyroan, Maryborough and Stradbally, Mountmellick, Mountrath, Portarlington, and Rathdowney.

1894

Slater's *Royal National Directory of Ireland* lists traders, police, teachers, farmers, and private residents in each of the towns, villages, and parishes of the county.

Family History

Surnames of Co. Laois. *Irish Roots* 4 (1996): 21–22.

"Notes on Some Portarlington Families 1860–1893." *Ir. Anc.* 17 (2) (1985): 82–95.

Baldwin, William. *The Genealogy of Baldwins from Queen's County.* New York, 1918.

"Ballyadams in the Queen's County, and the Bowen Family." *J. Kildare Arch. Hist. Soc.* 7 (1912–14): 3–32.

"The Chetwoods of Woodbrook in the Queen's County." *J. Kildare Arch. Hist. Soc.* 9 (1918–21): 205–26.

"The Autobiography of Pole Cosby, of Stradbally, Queen's County" (1703–1737). *J. Kildare Arch. Hist. Soc.* 5 (1906–08).

Jolly, M.A. *Jolly—a Portarlington Settler and His Descendants.* London, 1935.

Eswyn, Ellinor Lyster. *Lyster pioneers of lower Canada and the West: the Story of the Lysters of the old Queen's County.* Qualicum Beach, B.C., Canada, 1984, pp. 335.

"Historical Notes on the O'Mores and Their Territory of Leix, to the End of the Sixteenth Century." *J. Kildare Arch. Hist. Soc.* 6 (1909–11): 1–88.

Impey, E. Adeir. *A Roberts Family, Quondam Quakers of Queen's County.* London, 1939.

Houston, J.R. *A History of the Standish Family in Ireland and Canada.* Toronto: Houston Publication Trust, 1979.

"Notes on an Old Pedigree of the O'More Family of Leix." *R.S.A.I.* 35 (1905): 53–59.

Gravestone Inscriptions

The Laois/Offaly Family History Research Centre (see Research Services at the end of the chapter) has indexed most of the gravestones in the county and will conduct a search for a fee. Published sources include:

Tombstone Inscriptions of Castlebrack, compiled by Rosaleen Campbell and Bridie Dunne (1990).

Newspapers

There are few papers which are specific to this county. Those in the surrounding counties should be consulted, depending on the area of interest. Note that the county was previously known as Queen's County, and that the town of Portlaoise was also officially known as Maryborough until 1922.

Title: *Leinster Express*
Published in: Portlaoise, 1831–current
NLI Holdings: 9.1831–in progress
BL Holdings: 9.1831–12.1927; 1.1929–3.1941; 6.1941–in progress

Title: *Leinster Independent*
Published in: Portlaoise, 1834–40
NLI Holdings: 12.1834–12.1840 (with gaps)
BL Holdings: 12.1834–12.1835; 7.1836–5.1839; 10.1839–4.1840

Wills and Administrations

A discussion of the types of records, where they are held, and their availability and value is given in the Wills section of the introduction. The availability of prerogative wills, administrations, and marriage license records is also described in the relevant parts of the same section. Where available, published sources of these records are given in the Miscellaneous Sources section.

Pre-1858 Wills and Administrations

Prerogative Wills. See the introduction.

Consistorial Wills. County Laois wills and administrations (pre-1858) were probated in the Church of Ireland dioceses of Ossory, Kildare, or Leighlin. The original records were destroyed in the 1922 fire; however, the indexes survive and are at the National Archives. The guide to Catholic parish records in this chapter shows the diocese to which each civil parish belonged. The wills of residents of each diocese were usually proven within that diocese (see the Wills section for exceptions). The following records survive:

Wills

See the introduction. An account of Kildare diocesan wills has been published in *J. Kildare Arch. Hist. Soc.* 12 (3) (1938): 115–123; 12 (4) (1939): 188–189; 12 (5) (1940–41): 222–225; 12 (6) (1940–41): 269–272. The Walsh-Kelly Papers in the GO (GO ms. 683–6) include mainly Ossory wills.

Carrigan Manuscripts (NLI P903): administrations, wills, and abstracts from Ossory and Leighlin; indexed in *Ir. Gen.* 4 (3) (1970): 221–42. Also, intestate administrations from Ossory (1660–1803) and Leighlin (1702–1802) are in *Ir. Gen.* 4 (5) (1972): 477–89.

Abstracts

See the introduction; also, the Betham Collection (NAI) has abstracts of most wills from 1661 to 1826 for names beginning A–K, and to 1824 for those beginning K–S. These are in the NAI (Ms. 1A 44 22); also abstracts of wills, 1661–1826 from Phillips Manuscripts, A–K and L–S, are in the Friends Historical Library (FHL) Mf. 101027.

Indexes

"Index to the Wills of the Diocese of Kildare, in the Public Records Office of Ireland" (now the National Archives, or NAI) by Sydney Cary (editor) in *J. Kildare Arch. Hist. Soc.* 4 (6) (1905): 473–491; also the indexes (1661–1800) to all dioceses are published in Phillimore and Thrift's *Indexes to Irish Wills*, Vol. 1 (also in FHL Mf. 1426012, item 11). Indexes to wills (1652–1858) for Leighlin diocese are in the FHL (Mf. 100916). Ossory indexes (1536–1858) to 1800 are published by Phillimore. Leighlin—see Co. Carlow; also, Leighlin (1642–1858): those to 1800 have been published in Phillimore and Thrift's *Indexes to Irish Wills*.

Administration bonds for Kildare diocese (1679–1840 and 1770–1848) are in the FHL (Ms. 100962); those for Leighlin Diocese (1694–1845) are also in the FHL (Mf. 100963).

Post-1858 Wills and Administrations

Laois was served by the District Registry of Kilkenny. The surviving records are: Kilkenny District Will Books (1858–1895). NAI; SLC film 100943–5.

Marriage Licenses

Indexes

Leighlin and Ferns (1691–1845). PRO; GO ms. 612–17 (more complete); SLC film 100169–172. Dublin—see Co. Dublin.

Original Marriage Records

Kildare (1845–65). NAI; SLC film 100873.

Indexes

Kildare (1740–1850). NAI; SLC film 100868. Dublin—see Co. Dublin. "Index to Kildare Marriage License Bonds." Transcribed by Guillamore O'Grady in *J. Kildare Arch. Hist. Soc.* (A–C) in 11 (2) (1931): 43–58; (D–I) in 11 (3) (1932): 114–133; (J–O) in 12 (1) (1935): 12–29; (P–) in 12 (2) (1937): 74–98.

Ossory Marriage Licenses

Ir. Gen. 8 (3) (1992): 393–428.

Miscellaneous Sources

Surnames of Co. Laois. *Irish Roots* 4 (1996): 21–22.

Hood, Susan. "Birr Co. Offaly—Its History and Records." *Irish Roots* 3 (1995): 27–29.

Coote, Charles. *General View of Agriculture and Manufactures of the Queen's County.* 1801.

"The Huguenots of Portarlington." *Studies* 61 (1972): 343–53.

"Huguenot Officers and Soldiers Settled at Portarlington." *J. Kildare Arch. Hist. Soc.* 11 (4): 177–200 (gives names, biography, and holdings on attached map). Addendum 12 (5) (1940/41): 227–29.

"Landholders in Co. Laois." Tenants of an unnamed estate citing leases from 1830s–1890s. *Dun Laoghaire Gen. Soc. J.* 3 (2) (1994): 54–63.

MacCaba, S. *Historical Notes on Laois.* Portlaoise, 1963.

MacSuibhne, P. *Parish of Killeshin, Graigecullen.* Naas, 1972.

O'Byrne, D. *History of the Queen's County.* Dublin, 1856.

O'Hanlon, J., and E. O'Leary. *History of the Queen's County.* 4 vols. Dublin, 1907–14. Reprint. Kilkenny: Roberts, 1981.

Research Sources and Services

Journals

Laois Heritage (bulletin of Laois Heritage Society)

Libraries and Information Sources

Laois County Library, County Hall, Portlaoise, Co. Laois. Ph: (0502) 22044. The library has a sizable collection of local history materials, including books, directories, newspapers, periodicals, photographs, estate papers, etc.

Research Services

Laois/Offaly Family History Research Centre, Bury Quay, Tullamore, Co. Offaly. Ph/Fax: (0506) 21421; e-mail: ohas@iol.ie; Internet site: http://ireland.iol.ie/~ohas/. This is the official IGP center for Laois and Offaly. It has indexed most of the church registers of both counties, but particularly Offaly. In addition, it has indexed the 1901 census for Offaly and is working on Laois. It also has an extensive list of gravestone inscriptions. Researchers are advised to contact the center for an updated list of registers, and other sources, indexed. A research service is provided for a fee.

See also Research Services in Dublin in the introduction.

Societies

Cuman Seandalaiochta Laoise, Mrs. Matilda Cooney, Monamanry, Luggacurran, Portlaoise, Co. Laois

Mountmellick Heritage Society, Ms. Michelle McEvoy, 9 Emmet Street, Mountmellick, Co. Laois

Portarlington People's Museum, Mrs. Eileen Powell, Spa Street, Portarlington, Co. Laois

Laois Civil Parishes as Numbered on Map

1. Castlebrack
2. Kilmanman
3. Rearymore
4. Rosenallis
5. Ardea
6. Coolbanagher
7. Lea
8. Offerlane
9. Clonenagh and Clonagheen
10. Borris
11. Straboe
12. Kilteale
13. Kilcolmanbane
14. Dysertenos
15. Killenny
16. Moyanna
17. Stradbally
18. Curraclone
19. Timogue
20. Tullamoy
21. Kyle
22. Skirk
23. Aghaboe
24. Rathdowney
25. Donaghmore
26. Rathsaran
27. Erke
28. Kildellig
29. Bordwell
30. Killermogh
31. Coolkerry
32. Aghmacart
33. Durrow
34. Rosconnell
35. Glashare
36. Aharney
37. Attanagh
38. Ballyroan
39. Kilcolmanbrack
40. Fossy (Timahoe)
41. Abbeyleix
42. Dysertgallen
43. Ballyadams
44. St. John's (Churchtown)
45. Tecolm
46. Tankarstown
47. Rathaspick
48. Monksgrange
49. Killaban
50. Shrule
51. Killeshin
52. Sleaty
53. Cloydagh

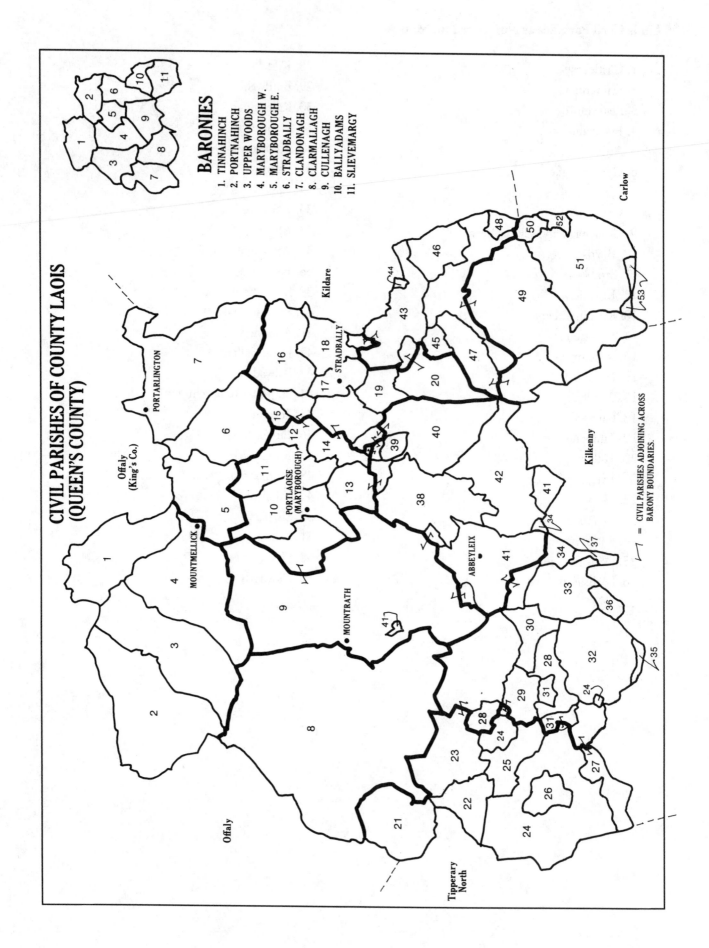

CIVIL PARISHES OF COUNTY LAOIS (QUEEN'S COUNTY)

BARONIES

1. TINNAHINCH
2. PORTNAHINCH
3. UPPER WOODS
4. MARYBOROUGH W.
5. MARYBOROUGH E.
6. STRADBALLY
7. CLANDONAGH
8. CLARMALLAGH
9. CULLENAGH
10. BALLYADAMS
11. SLIEVEMARGY

↵ = CIVIL PARISHES ADJOINING ACROSS
    BARONY BOUNDARIES.

Offaly (King's Co.)

Offaly

Kildare

Carlow

Kilkenny

Tipperary North

PORTARLINGTON
MOUNTMELLICK
PORTLAOISE (MARYBOROUGH)
MOUNTRATH
STRADBALLY
ABBEYLEIX

Laois Civil Parishes in Alphabetical Order

Abbeyleix (3 pts.): 41

Aghaboe: 23

Aghmacart: 32

Aharney: 36

Ardea: 5

Attanagh: 37

Ballyadams: 43

Ballyroan: 38

Bordwell: 29

Borris: 10

Castlebrack: 1

Clonenagh and Clonagheen: 9

Cloydagh: 53

Coolbanagher: 6

Coolkerry: 31

Curraclone: 18

Donaghmore: 25

Durrow: 33

Dysertenos: 14

Dysertgallen: 42

Erke: 27

Fossy (Timahoe): 40

Glashare: 35

Kilcolmanbane: 13

Kilcolmanbrack: 39

Kildellig: 28

Killaban: 49

Killenny: 15

Killermogh: 30

Killeshin: 51

Kilmanman: 2

Kilteale: 12

Kyle: 21

Lea: 7

Monksgrange: 48

Moyanna: 16

Offerlane: 8

Rathaspick: 47

Rathdowney: 24

Rathsaran: 26

Rearymore: 3

Rosconnell: 34

Rosenallis: 4

Shrule: 50

Skirk: 22

Sleaty: 52

St. John's (Churchtown): 44

Straboe: 11

Stradbally: 17

Tankarstown: 46

Tecolm: 45

Timogue: 19

Tullamoy: 20

County Leitrim

A Brief History

This Connaught county contains the towns of Dromahaire, Manorhamilton, Drumshanbo, Carrick-on-Shannon, and Ballinamore.

The northern and western parts of the county were once part of the old Gaelic kingdom of Breifne, which was ruled by the O'Rourkes. Other families associated with this part of the county are the McClancys and O'Meehans. In the southern part of the county, the major families are the McRannals (often Anglicized as Reynolds) and McMorrows. The other families of the county are Flynn, McLoughlin, Kelly, Gallagher, McKiernan, Rooney, Moran, McGowan, McGilheely, O'Gallon, O'Mulvey, McShanley, McColgan, McSharry, McWeeney, and McGovern.

Up to the Middle Ages, this county was densely wooded. The woods were gradually felled to provide charcoal and timber for local iron-mining operations. The county is now generally boggy and has a large proportion of wetlands and lakes.

The county was invaded by the Normans in the thirteenth century. Although they succeeded in taking the south of the county, they failed to conquer the northern portion. This remained under the control of the O'Rourkes until the sixteenth century.

Large portions of the county were confiscated from their owners in 1620 and given to English adventurers, including Villiers and Hamilton, who founded the town of Manorhamilton. The objective was to plant the county with English settlers, but this was largely unsuccessful. Further confiscations followed the unsuccessful 1641 rebellion of the Catholic Irish, when the Gaelic and Norman families of Leitrim joined the Catholic Confederacy (see Co. Kilkenny).

As the Gaelic and Norman families were predominantly Catholic, and the English were of the Protestant faith, the proportions of these religions among the population can, in very general terms, be used to estimate the origins of the inhabitants of the county and the success of the various attempts to "plant" the county. When religious affiliation was first determined in the census of 1861, the respective proportions of Catholic and Protestant were ninety percent and nine percent.

The county was very badly affected by the Great Famine of 1845-47. The population was 155,000 in 1841, and by 1851 it had fallen to 112,000. Of this reduction, almost 20,000 people died between 1845 and 1850, and the remainder emigrated to the cities or, more usually, abroad. Because of the poor agricultural productivity of the county, it has been a high-emigration county ever since these times, and the population is currently around 28,000.

Census and Census Substitutes

1659

"Census" of Ireland. Edited by S. Pender. Dublin: Stationery Office, 1939. NLI I6551. SLC film 924648.

1726-27

List of Protestant Householders in Parishes of Annaduffe, Kiltogher, Kiltubrid, Fenagh and Mohill. Edgeworth family papers, NAI M 1502. (Names-only list compiled for "the charitable distribution of religious books.")

1737-1825

Rental of the estate of Owen Wynne (civil parishes of Clooneclare, Cloonlougher, Killanummery, Killasnet and Rossinver). 1737-68 in NLI Ms. 5780-2; 1738-73 in NLI Ms. 5830-1; 1798-1825 in NLI Ms. 3311-31.

1791

Names of the Registered Freeholders of Co. Leitrim. GO Ms. 665; SLC film 100213.

1792

"List of Protestants in the Barony of Mohill." *Ir. Anc.* 16 (1): 35–36.

1798

List of Persons who Suffered Losses in '98 Rebellion. NLI JLB 94107 (approximately eighty names, addresses, and occupations).

1802

Printed list of larger tenants of the Tottenham estate (civil parishes of Clooneclare and Rossinver). NLI Ms. 10162.

1813

List of tenants of the estate of the Earl of Bessborough (parishes of Kiltubbrid and Fenagh). NAI M 3383, 3370. (Major tenants in 1805 in NAI M 3374.)

List of Freeholders of Barony of Mohill. NLI Ms 9628 (Clements Papers); also Leitrim County Library.

1812–28

List of tenants of the Clements estates: Parish of Carrigallen (1812–28) in NLI Ms. 3816–3827; Bohey townland, Cloone Parish (1812–24) in NLI Ms. 12805–7, 3828.

1820

A List of the Freeholders or Voters in Co. Leitrim, ca. 1820. Arranged alphabetically by barony. NLI Ms. 3830 (Leitrim Papers).

1821

Census of Parish of Carrigallen. NLI M 4646; SLC film 1279295; also in Leitrim Co. Library.

1822

List of larger tenants of the Viscount Newcomen's estate (parish of Drumlease). NAI M 2797.

1823–38

Tithe Applotment Survey (see introduction).

1827

Abstract of rental of the estate of the Earl of Bessborough, Co. Leitrim. (Twenty-six tenants in Fenagh and Kiltoghert.) NAI M 36206.

1833

List of tenants of the estate of Sir Humphrey Crofton

(civil parishes of Cloone, Kiltoghert, Oughteragh, and Mohill). NLI Ms. 4531.

1837–55

List of tenants of the Earl of Leitrim's estate (parishes of Carrigallen, Cloone, Clooneclare, Inishmagrath, Killasnet, Kiltoghert, and Mohill): 1837–42 in NLI Ms. 12787; 1838–65 in NLI Ms. 5728–5733; 1842–55 in NLI Ms. 5803–5; 1844–48 in NLI Ms. 12810–12; 1844 in NLI Ms. 179; 1854 in NLI Ms. 180.

1839

List of persons who obtained Game Certificates in Leitrim. PRONI T 688.

1842

Voters List. NAI 1842/4.

1845–56

List of tenants of the estate of William Johnson (mainly in parish of Inishmagrath). NLI Ms 9465.

1850

List of tenants (mainly large tenants) of the estate of Francis O'Beirne (mainly in parishes of Cloone, Kiltoghert, Oughteragh, and Mohill). NAI M 4531.

1852

"Leitrim Voters in Oughteragh and Cloonclare Parishes." *Breifne* 5 (20): 459–66. Leitrim County Library; SLC film 1279295.

1856

Griffith's Valuation (see introduction).

1901

Census. NAI (see introduction). Kiltoghert parish returns are in *Exploring Family Origins and Old Carrick-on-Shannon*. See Miscellaneous Sources.

1911

Census. NAI. (Kiltoghert parish returns as above.)

Church Records

Church of Ireland

See the introduction for a description of Church of Ireland records and their major repositories. Many C of I records were lost in the PRO fire of 1922. These are indicated as "Lost." However, as Church of Ireland records were effectively state records, the records of marriage (from 1845) are also in the General Registrar's Office. Many are still in local custody (LC), while oth-

COUNTY of LEITRIM,

And who have given in their Claims on or before the 6th of April, 1799, to the Commissioners for enquiring into the Losses sustained by such of his Majesty's *Loyal Subjects*, as have suffered in their Property by the Rebellion.

☞ This LIST is published for the Purpose of calling the Attention of all Persons well acquainted with the County of Leitrim, to the several Claims therein specified; and all such Persons are requested to communicate, as soon as possible, to the Commissioners (or any one of them) under Cover, to the Right Hon. the Chancellor of the Exchequer, Parliament House, Dublin, such Observations respecting the *Loyalty* or *Losses* of the several Persons mentioned therein, as may enable the Commissioners to ascertain their Title to Compensation.

CLAIMANT'S NAME.	ADDITION.	RESIDENCE.	County in which they reside	Place where Loss was sustained.	NATURE OF LOSS.	AMOUNT CLAIMED.
						£. s. d.
Abraham, Richard	—	Carrickban	Leitrim	Residence.	A mare	6 16 6
Acheson, John	—	Derrinacerrey	ditto	ditto	Cloaths, furniture, and provisions	5 2 2
Acheson, Mary	Widow	Dininoran	ditto	ditto	Provision, cloaths, furniture	8 9 0½
Acheson, George	—	Lavagh	ditto	ditto	Furniture, fowl, hay, and flax	4 7 4
Baker, Farrell	—	Drumahair	ditto	ditto	Cash, cloaths, a watch, linen, and arms	61 6 2½
Blair, James	—	Drumleafe	ditto	ditto	Cloaths, and shoebuckles	13 14 1½
Bragdon, David	—	Drumahair	ditto	ditto	A mare	2 10 0
Buchanan, Andrew	—	Shevdella	ditto	ditto	Cattle, fowl, and cloaths	15 4 5
Carty, George	—	Drumleafe	ditto	ditto	Cloaths and linen	2 4 7½
Carter, Thomas	—	Ditto	ditto	ditto	Wearing apparel	58 14 10½
Carter, Anne	—	Ditto	ditto	ditto	Cloaths, jewellery, and cash	14 2 3
Carter, John	—	Ditto	ditto	ditto	Cloaths, jewellery, and cash	92 2 3½
Carter, Patrick	Esquire	Ditto	ditto	ditto	Cash, wine, spirits, cloaths, and linen, &c.	849 19 10½
Carney, Martin	—	Drumahair	ditto	ditto	Spirits, wine, cloaths, and provisions	18 7 6
Clarke, Patrick	Yeoman	Ditto	ditto	ditto	Cloaths, provision, fowl, and books	10 13 0
Clarke, Hugh	—	Bawn	ditto	ditto	{ A horse, saddle and bridle, cloaths, and provisions	10 14 2
Conboy, Michael	—	Ardvarney	ditto	ditto	Yarn, furniture, cloaths	3 8 8
Crawford, Ann	—	Drumleafe	ditto	ditto	Cloaths, linen, and a saddle and bridle	50 1 1½
Cunian, John	—	Drumahair	ditto	ditto	A mare	6 16 6
Dodd, Roger	—	Ditto	ditto	ditto	Furniture, cloaths, plate, and watches	73 7 10½
Dogherty, Mary	—	Ditto	ditto	ditto	Cloaths	2 11 7
Elliott, John	—	Ardvardney	ditto	ditto	Furniture, cloaths, and provision	32 2 6
Elliotte, James	—	Ditto	ditto	ditto	{ A horse, saddle and bridle, windows broke, furniture, cloaths	33 19 10½
Gaffry, Patrick John	—	Ballinamore	ditto	ditto	Cloaths, and fire-arms	26 9 10
Gallagher, Hannah	Widow	Drumkerin	ditto	ditto	Watch, fowl, cloaths, and furniture	4 0 5
Hamilton, John	—	Ditto	ditto	ditto	Cloaths, furniture, provision, and a horse	55 7 7½
Hamilton, Wm. on behalf the children of Edw. Hamilton of Drumkerin, deceased.	—	Blackrock	ditto	Drumkerin, Co. Leitrim	Horses, spirits, oats, hay, and potatoes	71 10 3½
Huston, Joseph	—	Cornaugher	ditto	Residence	Saddle and bridle, cloaths, furniture	23 3 4½
Johnston, John	—	Ardvarney	ditto	ditto	A horse, and cloaths	7 1 1
Johnston, Robert	—	Aughnagallop	ditto	ditto	A horse	4 0. 0
Johnston, Andrew	—	Addergold.	ditto	Lands of Bawn, Co. Leitrim }	A horse, and a mare	22 0 0
Johnston, Andrew	—	Lodge	ditto	ditto	Cloaths, furniture, and groceries	44 10 4
Johnston, James	—	Gartermore	ditto	Lands of Belhovil, Co. Leitrim }	17 Sheep	17 0 0
Kelly, Ann	—	Drumleafe	ditto	Residence.	Cloaths, jewellery, and books	45 10 0
Keys, William	—	Derrinoran	ditto	ditto	Provision, fowl, and a saddle	4 3 2
Killcollum, Eleanor	Widow	Denbrisk	ditto	ditto	A horse and saddle	46 12. 9
M'Connell, Edward	—	Tullydall	ditto	ditto	Cloaths, furniture, fowl, and a gun	5 9 2
M'Loughlin, Farrell	—	Drumkeerin	ditto	ditto	Oats, spirits, furniture, and cloaths	42 9 4
M'Mullen, James	—	Drincoosra	ditto	ditto	A mare	5 13. 9
M'Sharry, Patrick	—	Drumahair	ditto	ditto	A horse, oats, and cloaths	12 17 2
M'Ternan, Charles	—	Corroder	ditto	ditto	Two saddles, and cloaths	9 19 1
Morrison, John	—	Cloen	ditto	ditto	A horse, cavalry saddle and bridle, and cloaths	17 3 4½
Moystyn, William	Yeoman	Drumahair	ditto	ditto	Cloaths, plate, fire-arms, fruit of orchard	29 4 5½
Moystyn, Henry	—	Cleenmore	ditto	ditto	Cloaths, furniture, and fowl	9 4 3½
Munroe, Thomas	—	Drumahair	ditto	ditto	Furniture, and cloaths	7 4 1
Murray, William	—	Ditto	ditto	ditto	Wearing apparel	2 19 8½
Nevill, Ann	—	Carrick-on-Shannon	ditto	Great road, leading from Dublin to Carrick-on-Shannon.	Millinery	46 14 11½
Newland, William	—	Gurteen	ditto	Residence	A horse, cloaths, damage to house	16 0 4
Palmer, John	—	Shibdella	ditto	ditto	{ Damage to windows, cloaths, furniture, and fowl	21 11 2
Palmer, James	—	Killargy	ditto	ditto	Horse, butter, meal, and cloaths	17 17 1
Patterson, William,	—	Kilmore	ditto	ditto	Cloaths, furniture, bank note, linen	10 6 4½
Patterson, George	—	Grosslodge	ditto	ditto	Fruit, furniture, hay, and butter	10 14 1½
Peyton, Tobias	—	Kesbcarigan	ditto	ditto	Cloaths, furniture, provisions, and windows broke	30 7 10½
Peyton, William	Gent.	Ditto	ditto	ditto	Damage to house, furniture, cloaths, and horse	16 15 1
Raycroft, Gilbert	—	Streamstown	ditto	Lands of Castill, Co. Leitrim }	Six bullocks	54 12 0.
Roarke, Bryan	—	Tullicooly	ditto	Residence	A colt	3 6 0
Roe, Pat. M'Dermott	—	Baraugh	ditto	ditto	Tools, cloaths, furniture, and oats	6 11 5
Ross, George	—	Drumahair	ditto	ditto	Oats, hay, cloaths, a pocket-book, and helmet	5 13 0½
Rutledge, Mary	Widow	Drumkerrin	ditto	ditto	Oats, furniture, cloaths, and crop	10 0 1
					Carried forward —	£ 2140 19 10

Extract from "A List of Persons Who Have Suffered Losses in Their Property in the County of Leitrim"—losses incurred during the Rebellion of 1798. NLI JLB 94107.

ers are in one of a variety of other archives (e.g., RCBL or NAI). Almost all of the parish registers of this county have been indexed by the Leitrim Heritage Centre (see Research Services at the end of the chapter). A search of the index will be conducted by the center for a fee. Those indexed are noted as "Indexed by LHC."

Annaduff
Earliest Records: b.1879–; m. 1845–; d. 1879–
Status: LC; Indexed by LHC (to 1900)

Aughavass
Status: Lost

Ballymeehan or Ballaghameehan
Earliest Records: b.1877–; m. 1859–; d. 1877–
Status: LC; RCBL (mf) (b/d. 1877–1985; m. 1859–1986); Indexed by LHC (to 1900)

Carrigallen
Earliest Records: b. 1883–; m. 1845–; d. 1874–
Status: LC; RCBL (mf) (b. 1883–1986; m. 1845–1941; d. 1874–1936)

Cloon
Earliest Records: b. 1880–; m. 1845–; d. 1880–
Status: LC; Indexed by LHC (to 1900)

Cloonclare
Earliest Records: b. 1816–1972; m. 1816–1921; d. 1816–1972
Status: LC; RCBL (mf) (b/m/d. 1816–1921, etc.); Indexed by LHC (to 1900)

Corawollen
Status: Lost

Drumkeeran
Earliest Records: b. 1873–; m. 1845–
Status: LC; RCBL (mf) (b. 1873–1944; m. 1845–1904)

Drumlease (Dromahare)
Earliest Records: b. 1827–; m. 1830–; d. 1827–
Status: LC; Indexed by LHC (to 1900)

Drumreilly
Earliest Records: b. 1877–; m. 1840–; d. 1877–
Status: LC; Indexed by LHC (to 1900)

Drumshanbo
Earliest Records: b. 1886–; m. 1845–; d. 1885–
Status: LC; Indexed by LHC (to 1900)

Farnaught
Earliest Records: b. 1883–; m. 1845–; d. 1892–
Status: LC; Indexed by LHC (b. and d. only to 1900)

Feenagh or Fenagh
Earliest Records: b. 1883–; m. 1854–; d. 1883–
Status: LC; Indexed by LHC (to 1900)

Glenlough (Killasnet Parish)
Status: Lost

Inismagrath
Earliest Records: b. 1877–; d. 1877–

Status: RCBL (mf) (b. 1877–1985; d. 1877–1983); Indexed by LHC (to 1900)

Killargue
Earliest Records: b. 1877–; m. 1859–; d. 1877–
Status: RCBL (mf) (b/d. 1877–1985; m. 1859–1986); Indexed by LHC (to 1900)

Killasnet (see also Glenlough)
Earliest Records: b. 1877–1984; m. 1846–1950; d. 1863–1956
Status: RCBL (mf) (b. 1877–1984; m. 1846–1950; d. 1863–1956); Indexed by LHC (to 1900)

Killenummery or Kilinummery
Earliest Records: b. 1884–1961; m. 1845–1905; d. 1856–1945
Status: LC; RCBL (mf) (b. 1884–1961; m. 1845–1905; d. 1856–1945); Indexed by LHC (to 1900)

Killigar
Status: Lost

Kiltoghert (see also Drumshanbo)
Earliest Records: b. 1810–; m. 1810–; d. 1810–
Status: LC; Indexed by LHC (to 1900)

Kiltubrid
Earliest Records: b. 1883–; m. 1845–; d. 1883–
Status: LC 1883–1900; Indexed by LHC (to 1900)

Kiltyclogher (see Manorhamilton for earlier entries)
Status: Lost

Manorhamilton or Cloonclare (see also Killasnet)
Earliest Records: b. 1816; m. 1816; d. 1816
Status: LC

Mogarban
Status: Lost

Mohill
Earliest Records: b/m. 1783; d. 1804
Status: LC; Indexed by LHC (to 1900)

Newtowngore or Newtown Gore
Earliest Records: b. 1877–; m. 1847–; d. 1877–
Status: RCBL (mf) (b/d. 1877–1921+; m. 1847–1950); Indexed by LHC (to 1900)

Outragh or Outeragh
Earliest Records: b. 1833–; m. 1833–; d. 1833–
Status: LC; Indexed by LHC (to 1900)

Rossinver
Earliest Records: b. 1876–; m. 1845–; d. 1876–
Status: LC; Indexed by LHC (to 1900)

Presbyterian

An account of Presbyterian records is given in the introduction. Many of the Presbyterian registers have been indexed by Leitrim Heritage Centre (see Research Services at the end of the chapter). A search of the index will be conducted for a fee. Those indexed are noted below as "Indexed by LHC."

Carrigallen
Earliest Records: b. 1829–; m. 1835–; d. 1880–
Status: LC; Indexed by LHC (to 1900)

Creevelea
Earliest Records: m. 1854–
Status: LC; Indexed by LHC (to 1900)

Drumkeerin (Co. Cavan)
Earliest Records: b. 1797–; m. 1835–; d. 1880–
Status: LC; Indexed by LHC (to 1900)

Methodist

Several of these registers have been indexed by Leitrim Heritage Centre (see Research Services at the end of the chapter). A search of the index will be conducted for a fee. Those indexed are noted below as "Indexed by LHC."

Boyle and Ballyfarnon (Co. Roscommon)
Earliest Records: m. 1883–
Status: LC; Indexed by LHC (to 1900)

Ballinamore
Earliest Records: m. 1805–
Status: LC; Indexed by LHC (to 1900)

Drumshanbo
Earliest Records: b. 1840–; m. 1866–
Status: LC; Indexed by LHC (to 1900)

Inismagrath
Earliest Records: m. 1886–
Status: LC; Indexed by LHC (to 1900)

Manorhamilton
Earliest Records: b. 1876–; m. 1865–
Status: LC; Indexed by LHC (to 1900)

Mohill
Earliest Records: b. 1882–; m. 1882–
Status: LC; Indexed by LHC (to 1900)

Newtowngore
Earliest Records: m. 1882–
Status: LC; Indexed by LHC (to 1900)

Roman Catholic

Note that most of the Catholic parish registers of this county have been indexed by Leitrim Heritage Centre (see Research Services at the end of the chapter). A search of the index will be conducted for a fee. Those indexed are noted below as "Indexed by LHC." Microfilm copies of all registers are also available in the National Library of Ireland (NLI), and through the LDS library system.

Civil Parish: Annaduff
Map Grid: 13
RC Parish: Annaduff
Diocese: AD
Earliest Record: b. 2.1849; m. 2.1849; d. 2.1849
Status: LC; NLI (mf); Indexed by LHC (to 1900)

Civil Parish: Carrigallen (1)
Map Grid: 15
RC Parish: Aughavas; also Carrigallen, see below
Diocese: KM
Earliest Record: b. 6.1845; m. 8.1845; d. 5.1845
Status: LC; NLI (mf); Indexed by LHC (to 1900)

Civil Parish: Carrigallen (2)
Map Grid: 15
RC Parish: Carrigallen
Diocese: KM
Earliest Record: b. 11.1829; m. 1.1841; d. 3.1842
Missing Dates: b. gaps 2.1830–12.1838; m. gaps 4.1848–1854; d. ends 6.1860
Status: LC; NLI (mf); Indexed by LHC (to 1900)

Civil Parish: Cloone (1)
Map Grid: 17
RC Parish: Cloone; see also below
Diocese: AD
Earliest Record: b. 2.1820; m. 1.1823; d. 1.1823
Missing Dates: b. 3.1820–1.1834, 1.1841–1.1843, 10.1849–1.1850; m. 1.1839–1.1843; d. 9.1845–1.1850
Status: LC; NLI (mf); Indexed by LHC (to 1900)

Civil Parish: Cloone (2)
Map Grid: 17
RC Parish: Gortletteragh
Diocese: AD
Earliest Record: b. 4.1830; m. 1.1826; d. 1.1826
Missing Dates: b. 8.1840–7.1848; m. 9.1827–2.1830, 4.1835–5.1848; d. 9.1826–3.1830, 2.1831–3.1839, 7.1839–8.1851, ends 7.1869
Status: LC; NLI (mf); Indexed by LHC (to 1900)

Civil Parish: Cloonclare
Map Grid: 5
RC Parish: Cloonclare
Diocese: KM
Earliest Record: b. 4.1841; m. 11.1850
Status: LC; NLI (mf); Indexed by LHC (to 1900)

Civil Parish: Cloonlogher
Map Grid: 4
RC Parish: part Drumlease; part Killarga
Diocese: KM

Civil Parish: Drumlease
Map Grid: 3
RC Parish: Drumlease or Drumlish
Diocese: KM
Earliest Record: b. 8.1859; m. 9.1859
Status: LC; NLI (mf); Indexed by LHC (to 1900)

Civil Parish: Drumreilly (1)
Map Grid: 9
RC Parish: Ballinglera; also Drumreilly Upper and Corlough, see below (2 and 3)
Diocese: KM
Earliest Record: b. 1883; m. 1887
Status: LC; NLI (mf); Indexed by LHC (to 1900)

Civil Parish: Drumreilly (2)
Map Grid: 9
RC Parish: Drumreilly Upper
Diocese: KM
Earliest Record: b. 1878; m. 1870
Status: LC; NLI (mf); Indexed by LHC (to 1900)

Civil Parish: Drumreilly (3)
Map Grid: 9
RC Parish: Corlough and Drumreilly Lower
Diocese: KM
Earliest Record: b. 3.1867; m. 1893
Status: LC; NLI (mf); Indexed by LHC (to 1900)

Civil Parish: Fenagh
Map Grid: 12
RC Parish: Fenagh
Diocese: AD
Earliest Record: b. 6.1825; m. 10.1826; d. 1825
Missing Dates: b. 10.1829–11.1834; m. 2.1832–1.1835, 3.1842–1.1844
Status: LC; NLI (mf); Indexed by LHC (to 1900)

Civil Parish: Inishmagrath
Map Grid: 8
RC Parish: Inishmagrath (Drumkeerin)
Diocese: KM
Earliest Record: b. 1834; m. 1834; d. 1834
Missing Dates: b. 1839–1880; m. 1839–1880; d. 1839–1880
Status: LC; NLI (mf); Indexed by LHC (to 1900)

Civil Parish: Killanummery
Map Grid: 6
RC Parish: Killenumerry and Ballintogher
Diocese: AD
Earliest Record: b. 5.1828; m. 6.1827; d. 5.1829
Missing Dates: b. 8.1846–11.1848; m. 8.1846–11.1848; d. ends 4.1846
Status: LC; NLI (mf); Indexed by LHC (to 1900)

Civil Parish: Killarga or Killargue
Map Grid: 7
RC Parish: Killarga and Dromahair
Diocese: KM
Earliest Record: b. 9.1852; m. 11.1853
Status: LC; NLI (mf); Indexed by LHC (to 1900)

Civil Parish: Killasnet
Map Grid: 2
RC Parish: Killasnet
Diocese: KM
Earliest Record: b. 3.1852; m. 3.1852; d. 3.1852
Missing Dates: b. 1.1869–11.1878; m. 5.1871–11.1878; d. ends 3.1868
Status: LC; NLI (mf); Indexed by LHC (to 1900)

Civil Parish: Kiltoghert (1)
Map Grid: 10
RC Parish: Murhaun; also Kiltoghert and Bornacoola, see below (2 and 3)

Diocese: AD
Earliest Record: b. 5.1861; m. 6.1868
Status: LC; NLI (mf); Indexed by LHC (to 1900)

Civil Parish: Kiltoghert (2)
Map Grid: 10
RC Parish: Kiltoghert
Diocese: AD
Earliest Record: b. 8.1826; m. 7.1832; d. 8.1832
Missing Dates: m. 6.1854; d. 6.1854–12.1866
Status: LC; NLI (mf); Indexed by LHC (to 1900)

Civil Parish: Kiltoghert (3)
Map Grid: 10
RC Parish: Bornacoola
Diocese: AD
Earliest Record: b. 1.1824; m. 6.1824; d. 6.1824
Missing Dates: m. 9.1837–5.1850
Status: LC; NLI (mf); Indexed by LHC (to 1900)

Civil Parish: Kiltubrid
Map Grid: 11
RC Parish: Kiltubrid
Diocese: AD
Earliest Record: b. 1.1841; m. 1.1841; d. 1.1847
Status: LC; NLI (mf); Indexed by LHC (to 1900)

Civil Parish: Mohill (see also Co. Longford)
Map Grid: 16
RC Parish: Mohill-Manachain
Diocese: AD
Earliest Record: b. 8.1836 (includes workhouse baptisms 1846–55); m. 7.1836; d. 7.1836
Missing Dates: m. 5.1854–8.1854
Status: LC; NLI (mf); Indexed by LHC (to 1900)

Civil Parish: Oughteragh
Map Grid: 14
RC Parish: Oughteragh (Ballinamore)
Diocese: KM
Earliest Record: b. 11.1841; m. 1.1841
Status: LC; NLI (mf); Indexed by LHC (to 1900)

Civil Parish: Rossinver (1)
Map Grid: 1
RC Parish: Kinlough; also Glenade and Rossinver, see below (2 and 3)
Diocese: KM
Earliest Record: b. 7.1835; m. 11.1840
Status: LC; NLI (mf); Indexed by LHC (to 1900)

Civil Parish: Rossinver (2)
Map Grid: 1
RC Parish: Glenade
Diocese: KM
Earliest Record: b. 11.1867; m. 1866
Status: LC; NLI (mf); Indexed by LHC (to 1900)

Civil Parish: Rossinver (3)
Map Grid: 1
RC Parish: Rossinver (Ballaghameehan)
Diocese: KM

Earliest Record: b. 8.1851; m. 8.1844
Status: LC; NLI (mf); Indexed by LHC (to 1900)

Commercial and Social Directories

1824

J. Pigot's *City of Dublin and Hibernian Provincial Directory* includes traders, nobility, gentry, and clergy lists of Ballinamore, Carrick-on-Shannon, Drumsna, Jamestown, and Manorhamilton.

1846

Slater's *National Commercial Directory of Ireland* lists nobility, clergy, traders, etc., in Carrick-on-Shannon, Dromahaire, Drumsna and Jamestown, Manorhamilton, and Mohill.

1856

Slater's *Royal National Commercial Directory of Ireland* lists nobility, gentry, clergy, traders, etc., in Ballinamore, Carrick-on-Shannon, Dromahaire, Drumsna and Jamestown, Manorhamilton, and Mohill.

1870

Slater's *Directory of Ireland* contains trade, nobility, and clergy lists for Ballinamore, Carrick-on-Shannon and Leitrim, Dromahaire, Drumsna, Manorhamilton, and Mohill.

1881

Slater's *Royal National Commercial Directory of Ireland* contains lists of traders, clergy, nobility, and farmers in adjoining parishes of the towns of Ballinamore, Carrick-on-Shannon, Manorhamilton and Dromahaire, and Mohill.

1894

Slater's *Royal National Directory of Ireland* lists traders, police, teachers, farmers, and private residents in each of the towns, villages, and parishes of the county.

Family History

The Leitrim-Roscommon Genealogy Home Page also has information on histories of families associated with the county (see Libraries and Information Sources below).

"Surnames of Co. Leitrim." Sean O'Suilleabhain. *Irish Roots* (4) (1994): 15–16.

Downey, L. A *History of the Protestant Downeys of Cos. Sligo, Leitrim, Fermanagh and Donegal* (also of the Hawksby family of Leitrim and Sligo). New York, 1931.

Breen, Fr. Mark. *The Gray Family of Co. Leitrim*. 1980.

Hawksby—see Co. Sligo.

"Notes on the MacRannals of Leitrim and Their Country: Being Introductory to a Diary of James Reynolds, Lough Scur, Co. Leitrim, for the Years 1658–1660." *R.S.A.I.* 35 (1905): 139–51.

"The Morans and the Mulveys of South Leitrim." *Ardagh and Clonmacnois Antiq. J.* 1 (3) (1932): 14–19.

"The Descendants of Col. Miles O'Reilly in Co. Leitrim (1650–1830) from Tradition." *Breifne* 2 (1) (1923): 15–19.

Reynolds—see MacRannal above.

Jones, W.G. *The Wynnes of Sligo and Leitrim*. Manorhamilton: Drumlin Publications, 1994. ISBN: I-873437-072.

Gravestone Inscriptions

Leitrim Heritage Centre has indexed the inscriptions from a large proportion of the graveyards in the county. These include eighty-five Catholic sites, twenty-seven Church of Ireland sites, and one Presbyterian site. For details on access to this source, see Research Services below.

Kiltubrid Churchyard: Anglican Record Project. (See Church of Ireland section in introduction.)

Newspapers

There are few papers which cover only this county. Those in the surrounding counties should be consulted, depending on the area of interest. All the papers listed below are also held in Leitrim County Library, and most have been indexed for the nineteenth century by the Leitrim Heritage Centre.

Title: *Leitrim and Longford Advertiser* (continued as *Leitrim Advertiser* in 1870)
Published in: Mohill, 1867–1924
NLI Holdings: 10.1867–12.1916; 6.1921–12.1924
BL Holdings: 10.1867–12.1916

Title: *Leitrim Gazette*
Published in: Mohill, 1858–67
NLI Holdings: 1858–67

Title: *Leitrim Journal*
Published in: Carrick-on-Shannon, 1850–72
NLI Holdings: 10.1850–3.1860; 11.1861–12.1872
BL Holdings: 10.1850–12.1857 (with gaps); 2.1858–3.1860; odd numbers 1861, 1870, and 1872

Title: *Leitrim Observer*
Published in: Carrick-on-Shannon, ca. 1890–current
NLI Holdings: 1904–in progress
BL Holdings: 1.1904–11.1920; 7.1959–in progress

2/-   Cen S/16/451   Application No. 3642

c/27941712

Date of receipt, 17.6.16   Disposed of,   ✓

EXTRACT FROM CENSUS RETURN OF 18 51

Full Name of Applicant, *Bridget McMorrow*

Address, *Mrs Bridget oRourke, Killarga, Dromahair.*
Co. Leitrim

Full Names of Father and Mother of Applicant, *James & Bridget McMorrow* ✓

Name of Head of Family (if other than Father)
with which Applicant resided in 18

Relationship and Occupation,

Residence in 18   :

County, *Leitrim*

Barony, *Drumahaire*   *? res in 51*

Parish, *Killarga*

Townland, *Fenagh* ✓

Street (if in a town),

Place in Record Treasury,   *L22-16*

Return searched by   *Jw 19/6/16 sheet 10*

Extract made by   *ZH 19.6.16*

Certified by   *HN 20.6.16*

Form replaced by   *Jw 20/6/16*

Copy despatched to Applicant's Address.   *Tju 21/6/16*

(7217.) Wt.5850—89.10,000.9/15.A.T.&Co.,Ltd.

A census search form. These were compiled as evidence of the occurrence of individuals in census returns, usually as proof of the age of the applicant.

Wills and Administrations

A discussion of the types of records, where they are held, and their availability and value is given in the Wills section of the introduction. The availability of prerogative wills, administrations, and marriage license records is also described in the relevant parts of the same section. Where available, published sources of these records are given in the Miscellaneous Sources section.

Pre-1858 Wills and Administrations

Prerogative Wills. See the introduction.

Consistorial Wills. County Leitrim is in the dioceses of Ardagh and Kilmore. The guide to Catholic parish records in this chapter shows the diocese to which each civil parish belonged. The wills of residents of each diocese were usually proven within that diocese (see the Wills section for exceptions). The following records survive:

Wills

See the introduction.

Abstracts

See the introduction.

Indexes

Index to Ardagh Wills (1695–1858). *Ir. Anc.* 1971 (Supplement) and SLC film 824242. Index to Kilmore Diocesan Wills published by Smyth-Wood; SLC film 990068.

Post-1858 Wills and Administrations

This county was served by the District Registries of Ballina (baronies of Rosclogher and Dromahaire) and Cavan (rest of the county). Ballina District Will Books (1865–1899). NAI; SLC films 100925 and 6. Cavan District Will Books (1858–1896). NAI; SLC films 100927 and 8.

Marriage Licenses

Indexes

Ardagh and Kilmore (1691–1845). NAI; SLC film 100869.

Miscellaneous Sources

O'Suilleabhain, Sean. "Surnames of Co. Leitrim." *Irish Roots* 4 (1994): 15–16.

Farrell, Noel. *Exploring Family Origins and Old Carrick-on-Shannon.* Longford Leader, 1994. (Contains 1901 and 1911 census data, electors lists, etc.)

Clancy, E., and P. Forde. *Ballinaglera Parish, Co. Leitrim: Aspects of its History and Traditions.* Dublin, 1980.

Clancy, P.S. *Historical Notices of the Parish of Inishmagrath, Co. Leitrim.* Carrick-on-Shannon, 1958.

"List of Sheriffs, Sub-Sheriffs, Jury Foremen, Lieutenants and M.P.s 1600–1868." Pub. 1869; NLI 2179.

MacParlan, J. *Statistical Survey of the County of Leitrim.* Royal Dublin Society, 1802.

O'Flynn, T. *History of Leitrim.* Dublin, 1937.

"Some Notes on the High Sheriffs of Co. Leitrim, 1701–1800." *Ir. Gen.* 1 (10) (1941): 301–09.

Jones Papers—Wills, deeds, and leases for Jones family of Leitrim. Leitrim County Library; SLC film 1279269.

Records of Manorhamilton Union Workhouse (1839–81). Leitrim County Library; SLC film 1279291–4.

Records of Carrick-on-Shannon Union Workhouse (1843–82). Leitrim County Library; SLC films 1279267–8 and 1279288–9.

Records of Mohill Union Workhouse (1839–83). Leitrim County Library; SLC films 1279269 and 1279287–92.

Research Sources and Services

Journals

Breifne (see Co. Cavan)

Libraries and Information Sources

Leitrim-Roscommon Genealogy Home Page (http://www.thecore.com/let-res/index.html) has sources for research in the counties, maps of different administrative divisions, and information on specific families associated with the county.

Leitrim County Library, The Courthouse, Ballinamore, Co. Leitrim. Ph: (078) 44012; fax: (353) 78 44425. The library has a sizable collection of local history materials, including books, directories, newspapers, periodicals, photographs, estate papers, and the papers of the Clements, Jones, Godley, and Crofton families. Their family history queries are generally referred to the Leitrim Heritage Centre, which is based within the library (see below).

Research Services

Leitrim Heritage Centre, County Library, Ballinamore, Co. Leitrim. Ph: (078) 44012; fax: (353) 78 44425. (See home page details above.) This is the official IGP center for Leitrim county. The center has compiled a comprehensive collection of family history material for the county and has indexed many of the relevant sources, including most church registers, gravestone inscriptions, etc. Researchers are advised to contact the center for an updated list of registers, and other sources, indexed. They also offer a full-time genealogical service on Leitrim families.

See also Research Services in Dublin in the introduction.

Societies

Breifne Historical Society (see Co. Cavan; mainly covers Cavan and West Leitrim)

Carrick-on-Shannon and District Historical Society, Ms. Evelyn McCabe-Kane, Drummaunroe, Jamestown, Carrick-on-Shannon, Co. Leitrim

Leitrim Civil Parishes as Listed on Map

1. Rossinver
2. Killasnet
3. Drumlease
4. Cloonlogher
5. Clooneclare
6. Killanummery
7. Killarga or Killargue
8. Inishmagrath
9. Drumreilly
10. Kiltoghert
11. Kiltubrid
12. Fenagh or Feenagh
13. Annaduff
14. Oughteragh
15. Carrigallen
16. Mohill
17. Cloone

Leitrim Civil Parishes in Alphabetical Order

Annaduff: 13
Carrigallen: 15
Cloone: 17
Clooneclare: 5
Cloonlogher: 4
Drumlease: 3
Drumreilly: 9
Fenagh or Feenagh: 12
Inishmagrath: 8
Killanummery: 6
Killarga or Killargue: 7
Killasnet: 2
Kiltoghert: 10
Kiltubrid: 11
Mohill: 16
Oughteragh: 14
Rossinver: 1

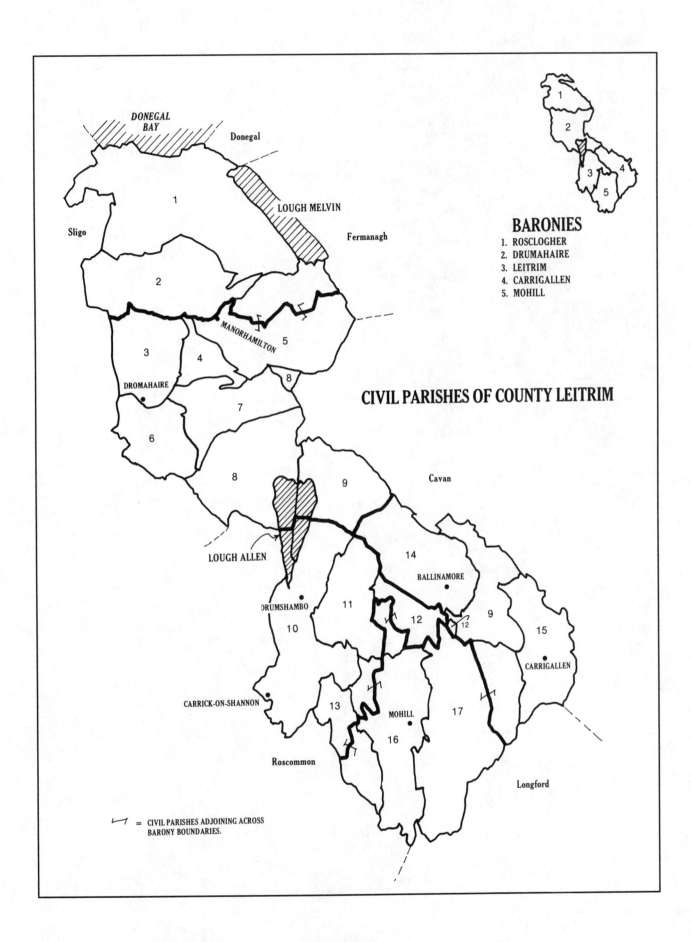

DONEGAL BAY

Donegal

LOUGH MELVIN

Sligo

Fermanagh

1

2

MANORHAMILTON

5

3

4

8

DROMAHAIRE

7

6

8

9

Cavan

CIVIL PARISHES OF COUNTY LEITRIM

LOUGH ALLEN

14

BALLINAMORE

DRUMSHAMBO

11

12

9

15

10

12

CARRIGALLEN

CARRICK-ON-SHANNON

13

MOHILL

17

16

Roscommon

Longford

BARONIES

1. ROSCLOGHER
2. DRUMAHAIRE
3. LEITRIM
4. CARRIGALLEN
5. MOHILL

1
2
3
4
5

⌐ = CIVIL PARISHES ADJOINING ACROSS
      BARONY BOUNDARIES.

County Limerick

A Brief History

Much of this county was part of the old Gaelic Kingdom of Thomond, while parts of the west of the county were in the Kingdom of Desmond. The major families in the county were the O'Briens, O'Ryans, O'Donovans, and O'Sheehans. Other families in the area included O'Hurley, MacSheehy, O'Gorman, O'Scanlan, and O'Hallinan.

In the mid-ninth century, the Vikings took control of Limerick City and retained it until the eleventh century, when they were defeated by the O'Brien chieftain, Brian Boru. From that time it became the seat of the O'Briens, rulers of Thomond. Because the Norse people did not use surnames, there is little evidence of the Viking heritage among the family names in the area. However, one of the few Norse names found in Ireland, Harold, is found in Limerick.

Following the Norman invasion, the county was granted to the De Burgos, ancestors of the Burkes, and to Fitzwalters and Fitzgeralds. The Norman influence is still evident in the names which are now common in Limerick, including Fitzgerald, Fitzgibbon, de Lacy, Woulfe, and Wall.

At the end of the sixteenth century, a rebellion by Fitzgerald, the Earl of Desmond (see Co. Kerry) led to a very bloody war, which devastated much of this area of Munster. Following the defeat of Desmond, his estates, some of which were in western Limerick, were granted to various adventurers and were planted with English settlers. The Plantation of Munster in 1598, which also included parts of Limerick, was largely a failure. Many of the settlers left during the O'Neill march through Munster in 1601, and others simply adopted Irish customs and assimilated into the native population. Further confiscations, which followed the 1641 and 1688 wars, increased the numbers of English landowners, but did not greatly increase the numbers of English settlers.

In 1709, families of German settlers from the Rhine Palatinate were brought to Limerick and settled around Rathkeale. These people were of the Moravian faith and came to be known as Palatines. Of the original eight hundred families who were brought to the county, only two hundred (approximately 1,200 people) remained in Ireland. Later in the century, groups of the remaining Palatine families moved to other colonies in Adare and in Castleisland in County Kerry. The commoner names among these people included Shouldice, Switzer, and Cole (see Miscellaneous Sources section for further references).

The county was badly affected by a local famine in 1820, caused by an outbreak of potato blight, and by the Great Famine of 1845-47. Almost seventeen percent of the county's population emigrated between 1851 and 1855, and almost 30,000 died between 1847 and 1850. The population was 330,000 in 1841, and by 1851 had fallen by twenty-one percent. By 1891 it had fallen to about 160,000, and is currently approximately 122,000.

Limerick is now an important industrial city and port. The other major towns in the county include Kilmallock, Newcastle West, Rathkeale, Abbeyfeale, and Adare.

Census and Census Substitutes

1570

List of the Freeholders and Gentlemen in Co. Limerick. NLI P1700; *N. Munster Arch. and Hist. Soc. J.* 9 (3) (1964): 108–12.

1586

Survey of Leaseholders on the Desmond Estates. NAI M 5037.

1654–56

Civil Survey. Vol. 4. Simington, R.C. Co. Limerick, with a section of Clanmaurice Baroney, Co. Kerry. Dublin: Stationery Office, 1938; SLC film 973122.

1659

"Census" of Ireland. Edited by S. Pender. Dublin: Stationery Office, 1939. NLI I6551. SLC film 924648.

1664

Hearth Money Roll for Askeaton. *N. Munster Antiq. J.* 1965.

1715–94

Freemen of the City of Limerick. PRO–London; SLC film 477000.

1746–1836

"Index of Freemen of Limerick." *N. Munster Antiq. J.* 4 (3) (1945): 103–30 (gives name, address, occupation in some cases, and date freedom attained).

1761

Militia List. Counties Limerick . . . . etc. GO Ms. 680.

Names and Addresses of Freeholders Voting in a Parliamentary Election. NLI ms. 16093.

1766

Householders of Parishes of Abington, Ardcanny, Cahircomey, Cahirelly, Carrigparson, Clonkeen, Kilkellane and Tuogh. NAI Parliamentary Papers 681/684. (Ardcanny also in NAI M 147.)

Protestant householders of Parishes of Clonagh, Croagh, Dondaniel, Kilscannel, Nantinan and Rathkeale. GO 537; RCB Ms. 37; SLC film 258517; also in *Ir. Anc.* 9 (2) (1977): 77–78.

List of Protestants and Papists in Limerick Diocese. GO 540; SLC film 100212.

1776

Names of the Owners of Freeholds Entitled to Vote. NAI Mf. 1321–22.

1793

"Two Lists of Persons Resident in the Vicinity of Newcastle in 1793 and 1821." *Ir. Anc.* 16 (1) (1984): 40–44.

1798

"List of Rebel Prisoners in Limerick Gaol." *N. Munster*

Antiq. J. 10 (1) (1966): 79–82.

1799

"Gentlemen of the Counties Clare and Limerick Who Were in Favour of the Union in 1799." *Ir. Anc.* 14 (1) (1982): 30–35.

1813

"The Chief Inhabitants of the Parishes of St. Mary's and St. John's Limerick in 1813." *Ir. Anc.* 17 (2) (1985): 75–76.

1816–28

"List of Freeholders for the County of Limerick." SLC film 100224; GO M623.

1817

"Voters in the Limerick City Election of 1817." NLI IR324L1; *Ir. Anc.* 17 (1) (1985): 49–57.

1821

Newcastle—see 1793.

"Fragments of Census Returns for Kilfinane District." *N. Munster Antiq. J.* 17 (1975): 83–90.

1823–38

Tithe Applotment Survey (see introduction).

1829

Limerick's Freeholders with Addresses and Occupations. GO M623.

1834

"Heads of Households in the Parish of Templebredon and Numbers in Each." *N. Munster Arch. and Hist. Soc. J.* 17 (1975): 91–101.

1835–39

Lists of residents of Limerick in Waterworks accounts. NLI P. 3451.

1836

Freemen—see 1746.

1840

List of Freeholders in the Barony of Coshlea. NLI ms. 9452.

1841

"Emigration to North America from Limerick Port, 1841." *N. Munster Antiq. J.* 23 (1981): 67–76 (includes the passenger list for the *Shelmalere,* 26 May 1841 to New York).

Delivery he is Intitled to 13s. 4d. fees on each Man for such Crimes. The following is a list disposed of as underneath mentioned—

Death, Executed

No. 1 Mathew Kennedy
2 John Moore
3 Stephen Dundon
4 Thomas Mullanny
5 John Hayes
6 Thomas McInerney
7 Thomas Kennedy
8 William Ryan Stephens
9 Patrick O Neill
10 Patrick Wallace

Transported

No. 1 Owen Ryan
2 Thomas Gorman
3 James Ryan
4 Edmond Ryan
5 James Keagh
6 John Dwyer
7 Thomas Dwyer
8 Charles Nolan
9 David Leahy
10 James Kennedy
11 John Moroney
12 Richard Kelly
13 Michael McInerney
14 Owen Ryan
15 James Brohane
16 John Cunningham
17 Wm. Higgins Enlisted in 54th Regt.
18 Andrew Ryan
19 Philip Hogan
20 John Cowney
21 Daniel Carroll
22 James Ryan Stephens
23 Daniel Hayes
24 James Kelly
25 Thomas Frost
26 John Connor
27 John Mawn
28 James Casey
29 Maurice Shea
30 Francis Arthur
31 John Kerin
32 Michael Conry
33 Ells. Allum
34 John Abraham

35 James Mahon
36 Thomas Lawler
37 Michael Timmen
38 Michael Daley
39 Michael Mulconry
40 Richd. Robinson Enlisted in the 54th Regt. Foot

Persons discharged on Bail

No. 1 Joseph O Loughlin
2 John FitzGerald
3 Daniel Bohan
4 James Hillard
5 Patrick Carroll
6 Michael Callaghan
7 Thomas Butler
8 Denis Halloran
9 Patrick Halloran
10 John Ryan
11 Darby Ward
12 Mathew Hayes
13 David Twohy
14 Michael Callaghan
15 Thomas Ryan
16 Michael Donegan
17 James Dundon
18 Martin Kelly
19 George Murphy
20 Wm. Gleeson
21 John Flinn
22 Hugh Dwyer
23 James Crough
24 George Hardgrove
25 Robert Cross
26 Martin Howard
27 Thomas Collopy
28 Wm. Tubbs
29 Richard Welsh
30 John Murphy
31 John O Hogan
32 Wm. Crowe
33 Edmond Dunn
34 Andrew Kennedy
35 Michael Considine
36 Mathew Dea
37 John Twohy
38 Thomas McKnight
39 Theobald Barry

40 Wm. Healy
41 Thomas Dunn
42 John Murphy
43 Wm. Gorman
44 James Grant
45 David Callon
46 Richd. McElligott
47 Wm. Hannabury
48 John Sullivan
49 Edward Riely
50 Edmond Sheehan
51 James Hackett
52 Daniel O Brien
53 Denis McNamara
54 John Meade
55 James Hayes

Prisoners discharged by the Court Martial

No. 1 Peter O Keeffe
2 Denis Ryan
3 John Clume
4 Edmond Ryan
5 Patrick Ryan
6 James Cowney
7 Thomas Lane
8 Charles Small
9 Michael McCormack
10 John Coraghan
11 John Ryan
12 Frans. McNamara
13 Martin Kelly
14 Patrick Connor
15 Barthw. Clanchy
16 Lieut. Harrass
17 Lieut. Rice
18 John Sullivan
19 Quarter Master Holmes
20 Thomas Doe
21 John Burke
22 Lieut. O Dwyer
23 Thomas Madagan
24 Chas. Strudgeon
25 Timothy Tierney
26 John Cloghessy
27 Danl. Shaughnessy
28 John McInerney
29 Edward Hastings
30 Michael Hastings
31 John Garvey

The Petition

To his Excellency Lord Marquis of Cornwallis,
Lieutenant General and General Governor & Commander in Chief of the Kingdom of Ireland—

A list of rebel prisoners held in Limerick Jail following the Rebellion of 1798, with their sentences. From *North Munster Antiquarian Journal* 10 (1) (1966).

1843

Voters List. NAI 1843/66.

1846

Survey of Households in Connection with Famine Relief. NLI ms. 582 (Loughill, Foynes, and Shanagolden area).

1848

Petitioners for William Smith O'Brien. Names of male petitioners in Abbeyfeale and Limerick City. NAI 1848/180.

1851

Kilfinane—see 1821 re: census fragments.

1851–52

Griffith's Valuation (see introduction).

1867

"List of Active Fenians in Co. Limerick." *N. Munster Antiq. J.* 10 (2) (1967): 169–72.

Marchers in memory of Allen, Larkin, O'Brien. *Old Limerick J.* 22 (1987). City of Limerick—Name, Occupation, Address of 437 marchers.

"Persons Attending Fenian Memorial Procession" (437 people named, with occupation and residence). *N. Munster Antiq. J.* 10 (2) (1967): 173–205.

1901

Census. NAI (see introduction).

1911

Census. NAI.

Church Records

Church of Ireland

See the introduction for a description of Church of Ireland records and their major repositories. Many C of I records were lost in the PRO fire of 1922. These are indicated as "Lost." However, as Church of Ireland records were effectively state records, the records of marriage (from 1845) are also in the General Registrar's Office. Many are still in local custody (LC), while others are in one of a variety of other archives (e.g., RCBL or NAI). Many of the parish registers of this county have been indexed by Limerick Archives (see Research Services at the end of the chapter). A search of the index will be conducted by the center for a fee. Those indexed are noted as "Indexed by LA." An index to the marriages in Co. Limerick before 1845 is available on SLC film 874438.

Abington

Earliest Records: b. 1811–; m. 1813–; d. 1810–
Status: LC; NAI MFCI 2, M5222 (b. 1811–98; m. 1813–45; d. 1810–92)

Adare

Earliest Records: b. 1826–; m. 1826–; d. 1826–
Status: LC; NLI P1994 (b. 1845–89); Indexed by LA (to 1980); SLC film 874437 (b. 1826–66; m. 1826–45; d. 1826–78)

Aney

Earliest Records: b. 1760–; m. 1761–; d. 1759–
Status: *J. Ir. Mem. Assoc.* 12 (b/m/d. to 1802 with index to deaths)

Ardcanny and Chapelrussell

Earliest Records: b. 1802–; m. 1802–; d. 1805–
Status: LC; NLI P 2761 (b. 1802–48; m. 1802–44; d. 1805–44); NAI M5072 5 (b/m. 1802–1920+; d. 1805–1940); Indexed by LA (to 1980); SLC film 928607 (b. 1802–1927; m. 1802–44; d. 1805–94)

Askeaton

Earliest Records: b. 1877–; m. 1845–; d. 1877–
Status: LC; Indexed by LA (to 1980)

Athlacca and Dromin

Status: Lost

Ballingarry

Earliest Records: b. 1785–; m. 1785–; d. 1785–
Status: LC; NAI MFCI 16 (b. 1785–1872; m. 1809–46; d. 1809–75); GO 701 (extracts); SLC film 257807 (extracts b/m/d. 1698–1736); SLC film 101780 (1785–1843); Indexed by LA (to 1980)

Ballinlanders

Earliest Records: m. 1852–77
Status: RCBL

Ballybrood

Status: Lost

Ballycahane

Status: Lost

Bruff

Earliest Records: b. 1859–; m. 1845–; d. 1859–
Status: LC; NAI M5975/6 (b. 1859–71; d. 1859–71); Indexed by LA (to 1980)

Caherconlish

Earliest Records: b. 1888–; m. 1845–; d. 1890–
Status: LC; Indexed by LA (to 1980)

Cahercorney

Status: Lost

Cahernarry (also see St. Mary)

Earliest Records: b. 1855–; m. 1847–; d. 1877–
Status: LC; NAI M5112 (b. 1855–77); Indexed by LA (to 1980)

Cappamore and Tuogh (see also Abington)

Earliest Records: b. 1859–; m. 1845–; d. 1859–

Status: LC; Indexed by LA (to 1980)

Chapelrussell—see Ardcanny

Corcomhide
Earliest Records: b. 1805-; m. 1805-; d. 1805-
Status: LC; NAI MFCI 16, M5987 (b/m/d. 1805-95)

Croagh
Status: Lost

Croom
Earliest Records: b. 1877-; m. 1848-; d. 1880-
Status: LC; Indexed by LA (to 1980)

Doon
Earliest Records: b. 1804; m. 1812; d. 1812
Status: LC and NAI; SLC film 990092 (b. 1812-77; m. 1812-45; d. 1812-73)

Drehidtarsna (see also St. Munchin)
Status: Lost

Dromkeen
Status: Lost

Fedamore
Earliest Records: b. 1840-; m. 1845-
Status: LC; NAI M5112 (b. 1840-91); Indexed by LA (to 1980)

Grean
Status: Lost

Kilbeheney
Status: Lost

Kilcornan
Earliest Records: b. 1892-; m. 1845-; d. 1893-
Status: LC; Indexed by LA (to 1980)

Kildimo
Earliest Records: b. 1809-; m. 1809-; d. 1809-
Status: LC

Kilfergus and Kilmoylan
Earliest Records: b. 1812-; m. 1815-; d. 1836-
Status: LC; NAI MFCI 17 (b. 1812-58; m. 1815-43; d. 1836-49); Indexed by LA (to 1980)

Kilfinane
Earliest Records: b. 1804-; m. 1804-; d. 1798-
Status: LC; NAI MFCI 16 (b. 1804-71; m. 1804-41; d. 1798-1871); Indexed by LA (to 1980); SLC film 897422 (b. 1804-07 and '44-65; m. 1804-45)

Kilflyn
Earliest Records: b. 1813-; m. 1813-; d. 1813-
Status: LC; Indexed by LA (to 1980)

Kilkeedy
Earliest Records: b. 1802-; m. 1802-; d. 1799-
Status: LC; Indexed by LA (to 1980)

Killaliathan
Earliest Records: b. 1879-; m. 1851-; d. 1883-
Status: LC; Indexed by LA (to 1980)

Killeedy
Earliest Records: b. 1879-; m. 1846-
Status: LC; Indexed by LA (to 1980)

Killeely
Status: Lost

Kilmallock
Earliest Records: b. 1883-; m. 1846-; d. 1883-
Status: LC; Indexed by LA (to 1980)

Kilmeedy
Earliest Records: b. 1805-; m. 1805-; d. 1805-
Status: LC; NAI MFCI 16, M5987 (b/m/d. 1805-95); Indexed by LA (to 1980); SLC film 897422 (b/m. 1805-1900 and '44-65; d. 1845-1900)

Kilmurry
Status: Lost

Kilpeacon (also see Rathkeale)
Earliest Records: b 1892-; m 1845-; d. 1895-
Status: LC; Indexed by LA (to 1980)

Kilscannell
Earliest Records: b. 1824-; m. 1825-; d. 1860-
Status: LC; NAI MFCI 16, M5987 (b. 1824-74; m. 1825-59; d. 1860-87); Indexed by LA (to 1980)

Knockainy
Earliest Records: b. 1883-; m. 1845-; d. 1883-
Status: LC; Indexed by LA (to 1980)

Limerick City—Garrison
Earliest Records: b. 1858-; d. 1865-
Status: LC; NAI MFCI 17, M5789/80 (b. 1858-71; d. 1865-71)

Limerick City—St. John's
Earliest Records: b. 1697-; m. 1697-; d. 1697-
Status: LC; NAI MFCI 14, 15 (b. 1697-1883; m. 1697-1845; d. 1697-1876); Indexed by LA (to 1980); SLC film 874438 (b. 1698-1827; m. 1697-1837; d. 1697-1837)

Limerick City—St. Laurence
Earliest Records: b. 1863-; d. 1697-
Status: LC

Limerick City—St. Mary's
Earliest Records: b. 1726-; m. 1726-; d. 1726-
Status: LC; NAI MFCI 15, M5978 (b. 1726-1871; m. 1726-1845; d. 1726-1942); Indexed by LA (to 1980); SLC film 897365 (b. 1726-1796; m. 1726-1842; d. 1726-1842)

Limerick City—St. Michael's
Earliest Records: b. 1803-; m. 1799-; d. 1803-
Status: LC; NAI MFCI 17, M5991 (b. 1803-71; m. 1803-45; d. 1803-89); Indexed by LA (to 1980, from 1827 for d.); SLC film 897422 (b. 1803-45; m/d. 1827-45)

Limerick City—St. Munchin
Earliest Records: b. 1700-; m. 1700-; d. 1700-

Missing Dates: b. 1705-34; m. 1769-97; d. 1705-34
Status: LC; Indexed by LA (1734-1980); SLC film
897365 (b/m/d. 1734-1840)

Loughill
Earliest Records: m. 1846-; d. 1883-
Status: LC; Indexed by LA (to 1980)

Mahoonagh
Earliest Records: b. 1861-
Status: LC; NAI M5977 (b. 1861-64)

Mungret
Earliest Records: b. 1852-; m. 1845; d. 1843-
Status: LC; NAI M5981/5986 (b. 1852-56; d. 1843-
72); Indexed by LA (to 1980)

Nantinan
Earliest Records: b. 1877-; m. 1845; d. 1848-
Status: LC; Indexed by LA (to 1980)

Newcastle or Newcastle West
Earliest Records: b. 1842-; m. 1845-; d. 1848-
Status: LC; NAI M5983/4 (b. 1848-70; d. 1848-76);
Indexed by LA (to 1980)

Particles (with Kilflyn)
Earliest Records: b. 1841-; m. 1800-; d. 1812-
Status: LC; NAI MFCI 16, M5987 (b. 1841-71);
Indexed by LA (to 1980)

Rathkeale
Earliest Records: b. 1742-; m. 1742-; d. 1742-
Status: LC; NAI MFCI 16, M5987, M5120/1 (b/d.
1781-1871; m. 1781-1836); Indexed by LA (to
1980); SLC film 897365 (b. 1742-1899; m. 1744-
1845; d. 1742-1901)

Rathronan and Ardagh
Earliest Records: b. 1720-; m. 1722-; d. 1722-
Status: LC; NAI MFCI 16, M5987 (b. 1818-71; d.
1824-71)

St. Patrick and Kilquane
Status: Lost

Shanagolden
Earliest Records: b. 1879-; m. 1847-; d. 1881-
Status: LC; Indexed by LA (to 1980)

Stradbally
Earliest Records: b. 1792-; m. 1787-; d. 1789-
Status: LC; NAI MFCI 3, M5222/M5249-52 (b.
1792-1881; m. 1787-1844; d. 1791-1850); Indexed
by LA (to 1980)

Tullybracky
Status: Lost

Roman Catholic

Note that most of the Catholic parish registers of this
county have been indexed by either Limerick Archives
(LA) or by Tipperary Heritage Unit (THU; see Research
Services at the end of the chapter). A search of their
indexes will be conducted for a fee. Microfilm copies of
all registers (except those for the Catholic diocese of
Cashel and Emly) are also available in the National Library of Ireland (NLI), and through the LDS library
system.

Civil Parish: Abbeyfeale
Map Grid: 74
RC Parish: Abbeyfeale
Diocese: LK
Earliest Record: b. 2.1829; m. 11.1856
Missing Dates: b. 10.1843-8.1856 (records exist, but
not on microfilm)
Status: LC; NLI (mf); Indexed by LA (to 1900)

Civil Parish: Abington (see also Co. Tipperary)
Map Grid: 61
RC Parish: Murroe and Boher
Diocese: EM
Earliest Record: b. 6.1814; m. 11.1815
Status: LC; NLI (mf); Indexed by LA (to 1900) and
by THU (to 1899)

Civil Parish: Adare
Map Grid: 89
RC Parish: Adare
Diocese: LK
Earliest Record: b. 7.1832; m. 7.1832
Status: LC; NLI (mf); Indexed by LA (to 1900)

Civil Parish: Aglishcormick
Map Grid: 60
RC Parish: see Kilteely
Diocese: EM

Civil Parish: Anhid
Map Grid: 93
RC Parish: see Croom
Diocese: LK

Civil Parish: Ardagh
Map Grid: 11
RC Parish: Ardagh
Diocese: LK
Earliest Record: b. 3.1845; m. 10.1841
Status: LC; NLI (mf); Indexed by LA (to 1900)

Civil Parish: Ardcanny
Map Grid: 17
RC Parish: see Kildimo
Diocese: LK

Civil Parish: Ardpatrick
Map Grid: 121
RC Parish: Ardpatrick
Diocese: LK
Earliest Record: b. 7.1861; m. 8.1861
Status: LC; NLI (mf); Indexed by LA (to 1900)

Civil Parish: Askeaton
Map Grid: 14
RC Parish: Askeaton (previously part of Kilfinane)

Diocese: LK
Earliest Record: b. 1.1829; m. 1.1829
Missing Dates: m. 7.1861–10.1861
Status: LC; NLI (mf); Indexed by LA (to 1900)

Civil Parish: Athlacca
Map Grid: 95
RC Parish: see Dromin
Diocese: LK

Civil Parish: Athneasy
Map Grid: 116
RC Parish: Bulgaden, see Kilbreedy Major
Diocese: LK

Civil Parish: Ballinard
Map Grid: 109
RC Parish: see Hospital
Diocese: EM

Civil Parish: Ballingaddy
Map Grid: 122
RC Parish: Kilmallock, see SS Peter and Paul
Diocese: LK

Civil Parish: Ballingarry (1)
Map Grid: 81
RC Parish: Ballingarry
Diocese: LK
Earliest Record: b. 1.1825; m. 1.1825
Missing Dates: b. 5.1828–12.1849; m. 2.1836–1.1850
Status: LC; NLI (mf); Indexed by LA (to 1900)

Civil Parish: Ballingarry (2)
Map Grid: 125
RC Parish: see Knocklong
Diocese: EM

Civil Parish: Ballinlough
Map Grid: 111
RC Parish: see Hospital
Diocese: EM

Civil Parish: Ballybrood
Map Grid: 57
RC Parish: see Caherconlish
Diocese: EM

Civil Parish: Ballycahane
Map Grid: 38
RC Parish: see Fedamore
Diocese: LK

Civil Parish: Ballylanders
Map Grid: 126
RC Parish: Ballylanders
Diocese: EM
Earliest Record: b. 3.1849; m. 1.1857
Status: LC; NLI (mf); Indexed by LA (to 1900) and by THU (to 1899)

Civil Parish: Ballynaclough
Map Grid: 66

RC Parish: Pallasgreen, see Grean
Diocese: EM

Civil Parish: Ballynamona
Map Grid: 110
RC Parish: see Hospital
Diocese: EM

Civil Parish: Ballyscaddan
Map Grid: 119
RC Parish: see Emly, Co. Tipperary
Diocese: EM

Civil Parish: Bruff
Map Grid: 96
RC Parish: Bruff
Diocese: LK
Earliest Record: b. 11.1781; m. 2.1781
Missing Dates: b. 9.1792–12.1807
Status: LC; NLI (mf); Indexed by LA (to 1900)

Civil Parish: Bruree
Map Grid: 84
RC Parish: Rockhill
Diocese: LK
Earliest Record: b. 1.1842; m. 7.1861
Status: LC; NLI (mf); Indexed by LA (to 1900)

Civil Parish: Cahervally
Map Grid: 50
RC Parish: see Donaghmore
Diocese: LK

Civil Parish: Caherconlish
Map Grid: 53
RC Parish: Caherconlish
Diocese: EM
Earliest Record: b. 1.1841; m. 2.1841
Status: LC; NLI (mf); Indexed by LA (to 1900) and by THU (to 1899)

Civil Parish: Cahercorney
Map Grid: 106
RC Parish: see Hospital
Diocese: EM

Civil Parish: Caherelly
Map Grid: 55
RC Parish: Ballybricken, see Ludden
Diocese: EM

Civil Parish: Cahernarry
Map Grid: 51
RC Parish: see Donaghmore
Diocese: LK

Civil Parish: Cappagh
Map Grid: 17
RC Parish: Cappagh, see also Kilcornan
Diocese: LK
Earliest Record: b. 1.1841; m. 1.1841
Status: LC; NLI (mf); Indexed by LA (to 1900)

Civil Parish: Carrigparson
Map Grid: 49
RC Parish: part Caherconlish; part Ballybricken, see Ludden
Diocese: EM

Civil Parish: Castletown
Map Grid: 64
RC Parish: see Doon
Diocese: CA

Civil Parish: Chapelrussel
Map Grid: 26
RC Parish: see Kildimo
Diocese: LK

Civil Parish: Clonagh
Map Grid: 19
RC Parish: see Kilcolman
Diocese: LK

Civil Parish: Cloncagh
Map Grid: 80
RC Parish: Knockaderry and Cloncagh
Diocese: LK
Earliest Record: b. 2.1838; m. 2.1838
Status: LC; NLI (mf); Indexed by LA (to 1900)

Civil Parish: Cloncrew
Map Grid: 86
RC Parish: see Dromcolliher
Diocese: LK

Civil Parish: Clonelty or Clonulty
Map Grid: 73
RC Parish: see Cloncagh
Diocese: LK

Civil Parish: Clonkeen
Map Grid: 47
RC Parish: Murroe, see Abington
Diocese: EM

Civil Parish: Clonshire
Map Grid: 18
RC Parish: see Adare
Diocese: LK

Civil Parish: Colmanswell
Map Grid: 87
RC Parish: Ballyagran and Colmanswell
Diocese: LK
Earliest Record: b. 9.1841; m. 9.1841
Missing Dates: b. 11.1844-1.1847, 8.1847-9.1850; m. 9.1844-1.1847, 10.1847-1.1851, 11.1859-9.1860
Status: LC; NLI (mf); Indexed by LA (to 1900)

Civil Parish: Corcomohide
Map Grid: 83
RC Parish: Ballyagran, see Colmanswell
Diocese: LK

Civil Parish: Crecora
Map Grid: 35
RC Parish: Crecora, see Mungret
Diocese: LK

Civil Parish: Croagh
Map Grid: 22
RC Parish: Croagh and Kilfinny
Diocese: LK
Earliest Record: b. 8.1836; m. 1.1844
Missing Dates: b. 6.1843-11.1843
Status: LC; NLI (mf); Indexed by LA (to 1900)

Civil Parish: Croom
Map Grid: 91
RC Parish: Croom
Diocese: LK
Earliest Record: b. 10.1828; m. 12.1770; d. 12.1770
Missing Dates: m. 7.1794-8.1807; d. ends 7.1794
Status: LC; NLI (mf); Indexed by LA (to 1900)

Civil Parish: Darragh
Map Grid: 129
RC Parish: Glenroe and Ballyorgan
Diocese: LK
Earliest Record: b. 6.1853; m. 8.1853
Status: LC; NLI (mf); Indexed by LA (to 1900)

Civil Parish: Derrygalvin
Map Grid: 46
RC Parish: Limerick, St. Patrick's; also part Fedamore
Diocese: LK

Civil Parish: Donaghmore
Map Grid: 48
RC Parish: Donaghmore and Knockea
Diocese: LK
Earliest Record: b. 1.1830; m. 7.1827
Status: LC; NLI (mf); Indexed by LA (to 1900)

Civil Parish: Doon
Map Grid: 63
RC Parish: Doon and Castletown; also part Cappamore, see Tuogh
Diocese: EM
Earliest Record: b. 3.1824; m. 1.1839
Status: LC; NLI (mf); Indexed by LA (to 1900) and by THU (to 1899)

Civil Parish: Doondonnell
Map Grid: 20
RC Parish: Coolcappa, see Kilcolman
Diocese: LK

Civil Parish: Drehidtarsna
Map Grid: 90
RC Parish: see Adare
Diocese: LK

Civil Parish: Dromin
Map Grid: 97
RC Parish: Dromin and Athlacca
Diocese: LK

Earliest Record: b. 5.1817; m. 6.1817
Missing Dates: b. 9.1837–3.1849; m. 12.1837–11.1849
Status: LC; NLI (mf); Indexed by LA (to 1900)

Civil Parish: Dromkeen
Map Grid: 58
RC Parish: part Kilteely; also part Pallasgreen, see Grean
Diocese: EM

Civil Parish: Drumcolliher
Map Grid: 85
RC Parish: Drumcolliher and Broadford
Diocese: LK
Earliest Record: b. 3.1830; m. 1.1830
Missing Dates: b. 9.1850–11.1851; m. 9.1850–10.1851, 10.1864–5.1866
Status: LC; NLI (mf); Indexed by LA (to 1900)

Civil Parish: Dunmoylan
Map Grid: 7
RC Parish: Coolcappa, see Clonagh
Diocese: LK

Civil Parish: Dysert
Map Grid: 92
RC Parish: see Croom
Diocese: LK

Civil Parish: Effin
Map Grid: 102
RC Parish: Effin and Garrenderk
Diocese: LK
Earliest Record: b. 3.1843; m. 4.1843
Status: LC; NLI (mf); Indexed by LA (to 1900)

Civil Parish: Emlygreenan
Map Grid: 117
RC Parish: Ballinvana, see Kilbreedy Major
Diocese: LK

Civil Parish: Fedamore
Map Grid: 104
RC Parish: Fedamore, see also Monasteranenagh
Diocese: LK
Earliest Record: b. 10.1806; m. 10.1806
Missing Dates: b. 7.1813–1.1814, 1.1822–7.1854; m. 7.1813–1.1814, 11.1825–8.1854
Status: LC; NLI (mf); Indexed by LA (to 1900)

Civil Parish: Galbally
Map Grid: 120
RC Parish: Galbally and Aherhon
Diocese: EM
Earliest Record: b. 3.1810; m. 10.1809
Missing Dates: b. 7.1820–7.1821, 7.1812–12.1828; m. 3.1820–7.1821
Status: LC; NLI (mf); Indexed by LA (to 1900) and by THU (to 1899)

Civil Parish: Glenogra
Map Grid: 105

RC Parish: part Dromin; part Bruff
Diocese: LK

Civil Parish: Grange
Map Grid: 72
RC Parish: see Bruff
Diocese: LK

Civil Parish: Grean
Map Grid: 65
RC Parish: Pallasgreen
Diocese: EM
Earliest Record: b. 1.1811; m. 1.1811
Status: LC; NLI (mf); Indexed by THU (to 1899)

Civil Parish: Hackmys (see Co. Cork)
Map Grid: 100
RC Parish: Charleville, see Rathgoggan, Co. Cork
Diocese: LK

Civil Parish: Hospital
Map Grid: 112
RC Parish: Hospital and Herberstown
Diocese: EM
Earliest Record: b. 1.1810; m. 2.1812
Status: LC; NLI (mf); Indexed by THU (to 1899)

Civil Parish: Inch St. Laurence or Isertlawrence
Map Grid: 56
RC Parish: see Caherconlish
Diocese: EM

Civil Parish: Iveruss
Map Grid: 24
RC Parish: see Askeaton
Diocese: LK

Civil Parish: Kilbeheny
Map Grid: 130
RC Parish: Kilbehenny; also part Mitchelstown, see Brigown, Co. Cork
Diocese: EM
Earliest Record: b. 12.1824; m. 1.1825
Missing Dates: m. 2.1843–5.1843
Status: LC; NLI (mf); Indexed by LA (to 1900) and by THU (to 1899)

Civil Parish: Kilbolane
Map Grid: 88
RC Parish: see Kilbolane, Co. Cork
Diocese: CY

Civil Parish: Kilbradran
Map Grid: 9
RC Parish: Coolcappa, see Kilcolman
Diocese: LK

Civil Parish: Kilbreedy Major
Map Grid: 115
RC Parish: Bulgaden and Ballinvana
Diocese: LK
Earliest Record: b. 3.1812; m. 6.1812

Missing Dates: m. 11.1853–2.1854
Status: LC; NLI (mf); Indexed by LA (to 1900)

Civil Parish: Kilbreedy Minor
Map Grid: 101
RC Parish: see Effin
Diocese: LK

Civil Parish: Kilcolman
Map Grid: 8
RC Parish: Kilcolman and Coolcappa
Diocese: LK
Earliest Record: b. 10.1827; m. 1.1828
Status: LC; NLI (mf); Indexed by LA (to 1900)

Civil Parish: Kilcornan
Map Grid: 25
RC Parish: Kilcornan (Stonehall), see also Cappagh
Diocese: LK
Earliest Record: b. 4.1825; m. 4.1825
Missing Dates: m. 3.1848–9.1848
Status: LC; NLI (mf); Indexed by LA (to 1900)

Civil Parish: Kilcullane
Map Grid: 108
RC Parish: see Hospital
Diocese: EM

Civil Parish: Kildimo
Map Grid: 28
RC Parish: Kildimo and Chapel Russell
Diocese: LK
Earliest Record: b. 1.1831; m. 1.1831
Status: LC; NLI (mf); Indexed by LA (to 1900)

Civil Parish: Kilfergus
Map Grid: 2
RC Parish: Glin
Diocese: LK
Earliest Record: b. 10.1851; m. 10.1851
Status: LC; NLI (mf); Indexed by LA (to 1900)

Civil Parish: Kilfinane
Map Grid: 124
RC Parish: Kilfinane
Diocese: LK
Earliest Record: b. 6.1832; m. 8.1832
Status: LC; NLI (mf); Indexed by LA (to 1900)

Civil Parish: Kilfinny
Map Grid: 79
RC Parish: see Croagh
Diocese: LK

Civil Parish: Kilflyn
Map Grid: 128
RC Parish: see Darragh
Diocese: LK

Civil Parish: Kilfrush
Map Grid: 113
RC Parish: see Hospital
Diocese: EM

Civil Parish: Kilkeedy
Map Grid: 29
RC Parish: Patrickswell (Lurriga)
Diocese: LK
Earliest Record: b. 10.1801; m. 4.1802
Status: LC; NLI (mf); Indexed by LA (to 1900)

Civil Parish: Killagholehane (Killaliathan)
Map Grid: 78
RC Parish: see Drumcolliher
Diocese: LK

Civil Parish: Killeedy
Map Grid: 77
RC Parish: Tournafulla; also part Newcastle
Diocese: LK
Earliest Record: b. 8.1840; m. 12.1840
Status: LC; NLI (mf); Indexed by LA (to 1900)

Civil Parish: Killeely
Map Grid: 30
RC Parish: see Killeely, Co. Clare
Diocese: LK

Civil Parish: Killeengarriff
Map Grid: 43
RC Parish: see Fedamore
Diocese: LK

Civil Parish: Killeenoghty
Map Grid: 37
RC Parish: see Mungret
Diocese: LK

Civil Parish: Killonahan (Killelonahan)
Map Grid: 34
RC Parish: see Mungret
Diocese: LK

Civil Parish: Kilmeedy
Map Grid: 82
RC Parish: Feenagh and Kilmeedy
Diocese: LK
Earliest Record: b. 8.1833; m. 7.1854
Status: LC; NLI (mf); Indexed by LA (to 1900)

Civil Parish: Kilmoylan
Map Grid: 6
RC Parish: see Shanagolden
Diocese: LK

Civil Parish: Kilmurry
Map Grid: 42
RC Parish: see Limerick—St. Patrick's
Diocese: LK

Civil Parish: Kilpeacon
Map Grid: 103
RC Parish: see Fedamore
Diocese: LK

Civil Parish: Kilquane (see also Co. Cork)
Map Grid: 127

RC Parish: Kilmallock, see SS Peter and Paul
Diocese: LK

Civil Parish: Kilscannell
Map Grid: 23
RC Parish: part Ardagh; part Rathkeale
Diocese: LK

Civil Parish: Kilteely
Map Grid: 69
RC Parish: Kilteely and Dromkeen
Diocese: EM
Earliest Record: b. 12.1815; m. 11.1832
Missing Dates: b. 4.1829–9.1832
Status: LC; NLI (mf); Indexed by LA (to 1900) and by THU (to 1899)

Civil Parish: Knockaney or Aney
Map Grid: 107
RC Parish: Knockainy and Patrickswell
Diocese: EM
Earliest Record: b. 3.1808; m. 4.1808; d. 6.1819
Missing Dates: m. 10.1821–1.1822, 2.1841–5.1841; d. ends 3.1821
Status: LC; NLI (mf); Indexed by LA (to 1900) and by THU (to 1899)

Civil Parish: Knocklong
Map Grid: 118
RC Parish: Knocklong and Glenbrohane
Diocese: EM
Earliest Record: b. 4.1809; m. 4.1809
Missing Dates: b. 6.1819–9.1823, 6.1830–1.1832, 7.1854–11.1854; m. 10.1819–1.1824, 10.1831–1.1836, 2.1854–8.1854
Status: LC; NLI (mf); Indexed by LA (to 1900) and by THU (to 1899)

Civil Parish: Knocknagaul
Map Grid: 36
RC Parish: see Mungret
Diocese: LK

Civil Parish: Limerick—St. John's
Map Grid: 1
RC Parish: St. John's
Diocese: LK
Earliest Record: b. 5.1788; m. 7.1821
Missing Dates: b. 12.1797–1.1825
Status: LC; NLI (mf); Indexed by LA (to 1900)

Civil Parish: Limerick—St. Lawrence's
Map Grid: 44
RC Parish: see St. John's
Diocese: LK

Civil Parish: Limerick—St. Mary's (see Limerick—St. Nicholas)

Civil Parish: Limerick—St. Michael's
Map Grid: 33
RC Parish: St. Michael; also part St. John's
Diocese: LK

Earliest Record: b. 8.1776; m. 2.1772
Missing Dates: b. 10.1801–1.1803, 2.1807–10.1807, 4.1813–1.1814, 9.1819–1.1820; m. 9.1802–3.1803, 7.1804–10.1807, 5.1813–6.1814, 11.1819–5.1821, 10.1861–1.1863
Status: LC; NLI (mf); Indexed by LA (to 1900)

Civil Parish: Limerick—St. Munchin's (see also Co. Clare)
Map Grid: 31
RC Parish: St. Munchin; also St. Mary's, see St. Nicholas
Diocese: LK
Earliest Record: b. 11.1764; m. 11.1764
Missing Dates: b. 5.1792–10.1798; m. 5.1792–10.1798, 5.1819–9.1819

Civil Parish: Limerick—St. Nicholas; see St. Mary's
Map Grid: 45
RC Parish: St. Mary's; also part St. Munchin's
Diocese: LK
Earliest Record: b. 1.1745; m. 10.1745
Status: LC; NLI (mf); Indexed by LA (to 1900)

Civil Parish: Limerick—St. Patrick's (see also Co. Clare)
Map Grid: 41
RC Parish: St. Patrick's
Diocese: LK
Earliest Record: b. 1.1805; m. 1.1806
Missing Dates: m. 9.1840–2.1841
Status: LC; NLI (mf); Indexed by LA (to 1900)

Civil Parish: Lismakeery
Map Grid: 15
RC Parish: see Askeaton
Diocese: LK

Civil Parish: Loughill
Map Grid: 3
RC Parish: Loughill (previously part of Glin) and Ballyhahill (previously part of Shanagolden)
Diocese: LK
Earliest Record: b. 10.1855; m. 11.1855
Status: LC; NLI (mf); Indexed by LA (to 1900)

Civil Parish: Ludden
Map Grid: 52
RC Parish: Ballybricken (and Bohermore)
Diocese: EM
Earliest Record: b. 11.1800; m. 8.1805
Status: LC; NLI (mf); Indexed by LA (to 1900) and by THU (to 1899)

Civil Parish: Mahoonagh
Map Grid: 76
RC Parish: Mahoonagh
Diocese: LK
Earliest Record: b. 3.1812; m. 8.1810
Missing Dates: b. 8.1830–6.1832, 7.1838–11.1839;

m. 5.1839–2.1840
Status: LC; NLI (mf); Indexed by LA (to 1900)

Civil Parish: Monagay (1)
Map Grid: 75
RC Parish: Monagea; also part Templeglantine, see below
Diocese: LK
Earliest Record: b. 1776; m. 1.1777
Missing Dates: b. 7.1813–3.1829, 12.1831–8.1833; m. 2.1792–1.1829
Status: LC; NLI (mf); Indexed by LA (to 1900)

Civil Parish: Monagay (2)
Map Grid: 75
RC Parish: Templeglantine
Diocese: LK
Earliest Record: b. 12.1864; m. 1.1865
Status: LC; NLI (mf); Indexed by LA (to 1900)

Civil Parish: Monasteranenagh
Map Grid: 39
RC Parish: Manister
Diocese: LK
Earliest Record: b. 1.1826; m. 1.1826
Status: LC; NLI (mf); Indexed by LA (to 1900)

Civil Parish: Morgans
Map Grid: 12
RC Parish: see Shanagolden
Diocese: LK

Civil Parish: Mungret
Map Grid: 32
RC Parish: Mungret and Crecora
Diocese: LK
Earliest Record: b. 11.1844; m. 11.1844
Status: LC; NLI (mf); Indexed by LA (to 1900)

Civil Parish: Nantinan
Map Grid: 16
RC Parish: see Cappagh
Diocese: LK

Civil Parish: Newcastle
Map Grid: 71
RC Parish: Newcastle West
Diocese: LK
Earliest Record: b. 5.1815; m. 4.1815 (also workhouse records from 11.1852)
Missing Dates: m. 11.1831–2.1834
Status: LC; NLI (mf); Indexed by LA (to 1900)

Civil Parish: Oola
Map Grid: 68
RC Parish: Oola and Solohead
Diocese: EM
Earliest Record: b. 10.1809; m. 1.1810
Missing Dates: b. 4.1828–2.1837; m. 11.1828–10.1832
Status: LC; NLI (mf); Indexed by LA and by THU (to 1900)

Civil Parish: Particles
Map Grid: 123
RC Parish: see Kifinane
Diocese: LK

Civil Parish: Rathjordan
Map Grid: 59
RC Parish: see Hospital
Diocese: EM

Civil Parish: Rathkeale
Map Grid: 21
RC Parish: Rathkeale
Diocese: LK
Earliest Record: b. 1.1811; m. 1.1811
Missing Dates: b. 7.1823–9.1831
Status: LC; NLI (mf); Indexed by LA (to 1900)

Civil Parish: Rathronan (1)
Map Grid: 10
RC Parish: Athea; also part Ardagh; also part Cratloe, see below
Diocese: LK
Earliest Record: b. 4.1830; m. 11.1827
Status: LC; NLI (mf); Indexed by LA (to 1900)

Civil Parish: Rathronan (2)
Map Grid: 10
RC Parish: Cratloe (see Co. Clare)
Diocese: LK
Earliest Record: b. 11.1802; m. 1.1822
Status: LC; NLI (mf); Indexed by LA (to 1900)

Civil Parish: Robertstown
Map Grid: 5
RC Parish: see Shanagolden
Diocese: LK

Civil Parish: Rochestown
Map Grid: 54
RC Parish: Ballybricken, see Ludden
Diocese: EM

Civil Parish: St. John's
Map Grid: 1
RC Parish: see Limerick—St. John's
Diocese: LK

Civil Parish: St. Lawrence's
Map Grid: 44
RC Parish: see Limerick—St. Lawrence's
Diocese: LK

Civil Parish: St. Mary's
Map Grid: between 41 and 45
RC Parish: see Limerick—St. Mary's
Diocese: LK

Civil Parish: St. Michael's
Map Grid: 33
RC Parish: see Limerick—St. Michael's
Diocese: LK

Civil Parish: St. Munchin's
Map Grid: 31
RC Parish: see Limerick–St. Munchin's
Diocese: LK

Civil Parish: St. Nicholas
Map Grid: 45
RC Parish: see Limerick–St. Nicholas
Diocese: LK

Civil Parish: St. Patrick's
Map Grid: 41
RC Parish: see Limerick–St. Patrick's
Diocese: LK

Civil Parish: St. Peter's and St. Paul's
Map Grid: 114
RC Parish: Kilmallock
Diocese: LK
Earliest Record: b. 10.1837; m. 11.1837
Status: LC; NLI (mf); Indexed by LA (to 1900)

Civil Parish: Shanagolden
Map Grid: 4
RC Parish: Shanagolden and Foynes
Diocese: LK
Earliest Record: b. 4.1824; m. 4.1824
Status: LC; NLI (mf); Indexed by LA (to 1900)

Civil Parish: Stradbally
Map Grid: 40
RC Parish: Castleconnell
Diocese: KL
Earliest Record: b. 2.1850; m. 8.1863
Status: LC; NLI (mf); Indexed by LA (to 1900)

Civil Parish: Tankardstown
Map Grid: 99
RC Parish: Kilmallock, see SS Peter and Paul
Diocese: LK

Civil Parish: Templebredon (see also Co. Tipperary)
Map Grid: 70
RC Parish: Pallasgreen, see Grean
Diocese: EM

Civil Parish: Tomdeely
Map Grid: 13
RC Parish: see Askeaton
Diocese: LK

Civil Parish: Tullabracky
Map Grid: 94
RC Parish: see Bruff
Diocese: LK

Civil Parish: Tuogh
Map Grid: 62
RC Parish: Cappamore
Diocese: EM
Earliest Record: b. 4.1845; m. 2.1843

Status: LC; NLI (mf); Indexed by LA and by THU (to 1899)

Civil Parish: Tuoghcluggin
Map Grid: 67
RC Parish: part Pallasgreen, see Grean; part Doon
Diocese: EM

Civil Parish: Uregare
Map Grid: 98
RC Parish: part Dromin; part Bruff
Diocese: LK

Society of Friends (Quakers)

See the introduction for an account of Quaker sources, which are extensive. A specific source for Limerick is:

Limerick Meeting: b/m/d. 1623-1863. OCM 14: 564-626 and SLC film 571396.

Commercial and Social Directories

1769

John Ferrar's *Directory of Limerick* contains an alphabetical list of merchants, traders, city officials, military personnel, Anglican clergy, and church wardens; also lists of revenue officers at Limerick, Scattery, Kilrush, and Tarbert; lists of barristers, attorneys, and public notaries; a list of guilds officers, physicians, surgeons, and apothecaries; and a list of Freemason officers. Also published in *Ir. Gen.* 3 (9) (1964): 329-40. Can also be accessed on the Internet at http://members.aol.com/LABATH/limerick.htm. SLC 941.5 A1.

1788

Richard Lucas's *General Directory of the Kingdom of Ireland* contains lists of traders in Limerick. Also reprinted in *The Irish Genealogist* 3 (12) (1967): 529-37. Can also be accessed on the Internet at http://members.aol.com/LABATH/lim1788.htm.

1809

Holden's *Triennial Directory* has alphabetical lists of traders in Limerick City. SLC films 100179 and 258722.

1820

J. Pigot's *Commercial Directory of Ireland* contains information on the gentry, nobility, and traders in and around the city of Limerick.

1824

J. Pigot's *City of Dublin and Hibernian Provincial Directory* includes traders, nobility, gentry, and clergy lists of Castleconnell, Kilmallock, Limerick, Newcastle, and Rathkeale.

1840

F. Kinder's *New Triennial and Commercial Directory for 1840, '41 and '42* gives traders, nobility, etc., for Limerick City (rare volume).

1846

Slater's *National Commercial Directory of Ireland* lists nobility, clergy, traders, etc., in Adare, Bruff, Castleconnell and O'Brien's Bridge, Croom, Kilmallock, Limerick, Newcastle, and Rathkeale.

1856

Slater's *Royal National Commercial Directory of Ireland* lists nobility, gentry, clergy, traders, etc., in Adare, Bruff, Castleconnell and O'Brien's Bridge, Croom, Kilmallock, Limerick, Newcastle, and Rathkeale.

1866

G.H. Bassett's *Directory of the City and County of Limerick and of the Principal Towns in the Cos. of Tipperary and Clare* has traders lists for Adare, Castleconnell, Kilmallock, Limerick, Newcastle, and Rathkeale and an alphabetical list of the gentry in the county.

1870

Slater's *Directory of Ireland* contains trade, nobility, and clergy lists of Adare, Askeaton, Bruff, Castleconnell, Croom, Kilmallock, Limerick, Newcastle, and Rathkeale.

1879

G.H. Bassett's *Limerick Directory* has a list of residents, professions, and traders in Limerick City and a list of traders in the towns of Abbeyfeale, Adare, Ardagh, Ashford, Askeaton, Athea, Broadford, Bruff, Caherconlish, Castleconnell, Croom, Drumcollogher, Foynes, Glin, Hospital, Kilmallock, Murroe, Newcastle West, Oola, Pallaskenry, Rathkeale, Shanagolden, and Tournafulla. There is also a list of gentlemen in the county.

1881

Slater's *Royal National Commercial Directory of Ireland* contains lists of traders, clergy, nobility, and farmers in adjoining parishes of the towns of Adare and Croom, Askeaton, Castleconnell and O'Brien's Bridge, Foynes (see Tarbert, Commercial and Social Directories section, Co. Kerry), Kilmallock, Limerick, Newcastle West, and Rathkeale.

1886

Francis Guy's *Postal Directory of Munster* lists gentry, clergy, traders, principal farmers, teachers, and police sergeants in each postal district of the county and has a listing of magistrates, clergy, and the professions. SLC film 1559399.

1893

Francis Guy's *Directory of Munster* lists traders and farmers in each of the postal districts of the county and a general alphabetical index to persons in the whole county.

1894

Slater's *Royal National Directory of Ireland* lists traders, police, teachers, farmers, and private residents in each of the towns, villages, and parishes in the county.

Note also that there are national directories for some of the professions, including medicine and the clergy.

Family History

Pedigrees of Clare, Galway, and Limerick families. GO Ms. 520; SLC film 257821.

"Bevan of Co. Limerick." *Ir. Anc.* 6 (1) (1974): 1–5.

"Carrigogunnell Castle and the O'Briens of Pubblebrien in the Co. Limerick." *R.S.A.I.* 37 (1907): 374–92; 38 (1908): 141–59.

"The Desmonds Castle at Newcastle Oconyll, Co. Limerick." *R.S.A.I.* 39 (1909): 42–58, 350–68.

"The Family Bible of John Ganley, William St., Limerick." *Ir. Anc.* 9 (2) (1979): 84–85.

Going—see Co. Tipperary.

"O'Grady of Cappercullen (Co. Limerick)." *N. Munster Antiq. J.* 7 (4) (1957): 20–22.

"O'Grady Papers (Kilballyowen, Co. Limerick)." *Anal. Hib.* 15: 35–62.

"Harte of Co. Limerick." Pedigree in *Swanzy Notebooks.* RCB Library, Dublin.

"Families of Hodges and Morgan of Old Abbey, Co. Limerick." *Ir. Anc.* 11 (2) (1979): 77–84.

Ferrar, Michael Lloyd. *The Limerick Huntingdon Ferrars by One of Them.* Plymouth, n.d.

"The MacSheehys of Connelloe, Co. Limerick." *Ir. Gen.* 4 (1970): 560–77.

"Monckton of Co. Limerick." *Ir. Anc.* 4 (1) (1972): 15–21.

Morgan—see Hodges.

"Nihell of Clare and Limerick." *Ir. Gen.* 4 (5) (1972): 496–506.

"The Peppards of Cappagh, Co. Limerick." *Ir. Anc.* 16 (2) (1984): 68–70.

"Roches of Newcastlewest, Co. Limerick." *Ir. Gen.* 2 (1950): 244–45.

"Scanlan of the Barony of Upper Connello, Co. Limerick." *Ir. Anc.* 4 (2) (1972): 71–80.

"Limerick O'Shaughnessy's." *Irish Family History* 9 (1993): 10–16.

The O'Shaughnessys of Munster. See Family History—Co. Galway.

Tuthill, P.B. *Pedigrees of Families of Tuthill and Villiers of Co. Limerick* (with notes). London, 1907-08.

Villiers—see Tuthill.

"The Vincent Family of Limerick and Clare." *Ir. Gen.* 4 (4) (1971): 347-48.

White, J.D. *The History of the Family of White of Limerick, Cappawhite.* Cashel, 1887.

Gravestone Inscriptions

Ardcanny: *Ir. Anc.* 9 (1) (1977): 3-5.

Ardpatrick: Fleming, John. *Reflections, Historical and Topographical, on Ardpatrick, Co. Limerick.* 1979.

Askeaton: IGRS Collection. GO.

Athlacca: Seoighe, Mainchin. *Dromin and Athlacca.* 1978.

Ballingarry: Hamilton, Rev. G.F. *Records of Ballingarry.* 1930. SLC film 990178.

Bruree: Mannix, Joyce. *Bruree (Brú Rí)—History of the Parish of Bruree and its Old Parish of Tankardstown.* Bruree-Rockwell Development Association, 1973.

Dromin: Seoighe, Mainchin. *Dromin and Athlacca.* 1978.

Grange: *Ir. Anc.* 10 (1) (1978): 49-51.

Kilbehenny: *Ir. Gen.* 2 (11) (1954): 349-54.

Knockainey (Lough Gur): *L. Gur. Hist. Soc. J.* 1 (1985): 51-61.

Knockainey (Patrickswell): *L. Gur. Hist. Soc. J.* 2 (1986): 71-79.

Limerick City Cemetery: Indexed by Limerick Archives (see Research Services).

Lough Gur—see Knockainey.

Mount St. Laurence (1855-1982): SLC films 1419439-41.

Nantinan: *Ir. Anc.* 7 (1980).

Patrickswell—see Knockainey.

Plassey: GO Ms. 622, 85.

Rathkeale, C of I: *Ir. Anc.* 14 (2) (1982): 105-20.

St. Mary's Cathedral: Talbot, Very Rev. M. *The Monuments of St. Mary's Cathedral, Limerick.* 1976 (available from the cathedral).

Stradbally: IGRS Collection, GO.

Tankardstown: Mannix, Joyce. *Bruree (Brú Rí)—History of the Parish of Bruree and its Old Parish of Tankardstown.* Bruree-Rockwell Development Association, 1973.

Newspapers

A card index to biographical notices in Limerick, Ennis, Clonmel, and Waterford newspapers up to 1821 (50,000 items) is in the library of University College, Cork. Microfiche copies of this are in Limerick Archives, the NLI, the library of University College, Dublin, and the New York Public Library. Albert O'Casey's *O'Kief, Coshe Mang and Slieve Luachra (OCM)* also has indexed (mainly Kerry) notices from some Limerick papers. In addition, papers from surrounding counties of Kerry, Cork, and Tipperary also extensively reported Limerick events and people. These should also be consulted. The newspaper sections in these chapters provide information about indexes available.

Title: *General Advertiser* or *Limerick Gazette*
Published in: Limerick, 1804-20 (index 1822-40)
NLI Holdings: 9.1809-9.1818
BL Holdings: 9.1804-11.1820
Indexed (1756-1827) in ffolliot Index; Indexed (1822-40) in OCM 11

Title: *Limerick and Clare Examiner*
Published in: Limerick, 1846-55
BL Holdings: 1.1846-6.1855

Title: *Limerick Chronicle*
Published in: Limerick, 1766-current (index 1822-40)
NLI Holdings: odd numbers 1768-1831; 1841-42; 1844-45; 1847-48; 1852; 1855; 1859-8.1921; 8.1927-12.1981; 1.1982-in progress
BL Holdings: odd numbers 1768-1869; 1.1879-in progress
Indexed (1756-1827) in ffolliot Index; Indexed (1822-40) in OCM 11

Title: *Limerick Evening Post* (continued as *Limerick Evening Post and Clare Sentinel* in 1828)
Published in: Limerick, 1811-33
NLI Holdings: 10.1811-12.1813; 3.1814-12.1818; 3.1828-12.1833
BL Holdings: 1-4.1828; 10.1832-3.1833; 8-12.1833
Indexed (1756-1827) in ffolliot Index; Indexed (1822-40) in OCM 11

Title: *Limerick Gazette*—see *General Advertiser*

Title: *Limerick Herald* (continued as *Limerick Evening Herald* in 1833)
Published in: Limerick, 1831-35
NLI Holdings: 4.1831-4.1835
BL Holdings: 4.1831-4.1835
Indexed (1756-1827) in ffolliot Index

Title: *Limerick Journal* (continued as *Munster Journal* in 1774)
Published in: Limerick, 1739-44
NLI Holdings: 11.8.1741 (one issue)
BL Holdings: odd numbers 1761; 1766-77
Indexed (1756-1827) in ffolliot Index

Title: *Limerick Leader*
Published in: Limerick, 1889-current
NLI Holdings: 6.1893-in progress
BL Holdings: 6.1893-12.1925; 8.1926-in progress
Other Holdings: *The Limerick Leader*, a current

Limerick newspaper, has an almost complete run of this paper.

Title: *Limerick Reporter* (continued as *Limerick Reporter and Tipperary Vindicator* in 1850)
Published in: Limerick, 1839–99 (index 1839)
NLI Holdings: 7.1839–12.1855; 4.1856–12.1895
BL Holdings: 7.1839–10.1871; 1.1872–1.1896
Indexed (1839) in OCM 11

Title: *Munster Journal*
Published in: Limerick, ca. 1737–77 (index 1939)
NLI Holdings: 5.1749–1.1755
BL Holdings: 5.1749–1.1755
Indexed (1749–1750) in OCM 11

Title: *Munster News*
Published in: Limerick, 1851–1935
NLI Holdings: 6.1851–1.1871; 6.1873–8.1922; 2.1925–6.1935
BL Holdings: 6.1851–1.1871; 5.1873–6.1920; 1.1921–12.1925; 1.1927–6.1935

Title: *Southern Advertiser*
Published in: Limerick, ca. 1889–93
BL Holdings: 4.1889–3.1893

Title: *Southern Chronicle* (called *Limerick Southern Chronicle* from 1864 and *Bassett's Chronicle* from 1875)
Published in: Limerick, 1863–85
NLI Holdings: 1.1865–12.1867; 1871–72
BL Holdings: 4.1863–5.1873; 4.1874–8.1875; 10.1875–12.1885

Wills and Administrations

A discussion of the types of records, where they are held, and their availability and value is given in the Wills section of the introduction. The availability of prerogative wills, administrations, and marriage license records is also described in the relevant parts of the same section. Where available, published sources of these records are given in the Miscellaneous Sources section.

Pre-1858 Wills and Administrations

Prerogative Wills. See the introduction.

Consistorial Wills. County Limerick is in the dioceses of Emly and Limerick, with a few parishes in Cashel, Killaloe, and Cloyne. The guide to Church of Ireland parish records in this chapter shows the diocese to which each civil parish belonged. The wills of residents of each diocese were usually proven within that diocese (see the Wills section for exceptions). The following records survive:

Wills

See the introduction.

Abstracts

See the introduction. The Westropp manuscripts in the RIA have many abstracts of wills and administrations from counties Clare and Limerick.

Indexes

Limerick (1615–1858). Up to 1800 published by Phillimore. Killaloe—see Co. Clare. Cloyne—see Co. Cork.

Post-1858 Wills and Administrations

This county was served by the District Registry of Limerick. The surviving records are kept in the NAI and are on microfilm in Mid-West Regional Archives (see Research Sources and Services section). Limerick District Will Books (1858–88): NAI; SLC film 100946–7.

Marriage Licenses

Indexes

Emly (1664–1857). NAI; SLC film 100861. Limerick (1691–1845). NAI; SLC film 100869. Cashel—see Co. Tipperary. Killaloe—see Co. Clare.

Miscellaneous Sources

"The Arthur Manuscripts" (medical records, wills and mortgages, accounts, and other records kept by Dr. Arthur of Limerick, 1590–1675). *N. Munster Antiq. J.* 6 (2) (1950): 29–40; continued in 6 (3) (1951): 67–82; 7 (1) (1953): 168–82; 7 (4) (1957): 4–10; 8 (1) (1958): 2–19.

White, Rev. P. *History of Clare and Dalcassian Clans of Tipperary, Limerick and Galway.* Dublin, 1893.

O'Mahony, S.C. *Poor Law Records of County Limerick, Clare and Tipperary. N. Munster Antiq. J.* Supplement to Vol. 21, 1979.

"An Elizabethan Map of Kilmallock." *N. Munster Antiq. J.* 11 (1968): 27–35.

"Emigration from Kilmallock Workhouse, 1848–1860." *L. Gur Hist. Soc. J.* 3 (1987); also *Ir. Anc.* 14 (2) (1982): 83–94.

Ferrar, J. *The History of Limerick to the Year 1787.* Limerick, 1787.

Fitzgerald, P., and J. McGregor. *The History, Topography and Antiquities of the County and City of Limerick.* 2 vols. Limerick, 1825–27.

"The German Colony in Co. Limerick." *N. Munster Antiq. J.* 1 (2) (1937): 42–53.

Hamilton, G.F. *Records of Ballingarry.* Limerick, 1930.

Herbert, R. *Worthies of Thomond. A compendium of short lives of the most famous men and women of Limerick and Clare to the present day.* Third Series. Limerick: The Leader, 1946.

Nash, Roisin. *A Bibliography of Limerick.* Limerick, 1962.

"Limerick Shop Signs of the Eighteenth Century." *N. Munster Antiq. J.* 2 (4) (1941): 156-66 (lists proprietors names, occupations, and relationships in some cases).

Tierney, Dom Mark. "Murroe and Boher." The history of an Irish country parish.

"The Silvermakers of Limerick." *Ir. Anc.* 10 (2) (1978): 99-107.

"The Trade Guilds of Limerick." *N. Munster Antiq. J.* 2 (3) (1941): 121-34 (names officials and members in some cases).

Mannix, Joyce. *Bruree (Brú Rí)–History of the Parish of Bruree and its Old Parish of Tankardstown.* Bruree-Rockwell Development Association, 1973 (includes abstracts from *Tithe Applotment* books, *Griffith's Valuation,* and other local sources; memorial inscriptions from Bruree and Tankardstown churchyards).

Kenmare Estates: Rent Rolls for Lord Viscount Kenmare's Estates in Kerry, Limerick, and Bantry, Co. Cork. NAI; SLC films 101772-9.

Register of Congregational Church, Henry St., Limerick (b. 1817-71; m. 1819-60). Mulligan & Vance, 1965; SLC film 496750.

St. John's Hospital Register (1816-26). SLC film 1279251.

Research Sources and Services

Journals

North Munster Antiquarian Society Journal
Old Limerick Journal
Limerick Field Journal

Libraries and Information Sources

Limerick County Library, 58 O'Connell Street, Limerick. Ph: (061) 318692/318477. The library has a local history section and bibliography of Limerick.

Limerick City Library, The Granary, Limerick. Ph: (061) 314668. This library has a local history section.

Research Services

Limerick Archives, The Granary, Michael St., Limerick. Contact: Dr. Chris O'Mahony. Ph: (061) 41077. This is the official IGP center for county Limerick. It is a long-established service, originally known as Mid-West Archives. It has indexed all of the records for Limerick and has also indexed many other local sources. Researchers are advised to contact the archives for an updated list of registers, and other sources, indexed. A research service is provided for a fee.

Tipperary Heritage Unit, The Bridewell, St. Michael St., Tipperary Town, Ireland. Ph/Fax: (062) 52725; e-mail: thu@iol.ie. This center has exclusive access to Catholic records of the RC Diocese of Cashel and Emly. They have indexed the baptismal and marriage records and *Griffith's Valuation,* and have access to the 1901 census. A search service will be provided for a fee.

See also Research Services in Dublin in the introduction.

Societies

Knockfierna Heritage and Folklore Group, Mr. David O'Riordan, Kilmore, Cranagh, Co. Limerick

Lough Gur and District Historical Society, Ms. Elizabeth Clifford, Crean, Bruff, Co. Limerick

Newcastle Historical Society, Mr. John Cussen, Cloneen, Gortboy, Newcastle West, Co. Limerick

Thomond Archaeological Society, Ms. Anne Yeoman, 9 Ashbrook, Ennis Road, Limerick

Limerick Civil Parishes as Numbered on Map

1. St. John's (parts of other Limerick city parishes)
2. Kilfergus
3. Loughill (3 pts.)
4. Shanagolden
5. Robertstown
6. Kilmoylan
7. Dunmoylan (3 pts.)
8. Kilcolman
9. Kilbradran (2 pts.)
10. Rathronan (2 pts.)
11. Ardagh (3 pts.)
12. Morgans
13. Tomdeely
14. Askeaton
15. Lismakeery
16. Nantinan (3 pts.)
17. Cappagh
18. Clonshire
19. Clonagh
20. Doondonnell
21. Rathkeale (2 pts.)
22. Croagh (2 pts.)
23. Kilsconnell
24. Iveruss
25. Kilcornan
26. Chapelrussell
27. Ardcanny
28. Kildimo
29. Kilkeedy
30. Killeely (2 pts.)
31. St. Munchin's
32. Mungret
33. St. Michael's
34. Killonahan
35. Crecora
36. Knocknagaul
37. Killeenoghty
38. Ballycahane
39. Monasteranenagh (2 pts.)
40. Stradbally
41. St. Patrick's
42. Kilmurry

43. Killeenagarriff
44. St. Lawrence's
45. St. Nicholas
46. Derrygalvin (2 pts.)
47. Clonkeen
48. Donaghmore
49. Carrigparson
50. Caheravally (2 pts.)
51. Cahernarry
52. Ludden
53. Caherconlish
54. Rochestown
55. Caherelly
56. Inch St. Lawrence
57. Ballybrood
58. Dromkeen
59. Rathjordan
60. Aglishcormick
61. Abington
62. Tuogh
63. Doon (4 pts.)
64. Castletown
65. Grean
66. Ballynaclough (3 pts.)
67. Tuoghcluggin (2 pts.)
68. Oola
69. Kilteely
70. Templebredon
71. Newcastle
72. Grange
73. Clonulty
74. Abbeyfeale
75. Monagay (3 pts.)
76. Mahoonagh
77. Killeedy (4 pts.)
78. Killagholane
79. Kilfinny
80. Cloncagh
81. Ballingarry (2 pts.)
82. Kilmeedy
83. Corcomohide

84. Bruree
85. Drumcolliher
86. Cloncrew
87. Colmanswell
88. Kilbolane
89. Adare
90. Drehidtarana
91. Croom (2 pts.)
92. Dysert
93. Anhid
94. Tullabracky
95. Athlacca
96. Bruff
97. Dromin
98. Uregare
99. Tankardstown
100. Hackmys
101. Kilbreedy Minor
102. Effin
103. Kilpeacon
104. Fedamore
105. Glenogra
106. Cahercorney
107. Knockainy (2 pts.)

108. Kilcullane
109. Ballinard
110. Ballynamona
111. Ballinlough
112. Hospital
113. Kilfrush
114. St. Peter's and St. Paul's
115. Kilbreedy Major
116. Athneasy
117. Emlygreenan
118. Knocklong
119. Ballyscadden
120. Galbally
121. Ardpatrick (2 pts.)
122. Ballingaddy
123. Particles
124. Kilfinnane
125. Ballingarry
126. Ballylanders
127. Kilquane
128. Kilflyn
129. Darragh
130. Kilbeheny

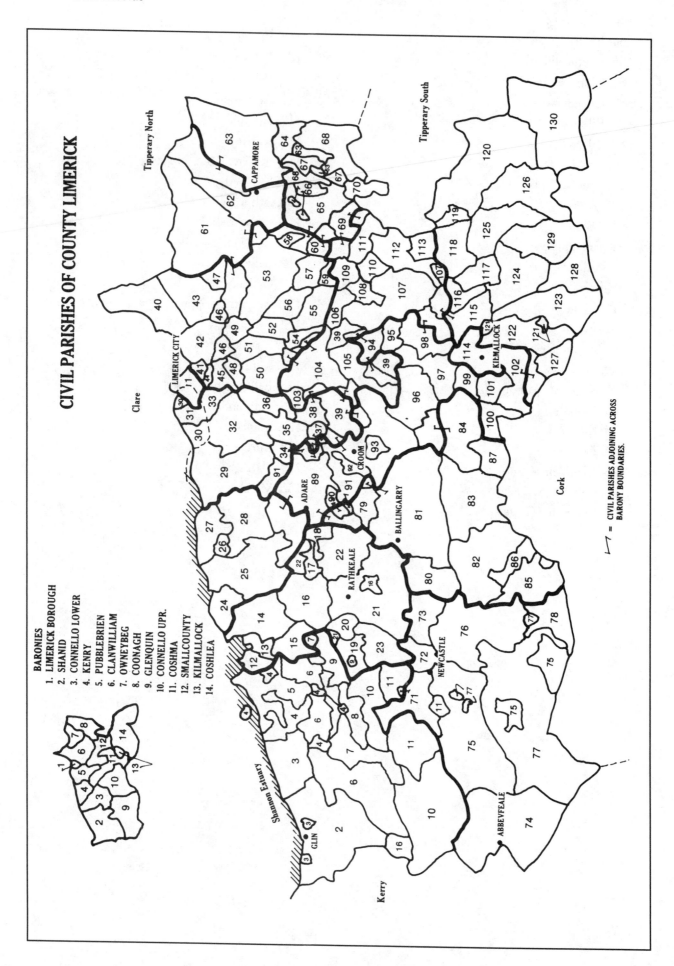

CIVIL PARISHES OF COUNTY LIMERICK

BARONIES
1. LIMERICK BOROUGH
2. SHANID
3. CONNELLO LOWER
4. KENRY
5. PUBBLEBRIEN
6. CLANWILLIAM
7. OWNEYBEG
8. COONAGH
9. GLENQUIN
10. CONNELLO UPR.
11. COSHMA
12. SMALLCOUNTY
13. KILMALLOCK
14. COSHLEA

= CIVIL PARISHES ADJOINING ACROSS
BARONY BOUNDARIES.

Limerick Civil Parishes in Alphabetical Order

Abbeyfeale: 74

Abington: 61

Adare: 89

Aglishcormick: 60

Anhid: 93

Ardagh (3 pts.): 11

Ardcanny: 27

Ardpatrick (2 pts.): 121

Askeaton: 14

Athlacca: 95

Athneasy: 116

Ballinard: 109

Ballingaddy: 122

Ballingarry (2 pts.): 81

Ballingarry: 125

Ballinlough: 111

Ballybrood: 57

Ballycahane: 38

Ballylanders: 126

Ballynaclough (3 pts.): 66

Ballynamona: 110

Ballyscadden: 119

Bruff: 96

Bruree: 84

Caheravally (2 pts.): 50

Caherconlish: 53

Cahercorney: 106

Caherelly: 55

Cahernarry: 51

Cappagh: 17

Carrigparson: 49

Castletown: 64

Chapelrussell: 26

Clonagh: 19

Cloncagh: 80

Cloncrew: 86

Clonkeen: 47

Clonshire: 18

Clonulty: 73

Colmanswell: 87

Corcomohide: 83

Crecora: 35

Croagh (2 pts.): 22

Croom (2 pts.): 91

Darragh: 129

Derrygalvin (2 pts.): 46

Donaghmore: 48

Doon (4 pts.): 63

Doondonnell: 20

Drehidtarana: 90

Dromin: 97

Dromkeen: 58

Drumcolliher: 85

Dunmoylan (3 pts.): 7

Dysert: 92

Effin: 102

Emlygreenan: 117

Fedamore: 104

Galbally: 120

Glenogra: 105

Grange: 72

Grean: 65

Hackmys: 100

Hospital: 112

Inch St. Lawrence: 56

Iveruss: 24

Kilbeheny: 130

Kilbolane: 88

Kilbradran (2 pts.): 9

Kilbreedy Major: 115

Kilbreedy Minor: 101

Kilcolman: 8

Kilcornan: 25

Kilcullane: 108

Kildimo: 28

Kilfergus: 2

Kilfinnane: 124

Kilfinny: 79

Kilflyn: 128

Kilfrush: 113

Kilkeedy: 29

Killagholane: 78

Killeedy (4 pts.): 77

Killeely (2 pts.): 30

Killeenagarriff: 43

Killeenoghty: 37

Killonahan: 34

Kilmeedy: 82

Kilmoylan: 6

Kilmurry: 42

Kilpeacon: 105

Kilquane: 127

Kilsconnell: 23

Kilteely: 69

Knockainy (2 pts.): 107

Knocklong: 118

Knocknagaul: 36

Lismakeery: 15

Loughill (3 pts.): 3

Ludden: 52

Mahoonagh: 76

Monagay (3 pts.): 75

Monasteranenagh (2 pts.): 39

Morgans: 12

Mungret: 32

Nantinan (3 pts.): 16

Newcastle: 71

Oola: 68

Particles: 123

Rathjordan: 59

Rathkeale (2 pts.): 21

Rathronan (2 pts.): 10

Robertstown: 5

Rochestown: 54

Shanagolden: 1

St. John's (parts of other Limerick City parishes): 44

St. Lawrence's: 33

St. Michael's: 31

St. Munchin's: 45

St. Nicholas: 41

St. Patrick's: 11

St. Peter's and St. Paul's: 4

Stradbally: 40

Tankardstown: 99

Templebredon: 70

Tomdeely: 13

Tullabracky: 94

Tuogh: 62

Tuoghcluggin (2 pts.): 67

Uregare: 98

County Longford

A Brief History

This Leinster county contains the towns of Longford, Granard, Ballymahon, Edgeworthstown, and Ballinamuck.

At the beginning of the Christian era, the area now forming County Longford was part of the Kingdom of Conmaicne. From the ninth to the fifteenth centuries, it was known as "Annaly." The county was mainly the territory of the O'Farrells. Other Irish families associated with the county are O'Quinns, (Mc)Gilna, Leavy, Mulroy, and (Mac)Gaynor.

Although Longford was nominally granted to Hugh de Lacy after the Norman conquest in the twelfth century, there was little real Norman influence in the county due to the power of the O'Farrells. The family of Tuite was one of the few to establish a settlement in the county.

In the sixteenth and early seventeenth century, parts of Longford were planted with English settlers, including Aungier, Forbes, Newcomen, King, Harman, Lane, and Edgeworth. The Edgeworths were major landowners in the county and were very popular because of their efforts on the tenant's behalf.

In 1641, the O'Farrells joined the rebellion by the Catholic Confederacy (see Co. Kilkenny). On the Confederacy's defeat by Cromwell in 1649, the family lost its remaining estates and influence in the county.

This largely agricultural county was badly affected by the Great Famine of 1845-47. The population, which was 115,000 in 1841, had fallen by twenty-nine percent in 1851. Over 14,000 Longford people died between 1845 and 1850 of starvation and disease, and the remainder emigrated to the cities or, more usually, abroad. The county continued to have a high rate of emigration throughout the remainder of the century and beyond. The current population is 31,000.

Census and Census Substitutes

1659

"Census" of Ireland. Edited by S. Pender. Dublin: Stationery Office, 1939. NLI I6551. SLC film 924648.

1726-27

List of Protestant Householders in Abbeylara, Ardagh, Clonbroney, Cloongish, Kilcomack, Killashee, Rathaspick, Rathreagh, Russan, Shrule, Street, Taghshinee, and Abbyshrule. Edgeworth family papers NAI M 1502. (Names-only list compiled for "the charitable distribution of religious books.")

1731

Protestants in the Parishes of Shrule, Rathaspick, and Rathreagh. RCB GS 2/7/3/25.

1747-1806

Freeholders of Co. Longford. NAI M2745.

1766

Protestants in the Parishes of Abbeylara and Russagh. RCBL Ms. 23; GO 537. Abbeylara on SLC film 258517 and NAI M2476.

1790

Names of the Owners of Freeholds in Co. Longford, ca. 1790. NAI film 2486-88; NLI P 1897; SLC film 100888.

1796

Spinning Wheel Premium List (see introduction).

1800-35

Printed List of Co. Longford Freeholders. GO Ms. 444; SLC film 100181.

1823–38

Tithe Applotment Survey (see introduction).

1829–36

Freeholders List of Co. Longford. GO Ms. 444; SLC film 100181.

1834

List of Heads of Households in the Parish of Granard, showing numbers of males and females of each religion (i.e., Catholic, Protestant, or Presbyterian) in each household. In the Catholic parish register for Granard. NLI P 4237; SLC film 926027.

1838

"Householders in the Catholic Parish of Mullinalaghta [part of civil parish of Scrabby and Columbkille East]" (gives names of householders in each of twelve townlands who contributed to a new church at Cloonagh). In Mullinalaghta parish records; *Teathbha* 1 (3) (1973): 244–51.

1839

List of persons who obtained Game Certificates in . . . Longford, etc. PRONI T 688.

1843

Voters List. NAI 1843/62.

1848

Petitioners for William Smith O'Brien. Names of male petitioners in Longford. NAI 1848/180.

1853–1901

Cash receipts from sundry persons to various Longford estates. Longford/Westmeath Library; SLC films 1279279-80.

1854

Griffith's Valuation (see introduction). Full index published as Co. *Longford Survivors of the Great Famine* by David Leahy. Limerick: Derryvin Press, 1996. ISBN: 0-952865-0-9.

1901

Census. NAI. Complete index in *Longford and Its People* by David Leahy. Dublin: Flyleaf Press, 1990. ISBN: 0-9508466-2-7. Also, Harry Farrell's *Exploring Family Origins and Old Longford Town* (see Miscellaneous Sources) has a street-by-street listing of Longford Town residents.

1911

Census. NAI.

Church Records

Church of Ireland

See the introduction for a description of Church of Ireland records and their major repositories. Many C of I records were lost in the PRO fire of 1922. These are indicated as "Lost." However, as Church of Ireland records were effectively state records, the records of marriage (from 1845) are also in the General Registrar's Office. Some are still in local custody (LC), while others are in one of a variety of other archives (e.g., RCBL or NAI). Many of the parish registers of this county have been indexed by the Longford Museum and Genealogical Centre (see Research Services at the end of the chapter). A search of the index will be conducted by the center for a fee. Those indexed are noted as "Indexed by LMGC."

Abbeylara
Earliest Records: b. 1877–; m. 1846–; d. 1886–
Status: LC; Indexed by LMGC (to 1899)

Ardagh
Earliest Records: b. 1811–; m. 1811–; d. 1811–
Status: LC

Ballymacormick
Status: Lost

Cashel
Status: Lost

Clonbroney
Earliest Records: b. 1821; m. 1823; d. 1822
Status: LC; Indexed by LMGC (to 1899)

Clonguish and Clongishkilloe
Earliest Records: b. 1821; m. 1820; d. 1820
Status: LC; Indexed by LMGC (to 1899)

Columbkille
Earliest Records: b. 1894–; m. 1845–; d. 1896–
Status: LC; RCBL (mf) (b. 1894-1985; m. 1845-1934; d. 1896-1983)

Drumhish
Earliest Records: m. 1846-1887
Status: Indexed by LMGC

Edgeworthstown
Earliest Records: b. 1801; m. 1801; d. 1802
Status: LC; Indexed by LMGC (to: b. 1899, m. 1896, d. 1891)

Forgney
Earliest Records: b. 1808–; m. 1804–; d. 1804–
Status: LC; NAI MFCI 61 (b. 1808-1918; m. 1804-71; d. 1804-1914)

Granard
Earliest Records: b. 1820–; m. 1820–; d. 1820–
Status: LC; Indexed by LMGC (to 1899)

Kilcormick
Earliest Records: b. 1795–; m. 1795–; d. 1795–
Status: LC

Kilglass
Earliest Records: b. 1877–; m. 1845–; d. 1881–
Status: LC; Indexed by LMGC (to: b. 1899, m. 1896, d. 1898)

Killashee
Earliest Records: b. 1772–; m. 1772–; d. 1778–
Status: LC; Indexed by LMGC (to 1899)

Killoe
Earliest Records: b. 1825–; m. 1825–; d. 1825–
Status: LC; Indexed by LMGC (to: b. 1896, m. 1899, d. 1898)

Mothel
Status: Lost

Moydow
Earliest Records: b. 1821–; m. 1821–; d. 1821–
Status: LC

Rathcline
Earliest Records: b. 1846–; d. 1847–
Status: LC

Shrule
Earliest Records: b. 1854–63
Status: RCBL

Templemichael
Earliest Records: b. 1796–; m. 1770; d. 1796–
Status: LC; NAI M5724-6 (b. 1796-1835; m. 1777-1838; d. 1796-1838); Indexed by LMGC (to 1899)

Termonbarry
Earliest Records: m. 1846-1879
Status: Indexed by LMGC

Presbyterian

An account of Presbyterian records is given in the introduction. These registers rarely contain death records, and occasionally have only records of births.

Tully (Edgeworthstown)
Starting Date: 1844

Roman Catholic

Many of the parish registers of this county have been indexed by the Longford Museum and Genealogical Centre (see Research Services at the end of the chapter). A search of the index will be conducted by the center for a fee. Those indexed are noted as "Indexed by LMGC." Microfilm copies of all registers are also available in the National Library of Ireland (NLI), and through the LDS library system.

Civil Parish: Abbeylara
Map Grid: 7
RC Parish: Abbeylara

Diocese: AD
Earliest Record: b. 1822; m. 1855; d. 1854
Status: LC; NLI (mf); Indexed by LMGC

Civil Parish: Abbeyshrule
Map Grid: 23
RC Parish: see Taghshinny
Diocese: AD

Civil Parish: Agharra
Map Grid: 24
RC Parish: see Kilglass
Diocese: AD

Civil Parish: Ardagh
Map Grid: 9
RC Parish: Ardagh and Moydow
Diocese: AD
Earliest Record: b. 1793; m. 1793; d. 1822
Missing Dates: b. 1.1816-10.1822
Status: LC; NLI (mf); Indexed by LMGC (to 1895)

Civil Parish: Ballymacormick
Map Grid: 14
RC Parish: see Templemichael
Diocese: AD

Civil Parish: Cashel
Map Grid: 19
RC Parish: Cashel (Newtowncashel)
Diocese: AD
Earliest Record: b. 1866; m. 1830; d. 1830
Status: LC; NLI (mf); Indexed by LMGC (to 1899)

Civil Parish: Clonbroney
Map Grid: 5
RC Parish: Clonbroney
Diocese: AD
Earliest Record: b. 1828; m. 1828; d. 1828
Status: LC; NLI (mf); Indexed by LMGC (to 1901/1899)

Civil Parish: Clongesh
Map Grid: 3
RC Parish: Clonguish (Newtownforbes)
Diocese: AD
Earliest Record: b. 1829; m. 1829; d. 1829
Status: LC; NLI (mf); Indexed by LMGC (to 1888/1880)

Civil Parish: Columbkille (1)
Map Grid: 4
RC Parish: Columbkille; also Scrabby, see below
Diocese: AD
Earliest Record: b. 1833; m. 1833; d. 1836
Status: LC; NLI (mf); Indexed by LMGC (to 1899, 1858, 1858)

Civil Parish: Columbkille (2)
Map Grid: 4
RC Parish: Scrabby and Columbkille East
Diocese: AD

Earliest Record: b. 1870; m. 1877
Status: LC; NLI (mf); Indexed by LMGC (to 1895)

Civil Parish: Forgney
Map Grid: 25
RC Parish: Moyvore
Diocese: ME
Earliest Record: b. 1832; m. 1832; d. 1831
Status: LC; NLI (mf); Indexed by Dun na Si HC (see
Westmeath–Research Services)

Civil Parish: Granard
Map Grid: 6
RC Parish: Granard
Diocese: AD
Earliest Record: b. 1779; m. 1782; d. 1811
Status: LC; NLI (mf); Indexed by LMGC (to 1894,
1869, 1865)

Civil Parish: Kilcommock
Map Grid: 20
RC Parish: Kilcomogue (Kilcommac) or Kenagh
Diocese: AD
Earliest Record: b. 1859; m. 1859; d. 1859
Status: LC; NLI (mf); Indexed by LMGC (to 1880)

Civil Parish: Kilglass
Map Grid: 16
RC Parish: Legan (Kilglass and Rathreagh)
Diocese: AD
Earliest Record: b. 1855; m. 1855; d. 1855
Status: LC; NLI (mf); Indexed by LMGC (to 1899,
1896, 1890)

Civil Parish: Killashee
Map Grid: 13
RC Parish: Killashee (and Cluain-a-Donald from
1864)
Diocese: AD
Earliest Record: b. 1840; m. 1828; d. 1841
Missing Dates: b. 12.1843-4.1848; m. 10.1843-
6.1848; d. 8.1843-11.1858
Status: LC; NLI (mf); Indexed by LMGC (to 1898)

Civil Parish: Killoe (1)
Map Grid: 1
RC Parish: Drumlish; also Killoe, see below
Diocese: AD
Earliest Record: b. 1834; m. 1834; d. 1834
Missing Dates: b. 3.1868-3.1874; m. 3.1868-1.1870,
6.1872-1.1870; d. 3.1868-2.1870, 7.1872-8.1876
Status: LC; NLI (mf); Indexed by LMGC (to 1899)

Civil Parish: Killoe (2)
Map Grid: 1
RC Parish: Killoe
Diocese: AD
Earliest Record: b. 1826; m. 1826; d. 1826
Missing Dates: b. 8.1852-2.1853, 10.1868-4.1869;
m. 10.1852-9.1854; d. 6.1853-8.1853
Status: LC; NLI (mf); Indexed by LMGC (to 1895)

Civil Parish: Mohill
Map Grid: 2
RC Parish: see Mohill, Co. Leitrim
Diocese: AD

Civil Parish: Mostrim
Map Grid: 10
RC Parish: Mostrim (Edgeworthstown)
Diocese: AD
Earliest Record: b. 1837; m. 1838; d. 1838
Status: LC; NLI (mf); Indexed by LMGC (to 1895)

Civil Parish: Moydow
Map Grid: 15
RC Parish: see Ardagh
Diocese: AD

Civil Parish: Noughaval
Map Grid: 26
RC Parish: see Drumraney, Co. Westmeath
Diocese: ME

Civil Parish: Rathcline
Map Grid: 18
RC Parish: Rathcline (Lanesboro)
Diocese: AD
Earliest Record: b. 1840; m. 1840; d. 1841
Status: LC; NLI (mf); Indexed by LMGC (to 1895)

Civil Parish: Rathreagh
Map Grid: 12
RC Parish: see Kilglass
Diocese: AD

Civil Parish: Shrule
Map Grid: 21
RC Parish: Ballymahon or Shrule
Diocese: AD
Earliest Record: b. 1820; m. 1829; d. 1820
Missing Dates: b. 11.1830; d. 10.1830
Status: LC; NLI (mf); Indexed by LMGC (to 1887)

Civil Parish: Street
Map Grid: 11
RC Parish: Streete
Diocese: AD
Earliest Record: b. 1820; m. 1820; d. 1823
Missing Dates: b. 7.1827-12.1834; m. 1.1828-
1.1835; d. 8.1829-12.1834, 1.1841-7.1842
Status: LC; NLI (mf); Indexed by LMGC

Civil Parish: Taghsheenod
Map Grid: 17
RC Parish: see Taghshinny
Diocese: AD

Civil Parish: Taghshinny
Map Grid: 22
RC Parish: Taghshinney, Taghshinod, and
Abbeyshrule
Diocese: AD
Earliest Record: b. 1835; m. 1835; d. 1835
Missing Dates: b. 3.1844-5.1848; m. 8.1842-5.1848;

d. 11.1842–5.1848
Status: LC; NLI (mf); Indexing by LMGC in progress

Civil Parish: Templemichael
Map Grid: 8
RC Parish: Templemichael and Ballymacormack
Diocese: AD
Earliest Record: b. 1802; m. 1802; d. 1802
Missing Dates: b. 1.1808–6.1808
Status: LC; NLI (mf); Indexed by LMGC (to 1885, 1897, 1829)

Commercial and Social Directories

1824

J. Pigot's *City of Dublin and Hibernian Provincial Directory* includes traders, nobility, gentry, and clergy lists of Granard, Lanesborough, and Longford.

1846

Slater's *National Commercial Directory of Ireland* lists nobility, clergy, traders, etc., in Ballymahon, Granard, Longford, and Mostrim (Edgeworthstown).

1856

Slater's *Royal National Commercial Directory of Ireland* lists nobility, gentry, clergy, traders, etc., in Ballymahon, Granard, Longford and Newtown-Forbes, and Mostrim (Edgeworthstown).

1870

Slater's *Directory of Ireland* contains trade, nobility, and clergy lists for Ballymahon, Edgeworthstown, Granard, and Longford.

1881

Slater's *Royal National Commercial Directory of Ireland* contains lists of traders, clergy, nobility, and farmers in adjoining parishes of the towns of Ballymahon, Edgeworthstown, Granard, and Longford.

1894

Slater's *Royal National Directory of Ireland* lists traders, police, teachers, farmers, and private residents in each of the towns, villages, and parishes of the county.

Family History

Papers relating to the Bond family and Barbor family, Longford. NAI 8462–8562: T 768–773.

"Burrowes of Fernsborough." Pedigree in *Swanzy Notebooks*. RCB Library, Dublin.

"The Davys Family Records." S.F. O'Cianain. Records kept by members of the Davys family from 1693–1832. Longford: Longford Printing Co., 1931.

Copies of census returns of the Egan family, Co. Longford, 1851. NAI M 5249 (65).

"Entries from the Family Bible of James Hyde of Longford." *Ir. Anc.* 2 (1) (1970): 23.

"The Fetherton Family of Ardagh." *Teathbha* 2 (1) (1980): 17–32.

Forbes, John. *Memoirs of the Earls of Granard*. London, 1868.

Copies of census returns of the Geraghty family, Co. Longford, 1841. NAI 5248 (21).

"Grier of Gurteen." Pedigree in *Swanzy Notebooks*. RCB Library, Dublin.

Lefroy, Sir J.H. *Notes and Documents Relating to Lefroy of Carrickglass, Co. Longford*. 1868.

Copies of census returns of the Reilly family, Co. Longford, 1851. NAI M 5349 (65).

Gravestone Inscriptions

Ballymacormack (RC)–Longford Town: in Harry Farrell's *Exploring Family Origins and Old Longford Town*. Longford Leader, 1986.

Ballymacormack (C of I)–Longford Town: in Harry Farrell's *Exploring Family Origins and Old Longford Town*. Longford Leader, 1986.

Granard–St. Patrick's (C of I): in R.W. Stafford's *St. Patrick's Church of Ireland, Granard: Notes of Genealogical and Historical Interest*. 1983.

Longford Town (Presbyterian): in Harry Farrell's *Exploring Family Origins and Old Longford Town*. Longford Leader, 1986.

St. John's (C of I)–Longford Town: in Harry Farrell's *Exploring Family Origins and Old Longford Town*. Longford Leader, 1986.

Newspapers

There were no early papers published within the county. Those in the surrounding counties should be consulted, depending on the area of interest.

Title: *Longford Independent*
Published in: Longford, 1868–1918
NLI Holdings: 1888–1913; 1921–1.1925
BL Holdings: 9.1869–12.1918

Title: *Longford Journal*
Published in: Longford, 1839–1914
NLI Holdings: odd numbers 1842–66
BL Holdings: 1.1839–7.1869; 1.1870–9.1888; odd numbers 1889, 1890; 1.1899–8.1914

Title: *Longford Leader and Cavan, Leitrim, Roscommon and Westmeath News*
Published in: Longford, 1897–current
NLI Holdings: 4.1907–7.1910; 7.1927–in progress
BL Holdings: 4.1907–in progress (except 1–2.1926)

Title: *Midland Counties Gazette*
Published in: Longford, 1853–63
BL Holdings: 6.1853–4.1863

Wills and Administrations

A discussion of the types of records, where they are held, and their availability and value is given in the Wills section of the introduction. The availability of prerogative wills, administrations, and marriage license records is also described in the relevant parts of the same section. Where available, published sources of these records are given in the Miscellaneous Sources section.

Pre-1858 Wills and Administrations

Prerogative Wills. See the introduction.

Consistorial Wills. County Longford is mainly in the diocese of Ardagh, with two parishes in Meath. The guide to Catholic parish records in this chapter shows the diocese to which each civil parish belonged. The wills of residents of each diocese were usually proven within that diocese (see the Wills section for exceptions). The following records survive:

Wills

See the introduction.

Abstracts

See the introduction. The RIA's Upton Papers also contain abstracts to Longford wills. RIA Library.

Indexes

Ardagh (1695–1858). *Ir. Anc.* (1971); SLC film 824242. Meath—see Co. Meath.

Post-1858 Wills and Administrations

This county was served by the District Registry of Cavan. The surviving records are kept in the NAI, and include: Cavan District Will Books (1858–1896). NAI and SLC films 100927–8.

Marriage Licenses

Indexes

Meath (1691–1845). NAI; SLC film 100869.

Miscellaneous Sources

Brady, G. *In Search of Longford Roots.* Birr: Offaly Historical Society, 1987.

Farrell, Harry. *Exploring Family Origins and Old Longford Town.* Longford Leader, 1986.

Farrell, J.P. *Historical Notes and Stories of the County Longford.* Longford, 1979.

Farrell, J.P. *History of the County of Longford.* Dublin, 1891.

Leahy, David. *Longford and Its People.* Dublin: Flyleaf Press, 1990. ISBN: 0-9508466-2-7 (complete index to 1901 census).

Murray, C. *Bibliography of Co. Longford.* Longford, 1961. SLC film 1279275.

"Some Notes on the High Sheriffs of Co. Longford 1701–1800." *Ir. Gen.* 2 (1) (1943): 13–21.

McGivney, J. *Place-names of the County Longford.* Longford, 1908.

Leitrim Sheriffs, 1605–1799. *Roscommon Herald* 2/9/1991 (names only).

Research Sources and Services

Journals

Teathbha (journal of Longford Historical Society)
Ardagh and Clonmacnoise Historical Society Journal

Libraries and Information Sources

Longford/Westmeath Joint Library, Dublin Road, Mullingar, Co. Westmeath. Ph: (044) 40781/2/3. The library has indexes to six Longford parishes and answers research queries.

Research Services

Longford Museum and Genealogical Centre, Old VEC, Battery Rd., Longford, Co Longford. Ph: (043) 41235. This is the official IGP center for the county. It has indexed a large proportion of the church registers of the county and is working on further indexing. Researchers are advised to contact the center for an updated list of registers, and other sources, indexed. It will conduct searches of the database for a fee.

See also Research Services in Dublin in the introduction.

Societies

Longford Historical Society, Mr. Luke Baxter, Main Street, Longford, Co. Longford (publishers of *Teathbha*)

Longford Civil Parishes as Listed on Map

1. Killoe
2. Mohill
3. Clongesh
4. Columbkille
5. Clonbroney
6. Granard
7. Abbeylara
8. Templemichael
9. Ardagh
10. Mostrim
11. Street
12. Rathreagh
13. Killashee
14. Ballymacormick
15. Moydow
16. Kilglass
17. Taghsheenod
18. Rathcline
19. Cashel
20. Kilcommock
21. Shrule
22. Taghshinny
23. Abbeyshrule
24. Agharra
25. Forgney
26. Noughaval

Longford Civil Parishes in Alphabetical Order

Abbeylara: 7
Abbeyshrule: 23
Agharra: 24
Ardagh: 9
Ballymacormick: 14
Cashel: 19
Clonbroney: 5
Clongesh: 3
Columbkille: 4
Forgney: 25
Granard: 6
Kilcommock: 20
Kilglass: 16
Killashee: 13
Killoe: 1
Mohill: 2
Mostrim: 10
Moydow: 15
Noughaval: 26
Rathcline: 18
Rathreagh: 12
Shrule: 21
Street: 11
Taghsheenod: 17
Taghshinny: 22
Templemichael: 8

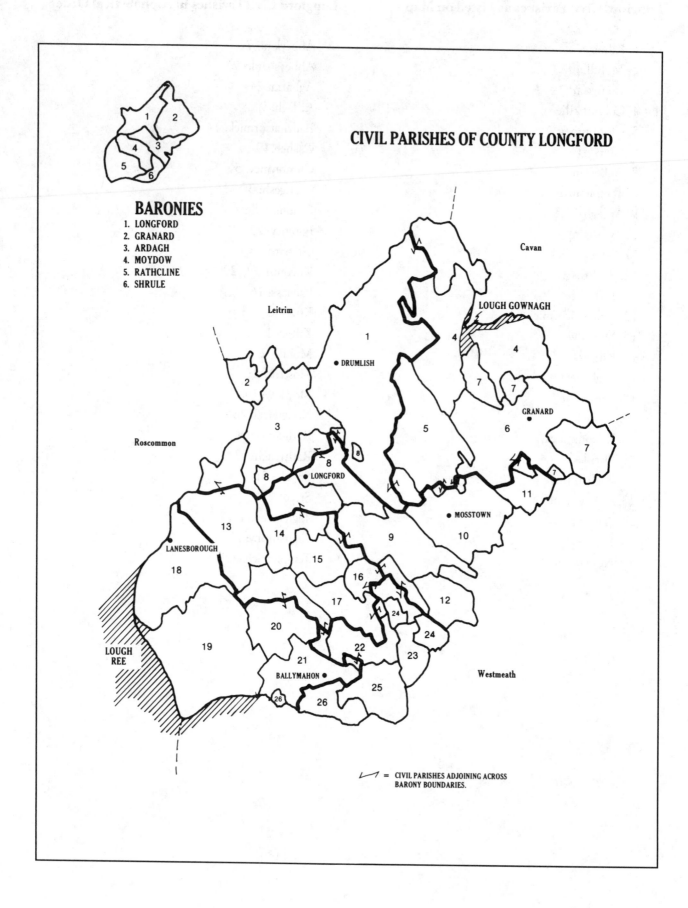

CIVIL PARISHES OF COUNTY LONGFORD

BARONIES

1. LONGFORD
2. GRANARD
3. ARDAGH
4. MOYDOW
5. RATHCLINE
6. SHRULE

Cavan

Leitrim

LOUGH GOWNAGH

Roscommon

DRUMLISH

GRANARD

LONGFORD

MOSSTOWN

LANESBOROUGH

LOUGH REE

BALLYMAHON

Westmeath

⌐⌐ = CIVIL PARISHES ADJOINING ACROSS BARONY BOUNDARIES.

County Louth

A Brief History

Louth is the smallest county in Ireland, comprising only 200,000 acres. It contains the towns of Drogheda, Dundalk, Ardee, Carlingford, and Castlebellingham.

Before the arrival of the Normans, it formed part of the Kingdom of Oriel. The territory within the present county of Louth was then ruled by the O'Carrolls. Other Gaelic families in the area included McArdle, McSorly, (Mc)Barron, and McScanlan. The main town in the county, Drogheda, was founded by the Norse Vikings under Turgesius in 911.

Following the Norman invasion, this area was overtaken in 1183 by John de Courcey, and the area now forming the county of Louth was immediately settled with English farmers. Among these were the families of Verdon, Bellew, Taaffe, Dowdall, Peppard, and Plunkett. The county was one of the first four established in 1210 by King John of England.

Louth was part of the "Pale," the English-controlled part of Ireland, for most of the succeeding centuries, and was fortified against attack from the surrounding areas. The county was overrun in the rebellion of O'Neill and the Ulster chieftains in the 1590s, but reverted to English control afterwards.

In the rebellion of the Catholic Confederacy of 1641 (see Co. Kilkenny), Drogheda was one of the rebel strongholds. In 1649 it was besieged by the army of Oliver Cromwell, who, on its surrender, massacred two thousand of the garrison of the town and transported the few survivors to Barbados.

The county was less affected than many by the Great Famine of 1845–47. The population was 128,000 in 1845, and by 1851 it had fallen to 108,000. Approximately 14,000 people died between 1845 and 1850.

Further thousands emigrated in this period and in the succeeding decades.

The county is agriculture-based and also has major brewing, fishing, cement, and shipping industries. The current population is around 90,000.

Census and Census Substitutes

1575

A 1575 Rent Roll (with contemporaneous maps of the Bagenal Estate in Carlingford lough district). *Louth Arch. J.* 21 (1) (1985): 31–47.

1600

"Gentlemen of Co. Louth." *Louth Arch. J.* 4 (4) (1919/20): 308–10 (names, residences, and some biographical details).

1659

"Census" of Ireland. Edited by S. Pender. Dublin: Stationery Office, 1939. NLI I6551. SLC film 924648.

"Rent Roll of Some Parts of Dundalk Town and Adjoining Lands." *Louth Arch. J.* 19 (1) (1977): 24–58 (lists tenants, subtenants, description of property, and rent).

1659–60

"Census of Louth County and Drogheda" (based on poll money returns). *Louth Arch. J.* 1 (2) (1905): 61–73; GO Ms. 541; SLC film 100225 (gives townlands, tituladoes, numbers of English and Irish, and principal Irish names in each barony).

1663–64

"Hearth Money Rolls—Baronies of Ferrard, Ardee, Louth, and Dundalk" (part). *Louth Arch. J.* 6 (4) (1928): 181–89.

"Hearth Money Roll for Drogheda." *Louth Arch. J.* 6 (2) (1926): 79–88.

"Hearth Money Roll for Orior Barony." *Louth Arch. J.* 7 (3) (1931): 419–31.

1664–66

"Hearth Money Roll for Barony of Dundalk." *Louth. Arch. J.* 7 (4) (1932): 500–15; SLC film 990411. Supplement in *Louth Arch. J.* 12 (4): 276–77.

1666–67

"Hearth Money Roll of Dunleer Parish." *Ir. Gen.* 4 (2) (1969): 142–44.

1683

"Co. Louth Brewers and Retailers." *Louth Arch. J.* 3 (3) (1914): 261–66 (names and barony/town of residence).

"Drogheda Trade and Customs Records." *Louth Arch. J.* 3 (1) (1912): 83–104; 3 (3) (1914): 250–58 (lists names of merchants).

1715

"Freemen of the Corporation of Dunleer." *Ir. Gen.* 4 (1): 10–13; SLC film 100225.

1739–41

"Corn Census of Co. Louth." *Louth. Arch. J.* 11 (4) (1948): 254–86; SLC film 990411 (lists over 1,600 persons, with addresses and their stocks of corn).

1760

"Census of Ardee Parish." *Ir. Gen.* 3 (5): 179–84.

1761

Militia List: County Louth. GO Ms. 680.

1765

"Tenants of Bayly Estate, Lordship of O'Meath." *Louth Arch. J.* 18 (1) (1973): 43–45 (ninety names with notes in text).

1766

Census: Entries for parishes of Ballymackenny, Charlestown, Clonkeehan, and Mapastown. *Louth Arch. J.* 1958.

1766

Religious Census. "Catholic and Protestants in Ardee and United Parishes" (parishes of Ardee, Ballymachkinny, *Beaulieu, Carlingford,* Charlestown, Clonkeehan, Creegan, *Darver,* Drogheda, *Dromiskin,* Kildemock, Kileshiel, *Louth,* Mapastown, *Phillipstown,* Shanlis, Smarmore, Stickallen, *Tallonstown,* and *Termonfecken*). NAI 1A 41 100; SLC film 990411 (except Charlestown, Clonkeehan, Killeshiel, and Mapastown).

"Census of Louth Parishes" (parishes *italicized* above). *Louth Arch. J.* 14 (2) (1958): 103–17.

Parish of Creggan. In Rev. L. P. Murray, *History of the Parish of Creggan.* Dundalk, 1940; *Louth Arch. J.* 8 (2) (1934): 156–62; NAI 1A 46 49. SLC film 1279330.

"Families Around Ardee" (census of parishes of Ardee, Kildemock, Shanlis, Smarmore, Stichillen). *Louth Arch. J.* 10 (1) (1941): 72–76.

1775

"Catholic Qualification Roll Extracts" (forty-nine names, addresses, and occupations). 59th Report DKPRI: 50–84.

1777

"Jurors of Co. Louth." *Louth Arch. J.* 6 (4) (1928): 275–76 (thirty-seven names and addresses).

1779–81

"Rental and Accounts of Collon Estate (Hon. John Foster)." *Louth Arch. J.* 10 (3) (1943): 222–29 (lists tenants by townland, holdings, etc.).

1782–88

"Tenants on Two Clanbrassil Estate Maps of Dundalk." *Louth Arch. J.* 15 (1) (1961): 39–87 (gives tenants on 425 holdings in twenty-five townlands around Dundalk and tenants of 305 holdings in the town, with description of holdings).

1786–92

"Cess Payers in Dunleer Union" (i.e., parishes of Dunleer, Cappagh, Drumcar, Dysart, Moylary, and Monasterboice). *Louth Arch. J.* 9 (1) (1937–40): 42–45.

1791

"Names of Landholders in the Parish of Dromiskin." In Rev. J. B. Leslie, *History of Kilsaran Union of Parishes.* Dundalk, 1908.

1798–1802

"Voters List of Drogheda." *Louth Arch. J.* 20: 319–33.

1801

"*Tithe Applotment Survey* of the Parishes of Stabannon and Roodstown." In Rev. J. B. Leslie, *History of Kilsaran Union of Parishes.* Dundalk, 1908.

1802

"Protestant Parishioners of Carlingford." *Louth Arch. J.* 16 (3) (1967): 161–62.

1809

"Tenants in Culver House Park, Drogheda." *Louth Arch. J.* 11 (3) (1947): 206-08 (lists thirty tenants and addresses, with map).

1810

"Tenants List for Anglesey Estate" (seventeen townlands in parish of Carlingford—name, townland, lease status, etc.). *Louth Arch. J.* 12 (2) (1950): 136-43.

1810-17

"Tenants on Caraher of Cardistown Potato Land." *Louth Arch. J.* 16 (3) (1967): 177-83.

1821

Registered Freeholders of Co. Louth. Dublin: Shaw, 1820; NLI Ir 94132 L3 (gives name, residence, location of freehold, and landlord's name).

1823-38

Tithe Applotment Survey (see introduction).

1824-27

Lists of Freeholders in County Library, Dundalk.

1830

"Subscribers to School at Drakestown" (parish of Kildemock). *Louth Arch. J.* 12 (1) (1949): 38 (fifty-two names and addresses).

1832-36

"List of Holders of, and Applicants for, Licenses to Sell Liquor in Drogheda and Dundalk" (names and addresses). *Parl. Papers* 1837, 13 (2): Appendix 10.

1834

"Census of the Parish of Tallanstown." *Louth Arch. J.* 14 (1) (1957): 14-25; SLC film 990411 (gives householders in each townland and number of Catholics and Protestants in each house).

1837

"Occupants of Drogheda, Arranged by Street Within Each Parish, Giving Description of Premises and Valuation." *Parl. Papers* 1837, 11 (2): 265-71.

"Tithe Census of Parishes of Kilsaran and Gormanstown." *Louth Arch J.* 12 (3) (1951): 197-204 (landlords' names in each townland). Addendum in 12 (4) (1952): 281.

"Occupants of Dundalk Arranged by Street, Giving Valuation of Property." *Parl. Papers* 1837, 11 (2): 272-79.

"List of Those Made Freemen of Drogheda and Dundalk Since 1831" (names, occupations, and addresses). *Parl. Papers* 1837, 11 (1): Appendix B1; 1837/ 38, 13 (2): Appendix 3.

1838

"Lists of Marksmen (illiterate voters) in Drogheda and Dundalk" (names, addresses, and occupations). *Parl. Papers* 1837, 11 (1): Appendix A3; 1837/38, 13 (2): Appendix 4.

"Tenants on Balfour Estates" (part of Ardee; townlands of Dromin, Dunbin, Hacklim, Listulk, Keeron, Little Grange, Mellifont, Sheepgrange). *Louth Arch. J.* 12 (3) (1951): 188-90.

1842

Voters List. NAI 1842/70.

1847

"Voters Lists for Borough of Dundalk." *Louth Arch. J.* 16 (4) (1968): 224-32 (names, addresses, occupations, and political persuasion).

"Voters in Drogheda Parliamentary Elections." *Louth Arch. J.* 21 (3) (1986) (name, address, and status—freeman, householder, etc.).

1852

"Tenants on McClintock Estate, Drumcar." *Louth Arch. J.* 16 (4) (1968): 230-32 (114 names and addresses; mainly townlands of Drumcar, Greenmount, Adamstown, Annagassan, and Dillonstown).

"Families in the Townlands of Mosstown and Phillipstown (parish of Mosstown)." *Louth Arch. J.* 18 (3) (1975): 232-37; SLC film 990411 (lists thirty-eight families, including names, ages, and notes on each).

List of Electors of Co. Louth who voted in the general election of 1852 . . . Dundalk: Patrick Dowdall, 1852, pp. 56. NLI ms. 1660. (Gives names and addresses of voters in 1852 and in the by-election of 1854.)

1854

Griffith's Valuation (see introduction).

1856

"Tenants on Anglesey Estate" (parish of Carlingford: twenty-two townlands). *Louth Arch. J.* 12 (2) (1950): 143-51.

1857

A list of the several baronies of Co. Louth who voted at the general election of 1857 (also shows how they voted). Dundalk: Patrick Dowdall, 1857, pp. 64. NLI mss. 3538-45.

1865

Parliamentary Register of Workers for Co. Louth, showing Landlords and their Tenants on the register and how they voted. (Gives tenant's name, address, and landlord in each barony.) Dublin: Peter Roe, 1865. NLI P 2491. Dundalk: W. Tempest, 1865, pp. 75.

1901

Census. NAI (see introduction).

1911

Census. NAI.

Church Records

Church of Ireland

See the introduction for a description of Church of Ireland records and their major repositories. Many C of I records were lost in the PRO fire of 1922. These are indicated as "Lost." However, as Church of Ireland records were effectively state records, the records of marriage (from 1845) are also in the General Registrar's Office. Many are still in local custody (LC), while others are in one of a variety of other archives (e.g., RCBL or NAI). Indexing by AA and/or MHC is planned.

Ardee
Earliest Records: b. 1735–; m. 1744–; d. 1732–
Missing Records: 1753–1798
Status: LC; and RCBL (mf) (b. 1799–1868; m. 1802–49; d. 1801–1981)

Ballymakenny
Status: Lost

Barronstown
Earliest Records: b. 1878–; m. 1846–; d. 1878–
Status: LC; RCBL (mf) (b. 1878–1952; m. 1846–1951; d. 1878–1956)

Ballymascanlon
Earliest Records: b. 1801–; m. 1805–; d. 1817–
Status: Lost

Beaulieu
Status: Lost

Carlingford
Status: Lost

Carlingford Rathcorr
Status: Lost

Carrick or Carrick-baggot (see Rathdrumin)

Charlestown
Earliest Records: b. 1822–; m. 1822–; d. 1822–
Status: LC; NAI and RCBL (mf) (b. 1822–36; m. 1824–1911; d. 1823–1912); SLC film 990487

Clogher
Earliest Records: b. 1811–91; m. 1792–1910; d. 1810–1986
Status: LC; RCBL (mf) (b. 1811–91; m. 1792–1910; d. 1810–1986)

Clonkeen
Earliest Records: b. 1808–41; m. 1808–72; d. 1808–1904
Status: NAI

Clonmore
Status: Lost

Collon
Earliest Records: b. 1790–; m. 1790–; d. 1791–
Status: LC; RCBL (mf) (b. 1790–1969; m. 1790–1845; d. 1791–1950); SLC 941.825/k29c (1790–1823)

Dromin (Armagh)—see Collon

Darver
Earliest Records: m. 1870–75
Status: RCBL (mf)

Dromiskin
Earliest Records: b. 1791–; m. 1791–; d. 1791–
Status: LC; SLC film 973045 (b. 1799–1840; m. 1805–42; d. 1802–1900)

Drogheda
Earliest Records: b. 1654–; m. 1654–; d. 1653–
Status: LC; RCBL (mf) (b. 1654–1886; m. 1654–1956; d. 1653–1864); and NAI M5127 (b/m/d. 1747–72); SLC 941.825/D2 v26d (1747–1772)

Drumcar
Earliest Records: b. 1841–; m. 1841–; d. 1841–
Status: LC

Dunany
Status: Lost

Dundalk
Earliest Records: b. 1729–; m. 1755–; d. 1727–
Status: LC; RCBL (mf) (b. 1729–1924; m. 1750–1929; d. 1727–1985); SLC film 962930 (b. 1729–1803; m. 1755–1803; d. 1752–1803)

Dunleer
Earliest Records: b. 1787–92; m. 1738–96; d. 1729–95
Status: LC; RCBL (extracts) (b. 1787–92; m. 1738–96; d. 1729–95)

Faughart
Earliest Records: m. 1848–
Status: RCBL (mf) (m. 1848–64)

Haggardstown
Status: Lost

Haynestown
Earliest Records: b. 1865–; m. 1855–; d. 1871–
Status: LC; RCBL (mf) (b. 1865–1984; m. 1855–1951; d. 1871–1983)

Jonesboro
Earliest Records: b. 1802–; m. 1821–; d. 1826–
Status: LC

Killanney
Earliest Records: b. 1825–; m. 1825–; d. 1825–
Status: LC

Killencoole
Earliest Records: b. 1877–; m. 1849–; d. 1886–
Status: LC; RCBL (mf) (b. 1877–1954; m. 1849–1944; d. 1886–1965)

Kilsaran
Earliest Records: b. 1818–; m. 1818–; d. 1818–
Status: LC; b. 1818–1840 indexed by Anglican Rec. Proj.—available at RCBL and Soc. Gen. (London); SLC film 897365 (b. 1818–1840; m. 1818–1845; d. 1818–1900)

Louth
Earliest Records: b. 1889–; m. 1849–; d. 1886–
Status: LC; RCBL (mf) (b. 1889–1904; m. 1849–1944; d. 1886–1965)

Mansfieldstown
Earliest Records: b. 1824–; m. 1824–; d. 1824–
Status: SLC film 973045 (b. 1825–1884; m. 1824–1884; d. 1838–1884)

Moylary
Status: Lost

Omeath
Earliest Records: b. 1883–; d. 1845–; m. 1883–
Status: LC; RCBL (mf) (b. 1883–1936; d. 1845–1930; m. 1883–1936)

Rathdrumin
Status: Lost

St. Mary, Drogheda
Earliest Records: b. 1763–; m. 1763–; d. 1763–
Missing Dates: b. 1775–1820; m. 1775–1820; d. 1775–1820
Status: LC

St. Peter, Drogheda
Earliest Records: b. 1654–; m. 1654–; d. 1654–
Missing Dates: b. 1747–1772; m. 1747–1772; d. 1747–1772
Status: LC

Stabannon
Earliest Records: b. 1688–; m. 1688–; d. 1688–
Status: SLC film 874438 (b. 1668–1754 and 1782–1847; m. 1668–1754 and 1782–1845; d. 1668–1754 and 1782–1859)

Termonfeckin
Status: Lost

Tullyallen and Mellifont
Earliest Records: b. 1812–; m. 1815–; d. 1814–
Status: LC

Presbyterian
An account of Presbyterian records is given in the introduction. These registers rarely contain death records, and occasionally have only records of births. Registers are in local custody. Indexing by AA and/or MHC is planned.

Corvally (Dundalk)
Starting date: 1840

Dundalk
Starting date: 1819

Methodist
Methodist churches are known to have existed at Drogheda, Dundalk, Carlingford, and Castlebellingham. No death records were maintained. See the introduction for information on sources and access. The records available are:

Dundalk
Starting date: 1837–
Status: LC

Drogheda
Starting date: 1829–
Status: LC

Roman Catholic
Note that some of the Catholic parish registers of this county have been indexed by Meath Heritage Centre (see Research Services at the end of the Meath chapter) and by Armagh Ancestry (see Armagh chapter). A search of the index will be conducted by these centers for a fee. Those indexed by Armagh Ancestry are indicated as "Indexed by AA." Microfilm copies of all registers are also available in the National Library of Ireland (NLI), and through the LDS library system.

Civil Parish: Ardee
Map Grid: 29
RC Parish: Ardee
Diocese: AM
Earliest Record: b. 4.1763; m. 1763; d. 7.1765
Missing Dates: b. 10.1810–4.1821; m. 10.1810–4.1821, ends 2.1826; d. 10.1810–3.1821, ends 2.1825
Status: LC; NLI (mf); Indexed by AA (b/m. to 1900; d. 1810–1821)

Civil Parish: Ballybarrack
Map Grid: 14
RC Parish: Kilkerley, see Dunbin
Diocese: AM

Civil Parish: Ballyboys
Map Grid: 3
RC Parish: Lordship, see Ballymascanlon
Diocese: AM

Civil Parish: Ballymakenny
Map Grid: 62
RC Parish: part Monasterboice; part Termonfeckin
Diocese: AM

Civil Parish: Ballymascanlon
Map Grid: 1
RC Parish: Lordship (Ravensdale); also part Faughart
Diocese: AM
Earliest Record: b. 1.1838; m. 1.1838
Status: LC; NLI (mf); Indexed by AA (to 1900)

Civil Parish: Barronstown
Map Grid: 10
RC Parish: Kilkerley, see Dunbin
Diocese: AM

Civil Parish: Beaulieu
Map Grid: 61
RC Parish: see Termonfeckin
Diocese: AM

Civil Parish: Cappoge
Map Grid: 38
RC Parish: see Dunleer
Diocese: AM

Civil Parish: Carlingford
Map Grid: 2
RC Parish: Carlingford and Clogherny
Diocese: AM
Earliest Record: b. 4.1835; m. 4.1835; d. 4.1835
Missing Dates: d. 8.1848-10.1867
Status: LC; NLI (mf); Indexed by AA (b/m. to 1900)

Civil Parish: Carrickbaggot
Map Grid: 51
RC Parish: Clogherhead, see Clogher
Diocese: AM

Civil Parish: Castletown
Map Grid: 11
RC Parish: see Dundalk
Diocese: AM

Civil Parish: Charlestown
Map Grid: 27
RC Parish: see Tallanstown
Diocese: AM

Civil Parish: Clogher
Map Grid: 57
RC Parish: Clogherhead (Walshestown and Clogher)
Diocese: AM
Earliest Record: b. 11.1744; m. 2.1742; d. 1744
Missing Dates: b. 10.1777-4.1780, 12.1799-3.1833, 10.1836-8.1837; m. 8.1771-4.1780, 9.1799-4.1833, 10.1836-8.1837
Status: LC; NLI (mf); Indexed by AA (to 1900)

Civil Parish: Clonkeehan
Map Grid: 21

RC Parish: see Tallanstown
Diocese: AM

Civil Parish: Clonkeen
Map Grid: 26
RC Parish: see Tallanstown
Diocese: AM

Civil Parish: Clonmore
Map Grid: 46
RC Parish: Togher
Diocese: AM
Earliest Record: b. 11.1791; m. 7.1791; d. 1791
Missing Dates: b. 4.1828-8.1869; m. 3.1828-2.1873; d. ends 1817
Status: LC; NLI (mf); Indexed by AA (b/m. to 1900; d. to 1817)

Civil Parish: Collon
Map Grid: 48
RC Parish: Collon
Diocese: AM
Earliest Record: b. 4.1789; m. 1.1789
Missing Dates: b. 3.1807-8.1819; m. 2.1807-12.1817, 9.1845-3.1848
Status: LC; NLI (mf)

Civil Parish: Creggan
Map Grid: 6
RC Parish: see Creggan, Co. Armagh
Diocese: AM

Civil Parish: Darver
Map Grid: 20
RC Parish: see Dromiskin
Diocese: AM

Civil Parish: Dromin
Map Grid: 37
RC Parish: see Dunleer
Diocese: AM

Civil Parish: Dromiskin
Map Grid: 19
RC Parish: Darver (Dromiskin)
Diocese: AM
Earliest Record: b. 6.1787; m. 7.1787; d. 1871
Missing Dates: m. 6.1836-5.1837
Status: LC; NLI (mf); Indexed by AA (b/m. to 1900; d. to 1879)

Civil Parish: Drumcar
Map Grid: 35
RC Parish: Togher, see Clonmore
Diocese: AM

Civil Parish: Drumshallon
Map Grid: 55
RC Parish: part Monasterboice; part Termonfeckin
Diocese: AM

Civil Parish: Dunany
Map Grid: 43

RC Parish: Togher, see Clonmore
Diocese: AM

Civil Parish: Dunbin
Map Grid: 13
RC Parish: Kilkerley (Haggardstown/Blackrock)
Diocese: AM
Earliest Record: b. 1.1752; m. 1.1752; d. 1.1752
Missing Dates: d. 3.1806–9.1831, ends 8.1838
Status: LC; NLI (mf); Indexed by AA (to 1900)

Civil Parish: Dundalk
Map Grid: 12
RC Parish: Dundalk
Diocese: AM
Earliest Record: b. 8.1790; m. 8.1790; d. 8.1790
Missing Dates: b. 9.1802–5.1814; m. 11.1802–
10.1817, ends 8.1831; d. ends 11.1802
Status: LC; NLI (mf); Indexed by AA (to 1900)

Civil Parish: Dunleer
Map Grid: 44
RC Parish: Dunleer
Diocese: AM
Earliest Record: b. 1798; m. 1772; d. 1832
Missing Dates: d. 12.1858–1.1877
Status: LC; NLI (mf); Indexed by AA (to 1900)

Civil Parish: Dysart
Map Grid: 45
RC Parish: Togher, see Clonmore
Diocese: AM

Civil Parish: Faughart
Map Grid: 5
RC Parish: Faughart
Diocese: AM
Earliest Record: b. 4.1851; m. 4.1851
Status: LC; NLI (mf); Indexed by AA (to 1900)

Civil Parish: Gernonstown
Map Grid: 32
RC Parish: see Kilsaran
Diocese: AM

Civil Parish: Haggardstown
Map Grid: 15
RC Parish: see Dundalk
Diocese: AM

Civil Parish: Haynestown
Map Grid: 16
RC Parish: Kilkerley, see Dunbin
Diocese: AM

Civil Parish: Inishkeen
Map Grid: 9
RC Parish: see Inishkeen, Co. Monaghan
Diocese: AM

Civil Parish: Kane
Map Grid: 8

RC Parish: see Dundalk
Diocese: AM

Civil Parish: Kildemock
Map Grid: 40
RC Parish: see Ardee
Diocese: AM

Civil Parish: Killany
Map Grid: 23
RC Parish: see Louth
Diocese: AM

Civil Parish: Killincoole
Map Grid: 18
RC Parish: Darver, see Dromiskin
Diocese: AM

Civil Parish: Kilsaran
Map Grid: 31
RC Parish: Kilsaran
Diocese: AM
Earliest Record: b. 1.1809; m. 1.1809
Missing Dates: b. 5.1824–8.1831, 6.1836–7.1853; m.
10.1826–8.1831, 11.1836–9.1853
Status: LC; NLI (mf); Indexed by AA (to 1900)

Civil Parish: Louth
Map Grid: 17
RC Parish: Louth
Diocese: AM
Earliest Record: b. 3.1833; m. 4.1833
Missing Dates: b. 9.1871–10.1873
Status: LC; NLI (mf); Indexed by AA (to 1900)

Civil Parish: Mansfieldstown
Map Grid: 22
RC Parish: Darver, see Dromiskin
Diocese: AM

Civil Parish: Mapastown
Map Grid: 28
RC Parish: see Ardee
Diocese: AM

Civil Parish: Marlestown
Map Grid: 50
RC Parish: see Dunleer
Diocese: AM

Civil Parish: Mayne
Map Grid: 56
RC Parish: Clogherhead, see Clogher
Diocese: AM

Civil Parish: Monasterboice
Map Grid: 54
RC Parish: Monasterboice
Diocese: AM
Earliest Record: b. 1814; m. 1814; d. 1814
Missing Dates: b. 1831–33; d. ends 1822
Status: LC; NLI (mf); Indexed by AA (to 1900)

Civil Parish: Mosstown
Map Grid: 41
RC Parish: see Dunleer
Diocese: AM

Civil Parish: Mullary
Map Grid: 49
RC Parish: see Monasterboice
Diocese: AM

Civil Parish: Parsonstown
Map Grid: 53
RC Parish: Clogherhead, see Clogher
Diocese: AM

Civil Parish: Philipstown (1) (near Barronstown)
Map Grid: 7
RC Parish: Kilkerley, see Dunbin
Diocese: AM

Civil Parish: Philipstown (2) (near Clonkeen)
Map Grid: 24
RC Parish: see Tallanstown
Diocese: AM

Civil Parish: Philipstown (3) (near Drogheda)
Map Grid: 59
RC Parish: see St. Peter's, Drogheda
Diocese: AM

Civil Parish: Port
Map Grid: 47
RC Parish: Togher, see Clonmore
Diocese: AM

Civil Parish: Rathdrumin
Map Grid: 52
RC Parish: Clogherhead, see Clogher
Diocese: AM

Civil Parish: Richardstown
Map Grid: 34
RC Parish: see Dunleer
Diocese: AM

Civil Parish: Roche
Map Grid: 4
RC Parish: see Dundalk; also part Faughart
Diocese: AM

Civil Parish: St. Mary's, Drogheda (see also Co. Meath)
Map Grid: 64
RC Parish: Drogheda, see St. Peter's, below
Diocese: AM

Civil Parish: St. Peter's, Drogheda
Map Grid: 63
RC Parish: Drogheda
Diocese: AM
Earliest Record: b. 1.1744; m. 1804
Missing Dates: b. 5.1757–8.1764, 10.1771–4.1777, 2.1778–6.1781, 4.1795–10.1803, 12.1804–11.1815;

m. 1805–1818
Status: LC; NLI (mf); Indexed by AA (to 1900)

Civil Parish: Salterstown
Map Grid: 42
RC Parish: Togher, see Clonmore
Diocese: AM

Civil Parish: Shanlis
Map Grid: 36
RC Parish: see Ardee
Diocese: AM

Civil Parish: Smarmore
Map Grid: 39
RC Parish: see Ardee
Diocese: AM

Civil Parish: Stabannon
Map Grid: 30
RC Parish: see Kilsaran
Diocese: AM

Civil Parish: Stickillin
Map Grid: 33
RC Parish: see Ardee
Diocese: AM

Civil Parish: Tallanstown
Map Grid: 25
RC Parish: Tallanstown
Diocese: AM
Earliest Record: b. 11.1817; m. 4.1804
Missing Dates: b. 4.1825–9.1830; m. 6.1863–8.1867
Status: LC; NLI (mf); Indexed by AA (to 1900)

Civil Parish: Termonfeckin
Map Grid: 60
RC Parish: Termonfeckin
Diocese: AM
Earliest Record: b. 4.1823; m. 1799; d. 1799
Missing Dates: d. ends 10.1833
Status: LC; NLI (mf); Indexed by AA (to 1900)

Civil Parish: Tullyallen (1) (also in Co. Meath)
Map Grid: 58
RC Parish: Tullyallen, Kilichel, Donoghmore and Killishall, see also Mellifont below
Diocese: AM
Earliest Record: b/m/d. 1.1816
Missing Dates: b. 1.1834–3.1837, 8.1844–8.1845; m. 1.1834–4.1837, 7.1844–9.1845; d. 5.1834–3.1837, 8.1844–8.1845
Status: LC; NLI (mf)

Civil Parish: Tullyallen (2)
Map Grid: 58
RC Parish: Mellifont
Diocese: AM
Earliest Record: b. 12.1821; m. 12.1821
Status: LC; NLI (mf); Indexed by AA (to 1900)

Commercial and Social Directories

1820

J. Pigot's *Commercial Directory of Ireland* contains information on the gentry, nobility, and traders in and around the towns of Drogheda and Dundalk.

1824

J. Pigot's *City of Dublin and Hibernian Provincial Directory* includes traders, nobility, gentry, and clergy lists of Ardee, Carlingford, Castlebellingham, Drogheda, and Dundalk.

1830

McCabe's *Directory of Drogheda*.

1846

Slater's *National Commercial Directory of Ireland* lists nobility, clergy, traders, etc., in Ardee and Louth, Carlingford, Castlebellingham and Dunleer, Drogheda, and Dundalk.

1856

Slater's *Royal National Commercial Directory of Ireland* lists nobility, gentry, clergy, traders, etc., in Ardee and Louth, Carlingford, Castlebellingham and Dunleer, Drogheda, and Dundalk.

1866

G.H. Bassett's *Louth County Guide and Directory*.

1870

Slater's *Directory of Ireland* contains trade, nobility, and clergy lists for Ardee, Carlingford, Castlebellingham, Drogheda, and Dundalk.

1881

Slater's *Royal National Commercial Directory of Ireland* contains lists of traders, clergy, nobility, and farmers in adjoining parishes of the towns of Ardee and Louth, Carlingford, Castlebellingham and Dunleer, Drogheda, and Dundalk.

1894

Slater's *Royal National Directory of Ireland* lists traders, police, teachers, farmers, and private residents in each of the towns, villages, and parishes of the county.

1896

Tempest's *Almanac and Directory of Dundalk*. The 1890-95 editions have no lists of traders. <u>Published annually from 1896.</u> SLC 941.825/c3 k2c.

Family History

Ball of Ball's Grove, Drogheda. *Burke's Irish Family Records*, 1976.

Bolton of Bective House. *Burke's Landed Gentry*, 1863.

Boylan of Hilltown, Drogheda, Co. Louth. *Burke's Irish Family Records*, 1976.

"Butler, The Barony of Dunboyne" by T. Blake Butler. *Irish Genealogist* 2 (1945): 66; (1946): 107; (1947): 130; (1948): 162.

"The Byrnes of Co. Louth." *J. Louth Arch. and Hist. Soc.* 2 (1908-11): 45-49.

"The Clinton Family of Co. Louth." *J. Louth Arch. and Hist. Soc.* 3 (1912): 1-15.

"Clinton Records." *J. Louth Arch. and Hist. Soc.* 12 (1950): 109-16.

"The Dawsons of Ardee." *J. Louth. Arch. and Hist. Soc.* 8 (1933): 22-33.

"The De Verdons of Louth." *R.S.A.I.* 25 (1895): 317-28.

"The De Verdons of Louth." *R.S.A.I.* 29 (1899): 417-19.

"Family Names in Louth." *J. Louth Arch. and Hist. Soc.* 1 (3) (1906): 64-76.

"Genealogy of a North Louth Family (Murphy)." *J. Louth Arch. and Hist. Soc.* 18 (2) (1974): 105-09.

"In Search of a Louth Family, the Nearys." *J. Louth Arch. and Hist. Soc.* 15 (1968): 239-50.

"Moore of Mooremount." Pedigree in *Swanzy Notebooks*. RCB Library, Dublin.

"The Moores of the City of Drogheda." *Gen.* 33, N.S. (1916): 127-28.

The Family of Moore by the Countess of Drogheda. Dublin, 1906.

O'Boyle, Edward. *The Warren Saga*. Londonderry, 1947.

"Potters of Ardee." *J. Louth Arch. and Hist. Soc.* 18 (2) (1974): 165-70.

"Smiths of Cos. Louth and Down." Pedigree in *Swanzy Notebooks*. RCB Library, Dublin.

Amory, T.C. *Materials for a History of the Family of Sullivan . . . of Ardee, Ireland*. Cambridge, Mass., 1893.

"Some Early Documents Relating to English Uriel, and the Towns of Drogheda and Dundalk." In Charles McNeill, *The Draycott Family*; and *J. Louth Arch. and Hist. Soc.* 5 (1924): 270-75.

"Some Notes on the Family of Bellew of Thomastown, Co. Louth." *J. Louth Arch. and Hist. Soc.* 5 (1923): 193-97.

"Some Notes on the Family of Warren of Warrenstown, Co. Louth." *J. Louth Arch. and Hist. Soc.* 4 (1916): 26-34.

"Taaffe of Co. Louth." *J. Louth Arch. and Hist. Soc.* 14 (1960): 55-67.

Warren, Thomas. *History of the Warren Family.* 1902.

Gravestone Inscriptions

Ardee: *Ir. Gen.* 3 (1) (1956): 36–40.

Ballymakenny: *Seanchas Ardmhacha* 2 (1) (1983/84): 107–27.

Ballymascanlon: *Louth Arch. J.* 17 (4) (1972): 215–27.

Ballypousta (Kildemock, C of I): *Louth Arch. J.* 12 (1) (1949): 37.

Bannteale—see Rathdrummin.

Beaulieu: *Louth Arch. J.* 10 (1): 1981.

Cappoge—see Dysart.

Carlingford: *Louth Arch. J.* 19 (2) (1978): 149–65.

Castlebellingham: Leslie, Rev. James B. *History of Kilsaran Union of Parishes in the Co. of Louth.* 1908.

Castletown (Dundalk): *Tombstone Inscriptions in Castletown Graveyard, Dundalk.* Old Dundalk Society, 1992.

Charlestown: L'Estrange, G.W. *Notes and Jottings Concerning the Parish of Charlestown Union.* 1912.

Clogher: SLC 941.825/C2 v3g.

Clonkeen: L'Estrange, G.W. *Notes and Jottings Concerning the Parish of Charlestown Union.* 1912.

Clonmore (near Dunleer): *Louth Arch. J.* 20 (2) 1982.

Collon, Mosstown, and Dromin: by James Garry (1985); SLC 941.825/k29c.

Drogheda, St. Mary's Churchyard: SLC 941.825/D2 v3gj.

Dromiskin: Leslie, Rev. James B. *History of Kilsaran Union of Parishes in the Co. of Louth.* 1908.

Dundalk (St. Leonard's Garden): *Irish-American Genealogist* (1978): 174–75, 179–80.

Dunleer: *Louth Arch. J.* 22 (4) (1992): 446–452 (fifty-three inscriptions).

Dysart, Cappoge, and Drumshallon: *Louth Arch. J.* 19 (3) (1979): 240–48.

Drumshallon—see Dysart.

Faughart: *Tombstone Inscriptions from Fochart.* Dundalgan Press, 1968.

Faughart: Maclomhair, Rev. D. *Urnai.* Dundalk: Dundalgan Press, 1969; SLC 94.5 A150 (cemetery).

Kildemock: *Louth Arch J.* 13 (1) (1953): 81–82.

Killanny: *Clogher Record* 6 (1) 1966.

Kilsaran: Leslie, Rev. James B. *History of Kilsaran Union of Parishes in the Co. of Louth.* 1908.

Louth Village: "St. Mary's Abbey." *Louth Arch. J.* 19 (4) (1980): 297–317.

Mansfieldstown: Leslie, Rev. James B. *History of Kilsaran Union of Parishes in the Co. of Louth.* 1908.

Mayne: *Louth Arch. J.* 20 (4) (1984); SLC 941.825/M1 v3g.

Newtownstalaban: *Louth Arch. J.* 17 (2) 1970.

Port: *Louth Arch. J.* 21 (2) (1986): 208–218 (over seventy inscriptions).

Rathdrumin and Banntaaffe (Glebe Townland): *Louth Arch. J.* 19 (1) (1977): 74–76.

Seatown, Dundalk: *Tempest's Annual Directory and Guide for the Town of Dundalk.* Dundalgan Press, 1967, 1971–72.

Shanalis—see Smarmore.

Smarmore, Stickillin, and Shanalis. *Louth Arch. J.* 22 (1) (1989): 82–89.

Stabannon: Leslie, Rev. James B. *History of Kilsaran Union of Parishes in the Co. of Louth.* 1908.

Stagrennan: *J. Old Drogheda Soc.* 2 (1977): 31–36.

Stickillin—see Smarmore.

Termonfeckin: *Ir. Gen.* 8 (2): 293–305; 8 (3): 436–452.

Tullyallen: *Seanchas Ardmhacha* 8 (2) (1977): 308–43.

Newspapers

Title: *Drogheda Argus* (continued as *Argus* in 1951)
Published in: Drogheda, 1835–current
NLI Holdings: 1.1859–12.1913; 7.1927–in progress
BL Holdings: 9.1835–12.1921; 1.1923–11.1936

Title: *Drogheda Conservative Journal*
Published in: Drogheda, 1837–48
NLI Holdings: 6.1837–12.1848
BL Holdings: 6.1837–12.1848

Title: *Drogheda Independent*
Published in: Drogheda, 1884–current
NLI Holdings: odd numbers 12.1884–8.1889; 1889–in progress
BL Holdings: 1.1890–in progress

Title: *Drogheda Journal*
Published in: Drogheda, 1788–1843
NLI Holdings: 1.1823–5.1840; 7.1841–3.1843
BL Holdings: 1.1823–5.1840; 7.1841–3.1843

Title: *Dundalk and Newry Express*
Published in: Dundalk, 1860–70
BL Holdings: 6–10.1860; 10–11.1861; 12.1861–1.1870

Title: *Dundalk Democrat*
Published in: Dundalk, 1849–current
NLI Holdings: 10.1849–in progress
BL Holdings: 10.1849–10.1948 (except 1926)

Title: *Dundalk Examiner*
Published in: Dundalk, 1881–1960
NLI Holdings: odd numbers 1920; 1929–30
BL Holdings: 1.1881–6.1930

Title: *Dundalk Herald*
Published in: Dundalk, 1868–1921
NLI Holdings: 1880 (two issues)
BL Holdings: 10.1868–1.1921

Title: *The Conservative* (continued as *Drogheda Conservative* in 1864)
Published in: Drogheda, 1849–1908
NLI Holdings: odd numbers 4.1855–3.1901
BL Holdings: 6.1849–10.1908

Wills and Administrations

A discussion of the types of records, where they are held, and their availability and value is given in the Wills section of the introduction. The availability of prerogative wills, administrations, and marriage license records is also described in the relevant parts of the same section. Where available, published sources of these records are given in the Miscellaneous Sources section.

Pre-1858 Wills and Administrations

Prerogative Wills. See the introduction.

Consistorial Wills. County Louth is mainly in the diocese of Armagh, with two parishes in Clogher. The guide to Catholic parish records in this chapter shows the diocese to which each civil parish belonged. The wills of residents of each diocese were usually proven within that diocese (see the Wills section for exceptions). The following records survive:

Wills

See the introduction. There are eighty-six wills in the Townley Hall papers. NLI D 15093–15178.

"Indexed List of Wills of Dundalk Residents." *Louth Arch. J.* 10 (2) (1942): 113–15 (some 250 names, addresses, dates, and a few occupations).

Abstracts

See the introduction.

Indexes

Armagh—see Co. Armagh Clogher—see Co. Monaghan.

Post-1858 Wills and Administrations

This county was served by the District Registry of Armagh. The surviving records are kept in the PRONI and NAI. Records include: Armagh District Will Books (1858–1900). NAI; SLC films 917201, 917484–92, 917906–16.

Marriage Licenses

Indexes

Armagh (1727–1845). NAI; SLC film 100859–860. Clogher (1709–1866). NAI; SLC film 100862; see also Miscellaneous Sources below.

Miscellaneous Sources

"A Census of Ardee, Co. Louth in 1760." *Ir. Gen.* 3 (5): 179–84.

"Clergy and Churchwardens of Termonfeckin Parish (1725–1804)." *Louth Arch. J.* 17 (2) (1970): 84–86.

D'Alton, John. *A History of Drogheda.* 2 vols. 1844.

"Dowdall Deeds." Irish Manuscripts Commission. Dublin: Stationery Office, 1960.

"Drogheda Census, 1798" (numbers on each street). *Louth Arch. J.* 17 (2) (1970): 91–95.

"Farm Account Books from Gaulstown, Monasterboice 1802–1860." *Louth Arch. J.* 17 (4) (1972): 235–49 (lists over two hundred names of laborers, tenants, etc., and financial dealings—including loans to send family members to America).

Leslie, Rev. J.B. "History of Kilsaran (Co. Louth)." Dundalk: Dundalgan Press, 1986.

"Old Title Deeds of Co. Louth." *Louth Arch. J.* 7 (2) (1930): 168–74; 7 (3) (1931): 402–05; 7 (4) (1932): 488–96; 8 (1) (1933): 52–60; 8 (2) (1934): 193–209; 8 (3) (1935): 283–88; 10 (1) (1941): 63–66; 10 (3) (1943): 245–50; 11 (1) (1945): 58–62.

"Roll of the Sovereigns and Burgesses of Carlingford 1706–1828." *Louth Arch. J.* 3 (3) (1914): 273–82.

"Some (Nineteen) Dundalk leases (1715–1815)." *Louth Arch. J.* 6 (4) (1928): 213–28. Gives 1,544 tenants on the primates lands in Clonfeacle, Kilmore, O'Neilland, Deanery of Dundalk, Drumyskyn (Dromiskin), Primatestown, Kilmone, and the Newton of Monasterboyde.

"Title Deed Extracts: Drakestown and Kilpatrick (part of Kildemock) 1669–1852." *Louth Arch. J.* 12 (1) (1949): 61–81.

"Title Deed Extracts: Paughanstown, Hacklim and Roestown." *Louth Arch. J.* 12 (3) (1951): 157–96.

"Title Deed Extracts: Millockstown and Blakestown." *Louth Arch. J.* 13 (1) (1953): 102–23.

"The Landless in Mid-Nineteenth-Century Louth." *Louth Arch. J.* 16 (2) (1966): 103–10.

Ua Dubhthaigh, Padraic. "The Book of Dundalk." Sligo: Champion Publications, 1946.

"Volunteers, Militia, Yeomanry, and Orangemen (1726–1825)." *Louth Arch. J.* 18 (4) (1976): 279–94 (officers' names).

Research Sources and Services

Journals

County Louth Archaeological and Historical Journal
Seanchas Ardmhacha
Clogher Record
Tempest's Annual (to 1976 only)
Journal of the Old Drogheda Society

Libraries and Information Sources

Louth County Library, Chapel Street, Dundalk, Co. Louth. Ph: (042) 35457. The library has a sizable collection of local history materials, including books, directories, newspapers, periodicals, photographs, estate papers, etc.

Research Services

Armagh Ancestry, 42 English Street, Armagh, N. Ireland, BT61 7AB. Ph: (0861) 521802; fax: (0861) 510033. This organization has computer-indexed all of Armagh and some of the Louth Catholic church registers pre-1900, and some Presbyterian church registers pre-1900. Further Presbyterian registers, Church of Ireland registers, and pre-1922 death records are being indexed. Researchers are advised to contact the center for an updated list of registers, and other sources, indexed. Research services are conducted for a fee.

Armagh Record Centre, Ara Coeli, Armagh BT61 7GY. Ph: (01861) 522981. This is the record center for the Catholic Archdiocese of Armagh. They have indexed all of the Catholic records of the diocese, which covers both the counties Armagh and Louth.

See also Meath Heritage Centre—Co. Meath chapter.

See also Research Services in Dublin in the introduction.

Societies

County Louth Archaeological and Historical Society, Mr. Noel Ross, 5 Oliver Plunkett Park, Dundalk, Co. Louth

Old Drogheda Society, Ms. Peggy O'Reilly, 8 The Pines, Dublin Road, Drogheda, Co. Louth

Old Dundalk Society, Ms. Imelda Hanratty, 29 Culhane Street, Dundalk, Co. Louth

Louth Civil Parishes as Numbered on Map

1. Ballymascanlon (2 pts.)
2. Carlingford
3. Ballyboys
4. Roche
5. Faughart
6. Creggan
7. Philipstown (see also 24 and 59)
8. Kane
9. Inishkeen (2 pts.)
10. Barronstown
11. Castletown (2 pts.)
12. Dundalk
13. Dunbin
14. Ballybarrack
15. Haggardstown
16. Haynestown
17. Louth
18. Killincoole
19. Dromiskin
20. Darver
21. Clonkeehan
22. Mansfieldstown
23. Killanny (2 pts.)
24. Philipstown (see also 7 and 59)
25. Tallanstown
26. Clonkeen
27. Charlestown
28. Mapastown
29. Ardee
30. Stabannon
31. Kilsaran
32. Gernonstown
33. Stickillin
34. Richardstown
35. Drumcar
36. Shanlis (2 pts.)
37. Dromin
38. Cappoge
39. Smarmore
40. Kildemock
41. Mosstown
42. Salterstown
43. Dunany
44. Dunleer
45. Dysart
46. Clonmore
47. Port
48. Collon
49. Mullary
50. Marlestown

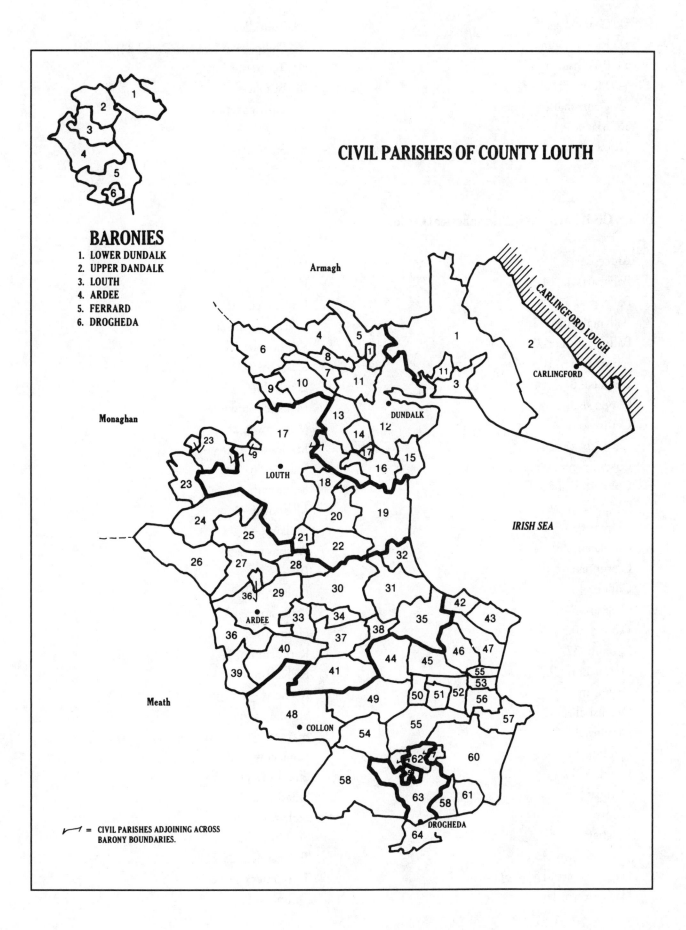

CIVIL PARISHES OF COUNTY LOUTH

BARONIES

1. LOWER DUNDALK
2. UPPER DANDALK
3. LOUTH
4. ARDEE
5. FERRARD
6. DROGHEDA

Armagh

Monaghan

Meath

CARLINGFORD LOUGH

CARLINGFORD

DUNDALK

IRISH SEA

LOUTH

ARDEE

COLLON

DROGHEDA

⌐ = CIVIL PARISHES ADJOINING ACROSS
      BARONY BOUNDARIES.

51. Carrickbaggot
52. Rathdrumin
53. Parsonstown
54. Monasterboice
55. Drumshallon (2 pts.)
56. Mayne
57. Clogher

58. Tullyallen (2 pts.)
59. Philipstown (see also 7 and 24)
60. Termonfeckin
61. Beaulieu
62. Ballymakenny
63. St. Peter's
64. St. Mary's

Louth Civil Parishes in Alphabetical Order

Ardee: 29
Ballybarrack: 14
Ballyboys: 3
Ballymakenny: 62
Ballymascanlon (2 pts.): 1
Barronstown: 10
Beaulieu: 61
Cappoge: 38
Carlingford: 2
Carrickbaggot: 51
Castletown (2 pts.): 11
Charlestown: 27
Clogher: 57
Clonkeehan: 21
Clonkeen: 26
Clonmore: 46
Collon: 48
Creggan: 6
Darver: 20
Dromin: 37
Dromiskin: 19
Drumcar: 35
Drumshallon (2 pts.): 55
Dunany: 43
Dunbin: 13
Dundalk: 12
Dunleer: 44
Dysart: 45
Faughart: 5
Gernonstown: 32
Haggardstown: 15
Haynestown: 16

Inishkeen (2 pts.): 9
Kane: 8
Kildemock: 40
Killanny (2 pts.): 23
Killincoole: 18
Kilsaran: 31
Louth: 17
Mansfieldstown: 22
Mapastown: 28
Marlestown: 50
Mayne: 56
Monasterboice: 54
Mosstown: 41
Mullary: 49
Parsonstown: 53
Port: 47
Philipstown: 7
Philipstown: 24
Philipstown: 59
Rathdrumin: 52
Richardstown: 34
Roche: 4
St. Mary's: 64
St. Peter's: 63
Salterstown: 42
Shanlis (2 pts.): 36
Smarmore: 39
Stabannon: 30
Stickillin: 33
Tallanstown: 25
Termonfeckin: 60
Tullyallen (2 pts.): 58

County Mayo

A Brief History

Situated on the northwestern shore of Connaught, County Mayo contains the towns of Killala, Castlebar, Crossmolina, Westport, and Ballina.

The main Gaelic families in the area were O'Malley, O'Flaherty, McEvilly, O'Henaghan, and O'Flannery. Among the Norman families who settled in this county were the Burkes, Barretts, Nangles, Costelloes, and Jordans. Other septs related to these Norman families and now found in the county include the McPhilbins, McAndrews, Prendergasts, and Fitzmaurices.

After the seventeenth-century redistribution of Mayo land to English adventurers, the major estate-holders included Browne, Altamont, and Cuffe. During the seventeenth century, there were a few attempts to settle parts of Mayo with people from England or northern Ireland. One such settlement was that of the Mullett Peninsula, with families from Ulster. Several of these, including the Dixons, established themselves in the area. Many families who were forced to leave the northern counties because of the sectarian fighting of the 1790s also settled in Mayo. These incidents have been relatively well documented.

In 1798, the French landed 1100 men in Mayo under General Humbert to assist the rebellion of United Irishmen. This invasion was too late to be effective, however, as the main rebellion had been defeated earlier in the year. Assisted by local rebels, this army took control of Mayo, but was eventually defeated at Ballinamuck.

The land in Mayo is relatively poor. In spite of this, the county was one of the most densely populated at the beginning of the nineteenth century, when there were 474 people per square mile of arable land in the county. This dense population was very badly affected by the Great Famine of 1845–47. The population dropped from almost 390,000 in 1841 to 274,000 in 1851. Approximately 45,000 people died between 1845 and 1850, and huge numbers emigrated. Between 1850 and 1855 alone, over 21,000 people emigrated. By 1891 the population had dropped to 219,000, and is currently around 115,000.

Census and Census Substitutes

1600–1700

Mayo Landowners in the Seventeenth Century. *R.S.A.I.* (1962): 153–162; 95 (1965): 237–47.

1636–1703

Books of Survey and Distribution, Vol. II. Co. Mayo. R.C. Simington. Dublin: Stationery Office, 1956. SLC film 962524.

1783

Register of the Householders of the Parish of Ballinrobe Showing Residence. *Anal. Hib.* 14: 113–17.

1787

Rental of the Altamont Estate in Thirteen Civil Parishes, including Westport town. NAI M 5788 (2). Westport town extracts published in *Cathair na Mairt* (2) 1.

1790–1810

Rental of the Dillon Estate. Indexed by South Mayo Family Research Centre (see Research Services at the end of the chapter).

1796

"Lists of Catholics Emigrating from Ulster to Mayo" (arranged by parish and counties of origin, i.e., Antrim,

374   MARKET-WOMEN.

which they remained from the 26th of August to the 26th of September. The Earl of Lucan, the owner of the town, has a residence in the suburbs, but it does not possess any particular attractions.

It was market day at Castlebar when I arrived there, and I strolled for a couple of hours among the market people. Great numbers of women, holding a hank or two of yarn of their own spinning, stood in the streets and offered their trifling commodities for sale. Very few of those whom I addressed could speak English; but some of the men about, seeing the disadvantages under which I laboured, very obligingly stepped forward, and offered assistance as interpreters. This sort of politeness is common to the Irish. I ascertained that the women could not earn by spinning more than a penny or two-pence a day, and hundreds of them attended the market whose earnings for the whole week did not exceed sixpence or ninepence; yet notwithstanding this inadequate reward of long and hard labour, their honest countenances wore the habi-

RENTS—LABOURERS' WAGES.   375

tual impress of cheerfulness and perfect good humour. Scarcely any of the women had shoes, and I felt considerable alarm while threading my way through a dense crowd, lest I should step upon their feet.

The corn and meal were brought into the town by horses, mules, and asses, many of which remained in the market with their loads upon their backs. Oats were selling at 5d. and 6d. per stone. But little wheat is produced in the neighbourhood, nor is barley much grown, except to supply the potheen manufactories in the mountains. Rents are about 20s. an acre; and wages from 6d. to 8d. a day; but if regular work is afforded, 6d., without diet, is the usual amount. Although their agriculture and customs seem better adapted to the last century, yet if we may draw a comparison between their present practises, and the account given by Arthur Young in 1779, some improvement has actually taken place. "To Castlebar," says he, "over an indifferent country and a vile stony road; about that town the husbandry is admirable. They have three customs,

A description of Fair Day in Castlebar, County Mayo, in 1835. From *The Miseries and Beauties of Ireland* by Jonathan Binns (London, 1837).

Armagh, Cavan, Down, Fermanagh, Derry, Monaghan, and Tyrone). *Seanchas Ardmhacha* 3 (1) (1958): 17–50.

"Lists of Northern Catholics Recently Settled in Mayo Compiled by Landlords Browne, Altamont, and Cuffe." SPO Reb. Papers 620 (series for 1796). Cuffe list: SPO/620/26/145. Altamont list: SPO 620/26/82–only twenty-two names, plus numbers of children and county and parish of origin.

Spinning Wheel Premium List (see introduction). Published in *Cathair na Mairt* 11 (1) (1991): 93–97.

1798

List of Persons Who Suffered Losses in '98 Rebellion. NLI JLB 94107 (approximately 650 names, addresses, and occupations).

1815

Rental of the Altamont Estate for Westport Town. NAI M 5788 (2). Also published in *Cathair na Mairt* (2) 1.

1820

Protestant householders in Killala. NAI MFCI 32.

1823–38

Tithe Applotment Survey (see introduction).

1825

Rental of the Browne Estate. Indexed by South Mayo Family Research Centre (see Research Services at the end of the chapter).

1826–27

Mayo Assizes Quaere Book. NLI IR 94123 M3 (names contractors, public employees, jurymen, etc.).

1830–60

Pupils at Lehinch National School (Parish of Kilcommon). *Journal of South Mayo Family Research* 1989, pp. 39–49.

1832

Protestant residents of Foxford. NLI Ms. 8295.

1833

Memorial of cess-payers of the parish of Crossmolina. NAI OP 1833/77 (approximately 170 names).

Rental of the Clanmorris Estate (Parishes of Kilcommon, Kilmainemore, Mayo, Robeen, Rosslee, Tonaghty, and Toomour). NLI Ms. 3279.

1839

List of Persons who obtained Game Certificates in . . . Mayo, etc. PRONI T 688.

1848

Rental of the Lindsey Estate. Indexed by South Mayo Family Research Centre (see Research Services at the end of the chapter).

1851

Rental of lands under care of a Court Receiver in Castleleaffy Estate, Rosehill, Carrowmore and Cahir, Clare Island, Ballynew Estate, Kilboyne Estate and Kilmacarrow, Co. Mayo. NAI M 2795.

1852–54 and 1878–82

Tenants of John Hearne, Agent to De Montmorency Estate, Ballinrobe. *Journal of South Mayo Family Research* 1989, pp. 23–27 (240 tenants).

1856–57

Griffith's Valuation (see introduction).

1856–57

Persons entitled to vote in Co. Mayo, listing names, addresses, nature of qualification, etc. Barony of Tyrawley (535 persons) NAI M 2782; Kilmaine (370 persons) NAI M 2783; Gallen (372 persons) NAI M 2784.

1878–79

Rental of the Moore Estate. Indexed by South Mayo Family Research Centre (see Research Services at the end of the chapter).

1878–82 (Ballinrobe)—see 1852–54

1901

Census. NAI (see introduction). SLC film 846215–62.

Mayo-born people in Kingstown, Co. Dublin, 1901 census. *Dun Laoghaire Gen. Soc. J.* 5 (2) (1996): 71–74.

Achill Parish Index. Indianapolis: W.G. Masterson, 1994.

1908

Tenants of Fitzgerald Estate, Turlough Park, Castlebar. *Journal of South Mayo Family Research* 1989, p. 30–37. (Name index of 380 tenants.)

1911

Census. NAI.

Church Records

Church of Ireland

See the introduction for a description of Church of Ireland records and their major repositories. Many C of I records were lost in the PRO fire of 1922. These are indicated as "Lost." However, as Church of Ireland records were effectively state records, the records of marriage (from 1845) are also in the General Registrar's Office. Many are still in local custody (LC), while others are in one of a variety of other archives (e.g., RCBL or NAI).

Many of the parish registers of this county have been indexed by the two local heritage centers, Mayo North Family History Research Centre and South Mayo Family Research Centre (see Research Services at the end of the chapter). Searches of the indexes will be conducted by the centers for a fee. Those indexed are noted as "Indexed by MNFHRC" or "by SMFRC" as appropriate.

Achill
Earliest Records: b. 1854–; m. 1855–
Status: LC; RCBL; NAI MFCI 33 (d. 1854–77)

Aghaslee or Aasleagh
Earliest Records: b. 1875–; m. 1859–; d.1879–
Status: RCBL (b. 1875–1956); Indexed by SMFRC (to 1900)

Aglish—see Castlebar

Aughagower and Knappagh
Earliest Records: b. 1810–; m. 1810–; d. 1825
Status: LC; NAI MFCI 33 (b. 1825–92; m. 1828–46; d. 1828–93); Indexed by SMFRC (to 1900)

Aughaval (Westport)
Earliest Records: b. 1801–; m. 1802–; d. 1820–
Status: RCBL; NAI MFCI 33 (b. 1801–72; m. 1802–45; d. 1820–1908); Indexed by SMFRC (to 1900)

Ayle
Earliest Records: b. 1825–; m. 1828–; d. 1828–
Status: RCBL

Balla
Earliest Records: b. 1871–; m. 1878–; d. 1887–
Status: LC; Indexed by SMFRC (to 1900)

Ballina
Earliest Records: b. 1770–; m. 1770–; d. 1871–
Status: LC; Indexed by MNFHRC (to 1900)

Ballinakill
Earliest Records: b. 1852–; d. 1852–
Status: NAI MFCI 31 and LC (b/d. 1852)

Ballinchalla or The Neale
Earliest Records: b. 1831–; m. 1832–; d. 1831–
Status: LC; RCBL (b. 1831–35; m. 1832–1917; d. 1831–36); Indexed by SMFRC (to 1900)

Ballinrobe
Earliest Records: b. 1796–; m. 1809–; d. 1809–
Status: LC; RCBL (b. 1796–1912; m. 1809–62; d.

1809–1974); NAI MFCI 35 (b. 1796–1872; m. 1809–46; d. 1809–75); Indexed by SMFRC (to 1900)

Ballycastle
Earliest Records: b. 1842–; m. 1844–; d. 1877–
Status: LC; Indexed by MNFHRC (to 1899)

Ballycroy (Kilcommon Erris)
Earliest Records: m. 1855–98; d. 1883–1962
Status: RCBL

Ballyhane or Ballyhean
Earliest Records: m. 1875–; d. 1855–
Status: LC; Indexed by SMFRC (to 1900)

Ballyovey
Earliest Records: b. 1879–; m. 1854–; d. 1880–
Status: RCBL; Indexed by SMFRC (to 1900 for m., 1880 for d.)

Ballysakeery
Earliest Records: b. 1802–; m. 1802–; d. 1802–
Status: LC; NAI MFCI 32

Belcarra Church (Drum Parish)
Earliest Records: b. 1877–; m. 1845–; d. 1879–
Status: LC; Indexed by SMFRC (to 1900)

Belmullet (see also Kilcommon Erris)
Earliest Records: b.1877–;
Status: LC; Indexed by MNFHRC (to 1900)

Binghamstown (see Kilcommon Erris)

Bulnahinich
Earliest Records: m. 1854–
Status: RCBL

Burriscarra (see Ballyhane)

Burrishoole
Status: Lost

Castlebar (Aglish)
Earliest Records: b. 1835–; m. 1835–; d. 1834–
Status: LC; NAI MFCI 33 (b. 1835–72; m. 1835–72; d. 1834–67); Indexed by SMFRC (b. 1840–; m. 1845–; d. 1848–; all to 1900)

Castlekirk
Earliest Records: b. 1879–; m. 1876–; d. 1879–
Status: LC; Indexed by SMFRC (to 1925, 1905, and 1963, respectively)

Castlemore
Earliest Records: b. 1890–; m. 1847–
Status: RCBL

Claremorris (see Kilcoleman)

Cong
Earliest Records: b. 1746–; m. 1745–; d. 1745–
Status: LC; RCBL (b. 1746–1863; m. 1745–1956; d. 1745–1863); NAI MFCI 32 (b. 1746–1863; m. 1745–1956); Indexed by SMFRC (to 1900)

Cooneal
Earliest Records: b. 1802-; m. 1802-
Status: LC; Indexed by MNFHRC (to 1900)

Crossboyne
Earliest Records: b. 1747-; m. 1854-; d. 1873-
Status: LC; RCBL (b. 1877-1924; m. 1854-1937; d. 1879-1973); Indexed by SMFRC (to 1900)

Crossmolina
Earliest Records: b. 1768-; m. 1769-; d. 1779-
Status: LC; NAI MFCI 6; Indexed by MNFHRC (b/m. to 1899); SLC film 897365 (b. 1768-1817; m/d. 1758-1823)

Drum (see Belcarra)

Dugort (Achill)
Earliest Records: b. 1838-; m. 1838-; d. 1838-
Status: LC; NAI MFCI 33/4; RCBL (m. 1845-88)

Dunfeeny and Kilbride
Status: Lost

Foxford
Earliest Records: b. 1844-; m. 1844-
Status: LC; Indexed by MNFHRC (to 1900)

Hollymount (see Kilcommon)

Kilcolman (Claremorris)
Earliest Records: b. 1877-; m. 1846-; d. 1878-
Status: RCBL; Indexed by SMFRC (all records)

Kilcommon Erris
Status: Lost

Kilcommon Hollymount Union
Earliest Records: b. 1921-; m. 1845-; d. 1920-
Status: RCBL; Indexed by SMFRC (m. to 1937)

Kilconduff
Status: Lost

Kilgeever (see Louisburgh)

Killala
Earliest Records: b. 1757-; m. 1704-; d. 1758-
Status: NAI MFCI 31/2 (b. 1757-1871; m. 1759-1842; d. 1758-1877); Indexed to 1900 by MNFHRC (b. 1810-; m. 1704-; d. 1838-); SLC film 897365 (b. 1757-1769; m. 1757-1767; d. 1757-1772)

Killedan
Status: Lost

Kilmainemore
Earliest Records: b. 1744-; m. 1744-; d. 1774-; (also Vestry Book, 1812-19, containing some entries of baptisms, marriages, and burials, 1811-23)
Missing Dates: b/m/d. 1779-1820
Status: LC; RCBL (b. 1744-1927; m. 1744-1891; d. 1744-1958); NAI MFCI 35, M6088 (as for RCBL, except d. 1744-1908); Indexed by SMFRC (to 1900 for b. and m., 1948 for d.)

Kilmina (Kilmeena)
Earliest Records: b. 1887-1904; m. 1845-1917
Status: RCBL

Kilmore Erris and Kilcommon
Earliest Records: b. 1877-
Status: LC; Indexed by MNFHRC (to 1900)

Kilmoremoy
Earliest Records: b. 1793-1874; m. 1793-1846; d. 1769-1875
Status: NAI MFCI 35/6; SLC film 897365 (b. 1768-1817; m. 1768-1815; d. 1768-1821)

Knappagh
Earliest Records: b. 1855-; d. 1855-
Status: LC; NAI MFCI 32 (d. 1855-71) and RCBL (m. 1855-1952)

Lackan
Status: Lost

Louisburgh or Kilgeever
Earliest Records: b. 1846-; m. 1846-; d. 1810-
Status: RCBL (b/m. 1846-1952); Indexed by SMFRC (to 1900 for b. and m., 1970 for d.)

Mayo
Earliest Records: m. 1849-
Status: RCBL (1849-62)

Moygounagh (see also Crossmolina)
Earliest Records: b. 1856-
Status: LC

Straid (see Templemore)

Swineford (see Kilconduff)

Toomore (see Straid)

Templemore
Earliest Records: b. 1755-; m. 1758-; d. 1755-
Status: LC

Turlough (see also Castlebar)
Earliest Records: b. 1810-; m. 1810-; d. 1810-
Status: LC; NAI MFCI 36 (b. 1821-72; m. 1822-56; d. 1822-73); Indexed by SMFRC (to 1900)

Westport (see Aughaval)

Methodist

Methodist churches were located in several parts of the county. No death records were maintained. Several of the Methodist registers have been indexed by Mayo North Family History Research Centre (see Research Services at the end of the chapter). A search of their index will be conducted for a fee. Those indexed are noted below as "Indexed by MNFHRC."

Ballina
Starting Date: b. 1838-; m. 1864-
Status: LC; Indexed by MNFHRC (to 1900)

Castlebar
Starting Date: b. 1829-; m. 1868-
Status: LC; Indexed by MNFHRC (to 1900)

Crossmolina
Starting Date: m. 1866-1871
Status: LC; Indexed by MNFHRC

Erris
Starting Date: b. 1851-61
Status: LC; Indexed by MNFHRC

Killala
Starting Date: b. 1852-1864; m. 1864-
Status: LC; Indexed by MNFHRC (b. 1852-1864; m. 1864-1900)

Westport
Starting Date: b. 1851-; m. 1864-
Status: LC; Indexed by MNFHRC (b. 1851-1900; m. 1864-1897)

Presbyterian

An account of Presbyterian records is given in the introduction. These registers rarely contain death records, and occasionally have only records of births. This is indicated where appropriate. The Mayo registers have been indexed by the two local heritage centers, Mayo North Family History Research Centre and South Mayo Family Research Centre (see Research Services at the end of the chapter). Searches of the indexes will be conducted by the centers for a fee. Those indexed are noted as "Indexed by MNFHRC" or "by SMFRC" as appropriate.

Aglish (Castlebar)
Starting Date: m. 1897
Status: LC; Indexed by SMFRC

Aughaval (Westport)
Starting Date: b. 1859-; m. 1853-
Status: LC; Indexed by SMFRC (to 1900)

Ballysakeery
Starting Date: b. 1848-; m. 1837-
Status: LC; Indexed by MNFHRC (to 1900)

Burrishoole
Starting Date: b. 1850-; m. 1859-
Status: LC; Indexed by MNFHRC (b. 1850-1900; m. 1859-1890)

Doonfeeney
Starting Date: b. 1849-; m. 1851-
Status: LC; Indexed by MNFHRC (b. 1849-1900; m. 1851-1896)

Kilmascanlon
Starting Date: b. 1849-1897; m. 1857-1897
Status: LC; Indexed by MNFHRC

Kilmoremoy
Starting Date: b. 1846-; m. 1851-

Status: LC; Indexed by MNFHRC (to 1900)

Turlough
Starting Date: b. 1819-; m. 1819-
Status: LC; Indexed by MNFHRC (to 1900 and 1898, respectively)

Roman Catholic

Note that the Catholic parish registers of this county have been indexed by the two local heritage centers, Mayo North Family History Research Centre and South Mayo Family Research Centre (see Research Services at the end of the chapter). Searches of the indexes will be conducted by the centers for a fee. Those indexed are noted as "Indexed by MNFHRC" or "by SMFRC" as appropriate. Microfilm copies of all registers are also available in the National Library of Ireland (NLI), and through the LDS library system.

Civil Parish: Achill
Map Grid: 19
RC Parish: Achill
Diocese: TU
Earliest Record: b. 12.1867; m. 10.1821
Status: LC; NLI (mf); Indexed by MNFHRC

Civil Parish: Addergoole
Map Grid: 16
RC Parish: Addergoole (Lahardane)
Diocese: KA
Earliest Record: b. 1.1840; m. 1.1840
Status: LC; NLI (mf); Indexed by MNFHRC

Civil Parish: Aghagower
Map Grid: 48
RC Parish: Aghagower (Westport)
Diocese: TU
Earliest Record: b. 4.1828; m. 11.1821
Missing Dates: b. 5.1836-3.1842
Status: LC; NLI (mf); Indexed by SMFRC

Civil Parish: Aghamore
Map Grid: 70
RC Parish: Aghamore
Diocese: TU
Earliest Record: b. 2.1864; m. 12.1864
Status: LC; NLI (mf); Indexed by SMFRC

Civil Parish: Aglish
Map Grid: 24
RC Parish: Aglish, Ballyhean, and Breaghy
Diocese: TU
Earliest Record: b. 1.1838; m. 6.1824
Status: LC; NLI (mf); Indexed by SMFRC

Civil Parish: Annagh
Map Grid: 73
RC Parish: Ballyhaunis (Annagh)
Diocese: TU
Earliest Record: b. 11.1851; m. 6.1821
Status: LC; NLI (mf); Indexed by SMFRC

Civil Parish: Ardagh
Map Grid: 14
RC Parish: Ardagh
Diocese: KA
Earliest Record: b. 1866; m. 1882
Status: LC; NLI (mf); Indexed by MNFHRC

Civil Parish: Athymass
Map Grid: 36
RC Parish: Attymass
Diocese: KA
Earliest Record: b. 6.1875; m. 2.1874
Status: LC; NLI (mf); Indexed by MNFHRC

Civil Parish: Balla
Map Grid: 59
RC Parish: Balla, Belcarra, and Manulla
Diocese: TU
Earliest Record: b. 5.1837; m. 7.1821
Status: LC; NLI (mf); Indexed by SMFRC

Civil Parish: Ballinchalla
Map Grid: 52
RC Parish: see Cong
Diocese: TU

Civil Parish: Ballinrobe
Map Grid: 50
RC Parish: Ballinrobe
Diocese: TU
Earliest Record: b. 8.1843; m. 10.1821
Missing Dates: 4.1856–1.1861; 4.1856–1.1861
Status: LC; NLI (mf); Indexed by SMFRC

Civil Parish: Ballintober
Map Grid: 30
RC Parish: Burriscarra and Ballintubber
Diocese: TU
Earliest Record: b. 9.1839; m. 9.1839
Status: LC; NLI (mf); Indexing planned by SMFRC

Civil Parish: Ballyhean
Map Grid: 27
RC Parish: see Aglish, etc.
Diocese: TU

Civil Parish: Ballynahaglish
Map Grid: 18
RC Parish: Backs (Knockmore)
Diocese: KA
Earliest Record: b. 1825; m. 1815
Missing Dates: b. 1860; m. 4.1860–1.1865, 12.1869–2.1874
Status: LC; NLI (mf); Indexed by MNFHRC

Civil Parish: Ballyovey
Map Grid: 34
RC Parish: Partry and Tourmakeady; see Ballinrobe for pre-1869 records
Diocese: TU
Earliest Record: b. 10.1869; m. 1847
Status: LC; NLI (mf); Indexed by SMFRC

Civil Parish: Ballysakeery
Map Grid: 12
RC Parish: Ballysakeery (Cooneal)
Diocese: KA
Earliest Record: b. 11.1843; m. 10.1843
Status: LC; NLI (mf); Indexed by MNFHRC

Civil Parish: Bekan
Map Grid: 72
RC Parish: Bekan
Diocese: TU
Earliest Record: b. 8.1832; m. 5.1832
Missing Dates: b. 2.1844–12.1844; m. pages missing
Status: LC; NLI (mf); Indexed by SMFRC

Civil Parish: Bohola
Map Grid: 43
RC Parish: Bohola
Diocese: AC
Earliest Record: b. 10.1857; m. 10.1857
Status: LC; NLI (mf); Indexed by MNFHRC

Civil Parish: Breaghwy
Map Grid: 26
RC Parish: see Aglish, etc.
Diocese: TU

Civil Parish: Burriscarra
Map Grid: 31
RC Parish: Burriscarra, etc., see Ballintober
Diocese: TU

Civil Parish: Burrishoole
Map Grid: 20
RC Parish: Burrishoole (Newport)
Diocese: TU
Earliest Record: b. 1.1872; m. 1872
Status: LC; NLI (mf); Indexed by MNFHRC

Civil Parish: Castlemore
Map Grid: 69
RC Parish: see Balla
Diocese: TU

Civil Parish: Cong (see also Co. Galway)
Map Grid: 55
RC Parish: Cong and The Neale
Diocese: TU
Earliest Record: b. 2.1870; m. 1870
Status: LC; NLI (mf); Indexed by SMFRC

Civil Parish: Crossboyne
Map Grid: 63
RC Parish: Crossboyne and Taugheen
Diocese: TU
Earliest Record: b. 1835; m. 1791
Status: LC; NLI (mf); Indexed by SMFRC

Civil Parish: Crossmolina
Map Grid: 13
RC Parish: Crossmolina
Diocese: KA
Earliest Record: b. 8.1831; m. 11.1832

Missing Dates: b. 8.1841–4.1845; m. 2.1841–3.1846
Status: LC; NLI (mf); Indexed by MNFHRC

Civil Parish: Doonfeeny
Map Grid: 3
RC Parish: Ballycastle (Kilbride and Doonfeeny)
Diocese: KA
Earliest Record: b. 1853; m. 1.1869
Status: LC; NLI (mf); Indexed by MNFHRC

Civil Parish: Drum
Map Grid: 29
RC Parish: see Balla
Diocese: TU

Civil Parish: Islandeady
Map Grid: 23
RC Parish: Islandeady
Diocese: TU
Earliest Record: b. 9.1839; m. 9.1839
Status: LC; NLI (mf); Indexed by SMFRC

Civil Parish: Kilbeagh
Map Grid: 66
RC Parish: Kilbeagh (Charlestown)
Diocese: AC
Earliest Record: b. 1847; m. 1844
Status: LC; NLI (mf); Indexed by MNFHRC

Civil Parish: Kilbelfad
Map Grid: 17
RC Parish: Backs, see Ballynahaglish
Diocese: KA

Civil Parish: Kilbride
Map Grid: 4
RC Parish: see Doonfeeny
Diocese: KA

Civil Parish: Kilcolman (1) (near Crossboyne)
Map Grid: 61
RC Parish: Kilcolman (Claremorris)
Diocese: TU
Earliest Record: b. 4.1835; m. 1805
Missing Dates: b. 1.1838–3.1839; m. 2.1830–1.1835, 3.1836–12.1838
Status: LC; NLI (mf); Indexed by SMFRC

Civil Parish: Kilcolman (2)
Map Grid: 67
RC Parish: see Co. Sligo
Diocese: TU

Civil Parish: Kilcommon (Erris Barony)
Map Grid: 2
RC Parish: Belmullet; also Aughoose/Bangor records (1853–61)
Diocese: KA
Earliest Record: b. 2.1841; m. 1.1836
Missing Dates: m. 5.1845–8.1857
Status: LC; NLI (mf); Indexed by MNFHRC

Civil Parish: Kilcommon (Kilmaine Barony)
Map Grid: 51
RC Parish: Kilcommon and Robeen (Hollymount)
Diocese: TU
Earliest Record: b. 12.1865; m. 11.1865
Status: LC; NLI (mf); Indexed by SMFRC

Civil Parish: Kilconduff
Map Grid: 41
RC Parish: Kilconduff and Meelick
Diocese: AC
Earliest Record: b. 1822; m. 1808
Status: LC; NLI (mf); Indexed by SMFRC

Civil Parish: Kilcummin
Map Grid: 5
RC Parish: see Lackan
Diocese: KA

Civil Parish: Kildacommoge
Map Grid: 42
RC Parish: Keelogues
Diocese: TU
Earliest Record: b. 8.1847; m. 8.1847
Status: LC; NLI (mf); Indexed by MNFHRC

Civil Parish: Kilfian
Map Grid: 7
RC Parish: Kilfian
Diocese: KA
Earliest Record: b. 10.1826; m. 7.1826; d. 10.1826
Missing Dates: b. ends 7.1836; m. ends 10.1844; d. ends 2.1832
Status: LC; NLI (mf); Indexed by MNFHRC

Civil Parish: Kilgarvan
Map Grid: 35
RC Parish: Kilgarvan (Bonniconlon)
Diocese: KA
Earliest Record: b. 8.1870; m. 11.1844
Status: LC; NLI (mf); Indexed by MNFHRC

Civil Parish: Kilgeever (1)
Map Grid: 47
RC Parish: Clare Island; also Kilgeever, see below
Diocese: TU
Earliest Record: b. 10.1851
Status: LC; NLI (mf); Indexed by SMFRC

Civil Parish: Kilgeever (2)
Map Grid: 47
RC Parish: Kilgeever (Louisburgh)
Diocese: TU
Earliest Record: b. 2.1850; m. 1850
Missing Dates: b. 3.1869–8.1872
Status: LC; NLI (mf); Indexed by SMFRC

Civil Parish: Killala
Map Grid: 10
RC Parish: Killala
Diocese: KA

Earliest Record: b. 4.1852; m. 12.1873
Status: LC; NLI (mf); Indexed by MNFHRC

Civil Parish: Killasser
Map Grid: 38
RC Parish: Killasser
Diocese: AC
Earliest Record: b. 11.1847; m. 12.1847; d. 11.1847
Missing Dates: d. ends 6.1848
Status: LC; NLI (mf); Indexed by MNFHRC

Civil Parish: Killedan
Map Grid: 44
RC Parish: Killedan (Kiltimagh)
Diocese: AC
Earliest Record: b. 2.1861; m. 5.1834
Status: LC; NLI (mf); Indexed by SMFRC

Civil Parish: Kilmaclasser
Map Grid: 22
RC Parish: Kilmeena
Diocese: TU
Earliest Record: not on microfilm
Status: LC; NLI (mf); Indexed by SMFRC

Civil Parish: Kilmainebeg
Map Grid: 56
RC Parish: Kilmaine (Kilmeine)
Diocese: TU
Earliest Record: b. 6.1854; m. 5.1855
Status: LC; NLI (mf); Indexed by SMFRC

Civil Parish: Kilmainemore
Map Grid: 54
RC Parish: Kilmaine, see Kilmainbeg
Diocese: TU

Civil Parish: Kilmeena
Map Grid: 21
RC Parish: Kilmeena, see Kilmaclasser
Diocese: TU

Civil Parish: Kilmolara
Map Grid: 53
RC Parish: Neale, see Cong
Diocese: TU

Civil Parish: Kilmore
Map Grid: 1
RC Parish: Kilmore-Erris
Diocese: KA
Earliest Record: b. 1859; m. 9.1860
Status: LC; NLI (mf); Indexed by MNFHRC

Civil Parish: Kilmoremoy
Map Grid: 15
RC Parish: Kilmoremoy (Ballina)
Diocese: KA
Earliest Record: b. 5.1823; m. 5.1823; d. 4.1823
Missing Dates: b. 10.1836–5.1849, 7.1849–7.1857;
m. 10.1842–10.1850; d. 8.1836–9.1840, ends 5.1844
Status: LC; NLI (mf); Indexed by MNFHRC

Civil Parish: Kilmovee
Map Grid: 68
RC Parish: Kilmovee
Diocese: AC
Earliest Record: b. 2.1854 (two registers); m. 11.1824
Missing Dates: m. 8.1848–10.1854
Status: LC; NLI (mf); Indexed by SMFRC

Civil Parish: Kilturra (see also Co. Sligo)
Map Grid: 65
RC Parish: Kilshalvey, Kilturra, and Cloonoghill
Diocese: AC
Earliest Record: b. 1.1842; m. 4.1833
Missing Dates: b. incomplete pre-1852
Status: LC; NLI (mf); Indexed by MNFHRC

Civil Parish: Kilvine
Map Grid: 64
RC Parish: Kilvine
Diocese: TU
Earliest Record: no registers pre-1880
Status: LC; NLI (mf); Indexed by SMFRC

Civil Parish: Knock
Map Grid: 71
RC Parish: Knock
Diocese: TU
Earliest Record: b. 12.1868; m. 9.1875
Status: LC; NLI (mf); Indexed by SMFRC

Civil Parish: Lackan
Map Grid: 6
RC Parish: Lackan or Lacken
Diocese: KA
Earliest Record: b. 8.1852; m. 3.1854
Status: LC; NLI (mf); Indexed by MNFHRC

Civil Parish: Manulla
Map Grid: 28
RC Parish: Balla and Manulla, see Balla
Diocese: TU

Civil Parish: Mayo
Map Grid: 60
RC Parish: Mayo Abbey and Roslea, see also Balla
Diocese: TU
Earliest Record: b. 4.1841; m. 9.1841
Status: LC; NLI (mf); Indexed by SMFRC

Civil Parish: Meelick
Map Grid: 40
RC Parish: Kilconduff and Meelick, see Kilconduff
Diocese: AC

Civil Parish: Moorgagagh
Map Grid: 57
RC Parish: Kilmaine, see Kilmainebeg
Diocese: TU

Civil Parish: Moygownagh
Map Grid: 11
RC Parish: Moygownagh

Diocese: KA
Earliest Record: b. 1887; m. 1881
Status: LC; NLI (mf); Indexed by MNFHRC

Civil Parish: Oughaval
Map Grid: 45
RC Parish: Aughaval (Westport)
Diocese: TU
Earliest Record: b. 1823 (two registers); m. 4.1823
Missing Dates: m. 5.1857-1.1959
Status: LC; NLI (mf); Indexed by SMFRC

Civil Parish: Rathreagh
Map Grid: 8
RC Parish: Kilfian, see Kilfian
Diocese: KA

Civil Parish: Robeen
Map Grid: 49
RC Parish: Kilcommon and Robeen
Diocese: TU
Earliest Record: b. 10.1857; m. 10.1857
Status: LC; NLI (mf); Indexed by SMFRC

Civil Parish: Rosslee
Map Grid: 32
RC Parish: Mayo and Rosslea, see Mayo
Diocese: TU

Civil Parish: Shrule
Map Grid: 58
RC Parish: Shrule
Diocese: TU
Earliest Record: b. 7.1831; m. 7.1831
Missing Dates: b. ends 8.1864; m. 6.1848-10.1855, ends 5.1864
Status: LC; NLI (mf); Indexed by SMFRC

Civil Parish: Tagheen
Map Grid: 62
RC Parish: Crossboyne and Tagheen, see Crossboyne
Diocese: TU

Civil Parish: Templemore
Map Grid: 39
RC Parish: Templemore (Straide)
Diocese: KA
Earliest Record: b. 1888; m. 5.1872
Status: LC; NLI (mf); Indexed by MNFHRC

Civil Parish: Templemurry
Map Grid: 9
RC Parish: Killala, see Killala
Diocese: AC

Civil Parish: Toomore
Map Grid: 37
RC Parish: part Toomore (Foxford); part Kilturra
Diocese: AC
Earliest Record: b. 4.1833; m. 12.1871
Missing Dates: b. 3.1840-1.1870
Status: LC; NLI (mf); Indexed by MNFHRC

Civil Parish: Touaghty
Map Grid: 33
RC Parish: see Mayo
Diocese: TU

Civil Parish: Turlough
Map Grid: 25
RC Parish: Turlough (Parke)
Diocese: TU
Earliest Record: b. 8.1847; m. 8.1847
Status: LC; NLI (mf); Indexed by MNFHRC

Commercial and Social Directories

1824

J. Pigot's *City of Dublin and Hibernian Provincial Directory* includes traders, nobility, gentry, and clergy lists of Ballina, Ballinrobe, Castlebar, Killala, Swinford, and Westport.

1846

Slater's *National Commercial Directory of Ireland* lists nobility, clergy, traders, etc., in Ballina, Ballinrobe, Castlebar, Claremorris, Killala, Newport, Swinford, and Westport.

1856

Slater's *Royal National Commercial Directory of Ireland* lists nobility, gentry, clergy, traders, etc., in Ballina, Ballinrobe, Castlebar, Claremorris, Killala, Newport, Swinford, and Westport.

1870

Slater's *Directory of Ireland* contains trade, nobility, and clergy lists for Ballina, Ballinrobe and Hollymount, Castlebar, Claremorris and Ballyhaunis, Killala, Newport, Swinford, and Westport.

1881

Slater's *Royal National Commercial Directory of Ireland* contains lists of traders, clergy, nobility, and farmers in adjoining parishes of the towns of Ballina and Killala, Ballinrobe and Hollymount, Castlebar, Claremorris, Ballyhaunis and Knock, Swinford and Bellaghy, Westport, and Newport.

1894

Slater's *Royal National Directory of Ireland* lists traders, police, teachers, farmers, and private residents in each of the towns, villages, and parishes of the county.

Family History

Baird, S. Dennie, and Jennie M. Baird. *The Bairds. A condensed chronology of an ancient house with genealogi-*

cal tracings of its American descendants. Wisconsin: Stephen A. Baird, 1909.

Burtchaell, G.D. "The Moore Family of Brize Castle, Co. Mayo." *R.S.A.I.* (1901).

"The Elwood Family." *Ir. Gen.* 6 (4) (1983): 477–86.

"The Gray Family of Claremorris." *Ir. Gen.* 7 (4): 551–562.

"The MacDonalds of Mayo." *J. Galway Arch. Hist. Soc.* 17 (1936–37): 65–82.

"Sir Thomas More—Descendants in the Male Line: The Moores of Moorehall, Co. Mayo." *R.S.A.I.* 36 (1906): 224–30.

Chapman, E. *Memoirs of My Family: Together with Some Researches into the Early History of the Morris Families of Tipperary, Galway, and Mayo.* Frome, 1928.

Mulloy, Sheila. *O'Malley People and Places.* Whitegate & Carrowbawn, 1988.

"Notes on the Lineage of Lambert of Brookhill, Co. Mayo." *Ir. Gen.* 3 (10) (1965): 372–79.

"O'Malley Papers (Co. Mayo)." *Anal. Hib.* 25: 185–202.

"O'Malleys Between 1651 and 1725." *J. Galway Arch. Hist. Soc.* 25 (1952).

"The Ormsbys of Tobervaddy (Co. Mayo)." *Ir. Gen.* 1 (1941): 284–86.

"The Ruttledge Families of Co. Mayo." *Ir. Gen.* 7 (3): 433–453.

Gravestone Inscriptions

An account of some graveyards is given in "The Graveyards of West Mayo" in *Irish Family History* 6 (1990): 15–20. All of the gravestones of Mayo have been indexed by either the Mayo North Family History Research Centre or the South Mayo Family Research Centre (see Research Services at the end of the chapter). These can be searched by the relevant center for a fee. Other sources are:

Kilcommon (Hollymount): *South Mayo Family Res. Soc.* 1989, pp. 3–8.

Killedan Churchyard (C of I): *South Mayo Family Res. Soc.* 1989, pp. 9–14.

Castlebar (Old): Held by Mayo County Library.

Newspapers

Title: *Ballina Advertiser*
Published in: Ballina, 1840–43
NLI Holdings: 1.1840–11.1843
BL Holdings: 1.1840–11.1843

Title: *Ballina Chronicle*
Published in: Ballina, 1849–51
BL Holdings: 5.1849–8.1851

Title: *Ballina Herald* (incorporated with *Western People*)
Published in: Ballina, ca. 1866–1962
NLI Holdings: 8.1927–4.1962
BL Holdings: 10.1891–11.1892; 4.1913–4.1962

Title: *Ballina Impartial* or *Tyrawly Advertiser*
Published in: Ballina, 1823–35
NLI Holdings: 1.1823–12.1825; 1.1827–11.1835
BL Holdings: 1.1823–12.1825; 1.1827–11.1835

Title: *Ballina Journal and Connaught Advertiser*
Published in: Ballina, 1882–95
BL Holdings: 11.1882–3.1895

Title: *Ballinrobe Chronicle* (and *Mayo Advertiser*)
Published in: Ballinrobe, 1866–1903
NLI Holdings: 9.1866–10.1903 (none published 12.1867–4.1868)
BL Holdings: 9.1866–10.1903 (none published 12.1867–4.1868)

Title: *Connaught Telegraph*
Published in: Castlebar, 1828–current
NLI Holdings: 6.1879–12.1913; 6.1919–in progress
BL Holdings: 5.1876–in progress

Title: *Connaught Watchman*
Published in: Ballina, 1851–63
BL Holdings: 8.1851–10.1863

Title: *Mayo Constitution* (and *Roscommon Intelligencer*)
Published in: Castlebar, 1812–72
NLI Holdings: 1.1828–11.1871
BL Holdings: 1.1828–11.1871

Title: *Mayo Examiner*
Published in: Castlebar, 1868–1903
BL Holdings: 7.1868–6.1903

Title: *Mayo News*
Published in: Westport, 1893–current
BL Holdings: 1.1893–in progress

Title: *Telegraph* or *Connaught Ranger*
Published in: Castlebar, 1830–70
BL Holdings: 8.1830–12.1855; 2.1856–12.1869, odd numbers 1870

Title: *Tyrawly Herald* or *Mayo and Sligo Intelligencer*
Published in: Ballina, 1844–70
NLI Holdings: 1.1844–9.1870
BL Holdings: 1.1844–9.1870

Title: *Western Gem*
Published in: Ballina, 1843
NLI Holdings: 4–12.1843
BL Holdings: 4–12.1843

Title: *Western People*
Published in: Ballina, 1883–current
NLI Holdings: 5.1889–in progress
BL Holdings: 5.1889–in progress

Wills and Administrations

A discussion of the types of records, where they are held, and their availability and value is given in the Wills section of the introduction. The availability of wills, administrations, and marriage license records is also described in the relevant parts of the same section. Where available, published sources of these records are given in the Miscellaneous Sources section.

Pre-1858 Wills and Administrations

Prerogative Wills. See the introduction.

Consistorial Wills. County Mayo is in the dioceses of Killala, Achonry, and Tuam. The guide to Catholic parish records in this chapter shows the diocese to which each civil parish belonged. The wills of residents of each diocese were usually proven within that diocese (see the Wills section for exceptions). The following records survive:

Wills

See the introduction.

Abstracts

See the introduction.

Indexes

"Killala and Achonry: 1698–1838." *Ir. Gen.* 3 (12): 506–19.

Tuam—see Co. Galway.

Post-1858 Wills and Administrations

This county was served by the District Registry of Ballina. The surviving records are kept in the NAI. Records include: Ballina District Will Books (1865–1899). NAI; SLC film 100925-6.

Marriage Licenses

Indexes

Tuam (1661–1750). NAI; SLC film 100872.

Miscellaneous Sources

Delaney, G. "Surnames of Co. Mayo." *Irish Roots* 1 (1995): 21–22.

Murphy, M., and J.R. Reilly. *Marriages in the Roman Catholic Diocese of Tuam, Ireland, 1821–1829.* USA: Heritage Books, 1993.

Tuam RC Diocese. Register of marriages in each Deanery for parts of 1821 and 1822, with additions in many parishes to 1829. NLI film P4222.

"A Map of Part of the County of Mayo in 1584; With Notes Thereon, and an Account of the Author (John Browne), and His Descendants." *J. Galway Arch.*

Hist. Soc. 5 (1907–08): 145–58.

"Crossmolina—An Historical Survey." Available from Crossmolina Historical and Archaeological Society.

D'Alton, Rev. M. *A Short History of Ballinrobe Parish.* Browne & Nolan, 1931.

"The Ethnography of Ballycroy, Co. Mayo." *Proc. R. Ir. Acad.* 3rd ser. 4 (1896–98): 110–11.

"The Ethnography of Clare Island and Inishturk, Co. Mayo." *Proc. R. Ir. Acad.* 5 (1898–1900): 72.

"The Ethnography of The Mullet, Inishkea Islands and Portnacloy, Co. Mayo." *Proc. R. Ir. Acad.* 3 (1893–96): 648–49.

"Mayo Landowners in the Seventeenth Century." *R.S.A.I.* 95 (1965): 237–47.

Moran, G.P. "The Mayo Evictions of 1860." Westport. F.N.T., 1986.

O'Connell, C. "Index of pupils at Lehinch School (1855–72)." Townland of Lissatana, c.p. of Kilcommon. *South Mayo Family Res. Soc. J.* 1989: 39–49. Gives child's name, year of birth, address, and parents' occupations.

Knox, H. *History of Co. Mayo from Earliest Times to the Close of the Sixteenth Century.* Dublin, 1915.

"The Graveyards of West Mayo." *Irish Family History* 6 (1990): 15–20.

"A List of the Yeomanry Corps of Connaught, 1803." *Irish Sword* 3 (12) 1958.

"Mayomen Who Died Serving with Connaught Rangers 1914–18." *Cathair na Mairt* 7 (1) (1987): 21–31.

Quinn, J.F. *History of Mayo.* Dublin: Brendan Quinn. Vol. 1—ISBN: 0-9519-280-07; Vol. 2—ISBN: 0-9519 280-15 (originally published in weekly parts in *Western People* in the 1930s).

Newport Area Families 1864–1880. Indianapolis: W.G. Masterson, 1994.

Research Sources and Services

Journals

Cathair na Mairt (journal of the Westport Historical Society, 1981–)

North Mayo Historical Journal (published by North Mayo Historical and Archaeological Society, 1982–)

Journal of South Mayo Family Research (published by South Mayo Family Research Centre, 1988–)

Libraries and Information Sources

Mayo County Library, Mountain View, Castlebar, Co. Mayo. Ph: (094) 24444; fax: (353) 94 24774. The library has a range of local history materials, including maps, estate records, periodicals, newpapers, the 1901 census, *Griffith's Valuation*, and a collection of local folklore compiled in 1937/38.

Research Services

Mayo North Family History Research Centre, Enniscoe, Castlehill, Ballina, Co. Mayo. Ph: (096) 31809; fax: (096) 31885. This is the official IGP center for the north of the county. It has indexed most of the Catholic and Church of Ireland church registers. The center can provide a research service using these indexes, and also other local sources, such as the 1901 census, *Griffith's Valuation*, inscriptions of all local graveyards, the civil records of birth and marriage, school and estate records, and other local sources. Church records indexed by this center are noted (as MNFHRC) in the lists above.

South Mayo Family Research Centre, Main Street, Ballinrobe, Co Mayo. Ph/Fax: (353) 92 41214; e-mail: soumay@iol.ie. Internet: http://www.mayo-ireland.ie/roots.htm. This is the official IGP center for the south of the county. It has indexed all of the registers of churches of all denominations; the 1901 census; *Griffith's Valuation*; inscriptions of all local graveyards to 1994; the civil records of birth, marriage, and death to 1902; records of the Dillon, Moore, Lindsey, and Browne estates; and other unique local sources. Researchers are advised to contact the center for an updated list of registers, and other sources, indexed. Searches will be conducted for a fee. Church records indexed by this center are noted (as SMFRC) in the lists above.

See also Research Services in Dublin in the introduction.

Societies

Crossmolina Historical and Archaeological Society, Ms. Bernadette Lynn, Enniscoe, Castlehill, Ballina, Co. Mayo

Crossmolina Historical Society, Mrs. Susan Kellett, Enniscoe, Ballina, Co. Mayo. Ph: (096) 31112

Kiltimagh Historical Society, Ms. Vera Carney, James' Street, Kiltimagh, Co. Mayo

South Mayo Family History Research Society, Bushfield House, Hollymount, Co. Mayo

Westport Historical Society, The Secretary, Clew Bay Heritage Centre, The Quay, Westport, Co. Mayo

Mayo Civil Parishes as Numbered on Map

1. Kilmore
2. Kilcommon (Erris)
3. Doonfeeny
4. Kilbride
5. Kilcummin
6. Lackan
7. Kilfian
8. Rathreagh
9. Templemurry
10. Killala
11. Moygawnagh
12. Ballysakeery
13. Crossmolina
14. Ardagh
15. Kilmoremoy
16. Addergoole
17. Kilbelfad
18. Ballynahaglish
19. Achill
20. Burrishoole
21. Kilmeena
22. Kilmaclasser
23. Islandeady (2 pts.)
24. Aglish
25. Turlough
26. Breaghwy
27. Ballyhean
28. Manulla
29. Drum
30. Ballintober (2 pts.)
31. Burriscarra
32. Rosslee
33. Touaghty
34. Ballyovey
35. Kilgarvan
36. Attymass
37. Toomore

38. Killasser
39. Templemore
40. Meelick
41. Kilconduff
42. Kildacommoge (3 pts.)
43. Bohola
44. Killedan
45. Oughaval
46. Inishboffin
47. Kilgeever
48. Aghagower
49. Robeen
50. Ballinrobe
51. Kilcommon (Kilmaine)
52. Ballinchalla
53. Kilmolara
54. Kilmainemore (2 pts.)
55. Cong
56. Kilmainebeg (2 pts.)
57. Moorgagagh
58. Shrule
59. Balla
60. Mayo
61. Kilcolman
62. Tagheen
63. Crossboyne
64. Kilvine
65. Kilturra
66. Kilbeagh
67. Kilcolman
68. Kilmovee
69. Castlemore
70. Aghamore
71. Knock
72. Bekan
73. Annagh

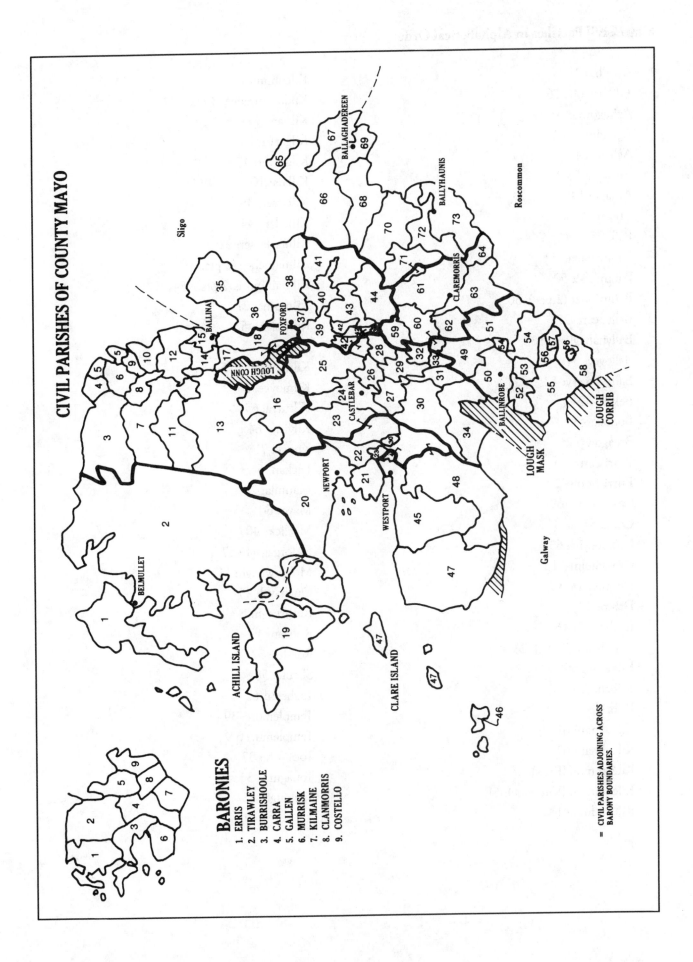

CIVIL PARISHES OF COUNTY MAYO

BARONIES
1. ERRIS
2. TIRAWLEY
3. BURRISHOOLE
4. CARRA
5. GALLEN
6. MURRISK
7. KILMAINE
8. CLANMORRIS
9. COSTELLO

= CIVIL PARISHES ADJOINING ACROSS
BARONY BOUNDARIES.

Mayo Civil Parishes in Alphabetical Order

Achill: 19
Addergoole: 16
Aghagower: 48
Aghamore: 70
Aglish: 24
Annagh: 73
Ardagh: 14
Attymass: 36
Balla: 59
Ballinchalla: 52
Ballinrobe: 50
Ballintober (2 pts.): 30
Ballyhean: 27
Ballynahaglish: 18
Ballovey: 34
Ballysakeery: 12
Bekan: 72
Bohola: 43
Breaghwy: 26
Burriscarra: 31
Burrishoole: 20
Castlemore: 69
Cong: 55
Crossboyne: 63
Crossmolina: 13
Doonfeeny: 3
Drum: 29
Inishbofin: 46
Islandeady (2 pts.): 23
Kilbeagh: 66
Kilbelfad: 17
Kilbride: 4
Kilcolman: 61
Kilcolman: 67
Kilcommon (Erris): 2
Kilcommon (Kilmaine): 51
Kilconduff: 41

Kilcummin: 5
Kildacommoge (3 pts.): 42
Kilfian: 7
Kilgarvan: 35
Kilgeever: 47
Killala: 10
Killasser: 38
Killedan: 44
Kilmaclasser: 22
Kilmainebeg (2 pts.): 56
Kilmainmore (2 pts.): 54
Kilmeena: 21
Kilmolara: 53
Kilmore: 1
Kilmoremoy: 15
Kilmovee: 68
Kilturra: 65
Kilvine: 64
Knock: 71
Lackan: 6
Manulla: 28
Mayo: 60
Meelick: 40
Moorgagagh: 57
Moygownagh: 11
Oughaval: 45
Rathreagh: 8
Robeen: 49
Rosslee: 32
Shrule: 58
Tagheen: 62
Templemore: 39
Templemurry: 9
Toomore: 37
Touaghty: 33
Turlough: 25

County Meath

A Brief History

This Leinster county contains the towns of Navan, Trim, Kells, Oldcastle, and Athboy.

In the old Irish system of administration, the present county of Meath was part of a larger area of the same name, which was the territory of the High King of Ireland. The High King's residence was situated on the Hill of Tara, which is within the present county of Meath.

The major Irish families in the county were O'Melaghlin or McLoughlin, McGogarty, O'Loughnane, Hayes, (O')Kelly, (O')Hennessy, and O'Reilly.

Following the Norman conquest of Leinster, the county was given to Hugh de Lacy, who built an extensive castle on the site of the present town of Trim. The Normans also built castles at Navan and Kells. Over the succeeding centuries, however, the effective control of the English administration in the county waned as the Normans assimilated into the Irish way of life and the native families became more powerful. The area controlled by England gradually shrank to an area around Dublin, the Pale, which included the eastern parts of the present County Meath. It was in this area of rich farmland that many Norman families settled. The main families which settled were those of Preston, Plunkett, Cusack, Darcy, Dillon, Nangle, Dowdall, Fleming, and Barnewall.

Some of the native families migrated from the county as a result of the Norman conquest, but most remained either as tenants or servants of the Normans or on their own lands.

During the 1641 rebellion, most of the Irish and Norman families of the county, led by a Preston, rebelled against English rule. This rebellion was defeated, and the lands of many of the rebels were confiscated and given to soldiers and officers of Cromwell's army.

Once described as "the great grazing ground" of Ireland, County Meath has an abundance of pastureland. Large farms prospered on these lands, but few small farmers were able to earn a sufficient living.

The population of the county dropped dramatically during the 1840s, the period of the Great Famine. The population was 183,000 in 1841, making Meath one of the least densely populated counties in the country (two hundred people per square mile). By 1857 this population had dropped to 141,000. Almost 20,000 died between 1845 and 1850 from starvation and disease, and further thousands emigrated. The population is currently around 96,000.

Census and Census Substitutes

1654–56

"The Civil Survey." R.C. Simington. With returns of titles for the Meath Baronies. Dublin: Stationery Office, 1940.

1659

"Census" of Ireland. Edited by S. Pender. Dublin: Stationery Office, 1939. NLI 16551. SLC film 924648. Covers parishes of Abbey, Athlumney, Ardcath, Ardmulchan, Ballygart, Ballymagarvey, Ballymaglassan, Brownstown, Clonalvy, Colpe, Crookstown, Donoghmore, Dowestown, Duleek, Dunshaughlin, Dunowre, Dunsany, Fennor, Grenock, Julianstown, Kentstown, Kilbrew, Kilcarne, Kilkervan, Killeen, Killegan, Kilmoon, Knockamon, Macestown, Moorchurch, Monkstown, Paynstown, Rathbeggan, Rathfeagh, Rathregan, Ratoath, Skryne, Staffordstown, Stamullen, Tara, Trevett, and Templekeran. SLC film 924648.

1710

List of Voters in Kells. NLI (Headfort Papers); PRONI T 3163.

1761–88

"Lists of Freeholders in Co. Meath." NLI ms. 787/8.

1766

Protestant householders in the Parish of Ardbraccan, Churchtown, Liscartan, Martry, and Rataine. RCBL Ms. 37 (and Ms. 23 for Ardbraccan); SLC films 258517 and 100173; GO 537.

1770

List of Freeholders of Co. Meath, Compiled for Election Purposes. NLI ms. 787/8; SLC film 100181.

1775

"Catholic Qualification Roll Extracts" (seventy names, addresses, and occupations). 59th Report DKPRI: 50-84.

1775–80

Freeholders of Co. Meath. GO ms. 442 and SLC film 100181.

1781

List of Voters. NAI M 4878, 4910-12. (M 4911 lists approximately 2,500 names, addresses, and landholdings.)

1783

List of Meath Voters. NLI (Headfort Papers); PRONI T 3163.

1792

Alphabetical list of the Freeholders of Co. Meath. RIA; Upton Papers No. 12.

1792/3

Hearth Tax Collectors account books. NAI Ms 26735-9 (Headfort Papers). Names, residences, and observations.

1796

Spinning Wheel Premium List (see introduction).

1798

List of Persons who Suffered Losses in '98 Rebellion. NLI JLB 94107 (approximately 120 names, addresses, and occupations).

1802–13

"Protestants in Parishes of Agher, Ardagh, Castlerickard, Castletown-Kilpatrick, Clonard, Clongill (with ages), Drumconrath (with some ages), Duleek, Emlagh, Julianstown, Kells, Kentstown, Kilbeg, Kilmainhamwood, Kilskyre, Knockmark, Laracor, Moynalty, Navan, Newtown, Raddenstown, Rathcore, Rathkenny, Rathmolyon, Ratoath, Robertstown, Skryne, Slane, Syddan, Tara, and Trim." *Ir. Anc.* 5 (1) (1973): 37-52.

1813

"Protestant Children at Ardbraccan School." *Ir. Anc.* 5 (1) (1973): 38.

1815

List of Meath Voters. NLI (Headfort Papers); PRONI T 3163.

1816

"Tenants of the Wellesley Estates at Dengan, Ballymaglossan, Moyare, Mornington, and Trim." *Riocht na Midhe* 4 (4) (1967): 10-25.

1821

Government Census Remnants for . . . Parishes of Ardbraccan, Ardsallagh, Balrathboyne, Bective, Churchtown, Clonmacduff, Donaghmore, Donaghpatrick, Kilcooly, Liscartan, Martry, Moymet, Navan, Newtownclonbun, Rataine, Rathkenny, Trim, Trimlestown, Tullaghanoge. SLC film 597735, NAI CEN 1821/35-53.

Smith/Smyth households abstracted from the 1821 census returns. *Dun Laoghaire Gen. Soc. J.* 3 (4), 1994. (Seventy-seven households.)

1823–38

Tithe Applotment Survey (see introduction).

1830

"Census of Landowners in Julianstown, Moorchurch, Stamullen, and Clonalvy." *Riocht na Midhe* 3 (4) (1966): 354-58 (gives name and holding in each townland of each parish, except townlands of Ballygarth, Corballis, and Whitecross).

1831

Canvas Book of the Meath Election. *Ir. Gen.* 7 (2) (1987): 278-288.

1833

"List of Protestant Parishioners Paying Church Cess in Colpe and Kilsharvan Parishes." *Riocht na Midhe* 4 (3) (1969): 61-62.

1835

"Meath Election, January 1835." NAI–SPO (Outrage Papers), 1835/148. (Names of those who voted only.)

```
┌─────────────────────────────────────────────────────────────┐
│                         MEATH                                │
│                                                              │
│       (*The following persons, in the baronies of Upper      │
│    and Lower Duleek, have this day taken the Oath of         │
│    Allegiance):                                              │
│                                                              │
│    Richard Aylward (*Aylmer), Par. Pr. & Vic. Genl. Diocese  │
│       Meath, Stamullin residg. therein.                      │
│                                                              │
│    Wm. Coleman    ..    .. Balltray        .. Farmer         │
│    James Mackey   ..    .. Ninch           ..     ,,         │
│    Ignatius Farrell     .. Balloy          ..     ,,         │
│    Geo. Ennis     ..    .. Claristown      ..     ,,         │
│    John Murphy    ..    .. Rogerstn.       ..     ,,         │
│    John Tuite     ..    .. Minnetstown     ..     ,,         │
│    Richd. Callaghan     .. Smithstn.       ..     ,,         │
│    Wm. Boylan     ..    .. Legdoory        ..     ,,         │
│    Corns. Dempsey       .. Stamulon (*Stamullen)  ,,         │
│    Nichs. Pentony ..    .. Gormanstn.      ..     ,,         │
│    Patt. Caulfield ..   .. Dananestn.                        │
│                            (*Demanestown)  ..     ,,         │
│    Nichs. Rafferty ..   .. Millmurderry    ..     ,,         │
│    Thos. Caulief  ..    .. Demanestn.      ..     ,,         │
│    Bryan McEnally       .. Bryerlays       ..     ,,         │
│    Patrick McEnally     .. Sarsfieldstn.   ..     ,,         │
│                                                              │
│       Before James Brabazon—11 Dec. 1775. (*Mornington).     │
└─────────────────────────────────────────────────────────────┘
```

An extract from the "Catholic Qualification Rolls" for County Meath, 1775. The persons listed were Catholics who took an oath of allegiance to the British sovereign and thereby qualified for certain benefits which had previously been denied under the Penal Laws. From the 59th Report of the Deputy Keeper of Public Records of Ireland.

1838

"Balfour Tenants in Townlands of Belustran, Cloughmacow, and Doe and Hurtle." *Louth Arch. J.* 12 (3) (1951): 190.

1843

Voters List. NAI 1843/58.

1848

"Petitioners for William Smith O'Brien." NAI 1848/180 (names of male petitioners in Oldcastle).

1854

Griffith's Valuation (see introduction).

1866–73

Emigrants from Stamullen RC Parish. *Ir. Gen.* 8 (2) (1991): 290-292. (Name, age, occupation, marital status, residence, and intended destination.)

1871

Census of the Parishes of Drumcondra and Loughbrackan. (Included in the Catholic Parish Register.) NAI P 4184.

1901

Census. NAI (see introduction), and SLC films 846263-81, 846418-9. Indexed by Meath Heritage Centre (see Research Services at end of chapter).

1911

Census. NAI. Indexed by Meath Heritage Centre (see Research Services at the end of the chapter).

Church Records

Church of Ireland

See the introduction for a description of Church of Ireland records and their major repositories. Many C of I records were lost in the PRO fire of 1922. These are indicated as "Lost." However, as Church of Ireland records were effectively state records, the records of marriage (from 1845) are also in the General Registrar's Office. Many are still in local custody (LC), while others are in one of a variety of other archives (e.g., RCBL or NAI). All of the Church of Ireland registers of this county have been indexed by the Meath Heritage Centre (see Research Services at the end of the chapter). A search of the index will be conducted by the center for a fee. Those indexed are noted as "Indexed by Meath HC."

Agher
Earliest Records: b. 1796–; m. 1807–; d. 1798–
Status: LC; NAI MFCI 51 (b. 1796-1874; m. 1807-39; d. 1798-1875); Indexed by Meath HC (to b/d. 1847; m. 1900)

Ardagh
Status: Indexed by Meath HC (m. 1845 to 1900 only)

Ardbraccan
Earliest Records: b. 1884–; m. 1845–; d. 1884–
Status: LC; Indexed by Meath HC (to 1900)

Ardmulchan (see Painestown)

Athboy
Earliest Records: b. 1736–; m. 1736–; d. 1736–
Missing Dates: b. 1749-97; m. 1748-98; d. 1740-98
Status: LC; NAI MFCI 53/4 (b/d. 1736-1877; m. 1736-1845); Indexed by Meath HC (to 1900)

Athlumney (see Navan)

Ballivor (see Killachonagan)

Ballymaglasson
Earliest Records: b. 1877–; m. 1866–; d. 1877–
Status: LC; Indexed by Meath HC (to 1900)

Balrathboyne
Earliest Records: b. 1877–; m. 1875–; d. 1878–
Status: LC; Indexed by Meath HC (to 1900)

Bective
Earliest Records: b. 1853–; m. 1853–; d. 1857–
Status: NAI MFCI 48 (b. 1853-73; d. 1857-79); Indexed by Meath HC (to 1900)

Castlepollard
Earliest Records: b. 1890–; m. 1851–
Status: LC; Indexed by Meath HC (to 1900)

Castlepollard/Rathgraffe
Earliest Records: b. 1869–; m. 1846–; d. 1899–
Status: LC; Indexed by Meath HC (to 1900)

Castlerickard
Earliest Records: b. 1869–; m. 1846–; d. 1878–
Status: LC and NAI M5137 (b. 1869-77); Indexed by Meath HC (to 1900)

Castletown
Earliest Records: d. 1885–
Status: LC; Indexed by Meath HC (to 1900)

Castletown and Nobber
Earliest Records: b. 1883–
Status: LC; Indexed by Meath HC (to 1900)

Churchtown (see Ardbraccan)

Clonard
Earliest Records: b. 1792–; m. 1793–; d. 1793–

Status: LC; RCBL (m. 1846-50); NAI M5232/3 (b. 1792-1880; m. 1836-76; d. 1838-90)

Clongill
Earliest Records: b. 1795–; d. 1795–
Status: LC; NAI MFCI 43/4 (b/d. 1795-1804); Indexed by Meath HC (to 1900)

Clonmellon
Earliest Records: b. 1855–; m. 1845–; d. 1851–
Status: LC; Indexed by Meath HC (to 1900)

Collinstown
Earliest Records: b. 1888–; m. 1860–; d. 1886–
Status: LC; Indexed by Meath HC (to 1900)

Colpe
Earliest Records: b. 1880–; m. 1851–
Status: LC; Indexed by Meath HC (to 1900)

Delvin
Earliest Records: b. 1817–; m. 1895–; d. 1847–
Status: LC; Indexed by Meath HC (to 1900)

Donoghpatrick
Earliest Records: b. 1878–; m. 1845–; d. 1880–
Status: LC; Indexed by Meath HC (to 1900)

Drakestown
Earliest Records: b. 1884–; m. 1899–; d. 1885–
Status: LC; Indexed by Meath HC (to 1900)

Drogheda (St. Mary's)
Earliest Records: b. 1763–; m. 1763–; d. 1763–
Status: LC; NAI MFCI 39 (b. 1763-1871; m. 1763-1845; d. 1763-1872); Indexed by Meath HC (to 1900)

Drumconrath
Earliest Records: b. 1799–; m. 1820–; d. 1821–
Status: LC; RCBL (b. 1799-1826; m. 1820-1956; d. 1821-26); NAI MFCI 45 (b. 1799-1983; m. 1820-44; d. 1821-98); Indexed by Meath HC (to 1900)

Drumcree
Earliest Records: b. 1818–; m. 1869–; d. 1841–
Status: LC; Indexed by Meath HC (to 1900)

Duleek
Earliest Records: b. 1880–; m. 1845–; d. 1881–
Status: LC; Indexed by Meath HC (to 1900)

Dunboyne
Earliest Records: b. 1879–; m. 1845–; d. 1877–
Status: LC; Indexed by Meath HC (to 1900)

Dunshaughlin
Earliest Records: b. 1839–; m. 1846–; d. 1839–
Status: LC; NAI MFCI 41 (b. 1839-74; d. 1839-77); Indexed by Meath HC (to 1900)

Enniskeen
Earliest Records: b. 1881–; m. 1845–; d. 1895–
Status: LC; Indexed by Meath HC (to 1900)

Foyran
Earliest Records: m. 1898–
Status: LC; Indexed by Meath HC (to 1900)

Galtrim
Earliest Records: b. 1878-; m. 1845-; d. 1878-
Status: LC; Indexed by Meath HC (to 1900)

Girley
Earliest Records: m. 1874-
Status: LC; Indexed by Meath HC (to 1900)

Julianstown
Earliest Records: b. 1787-; m. 1791-; d. 1778-
Status: LC; NAI MFCI 39 (b. 1787-1869; m. 1797-1837; d. 1778-1873); Indexed by Meath HC (to 1900)

Kells
Earliest Records: b. 1773-; m. 1773-; d. 1773-
Status: LC; NAI MFCI 46/7 (b. 1773-1876; m. 1773-1844; d. 1773-1904); Indexed by Meath HC (to 1900)

Kentstown
Earliest Records: b. 1877-; m. 1848-; d. 1878-
Status: LC; Indexed by Meath HC (to 1900)

Kilbrew (see also Kilmoon)
Earliest Records: m. 1850-
Status: LC; Indexed by Meath HC (to 1900)

Kilbride (see Dunboyne)

Kilbride/Castlecor (Oldcastle)
Earliest Records: b. 1886-; m. 1848-; d. 1878-
Status: LC; Indexed by Meath HC (to 1900)

Kilcock
Earliest Records: b. 1884-; m. 1877-; d. 1886-
Status: LC; Indexed by Meath HC (to 1900)

Kildalkey
Earliest Records: b. 1878-; m. 1859-
Status: LC; Indexed by Meath HC (b. to 1900; m. to 1873)

Killeagh
Earliest Records: b. 1886-; m. 1846-
Status: LC; Indexed by Meath HC (to 1900)

Killachonagan or Killaconegan (Ballivor)
Earliest Records: b. 1853-; m. 1853-; d. 1853-
Status: LC; NAI M5117 (b. 1853-77; m. 1853-62; d. 1853-63); Indexed by Meath HC (b. 1877-1900; m. 1845-1873; d. 1879-1900)

Kilmainhamwood
Earliest Records: b. 1881-; m. 1852-
Status: RCBL (b. 1881-92; m. 1852-76); Indexed by Meath HC (to 1900)

Kilmessan
Earliest Records: b. 1886-; m. 1848-; d. 1890-
Status: LC; Indexed by Meath HC (to 1900)

Kilmoon
Earliest Records: b. 1873-; m. 1855-; d. 1877-
Status: LC; Indexed by Meath HC (to 1900)

Kilmore
Earliest Records: m. 1834-; d. 1827-

Status: LC; NAI MFCI 42 (m. 1834-42; d. 1827-42); m. indexed by Meath HC (b. to 1900; m. to 1842)

Kilshine
Earliest Records: b. 1875-; m. 1846-; d. 1895-
Status: LC; Indexed by Meath HC (to 1900)

Kingscourt/Enniskeen
Earliest Records: b. 1881-; m. 1845-; d. 1895-
Status: LC; Indexed by Meath HC (to 1900)

Kilskeer/Crossakeel
Earliest Records: m. 1845-
Status: Indexed by Meath HC (to 1900)

Knockmark
Earliest Records: b. 1825-; m. 1837-; d. 1825-
Status: LC

Laracor
Earliest Records: b. 1881-; m. 1845-; d. 1881-
Status: LC; Indexed by Meath HC (to 1900)

Loughan or Castlekieran
Status: Lost

Loughcrew
Earliest Records: b. 1800-; m. 1800-; d. 1800-
Status: LC; NAI MFCI 51 (b/m/d. 1800-21); Indexed by Meath HC (to 1900)

Mayne
Earliest Records: b. 1840-; m. 1888-; d. 1823-
Status: LC; Indexed by Meath HC (to 1900)

Maynooth
Earliest Records: b. 1871-; m. 1871-; d. 1871-
Status: LC; Indexed by Meath HC (to 1900)

Mountnugent
Earliest Records: m. 1857-
Status: LC; Indexed by Meath HC (to 1900)

Moybolgue
Earliest Records: b. 1869-; m. 1878-; d. 1896-
Status: LC; Indexed by Meath HC (to 1900)

Moyglare
Earliest Records: b. 1879-; m. 1856-; d. 1879-
Status: LC; Indexed by Meath HC (to 1900)

Moynalty
Earliest Records: b. 1893-; m. 1845-; d. 1894-
Status: LC; Indexed by Meath HC (to 1900)

Navan
Earliest Records: b. 1880-; m. 1845-; d. 1879-
Status: LC; Indexed by Meath HC (to 1900)

Newtown
Earliest Records: m. 1845-
Status: LC; Indexed by Meath HC (to 1900)

Nobber
Earliest Records: b. 1828-; m. 1828-; d. 1831-
Status: LC; RCBL (m. 1850-1945); NAI M5062 and

SLC film 597159 (b. 1828–68; m. 1828–44; d. 1831–61); Indexed by Meath HC (to 1900)

Oldcastle
Earliest Records: b. 1814–; m. 1815–; d. 1814–
Status: LC; NAI MFCI 52 (b. 1814–84; m. 1815–45; d. 1814–90); Indexed by Meath HC (to 1900)

Painestown (Ardmulchan)
Earliest Records: b. 1698–; m. 1698–; d. 1698–
Status: LC; RCBL (b. 1833–1917; m. 1835–1919; d. 1834–1908); NAI MFCI 40/I (extracts—b. 1704–1901; m. 1704–1901; d. 1704–1901); b/m. indexed by Meath HC (to 1900)

Painestown–St. Anne
Earliest Records: b. 1859–1919; m. 1864–1913
Status: RCBL

Piercetown (see Kilmoon)
Status: Lost

Raddanstown
Earliest Records: b. 1877–; m. 1870–; d. 1879–
Status: LC; Indexed by Meath HC (to 1900)

Rathbeggan
Status: Lost

Rathcore
Earliest Records: b. 1810–; m. 1811–; d. 1810–
Status: LC; NAI MFCI 51 (b. 1810–1983; m. 1811–35; d. 1810–71); Indexed by Meath HC (to 1900)

Rathkenny
Status: Lost

Rathmolyon
Earliest Records: b. 1733–; m. 1734–; d. 1734–
Status: LC; NAI MFCI 51 (b. 1733–1876; m. 1834–56; d. 1834–77); Indexed by Meath HC (to 1900)

Ratoath
Earliest Records: b. 1878–; m. 1846–; d. 1879–
Status: LC; Indexed by Meath HC (b/d. to 1900; m. to 1885)

Robertstown (see Newtown)

St. Mary, Drogheda
Earliest Records: b. 1763; m. 1763; d. 1763
Missing Dates: b. 1776–1801; m. 1776–1801; d. 1776–1801
Status: LC

Skryne and Lismullan
Earliest Records: b. 1877–; m. 1846–; d. 1877
Status: LC; Indexed by Meath HC (to 1900)

Slane
Earliest Records: m. 1845–
Status: LC; Indexed by Meath HC (to 1900)

Stackallen
Earliest Records: b. 1885–; m. 1845–; d. 1886
Status: LC; Indexed by Meath HC (to 1900)

Syddan
Earliest Records: b. 1720–; m. 1721–; d. 1725–
Status: LC; RCBL (b. 1720–1825; m. 1721–1949; d. 1725–1824); NAI MFCI 46 (b. 1720–1983; m. 1721–1865; d. 1725–1983); Indexed by Meath HC (to 1900)

Tara
Earliest Records: b. 1877–; m. 1847–; d. 1877–
Status: LC; Indexed by Meath HC (to 1900)

Tessauran
Earliest Records: b. 1819; m. 1820–; d. 1819–
Status: LC; Indexed by Meath HC (to 1900)

Trim
Earliest Records: b. 1782–; m. 1792–; d. 1792–
Status: LC; NAI MFCI 49 (b. 1782–1876; m. 1792–1849; d. 1792–1871); Indexed by Meath HC (to 1900)

Roman Catholic

Note that all of the Catholic parish registers of this county have been indexed by Meath Heritage Centre (see Research Services at the end of the chapter). A search of the index will be conducted by the center for a fee. Those indexed are noted as "Indexed by Meath HC." Microfilm copies of all registers are also available in the National Library of Ireland (NLI), and through the LDS library system.

Civil Parish: Agher
Map Grid: 138
RC Parish: see Laracor
Diocese: ME

Civil Parish: Ardagh
Map Grid: 17
RC Parish: see Drumcondra
Diocese: ME

Civil Parish: Ardbraccan
Map Grid: 50
RC Parish: Bohermeen
Diocese: ME
Earliest Record: b. 6.1832; m. 4.1831; d. 1.1833
Missing Dates: 5.1842–1.1865, ends 3.1868
Status: LC; NLI (mf); Indexed by Meath HC (to 1900)

Civil Parish: Ardcath
Map Grid: 102
RC Parish: Ardcath
Diocese: ME
Earliest Record: b. 10.1795; m. 6.1797
Status: LC; NLI (mf); Indexed by Meath HC (to 1900)

Civil Parish: Ardmulchan
Map Grid: 79
RC Parish: Blacklion or Beaupark and Yellow Furze
Diocese: ME
Earliest Record: b. 12.1815; m. 1.1816; d. 1816
Status: LC; NLI (mf)

Civil Parish: Ardsallagh
Map Grid: 57
RC Parish: see Navan
Diocese: ME

Civil Parish: Assey
Map Grid: 116
RC Parish: Dunsany and Kilmessan, see Kilmessan
Diocese: ME

Civil Parish: Athboy
Map Grid: 70
RC Parish: Athboy
Diocese: ME
Earliest Record: b. 4.1794; m. 5.1794; d. 4.1794
Missing Dates: b. 11.1799-3.1807, 5.1826-1.1827; m. 11.1799-3.1807, 10.1864-2.1865; d. 3.1798-3.1807, 2.1826-1.1827, 1.1848-1.1865
Status: LC; NLI (mf)

Civil Parish: Athlumney
Map Grid: 80
RC Parish: Johnstown, see Monktown
Diocese: ME

Civil Parish: Balfeaghan
Map Grid: 141
RC Parish: Kilcloon, see Rathregan
Diocese: ME

Civil Parish: Ballyboggan
Map Grid: 110
RC Parish: see Castlejordan, Co. Offaly
Diocese: ME

Civil Parish: Ballygarth
Map Grid: 100
RC Parish: see Stamullen
Diocese: ME

Civil Parish: Ballymagarvey
Map Grid: 68
RC Parish: Blacklion, see Ardmulchan
Diocese: ME

Civil Parish: Ballymaglassan
Map Grid: 135
RC Parish: Kilcloon, see Rathregan
Diocese: ME

Civil Parish: Balrathboyne
Map Grid: 36
RC Parish: Bohermeen, see Ardbraccan
Diocese: ME

Civil Parish: Balsoon
Map Grid: 117
RC Parish: Dunsany and Kilmessan, see Kilmessan
Diocese: ME

Civil Parish: Bective
Map Grid: 76
RC Parish: see Navan
Diocese: ME

Civil Parish: Brownstown
Map Grid: 84
RC Parish: Blacklion, see Ardmulchan
Diocese: ME

Civil Parish: Burry
Map Grid: 35
RC Parish: see Kells
Diocese: ME

Civil Parish: Castlejordan
Map Grid: 111
RC Parish: see Castlejordan, Co. Offaly
Diocese: ME

Civil Parish: Castlekeeran (see Loughan)

Civil Parish: Castlerickard
Map Grid: 108
RC Parish: Killyon and Longwood
Diocese: ME
Earliest Record: b. 1.1829; m. 1.1829; d. 1.1829
Missing Dates: d. ends 2.1855
Status: LC; NLI (mf); Indexed by Meath HC (b/m. to 1900; d. to 1880)

Civil Parish: Castletown
Map Grid: 11
RC Parish: Castletown-Kilpatrick
Diocese: ME
Earliest Record: b. 12.1805; m. 5.1816
Missing Dates: b. 5.1822-1.1826; m. 5.1822-1.1824; 4.1841-11.1842
Status: LC; NLI (mf); Indexed by Meath HC (to 1900)

Civil Parish: Churchtown
Map Grid: 55
RC Parish: Dunderry
Diocese: ME
Earliest Record: b. 10.1837; m. 10.1841
Missing Dates: b. 7.1869-5.1870; m. 5.1869-5.1871
Status: LC; NLI (mf); Indexed by Meath HC (to 1900)

Civil Parish: Clonalvy
Map Grid: 106
RC Parish: see Ardcath
Diocese: ME

Civil Parish: Clonard
Map Grid: 109
RC Parish: Kinnegad, see Killucan, Co. Westmeath; also part Longwood, see Castlerickard
Diocese: ME

Civil Parish: Clongil
Map Grid: 15
RC Parish: Castletown-Kilpatrick, see Castletown
Diocese: ME

Civil Parish: Clonmacduff
Map Grid: 73
RC Parish: see Churchtown
Diocese: ME

Civil Parish: Collon
Map Grid: 43
RC Parish: see Collon, Co. Louth
Diocese: AM

Civil Parish: Colp
Map Grid: 61
RC Parish: St. Mary's, Co. Louth
Diocese: ME

Civil Parish: Cookstown
Map Grid: 129
RC Parish: see Ratoath
Diocese: ME

Civil Parish: Crickstown (or Creekstown)
Map Grid: 128
RC Parish: Curraha (see also Ratoath and
Donaghmore)
Diocese: ME
Earliest Record: b. 4.1802; m. 6.1802; d. 6.1802
Missing Dates: d. 4.1823–11.1833, ends 4.1863
Status: LC; NLI (mf); Indexed by Meath HC (to 1900)

Civil Parish: Cruicetown
Map Grid: 5
RC Parish: see Nobber
Diocese: ME

Civil Parish: Culmullin
Map Grid: 137
RC Parish: see Dunshaughlin
Diocese: ME

Civil Parish: Cushinstown
Map Grid: 99
RC Parish: see Duleek
Diocese: ME

Civil Parish: Danestown
Map Grid: 88
RC Parish: Blacklion, see Ardmulchan
Diocese: ME

Civil Parish: Derrypatrick
Map Grid: 123
RC Parish: Moynalty and Galtrim
Diocese: ME
Earliest Record: b. 10.1811; m. 11.1783; d. 10.1811
Missing Dates: b. 10.1828–3.1831; m. 11.1786–
10.1811, 9.1828–4.1831; d. 9.1828–10.1877
Status: LC; NLI (mf); Indexed by Meath HC (to 1900)

Civil Parish: Diamor
Map Grid: 29
RC Parish: Kilskyre, see Kilskeer
Diocese: ME

Civil Parish: Donaghmore (near Navan)
Map Grid: 52
RC Parish: see Navan
Diocese: ME

Civil Parish: Donaghmore (near Ratoath)
Map Grid: 133
RC Parish: see Crickstown
Diocese: ME

Civil Parish: Donaghpatrick
Map Grid: 38
RC Parish: Kilberry and Telltown, see Kilberry
Diocese: ME

Civil Parish: Donore
Map Grid: 59
RC Parish: Donore or Rosnaree
Diocese: ME
Earliest Record: b. 1.1840; m. 4.1840
Missing Dates: m. 7.1841–11.1850
Status: LC; NLI (mf); Indexed by Meath HC (to 1900)

Civil Parish: Dowdstown
Map Grid: 85
RC Parish: Skryne, see Skreen
Diocese: ME

Civil Parish: Dowth
Map Grid: 48
RC Parish: see Slane
Diocese: AM

Civil Parish: Drakestown
Map Grid: 12
RC Parish: see Castletown
Diocese: ME

Civil Parish: Drumcondra
Map Grid: 18
RC Parish: Drumconrath
Diocese: ME
Earliest Record: b. 10.1811; m. 9.1811; d. 8.1813
Status: LC; NLI (mf); Indexed by Meath HC (to 1900)

Civil Parish: Drumlargan
Map Grid: 139
RC Parish: Summerhill, see Laracor
Diocese: ME

Civil Parish: Dulane
Map Grid: 33
RC Parish: Carnaross, see Loughan
Diocese: ME

Civil Parish: Duleek
Map Grid: 64
RC Parish: Duleek
Diocese: ME
Earliest Record: b. 2.1852; m. 2.1852
Status: LC; NLI (mf); Indexed by Meath HC (to 1900)

Civil Parish: Duleek Abbey
Map Grid: 103
RC Parish: see Duleek
Diocese: ME

Civil Parish: Dunboyne
Map Grid: 145

RC Parish: Dunboyne
Diocese: ME
Earliest Record: b. 9.1798; m. 6.1787; d. 6.1787
Status: LC; NLI (mf)

Civil Parish: Dunmoe
Map Grid: 53
RC Parish: see Slane
Diocese: ME

Civil Parish: Dunsany
Map Grid: 95
RC Parish: see Kilmessan
Diocese: ME

Civil Parish: Dunshaughlin
Map Grid: 126
RC Parish: Dunshaughlin
Diocese: ME
Earliest Record: b. 1.1789; m. 10.1800; d. 1.1789
Missing Dates: b. 1.1843-1.1849; m. 2.1834-2.1849;
d. 1.1828-1.1863, ends 12.1872
Status: LC; NLI (mf); Indexed by Meath HC (to 1900)

Civil Parish: Emlagh
Map Grid: 7
RC Parish: Staholmog, see Kilbeg
Diocese: ME

Civil Parish: Enniskeen
Map Grid: 9
RC Parish: Kingscourt, see Enniskeen, Co. Cavan
Diocese: ME

Civil Parish: Fennor
Map Grid: 58
RC Parish: see Slane
Diocese: ME

Civil Parish: Follistown
Map Grid: 82
RC Parish: Johnstown, see Monktown
Diocese: ME

Civil Parish: Gallow
Map Grid: 140
RC Parish: Summerhill, see Laracor
Diocese: ME

Civil Parish: Galtrim
Map Grid: 121
RC Parish: Moynalvy, see Derrypatrick
Diocese: ME

Civil Parish: Gernonstown
Map Grid: 41
RC Parish: see Slane
Diocese: ME

Civil Parish: Girley
Map Grid: 39
RC Parish: see Kells
Diocese: ME

Civil Parish: Grangegeeth
Map Grid: 42
RC Parish: see Slane
Diocese: ME

Civil Parish: Greenoge
Map Grid: 134
RC Parish: see Crickstown
Diocese: ME

Civil Parish: Inishmot
Map Grid: 20
RC Parish: Lobinstown, see Killary
Diocese: ME

Civil Parish: Julianstown
Map Grid: 66
RC Parish: see Stamullen
Diocese: ME

Civil Parish: Kells
Map Grid: 34
RC Parish: Kells
Diocese: ME
Earliest Record: b. 7.1791; m. 8.1791; d. 6.1794
Missing Dates: b. 12.1827-7.1828; d. ends 3.1824
Status: LC; NLI (mf); Indexed by Meath HC (to 1900)

Civil Parish: Kentstown
Map Grid: 67
RC Parish: Blacklion, see Ardmulchan
Diocese: ME

Civil Parish: Kilbeg
Map Grid: 4
RC Parish: Kilbeg or Staholmog
Diocese: ME
Earliest Record: b. 12.1817; m. 1.1810; d. 1830
Missing Dates: b. 1.1852-3.1858; m. 6.1813-1.1830,
5.1852-5.1858
Status: LC; NLI (mf); Indexed by Meath HC (to 1900)

Civil Parish: Kilberry
Map Grid: 16
RC Parish: Oristown and Kilberry
Diocese: ME
Earliest Record: b. 12.1757; m. 11.1763; d. 1771
Missing Dates: b. 7.1784-4.1797, 5.1814-2.1831,
12.1840-11.1847; m. 5.1780-1.1783, 6.1784-4.1797,
4.1801-9.1801, 8.1842-3.1848; d. various dates to
1881
Status: LC; NLI (mf); Indexed by Meath HC (to 1900)

Civil Parish: Kilbrew
Map Grid: 125
RC Parish: see Crickstown
Diocese: ME

Civil Parish: Kilbride (1) (near Oldcastle)
Map Grid: 24
RC Parish: Killeagha and Kilbride (Mount Nugent),
see Co. Cavan

Diocese: ME
Earliest Record: b. 1.1832; m. 1.1832
Status: LC; NLI (mf)

Civil Parish: Kilbride (2) (near Dunboyne)
Map Grid: 146
RC Parish: Dunboyne and Kilbride, see Dunboyne
Diocese: ME

Civil Parish: Kilcarn
Map Grid: 81
RC Parish: Johnstown, see Monkstown
Diocese: ME

Civil Parish: Kilclone
Map Grid: 143
RC Parish: Kilcloon, see Rathregan
Diocese: ME

Civil Parish: Kilcooly
Map Grid: 78
RC Parish: see Trim
Diocese: ME

Civil Parish: Kildalkey
Map Grid: 71
RC Parish: Ballivor, see Killaconnigan
Diocese: ME

Civil Parish: Killaconnigan
Map Grid: 72
RC Parish: Ballivor
Diocese: ME
Earliest Record: b. 2.1837; m. 4.1837; d. 2.1837
Status: LC; NLI (mf); Indexed by Meath HC (to 1900)

Civil Parish: Killallon
Map Grid: 30
RC Parish: Clonmellon, see Killua, Co. Westmeath
Diocese: ME

Civil Parish: Killary
Map Grid: 23
RC Parish: Lobinstown
Diocese: ME
Earliest Record: b. 10.1823; m. 9.1823
Status: LC; NLI (mf); Indexed by Meath HC (to 1900)

Civil Parish: Killeagh
Map Grid: 26
RC Parish: see Oldcastle
Diocese: ME

Civil Parish: Killeen
Map Grid: 94
RC Parish: Dunsany, see Kilmessan
Diocese: ME

Civil Parish: Killegland
Map Grid: 130
RC Parish: see Ratoath
Diocese: ME

Civil Parish: Killyon
Map Grid: 107

Civil Parish: Longwood, see Castlerickard
RC Parish: Longwood, see Castlerickard
Diocese: ME

Civil Parish: Kilmainham
Map Grid: 2
RC Parish: Kilmainhamwood and Moybologue; see
Co. Cavan
Diocese: ME
Earliest Record: b. 1.1869; m. 1.1869
Status: LC; NLI (mf); Indexed by Meath HC (to 1900)

Civil Parish: Kilmessan
Map Grid: 120
RC Parish: Kilmessan
Diocese: ME
Earliest Record: b. 7.1742; m. 7.1742; d. 10.1756
Missing Dates: b. 8.1750–10.1756, 6.1768–1.1791; m.
8.1750–10.1756, 6.1768–1.1791
Status: LC; NLI (mf)

Civil Parish: Kilmoon
Map Grid: 98
RC Parish: see Crickstown
Diocese: ME

Civil Parish: Kilmore
Map Grid: 136
RC Parish: Moynalty, see Derrypatrick
Diocese: ME

Civil Parish: Kilsharvan
Map Grid: 65
RC Parish: St. Mary's, Drogheda, see St. Mary's
Diocese: ME

Civil Parish: Kilshine
Map Grid: 14
RC Parish: Castletown-Kilpatrick, see Castletown
Diocese: ME

Civil Parish: Kilskeer
Map Grid: 31
RC Parish: Kilskeer
Diocese: ME
Earliest Record: b. 4.1784; m. 1.1784; d. 1.1784
Missing Dates: m. 11.1790–6.1808, 7.1841–1.1842; d.
8.1790–11.1859
Status: LC; NLI (mf); Indexed by Meath HC (to 1900)

Civil Parish: Kiltale
Map Grid: 122
RC Parish: Moynalvy, see Derrypatrick
Diocese: ME

Civil Parish: Knock
Map Grid: 13
RC Parish: Castletown-Kilpatrick, see Castletown
Diocese: ME

Civil Parish: Knockcommon
Map Grid: 63
RC Parish: see Donore
Diocese: ME

Civil Parish: Knockmark
Map Grid: 124
RC Parish: see Dunshaughlin
Diocese: ME

Civil Parish: Laracor
Map Grid: 113
RC Parish: Summerhill
Diocese: ME
Earliest Record: b. 4.1812; m. 4.1812; d. 4.1812
Missing Dates: m. 2.1854–7.1854; d. ends 11.1836
Status: LC; NLI (mf); Indexed by Meath HC (to 1900)

Civil Parish: Liscartan
Map Grid: 51
RC Parish: see Ardbraccan
Diocese: ME

Civil Parish: Lismullin
Map Grid: 90
RC Parish: see Skreen
Diocese: ME

Civil Parish: Loughan or Castlekeeran (see also Co. Cavan)
Map Grid: 32
RC Parish: Carnaross
Diocese: ME
Earliest Record: b. 8.1806; m. 6.1805; d. 6.1805
Missing Dates: b. 10.1807–5.1808, 9.1815–6.1827; m. 2.1820–2.1823, 2.1825–1.1828, 4.1861–7.1861; d. ends 9.1856
Status: LC; NLI (mf)

Civil Parish: Loughbrackan
Map Grid: 19
RC Parish: see Drumcondra
Diocese: ME

Civil Parish: Loughcrew
Map Grid: 28
RC Parish: see Oldcastle
Diocese: ME

Civil Parish: Macetown
Map Grid: 97
RC Parish: see Skreen
Diocese: ME

Civil Parish: Martry
Map Grid: 49
RC Parish: see Ardbraccan
Diocese: ME

Civil Parish: Mitchelstown
Map Grid: 21
RC Parish: Lobinstown, see Killary
Diocese: ME

Civil Parish: Monknewtown
Map Grid: 47
RC Parish: see Grangegeeth
Diocese: ME

Civil Parish: Monktown
Map Grid: 87
RC Parish: Johnstown
Diocese: ME
Earliest Record: b. 1.1839; m. 1.1839
Status: LC; NLI (mf); Indexed by Meath HC (to 1900)

Civil Parish: Moorechurch
Map Grid: 101
RC Parish: see Stamullen
Diocese: ME

Civil Parish: Moybolgue (see also Co. Cavan)
Map Grid: 1
RC Parish: see Kilmainham (also Moynalty)
Diocese: ME

Civil Parish: Moyglare
Map Grid: 144
RC Parish: Kilcloon, see Rathregan
Diocese: ME

Civil Parish: Moylagh
Map Grid: 27
RC Parish: see Oldcastle
Diocese: ME

Civil Parish: Moymet
Map Grid: 75
RC Parish: see Churchtown
Diocese: ME

Civil Parish: Moynalty
Map Grid: 3
RC Parish: Moynalty
Diocese: ME
Earliest Record: b. 7.1830; m. 12.1829; d. 3.1830
Status: LC; NLI (mf); Indexed by Meath HC (to 1900)

Civil Parish: Navan
Map Grid: 54
RC Parish: Navan
Diocese: ME
Earliest Record: b. 1.1782; m. 2.1852; d. 6.1868
Missing Dates: b. 5.1813–9.1842
Status: LC; NLI (mf); Indexed by Meath HC (to 1900)

Civil Parish: Newtown
Map Grid: 6
RC Parish: Staholmog, see Kilbeg
Diocese: ME

Civil Parish: Newtownclonbun
Map Grid: 77
RC Parish: see Trim
Diocese: ME

Civil Parish: Nobber
Map Grid: 10
RC Parish: Nobber
Diocese: ME
Earliest Record: b. 7.1754; m. 2.1757; d. 1.1757

Missing Dates: records end 1865
Status: LC; NLI (mf); Indexed by Meath HC (to 1900)

Civil Parish: Oldcastle
Map Grid: 25
RC Parish: Oldcastle
Diocese: ME
Earliest Record: b. 1.1789; m. 4.1789; d. 3.1789
Missing Dates: b. 2.1807–11.1808; m. 2.1807–
11.1808; d. 2.1807–11.1808, ends 1.1809
Status: LC; NLI (mf); Indexed by Meath HC (to 1900)

Civil Parish: Painestown
Map Grid: 62
RC Parish: Blacklion, see Ardmulchan
Diocese: ME

Civil Parish: Piercetown
Map Grid: 105
RC Parish: see Ardcath
Diocese: ME

Civil Parish: Rataine
Map Grid: 56
RC Parish: Dunderry, see Churchtown
Diocese: ME

Civil Parish: Rathbeggan
Map Grid: 132
RC Parish: see Ratoath
Diocese: ME

Civil Parish: Rathcore
Map Grid: 115
RC Parish: see Laracor
Diocese: ME

Civil Parish: Rathfeigh
Map Grid: 92
RC Parish: see Skreen
Diocese: ME

Civil Parish: Rathkenny
Map Grid: 40
RC Parish: see Slane
Diocese: ME

Civil Parish: Rathmolyon
Map Grid: 114
RC Parish: Summerhill, see Laracor
Diocese: ME

Civil Parish: Rathmore
Map Grid: 69
RC Parish: see Athboy
Diocese: ME

Civil Parish: Rathregan
Map Grid: 131
RC Parish: Kilcloon
Diocese: ME
Earliest Record: b. 2.1836; m. 4.1836
Status: LC; NLI (mf); Indexed by Meath HC (to 1900)

Civil Parish: Ratoath
Map Grid: 127
RC Parish: Ratoath
Diocese: ME
Earliest Record: b. 1781; m. 1780; d. 1789
Status: LC; NLI (mf); Indexed by Meath HC (to 1900)

Civil Parish: Rodanstown (Robanstown)
Map Grid: 142
RC Parish: Kilcloon, see Rathregan
Diocese: ME

Civil Parish: St. Mary's
Map Grid: 60
RC Parish: see St. Mary's, Drogheda, Co. Louth
Diocese: ME

Civil Parish: Scurlockstown
Map Grid: 119
RC Parish: see Kilmessan
Diocese: ME

Civil Parish: Siddan
Map Grid: 22
RC Parish: Lobinstown, see Killary
Diocese: ME

Civil Parish: Skreen
Map Grid: 91
RC Parish: Skryne
Diocese: ME
Earliest Record: b. 11.1841; m. 1.1842
Status: LC; NLI (mf); Indexed by Meath HC (to 1900)

Civil Parish: Slane (1)
Map Grid: 44
RC Parish: Slane
Diocese: ME
Earliest Record: b. 1851; m. 1851
Status: LC; NLI (mf); Indexed by Meath HC (to 1900)

Civil Parish: Slane (2)
Map Grid: 44
RC Parish: Rathkenny
Earliest Record: b. 11.1784; m. 11.1784
Missing Dates: b. 12.1815–7.1818, 2.1861–8.1866; m.
1.1788–8.1818, 12.1844–5.1846, 11.1857–10.1866
Status: LC; NLI (mf); Indexed by Meath HC (to 1900)

Civil Parish: Stackallen
Map Grid: 46
RC Parish: part Rathkenny; part Slane, see Slane (2)
Diocese: ME

Civil Parish: Staffordstown
Map Grid: 83
RC Parish: Johnstown, see Monktown
Diocese: ME

Civil Parish: Staholmog
Map Grid: 8
RC Parish: Staholmog, see Kilbeg
Diocese: ME

Civil Parish: Stamullin
Map Grid: 104
RC Parish: Stamullen
Diocese: ME
Earliest Record: b. 1.1831; m. 5.1830; d. 1.1834
Status: LC; NLI (mf); Indexed by Meath HC (to 1900)

Civil Parish: Tara
Map Grid: 89
RC Parish: see Skreen
Diocese: ME

Civil Parish: Teltown
Map Grid: 37
RC Parish: see Kilberry
Diocese: ME

Civil Parish: Templekeeran
Map Grid: 86
RC Parish: see Skreen
Diocese: ME

Civil Parish: Timoole
Map Grid: 93
RC Parish: see Duleek
Diocese: ME

Civil Parish: Trevet
Map Grid: 96
RC Parish: see Skreen
Diocese: ME

Civil Parish: Trim
Map Grid: 112
RC Parish: Trim
Diocese: ME
Earliest Record: b. 7.1829; m. 7.1829; d. 1.1831
Missing Dates: d. ends 4.1841
Status: LC; NLI (mf); Indexed by Meath HC (to 1900)

Civil Parish: Trubley (Tubberville)
Map Grid: 118
RC Parish: Dunsany, see Kilmessan
Diocese: ME

Civil Parish: Tullaghanoge
Map Grid: 74
RC Parish: see Churchtown
Diocese: ME

Civil Parish: Tullyallen
Map Grid: 45
RC Parish: see Tullyallen (1), Co. Louth
Diocese: AM

Commercial and Social Directories

1824

J. Pigot's *City of Dublin and Hibernian Provincial Directory* includes traders, nobility, gentry, and clergy lists of Athboy, Duleek, Kells, Navan, Ratoath, Summerhill, and Trim.

1846

Slater's *National Commercial Directory of Ireland* lists nobility, clergy, traders, etc., in Athboy, Duleek, Kells, Navan, Ratoath, Ashbourne and Dunshaughlin, Trim, and Summerhill.

1856

Slater's *Royal National Commercial Directory of Ireland* lists nobility, gentry, clergy, traders, etc., in Athboy, Duleek, Kells, Navan, Oldcastle, Ratoath, Ashbourne and Dunshaughlin, Slane, Trim, and Summerhill.

1870

Slater's *Directory of Ireland* contains trade, nobility, and clergy lists for Athboy, Duleek, Kells, Navan, Oldcastle, Ratoath, Slane, and Trim.

1881

Slater's *Royal National Commercial Directory of Ireland* contains lists of traders, clergy, nobility, and farmers in adjoining parishes of the towns of Duleek, Kells, Navan, Oldcastle, Ratoath, Ashbourne and Dunshaughlin, Trim, and Athboy.

1894

Slater's *Royal National Directory of Ireland* lists traders, police, teachers, farmers, and private residents in each of the towns, villages, and parishes of the county.

Family History

Aylmer, Sir F.J. *The Aylmers of Ireland.* 1931.
"Barnewall of Rowestown, Co. Meath." *Ir. Gen.* 4 (1978): 174-82.
"The Barnwalls." *Riocht na Midhe* 1 (1957): 64-68.
"Barnwell of Kilbrew, Co. Meath." *Ir. Gen.* 6 (1) (1980): 9-17.
"The Family of Barnewall." *Ir. Gen.* 3 (1959-66): 124-35, 173-76, 198-209, 249-56, 311-21, 384-88, 445-54.
"The Berfords of Kilrue." *Riocht na Midhe* 6 (4) (1978/79): 89-118.
Strange, Mary A. *The Bourne(s) Families of Ireland.* USA: Stramer Corporation, 1970.
"The Briens of Brawney." *Riocht na Midhe* 7 (4) (1980/81): 80-98.
"The MacCoghlans of Delvin." *Ir. Gen.* 4 (6) (1973): 534-46; 5 (1) (1974): 21-32.
"The MacCoghlans of Delvin Eathra" by Liam Cox. *Irish Genealogist* 4 (1970): 534-546; 5 (1971): 21-32.
"William Burton Conyngham, 1733-1796" by C.E.F. Trench. *Riocht na Midhe* 8 (1987): 113-129.
"The Cusacks of Killeen, Co. Meath." *Riocht na Midhe* 7 (4) (1980/81): 3-35.

Cusack—see Co. Dublin.

"The Cusacks of Portraine and Rathaldron." *Riocht na Midhe* 4 (4) (1970): 58-61.

"Darcy of Platten." *Ir. Gen.* 6 (4) (1983): 403-22.

"Dillon, Cnoc Diolun, a Genealogical Survey of the Dillon Family in Ireland" by Gerald Dillon. *Ir. Gen.* 2 (1955): 361.

"Dowdalls of Athlumney." *Riocht na Midhe* 3 (3) (1965): 205-10.

"Draycott of Mornington." *Riocht na Midhe* 6 (3).

Duffy, Walter Leonard, and Bridget Duffy. *From Meath to Balmain—The story of a convict couple and their family by Patricia Stemp*. New South Wales, Australia, 1989.

Fagan, Co. Meath. *Irish Builder* 30: 78.

"ffolliott of Co. Meath." *Ir. Anc.* 1 (1): 27-33.

"Fleming and Conyngham of Slane." *Riocht na Midhe* 7 (2) (1982/83): 69-75.

Betham, Sir W. *Fleming, Historical and genealogical memoir of the family of Fleming of Slane*. 1829.

"The Foxes of Muintir Thaidgean." *Riocht na Midhe* 4 (4) (1970): 6-23.

Trench, C.E.F. *The families of Gaughran and Vaughey of Slane, Co. Meath as recorded in the Slane Vestry Books 1738-1862*.

"The Griersons of Co. Meath." *Ir. Gen.* 3 (4) (1959): 136-43.

O'Hart, J. *The last princes of Tara, or a brief sketch of the O'Hart ancient royal family*. Dublin, 1873.

Magan, William. *Umma-More: The Story of an Irish Family*. Dorset, England: 1983.

"The Mageoghans." *Riocht na Midhe* 4 (3) (1969): 63-86.

Burke, Sir B. "The O'Melaghlins, Kings of Meath" in *Viscissitudes of Families*, vol. 2. London, 1883: p. 336-51.

"The Molloy Family of Kells." *Ir. Gen.* 3 (1961): 187-89.

"O'Molloys of Fircall." *Riocht na Midhe* 5 (3) (1973): 14-45.

"A short account of the Nangle Family" compiled by F.E. Nangle in collaboration with J.F.T. Nangle. Privately published. Ardglass, Co. Down, 1986.

"Piers of Tristernagh." *Riocht na Midhe* 7 (4) (1980/81): 52-76.

"Plunkett of Loughcrew." *Ir. Gen.* 5 (4) (1977): 422-27.

"The Plunkett Family of Loughcrew." *Riocht na Midhe* 1 (4) (1958): 49-53.

Crisp, F.A., ed. *O'Reilly, formerly of Baltrasna, Co. Meath in visitation of Ireland*, vol. 4. Privately printed, 1911.

"Tandy of Drewstown." Pedigree in *Swanzy Notebooks*. RCB Library, Dublin.

"Tandy of Johnsbrook." Pedigree in *Swanzy Notebooks*. RCB Library, Dublin.

"Tucker of Petersville." Pedigree in *Swanzy Notebooks*. RCB Library, Dublin.

Tyrrell—see Co. Dublin.

Vaughey—see Gaughran.

"The Wakelys of Navan and Ballyburly." *Riocht na Midhe* 5 (4) (1974): 3-19.

Gravestone Inscriptions

A series of records of gravestone inscriptions made by the late Dr. Beryl Moore are held in Meath County Library and on SLC film 1596994. These are denoted below as "Moore Transcriptions." Some are also published in *Memorial Inscriptions of Some Graveyards in Co. Meath* by Noel E. French, published by the author (1987).

In addition, Meath Heritage Centre has indexed further gravestones, and will conduct a search for a fee (see Research Services at the end of the chapter).

Agher: Moore Transcriptions; *Ir. Anc.* 10 (2) (1978): 129-38.

Ardmulchan: Meath Heritage Centre.

Ardsallagh: Meath Heritage Centre.

Arodstown: *Riocht na Midhe* 6 (1) (1975): 38-49; Moore Transcriptions.

Assey: Moore Transcriptions.

Athboy: *Ir. Anc.* 13 (1), (2): 113-24.

Athlumney: Moore Transcriptions.

Balfeaghan: Moore Transcriptions.

Balsoon: *Ir. Anc.* 8 (2) (1976): 94-95.

Castlejordan: Moore Transcriptions.

Castlekieran: Moore Transcriptions.

Churchtown: Moore Transcriptions.

Clady (Parish of Bective): *Ir. Anc.* 16 (1) (1984): 9-13.

Clonabreany: Moore Transcriptions; *Riocht na Midhe* 6 (2) (1976): 16-36.

Clonmacduff (alias Courtown or Blackchurch): *Riocht na Midhe* 7 (4) (1980/81): 111-28.

Colp: Transcribed by James Garry; SLC 941.82/C1 v3g.

Courtown: Moore Transcriptions.

Danestown: *Riocht na Midhe* 5 (4) (1974): 87-97; Moore Transcriptions.

Donaghmore: Meath Heritage Centre.

Dowdstown: Meath Heritage Centre.

Drogheda—St. Mary's: *J. Old Drogheda Society* 1986.

Drumlargan: *Ir. Anc.* 12 (1), (2): 1980; Moore Transcriptions.

Duleek: *Ir. Gen.* 3 (12) (1967): 538-40.

Dunboyne, C of I: *Ir. Anc.* 11 (1) (1979): 54-68; (2): 137-53.

Dunmoe: Meath Heritage Centre.

Gallow: Moore Transcriptions.

Gernonstown: Meath Heritage Centre.

Girley: Meath Heritage Centre.

Girley (C of I): Meath Heritage Centre.

Hermitage of Erc: Meath Heritage Centre.

Hill of Ward: Meath Heritage Centre.

Kells: *Ir. Gen.* 3 (12) (1966): 439–44.

Kilbride: *Riocht na Midhe* 6 (3) (1977): 23–38; Moore Transcriptions.

Kilcarn: Meath Heritage Centre.

Killaconnigan: *Ir. Anc.* 16 (2) (1984): 107–17.

Killeen: *Riocht na Midhe* 4 (4) (1970): 24–29.

Kilmore: *Riocht na Midhe* 6 (1) (1975): 38–49; Moore Transcriptions.

Kilsharvan: *Riocht na Midhe* 1988/89.

Loughcrew: *Ir. Anc.* 9 (2) (1977): 85–101.

Loughcrew, Old: Moore Transcriptions.

Macetown: Moore Transcriptions.

Monkstown: *Riocht na Midhe* 1987.

Mornington: *J. Old Drogheda Society* 1989. Transcribed by James Garry; SLC 941.82/M1 v3m.

Moy (Summerhill): Moore Transcriptions; *Ir. Anc.* 6 (2) (1974): 85–96.

Moyagher: Moore Transcriptions; *Ir. Anc.* 8 (1) (1976): 9–12.

Newton: Meath Heritage Centre.

Oldcastle: *Riocht na Midhe* 4 (2) (1968): 11–19.

Rathkenny: Meath Heritage Centre.

Rathmore: *Ir. Anc.* 7 (2) (1975): 70–82; Moore Transcriptions.

Scullockstown: Moore Transcriptions.

Skryne: Meath Heritage Centre.

St. Fechin's Church: Moore Transcriptions.

St. Mary's, Killeen: Moore Transcriptions.

Stagrennan, Mornington: *J. Old Drogheda Society* 1977.

Tara: Meath Heritage Centre.

Trim—St. Patrick's (C of I): Meath Heritage Centre.

Trimblestown: Meath Heritage Centre.

Tullaghanogue: Meath Heritage Centre.

Tyrcogan or Tyrcroghan: Moore Transcriptions.

Newspapers

There were no newspapers published in this county before 1845. Papers from the surrounding counties should be searched, starting with those in the county adjacent to the area of interest. An index to Meath births and deaths (1800–1816) in *Faulkner's Dublin Journal* was compiled by Michael Breen of the National Library. Copies are in the NLI, Meath Heritage Centre, and the Meath County Library.

Title: *Meath Chronicle*
Published in: Navan, 1897–current
BL Holdings: 5.1906–9.1907; 1.1909–1.1924
Co. Library: 1904–in progress

Title: *Meath Herald and Cavan Advertiser*
Published in: Kells, 1845–1936
NLI Holdings: 2.1845–9.1913; 1.1928–11.1936
BL Holdings: 2.1845–12.1921; 4.1924–9.1933

Title: *Meath People*
Published in: Navan, 1857–63
NLI Holdings: 8.1857–11.1863
BL Holdings: 8.1857–11.1863

Title: *Meath Reporter*
Published in: Trim, 1870–1901
NLI Holdings: 1.1888–6.1901
BL Holdings: 3–10.1871

Wills and Administrations

A discussion of the types of records, where they are held, and their availability and value is given in the Wills section of the introduction. The availability of prerogative wills, administrations, and marriage license records is also described in the relevant parts of the same section. Where available, published sources of these records are given in the Miscellaneous Sources section.

Pre-1858 Wills and Administrations

Prerogative Wills. See the introduction.

Consistorial Wills. County Meath is mainly in the diocese of Meath, with three parishes in Armagh. The guide to Catholic parish records in this chapter shows the diocese to which each civil parish belonged. The wills of residents of each diocese were usually proven within that diocese (see the Wills section for exceptions). The following records survive:

Wills

See the introduction.

Abstracts

See the introduction.

Indexes

Meath (fragment of 1572–1858 with index) is in the NAI. A transcript for 1635–1838 provides name of testator and year of probate only—NAI T 7431 (Betham Papers); Kilmore—see Co. Cavan; Armagh—see Co. Armagh.

Administrations

An index to diocesan administration bonds (1663–1857) is in the NAI.

Post-1858 Wills and Administrations

This county was served by the District Registry of Dublin. The surviving records are kept in the NAI. Records include: Principal Probate Registry Will Books (1858-1891). NAI and SLC film 100918-24.

Marriage Licenses

Indexes. Meath and Kilmore (1691-1845). NAI; SLC film 100869. Armagh—see Co. Armagh.

Miscellaneous Sources

French, Noel. *Meath Ancestors.* Trymme Press, 1993.

"Aspects of Navan History." *Riocht na Midhe* 3 (1) (1963): 33-56.

Cogan, A. *The Ecclesiastical History of the Diocese of Meath.* 3 vols. Dublin, 1874.

Connell, P. *Changing Forces Shaping a Nineteenth-Century Town: A Case Study of Navan.* Maynooth, 1978.

Brady, J. *A Short History of the Parishes of the Diocese of Meath 1867.* Published 1937-1944.

Conlon, L. *The Heritage of Collon 1764-1984.* 1984.

Coogan, O. *A Short History of South-East Meath.* 1979.

Coogan, O. *A Short History of Dunshaughlin, Culmullen and Knockmark.* The author, 1989.

Coogan, T., and J. Charlesfort Gaughran. *The story of a Meath Estate and its people 1668-1968.* 1991.

Fitzsimons, J. *The Parish of Kilbeg.* 1974.

French, N. *A Short History of Athboy.* 1985.

French, N. *Trim, Traces and Places.* 1987.

Johnstown's I.C.A. *A Local History of Johnstown Parish.* 1985.

Julianstown I.C.A. *A History of Julianstown.* E. Delaney, ed. 1985.

O'Boyle, E. *A History of Duleek.* 1989.

O'Meachair, D. *A Short History of County Meath.* 1928.

Thompson, R. *Statistical Survey of County Meath.* 1802.

"The Great Landowners of Meath 1879." *Riocht na Midhe* 7 (4) (1980/81): 99-110.

"Land Tenure in East Westmeath and Agriculture 1820-4." *Riocht na Midhe* 5 (4) (1978/79): 33-48.

O'Meachair, Donnchadh. "A Short History of County Meath." Royal Meath. Navan, 1928.

"Register of Pupils at Donacarney School, Co. Meath, 1873." *Ir. Anc.* 16 (2) (1984): 75-77.

"State of the Poor in Oldcastle 1834." *Riocht na Midhe* 1 (4) (1958): 69-74.

"Yeomanry, Militia, and Orangemen of Co. Meath." *Riocht na Midhe* 5 (4) (1978/79): 3-32 (names of officers only).

Research Sources and Services

Journals

Riocht na Midhe (published by Meath Archaeological and Historical Society)

Annala Dhamhliag (The Annals of Duleek)

Libraries and Information Sources

Meath County Library, Railway Street, Navan, Co. Meath. Ph: (046) 21134/21451. The local studies section of the library has all standard sources, plus other local material and an index to *Riocht na Midhe.* It also houses the Board of Guardian minutes and workhouse records for the county (1839-1921), and the County Infirmary records (1809-1960).

Research Services

Meath Heritage Centre, Mill Street, Trim, Co. Meath. Ph: (353 46) 36633; fax: (353 46) 37502. This is the official IGP center for County Meath, and previously offered services for Louth as well. They have fully indexed all RC and C of I registers, the 1901 census, *Griffith's Valuation* and tithe books, and also have access to a wide range of other local records. Researchers are advised to contact the center for an updated list of registers, and other sources, indexed. A research service is provided for a fee.

See also Research Services in Dublin in the introduction.

Societies

Duleek Historical Society, Mr. Enda O'Boyle, "Endevere," Duleek, Co. Meath (publishers of *Annala Dhamhliag*)

Meath Archaeological and Historical Society, Mr. Joe Gogarty, Eden, Kilmainham Wood, Kells, Co. Meath (publishers of *Riocht na Midhe*)

Old Dunboyne Society, Mr. Denis Kenny, Dunboyne, Co. Meath

Oldcastle Historical and Archaeological Society, Mrs. Anne Fox, Patrickstown, Ballinlough, Kells, Co. Meath

Rathfeigh Historical Society, Mr. Gerald Perry, Rathfeigh, Tara, Co. Meath

Slane Historical Society, Ms. Sheila Crehan, Slane, Co. Meath

Meath Civil Parishes as Numbered on Map

1. Moybolgue	43. Collon
2. Kilmainham	44. Slane
3. Moynalty	45. Tullyallen
4. Kilbeg	46. Stackallen
5. Cruicetown	47. Monknewtown
6. Newtoen	48. Dowth
7. Emlagh	49. Martry
8. Staholmog	50. Ardbraccan
9. Enniskeen	51. Liscartan
10. Nobber	52. Donaghmore
11. Castletown	53. Dunmoe
12. Drakestown	54. Navan
13. Knock	55. Churchtown
14. Kilshine (2 pts.)	56. Rataine
15. Clongill	57. Ardsallagh
16. Kilberry	58. Fennor
17. Ardagh	59. Donnore
18. Drumcondra	60. St. Mary's
19. Loughbrackan	61. Colp
20. Inishmot	62. Painestown
21. Mitchelstown	63. Knockcommon
22. Siddan	64. Duleek
23. Killary	65. Kilsharvan
24. Kilbride	66. Julianstown
25. Oldcastle	67. Kentstown
26. Killeagh	68. Ballymagarvey
27. Moylagh	69. Rathmore
28. Loughcrew	70. Athboy
29. Diamor	71. Kildalkey
30. Killallon	72. Killaconnigan
31. Kilskeer	73. Clonmacduff
32. Loughan (Castlekeeran)	74. Tullaghanoge
33. Dulane	75. Moymet
34. Kells	76. Bactive
35. Burry	77. Newtownclonbun
36. Balrathboyne	78. Kilcooly
37. Teltown	79. Ardmulchan
38. Donaghpatrick (2 pts.)	80. Athlumney
39. Girley	81. Kilcarn
40. Rathkenny	82. Follistown
41. Geronstown	83. Staffordstown
42. Grangegeeth	84. Brownstown

85. Dowdstown
86. Templekeeran (2 pts.)
87. Monktown
88. Danestown (2 pts.)
89. Tara
90. Lismullin
91. Skreen
92. Rathfeigh
93. Timoole
94. Killeen
95. Dunsany
96. Trevet
97. Macetown
98. Kilmoon
99. Cushinstown
100. Ballygarth
101. Moorechurch
102. Ardcath
103. Duleek Abbey
104. Stamullen
105. Piercetown (2 pts.)
106. Clonsalvy
107. Killyon
108. Castlerickard
109. Clonard
110. Ballyboggan
111. Castlejordan
112. Trim
113. Laracor
114. Rathmolyon
115. Rathcore
116. Assey

117. Balsoon
118. Trubley
119. Scurlockstown
120. Kilmessan
121. Galtrim
122. Kiltale
123. Derrypatrick
124. Knockmark
125. Kilbrew
126. Dunshaughlin
127. Ratoath
128. Crickstown
129. Cookstown
130. Killegland
131. Rathregan
132. Rathbeggan
133. Donaghmore
134. Greenoge
135. Ballymaglass
136. Kilmore
137. Culmullin
138. Agher (2 pts.)
139. Drumlargan
140. Gallow
141. Balfeaghan
142. Rodanstown
143. Kilclone
144. Moyglare
145. Dunboyne
146. Kilbride

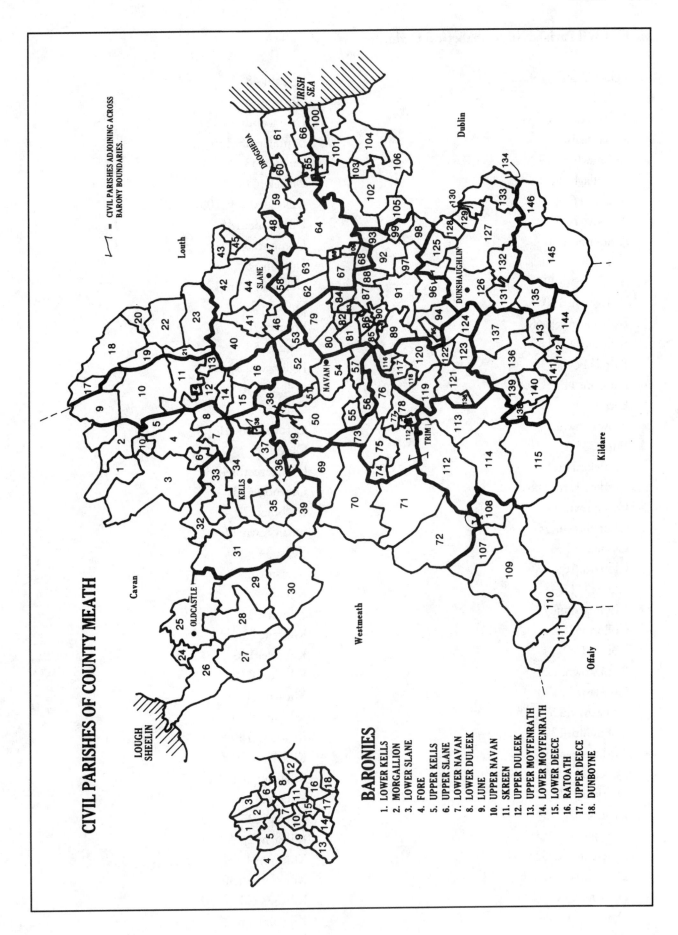

CIVIL PARISHES OF COUNTY MEATH

IRISH SEA

DROGHEDA

Dublin

Louth

Cavan

• OLDCASTLE

LOUGH
SHEELIN

• KELLS

SLANE •

NAVAN •

TRIM

Westmeath

Kildare

DUNSHAUGHLIN •

Offaly

BARONIES
1. LOWER KELLS
2. MORGALLION
3. LOWER SLANE
4. FORE
5. UPPER KELLS
6. UPPER SLANE
7. LOWER NAVAN
8. LOWER DULEEK
9. LUNE
10. UPPER NAVAN
11. SKREEN
12. UPPER DULEEK
13. UPPER MOYFENRATH
14. LOWER MOYFENRATH
15. LOWER DEECE
16. RATOATH
17. UPPER DEECE
18. DUNBOYNE

Meath Civil Parishes in Alphabetical Order

Agher (2 pts.): 138

Ardagh: 17

Ardbraccan: 50

Ardcath: 102

Ardmulchan: 79

Ardsallagh: 57

Assey: 116

Athboy: 70

Athlumney: 80

Balfeaghan: 141

Ballyboggan: 110

Ballygarth: 100

Ballymagarvey: 68

Ballymaglass: 135

Balrathboyne: 36

Balsoon: 117

Bective: 76

Brownstown: 84

Burry: 35

Castlejordan: 111

Castlerickard: 108

Castletown: 11

Churchtown: 55

Clonalvy: 106

Clonard: 109

Clongill: 15

Clonmacduff: 73

Collon: 43

Colp: 61

Cookstown: 129

Crickstown: 128

Cruicetown: 5

Culmullin: 137

Cushinstown: 99

Danestown (2 pts.): 88

Derrypatrick: 123

Diamor: 29

Donaghmore: 133

Donaghmore: 52

Donaghpatrick (2 pts.): 38

Donore: 59

Dowdstown: 85

Dowth: 48

Drakestown: 12

Drumcondra: 18

Drumlargan: 139

Dulane: 33

Duleek: 64

Duleek Abbey: 103

Dunboyne: 145

Dunmoe: 53

Dunsany: 95

Dunshaughlin: 126

Emlagh: 7

Enniskeen: 9

Fennor: 58

Follistown: 82

Gallow: 140

Galtrim: 121

Geronstown: 41

Girley: 39

Grangegeeth: 42

Greenoge: 134

Inishmot: 20

Julianstown: 66

Kells: 34

Kentstown: 67

Kilbeg: 4

Kilberry: 16

Kilbrew: 125

Kilbride: 146

Kilbride: 24

Kilcarn: 81

Kilclone: 143

Kilcooly: 78

Kildalkey: 71

Killaconnigan: 72

Killallon: 30

Killary: 23

Killeagh: 26

Killeen: 94

Killegland: 130

Killyon: 107

Kilmainham: 2

Kilmessan: 120

Kilmoon: 98

Kilmore: 136

Kilsharvan: 65

Kilshine (2 pts.): 14

Kilskeer: 31

Kiltale: 122

Knock: 13

Knockcommon: 63

Knockmark: 124

Laracor: 113

Liscartan: 51

Lismullin: 90

Loughan (Castlekeeran): 32

Loughbrackan: 19

Loughcrew: 28

Macetown: 97

Martry: 49

Mitchelstown: 21

Monknewtown: 47

Monktown: 87

Moorechurch: 101

Moybolgue: 1

Moyglare: 144

Moylagh: 27

Moymet: 75

Moynalty: 3

Navan: 54

Newtown: 6

Newtownclonbun: 77

Nobber: 10

Oldcastle: 25

Painestown: 62

Piercetown (2 pts.): 105

Rataine: 56

Rathbeggan: 132

Rathcore: 115

Rathfeigh: 92

Rathkenny: 40

Rathmolyon: 114

Rathmore: 69

Rathregan: 131

Ratoath: 127

Rodanstown: 142

Scurlockstown: 119

Siddan: 22

Skreen: 91

Slane: 44

St. Mary's: 60

Stackallen: 46

Staffordstown: 83

Staholmog: 8

Stamullen: 104

Tara: 89

Teltown: 37

Templekeeran (2 pts.): 86

Timoole: 93

Trevet: 96

Trim: 112

Trubley: 118

Tullaghanoge: 74

Tullyallen: 45

County Monaghan

A Brief History

This Ulster county contains the towns of Monaghan, Clones, Castleblayney, and Carrickmacross.

In the old Gaelic system of land division, Monaghan was part of the Kingdom of Oriel. It was also known as McMahon's country, after the dominant family in the area. The McMahons and their allies, the McKennas and O'Connollys, maintained effective domination of the county even after the arrival of the Normans in the twelfth century. The county boundaries were not established by the English administration until the late sixteenth century.

After the defeat of the rebellion of O'Neill and the Ulster chieftains in 1603, the county was not planted, as were the other counties of Ulster. The lands were instead left in the hands of the native chieftains. In 1641, the McMahons and their allies joined the general rebellion of Irish Catholics, and, following their defeat, there was some plantation of the county with Scottish and English families.

Analysis of the Hearth Money Rolls of 1663 shows that the commonest names in the county at the time (in descending order) were McMahon, McKenna, O'Duffy, O'Connolly, McCabe, McWard, McArdle, McIlmartin, O'Byrne, O'Callan, McCallan, O'Kelly, O'Murphy, McNaney, McTreanor, O'Gowan or McGowan, O'Boylan, McIlcollin, O'Finnegan, O'Cassidy, and McPhilip.

The McCabes were a gallowglass, or mercenary, family, probably brought into the county by the McMahons following the Norman invasion. The O'Byrnes, who are relatively numerous in the county, are probably descendants of the Kildare or Wicklow O'Byrnes. This family was driven from its Kildare territories by the Normans in the late twelfth century. It is suggested that part of this clan may have migrated into Monaghan.

The major settlers in the county were Scottish farmers brought over from the area of Strathclyde. Common names among these settlers were McAndrew, Mackay, Sinclair, Stewart, Buchanan, McKenzie, Davidson, Ferguson, Blackshaw, McCaig, Walker, Cameron, Gordon, Patterson, and McCutcheon.

A general indication of the proportions of the population of Irish or Norman extraction, or of English or Scottish descent, can be derived from the statistics on religious persuasions of the inhabitants. These groups were, respectively, predominantly Catholic, Church of Ireland, or Presbyterian. In 1861, when the census first determined religion, the respective proportions were seventy-three, fourteen, and twelve percent.

In the late eighteenth and early nineteenth centuries, the county became increasingly more densely populated. In 1841 there were 428 people per square mile, making the county one of the most densely populated in the country. The Great Famine of 1845–47 affected the county very badly. In 1841 the population was 200,000, but by 1851 it had fallen by thirty percent, to 142,000. Over 25,000 people died in the same decade, and a further 30,000 emigrated.

The county is currently mainly dependent on agriculture and related industry, and has a population of approximately 52,000.

Census and Census Substitutes

1632–36

"The Balfour Rentals of 1632 and 1636" (with tenant list). *Clogher Record* 12 (1) (1985): 92–109.

1641

An index to the rebels of 1641 in the Co. Monaghan depositions. *Clogher Record* 15 (2) (1995): 69–89 (gives names, addresses, and notes).

1659

"Census" of Ireland. Edited by S. Pender. Dublin: Stationery Office, 1939. NLI I6551. SLC film 924648.

1666

Hearth Money Roll. In D. Rushe, *A History of Monaghan*, pp. 291–338.

1738

"Some Clones Inhabitants." *Clogher Record* 2 (3) (1959): 512–14.

1751–80

Rent rolls of Glasslough and Emy Estates in Co. Monaghan (Leslie Estate). NLI Ms. 13719 part 3 (1751–52); Ms. 5783 (1751–66); Ms. 5809 (1764–80); and Ms. 13719 part 3 (1767–79).

1761

Militia list for Co. Monaghan, etc. GO Ms. 680.

1764

Rentals and Reports of the Kane Estate, Errigal Truagh. *Clogher Record* 13 (3) (1990). Includes alphabetical list of tenants and comments for years 1764, 1801, and 1819–21.

1772

"Castleblayney Rent Book 1772." *Clogher Record* 11 (1) (1982): 414–18.

1777

"Some Protestant Inhabitants of Carrickmacross 1777." *Clogher Record* 6 (1) (1966): 119–25.

1778–96

"Catholic Qualification Rolls Index: Fermanagh and Monaghan." *Clogher Record* 2 (3) (1959): 544–51 (Catholics taking oath of loyalty; gives name, occupation, and residence).

1784–89

"A Rental of the Anketell Estate, Co. Monaghan 1784–89" (with indexed list of tenants). *Clogher Record* 11 (3) (1984): 403–20.

1785

Male Protestants of Seventeen Years and Over in the Diocese of Clogher (i.e., parishes of Errigal, Trough,

and Magheracloone). SLC film 258517.

1786

"The Ballybay Estate 1786" (including list of tenants). *Clogher Record* 11 (1) (1982): 71–76.

1790–c.1830

"The Ker Estate, Newbliss, Co. Monaghan 1790–c.1830" (with list of four hundred tenants). *Clogher Record* 12 (1) (1985): 110–26.

1796

Spinning Wheel Premium List (see introduction; six thousand names). SLC film 1279328.

See also Mayo 1796 (List of Catholics).

1801

Errigal Truagh—see 1764.

1819/20

Errigal Truagh—see 1764.

1821

Extracts from 1821 census. *Clogher Record* 14 (1) (1991): 89–91.

A Clones Rent Roll. *Clogher Record* 13 (1) (1988): 32–37 (townland, street, and name).

1823

Some Church of Ireland members in Aghadrumsee area (Clones Parish). *Clogher Record* 15 (1) (1994): 107–121 (gives names and family details).

1823–38

Tithe Applotment Survey (see introduction).

1824

Protestant householders in parish of Aghabog. RCBL D1/1/1.

1839

List of persons who obtained Game Certificates in Ulster. PRONI T 688.

1843

Magistrates, Landed Proprietors, etc. NLI Ms. 12,767.

1843–54

Assisted emigration from Shirley Estate. *Clogher Record* 14 (2) (1992): 7–62 (lists emigrants, ages, and addresses; includes children).

1847

"Castleblayney Poor Law Rate Book (1847)." *Clogher Record* 5 (1) (1963): 131–48 (ratepayers in each townland in Castleblayney Poor Law Union).

1848

Petitioners for William Smith O'Brien. NAI 1848/180 (names of male petitioners in Carrickmacross and Castleblaney). Carrickmacross only in *Clogher Record* (1995).

1858–60

Griffith's Valuation (see introduction).

1901

Census. NAI (see introduction). SLC films 846420-328 and 850445-54.

1911

Census. NAI.

Church Records

Church of Ireland

See the introduction for a description of Church of Ireland records and their major repositories. Many C of I records were lost in the PRO fire of 1922. These are indicated as "Lost." However, as Church of Ireland records were effectively state records, the records of marriage (from 1845) are also in the General Registrar's Office. Many are still in local custody (LC), while others are in one of a variety of other archives (e.g., RCBL or NAI). All of the Church of Ireland registers of this county have been indexed by Monaghan Ancestry (see Research Services at the end of the chapter). A search of the index will be conducted by the center for a fee. Those indexed are noted as "Indexed by Mon. Anc."

Aghadrumsee
Earliest Records: b. 1821–; m. 1821–; d. 1822–
Status: LC

Ardragh (St. Patrick's)
Status: Lost

Aughnamullen
Status: Lost

Ballybay
Earliest Records: b. 1811; m. 1813; d. 1813
Status: LC; b. only indexed by Mon. Anc. (to 1900)

Carrickmacross or Magheross
Earliest Records: b. 1797–; m. 1798–; d. 1831–
Status: LC; RCBL (mf) (b. 1797-1984; m. 1798-1920; d. 1831-1981)

Castleblayney (see Mucknoe)

Clones (Adhadrimsee)
Earliest Records: b. 1829–; m. 1829–; d. 1829–
Status: LC; RCBL (mf) (b. 1829-1927; m. 1829-1935; d. 1829-90); SLC film 897416 (b. 1682-1733, 1755-1873; m. 1682-1704; d. 1682-1704, 1722-1744, 1796-1900)

Clontibret
Earliest Records: b. 1864–; d. 1864–
Status: LC; RCBL (mf) (b. 1864-1865; d. 1864-1865)

Clough
Earliest Records: b. 1811–; m. 1811–; d. 1811–
Status: LC

Cooneen
Earliest Records: b. 1872–; m. 1887–
Status: LC; RCBL (mf) (b. 1872-1975; m. 1887-1935)

Crossduff (Aughnamullen East)
Status: Lost

Currin (Rockcorry)
Earliest Records: b. 1810; m. 1812; d. 1810
Status: LC

Currin Drum
Earliest Records: b. 1828; m. 1828; d. 1828
Status: LC

Donagh
Earliest Records: b. 1796–; m. 1796–; d. 1796–
Status: LC; SLC film 1279239 (b/m/d. 1796-1815)

Donaghmoyne
Earliest Records: d. 1878–
Status: LC; RCBL (mf) (d. 1878-1969)

Drumsnat
Earliest Records: b. 1825–; m. 1825–; d. 1825–
Status: LC

Errigle-Shanco
Status: Lost

Errigle-Trough
Earliest Records: b. 1809–; m. 1803–; d. 1802–
Status: LC

Inniskeen
Status: Lost

Killanney
Earliest Records: b. 1825–; m. 1825–; d. 1825–
Status: LC

Killeevan
Earliest Records: b. 1811–; m. 1811–; d. 1811–
Status: LC

Kilmore (also see St. Ranoodan)
Earliest Records: b. 1826–; m. 1826–; d. 1826–
Status: LC; RCBL (mf) (b. 1826-1984; m. 1826-1956; d. 1826-1982)

Magheracloone
Earliest Records: b. 1806–1984; m. 1813–1985; d. 1806–1984
Status: LC; RCBL (mf) (b/d. 1806–1984; m. 1813–1985)

Monaghan
Earliest Records: b. 1802–; m. 1802–; d. 1802–
Status: LC; RCBL (mf) (b. 1802–1907; m. 1802–1910; d. 1802–57)

Mucknoe or Castleblayney
Earliest Records: b. 1810–; m. 1810–; d. 1810–
Status: LC

Mullaghfad
Earliest Records: b. 1836–; m. 1837– (four entries of marriages 1868–69 in burial register); d. 1850–
Status: LC; RCBL (mf) (b. 1878–1971; m. 1906–62)

Newbliss
Earliest Records: b. 1841; d. 1837
Status: LC

Rockcorry
Status: Lost

St. Mark, Augher
Earliest Records: b. 1866–
Status: LC

St. Ranoodan
Earliest Records: b. 1861–; d. 1867–
Status: LC

Tullycorbet
Status: Lost

Tydavnet
Earliest Records: b. 1822–; m. 1822–; d. 1822–
Status: LC; RCBL (mf) (b. 1822–83; m. 1822–1950; d. 1822–67)

Tyholland
Earliest Records: b. 1806–; m. 1806–; d. 1806–
Status: LC

Presbyterian

An account of Presbyterian records is given in the introduction. These registers rarely contain death records, and occasionally have only records of births. This is indicated where appropriate.

Ballyalbany
Starting Date: 1802

Ballybay
Starting Date: 1833
Status: LC; SLC film 1279329 (b. 1834–1984; m. 1834–1970)

Ballyhobridge (Clones)
Starting Date: 1846

Broomfield (Castleblaney)
Starting Date: 1841

Cahans (Ballybay)
Starting Date: 1752
Status: LC; SLC film 1279329 (1752–1901 indexed)

Castleblaney
Starting Date: 1832

Clones
Starting Date: 1856

Clontibret
Starting Date: 1825

Corlea
Starting Date: 1835

Creeve
Starting Date: 1845
Status: LC; SLC film 1279239 (b/m. 1819–1964)

Derryvalley (Ballybay)
Starting Date: 1816
Status: LC; SLC film 1279329 (b. 1816–1931; m. 1833–1945 and index to marriages 1846–1953)

Drumkeen (Newbliss)
Starting Date: 1856

Frankford (Castleblaney)
Starting Date: 1820

Glennan (Glasslough)
Starting Date: 1829

Loughmorne
Starting Date: 1846
Status: LC; SLC film 1279239 (b. 1846–93)

Middletown (Glasslough)
Starting Date: 1829

Monaghan
Starting Date: 1824

Newbliss
Starting Date: 1856

Scotstown
Starting Date: 1856

Stonebridge (Newbliss)
Starting Date: 1821

Tullycorbet
Starting Date: 1796
Status: LC; SLC film 1279323 (b. 1796–1831)

Methodist

An account of Methodist records is given in the introduction. Early churches were in Clones, Monaghan, Newbliss, and Rockcurry.

Roman Catholic

Note that all of the Catholic parish registers of this county have been indexed by Monaghan Ancestry (see Research Services at the end of the chapter). A search of the index will be conducted by the center for a fee.

Those indexed are noted as "Indexed by Mon. Anc." Microfilm copies of all registers are also available in the National Library of Ireland (NLI), and through the LDS library system.

Civil Parish: Aghabog
Map Grid: 12
RC Parish: Aghabog, see Killeevan
Diocese: CG

Civil Parish: Aghnamullen (1)
Map Grid: 18
RC Parish: Aghnamullen East; also Aghnamullen West, see below
Diocese: CG
Earliest Record: b. 7.1857; m. 7.1857; d. 7.1857
Missing Dates: b. 10.1876-8.1878; m. 10.1876-8.1878
Status: LC; NLI (mf); Indexed by Mon. Anc.

Civil Parish: Aghnamullen (2)
Map Grid: 18
RC Parish: Aghnamullen West
Diocese: CG
Earliest Record: b. 2.1841; m. 2.1841
Status: LC; NLI (mf); Indexed by Mon. Anc.

Civil Parish: Ballybay
Map Grid: 17
RC Parish: part Tullycorbet; part Aghnamullen (2)
Diocese: CG

Civil Parish: Clones (see also Co. Fermanagh)
Map Grid: 9
RC Parish: Clones
Diocese: CG
Earliest Record: b. 7.1848; m. 5.1821
Missing Dates: b. 4.1854-4.1855; m. 3.1840-10.1840
Status: LC; NLI (mf); Indexed by Mon. Anc.

Civil Parish: Clontibret
Map Grid: 15
RC Parish: Clontibret
Diocese: CG
Earliest Record: b. 2.1861
Status: LC; NLI (mf); Indexed by Mon. Anc.

Civil Parish: Currin
Map Grid: 13
RC Parish: see Killeevan
Diocese: CG

Civil Parish: Donagh
Map Grid: 2
RC Parish: Donagh
Diocese: CG
Earliest Record: b. 5.1836; m. 5.1836
Status: LC; NLI (mf); Indexed by Mon. Anc.

Civil Parish: Donaghmoyne
Map Grid: 20
RC Parish: Donaghmoyne

Diocese: CG
Earliest Record: b. 1.1840; m. 10.1840; LC: 1840-63
Status: LC; NLI (mf); Indexed by Mon. Anc.

Civil Parish: Drummully (see also Co. Fermanagh)
Map Grid: 11
RC Parish: see Galloon, Co. Fermanagh; see also Killeevan
Diocese: CG

Civil Parish: Drumsnat
Map Grid: 5
RC Parish: Drumsnat and Kilmore
Diocese: CG
Earliest Record: b. 2.1836; m. 2.1836; d. 2.1836
Missing Dates: b. 6.1872-3.1875; m. 6.1872-3.1875; d. 6.1872-3.1875
Status: LC; NLI (mf); Indexed by Mon. Anc.

Civil Parish: Ematris
Map Grid: 14
RC Parish: Ematris
Diocese: CG
Earliest Record: b. 5.1848; m. 2.1850
Missing Dates: b. 3.1860-3.1861
Status: LC; NLI (mf); Indexed by Mon. Anc.

Civil Parish: Errigal Trough (see also Co. Tyrone)
Map Grid: 1
RC Parish: Errigal Trough
Diocese: CG
Earliest Record: b. 11.1835; m. 12.1837
Missing Dates: b. 3.1852-3.1861; m. 7.1849-1.1862
Status: LC; NLI (mf); Indexed by Mon. Anc.

Civil Parish: Inishkeen
Map Grid: 21
RC Parish: Inishkeen
Diocese: CG
Earliest Record: b. 7.1837; m. 4.1839
Missing Dates: b. 10.1862-7.1863; m. ends 11.1850
Status: LC; NLI (mf); Indexed by Mon. Anc.

Civil Parish: Killanny
Map Grid: 23
RC Parish: Carrickmacross, see Magheross
Diocese: CG

Civil Parish: Killeevan
Map Grid: 10
RC Parish: Killeevan
Diocese: CG
Earliest Record: b. 1.1871; m. 1.1871
Status: LC; NLI (mf); Indexed by Mon. Anc.

Civil Parish: Kilmore
Map Grid: 6
RC Parish: see Drumsnat
Diocese: CG

Civil Parish: Magheracloone
Map Grid: 22
RC Parish: Magheracloone

Diocese: CG
Earliest Record: b. 5.1836; m. 10.1826
Missing Dates: b. 11.1863-1.1865; m. 3.1959-4.1866
Status: LC; NLI (mf); Indexed by Mon. Anc.

Civil Parish: Magheross
Map Grid: 19
RC Parish: Carrickmacross
Diocese: CG
Earliest Record: b. 1.1858; m. 2.1838
Missing Dates: m. 1.1844-1.1858
Status: LC; NLI (mf); Indexed by Mon. Anc.

Civil Parish: Monaghan
Map Grid: 7
RC Parish: Monaghan
Diocese: CG
Earliest Record: b. 11.1835; m. 2.1827
Missing Dates: b. 12.1847-6.1849, 4.1850-1.1857; m. 6.1850-1.1857
Status: LC; NLI (mf); Indexed by Mon. Anc.

Civil Parish: Muckno
Map Grid: 16
RC Parish: Muckno
Diocese: CG
Earliest Record: b. 11.1835; m. 10.1835
Status: LC; NLI (mf); Indexed by Mon. Anc.

Civil Parish: Tedavnet
Map Grid: 3
RC Parish: Tydavnet
Diocese: CG
Earliest Record: b. 11.1835; m. 4.1825
Missing Dates: m. 10.1865-1.1876
Status: LC; NLI (mf); Indexed by Mon. Anc.

Civil Parish: Tehallan
Map Grid: 4
RC Parish: Tyholland
Diocese: CG
Earliest Record: b. 5.1835; m. 1.1827; d. 1.1851
Missing Dates: b. 12.1863-12.1863; m. 12.1865-2.1866; d. ends 12.1863
Status: LC; NLI (mf); Indexed by Mon. Anc.

Civil Parish: Tullycorbet
Map Grid: 8
RC Parish: Tullycorbet
Diocese: CG
Earliest Record: b. 4.1862; m. 5.1862
Status: LC; NLI (mf); Indexed by Mon. Anc.

Commercial and Social Directories

1824

J. Pigot's *City of Dublin and Hibernian Provincial Directory* includes traders, nobility, gentry, and clergy lists of Ballybay, Carrickmacross, Castleblayney, Clones, and Monaghan.

1846

Slater's *National Commercial Directory of Ireland* lists nobility, clergy, traders, etc., in Ballybay, Carrickmacross, Castleblayney, Clones and Newtown-Butler, and Monaghan.

1852

Henderson's *Belfast and Province of Ulster Directory* has lists of inhabitants, traders, etc., in and around the towns of Ballybay, Clones, and Monaghan.

1854

Further edition of the above extended to cover Carrickmacross and Castleblayney. Further editions were issued in 1856, 1858, 1861, 1863, 1865, 1868, 1870, 1877, 1880, 1884, 1890, 1894, 1900.

1856

Slater's *Royal National Commercial Directory of Ireland* lists nobility, gentry, clergy, traders, etc., in Ballybay, Carrickmacross, Castleblayney, Clones and Newtown-Butler, and Monaghan.

1865

R. Wynne's *Business Directory of Belfast* covers Clones and Monaghan.

1870

Slater's *Directory of Ireland* contains trade, nobility, and clergy lists for Ballybay, Carrickmacross and Shercock, Castleblayney, Clones, and Monaghan.

1881

Slater's *Royal National Commercial Directory of Ireland* contains lists of traders, clergy, nobility, and farmers in adjoining parishes of the towns of Ballybay, Carrickmacross and Shercock, Castleblayney, Clones, and Monaghan.

1894

Slater's *Royal National Directory of Ireland* lists traders, police, teachers, farmers, and private residents in each of the towns, villages, and parishes of the county.

Family History

"Families of Medieval Clones." *Clogher Record* 2 (3) (1959): 385-414.

"Notes on the Families of Blaney, Co. Monaghan, and Denny of Tralee, Co. Kerry." *J. Ass. Pres. Mem. Dead* 7 (1907-09): 373.

"Campbell of Co. Monaghan." Pedigree in *Swanzy Notebooks*. RCB Library, Dublin.

Carson, T.W. *Carson of Shanroe, Co. Monaghan.* Dublin, 1879.

Carson, James. *A Short History of the Carson Family of Monanton, Co. Monaghan.* Belfast, 1879.

"Dawson of Co. Monaghan." Pedigree in *Swanzy Notebooks.* RCB Library, Dublin.

McCluskey, Seamus. *Emyvale–McKenna Country.* N.p., 1996.

"The MacMahons of Monaghan (1500–1603)." *Clogher Record* 1 (1955–62): 22–38, 85–107; 2: 490–503; 4: 190–94.

Belfast, G.S. *A Family History of Montgomery of Ballyleck, Co. Monaghan.* Belfast, 1887.

"Noble of Co. Monaghan." Pedigree in *Swanzy Notebooks.* RCB Library, Dublin.

"Pockrick of Co. Monaghan." Pedigree in *Swanzy Notebooks.* RCB Library, Dublin.

"Rogers of Co. Monaghan." Pedigree in *Swanzy Notebooks.* RCB Library, Dublin.

Williams, J.F. *The Groves and Lappan; Monaghan County, Ireland–An account of . . . the Genealogy of the Williams.* Saint Paul, 1889.

"Wray of Co. Monaghan." Pedigree in *Swanzy Notebooks.* RCB Library, Dublin.

"Wright of Co. Monaghan." Pedigree in *Swanzy Notebooks.* RCB Library, Dublin.

Gravestone Inscriptions

Some of the gravestone inscriptions for the county have been abstracted and indexed by Monaghan Ancestry (see Research Services at the end of the chapter). These are indicated as "Indexed by Mon. Anc."

Aghabog: see Killeevan.

Cahans (Presbyterian): Indexed by Mon. Anc.

Clones Abbey and Round Tower Graveyard: *Clogher Record* 11 (3) (1984): 421–48.

Clones (St. Tigherneach's C of I): *Clogher Record* 13 (1) 1988.

Clontibret: *Clogher Record* 8 (2) 1974.

Cahans (C of I): Indexed by Mon. Anc.

Clontibret (Presbyterian): Indexed by Mon. Anc.

Coolshannagh (Monaghan): Indexed by Mon. Anc.

Donagh: *Clogher Record* 2 (1) (1957): 192–204.

Donaghmayne: GO Ms. 745; SLC film 257809.

Drumsnat: *Clogher Record* 6 (1) (1966): 71–103.

Drumswords: *Clogher Record* 12 (1) (1985): 18–22.

Edergole (Ematris): Indexed by Mon. Anc.

Errigal (Old) Cemetery: *Clogher Record* 12 (3) (1987): 372–387.

Glaslough: *Clogher Record* 9 (3) (1978): 77–85.

Killanny: *Clogher Record* 6 (1) (1966): 191–96.

Killeevan and Aghabog: *Clogher Record* 11 (1) (1982): 119–49.

Kilmore: *Clogher Record* 11 (3) (1983): 184–86; 12 (1) (1985): 127–31.

Macalla: *Clogher Record* 3 (4) 1978.

Magheross: *Clogher Record* 5 (1) (1963): 123–30.

Mullandoy: *Clogher Record* 6 (1) 1966.

Rackwallace: *Clogher Record* 4 (3) (1962): 155–62.

Roslea (St. Tierney's RC): *Clogher Record* 13 (1) (1984): 421–48.

Tehallen: GO Ms. 745; SLC film 257809.

Tighernachs (C of I, Clones): *Clogher Record* 13 (1) (1988): 20–115.

Tydavnet (Old Cemetery): *Clogher Record* 1 (2) (1954): 43–55.

Urbleshanny (Tydavnet): Indexed by Mon. Anc.

Newspapers

There were no newspapers published in this county before 1839. Papers from the surrounding counties should be searched, starting with those in the county adjacent to the area of interest.

Title: *The Argus*
Published in: Monaghan, 1875–81
BL Holdings: odd numbers 1875; 10.1875–11.1877; 2.1878–7.1881

Title: *Northern Standard*
Published in: Monaghan, 1839–current
NLI Holdings: 1.1885–12.1913; 6.1921–in progress
BL Holdings: 1.1839–in progress

Title: *People's Advocate*
Published in: Monaghan, 1876–1906
NLI Holdings: 12.1904–4.1906
BL Holdings: 2.1876–4.1906

Title: *Weekly Chronicle*
Published in: Clones, 1883
BL Holdings: 7–11.1883

Wills and Administrations

A discussion of the types of records, where they are held, and their availability and value is given in the Wills section of the introduction. The availability of prerogative wills, administrations, and marriage license records is also described in the relevant parts of the same section. Where available, published sources of these records are given in the Miscellaneous Sources section.

Pre-1858 Wills and Administrations

Prerogative Wills. See the introduction.

Consistorial Wills. County Monaghan is entirely in the diocese of Clogher. The guide to Catholic parish records in this chapter shows the diocese to which each civil parish belonged. The wills of residents of each diocese were usually proven within that diocese (see the Wills section for exceptions). The following records survive:

Wills

See the introduction.

Abstracts

Swanzy Will Abstracts (mainly from Clogher and Kilmore) are in the RCB Library.

Indexes

Clogher (1661–1858). Published by Phillimore. NAI.

Post-1858 Wills and Administrations

This county was served by the District Registry of Armagh. The surviving records are kept in the NAI. Records include: Armagh District Will Books (1858–1900). NAI; SLC films 917201, 917484–92, 917906–16.

Marriage Licenses

Indexes

Clogher (1709–1866). NAI; SLC film 100862.

Miscellaneous Sources

Old Monaghan 1775–1995. Clogher Historical Soc., Monaghan, 1995.

"Rentals and Reports of the Kane Estate, Errigal Truagh 1764–1821." *Clogher Record* 13 (3) (1990). (Includes alphabetical list of tenants and comments for years 1764, 1801, and 1819–21.)

"Assisted emigration from Shirley Estate—1843–54." *Clogher Record* 14 (2) (1992): 7–62.

"Clogherici—Catholic Clergy of the Diocese of Clogher (1535–1835): The McMahon Clergy." *Clogher Record* 11 (1) (1982): 43–59.

"Farney in 1634: An Examination of John Raven's Survey of the Essex Estate." *Clogher Record* 11 (3) (1983): 245–56 (no residents).

Livingstone, Peadar. *The Monaghan Story. A documented history of the Co. Monaghan from the earliest times to 1976*. Enniskillen: Clogher Historial Society, 1980.

Miscellaneous land and probate records for Monaghan: late nineteenth–early twentieth century—SLC film 1279320; seventeenth–twentieth century—SLC film 1279322; 1871–1900—SLC film 1279320. All the above are at Monaghan Co. Museum.

Moffett, Rev. B. *A List of Pupils of Viscount Weymouth's School, Carrickmacross, Who Entered Trinity College, Dublin, from 1706 to 1909*. Dundalk: Tempest, 1911.

"Summary of Inquests held on Currin, Co. Monaghan victims 1846–1855." *Clogher Record* (1995): 90–100.

Rushe, D. *Monaghan in the Eighteenth Century*. Dundalk: Gill, 1919.

Rushe, D. *History of Monaghan for 200 Years: 1660–1860*. Dundalk: Tempest, 1921. Details the political and social history of the county, mentioning the names of persons on the Grand Juries, tenant farms, surveyors, rioters, persons charged at the Assizes, and many others.

Shirley, E.P. "Some Account of the Territory or Dominion of Farney, in the Province and Earldom of Ulster." London: Wm. Pickering (Whittingham), 1845.

Shirley, E.P. *The History of the County of Monaghan*. London, 1879. Reprinted. Bangor: Fox, 1988.

"The Volunteer Companies of Ulster 1778–1793: 7, Monaghan." *Irish Sword* 8 (31) (1967): 95–97 (some officers' and prisoners' names only).

"The National School System in Co. Monaghan 1831–1850." *Clogher Record* 12 (2) (1986): 209–232.

Workhouse Records: Records of Castleblaney Union Workhouse (1840–1852). Monaghan Co. Museum; SLC film 1279319–20.

Research Sources and Services

Journals

Clogher Record (published by Clogher Historical Society, 1953–)

The Drumlin

Libraries and Information Sources

Monaghan County Library, The Diamond, Clones, Co. Monaghan. Ph: Clones 143

Monaghan County Museum, The Courthouse, Monaghan

Research Services

Monaghan Ancestry, 6 Tully, Monaghan, Co. Monaghan. Ph: (047) 82304; fax: (353) 47 82304. (Abbreviated "Mon. Anc." in this chapter.) This is the official IGP center for Monaghan. They have indexed over half of the Catholic registers of the county, a few of the Church of Ireland registers, and all of the *Griffith's Valuation* and *Tithe Applotment* records. Indexing of all further records is in progress. Researchers are advised to contact the center for an updated list of registers, and other sources, indexed. They also have access to school attendance records, estate records, and to the extensive material collected since 1952 by the Clogher Historical Society (see below). Monaghan Ancestry has also published several books, e.g., *Old Monaghan 1785–1995* (published 1995). Searches for Monaghan families (by post only) will be conducted for a fee.

See also Research Services in Dublin or Belfast in the introduction.

Societies

Clogher Historical Society, Mr. J.I.D. Johnston, Corick, Clogher, Co. Tyrone. This society publishes *Clogher Record*, which deals with the social, church, political, archaeological, and genealogical history of the diocese of Clogher. This covers the counties of Monaghan, Fermanagh, South Tyrone, and a small part of Donegal around Ballyshannon. The journal is a particularly important source of information on these counties, as can be seen from the number of references to its pages in this chapter. The society also published *Old Monaghan 1775–1995* in 1995, and *Clones in McMahon Country* is planned for 1997.

Monaghan Civil Parishes as Numbered on Map

1. Errigal Trough
2. Donagh
3. Tedavnet
4. Tehallen
5. Drumsnat
6. Kilmore (2 pts.)
7. Monaghan
8. Tullycorbet
9. Clones
10. Killeevan (2 pts.)
11. Drummully (2 pts.)
12. Aghabog
13. Currin (2 pts.)
14. Ematris
15. Clontibret
16. Muckno
17. Ballybay
18. Aghnamullen
19. Magheross
20. Donaghmoyne
21. Inishkeen
22. Magheracloone
23. Killanny

Monaghan Civil Parishes in Alphabetical Order

Aghabog: 12
Aghnamullen: 18
Ballybay: 17
Clones: 9
Clontibret: 15
Currin (2 pts.): 13
Donagh: 2
Donaghmoyne: 20
Drummully (2 pts.): 11
Drumsnat: 5
Ematris: 14
Errigal Trough: 1
Inishkeen: 21
Killanny: 23
Killeevan (2 pts.): 10
Kilmore (2 pts.): 6
Magheracloone: 22
Magheross: 19
Monaghan: 7
Muckno: 16
Tedavnet: 3
Tehallen: 4
Tullycorbet: 8

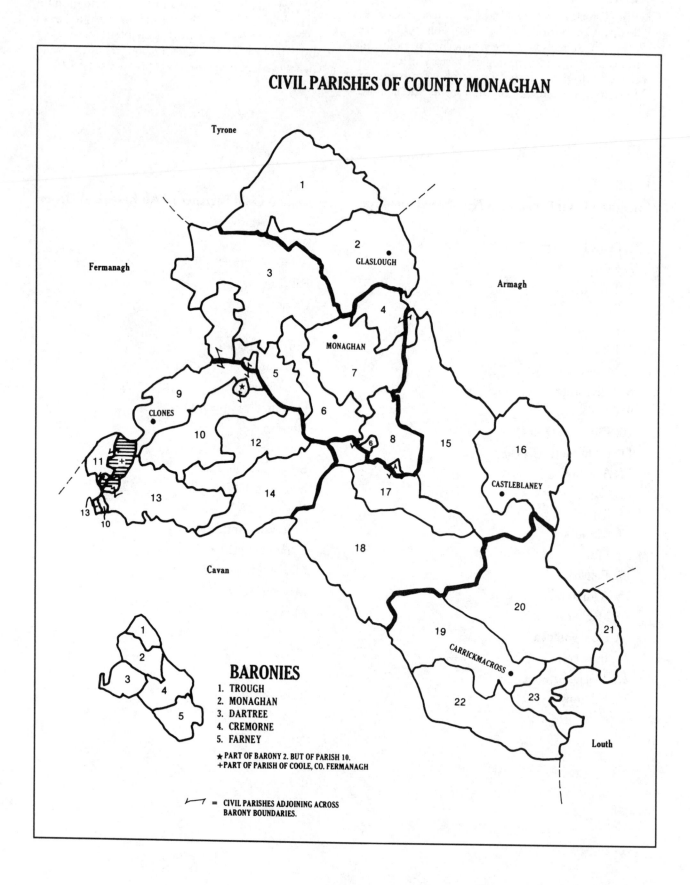

CIVIL PARISHES OF COUNTY MONAGHAN

Tyrone

Fermanagh

Armagh

GLASLOUGH

MONAGHAN

CLONES

CASTLEBLANEY

Cavan

CARRICKMACROSS

Louth

BARONIES

1. TROUGH
2. MONAGHAN
3. DARTREE
4. CREMORNE
5. FARNEY

★ PART OF BARONY 2. BUT OF PARISH 10.
+ PART OF PARISH OF COOLE, CO. FERMANAGH

⊢┐ = CIVIL PARISHES ADJOINING ACROSS
BARONY BOUNDARIES.

County Offaly

A Brief History

Located in the midlands of Ireland, this small county contains the towns of Tullamore, Birr, Portarlington, Ferbane, and Daingean. In the old Gaelic system, the county was part of the Kingdom of Ui Failghe, or Offaly. It was named King's County when the English re-divided the country into counties in 1547. The name was changed back to Offaly on the foundation of the Irish state in 1922.

Within the ancient territory, the major Gaelic families were the O'Carrolls, O'Delaneys, MacCoghlans, O'Molloys, and O'Connors. Although conquered by the Normans in the twelfth century, English rule gradually waned in the county. In the fifteenth and sixteenth centuries, Offaly and neighbouring Laois were among the most rebellious counties in the country. Continued raids by the Irish from these counties on the English-controlled area around Dublin finally caused the English to invade Laois and Offaly in 1547. The native families were driven back, and several garrisons and forts were built. In Offaly, the O'Connor's fort of Daingean was garrisoned by the English and renamed Philipstown (now renamed Daingean). The lands confiscated from the native families were granted to officers and settlers.

However, as resistance to the English garrisons by the native population continued, the English authorities decided to clear the counties of the native people and bring in settlers from England. This was begun in 1556, making it the first plantation of Ireland. Two-thirds of tribal lands were confiscated at this time. The plantation was fiercely resisted and only partially successful. However, it did result in the introduction of a large number of English families to the area.

Since the native population is predominantly Catholic, and English settlers were mainly of the Protestant faith, the proportions of these religions among the population can, in very general terms, be used to estimate the origins of the inhabitants of the county. When religious affiliation was first determined in the census of 1861, the proportions of Catholic and Protestant in County Offaly were eighty-nine and ten percent, respectively.

The county was badly affected by the Great Famine of 1845-47. The population, which was 147,000 in 1841, fell to 112,000 in 1851. Of this, some 22,000 died between 1845 and 1851, and a high proportion emigrated. The population continued to fall for the rest of the century and beyond, and is now approximately 58,000.

Census and Census Substitutes

1659

"Census" of Ireland. Edited by S. Pender. Dublin: Stationery Office, 1939. NLI I6551. SLC film 924648.

1763

Tullamore tenants of the Earl of Charleville. SLC 941.5 A1.

1766

Religious Census (Protestant and Catholic) of the "Parish of Ballycommon." *J. Kildare Arch. Hist. Soc.* 7: 274-76; (1912-14) GO ms. 537; SLC film 100173, 258517, and RCB Ms. 37.

1802

"Protestants in Parishes of Ballyboggan, Ballyboy, Castlejordan and Ballybeg, Clonmacnoise, Drumcullen, Eglish, Gallen, Killoughey, Lynally, Reynagh, Tullamore-Kilbride." *Ir. Anc.* 5 (2) (1973): 113-20.

1821

Government Census of Parishes of Aghancon, Birr, Ettagh, Kilcolman, Kinnitty, Letterluna, Roscomroe, Roscrea, Seirkieran. SLC film 100818. NAI CEN 1821/26-34.

1823-38

Tithe Applotment Survey (see introduction).

1824

List of Catholic Householders in Each Townland of Lusmagh Parish on November 1st. Included in the Catholic registers of Lusmagh (see Roman Catholic records section).

1830

List of Contributors to a New Catholic Church at Wherry (gives only townland and sum subscribed by each person). Included in the Catholic registers of Lusmagh Church.

1835

Census of Tubber Parish (arranged by townland, giving age, occupation, and religion of each person, but no relationships). NLI P 1994.

1840

Census of Parishes of Eglish and Drumcullen. Arranged by townland, gives heads of households, occupations, numbers of males and females in each household, numbers over and under fifteen, numbers of male and female servants. Included in the Catholic parish register of Eglish NLI p. 4175 (see Roman Catholic records section). Another undated census is also included in the register.

1840-50

Rental of Offaly Estate. Parish of Clonsast: Townlands of Brackna, Clonsast, Clonbrock, Ballinoulart, Cappa, Ballyshane, Ballinrahan—154 tenants with rents and some comments. NLI Ms. 4337.

1842

Voters List. NAI 1842/27.

1852

"Emigrants from Kilconcouse (parish of Kinnitty)" (names, ages, and relationships of fifty-six people with dates of departure, arrival, etc.). In E. Ellis, *Migrants from Ireland 1847-52*. Baltimore: Genealogical Publishing Co., 1977, pp. 57-59.

1854

Griffith's Valuation (see introduction).

1855

Rental of Ballyfarrell (fourteen tenants) and Derrymore (twelve tenants) in Parish of Killoughy, Co. Offaly, and maps of their holdings. NAI M 601.

1901

Census. NAI. Indexed by LOFHC. SLC film 843007-20.

1911

Census. NAI.

Church Records

Church of Ireland

See the introduction for a description of Church of Ireland records and their major repositories. Many C of I records were lost in the PRO fire of 1922. These are indicated as "Lost." However, as Church of Ireland records were effectively state records, the records of marriage (from 1845) are also in the General Registrar's Office. Many are still in local custody (LC), while others are in one of a variety of other archives (e.g., RCBL or NAI). Most of the parish registers of this county have been indexed by the Laois/Offaly Family History Research Centre (see Research Services at the end of the chapter). A search of the index will be conducted by the center for a fee.

Aghancon
Status: Lost

Ballyboy (Frankford)
Earliest Records: b. 1709-; m. 1709-; d. 1709-
Status: LC; RCBL (b. 1709-1847; m. 1709-1819; d. 1709-1863) and NAI (b. 1710)

Ballyburley (see Primult)

Ballycommon
Status: Lost

Ballykean
Status: Lost

Ballymacwilliam (see Monasteroris, RC records section)

Birr
Earliest Records: b. 1760-; m. 1760-; d. 1786-
Status: NAI MFCI 2, 3, M5221; LC (b/m/d. 1772) and GO 578 (extracts—b. 1760-1806; m. 1762-1804; d. 1792-1856)

Borrisnafarney
Earliest Records: b. 1827-; m. 1827-; d. 1827-
Status: LC and NAI MFCI 4 (b. 1828-77; m. 1827-51; d. 1827-76)

Castlejordan
Earliest Records: b. 1702–; m. 1707–; d. 1704–
Status: RCBL (b. 1702–1964; m. 1707–1941; d. 1704–1863); NAI MFCI 50 (b. 1702–1877; m. 1707–1845; d. 1704–1877); (also curacy of Ballyboggan: register of b/m/d. for 1702–68 also exists)

Clara and Kilmonaghan
Status: Lost

Cloneyburke
Earliest Records: b. 1824–; d. 1834–
Status: LC; NAI MFCI 72 (b. 1824–1982; d. 1834–1983)

Clonmacnois
Earliest Records: b. 1828–; m. 1830–; d. 1818–
Status: LC; RCBL (m. 1845–1893); NAI MFCI 57 (b. 1828–74; d. 1818–1977)

Drumraney
Earliest Records: m. 1847–
Status: RCBL (m. 1847–1860)

Dunkerrin
Earliest Records: b. 1825; m. 1826; d. 1825
Status: LC; NAI MFCI 4, and M 5222 (b. 1825–73; m. 1826–45; d. 1825–73)

Durrow
Earliest Records: b. 1706; m. 1797; d. 1706
Missing Records: b. 1801–15; m. 1802–15; d. 1801–15
Status: LC; NAI MFCI 55 (b. 1816–83; m. 1818–75; d. 1817–83); SLC film 990092 (b. 1731–1841; m/d. 1731–1836)

Eglish
Status: Lost

Ettagh
Earliest Records: b. 1825; m. 1820; d. 1826
Status: LC and NAI MFCI 4, M5222 (b. 1825–67; m. 1826–68; d. 1826–73)

Ferbane (Whirry)—see also Gallen
Earliest Records: b. 1797–; m. 1797–; d. 1797–
Status: LC; NLI Ms. 4122 (b. 1797–1822; m. 1797–1822; d. 1797–1822); NAI MFCI 57 (b. 1819–75; d. 1821–57)

Gallen (see also Reynagh)
Earliest Records: b. 1842; m. 1842; d. 1844
Status: LC

Geashill
Earliest Records: b. 1713; m. 1713; d. 1713
Status: LC and NAI MFCI 65 (b. 1713–1905; m. 1713–1846; d. 1713–1907)

Kilbride (see Clara)

Kilbride, Tullamore
Earliest Records: b. 1805; m. 1805; d. 1805
Status: LC

Kilcoleman
Earliest Records: b. 1829–; d. 1839–
Status: LC; NAI MFCI 4, M5235 (b. 1829–75; d. 1839–72)

Killaderry or Philipstown
Status: Lost

Killeigh (see also Geashill)
Earliest Records: b. 1808–; m. 1809–; d. 1808–
Status: LC; NAI M5115/6 (b. 1808–23; m. 1809–32; d. 1808–35); NLI Ms. 7974 (b/m/d. 1808–35) (transcript) and NAI MFCI 65 (b. 1808–71; m. 1808–82; d. 1808–71); SLC film 990092 (b/m. 1808–1813; d. 1808–1835)

Killoughy
Earliest Records: b. 1818; m. 1816; d. 1877
Status: LC

Kilmurryely (see Shinrone)

Kilnegarenagh or Lemanaghan
Status: Lost

Kinnitty
Earliest Records: b. 1800; m. 1801; d. 1802
Status: LC and NAI MFCI 57 (b. 1850–78; d. 1850–83)

Lemanaghan
Earliest Records: b. 1885–; m. 1845–; d. 1884–
Status: RCBL (b. 1885–1975; m. 1845–1951; d. 1884–1988)

Lynally
Status: Lost

Primult or Ballyburley
Status: Lost

Rahan
Status: Lost

Reynagh
Status: Lost

Roscrea
Earliest Records: b. 1784; m. 1784; d. 1784
Status: LC and NAI MFCI 3, M5222 (b. 1784–1878; m. 1791–1845; d. 1792–1872)

Seirkieran
Status: Lost

Shinrone
Earliest Records: b. 1741–; m. 1741–; d. 1741–
Status: LC and NAI MFCI 4, M5222 (b. 1741–1877; m. 1741–1844; d. 1741–1876)

Templeharry
Earliest Records: b. 1800; m. 1800; d. 1800
Status: LC and NAI MFCI 24, M6048 (b/d. 1845–79)

Tessauran
Earliest Records: b. 1819–; d. 1819–
Status: LC; NAI MFCI 57 (b. 1819–77; d. 1819–77)

Tullamore

Earliest Records: b. 1805–; m. 1805–; d. 1805–
Status: LC; NAI MFCI 55 (b. 1805-1902; m. 1805-50; d. 1805-70)

Methodist

Methodist churches were located in several parts of the county (see the introduction). No death records were maintained. Some of the Methodist registers have been indexed by Laois/Offaly Heritage Centre (see Research Services at the end of the chapter). A search of the index will be conducted by the center for a fee. Those indexed are noted as "Indexed by LOFHS."

Birr

Earliest Records: b. 1877
Status: LC; Indexed by LOFHS (to 1900)

Tullamore

Earliest Records: b. 1830
Status: LC; Indexed by LOFHS (to 1900)

Athlone

Earliest Records: b. 1842
Status: LC; Indexed by LOFHS (to 1900)

Society of Friends (Quaker)

See the introduction for an account of Quaker records. The records for Offaly include: Edenderry Monthly Meeting Register (1612-1910). FHL, Dublin (b. 1612-1846; m. 1652-1910; d. 1680-1860).

Roman Catholic

Note that most of the Catholic parish registers of this county have been indexed by the Laois/Offaly Heritage Centre (see Research Services at the end of the chapter), and a few by the Dun na Si Heritage Centre (see Research Services at the end of the Co. Westmeath chapter). Searches of the indexes will be conducted by the centers for a fee. Those indexed are noted as "Indexed by LOFHS" or "by Dun na Si HC" as appropriate. Microfilm copies of all registers are also available in the National Library of Ireland (NLI), and through the LDS library system.

Civil Parish: Aghancon

Map Grid: 38
RC Parish: see Seirkieran, also Roscrea
Diocese: K and K

Civil Parish: Ardnurcher (or Horseleap, see also Co. Westmeath)

Map Grid: 3
RC Parish: Clara, see Kilbride (1)
Diocese: ME

Civil Parish: Ballyboy

Map Grid: 27

RC Parish: Ballyboy and Killoughy (Kilcormac)
Diocese: ME
Earliest Record: b. 1.1821; m. 6.1821; d. 2.1826
Status: LC; NLI (mf); Indexed by LOFHS (to 1900)

Civil Parish: Ballyburly

Map Grid: 6
RC Parish: Rhode
Diocese: KD
Earliest Record: b. 1.1829; m. 8.1829
Missing Dates: m. gaps 2.1878-12.1880
Status: LC; NLI (mf); Indexed by LOFHS (to 1900)

Civil Parish: Ballycommon

Map Grid: 21
RC Parish: part Daingean, see Killaderry; also part Tullamore, see Kilbride (2)
Diocese: KD

Civil Parish: Ballykean

Map Grid: 29
RC Parish: Killeigh
Diocese: KD
Earliest Record: b. 1844; m. 1844
Status: LC; NLI (mf); Indexed by LOFHS (to 1899)

Civil Parish: Ballymacwilliam

Map Grid: 7
RC Parish: Edenderry, see Monasteroris; also part Rhode, see Ballyburly
Diocese: KD

Civil Parish: Ballynakill

Map Grid: 24
RC Parish: Edenderry, see Monasteroris; also Daingean, see Killaderry
Diocese: KD

Civil Parish: Birr

Map Grid: 34
RC Parish: Birr and Loughkeen
Diocese: K and K
Earliest Record: b. 5.1838 (two record books in some periods); m. 5.1838
Missing Dates: 12.1846
Status: LC; NLI (mf); Indexed by LOFHS (to 1899)

Civil Parish: Borrisnafarney (see also Co. Tipperary)

Map Grid: 51
RC Parish: Couraganeen (Bourney and Corbally)
Diocese: K and K
Earliest Record: b. 7.1836; m. 6.1836
Missing Dates: b. 8.1866-1.1867, 1873; m. 12.1866-1.1867, 1873
Status: LC; NLI (mf); Indexed by TNFHF (to 1866)
(see Co. Tipperary—Research Services)

Civil Parish: Castlejordan (in two parts—see also Co. Meath)

Map Grid: 5
RC Parish: Ballinabrackey; also Rhode, see Ballyburly

Diocese: ME
Earliest Record: b. 11.1826; m. 11.1826; d. 11.1848
Missing Dates: d. 7.1849–1880
Status: LC; NLI (mf); Indexed by Dun na Si HC (b/m. to 1900; d. 1900–1993); see Co. Westmeath

Civil Parish: Castletownely
Map Grid: 48
RC Parish: see Dunkerrin
Diocese: K and K

Civil Parish: Clonmacnoise
Map Grid: 8
RC Parish: Clonmacnoise (also part Lemanaghan)
Diocese: ME
Earliest Record: b. 4.1826 (two separate record books for some periods); m. 4.1826; d. 2.1841
Missing Dates: b. 7.1842–2.1848; m. 2.1842–2.1848; d. 2.1842–2.1848
Status: LC; NLI (mf); Indexed by LOFHS (b. to 1908; m. to 1899 only)

Civil Parish: Clonsast
Map Grid: 25
RC Parish: Clonbulloge
Diocese: KD
Earliest Record: b. 11.1819; m. 1.1808
Status: LC; NLI (mf); Indexed by LOFHS (to 1899)

Civil Parish: Clonyhurk
Map Grid: 30
RC Parish: Portarlington
Diocese: KD
Earliest Record: b. 1.1820; m. 11.1822
Status: LC; NLI (mf); Indexed by LOFHS (to 1899)

Civil Parish: Corbally (see also Co. Tipperary)
Map Grid: 40
RC Parish: Roscrea, see Co. Tipperary
Diocese: K and K

Civil Parish: Croghan
Map Grid: 19
RC Parish: Rhode—see Ballyburly
Diocese: K and K

Civil Parish: Cullenwaine
Map Grid: 50
RC Parish: see Dunkerrin
Diocese: K and K

Civil Parish: Drumcullen
Map Grid: 32
RC Parish: see Eglish
Diocese: ME

Civil Parish: Dunkerrin
Map Grid: 46
RC Parish: Dunkerrin (Moneygall and Barna)
Diocese: K and K
Earliest Record: b. 1.1820; m. 1.1820
Status: LC; NLI (mf); Indexed by LOFHS (b. to 1911; m. to 1899)

Civil Parish: Durrow (see also Co. Westmeath)
Map Grid: 15
RC Parish: Tullamore, see Kilbride (2)
Diocese: ME

Civil Parish: Eglish
Map Grid: 31
RC Parish: Eglish and Drumcullen
Diocese: ME
Earliest Record: b. 1.1809; m. 2.1819; d. 1807
Missing Dates: b. 12.1810–2.1819; m. 3.1829–6.1829; d. 4.1829–6.1837, 5.1846–1.1848
Status: LC; NLI (mf); Indexed by LOFHS (to 1899)

Civil Parish: Ettagh
Map Grid: 43
RC Parish: see Kilcolman
Diocese: K and K

Civil Parish: Finglass
Map Grid: 49
RC Parish: see Dunkerrin
Diocese: K and K

Civil Parish: Gallen
Map Grid: 12
RC Parish: Cloghan and Banagher (or Gallen and Reynagh)
Diocese: ME
Earliest Record: b. 11.1811; m. 10.1797; d. 11.1803
Missing Dates: b. several gaps 1812–1829 (two record books for some periods); m. 7.1837–2.1838; d. few records to 1820
Status: LC; NLI (mf); Indexed by LOFHS (b/m. to 1899)

Civil Parish: Geashill
Map Grid: 28
RC Parish: Killeigh, see Ballykeane

Civil Parish: Horseleap (see Ardnurcher)
Map Grid: 3
RC Parish: Clara, see Kilbride (1)

Civil Parish: Kilbride (1) (near Kilmanaghan)
Map Grid: 4
RC Parish: Clara
Diocese: ME
Earliest Record: b. 2.1845; m. 11.1821; d. 1.1825
Missing Dates: d. 2.1854–10.1864, ends 10.1868
Status: LC; NLI (mf); Indexed by LOFHS (b. to 1910; m. to 1899; d. to 1865)

Civil Parish: Kilbride (2) (near Lynally)
Map Grid: 17
RC Parish: Tullamore
Diocese: ME
Earliest Record: b. 6.1809; m. 4.1801
Missing Dates: b. 2.1810–11.1820, 2.1822–2.1827, 2.1836; m. 10.1807–11.1820, 2.1822–2.1827
Status: LC; NLI (mf); Indexed by LOFHS (to 1899)

Civil Parish: Kilclonfert
Map Grid: 20
RC Parish: Daingean, see Killaderry
Diocese: KD

Civil Parish: Kilcolman
Map Grid: 41
RC Parish: Kilcolman
Diocese: K and K
Earliest Record: b. 3.1830; m. 4.1830
Missing Dates: b. 11.1869–1880; m. 2.1868–1880
Status: LC; NLI (mf); Indexed by LOFHS (to 1899)

Civil Parish: Kilcomin
Map Grid: 45
RC Parish: see Shinrone
Diocese: K and K

Civil Parish: Kilcumreragh
Map Grid: 1
RC Parish: Tobber, see Kilmanaghan
Diocese: ME

Civil Parish: Killaderry
Map Grid: 22
RC Parish: Daingean
Diocese: KD
Earliest Record: b. 8.1795; m. 1.1820; d. 1880 (there are two separate books for Daingean in the period 1850–55)
Missing Dates: b. 9.1798–1.1820; m. 12.1866–2.1867
Status: LC; NLI (mf); Indexed by LOFHS (1820 to 1899)

Civil Parish: Killagally (see Wherry)

Civil Parish: Killoughy
Map Grid: 26
RC Parish: Kilcormac, see Ballyboy
Diocese: ME

Civil Parish: Kilmanaghan (see also Co. Westmeath)
Map Grid: 2
RC Parish: Tobber (or Tubber) and Rosemount
Diocese: ME
Earliest Record: b. 11.1821; m. 11.1824; d. 1824
Status: LC; NLI (mf); Indexed by Dun na Si HC (b/m. to 1900; d. 1824–1873) and by LOFHS (b/m. to 1899; d. to 1845)

Civil Parish: Kilmurryely
Map Grid: 42
RC Parish: see Shinrone
Diocese: K and K

Civil Parish: Kinnitty
Map Grid: 36
RC Parish: Kinnitty (Kinnety)
Diocese: K and K
Earliest Record: b. 2.1833; m. 1.1833
Missing Dates: m. 12.1871–1.1872
Status: LC; NLI (mf); Indexed by LOFHS (to 1899)

Civil Parish: Lemanaghan
Map Grid: 9
RC Parish: Balnahowen and Lemanaghan
Diocese: ME
Earliest Record: b. 8.1821; m. 1.1822; d. 11.1821
Missing Dates: b. 12.1824–2.1826, 2.1839–2.1841, 9.1845–7.1854; m. 8.1845–10.1854; d. 9.1845–9.1854
Status: LC; NLI (mf); Indexed by Dun na Si HC (to 1900, 1899, and 1846, respectively—see Co. Westmeath); and by LOFHS (b/m. to 1899; d. to 1846)

Civil Parish: Letterluna
Map Grid: 33
RC Parish: see Kinnitty
Diocese: K and K

Civil Parish: Lusmagh
Map Grid: 14
RC Parish: Lusmagh
Diocese: ME
Earliest Record: b. 12.1827; m. 1824; d. 1.1837
Missing Dates: b. 5.1829–4.1833; m. 3.1829–7.1832
Status: LC; NLI (mf); Indexed by LOFHS (b/m. to 1899; d. to 1882)

Civil Parish: Lynally
Map Grid: 18
RC Parish: Killina, see Rahan
Diocese: ME

Civil Parish: Monasteroris or Castropetre
Map Grid: 23
RC Parish: Edenderry
Diocese: KD
Earliest Record: b. 1.1820; m. 1.1820
Missing Dates: m. 11.1837–9.1838
Status: LC; NLI (mf); Indexed by LOFHS (to 1899)

Civil Parish: Rahan
Map Grid: 16
RC Parish: Rahan or Killina
Diocese: ME
Earliest Record: b. 7.1810; m. 7.1810
Missing Dates: b. 5.1816–1.1822; m. 3.1816–1.1822
Status: LC; NLI (mf); Indexed by LOFHS (to 1899)

Civil Parish: Reynagh
Map Grid: 13
RC Parish: see Gallen
Diocese: ME

Civil Parish: Roscomroe
Map Grid: 37
RC Parish: see Kinnitty
Diocese: K and K

Civil Parish: Roscrea
Map Grid: 39
RC Parish: see Roscrea, Co. Tipperary
Diocese: KL

Civil Parish: Seirkieran
Map Grid: 35
RC Parish: Seirkieran
Diocese: OS
Earliest Record: b. 4.1830; m. 7.1830; d. 1877
Status: LC; NLI (mf); Indexed by LOFHS (to 1899)
(b. to 1901; m. to 1899; d. to 1902)

Civil Parish: Shinrone
Map Grid: 44
RC Parish: Shinrone and Ballinagarry
Diocese: K and K
Earliest Record: b. 2.1842; m. 4.1842
Status: LC; NLI (mf); Indexed by LOFHS (to 1899)

Civil Parish: Templeharry
Map Grid: 47
RC Parish: see Dunkerrin
Diocese: K and K

Civil Parish: Tisaran
Map Grid: 10
RC Parish: see Wherry
Diocese: ME

Civil Parish: Wherry or Killagally
Map Grid: 11
RC Parish: Ferbane or Wherry (Tisaran and Fuithre)
Diocese: ME
Earliest Record: b. 10.1819; m. 11.1819; d. 12.1821
Missing Dates: b. 7.1865-6.1876; m. ends 11.1833;
d. 8.1835-3.1855
Status: LC; NLI (mf); Indexed by LOFHS (b/m. to 1899)

Commercial and Social Directories

1824

J. Pigot's *City of Dublin and Hibernian Provincial Directory* includes traders, nobility, gentry, and clergy lists of Banagher, Birr, Cloghan, Edenderry, Frankford, Philipstown, and Tullamore.

1846

Slater's *National Commercial Directory of Ireland* lists nobility, clergy, traders, etc., in Banagher, Birr, Clara, Cloghan, Edenderry, Frankford and Ballyboy, Philipstown, and Tullamore.

1856

Slater's *Royal National Commercial Directory of Ireland* lists nobility, gentry, clergy, traders, etc., in Banagher, Birr, Clara, Cloghan and Ferbane, Edenderry, Frankford and Ballyboy, Philipstown, and Tullamore.

1870

Slater's *Directory of Ireland* contains trade, nobility, and clergy lists for Banagher, Birr, Cloghan and Ferbane, Clara, Edenderry, Frankford, Philipstown, and Tullamore.

1881

Slater's *Royal National Commercial Directory of Ireland* contains lists of traders, clergy, nobility, and farmers in adjoining parishes of the towns of Banagher, Cloghan and Ferbane, Birr, Edenderry, Frankford, and Tullamore.

1890

King's County Directory contains lists of electors for each polling district; residents (by street) of Parsonstown (Birr) with occupations, and Tullamore; also tradesmen for other towns. Also lists of jurymen, etc., and notes on the principal families and parishes, published in Parsonstown, 1890. NLI I655l.

1894

Slater's *Royal National Directory of Ireland* lists traders, police, teachers, farmers, and private residents in each of the towns, villages, and parishes of the county.

Family History

"The Fitzgeralds, Barons of Offaly." *R.S.A.I.* 44 (1914): 99-113.

Stone, M.E. *Some Notes on the Fox Family of Kilcoursey in King's Co.* Chicago, 1890.

"The Hopper Family." *Ir. Anc.* 149 (2) (1982): 13-19, 59-73.

"The Moone Family of Doon." *Irish Family Hist. Soc. J.* 2 (1986): 71-81.

"Odlums of Offaly." *Irish Family History* 5 (1989): 71-79.

"Pierce Family of Offaly." *Irish Family History* 8 (1992): 78-83.

Smith—see also Co. Tipperary.

Nuttall-Smith, G.N. "Narrative Pedigree of the Family of Smith of Co. Offaly." 1921. GO Ms. 556.

"The Turpin Family of Tullamore, Co. Offaly." *Ir. Anc.* 16 (1) (1984): 1-5.

"The Ushers of Birr." *Ir. Gen.* 5 (5) (1978): 606-24.

Memoir of the Warburton Family of Garryhinch, King's Co. Dublin, 1848. 2nd ed. 1881.

Gravestone Inscriptions

The major printed source is the series on Offaly Tombstone Inscriptions (numbers 1-4) published by Offaly Historical Society (see Research Sources and Services). This society has indexed most of the gravestones in the county and will conduct a search for a fee. The published sources are:

Daingean: No. 4.
Kilclonfert: In *Towards a History of Kilclonfert*. Offaly Historical Society, 1984.
Lusmagh: No. 3.
Monasteroris: No. 2.
Rahan: No. 1.

Newspapers

There were no newspapers published in this county before 1839. Papers from the surrounding counties should be searched, starting with those in the county adjacent to the area of interest. The *Kings County Chronicle* (from 1845 to 1865) has been indexed by the Offaly Historical Society (see Research Sources and Services).

Title: *Kings County Chronicle* (continued as *Offaly Chronicle*, then *Midland Chronicle*)
Published in: Birr, 1845–1922
NLI Holdings: 9.1845–2.1920; 10.1921–6.1963
BL Holdings: 9.1845–6.1963 (except 1–3.1926; 1930)

Title: *Leinster Reporter and Midland Counties Advertiser*
Published in: Tullamore, 1859–1929
BL Holdings: 1.1859–11.1881; 6.1889–11.1892; 1.1893–12.1914; 1.1916–1.1920; 3.1920–12.1925; 1.1927–12.1929

Title: *Midland Tribune*
Published in: Birr, 1881–current
NLI Holdings: 8.1882–in progress
BL Holdings: odd numbers 9.1881; 8.1882–in progress (except 1926)

Wills and Administrations

A discussion of the types of records, where they are held, and their availability and value is given in the Wills section of the introduction. The availability of prerogative wills, administrations, and marriage license records is also described in the relevant parts of the same section. Where available, published sources of these records are given in the Miscellaneous Sources section.

Pre-1858 Wills and Administrations

Prerogative Wills. See the introduction.
Consistorial Wills. County Offaly is in the dioceses of Meath, Kildare, and Killaloe, with one parish in Clonfert and one in Ossory. The guide to Catholic parish records in this chapter shows the diocese to which each civil parish belonged. The wills of residents of each diocese were usually proven within that diocese (see the Wills section for exceptions). The following records survive:

Wills

See the introduction.

Abstracts

See the introduction.

Indexes

Meath: fragments from 1572 to 1858. Killaloe—see Co. Clare. Clonfert—see Co. Galway. Ossory—see Co. Kilkenny.

Post-1858 Wills and Administrations

This county was served by the District Registry of Kilkenny. The surviving records are kept in the NAI.

Marriage Licenses

Original Records

Kildare—see Co. Kildare.

Indexes

Kildare (1740–1850). NAI; SLC film 100868. Meath, Killaloe, and Clonfert (1691–1845). NAI; SLC film 100869. Ossory—see Co. Kilkenny.

Miscellaneous Sources

Byrne, Michael. *Sources for Offaly History*. Tullamore: Offaly Research Library, 1978.

Byrne, Michael. *Tullamore Catholic Parish: A Historical Survey*. Tullamore: Tullamore Parish Committee, 1987.

Feehan, J. *The Landscape of Slieve Bloom—A Study of its Natural and Human Heritage*. Dublin, 1979.

Hitchcock, F.R.M. *The Midland Sept and The Pale. An account of the early septs and later settlers of the King's County and of life in the English Pale*. Dublin: Sealy, 1908.

"High Sheriffs of King's Co. 1655–1915" (with biographical notes to 1860). *J. Kildare Arch. Hist. Soc.* 8 (1) (1915): 30–50.

"Register of Tenants who Planted Trees: Geashill Parish 1793–1907; Eglish Parish 1809–1837." *J. Kildare Arch. Hist. Soc.* 15 (3) (1973/74): 310–18.

Research Sources and Services

Libraries and Information Sources

Offaly County Library, O'Connor Square, Tullamore, Co Offaly. Ph: (0506) 21419/21113. This library has a sizable collection of local history materials, including books, directories, newspapers, periodicals, photographs, estate papers, etc.

Research Services

Laois/Offaly Family History Research Centre, Bury Quay, Tullamore, Co. Offaly. Ph./fax: (0506) 21421; e-mail: ohas@iol.ie; Internet site: http://ireland.iol.ie/~ohas/. This is the official IGP center for Laois and Offaly. It has indexed most of the church registers of both counties, but particularly Offaly. In addition, it has indexed the 1901 census for Offaly and is working on Laois. It also has an extensive list of gravestone inscriptions. Researchers are advised to contact the center for an updated list of registers, and other sources, indexed. A research service is provided for a fee.

See also Research Services in Dublin in the introduction.

Societies

Birr Historical Society, Ms. P. Kavanagh-Neavyn, Casa Jesu, Lisheen, Birr, Co. Offaly

Edenderry Historical Society, Patience Pollard, Ballygibbon, Edenderry, Co. Offaly

Offaly Historical Society, Mr. John Kearney, Bury Quay, Tullamore, Co. Offaly

Offaly Civil Parishes as Listed on Map

1. Kilcumreragh
2. Kilmanaghan
3. Ardnurcher (Horseleap)
4. Kilbride
5. Castlejordan
6. Ballyburly
7. Ballymacwilliam
8. Clonmacnoise
9. Lemanaghan
10. Tisaran
11. Killagally (Wherry)
12. Gallen
13. Reynagh
14. Lusmagh
15. Durrow
16. Rahan
17. Kilbride
18. Lynally
19. Croghan
20. Kilclonfert
21. Ballycommon
22. Killaderry
23. Monasteroris
24. Ballynakill
25. Clonsast
26. Killoughy
27. Ballyboy
28. Geashill
29. Ballykean
30. Clonyhurk
31. Eglish
32. Drumcullen
33. Letterluna
34. Birr
35. Seirkieran
36. Kinnitty
37. Roscomroe
38. Aghancon
39. Roscrea
40. Corbally
41. Kilcolman
42. Kilmurryely
43. Ettagh
44. Shinrone
45. Kilcomin
46. Dunkerrin
47. Templeharry
48. Castletownely
49. Finglas
50. Cullenwaine
51. Borrisnafarney

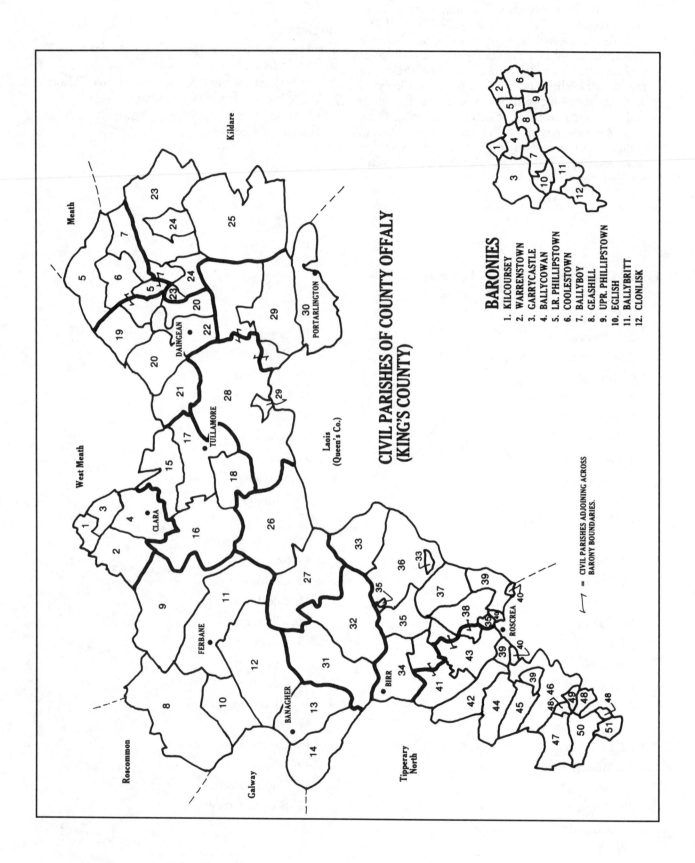

CIVIL PARISHES OF COUNTY OFFALY (KING'S COUNTY)

BARONIES

1. KILCOURSEY
2. WARRENSTOWN
3. GARRYCASTLE
4. BALLYCOWAN
5. LR. PHILLIPSTOWN
6. COOLESTOWN
7. BALLYBOY
8. GEASHILL
9. UPR. PHILLIPSTOWN
10. EGLISH
11. BALLYBRITT
12. CLONLISK

⌐ = CIVIL PARISHES ADJOINING ACROSS BARONY BOUNDARIES.

Kildare

Meath

West Meath

Roscommon

Galway

Tipperary North

Laois (Queen's Co.)

DAINGEAN

CLARA

TULLAMORE

FERBANE

BANAGHER

BIRR

ROSCREA

PORTARLINGTON

Offaly Civil Parishes in Alphabetical Order

Aghancon: 38

Ardnurcher (Horseleap): 3

Ballyboy: 27

Ballyburly: 6

Ballycommon: 21

Ballykean: 29

Ballymacwilliam: 7

Ballynakill: 24

Birr: 34

Borrisnafarney: 51

Castlejordan: 5

Castletownely: 48

Clonmacnoise: 8

Clonsast: 25

Clonyhurk: 30

Corbally: 40

Croghan: 19

Cullenwaine: 50

Drumcullen: 32

Dunkerrin: 46

Durrow: 15

Eglish: 31

Ettagh: 43

Finglas: 49

Gallen: 12

Geashill: 28

Horseleap (Ardnurcher): 3

Kilbride: 4

Kilbride: 17

Kilclonfert: 20

Kilcolman: 41

Kilcomin: 45

Kilcumreragh: 1

Killaderry: 22

Killagally (Wherry): 11

Killoughy: 26

Kilmanaghan: 2

Kilmurryely: 42

Kinnitty: 36

Lemanaghan: 9

Letterluna: 33

Lusmagh: 14

Lynally: 18

Monasteroris: 23

Rahan: 16

Reynagh: 13

Roscomroe: 37

Roscrea: 39

Seirkieran: 35

Shinrone: 44

Templeharry: 47

Tisaran: 10

Wherry (Killagally): 11

County Roscommon

A Brief History

This Connaught county contains the towns of Boyle, Roscommon, Strokestown, and Castlerea.

Under the old Gaelic system, the ruling families in this area were the O'Conors and McDermotts in the north, and O'Kellys in the south. Other names associated with the county include McGreevy, O'Beirne, Duignan, O'Gormley, O'Cooney, McAneeny, Hayes, O'Clabby, and McDockery.

The Norman invasion had little effect on this county due to the power of the native inhabitants.

The boundaries of the county were established in 1565 by Sir Henry Sidney. In 1641, the Gaelic families joined the Rebellion of the Catholic Confederacy, but were defeated; their lands were confiscated and granted to English and Scottish settlers. In the Cromwellian resettlement of Ireland, the county was one of those set aside for occupation by the "delinquent proprietors," i.e., those landowners who had been dispossessed of their lands in other parts of the country. The number of non-native settlers in the county has therefore been very low. As a rough indication of this, the Roman Catholic proportion of the population has been over ninety-six percent since census records began.

The county was densely wooded in the Middle Ages. Most of these woods were gradually cut down and used for charcoal in local iron-mining operations during this time, and also in an iron works established in the county in 1788. The county has generally wet and marshy land which is not ideally suited to agriculture. The major agricultural produce of the county were cattle and sheep, and it was famed for the quality of its cattle in the eighteenth century.

The county suffered relatively badly during the Great Famine of 1845–47. There were 13,000 deaths in the county in these three years, and further thousands emigrated. From a peak of 253,000 in 1841, the population in 1851 had dropped by 80,000. Because of the poor agricultural nature of the area and the tradition of emigration which remained in the county, the population continued to decrease for the remainder of the century. In 1891, the population had fallen to only 114,000, and is currently approximately 54,000.

Census and Census Substitutes

1654–56

Books of Survey and Distribution, Co. Roscommon. Vol 1. R.C. Simington. Dublin: Stationery Office, 1949. SLC film 96524.

1659

"Census" of Ireland. Edited by S. Pender. Dublin: Stationery Office, 1939. NLI I6551. SLC film 924648.

1749

Religious Census of Elphin Diocese—householders, occupations, religion, number of children, and number of servants: Parishes of Aughrim, Ardcarne, Athleague, Ballintober, Ballynakill, Baslick, Boyle, Bumlin, Cam, Clontuskert, Clooncraff, Cloonfinlough, Cloonygormican, Creive, Drimatemple, Dunamon, Dysart, Estersnow, Elphin, Fuerty, Kilbride, Kilbryan, Kilcolagh, Kilcooley, Kilcorkey, Kilgefin, Kilglass, Kilkeevin, Killinvoy, Killuken, Killumnod, Kilmacallan, Kilmacumsy, Kilmore, Kilnamanagh, Kilronan, Kiltoom, Kiltrustan, Lissonuffy, Ogulla, Oran, Rahara, Roscommon, St. John's Athlone, St. Peter's Athlone, Shankill, Taghboy, Termonbarry, Tibohine, Tisrara, and Tumna. NAI M 2466; SLC film 101781.

1760–86

Rental of the Boswell Estate—Kilronan Parish. NLI P4937 (major tenants only).

1761

Militia List for Co. Roscommon, etc. GO Ms. 680.

1778

Rental of the Crofton Estate—in nine different parishes. NLI Ms. 19672.

1780

List of Freeholders. SLC film 100181; GO Ms. 442.

1790–99

Several lists of Freeholders. NLI Ms. 10130.

ca. 1790

Rentals and Leases of Walker Evans Estate. NLI Ms. 10152 (tenants in civil parish of Creeve).

1792

Rentals of the Gunning Estate. NLI Ms. 10152 (major tenants only, in townlands in the civil parishes of Athleague, Fuerty, and Kilcooley).

1792 and 1804

Rentals of Sir Thomas Dundas' Estate: NLI Ms. 2787 (major tenants in townlands in civil parishes of Boyle, Estersnow, Kilnamanagh, and Tumna).

1796

Spinning Wheel Premium List (see introduction; approximately three thousand names).

1801–06

Tenant list of the Clonbrock Estate—Taughmaconnell Parish. NLI Ms. 19501.

1813–21

Registers of Freeholders (alphabetically arranged within each barony; gives names, addresses, location of freehold, etc.). NLI ILB 324.

1823–38

Tithe Applotment Survey (see introduction).

1833

Rental of the Crofton Estate—Tumna Parish. NLI Ms. 4531.

1834

List of tenants in Moore Parish. NLI Ms. 24880.

1836–40

Rental of the Tenison Estate—Parishes of Ardcarn and Kilronan. NLI Ms. 5101.

1836–44

List of Qualified Voters (arranged alphabetically within each barony; gives address). NLI IR 32341 R 20.

1839

Persons who obtained Game Certificates in Roscommon, etc. PRONI T 688.

1843

Voters List for Roscommon. NAI 1843/59.

1847–48

"Tenants From Ballykilcline (Kilglass parish) Who Emigrated Under State-aided Scheme" (names, ages, and relationships of 336 people, and dates of departure, arrival, and name of ship). In E. Ellis, *Emigrants from Ireland 1847–52*. Baltimore: Genealogical Publishing Co., 1977, pp. 10–21.

1848

Male Catholics resident in the Parish of Boyle. NLI P 4692.

1857–58

Griffith's Valuation (see introduction).

1865–98

Athlone Loan Society—Loans and Repayments Accounts. Longford/Westmeath Library and SLC films 1279277–81.

1901

Census. NAI. SLC films 850470–85, 851571–81.

1911

Census. NAI.

Church Records

Church of Ireland

See the introduction for a description of Church of Ireland records and their major repositories. Many C of I records were lost in the PRO fire of 1922. These are indicated as "Lost." However, as Church of Ireland records were effectively state records, the records of marriage (from 1845) are also in the General Registrar's Office. Many are still in local custody (LC), while others are in one of a variety of other archives (e.g., RCBL or NAI). Most of the Church of Ireland registers of this county have been indexed by the Roscommon Heritage and Genealogical Society (see Research Services at the end of the chapter). A search of the index will be conducted by the center for a fee. Those indexed are noted as "Indexed by RHGS."

Ahanagh
Earliest Records: b. 1856
Status: LC

Ardcarne
Earliest Records: b. 1825–; m. 1814–; d. 1825–
Status: LC; Indexed by RHGS (to 1939+)

Ardclare
Earliest Records: b. 1880–; m. 1860–
Status: LC; Indexed by RHGS (to 1900, 1919 respectively)

Athleague
Earliest Records: b. 1876–; m. 1846–
Status: LC; Indexed by RHGS (to 1900, 1888 respectively)

Athlone
Earliest Records: b. 1845; m. 1845
Status: LC; Indexed by RHGS (1845 only)

Aughrim
Earliest Records: b. 1879–; m. 1849–
Status: LC; Indexed by RHGS (to 1977, 1952 respectively)

Ballinlough
Earliest Records: b. 1822–; m. 1822–; d. 1831–
Status: LC; Indexed by RHGS (to 1951+)

Ballyforan
Earliest Records: b. 1847–; m. 1851–
Status: LC; Indexed by RHGS (to 1900)

Ballygar
Earliest Records: b. 1880
Status: LC; Indexed by RHGS (1880 only)

Battlebridge (see Toomna)

Boyle
Earliest Records: b. 1796–; m. 1793–; d. 1819–
Status: LC; Indexed by RHGS (to 1979+)

Bumlin (Strokestown)
Earliest Records: b. 1811–; m. 1811–; d. 1811–
Status: LC; Indexed by RHGS (to 1933, 1863, and 1976, respectively)

Cam (see Kiltoom)

Cashel (see also Rathcline)
Earliest Records: b. 1877–
Status: LC; Indexed by RHGS (to 1899)

Castleblakney
Earliest Records: m. 1860–
Status: LC; Indexed by RHGS (to 1898)

Castlerea
Earliest Records: m. 1785–
Status: LC; Indexed by RHGS (to 1897)

Croghan
Earliest Records: b. 1860–; m. 1869–; d. 1860–
Status: LC; Indexed by RHGS (to 1977+)

Donamon and Fuerty (Donamon and Fuerty united in 1866)
Earliest Records: b. 1881–; m. 1847–
Status: LC; Indexed by RHGS (to 1900 and 1890 respectively)

Estersnow
Earliest Records: b. 1800–; m. 1808–; d. 1807–
Status: LC; Indexed by RHGS (to 1902, 1959, and 1886, respectively)

Elphin
Earliest Records: b. 1896–; m. 1845–; d. 1838–
Status: LC; Indexed by RHGS (to 1944+)

Fuerty (see Donamon)

Kilbride (see Roscommon)

Kilbryan
Earliest Records: b. 1853–; m. 1857–
Status: LC; Indexed by RHGS (to 1858+)

Kilcorkey (no inventory)

Kilgeffin
Earliest Records: d. 1845–
Status: LC; Indexed by RHGS (to 1869)

Kilglass
Earliest Records: b. 1822–; m. 1825–
Status: LC; Indexed by RHGS (to 1842 and 1880 respectively)

Kilkeevin
Earliest Records: b. 1748; m. 1748; d. 1748
Status: LC

Killenvoy or Kilenvoy
Earliest Records: b. 1878–; d. 1879–
Status: LC; Indexed by RHGS (to 1899 and 1963 respectively)

Killeroran
Earliest Records: m. 1856–; d. 1883–
Status: LC; Indexed by RHGS (to 1904 and 1961 respectively)

Killukin (see Ardclare)
Status: Lost

Kilmore
Status: Lost

Kilronan
Earliest Records: b. 1877–; m. 1848–; d. 1878–
Status: LC; Indexed by RHGS (to 1937–)

Kiltoom and Cam
Earliest Records: b. 1797–; m. 1797–; d. 1797–
Status: LC; NL Pos. 5309 (b. 1797–1943; m. 1822–1910; d. 1801–1943) and NA MFCI 61 (b. 1797–1943; m. 1802–43; d. 1801–73); Indexed by RHGS (b. 1797–

1894; m. 1800–1890; d. 1801–1840); SLC film 989751 (b. 1834–64; m. 1835–64; d. 1837–65–with gaps)

Kiltullagh
Earliest Records: b. 1822
Status: LC; Indexed by RHGS (1822 only)

Knockcroghery
Earliest Records: m. 1847–
Status: LC; Indexed by RHGS (to 1890)

Lanesboro
Earliest Records: b. 1848–; m. 1848–
Status: LC; Indexed by RHGS (to 1855 and 1885 respectively)

Loughglinn
Earliest Records: b. 1877–; m. 1845–
Status: LC; Indexed by RHGS (to 1908 and 1874 respectively)

Moore and Drum
Status: Lost

Mount Talbot
Earliest Records: d. 1847–
Status: LC; Indexed by RHGS (to 1930)

Rathcline and Cashel
Earliest Records: b. 1804–; m. 1806–; d. 1807–
Status: LC; Indexed by RHGS (to 1844, 1839, and 1832, respectively)

Roscommon and Kilbride
Earliest Records: b. 1882–; m. 1847–; d. 1888–
Status: LC; Indexed by RHGS (to 1898, 1898, and 1985, respectively)

St. Mary's (Athlone)
Earliest Records: b. 1746–1903; m. 1754–1860; d. 1747–1892
Status: NA MFCI–57 and NL Pos. 5309 (b. 1849–1903; m. 1845–90; d. 1849–1901)

St. Peter (Athlone)
Earliest Records: m. 1845–70
Status: NL Pos. 5309

Strokestown (see Bumlin)

Tarmonbarry
Status: Lost

Tessaragh, Taughboy, and Dysart
Status: Lost

Tibohine
Earliest Records: b. 1811–; m. 1811–; d. 1811–
Status: LC

Toomna (Battlebridge)
Earliest Records: b. 1865–; m. 1846–; d. 1818–
Status: LC; Indexed by RHGS (to 1849+)

Methodist

An account of Methodist records is given in the introduction. Several of these registers have been indexed by Roscommon Heritage and Genealogical Society (see Research Services at the end of the chapter) and one by Leitrim Heritage Centre (see Leitrim chapter). These are indicated as "Indexed by RHGS" or "by LHC" as appropriate.

Athlone
Earliest Records: b. 1842–; m. 1873–
Status: LC; Indexed by RHGS (to 1900)

Ballyfarnon
Earliest Records: m. 1883–
Status: LC; Indexed by RHGS (to 1918)

Boyle and Ballyfarnon
Earliest Records: m. 1883–
Status: LC; Indexed by LHC (to 1900)

Boyle and Drumshanbo
Earliest Records: b. 1840–; m. 1906–
Status: LC; Indexed by RHGS (to 1974 and 1939 respectively)

Presbyterian

An account of Presbyterian records is given in the introduction. These registers rarely contain death records, and occasionally have only records of births. This is indicated where appropriate. Several of these registers have been indexed by Leitrim Heritage Centre (see Research Services at the end of the Leitrim chapter). A search of the index will be conducted for a fee. Those indexed are noted below as "Indexed by LHC."

Boyle
Earliest Records: m. 1861–
Status: LC; Indexed by LHC (to 1939)

Clogher and Ballaghadereen
Earliest Records: m. 1857–
Status: LC; Indexed by LHC (to 1917)

Roman Catholic

Most of the Catholic parish registers of this county have been indexed by Roscommon Heritage and Genealogical Society (see Research Services at the end of the chapter). A search of the index will be conducted by the center for a fee. Those indexed are noted as "Indexed by RHGS." Microfilm copies of all registers are also available in the National Library of Ireland (NLI), and through the LDS library system.

Civil Parish: Ardcarn
Map Grid: 4
RC Parish: Ardcarn (Cootehall)
Diocese: EL
Earliest Record: b. 3.1843; m. 3.1843
Missing Dates: m. 6.1860–4.1861
LC; NLI (mf); Indexed by RHGS

Civil Parish: Athleague
Map Grid: 44
RC Parish: Athleague and Fuerty
Diocese: EL
Earliest Record: b. 1.1808; m. 7.1808; d. 1.1807
Missing Dates: b. 5.1828–8.1834, 7.1864–1.1865; m. 2.1834–3.1836; d. ends 1837
LC; NLI (mf); Indexed by RHGS

Civil Parish: Aughrim
Map Grid: 19
RC Parish: Aughrim (see also Kilmore)
Diocese: EL
Earliest Record: b. 8.1816; m. 8.1816
Missing Dates: b. 12.1837–1.1865; m. 12.1837–1.1865
LC; NLI (mf); Indexed by RHGS

Civil Parish: Ballintober
Map Grid: 18
RC Parish: Ballintober
Diocese: EL
Earliest Record: b. 12.1831; m. 7.1831
LC; NLI (mf); Indexed by RHGS

Civil Parish: Ballynakill
Map Grid: 35
RC Parish: see Ballynakill (2) (Ballymoe), Co. Galway
Diocese: EL

Civil Parish: Baslick
Map Grid: 16
RC Parish: see Ogulla
Diocese: EL

Civil Parish: Boyle
Map Grid: 2
RC Parish: Boyle
Diocese: EL
Earliest Record: b. 9.1827; m. 9.1828; d. 7.1848
Missing Dates: m. 6.1846–10.1864; d. ends 11.1864
LC; NLI (mf); Indexed by RHGS

Civil Parish: Bumlin
Map Grid: 26
RC Parish: see Lissonuffy
Diocese: EL

Civil Parish: Cam or Camma
Map Grid: 51
RC Parish: see Kiltoom
Diocese: EL

Civil Parish: Castlemore
Map Grid: 9b
RC Parish: Castlemore and Kilcolman
Diocese: AC
Earliest Record: b. 11.1851; m. 8.1830
Missing Dates: m. 10.1867–2.1868
LC; NLI (mf); Indexed by RHGS

Civil Parish: Clooncraff
Map Grid: 21

RC Parish: Kiltrustan, etc., see Lissonuffy
Diocese: EL

Civil Parish: Cloonfinlough
Map Grid: 28
RC Parish: Lissonuffy, see Lissonuffy
Diocese: EL

Civil Parish: Cloontuskert
Map Grid: 40
RC Parish: Cloontuskert
Diocese: EL
Earliest Record: b. 1.1865; m. 2.1865
LC; NLI (mf); Indexed by RHGS

Civil Parish: Cloonygormican
Map Grid: 34
RC Parish: Glinsk; see Ballynakill (2) (Ballymoe), Co. Galway
Diocese: EL

Civil Parish: Creagh
Map Grid: 57
RC Parish: see Kilcloony, Co. Galway
Diocese: CF

Civil Parish: Creeve
Map Grid: 13
RC Parish: Creeve, see Elphin

Civil Parish: Drum
Map Grid: 56
RC Parish: see St. Peter's (Athlone)
Diocese: TU

Civil Parish: Drumatemple (see also Co. Galway)
Map Grid: 33
RC Parish: see Ballintober
Diocese: EL

Civil Parish: Dunamon
Map Grid: 37
RC Parish: Kilbegnet, see Ballynakill (2) (Ballymoe), Co. Galway
Diocese: EL

Civil Parish: Dysart
Map Grid: 53
RC Parish: Dysart and Tissara
Diocese: EL
Earliest Record: b. 7.1850 (two registers); m. 12.1862; d. 12.1862
Missing Dates: d. ends 1.1867
LC; NLI (mf); Indexed by RHGS

Civil Parish: Eastersnow or Estersnow
Map Grid: 6
RC Parish: part Killukin (1); part Kilnamanagh
Diocese: EL

Civil Parish: Elphin
Map Grid: 22
RC Parish: Elphin and Creeve
Diocese: EL

Earliest Record: b. 6.1807; m. 5.1807
Missing Dates: b. 12.1808–5.1810, 7.1860–1.1866; m. 10.1830–3.1864
LC; NLI (mf); Indexed by RHGS

Civil Parish: Fuerty
Map Grid: 43
RC Parish: see Athleague
Diocese: EL

Civil Parish: Kilbride
Map Grid: 38
RC Parish: Kilbride
Diocese: EL
Earliest Record: b. 7.1835; m. 9.1838
Missing Dates: b. 9.1849–4.1868; m. ends 1846
LC; NLI (mf); Indexed by RHGS

Civil Parish: Kilbryan
Map Grid: 3
RC Parish: see Boyle
Diocese: EL

Civil Parish: Kilcolagh
Map Grid: 11
RC Parish: see Killukin (1)
Diocese: EL

Civil Parish: Kilcolman (see also Co. Mayo and Co. Sligo)
Map Grid: 9a
RC Parish: see Castlemore
Diocese: AC

Civil Parish: Kilcooly
Map Grid: 25
RC Parish: see Ogulla
Diocese: EL

Civil Parish: Kilcorkey
Map Grid: 14
RC Parish: Kilcorkey and Frenchpark
Diocese: EL
Earliest Record: b. 1.1865
LC; NLI (mf); Indexed by RHGS

Civil Parish: Kilgefin
Map Grid: 39
RC Parish: see Cloontuskert
Diocese: EL

Civil Parish: Kilglass
Map Grid: 31
RC Parish: Kilglass and Rooskey
Diocese: EL
Earliest Record: b. 10.1865
LC; NLI (mf); Indexed by RHGS

Civil Parish: Kilkeevan
Map Grid: 15
RC Parish: Kilkeevan
Diocese: EL
Earliest Record: b. 11.1804; m. 11.1804; d. 2.1805

Missing Dates: b. 5.1809–1.1816, 8.1819–1.1826; m. 7.1809–1.1816, 4.1820–10.1838; d. 5.1809–1.1816, 10.1819–1.1852, ends 1855
LC; NLI (mf); Indexed by RHGS

Civil Parish: Killinvoy
Map Grid: 46
RC Parish: see St. John's
Diocese: EL

Civil Parish: Killukin (1) (Boyle)
Map Grid: 7
RC Parish: Killukin and Killumod
Diocese: EL
Earliest Record: b. 6.1811; m. 4.1825; d. 10.1820
Missing Dates: d. ends 3.1826
LC; NLI (mf); Indexed by RHGS

Civil Parish: Killukin (2) (Roscommon)
Map Grid: 27
RC Parish: part Ogulla; part Cloonfinlough, see Lissonuffy
Diocese: EL

Civil Parish: Killumod
Map Grid: 8
RC Parish: Killumod, see Killukin (1)
Diocese: EL

Civil Parish: Kilmacumsy
Map Grid: 12
RC Parish: see Elphin
Diocese: EL

Civil Parish: Kilmeane
Map Grid: 45
RC Parish: see St. John's
Diocese: EL

Civil Parish: Kilmore
Map Grid: 30
RC Parish: Kilmore
Diocese: EL
Earliest Record: b. 2.1825; m. 3.1825
Missing Dates: b. 2.1860–1.1865; m. 11.1859–2.1865
LC; NLI (mf); Indexed by RHGS

Civil Parish: Kilnamanagh
Map Grid: 9
RC Parish: Kilnamanagh (Breedogue and Ballinameen)
Diocese: EL
Earliest Record: b. 11.1859; m. 2.1860
LC; NLI (mf); Indexed by RHGS

Civil Parish: Kilronan
Map Grid: 1
RC Parish: Kilronan (Keadue, Arigna, and Ballyfarnon)
Diocese: TU
Earliest Record: b. 1.1824; m. 10.1823; d. 6.1835
Missing Dates: b. 7.1829–1.1835; m. 6.1829–1.1835
LC; NLI (mf); Indexed by RHGS

Civil Parish: Kilteevan
Map Grid: 42
RC Parish: see Roscommon
Diocese: EL

Civil Parish: Kiltoom
Map Grid: 52
RC Parish: Kiltoom (Ballybay)
Diocese: EL
Earliest Record: b. 10.1835; m. 10.1835; d. 7.1837
Missing Dates: b. 5.1845-4.1848; m. 7.1846-1.1848;
d. 3.1845-1.1857, ends 1865
LC; NLI (mf); Indexed by RHGS

Civil Parish: Kiltrustan
Map Grid: 23
RC Parish: see Lissonuffy
Diocese: EL

Civil Parish: Kiltullagh
Map Grid: 17
RC Parish: Kiltullagh
Diocese: TU
Earliest Record: b. 9.1839; m. 8.1839
Missing Dates: m. 4.1874-1.1877
LC; NLI (mf); Indexed by RHGS

Civil Parish: Lissonuffy
Map Grid: 29
RC Parish: Kiltrustan, Lissonuffy, and Cloonfinlough
(Strokestown)
Diocese: EL
Earliest Record: b. 10.1830 (several different registers);
m. 10.1830
Missing Dates: b. 1.1846-12.1851; m. 11.1852-
11.1853
LC; NLI (mf); Indexed by RHGS

Civil Parish: Moore
Map Grid: 58
RC Parish: Moore
Diocese: TU
Earliest Record: b. 9.1876; m. 1.1877
LC; NLI (mf); Indexed by RHGS

Civil Parish: Ogulla
Map Grid: 24
RC Parish: Ogulla and Baslic (Tulsk)
Diocese: EL
Earliest Record: b. 1.1865; m. 1.1864
LC; NLI (mf); Indexed by RHGS

Civil Parish: Oran
Map Grid: 36
RC Parish: Oran (Cloverhill)
Diocese: EL
Earliest Record: b. 1.1845; m. 1.1845
LC; NLI (mf); Indexed by RHGS

Civil Parish: Rahara or Raharrow
Map Grid: 48

RC Parish: see St. John's
Diocese: EL

Civil Parish: Roscommon
Map Grid: 41
RC Parish: Roscommon and Kilteevan
Diocese: EL
Earliest Record: b. 10.1837; m. 1.1820
LC; NLI (mf); Indexed by RHGS

Civil Parish: St. John's or Ivernoon
Map Grid: 49
RC Parish: St. John's
Diocese: EL
Earliest Record: b. 7.1841 (several different registers);
m. 7.1841; d. 1854
Missing Dates: d. 1858-1859
LC; NLI (mf); Indexed by RHGS

Civil Parish: St. Peter's (Athlone)
Map Grid: 55
RC Parish: St. Peter's Athlone
Diocese: EL
Earliest Record: b. 1.1789; m. 1.1789; d. 1.1789
LC; NLI (mf); Indexed by RHGS

Civil Parish: Shankill
Map Grid: 20
RC Parish: see Elphin
Diocese: EL

Civil Parish: Taghboy (see also Co. Galway)
Map Grid: 50
RC Parish: see Dysart
Diocese: EL

Civil Parish: Taghmaconnell
Map Grid: 54
RC Parish: Taghmaconnell
Diocese: CF
Earliest Record: b. 7.1842; m. 1.1863
LC; NLI (mf); Indexed by RHGS and by East GFHS
(see Co. Galway)

Civil Parish: Termonbarry
Map Grid: 32
RC Parish: Rooskey, see Kilglass
Diocese: EL

Civil Parish: Tibohine (1)
Map Grid: 10
RC Parish: Tibohine; also Loughglynn, see below; also
part Frenchpark, see Kilcorkey
Diocese: EL
Earliest Record: b. 1.1833; m. 1.1833
Missing Dates: b. 9.1864-5.1875; m. 6.1864-2.1865
LC; NLI (mf); Indexed by RHGS

Civil Parish: Tibohine (2)
Map Grid: 10
RC Parish: Loughglynn and Lisacul
Diocese: EL
Earliest Record: b. 3.1817; m. 4.1817; d. 1.1850

Missing Dates: b. 11.1826–12.1829, 4.1863–1.1865;
m. 3.1827–2.1836, 4.1837–12.1849, 2.1858–1.1865;
d. 6.1854–1.1868
LC; NLI (mf); Indexed by RHGS

Civil Parish: Tisrara
Map Grid: 47
RC Parish: see Dysart
Diocese: EL

Civil Parish: Tumna
Map Grid: 5
RC Parish: part Killukin (1); also part Ardcarn
Diocese: EL

Commercial and Social Directories

1824

J. Pigot's *City of Dublin and Hibernian Provincial Directory* includes traders, nobility, gentry, and clergy lists of Boyle, Castlerea, Elphin, Roscommon, and Strokestown.

1846

Slater's *National Commercial Directory of Ireland* lists nobility, clergy, traders, etc., in Boyle, Castlerea, Elphin, Roscommon, and Strokestown.

1856

Slater's *Royal National Commercial Directory of Ireland* lists nobility, gentry, clergy, traders, etc., in Boyle, Castlerea, Elphin, Roscommon, and Strokestown.

1870

Slater's *Directory of Ireland* contains trade, nobility, and clergy lists for Boyle, Castlerea, Elphin, Roscommon, and Strokestown.

1881

Slater's *Royal National Commercial Directory of Ireland* contains lists of traders, clergy, nobility, and farmers in adjoining parishes of the towns of Boyle, Castlerea, Elphin, Roscommon, and Strokestown.

1894

Slater's *Royal National Directory of Ireland* lists traders, police, teachers, farmers, and private residents in each of the towns, villages, and parishes of the county.

Family History

The Leitrim-Roscommon genealogy home page has information on histories of families associated with the county (see Libraries and Information Sources below).

Crofton, H. *Crofton Memoirs: Account of John Crofton of Ballymurray, Co. Roscommon, his Ancestors and Descendants and Others Bearing his Name.* York, 1911.

O'Cianain, S.F. "The Davys Family Records." Records kept by members of the Davys family, formerly of Cloonbonny, near Lanesborough, and of Martinstown, near Roscommon, from 1693 to 1832. Printed from the originals in the possession of the family. Longford: Longford Printing Co., 1931.

"Notes on the Dodwells of Manor Dodwell, Co. Roscommon." *Ir. Gen.* 1 (1941): 315–17.

Ellison—see Wexford.

"The Irwins of Roxborough, Co. Roscommon and Streamstown, Co. Sligo." *Ir. Gen.* 1 (2) (1937): 19–24.

Memoir Regarding the Family of Irwin of Rathmoyle. N.p., 1964.

"Notes on the Lloyd Family of Ardnagowen, Co. Roscommon." *J. Ass. Pres. Mem. Dead* 6 (1904–06): 403.

"Mahon of Strokestown, Co. Roscommon." *Ir. Anc.* 10 (2) (1978): 77–80.

Mills—see Co. Galway.

"Nicholas Mahon and Seventeenth-Century Roscommon." *Ir. Gen.* 3 (6) (1963): 228–35.

Connellan, M.J. "Ballmulconry and the Mulconrys" (Co. Roscommon). Dublin.

O'Conor, Don C. *The O'Connors of Connaught.* Dublin, 1891.

O'Conor, R. *Memoir of the O'Connors of Ballintubber, Co. Roscommon.* Dublin, 1859.

O'Connor, Roderic. *Lineal Descent of the O'Connors of Co. Roscommon.* Dublin, 1862.

O'Connor, R. *Historical and Genealogical Memoir of the O'Connors, Kings of Connaught.* Dublin, 1861.

Dunleavy, G.W., and J.E. Dunleavy. "The O'Connor Papers: Their Significance to Genealogists." *Eire-Ir* 11 (2) (1976): 104–18.

"O'Hanly and the Townland of Kilmacough." *Ir. Gen.* 3 (3) (1963): 101–08.

"Pedigree of Walsh of Crannagh, Co. Roscommon." *J. Ass. Pres. Mem. Dead* 7 (1907–09): 700.

Gravestone Inscriptions

Gravestone inscriptions for this county are available in the county library.

Aughrim (Old): *Roscommon Heritage and Genealogical Society.*

Cam: GO IGRS Collection 138.

Cloonfinlough: *Roscommon Heritage and Genealogical Society.*

Dysert: *Roscommon Heritage and Genealogical Society;* also GO IGRS Collection 138.

Elphin: GO Ms. 622, 151.

Fuerty: *Roscommon Heritage and Genealogical Society.*

Jamestown: GO Ms. 622, 170.

Kiltrustan: *Roscommon Heritage and Genealogical Society.*

Kilverdin: *Roscommon Heritage and Genealogical Society.*

Lisoonuffy: *Roscommon Heritage and Genealogical Society.*

Roscommon (C of I): *Roscommon Heritage and Genealogical Society.*

Strokestown: *Roscommon Heritage and Genealogical Society*; also GO Ms. 622, 174, and 182.

Taughmaconnell: GO IGRS Collection 71.

Tisrara: GO IGRS Collection 144.

Newspapers

There were no newspapers published in this county before 1828. Papers from the surrounding counties should be searched, starting with those in the county adjacent to the area of interest.

Title: *Boyle Gazette*
Published in: Boyle, 1891
NLI Holdings: 1–7.1891
BL Holdings: 2–7.1891

Title: *Roscommon and Leitrim Gazette*
Published in: Boyle, 1822–82
NLI Holdings: 1.1841–12.1844
BL Holdings: 4.1822–6.1882

Title: *Roscommon Constitutionalist*
Published in: Boyle, 1886–ca. 1891
NLI Holdings: 1.1889–11.1891
BL Holdings: 4.1889–11.1891

Title: *Roscommon Herald*
Published in: Boyle, 1859–current
NLI Holdings: 1.1882–11.1920; 1.1921–in progress
BL Holdings: 4.1859–11.1920; 1921–in progress

Title: *Roscommon Journal*
Published in: Roscommon, 1828–1927
NLI Holdings: 11.1841–12.1927 (with gaps)
BL Holdings: 7.1828–9.1832; 11.1832–10.1848; 8.1849–12.1918; 3.1919–12.1925

Title: *Roscommon Reporter*
Published in: Roscommon, 1850–60
BL Holdings: 3.1850–3.1851; 2.1856–3.1859; 10.1860

Title: *Roscommon Weekly Messenger* (continued as *Roscommon Messenger* in 1861)
Published in: Roscommon, 1848–1935
NLI Holdings: 1.1902–12.1935
BL Holdings: 5.1845–12.1886; 1.1888–12.1935

Wills and Administrations

A discussion of the types of records, where they are held, and their availability and value is given in the Wills section of the introduction. The availability of prerogative wills, administrations, and marriage license records is also described in the relevant parts of the same section. Where available, published sources of these records are given in the Miscellaneous Sources section.

Pre-1858 Wills and Administrations

Prerogative Wills. See the introduction.

Consistorial Wills. County Roscommon is in the dioceses of Elphin, Achonry, Clonfert, Tuam, and Ardagh. The guide to Catholic parish records in this chapter shows the diocese to which each civil parish belonged. The wills of residents of each diocese were usually proven within that diocese (see the Wills section for exceptions). The following records survive:

Wills
See the introduction.

Abstracts
See the introduction.

Indexes
Elphin (1650–1858); Tuam (1648–1858); Index to Clonfert Marriage License Bonds, Wills, and Administrations: SLC film 990403. Index to Clonfert and Kilmacduagh Wills: pub. by Smyth-Wood (1977); SLC 941.5 A1. Achonry—see Co. Mayo; Ardagh—see Co. Longford.

Post-1858 Wills and Administrations

This county was served by the District Registry of Tuam. The surviving records are kept in the NAI. Records include: Tuam District Will Books (1858–1901). NAI; SLC film 100949–50.

Marriage Licenses

Indexes
Elphin and Achonry (1740–1850). NAI; SLC film 100868. Clonfert and Ardagh (1691–1845). NAI; SLC film 100869. Tuam (1661–1750). NAI; SLC film 100872.

Miscellaneous Sources

McGowan, Eileen. "Surnames of Co. Roscommon." *Irish Roots* 1 (1993): 20–21.

Murphy, M., and J.R. Reilly. *Marriages in the Roman Catholic Diocese of Tuam, Ireland, 1821–1829.* USA: Heritage Books, 1993.

Tuam RC Diocese. Register of marriages in each Deanery for parts of 1821 and 1822, with additions in many parishes to 1829. NLI film P4222.

Gacquin, William. *Roscommon before the Famine–The Parishes of Kilmoon and Cam 1749–1845.* Dublin: Irish

Academic Press, 1996.

Burke, F. *Loch Ce, and Its Annals, North Roscommon and the Diocese of Elphin in Times of Old.* Dublin, 1895.

Carthy, P. *Landholding and Settlement in Co. Roscommon.* M.A. Thesis, University College, Dublin, 1970 (unpublished).

Dunleavy, J.E., and G.W. Dunleavy. "Catalogue of the O'Conor Papers." *Studies* (Autumn/Winter 1973).

Dunleavy, G.W., and J.E. Dunleavy. *The O'Conor Papers: A Descriptive Catalogue and Surname Register of the Materials at Clonalis House.* Madison: University of Wisconsin Press, 1977.

Weld, I. *Statistical Survey of the County of Roscommon.* Dublin: Royal Dublin Society, Graisberry, 1832.

John Browne: Map of Carronaskeagh, Cloonfinlought, May 1811. NLI Ms. 16 1 14 (8) (gives tenants' names).

Leases of the Lord Lorton Estate: NLI Mss. 3104/5, Lease Books, 1740–1900. (Major and small tenants in townlands of the civil parishes of Ardcarn, Aughrim, Boyle, Creeve, Elphin, Estersnow, Kilbryan, Kilnamanagh.)

Accounts and rentals of the Charles Manners St. George Estate: NLI Ms. 4001-22. 1842–46, 1850–55, 1861–71. (Deals with holdings in the townlands in the civil parishes of Ardcarn, Killukin, Killumod.)

Leases of the Rev. Rodney Ormsby: NLI Ms. 10152 ca. 1803. (Grange townland.)

Rent Roll of the Pakenham-Mahon Estate. NLI Ms. 10152 (1765–54; covering townlands in civil parishes of Bumlin, Cloonfinlough, Elphin, Kilgefin, Kilglass, Kilnamanagh, Kiltrustan, Lisonuffy, Shankill).

Rentals and Leases of the Sandford Estate. NLI Ms. 10152. 1718–1845 (major tenants only in townlands in the civil parishes of Ballintober, Baslick, Kilkeevin, Boyle, Kiltullagh and Tibohine).

Records of Athlone and District (1690–1900). Compiled by Maladry Moran. GO 674–678 and SLC films 100214-6 (index to people, places, and subjects, newspaper cuttings, etc.).

Deed Extracts (Athlone 1836–61; Roscommon 1720–1828). Longford/Westmeath Library (Burgess Papers); SLC film 1279274.

Research Sources and Services

Journals

Journal of County Roscommon Historical and Archaeological Society (1986–present)

Journal of Old Athlone Society (1969–)

Libraries and Information Sources

Roscommon County Library, Abbey Street, Roscommon. Ph: (0903) 6203

Research Services

The Leitrim-Roscommon genealogy home page (http://www.thecore.com/let-res/index.html) has sources for research in the counties, maps of different administrative divisions, and information on specific families associated with the county.

County Roscommon Heritage and Genealogical Society, County Heritage Centre, Strokestown, Co. Roscommon. Ph: (078) 33380. This is the official IGP center for the county. It has access to all of the records of all denominations up to 1900, the 1901 census, *Griffith's Valuation*, *Tithe Applotment Books*, and a range of other local sources for the county. Researchers are advised to contact the center for an updated list of registers, and other sources, indexed. Searches of the database will be conducted for a fee.

See also Research Services in Dublin in the introduction.

Societies

Aughrim and Kilmore History Group, Mrs. Kathleen O'Dowd, Kilcroy, Hillstreet, via Carrick-on-Shannon, Co. Roscommon

Ballaghadereen Museum and Art Centre, Ms. Bernadette Jordan, Cortoon, Ballaghaderreen, Co. Roscommon

Roscommon Historical Society, Mr. Albert Siggins, Castlestrange, Castlecoote, Co. Roscommon

Tisrara Heritage Society, Ms. Eileen Healy, Carroward, Mount Talbot, Co. Roscommon

Roscommon Civil Parishes as Numbered on Map

1. Kilronan
2. Boyle
3. Kilbryan
4. Ardcarn
5. Tumna
6. Eastersnow or Estersnow
7. Killukin (see also 27)
8. Killumod
9. Kilnamanagh
9a. Kilcolman
9b. Castlemore
10. Tibohine
11. Kilcolagh
12. Kilmacumsy
13. Creeve
14. Kilcorkey
15. Kilkeevan
16. Baslick
17. Kiltullagh
18. Ballintober
19. Aughrim
20. Shankill
21. Clooncraff
22. Elphin
23. Kiltrustan
24. Ogulla
25. Kilcooly
26. Bumlin
27. Killukin (see also 7)
28. Cloonfinlough
29. Lissonuffy
30. Kilmore
31. Kilglass
32. Termonbarry
33. Drumatemple
34. Cloonygormican
35. Ballynakill
36. Oran
37. Dunamon
38. Kilbride
39. Kilgefin
40. Cloontuskert
41. Roscommon
42. Kilteevan
43. Fuerty
44. Athleague
45. Kilmeane
46. Killinvoy or Killenvoy
47. Tisrara
48. Rahara
49. St. John's or Ivernoon
50. Taghboy
51. Cam or Camma
52. Kiltoom
53. Dysart or Dysert
54. Taghmaconnell or Taughmaconnell
55. St. Peter's
56. Drum
57. Creagh
58. Moore

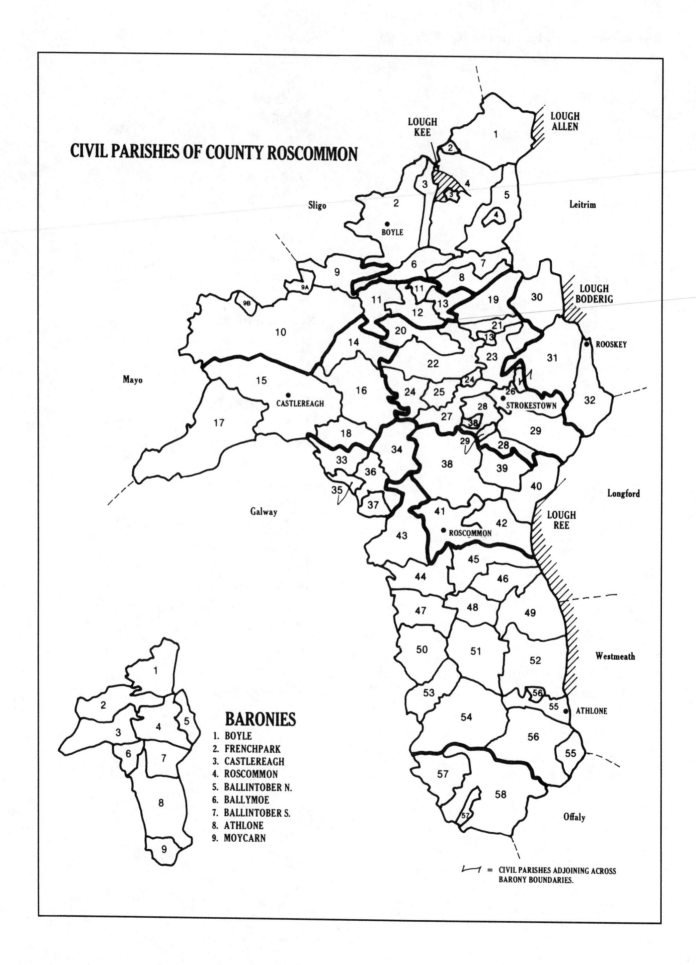

CIVIL PARISHES OF COUNTY ROSCOMMON

LOUGH
KEE

LOUGH
ALLEN

Sligo

Leitrim

BOYLE

LOUGH
BODERIG

ROOSKEY

Mayo

CASTLEREAGH

STROKESTOWN

Longford

Galway

ROSCOMMON

LOUGH
REE

Westmeath

ATHLONE

Offaly

BARONIES
1. BOYLE
2. FRENCHPARK
3. CASTLEREAGH
4. ROSCOMMON
5. BALLINTOBER N.
6. BALLYMOE
7. BALLINTOBER S.
8. ATHLONE
9. MOYCARN

⌐ = CIVIL PARISHES ADJOINING ACROSS
BARONY BOUNDARIES.

Roscommon Civil Parishes in Alphabetical Order

Ardcarn: 4
Athleague: 44
Aughrim: 19
Ballintober: 18
Ballynakill: 35
Baslick: 16
Boyle: 2
Bumlin: 26
Cam or Camma: 51
Castlemore: 9b
Clooncraff: 21
Cloonfinlough: 28
Cloontuskert: 40
Cloonygormican: 34
Creagh: 57
Creeve: 13
Drum: 56
Drumatemple: 33
Dunamon: 37
Dysart or Dysert: 53
Eastersnow or Estersnow: 6
Elphin: 22
Fuerty: 43
Kilbride: 38
Kilbryan: 3
Kilcolagh: 12
Kilcolman: 9a
Kilcooly: 25
Kilcorkey: 14
Kilgefin: 39

Kilglass: 31
Kilkeevan: 15
Killinvoy or Killenvoy: 46
Killukin (1): 7
Killukin (2): 27
Killumod: 8
Kilmacumsy: 12
Kilmeane: 45
Kilmore: 30
Kilnamanagh: 9
Kilronan: 1
Kilteevan: 42
Kiltoom: 52
Kiltrustan: 23
Kiltullagh: 17
Lissonuffy: 29
Moore: 58
Ogulla: 24
Oran: 36
Rahara: 48
Roscommon: 41
Shankill: 20
St. John's or Ivernoon: 49
St. Peter's: 55
Taghboy: 50
Taghmaconnell or Taughmaconnell: 54
Termonbarry: 32
Tibohine: 10
Tisrara: 47
Tumna: 5

County Sligo

A Brief History

This Connaught county contains the towns of Sligo, Ballymote, Collooney, Ballysodare, and Enniscrone.

Sligo was the ancestral territory of a branch of the O'Connors, called O'Connor Sligo. Other Gaelic families associated with the county include O'Dowd, O'Hara, O'Hart, McDonagh, Mac Firbis, and O'Colman. The site of the town of Sligo has been of strategic importance since ancient times, since all traffic on the coastal route between south and north had to ford the river here. A fortress which guarded this ford was plundered by Norse pirates as early as A.D. 807.

After the Norman invasion of Connacht in 1235, Sligo was granted to Maurice Fitzgerald, who effectively founded Sligo town by building a castle there in 1245 and making it his residence. The Taaffe family was among the Norman families who settled in the county. Further settlers were brought into the county at various periods, including weavers from the north of Ireland brought in by Lord Shelbourne in 1749.

As the native Irish and Norman population were predominantly Catholic, the Scottish usually Presbyterian, and the English of the Protestant faith, the proportions of these religions among the population can, in very general terms, be used to estimate the origins of the inhabitants of the county. When religious affiliation was first determined in the census of 1861, the respective proportions of Catholic, Presbyterian, and Protestant in Sligo were ninety, eight, and one percent.

Apart from the weaving industry and some mining operations, Sligo is basically an agricultural county. The town of Sligo was an important port in the eighteenth and nineteenth centuries, particularly as the River Erne and its lake systems facilitated inland trading and transport. It was also an important port of emigration. The peak of population was reached in 1841 at 181,000. The Great Famine of 1845-47 badly affected the county, and the population had dropped by 52,000 in ten years, including some 20,000 deaths. By 1901 the population had fallen to 84,000, and is currently 56,000.

Census and Census Substitutes

1659

"Census" of Ireland. Edited by S. Pender. Dublin: Stationery Office, 1939. NLI I6551. SLC film 924648.

1665

Hearth Money Rolls. Printed by Stationery Office for the Irish Manuscripts Commission, 1967; also in *Anal. Hib.* 24.

1749

Religious Census of Elphin Dioceses—lists householders, occupation, religion, number of children, and servants: parishes of Aghanagh, Ahamlish, Ballynakill, Ballysumaghan, Drumcliff, Drumcolumb, Killadoon, Kilmacallan, Kilmactranny, Kilross, Shancough, Sligo, Tawnagh. NAI 1A 3613; SLC film 101781.

1760-86

Major tenants of the Strafford Estate—covering eighteen parishes, including Sligo town. NLI Ms. 10223.

Rental of the Boswell Estate—Ahamlish and Drumrat Parishes. NLI P4937 (major tenants only).

Rental of the O'Hara Estate—Parishes of Achonry, Ballysadare, Killoran and Killvarnet. NLI Pos. 1923 (rent roll plus names in leases).

```
        SLIGO (or 22d) Batt.
Col.    John Irwin      4 June 1807
Lt.Col. Roger Parke    20 July do.
Majors  Alex. Perceval 12 Feb. 1807
        Chas. K. O'Hara 23 J ly do.
Capts.  Rob. Lindfay   13 May 1801
        John Tyler     21 May 1803
        Wm. Lindfey    18 Aug. 1803
        Rob. Powell     1 Dec.   do.
        James Jones    26 Apr. 1804
        Wm. Furey      30 Sept. 1805
Lieuts. Wm. Clarke     26 Oct. 1798
        Tho. Trumble   13 May 1801
        Booth Jones    25 Oct. 1803
        Harloe Elwood  30 Sept.1805
        Wm. Barrett     1 Oct. do.
        John Coen      20 Feb. 1806
        James Burrowes       do.
        James Light          do.
        Geo. Powell     5 May do.
        Hen. Fawcett   18. Nov. do.
        Francis Knox         do.
        Jones T. Irwin  4 May 1807
        Thos. P. Jones 24 June do.
Enfigns Wm. Hamilton  18 Nov. 1806
        John Ormfby          do.
        Richard Eagar        do.
        Andw. Parke     4 May 1807
        Wm. Dennis     24 June  do.
Paym.   Rob. Ormfby     1 Apr. 1799
Adjut.  Capt. S. Goodwin 10 July 1798
2.Maf.  Ja. Burrowes   22 Aug. 1803
Surg.   John Fawcett   15 July 1793
Affift. do. Geo. Smith   5 Aug. 1807
Agents  Cane and Son
```

The Officers of the Sligo Militia, or 22nd Battalion, in 1808. Extract from *The Gentlemans and Citizens Almanack*, compiled by John Watson Stewart (Dublin, 1908).

1792 and 1804

Rental records of the Sir Thomas Dundas Estate: NLI Mss. 2787, 2788. (Major tenants in townlands in the civil parishes of Aghanagh, Drumrat, Emlaghfad, Kilcolman, Kilfree, Kilglass, Kilmacallan, Kilmacteigue, Kilmactranny, Kilmoremoy, Kilshalvey, and Skreen.)

1795–96

Alphabetical list of Sligo Freeholders (from Markree Library). NLI Ms. 3136.

1795–97

Voters List for Co. Sligo (transcribed from NLI ms. 3075). McDonagh Ms. No. 21, Sligo Co. Library.

1796

Spinning Wheel Premium List (see introduction).

1798

List of Persons who Suffered Losses in '98 Rebellion. NLI JLB 94107 (approximately 250 names, addresses, and occupations).

1813

Petition by Sligo Protestants. NLI P 504.

1823–37

Tithe Applotment Survey (see introduction).

1832–37

"List of Voters Registered in the Borough of Sligo." *Parl. Papers* 1837, 11 (2): 205-16 (835 names, occupations, and addresses).

1839

List of persons who obtained Game Certificates in Sligo, etc. PRONI T 688.

1843

Voters List. NAI 1843/61.

1852

Names of electors for Co. Sligo at 1852 general election. NLI Ms. 3064 (three manuscripts poll books, each 49 pp., giving names, addresses and qualifications).

1853

Rental of the Crofton Estate—Dromard and Templeboy Parishes. NAI M 938X and 940X.

1858

Griffith's Valuation (see introduction).

1876

Owners of Land in Co. Sligo, compiled by Local Government Board (lists owners of land of one acre and over). Sligo Co. Library.

1901

Census. NAI (see introduction). The returns for the parish of Achonry are in *From Plain to Hill*, Mayo, 1995; Sligo people in the Dun Laoghaire Co. Dublin census are in *Dun Laoghaire Gen. Soc. J.* 5 (3) (1996): 114-116. SLC films 851582-851605.

1911

Census. NAI.

Church Records

Church of Ireland

See the introduction for a description of Church of Ireland records and their major repositories. Many C of I records were lost in the PRO fire of 1922. These are indicated as "Lost." However, as Church of Ireland records were effectively state records, the records of marriage (from 1845) are also in the General Registrar's Office. Many are still in local custody (LC), while others are in one of a variety of other archives (e.g., RCBL or NAI). All of the Church of Ireland registers of this county have been indexed by the County Sligo Heritage and Genealogy Society (see Research Services at the end of the chapter). A search of the index will be conducted by the center for a fee. Those indexed are noted as "Indexed by SHGS."

Achonry
Earliest Records: m. 1845-
Status: LC; Indexed by SHGS (to 1949)

Aghanagh
Earliest Records: b. 1856-; m. 1857-; d. 1856-
Status: LC; Indexed by SHGS (to 1937+)

Ahamlish
Earliest Records: b. 1882-; m. 1847-; d. 1877-
Status: LC; Indexed by SHGS (to 1899)

Ballisodare (or Ballysadare)
Earliest Records: m. 1845-1954
Status: RCBL

Ballysumaghan and Killery
Earliest Records: b. 1844-; m. 1846-; d. 1850-
Status: LC; Indexed by SHGS (to 1974, 1956 and 1956 respectively)

Castleconnor (and Killanley)
Earliest Records: b. 1800-; m. 1800-; d. 1800-
Status: LC; NAI MFCI 33 (b/m/d. 1800-21); Indexed by SHGS (from 1835 to 1900, 1896, and 1988, respectively); SLC film 897365 (b. 1867-72; d. 1867-73)

Drumard or Dromard (including Beltra)
Earliest Records: b. 1895-; m. 1845-; d. 1895-
Status: LC; Indexed by SHGS (to 1901, 1899 and 1987 respectively)

Drumcliff
Earliest Records: b. 1805-; m. 1845-; d. 1805-
Status: LC; NAI M5094-5107 (b. 1805-87; m. 1805-66; d. 1805-58); Indexed by SHGS (to 1890, 1899 and 1902 respectively); SLC film 982173 (b. 1805-64; m. 1805-34; d. 1805-58)

Easkey
Earliest Records: b. 1822-; m. 1822-; d. 1827-
Status: LC; NAI MFCI 33 (b/d. 1822-71; m. 1822-45); Indexed by SHGS (to 1900, 1898 and 1988 respectively)

Emlafad (or Emlaghfad) and Kilmorgan
Earliest Records: b. 1762-; m. 1762-; d. 1762-
Status: RCBL (b. 1762-1882; m. 1762-1875; d. 1762-1941); and NAI MFCI 33 (b. 1808-80; m/d. 1831-73); Indexed by SHGS (to 1921, 1895 and 1893 respectively)

Kilglass
Earliest Records: b. 1886-; m. 1845-; d. 1886-
Status: LC; Indexed by SHGS (to 1900, 1898 and 1908 respectively)

Killanley (see Castleconnor)

Killaraght
Status: Lost

Killaspicbrone (see St. John, Sligo)

Killerry
Status: Lost

Killoran (see Rathbarron)

Kilmacowen (see St. John, Sligo)

Kilmacshalgan
Earliest Records: b. 1880-; m. 1846-; d. 1883-
Status: LC; Indexed by SHGS (to 1900, 1899 and 1988 respectively)

Kilmacteigue
Earliest Records: b. 1877-; m. 1851-
Status: LC; Indexed by SHGS (to 1900 and 1953 respectively)

Kilmactranny
Earliest Records: b. 1817-; m. 1817-; d. 1817-
Status: LC; Indexed by SHGS (to 1919, 1954 and 1983 respectively)

Knocknarea (St. Anne's)
Earliest Records: b. 1842-; m. 1843-; d. 1842-
Status: LC; Indexed by SHGS (to 1899)

Lissadill
Earliest Records: b. 1836; m. 1842
Status: LC

Rathbarron, Coolaney and Killoran
Earliest Records: b. 1845-; m. 1896-
Status: LC; Indexed by SHGS (to 1986)

Rosses
Status: Lost

St. Johns, Sligo
Earliest Records: b. 1802-; m. 1802-; d. 1844-
Status: LC; Indexed by SHGS (to 1902, 1901 and 1981 respectively)

Skreen
Earliest Records: b. 1877-; m. 1846-; d. 1877-
Status: LC; Indexed by SHGS (to 1899)

Taunagh or Tawnagh (including Riverstown, Kilmacalane, Drumcollum)
Earliest Records: b. 1877-; m. 1845-; d. 1877-
Status: LC; Indexed by SHGS (to 1900, 1901 and 1988 respectively)

Tobbercurry or Tubbercurry
Earliest Records: b. 1877-; m. 1846-
Status: LC; Indexed by SHGS (to 1899)

Toomour-Sligo (see Emlafad)

Presbyterian

An account of Presbyterian records is given in the introduction. These registers rarely contain death records, and occasionally have only records of births. This is indicated where appropriate. Some of the Presbyterian registers of Sligo have been indexed by the County Sligo Heritage and Genealogy Society (see Research Services at the end of the chapter). A search of the index will be conducted for a fee. Those indexed are noted below as "Indexed by SHGS."

Sligo Circuit
Earliest Records: b. 1806-; m. 1845-
Status: LC; Indexed by SHGS (to 1899)

Methodist

See the introduction for an account of Methodist records and their accessibility. A Methodist church was located in Sligo, and the register has been indexed by the County Sligo Heritage and Genealogy Society (see Research Services at the end of the chapter). A search of the index will be conducted for a fee. No death records were maintained.

Sligo Circuit
Earliest Records: b. 1819-; m. 1846-
Status: LC; Indexed by SHGS (to 1899)

Roman Catholic

Note that all of the Catholic parish registers of this county have been indexed by the County Sligo Heritage and Genealogy Society (see Research Services at the end of the chapter). A search of the index will be conducted by the center for a fee. Those indexed are noted as "Indexed by SHGS." Microfilm copies of all registers are also available in the National Library of Ireland (NLI), and through the LDS library system.

Civil Parish: Achonry (1)
Map Grid: 19
RC Parish: Clonacool; also Achonry and Curry, see below
Diocese: AC
Earliest Record: b. 10.1859; m. 10.1859
Status: LC; NLI (mf); Indexed by SHGS

Civil Parish: Achonry (2)
Map Grid: 19
RC Parish: Achonry
Diocese: AC
Earliest Record: b. 1878; m. 8.1865
Status: LC; NLI (mf); Indexed by SHGS

Civil Parish: Achonry (3)
Map Grid: 19
RC Parish: Curry
Diocese: AC
Earliest Record: b. 10.1867; m. 11.1867
Status: LC; NLI (mf); Indexed by SHGS

Civil Parish: Aghanagh
Map Grid: 38
RC Parish: Aghanagh
Diocese: EL
Earliest Record: b. 6.1803; m. 1.1800; d. 3.1800
Missing Dates: b. 1.1808-10.1816, 1.1819-1.1821, 11.1841-1.1844; m. 6.1802-4.1829, 3.1850-11.1858; d. 3.1802-11.1822, 9.1846-11.1858
Status: LC; NLI (mf); Indexed by SHGS

Civil Parish: Ahamlish
Map Grid: 1
RC Parish: Ahamlish
Diocese: EL
Earliest Record: b. 11.1796; m. 12.1796; d. 11.1796
Missing Dates: b. 5.1829-1.1831, 11.1835-9.1836; d. 10.1822-1.1827, ends 7.1845
Status: LC; NLI (mf); Indexed by SHGS

Civil Parish: Ballynakill
Map Grid: 31
RC Parish: Sowey, see Kilmacallan
Diocese: EL

Civil Parish: Ballysadare
Map Grid: 16
RC Parish: Balysodare and Kilvarnet
Diocese: AC

Earliest Record: b. 4.1842; m. 1.1858
Missing Dates: b. 8.1853–2.1858
Status: LC; NLI (mf); Indexed by SHGS

Civil Parish: Ballysumaghan
Map Grid: 30
RC Parish: Sowey, see Kilmacallan
Diocese: EL

Civil Parish: Calry
Map Grid: 4
RC Parish: Sligo, see St. John's
Diocese: EL

Civil Parish: Castleconor
Map Grid: 14
RC Parish: Castleconor
Diocese: KA
Earliest Record: b. 1.1855; m. 10.1854
Status: LC; NLI (mf); Indexed by SHGS

Civil Parish: Cloonoghil
Map Grid: 23
RC Parish: Kilshalvey, etc., see Kilturra, Co. Mayo
Diocese: AC

Civil Parish: Dromard
Map Grid: 13
RC Parish: see Skreen
Diocese: KA

Civil Parish: Drumcliff
Map Grid: 3
RC Parish: Drumcliff
Diocese: EL
Earliest Record: b. 5.1841; m. 1.1865
Status: LC; NLI (mf); Indexed by SHGS

Civil Parish: Drumcolumb
Map Grid: 32
RC Parish: Riverstown, see Kilmacallan
Diocese: EL

Civil Parish: Drumrat
Map Grid: 27
RC Parish: Drumrat
Diocese: AC
Earliest Record: b. 11.1843; m. 1.1842
Missing Dates: b. 3.1855–1.1874; m. 5.1851–12.1872
Status: LC; NLI (mf); Indexed by SHGS

Civil Parish: Easky
Map Grid: 9
RC Parish: Easky; also part Kilglass
Diocese: KA
Earliest Record: b. 6.1864
Status: LC; NLI (mf); Indexed by SHGS

Civil Parish: Emlaghfad
Map Grid: 21
RC Parish: Emlefad and Kilmorgan
Diocese: AC

Earliest Record: b. 7.1856; m. 8.1824
Status: LC; NLI (mf); Indexed by SHGS

Civil Parish: Kilcolman (see also Co. Roscommon and Co. Mayo)
Map Grid: 40
RC Parish: see Castlemore, Co. Roscommon
Diocese: AC

Civil Parish: Kilfree
Map Grid: 39
RC Parish: see Killaraght
Diocese: AC

Civil Parish: Kilglass
Map Grid: 8
RC Parish: Kilglass
Diocese: KA
Earliest Record: b. 10.1825; m. 11.1825; d. 11.1825
Missing Dates: m. 5.1867–11.1867; d. ends 6.1867
Status: LC; NLI (mf); Indexed by SHGS

Civil Parish: Killadoon
Map Grid: 35
RC Parish: Geevagh, see Kilmactranny
Diocese: EL

Civil Parish: Killaraght
Map Grid: 41
RC Parish: Kilfree and Killaraght
Diocese: AC
Earliest Record: b. 5.1873; m. 2.1844
Status: LC; NLI (mf); Indexed by SHGS

Civil Parish: Killaspugbrone
Map Grid: 5
RC Parish: Sligo, see St. John's
Diocese: EL

Civil Parish: Killerry
Map Grid: 28
RC Parish: see Killanummery, Co. Leitrim
Diocese: AD

Civil Parish: Killoran
Map Grid: 17
RC Parish: Killoran
Diocese: AC
Earliest Record: b. 4.1878; m. 4.1846
Status: LC; NLI (mf); Indexed by SHGS

Civil Parish: Kilmacallan
Map Grid: 34
RC Parish: Riverstown (Taunagh)
Diocese: EL
Earliest Record: b. 11.1803; m. 11.1803
Missing Dates: b. 12.1834–5.1836; m. 1.1829–5.1836
Status: LC; NLI (mf); Indexed by SHGS

Civil Parish: Kilmacowen
Map Grid: 7
RC Parish: Sligo, see St. John's
Diocese: EL

Civil Parish: Kilmacshalgan
Map Grid: 10
RC Parish: Kilmacshalgan (see Templeboy for pre-1808 records)
Diocese: KA
Earliest Record: b. 6.1868; m. 1.1868
Status: LC; NLI (mf); Indexed by SHGS

Civil Parish: Kilmacteige
Map Grid: 20
RC Parish: Kilmacteige (Tourlestrane)
Diocese: AC
Earliest Record: b. 4.1845; m. 1.1848
Status: LC; NLI (mf); Indexed by SHGS

Civil Parish: Kilmactranny
Map Grid: 37
RC Parish: Geevagh
Diocese: EL
Earliest Record: b. 2.1873; m. 1.1851
Status: LC; NLI (mf); Indexed by SHGS

Civil Parish: Kilmoremoy
Map Grid: 15
RC Parish: see Kilmoremoy, Co. Mayo
Diocese: KA

Civil Parish: Kilmorgan
Map Grid: 22
RC Parish: see Emlaghfad
Diocese: AC

Civil Parish: Kilross
Map Grid: 29
RC Parish: Sowey, see Kilmacallan
Diocese: EL

Civil Parish: Kilshalvy
Map Grid: 26
RC Parish: see Kilturra, Co. Mayo
Diocese: AC

Civil Parish: Kilturra
Map Grid: 25
RC Parish: see Co. Mayo
Diocese: AC

Civil Parish: Kilvarnet
Map Grid: 18
RC Parish: see Ballysadare
Diocese: AC

Civil Parish: Rossinver
Map Grid: 2
RC Parish: see Rossinver (3), Co. Leitrim
Diocese: KM

Civil Parish: St. John's
Map Grid: 6
RC Parish: Sligo
Diocese: EL
Earliest Record: b. 10.1858; m. 10.1858
Status: LC; NLI (mf); Indexed by SHGS

Civil Parish: Shancough
Map Grid: 36
RC Parish: Geevagh, see Kilmactranny
Diocese: EL

Civil Parish: Skreen
Map Grid: 12
RC Parish: Skreen and Dromard
Diocese: KA
Earliest Record: b. 7.1848; m. 7.1848
Missing Dates: m. 8.1869–7.1878
Status: LC; NLI (mf); Indexed by SHGS

Civil Parish: Tawnagh
Map Grid: 33
RC Parish: Riverstown, see Kilmacallan
Diocese: EL

Civil Parish: Templeboy
Map Grid: 11
RC Parish: Templeboy and Kilmacshalgan
Diocese: KA
Earliest Record: b. 9.1815; m. 10.1815; d. 11.1815
Missing Dates: b. 11.1816–5.1826, 11.1838–6.1868;
m. 12.1837–1.1868; d. 11.1816–10.1824, 12.1833
Status: LC; NLI (mf); Indexed by SHGS

Civil Parish: Toomour
Map Grid: 24
RC Parish: part Drumrat; part Toomore, Co. Mayo
Diocese: AC

Commercial and Social Directories

1824

J. Pigot's *City of Dublin and Hibernian Provincial Directory* includes traders, nobility, gentry, and clergy lists of Ballisodare, Ballymote, Collooney, and Sligo.

1839

"Sligo Independent's" *Sligo-Derry Directory* lists traders, gentry, etc. SLC film 100179.

1846

Slater's *National Commercial Directory of Ireland* lists nobility, clergy, traders, etc., in Ballymote, Collooney and Ballysodare, and Sligo.

1856

Slater's *Royal National Commercial Directory of Ireland* lists nobility, gentry, clergy, traders, etc., in Ballymote, Collooney and Ballysodare, and Sligo.

1865

Sligo Independent Almanac.

1870

Slater's *Directory of Ireland* contains trade, nobility, and clergy lists for Ballymote, Collooney and Ballysodare, and Sligo.

1881

Slater's *Royal National Commercial Directory of Ireland* contains lists of traders, clergy, nobility, and farmers in adjoining parishes of the towns of Ballymote, Collooney and Ballysodare, Enniscrone and Easkey (see Ballina, Co. Mayo), and Sligo.

1889

Sligo Independent Directory of Ballymote, Cliffoney, Easkey, Coolaney, Drumcliff, Collooney, Carney, Dromore West, Riverstown and Bunnemadden, Rosses Point and Enniscrone, Sligo, and Tubbercurry.

1894

Slater's *Royal National Directory of Ireland* lists traders, police, teachers, farmers, and private residents in each of the towns, villages, and parishes of the county.

Family History

Pedigrees of Co. Sligo Families. McDonagh Mss. No. 23, Sligo Co. Library.

Downey, L. *A History of the Protestant Downeys of Cos. Sligo, Leitrim, Fermanagh and Donegal* (also of the Hawksby family of Leitrim and Sligo). New York, 1931.

Byrne, Celeste. "Hillas of Co. Sligo." *Ir. Anc.* 4 (1972): 26–29.

Irwin—see Co. Roscommon.

The McDermots of Moylurg. Typescript in Sligo Co. Library.

Pedigrees of the McDonagh Clan of Corann and Tirerill and Other Families of Co. Sligo. McDonagh Mss. No. 1, Sligo Co. Library.

The McDonagh Family of Co. Sligo. McDonagh Mss. No. 5, Sligo Co. Library.

O'Connor, Watson B. *The O'Connor Family: Families of Daniel and Matthias O'Connor of Corsallagh House, Achonry, Co. Sligo, Ireland, A.D. 1750*. Brooklyn, 1914.

Internet information on O'Kelly is at http://shaw.iol.ie/~okelly/oksligo.htm.

"The Family of Wood, Co. Sligo." *Ir. Gen.* 3 (8) (1963): 300–09; 3 (9) (1964): 364–65.

Jones, W.G. "The Wynnes of Sligo and Leitrim." Manorhamilton: Drumlin Publications, 1994. ISBN: I-873437-07-2.

Gravestone Inscriptions

Most gravestone inscriptions for this county have been indexed by the Co. Sligo Heritage and Genealogy Society (see Research Services at the end of the chapter).

Calry: GO IGRS Collection.

Sligo-St. John's (C of I): *Church and Parish of St. John*, Tyndall.

Sligo Abbey: GO IGRS Collection.

Newspapers

Although there was a Sligo paper, *The Sligo Journal*, published as early as 1807, there are no copies of it before 1822. Mayo, Galway, and other county papers may also be consulted for early notices of relevance to this county.

Title: *The Champion* or *Sligo News* (continued as *Sligo Champion* from 1853)
Published in: Sligo, 1836–current
NLI Holdings: 10.1879–in progress (with gaps)
Sligo Co. Library Holdings: 1836–70; 1897–1925
BL Holdings: 6.1836–in progress

Title: *Sligo Chronicle*
Published in: Sligo, 1850–93
Sligo Co. Library Holdings: 4.1850–4.1893

Title: *Sligo Independent*
Published in: Sligo, 1855–1961
NLI Holdings: 1.1879–12.1961 (with gaps)
Sligo Co. Library Holdings: 9.1855–12.1859 (with gaps)
BL Holdings: 9.1855–7.1869; odd numbers 1870; 1.1875–7.1876; 2–9.1877; 3.1879–9.1921

Title: *Sligo Journal*
Published in: Sligo, ca. 1807–66
NLI Holdings: 3–12.1823
Sligo Co. Library Holdings: 3–7.1822; 1828–3.1866
BL Holdings: 1.1828–3.1866

Title: *Sligo Observer*
Published in: Sligo, 1828–31
NLI Holdings: 10.1828–2.1831
Sligo Co. Library Holdings: 10.1828–2.1831
BL Holdings: 10.1828–2.1831

Wills and Administrations

A discussion of the types of records, where they are held, and their availability and value is given in the Wills section of the introduction. The availability of prerogative wills, administrations, and marriage license records is also described in the relevant parts of the same section. Where available, published sources of these records are given in the Miscellaneous Sources section.

Pre-1858 Wills and Administrations

Prerogative Wills. See the introduction.

Consistorial Wills. County Sligo is in the dioceses of Killala, Elphin, and Achonry, with one parish in Ardagh and one in Kilmore. The guide to Catholic parish records in this chapter shows the diocese to which each civil parish belonged. The wills of residents of each diocese were usually proven within that diocese (see the Wills section for exceptions). The following records survive:

Wills

See the introduction. County Sligo Wills (1705–32): NLI ms. 2164.

Abstracts

See the introduction.

Indexes

Killala and Achonry (1698–1838). *Ir. Gen.* 3 (2): 506–19; *Ir. Anc.* 7: 55–61. Ardagh—see Co. Longford. Kilmore—see Co. Cavan. Index to Ardagh Wills and Administrations. SLC film 824242. Index to Killala and Achonry Wills, pub. by Smyth-Wood. SLC 941.5 A1.

Post-1858 Wills and Administrations

This county was served by the District Registry of Ballina. The surviving records are kept in the NAI. Records include: Ballina District Will Books (1865–1899). NAI; SLC film 100925-6.

Marriage Licenses

Indexes

Elphin, Killala, and Achonry (1740–1850). NAI; SLC film 100868. Kilmore and Ardagh (1691–1845). NAI; SLC film 100869.

Miscellaneous Sources

"Further Notes on the High Sheriffs of Co. Sligo." *Ir. Gen.* 1 (1) (1937): 16–18; 2 (7) (1949): 197–203; 2 (9) (1952): 269–75.

McDonagh, J. *History of Ballymote and the Parish of Emlaghfad.* 1936.

From Plain to Hill—A Short History of the Parish of Achonry. Achonry/Mullinabreena Developing West Group, Mayo, 1995. Contains school rolls, census returns, and other local material.

Farry, M. *Killoran and Coolaney; a Local History.* 1985.

McGuinn, J. *Curry.* 1984. Well-researched parish history.

McPartlan, J. *Statistical Survey of Co. Sligo.* Dublin Society, 1801.

McTernan, J. *Historic Sligo: A Bibliographical Introduction to the Antiquities and History of Co. Sligo.* 1965.

O'Rourke, Rev. T. *History of the Parishes of Ballysadare and Killarnet.* 1878.

O'Rourke, Rev. T. *History of Sligo, Town and County.* 2 vols. 1889.

Wood-Martin, W.G. *History of Sligo.* 3 vols. 1882–1892.

McGuinn, J. *Sligo Men in the Great War–1914–1918.* Belturbet, Co. Cavan: Naughan Press, 1994. List of Sligo men killed (with addresses).

Estate records of the Cooper family, 1775–1872: NLI Mss. 3050–3060 and NLI Mss. 9753–57. Rentals and accounts of tenants in townlands of the civil parishes of Achonry, Ahamlish, Ballsadare, Ballysumaghan, Drumcolumb, Drumcliff, and Killery.

Estate records of the Lord Lorton Estate, 1740–1900: NLI Mss. 3104, 3105. Leases of small and large tenants in the civil parishes of Aghanagh, Drumcolomb, Kilfree, Killaraght, Kilmacallan, Kilshalvey, and Toomour.

Estate records of Owen Wynne's Estate, 1737–1825: NLI Mss. 5780–5782 and NLI Mss. 3311–13. Rentals and expense books of tenants in the civil parishes of Ahamlish, Ballysadare, Calry, Drumcliff, Killoran, St. John's, Tawnagh, and Templeboy.

Research Sources and Services

Libraries and Information Sources

Sligo County Library, The Courthouse, Sligo. Ph: (071) 42212. This library has a very extensive collection of local history material, including maps, periodicals, books, the 1901 census, *Griffith's Valuation*, *Tithe Applotment* books, and various other local sources.

Research Services

Co. Sligo Heritage and Genealogy Society, Aras Reddan, Temple St., Sligo, Ireland. Ph: (071) 43728. This is the official IGP center for the county. It has indexed all of the church registers of the county and also has access to the usual local history sources. Researchers are advised to contact the center for an updated list of registers, and other sources, indexed. A research service is provided for a fee.

See also Research Services in Dublin in the introduction.

Societies

Co. Sligo Heritage and Genealogy Society (see address above)

Ballymote Heritage Society, Ms. Betty Conlon, Graniamore P.Q., Ballymote, Co. Sligo

Sligo Field Club, Mr. Martin Timoney, Keash, Co. Sligo

Sligo Civil Parishes as Numbered on Map

1. Ahamlish
2. Roseinver
3. Drumcliff
4. Calry
5. Killaspugbrone
6. St. John's
7. Kilmacowen
8. Kilglass
9. Easky
10. Kilmacshalgan
11. Templeboy (2 pts.)
12. Skreen
13. Dromard
14. Castleconor
15. Kilmoremoy
16. Ballysadare
17. Killoran
18. Kilvarnet
19. Achonry
20. Kilmacteige
21. Emlaghfad
22. Kilmorgan
23. Cloonoghil
24. Toomour
25. Kilturra
26. Kilshalvy (2 pts.)
27. Drumrat (2 pts.)
28. Killerry
29. Kilross
30. Ballysumaghan
31. Ballynakill
32. Drumcolumb (4 pts.)
33. Tawnagh
34. Kilmacallan
35. Killadoon
36. Shancough
37. Kilmactranny
38. Aghanagh
39. Kilfree
40. Kilcolman
41. Killaraght

Sligo Civil Parishes in Alphabetical Order

Achonry: 19
Aghanagh: 38
Ahamlish: 1
Ballynakill: 31
Ballysadare: 16
Ballysumaghan: 30
Calry: 4
Castleconor: 14
Cloonoghil: 23
Dromard: 13
Drumcliff: 3
Drumcolumb (4 pts.): 32
Drumrat (2 pts.): 27
Easky: 9
Emlaghfad: 21
Kilcolman: 40
Kilfree: 39
Kilglass: 8
Killadoon: 35
Killaraght: 41
Killaspugbrone: 5
Killerry: 28
Killoran: 17
Kilmacallan: 34
Kilmacowen: 7
Kilmacshalgan: 10
Kilmacteige: 20
Kilmactranny: 37
Kilmoremoy: 15
Kilmorgan: 22
Kilross: 29
Kilshalvy (2 pts.): 26
Kilturra: 25
Kilvarnet: 18
Roseinver: 2
Shancough: 36
Skreen: 12
St. John's: 6
Tawnagh: 33
Templeboy (2 pts.): 11
Toomour: 24

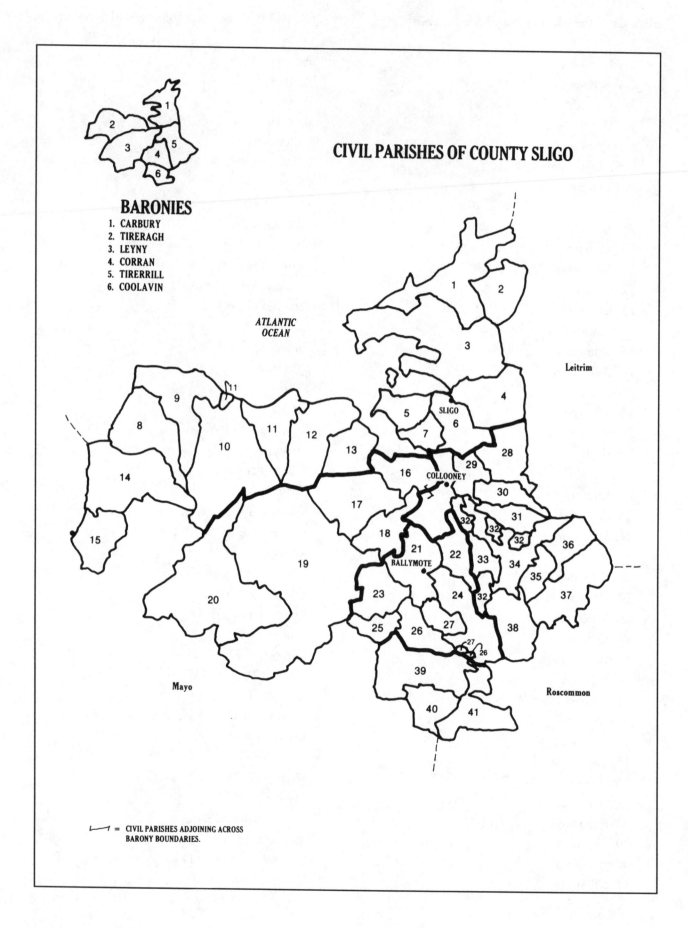

CIVIL PARISHES OF COUNTY SLIGO

BARONIES

1. CARBURY
2. TIRERAGH
3. LEYNY
4. CORRAN
5. TIRERRILL
6. COOLAVIN

ATLANTIC
OCEAN

Leitrim

SLIGO

COLLOONEY

BALLYMOTE

Mayo

Roscommon

⌐ = CIVIL PARISHES ADJOINING ACROSS
BARONY BOUNDARIES.

County Tipperary

A Brief History

Tipperary is an inland county with an area of just over one million acres, eighty percent of which is arable agricultural land. The county contains the towns of Clonmel, Nenagh, Thurles, Roscrea, Tipperary, Cashel, Cahir, Templemore, Carrick-on-Suir, and Fethard.

Historically, the county was partly in the old Gaelic territory of Ormond and partly in Thomond. The major Irish families included the O'Fogartys, O'Briens, and O'Kennedys. Other names associated with the county are O'Moloney, O'Mulryan or Ryan, Meagher or Maher, Hourigan, Hayes, and Gleeson.

The county was invaded by the Normans in 1172. It was subsequently granted to Theobald Walter, who was given the title Chief Butler of Ireland, from which the family took the surname "Butler." Among the Norman names now found in the county are Prendergast, Burke, Purcell, Fitzgerald, Everard, St. John, and Grace.

As elsewhere in the country, the Norman families assimilated into the local population, and British cultural and administrative influence gradually waned. Among the vast majority of the people, English influence was negligible until the seventeenth century. Gaelic was the common language of the people, and even as late as 1841, approximately eight percent of the population spoke only Gaelic.

In 1641, the Irish and Norman chieftains of Tipperary joined the rebellion of the Catholic Confederacy, but were defeated by Oliver Cromwell in 1649. The lands of those who had rebelled were divided among English adventurers and among the soldiers of Cromwell's army. Most of these soldiers had no interest in the land and sold it to their officers and others who thereby managed to put together large estates in the county. There was little settlement by soldiers in the county.

Tipperary was relatively badly affected by the Great Famine of 1845–47. The population reached a peak of 436,000 in 1841. Following the large-scale failure of the potato crop, the population declined rapidly. Almost 70,000 people died in the county between 1845 and 1850, particularly in the years 1849 and 1850.

Huge numbers of people are known to have emigrated from the county during the nineteenth century. About 190,000 people are estimated to have emigrated from Tipperary between 1841 and 1891, particularly in the 1840s, '50s, and '60s. In the same period, the rural population fell from 364,000 to 134,000 and the town population from 71,000 to 39,000.

County Tipperary is a largely agricultural county, with industries in the larger towns. It has a current population of 135,000.

Census and Census Substitutes

1551

Lists of Jurors in Various Towns in Co. Tipperary and of the County Generally, With a Writ to the Sheriff for Summoning Juries. NLI D 2553.

1595

Names of the Freeholders in Co. Tipperary, 1595. NLI P1700.

1641

Book of Survey and Distribution. NLI Ms. 977; SLC film 973121.

1641–63

"Proprietors of Fethard, Co. Tipperary." *Ir. Gen.* 6 (1) (1980): 5–8.

1653

"The Names of Soldiers and Adventurers who Received Land in Co. Tipperary Under the Cromwellian Settlement, 1653." In Prendergast, John, *The Cromwellian Settlement of Ireland.* Dublin, 1922, pp. 386–400.

1654–56

Simington, R.C. The Civil Survey A.D. 1654-1656. County of Tipperary. Vol. 1: Eastern and Southern parts; vol. 2: Western and Northern Baronies. Dublin: Stationery Office, 1934. NLI I 6551; SLC film 0973121.

1659

"Census" of Ireland. Edited by S. Pender. Dublin: Stationery Office, 1939. NLI I6551. SLC film 924648.

1662–90

Cause list of Chancery Pleadings at the Palatine Court. DKPRI 6th Report, p. 47–72 (gives plaintiffs, defendants, and dates).

1664

"The Dispossessed Landowners of Ireland: Co. Tipperary." *Ir. Gen.* 4 (5) (1972): 429–34.

1666–68

Three Hearth Money Rolls. Printed as *Tipperary's Families*, edited by Thomas Laffan, p. 9–193. Dublin, 1911.

1750

"Catholics in Parishes of Barnane, Bourney, Corbally, Killavanough, Killea, Rathnaveoge, Roscrea, Templeree, Templetouhy." *Ir. Gen.* 4 (6) (1973): 578–83; NLI ms. 8913.

1761

Militia List of Counties . . . Tipperary, etc. GO Ms. 680.

1766

Householders of the Parishes of Ardmayle, Athassel,* Ballintemple, Ballingarry, Ballygriffin,* Ballysheehan, Boytonrath, Brickendown,* Bruis, Cashel (St. John), Cashel (St. Patrick's Rock), Castletownarra (Protestants only), Clerihan, Clonbeg, Cloneen, Clonoulty, Cloonbulloge, Clonpet, Colman, Cordangan, Corrogue, Cullen, Dangandargan,* Drum (Ballycahill and Templebeg-United), Duntryleague, Erry, Fethard (Crompes and Coolmunddry), Gaile, Grean, Horeabbey,* Killardry, Killbrugh, Killea,* Kilconnell,

Kilfeacle, Killevinogue,* Knockgraffon,* Killnerath,* Kiltynan, Lattin, Magorban, Mealiffe,* New Chapel* (also specifies members of households, e.g., wife, son, etc.), Oughterliege, Pepperstown, Railstown, Rathcoole, Rathleyny, Relickmurry,* Redcity, Shronell, Solloghodmore and Solloghodbeg, Templemore,* Templeneiry, Templenoe, Tipperary, Toom (Doon and Donaghill), Uskeane, Youghalarra (Protestants only). NAI 1A 46 49. NAI Parl. Returns, 682–701.

Parishes of Ballingarry and Uskeane. GO 536 and GO Ms. 665; SLC film 100213. Killea* is also on NAI M3585 and RCB Ms. 37. Youghalarra and Uskeane are on RCB Ms. 37. GO 572; SLC film 100224.

*Numbers in the household are also given in these parishes.

1775

Catholic Qualification Roll Extracts (368 names, addresses, and occupations). 59th Report DKPRI: 50–84.

Landowners and their representatives; also freeholders in Co. Tipperary. GO Ms. 442.

1776

Lists of Voters. NAI M4878 and NAI mf 4912; GO 536.

A Register of the Freeholders in Co. Tipperary. NAI film 1321–2; GO Ms. 442; SLC film 100181.

1786

Some Catholic inhabitants of Thurles town and parish. *Dublin Evening Post,* 28 October 1786.

1799

Census of Carrick-on-Suir (gives name, age, religion, and occupation of all inhabitants). NLIP 28; BM ms. 11,722. A descriptive note on the census is in *Ir. Gen.* 5 (2) (1975): 271–72; *Decies* 21 (1982): 29–31.

1802

"Some Game Licenses of 1802." *Ir. Anc.* 8 (1): 38–47 (lists names and addresses of licensees in Clonmel, Cashel, and Tipperary).

1821

Householders in parish of Killinafe (East and West Curroghaneddy townlands only). NAI M 242 and M 346. SLC film 100181.

Extracts (selected surnames) from parishes of St. Nicholas, Grangemockler, Newchapel, Tipperary. GO Ms. 685; SLC film 100158.

1823–38

Tithe Applotment Survey (see introduction). List of tithe

defaulters for 1831 (compiled by S. McCormac) is in NAI and NLI; see *Irish Roots* 1 (1997): 25-28.

1832-36

"Names of Excise License Holders and Applicants in Cashel and Clonmel" (180 names and addresses). *Parl. Papers* 1837/38, 13 (2): Appendix 10, 13.

1832-37

"List of Voters Registered in the Boroughs of Clonmel and Cashel." *Parl. Papers* 1837, 11 (2): 217-33 (approximately nine hundred names, occupations, and residences in Clonmel; over 350 names and occupations in Cashel).

1834

"Census of Parish of Templebredon." *J. N. Munster Arch. and Hist. Soc.* 17 (1975): 91-101 (lists the heads of households in each townland, with numbers of males and females).

1835

Census of Parishes of Birdhill and Newport (gives the name of the householder in each townland or street with numbers of males and females in each household). NLI P 1561.

1837

"Lists of Freemen (since 1831) of Cashel and Clonmel" (120 names, occupations, and residences). *Parl. Papers* 1837/38, 13 (2): Appendix 3.

"Occupants of Clonmel, by Street, Giving Description of Premises and Valuation." *Parl. Papers* 1837, 11 (2): 247-64.

1840-44

"Names of All Persons Qualified to Serve as Jurors in the Northern Division of the County of Tipperary." *Parl. Papers* 1844, 43 (380): 1-29.

1845

List of Subscribers to Roscrea Chapel. In Catholic parish register of Roscrea and Kyle (see civil parish of Roscrea and Kyle in Roman Catholic records section).

1848

Petitioners for William Smith O'Brien. Names of male petitioners in Borrisokane, Carrick-on-Suir, Cashel, and Clonmel. NAI 1848/180.

1851

Griffith's Valuation (see introduction).

1864-70

"Census of Protestants in the parishes of Shanrahan and Tullagherton, Co. Tipperary, in 1864-1870." *Ir. Anc.* 16 (2) (1984): 61-67.

1873-80

"Census of Protestant Parishioners in Clogheen Union, Co. Tipperary, in 1873, '77, and '80." *Ir. Anc.* 17 (1) (1985): 25-30.

1901

Census. NAI (see introduction). SLC (mf).

1911

Census. NAI.

Church Records

Church of Ireland

See the introduction for a description of Church of Ireland records and their major repositories. Many C of I records were lost in the PRO fire of 1922. These are indicated as "Lost." However, as Church of Ireland records were effectively state records, the records of marriage (from 1845) are also in the General Registrar's Office. Many are still in local custody (LC), while others are in one of a variety of other archives (e.g., RCBL or NAI). Many of the Church of Ireland registers have been indexed by the heritage centers which operate in the county (see Research Services at the end of the chapter). These include Tipperary North Family History Foundation and the Bru Boru Heritage Centre. Searches of the indexes will be conducted by the centers for a fee. Those indexed are noted as "Indexed by TNFHF" or "by BBHC" as appropriate.

Abington (or Tuogh)
Earliest Records: b. 1811; m. 1813; d. 1810
Status: LC; Indexed by TNFHF (b/m. to 1911; d. to 1984)

Aghnameadle
Earliest Records: b. 1834; m. 1834; d. 1834
Status: LC; Indexed by TNFHF (b/m. to 1911; d. to 1984)

Aghlishcloghane
Earliest Records: b. 1828; m. 1845; d. 1828
Status: LC; Indexed by TNFHF (b/m. to 1911; d. to 1985)

Ardcroney
Earliest Records: b. 1834; m. 1834; d. 1834
Status: LC; Indexed by TNFHF (m. 1845-1911)

Ardfinnan
Earliest Records: b. 1877-
Status: RCBL (b. 1877-1937)

Ardmayle
Earliest Records: b. 1815-; d. 1815-
Status: LC; NAI M5889, 5890 (b. 1815-71; d. 1815-77)

Athassel or Relickmurry
Status: Lost

Ballinaclough
Earliest Records: b. 1877; m. 1845; d. 1877
Status: LC; Indexed by TNFHF (to 1911)

Ballingarry
Earliest Records: b. 1785; m. 1785; d. 1785
Missing Dates: b. 1803-15; m. 1803-15; d. 1803-1815
Status: LC; NAI M5131 (b. 1816-18); Indexed by TNFHF (b/d. 1877-1911; m. 1845-1911)

Ballintemple
Earliest Records: b. 1805-; m. 1805-; d. 1805-
Status: LC; NAI MFCI 13, M5880, M5931 (b. 1805-71; m. 1805-43; d. 1805-75)

Ballymackey
Earliest Records: b. 1877; m. 1845; d. 1877
Status: LC; Indexed by TNFHF (to 1911)

Ballysheehan
Status: Lost

Bansha (see Templeneiry)

Borrisnafarney
Earliest Records: b. 1828-; m. 1827-; d. 1827-
Status: LC; NAI MFCI 4 (b. 1828-77; m. 1827-51; d. 1827-76)

Borrisokane
Earliest Records: b. 1877; m. 1845; d. 1877
Status: LC; Indexed by TNFHF (b/m. to 1911; d. to 1985)

Borrisoleigh
Status: Lost

Cahir
Earliest Records: b. 1801; m. 1802; d. 1804
Status: LC; NAI MFCI 9, M5366 (b. 1805-73; m. 1802-48; d. 1825-72)

Carrick-on-Suir
Earliest Records: b. 1803-; m. 1804-; d. 1803-
Status: LC; NAI MFCI 9 (b. 1803-74; m. 1804-65; d. 1803-75)

Cashel
Earliest Records: b. 1668-; m. 1654-; d. 1668-
Status: LC; NLI P 1390 (b/d. 1668-1786; m. 1654-1842); NAI MFCI 7, M5366 (b/d. 1668-1842, m. 1654-1842)

Cashel Liberties
Earliest Records: m. 1654-57
Status: published by Parish Rec. Soc., vol. I

Castletownarra
Earliest Records: b. 1802-; m. 1803-; d. 1802-
Status: LC; NAI MFCI 5 (b. 1802-72; m. 1803-46; d. 1802-79); Indexed by TNFHF (b. 1802-1911; m. 1846-1911; d. 1850-1973)

Clogheen (see Shanrahan)

Clonbeg
Status: Lost

Clonmel-St. Mary
Earliest Records: b. 1766-; m. 1768-; d. 1767-
Status: LC; RCBL (b. 1791-1807); NAI MFCI 8 and 9 (b. 1766-1874; m. 1768-1847; d. 1767-1873)

Clonoulty
Earliest Records: b. 1766-; m. 1768-; d. 1767-
Status: NAI MFCI 13 (b. 1766-1874; m. 1768-1847; d. 1767-1873)

Cloughjordan
Earliest Records: b. 1846-72
Status: NAI MFCI 4

Corbally
Earliest Records: b. 1834; d. 1849
Status: LC; NAI MFCI 4 (b. 1834-49, d. 1849)

Cullen
Earliest Records: b. 1770; m. 1770; d. 1770
Status: LC

Derrygrath
Status: Lost

Donoghill (see also Templeneiry)
Earliest Records: b. 1856-; d. 1859-
Status: LC; NAI M5887, 5888 (b. 1856-74; d. 1859-78)

Dorrha
Earliest Records: b. 1880; m. 1848; d. 1884
Status: LC; Indexed by TNFHF (b/m. to 1911; d. to 1982)

Dunkerrin
Earliest Records: b. 1825-; m. 1826-; d. 1825-
Status: LC; NAI MFCI 4, M5888 (b. 1825-73; m. 1826-45; d. 1825-73)

Emly
Status: Lost

Fennor
Status: Lost

Fethard
Earliest Records: b. 1804-; m. 1804-; d. 1804-
Status: LC; NAI MFCI 12 (b. 1804-50; m. 1804-43; d. 1804-50)

Finnoe and Cloughprior
Earliest Records: b. 1886; m. 1846; d. 1886
Status: LC; Indexed by TNFHF (b/m. to 1911; d. to 1981)

Galbally
Status: Lost

Glankeen
Status: Lost

Holy Cross
Earliest Records: b. 1800–; d. 1876–
Status: LC; NAI M5930 (b. 1800–80; d. 1876–80)

Innislonnagh
Status: Lost

Kilbarron
Earliest Records: b. 1878; m. 1845
Status: LC; Indexed by TNFHF (to 1911)

Kilcooly
Status: Lost

Kilfithnone
Status: Lost

Kilkeary
Status: Lost

Killaloan
Status: Lost

Killenaule
Earliest Records: b. 1742–1801
Status: NL MS 2048

Killodiernan
Earliest Records: b. 1880; m. 1847; d. 1880
Status: LC; Indexed by TNFHF (to 1911)

Killoscully
Earliest Records: b. 1884; m. 1846; d. 1886
Status: LC; Indexed by TNFHF (to 1911)

Kilmastulla and Templeachally
Earliest Records: b. 1755; m. 1845; d. 1879
Status: LC; Indexed by TNFHF (b/m. to 1911; d. to 1969)

Kilmore
Earliest Records: b. 1886; m. 1847; d. 1886
Status: LC; Indexed by TNFHF (to 1911)

Kilruane
Earliest Records: b. 1880; m. 1845; d. 1877
Status: LC; Indexed by TNFHF (to 1911)

Kilshane
Status: Lost

Kilvemnon
Status: Lost

Kyle and Knock
Earliest Records: b. 1845; m. 1846
Status: LC; Indexed by TNFHF (to 1880)

Knockgraffon
Status: Lost

Lismalin
Status: Lost

Lisronagh
Status: Lost

Lockeene or Loughkeen
Earliest Records: b. 1879; m. 1848; d. 1880
Status: LC; Indexed by TNFHF (b/m. to 1911; d. to 1985)

Lorrha
Earliest Records: b. 1877; m. 1846; d. 1880
Status: LC; Indexed by TNFHF (b/m. to 1911; d. to 1985)

Loughmoe
Status: Lost

Magarban
Earliest Records: b. 1804–; m. 1804–; d. 1805–
Status: LC; NAI M5278, 5280/1 (b. 1804–78; m. 1804–14; d. 1805–73)

Magorban
Status: Lost

Mealiffe
Earliest Records: b. 1791; m. 1795; d. 1792
Status: LC and NAI M5930

Modreeny
Earliest Records: b. 1842–; m. 1841–; d. 1827–
Status: LC; NAI NFCI 30 (b. 1842–73; m. 1841–44; d. 1842–1903); Indexed by TNFHF (to 1911); SLC film 992663 (extracts 1786–1827)

Monsea (Dromineer, Knigh, and Cloghprior)
Earliest Records: b. 1886; m. 1845; d. 1880
Status: LC; Indexed by TNFHF (to 1911)

Moyne
Status: Lost

Nenagh
Earliest Records: b. 1877; m. 1845; d. 1877
Status: LC; Indexed by TNFHF (to 1911)

Newchapel
Status: Lost

Newport (St. John's) or Newport Union
Earliest Records: b. 1755–; m. 1755–; d. 1756–
Status: NAI MFCI 2, M222 (b. 1755–1842; m. 1789–1872; d. 1783–1836); Indexed by TNFHF (b/m. to 1911; d. to 1985)

Rathronan
Status: Lost

Relickmurry (see Athassel)

Roscrea
Earliest Records: b. 1784–; m. 1791–; d. 1792–
Status: LC; NAI MFCI 3, M5222 (b. 1784–1878; m. 1791–1845; d. 1792–1872); Indexed by TNFHF (b. 1810–1830; m. 1810–1880)

St. John Baptist (Cashel)
Earliest Records: b. 1668; m. 1668; d. 1668

Status: LC

St. John Newport
Earliest Records: b. 1782; m. 1782; d. 1782
Status: LC

St. Mary-Clonmel (see Clonmel, St. Mary)

Shanrahan and Templetenny
Status: Lost

Shronell and Lattin
Status: Lost

Templederry
Earliest Records: b. 1874; m. 1875; d. 1845
Status: LC; Indexed by TNFHF (to 1911)

Templemichael (no church, no records)

Templemore
Earliest Records: b. 1812; m. 1812; d. 1812 (entries of b/m/d. 1791–1809 in vestry book for 1789–1872)
Status: LC; NAI MFCI 7, M5364 (b. 1791–1877; m. 1812–45; d. 1791–1891)

Templeneiry or Bansha
Status: Lost

Templenor (see Tipperary)

Templetenny (see also Shanrahan)
Status: Lost

Templetuohy
Status: Lost

Terryglass
Earliest Records: b. 1809–; m. 1809–; d. 1809–
Status: RCBL (b. 1809–1862; m. 1809–1916; d. 1809–1882); NAI MFCI 3, M5222 (b/d. 1809–77; m. 1809–53); Indexed by TNFHF (b/m. to 1911; d. to 1982)

Thurles
Status: Lost

Tipperary
Earliest Records: b. 1779–; m. 1779–; d. 1779–
Status: LC; NAI MFCI 6 (b. 1779–1873; m. 1779–1845; d. 1779–1875)

Toem (includes entries from Holyford Mines)
Earliest Records: b. 1802–; m. 1804–; d. 1803–
Status: LC; NAI M5130 (b. 1802–66; m. 1804–45; d. 1803–77); SLC film 924692 (b. 1802–65; m. 1802–45; d. 1802–77)

Tubrid
Earliest Records: b. 1892–
Status: RCBL (b. 1892–1905)

Tullamelan/Tullmellin
Earliest Records: b. 1818–; m. 1831–; d. 1829–
Status: LC; NAI MFCI 7, M5351/2 (b. 1818–77; m. 1831–40; d. 1829–75)

Whitechurch (see Tubrid)

Youghalarra
Status: Lost

Society of Friends (Quaker)
See the introduction for an account of Quaker records. The records for Tipperary include: Tipperary Monthly Meeting Register (1618–1860). FHL, Dublin (b. 1618–1860; m. 1636–1858; d. 1657–1859).

Roman Catholic
Many of the Catholic registers have been indexed by the three heritage centers which operate in the county (see Research Services at the end of the chapter). These are Tipperary North Family History Foundation (TNFHF), the Bru Boru Heritage Centre (BBHC), and Tipperary Heritage Unit (THU). Searches of the indexes will be conducted by these centers for a fee. Some parishes which are on the borders of Co. Waterford are also indexed by Waterford Heritage Ltd. (see Waterford chapter). Those indexed are noted as "Indexed by . . ." as appropriate. Microfilm copies of all registers (except those for the Catholic diocese of Cashel and Emly) are also available in the National Library of Ireland (NLI), and through the LDS library system.

Civil Parish: Abington
Map Grid: N28
RC Parish: Murroe, see Abington, Co. Limerick
Diocese: EM

Civil Parish: Aghacrew
Map Grid: S4
RC Parish: Annacarty, see Donohill
Diocese: CA

Civil Parish: Aghnameadle
Map Grid: N38
RC Parish: Toomevara
Diocese: KL
Earliest Record: b. 3.1831; m. 8.1830
Missing Dates: b. 6.1856–5.1861; m. 9.1836–6.1861
Status: LC; NLI (mf); Indexed by TNFHF (to 1911)

Civil Parish: Aglishcloghane
Map Grid: N4
RC Parish: see Borrisokane
Diocese: KL

Civil Parish: Ardcrony
Map Grid: N13
RC Parish: Cloughjordan, see Modreeny
Diocese: KL

Civil Parish: Ardfinnan
Map Grid: S94
RC Parish: Ardfinnan
Diocese: LS
Earliest Record: b. 12.1809; m. 4.1817
Missing Dates: m. 2.1822–1.1827

William Scurlocke of Ballyngronty and Juane Kenedy of the same
in the Barrony of Clañwilliam married 13° January 1656°.

Teige Mulcroe of Boytonrath and Margarett Dooly of Woodins-
towne in the Barrony of Middlethird married 14° January
1656°.

Morgan Mackan of Darrymore and Catherin Ryane of the same
in the Barrony of Kilnemañagh married 16° January 1656°.

John Breanagh of Shanbally Duffe and Catherin Purcell of the
same in the Barrony of Middlethird married 20° Januarii
1656°.

Richard Ryane of Rathkenane and Margarett Dwyer of the same
in the Barrony of Kilnemannagh married 20° Januarij 1656°.

Edward Coñill of Kylltane and Margarett ny Danniell of Bansagh
in the Barrony of Clañwilliam married 20° Januarii 1656°.

Thomas Hiffernane of Ballynry and Gyles Meagher of the same
in the Barrony of Middlethird married 1° ffebr. 1656°.

Redmond Magrath of Ballymore and Ellis Butler of Culinure
in the Barrony of Kyllnemañagh married 17° Oct. 1656.

Donnogh Ryane of Cashell and Catherin Meehane of the same
married 4° Nov. 1656.

Teige mcConnor of Culinure and Uny Ryane of Clonisbeo in the
Barrony of Kylnemannagh married 4° Nov. 1656°.

Edmond Magrath of Cashell and Catherin Donoghie of Croghtina-
bluolie in the Barrony of Middlethird married 4° Nov. 1656°.

Teige Ryane of Dundrome and Margarett Ryane of Ballisidie
in the Barrony of Kylnemañagh married 12° Novbris 1656°.

Roger Higgin of Clounoultie in the Barrony of Kylnemañagh &
Honnora Devane of Ardmaile in the Barrony of Middlethird
married 13° Nov. 1656°.

Edmond Meagher of Cashell & Ellan Hacckett of the same married
13° Nov. 1656°.

Edmond Wailsh of Clounoultie and Sara Ryane of the same in
the Barrony of Middlethird married 15° Nov. 1656°.

Donnogh Arra of Ardmayle and Juane Dooly of the same in the
Barrony of Middlethird married 25° Nov. 1656°.

John fflood of Clonoultie in the Barrony of Kylnemañagh & Juane
Boorke of Collaghill in the Barrony of Eliogertie married
21 Dec. 1656°.

John Hickie of Boytonrath and Juane Hyffernane of the same
in the Barrony of Middlethird married 26° Decembr. 1656°.

Thomas Meagher of Cashell and Margarett ny Danniell of the
Barrony of Middlethird married 31° Dec. 1656°.

Willm Pemerton of Killteynane troop, and Añ Coogiñ of the Towne
of ffithard spinster married 5° Martij 1656.

Daniell ò Hallurane of Greistowne in the Barrony of Slyevardagh,
& Margarett Lemeasny of the same married March the 20th
1656.

John Henes of the parrish of Drañgane in the Barrony of Middlethird, & Catherin Bryen of the same married March the 16th
1656.

Derby Dalloghonty of Drañgane aforesd, & Juañ Carroll of the
same married die predicto

John Shea & Juañ Haly of Drañgane aforesd married the day
aforesd.

John Meagher of Priestowne in the sd Barrony, & Ellis Mahuny
of the same married March the 16th 56.

A page of 1656 marriage records from a published copy of the *Register of
the Liberties of Cashel* (County Tipperary), Parish Register Society of
Ireland, Vol. 4 (Dublin, 1907).

Status: LC; NLI (mf); Indexed by WHL (to 1900)

Civil Parish: Ardmayle
Map Grid: S37
RC Parish: Boherlahan and Dualla
Diocese: CA
Earliest Record: b. 1736; m. 1736
Missing Dates: b. 1740-4.1810; m. 1740-4.1810;
2.1822-1.1827
Status: LC; NLI (mf); Indexed by THU (to 1900)

Civil Parish: Athnid
Map Grid: N71
RC Parish: see Thurles
Diocese: CA

Civil Parish: Ballingarry (1) (Lower Ormond)
Map Grid: N10
RC Parish: Ballingarry (see also Borrisokane)
Diocese: KL
Earliest Record: b. 1842; m. 1842
Status: LC; NLI (mf); Indexed by TNFHF (to 1911)

Civil Parish: Ballingarry (2) (Slieveardagh)
Map Grid: S77
RC Parish: Ballingarry
Diocese: CA
Earliest Record: b. 6.1814; m. 4.1814
Missing Dates: b. 5.1827-8.1827; m. 2.1822-1.1826
Status: LC; NLI (mf); Indexed by THU

Civil Parish: Ballintemple
Map Grid: S6
RC Parish: Knockavilla, see Oughterleague
Diocese: CA

Civil Parish: Ballybacon
Map Grid: S97
RC Parish: see Ardfinnan
Diocese: LS

Civil Parish: Ballycahill
Map Grid: N68
RC Parish: see Holycross
Diocese: CA

Civil Parish: Ballyclerahan
Map Grid: S101
RC Parish: Clerihan
Diocese: CA
Earliest Record: b. 4.1852; m. 8.1852
Status: LC; NLI (mf); Indexed by THU (to 1900)

Civil Parish: Ballygibbon
Map Grid: N29
RC Parish: Cloughjordan, see Modreeny
Diocese: KL

Civil Parish: Ballygriffin
Map Grid: S14
RC Parish: Annacarty, see Donohill
Diocese: CA

Civil Parish: Ballymackey

Map Grid: N31
RC Parish: see Caher
Diocese: KL

Civil Parish: Ballymurreen
Map Grid: N79
RC Parish: see Moycarkey
Diocese: CA

Civil Parish: Ballynaclogh
Map Grid: N36
RC Parish: Silvermines, see Kilmore (2)
Diocese: KL

Civil Parish: Ballysheehan
Map Grid: S38
RC Parish: Boherlahan, etc., see Ardmayle
Diocese: CA

Civil Parish: Baptistgrange
Map Grid: S68
RC Parish: Powerstown, see Kilgrant
Diocese: LS

Civil Parish: Barnane-Ely
Map Grid: N51
RC Parish: see Drom and Inch
Diocese: CA

Civil Parish: Barretsgrange
Map Grid: S60
RC Parish: Fethard and Killusty, see Fethard
Diocese: CA

Civil Parish: Borrisnafarney
Map Grid: N47
RC Parish: Couraganeen, see Bourney
Diocese: KL

Civil Parish: Borrisokane
Map Grid: N8
RC Parish: Borrisokane-Aglish
Diocese: KL
Earliest Record: b. 6.1821; m. 7.1821
Missing Dates: m. 1.1844-10.1844
Status: LC; NLI (mf); Indexed by TNFHF (to 1911)

Civil Parish: Bourney
Map Grid: N45
RC Parish: Couraganeen, or Bourney and Corbally
Diocese: KL
Earliest Record: b. 7.1836; m. 6.1836
Missing Dates: b. 1873; m. 1873
Status: LC; NLI (mf); Indexed by TNFHF (to 1866)

Civil Parish: Boytonrath
Map Grid: S56
RC Parish: Golden, see Relickmurry
Diocese: CA

Civil Parish: Brickendown
Map Grid: S43
RC Parish: Boherlahan and Dualla, see Ardmayle
Diocese: CA

Civil Parish: Bruis
Map Grid: S27
RC Parish: see Lattin
Diocese: EM

Civil Parish: Buolick
Map Grid: S72
RC Parish: Gortnahoe
Diocese: CA
Earliest Record: b. 9.1805; m. 10.1805
Missing Dates: b. 12.1830–3.1831; m. 11.1830–10.1831
Status: LC; NLI (mf); Indexed by THU (to 1900)

Civil Parish: Burgesbeg
Map Grid: N22
RC Parish: Youghalarra-Burgess (or Burgess and Youghal)
Diocese: KL
Earliest Record: b. 10.1828; m. 10.1820
Status: LC; NLI (mf); Indexed by TNFHF (to 1911)

Civil Parish: Caher
Map Grid: S91
RC Parish: Caher
Diocese: LS
Earliest Record: b. 6.1776; m. 7.1776
Missing Dates: b. 3.1793–8.1809
Status: LC; NLI (mf); Indexed by WHL (b/m. 1776–1900)

Civil Parish: Carrick
Map Grid: S116
RC Parish: Carrick-on-Suir
Diocese: LS
Earliest Record: b. 9.1784; m. 1.1788
Missing Dates: b. 4.1803–5.1805, 7.1819–1.1823; m. 10.1803–1.1806, 2.1815–1.1823, 10.1825–1.1826
Status: LC; NLI (mf); Indexed by WHL (to 1900)

Civil Parish: Castletownarra
Map Grid: N19
RC Parish: Castletownarra
Diocese: KL
Earliest Record: b. 11.1849; m. 11.1849
Status: LC; NLI (mf); Indexing planned by TNFHF

Civil Parish: Clogher
Map Grid: S1
RC Parish: see Clonoulty
Diocese: CA

Civil Parish: Cloghprior
Map Grid: N12
RC Parish: Cloghprior and Monsea (Puckane)
Diocese: KL
Earliest Record: b. 2.1834; m. 2.1834
Missing Dates: b. ends 12.1865
Status: LC; NLI (mf); Indexed by TNFHF (to 1911)

Civil Parish: Clonbeg
Map Grid: S33

RC Parish: see Galbally, Co. Limerick
Diocese: CA

Civil Parish: Clonbullogue
Map Grid: S32
RC Parish: Bansha and Kilmoyler, see Templeneiry
Diocese: CA

Civil Parish: Cloneen or Cloyne
Map Grid: S54
RC Parish: see Drangan
Diocese: CA

Civil Parish: Clonoulty
Map Grid: S3
RC Parish: Clonoulty and Rossmore
Diocese: CA
Earliest Record: b. 10.1804; m. 10.1804
Missing Dates: m. 6.1809–10.1809
Status: LC; NLI (mf); Indexed by THU (to 1900)

Civil Parish: Clonpet
Map Grid: S28
RC Parish: part Lattin; part Tipperary
Diocese: EM

Civil Parish: Colman
Map Grid: S66
RC Parish: Clerihan, see Ballyclerahan
Diocese: CA

Civil Parish: Cooleagh
Map Grid: S45
RC Parish: see Killenaule
Diocese: CA

Civil Parish: Coolmundry
Map Grid: S63
RC Parish: Fethard and Killusty, see Fethard

Civil Parish: Corbally (see also Co. Offaly)
Map Grid: N43
RC Parish: Couraganeen, see Bourney
Diocese: KL

Civil Parish: Cordangan (or Cardangan)
Map Grid: S29
RC Parish: Lattin and Cullen, see Lattin; see also Tipperary
Diocese: EM

Civil Parish: Corroge
Map Grid: S25
RC Parish: see Tipperary
Diocese: EM

Civil Parish: Crohane
Map Grid: S78
RC Parish: see Ballingarry (2)
Diocese: CA

Civil Parish: Cullen
Map Grid: S17
RC Parish: Lattin and Cullen, see Lattin
Diocese: EM

Civil Parish: Cullenwaine
Map Grid: N46
RC Parish: see Dunkerrin, Co. Offaly
Diocese: KL

Civil Parish: Dangandargan
Map Grid: S49
RC Parish: Golden, see Relickmurry
Diocese: CA

Civil Parish: Derrygrath
Map Grid: S92
RC Parish: see Ardfinnan
Diocese: LS

Civil Parish: Dogstown
Map Grid: S57
RC Parish: part New Inn, see Knockgraffon; part
Golden, see Relickmurry
Diocese: CA

Civil Parish: Dolla
Map Grid: N35
RC Parish: part Silvermines, see Kilmore (2); part
Killanave, etc., see Kilnaneave
Diocese: KL

Civil Parish: Donaghmore
Map Grid: S67
RC Parish: Powerstown, see Kilgrant
Diocese: LS

Civil Parish: Donohill
Map Grid: S2
RC Parish: Annacarty and Donohill
Diocese: CA
Earliest Record: b. 5.1821; m. 5.1821
Status: LC; NLI (mf); Indexed by THU

Civil Parish: Doon
Map Grid: N57
RC Parish: see Co. Limerick
Diocese: EM

Civil Parish: Dorrha
Map Grid: N2
RC Parish: Lorrha and Dorrha, see Lorrha
Diocese: KL

Civil Parish: Drangan
Map Grid: S48
RC Parish: Drangan (and Cloyne)
Diocese: CA
Earliest Record: b. 1.1811; m. 1.1812
Missing Dates: m. 10.1846-1.1847
Status: LC; NLI (mf); Indexed by THU (to 1898)

Civil Parish: Drom
Map Grid: N62
RC Parish: Drom and Inch
Diocese: CA
Earliest Record: b. 1809; m. 1807
Status: LC; NLI (mf); Indexed by THU (to 1900)

Civil Parish: Dromineer
Map Grid: N15
RC Parish: Cloghprior and Monsea, see Cloghprior
Diocese: KL

Civil Parish: Emly
Map Grid: S22
RC Parish: Emly
Diocese: EM
Earliest Record: b. 7.1810; m. 4.1809
Missing Dates: m. 10.1838-1.1839
Status: LC; NLI (mf); Indexed by THU (to 1899)

Civil Parish: Erry
Map Grid: S39
RC Parish: Boherlahan, etc., see Ardmayle
Diocese: CA

Civil Parish: Fennor
Map Grid: S71
RC Parish: Gortnahoe, see Buolick
Diocese: CA

Civil Parish: Fertiana
Map Grid: N74
RC Parish: see Moycarky
Diocese: CA

Civil Parish: Fethard
Map Grid: S62
RC Parish: Fethard and Killusty
Diocese: CA
Earliest Record: b. 1.1806; m. 1.1806
Missing Dates: b. 1.1847-12.1847; m. 4.1820-1.1824
Status: LC; NLI (mf); Indexed by THU (to 1900)

Civil Parish: Finnoe
Map Grid: N7
RC Parish: see Kilbarron
Diocese: KL

Civil Parish: Gaile or Geale
Map Grid: S36
RC Parish: Boherlahan, etc., see Ardmayle
Diocese: CA

Civil Parish: Galbooly or Boly
Map Grid: N75
RC Parish: see Moycarky
Diocese: CA

Civil Parish: Garrangibbon
Map Grid: S106
RC Parish: Ballyneale, see Grangemockler
Diocese: LS

Civil Parish: Glenkeen
Map Grid: N54
RC Parish: Borrisoleigh
Diocese: CA
Earliest Record: b. 11.1814; m. 11.1814
Status: LC; NLI (mf); Indexed by THU (to 1900)

Civil Parish: Glenbane
Map Grid: S23
RC Parish: see Lattin
Diocese: EM

Civil Parish: Grangemockler
Map Grid: S84
RC Parish: Ballyneale and Grangemockler
Diocese: LS
Earliest Record: b. 1839; m. 1839
Status: LC; NLI (mf); Indexed by WHL (to 1900)

Civil Parish: Grange St. John (see Baptistgrange)

Civil Parish: Graystown
Map Grid: S74
RC Parish: see Cashel
Diocese: CA

Civil Parish: Holycross
Map Grid: N73
RC Parish: Holycross and Ballycahill
Diocese: CA
Earliest Record: b. 1.1835; m. 1.1835
Status: LC; NLI (mf); Indexed by THU (to 1900)

Civil Parish: Horeabbey
Map Grid: S41
RC Parish: Cashel, see St. John Baptist
Diocese: CA

Civil Parish: Inch
Map Grid: N66
RC Parish: Drom and Inch, see Drom
Diocese: CA

Civil Parish: Inish-Lounaght
Map Grid: S102
RC Parish: Clonmel, St. Mary's, see St. Mary's
Clonmel
Diocese: LS

Civil Parish: Isert-Kieran
Map Grid: S82
RC Parish: Mullinahone, see Kilvemnon
Diocese: CA

Civil Parish: Kilbarron
Map Grid: N6
RC Parish: Kilbarron and Terryglass
Diocese: KL
Earliest Record: b. 7.1827; m. 9.1827
Status: LC; NLI (mf); Indexed by TNFHF (to 1911)

Civil Parish: Kilbragh
Map Grid: S59
RC Parish: Cashel, see St. John Baptist
Diocese: CA

Civil Parish: Kilcash
Map Grid: S107
RC Parish: part Kilsheelan; part Powerstown, see
Kilgrant
Diocese: LS

Civil Parish: Kilclonagh
Map Grid: N67
RC Parish: see Templetuohy
Diocese: CA

Civil Parish: Kilcomenty
Map Grid: N24
RC Parish: Ballinahinch or Killoscully
Diocese: CA
Earliest Record: b. 7.1839; m. 1.1853
Status: LC; NLI (mf); Indexed by TNFHF (to 1899);
Indexed by THU

Civil Parish: Kilconnell
Map Grid: S51
RC Parish: part Killenaule; also part Boherlahan, see
Ardmayle
Diocese: CA

Civil Parish: Kilcooly (near Fennor)
Map Grid: N77
RC Parish: Gortnahoe, see Buolick
Diocese: CA

Civil Parish: Kilcooly (near Moyne, see also Co. Kilkenny)
Map Grid: S73
RC Parish: part Killenaule; also part Gortnahoe, see
Buolick
Diocese: CA

Civil Parish: Kilcornan
Map Grid: S16
RC Parish: Pallasgreen, see Grean, Co. Limerick
Diocese: EM

Civil Parish: Kilfeakle
Map Grid: S20
RC Parish: Golden, see Relickmurry
Diocese: CA

Civil Parish: Kilfithmone
Map Grid: N61
RC Parish: Drom and Inch, see Drom
Diocese: CA

Civil Parish: Kilgrant
Map Grid: S110
RC Parish: Powerstown
Diocese: LS
Earliest Record: b. 9.1808; m. 8.1808
Status: LC; NLI (mf); Indexed by WHL (to 1900)

Civil Parish: Kilkeary
Map Grid: N37
RC Parish: Toomevara, see Aghnameadle
Diocese: KL

Civil Parish: Killaloan (see Co. Waterford)
Map Grid: S115
RC Parish: part Powerstown, see Kilgrant; part St.
Mary's Clonmel

Civil Parish: Killardry (2 parts)
Map Grid: S31
RC Parish: Kilmoyler, see Templeneiry
Diocese: CA

Civil Parish: Killavinoge
Map Grid: N49
RC Parish: see Templemore
Diocese: CA

Civil Parish: Killea
Map Grid: N48
RC Parish: see Templemore
Diocese: CA

Civil Parish: Killeenasteena
Map Grid: S55
RC Parish: Golden, see Relickmurry
Diocese: CA

Civil Parish: Killenaule
Map Grid: S75
RC Parish: Killenaule
Diocese: CA
Earliest Record: b. 12.1742; m. 8.1812
Missing Dates: b. 1.1802–1.1814; m. 11.1851–2.1852
Status: LC; NLI (mf); Indexed by THU (to 1900)

Civil Parish: Killodiernan
Map Grid: N11
RC Parish: Monsea, see Cloghprior
Diocese: KL

Civil Parish: Killoscully
Map Grid: N25
RC Parish: part Ballinahinch, see Kilcomenty; part
Newport, see Kilvellane
Diocese: CA

Civil Parish: Killoskehan
Map Grid: S50
RC Parish: part Upperchurch; also part Cappawhite,
see Toem
Diocese: CA

Civil Parish: Kilmastulla
Map Grid: N23
RC Parish: Ballina, see Templeachally
Diocese: EM

Civil Parish: Kilmore (1) (Upper Ormond)
Map Grid: N34
RC Parish: Youghalarra, see Burgesbeg
Diocese: CA

Civil Parish: Kilmore (2) (Kilnemanagh)
Map Grid: S7
RC Parish: Silvermines or Ballinaclough
Diocese: KL
Earliest Record: b. 11.1840; m. 1.1841
Status: LC; NLI (mf); Indexed by TNFHF (to 1911)

Civil Parish: Kilmucklin
Map Grid: S12

RC Parish: Oola and Sohohead, see Oola, Co.
Limerick
Diocese: CA

Civil Parish: Kilmurry
Map Grid: S112
RC Parish: part Ballyneale, see Grangemockler; also
part Carrick-on-Suir, see Carrick
Diocese: LS

Civil Parish: Kilnaneave
Map Grid: N39
RC Parish: see Templederry

Civil Parish: Kilnarath
Map Grid: N27
RC Parish: part Ballinahinch, see Kilcomenty; part
Newport, see Kilvellane
Diocese: CA

Civil Parish: Kilpatrick
Map Grid: S5
RC Parish: Knockavilla, see Oughterleague
Diocese: CA

Civil Parish: Kilruane
Map Grid: N30
RC Parish: Cloghjordan, see Modreeny
Diocese: KL

Civil Parish: Kilshane
Map Grid: S30
RC Parish: see Tipperary
Diocese: EM

Civil Parish: Kilsheelan
Map Grid: S111
RC Parish: Gambonsfield and Kilcash (Kilsheelan)
Diocese: LS
Earliest Record: b. 1840; m. 1840
Status: LC; NLI (mf); Indexed by WHL (to 1900)

Civil Parish: Kiltegan
Map Grid: S109
RC Parish: Powerstown, see Kilgrant
Diocese: LS

Civil Parish: Kiltinan
Map Grid: S69
RC Parish: Fethard and Killusty, see Fethard
Diocese: EL

Civil Parish: Kilvellane
Map Grid: N26
RC Parish: Newport/Birdhill
Diocese: CA
Earliest Record: b. 1785; m. 1795; d. 2.1813
Missing Dates: b. 7.1859–11.1859; m. 2.1859–
11.1859; d. ends 5.1839
Status: LC; NLI (mf); Indexed by TNFHF and by
THU (to 1911)

Civil Parish: Kilvemnon
Map Grid: S83

RC Parish: Mullinahone; also Ballyneale, see Grangemockler
Diocese: CA
Earliest Record: b. 7.1809; m. 2.1810
Status: LC; NLI (mf); Indexed by THU (to 1900)

Civil Parish: Knigh
Map Grid: N16
RC Parish: see Cloghprior
Diocese: KL

Civil Parish: Knockgraffon
Map Grid: S64
RC Parish: New Inn
Diocese: CA
Earliest Record: b. 3.1820; m. 6.1798
Status: LC; NLI (mf); Indexed by THU (to 1900)

Civil Parish: Latteragh
Map Grid: N40
RC Parish: see Aghnameadle
Diocese: KL

Civil Parish: Lattin
Map Grid: S26
RC Parish: Lattin and Cullen
Diocese: EM
Earliest Record: b. 12.1846; m. 9.1846
Status: LC; NLI (mf); Indexed by THU (to 1900)

Civil Parish: Lickfinn
Map Grid: S76
RC Parish: see Killenaule
Diocese: CA

Civil Parish: Lisbunny
Map Grid: N32
RC Parish: Bansha, see Templeneiry
Diocese: KL

Civil Parish: Lismalin
Map Grid: S80
RC Parish: Ballingarry, see Ballingarry (2)
Diocese: CA

Civil Parish: Lisronagh
Map Grid: S104
RC Parish: Powerstown, see Kilgrant
Diocese: LS

Civil Parish: Lorrha
Map Grid: N1
RC Parish: Lorrha and Dorrha
Diocese: KL
Earliest Record: b. 10.1829; m. 10.1829
Status: LC; NLI (mf); Indexed by TNFHF (to 1911)

Civil Parish: Loughkeen
Map Grid: N5
RC Parish: see Birr, Co. Offaly
Diocese: KL

Civil Parish: Loughmoe East (Callabeg)
Map Grid: N64

RC Parish: Loughmore, see Loughmoe West
Diocese: CA

Civil Parish: Loughmoe West (Loughmoe)
Map Grid: S63
RC Parish: Loughmore
Diocese: CA
Earliest Record: b. 3.1798; m. 4.1798
Missing Dates: m. 6.1840–9.1840
Status: LC; NLI (mf); Indexed by THU (to 1900)

Civil Parish: Magorban
Map Grid: S44
RC Parish: see Killenaule
Diocese: CA

Civil Parish: Magowry
Map Grid: S47
RC Parish: see Killenaule
Diocese: CA

Civil Parish: Modeshil
Map Grid: S81
RC Parish: Mullinahone, see Kilvemnon
Diocese: CA

Civil Parish: Modreeny
Map Grid: N14
RC Parish: Cloughjordan
Diocese: KL
Earliest Record: b. 8.1833; m. 5.1833
Status: LC; NLI (mf); Indexed by TNFHF (to 1911)

Civil Parish: Molough
Map Grid: S99
RC Parish: see Newcastle, Co. Waterford
Diocese: LS

Civil Parish: Monsea
Map Grid: N17
RC Parish: see Cloghprior
Diocese: KL

Civil Parish: Mora
Map Grid: S65
RC Parish: Clerihan, see Ballyclerahan
Diocese: LS

Civil Parish: Mortlestown
Map Grid: S86
RC Parish: see Caher
Diocese: LS

Civil Parish: Mowney
Map Grid: S79
RC Parish: Ballingarry, see Ballingarry (2)
Diocese: CA

Civil Parish: Moyaliff
Map Grid: N59
RC Parish: see Upperchurch
Diocese: CA

Civil Parish: Moycarky
Map Grid: N78

RC Parish: Moycarky and Borris
Diocese: CA
Earliest Record: b. 10.1793; m. 10.1793
Missing Dates: b. 11.1796–1.1801, 10.1809–6.1810, 11.1810–1.1817, 4.1818–1.1830; m. 10.1796–1.1810, 11.1817–1.1830, 5.1854–9.1854
Status: LC; NLI (mf); Indexed by THU (to 1900)

Civil Parish: Moyne
Map Grid: N65
RC Parish: see Templetuohy
Diocese: CA

Civil Parish: Neddans
Map Grid: S98
RC Parish: see Ardfinnan
Diocese: LS

Civil Parish: Nenagh
Map Grid: N18
RC Parish: Nenagh
Diocese: KL
Earliest Record: b. 1.1792; m. 1.1792
Missing Dates: b. 11.1809–11.1830, 12.1842–1.1845, 4.1858–1.1859; m. 2.1794–9.1818
Status: LC; NLI (mf); Indexed by TNFHF (to 1911)

Civil Parish: Newcastle
Map Grid: S100
RC Parish: see Newcastle, Co. Waterford
Diocese: LS

Civil Parish: Newchapel
Map Grid: S103
RC Parish: Clerihan, see Ballyclerahan
Diocese: CA

Civil Parish: Newtownlennan
Map Grid: S113
RC Parish: Carrick-on-Suir, see Carrick; also part Ballyneale, see Grangemockler
Diocese: LS

Civil Parish: Oughterleague
Map Grid: S8
RC Parish: Knockavilla
Diocese: CA
Earliest Record: b. 5.1834; m. 7.1834
Status: LC; NLI (mf); Indexed by THU (to 1900)

Civil Parish: Outeragh
Map Grid: S70
RC Parish: see Caher
Diocese: LS

Civil Parish: Peppardstown
Map Grid: S53
RC Parish: Drangan, see Drangan
Diocese: CA

Civil Parish: Rahelty
Map Grid: N72
RC Parish: see Thurles
Diocese: CA

Civil Parish: Railstown
Map Grid: S50
RC Parish: Cashel, see St. John Baptist
Diocese: CA

Civil Parish: Rathcool
Map Grid: S52
RC Parish: see Killenaule
Diocese: CA

Civil Parish: Rathkennan
Map Grid: S1a
RC Parish: see Clonoulty
Diocese: CA

Civil Parish: Rathlynan or Rathliney
Map Grid: S13
RC Parish: Knockavilla, see Oughterleague
Diocese: CA

Civil Parish: Rathnaveoge
Map Grid: N44
RC Parish: Dunkerrin, see Dunkerrin, Co. Offaly
Diocese: KL

Civil Parish: Rathronan
Map Grid: S108
RC Parish: Powerstown, see Kilgrant
Diocese: LS

Civil Parish: Redcity
Map Grid: S61
RC Parish: Fethard and Killusty, see Fethard
Diocese: CA

Civil Parish: Relickmurry and Athassel
Map Grid: S21
RC Parish: Golden
Diocese: CA
Earliest Record: b. 5.1833; m. 5.1833
Status: LC; NLI (mf); Indexed by THU (to 1900)

Civil Parish: Rochestown
Map Grid: S93
RC Parish: see Ardfinnan
Diocese: LS

Civil Parish: Roscrea (see also Co. Offaly)
Map Grid: N42
RC Parish: Roscrea and Kyle
Diocese: KL
Earliest Record: b. 1.1810; m. 2.1810
Missing Dates: m. 8.1822–4.1823
Status: LC; NLI (mf); Indexing planned by TNFHF

Civil Parish: St. John Baptist
Map Grid: S42
RC Parish: Cashel
Diocese: CA
Earliest Record: b. 11.1793; m. 1.1793
Missing Dates: m. 6.1831
Status: LC; NLI (mf); Indexed by THU (to 1903)

Civil Parish: St. Johnstown or Scaddanstown
Map Grid: S46
RC Parish: Killenaule, see Killenaule
Diocese: CA

Civil Parish: St. Mary's (Clonmel) (also in Co. Waterford)
Map Grid: S114
RC Parish: Clonmel (St. Mary's); also SS. Peter and Paul, Clonmel, see St. Mary's below; also Powerstown, see Kilgrant
Diocese: LS
Earliest Record: b. 2.1790; m. 4.1797
Missing Dates: b. 12.1790-3.1793, 12.1793-1.1795, ends 1.1864; m. ends 1.1836
Status: LC; NLI (mf); Indexed by WHL (to 1900)

Civil Parish: St. Mary's
Map Grid: S114
RC Parish: St. Peter's and St. Paul's, Clonmel
Diocese: LS
Earliest Record: b. 2.1836; m. 2.1836
Status: LC; NLI (mf); Indexed by WHL (to 1900)

Civil Parish: St. Patricksrock
Map Grid: S40
RC Parish: Cashel, see St. John Baptist
Diocese: CA

Civil Parish: Shanrahan
Map Grid: S88
RC Parish: Clogheen, also Templetenny
Diocese: LS
Earliest Record: b. 6.1815; m. 7.1814
Missing Dates: m. ends 4.1867
Status: LC; NLI (mf); Indexed by WHL (to 1900)

Civil Parish: Shronell
Map Grid: S24
RC Parish: Lattin and Cullen, see Lattin
Diocese: EM

Civil Parish: Shyane
Map Grid: N70
RC Parish: see Thurles
Diocese: CA

Civil Parish: Solloghodbeg
Map Grid: S11
RC Parish: Oola and Solohead, see Oola, Co. Limerick
Diocese: EM

Civil Parish: Solloghodmore
Map Grid: S10
RC Parish: Oola and Solohead, see Oola, Co. Limerick
Diocese: EM

Civil Parish: Templeachally
Map Grid: N21
RC Parish: Ballina and Boher
Diocese: EM

Earliest Record: b. 3.1832; m. 5.1832
Status: LC; NLI (mf); Indexed by TNFHF (to 1903); Indexed by THU

Civil Parish: Templebeg
Map Grid: N56
RC Parish: Kilcommon/Hollyford
Diocese: CA
Earliest Record: b. 3.1813; m. 6.1813
Missing Dates: m. 1.1840-5.1840
Status: LC; NLI (mf); Indexed by TNFHF (to 1900); Indexed by THU (to 1895)

Civil Parish: Templebredon
Map Grid: S15
RC Parish: Pallasgreen, see Grean, Co. Limerick
Diocese: EM

Civil Parish: Templederry
Map Grid: N41
RC Parish: Kilnaneave and Templederry
Diocese: KL
Earliest Record: b. 9.1840; m. 2.1839
Missing Dates: m. ends 2.1869
Status: LC; NLI (mf); Indexed by TNFHF (to 1911)

Civil Parish: Templedowney
Map Grid: N33
RC Parish: Toomevara, see Aghnameadle
Diocese: KL

Civil Parish: Temple-etney
Map Grid: S105
RC Parish: see Kilsheelan
Diocese: LS

Civil Parish: Templemichael
Map Grid: S85
RC Parish: Ballyneale, see Grangemockler
Diocese: LS

Civil Parish: Templemore
Map Grid: N60
RC Parish: Templemore
Diocese: CA
Earliest Record: b. 8.1807; m. 11.1807
Missing Dates: m. 1.1820-2.1834
Status: LC; NLI (mf); Indexed by TNFHF (to 1911) and by THU (to 1900)

Civil Parish: Templeneiry
Map Grid: S34
RC Parish: Bansha and Kilmoyler
Diocese: CA
Earliest Record: b. 11.1820; m. 1.1822
Status: LC; NLI (mf); Indexed by THU (to 1899)

Civil Parish: Templenoe
Map Grid: S19
RC Parish: see Tipperary
Diocese: CA

Civil Parish: Templeree
Map Grid: N52
RC Parish: Loughmore, see Loughmoe West
Diocese: CA

Civil Parish: Templetenny
Map Grid: S87
RC Parish: Ballyporeen (Templetenny)
Diocese: LS
Earliest Record: b. 11.1817; m. 1.1818
Status: LC; NLI (mf); Indexed by WHL (to 1900)

Civil Parish: Templetuohy
Map Grid: N53
RC Parish: Moyne and Templetuohy
Diocese: CA
Earliest Record: b. 1.1809; m. 2.1804
Status: LC; NLI (mf); Indexed by THU (to 1900)

Civil Parish: Terryglass
Map Grid: N3
RC Parish: see Kilbarron
Diocese: KL

Civil Parish: Thurles
Map Grid: N69
RC Parish: Thurles
Diocese: CA
Earliest Record: b. 3.1795; m. 4.1795
Missing Dates: b. 11.1821–8.1822; m. 2.1820–8.1822
Status: LC; NLI (mf); Indexed by THU (to 1927)

Civil Parish: Tipperary
Map Grid: S18
RC Parish: Tipperary
Diocese: CA
Earliest Record: b. 1.1810; m. 2.1793
Missing Dates: m. 5.1809–1.1810
Status: LC; NLI (mf); Indexed by THU (to 1899)

Civil Parish: Toem
Map Grid: S9 and N58
RC Parish: Cappawhite
Diocese: CA
Earliest Record: b. 10.1815; m. 2.1804
Status: LC; NLI (mf); Indexed by THU (to 1900)

Civil Parish: Tubbrid
Map Grid: S89
RC Parish: Ballylooby
Diocese: LS
Earliest Record: b. 5.1828; m. 5.1828
Status: LC; NLI (mf); Indexed by WHL (to 1900)

Civil Parish: Tullaghmelan
Map Grid: S95
RC Parish: see Ardfinnan
Diocese: LS

Civil Parish: Tullaghorton
Map Grid: S96
RC Parish: Ballylooby, see Tubbrid
Diocese: LS

Civil Parish: Tullamain
Map Grid: S58
RC Parish: part Cashel, see St. John Baptist; part Fethard

Civil Parish: Twomileborris
Map Grid: N76
RC Parish: see Moycarkey
Diocese: CA

Civil Parish: Upperchurch or Templeoutragh
Map Grid: N55
RC Parish: Upperchurch
Diocese: CA
Earliest Record: b. 10.1829; m. 2.1829
Status: LC; NLI (mf); Indexed by THU (to 1900)

Civil Parish: Uskane
Map Grid: N9
RC Parish: see Borrisokane
Diocese: KL

Civil Parish: Whitechurch
Map Grid: S90
RC Parish: Ballylooby, see Tubbrid
Diocese: KL

Civil Parish: Youghalarra
Map Grid: N20
RC Parish: see Burgesbeg
Diocese: KL

Commercial and Social Directories

1788

Richard Lucas's *General Directory of the Kingdom of Ireland* contains lists of traders in Borrisoleigh, Carrick-on-Suir, Cashel, Clonmel, Nenagh, Thurles, Tipperary. Reprinted in *Ir. Gen.* 3 (11) (1966): 468–76.

1820

J. Pigot's *Commercial Directory of Ireland* contains information on the gentry, nobility, and traders in and around the town of Clonmel.

1824

J. Pigot's *City of Dublin and Hibernian Provincial Directory* includes traders, nobility, gentry, and clergy lists of Cahir, Carrick-on-Suir, Cashel, Clogheen, Clonmel, Fethard, Killenaule, Nenagh, Roscrea, Templemore, Thurles, and Tipperary.

1839

T. Shearman's *New Commercial Directory for the Cities of Waterford and Kilkenny, Towns of Clonmel, Carrick-on-Suir, New Ross and Carlow* lists traders, gentry, etc., in Carrick-on-Suir and Clonmel.

1840

F. Kinder's *New Triennial and Commercial Directory for 1840, '41 and '42* contains lists of traders, nobility, and others for Clonmel and Carrick-on-Suir (rare volume).

1846

Slater's *National Commercial Directory of Ireland* lists nobility, clergy, traders, etc., in Borrisoleigh, Cahir, Carrick-on-Suir, Cashel, Clogheen, Clonmel, Fethard, Killenaule, Nenagh, Newport, Roscrea, Templemore, Thurles, and Tipperary.

1856

Slater's *Royal National Commercial Directory of Ireland* lists nobility, gentry, clergy, traders, etc., in Borrisoleigh, Cahir, Carrick-on-Suir, Cashel and Golden, Clogheen, Clonmel, Fethard, Killenaule, Nenagh, Newport, Roscrea, Templemore, Thurles, and Tipperary.

1866

G.H. Bassett's *Directory of the City and County of Limerick and of the Principal Towns in the Cos. of Tipperary and Clare* has traders lists for Clonmel, Cashel, Nenagh, Newport, Thurles, and Tipperary, and an alphabetical list of the gentry in the county.

1870

Slater's *Directory of Ireland* contains trade, nobility, and clergy lists for Borrisoleigh, Caher, Carrick-on-Suir, Cashel, Clogheen, Clonmel, Fethard, Killenaule, Nenagh, Newport, Roscrea, Templemore, Thurles, and Tipperary.

1881

Slater's *Royal National Commercial Directory of Ireland* contains lists of traders, clergy, nobility, and farmers in adjoining parishes of the towns of Borrisoleigh, Cahir, Carrick-on-Suir, Cashel, Clogheen, Clonmel, Fethard, Killenaule, Nenagh, Newport, Roscrea, Templemore, Thurles, and Tipperary.

1886

Slater's *Royal National Commercial Directory of Ireland* contains lists of traders, clergy, nobility, and farmers in adjoining parishes of the towns of Cahir and Ballylooby, Carrick-on-Suir, Cashel, Clogheen, Clonmel, Fethard, Killenaule, Nenagh, Newport, Roscrea, Templemore, Thurles, and Tipperary.

Francis Guy's *Postal Directory of Munster* lists gentry, clergy, traders, principal farmers, teachers, and police sergeants in each postal district of the county, and has a listing of magistrates, clergy, and the professions for the whole county.

1889

Bassett's *Book of Co. Tipperary* lists traders, farmers, and prominent residents in even small villages in the county.

1893

Francis Guy's *Postal Directory of Munster* lists traders and farmers in each of the postal districts and has a general alphabetical index to prominent persons in the county. SLC film 1559399.

1894

Slater's *Royal National Directory of Ireland* lists traders, police, teachers, farmers, and private residents in each of the towns, villages, and parishes of the county.

Family History

"Armstrong of Tipperary." *Swanzy Notebooks.* RCB Library, Dublin.

"Bell of Tipperary." *Swanzy Notebooks.* RCB Library, Dublin.

"The Bourkes of Illeagh." *N. Munster Antiq. J.* 1 (2) (1937): 67–77.

Carden, J. *Some Particulars Relating to the Family and Descendants of John Carden of Templemore.* 1912.

"The Family of Everard" (of Fethard). *Ir. Gen.* 7 (3): 328–348; 7 (4): 505–542; 8 (2): 175–206; 8 (4): 575–601; 9 (1): 43–72.

"Going of Munster." *Ir. Anc.* 9 (1) (1977): 21–43.

"The Grant Families of Co. Tipperary." *J. Cork Arch. and Hist. Soc.* 226 (1972): 65–75.

The Grubbs of Tipperary: Studies in Heredity and Character. Cork: Mercier, 1972 (a good bibliography on pages 229–31).

"Limerick and Gerald Griffin." *N. Munster Antiq. J.* 2 (1) (1940): 4–13.

Matthew, David. "Father Mathew's Family: The Mathews in Tipperary." *Capuchin Annual* (1957): 143–52.

Chapman, E. *Memoirs of My Family: Together with Some Researches into the Early History of the Morris Families of Tipperary, Galway, and Mayo.* Frome, 1928.

"The Family Register of the O'Briens of Newcastle, Ballyporeen." *Ir. Gen.* 2 (1953): 308–10.

"Family Register of the O'Briens of Newcastle, Co. Tipperary." *Ir. Gen.* 2 (1953): 308–10.

Callanan, M. *Records of Four Tipperary Septs: The O'Kennedys, O'Dwyers, O'Mulryans, O'Meaghers.* Galway, 1938.

The O'Shaughnessys of Munster. See Family History—Co. Galway.

"The Powells of Templederry." *J. Ballinteer FHS* 1 (3): 134–139.

"Power Papers (Kilsheelan, Co. Tipperary)." *Anal. Hib.* 25: 57–75.

"The Prendergast Family." Notes on the family collected for John P. Prendergast. This and other Prendergast papers relative to Tipperary and Waterford are in Kings Inn Library, Dublin.

Seymour, St. John D. "Family Papers Belonging to the Purcells of Loughmoe, Co. Tipperary." *N. Munster Antiq. J.* 3 (1914): 124–29, 191–203.

Reade—see Kilkenny.

"Pedigree of Smith Family of King's Co. and Co. Tipperary 1666–1881." *J. Ass. Pres. Mem. Dead* 8 (1910–12): 208.

"Tobin of Kilnagranagh, Co. Tipperary." *Ir. Gen.* 5 (4) (1977): 491–95.

"Traceys of Tipperary." *Irish Family History* 8 (1992): 33–34.

"The Trehy Family (Tipperary)." *Irish Family History* 8 (1992): 69–77.

Wolfe—see Kildare.

Gravestone Inscriptions

The major series of published gravestone inscriptions for this county is that published by Ormond Historical Society (see Research Sources and Services section).

Ballygibbon: published by Ormond Historical Society.

Ballynaclogh: published by Ormond Historical Society.

Borrisokane: published by Ormond Historical Society.

Castletownarra: published by Ormond Historical Society.

Cloughprior: published by Ormond Historical Society.

Dolla: published by Ormond Historical Society.

Kilbarron: published by Ormond Historical Society.

Kilfeacle: Reference guide to Kilfeacle Cemetery. Senator Willie Ryan, 1985, self-published.

Kilkeary: published by Ormond Historical Society.

Killaneave: published by Ormond Historical Society.

Kilmore: *Ir. Gen.* 2 (10) (1953): 317–21.

Kilruane: published by Ormond Historical Society.

Knygh: published by Ormond Historical Society.

Nenagh: published by Ormond Historical Society.

Uskane: *Ir. Gen.* 3 (2) (1957): 74–75.

Newspapers

Tipperary is a large county which published many newspapers. For the south of the county, Clonmel is the major center of publication. The towns of Nenagh, Thurles, Roscrea, and Cashel also produced newspapers at various times.

Limerick and Waterford newspapers also contain notices regarding the parts of county Tipperary that are adjacent to them. The *Kings County Chronicle* (see Co. Offaly) also contains notices of relevance to the north of the county.

An index to the biographical notices up to 1821 in newspapers from Clonmel, Limerick, Ennis, and Waterford, which contains 50,000 items, is available on microfiche in the library of University College, Dublin. Microfiche copies are available from the compiler, Ms. R. ffolliott, Glebe House, Fethard, Co. Tipperary.

Title: *Cashel Gazette*
Published in: Cashel, 1864–93
BL Holdings: 5.1864–7.1866; 10.1868–9.1871; 10.1871–7.1893

Title: *Clonmel Advertiser*
Published in: Clonmel, ca. 1811–38
NLI Holdings: 7.1813–7.1819; 1.1828–4.1838
BL Holdings: 1.1828–4.1838

Title: *Clonmel Gazette, Powers*
Published in: Clonmel, ca. 1792
NLI Holdings: 6.1802–11.1804 (incomplete)

Title: *Clonmel Gazette* or *Hibernian Advertiser*
Published in: Clonmel, 1788–93
NLI Holdings: 4.1788–2.1795; one volume of old issues from 1788 to 1793
BL Holdings: odd numbers 9–12.1792

Title: *Clonmel Herald*
Published in: Clonmel, 1813–41
NLI Holdings: 5.1813; 1.1828–3.1841
BL Holdings: 5.1813; 1.1828–3.1841

Title: *County Tipperary Independent and Tipperary Free Press*
Published in: Clonmel, 1882–91; Waterford, 1891–1907
BL Holdings: 11.1882–4.1905; 5.1907–11.1907

Title: *Midland Counties Advertiser*
Published in: Roscrea, 1854–1948
NLI Holdings: 8.1927–6.1947
BL Holdings: 1.1854–11.1881; 9.1882–1.1893; 3.1893–9.1948

Title: *Nationalist and Tipperary Advertiser* (continued as *Nationalist and Munster Advertiser* in 1908)
Published in: Thurles, 1881; Clonmel, 1886–present
NLI Holdings: 1.1892; 1.1905–2.1908
BL Holdings: 2.1890–2.1908

Title: *Nenagh Gazette*
Published in: Nenagh, 1841–42
NLI Holdings: 1.1841–6.1842
BL Holdings: 1.1841–6.1842

Title: *Nenagh Guardian* or *Tipperary (North Riding) and Ormond Advertiser* (continued as *The Nenagh Guardian*)
Published in: Nenagh, 1838–in progress

NLI Holdings: 4.1860; 6.1859–1861; 1.1862–12.1868; 1.1875–12.1876; 12.1899
BL Holdings: 7.1838–12.1925; 1.1927–in progress

Title: *Nenagh News and Tipperary Vindicator*
Published in: Nenagh, 1898–1924
NLI Holdings: several issues in 1921
BL Holdings: 7.1898–2.1923; 4.1923–12.1924

Title: *Tipperary Advocate*
Published in: Nenagh, 1858–89
NLI Holdings: 1.1860–10.1889
BL Holdings: 3.1858–9.1869; two numbers for 10.1889

Title: *Tipperary and Clare Independent*
Published in: Nenagh, 1867–69
BL Holdings: 4.1867–9.1869

Title: *Tipperary Champion*
Published in: Clonmel, ca. 1898–1910
BL Holdings: 8.1903; 1.1904–12.1910

Title: *Tipperary Constitution*
Published in: Clonmel, 1835–48
NLI Holdings: 12.1835–5.1848
BL Holdings: 12.1835–5.1848

Title: *Tipperary Examiner* (includes Limerick, Waterford, and Kilkenny)
Published in: Clonmel, 1858–59
BL Holdings: 4.1858–5.1859

Title: *Tipperary Free Press*
Published in: Clonmel, 1826–81
NLI Holdings: 12.1826–7.1881
BL Holdings: 12.1826–7.1881

Title: *Tipperary Leader*
Published in: Thurles (first series), 1855–85; (second series), 9.1822–4.1885
NLI Holdings: 9.1882–4.1885
BL Holdings: 1.1855–3.1856; 9.1882–4.1885

Title: *Tipperary Nationalist and Southern Irishman*
Published in: Clonmel, ? to 1890
BL Holdings: 5.1889–2.1890

Title: *Tipperary People*
Published in: Clonmel, 1865–66
NLI Holdings: 1920–21
BL Holdings: 7.1865–7.1866; 8.1876–12.1877; 1.1879–12.1891; 1.1893–12.1904; 1.1906–11.1918

Title: *Tipperary Vindicator* (continued as *Limerick Reporter and Tipperary Vindicator* in 1849)
Published in: Nenagh, 1844–49
NLI Holdings: 12.1844–12.1849; 4.1856–12.1895
BL Holdings: 1.1844–12.1849; 4.1859–10.1877

Title: *Tipperary Weekly News and Advertiser*
Published in: Tipperary, ca. 1857–58
BL Holdings: 1–2.1858

Wills and Administrations

A discussion of the types of records, where they are held, and their availability and value is given in the Wills section of the introduction. The availability of prerogative wills, administrations, and marriage license records is also described in the relevant parts of the same section. Where available, published sources of these records are given in the Miscellaneous Sources section.

Pre-1858 Wills and Administrations

Prerogative Wills. See the introduction.

Consistorial Wills. This county is in the dioceses of Cashel, Emly, Killaloe, and Lismore. The guide to Roman Catholic parish records in this chapter shows the diocese to which each civil parish belonged. The wills of residents of each diocese were usually proven within that diocese (see the Wills section for exceptions). The following records survive:

Wills

See the introduction.

Abstracts

See the introduction.

The Welply Will Abstracts in the RCBL contain extracts from 1,682 Munster wills, mainly from Cork. Index contains name, date of will, and (usually) probate and residence. Index in *Ir. Gen.* from 6 (6) 1985 to 7 (1) 1986.

Indexes

Cashel and Emly (1618–58 and up to 1800) published by Phillimore. Killaloe (1704–1857). Lismore (1648–1858) published to 1800 by Phillimore.

Post-1858 Wills and Administrations

This county was served by the District Registries of Limerick (North County) and Waterford (South County). The surviving records are kept in the NAI. Records include: Limerick District Will Books (1858–1894). NAI; SLC film 100951–4.

Marriage Licenses

Marriage Licenses—Diocese of Killaloe (1680–1762). GO 688; SLC film 100239.

Indexes

Cashel and Emly (1664–1857). NAI; SLC film 100861. Killaloe (1691–1845). NAI; SLC film 100869. Lismore (1661–1750). NAI; SLC film 100872.

Miscellaneous Sources

Bassett, G.H. *The Book of Co. Tipperary.* Dublin, 1889.

Burke, W.P. *History of Clonmel.* Dublin, 1907. Reprint. Kilkenny, 1983.

Poor Law Records of County Limerick, Clare and Tipperary. *N. Munster Antiq. J.* Supplement to Vol. 21, 1979.

"Cahir Estate Records," 1826–1966. Records of the Cahir Estate Co., which managed several estates in Tipperary, particularly those of Charteris, Earl of Glengall, R.P. Maxwell, Solomon Watson, Cole Baker, etc. NAI 796.

White, Rev. P. *History of Clare and Dalcassian Clans of Tipperary, Limerick and Galway.* Dublin, 1893.

Cunningham, G. *Roscrea and District.* Roscrea, 1976.

"Emigration from the Workhouse of Nenagh Union, Co. Tipperary 1849–1860." *Ir. Anc.* 17 (1) (1985): 10–17.

"Extracts from the Minutes of the Corporation of Fethard, Co. Tipperary: Freemen of the Corporation." *Ir. Gen.* 5 (3) (1976): 370–82.

"Proprietors of Fethard, Co. Tipperary, 1641–1663." *Ir. Gen.* 6 (1) (1980): 5–8.

Murphy, Nancy. *Tracing Northwest Tipperary Roots.* Nenagh, 1982.

Nolan, W., and T. McGrath, eds. *Tipperary History and Society: Interdisciplinary Essays on the History of an Irish County.* Dublin: Geography Publications, 1985.

Nolan, W., and W. Corbett. *Thurles–The Cathedral Town.* Dublin: Geography Publications, 1989.

"The Seneschals of the Liberty of Tipperary." *Ir. Gen.* 52 (10): 294–302; 2 (11): 326–36; 2 (12): 368–76; 3 (2): 46–59; 3 (3): 109–15; 3 (4): 120–23.

Research Sources and Services

Journals

Cork Historical and Archaeological Society Journal (for south Tipperary, see Research Sources and Services section, Co. Cork)

Eile (published by Roscrea Heritage Society)

North Munster Antiquarian Journal

Tipperary Historical Journal (accessible on the Internet at http://www.iol.ie/~tipplibs/Welcome.htm)

Libraries and Information Sources

Tipperary County Library, Castle Avenue, Thurles, Co. Tipperary. Ph: (0504) 21102

Research Services

Tipperary North Family History Foundation, The Gatehouse, Kickham St., Nenagh, Co. Tipperary. Ph:

(067) 33850; fax: (353) 67 33586. The foundation runs Nenagh District Heritage Centre and is the official IGP center for the northern parts of Co. Tipperary. Its sources include indexed parish records, gravestone inscriptions, land records, the 1901 census, civil records, directories, and local maps. Researchers are advised to contact the center for an updated list of registers, and other sources, indexed. The foundation will provide a search of its database for a fee.

Brú Ború Heritage Group (BBHC), Bohereenglas, Cashel, Co. Tipperary. Ph: (062) 61552. This is the official IGP center for the south of the county. They have indexed many of the church records of the area, and also have access to other relevant records. Researchers are advised to contact the center for an updated list of registers, and other sources, indexed. They will conduct a search for a fee.

Tipperary Heritage Unit (THU), The Bridewell, St. Michael St., Tipperary Town, Ireland. Ph/Fax: (062) 52725; e-mail: thu@iol.ie. This center has exclusive access to Catholic records of the RC Diocese of Cashel and Emly. They have indexed the baptismal and marriage records and *Griffith's Valuation*, and have access to the 1901 census. A search service will be provided for a fee.

Irish Origins Research Agency, College Road, Kilkenny. Ph: (056) 21483; fax: (056) 64777. Genealogical research service, specializing in counties Kilkenny, Carlow, Tipperary, Wexford, and Waterford.

Societies

Clonmel and District Historical Society, Mr. Tony Butler, 110 Irishtown, Clonmel, Co. Tipperary

County Tipperary Historical Society, Dr. Denis G. Marnane, 20 Main Street, Tipperary, Co. Tipperary; Web page: http://www.iol.ie/~tipplibs/Welcome.htm

Fethard Historical Society, Ms. Doirin Saurus, Cramps Castle, Fethard, Co. Tipperary

Nenagh District Heritage Society, Mrs. Nancy Murphy, Governor's House, Nenagh, Co. Tipperary

Newport Archaeological and Historical Society, Mr. Gerard Lenehan, Ahane, Newport, Co. Tipperary

Ormond Historical Society, Mr. James Slattery, Ballyanny, Nenagh, Co. Tipperary

Roscrea Heritage Society, Mr. Coll Carmody, Rosemary Street, Roscrea, Co. Tipperary

Templemore Historical Society, Mr. Jeramiah O'Keeffe, Borrisbeg, Templemore, Co. Tipperary

Tipperary Town Heritage Society, Ms. Mary O'Connor, Golden, Co. Tipperary

Tipperary North Civil Parishes as Numbered on Map

1. Lorrha
2. Dorrha
3. Terryglass
4. Aglishcloghane
5. Loughkeen
6. Kilbarron
7. Finnoe
8. Borrisokane
9. Uskane
10. Ballingarry
11. Killodieran
12. Cloghprior
13. Ardcrony
14. Modreeny
15. Dromineer
16. Knigh
17. Monsea (2 pts.)
18. Nenagh
19. Castletownarra
20. Youghalarra
21. Templeachally
22. Burgesbeg
23. Kilmastulla
24. Kilcomenty
25. Killoscully
26. Kilvellane
27. Kilnarath (2 pts.)
28. Abington
29. Ballygibbon
30. Kilruane (2 pts.)
31. Ballymackey
32. Lisbunny
33. Templedowney (3 pts.)
34. Kilmore
35. Dolla
36. Ballynaclough
37. Kilkeary (2 pts.)
38. Aghnameadle (2 pts.)
39. Kilnaneave
40. Latteragh

41. Templederry
42. Roscrea
43. Corbally
44. Rathnaveoge
45. Bourney (2 pts.)
46. Cullenwaine
47. Borrisnafarney
48. Killea
49. Killavinoge
50. Killoskehan
51. Barnane Ely
52. Templeree
53. Templetuohy
54. Glenkeen
55. Upperchurch
56. Templebeg (2 pts.)
57. Doon
58. Toem
59. Moyaliff
60. Templemore
61. Kilfithmone
62. Drom
63. Loughmoe West
64. Loughmoe East
65. Moyne
66. Inch
67. Kilclonagh
68. Ballycahill
69. Thurles
70. Shyane
71. Athnid
72. Rahelty (2 pts.)
73. Holycross
74. Fertiana
75. Galbooly
76. Twomileborris
77. Kilcooly
78. Moycarky
79. Ballymurreen (2. pts)

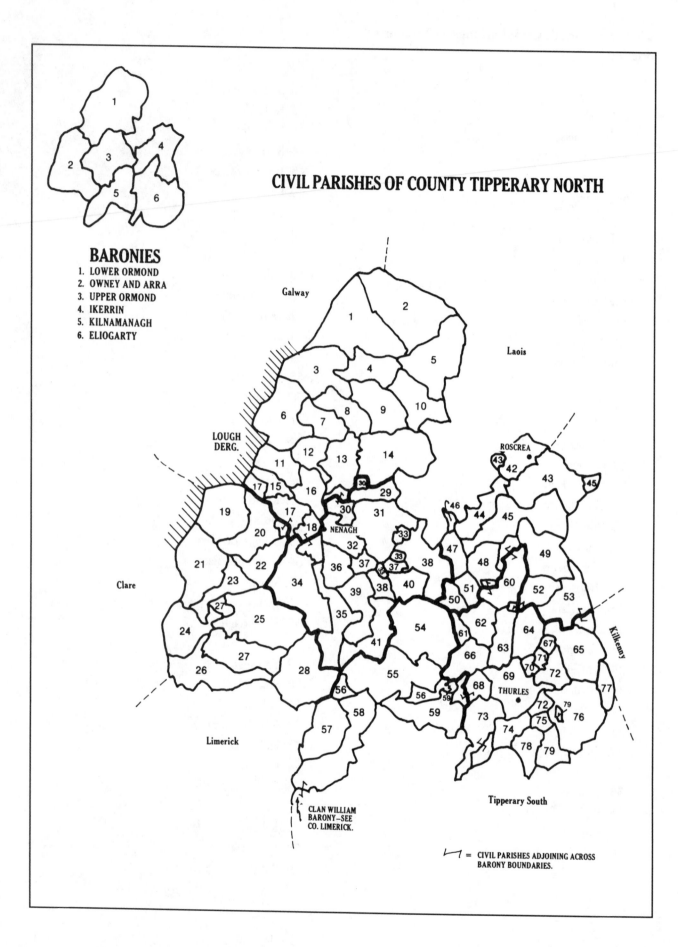

CIVIL PARISHES OF COUNTY TIPPERARY NORTH

BARONIES

1. LOWER ORMOND
2. OWNEY AND ARRA
3. UPPER ORMOND
4. IKERRIN
5. KILNAMANAGH
6. ELIOGARTY

Galway

Laois

LOUGH DERG.

ROSCREA

Clare

NENAGH

Kilkenny

THURLES

Limerick

CLAN WILLIAM BARONY—SEE CO. LIMERICK.

Tipperary South

⌐ = CIVIL PARISHES ADJOINING ACROSS BARONY BOUNDARIES.

Tipperary North Civil Parishes in Alphabetical Order

Abington: 28

Aghnameadle (2 pts.): 38

Aglishcloghane: 4

Ardcrony: 13

Athnid: 71

Ballingarry: 10

Ballycahill: 68

Ballygibbon: 29

Ballymackey: 31

Ballymurreen (2 pts.): 79

Ballynaclough: 36

Barnane Ely: 51

Borrisnafarney: 47

Borrisokane: 8

Bourney (2 pts.): 45

Burgesbeg: 22

Castletownarra: 19

Cloghprior: 12

Corbally: 43

Cullenwaine: 46

Dolla: 35

Doon: 57

Dorrha: 2

Drom: 62

Dromineer: 15

Fertiana: 74

Finnoe: 7

Galbooly: 75

Glenkeen: 54

Holycross: 73

Inch: 66

Kilbarron: 6

Kilclonagh: 67

Kilcomenty: 24

Kilcooly: 77

Kilfithmone: 61

Kilkeary (2 pts.): 37

Killavinoge: 49

Killea: 48

Killoskehan: 50

Killodieran: 11

Killoscully: 25

Kilmastulla: 23

Kilmore: 34

Kilnaneave: 39

Kilnarath (2 pts.): 27

Kilruane (2 pts.): 30

Kilvellane: 26

Knigh: 16

Latteragh: 40

Lisbunny: 32

Lorrha: 1

Loughkeen: 5

Loughmoe East: 64

Loughmoe West: 63

Modreeny: 14

Monsea (2 pts.): 17

Moyaliff: 59

Moycarky: 78

Moyne: 65

Nenagh: 18

Rahelty (2 pts.): 72

Rathnaveoge: 44

Roscrea: 42

Shyane: 70

Templeachally: 21

Templebeg (2 pts.): 56

Templederry: 41

Templedowney (3 pts.): 33

Templemore: 60

Templeree: 52

Templetuohy: 53

Terryglass: 3

Thurles: 69

Toem: 58

Twomileborris: 76

Upperchurch: 55

Uskane: 9

Youghalarra: 20

Tipperary South Civil Parishes as Numbered on Map

1. Clogher
1a. Rathkennan
2. Donohill
3. Clonoulty (2 pts.)
4. Aghacrew
5. Kilpatrick
6. Ballintemple
7. Kilmore
8. Oughterleague (2 pts.)
9. Toem
10. Solloghodmore
11. Solloghodbeg
12. Kilmucklin
13. Rathlynin
14. Ballygriffin
15. Templebredon
16. Kilcornan
17. Cullen
18. Tipperary
19. Templenoe
20. Kilfeakle
21. Relickmurry and Athassel
22. Emly
23. Glenbane
24. Shronell
25. Corroge
26. Lattin
27. Bruis
28. Clonpet
29. Cordangan
30. Kilshane
31. Killardry
32. Clonbulloge
33. Clonbeg
34. Templeneiry
35. Holycross
36. Gaile
37. Ardmayle
38. Ballysheehan
39. Erry
40. St. Patricksrock (2 pts.)

41. Horeabbey
42. St. John Baptist (4 pts.)
43. Brickendown
44. Magorban
45. Cooleagh
46. St. Johnstown
47. Magowry
48. Drangan
49. Dangandargan
50. Railstown
51. Kilconnell (3 pts.)
52. Rathcool
53. Peppardstown
54. Cloneen
55. Killeenasteena
56. Boytonrath
57. Dogstown
58. Tullamain (2 pts.)
59. Kilbragh
60. Barrett's grange
61. Redcity
62. Fethard
63. Coolmundry
64. Knockgraffon
65. Mora
66. Colman
67. Donaghmore
68. Baptistgrange (2 pts.)
69. Kiltinan
70. Outeragh
71. Fennor (2 pts.)
72. Buolick
73. Kilcooly (3 pts.)
74. Graystown
75. Killenaule
76. Lickfinn
77. Ballingarry
78. Crohane
79. Mowney
80. Lismalin
81. Modeshil

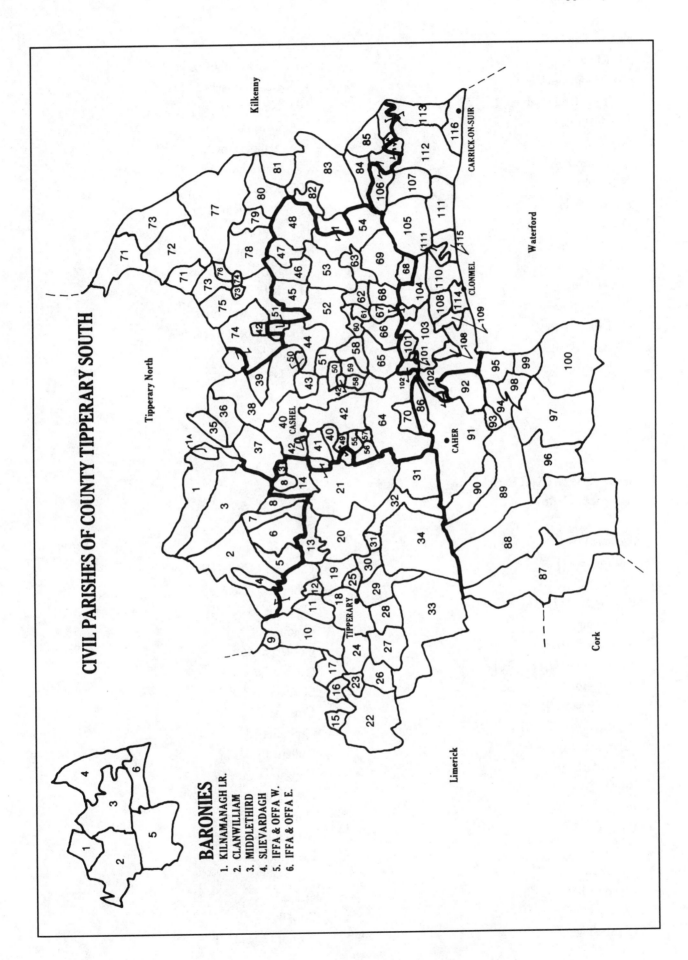

CIVIL PARISHES OF COUNTY TIPPERARY SOUTH

BARONIES

1. KILNAMANAGH LR.
2. CLANWILLIAM
3. MIDDLETHIRD
4. SLIEVARDAGH
5. IFFA & OFFA W.
6. IFFA & OFFA E.

Kilkenny

Tipperary North

Waterford

CARRICK-ON-SUIR

CLONMEL

CASHEL

CAHER

TIPPERARY

Limerick

Cork

82. Isertkieran
83. Kilvemnon
84. Grangemocklet
85. Templemichael
86. Mortlestown
87. Templetenny
88. Shanrahan
89. Tubbrid
90. Whitechurch
91. Caher
92. Derrygrath
93. Rochestown
94. Ardfinnan
95. Tullaghmelan
96. Tullaghorton
97. Ballybacon
98. Neddans
99. Molough

100. Newcastle
101. Ballyclerahan (2 pts.)
102. Inishlounaght (2 pts.)
103. Newchapel
104. Lisronagh
105. Temple-etny
106. Garrangibbon
107. Kilcash
108. Rathronan (2 pts.)
109. Kiltegan
110. Kilgrant
111. Kilsheelan (2 pts.)
112. Kilmurry
113. Newtownlennan
114. Clonmel (St. Mary's)
115. Killaloan
116. Carrick

Tipperary South Civil Parishes in Alphabetical Order

Aghacrew: 4
Ardfinnan: 94
Ardmayle: 37
Ballingarry: 77
Ballintemple: 6
Ballybacon: 97
Ballyclerahan (2 pts.): 101
Ballygriffin: 14
Ballysheehan: 38
Baptistgrange (2 pts.): 68
Barrett's grange: 60
Boytonrath: 56
Brickendown: 43
Bruis: 27
Buolick: 72
Caher: 91
Carrick: 116
Clogher: 1
Clonbeg: 33
Clonbulloge: 32

Cloneen: 54
Clonmel (St. Mary's): 114
Clonoulty (2 pts.): 3
Clonpet: 28
Colman: 66
Cooleagh: 45
Coolmundry: 63
Cordangan: 29
Corroge: 25
Crohane: 78
Cullen: 17
Dangandargan: 49
Derrygrath: 92
Dogstown: 57
Donaghmore: 67
Donohill: 2
Drangan: 48
Emly: 2
Erry: 39
Fennor (2 pts.): 71

Fethard: 62
Gaile: 36
Garrangibbon: 106
Glenbane: 23
Grangemocklet: 84
Graystown: 74
Holycross: 35
Horeabbey: 41
Inishlounaght (2 pts.): 102
Isertkieran: 82
Kilbragh: 59
Kilcash: 107
Kilconnell (3 pts.): 51
Kilcooly (3 pts.): 73
Kilcornan: 16
Kilfeakle: 20
Kilgrant: 110
Killaloan: 115
Killardry: 31
Killeenasteena: 55
Killenaule: 75
Kilmore: 7
Kilmucklin: 12
Kilmurry: 112
Kilpatrick: 5
Kilshane: 30
Kilsheelan (2 pts.): 111
Kiltegan: 109
Kiltinan: 69
Kilvemnon: 83
Knockgraffon: 64
Lattin: 26
Lickfinn: 76
Lismalin: 80
Lisronagh: 104
Magorban: 44
Magowry: 47
Modeshil: 81
Molough: 99

Mora: 65
Mortlestown: 86
Mowney: 79
Neddans: 98
Newcastle: 100
Newchapel: 103
Newtownlennan: 113
Oughterleague (2 pts.): 8
Outeragh: 70
Peppardstown: 53
Railstown: 50
Rathcool: 52
Rathkennan: 1a
Rathlynin: 13
Rathronan (2 pts.): 108
Redcity: 61
Relickmurry and Athassel: 21
Rochestown: 93
Shanrahan: 88
Shronell: 24
Solloghodbeg: 11
Solloghodmore: 10
St. John Baptist (4 pts.): 42
St. Johnstown: 46
St. Patricksrock (2 pts.): 40
Temple-etny: 105
Templebredon: 15
Templemichael: 85
Templeneiry: 34
Templenoe: 19
Templetenny: 87
Tipperary: 18
Toem: 9
Tubbrid: 89
Tullaghmelan: 95
Tullaghorton: 96
Tullamain (2 pts.): 58
Whitechurch: 90

County Tyrone

A Brief History

An inland Ulster county, Tyrone contains the towns of Strabane, Omagh, Clogher, Dungannon, and Ballygawley. Before the establishment of the present county, this area was part of the territory of Tirowen, from which the county was named. The ruling family in the area were the O'Neills, and other important families were O'Quinn, O'Donnelly, O'Hamill, McGurk, MacMurphy, O'Hegarty, O'Devlin, O'Lunney, McGilmartin, MacGettigan, MacCloskey, MacColgan, O'Mulvenna, MacGilligan, O'Laverty, and MacNamee.

The Norman invasion had little effect on this area because of the power of the O'Neills and the other chieftains. The O'Neills' base was at Dungannon, but all trace of their castle has now disappeared. In 1594, as a result of various attempts by the English to obtain control of Ulster land, Hugh O'Neill, the leader of the Irish in Ulster, began a rebellion. With Red Hugh O'Donnell of Donegal and the other major families of Ulster, he defeated successive armies sent to subdue the rebellion. In 1601, the Spanish sent an army to assist the Irish in this war. However, the Spanish army landed in Kinsale, in County Cork, forcing O'Neill to march the length of the country to link up with them. This proved to be a serious tactical mistake. O'Neill's army was forced to abandon this attempt and was subsequently defeated in 1603.

Shortly afterwards, O'Neill and many of his ally chieftains and their families left the country. This so-called "Flight of the Earls" marked the final breakdown of the old Gaelic order in Ulster. Most of the O'Neill territories and those of his allies were confiscated and divided into six of the present Ulster counties. Tyrone was divided up between various English and Scottish adventurers who undertook to bring over settlers to their estates. The native Irish were also allotted some por-tions of these lands, and others remained as laborers on the estates of the new settlers. The "armed men" of Ulster were forced to resettle in the province of Connaught.

The major undertakers and large tenants who arrived in Tyrone during this "Ulster Plantation" included Hamilton, Buchanan, Galbraith, Stewart, Newcomen, Drummond, Ridgwaie, Lowther, Burleigh, Leigh, Cope, Parsons, Sanderson, Lindsey, Caulfield, Ansley, Wingfield, and Chichester.

There was severe disturbance in this county during the 1641 rebellion. Sir Phelim O'Neill led the Catholic Irish in the county and successfully defeated several English armies. In 1649, however, the rebellion was finally defeated, and the lands of those taking part were confiscated. New proprietors took over the remaining lands of the Irish chieftains.

During the eighteenth century, many Ulster Presbyterians, the so-called Scots-Irish, left Ireland as a result of the discrimination against them in the Penal Laws. These laws had been instituted in the 1690s, primarily against Catholics. An indication of the origins of Tyrone inhabitants can generally be determined from the religious persuasions of its inhabitants. This is possible because the native Irish are predominantly Catholic, the Scottish are Presbyterian, and the English are Protestant (Episcopalian). In 1861, when the census first determined the religion of respondents, the relative proportions were fifty-seven, twenty-two, and twenty percent, respectively.

The county was relatively badly affected by the Great Famine of 1845–47. The population, which was 313,000 in 1841, fell to 256,000 by 1851. Of this drop, some 28,000 died between 1845 and 1850, and the remainder emigrated to the cities or abroad. The population continued to fall throughout the century, and by 1891 it was 171,000.

In 1921, this county was one of the six which remained within the United Kingdom on the establishment of the Irish Free State.

Census and Census Substitutes

1612-13

"Survey of Undertakers Planted in Tyrone" (names, acreages allotted, and account of the progress of each). Hist. Mss. Comm. Rep. (Hastings Mss.) 4 (1947): 159-82.

1630

Muster Roll. PRONI T808/15164; NLI mf. P 206.

1631

Muster Roll of Clogher and Strabane. PRONI T934; BL add. ms. 4770.

1654-56

Civil Survey, Vol 3. R.C. Simington. Dublin: Stationery Office, 1934. SLC film 0973121.

1659

"Census" of Ireland. Ed. by S. Pender. Dublin: Stationery Office, 1939. NLI I6551. SLC film 924648.

1662-63

Poll Tax Return for Aghaloo Parish. SLC film 258551.

1664-68

"Hearth Money and Subsidy Rolls for Barony of Dungannon." *Seanchas Ardmhacha* 6 (1) (1971): 24-45; SLC film 258551; NLI Ms 9583/4.

1666

Hearth Money Roll. NLI mss. 9584-85. The part of Tyrone in Clogher diocese is covered in *The Clogher Record* 5 (3) (1965): 379-87; SLC film 258551.

List of christenings, marriages, and burials in parish of Clogher. Clogher Diocesan Records D10.2/9/206; SLC film 993170.

1666-68

"Subsidy Rolls (for Clogher Diocese)." *The Clogher Record* 5 (3) (1965): 379-87.

1740

Protestants in the Parishes of Derryloran and Kildress. RCB Library; SLC film 1279327; GO 539; PRONI T808/15258.

1761

Militia List for Counties of . . . Tyrone, etc. GO Ms. 680.

1766

Householders of Parishes of Aghalow, Artrea, Carnteel, Derryloran, Drumglass, Dungannon, Kildress, and Tullyniskan. SLC film 258517; RCB MS 23; NAI Parliamentary Returns Nos. 648, 650, 665, and 667; also householders of Donaghhendry, Errigal Keerogue on NAI Parliamentary Returns Nos. 658 and 666; Tullyniskan, Dungannon, and Drumglass are also on NAI M2476. All of the above (except Carnteel, Donaghhendry, and Errigal Keerogue) on GO Ms. 536.

Religious Census of Parishes of Aghalow, Carnteel, Derryloran, Drumglass, Dungannon, and Tullaniskan. *Seanchas Ardmhacha* 4 (1) (1960/61): 147-70.

1780

Householders (all religions) of Termonmaguirk. RCBL GS 2/7/3/25 (several hundred names).

1796

See Mayo 1796 (List of Catholics).

Spinning Wheel Premium List (over 10,000 names; see introduction). SLC film 1419442.

Petition of Twenty-three Protestants. NAI-SPO 620/26/125.

1802

County of Tyrone 1802 by John McEvoy. 1802. Reprint. Friars Bush Press, 1991.

1821

Extract of Government Census of Ballygunner (Callaghane townland only). *Decies* 17 (1981): 67-70.

1823-38

Tithe Applotment Survey (see introduction).

1834

"Occupants of Dungannon Arranged by Street, Giving Property Values." *Parl. Papers* 1837, 11 (1), Appendix G, 203-06.

1839

List of persons who obtained Game Certficates in Ulster. PRONI T 688.

1842

Voters of Tyrone. NAI 1842/77.

1851/2

All Church of Ireland people in parish of Clogherny. PRONI D10 4/32C/9/4/2 and 5; also at PRONI in T877 (839). (Names and ages.)

1860

Griffith's Valuation (see introduction).

1901

Census. NAI (see introduction). A full index (on microfiche) to this census is available from Largy Books, PO Box 6023, Fort McMurray, Alberta T9H 4W1, Canada. Ph: (403) 791-1750. SLC films 855968-98, 856144-56.

1911

Census. NAI.

Church Records

Church of Ireland

See the introduction for a description of Church of Ireland records and their major repositories. Many C of I records were lost in the PRO fire of 1922. These are indicated as "Lost." However, as Church of Ireland records were effectively state records, the records of marriage (from 1845) are also in the General Registrar's Office. Many are still in local custody (LC), while others are in one of a variety of other archives (e.g., RCBL or NAI). All of the Church of Ireland registers of this county have been indexed by Irish World (see Research Services at the end of the chapter). A search of the index will be conducted by the center for a fee. Those indexed are noted as "Indexed by Irish World."

Aghalurcher
Earliest Records: b. 1788; m. 1788; d. 1788
Status: LC

Altedesert, Pomeroy Church
Status: Lost (earlier entries in Termonmaguirk)

Arboe
Earliest Records: b. 1773; m. 1773; d. 1773
Status: LC; SLC film 824282 (m. 1783-1845), film 933409 (b. 1777-1877)

Ardstraw
Status: Lost

Ardtrea
Earliest Records: b. 1811; m. 1811; d. 1811
Status: LC

Badoney Lower
Earliest Records: b. 1818; m. 1817; d. 1820
Status: LC

Badoney Upper
Status: LC; Indexed by Irish World (m. 1846-1889)

Ballinderry
Earliest Records: b. 1802; m. 1802; d. 1802
Status: LC; SLC film 6026027 (b/m/d. 1802-1870)

Ballyclog
Earliest Records: b. 1828; m. 1828; d. 1828
Status: LC

Ballygawley (see also Errigal Keerogue)
Status: LC; Indexed by Irish World (m. 1845-1921)

Baronscourt
Status: LC; Indexed by Irish World (m. 1858-1921)

Barr
Earliest Records: b. 1880-; m. 1845-; d. 1885-
Status: RCBL (mf) (b. 1880-1982; m. 1845-1934; d. 1885-1921); LC; Indexed by Irish World (m. 1845-1921)

Benburb (see Clonfeacle)

Caledon or Aghaloo
Earliest Records: b. 1791; m. 1791; d. 1791
Status: LC; Indexed by Irish World (m. 1858-1921)

Camus (Mourne)
Earliest Records: b. 1803; m. 1825; d. 1825
Status: LC; SLC film 824282 (m. 1804-1845), film 933419 (b. 1802-1873)

Cappagh
Earliest Records: b. 1758; m. 1758; d. 1758
Status: LC; Indexed by Irish World (m. 1845-1921)

Carnteel (Aughnactsy)
Earliest Records: b. 1805; m. 1805; d. 1805
Status: LC; SLC film (Vestry book extracts, 1711-1807)

Carrickmore (see Termonmaguirk)

Clanabogan
Earliest Records: b. 1863; d. 1863
Status: LC; Indexed by Irish World (m. 1865-1921)

Clogher
Earliest Records: b. 1763; m. 1763; d. 1763
Status: LC; Indexed by Irish World (m. 1845-1921)

Clogherny
Earliest Records: b. 1824; m. 1825; d. 1825
Status: LC; NAI M5049 (b. 1859-75); Indexed by Irish World (m. 1845-1921); NAI and SLC film (extracts 1859-75)

Clonfeacle
Status: LC; Indexed by Irish World (m. 1845-1921)

Clonoe
Earliest Records: b. 1824; m. 1812; d. 1824
Status: LC; Indexed by Irish World (m. 1845-1921)

Cooley or Sixmilecross
Earliest Records: b. 1836; m. 1836; d. 1836
Status: LC

Derg
Earliest Records: b. 1807; m. 1807; d. 1839
Status: LC; Indexed by Irish World (m. 1846-1921)

Derrygortrevy
Status: Lost

Derryloran
Earliest Records: b. 1796; m. 1796; d. 1796
Status: LC

Desertcreat
Earliest Records: b. 1812; m. 1812; d. 1812
Status: LC

Donacavey
Earliest Records: b. 1878-; m. 1845-; d. 1878-
Status: RCBL (mf) (b. 1878-1936; m. 1845-1902; d. 1878-1903); LC; Indexed by Irish World (m. 1845-1921)

Donagheady
Earliest Records: b. 1754; m. 1826; d. 1826
Missing Dates: b. 1766-1825
Status: LC; Indexed by Irish World (m. 1845-1855)

Donaghenry
Earliest Records: b. 1734; m. 1811; d. 1811
Missing Dates: b. 1769-1809
Status: LC

Donaghmore
Earliest Records: b. 1777; m. 1777; d. 1777
Status: LC; Indexed by Irish World (m. 1846-1921)

Donaghmore, Upper
Status: LC; Indexed by Irish World (m. 1845-1921)

Dromore
Status: Lost

Drumakilly
Status: Lost

Drumclamph
Status: Lost

Drumglass
Earliest Records: b. 1600; m. 1754; d. 1754
Missing Dates: b. 1767-1822; m. 1768-1813
Status: LC

Drumrath
Earliest Records: b. 1800; m. 1800; d. 1800
Status: LC

Dunnalong
Status: LC; Indexed by Irish World (m. 1868-1935)

Edenderry
Earliest Records: b. 1841; d. 1849
Status: LC; Indexed by Irish World (m. 1857-1921)

Errigal Keerogue
Earliest Records: b. 1812; m. 1812; d. 1812
Status: LC

Errigle-Portclare
Earliest Records: b. 1835; m. 1835; d. 1835
Status: LC

Errigle-Trough
Earliest Records: b. 1809; m. 1803; d. 1802
Status: LC

Finconagh or Donacavey
Earliest Records: b. 1777; m. 1800; d. 1800
Status: LC; Indexed by Irish World (m. 1845-1921)

Fivemiletown (see also Clogher)
Earliest Records: b. 1804; m. 1804; d. 1804
Status: LC; Indexed by Irish World (m. 1845-1921)

Kildress
Earliest Records: b. 1794; m. 1799; d. 1864
Status: LC

Killeeshill
Status: LC; Indexed by Irish World (m. 1845-1921)

Killyman
Earliest Records: b. 1741; m. 1741; d. 1741
Status: LC; Indexed by Irish World (m. 1845-1921)

Kilskeery
Earliest Records: b. 1772; m. 1772; d. 1772
Status: LC

Longfield Lower
Status: Lost

Longfield Upper
Status: Lost

Leckpatrick
Status: LC; Indexed by Irish World (m. 1845-1921)

Lislimnaghan
Earliest Records: b. 1862; d. 1864
Status: LC

Mountfield
Status: Lost

Moy
Status: LC; Indexed by Irish World (m. 1845-1921)

Newtownsaville
Earliest Records: b. 1877-1901; m. 1860-1935; d. 1877-1933
Status: RCBL (mf)

Pomeroy (see also Altedesert)
Status: LC; Indexed by Irish World (m. 1846-1921)

St. Mary, Portclare (see Errigle-Portclare)
Status: Lost

Sixmilecross or Cooley
Earliest Records: b. 1836; m. 1836; d. 1836
Status: LC

Termonamongan
Earliest Records: b. 1825; m. 1825; d. 1825
Status: LC

Termonmaguirk (see also Drumakilly)
Status: LC; Indexed by Irish World (m. 1846-1921)

Tullyniskin
Earliest Records: b. 1794; m. 1794; d. 1809
Status: LC

Urney (Strabane)
Earliest Records: b. 1813; m. 1814; d. 1815
Status: LC; Indexed by Irish World (m. 1845–1921)

Presbyterian

An account of Presbyterian records is given in the introduction. These registers rarely contain death records, and occasionally have only records of births. This is indicated where appropriate. Many of the Presbyterian registers of Tyrone have been indexed by Irish World (see Research Services at the end of the chapter). A search of the index will be conducted for a fee. Those indexed are noted below as "Indexed by Irish World."

Albany (Stewartstown)
Starting Date: b. 1814
Status: LC; PRONI MIC IP/48

Alt
Starting Date: m. 1845
Status: LC; Indexed by Irish World (m. 1845–1921); PRONI MIC IP/249

Ardstraw
Starting Date: 1837
Status: LC; Indexed by Irish World (m. 1886–1936); PRONI MIC IP/50

Aughataire (Fivemiletown)
Starting Date: 1836
Status: LC; PRONI MIC IP/

Aughnacloy/Carnteel
Starting Date: b/m. 1812
Status: LC; Indexed by Irish World (m. 1845–1921); PRONI MIC IP/38

Badoney
Starting Date: m. 1845
Status: PRONI MIC IP/278

Ballygawley
Starting Date: b. 1842; m. 1845
Status: LC; PRONI MIC IP/61

Ballygorey (Cookstown)
Starting Date: 1834
Status: LC; PRONI MIC IP/

Ballymagrave
Starting Date: b. 1851; m. 1845
Status: LC; PRONI MIC IP/39

Ballynahatty (Omagh)
Starting Date: b. 1845; m. 1843
Status: LC; PRONI MIC IP/97

Ballyreagh (Ballygawley)
Starting Date: 1843
Status: LC; PRONI MIC IP/

Benburb
Starting Date: b. 1874; m. 1845
Status: LC; PRONI MIC IP/60

Brigh (Stewartstown)
Starting Date: b/m. 1837
Status: LC; PRONI MIC IP/13; SLC film 933409 (b. 1808–1875)

Caledon
Starting Date: b. 1870; m. 1848
Status: LC; PRONI MIC IP/28

Carland (Castlecaulfield)
Starting Date: b. 1759; m. 1770
Status: LC; PRONI MIC IP/28

Castlecaulfield (Donaghonore Upper)
Starting Date: m. 1845
Status: LC; Indexed by Irish World (m. 1845–1921); PRONI MIC IP/121

Castlederg
Starting Date: b. 1823; m. 1845
Status: LC; Indexed by Irish World (m. 1845–1921); PRONI MIC IP/73

Cleggan (Cookstown)
Starting Date: 1848
Status: LC; PRONI MIC IP/

Clenanees (Castlecaulfield)
Starting Date: b. 1811; m. 1849; d. 1865
Status: LC; PRONI MIC IP/44 and 45

Clogher (Carntall)
Starting Date: b. 1819; m. 1829
Status: LC; PRONI MIC IP/96

Coagh
Starting Date: 1839
Status: LC; PRONI MIC IP/

Cookstown
Starting Date: b. 1836; m. 1845
Status: LC; PRONI MIC IP/43 and 139

Corrick
Starting Date: m. 1851
Status: LC; PRONI MIC IP/279

Creevan (see Ballymatty 2nd)

Crockantanty
Starting Date: m. 1876
Status: LC; PRONI MIC IP/254

Crossroads (see under Mountjoy)
Starting Date: b. 1821; m. 1845
Status: LC

Donagheady (Strabane)
Starting Date: 1838
Status: LC; PRONI MIC IP/

Douglas
Starting Date: b. 1840; m. 1832

Status: LC; PRONI MIC IP/50

Dromore
Starting Date: b. 1863; m. 1835
Status: LC; PRONI MIC IP/247

Drumleagh
Starting Date: b. 1863; m. 1845
Status: LC; PRONI MIC IP/303

Drumguin
Starting Date: b/m. 1845
Status: LC; PRONI MIC IP/65

Dungannon
Starting Date: b. 1790; m. 1785
Status: LC; PRONI MIC IP/3a

Edenderry (Omagh)
Starting Date: b/m. 1845
Status: LC; PRONI MIC IP/108

Eglish (Dungannon)
Starting Date: b. 1856; m. 1846; d. 1858
Status: LC; PRONI MIC IP/122

Fintona
Starting Date: b/m. 1836
Status: LC; PRONI MIC IP/283

Gillygooly (Omagh)
Starting Date: b. 1848; m. 1845
Status: LC; PRONI MIC IP/234

Glenelly
Starting Date: b. 1848; m. 1845
Status: LC; PRONI MIC IP/234

Glenhoy
Starting Date: b. 1832; m. 1869
Status: LC; PRONI MIC IP/255

Gortin
Starting Date: b. 1843; m. 1845
Status: LC; PRONI MIC IP/234

Killeter
Starting Date: b/m. 1839
Status: LC; PRONI MIC IP/252

Leckpatrick (Strabane)
Starting Date: b. 1838; m. 1835
Status: LC; PRONI MIC IP/49

Magheramason
Starting Date: b. 1878; m. 1881
Status: LC; PRONI MIC IP/369

Minterburn (Caledon)
Starting Date: b. 1829; m. 1845
Status: LC; PRONI MIC IP/26

Mountjoy
Starting Date: b. 1821; m. 1845
Status: LC; PRONI MIC IP/242

Moy
Starting Date: b. 1852; m. 1854

Status: LC; PRONI MIC IP/36

Newmills (Dungannon)
Starting Date: b. 1850; m. 1846
Status: LC; PRONI MIC IP/295

Omagh (1st and 2nd)
Starting Date: b. 1821; m. 1846
Status: LC; PRONI MIC IP/128 and 235

Orritor (Cookstown)
Starting Date: 1831
Status: LC; PRONI MIC IP/

Pomeroy
Starting Date: b. 1841; m. 1845
Status: LC; PRONI MIC IP/120

Sandholes (Cookstown)
Starting Date: b. 1863; m. 1845
Status: LC; PRONI MIC IP/42

Seskinore
Starting Date: b. 1863; m. 1843
Status: LC; PRONI MIC IP/245

Sion
Starting Date: b. 1866; m. 1866
Status: LC; PRONI MIC IP/251

Strabane (1st and 2nd)
Starting Date: b. 1828; m. 1845
Status: LC; PRONI MIC IP/10

Urney (Sion Mills) (2nd Castlederg)
Starting Date: b. 1837; m. 1861
Status: LC; Indexed by Irish World (m. 1861–1921);
PRONI MIC IP/250

Society of Friends (Quaker)

See the introduction for an account of Quaker records.
The records for Tyrone include: Grange Monthly Meeting Register (1653–1861, civil parish of Clonfeacle).
FHL, Dublin; SLC film 571396 (b. 1653–1861; m. 1678–1854; d. 1730–1858).

Roman Catholic

Note that most of the Catholic parish registers of this county have been indexed by Irish World (see Research Services at the end of the chapter). A search of the index will be conducted by the center for a fee. Those indexed are noted as "Indexed by Irish World." Microfilm copies of all registers are also available in the National Library of Ireland (NLI), and through the LDS library system.

Civil Parish: Aghaloo
Map Grid: 38
RC Parish: Aghaloo (Aughnacloy)
Diocese: AM
Earliest Record: b. 1.1846; m. 1826; d. 1868
Missing Dates: m. 5.1834–10.1837

Status: LC; Indexed by Irish World (to 1900); NLI (mf)

Civil Parish: Aghalurcher
Map Grid: 43
RC Parish: see Co. Fermanagh
Diocese: CG
Status: LC; Indexed by Irish World (to 1900); NLI (mf)

Civil Parish: Arboe (see also Co. Derry)
Map Grid: 27
RC Parish: Ardboe or Arboe
Diocese: AM
Earliest Record: b. 11.1827; m. 11.1827
Status: LC, NLI (mf)

Civil Parish: Ardstraw (1)
Map Grid: 6
RC Parish: Ardstraw East (Newtown Stewart); also Ardstraw West, see below
Diocese: DE
Earliest Record: b. 12.1861; m. 12.1860
Status: LC, NLI (mf)

Civil Parish: Ardstraw (2)
Map Grid: 6
RC Parish: Ardstraw West and Castlederg
Diocese: DE
Earliest Record: b. 6.1846; m. 5.1843
Missing Dates: b. 3.1850-1.1852
Status: LC, NLI (mf)

Civil Parish: Artrea
Map Grid: 22
RC Parish: Moneymore, see Artrea, Co. Derry
Diocese: AM

Civil Parish: Ballinderry
Map Grid: 24
RC Parish: see Co. Derry
Diocese: AM

Civil Parish: Ballyclog
Map Grid: 26
RC Parish: see Ardboe
Diocese: AM
Status: LC, NLI (mf); SLC film 933409 (b. 1808-1875)

Civil Parish: Bodoney Lower
Map Grid: 8
RC Parish: see Bodoney Upper
Diocese: DE

Civil Parish: Bodoney Upper
Map Grid: 7
RC Parish: Bodoney Upper (Plumbridge or Cranagh)
Diocese: DE
Earliest Record: b. 10.1866
Status: LC, NLI (mf)

Civil Parish: Camus
Map Grid: 5
RC Parish: Clonleigh and Camus (Strabane)
Diocese: DE
Earliest Record: b. 4.1773; m. 8.1788
Missing Dates: b. 2.1795-1.1836, 5.1837-3.1853; m. 9.1781-3.1843
Status: LC, NLI (mf)

Civil Parish: Cappagh
Map Grid: 9
RC Parish: Cappagh (Killyclogher)
Diocese: DE
Earliest Record: b. 7.1843; m. 7.1843; d. 7.1843
Status: LC, NLI (mf)

Civil Parish: Carnteel
Map Grid: 37
RC Parish: part Aghaloo; part Errigal Kieran
Diocese: AM

Civil Parish: Clogher
Map Grid: 40
RC Parish: Clogher
Diocese: CG
Earliest Record: b. 4.1856; m. 9.1825
Missing Dates: m. 11.1835-3.1840
Status: LC, NLI (mf)

Civil Parish: Clogherny
Map Grid: 15
RC Parish: Beragh (Ballintacker)
Diocese: AM
Earliest Record: b. 9.1832; m. 7.1834
Status: LC; NLI (mf); Indexed by Irish World (to 1900)

Civil Parish: Clonfeacle (see also Co. Armagh)
Map Grid: 35
RC Parish: Clonfeacle (Moy)
Diocese: AM
Earliest Record: b. 10.1814; m. 11.1814
Missing Dates: b. 3.1840-8.1840
Status: LC, NLI (mf); Indexed by Irish World (to 1900)

Civil Parish: Clonoe
Map Grid: 31
RC Parish: Clonoe
Diocese: AM
Earliest Record: b. 2.1810; m. 12.1806; d. 12.1806
Missing Dates: b. 5.1816-10.1822; m. 5.1816-1.1823; d. ends 5.1816
Status: LC, NLI (mf); Indexed by Irish World (to 1900) and AA (to 1900—see Armagh)

Civil Parish: Derryloran (see also Co. Derry)
Map Grid: 21
RC Parish: see Desertcreat
Diocese: AM

Civil Parish: Desertcreat
Map Grid: 25
RC Parish: Desertcreat and Derryloran (Cookstown)
Diocese: AM
Earliest Record: b. 1814; m. 1811
Status: LC, NLI (mf); Indexed by Irish World (to 1900)

Civil Parish: Donacavey
Map Grid: 39
RC Parish: Donaghcavey (Fintona)
Diocese: CG
Earliest Record: b. 11.1857; m. 10.1857
Status: LC, NLI (mf)

Civil Parish: Donaghedy
Map Grid: 1
RC Parish: Donaghedy (Dunamanagh)
Diocese: DE
Earliest Record: b. 4.1854; m. 11.1858; d. 12.1857
Missing Dates: m. 7.1859-12.1862, ends 5.1863; d. ends 7.1859
Status: LC, NLI (mf)

Civil Parish: Donaghenry
Map Grid: 28
RC Parish: Stewartstown (Coalisland)
Diocese: AM
Earliest Record: b. 2.1849; m. 5.1853; d. 1.1854
Status: LC, NLI (mf)

Civil Parish: Donaghmore
Map Grid: 32
RC Parish: Donaghmore (see also Killeeshil)
Diocese: AM
Earliest Record: b. 2.1837; m. 3.1837
Status: LC, NLI (mf); Indexed by Irish World (to 1900); SLC film 962187 (1741-1825), film 883727 (b. index 1748-1825), film 883818 (m. index 1741-1825)

Civil Parish: Dromore
Map Grid: 16
RC Parish: Dromore
Diocese: CG
Earliest Record: b. 11.1835; m. 10.1835
Status: LC, NLI (mf)

Civil Parish: Drumglass
Map Grid: 33
RC Parish: Drumglass, Killyman, and Tullyniskin (Dungannon)
Diocese: AM
Earliest Record: b. 1783; m. 1783; d. 10.1821
Missing Dates: b. 1791-1820; m. 1789-1820, 12.1829-5.1831, 5.1833-8.1833; d. 11.1829-4.1831
Status: LC, NLI (mf); Indexed by Irish World (to 1900)

Civil Parish: Drumragh
Map Grid: 13
RC Parish: Drumragh (Omagh)

Diocese: DE
Earliest Record: b. 5.1846; m. 6.1846; d. 5.1846
Missing Dates: b. 11.1846-11.1853; m. 8.1846-11.1853; d. 7.1846-11.1853
Status: LC, NLI (mf)

Civil Parish: Errigal Keerogue
Map Grid: 41
RC Parish: Errigal Kieran (Ballygawley or Ballymacelroy)
Diocese: AM
Earliest Record: b. 1834; m. 1.1864
Status: LC, NLI (mf); Indexed by Irish World (b. to 1897; m. to 1900)

Civil Parish: Errigal Trough (see Co. Monaghan)
Map Grid: 42
RC Parish: see Co. Monaghan
Diocese: CG

Civil Parish: Kildress
Map Grid: 20
RC Parish: Kildress
Diocese: AM
Earliest Record: b. 1.1835; m. 3.1835; d. 3.1835
Missing Dates: b. 12.1852-1.1857, 8.1859-1.1861, 2.1865-1.1878
Status: LC, NLI (mf); Indexed by Irish World (to 1900) and by AA (see Co. Armagh)

Civil Parish: Killeeshil
Map Grid: 36
RC Parish: Tullyallen, Killeeshil, and Donaghmore
Diocese: AM
Earliest Record: b. 1.1816; m. 1.1816; d. 1.1816
Status: LC, NLI (mf); Indexed by Irish World (to 1900)

Civil Parish: Killyman
Map Grid: 34
RC Parish: Dungannon, see Drumglass
Diocese: AM
Status: LC, NLI (mf)

Civil Parish: Kilskeery
Map Grid: 17
RC Parish: Kilskeery (Trillick)
Diocese: CG
Earliest Record: b. 10.1840; m. 8.1840
Status: LC, NLI (mf)

Civil Parish: Learmount
Map Grid: 3
RC Parish: see Cumber Upper, Co. Derry
Diocese: DE

Civil Parish: Leckpatrick
Map Grid: 2
RC Parish: Leckpatrick; also part Donaghedy
Diocese: DE
Earliest Record: b. 9.1863; m. 9.1863
Status: LC, NLI (mf)

Civil Parish: Lissan
Map Grid: 19
RC Parish: Lissan
Diocese: AM
Earliest Record: b. 1822; d. 1822
Status: LC, NLI (mf); Indexed by Irish World (to 1900)

Civil Parish: Longfield East
Map Grid: 12
RC Parish: see Longfield West
Diocese: DE

Civil Parish: Longfield West
Map Grid: 11
RC Parish: Drumquin (Longfield)
Diocese: DE
Earliest Record: b. 9.1846; m. 9.1846; d. 7.1853
Missing Dates: d. ends 2.1856
Status: LC, NLI (mf)

Civil Parish: Magheracross
Map Grid: 18
RC Parish: see Derryvullan, Co. Fermanagh
Diocese: CG

Civil Parish: Pomeroy
Map Grid: 29
RC Parish: Pomeroy
Diocese: AM
Earliest Record: b. 2.1837; m. 3.1837; d. 3.1837
Missing Dates: b. 11.1840-12.1841, 5.1852-4.1857, 8.1865-2.1869; m. 12.1840-12.1841, 6.1865-7.1869; d. 12.1840-4.1857, 4.1861-7.1871
Status: LC, NLI (mf); Indexed by Irish World (to 1900)

Civil Parish: Tamlaght (see also Co. Derry)
Map Grid: 23
RC Parish: see Arboe
Diocese: AM

Civil Parish: Termonamongan
Map Grid: 10
RC Parish: Termonamongan (Aghyaran)
Diocese: DE
Earliest Record: b. 3.1863; m. 9.1863
Status: LC, NLI (mf)

Civil Parish: Termonmaguirk (1)
Map Grid: 14
RC Parish: Termonmaguirc (also Carrickmore, see below)
Diocese: AM
Earliest Record: b. 12.1834; m. 10.1834
Missing Dates: b. ends 2.1857; m. ends 12.1857
Status: LC, NLI (mf); Indexed by Irish World (to 1857)

Civil Parish: Termonmaguirk (2)
Map Grid: 14
RC Parish: Carrickmore

Earliest Record: b. 1881; m. 1881
Status: LC; NLI (mf); Indexed by Irish World (to 1900)

Civil Parish: Tullyniskan
Map Grid: 30
RC Parish: see Drumglass
Diocese: AM

Civil Parish: Urney
Map Grid: 4
RC Parish: Urney, see Co. Donegal
Diocese: DE

Commercial and Social Directories

1819
Thomas Bradshaw's *General Directory of Newry* lists traders in Dungannon.

1820
Thomas Bradshaw's *General Directory.* Newry, 1819.

J. Pigot's *Commercial Directory of Ireland* contains information on the gentry, nobility, and traders in and around the town of Strabane.

1824
J. Pigot's *City of Dublin and Hibernian Provincial Directory* includes traders, nobility, gentry, and clergy lists of Aughnacloy, Cookstown, Dungannon, Moy and Charlemont, Newtown-Stewart, Omagh, Stewartstown, and Strabane.

1842
Martin's *Belfast Directory* lists residents of principal streets, gentry, and traders in Cookstown, Dungannon, and Stewartstown.

1846
Slater's *National Commercial Directory of Ireland* lists nobility, clergy, traders, etc., in Aughnacloy, Cookstown and Desertcreat, Dungannon, Coal Island and Donaghmore, Moy and Charlemont, Newtownstewart, Omagh, Stewartstown, and Strabane.

1852
Henderson's *Belfast and Province of Ulster Directory* has lists of inhabitants, traders, etc., in and around the towns of Aughnacloy, Cookstown, Dungannon, Moy, and Charlemont.

1854
Further edition of the above covers Aughnacloy, Bellaghy, Clogher, Cookstown, Dungannon, Moy and Charlemont, Omagh, Stewartstown, and Strabane. Fur-

ther editions issued in 1856, 1858, 1861, 1863, 1865, 1868, 1870, 1877, 1880, 1884, 1890, 1894, 1900.

1856

Slater's *Royal National Commercial Directory of Ireland* lists nobility, gentry, clergy, traders, etc., in Aughnacloy and Ballygawley, Clogher and Five-Mile-Town, Cookstown, Dungannon, Coal Island and Donaghmore, Moy and Charlemont, Newtown-Stewart, Omagh, Stewartstown, and Strabane.

1865

R. Wynne's *Business Directory of Belfast* covers Cookstown, Dungannon, Omagh, and Strabane.

1870

Slater's *Directory of Ireland* contains trade, nobility, and clergy lists for Aughnacloy, Caledon, Castlederg, Clogher and Five-Mile-Town, Cookstown, Moy, Newtownstewart and Gortin, Omagh, Stewartstown, and Strabane.

1881

Slater's *Royal National Commercial Directory of Ireland* contains lists of traders, clergy, nobility, and farmers in adjoining parishes of the towns of Aughnacloy, Castlederg, Clogher and Five-Mile-Town, Cookstown and Stewartstown, Dungannon, Newtownstewart and Gortin, Omagh, and Strabane.

1882

The *Omagh Almanac* has lists of clergy, school staff, medical practitioners, and gentry for the county. It also lists traders in Cookstown, Dungannon, Fintona, Omagh, and Strabane.

1885

Further edition of above.

1887

Derry Almanac of Castlederg, Fintona, Gortin, Newtown-Stewart, Omagh, and Strabane (issued annually from 1891).

1888

Further edition of *Omagh Almanac* (see 1882).

1891

Further edition of *Omagh Almanac* covering traders and lists of residents (with *): Aughnacloy,* Augher,* Ballygawley, Beragh, Clogher, Cookstown, Dromore, Drumquin,* Dungannon, Fintona, Gortin, Newtownstewart, Omagh,* Sixmilecross, Strabane, and Trillick.

Family History

A Web page for researchers in Tyrone is http://pw2.netcom.com/~vanessa1/from-tyrone.html.

Abercorn (Hamilton) Family Records (1611–1890). PRONI DOD 623; SLC (mf).

Campbell, F. *The Genealogy of Robert Campbell of Co. Tyrone.* New York, 1909.

Develin, J. *The O'Devlins of Tyrone: The Story of an Irish Sept.* Rutland, Vermont, 1938.

Godfrey, Earnest H., comp. *The Lindesays of Loughry, Co. Tyrone: A Genealogical History.* London, 1949.

Hamilton—see Fermanagh.

Macausland Family Papers (Strabane—1250–1942). PRONI DOD 669; SLC film 248300.

Marshall, John J., ed. *Vestry records of the Church of St. John, Parish of Aghalow with an account of the family of Hamilton of Caledon 1691–1807.* Dungannon, 1935 (NLI Ir 27411 a2).

"Irwin family, Altmore, Pomeroy." *Family Links* 1 (7) (1983): 17–20.

"Notes on the Family of Cairnes, Co. Tyrone." *J. Ass. Pres. Mem. Dead* 12 (1926-31): 297.

Steward Family Papers (1671–1720). PRONI DOD 459; SLC film 247311.

Gravestone Inscriptions

Irish World (see Research Services at the end of the chapter) has indexed a huge range of gravestone inscriptions from seven hundred graveyards in Tyrone and Fermanagh. The full list is not included here for reasons of space. This index can be searched for a fee.

Published sources of gravestone inscriptions are:

Clogher: Johnston, John I.D. *Clogher Cathedral Graveyard.* 1972.

Donaghcavey: *Clogher Record* 7 (2) (1970): 299–320.

Drumglass: *Seanchas Ardmhacha* 9 (2) (1974): 316-19.

Grange (Strabane): published by Sheelagh and David Dodd, 1993.

Kilskeery (Old): *Clogher Record* 8 (1) (1973): 51-57.

Newspapers

For biographical notices from 1772 onward, the *Londonderry Journal* (see Co. Derry) should also be consulted, as its circulation covered much of Tyrone.

Title: *Mid-Ulster Mail*
Published in: Cookstown, 1891–current
NLI Holdings: 1.1899–5.1915; 1.1950–in progress
BL Holdings: 2.1891–5.1915; 1.1923–12.1925; 1.1927–12.1940; 1.1942–in progress

Title: *Strabane Chronicle*
Published in: Strabane, 1896–current
NLI Holdings: 1.1950–in progress
BL Holdings: 1.1899–in progress

Title: *Strabane Morning Post*
Published in: Strabane, 1812–37
BL Holdings: 1.1823–4.1837

Title: *Tyrone Constitution*
Published in: Omagh, 1844–current
NLI Holdings: 1.1885–12.1941
BL Holdings: 11.1844–4.1853; 2.1854–3.1861;
3.1862–12.1927; 1.1929–in progress

Title: *Ulster Chronicle* (continued as *Tyrone Courier and Dungannon News* in 1921 and as *Dungannon News and Tyrone Courier* from 6.1968)
Published in: Dungannon, 1807–ca. 1824
NLI Holdings: 1.1885–12.1913; 6.1921–8.1947;
1.1954–5.1968
BL Holdings: 1.1880–12.1889; 1.1904–12.1916

Wills and Administrations

A discussion of the types of records, where they are held, and their availability and value is given in the Wills section of the introduction. The availability of prerogative wills, administrations, and marriage license records is also described in the relevant parts of the same section. Where available, published sources of these records are given in the Miscellaneous Sources section.

Pre-1858 Wills and Administrations

Prerogative Wills. See the introduction.

Consistorial Wills. County Tyrone is divided among the dioceses of Armagh, Derry, and Clogher. The guide to Catholic parish records in this chapter shows the diocese to which each civil parish belonged. The wills of residents of each diocese were usually proven within that diocese (see the Wills section for exceptions). The following records survive:

Wills

See the introduction.

Abstracts

See the introduction.

Indexes

Armagh—see Co. Armagh. Derry (1612–1858) published to 1858 by Phillimore. Clogher (1661–1858). Clogher Diocesan Marriage License Bonds (1709–1866). NAI and SLC film 100862.

Post-1858 Wills and Administrations

This county was served by the District Registries of Londonderry and Armagh. The surviving records are kept in the PRONI. Records include Armagh District Will Books (1858–1900). SLC films 917210, 917484–88, 917906–16.

Marriage Licenses

Indexes

Armagh (1727–1845). PRO; SLC film 100859–860.
Clogher (1709–1866). PRO; SLC film 100862.

Miscellaneous Sources

O'Kane, W. "Surnames of Co. Tyrone." *Irish Roots* 4 (1993): 28–29.

An Introduction to the Abercorn Letters (as Relating to Ireland, 1736–1816). Omagh, 1972 (correspondence of the Duke of Abercorn's family relating to their estates in Ireland).

Gebbie, Canon J.H. *Ardstraw (Newtownstewart): Historical Survey of a Parish (1600–1900).* Omagh: Strule Press, 1968.

"High Sheriffs of Tyrone 1606–1903." Appendix U. *The History of Two Ulster Manors.* Earl of Belmore, London/Dublin, 1903.

MacEvoy, J. *Statistical Survey of County Tyrone.* 1802. Reprint. Belfast: Friars Bush Press, 1991.

Provisional list of pre-1900 School Registers in the PRONI. *Ulster Gen. and Hist. Guild* 9 (1986): 60–71.

"The Survey of Armagh and Tyrone 1622." *Ulster J. Arch.* 23 (1960): 126–37; 27 (1964): 140–54.

"Volunteer Companies of Ulster 1778–1793." *Tyrone Irish Sword* 8 (1968): 210–17 (officers' names only).

County of Tyrone 1802 by John McEvoy. 1802. Reprint. Friars Bush Press, 1991.

Workhouse Records: Records of Strabane Union Workhouse (1862–1883). PRONI; SLC film 259164–5. Persons admitted to and discharged from Clogher Union Workhouse (1863–1881). PRONI; SLC film 993083.

Duffy, Patrick. *Landscapes of South Ulster (Parish Atlas of Diocese of Clogher).* Belfast: Institute of Irish Studies, 1993.

Research Sources and Services

Journals

Seanchas Ardmhacha
Clogher Record
North Irish Roots

Libraries and Information Sources

Western Education and Library Board, Library Headquarters, Dublin Road, Omagh, Co. Tyrone. Ph: (080662) 44821. This library has an extensive collection of local history materials, including newspapers, periodicals, maps, and other sources.

Ulster-American Folk Park Library, Mellon Road, Castletown, Omagh, Co. Tyrone, N. Ireland BT78 5QY. Ph: (01662) 243292; fax: (01662) 242241; e-mail: uafp@iol.ie. This library is primarily for migration studies. Its central theme is emigration to the New World between 1700 and 1900, with particular emphasis on the lives and experiences of Ulster emigrants. It holds an emigration database of information on all aspects of Irish emigration, including ship passenger lists, emigrants' letters, family papers, etc. The database may be accessed directly, or through the libraries of Northern Ireland.

Research Services

Irish World, 26 Market Sq., Dungannon, Co. Tyrone BT70 1AB. Ph: (018687) 24187; fax: (01868) 752141; e-mail: irishwld@gpo.iol.ie; home page: http://www.iol.ie/irishworld/. This organization is the official IGP indexing center for Fermanagh and Tyrone. It has compiled one of the largest databases of family history information in the country. This includes church records, gravestone inscriptions from seven hundred graveyards, civil records of birth, death, and marriage, census and land records, etc. Researchers are advised to contact the center for an updated list of registers, and other sources, indexed. A research service is provided for a fee. They have also published books on local history subjects, and produce coats of arms and related products.

See also Research Services in Belfast in the introduction.

Societies

North of Ireland Family History Society, Queens University of Belfast, Dept. of Education, 69 University Street, Belfast BT7 1HL. Publishers of *North Irish Roots*

Clogher Historical Society, Mr. J.I.D. Johnston, Corick, Clogher, Co. Tyrone. This society publishes *Clogher Record*, which deals with the social, church, political, archaeological, and genealogical history of the dio-

cese of Clogher. This covers South Tyrone, as well as the counties of Monaghan, Fermanagh, and a small part of Donegal around Ballyshannon.

Coalisland and District Historical Society, Mrs. Sheila Quinn, Marymount, Creenagh Hill, Dungannon, Co. Tyrone, BT71 6EY. Ph: (01868) 748616

Gortin and District Historical Society, Ms. Kathleen McSwiggan, 106 Gorticashel Road, Gortin, Omagh, Co. Tyrone, BT79 8NT. Ph: (01662) 648436

Killester and District Historical Society, Mr. Daniel McSorley, 15 Meenamullen Road, Killeter, Castlederg, Co. Tyrone, BT81 8HQ. Ph: (01662) 670331

Muintirevlin Historical Society, Mrs. Mary McCann, 144 Ardboe Road, Coagh, Cookstown, Co. Tyrone, BT80 OHU. Ph: (01648) 736014

O'Neill Country Historical Society, Mr. Brendan J. McAnallen, Tullygiven, Brantry, Dungannon, Co. Tyrone. Ph: (01861) 548387

Rock and District Historical Society, Miss Ellen Doris, Clare, Cookstown, Co. Tyrone, BT80 8RJ. Ph: (016487) 62035

Stewartstown and Dist. Local History Society, Mrs. Joan Laverty, The Castle Farm, Stewartstown, Dungannon, Co. Tyrone, BT71 5LD. Ph: (01868) 738668

Strabane History Society, Mr. Brian Carlin, 35 Carricklynn Avenue, Urney Road, Strabane, Co. Tyrone, BT82 9BF. Ph: (01504) 884979

Tempo Historical Society, Mrs. Mary Hamilton, Furnish, Fivemiletown, Co. Tyrone, BT75 OQY. Ph: (01365) 521416

Termonmaguire Historical Society, Mr. Michael Haughey, Granagh, Carrickmore, Sixmilecross, Omagh, Co. Tyrone. Ph: (01662) 761525

West Tyrone Historical Society, Mr. Harry B. McCartney, 32 Lisanelly Park, Omagh, Co. Tyrone, BT79 7DE. Ph: (01662) 243113

Donaghmore Historical Society, Miss Evelyn Cardwell, Augharan, Carland, Dungannon, Co. Tyrone, BT71 4HG. Ph: (01868) 767388

Tyrone Civil Parishes as Numbered on Map

1. Donaghedy
2. Leckpatrick
3. Learmount
4. Urney (2 pts.)
5. Camus

6. Ardstraw
7. Bodoney Upper
8. Bodoney Lower
9. Cappagh
10. Termonamongan

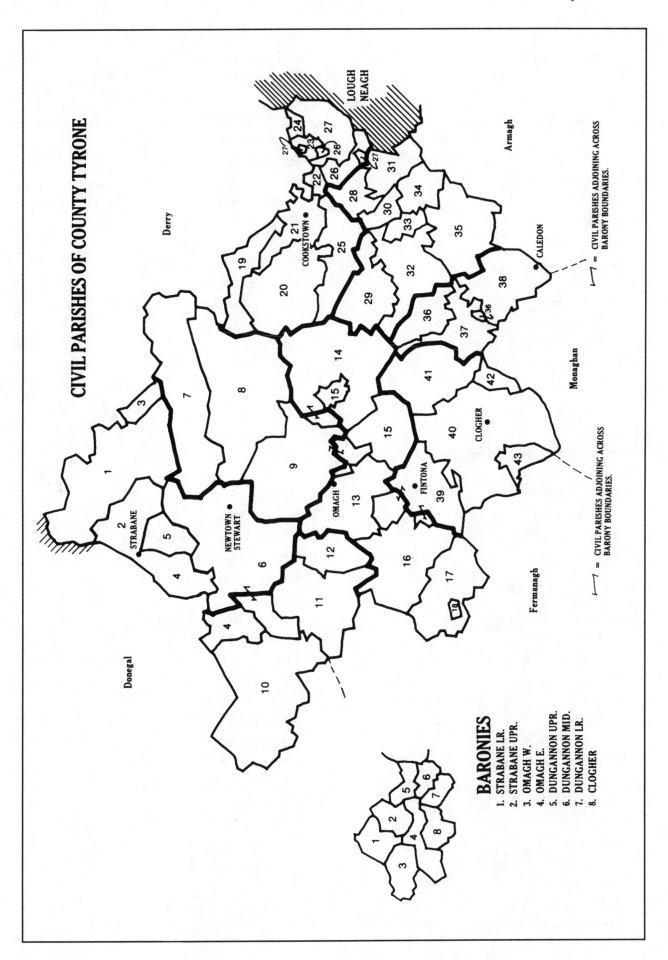

CIVIL PARISHES OF COUNTY TYRONE

LOUGH NEAGH

Derry

Armagh

Monaghan

Fermanagh

Donegal

COOKSTOWN

CALEDON

CLOGHER

FINTONA

OMAGH

NEWTOWN STEWART

STRABANE

⌐ = CIVIL PARISHES ADJOINING ACROSS BARONY BOUNDARIES.

⌐ = CIVIL PARISHES ADJOINING ACROSS BARONY BOUNDARIES.

BARONIES
1. STRABANE LR.
2. STRABANE UPR.
3. OMAGH W.
4. OMAGH E.
5. DUNGANNON UPR.
6. DUNGANNON MID.
7. DUNGANNON LR.
8. CLOGHER

11. Longfield West
12. Longfield East
13. Drumragh
14. Termonmaguirk
15. Clogherney (2 pts.)
16. Dromore
17. Kilskeery
18. Magheracross
19. Lissan
20. Kildress
21. Derryloran
22. Artrea
23. Tamlaght
24. Ballinderry
25. Desertcreat
26. Ballyclog (2 pts.)
27. Arboe (2 pts.)

28. Donaghenry
29. Pomeroy
30. Tullyniskan
31. Clonoe
32. Donaghmore
33. Drumglass
34. Killyman
35. Clonfeacle
36. Kileeshil (2 pts.)
37. Carnteel
38. Aghaloo (2 pts.)
39. Donaghcavey
40. Clogher
41. Errigal Keerogue
42. Errigal Trough
43. Aghalurcher

Tyrone Civil Parishes in Alphabetical Order

Aghaloo (2 pts.): 38
Aghalurcher: 43
Arboe (2 pts.): 27
Ardstraw: 6
Artrea: 22
Ballinderry: 24
Ballyclog (2 pts.): 26
Bodoney Upper: 7
Bodoney Lower: 8
Camus: 5
Cappagh: 9
Carnteel: 37
Clogher: 40
Clogherney (2 pts.): 15
Clonfeacle: 35
Clonoe: 31
Derryloran: 21
Desertcreat: 25
Donaghcavey: 39
Donaghedy: 1
Donaghenry: 28
Donaghmore: 32

Dromore: 16
Drumglass: 33
Drumragh: 13
Errigal Keerogue: 41
Errigal Trough: 42
Kildress: 20
Kileeshil (2 pts.): 36
Killyman: 34
Kilskeery: 17
Learmount: 3
Leckpatrick: 2
Lissan: 19
Longfield West: 11
Longfield East: 12
Magheracross: 18
Pomeroy: 29
Tamlaght: 23
Termonamongan: 10
Termonmaguirk: 14
Tullyniskan: 30
Urney (2 pts.): 4

County Waterford

A Brief History

Home of the manufacturer of the famous Waterford crystal, this coastal Munster county contains the city of Waterford and the towns of Dungarvan, Tramore, Lismore, and Cappoquin.

Most of the present county was originally in the Kingdom of Decies. The major families were the O'Phelans, McGraths, O'Briens, and O'Keanes.

The town of Waterford itself was founded by the Danish Vikings in A.D. 853. The Danes successfully defended the town against the local inhabitants and remained a powerful force in the county until the eleventh century, when the city was taken by the Normans. However, as the Danes did not use surnames, there is little evidence of the Viking heritage in the names now found in the county.

After the Norman invasion, the county was granted to Robert de Poer, whose family are the ancestors of the Powers. Other Norman names now common in the county are Aylward, Wyse, and Wall. Wadding, an Anglo-Saxon name, has also been found in Waterford since Norman times. The city of Waterford became a stronghold of the Normans and was second only to Dublin in its importance.

Following the unsuccessful insurrection of the Earl of Desmond (see Co. Kerry), part of Waterford was confiscated from its owners and planted with English settlers in 1583. Many of these left again in 1598 during the war with Hugh O'Neill (see Co. Tyrone). In the 1641 rebellion of the Catholic Confederacy (see Co. Kilkenny), the city sided with the Irish Catholics and successfully withstood a siege by Oliver Cromwell's army. The city finally surrendered the following year following a second siege by Cromwell's army, led by General Ireton. Neither the 1583 nor the 1650 settlements were very significant, however.

Waterford has been an important port since its establishment and has had extensive trading links with many countries. There is, for instance, a long-established link with eastern Canada, particularly Newfoundland. Considerable emigration to Canada from Waterford took place, and there is much evidence of Waterford people traveling to and from eastern Canadian ports, even to the extent of families bringing children back to Waterford to be baptized.

The county suffered considerably in the Great Famine of 1845-47. The population in 1841 was 196,000 and by 1851 had fallen twenty percent, to 164,000. Approximately 25,000 people died in the years 1845-50, and the remainder emigrated to the cities or, more usually, abroad. Between 1851 and 1855, for instance, over 28,000 people emigrated from the county. During the remainder of the century the population continued to decline through emigration, so that by 1891 it was only 98,000. It is currently 89,000.

The town is still an important port, and also has several major industries: a dairy industry, which processes the produce of the county's many dairy herds; engineering; and the previously mentioned Waterford crystal glass, which was first manufactured here in 1783.

Census and Census Substitutes

1542-1650

"The Freemen of Waterford." *Ir. Gen.* 5 (5) (1978): 560-72.

1641

"Proprietors of Waterford" (name and street). *J. Cork Hist. and Arch. Soc.* 51 (173) (1946): 10-30.

A 1783 map of the road from Waterford to Carrick-on-Suir. From Taylor and Skinner's *Maps of the Roads of Ireland* (Dublin, 1783).

1654–56

"The Civil Survey A.D. 1654-1656." R.C. Simington. Dublin: Stationery Office, 1942.

1659

"Census" of Ireland. Edited by S. Pender. Dublin: Stationery Office, 1939. NLI 16551. SLC film 924648.

1662

"Subsidy Roll" (taxpayers of over £1 annual land value or £3 annual goods value). *Anal. Hib.* 30 (1982): 47-96.

1663

"Inhabitants of Waterford City, Showing Trade or Profession." *J. Cork Hist. and Arch. Soc.* 51.

1663–64

"Tenants or Possessors of Waterford" (name and street). *J. Cork Hist. and Arch. Soc.* 51 (173) (1946): 10-30.

1664–66

Civil Survey, Vol. 6. SLC film 973123.

1700

"Members of Some Waterford Guilds." *J. Waterford and S.E. Ire. Arch. Soc.* 7 (1901): 61-65.

1760

"Tenants of Bellew Properties in and Adjoining Dungarvan." *J. Waterford and S.E. Ire. Arch. Soc.* 19 (4) (1911): 103-07 (index to estate map—some fifty-five names, addresses, property and lease details).

1766

Householders of Parish of Killoteran, Waterford City. NAI Parl. Returns 1413; SLC film 100158; GO ms. 684.

1772

Hearth Money Rolls for parts of Waterford. *J. Waterford and S.E. Ire. Arch. Soc.* 15 (1912).

1775

Catholic Qualification Roll Extracts (174 names, addresses, and occupations). 59th Report DKPRI: 50-84.

"Principal Gentry of Co. Waterford." *J. Waterford and S.E. Ire. Arch. Soc.* 16 (2) (1913): 49-55.

1778

"Inhabitants of Waterford City." *Freeman's J.* 16 (30) (29 October 1778); 16 (32) (3 November 1778); 16 (33) (5 November 1778); SLC film 993913.

1792

"The Leading Catholics of Waterford in 1792." *Ir. Anc.* 8 (2) (1976): 80-81.

1793

Tenants of Lands, etc., belonging to City of Waterford and Other Accounts. NLI; GO 1917 (gives original lessees, current tenants of described premises, plus names of suppliers or employees paid by city, with description of the service provided; over three hundred names).

1807

"How Waterford City Voted in 1807" (voter lists). *Ir. Anc.* 8 (11): 18-32.

1821

"Extracts from the Census of the City of Waterford." *Ir. Gen.* 4 (1) (1968): 17-26; 4 (2) (1969): 122-30; SLC film 100158.

"Transcript of 1821 Government Census Returns for Townland of Callaghane." *Decies* 17 (1981): 67-70.

The abstracts for Waterford city (2,188 records) have been indexed by Thomas Veale, who has placed copies in the NAI, Waterford City Library, and other archives.

Extracts (selected surnames) for Ballylaneen, Ballynakill, Clashmore, Clonagam, Crooke, Drumcannon, Dungarvan, Dunhill, Faithlegg, Fenagh, Kilgobnet, Kill St. Nicholas, Killea, Kilmacomb, Kilmeaden, Lisnakill, Newcastle, Rathmolyan, Reisk, Ringagonag, Stradbally, Waterford, and Whitechurch. GO Ms. 684; SLC film 100158.

1823–38

Tithe Applotment Survey (see introduction).

1831 and 1841

Extracts from Government Census for the Parish of Dungarvan, mainly for the names Walsh and Kelly. QUB; SLC film 100158; NAI; GO Ms. 684.

1835

A complete list of voters for Parliamentary election for city of Waterford. Waterford: Thomas Hanton, 1835. (Names and addresses of all the voters.)

1839

Waterford City Polling List, 1839. *Ir. Gen.* 8 (2) (1991): 275-289.

1841

Ratepayers, Contractors, and Suppliers to Waterford County. Statement of Accounts, Spring Assizes. NLI I 6551.

Extracts from 1841 census for Dungarvan (selected surnames). NAI; GO Ms. 684; SLC film 100158.

1843

Voters List. NAI 1843/65.

1846

Ratepayers, Contractors, and Suppliers to Waterford County. Statement of Accounts, Spring Assizes. NLI I 6551.

1847

"Names of Principal Fishermen in Ring, with Names of Boats, etc." Alcock, J. *Facts from the Fisheries 1848.* Waterford, 1848. NLI I6551.

1848–51

Griffith's Valuation (see introduction).

1849

"Ballysaggart Estate." *Decies* 27 (1984): 4–12 (account of evictions and trial; gives some tenants' names).

1851

Extracts from the Government Census of Drumcannon (Tramore), Mainly for the Names Walsh and Kelly. QUB; SLC film 100158.

1857

"The Estate of George Lane Fox." *Decies* 26 (1984): 52–59 (mainly parish of Kilbarry; gives tenants' names and holdings).

1901

Census. NAI.

1911

Census. NAI.

Church Records

Church of Ireland

See the introduction for a description of Church of Ireland records and their major repositories. Many C of I records were lost in the PRO fire of 1922. These are indicated as "Lost." However, as Church of Ireland records were effectively state records, the records of marriage (from 1845) are also in the General Registrar's Office. Many are still in local custody (LC), while others are in one of a variety of other archives (e.g., RCBL or NAI). All of the Church of Ireland registers of this county have been indexed by Waterford Heritage Limited (see Research Services at the end of the chapter). A search of the index will be conducted by the center for a fee. Those indexed are noted as "Indexed by WHL."

Ardmore and Ballymacart
Status: Lost

Ballylaneen
Earliest Records: b/m/d. 1800
Status: LC; SLC film 990092 (b/d. 1800–64; m. 1800–45)

Ballynakill
Status: Lost

Cappoquinn
Earliest Records: b. 1844
Status: LC

Carrickbeg (see Dysart)

Clashmore
Earliest Records: b. 1828–
Status: LC; NAI M5085 (b. 1828–76)

Clonegam
Earliest Records: b. 1741; m. 1742; d. 1743 (one register, 1820–25, in custody of rector of Fethard-on-Sea)
Status: LC; NAI MFCI 13, 15 (b. 1741–1870; m. 1742–1845; 1743–1875)

Colnea
Earliest Records: b/m/d. 1800
Status: LC; SLC film 990092 (b/d. 1800–64; m. 1800–45)

Dungarvan
Earliest Records: b. 1741; m. 1741; d. 1741
Status: LC; NAI MFCI 10 and M5056–8 (b/m/d. 1741–1875)

Dunhill
Status: Lost

Dysart
Status: Lost

Guilcagh
Status: Lost

Innislonagh
Earliest Records: b. 1801; m. 1800; d. 1805
Status: NAI

Kill St. Nicholas
Earliest Records: b. 1730; m. 1730; d. 1730
Status: LC; NAI MFCI 8 (b/m/d. 1730–1864); SLC film 897365 (b/d. 1730, 1735–1864; m. 1730, 1736–1862; d. 1730, 1736–1862)

Killea (see also Kill St. Nicholas)
Earliest Records: b. 1816–; m. 1816–; d. 1849–
Status: LC; NAI M5363 (b. 1816–54; m. 1816–49; d. 1849–52)

Killoteran
Earliest Records: b. 1770; m. 1768; d. 1758
Missing Dates: b. 1829–76; d. 1773–1838
Status: LC

Killrossanty
Earliest Records: b. 1838–; m. 1838–; d. 1843–
Status: LC; NA M5952 (b. 1838-76; m. 1838-41; d. 1843-71); SLC film 990092 (b/d. 1838-65; m. 1838-45; d. 1838-71)

Kilmeadon
Earliest Records: b. 1683; m. 1683; d. 1683
Status: LC

Kilronan
Status: Lost

Kilwatermoy (see also Tallow)
Earliest Records: b. 1860–; d. 1858–
Status: LC; NAI M5355, 5350 (b. 1860-72; d. 1858-80)

Kinsalebeg and Grange
Earliest Records: b. 1817; m. 1827; d. 1841
Status: LC

Lismore
Earliest Records: b. 1693–; m. 1692–; d. 1711–
Status: LC; NAI MFCI 1 and 18, and M5222, 5982 (b. 1693-1841; m. 1692-1847; d. 1711-1841); marriages (1692-1838) are in *Ir. Gen.* 6 (1) (1980): 38-47

Macollop
Status: Lost

Macully or Kilculliheen
Status: Lost

Monksland
Earliest Records: b. 1836; m. 1837; d. 1836
Status: LC

Mothel
Status: Lost

Ringagonagh
Status: Lost

Rossmire
Earliest Records: b. 1834; m. 1803; d. 1836
Status: LC; NAI M5370 (b. 1866-71; d. 1866-71)

Stradbally
Earliest Records: b. 1798; m. 1798; d. 1798
Status: LC and NAI; SLC film 990092 (b/d. 1800-64; m. 1800-45) and film 883875 (b. index)

Tallow (see also Kilwatermoy)
Earliest Records: b. 1772–; m. 1772–; d. 1772–
Missing Dates: b. 1810-28; m. 1810-28; d. 1810-28
Status: LC; NAI MFCI 9, M5357 (b. 1829-74; d. 1831-73); SLC film 924521 (b. 1772-1828; m. 1776-96; d. 1772-98); film 883740 (b. index); film 883818 (m. index)

Templemichael
Earliest Records: b. 1801–; m. 1804–; d. 1823–
Status: LC; NAI M5065/6, 5356 (b. 1801-72; m. 1804-65; d. 1823-1920); SLC film 924521 (b/d.

1821-1865; m. 1814-65); film 883662 (b. index); film 1001477 (m. index)

Waterford City-Holy Trinity
Earliest Records: b/m/d. 1655–
Status: LC; NAI MFCI 12, 13 (b. 1655-1857; m. 1655-1850; d. 1655-1892)

Waterford City-St. Olave
Earliest Records: b. 1741–; m. 1742–; d. 1744–
Status: LC; NAI MFCI 10, 11; M5366, 5368/9 (b. 1741-1872; m. 1742-1845; d. 1744-1838)

Waterford City-St. Patrick's
Earliest Records: b. 1723–; m. 1725–; d. 1723–
Status: LC; NAI MFCI 10, 11 (b. 1723-1872; m. 1725-1845; d. 1723-1855)

Whitechurch
Status: Lost

Presbyterian
An account of Presbyterian records is given in the introduction. These registers rarely contain death records, and occasionally have only records of births.

Waterford
Starting Date: 1770
Status: LC

Society of Friends (Quaker)
See the introduction for an account of Quaker records. The records for Waterford include: Waterford Monthly Meeting Register (1624-1860). FHL, Dublin; SLC film 571398 (b. 1624-1856; m. 1649-1860; d. 1656-1860).

Roman Catholic
Note that all of the Catholic parish registers of this county have been indexed by Waterford Heritage Limited (see Research Services at the end of the chapter). A search of the index will be conducted by the center for a fee. Those indexed are noted as "Indexed by WHL." Microfilm copies of all registers are also available in the National Library of Ireland (NLI), and through the LDS library system.

Civil Parish: Affane
Map Grid: 19
RC Parish: see Modeligo
Diocese: LS

Civil Parish: Aglish
Map Grid: 68
RC Parish: Aglish
Diocese: LS
Earliest Record: b. 1831; m. 1833
Status: LC; NLI (mf); Indexed by WHL (to 1900)

Civil Parish: Ardmore
Map Grid: 69
RC Parish: Ardmore; also part Aglish

Diocese: LS
Earliest Record: b. 1816; m. 1.1823
Status: LC; NLI (mf); Indexed by WHL (b. to 1900; m. 1857–1900)

Civil Parish: Ballygunner
Map Grid: 58
RC Parish: see Waterford City, Trinity Within
Diocese: WA

Civil Parish: Ballylaneen
Map Grid: 34
RC Parish: see Stradbally
Diocese: LS

Civil Parish: Ballymacart
Map Grid: 74
RC Parish: see Ardmore
Diocese: LS

Civil Parish: Ballynakill
Map Grid: 51
RC Parish: see Waterford City, St. John's Within
Diocese: WA

Civil Parish: Clashmore
Map Grid: 71
RC Parish: Clashmore
Diocese: LS
Earliest Record: b. 1.1811; m. 1.1810
Status: LC; NLI (mf); Indexed by WHL (to 1900)

Civil Parish: Clonea
Map Grid: 32
RC Parish: see Kilgobnet
Diocese: LS

Civil Parish: Clonegam
Map Grid: 11
RC Parish: Portlaw
Diocese: LS
Earliest Record: b. 1.1809 (three registers for some periods); m. 1.1805
Status: LC; NLI (mf); Indexed by WHL (to 1900)

Civil Parish: Colligan
Map Grid: 27
RC Parish: see Kilgobnet
Diocese: LS

Civil Parish: Corbally
Map Grid: 66
RC Parish: Tramore, see Drumcannon
Diocese: WA

Civil Parish: Crooke
Map Grid: 60
RC Parish: see Killea
Diocese: WA

Civil Parish: Drumcannon
Map Grid: 47
RC Parish: Tramore

Diocese: WA
Earliest Record: b. 1.1798; m. 1785
Status: LC; NLI (mf); Indexed by WHL (to 1900)

Civil Parish: Dungarvan (1)
Map Grid: 30
RC Parish: Dungarvan; also Abbeyside, see below
Diocese: LS
Earliest Record: b. 2.1787; m. 5.1809
Missing Dates: b. 4.1798–9.1811; m. 5.1823–7.1823
Status: LC; NLI (mf); Indexed by WHL (to 1900)

Civil Parish: Dungarvan (2)
Map Grid: 30
RC Parish: Abbeyside
Diocese: LS
Earliest Record: b. 7.1828; m. 7.1828
Missing Dates: m. 2.1842–5.1842
Status: LC; NLI (mf); Indexed by WHL (to 1900)

Civil Parish: Dunhill
Map Grid: 44
RC Parish: Dunhill and Fenor
Diocese: LS
Earliest Record: b. 4.1829 (two registers for period 1852–76); m. 11.1836; d. 1.1879
Missing Dates: d. ends 11.1881
Status: LC; NLI (mf); Indexed by WHL (to 1900)

Civil Parish: Dysert
Map Grid: 6
RC Parish: Carrickbeg, see Kilmoleran
Diocese: LS

Civil Parish: Faithlegg
Map Grid: 53
RC Parish: see Killea
Diocese: WA

Civil Parish: Fenoagh
Map Grid: 8
RC Parish: Carrickbeg, see Kilmoleran
Diocese: LS

Civil Parish: Fews
Map Grid: 25
RC Parish: see Kilrossanty
Diocese: LS

Civil Parish: Grange or Lisgrennan
Map Grid: 73
RC Parish: see Ardmore
Diocese: LS

Civil Parish: Guilcagh or Guilco
Map Grid: 12
RC Parish: Portlaw, see Clonegam

Civil Parish: Inish-Lounaght
Map Grid: 1
RC Parish: see Inish-Lounaght, Co. Tipperary

Civil Parish: Islandikane
Map Grid: 48

RC Parish: see Dunhill
Diocese: WA

Civil Parish: Kilbarry
Map Grid: 54
RC Parish: see Waterford City, Trinity Without
Diocese: WA

Civil Parish: Kilbarrymeaden
Map Grid: 36
RC Parish: Kill (Newtown)
Diocese: LS
Earliest Record: b. 3.1797; m. 4.1797
Missing Dates: b. 8.1830-2.1831
Status: LC; NLI (mf); Indexed by WHL (to 1900)

Civil Parish: Kilbride
Map Grid: 46
RC Parish: see Dunhill
Diocese: WA

Civil Parish: Kilburne
Map Grid: 42
RC Parish: see Waterford City, Trinity Without
Diocese: WA

Civil Parish: Kilcaragh
Map Grid: 57
RC Parish: see Waterford City, Trinity Within
Diocese: WA

Civil Parish: Kilcockan
Map Grid: 17
RC Parish: Knockanore
Diocese: LS
Earliest Record: b. 5.1816; m. 2.1854
Missing Dates: b. 4.1833-9.1833
Status: LC; NLI (mf); Indexed by WHL (to 1900)

Civil Parish: Kilcop
Map Grid: 59
RC Parish: see Killea
Diocese: WA

Civil Parish: Kilculliheen
Map Grid: 13
RC Parish: Slieverue, see Rathpatrick, Co. Kilkenny
Diocese: LS

Civil Parish: Kilgobnet
Map Grid: 23
RC Parish: Kilgobinet
Diocese: LS
Earliest Record: b. 4.1848; m. 10.1848
Missing Dates: b. 10.1872-3.1873
Status: LC; NLI (mf); Indexed by WHL (to 1900)

Civil Parish: Killaloan
Map Grid: 4
RC Parish: see St. Mary's Clonmel, Co. Tipperary
Diocese: LS

Civil Parish: Killea
Map Grid: 65

RC Parish: Killea and Crooke (Dunmore East)
Diocese: WA
Earliest Record: b. 1809; m. 1.1780
Missing Dates: b. 7.1820-10.1845; m. 10.1791-
1.1793, 2.1798-4.1815, 7.1820-8.1837, 7.1838-
10.1845
Status: LC; NLI (mf); Indexed by WHL (to 1900)

Civil Parish: Killoteran
Map Grid: 38
RC Parish: see Waterford City, Trinity Without
Diocese: WA

Civil Parish: Kill St. Lawrence
Map Grid: 55
RC Parish: see Waterford City, Trinity Within
Diocese: WA

Civil Parish: Kill St. Nicholas
Map Grid: 52
RC Parish: see Killea
Diocese: WA

Civil Parish: Killure
Map Grid: 56
RC Parish: see Waterford City, Trinity Within
Diocese: WA

Civil Parish: Kilmacleague
Map Grid: 62
RC Parish: see Killea
Diocese: WA

Civil Parish: Kilmacomb
Map Grid: 63
RC Parish: see Killea
Diocese: WA

Civil Parish: Kilmeaden
Map Grid: 37
RC Parish: Portlaw, see Clonegam
Diocese: LS

Civil Parish: Kilmolash
Map Grid: 28
RC Parish: part Cappoquin, see Lismore; part Aglish
Diocese: LS

Civil Parish: Kilmoleran
Map Grid: 7
RC Parish: Carrickbeg
Diocese: LS
Earliest Record: b. 1.1842; m. 1.1807
Missing Dates: b. 10.1846-2.1847
Status: LC; NLI (mf); Indexed by WHL (to 1900)

Civil Parish: Kilronan (1)
Map Grid: 2
RC Parish: part Inishlounaght, see Co. Tipperary;
part Touraneena, see Seskinan; part St. Mary's
Clonmel
Diocese: LS

Civil Parish: Kilronan (2)
Map Grid: 43
RC Parish: Ballybricken, see Waterford City, Trinity Without
Diocese: WA

Civil Parish: Kilrossanty
Map Grid: 24
RC Parish: Kilrossanty
Diocese: LS
Earliest Record: b. 7.1822; m. 1.1859
Missing Dates: b. 8.1858–1.1859
Status: LC; NLI (mf); Indexed by WHL (to 1900)

Civil Parish: Kilrush
Map Grid: 31
RC Parish: see Dungarvan
Diocese: LS

Civil Parish: Kilsheelan (also in Co. Tipperary)
Map Grid: 5
RC Parish: Kilsheelan (Gambonsfield and Kilcash)
Diocese: LS
Earliest Record: b. 1840; m. 1840
Status: LC; NLI (mf); Indexed by WHL (to 1900)

Civil Parish: Kilwatermoy
Map Grid: 16
RC Parish: Knockanore, see Kilcockan
Diocese: LS

Civil Parish: Kinsalebeg
Map Grid: 72
RC Parish: see Clashmore
Diocese: LS

Civil Parish: Leitrim
Map Grid: 13a
RC Parish: see Kilworth, Co. Cork
Diocese: CY

Civil Parish: Lickoran
Map Grid: 21
RC Parish: see Modelligo
Diocese: LS

Civil Parish: Lisgrennan (see Grange)

Civil Parish: Lismore and Mocollop (1)
Map Grid: 14
RC Parish: Ballyduff; also Lismore, see below (2); also Cappoquin, see below (3)
Diocese: LS
Earliest Record: b. 6.1849; m. 11.1853
Missing Dates: m. 1.1861–6.1861
Status: LC; NLI (mf); Indexed by WHL (to 1900)

Civil Parish: Lismore and Mocollop (2)
Map Grid: 14
RC Parish: Lismore
Diocese: LS
Earliest Record: b. 3.1820; m. 11.1822

Missing Dates: b. 2.1831–7.1840, 7.1848–2.1849, 4.1858–8.1866; m. 9.1839–2.1840
Status: LC; NLI (mf); Indexed by WHL (to 1900)

Civil Parish: Lismore and Mocollop (3)
Map Grid: 14
RC Parish: Cappoquin
Diocese: LS
Earliest Record: b. 4.1810; m. 1.1807
Status: LC; NLI (mf); Indexed by WHL (to 1900)

Civil Parish: Lisnakill
Map Grid: 41
RC Parish: see Waterford City, Trinity Without
Diocese: WA

Civil Parish: Modelligo
Map Grid: 20
RC Parish: Modelligo
Diocese: LS
Earliest Record: b. 7.1815; m. 1820
Status: LC; NLI (mf); Indexed by WHL (to 1900)

Civil Parish: Monamintra
Map Grid: 61
RC Parish: see Waterford City, Trinity Within
Diocese: WA

Civil Parish: Monksland
Map Grid: 35
RC Parish: see Inish-Lounaght, Co. Tipperary
Diocese: LS

Civil Parish: Mothel
Map Grid: 10
RC Parish: see Rathgormuck
Diocese: LS

Civil Parish: Newcastle
Map Grid: 40
RC Parish: Newcastle (and Fourmilewater)
Diocese: LS
Earliest Record: b. 7.1814; m. 1.1822
Status: LC; NLI (mf); Indexed by WHL (to 1900)

Civil Parish: Rathgormuck
Map Grid: 9
RC Parish: Clonea (Mothel and Rathgormack)
Diocese: LS
Earliest Record: b. 3.1831; m. 1852
Status: LC; NLI (mf); Indexed by WHL (to 1900)

Civil Parish: Rathmoylan
Map Grid: 67
RC Parish: see Killea
Diocese: WA

Civil Parish: Reisk
Map Grid: 45
RC Parish: see Dunhill
Diocese: WA

Civil Parish: Rinagonagh
Map Grid: 70
RC Parish: Ring and Old Parish
Diocese: LS
Earliest Record: b. 1813; m. 1813
Status: LC; NLI (mf); Indexed by WHL (to 1900)

Civil Parish: Rossduff
Map Grid: 64
RC Parish: see Killea
Diocese: WA

Civil Parish: Rossmire
Map Grid: 26
RC Parish: see Stradbally
Diocese: LS

Civil Parish: St. Mary's Clonmel (also in Co. Tipperary)
Map Grid: 3
RC Parish: Clonmel, St. Mary's
Diocese: LS
Earliest Record: b. 1790; m. 1798
Status: LC; NLI (mf); Indexed by WHL (to 1900)

Civil Parish: Seskinan
Map Grid: 22
RC Parish: Touraneena
Diocese: LS
Earliest Record: b. 7.1852; m. 7.1852
Status: LC; NLI (mf); Indexed by WHL (to 1900)

Civil Parish: Stradbally
Map Grid: 33
RC Parish: Stradbally
Diocese: LS
Earliest Record: b. 1797; m. 8.1805
Status: LC; NLI (mf); Indexed by WHL (to 1900)

Civil Parish: Tallow
Map Grid: 15
RC Parish: Tallow
Diocese: LS
Earliest Record: b. 4.1797; m. 4.1798
Missing Dates: b. 9.1842-1.1856; m. 4.1803-10.1808
Status: LC; NLI (mf); Indexed by WHL (to 1900)

Civil Parish: Templemichael
Map Grid: 18
RC Parish: Knockanore, see Kilcockan
Diocese: LS

Waterford City

Civil Parish: St. John's Within
Map Grid: 49
RC Parish: St. John's
Diocese: WA
Earliest Record: b. 4.1706; m. 4.1706
Missing Dates: b. 3.1730-3.1759, 3.1787-8.1807, 3.1816-6.1818 (microfilm ends in 1837); m. 3.1730-2.1760, 1.1817-9.1828

Status: LC; NLI (mf); Indexed by WHL (1759-1900)

Civil Parish: St. John's Without
Map Grid: 50
RC Parish: see St. John's Within
Diocese: WA

Civil Parish: St. Michael's
Map Grid: 49
RC Parish: part St. John's Within; part Trinity Within
Diocese: WA
Earliest Record: b. 12.1732; m. 6.1796
Missing Dates: m. ends 11.1796
Status: see St. John's Within

Civil Parish: St. Olave's
Map Grid: 49
RC Parish: see Trinity Within
Diocese: WA

Civil Parish: St. Patrick's
Map Grid: 49
RC Parish: St. Patrick's
Diocese: WA
Earliest Record: b. 4.1731; m. 4.1731
Missing Dates: b. 9.1791-5.1795, 3.1801-4.1827; m. 5.1791-1.1799, 12.1800-9.1826
Status: LC; NLI (mf); Indexed by WHL (to 1900)

Civil Parish: St. Peter's
Map Grid: 49
RC Parish: see Trinity Within
Diocese: WA
Earliest Record: b. 11.1737; m. 11.1743
Missing Dates: b. ends 8.1746; m. ends 1.1787
Status: see Trinity Within

Civil Parish: St. Stephen's Within
Map Grid: 49
RC Parish: part of St. John's
Diocese: WA
Earliest Record: b. 9.1731
Missing Dates: b. ends 3.1749
Status: see St. John's Within

Civil Parish: St. Stephen's Without
Map Grid: 49
RC Parish: see St. John's
Diocese: WA

Civil Parish: Trinity Within
Map Grid: 49
RC Parish: Trinity Within
Diocese: WA
Earliest Record: b. 1.1729; m. 9.1747
Missing Dates: b. 7.1775-2.1793; m. 12.1756-2.1761, 8.1777-1.1791, 6.1795-1.1797
Status: LC; NLI (mf); Indexed by WHL (to 1900)

Civil Parish: Trinity Without
Map Grid: 39

RC Parish: Trinity Without
Diocese: WA
Earliest Record: b. 1.1797; m. 1.1797
Status: LC; NLI (mf); Indexed by WHL (to 1900)

Civil Parish: Whitechurch
Map Grid: 29
RC Parish: see Aglish
Diocese: LS

Commercial and Social Directories

Many of the directories of this county have been indexed by Thomas Veale, who has placed copies in the National Archives; Waterford City Library; Irish Genealogical Research Society, London; and the Irish Genealogical Society, St. Paul, Minnesota. Those indexed have been marked "Indexed by Veale—see above."

1788

Richard Lucas's *General Directory of the Kingdom of Ireland* contains lists of traders in Dungarvan, Passage, and Waterford. Reprinted in *Ir. Gen.* 3 (10) (1965): 392–416. Indexed by Veale—see above.

1809

Holden's *Triennial Directory* has an alphabetical list of traders in the city of Waterford. SLC films 100179 and 258722.

1820

J. Pigot's *Commercial Directory of Ireland* contains information on the gentry, nobility, and traders in and around the towns of Dungarvan and Waterford.

1824

J. Pigot's *City of Dublin and Hibernian Provincial Directory* includes traders, nobility, gentry, and clergy lists of Cappoquin, Dungarvan, Kilmacthomas, Lismore, Tallow, Tramore, and Waterford. Indexed by Veale—see above.

1839

T.S. Harvey's *Directory of Waterford* contains alphabetical lists of gentry, merchants, and traders; it also has a house-by-house street directory.

T. Shearman's *New Commercial Directory for the Cities of Waterford . . .* lists traders, gentry, clergy, etc., in Waterford. Indexed by Veale—see above.

1840

F. Kinder's *New Triennial and Commercial Directory for 1840, '41, and '42* contains traders and other lists for Waterford City (rare volume).

1846

Slater's *National Commercial Directory of Ireland* lists nobility, clergy, traders, etc., in Dungarvan, Dunmore, Kilmacthomas, Lismore, Portlaw, Tallow, Tramore, and Waterford. Indexed by Veale—see above.

1856

Slater's *Royal National Commercial Directory of Ireland* lists nobility, gentry, clergy, traders, etc., in Bonmahon, Dungarvan, Dunmore, Kilmacthomas, Lismore and Cappoquin, Portlaw, Tallow, Tramore, and Waterford.

1866

T.S. Harvey's *Waterford Almanac and Directory* has an alphabetical list of residents and traders. It also has a useful period map of the city.

1869

Newenham Harvey's *Waterford Almanac and Directory* has a house-by-house directory, an alphabetical list of residents, and a list of traders.

1870

Slater's *Directory of Ireland* contains trade, nobility, and clergy lists for Bonmahon, Dungarvan, Dunmore, Kilmacthomas, Lismore and Cappoquin, Portlaw, Tallow, Tramore, and Waterford.

1881

Slater's *Royal National Commercial Directory of Ireland* contains lists of traders, clergy, nobility, and farmers in adjoining parishes of the towns of Dungarvan, Dunmore, Kilmacthomas, Lismore, Cappoquin and Tallow, Portlaw and Fiddown, Tramore, and Waterford.

1886

Francis Guy's *Postal Directory of Munster* lists gentry, clergy, traders, principal farmers, teachers, and police sergeants in each postal district of the county and has a listing of magistrates, clergy, and the professions for the whole county. SLC film 1559399.

1893

Francis Guy's *Postal Directory of Munster* lists traders and farmers in each of the postal districts of the county and has a general alphabetical index to persons in the whole county.

1894

Slater's *Royal National Directory of Ireland* lists traders, police, teachers, farmers, and private residents in each of the towns, villages, and parishes of the county.

P.M. Egan's *History, Guide and Directory of County and City of Waterford* lists householders and traders; also city mayors (1377–1891), city sheriffs (1575–1891), and high sheriffs of the county (1270–1891). Indexed by Veale—see above.

1909/10

Thom's *Commercial Directory*.

Family History

"The Ansons at Ardmore." *Ardmore* 5 (1988): 44–50.

"The Anthony Family of Carrigcastle and Seafield." *Decies* 16 (1981): 15–22.

Genealogical Account of the Bagge Family of Co. Waterford. Dublin, 1860.

"The Barkers of Waterford." *Decies* 17 (1981): 17–28.

"Distinguished Waterford Families: Baron." *J. Waterford and S.E. Ire. Arch. Soc.* 17 (1914): 47–65, 128–34, 137–52; 18 (1915): 69–87, 91–104.

"The Boltons of Co. Waterford." *Ir. Gen.* 7 (2): 186–200; 7 (3): 405–420; 7 (4): 615–641.

"Ancient and Illustrious Waterford Families: The Dobbyns and Waddings." *J. Waterford and S.E. Ire. Arch. Soc.* 4 (1955): 247–50.

"The Family of Everard." *Ir. Gen.* 7 (3): 328–348; 7 (4): 505–542; 8 (2): 175–206; 8 (4): 575–601; 9 (1): 43–72.

"The Fitzgeralds of Farnane, Co. Waterford, Redmond." *J. Waterford and S.E. Ire. Arch. Soc.* 14 (1911): 27–39, 72–81; 15 (1912): 168–76.

"Kavanagh Papers" (Borris, Co. Carlow). *Anal. Hib.* 25: 15–30.

Lloyd, A.R. *Genealogical Notes on Lloyd Family in Co. Waterford.* N.p., n.d.

"The Waterford Merrys." *J. Waterford and S.E. Ire. Arch. Soc.* 16 (1913): 30–35.

"The Nevins Family 1800–1840." *Decies* 37 (1988): 9–19.

"The O'Dells of Carriglea." *Ardmore* 3 (1986): 44–59.

O'Shee—see Power-O'Shee.

"Power-O'Shee Papers" (Gardenmorris, Co. Waterford). *Anal. Hib.* 20: 216–58.

"The Powers of Clashmore, Co. Waterford." *J. Cork Hist. and Arch. Soc.* 47 (1924): 121–22.

"The Prendergast Family." Notes on the family collected for John P. Prendergast. This and other Prendergast papers relative to Tipperary and Waterford are in Kings Inn Library, Dublin.

"The Rivers Family of Co. Waterford." *Decies* 12 (1979): 32–61.

"The Roberts Family of Waterford." *J. Waterford and S.E. Ire. Arch. Soc.* 2 (1896): 98–103.

"Pedigree of Ryland of Dungarvan and Waterford." *R.S.A.I.* 15 (1881): 562–65.

"The Thurstons and Ardmore." *Ardmore* 1 (1984): 26–30; 2 (1985): 32.

"Distinguished Waterford Families, I. Sherlock." *J. Waterford and S.E. Ire. Arch. Soc.* 9 (1906): 120–28, 171–75; 10 (1907): 42–44, 171–73.

"Sherlock of Butlerstown, Co. Waterford." *Ir. Gen.* 4 (2) (1969): 131–41.

Genealogia Dell' Antica e Nobile Famiglia Smyth di Ballynatray Nella Contea di Waterford in Irlanda. Estratta dagli antichi dal fu Cavaliere William Betham. Lucca, 1868.

"Tandy of Sion Lodge." Pedigree in *Swanzy Notebooks.* RCB Library, Dublin.

"Ussher Papers" (Cappagh, Co. Waterford). *Anal. Hib.* 15: 63–78.

Wright, W.B. *The Ussher Memoirs, or Genealogical Memoirs of the Ussher Families in Ireland.* London, 1899.

Wadding—see Dobbyn.

Higgins, P. "Ancient and Illustrious Waterford Families. The Wyses of the Manor of St. John's, Waterford." *J. Waterford and S.E. Ire. Arch. Soc.* 5 (1899): 199–206.

Gravestone Inscriptions

Some of the gravestone inscriptions of the county have been indexed by Waterford Heritage Limited (see Research Services at the end of the chapter); and others in Waterford City by Michael O'Sullivan (and indexed by Thomas Veale). Copies of the latter are in the National Archives; Waterford City Library; Irish Genealogical Research Society, London; and the Irish Genealogical Society, St. Paul, Minnesota.

Affane: *Ir. Gen.* 2 (9) (1952): 285–89.

Ballybricken: Recorded by M. O'Sullivan, indexing planned (see above).

Ballygunner, Old: GO-IGRS Collection No 56.

Ballynakill (C of I): GO-IGRS Collection No. 40.

Carbally: GO-IGRS Collection No. 153.

Churchtown (Dysert): *Decies* 25 (1984): 32–39.

Clashmore: *Ir. Gen.* 2 (8) (1950): 246–49.

Crook, Old: GO-IGRS Collection No. 138.

Crook (RC): GO-IGRS Collection No. 4.

Crumlin: *Ir. Gen.* 7 (3) (1988): 454–473.

Drumcannon: GO-IGRS Collection No. 86; and *Decies* 45 (1992): 49–61.

Dunhill, Old: GO-IGRS Collection No. 23.

Dunhill, East (C of I): GO-IGRS Collection No. 123.

Faha Chapel of Ease: *Decies* 17 (1981): 71–78.

Faithlegg: GO-IGRS Collection No. 166.

Fenough: GO-IGRS Collection No. 16.

French Church (Franciscan): *R.S.A.I.* (1973).

Guilcagh (C of I): GO-IGRS Collection No. 11.

Islandkane: GO-IGRS Collection No. 9.

Kilbarry: Recorded by M. O'Sullivan and indexed by T. Veale (see above).

Kilculliheen, Abbey Church: Recorded by M. O'Sullivan and indexed by T. Veale (see above).

Kill St. Lawrence: GO-IGRS Collection No. 170.

Killea (Old): GO-IGRS Collection No. 94.

Killoteran: GO-IGRS Collection No. 31.

Kilmedan: GO-IGRS Collection No. 122.

Knockeen: GO-IGRS Collection No. 6.

Lisnakill: GO-IGRS Collection No. 35.

Mothel: *Decies* 38 (1988): 17–27; 39 (1988): 45–53; 40 (Spring 1989): 46–55; 41 (Summer 1989): 46–51; 42 (Winter 1989): 33–39.

Mothel—Le Poer Family Plot: *Decies* 42 (1989): 40–43.

Newcastle: GO-IGRS Collection No. 38.

Passage: GO-IGRS Collection No. 1.

Portlaw (C of I): GO-IGRS Collection No. 7.

Rathmoylan: GO-IGRS Collection No. 10; and *Decies* 43 (1990): 9–11.

Rathcormack: *Decies* 37 (1988): 35–46 (120 inscriptions).

Reisk: GO-IGRS Collection No. 86.

Stradbally: *Decies* 16 (1981): 61–68; 17 (1982).

Waterford—Catholic Cathedral (St. John's, St. Olave's, St. Patrick's, St. Peter's): Recorded by M. O'Sullivan and indexed by T. Veale (see above).

Waterford—Christchurch Cathedral: Recorded by M. O'Sullivan and indexed by T. Veale (see above).

Waterford—French Church: Recorded by M. O'Sullivan, indexing planned (see above).

Waterford—John's Hill: Recorded by M. O'Sullivan, indexing planned (see above).

Waterford—St. John's Priory: Recorded by M. O'Sullivan and indexed by T. Veale (see above).

Waterford—St. Patrick's: Power, Rev. P. *Catholic Record of Waterford and Lismore.* Vol. 4. 1916.

Waterford—St. Thomas's: Recorded by M. O'Sullivan and indexed by T. Veale (see above).

Whitechurch: *Ir. Anc.* 5 (1) (1973).

Newspapers

A card index to biographical notices in Waterford, Ennis, Clonmel, and Limerick newspapers up to 1821 (50,000 items) is available on microfiche from Ms. R. ffolliott, Glebe House, Fethard, Co. Tipperary. A copy of this is held by NLI and Waterford City Library and some other archives. Note also that many of the biographical notices from *Ramsay's Waterford Chronicle* and the *Waterford Herald* have been abstracted and published. See the Miscellanous Sources section for details.

Title: *The Citizen* (see *The Waterford Citizen*)

Title: *The Mail* (see *The Waterford Mail*)

Title: *Mail and Waterford Daily Express*
Published in: Waterford, 1855–60
NLI Holdings: 1–11.1856; 1–12.1857; 1–6.1859
BL Holdings: 7.1855–6.1860

Title: *Munster Express* (and *Co. Tipperary Independent and Celt*)
Published in: Waterford, 1860–current
NLI Holdings: 1863–68 (with gaps); 1908–23 (with gaps); 1926–40
BL Holdings: 7.1860–7.1869; 1.1870–3.1905; 9.1906–in progress

Title: (Ramsey's) *Waterford Chronicle* (called *The Chronicle* from 1884)
Published in: Waterford, 1771–1910
NLI Holdings: 1771; 1777; 1811–12; 1.1814–12.1814; 1816–17; 1.1818–12.1818; 1819–23; 7.1827–12.1827; 1.1829–5.1849; 1.1905–12.1910
BL Holdings: 1771; 1.1811–12.1812; 1.1816–12.1817; 1.1819–12.1822; odd numbers 1826, 1827; 1.1829–5.1849; 8.1859–12.1875; 1.1889–12.1910
Indexed (1756–1827) in ffolliot Index; index for parts of 1776–96 published in *Irish Genealogist* (see Miscellaneous Sources section)

Title: *The Waterford Citizen and Waterford Commercial Record* (also *New Ross News* from 1902)
Published in: Waterford, 1859–1906
BL Holdings: 9.1859–6.1876; 12.1876–2.1906

Title: *Waterford Freeman*
Published in: Waterford, 1845–47
NLI Holdings: 7.1845–4.1847
BL Holdings: 7.1845–4.1847

Title: *Waterford Herald*
Published in: Waterford, ca. 1789–96
NLI Holdings: 6–11.1791; 1–11.1792; 1–10.1793; 11.1793–9.1794
BL Holdings: odd numbers 1793–96
Index for 1791–1796 published in *Irish Genealogist* (see Miscellaneous Sources section)

Title: *The Waterford Mail* (plus several additional titles from 1853–84)
Published in: Waterford, 1823–1908
BL Holdings: 8.1823–3.1905; 6.1907–9.1908

Title: *Waterford Mirror*
Published in: Waterford, ca. 1798–1843
NLI Holdings: 1804–40 (one volume, odd issues); 1–12.1807; 8.1808–7.1809; 2.1821–12.1824; 1.1827–9.1840
BL Holdings: 8.1808–7.1809; 1.1827–9.1843
Indexed (1756–1827) in ffolliot Index

Title: *Waterford Mirror and Tramore Visitor*
Published in: Waterford, 1860–1910

BL Holdings: 8.1860–7.1869; 4.1870–6.1873; 1–8.1875; 1.1884–12.1910

Title: *Waterford News*
Published in: Waterford, 1848–1958
NLI Holdings: 9.1848–3.1857; 1.1860–12.1883; 1.1885–12.1913; 5–12.1920; 8.1927–1.1959
BL Holdings: 9.1848–7.1869; 1.1870–12.1929; 1.1931–12.1958

Wills and Administrations

A discussion of the types of records, where they are held, and their availability and value is given in the Wills section of the introduction. The availability of prerogative wills, administrations, and marriage license records is also described in the relevant parts of the same section. Where available, published sources of these records are given in the Miscellaneous Sources section.

Pre-1858 Wills and Administrations

Prerogative Wills. See the introduction.

Consistorial Wills. County Waterford is mainly in the dioceses of Waterford and Lismore. One parish is in Cloyne diocese. The guide to Catholic parish records in this chapter shows the diocese to which each civil parish belonged. The wills of residents of each diocese were usually proven within that diocese (see the Wills section for exceptions). The following records survive:

Wills

See the introduction. NLI holds 1660 Waterford Wills and Administrations. NLI D 9248–9413. See Miscellaneous Sources for published references.

Abstracts

See the introduction and Miscellaneous Sources.

The Welply Will Abstracts in the RCBL contain extracts from 1,682 Munster wills, mainly from Cork. Index contains name, date of will, and (usually) probate, residence. Index in *Ir. Gen.* from 6 (6) 1985 to 7 (1) 1986.

"Old Wills." *J. Waterford and S.E. Ire. Arch. Soc.* 16 (4) (1913): 183–94 (extracts of biographical information, etc.); 17 (1) (1914): 17–32; 17 (2) (1914): 71–91; 17 (3) (1914): 170–81; 18 (1) (1915): 32–39; 18 (4) (1915): 152–74; 19 (1) (1920): 34–47.

"Wills Relating to Waterford" 3 (Index A–K). *Decies* 19 (1982): 39–52; 4 (Index L–Z). *Decies* 20 (1982): 51–60; *Decies* 22 (1983): 50–54; 6. *Decies* 23 (1983): 17–22.

Extracts relating to Waterford City and County in PRO. Compiled by Edmund Walsh Kelly. GO Ms. 684; SLC film 100158.

Indexes

Waterford and Lismore (1648–1858) up to 1800 published by Phillimore. Cloyne—see Co. Cork. "Index to Waterford Wills 1583–1810." *J. Waterford and S.E. Ire. Arch. Soc.* 8 (31) (1902): 24–29 (over four hundred names, dates, and occupations); 8 (32) (1903) (over three hundred names, dates, and addresses).

Post-1858 Wills and Administrations

This county was served by the District Registry of Waterford. The surviving records are kept in the NAI. Records include Waterford District Will Books (1858–1894). NAI; SLC film 100951–4.

Marriage Licenses

Indexes

Waterford and Lismore (1661–1750). NAI; SLC film 100872.

License Bonds

Jennings Mss. Published in "Marriage License Bonds, Chancery Bills, etc., in the Jennings Mss." *Decies* 24 (1983): 20–24 (mainly for the families Bray and Ronayne).

See Miscellaneous Sources for indexes.

Miscellaneous Sources

"Business Records Relating to Co. Waterford in the PRO." *Decies* 21 (1982): 43–55.

"Biographical Notes from Commonplace Book of Thomas Hayden. Carrickbeg, Co. Waterford." *Ir. Gen.* 9 (2) (1995): 195–201 (deaths, marriages, and miscellaneous items).

Nolan and Power, eds. *Waterford History and Society: Interdisciplinary Essays on the History of an Irish County.* Dublin: Geography Publications, 1986.

Egan, P.M. "History, Guide and Directory of County and City of Waterford." Kilkenny: the author, 1894. Intended to amplify the histories by Smith (1745) and Ryland (1824) by concentrating more on the history of Catholics.

"Genevese Exiles in County Waterford." *J. Cork. Hist. and Arch. Soc.* 75 (1970): 29–35.

"How Waterford City Voted in 1807." *Ir. Anc.* 8 (1) (1976): 18–32.

"Extracts from the *Waterford Herald* 1792." *Ir. Gen.* 6 (2) (1981): 154–58.

"Extracts from the *Waterford Herald* 1793, 1794, 1796." *Ir. Gen.* 6 (3) (1982): 334–52.

"Ramsay's *Waterford Chronicle* 1776. Births, Marriages and Deaths." *Ir. Gen.* 5 (3) (1976): 335–67.

"Ramsay's *Waterford Chronicle* 1777. Births, Marriages

and Deaths." *Ir. Gen.* 5 (4) (1977): 471–90; 5 (5) (1978): 625–42.

"Ramsay's *Waterford Chronicle* 1791. Births, Marriages and Deaths." *Ir. Gen.* 5 (6) (1979): 735–59.

"Ramsay's *Waterford Chronicle* 1778 and from the *Waterford Herald* 1650. Births, Marriages and Deaths." *Ir. Gen.* 6 (1) (1980): 22–37.

Smith, Charles. *The Ancient and Present State of the County and City of Waterford.* Containing a natural, civil, ecclesiastical, historical, and topographical description. Dublin: Wilson, 1774, pp. xx, 376. Reprint. Cork: Mercier, 1969.

"Some Seventeenth-Century Funeral Entries." *J. Waterford and S.E. Ire. Arch. Soc.* 6 (1900): 165–70.

"Village of Kill (Part of Kilbarrymeadon)" (all census and other surveys listed). Supplement to *Decies* 8 (1978): 19–42.

Cuffe, O.W. Records of the Waterford Militia, 1584–1885. (1885.) SLC 941.91. M27c.

Estates of Heathcote family in Cork and Waterford (tenant lists, rentals, and accounts). Hampshire Co. Record Office; SLC film 1471720.

Research Sources and Services

Journals

Journal of the Waterford and South East Ireland Archaeological Society

Decies (journal of the Old Waterford Society)

Ardmore

Libraries and Information Sources

Waterford City Library, Lady Lane, Waterford. Ph: (051) 73501. The local studies section has an extensive collection of local material on the county, including maps, family papers, periodicals, newspapers, etc.

Research Services

Waterford Heritage Limited, St. Patrick's Church, Jenkins Lane, Waterford. Ph: (051) 76123; fax: (353) 51 50645. This is the official IGP center for Co. Waterford. They have indexed most of the church registers and have access to many other genealogical sources for the county. Researchers are advised to contact the center for an updated list of registers, and other sources, indexed. Research on this database will be conducted for a fee.

Irish Origins Research Agency, College Road, Kilkenny. Ph: (056) 21483; fax: (056) 64777. Genealogical research service, specializing in counties Kilkenny, Carlow, Tipperary, Wexford, and Waterford.

See also Research Services in Dublin in the introduction.

Societies

Waterford Literary and Historical Society, 37 The Quay, Waterford

Old Waterford Society, Mr. Edward Synnott, Kilbride, Glenmore, via Waterford

Waterford Civil Parishes as Numbered on Map

1. Inishlounaght
2. Kilronan
3. St. Mary's Clonmel
4. Killaloan
5. Kilsheelan
6. Dysert
7. Kilmoleran
8. Fenoagh
9. Rathgormuck
10. Mothel
11. Clonegam
12. Guilcagh
13. Kilculliheen
13a. Leitrim
14. Lismore and Mocollop
15. Tallow
16. Kilwatermoy
17. Kilcockan
18. Templemichael
19. Affane
20. Modelligo
21. Lickoran
22. Seskinan
23. Kilgobnet (3 pts.)
24. Kilrossanty
25. Fews
26. Rossmire
27. Colligan
28. Kilmolash
29. Whitechurch
30. Dungarvan (2 pts.)
31. Kilrush
32. Clonea (2 pts.)
33. Stradbally
34. Ballylaneen
35. Monksland
36. Kilbarrymeadan
37. Kilmeadan
38. Killoteran
39. Trinity Without
40. Newcastle
41. Lisnakill
42. Kilburne
43. Kilronan
44. Dunhill
45. Reisk
46. Kilbride
47. Drumcannon (2 pts.)
48. Islandikane
49. Waterford City Parishes
50. St. John's Without
51. Ballynakill
52. Kill St. Nicholas (2 pts.)
53. Faithlegg
54. Kilbarry
55. Kill St. Lawrence
56. Killure
57. Kilcaragh
58. Ballygunner
59. Kilcop
60. Crooke
61. Monamintra
62. Kilmacleague
63. Kilmacomb
64. Rossduff
65. Killea
66. Corbally
67. Rathmoylan (2 pts.)
68. Aglish
69. Ardmore (2 pts.)
70. Ringagonagh
71. Clashmore (2 pts.)
72. Kinsalebeg (2 pts.)
73. Lisgrennan or Grange (2 pts.)
74. Ballymacart (3 pts.)

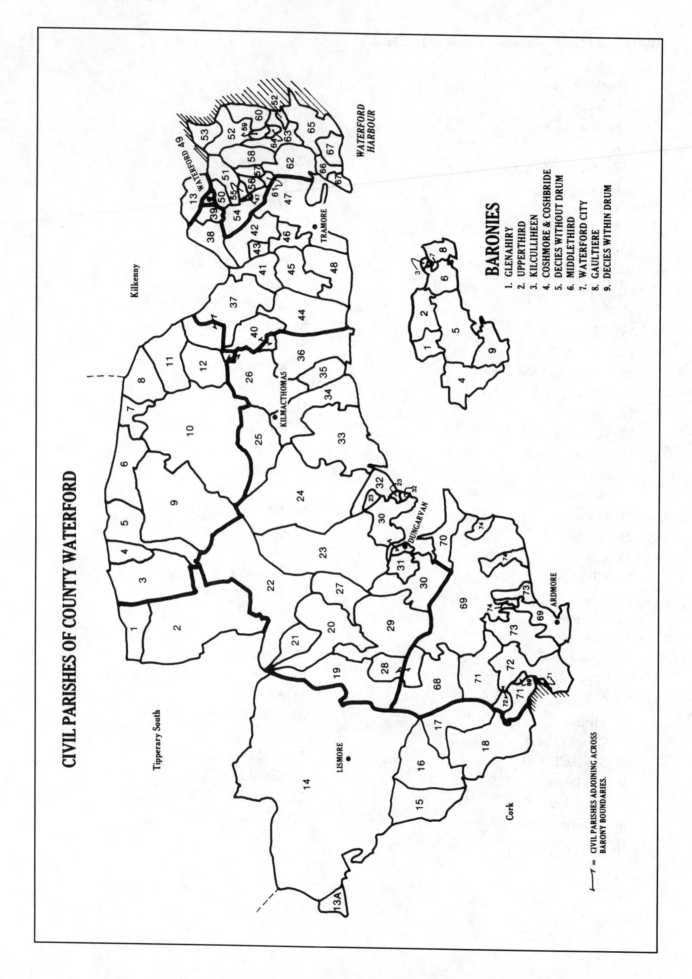

CIVIL PARISHES OF COUNTY WATERFORD

BARONIES

1. GLENAHIRY
2. UPPERTHIRD
3. KILCULLIHEEN
4. COSHMORE & COSHBRIDE
5. DECIES WITHOUT DRUM
6. MIDDLETHIRD
7. WATERFORD CITY
8. GAULTIERE
9. DECIES WITHIN DRUM

⌐ = CIVIL PARISHES ADJOINING ACROSS
BARONY BOUNDARIES.

Waterford Civil Parishes in Alphabetical Order

Affane: 19
Aglish: 68
Ardmore (2 pts.): 69
Ballygunner: 58
Ballylaneen: 34
Ballymacart (3 pts.): 74
Ballynakill: 51
Clashmore (2 pts.): 71
Clonea (2 pts.): 32
Clonegam: 11
Colligan: 27
Corbally: 66
Crooke: 60
Drumcannon (2 pts.): 47
Dungarvan (2 pts.): 30
Dunhill: 44
Dysert: 6
Faithlegg: 53
Fenoagh: 8
Fews: 25
Grange or Lisgrennan: 73
Guilcagh: 12
Inishlounaght: 1
Islandikane: 48
Kilbarry: 54
Kilbarrymeadan: 36
Kilbride: 46
Kilburne: 42
Kilcaragh: 57
Kilcockan: 17
Kilcop: 59
Kilculliheen: 13
Kilgobnet (3 pts.): 23
Kill St. Lawrence: 55
Kill St. Nicholas (2 pts.): 52
Killaloan: 4
Killea: 65
Killoteran: 38
Killure: 56
Kilmacleague: 62
Kilmacomb: 63
Kilmeadan: 37

Kilmolash: 28
Kilmoleran: 7
Kilronan: 2
Kilronan: 43
Kilrossanty: 24
Kilrush: 31
Kilsheelan: 5
Kilwatermoy: 16
Kinsalebeg (2 pts.): 72
Leitrim: 13a
Lickoran: 21
Lisgrennan or Grange (2 pts.): 73
Lismore and Mocollop: 14
Lisnakill: 41
Modelligo: 20
Monamintra: 61
Monksland: 35
Mothel: 10
Newcastle: 40
Rathgormuck: 9
Rathmoylan (2 pts.): 67
Reisk: 45; 64
Ringagonagh: 70
Rossduff: 64
Rossmire: 26
Seskinan: 22
St. John's Without: 50
St. Mary's Clonmel: 3
St. Michael's: 49
St. Olave's: 49
St. Patrick's: 49
St. Peter's: 49
St. Stephen's Within: 49
St. Stephen's Without: 49
Stradbally: 33
Tallow: 15
Templemichael: 18
Trinity Without: 39
Trinity Within: 49
Waterford City Parishes: 49
Whitechurch: 29

County Westmeath

A Brief History

This Leinster county contains the towns of Mullingar, Athlone, Castlepollard, Moate, and Kilbeggan.

In the old Irish administrative divisions, Westmeath was part of the Kingdom of Meath. This was the part of the country reserved as the territory of the High King. The major Irish families of the county were (Mc)Geoghegans, O'Growney, Brennan, O'Coffey, O'Mulleady, O'Malone, O'Curry, O'Daly, McAuley, O'Finlan, and McLoughlin.

After the arrival of the Normans in the late twelfth century, this area was given to Hugh de Lacy. Other Norman families who obtained lands and settled in the county were Nugent, Tyrrell, Petit, Tuite, Delamar, Dalton, Dillon, Fitzsimon(s), Hope, Ware, Ledwich, Dardis, and Gaynor.

The county was centrally involved in the rebellion of 1641 and was also active in the Williamite wars. There was very extensive confiscation of land following these wars, and very few of the Irish or Norman families who held land before 1641 retained their properties. The major families who obtained grants of land were those of Packenham, Wood, Cooke, Swift, Handcock, Gay, Handy, Winter, Levinge, Wilson, Judge, Rochfort, Ogle, Middleton, Burtle, and St. George. The families of Fetherston, Chapman, Smith, O'Reilly, Purdon, Nagle, Blacquiere, and North later obtained property by purchase.

In the eighteenth and early nineteenth centuries, the county was mainly composed of large farms under pasture. The Great Famine of 1845–47 did not affect the county as badly as others. In 1845 the population was 141,000. By 1851 it had fallen by twenty-one percent, to 111,000. Between 1845 and 1850 almost 16,000 people died, and further thousands emigrated. The population continued to decline for the remainder of the century and beyond, and is currently approximately 63,000.

Census and Census Substitutes

1636–1703

Book of Survey and Distribution–Westmeath. John Charles Lyons, 1852. SLC film 1279284.

1640

"Irish Proprietors in Moate and District." In Cox's *Moate, Co. Westmeath: A History of the Town and District.* Athlone, 1981. Appendix 11.

1659

"Census" of Ireland. Edited by S. Pender. Dublin: Stationery Office, 1939. NLI I6551. SLC film 924648.

1666

"Hearth Money Roll of Mullingar." *Franciscan College Journal* (1950); NAI.

1702–03

Alphabetical list of those acquiring land in Westmeath. RIA (Upton Papers); SLC film 101011.

1761–88

The Names of Owners of Freeholds in Co. Westmeath, Compiled for Electoral Purposes, 1761–1788. NLI mss. 787–788.

1761

Co. Westmeath Poll Book. GO ms. 443; SLC film 100181.

1766

Religious Census of the Parish of Russagh. SLC film 258517.

1802–03

"Census of Protestants in the Parishes of Ballyloughloe, Castletown Delvin, Clonarney, Drumraney, Enniscoffey, Kilbridepass, Killallon, Kilcleagh, Killough, Killua, Killucan, Leney, Moyliscar, and Rathconnell." *Ir. Anc.* 5 (2) (1973): 120–26.

1814

Major landholders of Westmeath (alphabetical by townland). RIA (Upton Papers); SLC film 101011.

1823–34

Tithe Applotment Survey (see introduction).

1832

Westmeath Voters for Baronies of: Brawney-Clonlona, Kilkenny W., Moycashel and Rathconrath. *Ir. Gen.* 5 (2) (1975): 234–49; continued in 6 (1): 90–98.

Corkaree, Delvin, Demifore, and Farbill. *Ir. Gen.* 5 (6) (1979): 772–89.

Fartullagh, Moycashel and Magherdernan, and Moygoish. *Ir. Gen.* 6 (1) (1980): 77–89.

Applicants to be registered as voters. Longford/Westmeath Library and SLC film 1279284.

1832–36

"List of Holders of, or Applicants for, Licenses to Sell Liquor in Athlone" (over one hundred names and addresses). *Parl. Papers* 1837, 13 (2): Appendix 10.

1835

Census of the Parish of Tubber (gives age, occupation, and religion of each person in each townland). NLI P 1994.

1837

"List of Those Made Freemen of Athlone Since 1831" (approximately 170 names, addresses, and occupations). *Parl. Papers* 1837, 11 (1): Appendix B1; 1837/38, 13 (2): Appendix 3.

1838

"Lists of Marksmen (illiterate voters) in Athlone" (forty-two names, occupations, and residences). *Parl. Papers* 1837, 11 (1): Appendix A3; and 1837/38, 13 (2): Appendix 4.

1839–59

Agents and Tenants of Robt. W. Lowry. Longford/Westmeath Library and SLC film 1279281.

1843

Voters List. NAI 1843/60.

1848

Petitioners for William Smith O'Brien. Names of male petitioners in Clonmellon. NAI 1848/180.

1854

Griffith's Valuation (see introduction).

1861

Athlone Voters. Longford/Westmeath Library and SLC film 1279285.

1865–98

Athlone Loan Society–Loans and Repayments Accounts. Longford/Westmeath Library and SLC films 1279277–81.

1871

Westmeath property owners. Longford/Westmeath Library and SLC film 1279285.

1873–91

Names and accounts of workmen on unidentified estate. Longford/Westmeath Library and SLC film 1279275.

1901

Census. NAI (see introduction).

1911

Census. NAI.

Church Records

Church of Ireland

See the introduction for a description of Church of Ireland records and their major repositories. Many C of I records were lost in the PRO fire of 1922. These are indicated as "Lost." However, as Church of Ireland records were effectively state records, the records of marriage (from 1845) are also in the General Registrar's Office. Many are still in local custody (LC), while others are in one of a variety of other archives (e.g., RCBL or NAI). Some of the Church of Ireland registers of this county have been indexed by the Dun na Si Heritage Centre (see Research Services at the end of the chapter). A search of the index will be conducted by the center for a fee. Those indexed are noted as "Indexed by Dun na Si HC."

Abbyshrule
Earliest Records: b. 1821; m. 1821; d. 1821
Status: LC

Almorita
Earliest Records: m. 1846-
Status: RCBL (m. 1846-1937)

Ardnurcher and Kilbeggan
Earliest Records: b. 1873-; m. 1819-
Status: NAI MFCI 62 (m. 1819-76); RCBL (b. 1873-1903 ; m. 1848-1974); Indexed by Dun na Si HC (b. 1873-1900; m. 1845-1900)

Athlone—St. Mary's
Earliest Records: b. 1746-; m. 1754-; d. 1747-
Status: NL Pos 5309 (b. 1746-1903; m. 1754-1860; d. 1747-1892); NAI MFCI 57 and LC (b/m/d. 1746); RCBL (b. 1768-1903; m. 1767-1890; d. 1747-1892); Extracts from Burgess Papers held by Dun na Si HC (b. 1842-86; m. 1835-60; d. 1710-1896); SLC films 1279272 and 4

Athlone—St. Peter's
Earliest Records: m. 1845
Status: NL Pos 5309 (m. 1845-1870); SLC film 1279274 (m. 1845-70; Vestry Minutes 1846-1941)

Ballyloughloe
Earliest Records: b. 1877 ; m. 1845; d. 1876
Status: RCBL (b. 1877-1955; m. 1845-1945; d. 1877-1970); Indexed by Dun na Si HC (to 1900)

Ballymore and Killare
Earliest Records: m. 1850
Status: RCBL (m. 1850-1923)

Balnalack (see Leney)
Status: Lost

Bunowen or Benown
Earliest Records: b. 1809; m. 1820-; d. 1820-
Status: LC; NLI Pos. 5309 (b/m/d. 1820-1941); NAI MFCI 61 (b. 1819-1876; d. 1829-1877); RCBL (m. 1847-1934); extracts from Burgess Papers held by Dun na Si HC (b. 1809-1859; d. 1830-1916); SLC film 1279272 (d. 1824-1941; Vestry Minutes 1820-1879, with index to persons)

Carrick (see Moylisker)

Castlelost
Status: Lost

Castlepollard
Earliest Records: m. 1845
Status: RCBL (m. 1845-1953)

Castletown Kindalen or Vastina
Earliest Records: b. 1850-
Status: NAI MFCI 54 (b. 1850-77)

Churchtown
Earliest Records: m. 1846-
Status: RCBL (m. 1846-1876)

Clonfadforan
Status: Lost

Clonmellon (see Killallon)

Collinstown
Earliest Records: b. 1838-; m. 1818-; d. 1837-
Status: NAI MFCI 51 (b. 1838-1963; m. 1818-51; d. 1837-1960); RCBL (b/m. 1838-1963; d. 1837-1960)

Delvin
Earliest Records: b. 1817-; m. 1817-; d. 1817-
Status: LC; NAI MFCI 51 (b. 1817-1947; m. 1817-1850; d. 1817-1943)

Drumcree (Kilcumney)
Earliest Records: b. 1816-; m. 1848-; d. 1816-
Status: NAI M5108/9 (b. 1816-1875; m. 1816-1881); RCBL (b. 1816-1983; m. 1848-1977); SLC film 1279272 (b/m/d. 1763-1862; Vestry Minutes 1795-1862 and 1860-1876, with index to persons)

Enniscoffey
Earliest Records: b. 1881-; m. 1845-; d. 1891-
Status: RCBL (b. 1881-1953; m. 1845-1925; d. 1891-1976)

Foyran
Earliest Records: b. 1890-; m. 1878-
Status: RCBL (b. 1890-1960; m. 1878-1939)

Kilbeggan
Earliest Records: b. 1881-; m. 1845-; d. 1882-
Status: RCBL (b. 1881-1959; m. 1845-1940; d. 1882-1988); Indexed by Dun na Si HC (to 1900)

Kilbixy
Earliest Records: b. 1815; m. 1814; d. 1816
Status: LC and RCBL (m. 1848-1947)

Kilbride (Veston) (no church, see Moylisker and Castlelost)

Kilcleagh (Moate)
Earliest Records: b. 1873-; m. 1845-; d. 1876-
Status: RCBL (b. 1873-1985; m. 1845-1990; d. 1876-1989); Indexed by Dun na Si HC (to 1899); extracts from Burgess Papers held by Dun na Si HC (d. 1830-1916)

Kilkenny West
Earliest Records: b. 1783-; m. 1783-; d. 1784-
Status: RCBL (b. 1783-1956; m. 1783-1913; d. 1784-1862); NAI MFCI 61 (b. 1783-1956; m. 1783-1855; d. 1784-1945); NL Pos. 5309 (b/m. 1762-83); extracts from Burgess Papers held by Dun na Si HC (b. 1785-1876; m. 1798-1855; d. 1811-1861); SLC film 990092 (b/d. 1816-65) and film 8838659 (b. index)

Killagh (see Drumcree)
Status: Lost

Killallon
Status: Lost

Killpatrick (see Rathconell)

Killucan
Earliest Records: b. 1696; m. 1696; d. 1696
Status: RCBL (b. 1696-1863; m. 1787-1857; d. 1700-1888); NLI Ms. 2049 (b/m/d. 1696-1786); GO 578 (b. 1696-1778; d. 1700-72); SLC film 992663 (transcripts: b. 1696-1795 and index; m. 1787-1929; d. 1700-72 and index); also on films 101011 and 100158

Kinnegad
Earliest Records: b. 1892-; m. 1845-; d. 1895-
Status: RCBL (b. 1892-1917; m. 1845-1894; d. 1895-1956)

Leney
Earliest Records: b. 1840-; m. 1845-; d. 1840-
Status: RCBL (b. 1840-1843; m. 1845-1945; d. 1840-1841); NAI MFCI 62 (b. 1840-72; d. 1860-71)

Mayne
Earliest Records: b. 1808-; m. 1809-; d. 1808-
Status: RCBL (b. 1808-1983; m. 1809-1980; d. 1808-1991); NAI MFCI 51 (b/d. 1808-70; m. 1809-70)

Moydrum (see also Willbrook)
Earliest Records: m. 1885
Status: RCBL (m. 1885-1954); extracts from Burgess Papers held by Dun na Si HC (b. 1756-1780; m. 1762-1769)

Moylisker
Earliest Records: m. 1845-
Status: RCBL (m. 1845-1956); SLC film 1279285 (m. 1846-1899; d. 1878-1900)

Mullingar
Earliest Records: m. 1845-
Status: RCBL (m. 1845-1956); SLC film 1279285

Newtown Fertullagh
Status: Lost

Portnashangan
Earliest Records: m. 1846-; d. 1880-
Status: RCBL (m. 1846-1979; d. 1880-1977); SLC film 1279272 (b/d. 1877-1900; m. 1846-1900-indexed)

Rathaspick
Earliest Records: b. 1879-; m. 1850-; d. 1878-
Status: Indexed by Dun na Si HC (to 1900)

Rathconell
Earliest Records: d. 1881-
Status: RCBL (d. 1881-1895)

Stonehall
Earliest Records: b. 1814-; m. 1814-; d. 1915-
Status: RCBL (b. 1878-1941); NAI MFCI 62 (b. 1814-57; m. 1814-54; d. 1915-54)

Streete
Earliest Records: b. 1827-; m. 1827-; d. 1827-
Status: Indexed by Dun na Si HC (to 1899, 1900 and 1897 respectively)

Willbrook (see also Moydrum)
Earliest Records: b. 1756-; m. 1762-
Status: RCBL (b. 1756-83; m. 1775); NL Pos 5309 (b. 1756-83; m. 1763-75); NAI MFCI 62 (b. 1756-83); extracts from Burgess Papers held by Dun na Si HC (b. 1756-1780; m. 1762-1769); SLC film 1279272 (b. 1756-83)

Presbyterian

An account of Presbyterian records is given in the introduction. These registers rarely contain death records, and occasionally have only records of births. Some of the Presbyterian registers have been indexed by Dun na Si Heritage Centre (see Research Services at the end of the chapter). A search of the index will be conducted by the center for a fee.

Society of Friends (Quaker)

See the introduction for an account of the records of Quakers, or Society of Friends. There was a meeting-house in Athlone, and some extracts of deaths (1809-1907) are in the Burgess Papers held by Dun na Si HC. Also, the Monthly Meeting Register for Moate (1605-1859) is in the FHL in Dublin, and on SLC film 571398 (b. 1605-1859; m. 1647-1840; d. 1660-1858).

Methodist

Methodist churches were located in several parts of the county (see the introduction). No death records were maintained. Some of the Methodist registers have been indexed by Dun na Si Heritage Centre (see Research Services at the end of the chapter). A search of the index will be conducted by the center for a fee.

Athlone
Earliest Records: m. 1873-
Status: LC; extracts from Burgess Papers held by Dun na Si HC (m. 1873-1896); SLC film 1279272

Roman Catholic

Note that most of the Catholic parish registers of this county have been indexed by Dun na Si Heritage Centre (see Research Services at the end of the chapter). A search of the index will be conducted by the center for a fee. Those indexed are noted as "Indexed by Dun na Si HC." Microfilm copies of all registers are also available in the National Library of Ireland (NLI), and through the LDS library system.

Civil Parish: Ardnurcher or Horseleap
Map Grid: 50
RC Parish: Clara, see Kilbride (1), Co. Offaly
Diocese: ME

Civil Parish: Ballyloughloe
Map Grid: 46

RC Parish: Ballyloughloe; also Moate, see Kilcleagh
(1)
Diocese: ME
Earliest Record: b. 1858; m. 1858; d. 1858
Status: LC; NLI (mf); Indexed by Dun na Si HC (to 1900)

Civil Parish: Ballymore
Map Grid: 36
RC Parish: Ballymore
Diocese: ME
Earliest Record: b. 9.1824; m. 4.1839
Missing Dates: m. 9.1870–2.1872
Status: LC; NLI (mf); Indexed by Dun na Si HC (b. to 1900; m. 1872–1900)

Civil Parish: Ballymorin
Map Grid: 38
RC Parish: Milltown, see Rathconrath
Diocese: ME

Civil Parish: Bunown
Map Grid: 30
RC Parish: see Drumraney
Diocese: ME

Civil Parish: Carrick
Map Grid: 59
RC Parish: part Rochfortbridge, see Castlelost; part Mullingar
Diocese: ME

Civil Parish: Castlelost
Map Grid: 63
RC Parish: Rochfortbridge
Diocese: ME
Earliest Record: b. 6.1823; m. 12.1816
Status: LC; NLI (mf)

Civil Parish: Castletownkindalen
Map Grid: 51
RC Parish: Castletown-Geoghegan
Diocese: ME
Earliest Record: b. 1819 (two registers from 1861–80); m. 2.1829 (two registers from 1861–80); d. 1819
Missing Dates: d. ends 1844
Status: LC; NLI (mf); Indexed by Dun na Si HC (to 1900, 1910 and 1844 respectively)

Civil Parish: Churchtown
Map Grid: 40
RC Parish: Dysart or Churchtown
Diocese: ME
Earliest Record: b. 8.1836; m. 2.1825
Status: LC; NLI (mf); Indexed by Dun na Si HC (b. 1846–1900; m. 1862–1900)

Civil Parish: Clonarney
Map Grid: 24
RC Parish: Clonmellon, see Killua
Diocese: ME

Civil Parish: Clonfad
Map Grid: 62
RC Parish: Rochfortbridge, see Castlelost
Diocese: ME

Civil Parish: Conry
Map Grid: 39
RC Parish: see Churchtown
Diocese: ME

Civil Parish: Delvin
Map Grid: 27
RC Parish: Delvin or Castletowndelvin
Diocese: ME
Earliest Record: b. 1783; m. 2.1785; d. 2.1785
Missing Dates: b. 3.1789–7.1792, 7.1812–7.1830; m. 3.1789–7.1792, 7.1812–9.1830; d. 3.1789–7.1792, 7.1812–1.1849, ends 4.1855
Status: LC; NLI (mf); Indexed by Dun na Si HC (b/m. only to 1900)

Civil Parish: Drumraney
Map Grid: 32
RC Parish: Drumraney (Noughaval)
Diocese: ME
Earliest Record: b. 4.1834; m. 5.1834
Status: LC; NLI (mf); Indexed by Dun na Si HC (to 1900)

Civil Parish: Durrow (see also Co. Offaly)
Map Grid: 54
RC Parish: see Durrow, Co. Offaly
Diocese: ME

Civil Parish: Dysart
Map Grid: 43
RC Parish: see Churchtown
Diocese: ME

Civil Parish: Enniscoffey
Map Grid: 58
RC Parish: Rochfortbridge, see Castlelost
Diocese: ME

Civil Parish: Faughalstown
Map Grid: 7
RC Parish: Turbotstown, see Mayne
Diocese: ME

Civil Parish: Foyran
Map Grid: 1
RC Parish: Castlepollard, see Rathgarve
Diocese: ME

Civil Parish: Kilbeggan
Map Grid: 52
RC Parish: Kilbeggan
Diocese: ME
Earliest Record: b. 11.1818; m. 10.1818; d. 1810
Missing Dates: b. 8.1824–4.1825; d. ends 12.1843
Status: LC; NLI (mf); Indexed by Dun na Si HC (to 1900)

Civil Parish: Kilbixy
Map Grid: 13
RC Parish: Sonna and Ballinacargy
Diocese: ME
Earliest Record: b. 9.1837; m. 11.1838; d. 1919-
Status: LC; NLI (mf); Indexed by Dun na Si HC (to 1892, 1900 and 1993 respectively)

Civil Parish: Kilbride
Map Grid: 60
RC Parish: Mountnugent, see Kilbride (1), Co. Meath
Diocese: ME

Civil Parish: Kilcleagh (1)
Map Grid: 47
RC Parish: Kilcleagh (Moate and Mount Temple); see also Kilcleagh (2)
Diocese: ME
Earliest Record: b. 1830; m. 1858-; d. 1858-
Status: LC; NLI (mf); Indexed by Dun na Si HC (to 1900)

Civil Parish: Kilcleagh (2)
Map Grid: 47
RC Parish: Lemanaghan or Balnahowen (also in Co. Offaly)
Diocese: ME
Earliest Record: b. 8.1821; m. 1.1830; d. 11.1829
Missing Dates: b. 12.1824-2.1826, 2.1839-2.1841; m. 8.1845-10.1854; d. 9.1845-9.1854
Status: LC; NLI (mf); Indexed by Dun na Si HC (to 1900, 1899 and 1846 respectively)

Civil Parish: Kilcumny
Map Grid: 23
RC Parish: Collinstown; see St. Feighin's
Diocese: ME

Civil Parish: Kilcumreragh
Map Grid: 49
RC Parish: see Kilmanaghan, Co. Offaly
Diocese: ME

Civil Parish: Kilkenny West
Map Grid: 31
RC Parish: Tubberclair (Glasson)
Diocese: ME
Earliest Record: b. 8.1829
Status: LC; NLI (mf); Indexed by Dun na Si HC (to 1900)

Civil Parish: Killagh
Map Grid: 28
RC Parish: Castletowndelvin, see Delvin
Diocese: ME

Civil Parish: Killare
Map Grid: 37
RC Parish: see Ballymore
Diocese: ME

Civil Parish: Killua
Map Grid: 25

RC Parish: Clonmellon
Diocese: ME
Earliest Record: b. 1.1759; m. 1.1757; d. 12.1757
Missing Dates: b. 11.1809-6.1819; m. 9.1809-7.1819, 7.1845-1.1846; d. 10.1809-11.1819, ends 7.1850
Status: LC; NLI (mf); Indexed by Dun na Si HC (to 1900; d. to 1993)

Civil Parish: Killucan (1)
Map Grid: 44
RC Parish: Killucan (Raharney); also Kinnegad, see Killucan (2)
Diocese: ME
Earliest Record: b. 5.1821; m. 5.1821
Status: LC; NLI (mf); Indexed by Dun na Si HC (to 1900)

Civil Parish: Killucan (2)
Map Grid: 44
RC Parish: Kinnegad
Diocese: ME
Earliest Record: b. 1824; m. 7.1844; d. 2.1869 (anointings from 1741-63; rents 1757)
Status: LC; NLI (mf); Indexed by Dun na Si HC (b/m. only to 1899)

Civil Parish: Killulagh
Map Grid: 26
RC Parish: see Delvin
Diocese: ME

Civil Parish: Kilmacnevan
Map Grid: 12
RC Parish: see Rathconrath
Diocese: ME

Civil Parish: Kilmanaghan
Map Grid: 48
RC Parish: Moate, see Kilcleagh; also Tubber, see Kilmanaghan, Co. Offaly
Diocese: ME

Civil Parish: Kilpatrick
Map Grid: 8
RC Parish: Collinstown, see St. Feighin's
Diocese: ME

Civil Parish: Lackan
Map Grid: 15
RC Parish: see Multyfarnham
Diocese: ME

Civil Parish: Leny
Map Grid: 17
RC Parish: see Multyfarnham
Diocese: ME

Civil Parish: Lickbla
Map Grid: 2
RC Parish: Castlepollard, see Rathgarve
Diocese: ME

Civil Parish: Lynn
Map Grid: 56
RC Parish: see Mullingar
Diocese: ME

Civil Parish: Mayne
Map Grid: 3
RC Parish: Turbotstown, Coole, or Mayne
Diocese: ME
Earliest Record: b. 8.1777; m. 11.1777; d. 8.1777
Missing Dates: b. 5.1796-1.1798, 11.1820-4.1824,
4.1835-2.1847; m. 4.1796-1.1798, 12.1820-5.1824,
7.1843-8.1846, 7.1863-11.1864; d. 11.1796-2.1803,
9.1820-4.1824, 8.1844-1.1846, ends 12.1850
Status: LC; NLI (mf); Indexed by Dun na Si HC (b/
m. to 1900; d. to 1990)

Civil Parish: Moylisker
Map Grid: 57
RC Parish: see Mullingar
Diocese: ME

Civil Parish: Mullingar
Map Grid: 42
RC Parish: Mullingar
Diocese: ME
Earliest Record: b. 7.1742; m. 10.1737; d. 7.1741
(anointings from 1741-63; rents 1757)
Missing Dates: b. 4.1816-1.1833, 11.1842-11.1843;
m. 7.1754-1.1779, 4.1824-1.1833, 4.1859-5.1860; d.
1797-1.1833, 5.1838-2.1843
Status: LC; NLI (mf); Indexed by Dun na Si HC (b/
m. to 1900)

Civil Parish: Multyfarnham
Map Grid: 16
RC Parish: Multyfarnham
Diocese: ME
Earliest Record: b. 2.1824; m. 2.1824; d. 1.1830
Missing Dates: d. ends 7.1844
Status: LC; NLI (mf); Indexed by Dun na Si HC (b/
m. to 1900; d. to 1844)

Civil Parish: Newtown
Map Grid: 53
RC Parish: see Castletownkindalen
Diocese: ME

Civil Parish: Noughaval
Map Grid: 29
RC Parish: Tang; see also Drumraney for earlier
records
Diocese: ME
Earliest Record: b. 1857; m. 1857
Status: LC; NLI (mf); Indexed by Dun na Si HC (b/
m. to 1900)

Civil Parish: Pass of Kilbride
Map Grid: 61
RC Parish: Rochfortbridge, see Castlelost
Diocese: ME

Civil Parish: Piercetown
Map Grid: 33
RC Parish: see Forgney, Co. Longford
Diocese: ME

Civil Parish: Portloman
Map Grid: 22
RC Parish: see Mullingar
Diocese: ME

Civil Parish: Portnashangan
Map Grid: 19
RC Parish: see Multyfarnham
Diocese: ME

Civil Parish: Rahugh
Map Grid: 55
RC Parish: see Kilbeggan
Diocese: ME

Civil Parish: Rathaspick
Map Grid: 11
RC Parish: Rathowen (Rathaspick and Russagh)
Diocese: AD
Earliest Record: b. 3.1822; m. 12.1819; d. 3.1822
Missing Dates: b. 9.1826-7.1832, 4.1833-5.1836,
10.1846-3.1847; m. 2.1826-10.1832, 10.1833-
1.1838; d. 2.1826-8.1832, 11.1833-8.1837
Status: LC; NLI (mf); Indexed by Dun na Si HC (to
1900)

Civil Parish: Rathconnell
Map Grid: 41
RC Parish: part Taghmon; part Mullingar
Diocese: ME

Civil Parish: Rathconrath
Map Grid: 34
RC Parish: Milltown
Diocese: ME
Earliest Record: b. 1.1781; m. 1.1781; d. 1.1781
Missing Dates: b. 9.1808-4.1809; m. 2.1805-4.1809;
d. 11.1808-4.1809, ends 10.1869
Status: LC; NLI (mf); Indexed by Dun na Si HC (b.
1791 to 1900 only)

Civil Parish: Rathgarve
Map Grid: 4
RC Parish: Castlepollard
Diocese: ME
Earliest Record: b. 1.1795; m. 3.1793; d. 1.1793
Missing Dates: b. 6.1825-11.1825; m. 8.1793-1.1795,
6.1825-11.1825; d. ends 6.1825
Status: LC; NLI (mf)

Civil Parish: Russagh
Map Grid: 10
RC Parish: see Rathaspick
Diocese: AD

Civil Parish: St. Feighin's
Map Grid: 5

RC Parish: Collinstown
Diocese: ME
Earliest Record: b. 2.1807; m. 6.1784; d. 4.1784
Missing Dates: b. 4.1815–3.1821, 11.1843–3.1844, ends 10.1849
Status: LC; NLI (mf); Indexed by Dun na Si HC (b/m. to 1900; d. to 1994)

Civil Parish: St. Mary's
Map Grid: 6
RC Parish: Collinstown, see St. Feighin's
Diocese: ME

Civil Parish: St. Mary's Athlone
Map Grid: 45
RC Parish: Athlone
Diocese: ME
Earliest Record: b. 1.1813; m. 1.1813; d. 1.1813
Missing Dates: b. 9.1826–5.1839, 4.1852–2.1853; m. 4.1827–1.1834, 12.1851–2.1854; d. ends 12.1826
Status: LC; NLI (mf); Indexed by Dun na Si HC (to 1867, 1868 and 1826 respectively)

Civil Parish: Stonehall
Map Grid: 18
RC Parish: see Rathconnell
Diocese: ME

Civil Parish: Street
Map Grid: 9
RC Parish: see Street, Co. Longford
Diocese: AD

Civil Parish: Taghmon
Map Grid: 21
RC Parish: Taghmon
Diocese: ME
Earliest Record: b. 9.1781; m. 1.1782; d. 1801
Missing Dates: b. 3.1790–3.1809, 12.1850–1.1864; m. 6.1791–8.1809, 5.1848–9.1868; d. ends 2.1848
Status: LC; NLI (mf); Indexed by Dun na Si HC (to 1886, 1848 and 1848 respectively)

Civil Parish: Templeoran
Map Grid: 14
RC Parish: Sonna, see Kilbixy
Diocese: ME

Civil Parish: Templepatrick
Map Grid: 35
RC Parish: Moyvore
Diocese: ME
Earliest Record: b. 9.1831; m. 2.1832; d. 8.1831
Missing Dates: d. 4.1852–5.1863, ends 9.1865
Status: LC; NLI (mf); Indexed by Dun na Si HC (b/m. to 1900; d. to 1865)

Civil Parish: Tyfarnham
Map Grid: 20
RC Parish: see Rathconnell
Diocese: ME

Commercial and Social Directories

1820

J. Pigot's *Commercial Directory of Ireland* has information on the gentry, nobility, and traders in and around the town of Athlone.

1824

J. Pigot's *City of Dublin and Hibernian Provincial Directory* includes traders, nobility, gentry, and clergy lists of Athlone, Ballymore, Castletowndelvin, Kilbeggan, Kinnegad, and Mullingar.

1846

Slater's *National Commercial Directory of Ireland* lists nobility, clergy, traders, etc., in Athlone, Castlepollard, Kilbeggan and Ballinagore, Kinnegad, and Mullingar.

1856

Slater's *Royal National Commercial Directory of Ireland* lists nobility, gentry, clergy, traders, etc., in Athlone, Castlepollard, Castletowndelvin, Kilbeggan and Ballinagore, Kinnegad, Moate, Mullingar, and Tyrrell's Pass.

1870

Slater's *Directory of Ireland* contains trade, nobility, and clergy lists for Athlone, Castlepollard, Castletowndelvin, Kilbeggan, Kinnegad, Moate, and Mullingar.

1881

Slater's *Royal National Commercial Directory of Ireland* contains lists of traders, clergy, nobility, and farmers in adjoining parishes of the towns of Athlone, Castlepollard, Castletowndelvin, Kilbeggan and Tyrrell's Pass, Moate, and Mullingar.

1894

Slater's *Royal National Directory of Ireland* lists traders, police, teachers, farmers, and private residents in each of the towns, villages, and parishes of the county.

1897

John Burgess's *Athlone, The Shannon and Lough Ree* has a directory of Athlone.

Family History

Papers (e.g., deeds, leases, and pedigrees) relating to following families: Daly; Dunne of Brittas; Fetherston; Hatfield of Killimor; Homan; Magan of Emoe; Percy; Tighe; Wilson of Piersfield. Longford/Westmeath Library (Upton Papers), and SLC film 101011.

Burgess, J.B. *Dictionary of Athlone Biography to 1871.*

Sheehan, J. *Worthies of Westmeath. A biographical dictionary of brief lives of famous Westmeath people.* Westmeath: Wellbrook Press, 1987.

Lyons family of Westmeath. Longford/Westmeath Library and SLC film 1279285.

"McKeoghs of Moyfinn." *J. Old Athlone Soc.* 1 (4) (1974/75): 234-37; 2 (5) (1978): 56-70.

Magan, William. *Umma-More. The Story of an Irish Family.* History of the Magan family of Umma, near Ballymore, Co. Westmeath, from ca. 1590. Salisbury: Element Books, 1983.

"Magawlys of Calry." *J. Old Athlone Soc.* 1 (2) (1970/71): 61-73; 1 (3) (1972/73): 147-60.

"Malones of Westmeath." *Gaelic Gleanings* 1 (1) (1981): 9-12; 1 (2): 46-48; 1 (3): 81-84; 1 (4): 127-30; 2 (1) (1982): 9-10.

Nugent and Rochfort families (biographies, property, and pedigrees). Longford/Westmeath Library and SLC film 1279285.

"Robinson of Killogeenaghan—a Westmeath Quaker Family." *Ir. Anc.* 14 (1) (1982): 1-5.

Rochfort—see Nugent.

"Smyth Papers" (Drumcree, Co. Westmeath). *Anal. Hib.* (20): 279-301.

Tuite family biographies and records. Longford/Westmeath Library and SLC film 1279285.

Tyrrell—see Co. Dublin.

Gravestone Inscriptions

Some graveyards have been indexed by Dun na Si Heritage Centre (see Research Services below), who should be contacted for an up-to-date list. Others are available in the following sources:

Athlone—Abbey Graveyard: Ryan, Hazel A. *Athlone Abbey Graveyard Inscriptions.* Mullingar, 1987. SLC 941.815/A1.

Ballyloughloe (Mount Temple): *Ir. Anc.* 4 (2): 1972. SLC film 1279227.

Castletown (Finea): GO Ms. 622, 107.

Delvin (St. Mary's Churchyard): *Ir. Anc* 14 (1) (1982): 39-57. SLC film 1596994.

Kilcleagh (C of I): Cox, Liam. *Moate, Co. Westmeath: A History of the Town and District.* 1981.

Killomenaghan (C of I): Cox, Liam. *Moate, Co. Westmeath: A History of the Town and District.* 1981.

Moate—St. Mary's (C of I) and Quaker graveyards: Cox, Liam. *Moate, Co. Westmeath: A History of the Town and District.* 1981. SLC film 1279227.

Multyfarnham Abbey: O'Gibeallain, P. *Multyfarnham Abbey: Monuments and Memories.* Multyfarnham, 1984.

Stonehall: GO Ms. 622, 183.

Streete: *Riocht na Midhe* 4 (3) (1969): 28-29.

Newspapers

Athlone is the major center for newspaper publishing in the county. For earlier notices relevant to the county, newspapers from neighboring counties should be searched, depending on the area of interest. Extracts from some Athlone newspapers are part of the Burgess Papers in Longford/Westmeath Library (see Miscellaneous Sources).

Title: *Athlone Conservative Advocate and Ballinasloe Reporter*
Published in: Athlone, 1837
NLI Holdings: 6-9.1837
BL Holdings: 6-9.1837

Title: *Athlone Independent*
Published in: Athlone, 1833-36
NLI Holdings: 11.1833-11.1836
BL Holdings: 11.1833-11.1836

Title: *Athlone Mirror, Westmeath and Roscommon Reformer*
Published in: Athlone, 1841-42
NLI Holdings: 9.1841-7.1842
BL Holdings: 9.1841-7.1842

Title: *Athlone Sentinel*
Published in: Athlone, 1834-61
NLI Holdings: odd numbers 1846-47
BL Holdings: 11.1834-7.1861

Title: *Athlone Times*
Published in: Athlone, 1889-1902
NLI Holdings: 1899
BL Holdings: 5.1889-1.1902

Title: *Westmeath Examiner*
Published in: Mullingar, 1882-current
NLI Holdings: 1.1906-in progress
BL Holdings: 9.1882-in progress

Title: *Westmeath Guardian and Longford Newsletter*
Published in: Mullingar, 1835-1928
NLI Holdings: 6.1921-10.1928
BL Holdings: 1.1835-10.1928

Title: *Westmeath Herald*
Published in: Athlone, 1859-60
BL Holdings: 4.1859-4.1860

Title: *Westmeath Independent*
Published in: Athlone, 1846-1968
NLI Holdings: 1.1885-12.1913; 2.1923-7.1968
BL Holdings: 6.1846-8.1880; odd numbers 1881-84; 2.1884-10.1920; 2.1922-7.1968

Title: *Westmeath Journal*
Published in: Mullingar, 1823-34
BL Holdings: 1.1823-5.1834

Title: *Westmeath Nationalist and Midland Reporter* (*Midland Reporter* from 1897)

Published in: Mullingar, 1891–1939
BL Holdings: 4.1891–12.1928; 1–10.1930; 1.1931–
9.1939

Wills and Administrations

A discussion of the types of records, where they are
held, and their availability and value is given in the
Wills section of the introduction. The availability of
prerogative wills, administrations, and marriage license
records is also described in the relevant parts of the
same section. Where available, published sources of these
records are given in the Miscellaneous Sources section.

Pre-1858 Wills and Administrations

Prerogative Wills. See the introduction.

Consistorial Wills. County Westmeath is mainly in the
diocese of Meath, with three parishes in Ardagh. The
guide to Catholic parish records in this chapter shows
the diocese to which each civil parish belonged. The
wills of residents of each diocese were usually proven
within that diocese (see the Wills section for exceptions).
The following records survive:

Wills

See the introduction.

Abstracts

See the introduction. The Upton papers also contain
Westmeath abstracts. RIA Library.

Indexes

Meath—see Co. Meath; Ardagh (1695–1858) published
in *Ir. Anc.* (1971). Index to Ardagh Wills and Administrations: Supplement to *Ir. Anc.* (1971) and SLC film
824242. Westmeath Wills Index (17th to 19th centuries): RIA (Upton Papers) and SLC film 101011.

Post-1858 Wills and Administrations

This county was served by the District Registry of
Mullingar. The surviving records are in the NAI.
Records include: Mullingar District Will Books (1859–
1887). NAI; SLC film 100948.

Marriage Licenses

Indexes

Meath and Ardagh (1691–1845). NAI; SLC film
100869.

Miscellaneous Sources

Keaney, M. "Surnames of Co. Westmeath." *Irish Roots*
4 (1992): 20–21.

"Athlone in the Civil War 1641–1652." *Irish Sword* 10
(38) (1977): 38–55.

"Constabulary Employed in the District of Moate, Co.
Westmeath." *Ir. Anc.* 7 (1) (1975): 35–38.

Sheehan, J. *Worthies of Westmeath. A biographical dictionary of brief lives of famous Westmeath people.*
Westmeath: Wellbrook Press, 1987.

Cox, Liam. *Moate, Co. Westmeath: A History of the Town
and District.* Athlone, 1981 (history of the area with
extensive family references).

"Early Nineteenth-Century Lists of Protestant Parishioners in the Dioceses of Meath." *Ir. Anc.* 5 (2) (1973):
113–26.

Grand Juries of Westmeath 1727 to 1853 with Their
Genealogies. NLI 34779.

Keaney, M. *Sources for Westmeath Studies.* Mullingar,
1982.

Kieran, K. *Bibliography of the History of Co. Westmeath.*
Mullingar, 1959.

Records of Athlone and District. M. J. Moran Mss. NLI
mss. 1543–1547. (Collection of news items for the
period 1690–1900.)

Walsh, Paul. *The Place-Names of Westmeath.* Dublin,
1957.

"Westmeath in the 1798 Period." *Irish Sword* 9 (34)
(1969): 1–15.

Records of Athlone and District (1690–1900). Compiled
by Maladry Moran. GO 674–678 and SLC films
100214-6 (index to people, places, and subjects, newspaper cuttings, etc.).

Deed Extracts (Athlone: 1836–61; Co. Westmeath:
1708–1828). Longford/Westmeath Library (Burgess
Papers); SLC film 1279274.

Rental lists of King-Harman Estate (1850–1916).
Longford/Westmeath Library and SLC films
1279273-5, 1279282.

Viscount Lorton Rent Ledger (n.d.). Longford/
Westmeath Library and SLC film 1279275.

Survey of Boyd and Countess Belvedere Estates (1818).
Longford/Westmeath Library and SLC film 1279276.

Temple Estate Rental (1888–95). Longford/Westmeath
Library and SLC film 1279275.

Extracts from Athlone Newspapers: *Athlone Independent*
(1833–36); *Athlone Sentinel* (1834–61); *Athlone Conservative Advocate* (1837); *Athlone Mirror* (1841–2);
Westmeath Herald (1859–60). Longford/Westmeath
Library (Burgess Papers) and SLC film 1279272.

Streets, buildings, and occupants of Athlone (1578–
1943). Longford/Westmeath Library (Burgess Papers)
and SLC film 1279274.

Rent book of Killynan House 1800–1820. Longford/
Westmeath Library (Burgess Papers) and SLC film
1279275.

Research Sources and Services

Journals
Riocht na Midhe (published by Meath Archaeological and Historical Society; see Research Sources and Services section, Co. Meath)

Journal of Old Athlone Society

Libraries and Information Sources
County Library, Dublin Road, Mullingar, Co. Westmeath. Ph: (044) 40781/2/3

Research Services
Dun na Si Heritage Centre, Moate, Co. Westmeath. Ph: (0902) 81183. This is the official IGP center for the county, and has indexed many of the church registers of several denominations. They also have ac-cess to a variety of other sources for the county. Researchers are advised to contact the center for an updated list of registers, and other sources, indexed. A research service is provided for a fee.

Laois/Offaly Heritage Centre (see Research Sources and Services section, Co. Offaly).

See also Research Services in Dublin in the introduction.

Societies
Moate Museum and Historical Society, Mrs. Teresa Sheehan, Avila, Moate, Co. Westmeath

Old Athlone Society, Mr. Liam Byrne, 44 Meadow Bank, Athlone, Co. Westmeath

Westmeath Archaeological and Historical Society, Mr. Paddy Raleigh, Bishopsgate, Mullingar, Co. Westmeath

Westmeath Civil Parishes as Numbered on Map

1. Foyran
2. Lickbla
3. Mayne
4. Rathgarve
5. St. Feighin's
6. St. Mary's
7. Faughalstown
8. Kilpatrick
9. Street
10. Russagh
11. Rathaspick
12. Kilmacnevan
13. Kilbixy
14. Templeoran
15. Lackan
16. Mulyfarnham
17. Leny
18. Stonehall
19. Portnashangan
20. Tyfarnham
21. Taghmon
22. Portloman
23. Kilcumny
24. Clonarney
25. Killua
26. Killulagh
27. Delvin
28. Killagh
29. Noughaval
30. Bunown
31. Kilkenny West
32. Drumraney
33. Piercetown

34. Rathconrath
35. Templepatrick
36. Ballymore
37. Killare
38. Ballymorin
39. Conry
40. Churchtown
41. Rathconnell
42. Mullingar
43. Dysart
44. Killucan (1)
44. Killucan (2)
45. St. Mary's Athlone
46. Ballyloughoe
47. Kilcleagh (1)
47. Kilcleagh (2)
48. Kilmanaghan
49. Kilcumreragh
50. Arnurcher or Horseleap
51. Castletownkindalen
52. Kilbeggan
53. Newtown
54. Durrow
55. Rahugh
56. Lynn
57. Moylisker
58. Enniscoffey
59. Carrick
60. Kilbride
61. Pass of Kilbride
62. Clonfad
63. Castlelost

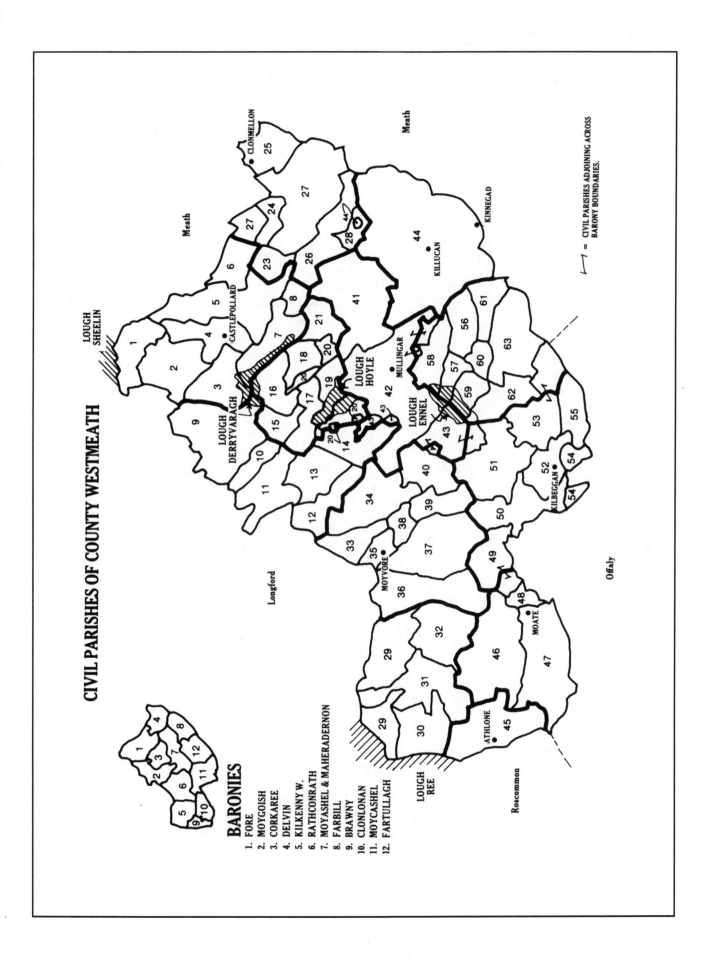

CIVIL PARISHES OF COUNTY WESTMEATH

BARONIES
1. FORE
2. MOYGOISH
3. CORKAREE
4. DELVIN
5. KILKENNY W.
6. RATHCONRATH
7. MOYASHEL & MAHERADERNON
8. FARBILL
9. BRAWNY
10. CLONLONAN
11. MOYCASHEL
12. FARTULLAGH

= CIVIL PARISHES ADJOINING ACROSS BARONY BOUNDARIES.

CLONMELLON

Meath

Meath

KINNEGAD

KILLUCAN

LOUGH SHEELIN

CASTLEPOLLARD

MULLINGAR

LOUGH HOYLE

LOUGH ENNEL

LOUGH DERRYVARAGH

Longford

KILBEGGAN

MOYVORE

Offaly

MOATE

ATHLONE

LOUGH REE

Roscommon

Westmeath Civil Parishes in Alphabetical Order

Arnurcher or Horseleap: 50
Ballyloughoe: 46
Ballymore: 36
Ballymorin: 38
Bunown: 30
Carrick: 59
Castlelost: 63
Castletownkindalen: 51
Churchtown: 40
Clonarney: 24
Clonfad: 62
Conry: 39
Delvin: 27
Drumraney: 32
Durrow: 54
Dysart: 43
Enniscoffey: 58
Faughalstown: 7
Foyran: 1
Kilbeggan: 52
Kilbixy: 13
Kilbride: 60
Kilcleagh (1): 47
Kilcleagh (2): 47
Kilcumny: 23
Kilcumreragh: 49
Kilkenny West: 31
Killagh: 28
Killare: 37
Killua: 25
Killucan (1): 44
Killucan (2): 44
Killulagh: 26

Kilmacnevan: 12
Kilmanaghan: 48
Kilpatrick: 8
Lackan: 15
Leny: 17
Lickbla: 2
Lynn: 56
Mayne: 3
Moylisker: 57
Mullingar: 42
Mulyfarnham: 16
Newtown: 53
Noughaval: 29
Pass of Kilbride: 61
Piercetown: 33
Portloman: 22
Portnaghangan: 19
Rahugh: 55
Rathaspick: 11
Rathconnell: 41
Rathconrath: 34
Rathgarve: 4
Russagh: 10
St. Feighin's: 5
St. Mary's: 6
St. Mary's Athlone: 45
Stonehall: 18
Street: 9
Taghmon: 21
Templeoran: 14
Templepatrick: 35
Tyfarnham: 20

County Wexford

A Brief History

Located in the southeastern corner of Ireland, County Wexford contains the towns of Wexford, Enniscorthy, New Ross, and Gorey. The county was traditionally the territory of the McMurroughs, Kavanaghs, and Kinsellas. Other Irish families in the county included O'Day, O'Leary, Murphy, O'Byrne, O'Dugan, and Bolger.

A settlement on the site of Wexford town was shown on the maps drawn by Ptolemy in the second century A.D. The modern town of Wexford was founded and named (Waesfjord) by the Norse Vikings as a trading settlement in the ninth or tenth century, and it became a large town and a major port. The steady arrival of the Normans and associated Flemish, French, and Welsh caused the the Norse to be driven from Wexford town to the area around Rosslare, where they gradually assimilated into the local population. However, because the Norse did not use surnames, there is little evidence of their heritage in the family names of the county.

It was in County Wexford that the first Norman armies, led by Robert Fitzstephen, landed in 1169. Evidence of their establishment in Wexford can be seen in the many Norman names now common in the county. These include Sinnott, Esmond, Stafford, Codd, Furlong, Wadding, Hore, and Devereux. The name Meyler, of Welsh origin, is also found in the county since Norman times. These Norman invaders gradually assimilated into the native population, except in the baronies of Bargy and Forth, where, cut off from the rest of the county, they developed a distinct culture and a dialect, called Yola, which is a mixture of Old English and Irish. This survived until the nineteenth to

In 1610, there was a small plantation of the county in which part of the land of the McMurroughs in the northern part of the county was confiscated and given to English settlers. The McMurroughs, in return, got full title to the remainder of their lands. As a result of local protests over this plantation, many local families were transported to Virginia. The records of contemporary Virginia settlements show many Murphy, Bolger, Kavanagh, and Byrne families.

Wexford joined the 1641 rebellion of the "Confederacy" of Irish Catholics (see Co. Kilkenny), and Wexford town became one of the major centers. In 1649, Oliver Cromwell besieged Wexford and, on its surrender, massacred the inhabitants. The lands of the rebel chieftains were confiscated and many were transported to the West Indies, or ordered to move west of the Shannon. Their lands were given either to those loyal to the English Parliament or as payment to Cromwell's soldiers and officers.

In 1661, many hundreds of English families were brought into Enniscorthy to man the iron works which were growing rapidly in that town. The county was not extensively involved in the Williamite/Jacobite conflict of the 1690s.

The county was a major center of the 1798 rebellion of the United Irishmen. A huge army of Wexfordmen took Wexford and Enniscorthy and controlled the entire county. The insurgents were finally defeated at Vinegar Hill, near Enniscorthy.

The county has always been noted for its prosperous farms and industrious farmers. Perhaps for this reason, it was less affected than many others by the Great Famine of 1845-47. The rural population density in 1841 was one of the lowest in the country, at 217 persons per square mile. The total population in 1841 was 202,000, and ten years later it had fallen to

180,000. There was considerable emigration, particularly from the north of the county. As elsewhere, emigration continued throughout the nineteenth century. The population by 1891 was 112,000 and is currently approximately 100,000.

Wexford is commonly regarded as an ethnically distinct part of the country because of the blend of Irish, Norse, and Norman blood.

Census and Census Substitutes

1640

"Wexford Privateers during the 1640s." *Wexford Hist. Soc. J.* 12 (1988–89): 23–49.

1654–56

Simington, R.C. "Civil Survey." County of Wexford. Vol. 9. Dublin: Stationery Office, 1954.

1659

"Census" of Ireland. Edited by S. Pender. Dublin: Stationery Office, 1939; NLI I6551; SLC film 924648; some baronies in *The Past*, vols. 4 and 5.

1740–63

Rental of the Shapland Carew Estate. NAI 1A 41 49.

1766

Householders of Parish of Ballynaslaney. NAI m. 2476; GO 537; RCB ms. 23.

Protestant householders in Parish of Edermine (names of householders, wives, and total number of children and servants). GO 537; SLC film 258517; RCB ms. 23.

1774

Tenants and Tradesmen from Baron Farnham's Estate of Newtownbarry. IFHS Newsletter No. 10 (1993): 5–7.

1775

Catholic Qualification Roll Extracts (twenty-three names, addresses, and occupations). 59th Report DKPRI: 50–84.

1775–1820

Rental of the Farnham Estate—Bunclody. NLI Ms. 787–8.

1776

"The Freemen of Wexford." *Ir. Gen.* 5 (1) (1973): 103–21; 5 (3) (1973): 314–34; 5 (4) (1973): 448–63.

1789

"Protestant Householders in the Parish of Ferns." *Ir. Anc.* 13 (2) (1981): 93–94.

1792

Some Protestant Householders in the Parishes of Ballycanew and Kiltrisk. *Ir. Anc.* 13 (2) (1981): 93–94.

1798

List of Persons Who Suffered Losses in '98 Rebellion. NLI JLB 94107 (over two thousand names, addresses, and occupations).

1820

Tenants of the Alcock estate in Clonmore. NLI Ms. 10169.

1821

Extracts from Government Census for St. Mary's Parish (New Ross) Rathaspick, mainly for surnames Walsh and Kelly. QUB; SLC film 100158.

1823–38

Tithe Applotment Survey (see introduction).

1842

Voters List. NAI 1842/82.

1851 and 1860

Presentments to the Grand Jury at the Spring Assizes in Co. Wicklow in 1851 and 1860 for provision for the care of deserted children (year, parish, child's name, age, nurse).

1853

Griffith's Valuation (see introduction).

1857

Deserted Children in Counties Wicklow and Wexford. *Dun Laoghaire Gen. Soc. J.* 3 (3) 1994. (Barony, parish, name of guardian, name of child.)

1861

Inhabitants of Catholic Parish of St. Mary's, Enniscorthy (included in the parish register, see RC records section; possibly a copy of official census, now destroyed). NAI P4250.

1867

Census of Catholics in RC parish of Marshalstown and Kilmeashal (in parish register: see Monart, RC records section). *Ir. Gen.* 6 (5) (1984): 652–669.

1870

"Wexford Supporters of the Pope." Catholics who signed a petition in support of the Pope. *Irish Family History* 8 (1992): 95–105 (approximately 1800 names and parishes of residence).

1901

Census. NAI (see introduction). SLC films 852478–2500, 863501–9, 857264–5.

1911

Census. NAI.

Church Records

Church of Ireland

See the introduction for a description of Church of Ireland records and their major repositories. Many C of I records were lost in the PRO fire of 1922. These are indicated as "Lost." However, as Church of Ireland records were effectively state records, the records of marriage (from 1845) are also in the General Registrar's Office. Many are still in local custody (LC), while others are in one of a variety of other archives (e.g., RCBL or NAI). Some of the Church of Ireland registers of this county have been indexed by Wexford Heritage Research Centre (see Research Services at the end of the chapter). A search of the index will be conducted by the center for a fee. Those indexed are noted as "Indexed by WHRC."

Adamstown
Earliest Records: b. 1814; m. 1851; d. 1814
Status: LC; Indexed by WHRC (to 1900)

Ardamine
Earliest Records: b. 1807; m. 1807; d. 1807
Status: LC

Ardcandrisk (see Wexford)

Ballycanew
Earliest Records: b. 1733; m. 1733; d. 1733
Status: LC; Indexed by WHRC (b/m/d. 1811–1900)

Ballycarney
Earliest Records: b. 1835; m. 1836; d. 1836
Status: LC

Ballyhuskard (see also St. Mary's Enniscorthy)
Status: Lost

Bannon
Status: Lost

Bunclody
Earliest Records: b. 1779; m. 1779; d. 1779
Missing Records: m/d. 1810–1836
Status: LC; Indexed by WHRC (to 1895)

Carne
Earliest Records: d. 1815–76
Status: NAI M1451

Carnew
Earliest Records: b. 1808; m. 1808; d. 1808
Status: LC

Carrig (see Wexford)

Castlebridge
Earliest Records: b. 1870; m. 1845; d. 1880
Status: LC; Indexed by WHRC (to 1900)

Churchtown
Earliest Records: d. 1835–77
Status: NAI M1451

Clone (see also Ferns and Kilbride)
Status: Lost

Clonegal or Moyacomb
Earliest Records: b. 1792; m. 1792; d. 1792
Status: LC; Indexed by WHRC (to 1900); b. 1792–1903, m. 1831–1906, and d. 1832–1903 indexed by Anglican Rec. Proj.—available at RCBL and Soc. Gen. (London)

Coolstuff
Status: Lost

Duncormick
Earliest Records: b. 1760; m. 1760; d. 1760
Status: LC

Edermine
Status: Lost

Ferns and Kilbride
Earliest Records: b. 1775; m. 1775; d. 1775
Status: LC

Fethard
Status: Lost

Glasscarrig
Earliest Records: b. 1835; m. 1835; d. 1807
Status: LC

Gorey
Earliest Records: b. 1827; m. 1827; d. 1827
Status: LC; Indexed by WHRC (to 1900)

Hollyforth
Earliest Records: b. 1817; m. 1845; d. 1877
Missing Records: b. 1836–1877
Status: LC; Indexed by WHRC (to 1900)

Hooke and Templetown
Status: Lost

Horetown
Status: Lost

Inch
Earliest Records: b. 1726–1866; m. 1726–1887; d. 1726–1986

Status: NAI M5059/60 and LC (b/m/d. 1726)
Also: b. 1866-1984, d. 1896-1984, NAI MFCI 82;
SLC film 883727 (b. 1722-1865–indexed) and film
883818 (m. 1726-1845–indexed)

Kilcormick
Status: Lost

Kildavin
Earliest Records: b. 1831; m. 1831; d. 1831
Status: LC; Indexed by WHRC (to 1879)

Killann
Earliest Records: b. 1835; m. 1835; d. 1835
Status: LC; Indexed by WHRC (to 1900)

Killegney
Earliest Records: b. 1802; m. 1802; d. 1802
Status: LC; Indexed by WHRC (to 1900)

Killesk
Earliest Records: b. 1788; d. 1788
Status: LC

Killinick and Ballybrennan
Earliest Records: b. 1804-20; m. 1804-20; d. 1805-19
Status: NAI M5063; SLC film 924521 (b/m/d. 1804-20); film 883662 (b. index); and film 1001477 (m. index)

Killurin
Earliest Records: m. 1845; d. 1880
Status: LC; Indexed by WHRC (to 1900)

Kilmallog
Earliest Records: b. 1813; m. 1813; d. 1813
Status: LC

Kilmeaden
Earliest Records: b. 1693-1873; m. 1683-1847; d. 1683-1882
Status: NAI MFCI 13, M5965

Kilmuckridge or Ballyvalden
Status: Lost

Kilnehue (see also Gorey)
Earliest Records: b. 1817; m. 1817; d. 1817
Status: LC

Kilnemanagh
Earliest Records: b. 1818; d. 1818
Missing Dates: b. ends 1836; d. ends 1836
Status: LC

Kilpatrick
Earliest Records: b. 1874; m. 1874; d. 1834-
Status: LC; NAI M1451 (d. 1834-64); Indexed by WHRC (1874 to 1900)

Kilrane (see Tacumshane)

Kilrush
Status: LC; b. 1878-1903 indexed by Anglican Rec. Proj.—available at RCBL and Soc. Gen. (London)

Kilscoran (see Tacumshane)

Kiltennell
Earliest Records: b. 1806; m. 1806; d. 1806
Status: LC

Leskinfere or Leskinfare
Earliest Records: b. 1836; m. 1803; d. 1836
Status: LC; Indexed by WHRC (to 1900)

Monamolin
Status: Lost

Monart
Status: Lost

Mulrankin
Earliest Records: b. 1786; m. 1786; d. 1786
Status: LC

Newtownbarry
Earliest Records: b. 1779; m. 1779; d. 1779
Status: LC

Old Ross (see also St. Mary, New Ross)
Earliest Records: b. 1802; d. 1814
Status: LC; Indexed by WHRC (to 1900)

Owenduff
Earliest Records: b. 1752; m. 1752; d. 1752 (with lists of baptisms, marriages, and burials 1806-29, and register of baptisms, marriages, and burials 1841-92)
Status: LC

Rathaspick or Rathaspeck
Earliest Records: b. 1844; m. 1844; d. 1844
Status: LC; Indexed by WHRC (m. 1845 to 1900)

Rathmacknee
Earliest Records: d. 1813-1866
Status: *J. Ir. Memorials Assoc.*

Rossdroit
Earliest Records: b. 1828; m. 1832; d. 1828
Status: LC; Indexed by WHRC (b. 1884-1900; m. 1845-1900; d. 1879-1900)

St. Iberius, Wexford (see Wexford)

St. Mary (see Wexford)

St. Mary, Enniscorthy
Earliest Records: b. 1798; m. 1798; d. 1798
Status: LC

St. Mary, New Ross
Earliest Records: b. 1763; m. 1764; d. 1764
Status: LC

St. Michael of Feagh (see Wexford)

St. Patrick (see Wexford)

St. Peter (see Wexford)

St. Selsker (see Wexford)

St. Tullogue (see Wexford)

Tacumshane (Union of Kilscoran)
Earliest Records: b. 1832; m. 1832; d. 1832
Status: LC

Taghmon
Status: Lost

Templescobin
Earliest Records: b. 1802; m. 1819; d. 1835
Status: LC and *J. Ir. Memorials Assoc.* (d. 1835–1864)

Templeshanbo
Earliest Records: b. 1827; m. 1800–14, 1827–; d. 1827
Status: LC; NAI M5729 (b. 1827–75; m. 1827–91; d. 1827–91); Indexed by WHRC (b. 1877–1900; m. 1845 to 1900); Anglican Rec. Proj. (m. 1800–14)

Templeshannon (see St. Mary, Enniscorthy)

Templetown (see Hooke)

Templeudigan (see also St. Mary, New Ross)
Earliest Records: b. 1877; m. 1840; d. 1877
Status: LC; Indexed by WHRC (to 1900)

Tomhaggard
Earliest Records: b. 1809; m. 1813; d. 1809
Status: LC

Toombe
Earliest Records: b. 1770; m. 1770; d. 1770
Missing Dates: b. 1819–20, ends 1821; m. 1819–20, ends 1821; d. 1819–20, ends 1821
Status: LC

Wexford
Earliest Records: b. 1674; m. 1674; d. 1674
Missing Dates: b. 1754–77; m. 1754–77; d. 1754–77
Status: LC; Indexed by WHRC (m. 1845–1900)

Whitechurch and Kilmokea
Status: GO 701 (extracts); SLC film 257807 (b/m/d. 1698–1736)

Presbyterian

An account of Presbyterian records is given in the introduction. These registers rarely contain death records, and occasionally have only records of births.

Wexford
Starting Date: 1844

Society of Friends (Quaker)

See the introduction for an account of Quaker records. The records for Wexford include: Wexford Monthly Meeting Register (1640–1862). FHL, Dublin; SLC film 571398 (b. 1646–1858; m. 1640–1862; d. 1656–1860).

Roman Catholic

Some of the registers of this county have been indexed by Wexford Heritage Research Centre (see Research Services at the end of the chapter). A search of the index will be conducted by the center for a fee. Those indexed are noted as "Indexed by WHRC." Microfilm copies of all registers are also available in the National Library of Ireland (NLI), and through the LDS library system.

Civil Parish: Adamstown
Map Grid: 50
RC Parish: Adamstown
Diocese: FE
Earliest Record: b. 1.1807 (two registers at some periods); m. 12.1849; d. 9.1823
Missing Dates: b. 10.1848–4.1849; d. ends 1.1832
Status: LC; NLI (mf); Indexed by WHRC (b. 1849–1900; m. 1892–1900)

Civil Parish: Allock
Map Grid: 65
RC Parish: Crossabeg, see Kilpatrick
Diocese: FE

Civil Parish: Ambrosetown
Map Grid: 102
RC Parish: part Bannow; part Rathangan, see Duncormick
Diocese: FE

Civil Parish: Ardamine
Map Grid: 30
RC Parish: Ballygarrett, see Kiltennell
Diocese: FE

Civil Parish: Ardcandrisk
Map Grid: 71
RC Parish: Glynn, see Killurin
Diocese: FE

Civil Parish: Ardcavan
Map Grid: 85
RC Parish: Castlebridge, see Ardcolm
Diocese: FE

Civil Parish: Ardcolm
Map Grid: 86
RC Parish: Castlebridge
Diocese: FE
Earliest Record: b. 10.1832; m. 12.1832
Status: LC; NLI (mf); Indexed by WHRC (to 1900)

Civil Parish: Artramont
Map Grid: 84
RC Parish: Crossabeg, see Kilpatrick
Diocese: FE

Civil Parish: Ballingly
Map Grid: 80
RC Parish: Ballymitty, see Bannow
Diocese: FE

Civil Parish: Ballyanne
Map Grid: 46
RC Parish: New Ross, see St. Mary (Bantry)
Diocese: FE

Civil Parish: Ballybrazil
Map Grid: 89
RC Parish: Suttons, see Kilmokea
Diocese: FE

Civil Parish: Ballybrennan
Map Grid: 126
RC Parish: Tagoat, see Rosslare
Diocese: FE

Civil Parish: Ballycanew
Map Grid: 24
RC Parish: Camolin, see Toome
Diocese: FE

Civil Parish: Ballycarney
Map Grid: 6
RC Parish: see Ferns
Diocese: FE

Civil Parish: Ballyconnick
Map Grid: 103
RC Parish: Rathangan, see Duncormick
Diocese: FE

Civil Parish: Ballyhoge
Map Grid: 53
RC Parish: Bree, see Clonmore
Diocese: FE

Civil Parish: Ballyhuskard
Map Grid: 58
RC Parish: part Oylegate, see Edermine; part Oulart, see Meelnagh
Diocese: FE

Civil Parish: Ballylannon
Map Grid: 79
RC Parish: see Clongeen
Diocese: FE

Civil Parish: Ballymitty
Map Grid: 81
RC Parish: see Bannow
Diocese: FE

Civil Parish: Ballymore
Map Grid: 129
RC Parish: Ballymore (and Mayglass)
Diocese: FE
Earliest Record: b. 1813; m. 1802
Status: LC; NLI (mf); Indexed by WHRC (to 1900)

Civil Parish: Ballynaslaney
Map Grid: 64
RC Parish: Oylegate, see Edermine
Diocese: FE

Civil Parish: Ballyvaldon
Map Grid: 62
RC Parish: Blackwater, see Killila
Diocese: FE

Civil Parish: Ballyvaloo
Map Grid: 68

RC Parish: Blackwater, see Killila
Diocese: FE

Civil Parish: Bannow
Map Grid: 105
RC Parish: Bannow or Carrick-on-Bannow
Diocese: FE
Earliest Record: b. 8.1832; m. 9.1830
Status: LC; NLI (mf); Indexed by WHRC (b. 1873–1900)

Civil Parish: Carne
Map Grid: 138
RC Parish: see Lady's Island
Diocese: FE

Civil Parish: Carnagh
Map Grid: 54
RC Parish: Carnagh (Cushinstown)
Diocese: FE
Earliest Record: b. 1.1759; m. 11.1752; d. 5.1794
Missing Dates: b. 8.1759–1.1778, 1.1830–7.1851; m. 2.1759–1.1778, 2.1824–8.1851, 9.1862–4.1863; d. 7.1808–5.1863
Status: LC; NLI (mf); Indexing planned by WHRC

Civil Parish: Carnew
Map Grid: 3
RC Parish: see Carnew, Co. Wicklow
Diocese: FE

Civil Parish: Carrick
Map Grid: 78
RC Parish: Glynn, see Killurin
Diocese: FE

Civil Parish: Castle-ellis
Map Grid: 60
RC Parish: part Oulart, see Meelnagh; part Blackwater, see Killila
Diocese: FE

Civil Parish: Chapel (Charon)
Map Grid: 44
RC Parish: Glynn, see Killurin; see also Killegney
Diocese: FE

Civil Parish: Clone
Map Grid: 11
RC Parish: Monageer (separate register for Boolavague, Monageer, for b. 1842 and m. 1847)
Diocese: FE
Earliest Record: b. 11.1838; m. 11.1838; d. 8.1838

Civil Parish: Clongeen
Map Grid: 72
RC Parish: Clongeen
Diocese: FE
Earliest Record: b. 1.1847; m. 4.1847
Status: LC; NLI (mf); Indexed by WHRC (to 1900)

Civil Parish: Clonleigh
Map Grid: 42

RC Parish: see Killegney
Diocese: FE

Civil Parish: Clonmines
Map Grid: 97
RC Parish: see Tintern
Diocese: FE

Civil Parish: Clonmore
Map Grid: 45
RC Parish: Bree; also part Davidstown, see
Templescoby
Diocese: FE
Earliest Record: b. 1.1837; m. 1.1837
Status: LC; NLI (mf); Indexed by WHRC (to 1900)

Civil Parish: Coolstuff
Map Grid: 76
RC Parish: part Glynn, see Killurin; part Taghmon
Diocese: FE

Civil Parish: Crosspatrick
Map Grid: 13
RC Parish: Tomacork, see Carnew, Co. Wicklow
Diocese: FE

Civil Parish: Donaghmore
Map Grid: 31
RC Parish: Ballygarrett, see Kiltennell
Diocese: FE

Civil Parish: Donowney
Map Grid: 51
RC Parish: part Taghmon; part Bree, see Clonmore
Diocese: FE

Civil Parish: Drinagh
Map Grid: 120
RC Parish: Piercestown, see Rathmacknee
Diocese: FE

Civil Parish: Duncormick
Map Grid: 106
RC Parish: Rathangan
Diocese: FE
Earliest Record: b. 1.1803; m. 6.1803
Missing Dates: b. 8.1805-1.1813; m. 6.1806-1.1813
Status: LC; NLI (mf); Indexed by WHRC (to 1850)

Civil Parish: Edermine
Map Grid: 63
RC Parish: Oylegate
Diocese: FE
Earliest Record: b. 3.1804; m. 4.1803; d. 1855
Missing Dates: b. 12.1820-8.1832; m. 10.1820-10.1832
Status: LC; NLI (mf); Indexed by WHRC (b/m. to
1900; d. to 1870)

Civil Parish: Ferns
Map Grid: 7
RC Parish: Ferns
Diocese: FE
Earliest Record: b. 5.1819; m. 5.1819; d. 1840

Missing Dates: b. 2.1840-9.1840; m. 1.1840-11.1840
Status: LC; NLI (mf); Indexed by WHRC (b. to 1900;
m. 1840-1900; d. 1840-1859)

Civil Parish: Fethard
Map Grid: 99
RC Parish: see Templetown
Diocese: FE

Civil Parish: Hook
Map Grid: 100
RC Parish: see Templetown
Diocese: FE

Civil Parish: Horetown
Map Grid: 74
RC Parish: part Adamstown; part Taghmon
Diocese: FE

Civil Parish: Inch (near Clongeen)
Map Grid: 73
RC Parish: see Clongeen
Diocese: DU

Civil Parish: Inch (near Kilgorman)
Map Grid: 16
RC Parish: Arklow, see Co. Wicklow
Diocese: FE

Civil Parish: Ishartmon
Map Grid: 133
RC Parish: see Ballymore
Diocese: FE

Civil Parish: Kerloge
Map Grid: 117
RC Parish: see Wexford
Diocese: FE

Civil Parish: Kilbride
Map Grid: 8
RC Parish: see Ferns
Diocese: FE

Civil Parish: Kilbrideglynn
Map Grid: 77
RC Parish: Glynn, see Killurin
Diocese: FE

Civil Parish: Kilcavan (near Gorey)
Map Grid: 19
RC Parish: Kilanieran, see Kilnenor
Diocese: FE

Civil Parish: Kilcavan (near Bannow)
Map Grid: 101
RC Parish: see Bannow
Diocese: FE

Civil Parish: Kilcomb
Map Grid: 4
RC Parish: see Ferns
Diocese: FE

Civil Parish: Kilcormick
Map Grid: 25
RC Parish: part Monageer, see Clone; part Oulart, see Meelnagh
Diocese: FE

Civil Parish: Kilcowan
Map Grid: 107
RC Parish: Rathangan, see Duncormick
Diocese: FE

Civil Parish: Kilcowanmore
Map Grid: 52
RC Parish: Bree, see Clonmore
Diocese: FE

Civil Parish: Kildavin
Map Grid: 118
RC Parish: Piercestown, see Rathmacknee
Diocese: FE

Civil Parish: Kilgarvan
Map Grid: 69
RC Parish: see Taghmon
Diocese: FE

Civil Parish: Kilgorman
Map Grid: 17
RC Parish: Arklow, see Co. Wicklow
Diocese: DU

Civil Parish: Killag
Map Grid: 109
RC Parish: Rathangan, see Duncormick
Diocese: FE

Civil Parish: Killann
Map Grid: 36
RC Parish: see Killegney
Diocese: FE

Civil Parish: Killegney
Map Grid: 43
RC Parish: Killegney (Cloughbawn)
Diocese: FE
Earliest Record: b. 3.1816; m. 3.1816; d. 3.1816
Missing Dates: b. 9.1850–1.1853; m. 9.1850–2.1853; d. 9.1850–2.1861
Status: LC; NLI (mf); Indexed by WHRC (to 1900)

Civil Parish: Killenagh
Map Grid: 29
RC Parish: part Ballygarrett, see Kiltennell; part Monamolin
Diocese: FE

Civil Parish: Killesk
Map Grid: 93
RC Parish: Sutton's, see Kilmokea
Diocese: FE

Civil Parish: Killiane
Map Grid: 122

RC Parish: Piercestown, see Rathmacknee
Diocese: FE

Civil Parish: Killila
Map Grid: 61
RC Parish: Blackwater
Diocese: FE
Earliest Record: b. 1.1815 (few legible entries pre-1818); m. 1.1815; d. 1.1843
Status: LC; NLI (mf); Indexed by WHRC (b. to 1900; m. to 1881; d. 1840–1883)

Civil Parish: Killincooly
Map Grid: 33
RC Parish: see Kilmuckridge
Diocese: FE

Civil Parish: Killinick
Map Grid: 125
RC Parish: Moyglass, see Ballymore
Diocese: FE

Civil Parish: Killisk
Map Grid: 59
RC Parish: part Castlebridge, see Ardcolm; part Oulart, see Meelnagh
Diocese: FE

Civil Parish: Killurin
Map Grid: 70
RC Parish: Glynn and Barntown
Diocese: FE
Earliest Record: b. 1.1817; m. 1.1817; d. 1.1823
Status: LC; NLI (mf); Indexed by WHRC (b. to 1900; d. 1867–1883)

Civil Parish: Kilmacree
Map Grid: 123
RC Parish: Piercestown, see Rathmacknee
Diocese: FE

Civil Parish: Kilmakilloge
Map Grid: 21
RC Parish: Gorey
Diocese: FE
Earliest Record: b. 5.1845; m. 6.1845
Status: LC; NLI (mf); Indexing planned by WHRC

Civil Parish: Kilmannon
Map Grid: 104
RC Parish: Rathangan, see Duncormick
Diocese: FE

Civil Parish: Kilmokea
Map Grid: 92
RC Parish: Suttons (Horeswood)
Diocese: FE
Earliest Record: (separate registers for Suttons, Ballykelly, from 1862) b. 11.1824; m. 2.1825; d. 5.1827
Missing Dates: d. 11.1836–1.1858
Status: LC; NLI (mf); Indexed by WHRC (b. to 1900; m. to 1894)

Civil Parish: Kilmore
Map Grid: 110
RC Parish: Kilmore
Diocese: FE
Earliest Record: b. 4.1752; m. 4.1752; d. 4.1752
Missing Dates: b. 3.1785-6.1790, 11.1794-1.1798,
3.1826-7.1828; m. 3.1785-6.1790, 11.1794-1.1798,
3.1826-11.1827; d. 3.1785-6.1790, 11.1794-1.1798,
ends 3.1826
Status: LC; NLI (mf); Indexed by WHRC (b. to 1900;
m/d. to 1850)

Civil Parish: Kilmuckridge
Map Grid: 34
RC Parish: Kilmuckridge (Litter)
Diocese: FE
Earliest Record: b. 10.1789; m. 1.1788
Missing Dates: m. 4.1798-9.1806
Status: LC; NLI (mf); Indexed by WHRC (b. 1818-
1900; m. 1876-1890)

Civil Parish: Kilnahue or Kilnehue or Lamogue
Map Grid: 18
RC Parish: Craanford, see Rossminoge
Diocese: FE

Civil Parish: Kilnamanagh
Map Grid: 32
RC Parish: Oulart, see Meelnagh
Diocese: FE

Civil Parish: Kilnenor
Map Grid: 15
RC Parish: Kilanieran
Diocese: FE
Earliest Record: b. 1.1852; m. 1.1852
Status: LC; NLI (mf); Indexing planned by WHRC

Civil Parish: Kilpatrick
Map Grid: 83
RC Parish: Crossabeg
Diocese: FE
Earliest Record: b. 1794; m. 1794; d. 1899
Status: LC; NLI (mf); Indexed by WHRC (to 1900)

Civil Parish: Kilpipe
Map Grid: 14
RC Parish: Killaveny, see Kilpipe, Co. Wicklow
Diocese: FE

Civil Parish: Kilrane
Map Grid: 131
RC Parish: Tagoat, see Rosslare
Diocese: FE

Civil Parish: Kilrush
Map Grid: 2
RC Parish: Kilrush
Diocese: FE
Earliest Record: b. 5.1841
Missing Dates: b. 11.1846-3.1855
Status: LC; NLI (mf); Indexing planned by WHRC

Civil Parish: Kilscanlan
Map Grid: 55
RC Parish: Cushinstown, see Carnagh
Diocese: FE

Civil Parish: Kilscoran
Map Grid: 130
RC Parish: Tagoat, see Rosslare
Diocese: FE

Civil Parish: Kiltennell
Map Grid: 28
RC Parish: Ballygarrett
Diocese: FE
Earliest Record: b. 11.1828; m. 8.1828; d. 8.1830
Missing Dates: b. ends 1863; m. ends 1865; d.
4.1857-10.1865, ends 4.1867
Status: LC; NLI (mf); Indexed by WHRC (to 1900)

Civil Parish: Kiltrisk
Map Grid: 27
RC Parish: Ballygarrett, see Kiltennell
Diocese: FE

Civil Parish: Kilturk
Map Grid: 111
RC Parish: see Kilmore
Diocese: FE

Civil Parish: Lady's Island
Map Grid: 136
RC Parish: Lady's Island
Diocese: FE
Earliest Record: b. 8.1737; m. 2.1753; d. 6.1868
Missing Dates: b. 5.1740-5.1752, 3.1763-1.1766,
12.1802-1.1807, 1.1818-10.1827; m. 12.1759-
2.1764, 5.1800-1.1807, 2.1818-10.1827; ends 2.1838
Status: LC; NLI (mf); Indexed by WHRC (b. to 1900;
m. 1838-1900; d. 1868-1900)

Civil Parish: Lamogue (see Kilnahue)

Civil Parish: Liskinfere
Map Grid: 23
RC Parish: Camolin, see Toome
Diocese: FE

Civil Parish: Maudlintown
Map Grid: 116
RC Parish: see Wexford
Diocese: FE

Civil Parish: Mayglass
Map Grid: 124
RC Parish: see Ballymore
Diocese: FE

Civil Parish: Meelnagh
Map Grid: 35
RC Parish: Oulart
Diocese: FE
Earliest Record: b. 10.1837; m. 11.1837

Missing Dates: b. 1.1853-10.1863; m. 11.1852-11.1874
Status: LC; NLI (mf); Indexing planned by WHRC

Civil Parish: Monamolin
Map Grid: 26
RC Parish: Monamolin; also part Kilmuckridge
Diocese: FE
Earliest Record: b. 3.1858; m. 10.1859
Status: LC; NLI (mf); Indexing planned by WHRC

Civil Parish: Monart
Map Grid: 10
RC Parish: Marshalstown; also part Ballindaggin, see Templeshanbo
Diocese: FE
Earliest Record: b. 5.1854; m. 11.1854; d. 10.1854
Status: LC; NLI (mf); Indexing planned by WHRC

Civil Parish: Moyacomb
Map Grid: 1
RC Parish: see Co. Wicklow and Co. Carlow
Diocese: FE

Civil Parish: Mulrankin
Map Grid: 108
RC Parish: see Kilmore
Diocese: FE

Civil Parish: Newbawn
Map Grid: 49
RC Parish: see Adamstown
Diocese: FE

Civil Parish: Oldross
Map Grid: 48
RC Parish: part Carnagh; part New Ross, see St. Mary (3)
Diocese: FE

Civil Parish: Owenduff
Map Grid: 91
RC Parish: see Tintern
Diocese: FE

Civil Parish: Rathaspick
Map Grid: 119
RC Parish: Piercestown, see Rathmacknee (separate register for Murrintown, 1839-54)
Diocese: FE

Civil Parish: Rathmacknee
Map Grid: 121
RC Parish: Piercestown
Diocese: FE
Earliest Record: b. 12.1811; m. 1.1812
Status: LC; NLI (mf); Indexed by WHRC (to 1900)

Civil Parish: Rathroe
Map Grid: 95
RC Parish: Hook, see Templetown
Diocese: FE

Civil Parish: Rossdroit
Map Grid: 38
RC Parish: Rathnure
Diocese: FE
Earliest Record: b/m/d. 10.1846
Status: LC; NLI (mf); Indexed by WHRC (to 1900)

Civil Parish: Rosslare
Map Grid: 128
RC Parish: Tagoat and Kilrane
Diocese: FE
Earliest Record: b. 1.1853; m. 2.1853; d. 10.1875
Status: LC; NLI (mf); Indexed by WHRC (to 1881)

Civil Parish: Rossminoge
Map Grid: 20
RC Parish: Craanford
Diocese: FE
Earliest Record: b. 8.1871; m. 11.1871
Status: LC; NLI (mf); Indexed by WHRC (to 1900)

Civil Parish: St. Bridget
Map Grid: 114
RC Parish: see Wexford
Diocese: FE

Civil Parish: St. Doologe
Map Grid: 116
RC Parish: see Wexford
Diocese: FE

Civil Parish: St. Helen
Map Grid: 132
RC Parish: Tagoat, see Rosslare
Diocese: FE

Civil Parish: St. Iberius
Map Grid: 135
RC Parish: see Lady's Island
Diocese: FE

Civil Parish: St. Iberius (Wexford Town)
Map Grid: 114
RC Parish: see Wexford
Diocese: FE

Civil Parish: St. James and Dunbrody
Map Grid: 94
RC Parish: see Templetown
Diocese: FE

Civil Parish: St. John (1) (near Wexford)
Map Grid: 113
RC Parish: Davidstown, see Wexford
Diocese: FE

Civil Parish: St. John (2) (near Enniscorthy)
Map Grid: 40
RC Parish: part Davidstown, see Templescoby; part St. Mary's (1)
Diocese: FE

Civil Parish: St. Margaret (1) (near Carne)
Map Grid: 137

RC Parish: see Lady's Island
Diocese: FE

Civil Parish: St. Margaret (2)
Map Grid: 87
RC Parish: Castlebridge, see Ardcolm

Civil Parish: St. Mary (1) (Wexford Town)
Map Grid: 114
RC Parish: see Wexford
Diocese: FE

Civil Parish: St. Mary (2) (Scarawalsh)
Map Grid: 12
RC Parish: St. Mary Enniscorthy
Diocese: FE
Earliest Record: b. 5.1794; m. 5.1794; d. 10.1815
Status: LC; NLI (mf); Indexed by WHRC (b/m. to 1900)

Civil Parish: St. Mary (3) (Bantry)
Map Grid: 47
RC Parish: New Ross
Diocese: FE
Earliest Record: b. 11.1789; m. 1817; d. 5.1794
Missing Dates: d. 4.1822–11.1851, ends 2.1849
Status: LC; NLI (mf); Indexed by WHRC (b/m. to 1900)

Civil Parish: St. Mary (4) (Bantry, near Bunclody)
Map Grid: 5
RC Parish: Newtownbarry
Diocese: FE
Earliest Record: b. 1834; m. 5.1834; d. 1834
Missing Dates: d. 1857–1858, 1872–1873
Status: LC; NLI (mf); Indexing planned by WHRC

Civil Parish: St. Michael (near Rosslare)
Map Grid: 127
RC Parish: Tagoat, see Rosslare
Diocese: FE

Civil Parish: St. Michael's of Feagh
Map Grid: 114
RC Parish: see Wexford
Diocese: FE

Civil Parish: St. Mullin
Map Grid: 41
RC Parish: see St. Mullins, Co. Carlow; also part New Ross, see St. Mary (3)
Diocese: FE

Civil Parish: St. Nicholas
Map Grid: 66
RC Parish: Castlebridge, see Ardcolm
Diocese: FE

Civil Parish: St. Patrick
Map Grid: 114
RC Parish: see Wexford
Diocese: FE

Civil Parish: St. Peter
Map Grid: 115
RC Parish: see Wexford
Diocese: FE

Civil Parish: St. Selskar
Map Grid: 114
RC Parish: see Wexford
Diocese: FE

Civil Parish: Skreen
Map Grid: 67
RC Parish: Castlebridge, see Ardcolm
Diocese: FE

Civil Parish: Tacumshin
Map Grid: 134
RC Parish: see Lady's Island
Diocese: FE

Civil Parish: Taghmon
Map Grid: 75
RC Parish: Taghmon
Diocese: FE
Earliest Record: b. 5.1801; m. 5.1801; d. 1.1828
Missing Dates: b. 12.1865–3.1866; m. 3.1835–4.1866; d. 12.1846–2.1866
Status: LC; NLI (mf); Indexed by WHRC (b. to 1900)

Civil Parish: Tellarought
Map Grid: 90
RC Parish: Cushinstown, see Carnagh
Diocese: FE

Civil Parish: Templescoby
Map Grid: 39
RC Parish: Davidstown
Diocese: FE
Earliest Record: b. 1801; m. 6.1808
Status: LC; NLI (mf); Indexed by WHRC (b. to 1900; m. 1840–1859)

Civil Parish: Templeshanbo
Map Grid: 9
RC Parish: Ballindaggin; also part St. Mary's Newtownbarry
Diocese: FE
Earliest Record: b. 7.1871; m. 7.1871
Status: LC; NLI (mf); Indexing planned by WHRC

Civil Parish: Templeshannon
Map Grid: 57
RC Parish: part St. Mary (2); part Monageer, see Clone
Diocese: FE

Civil Parish: Templetown
Map Grid: 98
RC Parish: Hook; also Templetown (2)
Diocese: FE
Earliest Record: b. 11.1835; m. 11.1875; d. 10.1835
Missing Dates: b. 8.1840–3.1844; d. ends 1854
Status: LC; NLI (mf); Indexed by WHRC (b. to 1873)

Civil Parish: Templetown (2)
Map Grid: 98
RC Parish: Templetown and St. James
Diocese: FE
Earliest Record: b. 12.1792; m. 11.1792; d. 1.1816
Missing Dates: b. 10.1793-1.1795, 11.1798-4.1805
Status: LC; NLI (mf); Partially indexed by WHRC (b. to 1894; m. to 1859; d. to 1879)

Civil Parish: Templeudigan
Map Grid: 37
RC Parish: see Killegney
Diocese: FE

Civil Parish: Tikillin
Map Grid: 82
RC Parish: Crossabeg, see Kilpatrick
Diocese: FE

Civil Parish: Tintern
Map Grid: 96
RC Parish: Tintern (Ballycullane)
Diocese: FE
Earliest Record: b. 9.1827 (in bad condition); m. 10.1827; d. 10.1828
Missing Dates: d. ends 1.1832
Status: LC; NLI (mf); Indexed by WHRC (to 1900)

Civil Parish: Tomhaggard
Map Grid: 112
RC Parish: see Kilmore
Diocese: FE

Civil Parish: Toome
Map Grid: 22
RC Parish: Camolin (Ballyoughter)
Diocese: FE
Earliest Record: b. 9.1810; m. 8.1815
Missing Dates: b. 12.1811-8.1815, 11.1832-8.1844; m. 2.1868-7.1871
Status: LC; NLI (mf); Indexing planned by WHRC

Civil Parish: Wexford
Map Grid: 114
RC Parish: Wexford
Diocese: FE
Earliest Record: b. 5.1671; m. 5.1671
Missing Dates: b. 1.1689-1.1694, 3.1710-2.1723, 8.1787-6.1815; m. 1.1685-4.1724
Status: LC; NLI (mf); Indexed by WHRC (to 1900)

Civil Parish: Wexford, St. Bridget
Map Grid: 114
RC Parish: see Wexford
Diocese: FE

Civil Parish: Wexford, St. Doologe
Map Grid: 114
RC Parish: see Wexford
Diocese: FE

Civil Parish: Wexford, St. Iberius
Map Grid: 114

RC Parish: see Wexford
Diocese: FE

Civil Parish: Wexford, St. Mary
Map Grid: 114
RC Parish: see Wexford
Diocese: FE

Civil Parish: Wexford, St. Michael's of Feagh
Map Grid: 114
RC Parish: see Wexford
Diocese: FE

Civil Parish: Wexford, St. Patrick
Map Grid: 114
RC Parish: see Wexford
Diocese: FE

Civil Parish: Wexford, St. Selskar
Map Grid: 114
RC Parish: see Wexford
Diocese: FE

Civil Parish: Whitechurch
Map Grid: 88
RC Parish: Horeswood, see Kilmokea
Diocese: FE

Civil Parish: Whitechurch-Glynn
Map Grid: 56
RC Parish: Glynn, see Killurin
Diocese: FE

Commercial and Social Directories

1788

Richard Lucas's *General Directory of the Kingdom of Ireland* contains lists of traders in Enniscorthy, Gorey, New Ross, Taghmon, and Wexford. Reprinted in *Ir. Gen.* 3 (10) (1965): 392-416.

1820

J. Pigot's *Commercial Directory of Ireland* contains information on the gentry, nobility, and traders in and around the towns of New Ross and Wexford.

1824

J. Pigot's *City of Dublin and Hibernian Provincial Directory* includes traders, nobility, gentry, and clergy lists of Enniscorthy, Gorey, New Ross, Taghmon, and Wexford.

1839

T. Shearman's *New Commercial Directory* lists traders, gentry, etc., in New Ross.

1840

F. Kinder's *New Triennial and Commerical Directory for 1840, '41 and '42* contains traders and other lists for New Ross.

1846

Slater's *National Commercial Directory of Ireland* lists nobility, clergy, traders, etc., in Enniscorthy and Ferns, Gorey, New Ross and Rossbercon, Taghmon, and Wexford.

1856

Slater's *Royal National Commercial Directory of Ireland* lists nobility, gentry, clergy, traders, etc., in Enniscorthy and Ferns, Fethard, Gorey, New Ross and Rossbercon, Newtownbarry, Taghmon, and Wexford.

1870

Slater's *Directory of Ireland* contains trade, nobility, and clergy lists for Enniscorthy, Fethard, Gorey, New Ross, Newtownbarry, Taghmon, and Wexford.

1872

Griffith's *County Wexford Almanac* has lists of traders in Enniscorthy and Ferns and an alphabetical list of medical doctors in the county.

1878

Griffith's Almanac. Directory and historical record of Co. Wexford. Wexford: Myles Doyle, 1878.

1881

Slater's *Royal National Commercial Directory of Ireland* contains lists of traders, clergy, nobility, and farmers in adjoining parishes of the towns of Enniscorthy and Ferns, Fethard, Gorey, New Ross, Newtownbarry, and Wexford.

1885

G.H. Bassett's *Wexford County Guide and Directory* has an alphabetical list of persons and traders for Wexford borough, and traders, farmers, and landholders in all postal districts in the county. Dublin: Sealy, 1885. Reprinted in 1991 by Hibernian Imprints, Dublin.

1894

Slater's *Royal National Directory of Ireland* lists traders, police, teachers, farmers, and private residents in each of the towns, villages and parishes of the county.

Family History

Murphy, Hilary. *Families of Co. Wexford.* Dublin: Geography Publications, 1986.

Kavanagh, Art, and Rory Murphy. *The Wexford Gentry.* 2 vols. Bunclody: Irish Family Names, 1994, 1996.

"Alcock Wilton of Wexford." *Irish Builder.* 1888.

"Byrnes and Wickhams of Wexford." *Irish Family History* 9 (1993): 55-58.

Codd—see Esmond.

"Devereux of the Leap." *Ir. Gen.* 4 (5) (1972): 450-60.

"The Dormer Family of New Ross." *R.S.A.I.* 19 (1889): 133-35.

"Doyle Wells of Gorey." *Irish Builder.* 1888.

"Dunne Papers (Brittas, Co. Wexford)." *Anal. Hib.* 30: 123-47.

"The Early Cullen Family." *Reportorium Novum* 2 (1) (1958): 185-202.

Ellison, J., and Henry Havelock. *In Search of My Family.* (Concerning the Ellison family.) Dublin: Dublin University Press, 1971.

"Frayne of Co. Wexford." *Ir. Gen.* 4 (3) (1970): 213-20.

Genealogies of Esmond, Codd, Jacob, and Redmond. GO film 279.

"Goodall of Wexford." *Ir. Gen.* 3 (12) (1967): 487-500.

"The Harvey-Waddy Connection." *J. Old Wexford Soc.* 8 (1980-81).

"Harvey Family of Co. Wexford, Sixteen Births 1798-1801." *J. Ass. Pres. Mem. Dead* 9 (1912-16): 572.

"Hatchell of Co. Wexford." *Ir. Gen.* 4 (5) (1972): 461-76.

"Houghton of Kilmannock." *Irish Builder.* 1888.

"The Ivory Family of New Ross." *R.S.A.I.* 80 (1950): 242-61.

Jacob—see Esmond.

Internet information on Keating is at http://www.vni.net/~kayk/keating.htm.

"Lambert of Wexford." *Past* 2 (1921): 129-38.

Lett, Katherine Lucy. "Records of the Lett Family in Ireland." 1925.

Loftus—see Co. Kilkenny.

Internet information on O'Kelly is at http://shaw.iol.ie/~okelly/okelly.htm.

"Notes on Brown of Mayglass (including pedigree)." *J. Ass. Pres. Mem. Dead* 9: 403.

"Notes on Cooke of Tomduff." *J. Ass. Pres. Mem. Dead* 1 (1888-91): 519.

"Notes on the Moore Family, Tinraheen, Co. Wexford." *J. Ass. Pres. Mem. Dead* 9: 189; and 10: 252.

Redmond—see Esmond.

Redmond, G.O. *Account of the Anglo-Norman Family of Devereux of Balmagir, Co. Wexford.* Dublin, 1891.

"Roches of Wexford." *J. Old Wexford Soc.* 2 (1969): 39-48.

"The Rossiters of Rathmacknee Castle (Co. Wexford), 1169-1881." *Past* 5 (1949): 103-16; 6 (1950): 13-44.

Waddy—see Harvey.

Wells—see Doyle.

West—see Co. Wicklow.

Wilton—see Alcock.

Gravestone Inscriptions

This is one of the most comprehensively recorded counties. The major source of inscriptions is the series *Memorials of the Dead*, volumes 5-7, compiled and published in a limited number of copies by Brian J. Cantwell. Copies are available in the NLI and NAI. They can also be searched by Wexford Heritage Research Centre (see Research Services). Glor na nGael has also added to this collection. This volume is listed at the end.

Memorials of the Dead, vol. 5 (North Wexford):

Ardamine
Askamore
Ballinclay (Quaker)
Ballindagen
Balloughter
Ballycanew
Ballycarney
Ballyduff
Ballyfad
Ballygarrett
Ballymore
Brideswell
Bunclody
Camolin
Castledockrill
Castletown
Clonatin
Clone
Craanford
Donoughmore
Ferns
Gorey
Holyfort
Inch
Kilanerin
Kilcashel
Kilcavan
Kilgorman
Killenagh
Kilmyshall
Kilnahue
Kilnenor
Kilrush
Kiltennel
Knockbrandon
Leskinfere
Limbrick
Monaseed
Prospect

Riverchapel
Rosminogue
Scarawalsh
Templeshanbo
Toberanierin
Toome

Memorials of the Dead, vol. 6 (Southeast Wexford):

Ardcavan Old
Ardcolm (C of I; Castlebridge)
Ardcolm Old
Artramont Old
Ballaghkeen (Church of St. John the Baptist) RC
Ballyfad
Ballyhuskard (C of I)
Ballymurn (RC)
Ballynaslaney, St. David's Well
Ballyvaldon Old
Ballyvaloo Old
Beggerin Island Old
Blackwater, St. Brigid (RC)
Boolavogue, St. Cormac (RC)
Carrig (Wexford) Old
Castlebridge (RC)
Castle Ellis Old
Clone, St. Paul's (C of I)
Cooladine (Quaker)
Crossabeg, SS Patrick and Brigid (RC)
Curracloe (RC)
Edermine Old
Enniscorthy, St. Aidan's Cathedral (RC)
Enniscorthy, St. Mary (C of I)
Enniscorthy, St. Senan (RC)
Enniscorthy, Templeshannon Old
Glascarrig (C of I)
Glenbrien, St. Peter (RC)
Kilcormack, St. Cormack (C of I)
Killilla Old
Killincooly Old
Kilmallock Old
Kilmuckridge (C of I)
Kilmuckridge (Litter) (RC)
Kilnamanagh, St. John's Church (C of I)
Kilpatrick (Saunderscourt) Old
Meelnagh Old
Monagear (RC)
Monamolin (RC)
Monamolin (C of I)
Oulart, St. Patrick (RC)
Oylegate (RC)
Screen (RC)

Solesborough Old (Quaker and C of I)

Tykillen Old

Wexford, Church of the Assumption (RC)

Wexford, Church of the Immaculate Conception (RC)

Wexford, Paupers Graveyard

Wexford, Redmond Memorial

Wexford, Church of St. Francis (Merchants') (RC)

Wexford, St. Iberius Church (C of I)

Wexford, St. John's Old

Wexford, St. Magdalen's Old

Wexford, St. Mary's Old

Wexford, St. Michael's Old

Wexford, St. Patrick's Old

Wexford, St. Selskar's Abbey

Memorials of the Dead, vol. 7 (Southwest Wexford):

Ambrosetown

Ballingly Old

Balloughton (C of I)

Ballybrennan Old

Ballyconnick Old

Ballylannen

Ballymitty, St. Peter (RC)

Ballymore (RC)

Ballymore Old

Bannow, per Dr. and Mrs. Hetherington

Barntown, Church of Blessed Virgin and St. Alphonsus

Broadway, St. Iberius

Carne, Churchtown (C of I)

Carne, St. Margaret

Carne, St. Vogus

Caroreigh, St. Garvan

Carrick-on-Bannow, Church of Immaculate Conception and St. Joseph

Cleriestown, St. Mannan (RC)

Coolstuff Old

Cullenstown (RC)

Cullenstown (near Cullenstown Strand)

Drinagh

Duncormick (C of I)

Grange

Grantstown Priory, O.S.A. (RC)

Horetown, St. James (C of I)

Isharton Old

Johnstown Castle Demesne

Kilcavan

Kilcowan

Kildavin

Kilgarvan

Killag

Killiane Old

Killinick (C of I)

Kilmacree

Kilmannan

Kilmore, St. Mary (RC)

Memorials to the Dead (compiled by Glor na nGael and published in 1990)

Ballindaggin Old Graveyard, Churchyard and Extension

Newspapers

The Wexford Heritage Research Centre (see Research Services) has indexes to some biographical notices in Wexford papers. In the following listings, "WCL" denotes holdings in the Wexford County Library (see Research Sources and Services section).

Title: *County of Wexford Express* (*Wexford and Kilkenny Express* from 1878)
Published in: Wexford, 1875–1907
BL Holdings: 5.1878–4.1905; 6–11.1907

Title: *Enniscorthy News* (and *Co. Wexford Advertiser*)
Published in: Enniscorthy, 1860–1912
BL Holdings: 3.1861–3.1902; 1.1911–5.1912

Title: *Gorey Correspondent* (*Arklow Standard* from 1876)
Published in: Gorey, ca. 1856–92
BL Holdings: 2.1861–12.1892

Title: *Guardian*
Published in: Wexford, 1847–56 (incorporated with *The People*)
NLI Holdings: 11.1847–12.1848; odd numbers 1849–55
BL Holdings: 11.1847–12.1856

Title: *New Ross Standard*
Published in: New Ross, 1889–current
NLI Holdings: 12.1904–in progress
BL Holdings: 8.1889–in progress

Title: *New Ross Reporter and Wexford (Carlow and Kilkenny) Advertiser*
Published in: New Ross, 1871–95; Waterford, 1895–1910
BL Holdings: 8.1874–6.1875; 6–11.1875; 1.1850–8.1910

Title: *The Watchman*
Published in: Enniscorthy, 1869–86
BL Holdings: 7.1869–9.1886
WCL Holdings: 7.1869–1.1870; 3.1870–9.1886

Title: *Wexford Advertiser* (see *New Ross Reporter*)

Title: *Wexford Evening Post*
Published in: Wexford, 1826–30
NLI Holdings: 3.1826–3.1830
WCL Holdings: five issues 9.1829–1.1830

Title: *Wexford Freeman*
Published in: Wexford, 1832–37
NLI Holdings: 5.1832–5.1837
BL Holdings: 5.1832–5.1837
WCL Holdings: seven issues 11.1806–7.1807; 4.1808–3.1810; 1.1817–7.1817

Title: *Wexford Herald*
Published in: Wexford, 1788–1865
NLI Holdings: 7.1788–6.1789; 7.1792–6.1793; 4.1806–7.1810; 4.1812–2.1814; 1.1828–8.1832
BL Holdings: 5.1813; 1.1828–8.1832; 1.1861–4.1865

Title: *Wexford Independent* (continued as *The Independent*, 1843–70, and *The Wexford Independent*, 1870–1906)
Published in: Wexford, 1830–1906
NLI Holdings: 8.1837 (bound in "Miscellaneous Newspapers," vol. 1); 1.1885–12.1905; 3.1906–8.1908
BL Holdings: 12.1830–7.1869; 7.1870–5.1873; 1.1874–8.1883; 1.1884–2.1906
WCL Holdings: 12.1830–12.1831

Title: *(Wexford) People*
Published in: Wexford, 1853–current
NLI Holdings: 1.1882–in progress
WCL Holdings: odd issues 10.1859; 1.1877; 3.1879; 7–11.1881; 6.1882; 9.1884–2.1887; 10.1888; 5.1891; 10.1892; 6.1893; 10.1898
Other Holdings: People Newspapers Ltd., Wexford holds all issues since 1861

Wills and Administrations

A discussion of the types of records, where they are held, and their availability and value is given in the Wills section in the introduction. The availability of prerogative wills, administrations, and marriage license records is also described in the relevant parts of the same section. Where available, published sources of these records are given in the Miscellaneous Sources section.

Pre-1858 Wills and Administrations

Prerogative Wills. See the introduction.

Consistorial Wills. County Wexford is mainly in the diocese of Ferns, with two parishes in Dublin and one in Leighlin. The guide to Catholic parish records in this chapter shows the diocese to which each civil parish belonged. The wills of residents of each diocese were usually proven within that diocese (see the Wills section for exceptions). The following records survive:

Wills

See the introduction.

Abstracts

See the introduction. Abstracts of Ferns Wills from

Phillips Manuscripts (surnames A–S for period 1661–1826). NAI; SLC film 101027.

Indexes

Ferns (1601–1858, badly mutilated), up to 1800 published by Phillimore. The NAI has a copy (1603–1838) for F–V, with unproved wills 1616–1842 for W only. NAI 1A 4 (16). A reconstructed copy of the index for 1800–57 (compiled by Ian Cantwell) is complete for F–T and fifty percent complete for the rest. This is also available in the NAI. Co. Wexford Wills: GO Ms. 685 and SLC film 100158. Ferns Administration Bonds (1679–1848): NAI; SLC film 100962. Leighlin Administration Bonds (1694–1845): NAI; SLC film 100963. Leighlin Wills (1652–1858): NAI; SLC film 100916.

Post-1858 Wills and Administrations

This county was served by the District Registry of Waterford. The surviving records are in the NAI. Records include Waterford District Will Books (1858–1894): NAI; SLC film 100951–4.

Marriage Licenses

See Miscellaneous Sources section.

Indexes

Ferns and Leighlin (1691–1845). NAI; SLC film 100870–71; GO ms. 612–617; SLC film 100169–72 (more complete copy). Marriage License Bonds for Ossory, Ferns, and Leighlin (1691–1845). GO Ms. 612–617 and SLC films 100169–72.

Miscellaneous Sources

"Ancient Gaelic Families of Co. Wexford." *Irish Family History* 6 (1990): 29–38.

Bassett, George H. *Wexford County Guide and Directory.* Dublin, 1885.

Browne, E., and T. Wickham, eds. *Lewis's Wexford.* Enniscorthy, 1983.

Butler, Thomas. *History of the Parish of Carrick-on-Bannow.* N.p., 1985.

Cantwell, Brian J. *Memorials of the Dead for County Wexford.* Vols. 5–10 (index).

County Wexford Almanac 1909. Wexford: John English and Co., 1909.

"Ferns Marriage Licenses 1662–1806 (except 1701–25 and 1693/94)." *J. Kildare Arch. Hist. Soc.* (A–B) 9 (1) (1918–21): 34–59; (C) 9: 178–90; (D–F) 9: 227–45; (G) 9: 292–300; (H) 9: 366–75, 9: 454–56, and 10: 29–31; (H contd.–P) 10: 61–99; (R–S) 10: 125–49; (T–Z) 10: 174–94.

Flood, W.H.G. *A History of Enniscorthy.* 1898.

Fraser, R. *Statistical Survey of the County of Wexford.* Royal Dublin Society, 1807.

Grattan-Flood, W. *History of the Diocese of Ferns.* Waterford, 1916.

Griffiths, George. *Chronicles of Co. Wexford to 1877.* Enniscorthy, 1877.

Hore, P.H. *The History of the Town and County of Wexford.* London, 1906.

Jeffrey, William H. *The Castles of Co. Wexford.* Old Wexford Society Presentation to Co. Library, Wexford, 1979.

Kinsella, A. *The Waveswept Shore—A History of the Courtown District.* Wexford, 1982.

Lacy, T. *Sights and Scenes in our Fatherland.* London, 1863.

Leslie, J.B. *Ferns Clergy and Parishes.* Dublin, 1936.

"Passenger List of Ticonderoga 1850" (many from Killaveney parish, Wexford; includes part of a group which founded New Wexford, Missouri). *The Past* 12 (1978): 49–52.

"Population Trends in Co. Wexford." *The Past* 6 (1950): 118–37.

"Quakers in Wexford." *Old Wexford Soc. J.* 3 (1) (1970): 36–41.

Hennessy, Patrick. *Davidstown, Courtnacuddy—A Wexford Parish.* Enniscorthy, 1986.

"Some Eighteenth-Century Petitions." *The Past* 9 (1972): 8–38.

Whelan, K., and W. Nolan, eds. *Wexford History and Society: Interdisciplinary Essays on the History of an Irish County.* Dublin: Geography Publications, 1987.

Whelan, K., ed. *A History of Newbawn.* Newbawn: Macra na Feirme, 1986.

Research Sources and Services

Journals

The Past (journal of the Ui Cinsealaigh Society)

Journal of the Wexford Historical Society

Journal of Waterford and South-East of Ireland Archaeological Society

Libraries and Information Sources

Wexford County Library, Abbey Street, Wexford. Ph: (053) 42211. The local studies section of the library has an extensive collection of local material, including books, directories, newspapers, periodicals, photographs, and estate papers. They also hold the records of local Methodist churches.

Research Services

Wexford Heritage Research Centre, Yola Farmstead, Tagoat, Co. Wexford. Ph: (053) 31177; fax: (353) 53 31177. This is the official IGP center for Wexford and has indexed most of the church registers of the county; they are actively working on the remainder. It also has an index to the 1901 census and *Griffith's Valuation*, and has access to a range of other family history sources for the county. Researchers are advised to contact the center for an updated list of registers, and other sources, indexed. Research is conducted for a fee.

St. Mullins Muintir Na Tire (see Research Sources and Services section, Co. Carlow).

Irish Origins Research Agency (see Research Sources and Services section, Co. Carlow).

See also Research Services in Dublin in the introduction.

Societies

Wexford Historical Society, Ms. Mary T. Kehoe, 27 Newlands, Wexford, Co. Wexford

Bunclody Historical Society, Mr. Rory Murphy, Ballinavocral, Bunclody, Co. Wexford

Taghmon Historical Society, Ms. Maria Colfer, The Rose, Camross, Foulksmills, Co. Wexford

Ui Cinsealaigh Historical Society, Rev. M. Glynn, St. Aidan's, Enniscorthy, Co. Wexford

New Ross Literary and Historical Society, Mr. James Doyle, Ard Ross, New Ross, Co. Wexford

Wexford Civil Parishes as Numbered on Map

1. Moyacomb
2. Kilrush
3. Carnew
4. Kilcomb
5. St. Mary's (Newtownbarry)
6. Ballycarney
7. Ferns
8. Kilbride
9. Templeshanbo
10. Monart
11. Clone
12. St. Mary's (2) (Scarawalsh)
13. Crosspatrick
14. Kilpipe
15. Kilnenor
16. Inch (Gorey)
17. Kilgorman
18. Kilnahue or Lamogue
19. Kilcavan (Gorey)
20. Rossminoge
21. Kilmakilloge
22. Toome
23. Liskinfere
24. Ballycanew
25. Kilcormick
26. Monamolin
27. Kiltrisk
28. Kiltennell
29. Killenagh
30. Ardamine
31. Donaghmore
32. Kilnamanagh
33. Killincooly
34. Kilmuckridge
35. Meelnagh
36. Killann
37. Templeudigan
38. Rossdroit
39. Templescoby
40. St. John (Bantry)
41. St. Mullin
42. Clonleigh
43. Killegney
44. Chapel
45. Clonmore
46. Ballyanne
47. St. Mary's (3) (Bantry)
48. Oldross
49. Newbawn
50. Adamstown
51. Donowney
52. Kilcowanmore
53. Ballyhoge
54. Carnagh
55. Kilscanlan
56. Whitechurch-Glynn
57. Templeshannon
58. Ballyhuskard
59. Killisk
60. Castle-ellis
61. Killila
62. Ballyvaldon
63. Edermine
64. Ballynaslaney
65. Allock
66. St. Nicholas
67. Skreen
68. Ballyvaloo
69. Kilgarvan
70. Killurin
71. Ardcandrisk
72. Clongeen
73. Inch (Shelmaliere W.)
74. Horestown
75. Taghmon
76. Coolstuff
77. Kilbrideglynn
78. Carrick
79. Ballylannon
80. Ballingly
81. Ballymitty
82. Tikillin
83. Kilpatrick
84. Artramont

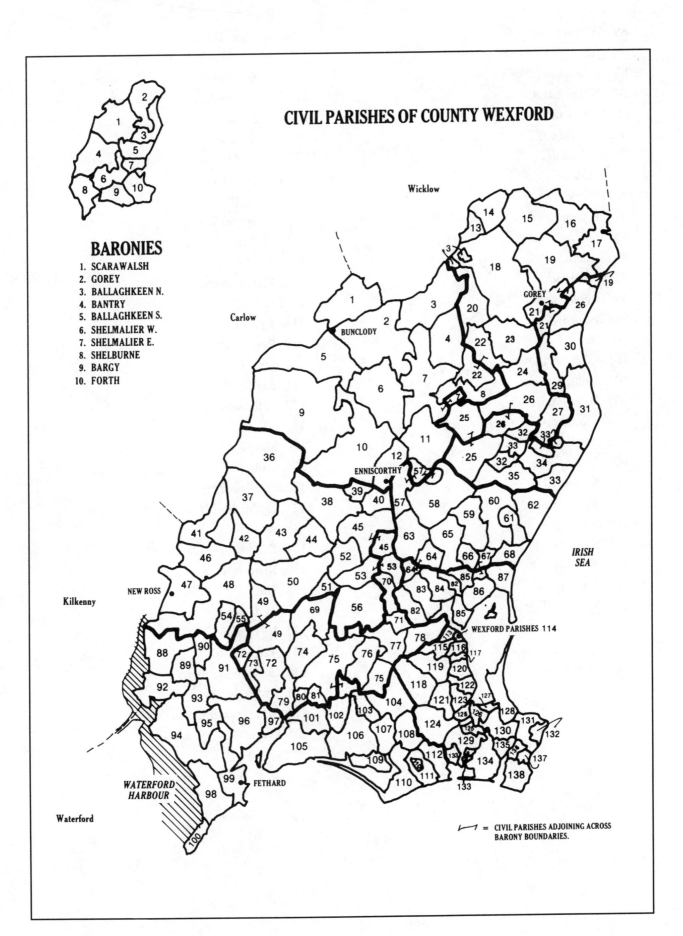

CIVIL PARISHES OF COUNTY WEXFORD

BARONIES

1. SCARAWALSH
2. GOREY
3. BALLAGHKEEN N.
4. BANTRY
5. BALLAGHKEEN S.
6. SHELMALIER W.
7. SHELMALIER E.
8. SHELBURNE
9. BARGY
10. FORTH

Wicklow

Carlow

BUNCLODY

Kilkenny

NEW ROSS

ENNISCORTHY

GOREY

IRISH SEA

WEXFORD PARISHES 114

WATERFORD HARBOUR

FETHARD

Waterford

⌐⌐ = CIVIL PARISHES ADJOINING ACROSS BARONY BOUNDARIES.

85. Ardcavan
86. Ardcolm
87. St. Margaret (Shelmaliere E.)
88. Whitechurch
89. Ballybrazil
90. Tellarought
91. Owenduff
92. Kilmokea
93. Killesk
94. St. James and Dunbrody
95. Rathroe
96. Tintern
97. Clonmines
98. Templetown
99. Fethard
100. Hook
101. Kilcavan (Bargy)
102. Ambrosetown
103. Ballyconnick
104. Kilmannon
105. Bannow
106. Duncormick
107. Kilcowan
108. Mulrankin
109. Killag
110. Kilmore
111. Kilturk
112. Tomhaggard
113. St. John (Forth)

114. Wexford Town
    Parishes:
    St. Bridget
    St. Doologe
    St. Iberius
    St. Mary
    St. Michael of Feagh
    St. Patrick
    St. Peter
    St. Selskar
115. St. Peter
116. St. Doologe
116. Maudlintown
117. Kerloge
118. Kildavin
119. Rathaspick
120. Drinagh
121. Rathmacknee
122. Killiane
123. Kilmacree
124. Mayglass
125. Killinick
126. Ballybrennan
127. St. Michael (Forth)
128. Rosslare
129. Ballymore
130. Kilscoran
131. Kilrane
132. St. Helen
133. Ishartmon
134. Tacumshin
135. St. Iberius
136. Lady's Island
137. St. Margaret (Forth)
138. Carne

Wexford Civil Parishes in Alphabetical Order

Adamstown: 50
Allock: 65
Ambrosetown: 102
Ardamine: 30
Ardcandrisk: 71
Ardcavan: 85
Ardcolm: 86
Artramont: 84
Ballingly: 80
Ballyanne: 46
Ballybrazil: 89
Ballybrennan: 126
Ballycanew: 24
Ballycarney: 6
Ballyconnick: 103
Ballyhoge: 53
Ballyhuskard: 58
Ballylannon: 79
Ballymitty: 81
Ballymore: 129
Ballynaslaney: 64
Ballyvaldon: 62
Ballyvaloo: 68
Bannow: 105
Carnagh: 54
Carne: 138
Carnew: 3
Carrick: 78
Castle-ellis: 60
Chapel: 44
Clone: 11
Clongeen: 72
Clonleigh: 42
Clonmines: 97
Clonmore: 45
Coolstuff: 76
Crosspatrick: 13
Donaghmore: 31
Donowney: 51
Drinagh: 120
Duncormick: 106
Edermine: 63

Ferns: 7
Fethard: 99
Hook: 100
Horestown: 74
Inch (Gorey): 16
Inch (Shelmaliere W.): 73
Ishartmon: 133
Kerloge: 117
Kilbride: 8
Kilbrideglynn: 77
Kilcavan (Bargy): 101
Kilcavan (Gorey): 19
Kilcomb: 4
Kilcormick: 25
Kilcowan: 107
Kilcowanmore: 52
Kildavin: 118
Kilgarvan: 69
Kilgorman: 17
Killag: 109
Killann: 36
Killegney: 43
Killenagh: 29
Killesk: 93
Killiane: 122
Killila: 61
Killincooly: 33
Killinick: 125
Killisk: 59
Killurin: 70
Kilmacree: 123
Kilmakilloge: 21
Kilmannon: 104
Kilmokea: 92
Kilmore: 110
Kilmuckridge: 34
Kilnahue or Lamogue: 18
Kilnamanagh: 32
Kilnenor: 15
Kilpatrick: 83
Kilpipe: 14
Kilrane: 131

Kilrush: 2
Kilscanlan: 55
Kilscoran: 130
Kiltennell: 28
Kiltrisk: 27
Kilturk: 111
Lady's Island: 136
Liskinfere: 23
Maudlintown: 116
Mayglass: 124
Meelnagh: 35
Monamolin: 26
Monart: 10
Moyacomb: 1
Mulrankin: 108
Newbawn: 49
Oldross: 48
Owenduff: 91
Rathaspick: 119
Rathmacknee: 121
Rathroe: 95
Rossdroit: 38
Rosslare: 128
Rossminoge: 20
Skreen: 67
St. Bridget: 114
St. Doologe: 114
St. Doologe: 116
St. Helen: 132
St. Iberius: 114
St. Iberius: 135
St. James and Dunbrody: 94

St. John (Bantry): 40
St. John (Forth): 113
St. Margaret (Forth): 137
St. Margaret (Shelmaliere E.): 87
St. Mary (1) (Wexford): 114
St. Mary (2) (Scarawalsh): 12
St. Mary (3) (Bantry): 47
St. Mary (4) (Bantry): 5
St. Michael (Forth): 127
St. Michael of Feagh: 114
St. Mullin: 41
St. Nicholas: 66
St. Patrick: 114
St. Peter: 114
St. Peter: 115
St. Selskar: 114
Tacumshin: 134
Taghmon: 75
Tellarought: 90
Templescoby: 39
Templeshanbo: 9
Templeshannon: 57
Templetown: 98
Templeudigan: 37
Tikillin: 82
Tintern: 96
Tomhaggard: 112
Toome: 22
Wexford Town: 114
Whitechurch-Glynn: 56
Whitechurch: 88

County Wicklow

A Brief History

This scenic, wooded Leinster coastal county contains the towns of Wicklow, Bray, Rathnew, Arklow, Rathdrum, Enniskerry, Greystones, and Baltinglass. Because of its scenery and fine woodlands, it is known as the "Garden of Ireland," and has been a popular resort area since the eighteenth century. The county has a wide coastal strip of fertile land, and the inland parts are mountainous.

In pre-Norman times this county was the territory of the O'Byrnes and O'Tooles. The families of O'Cullen, O'Kelly, O'Teige (Tighe), (O')Gahan, and McKeogh (or Kehoe) are also associated with the county. There were a number of Viking settlements on the Wicklow coast, including the towns of Arklow and Wicklow, whose names are of Danish origin. The family name of Doyle, which is common in the county (and elsewhere in Leinster), is also of Scandinavian origin.

After the Norman invasion, the coastal parts of the county came under the control of various Norman adventurers. These included the families of Archbold, Cosgrave, and Eustace. Wicklow town itself was granted to Maurice Fitzgerald, who fortified it against the constant attacks of the O'Byrnes and O'Tooles, who retained control of the more extensive mountainous parts of the county.

These families continued to rule most of Wicklow for many centuries afterwards, and made constant raids on the city of Dublin and on the Norman settlements in Wicklow. Their power was severely curtailed after the rebellion of the Irish Catholics in 1641, when Cromwell took every fort and stronghold in the county. However, the mountains of Wicklow continued to provide refuge for rebels until after the 1798 rebellion, when the so-called Military Road was built through the heart of the mountains to provide military access.

During the Great Famine of 1845-47, the county was not as badly affected as others. Nevertheless, the population dropped by over twenty percent between 1841 (126,000) and 1851 (99,000). Almost 13,000 people died in the county between 1845 and 1850.

The north of Wicklow, and particularly the towns of Bray, Greystones, and Enniskerry, have become increasingly populated during the last century. These towns are now large commuter areas for the city of Dublin. The population of the county is currently over 90,000.

Census and Census Substitutes

1659

"Census" of Ireland. Edited by S. Pender. Dublin: Stationery Office, 1939. NLI I6551. SLC film 924648.

1669

Taxpayers of Co. Wicklow, particularly containing Protestant families. GO (transcript) and SLC mf. 100248 item 4.

Hearth Money Roll. GO 667; NAI M4909; SLC film 100248; abbreviated copy published in *R.S.A.I.* 61: 165-78.

1745

Freeholders of Co. Wicklow who polled at an election. Stokes Mss. GO 537; NLI Ms. 3980; PRONI 2659 (Protestants only).

1761

Militia List for Co. Wicklow, etc. GO ms 680.

1766

Householders of the Parishes of Ballymaslaney,

Dunganstown, and Rathdrum; SLC mf. 100173 items 1–2. Also Drumkay, Dunganstown, Kilpoole, Rathdrum, and Rathnew; SLC film 258517 or 100173. GO 537; RCB ms. 37. Also available from Wicklow Heritage Centre.

1787–1812

Miners and Contractors at Avoca Mines. NLI Ms. 16, 304–16, 306.

1798

List of Persons Who Suffered Losses in the '98 Rebellion. NLI JB 94017 (approximately 950 names, addresses, and occupations).

1824–37

Tithe Applotment Survey (see introduction).

1843

Voters List. NAI 1843/64.

1847–1858

Coolatin Estate Emigration Papers. NLI Ms. 4974/75. Indexed by P. Gorry in *J. West Wicklow Hist. Soc.* 1988 et seq.

1848

Petitioners for William Smith O'Brien. Names of male petitioners in Bray. NAI 1848/180.

1850

Incomplete list of Freeholders (names alphabetically from Allen to Doyle only) for Barony of U. Talbotstown. NLI ms. 2661.

1852–53

Griffith's Valuation (see introduction). Full-name index compiled by Andrew J. Morris. Farmington, Mich.: A.J. Morris, 1989. 2 microfiches. NLI; SLC fiche 6342831.

1857

Deserted Children in Counties Wicklow and Wexford. *Dun Laoghaire Gen. Soc. J.* 3 (3) 1994. (Barony, parish, name of guardian, name of child.)

1864–1885

Vaccinations Register for the Registrar's Districts of Bray and Rathmichael 1864–1885. NAI L.B. G. 137 L2 (child's name, age, date of vaccination, parent or guardian, and address).

1901

Census. NAI (see introduction). Residents of St. Kevin's Reformatory, Glencree, are published in *Dun Laoghaire*

Gen. Soc. J. 5 (3): 86–92. (Gives name, age, and place of birth of 250 boys.)

1911

Census. NAI.

Church Records

Church of Ireland

See the introduction for a description of Church of Ireland records and their major repositories. Many C of I records were lost in the PRO fire of 1922. These are indicated as "Lost." However, as Church of Ireland records were effectively state records, the records of marriage (from 1845) are also in the General Registrar's Office. Many are still in local custody (LC), while others are in one of a variety of other archives (e.g., RCBL or NAI). Many of the Church of Ireland registers of this county have been indexed by the County Wicklow Heritage Centre (see Research Services at the end of the chapter). A search of the index will be conducted by the center for a fee.

Aghold
Earliest Records: b. 1714–; m. 1714–; d. 1714–
Status: LC; GO 578 (extracts–b. 1714–1863; m. 1714–1863; d. 1714–1863); SLC film 992663 (extracts 1714–1863)

Arklow
Status: Lost

Ashford (see Killiskey)

Ballinaclash (Rathdrum)
Earliest Records: b. 1839–; m. 1843–; d. 1842–
Status: LC; NAI MFCI 76 (b. 1839–1989; m. 1843–51; d. 1842–1984)

Ballintemple (Arklow)
Earliest Records: b. 1823–; m. 1823–
Status: LC; NAI MFCI 76 (b. 1823–51; m. 1823–54)

Ballynure
Earliest Records: b. 1815; m. 1818; d. 1818
Status: LC

Baltinglass
Status: Lost

Blessington
Earliest Records: b. 1695–; m. 1683–; d. 1683–
Status: LC; NAI MFCI 87 (b. 1695–1985; m. 1683–1878; d. 1683–1985)

Bray
Earliest Records: b. 1666; m. 1666; d. 1666
Status: LC

Calary
Status: Lost

Castlemacadam (Avoca)
Earliest Records: b. 1720-; m. 1719-; d. 1719-
Status: LC; NAI MFCI 76 (b. 1720-1904; m. 1719-
1860; d. 1719-1979)

Clonegal or Moyacomb—see Co. Wexford

Crosspatrick and Kilcommon
Earliest Records: b. 1830; m. 1830; d. 1830
Status: LC

Delgany
Earliest Records: b. 1666-; m. 1666-; d. 1666-
(entries for Newcastle, 1666-1777, in first volume of
Delgany records)
Status: LC; NAI MFCI 75 (b. 1666-1985; m. 1666-
1945; d. 1666-1985)

Derralossory
Status: Lost

Donard and Crehelp
Earliest Records: m. 1848-; d. 1888-
Status: RCBL (m. 1848-1955; d. 1888-1965)

Donoghmore or Donoughmore
Earliest Records: b. 1720-; m. 1720-; d. 1720-
Status: RCBL (b. 1720-1888; m. 1720-1856; d. 1720-
1929); NAI MFCI 89 (b. 1720-1888; m. 1720-1853;
d. 1720-1874)

Drumkey (see Wicklow)

Dunlavin
Earliest Records: b. 1697-; m. 1697-; d. 1697-
Status: RCBL (b. 1697-1934; m. 1697-1956; d. 1697-
1934); NAI MFCI 860 (b. 1697-1879; m. 1698-1844;
d. 1698-1879)

Enniskerry
Earliest Records: b. 1662-; m. 1662-; d. 1662-
Status: LC; NL Pos. 5484 (b. 1662-1874; m. 1662-
1852; d. 1662-1874)

Glenely or Glenealy
Earliest Records: b. 1808-; m. 1808-; d. 1817-
Status: LC; RCBL (b. 1808-80; m. 1808-64; d. 1817-
7); NAI MFCI 77LC (b/m/d. 1825)

Greystones
Status: LC

Hollywood
Status: Lost

Kilbride (1) (Blessington)
Status: Lost

Kilbride (2) (Bray)
Earliest Records: b. 1834-; m. 1845-; d. 1834-
Status: LC; NAI MFCI 82 (b. 1834-1970; m. 1845-
76; d. 1834-1984)

Kilbride (3) (Enorily)
Status: Lost

Kilcommon (see Glanely and Wicklow)
Status: Lost

Killiskey (see also Wicklow)
Earliest Records: b. 1818; m. 1818; d. 1824
Status: LC; NAI MFCI 83 (b. 1818-1905; m. 1818-
44; d. 1824-77)

Killoughter (see Wicklow)

Kiltegan and Kilranelagh
Status: Lost

Moyne
Earliest Records: b. 1838; m. 1841; d. 1836
Status: LC

Mullinacuff (Tinahely)
Earliest Records: b. 1698; m. 1698; d. 1797
Status: LC

Newcastle-Lyons
Earliest Records: b. 1677; m. 1662; d. 1663
Status: LC; NAI MFCI 85 (b. 1698-1954; m. 1697-
1846; d. 1699-1881); entries for Newcastle, 1666-
1777, in first volume of Delgany records

Powerscourt
Earliest Records: b. 1727; m. 1727; d. 1724
Status: LC; NAI MFCI 91 (b. 1677-1874; m. 1662-
1860; d. 1663-1873)

Preban (Tinahely)
Earliest Records: b. 1739; m. 1739; d. 1739
Status: LC

Rathdrum
Earliest Records: b. 1706-; m. 1706-; d. 1706-
Status: LC; RCBL (b. 1706-1845; m. 1706-1870; d.
1706-1916); NAI MFCI 77 (b. 1706-1865; m. 1706-
1855; d. 1706-1916)

Rathnew (see Wicklow)

Redcross
Earliest Records: b. 1830-
Status: NAI MFCI 79 (b. 1830-52)

Shillelagh
Earliest Records: b. 1833; m. 1833; d. 1833
Status: LC

Stratford-on-Slaney (Baltinglass)
Earliest Records: b. 1812; m. 1804; d. 1804
Status: LC

Wicklow
Earliest Records: b. 1655; m. 1729; d. 1729
Status: LC; NAI MFCI 83 (b. 1655-1983; m. 1729-
1869; d. 1729-1909)

Methodist

An account of Methodist records is given in the introduction. Many of the meetings in this county were
merged with those in the Dublin circuit. Their records

are now with these meetings. Transcripts of the baptism records (see below) are in the PRONI.

Arklow and Gorey
Starting Date: b. 1887
Status: LC (with Wicklow register); PRONI

Bray Church
Starting Date: b. 1863
Status: LC (part of Kingstown-Dun Laoghaire, Dublin); PRONI

Carlow
Starting Date: b. 1845
Status: LC; PRONI

Kingstown
Starting Date: b. 1843
Status: LC (now called Dun Laoghaire, Dublin); PRONI

Newtownbarry
Starting Date: b. 1833
Status: LC; PRONI

Rathdrum
Starting Date: b. 1856
Status: LC (with Wicklow register); PRONI

Wicklow
Starting Date: b. 1828
Status: LC; PRONI

Society of Friends (Quaker)

Quakers living in Wicklow were part of the Wicklow monthly meeting. Quakers from this meeting also resided in counties Dublin and Wexford. Many members were born in Northern Ireland and England. The records consist of b. 1627-1817, m. 1640-1862, d. 1654-1859, and can be accessed at the Friends Library (see the introduction). Transcripts on microfilm from SLC 571398, items 10-12.

Presbyterian

An account of Presbyterian records is given in the introduction. These registers rarely contain death records, and occasionally have only records of births.

Bray
Starting Date: b. 1836; m. 1853
Status: LC

Greystones
Starting Date: b. 1887; m. 1887
Status: LC

Roman Catholic

Almost all of the Catholic parish registers of this county have been indexed by County Wicklow Heritage Centre (see Research Services at the end of the chapter). A search of the index will be conducted by the center for a

fee. Those indexed have been indicated as "Indexed by Wicklow HC." Microfilm copies of all registers are also available in the National Library of Ireland (NLI), and through the LDS library system.

Civil Parish: Aghowle (Agharle)
Map Grid: 55
RC Parish: Clonmore, see Co. Carlow
Diocese: FE

Civil Parish: Ardoyne
Map Grid: 54
RC Parish: Clonmore, see Co. Carlow
Diocese: FE

Civil Parish: Arklow
Map Grid: 50
RC Parish: Arklow
Diocese: FE
Earliest Record: b. 5.1809; m. 1.1813
Missing Dates: b. 6.1809-12.1817; m. 10.1856-1.1857
Status: LC; NLI (mf); Indexed by Wicklow HC

Civil Parish: Ballinacor
Map Grid: 34
RC Parish: see Rathdrum
Diocese: FE

Civil Parish: Ballintemple
Map Grid: 47
RC Parish: see Arklow
Diocese: FE

Civil Parish: Ballykine
Map Grid: 37
RC Parish: see Rathdrum
Diocese: FE

Civil Parish: Ballynure
Map Grid: 15
RC Parish: part Baltinglass; part Dunlavin
Diocese: FE

Civil Parish: Baltinglass (see also Co. Carlow)
Map Grid: 20
RC Parish: Baltinglass
Diocese: FE
Earliest Record: b. 5.1807; m. 2.1810; d. 1824
Missing Dates: b. 2.1810-7.1810, 4.1811-10.1813; m. 4.1811-11.1813, 9.1815-4.1816, 2.1866-5.1866
Status: LC; NLI (mf)

Civil Parish: Blessington
Map Grid: 2
RC Parish: Blessington; also part Valleymount, see Boystown; part Ballymore Eustace, see Co. Kildare
Diocese: DU
Earliest Record: b. 1821; m. 1834
Missing Dates: b. 8.1825-5.1830, 6.1830-2.1833; m. 8.1825-8.1826
Status: LC; NLI (mf); Indexed by Wicklow HC (to 1900)

Civil Parish: Boystown
Map Grid: 4
RC Parish: Valleymount, (Baystown) or Blackditches
Diocese: DU
Earliest Record: b. 6.1810; m. 2.1810; d. 8.1824
Status: LC; NLI (mf); Indexed by Wicklow HC (to 1900)

Civil Parish: Bray
Map Grid: 12
RC Parish: Bray
Diocese: DU
Earliest Record: b. 1790; m. 1792
Status: LC; NLI (mf); Indexed by Wicklow HC (to 1900)

Civil Parish: Burgage
Map Grid: 3
RC Parish: see Blessington
Diocese: DU

Civil Parish: Calary
Map Grid: 23
RC Parish: see Derrylossary; part Bray; part Glendalough; part Kilquade, see Kilcoole
Diocese: DU

Civil Parish: Carnew (also in Co. Wexford)
Map Grid: 59
RC Parish: Tomacork (Carnew)
Diocese: FE
Earliest Record: b. 1.1785; m. 6.1793; d. 5.1794
Missing Dates: b. 5.1786–2.1791, 11.1797–1.1807; m. 2.1797–1.1807, 3.1845–6.1847; d. 12.1797–5.1847, 11.1856–5.1864, 1.1871–4.1873
Status: LC; NLI (mf); Indexed by Wicklow HC (1847 to 1900)

Civil Parish: Castlemacadam
Map Grid: 44
RC Parish: part Avoca, see Rathdrum; part Kilbride, see Dunganstown
Diocese: DU

Civil Parish: Crecrin
Map Grid: 53
RC Parish: Clonmore, see Co. Carlow
Diocese: DU

Civil Parish: Crehelp
Map Grid: 6
RC Parish: see Dunlavin
Diocese: DU

Civil Parish: Crosspatrick (see also Co. Wexford)
Map Grid: 57
RC Parish: Tomacork, see Carnew
Diocese: FE

Civil Parish: Delgany
Map Grid: 13
RC Parish: part Bray; part Kilquade, see Kilcoole
Diocese: DU

Civil Parish: Derrylossary
Map Grid: 24
RC Parish: Glendalough
Diocese: DU
Earliest Record: b. 6.1807; m. 1.1808
Missing Dates: b. 1.1838–8.1839; m. 6.1838–5.1840
Status: LC; NLI (mf); Indexed by Wicklow HC (to 1881)

Civil Parish: Donaghmore
Map Grid: 19
RC Parish: see Dunlavin; also part Baltinglass
Diocese: DU

Civil Parish: Donard
Map Grid: 9
RC Parish: see Dunlavin
Diocese: DU

Civil Parish: Drumkay
Map Grid: 41
RC Parish: Wicklow, see Kilpoole
Diocese: DU

Civil Parish: Dunganstown
Map Grid: 43
RC Parish: Kilbride and Barndarrig
Diocese: DU
Earliest Record: b. 1.1858; m. 2.1858
Status: LC; NLI (mf); Indexed by Wicklow HC (to 1900)

Civil Parish: Dunlavin
Map Grid: 8
RC Parish: Dunlavin and Donard
Diocese: DU
Earliest Record: b. 10.1815 (ink badly faded); m. 2.1831
Status: LC; NLI (mf); Indexed by Wicklow HC (to 1900)

Civil Parish: Ennereilly
Map Grid: 46
RC Parish: Avoca, see Rathdrum (2)
Diocese: DU

Civil Parish: Freynestown
Map Grid: 16
RC Parish: see Dunlavin
Diocese: DU

Civil Parish: Glenealy
Map Grid: 33
RC Parish: Wicklow, see Kilpoole
Diocese: DU

Civil Parish: Hacketstown
Map Grid: 35
RC Parish: see Hacketstown, Co. Carlow
Diocese: DU

Civil Parish: Hollywood
Map Grid: 7

RC Parish: Ballymore Eustace, see Co. Kildare
Diocese: DU

Civil Parish: Inch
Map Grid: 51
RC Parish: see Arklow
Diocese: DU

Civil Parish: Kilbride (1) (near Blessington)
Map Grid: 1
RC Parish: see Blessington
Diocese: DU

Civil Parish: Kilbride (2) (near Arklow)
Map Grid: 48
RC Parish: Avoca, see Rathdrum (2); also part Arklow
Diocese: DU

Civil Parish: Kilcommon (1) (near Rathdrum)
Map Grid: 32
RC Parish: Wicklow, see Kilpoole
Diocese: DU

Civil Parish: Kilcommon (2) (near Preban)
Map Grid: 38
RC Parish: Tomacork, see Carnew
Diocese: FE

Civil Parish: Kilcoole
Map Grid: 27
RC Parish: Kilquade and Kilmurray
Diocese: DU
Earliest Record: b. 8.1826; m. 8.1826
Missing Dates: b. 6.1855–12.1861
Status: LC; NLI (mf); Indexed by Wicklow HC (to 1900)

Civil Parish: Killahurler
Map Grid: 49
RC Parish: see Arklow
Diocese: DU

Civil Parish: Killiskey
Map Grid: 30
RC Parish: Wicklow, see Kilpoole
Diocese: DU

Civil Parish: Kilmacanoge
Map Grid: 11
RC Parish: see Bray
Diocese: DU

Civil Parish: Kilpipe (see also Co. Wexford)
Map Grid: 40
RC Parish: Killaveny
Diocese: FE
Earliest Record: b. 11.1800; m. 11.1800
Missing Dates: m. 9.1836–1.1837
Status: LC; NLI (mf); Indexed by Wicklow HC (to 1900)

Civil Parish: Kilpoole
Map Grid: 42
RC Parish: Wicklow

Diocese: DU
Earliest Record: b. 1.1748; m. 1.1747
Missing Dates: b. 6.1781–5.1796; m. 2.1778–2.1779, 10.1780–11.1795
Status: LC; NLI (mf); Indexed by Wicklow HC (to 1900)

Civil Parish: Kilranelagh
Map Grid: 21
RC Parish: Rathvilly, see Co. Carlow; also part Baltinglass
Diocese: LE

Civil Parish: Kiltegan
Map Grid: 22
RC Parish: Hacketstown, see Co. Carlow
Diocese: LE

Civil Parish: Knockrath
Map Grid: 25
RC Parish: see Rathdrum; also part Glendalough
Diocese: DU

Civil Parish: Liscolman
Map Grid: 52
RC Parish: Clonmore, see Co. Carlow
Diocese: LE

Civil Parish: Moyacomb
Map Grid: 58
RC Parish: Clonegal, see Moyacomb, Co. Carlow
Diocese: DU

Civil Parish: Moyne
Map Grid: 36
RC Parish: see Hacketstown, Co. Carlow
Diocese: DU

Civil Parish: Mullinacuff
Map Grid: 56
RC Parish: Clonmore, see Co. Carlow
Diocese: LE

Civil Parish: Newcastle Lower
Map Grid: 29
RC Parish: Kilquade and Kilmurray, see Kilcoole
Diocese: DU

Civil Parish: Newcastle Upper
Map Grid: 28
RC Parish: Kilquade and Kilmurray, see Kilcoole
Diocese: DU

Civil Parish: Powerscourt
Map Grid: 10
RC Parish: Enniskerry
Diocese: DU
Earliest Record: b. 10.1825; m. 11.1825
Status: LC; NLI (mf); Indexed by Wicklow HC (to 1900)

Civil Parish: Preban
Map Grid: 39
RC Parish: Killaveny, see Kilpipe

Diocese: FE

Civil Parish: Rathbran
Map Grid: 18
RC Parish: see Baltinglass
Diocese: LE

Civil Parish: Rathdrum (1)
Map Grid: 26
RC Parish: Rathdrum; also Avoca, see below
Diocese: DU
Earliest Record: b. 1.1795; m. 11.1810
Missing Dates: b. 1.1799–10.1816
Status: LC; NLI (mf); Indexed by Wicklow HC (to 1900)

Civil Parish: Rathdrum (2)
Map Grid: 26
RC Parish: Avoca
Diocese: DU
Earliest Record: b. 1778; m. 1778
Missing Dates: b. 2.1805–5.1809; m. 2.1805–11.1812, 2.1843–4.1844
Status: LC; NLI (mf); Indexed by Wicklow HC (to 1900)

Civil Parish: Rathnew
Map Grid: 31
RC Parish: Ashford; also part Wicklow, see Kilpoole
Diocese: DU
Earliest Record: b. 9.1864; m. 10.1864
Status: LC; NLI (mf); Indexed by Wicklow HC (to 1900)

Civil Parish: Rathsallagh
Map Grid: 14
RC Parish: see Dunlavin
Diocese: DU

Civil Parish: Rathtoole
Map Grid: 17
RC Parish: see Dunlavin
Diocese: DU

Civil Parish: Redcross
Map Grid: 45
RC Parish: Avoca, see Rathdrum
Diocese: DU

Civil Parish: Tober
Map Grid: 5
RC Parish: see Dunlavin
Diocese: DU

Commercial and Social Directories

1788

Richard Lucas's *General Directory of the Kingdom of Ireland* contains lists of traders in Arklow, Bray, and Wicklow. Reprinted in *Ir. Gen.* 3 (10) (1965): 392–416.

1824

J. Pigot's *City of Dublin and Hibernian Provincial Directory* includes traders, nobility, gentry, and clergy lists of Arklow, Baltinglass, Blessington, Bray, Newtown Mount Kennedy, Rathdrum, and Wicklow.

1846

Slater's *National Commercial Directory of Ireland* lists nobility, clergy, traders, etc., in Arklow, Baltinglass, Blessington, Bray, Newtown Mount Kennedy and Delgany, Rathdrum, and Wicklow.

1856

Slater's *Royal National Commercial Directory of Ireland* lists nobility, gentry, clergy, traders, etc., in Arklow, Baltinglass, Blessington, Bray and Enniskerry, Newtown Mount Kennedy, Delgany and Kilcoole, Rathdrum, Wicklow, and Ashford.

1870

Slater's *Directory of Ireland* contains trade, nobility, and clergy lists for Arklow, Baltinglass, Blessington, Bray, Newtown Mount Kennedy, Rathdrum, and Wicklow.

1881

Slater's *Royal National Commercial Directory of Ireland* contains lists of traders, clergy, nobility, and farmers in adjoining parishes of the towns of Arklow, Baltinglass, Donard and Dunlavin, Blessington, Bray and Enniskerry, Newtown Mount Kennedy, Greystones and Delgany, Rathdrum, and Wicklow.

1894

Slater's *Royal National Directory of Ireland* lists traders, police, teachers, farmers, and private residents in each of the towns, villages, and parishes of the county.

Family History

"Fitz-Eustace of Baltinglass." *J. Waterford and S.E. Ire. Arch. Soc.* 5 (1899): 190–95.

Fitzgerald, Lord Walter. "Hollywood, Co. Wicklow: With an Account of its Owners to the Commencement of the Seventeenth Century." *J. Kildare Arch. Hist. Soc.* 8 (1915–17): 185–96.

Batt, Elizabeth. *The Moncks and Charleville House. A Wicklow Family in the Nineteenth Century.* With ports and genealogical tables. Dublin: Blackwater, 1979.

O'Toole, P.L. *History of the Clan O'Byrne and Other Leinster Septs.* Dublin: Gill, 1890.

O'Byrne, G. *Historical Reminiscences of O'Byrnes, O'Tooles, O'Kavanaghs and Other Irish Chieftains.* London: M'Gowan, 1843.

O'Toole, P.L. *History of the Clan O'Toole and Other Leinster Septs.* Dublin, 1890.

O'Toole, John. *The O'Tooles, Anciently Lords of Powerscourt . . .* Dublin, n.d.

"Percy of Co. Wicklow." Pedigree in *Swanzy Notebooks.* RCB Library, Dublin.

"The Family of Saunders of Saunders' Grove, Co. Wicklow." *J. Kildare Hist. Arch. Soc.* 9 (1918-22): 125-33.

"The Valentine Family of Donard." *West Wicklow Hist Soc J.* 2 (1983/4): 63-69; 1 (1985/6): 22-26.

"The Wests of Ballydugan, Co. Down; the Rock, Co. Wicklow; and Ashwood, Co. Wexford." *Ulster J. Arch.* 2nd series 12 (1906): 135-41, 159-65.

Collection Concerning the Family of Yarner of Wicklow. N.p., 1870.

Gravestone Inscriptions

The following references may be found in Cantwell, Brian J., *Memorials of the Dead* (Vol. 1, Northeast Wicklow 1974; Vol. 2, Southeast Wicklow 1975; Vol. 3, Southwest Wicklow 1976; Vol. 4, Northwest Wicklow 1978). Copies are available in NAI, NLI, Wicklow Co. Library, and County Wicklow Heritage Centre.

Aghold: Vol. 3
Aghowle: Vol. 3
Annacurragh: Vol. 3
Ardoyne: Vol. 3
Arklow: Vol. 2
Ashford: Vol. 1
Askanagap: Vol. 3
Aughrim: Vol. 3
Avoca: Vol. 2
Ballinatone: Vol. 2
Ballintemple: Vol. 2
Ballycooge: Vol. 2
Ballycore: Vol. 4
Ballymaconnell: Vol. 3
Ballymaghroe: Vol. 3
Ballynure: Vol. 4
Baltinglass: Vol. 4
Baltyboys: Vol. 4
Barndarrig: Vol. 2
Barranisky: Vol. 2
Blacklion: Vol. 1
Blessington: Vol. 4
Bray: Vol. 1
Burgage: Vol. 4
Calary: Vol. 1
Carnew: Vol. 3
Castlemacadam: Vol. 2

Castletimon: Vol. 2
Cloghleagh: Vol. 4
Connary: Vol. 2
Coolafancy: Vol. 3
Coronation Plantation Obelisk: Vol. 4
Cranareen: Vol. 4
Crossbridge: Vol. 3
Crosschapel: Vol. 4
Crosspatrick: Vol. 3
Curraghlawn: Vol. 3
Curtlestown: Vol. 1
Davidstown: Vol. 4
Delgany: Vol. 1
Derralossary: Vol. 2
Donard: Vol. 4
Donoughmore: Vol. 4
Dunganstown: Vol. 2
Dunlavin: Vol. 4
Ennereilly: Vol. 2
Ennisboyne: Vol. 2
Enniskerry: Vol. 1
Glencree: Vol. 1
Glendalough: Vol. 4; "Monumental Inscription at Glendalough." *Ir. Gen.* 2 (3) (1945): 88-93
Glenealy: Vol. 2
Grangecon: Vol. 4
Greenan: Vol. 2
Greystones: Vol. 1
Hollywood: Vol. 4
Kilbride: Vols. 1, 2, and 4
Kilcarra: Vol. 2
Kilcommon: Vols. 2 and 3
Kilcoole: Vol. 1
Kilfea: Vol. 1
Killadreenan: Vol. 1
Killahurler: Vol. 2
Killamoat: Vol. 3
Killavany: Vol. 3
Killegar: Vol. 1
Killiskey: Vol. 1
Killoughter: Vol. 1
Kilmacanogue: Vol. 1
Kilmagig: Vol. 2
Kilmurry: Vol. 1
Kilpipe: Vol. 3
Kilquade: Vol. 1
Kilquiggan: Vol. 3
Kilranelagh: Vol. 4
Kiltegan: Vol. 3
Knockanana: Vol. 3

Knockanarrigan: Vol. 4
Knockarigg: Vol. 4
Knockloe: Vol. 3
Lackan: Vol. 4
Laragh: Vol. 4
Leitrim: Vol. 4
Liscolman: Vol. 3
Macreddin: Vol. 3
Moyne: Vol. 3
Mullinacuff: Vol. 3
Newcastle: Vol. 1
Newtown Mount Kennedy: Vol. 1
Nunscross: Vol. 1
Powerscourt: Vol. 1
Preban: Vol. 3
Rathbran: Vol. 4
Rathdrum: Vol. 2
Rathnew: Vol. 2
Redcross: Vol. 2
Redford: Vol. 1
Rossahane: Vol. 3
Scurlocks: Vol. 4
Shillelagh: Vol. 3
Stratford: Vol. 4
Templeboodin: Vol. 4
Templemichael: Vol. 2
Templerainy: Vol. 2
Tober: Vol. 4
Tomacrok: Vol. 3
Tornant: Vol. 4
Trinity: Vol. 1
Valleymount: Vol. 4
Whaley Abbey: Vol. 2
Wicklow: Vol. 2
Yewtree: Vol. 3

Newspapers

The earliest newspaper for this county is 1857. However, Dublin papers contain some relevant notices for the north of the county. For the other parts of the county, the relevant adjoining county newspapers should be consulted.

Title: *Bray Gazette* (continued as *Kingstown and The Bray Gazette* in 1872)
Published in: Bray, 1861–73
BL Holdings: 6.1861–3.1873

Title: *Bray Herald* (continued as *South Dublin Herald* in 1922, and as *Bray Herald* again 1923–27)
Published in: Bray, 1876–1927

NLI Holdings: 1.1905–4.1927
BL Holdings: 10.1876–1927

Title: *Wicklow Newsletter and County Advertiser*
Published in: Wicklow, 1857–1927
NLI Holdings: 1.1885–4.1927
BL Holdings: 1.1858–5.1873; 6.1874–12.1919; 1.1922–12.1926

Title: *Wicklow People*
Published in: Wicklow, 1886–current
NLI Holdings: 12.1904–8.1908; 3.1909–in progress
BL Holdings: 6.1889–in progress

Title: *Wicklow Star*
Published in: Wicklow, 1895–1900
BL Holdings: 10.1895–2.1900

Wills and Administrations

A discussion of the types of records, where they are held, and their availability and value is given in the Wills section in the introduction. The availability of prerogative wills, administrations, and marriage license records is also described in the relevant parts of the same section. Where available, published sources of these records are given in the Miscellaneous Sources section.

Pre-1858 Wills and Administrations

Prerogative Wills. See the introduction.

Consistorial Wills. County Wicklow is in the dioceses of Dublin, Ferns, and Leighlin, with one parish in Kildare. The guide to Catholic parish records in this chapter shows the diocese to which each civil parish belonged. The wills of residents of each diocese were usually proven within that diocese (see the Wills section for exceptions). The following records survive:

Wills

See the introduction.

Abstracts

See the introduction. The Lane-Poole Papers contain fifty-two will abstracts from the seventeenth to nineteenth centuries for Co. Wicklow. These are in NLI (ms. 5359) and also published in *Ir. Gen.* 8 (4) (1993): 610–617. Abstracts of Ferns Wills from Phillips Manuscripts (surnames A–S for period 1661–1826): NAI; SLC film 101027. Dublin Will Abstracts (surnames A–E for period 1560–1710): NAI; SLC film 100140.

Indexes

Dublin—see Co. Dublin. Ferns—see Co. Wexford. Leighlin—see Co. Carlow. Kildare—see Co. Kildare. Ferns Administration Bonds (1679–1848): NAI; SLC film 100962. Leighlin Administration Bonds (1694–1845):

NAI; SLC film 100963. Leighlin Wills (1652–1858): NAI; SLC film 100916. Dublin Administration Bonds (1697–1840): NAI; SLC film 100962.

Post-1858 Wills and Administrations

This county was served by the Principal Registry in Dublin. The surviving records are in the NAI. Records include: Waterford District Will Books (1858–1894). NAI; SLC film 100951–4. Principal Probate Registry Will Books (1858–91). NAI; SLC film 100918–24.

Marriage Licenses

Indexes and Abstracts

Dublin—see Co. Dublin. Ferns—see Co. Wexford. Kildare—see Co. Kildare. Dublin Diocesan Marriage Licenses (1638–1800): GO Ms. 134–138 and SLC film 100226. Marriage License Bonds for Ossory, Ferns, and Leighlin (1691–1845): GO Ms. 612–617 and SLC films 100169–72. Index to Leighlin Intestate Administrations: Supplement to *Ir. Anc.* (1972); SLC film 990403. Dublin Marriage License Abstracts (1638–1800) are in the Fisher Collection; GO and SLC film 100226.

Original Records

Kildare—see Co. Kildare.

Miscellaneous Sources

Gorry, Paul. "Surnames of Co. Wicklow." *Irish Roots* 1 (1997): 22–24.

A Hundred Years of Bray and Neighbourhood: 1770–1870. By "an old inhabitant." Blackrock, 1907, 1978.

"The Famine in Co. Wicklow." Educational packet produced by Co. Wicklow Heritage Society, 1996.

"The Last County—The Emergence of Wicklow as a County 1606–1845." Co. Wicklow Heritage Society, 1993.

Rees, Jim. "The Fitzwilliam Emigrants." *Irish Roots* 2 (1995): 8.

Hannigan, K., and W. Nolan. *Wicklow History and Society: Interdisciplinary Essays on the History of an Irish County.* Dublin: Geography Publications, 1994.

Price, Liam. *Place-Names of Co. Wicklow. The Irish form and meaning of parish, townland and local names.* Wexford: The People, 1953.

Cantwell, Brian J. *Memorials of the Dead in County Wicklow.* Tombstones from Co. Wicklow cemeteries transcribed in a four-volume set. Abstracts from Wicklow County Library, NAI, NLI, and Co. Wicklow Heritage Centre.

Vaccinations Register for the Registrar's Districts of Bray and Rathmichael 1864–1885. NAI L.B.G. 137 L2 (child's name, age, date of vaccination, parent or guardian, and address).

James, D., and S. O'Maitiu. *The Wicklow World of Elisabeth Smith 1840–1850.* Woodfield Press, 1996.

Coolatin Estate Emigration Records. In Coolatin Estate Papers; NLI Ms. 4974–5. Tenants willing to emigrate and details of their emigration. These papers are being indexed in successive issues of *J. West Wicklow Hist Soc.*

Records of Parish of Arklow by H. Hollingsworth (1971). SLC film 896641.

Research Sources and Services

Journals

Wicklow Roots (published by Wicklow County Genealogical Society)

Journal of the West Wicklow Historical Society

Bray Historical Record

Journal of Cualann Historical Society

Arklow Historical Society Journal

Libraries and Information Sources

Wicklow County Library, Greystones, Co. Wicklow. Ph: (01) 2874387. The library has a sizable collection of local history materials, including books, directories, newspapers, periodicals, photographs, estate papers, and the papers of the Clements, Jones, Godley, and Crofton families.

Bray Urban District Council, Public Library, Florence Road, Bray, Co. Wicklow. Ph: (01) 862600

Research Services

County Wicklow Heritage Society, The Courthouse, Wicklow, Co. Wicklow. Ph: (0404) 67324 ext. 126; fax: (353) 404 67792; e-mail: wickcoco@iol.ie. The County Wicklow Heritage Project was established in 1987 to provide a genealogical service on Wicklow families. It has indexed the majority of Catholic and Church of Ireland registers, and some of the Methodist and Presbyterian registers. Other local sources are also available. Researchers are advised to contact the center for an updated list of registers, and other sources, indexed. A research service is provided for a fee.

Societies

Wicklow County Genealogical Society, c/o 1 Summerhill, Wicklow Town, Co. Wicklow. Ph: (0404) 67442

Arklow Historical Society, Ms. Peggy Kelly, Upper Tinahask, Arklow, Co. Wicklow

Bray Cualann Historical Society, Ms. Kathleen Kinsella, 1 Alexandra Terrace, Novara Road, Bray, Co. Wicklow (publishers of *Wicklow Roots*)

Greystones Archaeological and Historical Society, Ms. Eileen Short, Brookfield, Glen Road, Delgany, Co. Wicklow

Hollywood Local History Group, Ms. Alice Corrigan, Hollywood, Co. Wicklow

Old Bray Society, Mr. Denis O'Sullivan, 5 Castle Street, Bray, Co. Wicklow

Rathdangan Historical Society, Killamoat, Rathdangan, Co. Wicklow

Roundwood Historical and Folklore Society, Ms. Monica Farrell, Old School, Roundwood, Co. Wicklow

Wicklow Historical Society, Miss Ann Carr, Ashtown Farm, Wicklow, Co. Wicklow

Wicklow Civil Parishes as Numbered on Map

1. Kilbride
2. Blessington
3. Burgage
4. Boystown
5. Tober
6. Crehelp
7. Hollywood
8. Dunlavin
9. Donard
10. Powerscourt
11. Kilmacanoge
12. Bray
13. Delgany
14. Rathsallagh
15. Ballynure
16. Freynestown
17. Rathtoole
18. Rathbran
19. Donaghmore
20. Baltinglass
21. Kilranelagh
22. Kiltegan
23. Calary
24. Derrylossary
25. Knockrath
26. Rathdrum
27. Kilcoole
28. Newcastle Upr.
29. Newcastle Lr.
30. Killiskey

31. Rathnew
32. Kilcommon
33. Glenealy
34. Ballinacor
35. Hacketstown
36. Moyne
37. Ballykine
38. Kilcommon
39. Preban
40. Kilpipe
41. Drumkay
42. Kilpoole
43. Dunganstown
44. Castlemacadam
45. Redcross
46. Ennereilly
47. Ballintemple
48. Kilbride
49. Killeburser
50. Arklow
51. Inch
52. Liscolman
53. Crecrin
54. Ardoyne
55. Aghowle or Agharle
55. Mullinacuff
57. Crosspatrick
58. Moyacomb
59. Carnew

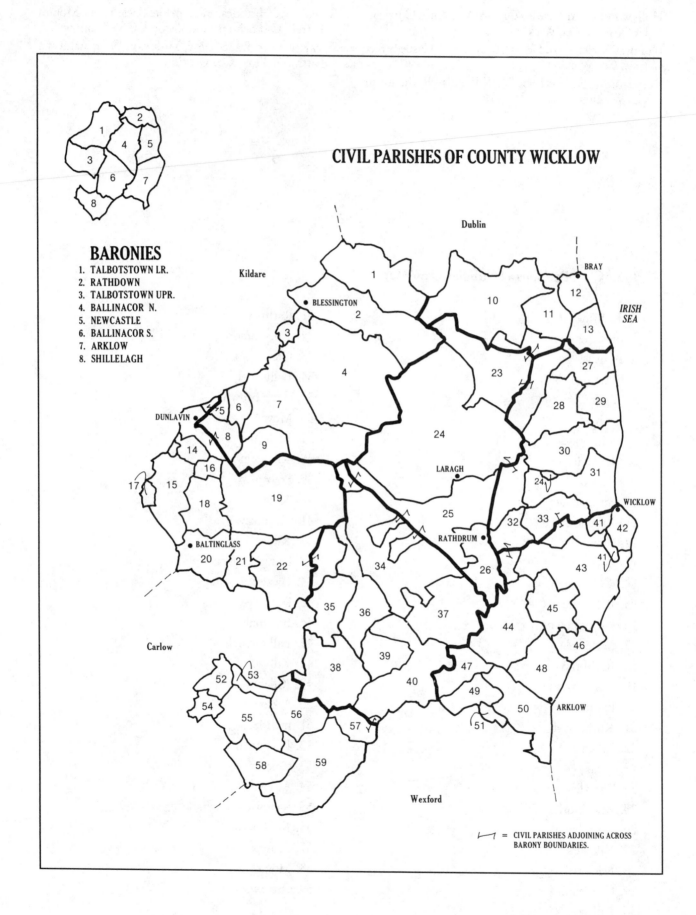

CIVIL PARISHES OF COUNTY WICKLOW

BARONIES

1. TALBOTSTOWN LR.
2. RATHDOWN
3. TALBOTSTOWN UPR.
4. BALLINACOR N.
5. NEWCASTLE
6. BALLINACOR S.
7. ARKLOW
8. SHILLELAGH

Dublin

Kildare

BLESSINGTON

BRAY

IRISH SEA

DUNLAVIN

LARAGH

BALTINGLASS

RATHDRUM

WICKLOW

Carlow

ARKLOW

Wexford

⊢⌐ = CIVIL PARISHES ADJOINING ACROSS
         BARONY BOUNDARIES.

Wicklow Civil Parishes in Alphabetical Order

Aghowle or Agharle: 55
Ardoyne: 54
Arklow: 50
Ballinacor: 34
Ballintemple: 47
Ballykine: 37
Ballynure: 15
Baltinglass: 20
Blessington: 2
Boystown: 4
Bray: 12
Burgage: 3
Calary: 23
Carnew: 59
Castlemacadam: 44
Crecrin: 53
Crehelp: 6
Crosspatrick: 57
Delgany: 13
Derrylossary: 24
Donaghmore: 19
Donard: 9
Drumkay: 41
Dunganstown: 43
Dunlavin: 8
Ennereilly: 46
Freynestown: 16
Glenealy: 33
Hacketstown: 35
Hollywood: 7

Inch: 51
Kilbride (1): 1
Kilbride (2): 48
Kilcommon (1): 32
Kilcommon (2): 38
Kilcoole: 27
Killeburser: 49
Killiskey: 30
Kilmacanoge: 11
Kilpipe: 40
Kilpoole: 42
Kilranelagh: 21
Kiltegan: 22
Knockrath: 25
Liscolman: 52
Moyacomb: 58
Moyne: 36
Mullinacuff: 56
Newcastle Lr.: 29
Newcastle Upr.: 28
Powerscourt: 10
Preban: 39
Rathbran: 18
Rathdrum: 26
Rathnew: 31
Rathsallagh: 14
Rathtoole: 17
Redcross: 45
Tober: 5

Appendix (Belfast)

Belfast Newspapers

The city of Belfast is in both County Down and County Antrim. These newspapers, therefore, are relevant in particular to Antrim and Down, but also to the other Ulster counties. The *Belfast Newsletter*, in particular, is of great value, since it is both early in publication (1737) and also covered a large part of northeast Ulster. The Linen Hall Library in Belfast has a good set of this paper, as well as a partial index.

Title: *Banner of Belfast*
Published in: Belfast, 1842–69
BL Holdings: 6.1842–8.1869

Title: *Belfast Advertiser* (continued as *Belfast Weekly Advertiser* in 1880)
Published in: Belfast, 1879–86
BL Holdings: 10.1879–2.1886

Title: *Belfast Commercial Chronicle*
Published in: Belfast, 1805–55
NLI Holdings: 4–8.1807; 2–10.1809
BL Holdings: odd numbers 1809, 1813, 1820–22, 1.1823–12.1827, 1.1832–8.1855

Title: *Belfast Daily Post*
Published in: Belfast, 1882
BL Holdings: 3–4.1882

Title: *Belfast Evening Star*
Published in: Belfast, 1890
BL Holdings: 1–5.1890

Title: *Belfast Evening Telegraph* (continued as *Belfast Telegraph* in 1918)
Published in: Belfast, 1870–current
BL Holdings: 3.1871–4.1918; 4.1918–in progress

Title: *Belfast Mercantile Register*
Published in: Belfast, old series ca. 1838–52; new series 1852–93
BL Holdings: 1.1840–3.1852; 3.1852–4.1893

Title: *Belfast Mercury* (continued as *Belfast Daily Mercury* in 1854)
Published in: Belfast, 1851–61
NLI Holdings: 1.1853–12.1857
BL Holdings: 3.1851–11.1861

Title: *Belfast Mercury or Freeman's Chronicle* (continued as *Belfast Evening Post* in 1786)
Published in: Belfast, 1783–86
NLI Holdings: 8.1783–8.1787
BL Holdings: 4.1784–3.1786

Title: *Belfast Morning News* (incorporated with *Irish News* in 1892)
Published in: Belfast, 1857–92
NLI Holdings: 1.1860–12.1865; 7.1882–8.1892
BL Holdings: 11.1857–8.1892

Title: *Belfast Newsletter*
Published in: Belfast, 1737–current
NLI Holdings: 10.1738–12.1835; 1.1837–9.1962
BL Holdings: odd numbers 1747, 1792, 1799, 1813, 1.1825–9.1962

Title: *Belfast Times* (also called *Belfast Daily Times*)
Published in: Belfast, 1872
BL Holdings: 1.1872–8.1872

Title: *Belfast Weekly Mail*
Published in: Belfast, 1852–54
BL Holdings: 11.1852–9.1854

Title: *Belfast Weekly News* (merged with *Belfast Newsletter* in 1942)
Published in: Belfast, 1855–1942
NLI Holdings: 6.1921–12.1924
BL Holdings: 7.1855–6.1942

Title: *Belfast Weekly Telegraph* (continued as *Cityweek* in 1964)
Published in: Belfast, 1873–1964
NLI Holdings: 1.1913–2.1916; 6–10.1964
BL Holdings: 8.1874–10.1964

Title: *Evening Press*
Published in: Belfast, 1870-74
BL Holdings: 5.1873-5.1874

Title: *Irish News*
Published in: Belfast, 1891-current
NLI Holdings: 8.1892-in progress
BL Holdings: 8.1891-in progress

Title: *Irish Weekly*
Published in: Belfast, 1891-1981
NLI Holdings: 6.1921-12.1922
BL Holdings: 8.1891-1981

Title: *Morning Post*
Published in: Belfast, 1855-58
BL Holdings: 1-4.1858

Title: *Northern Herald*
Published in: Belfast, 1833-36
BL Holdings: 9.1833-1.1836

Title: *Northern Star*
Published in: Belfast, 1792-96
NLI Holdings: 1.1792-12.1796
BL Holdings: 1.1792-12.1796

Title: *The Northern Star*
Published in: Belfast, 1868-72
NLI Holdings: 1.1870-11.1872
BL Holdings: 2.1868-11.1872

Title: *Northern Whig*
Published in: Belfast, 1824-1963
NLI Holdings: 1.1824-4.1829 (not published
8.1826-5.1827); 1.1839-12.1850; 3.1856-9.1963
BL Holdings: 1.1832-9.1963

Title: *Ulster Echo* (incorporated with *The Witness*)
Published in: Belfast, 1874-1916
BL Holdings: 5.1874-6.1916

Title: *Ulster Examiner* (incorporated with *Morning News*)
Note: called *Daily Examiner* (1870-82)
Published in: Belfast, 1868-82
NLI Holdings: 1.1870-6.1882
BL Holdings: 3.1868-7.1882

Title: *Ulster Observer*
Published in: Belfast, 1862-68
BL Holdings: 7.1862-1.1868

Title: *Ulster Times*
Published in: Belfast, 1836-43
NLI Holdings: 3.1836-8.1843
BL Holdings: 3.1836-8.1843

Title: *Ulster Weekly News* (incorporated with *Weekly Examiner*)
Published in: Belfast, 1873-82
BL Holdings: 3.1873-10.1881

Title: *Vindicator*
Published in: Belfast, 1839-48
NLI Holdings: 5.1839-2.1848
BL Holdings: 5.1839-2.1848

Title: *Weekly Examiner* (incorporated with *Irish Weekly News*)
Published in: Belfast, 1870-92
BL Holdings: 11.1870-8.1892

Title: *Weekly Northern Whig*
Published in: Belfast, 1858-1940
BL Holdings: 2.1858-4.1840

Title: *Weekly Observer*
Published in: Belfast, 1868-72
NLI Holdings: 1.1868-11.1872
BL Holdings: 1.1868-11.1872

Title: *Weekly Press*
Published in: Belfast, 1858-75
BL Holdings: 5.1858-6.1875

Title: *Weekly Vindicator*
Published in: Belfast, 1847-52
BL Holdings: 2.1847-8.1852

Title: *Witness*
Published in: Belfast, 1874-1941
NLI Holdings: 10.1906-1.1941
BL Holdings: 7.1875-1.1941

Church Records of Belfast

Church of Ireland

See the introduction for a description of Church of Ireland records and their major repositories. Many C of I records were lost in the PRO fire of 1922. These are indicated as "Lost." However, as Church of Ireland records were effectively state records, the records of marriage (from 1845) are also in the General Registrar's Office. Most are still in local custody (LC). The parish registers of Belfast are being indexed by the Ulster Historical Foundation, who will search their index for a fee. See Antrim and Down chapters for other C of I records in the surroundings of Belfast.

Parish: All Saints (University Street)
Existing Records: b. 1888; m. 1893; d. 1952
Status: LC

Parish: Antrim Road (see St. James and St. Peter)

Parish: Ballymacarrett (see St. Patrick)

Parish: Ballynafeigh (see St. Jude)

Parish: Ballysillan (see St. Mark)

Parish: Beersbridge Road (see St. Donard)

Parish: Belfast Cathedral (see St. Anne)

Parish: Christ Church (College Square North)
Existing Records: b. 1835; m. 1837; d. 1838
Missing Dates: b. 1859

Status: LC and PRONI

Parish: Cliftonville (see St. Silas)

Parish: Craven Street (Shankill, see St. Michael)

Parish: Cregagh (see St. Finnian)

Parish: Crumlin Road (see St. Mary)

Parish: Donegall Pass (see St. Mary Magdalene)

Parish: Drew Memorial (see St. Philip)

Parish: Duncairn Gardens (see St. Barnabas)

Parish: Dundela (see St. Mark)

Parish: Eglantine Avenue (see St. Thomas)

Parish: Falls (see St. Luke and St. John the Baptist)

Parish: Glencairn (see St. Andrew)

Parish: Grosvenor Road (see St. Philip)

Parish: Holy Trinity (Trinity St.)
Existing Records: b. 1844; m. 1855
Status: PRONI and LC

Parish: Knock (see St. Columba)

Parish: Knockbreda (Co. Down)
Existing Records: b. 1785; m. 1784; d. 1787
Status: PRONI and LC

Parish: Lisburn Road (see St. Nicholas and St. Thomas)

Parish: Lower Falls (see St. Luke)

Parish: Malone (see St. John)

Parish: Mariners Chapel (see also St. Anne)
Existing Records: b. 1868; m. 1868; d. 1868
Status: PRONI

Parish: Millfield (see St. Stephen)

Parish: Orangefield (see St. John the Evangelist)

Parish: St. Aidan (Blythe Street)
Existing Records: b. 1893; m. 1895
Status: LC

Parish: St. Andrew (Glencairn)
Existing Records: b. 1881; m. 1870
Status: LC

Parish: St. Anne (Shankill)
Existing Records: b. 1745; m. 1745; d. 1745
Status: PRONI and LC

Parish: St. Barnabas (Duncairn Gardens)
Existing Records: b. 1892; m. 1893
Status: LC

Parish: St. Clement (Templemore)
Existing Records: b. 1897; m. 1902
Status: LC

Parish: St. Columba (Knock)
Existing Records: b. 1890; m. 1896
Status: LC

Parish: St. Donard (Beersbridge Road)
Existing Records: b. 1900; m. 1903
Status: LC

Parish: St. Finnian (Cregagh)
Existing Records: b. 1928; m. 1834
Status: LC

Parish: St. George (High Street)
Existing Records: b. 1817; m. 1817
Status: PRONI and LC

Parish: St. James (Antrim Road)
Existing Records: b. 1871; m. 1871
Missing Dates: b. ends 1934; m. ends 1950
Status: LC

Parish: St. John (Malone)
Existing Records: b. 1842; m. 1842
Missing Dates: b. ends 1847; m. ends 1844
Status: PRONI

Parish: St. John the Baptist (Upper Falls)
Existing Records: b. 1855; m. 1863
Status: PRONI and LC

Parish: St. John the Evangelist (Orangefield)
Existing Records: b. 1853; m. 1853
Status: LC and PRONI (births only)

Parish: St. Jude (Ballynafeigh)
Existing Records: b. 1873; m. 1874; d. 1874
Status: LC

Parish: St. Luke (Northumberland Street, Lower Falls)
Status: Lost

Parish: St. Mark (1) (Ballysillan)
Existing Records: b. 1856: m. 1860
Status: LC and PRONI (baptisms only)

Parish: St. Mark (2) (Dundela)
Existing Records: b. 1869; m. 1879
Status: LC and PRONI (baptisms only)

Parish: St. Mary (Crumlin Road)
Existing Records: b. 1867; m. 1869; d. 1867
Status: LC and PRONI (baptisms and burials only)

Parish: St. Mary Magdalene
Existing Records: b. 1855; m. 1862
Status: LC and PRONI (baptisms only)

Parish: St. Mathew (Woodvale Road)
Existing Records: b. 1846; m. 1856; d. 1887
Status: LC and PRONI (baptisms only)

Parish: St. Michael (Craven Street)
Existing Records: b. 1893; m. 1900
Status: LC

Parish: St. Nicholas (Lisburn Road)
Existing Records: b. 1901; m. 1902
Status: LC

Parish: St. Patrick (Ballymacarrett)
Existing Records: b. 1827; m. 1827
Status: LC and PRONI

Parish: St. Paul (York Street)
Existing Records: b. 1851; m. 1921
Missing Dates: b. 1851-79
Status: LC

Parish: St. Peter (Antrim Road)
Existing Records: b. 1896; m. 1901
Status: LC

Parish: St. Philip (Drew Memorial)
Existing Records: b. 1871; m. 1872
Status: LC

Parish: St. Silas (Cliftonville)
Existing Records: b. 1899; m. 1902
Status: LC

Parish: St. Stephen (Millfield)
Existing Records: b. 1868; m. 1869
Status: LC

Parish: St. Thomas (Eglantine Avenue)
Existing Records: b. 1871; m. 1871
Status: LC

Parish: Shankill (see St. Anne and St. Mathew)

Parish: Templemore Avenue (see St. Clement)

Parish: Upper Falls (see St. John the Baptist)

Parish: Willowfield (Down)
Existing Records: b. 1872; m. 1872
Status: LC

Parish: Woodvale Road (see St. Mathew)

Parish: York Street (see St. Paul)

Presbyterian—Belfast City

An account of Presbyterian records is given in the introduction. These registers rarely contain death records, and occasionally have only records of births. This is indicated where appropriate. All are held in the local parish unless otherwise indicated. The Presbyterian registers of Down are being indexed by the Ulster Historical Foundation (see Research Services at the end of the appendix). A search of the index will be conducted for a fee. Copies of many are also held at the Public Record Office of Northern Ireland (PRONI). See Antrim and Down chapters for other Presbyterian records in the surroundings of Belfast.

Parish: Albert Street
Existing Records: b. 1852
Status: PRONI

Parish: Argyle
Existing Records: b. 1853
Status: LC

Parish: Ballymacarret
Existing Records: b. 1837
Status: PRONI

Parish: Ballysillan
Existing Records: b. 1839
Status: PRONI

Parish: Belmont
Existing Records: b. 1862
Status: PRONI

Parish: Berry Street
Existing Records: b. 1853
Status: PRONI

Parish: Carnmoney
Existing Records: b. 1708
Status: PRONI

Parish: Castlereagh
Existing Records: b. 1809
Status: LC

Parish: College Square North
Existing Records: b. 1845
Status: PRONI

Parish: Crescent
Existing Records: b. 1831
Status: PRONI

Parish: Donegall Street (Cliftonville)
Existing Records: b. 1824
Status: PHSA

Parish: Duncairn
Existing Records: b. 1861
Status: PRONI

Parish: Dundonald
Existing Records: b. 1678
Status: PHSA

Parish: Dunmurry
Existing Records: b. 1860
Status: LC

Parish: Ekenhead (Academy Street)
Existing Records: b. 1864
Status: PRONI

Parish: Eglinton
Existing Records: b. 1840
Status: PRONI

Parish: Fisherwick
Existing Records: b. 1810
Status: PRONI

Parish: Fitzroy
Existing Records: b. 1820
Status: PRONI

Parish: Gilnahirk
Existing Records: b. 1797
Status: LC

Parish: Great Victoria Street
Existing Records: b. 1860
Status: PRONI

Parish: Malone
Existing Records: b. 1845
Status: PRONI

Parish: May Street
Existing Records: b. 1835
Status: PRONI

Parish: Newtownbreda
Existing Records: b. 1845
Status: PRONI

Parish: Rosemary Street
Existing Records: b. 1718
Status: PRONI

Parish: St. Enoch
Existing Records: b. 1853
Status: LC

Parish: Sinclair Seamen's
Existing Records: b. 1854
Status: PRONI

Parish: Townsend Street
Existing Records: b. 1835
Status: LC

Parish: Westbourne
Existing Records: b. 1880
Status: PRONI

Parish: York Street
Existing Records: b. 1840
Status: PRONI

Non-Subscribing Presbyterian Churches

Parish: Dunmurry
Existing Records: b. 1807
Status: PRONI

Parish: Rosemary Street (1)
Existing Records: b. 1757
Status: PRONI

Parish: Rosemary Street (2)
Existing Records: b. 1817
Status: PRONI

Methodist

An account of the Methodist church in Ireland is given in the introduction.

Parish: Agnes Street
Existing Records: b. 1864; m. 1868
Status: LC

Parish: Carlisle Memorial
Existing Records: b. 1877; m. 1877
Status: LC

Parish: Crumlin Road
Existing Records: b. 1878; m. 1878
Status: LC

Parish: Donegal Square
Existing Records: b. 1815-1928; m. 1863-1911
Status: PRONI

Parish: Duncairn Gardens
Existing Records: b. 1890; m. 1895
Status: LC

Parish: Falls Road
Existing Records: b. 1882; m. 1863
Status: LC

Parish: Frederick Street
Existing Records: b. 1841-1904
Status: LC

Parish: Grosvenor Hall
Existing Records: b. 1895; m. 1896
Status: LC

Parish: Hydepark (North Belfast Mission)
Existing Records: b. 1834; m. 1868
Status: LC

Parish: Jennymount
Existing Records: b. 1873; m. 1913
Status: LC

Parish: Knock
Existing Records: b. 1874; m. 1872
Status: LC

Parish: Ligoniel
Existing Records: b. 1870; m. 1893
Status: LC

Parish: Mountpottinger (called Ballymacarret until 1891)
Existing Records: b. 1885; m. 1888
Status: LC

Parish: Ormeau Road
Existing Records: b. 1870; m. 1884
Status: LC

Parish: Osborne Park
Existing Records: b. 1894; m. 1878
Status: LC

Parish: Primitive Street
Existing Records: b. 1885; m. 1878
Status: LC

Parish: Salem New Connection
Existing Records: b. 1829; m. 1904
Status: LC

Parish: Sandy Row
Existing Records: b. 1885; m. 1878
Status: LC

Parish: Shankill Road
Existing Records: b. 1874; m. 1815
Status: LC

Parish: University Road
Existing Records: b. 1865; m. 1815
Status: LC

Index

A code letter or series of letters in parentheses after a proper name in the index indicates a type or denomination of parish. The codes for the types of parish are: B = Baptist; C = Civil; CI = Church of Ireland; M = Methodist; P = Presbyterian; Q = Quaker; RC = Roman Catholic. In cases where many parishes had the same name (for example, St. Mary's), these are distinguished both by denomination and by city or (in parentheses) county in which the parish is located.

A

Aasleagh (CI), 416
Abbey (C), 111
Abbey Church (P), 232
Abbey Historical Society, 63
Abbey (RC), 271
Abbey Street, Dublin (B), 228
Abbeydorney (RC), 293–95
Abbeyfeale (C,RC), 374
Abbeygormacan (C,RC), 270
Abbeyknockmoy (C), 270
Abbeyknockmoy (RC), 270, 276
Abbeylara (C), 391, 393
Abbeylara (CI), 392
Abbeylara (RC), 393
Abbeyleix (C), 10, 328, 347
Abbeyleix (CI), 344
Abbeyleix (RC), 328, 347
Abbeymahon (C), 133
Abbeymahon (CI), 127
Abbeyshrule (C), 393
Abbeyshrule (RC), 394
Abbeyside (RC), 544
Abbeystowry (C), 133
Abbeystrewery (CI), 127
Abbreviations, 44–46
Abbyshrule (CI), 558

Abercorn family, 534
Abercorn Papers, 178
Abington (C), 374, 502
Abington (CI), 372, 499
Abstracts
  of directories, 27
  of marriage records, 35, 248
  of wills, *illus.* 32, 34
    Antrim, 62
    Armagh, 78
    Cavan, 106
    Clare, 117
    Cork, 151
    Dublin, 248
    Galway, 280
    Kerry, 299
    Kildare, 316
    Kilkenny, 337
    Laois, 351
    Limerick, 384
    Longford, 396
    Monaghan, 458
    Tipperary, 515
    Waterford, 551
    Westmeath, 566
    Wicklow, 248, 601
Academy Street, Belfast (P), 610
Acheson family, 67
Achill (CI), 416, 417
Achill (C,RC), 418
Achonry (CI), 489
Achonry (C,RC), 490
Acton (CI), 72
Acton family, 243
Adams family, 104
Adamstown (C), 575
Adamstown (CI), 573
Adamstown (RC), 575, 577
Adare (CI), 372
Adare (C,RC), 374
Addergoole (C,RC), 270, 418

Addresses
  administrative divisions in relation to, 7
  in church records, 23
  in civil records, 10
  sources of, 2
  in will and administration abstracts, 30, 34
  in wills, 34
Aderrig (C), 233
Adhadrimsee (CI), 453
Administrations, 30, 34. *See also* Wills
Administrative divisions, 7, 10
Adventurers
  confiscated lands redistribution to, 41
    after O'Neill rebellion (1594-1603), 67
      in Cavan, 95
      in Derry, 165
      in Down, 203
      in Tyrone, 95
    after rebellion of 1580
      in Cork, 123
      in Limerick, 369
    after rebellion of 1641, 14
      in Kilkenny, 323
      in Tipperary, 497
    in Kerry, 287
    in Leitrim, 357
    in Mayo, 413
    in Tyrone, 525
Advertisements, in newspapers, 2
  vital data in, 30
Affane (C), 543
Age
  in census records, 14
  in civil records, 10
Agha (C), 85
Aghaboe (C), 344, 347
Aghaboe (RC), 347, 348
Aghabog (C), 452, 455
Aghabog (RC), 455
Aghabulloge (C), 133

D

E

U

Y